Literature and
Its Times

VOLUME 2
Civil Wars to Frontier Societies

(1800-1880s)

Literature and Its Times

Profiles of 300 Notable Literary Works and the Historical Events that Influenced Them

Joyce Moss • George Wilson

GALE

DETROIT NEW YORK TORONTO LONDON

**MAGNIFICAT HIGH SCHOOL
RESOURCE CENTER
ROCKY RIVER, OH 44116-3397**

Literature and Its Times

Profiles of 300 Notable Literary Works and the Historical Events that Influenced Them

VOLUME 2

Civil Wars to Frontier Societies (1800-1880s)

JOYCE MOSS • GEORGE WILSON

STAFF

Jeff Hill and Lawrence J. Trudeau, *Production Editors*
Susan Trosky, *Permissions Manager*
Kimberly F. Smilay, *Permissions Specialist*

Mary Beth Trimper, *Production Director*
Evi Seoud, *Production Manager*
Shanna Heilveil, *Production Assistant*

Cynthia Baldwin, *Product Design Manager*
Mary Claire Krzewinski, *Senior Art Director*

Barbara J. Yarrow, *Graphic Services Supervisor*
Randy Bassett, *Image Database Supervisor*
Robert Duncan, *Scanner Operator*
Pamela Hayes, *Photography Coordinator*

∞™ The paper used in this publication meets the minimum requirements of American National Standard for Information Sciences—Permanence Paper for Printed Library Materials, ANSI Z39.48-1984.

This publication is a creative work fully protected by all applicable copyright laws, as well as by misappropriation, trade secret, unfair competition, and other applicable laws. The authors and editors of this work have added value to the underlying factual material herein through one or more of the following: unique and original selection, coordination, expression, arrangement, and classification of the information.

All rights to this publication will be vigorously defended.

Copyright © 1997
Joyce Moss and George Wilson

All rights reserved including the right of reproduction in whole or in part in any form.

ISBN 0-7876-0606-5 (Set)
ISBN 0-7876-0608-1 (Volume 2)

Printed in the United States of America
10 9 8 7 6 5 4 3

Library of Congress Cataloging-in-Publication Data

Literature and its times : profiles of 300 notable literary works and the historical events that influenced them / [edited by Joyce Moss and George Wilson].
      p.   cm.
Includes bibliographical references and index.
Contents: v. 1. Ancient times to the American and French Revolutions, (pre-history-1790s) -- v. 2. Civil wars to frontier societies (1800-1880s) -- v. 3. Growth of empires to the Great Depression (1890-1930s) -- v. 4. World War II to the affluent fifties (1940-1950s) -- v. 5. Civil rights movements to future times (1960-2000).
    ISBN 0-7876-0607-3 (vol. 1 : alk. paper). -- ISBN 0-7876-0608-1 (vol. 2 : alk. paper). -- ISBN 0-7876-0609-X (vol. 3 : alk. paper). -- ISBN 0-7876-0610-3 (vol. 4 : alk. paper). -- ISBN 0-7876-0611-1 (vol. 5 : alk. paper)
    1. Literature and history. 2. History in literature. 3. Literature--History and criticism. I. Moss, Joyce, 1951- . II. Wilson, George, 1920- .
PN50.L574 1997
809'.93358--dc21

          97-34339
          CIP

Contents

Preface vii
Acknowledgments xi
Introduction xiii
Chronology of Relevant Events xvii
Contents by Title xxvii
Contents by Author xxix
Photo Credits xxxi
Entries 1
Index 429

Preface

"Even a great writer can be bound by the prejudices of his time . . . we cannot place Shakespeare in a sealed container. He belonged to his time," notes Alexander Leggatt in his essay "*The Merchant of Venice*: A Modern Perspective" (William Shakespeare, *The Merchant of Venice* [New York: Washington Square Press, 1992], 217). This reasoning, applicable to any work and its author, explains why *Literature and Its Times* fixes a wide range of novels, short stories, biographies, speeches, poems, and plays in the context of their particular historical periods.

In the process, the relationship between fact and fantasy or invention becomes increasingly clear. The function of literature is not necessarily to represent history accurately. Many writers aim rather to spin a satisfying tale or perhaps to convey a certain vision or message. Nevertheless, the images created by a powerful literary work—be it the Greek poem *Iliad,* the Spanish novel *The Adventures of Don Quixote,* or the American play *The Crucible*—leave impressions that are commonly taken to be historical. This is true from works that depict earlier eras to ones that portray more modern occurrences, such as the world wars or race relations. The fourteenth-century poem *Inferno* from the *Divine Comedy* by Dante Alighieri is probably the most powerful example. So vividly does *Inferno* describe Hell that for more than two centuries people took its description as truth, going so far as to map Hell according to the details of the poem.

In taking literature as fact, then, one risks acquiring a mistaken or an unverified notion of history. Yet, by the same token, history can be very well informed by literary works. An author may portray events in a way that for the first time aptly captures the fears and challenges of a period, enabling readers to better understand it and their own place in the historical continuum. This is easily illustrated by tracing novels that feature women's issues, from Nathaniel Hawthorne's *The Scarlet Letter* (1640s setting) to Leo Tolstoy's *Anna Karenina* (1870s) to Alice Walker's *The Color Purple* (1920s–40s) and Amy Tan's *The Joy Luck Club* (1940s–80s).

Placing a given work in historical context involves pinpointing conditions in the society in which it was written as well as set. Stephen Crane's *Red Badge of Courage* is set in the early 1860s. Published three decades later, it was written in a different social context and, in this case, in response to a literary trend of Crane's own era. Only by gaining insight into this era as well as the one in which the work takes place can it be fully appreciated; *Literature and Its Times* therefore addresses the author's time frame too.

The task of reconstructing the historical contexts of a work can be problematic. There are stories—the tales of England's King Arthur, for example—that defy any attempt to fit them neatly into a particular time. Living in a later era, their authors, consciously or not, mixed events that actually belong to two or more different pe-

Preface

riods. In some cases, this is an innocent mistake by a writer who did not have the benefit of accurate sources. In other cases, fidelity to the actual events of the time is of little concern to the writer; his or her main interest is the fictional world to be portrayed. In still other cases, the mixture of times is intentional. Happily, present-day knowledge makes it possible for this series to begin unweaving the historical mixture in these types of works.

Literature and Its Times relates history to literature on a case-by-case basis, intending to help readers respond fully to a work and to assist them in distinguishing fact from invention in the work. The series engages in this mission with a warm appreciation for the beauty of literature independent of historical facts, but also with the belief that ultimate regard is shown for a literary work and its author by positioning it in the context of pertinent events.

Selection of Literary Works

Literature and Its Times includes novels, short stories, plays, poems, biographies, essays, speeches, and documents. The works chosen for inclusion have been carefully selected on the basis of how frequently they are studied and how closely they are tied to pivotal historical events. Reflected in the selection are works not only by classic and still widely read authors but also by noteworthy ethnic and female authors. To finalize the selection, the complete list of titles was submitted to a panel of librarians, secondary teachers, and college professors. Please see "Acknowledgments" for a specific listing of these reviewers.

Format and Arrangement of Entries

The five volumes of *Literature and Its Times* are arranged chronologically from ancient times to the present. The set of entries within each volume is arranged alphabetically by title. As the series progresses, the range of years covered in each successive volume grows narrower due to the increasing number of works published in more recent times.

Each entry is organized according to the following sections.

1. **Introduction**—identifying information in three parts:

    The literary work—describes the genre, the time and place of the work, and the year(s) it was first performed or published;

    Synopsis—summarizes the storyline or contents;

    Introductory paragraph—introduces the literary work in relation to the author's life.

2. **Events in History at the Time the Literary Work Takes Place**—describes social and political events that relate to the plot or contents of the literary work and that occurred during the period the story takes place. Subsections vary depending on the literary work. The section takes a deductive approach, starting with events in history and telescoping inward to events in the literary work.

3. **The Literary Work in Focus**—describes in brief the plot or contents of the work. Generally this summary is followed by a subsection on one or more elements in the work that illuminate real events or attitudes of the period. The subsection takes an inductive approach, starting with the literary work and broadening outward to events in history. It is usually followed by a third subsection detailing the sources used by the author to create the work.

4. **Events in History at the Time the Literary Work Was Written**—describes social, political, and/or literary events in the author's lifetime that relate to the plot or contents of the work. When relevant, the section includes events in the author's life. Also discussed in the section are the initial reviews or reception accorded to the literary work.

5. **For More Information**—provides a list of all sources that have been cited in the entry as well as sources for further reading about the different issues or personalities featured in the entry.

If a literary work is set and written in the same time period, sections 2 and 4 of the entry on that work ("Events in History at the Time the Literary Work Takes Place" and "Events in History at the Time the Literary Work Was Written") are combined into the single section "Events in History at the Time of the Literary Work."

Additional Features

Whenever possible, primary source material is provided through quotations in the text and material in sidebars. There are also sidebars with historical details that amplify issues raised in the main text and with anecdotes that give readers a fuller understanding of the temporal context. Timelines appear in various entries to summarize intricate periods of history. To enrich and further clarify information, historically noteworthy illustrations have been included in the series. Maps as well as photographs provide visual images of potentially unfamiliar settings.

Comments and Suggestions

Your comments on this series and suggestions for future editions are welcome. Please write: Editors, *Literature and Its Times,* Gale Research, Inc., 835 Penobscot Building, Detroit, Michigan 48226-4094; or call toll-free: 1-800-877-4253.

Acknowledgments

For their careful review of entries in *Literature and Its Times*, the following professors and lecturers from the University of California at Los Angeles (UCLA) deserve the deepest appreciation:

English Department

Robert Aguirre
Martha Banta
Lynn Batten
A. R. Braunmuller
Daphne Brooks
King-Kok Cheung
Michael Colacurcio
Ed Condren
Jack Kolb
Jinqui Ling
Chris Mott
Michael North
Barbara Packer
David Rodes
Karen Rowe

Comparative Literature Department

Eric Gans
Kathryn King
Mary Kay Norseng
Ross Shideler

Slavic Languages and Literature Department

Micheal Heim
Peter Hodgson

Gratitude is also extended to professors from other institutions for their valuable review of selected entries, and to history department chairman Robert Sumpter for his guidance and reviews:

Rabbi Stanley Chyet, Hebrew Union College
Agnes Moreland Jackson, Pitzer College, English and Black Studies
Michael McGaha, Pomona College, Romance Languages and Literatures—Spanish Section
Robert Sumpter, Mira Costa High School, History Department

A host of contributers assisted in collecting and composing data for the entries in *Literature and Its Times*. Their painstaking hours of research and composition are deeply appreciated.

Diane R. Ahrens
Eric A. Besner
Suzanne C. Borghei
Luke Bresky
Anne Brooks
Corey Brettschneider
Thomas Cooper
Patricia Carroll
Terence Davis
Mark Druskoff
Shelby Fulmer
Betsy Hedberg-Keramidas

Acknowledgments

Ryan Hilbert
Lisa Gabbert
Anne Kim
Amy Merritt
Michael Le Sieur
Barbara A. Lozano
Michele Mednick
Michelle Miller
Larry Mowrey
Evan Porter
Edward R. OþNeill
David Riemer
Monica Riordan
Jane E. Roddy
George Ross
Rita Schepergerdes
Roberta Seid
Shira Tarrant
Benjamin Trefny
Pete Trujillo
Lorraine B. Valestuk
Colin Wells
Sandra Wade-Grusky
Allison Weisz
Jeannie Wilkinson
Denise Wilson
Brandon Wilson
Antoine Wilson

A special thank you is extended to Lorraine B. Valestuk, Ph.D., for her refinement of data and to Cheryl Steets, Ph.D., for her deft copy editing. Anne Leach indexed the volumes with proficiency and literary sensitivity. The editors also thank Larry Trudeau and Jeff Hill of Gale Research for their careful editorial management.

Lastly the editors express gratitude to those who guided the final selection of literary works included in the series:

Neil Anstead, Director of Humanities, Los Angeles Unified School District

William Balcolm, Librarian, Villa Park Public Library, Villa Park, IL

Marth Banta, Professor, University of California at Los Angeles

Carol Clark, Head Librarian, Robert E. Lee High School, Springfield, VA

Chris García, Head Librarian, Beverly Hills Children's Library, Beverly Hills, CA

Nancy Guidry, Young Adult Librarian, Santa Monica Public Library, Santa Monica, CA

Kenneth M. Holmes, Ph.D., Educational Consultant, Educational Concepts Unlimited, Bellville, IL

Carol Jago, Mentor Teacher, English Department, Santa Monica Public High School, Santa Monica, CA

Jim Merrill, Instructor, Oxnard Community College, Oxnard, CA

Mary Purucker, Head Librarian, Santa Monica High School, Santa Monica, CA

Karen Rowe, Professor, University of California at Los Angeles

Hilda K. Weisburg, Librarian, Sayreville War Memorial High School, Parlin, NJ

Dr. Brooke Workman, Teacher, West High School, Iowa City, IA

Richard Yarborough, Professor, University of California at Los Angeles

Introduction to Volume 2

Volume 2 of *Literature and Its Times* opens with works set during the aftermath of the French Revolution at the turn of the nineteenth century, and closes with literature that takes place at the turn of the twentieth century, as Americans put their own Civil War behind them and continued to spread westward. The American population increased greatly in the post-war years, with newcomers emigrating from Europe and with a rise in emigration from Asia. Across the continents, the century is characterized by war and insurrection. Included here is a collection of literary works that documents the struggle of peoples on both sides of the Atlantic Ocean to achieve a democratic society and to define the proper role of the individual within that society.

As the century unfolded, Napoleon Bonaparte conquered most of Europe and then lost it, Europeans overthrew their kings and governments, and United States citizens fought over frontiers with the British, the Spanish, the Mexicans, and the American Indians. Writers meanwhile pondered political concepts such as justice, social hierarchies, and the rights to which various members of society were entitled. In England, Charlotte Brontë (*Jane Eyre*) and Jane Austen (*Pride and Prejudice*) wrote novels featuring legally and socially powerless English women without money. In Russia, Leo Tolstoy examined gender inequalities (*Anna Karenina*). England's Charles Dickens (*Oliver Twist*) and France's Victor Hugo (*Les Misérables*) portrayed the plight of the urban poor. In America, nonfiction works produced in the period by Henry David Thoreau ("Civil Disobedience") and John Brown (John Brown's Last Speech) question the relative authorities of personal conviction and government legislation. Other works set in the period focus on the American West, raising equally troublesome questions about the legitimacy and moral implications of frontier justice, whether it involves tactics to subdue Indian tribes (Dee Brown's *Bury My Heart at Wounded Knee*), the hanging of accused thieves (Walter Val Tilburn Clark's *The Ox-Bow Incident*), or the blurred distinction between criminals and lawmen (Jack Schaefer's *Shane*).

In 1859 England's Charles Darwin published *On the Origin of Species by Means of Natural Selection*, a work that changed the way many people think about social structures. Darwin's study speaks of an evolutionary principle that has become known as "survival of the fittest" (a phrase coined by Herbert Spencer and one that Darwin himself used in the fifth edition of his work). The principle states that animals whose bodies are best adapted to their physical surroundings tend to be most successful. Applying Darwin's ideas to society resulted in the development of a school of thought known as *social* Darwinism. Its proponents taught that human beings divide naturally along lines of strength and power, and that the poor, weak, and powerless are simply less

Introduction

well equipped to adapt to the changes surging through society. Progress comes from human competition, the social Darwinists reasoned, which separates the strong from the weak, whom nature will eventually eliminate. Thus, charity and other efforts on behalf of the weak are pointless. Objecting to this reasoning, various writers have created literary works that are nevertheless affected by it, such as Bernard Pomerance's *The Elephant Man.*

The social Darwinists assumed that nature had made the white man superior to everyone else, an assumption that during the reign of Queen Victoria (1837–1901) led to potent social hierarchies and objections to them. Works of literature like W. E. B. Du Bois's *The Souls of Black Folk,* William Gibson's *The Miracle Worker,* and Charlotte Perkins Gilman's "The Yellow Wallpaper" all contest the idea that some people—blacks, the disabled, women—are naturally inferior to white men. Yet larger society stubbornly held onto the assumption of white male superiority well into the twentieth century.

Separate roles were prescribed for women and men in the Victorian Age, resulting in a gender hierarchy that, along with an ethnic hierarchy, would long determine the structure of Anglo-American culture. Around mid-century, however, on both sides of the Atlantic Ocean, women began struggling for emancipation. Issues of education, legal rights, profession, and freedom in courtship and marital choice run through the literature of and about the period, from Henrik Ibsen's *A Doll's House* to William Luce's *The Belle of Amherst* to Henry James's *Daisy Miller.* In fact, Darwin had suggested that women are the hardier, more necessary sex, who, as mothers, guarantee the preservation of the species. Others have used his work to argue both for and against the desirability of women leaving the home to pursue education and careers.

In the 1880s and 1890s social Darwinism began to take a different tack, focusing on competition between nations rather than among individuals. Proponents turned to dividing the world into advanced and less advanced races, assuming that white Europeans were superior and thus had the right to control the destinies of other peoples—whether they were Africans, Asians, or the formerly colonized white, black, and native Americans. This mind set gave rise to a missionary spirit, in which European white men and women felt obligated to bring their "superior" culture to "inferior" colonized peoples in, for example, Africa (as in Joseph Conrad's *Heart of Darkness*). Created from the perspective of native peoples, some of the literature set in their lands (in Africa—Chinua Achebe's *Things Fall Apart;* in America—Chief Joseph's "I Will Fight No More Forever") portrays just how unwelcome these whites often were.

For much of the century, another kind of tension loomed above such difficulties in the United States. The conflicts between North and South in the Civil War era dominated the history of the nation for some forty years. Prior to the war, concerns about racial relations and the nature of the American union escalated in light of the social revolutions sweeping through Europe; autobiographies by Southern black slaves (like Frederick Douglass and Harriet Jacobs) made their way north and found a sympathetic audience. During four years of Civil War and the troubled period of reconcilement and renewal known as Reconstruction, Americans faced the difficult chore of living up to their image as defenders of equality and freedom. What would the new America be like? In the South at least, the new America wound up resembling to a great extent the old America, as creative new ways of depriving black people of their civil rights emerged. Works like Booker T. Washington's *Up from Slavery* and Toni Morrison's *Beloved* reflect America's continuing debate about racial equality long after the postwar Thirteenth, Fourteenth, and Fifteenth amendments to the American constitution tried to put the matter to rest.

The collection closes during America's "Gilded Age," a time of increasing wealth and power, with its attendant technological innovations—the harnessing of electricity, the invention of the automobile and the telephone. Migrants flocked from rural areas, such as the one in which Edith Wharton's *Ethan Frome* is set, to the cities to labor in factories and benefit from the new inventions. For many, life improved in material comfort, but there was a seamy side to city living too, as shown in Theodore Dreiser's *Sister Carrie* and in the first part of Horatio Alger's poor-boy-succeeds tale, *Ragged Dick; or, Street Life in New York with the Boot-Blacks.* The so-called Gilded Age saw the spread of unscrupulous business practices and of unsanitary living and working conditions for people whose labor made life easier for the wealthy to enjoy.

One literary work, whose development spanned half a century, stands out in relation to nineteenth-century American history. From 1855 to 1892, Walt Whitman's poetic collection, *Leaves of Grass,* was published in nine different editions, each of which reflects the dominant concerns of the poet and the nation at the time of publication. Taken together, the collection reveals the moods, conflicts, and innovations of a people from their pre-Civil War decade, through the bloody years of the gruesome conflict, to the assassination of President Abraham Lincoln and the postwar promise of the Western frontier.

Chronology of Relevant Events

1800–1880s

THE ROMANTIC MOVEMENT

Romanticism refers to a pan-European movement that involved literature, the arts, and philosophy, and that heavily influenced pre-Civil War writings in the United States. The movement valued liberty over governmental and church authority, and the emotional and instinctive over the rational and deliberate. Romantics championed the weak and oppressed in society, took seriously dreams and the unconscious, and, in their bleaker moments, focused on death, evil, and pain. A reaction against the earlier Enlightenment era and its focus on the human intellect, Romanticism was above all a movement of rebellion. It was closely related to a movement among U.S. writers—transcendentalism.

	Historical Events	Literary Works Set in the Period
1790	1789 French Revolution ushers in a period of rebellion in politics and social life in various parts of Europe	
	1798 Romantic movement officially begins in England with the appearance of *Lyrical Ballads* by William Wordsworth and Samuel Taylor Coleridge	
1800	1799 William Wordsworth publishes first edition of *The Prelude*, another of English Romanticism's founding texts	early 1800s *Pride and Prejudice* by Jane Austen
	1804 Napoleon Bonaparte becomes emperor of France; Napoleonic Code becomes basis of French law	early 1800s "The Cask of Amontillado" by Edgar Allan Poe
	1805 Napoleon defeats Austrian and Russian troops at Austerlitz	
1810	1808 Napoleon defeats Spanish king Charles and exiles his heir Ferdinand VII; Spanish colonies in the Americas begin independence movements	
	1812 Napoleon invades Russia, retreats in disarray; U.S. declares war on Great Britain	

	Historical Events	Literary Works Set in the Period
	1813 Duke of Wellington invades France	
	1814 Spain, England, and Prussia attack France; Napoleon is exiled to Elba; the British burn Washington, D.C.; Francis Scott Key writes "Star-Spangled Banner"	
	1815 Napoleon returns to France; is defeated by the English and Prussians at Waterloo and exiled to St. Helena; United States defeats Britain in Battle of New Orleans	1815–35 *Les Misérables* by Victor Hugo 1815–38 *The Count of Monte Cristo* by Alexandre Dumas
	1816 Divorce, available since 1792, is outlawed in France	
1820	1818 Mary Shelley publishes *Frankenstein; or, The Modern Prometheus*, a Gothic-style novel, full of mystery and terror	1818 *Frankenstein* by Mary Shelley
	1821 Revolution breaks out in Greece	
	1823 Monroe Doctrine proclaims the Americas off-limits to European colonization	
	1825 Czar Nicholas I suppresses December Revolution in Russia	
1830	1830s Hudson River School, the first school of American landscape painting, is founded	1830s *Oliver Twist* by Charles Dickens 1830s "Self-Reliance" by Ralph Waldo Emerson
	1830 Charles X of France abolishes freedom of the press, dissolves lower house of French Parliament, and reduces the electorate drastically; Louis Philippe, Duke of Orleans, replaces him as "citizen king"; in America, Gothic architecture is in vogue and Joseph Smith publishes the *Book of Mormon*, inspiring the birth of a new religion	
	1832 Riot breaks out in Paris as Republicans try to dethrone Louis Philippe; cholera epidemic kills 20,000 in Paris	
	1834 New Poor Law in England cuts off aid to outdoor workers	
	1834–39 Spanish Civil War	
	1838 Ralph Waldo Emerson delivers "The American Scholar" address, heralding the transcendental movement	
1840		1840s *Jane Eyre* by Charlotte Brontë
	1843 Governesses' Benevolent Institution opens in London	1843 *The Turn of the Screw* by Henry James
	1845 Henry David Thoreau moves to Walden Pond	
1850		1851 *Walden* by Henry David Thoreau

THE VICTORIAN AGE

The Victorian Age (1837–1901) saw the height of European colonization of Africa and Asia, America's expansion west into territory owned or inhabited by Spanish-speaking mestizos and Indians, and persistent social hierarchies that distinguished conquerors from the conquered. While the Europeans continued to explore continents other than their own, Latin Americans, newly freed from Spanish rule, struggled to establish independent republics. On the home front, white society's females began to challenge the "separate spheres" philosophy that divided the domestic culture of women from the worldly culture of men.

	Historical Events	Literary Works Set in the Period
1830	1830 Colombia becomes an independent South American republic	1830s–1930s *One Hundred Years of Solitude* by Gabriel García Márquez

	Historical Events	**Literary Works Set in the Period**
1840	1837 Victoria crowned Queen of England; in United States, Oberlin College enrolls first (4) women; Georgia Female College, the first women's college in America, opens	
	1839 Opium War breaks out between England and China	
	1840 Queen Victoria marries Prince Albert; Samuel Cunard establishes trans-Atlantic steamship line	
	1842 England forms its first detective force; China gives Hong Kong to Great Britain in Treaty of Nanking	
	1844 British abolish imprisonment for debts less than £20	
	1845 Potato Famine decimates Ireland; Frederick Engels publishes *Condition of the Working Class in Great Britain*; Margaret Fuller publishes *Woman in the Nineteenth Century*, the first work of feminism in America	1845–86 *The Belle of Amherst* by William Luce
	1845–48 Britain annexes Punjab in India	
	1846 Smithsonian Institution opens in Washington, D.C.	
	1848 Lucretia Mott and Elizabeth Cady Stanton organize first women's rights meeting in America at Seneca Falls, New York	
1850	1849 Elizabeth Blackwell receives medical degree, the first American or European woman to do so	1850–1900 *Things Fall Apart* by Chinua Achebe
	1858 First trans-Atlantic telegraph cable links North America with Europe	
1860	1859 Darwin publishes *On the Origin of Species,* introducing the idea of survival of the fittest	
	1863 London's subway opens	1862 *Alice's Adventures in Wonderland* by Lewis Carroll
	1865 Leopold II becomes Belgian king	
	1869 John Stuart Mill publishes *The Subjection of Women,* an essay in support of domestic reform; Suez Canal begins operation	
1870	1870s Circus owner P. T. Barnum tours America with "Greatest Show on Earth"; Henry Morton Stanley explores Congo River	
	1870 French eliminate the monarchy, establish Republican France	
	1872 Susan B. Anthony is arrested for leading women voters to polls	
	1876 Queen Victoria is proclaimed "Empress of India"	
	1878 Afghanistan and Britain are at war	
1880	1880 Guy de Maupassant writes first acclaimed story, a tale about the Franco-Prussian War (1870–71), "Boule de Suif"	1880s "The Yellow Wallpaper" by Charlotte Perkins Gilman
		1880–1905(?) "The Open Window" by Saki
		1884–90 *The Elephant Man* by Bernard Pomerance
		1885 "The Necklace" by Guy de Maupassant
	1886 American poet Emily Dickinson dies	
	1887 Queen Victoria's Golden Jubilee celebrates her fifty-year rule	
		1889 *The Hound of the Baskervilles* by Arthur Conan Doyle
		late 1800s *Tess of the D'Urbervilles* by Thomas Hardy
		late 1800s *A Doll's House* by Henrik Ibsen
		late 1800s *Daisy Miller* by Henry James

	Historical Events	Literary Works Set in the Period
1900	1899 Charlotte Perkins Gilman publishes *Women and Economics*; civil war (the Thousand Days' War) erupts in Colombia 1901 Queen Victoria dies; Britain claims Nigeria, forming a protectorate from the Niger delta to the interior	1890s *Heart of Darkness* by Joseph Conrad late 1890s *Sons and Lovers* by D. H. Lawrence

MID- TO LATE NINETEENTH-CENTURY GLOBAL UNREST

Beginning in 1848, famine, unemployment, disease, and political oppression led Europeans to dethrone kings and dissolve governments; as in a huge game of dominoes, monarchies and governments across the continent toppled one after another. Across the Atlantic Ocean, the European revolutions were often seen as a confirmation of American ideals of heroic revolt and personal freedom. There was nonpolitical ferment around this time too. Cultures on both sides of the Atlantic saw the spread of challenges and innovations in literature and education.

	Historical Events	Literary Works Set in the Period
1840	1828–42 Thomas Arnold serves as headmaster of Rugby Public School in England, introducing policies that affect England's entire public school system 1840 American author Herman Melville pens essay contesting the idea that no author can surpass Shakespeare 1846–47 Great Potato Famine devastates Ireland 1846–48 Mexican-American War is fought 1848 Ferdinand II, tyrant of Naples and Sicily, is driven out; "Socialist" revolution in France drives out King Louis Philippe; more than 50 separate revolutions break out in Europe, from Ireland to Spain to Denmark, Prussia, Hungary, Austria, Switzerland, and Germany; Karl Marx and Frederick Engels publish *Communist Manifesto*	1830s–56 *Madame Bovary* by Gustave Flaubert 1834–42 *Tom Brown's Schooldays* by Thomas Hughes 1848 "Civil Disobedience" by Henry David Thoreau
1850	1852 Publication of *Uncle Tom's Cabin* fuels North-South rivalry in United States; Louis Napoleon (Napoleon III) becomes emperor of France 1853–56 Crimean War (Russia-Turkey) is fought 1855 Czar Alexander II assumes power in Russia 1857 Gustave Flaubert is charged with outraging public morals in *Madame Bovary*; Indian Mutiny occurs 1859 War of Italian Liberation erupts; John Stuart Mill publishes *On Liberty*	1850 *Uncle Tom's Cabin or, Life among the Lowly* by Harriet Beecher Stowe 1851 *Moby Dick* by Herman Melville 1851 *Leaves of Grass* (1st edition) by Walt Whitman 1856 *Leaves of Grass* (2nd edition) by Walt Whitman

	Historical Events	Literary Works Set in the Period
1860	1861 Serfs are emancipated in Russia	
	1861–65 American Civil War is fought	
	1863 Polish insurrection against Russia occurs	
	1865–69 Leo Tolstoy publishes *War and Peace*	
	1866 Fyodor Dostoevsky publishes *Crime and Punishment*	1866–1868 *Twenty Thousand Leagues under the Sea* by Jules Verne
	1867–94 Karl Marx publishes three volumes of *Das Kapital*	
1870	1870 Franco-Prussian War breaks out; fall of Napoleon III issues in French Third Republic	1870s *Anna Karenina* by Leo Tolstoy
	1875 Irish independence movement begins	
	1877 Russo-Turkish War is fought	
1880		

ANTEBELLUM AMERICA

The forces that would divide the United States were gathering strength in the decades immediately preceding the Civil War. Along with other factors, protests and uprisings about the nation's slave community helped carve a rift between North and South, despite juridical and political maneuvering to avoid confrontation.

	Historical Events	Literary Works Set in the Period
1800		1800s? *Uncle Remus: His Songs and His Sayings* by Joel Chandler Harris
	1804 Underground Railroad begins helping slaves escape to the North	
	1808 Federal law against importing slaves is passed	
		1809–1861 *Abraham Lincoln: The Prairie Years* by Carl Sandburg
1810		
		1813–58 *Incidents in the Life of a Slave Girl Written by Herself* by Harriet Jacobs
	1816 African Methodist Episcopal Church is founded in Philadelphia	
		1818–1838 *Narrative of the Life of Frederick Douglass, An American Slave* by Frederick Douglass
1820	1820s–30s Religious revival known as "Second Great Awakening" ushers in tide of reform throughout America	
	1820 Missouri Compromise bans slavery north of 36°30′; U.S. becomes world's largest cotton producer	
1830		
	1831 William Lloyd Garrison and Isaac Knapp establish antislavery journal *Liberator*; Nat Turner stages antislavery uprising	1831 *The Confessions of Nat Turner* by William Styron
	1833 American Anti-Slavery Society is founded	
	1834 Slavery is abolished in British Empire	
1840	1840s The "minstrel show" becomes popular in American theaters	1840 *The Adventures of Huckleberry Finn* by Mark Twain
		1848 "Civil Disobedience" by Henry David Thoreau

	Historical Events	**Literary Works Set in the Period**
1850	1850 Fugitive Slave Law mandates forcible return of runaway slaves to the South, raises accomplice's penalty to $1,000 for criminal damages and $1,000 for civil damages	
	1851 *The New York Times* is first printed	1851 "Ain't I a Woman?" by Sojourner Truth
	1854 Kansas-Nebraska Act leaves issue of slavery to territories' inhabitants; Republican Party is formed	
	1856 John Brown leads protest against Kansas-Nebraska Act; five proslavery people are killed	
	1856–61 "Bleeding Kansas": pro- and antislavery factions battle for control of the state	
	1857 Supreme Court hands down *Dred Scott* decision, saying that a slave is not a citizen and Congress does not have power to outlaw slavery, which makes Missouri Compromise invalid	
	1858 Abraham Lincoln battles Stephen Douglas in Illinois senatorial race and loses; the "Lincoln-Douglas Debates" prefigure Civil War conflict; Lincoln delivers "A House Divided" speech	
	1859 John Brown conducts raid on Harper's Ferry	1859 John Brown's Final Speech by John Brown
1860	1860 Abraham Lincoln is elected president; Oliver Winchester invents repeating rifle	1860 *Leaves of Grass* (3rd edition) by Walt Whitman

GOLD RUSH AND WESTERN EXPANSION

In 1804 Thomas Jefferson commissioned ex-soldiers Meriweather Lewis and William Clark to explore the upper Missouri region (now the Pacific Northwest), partly to establish relations with the Indians there who worked the lucrative fur trade with the British and the French in Canada. The pair reached the Pacific Ocean and returned with information about the West: which mountain passes to use, what the geography and climate were like, and who the Indians were. Other American explorers and settlers used this information to populate the resource-rich region that would soon become part of America. "Manifest Destiny," the philosophy that Anglo-Saxon Americans had a providential mission to spread throughout the continent, gained currency in the mid-1840s and remained popular for at least another fifty years.

	Historical Events	**Literary Works Set in the Period**
1800		
	1803 Louisiana Purchase	
	1805 Lewis and Clark reach Pacific Ocean	
1810		
	1811 John Jacob Astor's Pacific Fur Company establishes trading posts on the Columbia River	
1820		
	1825 Texas is opened to American settlers; Erie Canal begins operation	
1830		
		1834–36 *Two Years before the Mast* by Richard Henry Dana, Jr.

	Historical Events	Literary Works Set in the Period
	1836 Seige is conducted at the Alamo	
	1838 "Trail of Tears"—U.S. Government removes Cherokee people from Georgia to Indian Territory (today's Oklahoma)	
1840		1840s *The Story Catcher* by Mari Sandoz
	1842 First wagon trains move west along Oregon Trail	
	1844 United States annexes Texas	
	1848 Gold is discovered at Sutter's Mill, California	
	1849–60 200,000 people move to California	
1850		1850s "The Outcasts of Poker Flat" by Bret Harte
		1850 "The Notorious Jumping Frog of Calaveras County" by Mark Twain
		late 1850s–1930s *Thousand Pieces of Gold* by Ruthanne Lum McCunn
	1859 Oregon is admitted to Union	
1860	1860–61 Pony Express delivers mail to West	1860–67 *Leaves of Grass* (4th edition) by Walt Whitman
		1860–90 *Bury My Heart at Wounded Knee* by Dee Brown
		1860–90 *Black Elk Speaks* by John Neihardt
	1862 Homestead Act grants 160 acres of public land in the West to any adult citizen who heads a family	
	1867 U.S. buys Alaska from Russia	
1870	1872 Mark Twain publishes *Roughing It,* about his adventures in the West	
	1874 George Armstrong Custer discovers gold in the Black Hills of South Dakota	
	1876 Cheyenne-Sioux army defeats U.S. troops at Battle of Little Big Horn	
	1877 Nez Percé Indians are defeated at Bear Paw Mountain	1877 "I Will Fight No More Forever" by Chief Joseph
	late 1870s Population of San Francisco reaches 250,000	
1880	1880 Chinese Immigration Treaty limits Chinese immigrants to U.S.	1880–1916 *Ishi, Last of His Tribe* by Theodora Kroeber
	1880 Gold is discovered in Alaska	
	1881 Helen Hunt Jackson publishes *A Century of Shame* about scandalous treatment of American Indians by United States government	
	1883 Buffalo Bill Cody organizes first Wild West show	
		1885 *The Ox-Bow Incident* by Walter Van Tilburg Clark
	1887 General Allotment Act (Dawes Act) divides tribal land among individual tribesmen to ease assimilation into white culture	
	1889 North Dakota, South Dakota, Montana, Washington are admitted to union	1889 *Shane* by Jack Shaefer
1890	1890 Idaho and Wyoming are admitted to union	
	1890 U.S. Army massacres Sioux at Battle of Wounded Knee	

xxiii

| Historical Events | Literary Works Set in the Period |

AMERICAN CIVIL WAR

By mid-century, it was becoming clear that the economic, political, and social gulf between the industrial North and agricultural South was widening in the United States. As the nation grew, disagreements over the expansion of slave-holding territories, along with other points of contention, escalated. Southern states finally took drastic action, seceding from the Union to preserve their ways of life, including slavery. The North responded by entering into armed conflict to preserve the Union. The fighting erupted at Fort Sumter, South Carolina, launching a four-year war that would kill about 640,000 Americans.

Year	Historical Events	Literary Works Set in the Period
1860	1860 South Carolina is first state to secede from Union; ten others follow shortly thereafter	1860s–70s *Little Women* by Louisa May Alcott
1861	1861 Bombardment of Fort Sumter in Charleston, S.C., harbor initiates four years of civil war	1861–65 *Across Five Aprils* by Irene Hunt 1861–73 *Gone with the Wind* by Margaret Mitchell
1862	1862 Lincoln passes first military draft in American history; Union troops win Battle of Shiloh	
1863	1863 Emancipation Proclamation: after January 1, 1863, all slaves in rebel states are declared free by President Abraham Lincoln; hundreds of thousands of slaves become Union workers and soldiers; Union troops lose Battle of Chancellorsville, win Battle of Gettysburg; Lincoln announces "Ten Percent Plan," whereby a Southern state can form a new state government once 10 percent of its citizens take an oath of loyalty to the Union	1863 "An Occurrence at Owl Creek Bridge" by Ambrose Bierce 1863 *The Red Badge of Courage* by Stephen Crane 1863 Gettysburg Address by Abraham Lincoln
1864	1864 Ulysses Grant becomes commander of Union forces; General William Sherman marches to the sea at Savannah, Georgia, engaging in "total war," his troops burning fields and buildings on the way	
1865	1865 General Robert E. Lee surrenders—Civil War ends; Lincoln is assassinated; Ku Klux Klan is organized	

RECONSTRUCTION AND BEYOND

In 1865 the South stood in smoking rubble and Americans turned to the difficult task of rebuilding the nation. Deciding who would monitor the rebuilding proved difficult. Federal troops arrived to temporarily supervise the region, but Southern legislators were left mostly to their own devices concerning land and jobs. Southern whites quickly reverted to pre-Civil War habits, and the ex-slaves found themselves as discriminated-against as they had been before the war. Meanwhile, powerful agricultural interests managed to block industrialization of the region, and this kept much of it impoverished into the next century.

Year	Historical Events	Literary Works Set in the Period
1855		late 1850s–1900 *Up from Slavery* by Booker T. Washington
1865	1865 Thirteenth Amendment forbids slavery and involuntary servitude in the United States; Congress creates Bureau of Refugees, Freedmen, and Abandoned Lands 1865–67 "Presidential" Reconstruction under Andrew Johnson gives Southern governments free reign, provided that they abolish slavery, pay the Confederate war debt and prepare to rejoin the Union	

	Historical Events	Literary Works Set in the Period
	1867 Southern states (except Tennessee) reject proposed Fourteenth Amendment	
	1867–77 "Radical" or "Congressional" Reconstruction divides South into five military zones and draws up guidelines for government based on suffrage for all men	
	1868 Fourteenth Amendment grants citizenship to African Americans; President Johnson impeached and acquitted; Ulysses Grant becomes President	
	1870s Former Confederates return to power in the South; "Redeemers" try to scale down government, force all blacks to sign labor contracts, reduce funding for education and public projects, and tax farmers	
	1870 Fifteenth Amendment prohibits discrimination in voting because of "race, color, or previous condition of servitude"; all former Confederate states are now readmitted to Union	
	1873 Depression; cotton prices drop by 50 percent	1873 *Beloved* by Toni Morrison
1875		
	1877 Federal troops leave South, officially ending Reconstruction	
	1879 "Black Exodus"—20,000 African Americans migrate from the South to Kansas	
		1880s *The Miracle Worker* by William Gibson
	1881 Tuskegee Institute is founded	
		1883 "The Bear" by William Faulkner
1885		late 1800s "Barn Burning" by William Faulkner
	1890s "Great Migration"—rural Southern African Americans move to industrial cities of the North	late 1800s *Souls of Black Folk* by W. E. B. Du Bois
1895	1895 Booker T. Washington delivers "Atlanta Compromise" speech, advising blacks to learn useful skills and stop fighting racial segregation	

SECOND INDUSTRIAL REVOLUTION ("THE GILDED AGE")

The Second Industrial Revolution (the first began in Britain at the end of the eighteenth century) saw the "Americanization" of industry—the completion of the nation's modern transportation networks (rail and water), the harnessing of electricity, and the industrial production of new goods (packaged food and drugs, for example). Tycoons like John D. Rockefeller and Andrew Carnegie began to garner immense fortunes and brought American goods into the forefront of international markets. Cities flourished and small-town life began to disappear as men and women went to work in factories.

	Historical Events	Literary Works Set in the Period
1845	1845 Potato Famine in Ireland; Irish immigrants flood to America	
	1851 American Young Men's Christian Association (YMCA) is founded in Boston	

	Historical Events	Literary Works Set in the Period
1855		
		late 1850s *Ragged Dick; or Street Life in New York with the Boot-Blacks* by Horatio Alger
1865		
		1867–71 *Leaves of Grass* (5th edition) by Walt Whitman
	1869 Philadelphia garment workers form Knights of Labor Party	
	1870 New York's first elevated train line opens; Standard Oil is founded by thirty-one-year-old John D. Rockefeller	1870s–1900s *Ethan Frome* by Edith Wharton
	1873 Jay Cooke bank collapses; financial panic ensues throughout nation; typewriter is perfected by Remington Arms; first cable cars are used in San Francisco	1871–76 *Leaves of Grass* (6th edition) by Walt Whitman
1875	1875 Andrew Carnegie builds first Bessemer steel factory	
	1876 National Baseball League is founded; Melvil Dewey invents "Dewey Decimal Classification" for libraries	1876–81 *Leaves of Grass* (7th edition) by Walt Whitman
	1877 Workers conduct Great Railroad Strike; Marxist Socialist Labor Party is founded in United States	
	1879 Thomas Edison invents incandescent light; Henry George publishes *Progress and Poverty*, on inequality of wealth distribution in United States	
	1880s 70,000 miles of railroad are built in America; 164,000 miles in operation by 1894	1881–89 *Leaves of Grass* (8th edition) by Walt Whitman
	1880 Salvation Army is founded	
	1881 President James Garfield is assassinated	
1885	1887 First electric trolley line in America begins service in Richmond, Va.	late 1880s *Sister Carrie* by Theodore Dreiser
	1889 Andrew Carnegie publishes *The Gospel of Wealth*	1889–92 *Leaves of Grass* (9th edition) by Walt Whitman
	1892 Rudolf Diesel patents internal combustion engine; General Electric is founded	
	1893 Financial crash and depression	
	1894 Pullman strike pits workers against bosses and government; Antonin Dvorak's symphony "From the New World" is first performed in New York	
1895	1895 Guglielmo Marconi invents wireless telegraph	
	1896 Ford constructs first automobile	
	1897 First American subway line opens in Boston	

Contents by Title

Abraham Lincoln: The Prairie Years
  Carl Sandburg *1*

Across Five Aprils
  Irene Hunt *8*

Adventures of Huckleberry Finn, The
  Mark Twain *15*

"Ain't I a Woman?"
  Sojourner Truth *22*

Alice's Adventures in Wonderland
  Lewis Carroll *28*

Anna Karenina
  Leo Tolstoy *34*

"Barn Burning"
  William Faulkner *41*

"Bear, The"
  William Faulkner *47*

Belle of Amherst, The
  William Luce *54*

Beloved
  Toni Morrison *59*

Black Elk Speaks
  John Neihardt *66*

Bury My Heart at Wounded Knee
  Dee Brown *74*

"Cask of Amontillado, The"
  Edgar Allan Poe *81*

"Civil Disobedience" (Resistance to Civil Government)
  Henry David Thoreau *87*

Confessions of Nat Turner, The
  William Styron *93*

Count of Monte Cristo, The
  Alexandre Dumas *99*

Daisy Miller
  Henry James *105*

Doll's House, A
  Henrik Ibsen *111*

Elephant Man, The
  Bernard Pomerance *118*

Ethan Frome
  Edith Wharton *125*

Gettysburg Address
  Abraham Lincoln *130*

Gone with the Wind
  Margaret Mitchell *137*

Heart of Darkness
  Joseph Conrad *145*

Hound of the Baskervilles, The
  Arthur Conan Doyle *152*

"I Will Fight No More Forever"
  Chief Joseph *160*

Contents by Title

Incidents in the Life of a Slave Girl Written by Herself
   Harriet A. Jacobs **168**

Ishi, Last of His Tribe
   Theodora Kroeber. **174**

Jane Eyre
   Charlotte Brontë. **181**

John Brown's Final Speech
   John Brown **188**

Leaves of Grass
   Walt Whitman **195**

Little Women
   Louisa May Alcott. **202**

Madame Bovary
   Gustave Flaubert **209**

Miracle Worker, The
   William Gibson **216**

Misérables, Les
   Victor Hugo **223**

Moby Dick
   Herman Melville. **230**

Narrative of the Life of Frederick Douglass, An American Slave
   Frederick Douglass **236**

"Necklace, The"
   Guy de Maupassant **244**

"Notorious Jumping Frog of Calaveras County, The"
   Mark Twain. **249**

"Occurrence at Owl Creek Bridge, An"
   Ambrose Bierce **255**

Oliver Twist
   Charles Dickens **261**

One Hundred Years of Solitude
   Gabriel García Márquez. **268**

"Open Window, The"
   Saki **275**

"Outcasts of Poker Flat, The"
   Bret Harte **281**

Ox-Bow Incident, The
   Walter Van Tilburg Clark **288**

Pride and Prejudice
   Jane Austen **295**

Ragged Dick; or, Street Life in New York with the Boot-Blacks
   Horatio Alger **301**

Red Badge of Courage, The
   Stephen Crane **308**

"Self-Reliance"
   Ralph Waldo Emerson **314**

Shane
   Jack Schaefer **321**

Sister Carrie
   Theodore Dreiser **327**

Sons and Lovers
   D. H. Lawrence **334**

Souls of Black Folk, The
   W. E. B. Du Bois **340**

Story Catcher, The
   Mari Sandoz. **347**

Tess of the D'Urbervilles
   Thomas Hardy **353**

Things Fall Apart
   Chinua Achebe. **360**

Thousand Pieces of Gold
   Ruthanne Lum McCunn **366**

Tom Brown's Schooldays
   Thomas Hughes **372**

Turn of the Screw, The
   Henry James **378**

Twenty Thousand Leagues under the Sea
   Jules Verne **384**

Two Years before the Mast
   Richard Henry Dana, Jr. **391**

Uncle Remus: His Songs and His Sayings
   Joel Chandler Harris **397**

Uncle Tom's Cabin or, Life among the Lowly
   Harriet Beecher Stowe **403**

Up from Slavery
   Booker T. Washington **410**

Walden
   Henry David Thoreau **416**

"Yellow Wallpaper, The"
   Charlotte Perkins Gilman. **422**

Contents by Author

Achebe, Chinua
Things Fall Apart *360*

Alcott, Louisa May
Little Women *202*

Alger, Horatio
Ragged Dick; or, Street Life in New York with the Boot-Blacks *301*

Austen, Jane
Pride and Prejudice *295*

Bierce, Ambrose
"An Occurrence at Owl Creek Bridge" . . *255*

Brontë, Charlotte
Jane Eyre *181*

Brown, Dee
Bury My Heart at Wounded Knee *74*

Brown, John
John Brown's Final Speech *188*

Carroll, Lewis
Alice's Adventures in Wonderland *28*

Clark, Walter Van Tilburg
The Ox-Bow Incident *288*

Conrad, Joseph
Heart of Darkness *145*

Crane, Stephen
The Red Badge of Courage *308*

Dana, Richard Henry, Jr.
Two Years before the Mast *391*

Dickens, Charles
Oliver Twist *261*

Douglass, Frederick
Narrative of the Life of Frederick Douglass, An American Slave *236*

Doyle, Arthur Conan
The Hound of the Baskervilles *152*

Dreiser, Theodore
Sister Carrie *327*

Du Bois, W. E. B.
The Souls of Black Folk *340*

Dumas, Alexandre
The Count of Monte Cristo *99*

Emerson, Ralph Waldo
"Self-Reliance" *314*

Faulkner, William
"Barn Burning" *41*
"The Bear" *47*

Flaubert, Gustave
Madame Bovary *209*

Gibson, William
The Miracle Worker *216*

Gilman, Charlotte Perkins
"The Yellow Wallpaper" *422*

Contents by Author

Hardy, Thomas
 Tess of the D'Urbervilles 353

Harris, Joel Chandler
 *Uncle Remus: His Songs and
 His Sayings* 397

Harte, Bret
 "The Outcasts of Poker Flat" 281

Hughes, Thomas
 Tom Brown's Schooldays 372

Hugo, Victor
 Les Misérables 223

Hunt, Irene
 Across Five Aprils 8

Ibsen, Henrik
 A Doll's House 111

Jacobs, Harriet A.
 *Incidents in the Life of a Slave Girl
 Written by Herself* 168

James, Henry
 Daisy Miller 105
 The Turn of the Screw 378

Joseph, Chief
 "I Will Fight No More Forever" 160

Kroeber, Theodora
 Ishi, Last of His Tribe 174

Lawrence, D. H.
 Sons and Lovers 334

Lincoln, Abraham
 Gettysburg Address 130

Luce, William
 The Belle of Amherst 54

Márquez, Gabriel García
 One Hundred Years of Solitude 268

de Maupassant, Guy
 "The Necklace" 244

McCunn, Ruthanne Lum
 Thousand Pieces of Gold 366

Melville, Herman
 Moby Dick 230

Mitchell, Margaret
 Gone with the Wind 137

Morrison, Toni
 Beloved 59

Neihardt, John
 Black Elk Speaks 66

Poe, Edgar Allan
 "The Cask of Amontillado" 81

Pomerance, Bernard
 The Elephant Man 118

Saki
 "The Open Window" 275

Sandburg, Carl
 Abraham Lincoln: The Prairie Years 1

Sandoz, Mari
 The Story Catcher 347

Schaefer, Jack
 Shane 321

Stowe, Harriet Beecher
 *Uncle Tom's Cabin or, Life
 among the Lowly* 403

Styron, William
 The Confessions of Nat Turner 93

Thoreau, Henry David
 "Civil Disobedience" (Resistance to
 Civil Government) 87
 Walden 416

Tolstoy, Leo
 Anna Karenina 34

Truth, Sojourner
 "Ain't I a Woman?" 22

Twain, Mark
 The Adventures of Huckleberry Finn 15
 "The Notorious Jumping Frog of
 Calaveras County" 249

Verne, Jules
 *Twenty Thousand Leagues
 under the Sea* 384

Washington, Booker T.
 Up from Slavery 410

Wharton, Edith
 Ethan Frome 125

Whitman, Walt
 Leaves of Grass 195

Photo Credits

Abraham Lincoln, photograph. AP/Wide World Photos. Reproduced by permission. —Abraham Lincoln, manuscript. —Dr. Martin Luther King, Jr., photograph. AP/Wide World Photos. Reproduced by permission. —Samuel Clemens (Mark Twain), photograph. AP/Wide World Photos. Reproduced by permission. —Jim and Huck, illustration. From *The Adventures of Huckleberry Finn* by Mark Twain. —Sojourner Truth, photograph. The Granger Collection, New York. Reproduced by permission. —Alice Pleasance Liddell and Lorina Charlotte Liddell, photograph. —Alice and the Cheshire Cat, illustration. By John Tenniel. From *Alice's Adventures in Wonderland* by Lewis Carroll. Macmillan, 1865. —Nicola Pagett as Anna Karenina, photograph. From a BBC production of *Anna Karenina* by Leo Tolstoy. © BBC Picture Archives. Reproduced by permission. —Leo Tolstoy, photograph. Corbis-Bettmann. Reproduced by permission. —Four women picking cotton, photograph. By Charles Reich. Scope Associates, Inc. Reproduced by permission. —Men with skinned deer, photograph. By Charles Reich. Scope Associates, Inc. Reproduced by permission. —William Faulkner at barn door, photograph. By Charles Reich. Scope Associates, Inc. Reproduced by permission. —Emily Dickinson, photograph. The Granger Collection, Ltd, New York. Reproduced by permission. —Toni Morrison, photograph. AP/Wide World Photos. Reproduced by permission. —Toni Morrison, photograph. AP/Wide World Photos. Reproduced by permission. —Battle of Little Bighorn, pictograph. By Amos Bad Heart Bull. The Granger Collection, New York. Reproduced by permission. —Black Elk, manuscript. Western Historical Manuscript Collection. Reproduced by permission. —Dee Brown, photograph. By Dee Brown. Reproduced by permission. —Edgar Allan Poe, photograph. AP/Wide World Photos. Reproduced by permission. —Henry David Thoreau's birthplace, illustration. By Mary Wheeler, 1897. The Granger Collection, New York. Reproduced by permission. —Henry David Thoreau, photograph. By Benjamin D. Maxham, 1856. The Granger Collection, New York. Reproduced by permission. —Nat Turner captured in the forest, engraving. The Library of Congress. —Building where Nat Turner was confined, photograph.

Dumas, Alexandre, photograph. —Roman Coliseum, photograph. AP/Wide World Photos. Reproduced by permission. —Henrik Ibsen, illustration. The Library of Congress. —World premiere production of *A Doll's House* by Henrik Ibsen, photograph. —Joseph Carey Merrick, photograph. —Joseph Carey Merrick, photograph. —Edith Wharton, seated at her desk, photograph. —Edith Wharton, photograph. —Abraham Lincoln with Union troops, photograph. AP/Wide World Photos. Reproduced by permission. —William Tecumseh Sherman, photograph. —Joseph Conrad, manuscript. Beinecke Rare Book and Manuscript Library, Yale University. —Steamship *Roi des Belges*, photograph.

Photo Credits

Thames and Hudson Ltd. —Arthur Conan Doyle, painting. UPI/Bettmann. Reproduced by permission. —Jeremy Brett as Sherlock Holmes and Edward Hardwicke as Dr. Watson, photograph. Grenada Television International Ltd. Reproduced by permission of Grenada Television International Ltd. Conway Van Gelder Ltd. for Edward Hardwicke and William Morris Agency for the Estate of Jeremy Brett. —General Oliver Howard and Chief Joseph, photograph. —Nez Percé War of 1877, map. —Ishi, photograph. —Haworth Village, home of the Brontë family, engraving. —Lyric sheet to song "Old John Brown," broadside. —Walt Whitman, photograph. The Library of Congress. —Frontispiece and title page of *Leaves of Grass*, engraving. From a daguerreotype by Gabriel Harrison. —Louisa May Alcott writing at desk. Concord Free Public Library. —Gustave Flaubert's notebooks, photograph. —View of Rouen, 1847, illustration. —Anne Bancroft and Patty Duke, photograph. Scene from the film adaptation of *The Miracle Worker* by William Gibson. Copyright 1962 Playfilm Productions, Inc. Still courtesy of MGM Consumer Products. —Eleanor Roosevelt and Helen Keller, photograph. AP/Wide World Photos. Reproduced by permission. —Victor Hugo, photograph. By Nadar. —Sperm whale in its death throes, illustration. From *The Naturalist's Library,* 1837. —Cover of sheet music for "The Fugitive's Song," lithograph. By E. W. Bouve, 1845. —Frederick Douglass, engraving. The Library of Congress. —Biltmore Estate, photograph. AP/Wide World Photos. Reproduced by permission. —Cover of *Mark Twain's Sketches,* no. 1, illustration. By Daniel Webster, 1874.

Ruined railroad bridge at Fredericksburg, Virginia. Library of Congress. —"Oliver's Reception by Fagin and the Boys," illustration. By George Cruikshank. From *Oliver Twist* by Charles Dickens. —Gabriel García Márquez, photograph. AP/Wide World Photos. Reproduced by permission. —Cover of *One Hundred Years of Solitude* by Gabriel García Márquez, illustration. Avon Books. Reproduced by permission of William Morrow & Co., Inc. —H. H. Munro (Saki), photograph. —Bret Harte, daguerreotype. —The undesirables exiled from Poker Flat, illustration. By John Keely. From "The Outcasts of Poker Flat" by Bret Harte. Creative Education, Inc. Reproduced by permission. —Hanging scene, photograph. From the film adaptation of *The Ox-Bow Incident* by Walter Van Tilburg Clark. —Eighteenth-century family life, illustration. By John Harden. —Cover of *Ragged Dick* by Horatio Alger, illustration. The Library of Congress. —Title page of *The Red Badge of Courage* by Stephen Crane, 1895. —Stephen Crane, photograph. The Library of Congress. —Ralph Waldo Emerson, illustration. —Jack Schaefer, photograph. International Portrait Gallery. Reproduced by permission. —Bob and Shane, illustration. By John McCormack. From *Shane* by Jack Schaefer. © 1954 by John McCormack. Reproduced by permission of Houghton Mifflin Company. —Drexel Boulevard in Chicago, photograph. Chicago Historical Society. Reproduced by permission. —Theodore Dreiser, photograph. International Portrait Gallery. Reproduced by permission. —Jessie Chambers, photograph. —Lawrence family, photograph. —W. E. B. Du Bois, photograph. AP/Wide World Photos. Reproduced by permission. —W. E. B. Du Bois, photograph. AP/Wide World Photos. Reproduced by permission. —Death of Crazy Horse, pictograph. By Amos Bad Heart Bull. The Granger Collection, New York. Reproduced by permission. —Conrad Nagel and Blanche Sweet, photograph. From the film adaptation of *Tess of the D'Urbervilles* by Thomas Hardy. Collection Memory Shop. —Alec and Tess, illustration. By Hubert Herkomer. From *Tess of the D'Urbervilles* by Thomas Hardy. —Chinua Achebe, photograph. By Jerry Bauer. Reproduced by permission.

Chinese peddler, photograph. Idaho State Historical Society's Library and Archives, Boise. Reproduced by permission. —Thomas Hughes, engraving. —Henry James and William James, photograph. —The giant squid, illustration. By Edouard Riou. From *Vingt mille lieues sous les mers* by Jules Verne, 1870. —Jules Verne, photograph. —Richard Henry Dana, Jr., illustration. —Joel Chandler Harris, painting. Library of Congress. —Brer Rabbit and the Tar-Baby, illustration. Atlanta Constitution. Reproduced with permission. —Harriet Beecher Stowe, photograph. —Advertisement for *Uncle Tom's Cabin* by Harriet Beecher Stowe, illustration. New York Historical Society. —Booker T. Washington, photograph. The Library of Congress. —Henry David Thoreau, photograph. By Dunshee. —Recreation of Thoreau's room at Walden, photograph. —Charlotte Perkins Gilman, photograph. Corbis-Bettmann. Reproduced by permission.

Abraham Lincoln: The Prairie Years

by
Carl Sandburg

Although born over a decade after Abraham Lincoln's death, Carl Sandburg spent a large part of his life writing about the deeds and accomplishments of this American leader. *Abraham Lincoln: The Prairie Years,* commonly referred to as simply *The Prairie Years,* was the first of several works that Sandburg would publish about his favorite personality. Because of the inclusion of myths and unsubstantiated anecdotes about Lincoln along with its more factual content, the work is perhaps most aptly identified as folk biography rather than a genuine life story of the real man.

> **THE LITERARY WORK**
>
> A biography set on the American prairie (mainly in Kentucky, Indiana, and Illinois) from 1809 to 1861; published in 1926.
>
> **SYNOPSIS**
>
> The biography chronicles the life of America's sixteenth president from his humble birth in a log cabin until his departure for the White House in 1861.

Events in History at the Time the Biography Takes Place

The legal circuit. In the early 1800s, only a handful of law schools existed, primarily in the East, but most lawyers of the period preferred learning about the law through hands-on experience rather than in a classroom. Many were taken on as apprentices by more experienced practitioners who taught them firsthand how to effectively argue a case. Lincoln, however, taught himself the law without an apprenticeship, memorizing Blackstone's *Commentaries on the Laws of England.* He also learned by heart "Greenleaf on evidence, Chitty's *Pleadings,* and Story's *Equity,* rehearsing cases aloud, analyzing some legal point from various angles until he understood the essence of the problem" (Oates, *With Malice toward None,* p. 28).

After studying on his own, Lincoln became registered by the Sangamon County Court as a man of good moral character—a necessary step to becoming a lawyer in Illinois during the 1830s. He then summoned up the courage to take his bar exam—an oral questioning by practicing attorneys on the history and technical nuances of the law. Lincoln answered the questions without a fault, received his license (September 9, 1836), and immediately took on cases.

Because of their sparse population, many counties of the day could not yet sustain a full-time judge. Back in 1789 the first Congress of the United States had adopted a system whereby state supreme court justices would complete a circuit of local county seats twice a year to hear cases. In Illinois in the early 1800s, riding the circuit of local county seats took three months at a time, so that anyone who rode the circuit twice would be gone from home for roughly six months a year. Lawyers such as Lincoln, who lived in the larger centers, could earn money by traveling with the justices to help handle the local disputes. As a lawyer, Lincoln earned part of his income by traveling the Eighth Circuit, which, in the years between 1843 and 1853, contained as many as fourteen counties. He did his most effective legal work, however, in the Supreme Court of Illinois, where he won nearly all of the 243 cases he argued, earning a reputation as a lawyer's lawyer who was always admirably prepared. Lincoln also gained a reputation for honesty, which apparently mattered even more to him than the law. "Resolve to be honest at all events," he advised young attorneys, "and if in your own judgment you cannot be an honest lawyer, resolve to be honest without being a lawyer" (Lincoln in Oates, *With Malice toward None,* p. 105).

Campaign techniques. In an age devoid of television, many of the politicians of Lincoln's era were forced to campaign vigorously at the grassroots level. Although newspapers of the time published candidates' speeches in their entirety and supported a candidate with interests similar to their own, the most common form of politicking took place on the "stump" at sites used for campaigning oratory. People from miles around would come together to hear candidates debate their position on political matters. Oftentimes, these debates would last for hours with no sign of disinterest from the crowd. Such was the climate when Lincoln decided to run for United States Senate in 1858. One of the most famous political debates ever to take place occurred between Lincoln and his Democratic adversary in the campaign, Stephen A. Douglas. Because of the immense fame that accompanied Douglas prior to the debates, many initially believed him to be the overwhelming favorite. Douglas, a long-time congressman from Illinois, had been one of the engineers of the Compromise of 1850 (which, among other provisions, admitted California to the Union as a free state and made the Fugitive Slave Act stricter than before). He had also won renown for delivering fiery speeches. However, the gangly Lincoln proved to be a formidable opponent with strengths of his own. He displayed a clever wit and an adroit oratory talent that captured listeners. In all, the two squared off at nine different locations over a fourteen-week period. Although Douglas won the election, the exposure that Lincoln garnered during these debates helped catapult him onto the national scene.

Republican party. During the 1830s, American politics revolved around two prominent parties of the day: the Whigs and the Democrats. In time, unable to bear the internal divisiveness over the

Abraham Lincoln

issue of slavery, the Whig party fell apart. Arising in its place was the Republican party.

As Republicans began to organize themselves nationally, other competing parties were gradually absorbed into its fold. By 1856 the Republicans had garnered enough support to place their first candidate for the presidency on the ballot, John C. Fremont. Unfortunately for the party, Fremont lost to Democratic candidate James Buchanan, postponing its chance to take the White House for another four years.

In the years following Fremont's defeat, Abraham Lincoln campaigned vigorously on behalf of the Republican party, helping it secure the governorship in Illinois and emerging as its party leader in the state. He hoped to run again for the Senate in the election of 1860, but instead won the nomination for president. Armed with a platform that included opposition to the extension of slavery as well as support for economic measures such as higher tariff duties, federal aid for a transcontinental railroad, and encouragement of a national banking system, Lincoln made history by going on to win the election and taking office as the first Republican president.

Personal life. As a young man, Lincoln struggled with romantic relationships. He felt insecure in the presence of women and anxious about the possibility of being rejected in love. There are stories of a romance between Lincoln and Ann Rutledge, whose father provided board for Lincoln at his tavern in the early 1830s. Lincoln and Ann did indeed become friends, but she was engaged to another man at the time and there is no evidence that their friendship ever blossomed into a romance. Lincoln met Mary Todd in 1839, married her in 1842, and had two sons with her—Robert Todd in 1843 and Edward in 1845. The marriage was, in fact, relatively satisfying to both partners, who shared a respect for as well as a need for each other that superseded their differences in temperament. (He was loving, but withdrew at times; she was described as outspoken.) The newlyweds purchased a frame house, one and a half stories high, in downtown Springfield, within walking distance from Lincoln's office. Mary Todd was from a socially prominent and visible family, and Lincoln himself thrived in the citylike atmosphere. "The prevailing notion," says biographer Reinherd Luthin, "that Lincoln was a rural type is a misconception. Despite the legends that shroud his memory, Lincoln had left the rustic life behind him ... and he never cared to go back to it" (Luthin, p. 125).

The Biography in Focus

The contents. Sandburg chronicles the life of Abraham Lincoln from the time of his birth in a log cabin until his departure in 1861 for Washington, upon taking oath as America's sixteenth president. Spread out over two volumes numbering in excess of 900 pages, the biography carefully examines the personal as well as professional aspects of his life through historical examples as well as legendary anecdotes. Volume 1 covers the period of Lincoln's life from 1809 until 1853; volume 2 resumes with 1854 and continues through his success in the election of 1860 and his departure for the White House.

Volume 1. Sandburg's biography opens with a brief discussion of Lincoln's ancestry and continues with his birth in 1809 and his family's move two years later from their one-room, dirt-floor log cabin in central Kentucky's Nolin Creek to Knob Creek, eleven miles north. Sandburg speaks of Lincoln's education here, his daily trek of four miles to learn reading and writing in a log-cabin schoolhouse. In December of 1816, the family moves again, this time across the Ohio River to Little Pigeon Creek in southwestern Indiana, where they remain for fourteen years. Lincoln's mother dies and his father remarries during this stretch, then the family moves two more times before Lincoln strikes out on his own at age twenty-one, traveling to the village of New Salem, Illinois, where he remains for the next six years.

While residing in New Salem, Lincoln begins his career in politics and the military, running in 1832 for a seat in the Illinois House of Representatives and volunteering to fight in the Black Hawk War. Although the reply to the first military order he issues in his new post is, "Go to Hell" (Sandburg, *The Prairie Years,* vol. 1, p. 155), this becomes Lincoln's first experience as a leader in a wartime situation.

LINCOLN ON RACE

Douglas baited Lincoln on the issue of race, accusing him of regarding the black as his equal and of encouraging them to flood into Illinois and cover the prairies with black settlements. Blacks, Lincoln retorted, were not his equal or that of Douglas morally and intellectually but they were equal in their right to life, liberty, and the products of their own hard work. In his June 26, 1857, speech Lincoln included himself and his political party among the whites who felt "disgust" at and opposed the idea of a mixing of the races. On July 9, though, in another debate, he declared that yes, he had always hated slavery, as much as any abolitionist. It was a terrible moral evil. "Let us," pleaded Lincoln, "discard all this quibbling about ... this race and that race and the other race being inferior," and "once more stand up declaring that all men are created equal" (Lincoln in Oates, *With Malice toward None,* p. 150). Such remarks have led the biographer Stephen B. Oates to conclude that compared to the white supremacist attitudes of others in his era, Lincoln was an enlightened thinker in respect to race.

Lincoln loses his bid for office but runs again two years later and wins. Lincoln also begins to pursue a career in law. While still fulfilling his role as a representative, he opens a law office with John T. Stuart. In the legislature, he pushes a bill relocating the capital of the state from Vandalia to Springfield and moves there himself. Lincoln continues his life as both lawyer and legislator for the next five years, winning re-election three times.

Abraham Lincoln

> As I would not be a slave, so I would not be a master. This expresses my idea of democracy. Whatever differs from this, to the extent of the difference, is no democracy.
>
> A. Lincoln

A sample of Abraham Lincoln's handwriting.

LINCOLN'S MARRIAGE TO MARY TODD

Sandburg's biography claims that Lincoln's marriage to Mary Todd almost didn't take place. On the day of the original wedding, with the bride ready and the cakes ordered, Lincoln was nowhere to be found. Even after the two reconciled and decided to try again, Lincoln was still not without his doubts. According to rumors circulating on the day of the second attempt, the son of the man Lincoln rented a room from walked in while he was getting dressed for the ceremony. "Where are you going?" the child asked inquisitively. Lincoln replied: "To Hell, I suppose" (*The Prairie Years,* vol. 1, p. 291). There is, in fact, no evidence to support this tale, though the biography presents it as fact. Actually, Lincoln, stricken with low self-confidence because the Todd family frowned on him as a marriage partner, broke off his engagement to Mary and sank into a depression. He later renewed their relationship after friends informed him of her continuing affection.

The biography dips into Lincoln's personal life, which, it says, suffers tragedy when Ann Rutledge, a red-haired beauty whom Lincoln supposedly loves, dies from a fever. Lincoln later weds Mary Todd, a Kentuckian of proud heritage, who bears their first son, Robert Todd Lincoln, on August 1, 1843. Together, the couple purchases a modest one-and-a-half-story cottage "painted white, with green blinds, and white chimneys" (*The Prairie Years,* vol. 1, p. 426) on the corner of Eighth and Jackson Streets in Springfield. It proves to be the only home they ever own. Lincoln meanwhile continues practicing law, switching partners until he settles on William H. Herndon, with whom he would remain in business until winning the presidency.

In 1845 Lincoln campaigns vigorously as the Whig candidate for Congress and wins. Less than three weeks after taking his seat in Congress, he begins to stir up controversy. After listening to his colleagues describe their views on the ongoing war with Mexico, he concludes that the aggressor in the war is President Polk and the Democratic party. On January 12, 1848, Lincoln introduces the "spot" resolution, challenging Polk to clearly define the exact point in which the United States was, as Polk claims, drawn into war. This resolution gains Lincoln enemies, but shows his political tenacity. In 1849 his term expires and he returns home to Springfield, resuming his legal career. As volume one draws to a close, Lincoln is traveling on the Eighth Circuit Court, spending months away from his wife Mary and their children.

Volume 2. The second volume of Sandburg's biography opens with the passage of the Kansas-Nebraska Act in 1854, which rekindles Lincoln's interest in politics. Returning to the stump, he makes several poignant speeches against the controversial act, engaging thousands of listeners throughout Illinois. One man whose attention is especially piqued is Stephen A. Douglas, a senator from Illinois. In various locations, the two men meet and debate before large audiences about the merits and drawbacks of the Act. These clashes precede the famous Lincoln-Douglas debates that will take place four years later.

Lincoln's return to politics spurs his desire to run for the U.S. Senate in the next election. Until then, he continues to argue cases on a regular basis, becoming one of the most famous lawyers in Illinois.

Because of Lincoln's success against Stephen Douglas in their previous debates, Lincoln easily wins his party's nomination in 1858 to challenge the "Little Giant" for a seat in the U.S. Senate. At the nominating convention he delivers his famous "house divided" speech, which outlines the inevitably destructive consequences of maintaining a nation that is half-slave and half-free. He then meets with Douglas in a series of seven highly publicized debates. The debates prove immensely successful for Lincoln, drawing crowds as high as fifteen thousand. However, the Democratically controlled legislature, which decided such races at the time, elects Douglas, fifty-four to forty-six.

Following his defeat, Lincoln begins to tour the nation with a reprise of his earlier series of eloquent speeches regarding the fate of slavery. He draws enough attention to win the Republican nomination for president. Original tallies prove doubtful, but at the conclusion of the election the count shows "Lincoln winning with 1,866,452 votes, a majority of nearly a half-million over [the Democratic candidate Stephen] Douglas, the nearest contender" (*The Prairie Years,* vol. 2, p. 374). Volume 2 of Sandburg's biography closes as Lincoln bids farewell to his home town of Springfield before assuming his new role in Washington.

Sandburg's Lincoln. Sandburg's two-volume biography includes not only fact but also fictional passages presented as fact, with dialogue, scenes, and thoughts that are invented by Sandburg. As the biographer Stephen B. Oates points out, Sandburg accepts the legendary story about Lincoln and his young friend, Ann Rutledge, being involved romantically as if it were indisputable truth and then describes him sitting by the fire after her death on a storm-swept night. "The blowing weather woke some sort of lights in him," claims Sandburg. "And he went to the door and looked out into a night of fierce tumbling wind and black horizons. And he came back saying, 'I can't bear to think of her out there alone.' And he clenched his hands, mumbling, 'The rain and the storm shan't beat on her grave'" (Sandburg in Oates, *Our Fiery Trial,* p. 102). Certainly Lincoln grew melancholy after his friend Ann Rutledge's death at the tender age of twenty-two. But just as there is no evidence that he ever loved her in the romantic sense, there is no factual basis for the sense of grief and the dialogue about the storm and her grave that Sandburg attributes to Lincoln.

KANSAS-NEBRASKA ACT

Legislation passed by the U.S. Congress in 1854 provided for the creation of the Kansas and Nebraska territories. Seeking to solve the question of slavery peacefully, the act overturned an earlier policy, the 1820 Missouri Compromise, which had admitted Missouri to the Union as a slave state and Maine as a free state and prohibited slavery from the Louisiana Purchase north of 36°30′. If it had not been overturned, the Missouri Compromise would have barred slavery from the Kansas-Nebraska territories, and so Southern slaveowners, hoping to make the territories slave states, supported the Kansas-Nebraska Act. It allowed the territories to decide the issue for themselves through popular election, but this led both pro- and antislavery forces to try and forcefully manipulate the Kansas vote in their favor, creating strife in so-called "bleeding Kansas" in the mid-1850s.

Similarly, Sandburg's biography leaves out negative remarks made by Lincoln about race in the 1858 Lincoln-Douglas debates. The biography mentions only a couple of relatively gentle comments made by Lincoln, identifying blacks as inferior. Lincoln, Sandburg admits, did say "Certainly the Negro is not our equal in color—perhaps not in other respects" (*The Prairie Years,* vol. 2, p. 131). The omission of the more definite remarks made by Lincoln about white superiority and black inferiority reflects the biography's portrayal of the folk image of Lincoln as a nearly infallible shaper of American history.

The biography also presents Lincoln's religious beliefs in a way that encourages a misunderstanding of them. As a child growing up on the prairie, Sandburg writes fondly how Lincoln was accustomed to his mother reading from the Christian Bible on a regular basis. Sandburg also notes that later, while working as an attorney with William Herndon, Lincoln "believed in God and constantly mentioned God" (*The Prairie Years*, vol. 2, p. 254). Together, these two observations suggest Lincoln was an avid member of the Christian faith. But throughout his life, Lincoln claimed no denomination and failed to become a member of any church, an avoidance that occasionally hurt him politically.

SANDBURG DESCRIBES A LINCOLN-DOUGLAS DEBATE

Douglas was sitting by, in an overcoat, with a broad-brimmed white hat, smoking a cigar. When the time came for his half-hour of reply, he slipped out of his overcoat in a hurry, stepped to the front, denied Lincoln's charges, and four times walked up to Lincoln and shook his clenched fists close to Lincoln's nose. Lincoln kept his face solemn and looked Douglas in the eye, while some men in the audience got restless, started to pull off their coats, one Republican saying, 'Let them come on.' Then Douglas branched into another subject, and quiet came.

(*The Prairie Years*, vol. 2, p. 149)

Sources. When Carl Sandburg was approached by his publisher, Alfred Harcourt, to write a children's book about Lincoln, Sandburg was overjoyed. For decades, he had been collecting Lincoln lore, and the prospect of writing about a subject that had already captured his interest seemed ideal.

To begin his research, Sandburg first referred to previously published biographies of the former president. Of these, Ida Tarbell's thorough account, originally published as a series for *McClure's* magazine in 1895-96, and William Herndon's *Lincoln: The True Story of a Great Life*, authored by Lincoln's former law partner, proved invaluable. In addition, Sandburg traveled the nation collecting rare documents and interviewing those who had personally known the head of state. By the time Sandburg began writing, he had read over a thousand books on his subject and spoken with countless witnesses.

Sandburg also called upon several of his own experiences as well. Like Lincoln, Sandburg was born and raised in a small Midwestern town and spent his youth working in a myriad of jobs. As a result, much of the book reflects the personality of its author.

Events in History at the Time the Biography Was Written

Chicago race riots. Despite Lincoln's 1862 proclamation of emancipation for all slaves in confederate territory as of January 1, 1863, and the Union's subsequent victory in the Civil War, many blacks remained in the South even though they were free to live elsewhere. However, as a result of Northern employment shortages during World War I, large numbers of African Americans began to migrate northward, eventually causing increased competition in the work force and overcrowding in urban ghettos. Overall, this migration raised the tension between blacks and whites everywhere, particularly in Chicago.

One day in July of 1919, a young black boy swimming at the local bathing beach accidentally swam into an area restricted to whites only. Upon seeing this, some white boys on the beach began pelting him with stones, resulting in the drowning of the swimmer. When several black people approached a nearby officer and demanded he arrest those responsible, the officer refused. Eventually, more rocks were thrown from both sides until the fighting began to spread throughout the city. At the end of three days, twenty blacks and fourteen whites lay dead and several houses of blacks had been burned.

During these race riots, Sandburg was working as a journalist for the Chicago *Daily News*. In response to the riots, he decided to do a series of articles on the subject of racial strife in Chicago as well as the rest of the nation. The result was what some critics believe to be his best reporting ever, introducing him to the subject of racial strife, which he would later discuss in *The Prairie Years*.

Reviews of Sandburg's book. When *The Prairie Years* was finally published in 1926, it entered the literary world with mixed reviews. Some, such as the critic Edmund Wilson, attacked the work viciously on the ground that it was over-idealized. "There are moments when one is tempted to feel that the cruelest thing that has happened to Lincoln since he was shot by Booth has been to fall into the hands of Carl Sandburg," said the critic (Wilson in Callahan, p. 132). Others went the opposite route, praising Sandburg's biography as a masterpiece that managed to do justice to its subject. Still others sought the middle ground, complimenting the work for its brilliant prose and its content, but finding it to be sometimes invalid as historical biography. Sandburg himself said, "Among the biographers, I am a first-rate poet. And among the poets, a good biographer" (Sandburg in Callahan, p. 135).

A curious parallel. Because Lincoln was one of the greatest presidents in American history, many of his successors sought to invoke his image in the vain hope that some of the reverence that accompanied his name would enhance their public image. None were able to do so as successfully as Franklin Delano Roosevelt.

Upon first being elected president in 1932, Roosevelt assumed his role in an era unlike any the country had ever seen. After the stock market crash of 1929, unemployment was at a record high and the country's mood was grim. In response to this crisis, F.D.R. initiated bold new reforms that required the country's backing in order to prove effective. To gain this support, he drew parallels to the time of Lincoln, enlisting the aid of Carl Sandburg to his cause.

Because of the notoriety Sandburg had gained following the 1926 publication of *The Prairie Years,* many now linked his name inextricably with Lincoln's. By throwing his support behind F.D.R. in a series of campaign speeches and other writings, Sandburg brought his association with Lincoln into the political arena of the day. He lent the comparison between Lincoln and Roosevelt a sense of validity.

Nearly a decade later, Roosevelt called upon Sandburg once again. The president had been continually championed in Sandburg's syndicated newspaper column and through various speaking engagements, but Roosevelt once again needed Sandburg's talents on the stump. World War II was raging in Europe and American involvement seemed imminent. In order to gain support for F.D.R.'s policies, Sandburg made a series of speeches in which he compared the current state of history to the time when Lincoln was at the helm, describing F.D.R.'s actions as similar to ones Honest Abe would have taken.

Throughout his four terms as president, Franklin Delano Roosevelt invoked the image of Lincoln repeatedly. Without the assistance of America's Lincoln expert, Carl Sandburg, his efforts to compare his own presidency to that of the fallen leader might have been less successful.

For More Information

Callahan, North. *Carl Sandburg: His Life and Works.* University Park: Pennsylvania State University Press, 1987.

Friedman, Lawrence M. *A History of American Law.* 2nd ed. New York: Simon & Schuster, 1985.

Jones, Alfred Haworth. *Roosevelt's Image Brokers.* Port Washington, N.Y.: National University Publications, 1974.

Luthin, Reinhard H. *The Real Abraham Lincoln.* Englewood Cliffs, N.J.: Prentice-Hall, 1960.

Oates, Stephen B. *Our Fiery Trial: Abraham Lincoln, John Brown, and the Civil War Era.* Amherst: University of Massachusetts Press, 1979.

Oates, Stephen B. *With Malice toward None.* New York: Harper & Row, 1977.

Sandburg, Carl. *Abraham Lincoln: The Prairie Years.* 2 vols. New York: Harcourt, Brace & Company, 1926.

Across Five Aprils

by
Irene Hunt

Born in 1907, Irene Hunt lived in southern Illinois for most of her life. A number of her ancestors had lived in the region during the Civil War. Her grandfather, who was nine years old when the war began, told her many vivid stories about his childhood during this period. These stories, along with old family letters and records, provided part of the inspiration for her 1964 novel, *Across Five Aprils*. Its plot focuses on the experiences of one southern Illinois family during the Civil War. Though the story takes place in the 1860s, there are a number of similarities between its events and those that occurred in the 1960s, when the book was written.

Events in History at the Time the Novel Takes Place

Southern Illinois and its ties to the South. In 1861 Illinois was inhabited primarily by farm families such as the Creightons of *Across Five Aprils*. Illinois was one of the nation's "free" states, which meant that slavery was prohibited there. Even so, significant numbers of Illinois residents shared the racist attitudes held by many of their slaveholding neighbors to the south. State policy reflected these racist attitudes. The Illinois state constitution of 1848, for example, denied all blacks the right to vote, hold public office, or serve in the militia. In 1853 a bill was passed in the state legislature that prohibited free blacks from moving to the state, thus limiting the number of blacks in Illinois. The new law was triggered by white residents who feared that blacks

> **THE LITERARY WORK**
> A novel set in southern Illinois from 1861 to 1865; published in 1964.
>
> **SYNOPSIS**
> A young boy who has brothers fighting on both sides of the Civil War matures greatly during the years of conflict between the states.

would intermarry with white citizens, make what they believed to be unfair demands for social and political equality, and take jobs away from whites.

The southern part of Illinois in particular had a number of ties to the states where slavery was permitted. Illinois was bordered on its southern tip by two slave states, Missouri and Kentucky. Thousands of southern Illinois residents had originally come from these and other Southern states or had parents who had done so. This factor is illustrated in *Across Five Aprils;* the protagonist's mother, Ellen, had grown up in Kentucky, where most of her family continued to live.

In addition to family ties, southern Illinois had economic ties to the South. The region's farmers frequently sent their goods south along the Mississippi River, and they often traded Illinois products such as corn for Southern crops like cotton. Primarily an agricultural region, southern Illinois also shared with farmers in the South a distrust of northeastern commercial interests. Northern capitalists, or "Yankees," supported measures such as high tariffs on imports, which benefited their businesses but made prices on many items higher for farmers and everyone else. The term "Yankee," in fact, was considered an insult in southern Illinois. Because they shared similar views, many people in southern Illinois felt sympathetic toward the South before the Civil War.

Civil War in southern Illinois. In 1860 and 1861, eleven states seceded from the Union: North Carolina, South Carolina, Georgia, Alabama, Mississippi, Louisiana, Texas, Florida, Arkansas, Tennessee, and Virginia. This development sparked a fierce debate in the other slave states such as Missouri and Kentucky—and even in southern Illinois—over whether to secede from the Union and join the newly formed Confederacy. On January 31, 1861, one Illinois newspaper, the *Salem Advocate,* spoke of the possible secession of the southern part of the state. A public meeting in Pope County, in southern Illinois, endorsed secession. Ultimately, however, the majority of people in Illinois rejected the idea. A desire to remain in the Union prevailed.

Still, not everyone in Illinois agreed with the many Northerners who claimed that war was necessary to force their Southern neighbors back into the Union. Most of the state's whites, uninterested in improving the lives of blacks, disagreed with the abolitionists who insisted that it was time to fight for the freedom of black slaves. In Cairo, a community in southern Illinois, the *City Gazette* of December 6, 1860, advised readers to let South Carolina secede peacefully and admitted that the area's sympathies were mainly with the South.

When war finally broke out in April 1861, however, feelings of loyalty to the Union overcame the strong Southern sympathies of many of the state's residents. They had gradually come to fear that if the Union were dissolved into two separate nations, it might very well continue to break down into innumerable smaller confederacies. The United States of America would thus be replaced by a group of small, weak, and relatively vulnerable countries. The loyalty of the people of southern Illinois to the Union cause continued to be doubted by numerous people. In reality, however, the region sent thousands of local soldiers to fight for the North. A great many, like Tom and Eb in *Across Five Aprils,* were volunteers. Despite their ties to the South, the residents of southern Illinois were willing to fight for the preservation of the Union.

Life on the home front. Approximately 197,000 Illinois men joined the Union army over the course of the Civil War. The absence of so many sons, brothers, and husbands had a profound effect on families. On the great number of farms across Illinois, the most visible consequence of their departure was more work for those left at home. Since there was so much to do to keep a farm running, young men were an important source of labor for any family, and women and children had to assume many extra farm responsibilities as well. In *Across Five Aprils,* the boy Jethro works harder during the Civil War years than he ever had before.

A LETTER HOME

The following is an excerpt from a letter written by Lieutenant Samuel Edward Nichols of the Union army to his family in the North on October 17, 1862:

Dear Brother Fayette: Your letter ... was welcome, very so. Write often. Do not limit the number of your letters to that of mine ... do not mind if I do not respond as frequently as you write, and urge upon the folks the necessity of keeping me posted in all matters about home. All the matters, those even of minor importance; for everything about home multiplies in interest and in the same ratio as the distance from home and the time since separation have increased.... I always loved my home.... Some of my fondest dreams have for their location the sloping fields and rude woodland of my father's farm. But place is not all that constitutes happiness. No; it is the hearts that cluster around that place. I feel that at all times and through every circumstance, whether fortunate or adverse, the hearts which constitute our father's household in their beatings are ever true to those of their number who are so unfortunate as to be absent. I wish I could be with you at Thanksgiving time ... Write often ... Your affectionate Brother, Saml. E. Nichols.

(Nichols in Tapert, pp. 97-100)

The psychological and emotional impact of the Civil War on those left behind was less visible. Obviously families were quite affected by the absence of loved ones. Letters and journals from these years expressed great anxiety for the well-being of family members in the army. Those at home placed a great deal of importance on receiving letters on a regular basis from soldiers in the family. At the time letters were the only real form of long distance communication, and a great deal of feeling often went into them. Reg-

Across Five Aprils

ular mail kept those at home informed of the safety and health of their soldier relatives, and often included vivid accounts of various battles and the entire experience of war.

Some families were in the difficult position of having loved ones on both sides of the war. This is true of the Creightons in *Across Five Aprils*; one son chooses to join the Confederate army while the others fight for the Union. Such divisions were not limited to the border states and surrounding areas. For example, Connecticut native Katherine Hubbell married a man from Georgia in 1860. When the war came, her brother enlisted with the Union, while her husband and his four brothers fought for the Confederacy. Conflicting loyalties like these tore families apart throughout the war.

Many Americans in both the North and the South expected the Civil War to be brief, with quick victory for their side. In reality, it dragged on for four long years and became the bloodiest conflict in the nation's history. There were heavy casualties on both sides. Some 620,000 Americans never returned home, the victims of battle, prison camp, wounds, or disease. Thus, hundreds of thousands of families were changed forever by the Civil War.

The Novel in Focus

The plot. The novel opens in southern Illinois on an April day in 1861. Nine-year-old Jethro Creighton and his mother, Ellen, are working together out in the field. The possibility of civil war has been the main topic of conversation in their family lately. That night Ellen's nephew from Kentucky, Wilse, arrives at the farm unexpectedly for a visit. Over dinner, friendly conversation turns into a heated argument between Wilse and Jethro's brother Bill—who both sympathize with the South—and the rest of the family, who support the North. Later that night, they learn that Confederate forces have fired on Fort Sumter, South Carolina, an attack that marks the beginning of the Civil War.

That summer, patriotic enthusiasm for the war runs high. Many believe that it will be a short, easy victory for the North. With news of the Union defeat at Bull Run, Virginia, however, confidence diminishes. Soon Jethro's brother Tom and his cousin Eb leave home to fight for the Union. Jethro's favorite brother, Bill, has less enthusiasm for the war. He thinks deeply for weeks about what course of action he should take. Finally, he decides he cannot fight for the North and leaves home.

In February 1862 the North experiences its first real victory, a triumph at Fort Henry, Tennessee. The Creightons receive a letter from Tom. He has learned that serving as a soldier and fighting a war are not the glorious experiences he had expected. Jethro's brother John leaves to join the Union army, as does Shadrach Yale, a close family friend of the Creightons who is in love with Jethro's sister, Jenny.

One day in March, ten-year-old Jethro is entrusted with a great responsibility. He drives the family's cart fifteen miles away to the nearest town, Newton, to buy various supplies. At the general store, the young boy is questioned by a local man named Wortman as to his feelings about his brother Bill's Confederate sympathies. Jethro replies that Bill is still one of his favorite people in the world, which evokes a scornful and angry response from Wortman. That night, a local man named Budrow joins Jethro for part of the ride home, for he suspects that Wortman might try to make trouble for the boy. His suspicions prove true, but Budrow and Jethro and the supply-stocked cart remain safe.

When Jethro gets home and tells the story of his day, his parents grow worried. Jethro's father, Matt, who has been feeling somewhat ill, suffers a heart attack the next morning. With his father greatly weakened and his brothers away at war, young Jethro assumes many of the adult chores. One night a bundle of whips—which the family recognizes as a local symbol indicating a threat—and an ominous note are thrown on the Creightons' doorstep. They suspect the troublemakers are Wortman and other overzealous patriots. For weeks, the family members guard their property, fearful of an attack. After a month in which nothing happens, they become lax in their watchfulness. The Creightons awaken one night to witness their barn being destroyed by fire, but neighbors later help them raise a new barn. Soon afterward the Creightons learn that Tom has been killed.

By 1863 the war has dragged on so long that many are disillusioned; soldiers are deserting by the hundreds. Federal registrars arrive at the farm and inform the Creightons that cousin Eb has deserted; they then search the house for him. Shortly after this, Jethro finds Eb in the woods. He is ragged, filthy, gaunt, and desperate-looking. Jethro doesn't know whether to turn him in out of loyalty to the Union or to help him escape out of loyalty to his cousin. Confused, he writes a letter to President Lincoln. He receives a letter back informing him that a new policy implemented by the Union Army provides for limited forgiveness for deserters. Eb is thus able to return to the army with little punishment.

After May 1863, the family learns that their friend Shadrach has been seriously wounded at the Battle of Gettysburg, in Pennsylvania. Deeply concerned, Jenny travels to Washington, D.C., to see him. He gradually begins to recover, and the pair are wed. The Union captures Atlanta and Richmond from the Confederate forces and goes on to win the war. Lee surrenders to Grant in April of 1865. The news that President Lincoln has been assassinated, an event that saddens Jethro deeply, interrupts the victory celebrations. A degree of happiness returns, however, when Shadrach and Jenny come home.

Sympathy with the South. The main character of *Across Five Aprils*, the young boy Jethro, is mostly surrounded by people who strongly support the Union. Their main concern is to prevent the nation from splitting apart. Of secondary concern was a desire to prevent the spread of slavery into other states. For abolitionists, this desire was inspired by their moral outrage over the enslavement of fellow human beings. For the majority of Northerners, however, opposition to slavery stemmed from an economic concern. White farmers in Northern states were believed to be unable to successfully compete against slaveholders, whose operating costs were low because they employed slave labor. Many Northerners thus opposed slavery because they did not want to see what they believed to be an unfair economic system spread beyond the Southern states.

Meanwhile, Southerners saw their slaves as property and believed that people in the North had no right to interfere with their free possession of that property. They felt their constitutional rights were in danger. When the Southern states seceded, they broke away from a country in which they felt themselves oppressed. They believed they were fighting for independence from tyranny and subjugation, just as the American colonists had once fought for their independence from the domination of England.

Several characters in *Across Five Aprils* question the absolute righteousness of the Northern cause. When Ellen Creighton's nephew Wilse comes to visit from Kentucky, he makes arguments that reflect the viewpoint of the South. In so doing, he questions some of the Northern motivations for fighting the war. He disparages the North, contending that "a half of the country has growed rich ... but still jealous and fearful that the other half is apt to find good fortune too" (Hunt, *Across Five Aprils*, p. 33). Wilse further questions the underlying feelings of Northern abolitionists: "I'll ask you this: if tomorrow every slave in the South had his freedom and come up North, would yore abolitionists git the crocodile tears sloshed out of their eyes so they could take the black man by the hand? Would they say ... we want you to come to our churches and yore children to come to our schools...?" (*Across Five Aprils*, p. 35). In this passage, Wilse shares his view of the hypocrisy of Northerners who are opposed to the way blacks are treated in the South, yet would probably treat them little better if given an opportunity. Jethro's brother Bill insists that human nature is no purer in the North than in the South. Bill does not support slavery, but he decides that he cannot fight against the South, which he believes has been wronged by the North. Overall, *Across Five Aprils* is told from the perspective of Northerners. At the same time, arguments are presented that help explain their mixed motivations as well as those of Southerners. Neither side emerges as absolutely pure.

Sources. The story of *Across Five Aprils* was drawn from a number of different sources. Descriptions of the Civil War and associated events and attitudes were based upon scholarly research that utilized many books and written works about that time period. The story of the Creighton family was largely taken from the letters and records of Irene Hunt's own ancestors, who lived in southern Illinois during the war. Many of the situations related in the book were suggested to her by incidents that actually happened. Moreover, the author's grandfather, who was nine years old in 1861, just as Jethro is in the novel, told his granddaughter many detailed stories about the hardships and the triumphs of the war years. Aspects of the conflict that the author was unable to glean from family stories or historical sources were left out of her narrative. For example, Hunt did not name the exact date of the story's opening because she could not determine how long it would have taken for news of the first Southern shots fired on Fort Sumter, South Carolina, to reach a farm in southern Illinois. Mentioned throughout the book is another problematic detail: the baking of bread in the ashes of the family fireplace. Hunt was never quite sure how this was actually done and therefore never fully describes the process. She does incorporate, however, her grandfather's descriptions of that bread as the sweetest he had ever tasted. On the whole, *Across Five Aprils* is a novel

Across Five Aprils

Dr. Martin Luther King, Jr., just after being hit by a rock during a civil rights march through Chicago in August, 1966.

that is drawn from a rich combination of scholarly and personal resources.

Events in History at the Time the Novel Was Written

The Northern civil rights movement. During the Civil War, the main concern of people in Illinois and the rest of the North was to keep the Union from disintegrating. For many, the status of blacks in America was a secondary concern. Racism was common both in the South, where blacks were held in slavery, and in the North, where laws limiting the rights of free blacks were in place. By the 1960s, however, when *Across Five Aprils* was written, the rights of black people had become a central issue across the nation.

In the 1950s and early 1960s, the civil rights movement focused on attacking the most blatant denials of civil rights to blacks in the South, such as the right to vote. Before long, however, attention began to turn to the social and economic inequalities that existed for blacks in the North. Of particular concern were the inner-city ghettos, where impoverished blacks had lived for generations. These people were often forced by circumstances to live in rat-infested, overcrowded tenements and to send their children to inadequate schools. Another problem faced by blacks of every social class in the North was housing discrimination. Many whites who had no desire for black neighbors prevented blacks from moving into their neighborhoods.

The deep-seated prejudice that Northern whites felt for blacks showed itself in Chicago, Illinois, in the summer of 1966. There, Martin Luther King, Jr., led peaceful demonstrations into white neighborhoods to protest residential segregation. Whites responded to the marches with angry jeers and occasional violence. Rocks were thrown, and one hit King in the head, but he managed to continue walking. Thousands of whites tried to block the marches at different points in their routes or to directly assail the protesters. Police helped break up the mobs of whites, however.

These civil rights protests brought some gains to blacks. In the fight against housing discrimination in Chicago, for example, city officials agreed to intensify enforcement of the city's open-housing law and to provide low-cost public housing. Financial leaders promised to give mortgages on a nonracial basis. However, the civil rights movement in the North ultimately did little to change the extensive, deep-seated poverty experienced by blacks in urban centers like Chicago.

Vietnam. The Civil War divided the entire nation into two opposing sides, the North and the South. The Vietnam War, fought about a century later, in the 1960s, was a conflict that was fought on foreign ground. Still, it divided Americans as well. Although debate about American involvement in Vietnam never fully tore apart the country, it did split the population, and even some families, into opposing groups. On one side were those who supported the war as an essential part of the global struggle against communism. They believed that if the United States withdrew support from the anticommunist forces in Vietnam, the "domino theory" might become a reality: victorious communists would be encouraged to target their aggression at a widening circle of nations that would eventually fall into their sphere of power. Supporters of the war feared that the United States would eventually be left alone and vulnerable in a communist-dominated world. Furthermore, those in favor of the war were confident in American military power. If the United States continued to fight in Vietnam, they argued, eventual triumph would be inevitable.

> **DESERTION IN VIETNAM**
>
> Many American soldiers in both the North and the South deserted from the army during the Civil War. Even more deserted during the Vietnam War, for various reasons. The dangers soldiers faced in the war were too great for many of them to bear. The atrocities they saw there, and sometimes participated in, also drove many away. Innocent Vietnamese people were killed, women were raped, and whole villages full of civilians were destroyed. After seeing such horrors, some soldiers decided they could no longer fight. They abandoned their posts and made their way to cities like Saigon, where they hid in the back streets. Some soldiers left Vietnam on temporary leave and never returned. In all, 500,000 American soldiers deserted from Vietnam.

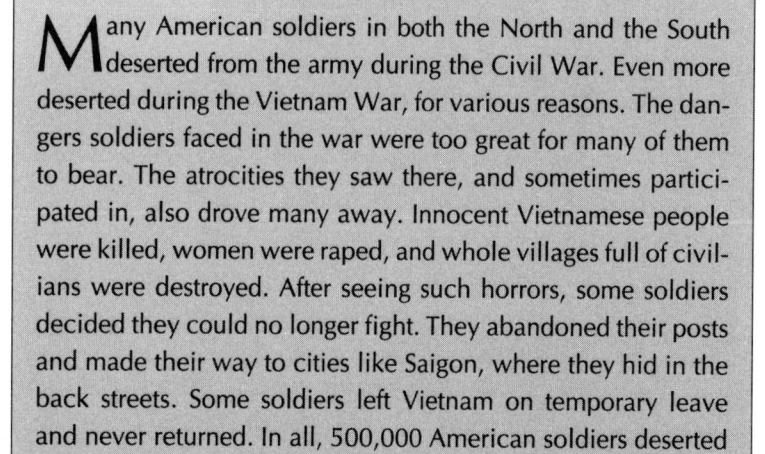

On the other side of the issue were those who opposed the war. Some believed that the anticommunist Vietnamese forces were corrupt and authoritarian in nature, and that for this reason, the United States should not support them. Critics also questioned the "domino theory," arguing

Across Five Aprils

that American troops were involved in a war that posed no compelling threat to the nation's security. Finally, many opponents of the war believed that it was diverting attention from more urgent problems at home. The number of opponents to the war increased throughout the 1960s and early 1970s in the United States. Antiwar pressure on the government eventually contributed to an official decision to withdraw American troops from Vietnam in 1975.

Reviews. *Across Five Aprils* has been called one of the finest books in the field of literature for young people. The object of much critical praise, it was described by John K. Bettersworth in the *New York Times Book Review* as "an intriguing and beautifully written book—a prize to those who take the time to read it, whatever their ages" (Bettersworth, pp. 8, 10). *The Booklist and Subscription Books Bulletin* praised the book as well, commenting that Irene Hunt had not only created a superb narrative with lifelike characters but had also reconstructed a vital piece of history. In 1965 the novel received the American Notable Book Award and the Clara Ingram Judson Award. It was also the sole runner-up for a Newbery Medal, the prize given to the most outstanding contribution to children's literature of the preceding year. The book was further honored in 1966 with the Lewis Carroll Shelf Award, which is given to books considered worthy to sit on a shelf next to *Alice in Wonderland* by a committee of librarians, teachers, parents, and writers. Singled out by the author as one of her own favorites, *Across Five Aprils* has remained popular with international as well as American readers. Since its initial release, the novel has been published in Canada, England, Italy, and South Africa.

For More Information

Bettersworth, John K. *New York Times Book Review* (May 10, 1964): 8, 10.

Hicken, Victor. *Illinois in the Civil War.* Chicago: University of Illinois Press, 1991.

Herring, George C. *America's Longest War: The United States and Vietnam, 1950-1975.* New York: John Wiley & Sons, 1979.

Hunt, Irene. *Across Five Aprils.* Chicago: Follett, 1964.

McPherson, James M. *What They Fought For: 1861-1865.* Baton Rouge: Louisiana State University Press, 1994.

Ralph, James R., Jr. *Northern Protest: Martin Luther King, Jr., Chicago, and the Civil Rights Movement.* Cambridge, Mass.: Harvard University Press, 1993.

Tapert, Annette, ed. *The Brothers' War: Civil War Letters to Their Loved Ones from the Blue and Gray.* New York: Random House, 1988.

The Adventures of Huckleberry Finn

by
Mark Twain

Samuel Clemens, who later took the pen name Mark Twain, spent his childhood in Hannibal, Missouri (model for the fictional town St. Petersburg), in the 1830s and '40s. The region had grown rapidly since the defeat of its Indian tribes in the War of 1812, becoming a destination of many Southerners, who moved there with their slaves. As the century progressed, events unfolded that would greatly affect the lives of both the new and old inhabitants of Missouri. Twain's *Huckleberry Finn* especially reflects the impact of these events on black-white relations in the region.

Events in History at the Time the Novel Takes Place

Missouri Compromise and slavery. The issue of slavery caused tension in Congress that surfaced in battles over the admission of new states. The Union was carefully balanced in 1820, comprised of twelve free states and twelve slave states. To maintain this balance, Congress worked out a compromise that year by admitting Maine as a free state and accepting Missouri's plan to enter as a slave state. Included in the compromise was a clause permitting Missouri slaveowners to recover any of their slaves who fled to nearby free states. Missouri tried also to exclude free blacks and mulattos from the state, but Congress would not permit such exclusions. Finally in 1821 Missouri abandoned its original plan and was admitted to the Union as a slave state.

> **THE LITERARY WORK**
> A novel set in St. Petersburg, Missouri, about 1840; published in 1885.
>
> **SYNOPSIS**
> A boy and a slave flee their hometown, heading down the Mississippi River toward the Ohio River and freedom.

The South, meanwhile, experienced success in agriculture. Cotton had replaced tobacco, rice, and indigo as its most profitable crop. By 1820 the United States had become the largest cotton producer in the world. Cotton would remain "king" from 1820 to 1860, with plantations springing up and spreading across the lower South through Alabama, Mississippi, and Louisiana. In need of slaves for field labor, the new farms of the lower South looked to upper South areas such as Missouri as a source, and owners here were sometimes tempted to accept the high prices offered for their slaves. In *The Adventures of Huckleberry Finn*, for example, Miss Watson, a Missouri slaveholder, is offered the enticing sum of $800 for her slave Jim by a buyer down in Louisiana.

Yet there also was a small but growing movement to abolish slavery elsewhere in the nation during these decades. The movement began in the North with the publication of the newspaper *The Liberator*. Other writings such as the

Huckleberry Finn

1845 *Narrative of the Life of Frederick Douglass* (also covered in *Literature and Its Times*) helped inspire resistance to and escape from the plantation system as well. In 1847 Missouri passed a law making it a crime to teach blacks how to read, largely to prevent them from being exposed to such writings.

The Underground Railroad. Northernmost among slave states in its region, Missouri was located close to a number of free states. In nearby Illinois and Indiana were escape paths used by runaway slaves. Known as the Underground Railroad, these paths were in fact located above ground and were part not of a railroad but of a network of houses and aid stations that supplied safe refuge to runaways along escape routes to the North and Canada. Most of these routes began at the Ohio River and cut northward across Indiana and Ohio territory.

The Mississippi River ran along the eastern border of Missouri, where it coursed southward to meet the Ohio River, which then coursed northward into free territory. The town Cairo was located at the rivers' intersection. For a slave fleeing from bondage in Missouri, Cairo lay at the start of the most promising escape path to freedom. The Ohio River led from there into the territory of Ohio, which had far more stations on the Underground Railroad than any other area in the Union.

Mark Twain

IF A SOUTHERNER HELPED A RUNAWAY

In those old slave holding days the whole community was agreed as to one thing, the awful sacredness of slave property. To help steal a horse or a cow was a low crime, but to help a hunted slave … was a much baser crime, & carried with it a stain, a moral smirch which nothing could wipe away.

(Twain, Explanatory Notes in *The Adventures of Huckleberry Finn*, p. 385)

Fugitive slave laws. Only a small fraction of fugitive or runaway slaves ever reached freedom, and those who assisted them risked punishment. A Fugitive Slave Act of 1793 stipulated a fine of $500 to anyone who helped a runaway. Increasing the penalty, the Fugitive Slave Act of 1850 raised the fine to $1000 to anyone who harbored or helped a runaway, added a six-month prison term, and charged such an accomplice another $1000 to be paid to the owner for damages caused by the absence of his or her slave.

Minstrel shows. Southerners convinced themselves that their slaves were content in bondage, and a performing art of the era—minstrel theater—encouraged them in this self-deception. The first minstrel show, staged in 1843, featured white male actors who blackened their faces with burnt cork, then sang, dance, and told jokes to a white audience. The early shows represented a variety of slaves and included a degree of realism, but performers soon dropped any attempt at honest representation. Their shows came to feature one stereotype: a lazy, loud-mouthed, flashily dressed black whose thick lips, said Twain, were painted to resemble slices of a ripe watermelon. The showman used poor grammar and was forever drinking gin, munching on chicken, and laughing his way through life. Performed across the country, minstrel shows spread this one image of the wide-grinning black without depth. They were orchestrated to provoke peals of laughter, and Twain found the shows musically superb. "It seems to me," he wrote, "that to the elevated mind and the sensitive spirit … the Negro show … [is] a standard and a summit … other forms of musical art may not hope to reach" (Twain in DeVoto, p. 110). That Twain regarded it primarily as entertainment, not as representative of real life, is clear from the depth of his black character Jim in *Huckleberry Finn*. It is a depth that surprises Jim's good-natured white companion in the novel, Huck. Taken aback by Jim's sensitivity, Huck reconsiders his own convictions.

> I do believe he cared just as much for his people as white folks does for theirn. It don't seem natural, but I reckon it's so.
> (Twain, *The Adventures of Huckleberry Finn*, p. 201)

The Mississippi as a thoroughfare. Lectures, circuses, and minstrel shows were virtually the only forms of entertainment that reached Southern small towns in the 1830s and '40s. Often the actors arrived on river craft. Traveling along the Mississippi in the early 1800s was a hodgepodge of vessels—steamboats, barges, rafts, canoes, and scows. Disasters were common. Besides the threat of a craft being consumed by fire, an especial hazard was presented by snags. These were great trees lodged firmly in the river. Hidden from sight, they gave no warning to oncoming voyagers. Vessels would crash and perhaps careen over, upsetting their own stoves, candles, and lamps, which started fires. Rescue was not always nearby. At times wide, the Mississippi measures 4,470 feet where it meets the Ohio River. Such a broad expanse made it possible in the 1830s and '40s for a river craft to travel for long stretches without encountering many other vessels, as Huck's raft did on its journey toward the juncture of the Mississippi and Ohio rivers.

The Novel in Focus

The plot. Told in first person, from Huckleberry Finn's point of view, the novel follows fourteen-year-old Huck in his escape from St. Petersburg, Missouri. He flees a widow who intends to make a civilized young man out of him and a drunken father who threatens to kill him. Soon after his escape, Huck encounters Jim, a slave escaping from St. Petersburg to avoid being sold farther south. The two float downstream on a raft, becoming intimate friends and encountering an assortment of humanity, from poor whites to rich gentlefolk, from con artists to middle-class townspeople.

On one occasion, Huck is adopted by a well-to-do family with a son about his own age who is killed in a family feud.

Sickened by the feud, Huck resumes his journey downriver with Jim. They miss their destination, Cairo, in the fog, then encounter two con men who claim to be royalty. The so-called "king" and "duke" try their hand at various scams, pretending to be actors, preachers, and the English uncles of three girls whose guardian has died and bequeathed them money.

The con men draw Huck into their schemes until he grows disgusted with their dishonesty. Huck lies too, telling stories of one kind or another throughout the novel, but never for greed or personal gain; one of the con men, on the other hand, resorts to betraying his rescuers by turning in Jim to collect the cash reward offered for the runaway slave's capture. Once caught, Jim is held prisoner at the Phelps farm. Huck rushes there to free him and encounters his old friend Tom Sawyer. The two set out to rescue Jim, but in the end he gains his freedom in a manner that neither he nor Huck ever expected. His owner, Miss Watson, has died and left a will that sets him free.

FOLK PUNISHMENTS IN NINETEENTH CENTURY AMERICA

Staying with the Grangerfords, a rich family that owns many farms and over a hundred slaves, Huck witnesses a blood feud against the Shepherdsons. A feud, he learns, happens when "a man has a quarrel with another man, and kills *him*, then that other man's brother kills him; then the other brothers, on both sides, goes for one another; then the *cousins* chip in—and by and by everybody's killed off" (*The Adventures of Huckleberry Finn*, p. 146). Feuds were common occurrences in the 1800s, especially in Kentucky, a state that bordered Missouri and site of the well-known Hatfield/McCoy feud. Another popular form of punishment was tarring and feathering, a fate that befalls two characters in the novel. Taking the law into its own hands, an angry mob would smear hot tar and shake feathers over its victim, a procedure that could cause serious injury, or even death.

The way Huck thinks. *Huckleberry Finn* was revolutionary for its time, in part because Twain wrote the way various Southern people talked, in dialects that both added realism and exposed prejudices. Huck's words reveal some of the prejudices:

> [Jim] was most always right; he had an uncommon level head for a nigger.

Huckleberry Finn

Jim disguising Huck in a dress.

I see it warn't no use wasting words—you can't learn a nigger to argue. So I quit.

Jim had a wonderful level head, for a nigger: he could most always start a good plan when you wanted one.
(*The Adventures of Huckleberry Finn*, pp. 93, 98, and 107)

Tom Sawyer concocts a mixed-up plan to help Jim escape. Though Jim sees no sense in the plan, the boys get him to go along with it because "he allowed we was white folks and knowed better than him" (*Adventures of Huckleberry Finn*, p. 309). Huck does not dispute such racist generalizations. Yet he acts according to his heart rather than the ideas put into his head by societal mores.

The triumph of the novel, and of Huck's character, is that though he is brought up with prejudices, he looks beyond them and reaches his own conclusions. Yet along the way, Huck is greatly troubled by the fact that his opinion differs from that of the society in which he was raised. In Huck's environment, slavery was not wrong but stealing property (slaves) certainly was. While Jim looks forward eagerly to being free, Huck is deeply troubled by the fact that he is to blame for it. He cannot get this out of his conscience.

It would get all around, that Huck Finn helped a nigger to get his freedom; and if I was to ever see anybody from that town again, I'd be ready to get down and lick his boots for shame.
(*The Adventures of Huckleberry Finn*, p. 268)

TWAIN'S MODELS FOR THE CHARACTERS IN *HUCKLEBERRY FINN*

Fictional Name	Real-life Source
St. Petersburg	Hannibal—Twain's hometown
Jackson's Island	Glassock's Island—located near Hannibal
Phelps's farm	Twain's uncle John Quarles's farm
Huckleberry Finn	Tom Blankenship—Twain's boyhood friend
Jim	Uncle Dan'l—a slave on John Quarles's farm
Pap Finn	Jimmy Finn—a town drunk
Aunt Polly	Jane Lampton Clemens—Twain's mother
Miss Watson	Mary Ann Newcomb—Twain's schoolteacher

Huck struggles over whether he should write to Jim's owner and tell her where he is. But then he reflects back on the journey downstream, seeing Jim and himself laughing, singing, and talking. Huck remembers his black companion standing his own watch and then Huck's too so that the fourteen-year-old boy can go on sleeping. In the end, he dismisses the idea of alerting Jim's owner, and this is no small decision, for Huck is convinced that he shall go to hell for failing to turn in the runaway. But he has traveled with Jim long enough to see beneath the minstrel-show stereotype and discover the complexities in the black man's character.

Early in the journey, Jim rebukes Huck for a practical joke the boy plays on the runaway. A frightening fog had separated them from each other in the dead of night. His anxious dread turning to joy, Huck finally finds Jim, who is fast asleep. When he awakens, the boy tries to fool him into believing the whole nasty experience never really happened and was only a dream. But Jim catches on and upbraids Huck. "All you wuz thinkin 'bout," he says, "wuz how you could make a fool uv ole Jim wid a lie." Pointing to some rubbish on the raft, he declares "dat truck dah is trash; en trash is what people is dat puts dirt on de head er dey fren's en makes 'em ashamed" (*The Adventures of Huckleberry Finn*, p. 105). It takes Huck fifteen minutes to decide he should apologize to a "nigger," but he does it and feels right about it too. Clearly their teamwork and time alone together has allowed the white boy to see beyond the black stereotype of his day.

Sources. Twain believed every fictional character had its real-life source. Over the years he kept notebooks describing people and places that found their way into *Huckleberry Finn*.

Huck and Jim are modeled on the real-life characters Tom Blankenship and Uncle Dan'l. "In *Huckleberry Finn*," explained its author, "I have drawn Tom Blankenship exactly as he was"; four years older than Twain, Tom "was ignorant, unwashed, insufficiently fed, but he had as good a heart as ever any boy had" (Explanatory Notes in *The Adventures of Huckleberry Finn*, p. 374). Tom Blankenship had an older brother, Benson, who stumbled upon a runaway on an island in 1847 and, forgoing a $50 reward for his capture, shuttled scraps of food to him all summer long. Like this runaway, the fictional Jim escapes to an island; his personality, however, is drawn from a slave named Daniel who lived on Twain's uncle's farm in Florida, Missouri.

> Uncle Dan'l, a middle-aged slave whose head was the best one in the negro-quarter, whose sympathies were wide and warm, and whose heart was honest and simple.... [I] have staged him in books under his own name and as "Jim" and carted him ... down the Mississippi on a raft...."
>
> (Explanatory Notes in *The Adventures of Huckleberry Finn*, p. 378)

An item from Twain's past helps explain the enormity of Huck's decision to aid Jim. In 1841 three whites were caught helping five slaves escape from Missouri. Twain's own father, John Clemens, served on the jury that sentenced the three to twelve years in jail.

Twain drew on experiences and viewpoints he encountered later in life as well, merging them into events in the novel. In 1857 he became a

Huckleberry Finn

steamboat pilot on the Mississippi. Twain came to know the turns and shapes of the river so well that he learned to steer in the dark of night. Given the hazards of river travel, he most likely witnessed some narrow escapes from disaster. His brother Henry, also a steamboat pilot, was not so lucky. Henry's vessel, *The Philadelphia,* exploded in June 1858, killing him. Despite the tragedy, Twain continued piloting a steamboat for four years until the Civil War broke out. His river boating gave him an intimate knowledge of the Mississippi, evident in the pages of *Huckleberry Finn.*

A NEW CIRCLE OF FRIENDS

By 1869 Twain was writing for the New York *Buffalo Express,* penning articles that lashed out at lynchings, or mob killings of blacks accused of crimes. He met the black leader Frederick Douglass, admiring this ex-slave's fight against segregation in public schools. And in 1870 Twain married Olivia (Livy) Langdon, whose parents had sheltered runaway slaves and welcomed the abolitionist William Lloyd Garrison into their home. In short, the adult Twain kept company with people whose views differed greatly from those he grew up with in Missouri.

Events in History at the Time the Novel Was Written

The Gilded Age. The last quarter of the nineteenth century was a time of great prosperity for many Americans. Industry thrived and great for-

---

MARK TWAIN TO HIS BUSINESS PARTNER CHARLES L. WEBSTER

Dear Charley,
The Committee of the Public Library of Concord, Mass. have ... expelled Huck from their library as "trash and suitable only for the slums." That will sell 25,000 copies for us sure.
(Twain in Neider, p. 176)

---

tunes were made. But while a few seemed to leap from rags into riches, hundreds of others sank into monotonous, dangerous jobs for miserable wages. Twain recognized the inequalities and co-authored the book *The Gilded Age,* thus naming the era for all its flash and glitter. It was known also as the Victorian age, after England's regent at the time, Queen Victoria. Its capital of London was the center of Victorian culture and a city that had become the trendsetter for high society on both continents. Spreading to America, the Victorian code of behavior promised that hard work and the avoidance of worldly pleasures would bring wealth and respect. There were carefully circumscribed ways of speaking, acting, and writing in Victorian society, limits that some novelists began to shake off toward the close of the century. Twain became one of these groundbreakers, and his novels suffered the consequences.

Published in 1876, Twain's *The Adventures of Tom Sawyer* was based on recollections of his own boyhood in Hannibal, Missouri. The novel was banned by libraries in both Brooklyn, New York, and Denver, Colorado. Its author nevertheless began work on a sequel, *The Adventures of Huckleberry Finn,* that same year and labored over it intermittently until 1883.

With his nephew Charles Webster, Twain created his own publishing firm whose first book was to be *Huckleberry Finn.* Twain proceeded cautiously, refusing to print the novel before he had 40,000 orders. His fears proved groundless. In the end *Huckleberry Finn* did well financially, but in 1894 Twain's company collapsed. Its downfall paralleled a severe depression in the nation, the Panic of 1893 to 1897, and Twain's family entered a period of great financial hardship.

Reviews. Twain published *The Adventures of Huckleberry Finn* in the United States in 1885. For a time, newspapers remained silent about the novel. They broke their silence after it was banned by a library committee in Concord, Massachusetts.

Although Twain seemed not to mind this setback, he was disturbed at other barbs thrown at the novel. Critics, including the celebrated author Louisa May Alcott as well as local newspaper writers, stoned the book with harsh words.

> If Mr. Clemens cannot think of something better to tell our pure-minded lads and lasses, he had best stop writing books for them.
> (Louisa May Alcott in Kaplan, p. 268)

Critics fought to keep the novel away from young readers, fearing that they, like Huck, might learn to steal, lie, use poor grammar, and run away. But others applauded the novel, pointing out that it painted a startlingly real picture of riverside life in the pre-Civil War era.

Reconstruction. Twain began work on *Huckleberry Finn* in 1876, eleven years after the American Civil War ended. The year 1876 also marked a change in conditions in the South. During Reconstruction—the period in which the rebel states were brought back into the Union—the region had experienced some progress. Congress, for example, passed a civil rights act in 1875 that guaranteed to all races equal use of trains, hotels, and other public places. Dominated by race-conscious white Southerners from pre-Civil War days, however, the old Democratic Party resumed control of the Southern states in 1876. Under its control, the new civil rights act was widely ignored, and the states began passing Jim Crow laws that required blacks to use separate schools, trains, bathrooms, drinking fountains, and other public facilities. (The name *Jim Crow* probably dates back to minstrel entertainer Thomas Rice, who in 1830 invented a famous song and jig in imitation of a misshapen old black man whom he saw dancing and singing a ditty that included the words "I jump Jim Crow.") In 1883 the Supreme Court declared the civil rights act of 1875 unconstitutional, which meant that it was lawful for private businesses to practice segregation. An 1896 Supreme Court decision, *Plessy v. Ferguson*, confirmed this ruling.

A curious parallel. Officially, blacks were free citizens after the Civil War. Yet deeply ingrained prejudices persisted, and it became lawful to ban black people from hotels, theaters, schools, and restaurants that catered to whites. Twain's novel ends with Tom Sawyer and Huck Finn overcoming various obstacles to rescue the captured slave Jim. In the misadventures that follow, Jim learns that his owner, Miss Watson, had died after he fled and in her will had released him from slavery. Huck and Tom, it seems, had been trying to free a black man who was already free. Looking back at the Jim Crow laws and other post-Civil War curbs on Southern blacks, the idea of freeing the freed slave described a very real need. But the parallel was probably unintentional on Twain's part, for in a notice at the beginning of the novel, the author warns readers not to look for a moral in this story.

For More Information

Child, Marquis W. *Mighty Mississippi: Biography of a River*. New Haven, Conn.: Ticknor & Fields, 1982.

DeVoto, Bernard, ed. *Mark Twain in Eruption*. New York: Harper & Brothers, 1922.

Foner, Eric. *Reconstruction*. New York: Harper & Row, 1988.

Jones, Virgil Carrington. *The Hatfields and the McCoys*. Chapel Hill: University of North Carolina Press, 1948.

Kaplan, Justin. *Mr. Clemens and Mark Twain*. New York: Simon and Schuster, 1966.

Neider, Charles. *The Selected Letters of Mark Twain*. New York: Harper & Row, 1982.

Toll, Robert C. *Blacking Up: The Minstrel Show in Nineteenth-Century America*. New York: Oxford University Press, 1974.

Twain, Mark. *Adventures of Huckleberry Finn*. Edited by Walter Blair and Victor Fischer. Berkeley: University of California Press, 1985.

"Ain't I a Woman?"

by
Sojourner Truth

Sojourner Truth was born in New York's Ulster County around 1797. Owned by several different families of New York, she was finally set free in 1827 after thirty years in slavery. Although she never learned to read or write, her personal magnetism and imposing presence made Truth a powerful champion of abolition and women's rights. Sojourner Truth staunchly believed that both slaves and women faced similar injustice and inequality. She devoted most of her adult years to speaking publicly about the wrongs of oppression and slavery in any form. Truth delivered her most famous speech on the issue at the Women's Rights Convention in Akron, Ohio, in May 1851.

Events in History at the Time of the Speech

Slavery. From 1820 to 1860 cotton production in the South soared to its highest level. The South relied heavily on slave labor to plant and harvest its cotton crops. By the mid-1800s, one out of every five Southern families owned slaves. Meanwhile, the Industrial Revolution, which spread throughout New England at this time, created factories that became the mainstay of the Northern economy. In contrast with the businesses of the South, which relied on black slaves, these factories depended mostly on white workers to succeed. The distinctions between North and South grew increasingly more pronounced.

Some slave owners were relatively gentle and understanding. Others, though, treated their

> **THE LITERARY WORK**
> A speech presented at the Akron, Ohio, Women's Rights Convention in 1851.
>
> **SYNOPSIS**
> In a passionately delivered speech, Sojourner Truth proclaims that all women deserve equality.

slaves with brutality and abuse. Hardly any laws existed to protect slaves, and the few that existed were seldom enforced. A slave, for example, could not hit a white person, even in self-defense. Conversely, the murder of a black slave by a white person was rarely considered a crime. The law regarded the rape of female slaves as criminal only because the act generally involved the trespassing of an outsider onto the slaveowner's property.

Abolition of slavery. Years before the appearance of militant abolitionists in the 1800s, convincing arguments against slavery had been developed. As early as the 1600s, America faced strong opposition to slave ownership from Quakers and other humanitarians.

During the 1780s several Northern states abolished slavery altogether. In 1808 Congress prohibited importing new slaves to the country, and the Missouri Compromise of 1820 forbade the creation of new slave states in the U.S. territories north of a certain geographical line. New

York, Sojourner Truth's home state, passed a law that the last of its slaves would become free on July 4, 1827. Despite many other attempts to outlaw the practice, however, slavery remained legal in the Southern states well into the 1800s. The longer slavery continued, the more the issue provoked tension between North and South.

The mid-1800s saw a growing interest in social and political reform in general, the aim being to improve the lot of humanity and create a more perfect society. Better public schools, cleaner jails, temperance (a movement against selling or drinking alcohol), and women's rights were among the important causes of the era. A religious surge known as the Second Great Awakening swept across the nation. In other parts of the world, countries such as England (1834) and France (1848) ended the practice of colonial slavery.

Humanitarian reforms, combined with the religious revival, produced a strong antislavery movement around this time in American history. In 1833 followers of William Lloyd Garrison, a well-known abolitionist, joined forces with other like-minded groups to form the American Anti-Slavery Society. Garrison quickly became the abolition movement's most outspoken member. In the first edition of his newspaper, *The Liberator,* Garrison wrote, "I *will* be as harsh as truth, and as uncompromising as justice. On this subject ... I will not retreat a single inch—AND I WILL BE HEARD" (Garrison in Franklin, p. 182). While objections to slavery were not new, Garrison's fiery words drew more attention to these issues. He adamantly refused to accept the idea of allowing it to continue for another minute.

As feelings about slavery grew stronger, violent uprisings became more frequent. Abolitionist tactics were often ugly, and Southerners responded with similar harshness. Finally, the ideological gap between the North and South regarding slavery and other issues reached the breaking point. The Civil War between North and South erupted in 1861.

Sojourner Truth, like other peaceful abolitionists, had long opposed violence in any form. By the time of the Civil War, however, Truth and several of her pacifist compatriots had experienced a change of heart. Militant abolitionists showed an increasing willingness to throw off the yoke of the white master by means of force if necessary. Truth reportedly said that if she was "ten years younger, I would fly to the battle-field ... and if it came to the pinch, put in a blow, now and then" (Truth in Mabee, p. 91).

Sojourner Truth

Women's role in the abolition movement. Women served vital functions in the abolition movement during the 1800s. They raised money, educated black children, and lectured on the wrongs of slavery. Despite their tireless work, though, women were excluded from taking active, decision-making roles in the antislavery movement. One stark example of this exclusion occurred at the 1840 international abolition convention. Abolitionists from around the globe convened in London for the World's Anti-Slavery Convention. Eight women delegates from America were refused seats on the floor merely on the ground that they were women. The entire first day of the convention was spent discussing whether women ought to be admitted as delegates. Some men argued that admitting women would lower the dignity of the convention. Others said that women were constitutionally unfit for public meetings. Nearly all of the men voted against admitting women delegates. In the end, the women were seated in the balcony while the male delegates proceeded to discuss the wrongs of slavery on the floor below.

The irony and injustice of their treatment at the World's Anti-Slavery Convention did not escape these women. Triggered in part by the mis-

"Ain't I a Woman?"

treatment they endured at the London convention, Elizabeth Cady Stanton, Lucretia Mott, and others went on to found the first American women's rights movement.

The fight for women's rights. Rights and opportunities were extremely limited for all women during the 1800s. In white society it was generally expected that women would marry, have children, and obey their husbands. The women found themselves barred from almost all professions except teaching; they earned far lower wages than men, and when women earned any money at all, their husbands were fully entitled to keep their earnings. White women suffered other inequalities, too. They could not own property, they were strongly discouraged from speaking in public, and, in the case of divorce, women could not be guardians of their own children. Like criminals, young people, and the insane, women were not allowed to vote. These rules reinforced the role that society felt white women should play, a role deemed proper for members of the so-called "cult of true womanhood." Meanwhile, society dismissed black women altogether, seeing them as having no place in this cult.

SOJOURNER TRUTH RIDES THE STREETCARS

In Washington, D.C., in 1865, many horse-car operators discriminated against black patrons. Ninety years before Rosa Parks's famous refusal to relinquish her bus seat to a white man (in Montgomery, Alabama, on December 1, 1955), Sojourner Truth valiantly insisted upon riding the streetcars whenever and wherever she pleased, and demanded an end to segregated public transportation.

The Seneca Falls Convention, held in July 1848, marked the official beginning of the women's rights movement, and it included mostly white women. Its official start came when three hundred concerned women and men gathered in upstate New York to discuss the wrongs faced by women. Using the language of the United States Declaration of Independence, they drafted a Declaration of Sentiments that listed the grievances and demands of women. The Seneca Falls Declaration stated "We hold these truths to be self-evident; that all men and women are created equal." Signers of the Declaration condemned the nation for requiring women to obey its laws but denying them the right to have a voice in the creation of those laws. In their view, the existing laws and practices in the realms of marriage, property, and education hindered a white woman's ability to pursue "life, liberty and happiness" (*Declaration of Sentiments*).

Included in the Declaration of Sentiments was the demand for women's suffrage, or the right to vote. Not all delegates present at Seneca Falls supported the right for women to vote. Several people abstained from signing the Declaration because they felt the right to vote was far too radical a demand.

The problems articulated at Seneca Falls were by no means solved during the convention. Participants hoped that subsequent meetings would take place across the country to continue the struggle for women's rights. In 1851 women's rights activists convened again in Akron, Ohio, to further discuss conditions for women in America. A clergyman began to speak, proclaiming that women should not be allowed to vote because they were helpless and weak. Sojourner Truth then took the podium to give her famous speech, becoming one of the few black women to be heard in this mostly white women's movement.

Sojourner Truth's speech at the Akron Women's Rights Convention in 1851 would not only answer the clergyman who spoke before her but would also link antislavery with feminist causes. As a result of Truth's speech, the issues of race and women's rights became firmly united, hinging on a common idea—that oppression of any individual was wrong. Some of the women's rights activists strongly disagreed with this strategy. Jane Swisshelm, a leader at Akron, had criticized Truth for bringing up the issue of race at an earlier women's rights meeting. "The convention," complained Swisshelm, "was not called to discuss the rights of color; and we think it altogether irrelevant and unwise to introduce the question" (Swisshelm in Painter, p. 123). Nevertheless Truth would continue to link the two issues at Akron and in subsequent years.

When the Civil War broke out, the women's rights movement slowed to a virtual stop for a period. Responding to the pressing need for supplies and other forms of aid on and off the battlefield, women turned their attention to the most immediate issues: abolishing slavery and helping the nation get through a violent war.

Black literacy in the nineteenth century. During the time when Sojourner Truth was a slave, most blacks in her home state of New York were illiterate. Literacy rates among blacks elsewhere in the nation were equally low. In the early 1800s, however, New York State planned to abolish slavery in gradual steps. Reasoning that slaves would be more capable of caring for themselves if they learned Christian values, New York passed a law in 1810 that directed slave owners to teach slave children on their property to read the scriptures.

By 1850 approximately 50 percent of black New Yorkers could read, but many blacks across the country remained illiterate. Sojourner Truth, though an intelligent woman, never learned to read or write herself. Instead, she relied upon friends to maintain her correspondence and record her autobiography. "I don't read such small stuff as letters," stated Truth, "I read men and nations" (Truth in Mabee, p. 66).

Religious connections to abolition and suffrage. Political speakers of the day, many of whom had their roots in various religious movements, often justified their arguments based on the authority of God. Quakers, a sect of Christians with a long tradition of speaking when the "spirit" moved them, supported through words and deeds the women's suffrage and antislavery drives.

In the 1830s Sojourner Truth became a wandering evangelist and religious mystic. For several years, she traveled from state to state speaking about her spiritual beliefs. For a time, Truth lived in various spiritual communities along the eastern seaboard. Since religious movements of the period emphasized preaching one's message as directed by God, they probably affected Sojourner Truth's speaking style. Certainly they help explain her frequent references to God to bolster her arguments. She heard voices she believed came from God, and felt that God had directed her to travel across the land, showing people their sins.

The belief that God was on their side most likely contributed to the willingness of abolition and women's rights activists to persevere in their struggle for equality. They did so in the face of open hostility from many who dismissed their message and believed that women should not speak in public. At the Akron convention, Sojourner Truth responded to hecklers in the audience who argued that God had made women naturally inferior to men. Reports indicated that several men argued that men were superior because Christ was a man and because Eve, a woman, caused the expulsion of humankind from Paradise. Sojourner Truth calmly rose to her feet and addressed the harassers: "Whar did your Christ come from?" asked Truth, then answered her own question. Christ was born "from God and a woman. Man had nothing to do with him." In defense of Eve, Truth retorted, "If de fust woman God ever made was strong enough to turn the world upside down, all 'lone, dese [women] togedder ought to be able to turn it back and get it right side up again" (Truth et al., *Narrative of Sojourner Truth,* p. 135).

THE TEMPERANCE MOVEMENT

The temperance movement, which called on Americans to abstain from drinking or selling liquor, flourished during the mid-1800s, drawing much of its strength from the women's movement. Women who fought for temperance did so in part for religious reasons, but also because they had no legal recourse against husbands who might become abusive or indebted as a result of a drunken spree.

Opposition to progressive women. Nineteenth-century women faced strong pressure to remain silent. Yet Sojourner Truth and other progressive women of her day courageously spoke out about their beliefs on abolition and women's rights. Standing alone at a public podium meant, for these women, risking ridicule, humiliation, and even assault. It was not uncommon for unsympathetic listeners to hurl rotten eggs or vegetables at the speaker. For example, Lucy Stone, a nineteenth-century women's rights activist, sustained a head injury from a prayer book thrown at her by a man in the audience during a speaking engagement. Another time, Stone was victimized when a hose of icy water was turned upon her by members of the audience during a speech she made in the dead of winter. Newspapers described women speakers as brazen female fanatics and foreign incendiaries. Many members of the clergy denounced women speakers as well, quoting the Bible to justify their insults. But Sojourner Truth, a striking and gaunt woman who stood nearly six feet tall, spoke out about women's suffering and their strengths with such spellbinding force that her voice silenced even the boldest hecklers. She seemed, moreover, to be addressing white women as well as men, insisting that the black woman be acknowledged as deserving of the same rights and

"Ain't I a Woman?"

respect as the white. One can visualize the insistent question, "Ain't I a Woman?" being directed not only at men in the audience but at her white coworkers in the women's movement.

The Speech in Focus

The contents. In what was to become her most renowned speech, Sojourner Truth argued that women deserved the same rights as men. If women were as strong as men and could carry an equal workload, she asked, then why shouldn't women have the rights they so deserve? Pushing up her sleeve to bare her strong and sinewy arm, Truth said, "I have plowed and reaped and husked and chopped and mowed, and can any man do more than that? I have heard much about the sexes being equal.... I am as strong as any man" (Truth, "Ain't I a Woman?," *Anti-Slavery Bugle,* p. 160).

CONTENDING RENDITIONS OF SOJOURNER TRUTH'S KEY PHRASES

Gage: "Den dey talks 'bout dis ting in de head. What dis dey call it?" "Intellect," whispered some one near. "Dat's it, honey. What's dat got to do with woman's rights or niggers' rights?"

Anti-Slavery Bugle: "As for intellect, all I can say is ... [y]ou need not be afraid to give us our rights for fear we will take too much."

Gage: "I tink dat 'twixt de niggers of de Souf and de women at de Norf all a talkin 'bout rights, de white men will be in a fix pretty soon."

Anti-Slavery Bugle: "But the women are coming up blessed be God and a few of the men are coming up with them. But man is in a tight place, the poor slave is on him, woman is coming on him, he is surely between a hawk and a buzzard."

(Stetson, pp. 116, 118)

Truth observed in her speech that men seemed to hold on dearly to their power over women. She contended, though, that men had nothing to fear by giving women their rights. "The poor men seem to be all in confusion and don't know what to do. Why children," Truth said, addressing the men in the audience, "if you have women's rights give it to her and you will feel better" ("Ain't I a Woman?," *Anti-Slavery Bugle,* p. 160). Women were not asking for more than what was rightfully theirs, claimed Truth. In fact, they were asking only for their fair share of liberty. If women have a pint of intellect and men have a quart, Truth questioned, then why can she not merely "have her little pint full?" ("Ain't I a Woman?," *Anti-Slavery Bugle,* p. 160).

According to one commonly accepted version of the famous speech, Sojourner Truth asked why a black woman should not be treated like any other woman. Truth turned towards a previous speaker and said, "Dat man ober dar say dat women needs to be helped into carriages, and lifted ober ditches, and to have de best place every whar. Nobody eber help me into carriages, or ober mud puddles, or gives me any best place, and ar'n't I a woman?" ("Ain't I a Woman?," *Narrative of Sojourner Truth,* p. 134).

The controversy over the speech. Because Sojourner Truth was never taught how to read or write, what is known about her life and her famous speech is available to us only through newspaper reports and accounts written by Truth's friends. There is considerable controversy over the factual accuracy of this information.

There exist at least two known versions of Truth's Akron address. The most widely accepted rendering comes from Frances Gage's report in *The Anti-Slavery Standard* of May 2, 1863. Gage's 1863 version of Truth's speech was incorporated into two important historical sources: Sojourner Truth's *Narrative* and Elizabeth Cady Stanton's *History of Woman Suffrage.* An alternative version of the speech was published in an 1851 issue of the abolition newspaper, *The Anti-Slavery Bugle,* published in Salem, Ohio. While both Gage and the newspaper convey similar messages about Truth's speech, the two renditions are different enough to raise significant questions about the accuracy of either account.

Gage wrote down Truth's speech twelve years after it was given, a length of time that gave rise to plausible concerns about whether Gage was able to recall precisely the words spoken by Sojourner Truth. In Gage's version of the speech, Truth reportedly repeated the phrase "Ain't I a Woman?" four times. This cadence and type of speech pattern is inconsistent with reports of Truth's numerous other speeches, but is highly consistent with Gage's own poetry and other writings. None of the four existing newspaper reports concerning the speech from 1851 mention Truth's use of the famous phrase. If Truth had in fact recited the haunting phrase "Ain't I a

Woman?" four times, as Gage reports, it seems unlikely that newspapers would neglect this fact.

Because Truth could not read, she was unable to check the accuracy of any written versions of her speech. Even if Truth was aware of any factual discrepancies, it is possible that she did not want to point out errors in Frances Gage's work and risk offending her, since Gage was a dear friend. On the other hand, it is questionable whether Truth spoke using the white dialect recorded in the *Anti-Slavery Bugle*.

To a large degree, Gage's rendition of Truth's speech has gone unquestioned. In any case, there is evidence that Sojourner Truth did not mind the folklore created about her speech and her life. "Her focus in telling the story of her life was not on factual truth about her life, but on the moral truth that could be learned from it.... Truth often seemed willing to let friendly myths develop about her, myths that might make her a more fascinating advocate of the causes she supported" (Mabee, p. 68). Later generations can be reasonably sure, however, that recorded accounts of key ideas in Truth's speech captured the spirit, if not the letter, of her words.

Sources. Sojourner Truth brought with her to the Akron Women's Rights Convention the power of her personal experience as both a woman and a freed black slave. Truth's physical presence was a strong reminder to her listeners about the oppression black women faced. Sojourner Truth was reportedly raped by a slave master and forced into marriage with her husband. She gave birth to five children while a slave, saw two daughters sold away from her, and had an owner who reneged on a promise to free her. (In response, she had simply left his farm, appealing to a Quaker neighbor who settled the matter so that Truth became free.) Who could better speak out on the issues of slavery and women's rights than one who had endured such a fate as Sojourner Truth?

How the speech was received. There is some controversy as to how Sojourner Truth's speech was received. According to Frances Gage, who was the presiding officer at the Akron Convention, white women were wary of Sojourner Truth. White men were far less charitable, booing and hissing as Truth approached the podium. In her report, Gage wrote that many of the leaders at the Akron Convention were "almost thrown into panic" at the sight of Sojourner Truth. They begged Gage not to let Truth speak because it would ruin the women's movement to have their cause "mixed with abolition and niggers" (Mabee, p. 69). Yet Gage claimed that Truth's powerful presence and charismatic speaking style were strong enough to calm even the most hostile crowd. According to at least twenty-seven other descriptions of the convention, however, the audience did not respond to Truth in as unruly a fashion as Gage reported.

Regardless of the conflicting descriptions of Sojourner Truth's reception at the Akron Women's Rights Convention, it is certain that she exerted a powerful influence on the abolition and women's rights movements of the nineteenth century. "Ain't I a Woman?," the title which later generations assigned to Sojourner Truth's speech, has survived to become a familiar slogan used by political activists to this day.

For More Information

Declaration of Sentiments. 1848. Reprint. Seneca Falls, N.Y.: Women's Rights National Historical Park, 1992.

Franklin, John Hope. *From Slavery to Freedom*. New York: Alfred A. Knopf, 1980.

Mabee, Carleton, with Susan Mabee Newhouse. *Sojourner Truth: Slave, Prophet, Legend*. New York: New York University Press, 1993.

Painter, Nell Irvin. *Sojourner Truth: A Life, a Symbol*. New York: W. W. Norton, 1996.

Robertson, James I., Jr. *Civil War! America Becomes One Nation*. New York: Alfred A. Knopf, 1992.

Stetson, Erlene. *Glorying in Tribulation: The Life of Sojourner Truth*. East Lansing: Michigan State University Press, 1994.

Truth, Sojourner. "Ain't I a Woman?" *The Anti-Slavery Bugle* (June 21, 1851): 160.

Truth, Sojourner, with Olive Gilbert and Frances Titus. *Narrative of Sojourner Truth*. Boston: For the Author, 1875.

Alice's Adventures in Wonderland

by
Lewis Carroll

Inspired by a boating excursion in 1862, Lewis Carroll's famous story *Alice's Adventures in Wonderland* was originally intended only to entertain three of his friends, who were children. The author set the oral story down in print so that the children might have it on hand to read for themselves. After showing it to another writer, Carroll was finally persuaded to publish his book. With the help of an illustrator, Sir John Tenniel, the author created his popular novel. Due to its fantasy setting, the only historical references in the work are those which pertain to Carroll's own times.

Events in History at the Time of the Novel

Queen Victoria (1819-1901). Victoria ascended to the British throne in 1837, after her uncle, King William IV, died without leaving a direct heir. At the time of her coronation, the English people had little respect for the monarchy, as it had previously been riddled with irresponsible conduct. Both William IV and Victoria's father lived openly with their mistresses, Mrs. Jordan (an actress) and Madame St. Laurent, respectively. Victoria's concern for the welfare of her people, however, soon gained her the respect of the nation. She and her husband Albert were able to restore some of the lustre that had faded from the royal throne. Some argue that "Great Britain might have become a republic [rather than a monarchy] if Victoria and Albert had not regained that respect by the display of their do-

> **THE LITERARY WORK**
> A children's novel set in a fantasy world; published in 1865.
>
> **SYNOPSIS**
> A young English girl dreams of traveling through a "wonderland" filled with magical creatures and nonsensical events.

mestic virtues and blameless private life" (Marshall, p. 94). Under the guidance of Victoria and her prime ministers, Britain developed its worldwide colonial empire. During Victoria's reign, the country increased its population by 50 percent and became, by some estimates, the richest nation in the world.

While Carroll's novel does not directly refer to England's reigning monarch, it does feature a prominent queen, the Queen of Hearts. She rules all of Wonderland, and her subjects bow to her wishes for fear of losing their heads. Like Queen Victoria, whose husband Prince Albert assisted her with royal duties, the king of Wonderland takes an active, if subservient, role with his queen. Carroll's Victorian audience would have been quite familiar and comfortable with this royal hierarchy.

Lewis Carroll and Alice Liddell. Lewis Carroll is actually the pen name of Charles Lutwidge Dodgson, a professor of mathematics at Christ Church College in Oxford University. Early in

Alice Liddell and her sister Lorina.

his university life, Carroll began contributing pieces of writing to various humorous journals. As he wanted to keep his two professions separate, he devised a pen name for his creative writings. Translating his first two names into Latin, he came up with "Carolus Lodovicus." He then anglicized these names and reversed their order, becoming "Lewis Carroll."

An avid and accomplished photographer, Carroll met Alice Liddell on the afternoon of April 25, 1856, as he attempted to take pictures of the Christ Church Cathedral. Only four years old at the time, Alice was one of three daughters of Reverend Henry George Liddell, the Dean of Christ Church. This meeting initiated a friendship that was to last several years. Carroll delighted in taking pictures of the three girls, and these photographs garnered such acclaim that he was given the title of the most outstanding photographer of children in the nineteenth century. Although he often met with all of the children at once, Carroll's favorite clearly was Alice. The little girl was "adept at asking challenging and disconcerting questions, [and] enjoyed teasing and ... logical argument" (Batey, p. 8). Carroll eventually developed this persona into the title character of *Alice's Adventures in Wonderland*.

Science vs. religion in Victorian England. The mid-Victorian period (1848-1870) often falls under the title of "The Age of Improvement." London, by the 1830s, had grown into a polluted, overcrowded metropolis. During Victoria's reign (1837-1901), the population of this city alone grew from 2 million to 6.5 million inhabitants. Although social change progressed slowly, a series of organizations and acts of the mid-Victorian period worked to regulate industrial growth. For instance, during the late 1860s the Nine Hours League was formed in Newcastle for the purpose of lobbying for a fifty-four-hour work week. The work week had previously gone unregulated.

In 1851 Prince Albert's Great Exhibition in Hyde Park displayed achievements of modern industry and science. The flourish of science and technology soon ignited a heated debate between the religious camps and the scientific ones. On one side, evolutionists argued under the principles set forth in Charles Darwin's *Origin of Species* (1859). Darwin suggested that every living creature produces offspring that in some way differs from itself. Certain of these differences give particular offspring a better chance for thriving in their environment, helping the species to survive the tests of "natural selection" imposed by climate, food, and predators. Darwin entitled this ancestral evolution the "survival of the fittest" (Darwin in Lindsay, p. 92). On the other side of the argument, members of the "Oxford movement" (so named for its birth at Oxford University) upheld the biblical concept that God had created the universe and that life did not evolve over time. This theory became known as "creationism." As a professor at Oxford, Lewis Carroll found himself caught in the middle of these sociological and theoretical debates. In 1860 the university played host to a famous British Association meeting at which the Darwinian scientist Thomas Henry Huxley argued with the creationist Bishop Samuel Wilberforce. Some scholars think that bits of these intellectual discussions surface in *Alice's Adventures in Wonderland*.

Carroll, word play, and Victorian humor. A mathematician by trade, Lewis Carroll had mixed feelings about words. He believed that their ambiguous nature led to infinite problems. Throughout his life, the author kept an exact copy of every correspondence sent or received. In this manner, he hoped to avoid misunderstandings of what he may or may not have said. This habit reflects a preoccupation and infatuation with words and puns that surface in the novel.

Like the Victorian society for which Carroll wrote, the author found endless humor in punning. The trial scene at the end of *Alice's Adventures in Wonderland* provides one such instance. When asked if she had ever had any fits, the Queen of Hearts replies, "Never!" (Carroll, *Alice's Adventures in Wonderland,* p. 100). Her husband, the King, retorts, "Then the words don't fit you.... It's a pun!" (*Alice's Adventures in Wonderland,* p. 101). This type of humor was quite popular in Victorian literature. As critic Donald Gray noted, Victorian "nonsense is full of a delight in the sounds of words, a delight which is also abundantly evident in the countless puns" (Gray, p. 168).

The novel also abounds with humorous references to poems typically taught to Victorian school children. Since education in the nineteenth century centered around endless memorization and recitation, most of the songs and poems in *Alice's Adventures in Wonderland* would have rung familiar to child readers. Alice's recitation of "You are old, Father William" (*Alice's Adventures in Wonderland,* p. 44), for instance, mocks a well-known poem by Robert Southey, England's poet laureate in 1813. Southey's poem, called "The Old Man's Comforts and How He Gained Them," begins with these two stanzas:

> "You are old, Father William," the young man cried;
> "The few locks which are left you are gray;
> You are hale, Father William,—a hearty old man:
> Now tell me the reason, I pray."
> "In the days of my youth," Father William replied,
> "I remembered that youth would fly fast,
> And abused not my health and my vigor at first,
> That I never might need them at last."
> (Southey, p. 171)

Compare these lines with the ones that Alice recalls:

> "You are old, Father William," the young man said,
> "And your hair has become very white;
> And yet you incessantly stand on your head—
> Do you think, at your age, it is right?"
> "In my youth," Father William replies to his son,
> "I feared it might injure the brain;
> But now that I'm perfectly sure I have none,
> Why, I do it again and again."
> (*Alice's Adventures in Wonderland,* p. 44)

Victorian education for girls. In Victorian England, the educational focus was on the manners a student acquired and the people with whom he or she associated. This emphasis was especially true for female students. A young girl's education often centered around "accomplishments" such as music, drawing, and other arts that would "make a man's home a bower of tasteful bliss" (McMurty, p. 189). Girls were usually educated at home by a governess and an assortment of masters on special subjects. Alice Liddell and her sisters, for instance, received drawing instruction under the guidance of John Ruskin. In the novel, Carroll's Alice remains continually concerned with the propriety of things. She sings and recites with the skill of any good Victorian child, and she even attempts to teach manners to the confused creatures of Wonderland. When affronted at the Mad Hatter's tea party, Alice remarks, "You shouldn't make personal remarks ... it's very rude" (*Alice's Adventures in Wonderland,* p. 59). Although the end of the century saw a trend toward educating women in those subjects taught to men (i.e., Latin, mathematics), this change affected only a small portion of the population, specifically the upper classes.

The Novel in Focus

The plot. Lying with her sister on the bank of a country river in England, Alice grows increas-

"Cheshire Puss!" said Alice (Wasn't that a pretty name for a cat?) "Would you tell me which way I ought to go from here?"

And so the Cheshire-Cat told her which way she ought to go to visit the Hatter, and which way to go, to visit the March Hare. "They're both mad!" said the Cat.

And then the Cat vanished away, just like the flame of a candle when it goes out!

Alice and the Cheshire Cat. Illustration from *The Nursery Alice*.

Alice in Wonderland

ingly bored with having "nothing to do" (*Alice's Adventures in Wonderland,* p. 7). Suddenly a white rabbit, wearing a waistcoat and talking to himself, startles the little girl out of her reverie. As she follows him down his rabbit hole, Alice has no idea that wild adventures await her in Wonderland.

Told in the third person, *Alice's Adventures in Wonderland* chronicles the journey of the novel's title character as she travels through a dreamlike world. At every bend in the road, Alice encounters new and exotic figures, from talking mice to animated playing cards. She even finds that the ingestion of certain foods alters her size. As she journeys, Alice attempts to make sense of a baby that turns into a pig, a caterpillar that speaks in riddles, and a cat that disappears and reappears without warning. Throughout the novel, Alice finds herself lost in this unreal setting, where standard convention does not apply.

The nonsensical adventure culminates with Alice's introduction to the Queen of Hearts and a trial concerning the theft of cherry tarts. Adhering to no apparent logic, the Queen commands the beheading of her subjects at frequent, whimsical intervals. Clearly, even the court system of Wonderland does not follow any rules or regulations. Alice soon finds herself wishing to return to the normalcy of her home in England. Soon enough the little girl awakens on the river bank she had left, and tells her sister of her curious dream.

Carroll and Darwinism. Lewis Carroll's interests pulled him simultaneously in the conflicting directions of science and religion. As a scholar, Carroll participated in the arguments about Darwinism that pervaded Oxford University, and he and most other members of the intellectual community attended the famous Huxley-Wilberforce debate.

Some reviewers believe that these dual passions are evident in *Alice's Adventures in Wonderland.* The subject of Darwinism, it is argued, can be found in a segment of the tale where, after falling down the white rabbit's hole, Alice finds herself quite alone. She does not meet other creatures until she cries so much that she creates a pool of tears. Eventually, a mouse, a duck, a Dodo, and several other animals emerge from the pool. Some critics think that this notion of life crawling forth from salt water echoes the Darwinian principles of evolution. Likewise, the Dodo character, according to these critics, refers to Darwin's studies of natural selection. The Dodo bird had been extinct since 1681, and the last known remains of the animal were preserved at Oxford. Still, while some assert that the book contains several Darwinian allusions, others contend that it does not deal with this scientific movement.

Carroll's interest in the creationist teachings of the church, meanwhile, were due in part to his family environment. His father, an ordained minister, greatly influenced his son's vocational aspirations. While growing up, Carroll had planned to seek a career in the church. Although he was ordained a deacon in 1861, for unknown reasons Carroll never took full holy orders. As a result, he could not lead church services. While some critics speculate that the author's slight stutter gave him an inferiority complex about public speaking, no one really knows why Carroll's religious career came to a halt. Despite the setback, he maintained a high degree of devotion to his religion.

For this reason, some feel that the "Pool of Tears" chapter comes solely from an autobiographical experience. After a rain shower ruined a boating expedition with his friend Robinson Duckworth and the Liddell children, Carroll was forced to lead the party to the safety of a shoreside home. Some readers say that he later retold this tale in his novel, casting Alice Liddell as Alice, her sisters Lorina and Edith as the Lory and the Eaglet, Duckworth as the Duck, and himself as the stuttering Dodo bird. This reading decidedly counters the Darwinian one. Mirroring the dualism of his own life, Carroll seems to leave the whole incident up to two very different but possible interpretations.

Sources. There is an exact genesis of *Alice's Adventures in Wonderland.* On July 4, 1862, Lewis Carroll, along with his friend Robinson Duckworth, took the three small Liddell daughters on a boat trip. As they traveled down the Thames River in England, Carroll entertained the children—Lorina, Alice, and Edith—with fantasy tales. It was at this point that he made Alice the protagonist of his story, using her curious, independent nature as the basis for his own fictional character.

The majority of references in Carroll's tale come from real-life acquaintances and events. For instance, the "bat" referred to in the Mad Hatter's rendition of "Twinkle, twinkle, little bat" (*Alice's Adventures in Wonderland,* p. 62) is Oxford's Professor Bartholomew Price, a figure known around campus as "the bat." Price's interest in astronomy led to Carroll's substituting his nickname for the word *star* in the poem.

The "treacle well" that the Dormouse talks of in the story also finds its roots in Oxford lore. Saint Frideswide of Oxford, the founder of Christ Church, was said to have been pursued by a suitor. For his boldness, the suitor was struck blind. Frideswide, however, took pity on the man and called forth a miraculous well of healing waters. It became known as the Treacle Well, and its history was quite familiar to Carroll.

Oxford also attracted a large share of entertainers. In 1860 the Ohio Minstrels visited the campus and sang "Oh Beautiful Star," among other songs. This tune appears in Carroll's work as "Oh Beautiful Soup," sung by the Mock Turtle. Traveling circuses showcased performers such as a ventriloquist who acted out "How doth the little busy bee" and a hypnotist who could make people behave like babies or sneeze violently. Carroll used these performances for inspiration when he had Alice recite "How dothe the little crocodile" (*Alice's Adventures in Wonderland*, p. 15) and when he wrote his chapter "Pig and Pepper."

Reception of the novel. Carroll first published his novel in 1865, but due to poor reproductions of Tenniel's illustrations, the work was immediately recalled. Although this edition never reached store shelves as a bound book, the unbound pages of text were retained by Carroll. In 1866 these sheets were sold to a different publisher and produced as a second issue of the first edition. Due to the printing problems associated with the 1865 publication, first editions of *Alice's Adventures in Wonderland* have become treasured collectibles.

Although a review in the highly respected journal *Athenaeum* complained that the story was stiff and overdone, it met with immediate commercial success. By 1900, 180,000 copies of the book had been sold. Carroll began his sequel, *Through the Looking Glass,* in 1867. According to an 1898 article in the *Pall Mall Gazette,* Carroll's Alice books were often quoted by newspapers and periodicals of the era, so much so that only Shakespeare's works were quoted with greater frequency.

For More Information

Batey, Mavis. *Alice's Adventures in Oxford.* London: Piktkin Pictorials, 1980.

Carroll, Lewis. *Alice's Adventures in Wonderland.* Edited by Penelope Lively. Rutland, Vt.: Everyman Classic, 1993.

Gray, Donald. "The Uses of Victorian Laughter." *Victorian Studies* 10 (October 1966): 1-4.

Lindsay, Donald, and E. S. Washington. *A Portrait of Britain between the Exhibitions.* Oxford: Clarendon Press, 1952.

Marshall, Dorothy. *The Life and Times of Victoria.* London: Weidenfeld and Nicolson, 1972.

McMurty, Jo. *Victorian Life and Victorian Fiction.* North Haven, Conn.: Archon, 1979.

Southey, Robert. *The Poetical Works of Robert Southey.* Vol. 2. Boston: Little, Brown, 1794.

Anna Karenina

by
Leo Tolstoy

Count Leo Nikolaevich Tolstoy was born into a noble family in 1828. Tolstoy's youth was spent among the world of the upper-class gentry during the last decades of serfdom in Russia. Throughout his life, Tolstoy felt torn between his own conflicting attitudes regarding the future of Russia and those of his noble class. By the time Tolstoy was in his early thirties he had discarded most of the trappings of gentry life and was spending much of his time working with and teaching the peasants of his estate, not unlike his character Levin in *Anna Karenina*. The writer also became concerned about other pressing social issues of his period, many of which appear in the pages of this novel.

Events in History at the Time of the Novel

The emancipation of the serfs. When Czar Alexander II came to power in 1855, he launched an era of reform. Under his influence, Russian politics made a marked turn toward more liberal policies. A central part of Alexander's reform efforts concerned the condition of the Russian peasants. These peasants or serfs worked and lived on the estates of the nobles. Essentially slaves, the serfs were considered the property of the landowner on whose estate they worked.

At an assembly of the marshals of the nobility, Alexander II stated his belief that it was better to "abolish serfdom from above, rather than wait for it to abolish itself from below" (Alexander in Troyat, p. 138). To accomplish this, he es-

> **THE LITERARY WORK**
>
> A novel set in Russia in the early 1870s; written and published between 1874 and 1877.
>
> **SYNOPSIS**
>
> Anna Karenina, a married woman of the upper class, falls in love with Count Vronsky, a dashing young army officer. After having a child by Vronsky, Anna supposes he does not love her and commits suicide. Her story is balanced by that of Konstantin Levin, a rural nobleman who finds joy in his marriage and comes to realize that the answers to life's most profound questions lie in a happy family life.

tablished a Committee for Peasant Affairs and instructed its members to draft reform legislation. Many upper-class politicians were against the reform, and this opposition caused the Committee to delay their work for the next five years. Leo Tolstoy, an ardent proponent of abolishing serfdom, was furious about this intentional stalling. He said of the situation, "Wherever one turns in Russia, one sees that everything is beginning to change—but the men in charge are old and therefore incompetent" (Tolstoy in Troyat, p. 139).

In 1861, after five years of political wrangling, an imperial manifesto was issued abolishing serfdom. On the surface the manifesto seemed promising; in reality it offered little reform. The manifesto stated that for a period of two years the serfs would be required to obey their owner as before, but the owner would no longer have the right to sell them, transfer them to another estate, or dispose of their children in any way. During the period of transition, the serfs would be required to pay a tithe of thirty rubles per man and ten rubles per woman each year. If they adhered to these provisions, the manifesto stated, they would receive freedom from their masters in 1863. They would then be given the use of their homes and enclosures as well as a measure of arable land in return for two types of payment. The first was the *obrok,* monetary payment of from eight to twelve rubles per person each year; the second was the *barshina,* payment in labor equal to forty days a year for men and thirty days for women. The implementation of the new measures was to be supervised by appointees from the nobility in each district.

Additional stipulations in the manifesto abolishing serfdom kept peasants bonded to their landlord until they had fully paid for their land, or until they reached a mutually satisfying agreement. The result was that even though the peasants could now work for themselves on land that, in some sense, belonged to them, the system had really not changed. Realizing this, the peasants in some areas began to riot. These uprisings were mercilessly quelled by government troops, and by 1865 they had ceased completely.

The ineffectiveness of the government reform is reflected in *Anna Karenina.* Though the story takes place about ten years after the emancipation, the peasants still work and live in poverty under legal conditions that keep them attached to the land of their masters.

Government and law in Russia. With the emancipation of the serfs in 1861 came important changes related to local government. Before the emancipation, the nobleman-landowner had been the sole and unlimited administrative power on his estate. Most of the police and judiciary positions in local government posts had also been filled by nobles. This system operated smoothly under bondage conditions, but under the new reforms, the government saw the necessity of reorganization. The main proponent of this administrative reform was N. A. Miliutin.

Miliutin's plan was to give local self-government more confidence, independence, and unity. Specifically, each of the local governments, or *zemstvos,* would consist of an elected assembly and an executive board. The county zemstvos were to elect the members of a provincial zemstvo, which would meet once a year. Once this plan was put into effect, both county and provincial zemstvos consisted of from ten to one hundred members. Their functions and powers were carefully defined and limited by Czar Alexander. The zemstvos were primarily responsible for satisfying the needs of the local community. Their key duties involved the upkeep of roads, the maintenance of prisons and hospitals, the promotion of industry and commerce, the betterment of public health and education, and the relief of the poor.

TOLSTOY: THE JUSTICE OF THE PEACE

In 1865 Tolstoy returned home from a trip abroad to discover that he had been appointed a Justice of the Peace for his locality. This made him responsible for supervising the new legislation for the emancipation of the serfs. In one case that came before his bench, Tolstoy gave a fair verdict in favor of a peasant's freedom and financial compensation from his owner. The local nobility were appalled that a fellow nobleman would side with the peasants, and Tolstoy's decision was overruled by the local officials.

The assemblies, however, suffered a lack of authority that handicapped their ability to carry out their duties. They had no control over police or government officials, whose assistance was needed to fulfill the zemstvos' duties. Also the zemstvos had limited funds and faced internal problems as different factions fought for power. Tolstoy highlights this last difficulty in his depiction of a provincial assembly meeting in *Anna Karenina.* Throughout the scene, the assembly pays almost no attention to the issues at hand, focusing instead on personal feuds between members of the council. The political maneuverings are so complicated that the character Konstantin Levin is unable to figure out what is happening or for whom he should vote. Despite all these problems, the zemstvos eventually proved successful. In time they turned into an efficient segment of government and developed public services to an unprecedented level across the land.

The decline of the Russian nobility. Meanwhile, large-scale farming, through which the nobles had attained their wealth, was in a state of decline. Among reasons for the decline, which began early in the nineteenth century, were a re-

Anna Karenina

Nicola Pagett as the title character in a film adaptation of *Anna Karenina*.

liance on outdated farming methods, a lack of new technology, and a shortage of capital. The emancipation of 1861, although designed to help the nobles financially, failed to do so. Under the provisions of the emancipation manifesto, a nobleman received subsidies for the loss of his lands if they were transferred to former serfs, yet this financial benefit went mostly unrealized. More than half of the 600 million rubles received by the nobility went to the treasury in settlement of outstanding mortgage loans. Only a small portion of this money wound up being reinvested in agricultural improvements, machinery, or livestock. The average yield per acre in Russia during this time was significantly lower than in the other European nations.

The decline of the nobility is most clearly shown by the rapid depletion of its landholdings. Between 1862 and 1872, the area owned by nobles declined by more than 10 percent. In the next decade, it would drop again, this time by more than 15 percent. Tolstoy depicts the decline of the noble class in *Anna Karenina* through the financial difficulties of the nobleman Oblonsky, and in the situations of several of the noblemen Levin meets at the provincial assembly.

Marriage and divorce in Russian society. Nineteenth-century Russia gave the husband complete legal power in a marriage. By imperial law, a wife had "to obey her husband as the head of the family, to live with him in love, respect, and unlimited obedience and to render him all pleasure and affection as mistress of the household" (Wagner, p. 62).

The law further regarded marriage as a religious institution. Since most Russians belonged to the Russian Orthodox Church, marriage usually fell under its dominion. Regarding marriage as a sacrament set up by God, the church made divorce extremely difficult to obtain. Dissolution of a marriage was possible only under a few circumstances—prolonged disappearance, sexual incapacity, exile to Siberia for a criminal act, or adultery if confirmed by at least two eyewitnesses. In cases of adultery, the church prohibited remarriage for the guilty spouse. Marriage partners could simply separate without getting a divorce, but a woman might easily fall into extreme financial difficulties. She had no legal right to support from her husband if she lived apart from him, yet still needed his consent before taking a job or attending a school of higher education. Furthermore, institutions offering this type of education did not even admit women until the 1870s.

Despite all these drawbacks, the number of divorces began to climb after the emancipation of the serfs, as the following figures indicate:

Year	Divorces	Marriages
1866	795	554,860
1870	696	602,278
1875	947	601,502
1880	879	654,496
1885	1,170	621,693

(Adapted from Wagner, p. 70)

With emancipation in 1861 came the emergence of a small women's rights movement led by radicals such as Nadezhda Vasilevna Stasova, who called for greater educational and job opportunities for females and founded societies to benefit them, including the Society for Cheap Lodgings, the Woman's Publishing Artel, and the Society for Woman's Work. Such women, a tiny minority, received a large boost from N. G. Cheryshevskii, whose novel *What Is To Be Done?* (1864) concerns a love triangle and a strong female character who studies medicine, becoming both self-fulfilled and useful to society. *What Is To Be Done?* had tremendous influence on Russian society. Other writers followed Cheryshevskii's lead, penning stories about strong females and love triangles in which one of the three characters steps out of the picture. To escape the laws and customs of Russian society, their characters sometimes resort to subterfuge, entering into a fictional, dishonest marriage, in which a woman fools others by wedding a man she does not love to escape a dreaded fate—the fate of marrying another man whom she despises. The fear of having to enter into such a marriage was realistic. In one gruesome incident, reported the journal *Otchestvennye zapiski* in 1868, a daughter was beaten by her mother until she agreed to marry a man she hated and then she was beaten by him. The daughter finally hanged herself.

There were heated opinions about how Russian women should deal with their problems. A controversy raged between novelists such as Cheryshevskii and others who wrote their own tales to counter his radical stories. The other novelists strongly disapproved of dishonest marriages and other such solutions to the problems confronting Russian women. While Tolstoy did not himself write a novel that openly attacked the radical solutions, he certainly disagreed with them and even accused Cheryshevskii's work of having a demoralizing effect on Russian society. Though on the surface the love triangle in *Anna Karenina* resembles the more radical works of the time, Tolstoy's plot promotes a real, rather than a dishonest, commitment to marriage, and the genuine happiness that this type of relationship can bring.

The Russo-Turkish War. In June of 1875, news began to reach the Russian public of troubling developments in the Balkans. In the Turkish territories of Bosnia and Herzegovina, the Christian (Russian Orthodox) Serbs were rising up against the Muslim Turks as a result of ethnic and religious tensions as well as the harshness of Turkish rule. The bulk of the population of Bosnia and Herzegovina was Slav by ethnic heritage, Serbian by language, and Russian Orthodox by religion, with a Roman Catholic minority. The upper landowning classes, however, were Muslim Turks. Further embittering the tensions between peasants and masters were their religious differences. The start of the peasant uprising is believed by many scholars to have been the visit of the Austrian Emperor Franz Josef to the region in 1875. His visit excited a great deal of Slav sympathy and radicalism and further exacerbated the existing tensions.

Anna Karenina

Historically, Russia had served as the protector of the Balkan Slavs, and so when reports of further Turkish atrocities reached Russia, tempers flared. Hundreds of Russian soldiers volunteered for service and unofficially served under the Russian General Cherniaev, who was controlling the Serbian army. In September 1876, this army was defeated by the Turks. Cherniaev's loss came as a shock to Russian nationalists. After Czar Alexander failed to enforce an effective armistice between the Serbs and the Turks, he declared war on Turkey on April 24, 1877. For the remainder of 1877, the war proved unpredictable, with both sides suffering defeats and gaining victories. Finally, after a crushing series of Russian victories, the Turkish army surrendered in January 1878.

From the beginning of the conflict, Tolstoy had been firmly against Russian intervention. When the czar made his declaration of war, Tolstoy responded by incorporating his own pacifist opinions into the concluding chapters of *Anna Karenina*. In these chapters, Levin argues with his brother and Katavasov, who both support Russia's entry into the conflict. When asked what he thinks of the volunteers leaving to fight the war, Levin responds, "In my opinion it means that in a nation of eighty million there will always be not hundreds, as now, but tens of thousands of men who have lost their social positions, happy-go-lucky people who are ready to go anywhere—into Pugachov's robber band or to Khiva, to Serbia" (Tolstoy, *Anna Karenina,* pp. 797-98). Levin also echoes Tolstoy's own pacifist opinions when he states that war is "bestial, cruel, and horrible" (*Anna Karenina,* p. 795). During its first publication in the periodical *Russian Herald,* Tolstoy's final chapters were removed and replaced by a simple epilogue written by the editor.

The Novel in Focus

The plot. The novel begins with a family crisis in the home of Stiva Oblonsky, a pampered and fun-loving nobleman, whose wife has just found out about his affair with a French governess. Stiva's sister, Anna Karenina, the wife of Alexei Karenin, a well-to-do bureaucrat, arrives to soothe the marital discord and dissuades Dolly from getting a divorce. Also arriving in Moscow at this time is Konstantin Levin, a friend of Stiva's who proposes to Dolly's sister Kitty Shtcherbatsky. She refuses his proposal because she is in love with Count Vronsky, a young army officer who has no plans of marriage.

When Vronsky meets Anna, he falls madly in love with her. At a ball a few nights later, Kitty's hopes for Vronsky are crushed when she witnesses the interaction between the Count and Anna. Anna cannot resist Vronsky's advances and enters into an affair with him. By the time she confesses her adultery to her husband, she is already pregnant with Vronsky's child.

Meanwhile, Levin has devoted himself to the rural life and to bettering the conditions of the peasants on his estate. He finally realizes that his dedication to work has been partially an attempt to forget his rejection from Kitty, whom he will always love.

Anna has by this time completely abandoned her husband and their eight-year-old son to be with Vronsky, although the young officer has not committed to a life with her. The uncertainty of the situation puts Anna into a desperate state as she approaches the end of her pregnancy.

Karenin finally grows frustrated enough with his unfaithful wife to hire a divorce lawyer. But Anna becomes deathly ill after the birth of her child, and her husband forgives her. The exchange leaves Vronsky, who is also present, feeling humiliated, and he unsuccessfully attempts suicide. Anna and Vronsky both recover and leave Moscow for a trip to Italy with their baby daughter. Karenin still wants a divorce, but Anna refuses because she fears the loss of her son, Sergei.

Meanwhile, Levin has returned to Moscow and become engaged to Kitty. The wedding has taken place and the couple have settled into a married life they both enjoy. Levin realizes that the key to happiness is the emotional satisfaction of a lifelong commitment. Following Levin's realization, the happy couple learn that Kitty is pregnant. Kitty gives birth to a son, and Levin makes another realization that the key to life is to dedicate oneself to the soul rather than pursue materialistic goals.

Before Levin's baby is born, Anna and Vronsky return from Italy. Their upper-class social circle welcomes Vronsky home but rejects Anna, scandalized by her behavior.

> [Vronsky] soon noticed that, though society was open to him personally, it was closed to Anna. As in a game of cat and mouse, the arms that were raised to allow him to get inside the circle were instantly lowered to prevent Anna from getting into it.
> (*Anna Karenina,* p. 530)

Anna grows increasingly desperate as Vronsky slips further away. Finally realizing that her love affair is over, Anna commits suicide by throwing herself under a train. Vronsky, also feel-

TOLSTOY'S MODELS FOR THE CHARACTERS IN *ANNA KARENINA*

Fictional name	Real-life source
Konstantin Levin	Leo Tolstoy himself
Nikolai Levin	Dmitry Tolstoy, Leo's brother
Kitty Shtcherbatsky	Sonya Bers—Tolstoy's wife
Anna Karenina	Pushkin's daughter—Marya Hartung
Alexei Karenin	Minister of Finance—Valuyev
Count Vronsky	Sonya's first suitor—Mitrofan Polivanov
Mikhailov	The painter Karmskoye

ing hopeless, volunteers for service in the Russo-Turkish war and leaves Moscow.

Women in transition. In *Anna Karenina,* Tolstoy provides three different models of wedlock: the marriages of Dolly and Stiva Oblonsky, Anna and Alexei Karenin, and Kitty and Konstantin Levin. A crucial aspect of the novel and of Tolstoy's system of belief is the position of the woman in marriage and in society. At the time that Tolstoy was writing his novel, men continued to dominate the family in Russia despite the fact that some women had begun to agitate for reform. The law still demanded unconditional obedience from a wife to her husband, and Russian custom gave men the right to use force to discipline their wives and children.

The only socially acceptable ways for Russian women to gain respect and prominence in society was through marriage, motherhood, and "appropriate" work. Marriage meant repeated childbearing. The average married woman of the 1800s bore four or five children in her lifetime, a respectable number. The other acceptable way for women to gain esteem was through family-related labor. Even more than in industrialized households of western Europe, Russian women performed a wide range of tasks. In peasant families, wives worked with their husbands in the fields and performed household chores. An upper-class woman, besides supervising household servants, was responsible for maintaining her family's social position through dinners, parties, and other gatherings.

Tolstoy subscribed to the belief that the greatest duty of women was to bear children and raise families. He depicts this belief through the fates of the females in *Anna Karenina.* Dolly and Kitty both achieve a certain degree of satisfaction through their children and family life. After abandoning her family for the illicit love of Vronsky, Anna realizes that she has no purpose in life and commits suicide. Marriage was losing significance among progressive Russians at the time, largely because the church so strongly opposed divorce. It is perhaps this social trend that Tolstoy's novel aims to combat.

Sources. *Anna Karenina* had its roots in a variety of sources. According to Tolstoy, the basic story was inspired by Aleksander Pushkin's *Tales of Belkin.* Like Pushkin, Tolstoy decided to write a novel concerning the private lives of contemporary people. Another source was a real-life tragedy that occurred near Tolstoy's estate. In 1872 a neighbor of Tolstoy's cast off his mistress, Anna Pirogova. The railroad had recently been extended into the province, and in her despair at the failed relationship, Anna rushed down to the tracks and threw herself under a train. The corpse was taken to a nearby engine shed, and Tolstoy, hearing of the incident, rode over to view the remains. Tolstoy had never known the woman, but her tragic suicide inspired the story of Anna Karenina's failed liaison with Vronsky and her subsequent suicide in the novel. Reinforcing this thread in the plot was another source, the novel *The Prime Minister* by the English writer Anthony Trollope. Tolstoy is known to have read the novel with keen interest and to have been inspired by the railroad suicide of the character Lopez in the novel.

Once he began writing, Tolstoy used real-life friends and relatives as the models for many of his characters.

Many incidents and ideas in the novel are also autobiographical. The death of Dmitry Tolstoy

Anna Karenina

Tolstoy dressed in peasant clothing, 1897.

from tuberculosis in the arms of his prostitute lover served as the model for the death of Nikolai Levin in the novel. Just like Levin and Kitty in the novel, Tolstoy and his fiancée, Sonya Bers, exchanged diaries prior to their wedding. The frantic scene in the novel in which Levin has no shirt to wear for his wedding is based on an incident that occurred on the day of Tolstoy's own wedding to Sonya. Also, the ideas of Levin in the novel concerning the condition of peasants and his enjoyment of farm life reflect Tolstoy's own experiences. Though he belonged to the most privileged class in society, Tolstoy spent most of his time at Yasnaya Polyana, his rural estate. Dressed in rough peasant clothing, he would work with the peasants in the field. Like Levin, Tolstoy dreamed of renouncing his title and wealth and living as they did.

Public reception of Anna Karenina. The publication of *Anna Karenina* drove Russian readers into a frenzy. The reading public was excited by the story of Anna's illicit love affair and was shocked by the scenes of her decline. Nicholas Strakhov, a literary critic and admirer of Tolstoy's work, wrote to Tolstoy about the reception of an installment of *Anna Karenina* in the *Russian Herald*: "Everyone is dumb with admiration for the February issue. The January one was less popular.... Now there is a roar of satisfaction. It's as though you were throwing food to starving men" (Strakhov in Troyat, p. 369). Strakhov wrote about the novel again to Tolstoy a year later: "Everyone is fascinated by your novel, it's incredible how many people are reading it. Only Pushkin and Gogol have ever been read like this, with people scrambling for every page and paying no attention to what anybody else is writing" (Strakhov in Troyat, p. 370). The novelist Fyodor Dostoyevsky, whose intense dislike for Tolstoy made any praise especially meaningful, called the novelist a god of the art. Dostoyevsky found a deeper significance in *Anna Karenina* than did most Russians. He wrote of the novel: "The reader felt that there was a living truth, a most real and inescapable truth, which has to be believed.... The Russian reader has to be often reminded of this eternal truth.... This reminder was a good act on the part of the author—to say nothing about the fact that he executed it as a sublime artist" (Dostoyesky in Hall, p. 447).

While the majority of Russians praised *Anna Karenina*, there were a few critics who denounced Tolstoy's novel. One of the greatest detractors of the work was the Russian Ivan Turgenev, whose love-hate relationship with Tolstoy was legendary. "I do not like *Anna Karenina*," wrote Turgenev, "despite some truly magnificent pages (the horse race, the hay-making, the hunt). But the whole thing is sour, it smells of Moscow and old maids, the Slavophilism and the narrow-mindedness of the nobility" (Turgenev in Troyat, p. 371). Even Turgenev's critique, though critical of the novel's themes, praises the power of Tolstoy's writing. It was with the publication of *Anna Karenina* that Tolstoy cemented his place as a key figure in Russian literature.

For More Information

Dukes, Paul. *A History of Russia: Medieval, Modern and Contemporary.* New York: McGraw-Hill, 1974.

Engel, Barbara Alpern. *Mothers and Daughters: Women of the Intelligentsia in Nineteenth-Century Russia.* London: Cambridge University Press, 1983.

Hall, Sharon K., ed. *Twentieth-Century Literary Criticism.* Vol. 4. Detroit: Gale Research, 1981.

Tolstoy, Leo, *Anna Karenina.* Translated by David Magarshack. New York: Signet Classic, 1981.

Troyat, Henri. *Tolstoy.* New York: Doubleday, 1967.

Wagner, William G. *Marriage, Property, and Law in Late Imperial Russia.* Oxford: Clarendon Press, 1994.

"Barn Burning"

by William Faulkner

Born in 1897, William Faulkner spent his very early years in the country villages of New Albany and Ripley, Mississippi. When he was five years old, his family moved to Oxford and settled there. From the vantage point of the partly restored old mansion his father and mother bought on the town's square, the young Faulkner was able to watch and listen to the parade of farmers that came into this town of little over a thousand citizens. Faulkner later bought his own estate just north of Oxford, where he continued to observe and reflect on the residents of the area. He also made use of his own family history, including ancestors who had led sometimes glorious, sometimes infamous lives in North Carolina and Mississippi. Drawing on these influences, he created many stories and novels set in the fictional county of Yoknapatawpha. Among them is the saga of the Snopes family, beginning with Abner Snopes in the short story, "Barn Burning."

THE LITERARY WORK
A short story set in Mississippi during the late 1800s; published in 1939.

SYNOPSIS
The ten-year-old son of a tenant farmer must choose between remaining loyal to his father and doing what he knows is morally right by alerting an intended victim of the crime his father is about to commit.

Events in History at the Time the Short Story Takes Place

Reconstruction and beyond. The Civil War virtually destroyed the economy of the South. The resources of even the smallest landowner had, in many cases, been seized by the Confederate government in support of the war effort, and the invading Union army had destroyed land and other property as a means of winning the war. The Thirteenth Amendment of 1865 freed the slaves but did not provide for their participation in land ownership. There was a plan in the U.S. Congress to confiscate all Southern farms larger than two hundred acres and divide them into forty-acre parcels for the ex-slaves, but this strategy never came to pass. After the war, lands were reclaimed by their former white owners without interference from Congress. Lawmakers insisted only on guaranteeing the ex-slaves the right to citizenship (the Fourteenth Amendment, ratified in 1868) and the vote (the Fifteenth Amendment, ratified in 1870).

In general, the federal government allowed issues concerning property and jobs to be worked out by the Southern people themselves. Since the breakup of the large plantations never did occur, Southern lands became concentrated into fewer and larger holdings than before the war, and Southern farmers restricted themselves more often to raising just one crop, usually cotton. In many cases, however, they no longer had resources to maintain the properties, and their slave labor force had disappeared.

New systems evolved. At a loss themselves, many ex-slaves at first signed work contracts and labored in gangs in the fields, but this system did not last long because of the ex-slaves' thirst for land of their own and their desire to send their children to school. "Many blacks ... broke contracts, ran away, engaged in work slowdowns or strikes, burned barns, and otherwise expressed their displeasure with the contract labor system" (Nash, p. 553). Replacing the contract labor system were the systems of sharecropping and tenant farming. In return for a plot of land, supplies, food, and clothing, the sharecropper pledged as much as 50 percent of his harvest to the landowner and used his own half to pay for goods purchased on credit at the landowner's store. In tenant farming, the farmer promised to sell his harvest to a local merchant from whom he rented land and supplies. He too had to purchase necessities on credit at the merchant's store. Both systems kept the farmers in debt from one year to the next, and at the end of their agreement with the owner, they found themselves once more landless. Moreover, since the terms of an agreement were from one crop to the next and there were frequent disputes, tenants often did not live long enough in a given area to gain any power by voting in local elections.

White tenants. Though tenant farming was undertaken by many former slaves, poor whites also became tenants in order to support their families after the war. They formed a large and resentful labor pool, possibly larger than that of the ex-slaves with whom they now competed. Oftentimes the white tenant clashed with landowners, convinced that he had been defrauded of his fair share. Like the black tenant farmers, the whites also tended to migrate from one area to another, and "after living a year or two on one place moved on" (Brooks, p. 17). As a result of the tenant system, the poverty and the self-esteem of many white farmers worsened after the Civil War. Prior to the conflict, the farmers had raised almost everything they ate. The greater amount of land devoted to growing cotton in the postwar years made it hard for them to produce food for their families; they had to purchase flour, meat, and other foods at the local store. The farmers tried to compensate by hunting, fishing, and raising corn and potatoes. Struggling to make ends meet, they often earned less than the black tenants.

The situation was a drastic comedown from conditions that existed before the war, when many of the poor whites lived in the "upcountry" region. The upcountry enveloped the mountains and hill lands where small communities of white families had lived under frontier conditions, largely isolated from the rest of the South until the Civil War. Self-sufficiency remained the primary goal of the area's farm families—a large majority of whom owned their land and worked it by themselves. These people were proud of their independence.

The destructive war, however, depleted or ruined the resources of the upcountry as well as other parts of the white South. Additionally, postwar demand for cotton stimulated large investments in the upcountry. The lands of the small farmers were sought by those who wanted to establish cotton plantations, and a depression in the mid-1870s made it necessary for many upcountry families to sell their land. By 1880 one third of the white farmers in the cotton states were tenants.

The plight of the poor tenant farmer can be seen in Abner Snopes's comment to his wife about his latest employer, Major de Spain: "I reckon I'll have a word with the man that aims to begin tomorrow owning me body and soul for the next eight months" (Faulkner, "Barn Burning," p. 10). Major de Spain confirms the helplessness of Abner's situation, doing nothing to sweeten Abner's temperament, when he says, "... you never had a hundred dollars. You never will. So, I'm going to charge you twenty bushels of corn against your crop" ("Barn Burning," p. 17). The charge is for some damage that Abner did to de Spain's costly rug, imported all the way from France. Though an atypical expense, the incident nevertheless illustrates the perpetual cycle of debt upon debt that shackled many tenant farmers, both white and black, to the service of one landowner.

Education. As early as 1801, Mississippi schools provided instruction for girls as well as boys. Parents who lived in the mountains and backwoods, however, generally had little or no education themselves and doubted that their children had a need for it. In any case, education interfered with such people's lifestyles, for it required some free time in which the children could study, a luxury that seemed unaffordable to many. Schoolwork would have taken time away from real chores that put food in their bellies, such as raising crops and hunting. It is for this reason and because the tenant-farming Snopes family in the story had moved at least a dozen times within the ten years of Colonel Sartoris Snopes's young life that education for him and his siblings was out of the question. They would more than likely have to move once again because of their father's illegal activities. The Snopes children had no home to speak of, no sense of stability or lasting friendships. All of their concentration was centered on mere day-to-day survival. Still, there were in young Colonel Sartoris, as in many poor whites, noble values—loyalty to his father but also individual integrity, a sense of honor and decency. A decade after "Barn Burning" was published, Faulkner would win the Nobel Prize for literature. In his acceptance speech he explained that his fiction was preoccupied with the human heart in conflict with itself, a condition that plagues the central character in "Barn Burning."

The Short Story in Focus

The plot. "Barn Burning" begins with ten-year-old Colonel Sartoris "Sarty" Snopes sitting in a makeshift court of the Justice of the Peace held in a dry goods store. Without sufficient evidence to convict Sarty's father, Abner Snopes, of burning the barn of his last landlord, the case is dismissed and the family moves on to yet another farm. This one, however, is much grander than the small farms and fields Sarty's family had lived on in the past. The boy has hope that maybe his father's anger against his fate—life as a tenant farmer—will abate. On the day of their arrival, though, his father deliberately steps in horse manure, then tracks it on his new landlord Major de Spain's hundred-dollar French rug.

In the background of the story are other family members—Sarty's two sisters, his mother, his aunt, and his older brother. The morose father, Abner, has the daughters clean the rug with a harsh lye, which ruins it. Outraged, Major de Spain charges him twenty bushels of corn to be taken from Abner's future harvest. Abner, placid on the outside, sues Major de Spain for leveling too severe a punishment. The Justice of the Peace reduces it to ten bushels, whereupon Sarty defiantly and loyally proclaims to his father that even that amount won't be taken from them. The boy has already suggested a strategy: "We'll gether hit and hide hit! I kin watch" (Faulkner, "Barn Burning," p. 16).

Aware of the exploitation in tenant farming, angered and outraged by the insult of it to him personally, Abner is not as impressed by the splendor of his new landlord's home as his son Sarty is. "Pretty and white, ain't it?" he tells the boy. "That's sweat. Nigger sweat. Maybe it ain't white enough yet to suit him. Maybe he wants to mix some white sweat with it" ("Barn Burning," p. 12). Sarty, however, perceives that it is wrong to hold Major de Spain responsible for the indignity his father suffers and to purposely destroy de Spain's property. Soon after the hearing, Abner Snopes sets out to claim justice for himself and burn down de Spain's barn in revenge for the punishment pronounced against him over the rug. Sarty, torn because of his loyalty to his father but driven by his own sense of justice, manages to warn de Spain of the impending fire, then runs away, presumably never to return home again.

Poor whites vs. blacks. In his book *William Faulkner and Southern History*, Joel Williamson makes an observation about Abner's penchant for burning barns and its possible roots. He compares it with the tactics that the slaves used, "the threat to burn the master's barn under the cover of darkness. Arson, it seems, has always been a favored form of retaliation by the powerless of the world" (Williamson, p. 329).

Though the tactic of barn burning may have been borrowed from the slaves, many poor whites had ill feelings for blacks in the late 1800s. This animosity resulted partly from the fact that the poor whites had to compete with blacks for sharecropping and tenant-farming jobs. Abner reflects this condition in his treatment of the black servant of his new landlord, Major de Spain. "Get out of my way, nigger," Abner barks, flinging the house servant aside ("Barn Burning," p. 11). His violence, though directed mostly at the landlord, finds a ready target in the black servant standing in his way.

White landowners often preferred black tenants to white ones, and "in very bad years in Mississippi . . . white tenants organized to drive black tenants off the land by violence" (Williamson, p. 154). When the violence escalated around the turn of the twentieth century, white landlords in Mississippi even hired some Pinkerton detectives to drive off poor whites. Property was at the heart of the frustrations of many poor whites and their dislike of blacks. Like the landowner, blacks interfered with the ability of poor whites to control property, which they equated with personal freedom. Limits on their power to transfer, acquire, or hold property were viewed as a personal affront, a destruction of their liberty.

Sources. Violence, frustration, and frequent moves marked the history of William Faulkner's family. This legacy became a source of inspiration for stories such as "Barn Burning." The fam-

"Barn Burning"

Picking cotton in the rural South.

ily's real-life saga included great-grandfather William Cuthbert Faulkner, who injured his brother in a fight in Missouri at age sixteen, suffered a beating from his own father, and ran away from home. He reappeared in Mississippi, hoping to live with an uncle who, at the time, was in jail. This great-grandfather became the first author in the family, writing a story about a real-life murderer that sold 2,500 copies the day the murderer was executed. The Old Colonel, as his family came to call him, went on to muster two regiments to fight in the Civil War, earned the respect of the community, and set up a successful law practice in Ripley, Mississippi. By 1868 William Cuthbert Faulkner had grown so prosperous that he decided not to have anything to do with the other Faulkners in the area, whom he considered "no-good." He therefore changed the spelling of his own name to Falkner.

William Faulkner, who would restore the *u* in his family name, was born to Murry and his wife, Miss Maud, in New Albany, near Oxford. Even as a youngster, he avowed that his ambition was to be a writer like his great-grandfather. Thus the Old Colonel became a model for his great-grandson, as well as a character in some of his stories. Certainly the experiences of Faulkner's family—its violent encounters, run-ins with Southern law, and uprootings from one place to another—fed the writer's imagination and helped provide background for his fictional tales.

In addition to his own family members, Faulkner was influenced by other residents of the Oxford area, especially struggling farmers. In fact, in 1938, the year before "Barn Burning" appeared in print, he bought a second farm, Greenfield, and leased it out to tenants. "Bill found more than just a farm out there," his brother recalled. "He found the kind of people he wrote about, hill people.... They fought over elections and settled their own disputes. We had a killing just across the creek from us, over redistricting a school zone" (John Faulkner in Blotner, p. 486).

Faulkner's daughter, Jill, has recounted the story of life on their own farm, Rowan Oak, and the commissary Faulkner ran that served as a store for the tenant farmers and some of the neighbors as well. She noted that the place "smelled of cheese" and mentioned the cans of sardines and the other foods in the commissary (Williamson, p. 272). Her description evokes a scene duplicated by Faulkner's description of what Sarty sees and smells as he sits in the general store awaiting the outcome of his father's hearing at the beginning of "Barn Burning."

Faulkner sets his story in the imaginary town of Jefferson in Yoknapatawpha County. (The town and county are not named in "Barn Burning," but other stories about the Sartoris and Snopes families place the action there.) Jefferson, in Faulkner's imagination, was a town of four thousand citizens with a few wealthy plantation homes still marking the outskirts, some abandoned and decaying. Such a setting was reminiscent of Faulkner's Oxford, Mississippi, with spots of wealth scattered among the ruins of plantations.

Events in History at the Time the Short Story Was Written

The Great Depression. Faulkner chronicled an era just after the Reconstruction, a period that held many similarities to the Depression years of the 1930s, when "Barn Burning" was written. During both time periods, some wealthy people took advantage of dismal economic circumstances to increase their own fortunes, while many poor people grew poorer and their situations grew more hopeless. Many farmers, who had long depended on government support, lost their lands to bankers during the Great Depression, and large farm syndicates began to dominate American farming, much as the plantation owners grew to dominate Southern agriculture in an earlier era.

William Faulkner was personally acquainted with financial hardships, although he never descended into total destitution. His hopes to be recognized as a writer met with continual frustration for more than a decade until shortly after the onset of the Great Depression in 1929.

The Depression meant the loss of jobs for millions of Americans. For Faulkner, it was an extension of his personal lack of fortune, but ironically he began to experience some professional success during the harsh decade. His novel *Sanctuary* appeared in the early 1930s. It was by Faulkner's own confession an idea deliberately conceived to make money, and it did. The success of this steamy novel brought Faulkner literary fame and financial reward. His earlier short stories, written and rejected, now began to sell, and offers came in to write for the film industry in Hollywood.

The Depression lingered in the United States, but Europe was edging toward war. By 1939, when Faulkner was writing seriously about his own Mississippi experiences and fantasies, conflict in Europe seemed imminent and the resultant preparations improved the American economy. These conditions bring to mind the effect the Civil War had on the financial status of a character in "Barn Burning." Sarty's father, Abner, had gone into the war, the story admits, to improve his fortune, "wearing no uniform . . . going to war . . . for booty" ("Barn Burning," pp. 24-25).

Publication and reception. "Barn Burning" was initially written as an introductory chapter to *The Hamlet,* the first in a trilogy of novels centered around the Snopes family. Faulkner later changed his mind and attempted to publish "Barn Burning" as an independent magazine story. First the *Post* rejected "Barn Burning," then *Redbook* and *The American Magazine* declined the chance to publish it on the grounds that it was too depressing. Other rejections poured in before *Harper's* purchased it for $400.

THE DISAPPEARING COLONEL SARTORIS SNOPES

Besides getting "Barn Burning" published in 1939, Faulkner managed also to complete the first volume of his trilogy about the Snopes family that year. Altogether it would take a decade to publish the trilogy, beginning with *The Hamlet* (1940), followed by *The Town* (1957), and *The Mansion* (1959). In none of these novels would Colonel Sartoris Snopes, who flees at the end of "Barn Burning," ever reappear.

Proud of the story, Faulkner later wrote a treatment to turn "Barn Burning" into a film, but nothing came of the project. Although various characters in "Barn Burning" resurfaced in other fiction by Faulkner, young Sarty never appeared again. In retrospect, some critics consider "Barn Burning" one of the finest short stories in Faulkner's entire repertoire. It was first printed in book form in the *Collected Stories of William Faulkner,* published in 1943. Many critics showered praise on the forty-two stories in the book, though some spoke of the variation in quality, singling out "Barn Burning" as a superior example. "These Collected Stories," said the *Atlantic,* "certainly strengthen the case of those critics who have steadily maintained that Faulkner is the greatest living American writer" (James, p. 298).

For More Information

Blotner, Joseph. *Faulkner: A Biography*. Vol. 2. New York: Random House, 1974.

Brooks, Cleanth. *William Faulkner: First Encounters*. New Haven, Conn.: Yale University Press, 1983.

Faulkner, William. "Barn Burning." In *Collected Stories of William Faulkner*. New York: Random House, 1943.

Foner, Eric. *Reconstruction*. New York: Harper & Row, 1988.

James, Mertice M., and Dorothy Brown, eds. *Book Review Digest*. Vol. 46. New York: H. W. Wilson, 1951.

McElvaine, Robert S. *The Great Depression*. New York: Times Books, 1984.

Nash, Gary B., et al., eds. *The American People: Creating a Nation and a Society*. Vol. 2. New York: Harper & Row, 1990.

Williamson, Joel. *William Faulkner and Southern History*. New York: Oxford University Press, 1993.

"The Bear"

by William Faulkner

THE LITERARY WORK

A short story set in fictional Yoknapatawpha County, Mississippi, in 1883 as well as a few years before and after; published in 1942.

SYNOPSIS

An annual bear hunt for "Old Ben" makes a man out of a boy who, upon reaching maturity, repudiates his share of the family farm.

William Faulkner grew up in Oxford, Mississippi, around the turn of the century. In 1929 he began his famous series of novels and short stories about the fictional Yoknapatawpha County, Mississippi, creating a complex set of characters who together formed a microcosm of the Deep South in the nineteenth and twentieth centuries. "The Bear" centers on Isaac "Ike" McCaslin, grandson of a Southern planter who ravaged his human relations as well as his wilderness property.

Events in History at the Time the Short Story Takes Place

Hunting in the South. Prior to and after the Civil War, hunting was a popular activity throughout the South, whether enjoyed as a pastime or employed for survival. Many Southern hunters used dogs to aid them in their search for prey and rode through the woods on horseback. They hunted to both obtain food and enjoy strictly masculine company since women as a rule were excluded. Faulkner himself joined a group of hunters every autumn to snare deer in the Mississippi Delta and partake of the sometimes drunken masculine camaraderie of the hunting camp. In his youth, he—like his main character in "The Bear"—would go hunting; Faulkner's companions were a man known as General Stone and his friends, who told tales of a seemingly uncatchable bear called Old Reel Foot.

Abundant throughout Mississippi was the black bear, a type threatening to dogs but deadly to men only in exceptional cases. Specially-trained hounds would follow the bear and bring it to bay—that is, bark it into a position of squaring off with the hunter. If the overeager dogs pounced on the bear, it would certainly destroy them, as Old Ben does to the great hound Lion in the story. With the help of two or three other dogs as fierce as he, Lion might have succeeded—there were examples of three or four fierce fighting dogs seizing and bringing a bear down together. Such cases were rare, though. More often a bear would disembowel dogs foolhardy enough to attack it, striking them with its paws or seizing them in its arms and biting through their spines and legs. So instead of using the dogs to kill a bear, hunters would shoot their quarry once it was cornered, using rifles, shotguns, revolvers, and sometimes a knife, the way the character Boon does on the fictional Old Ben. An actual Mississippi hunter, General Wade Hampton, would—after his dogs brought a bear to bay—rush in and stab it, reach-

Hunting scene in Mississippi.

ing over from behind a shoulder. He is known to have slain perhaps thirty bears this way, the largest weighing 410 pounds. There is a record of an even larger bear that roamed Mississippi, one weighing 640 pounds and a size worthy of Faulkner's fictional Old Ben.

Part black, part Chickasaw Indian, the character Sam Fathers helps raise Isaac McCaslin to manhood in Faulkner's story, teaching him how to hunt and survive in the wilderness. At the beginning of the 1800s, the Chickasaw, a nation inhabiting northern Mississippi, were esteemed as the Mississippi Valley's most skilled hunters. Their favorite game was deer, followed by bear. The Chickasaw would turn bearskin into heavy winter robes and bedcoverings, the tough hide into sturdy moccasins, the dried gut into bowstrings, slabs of fat from the carcass into oil for cooking or a nutrient for their hair, and the bear's claws into jewelry. By the time "The Bear" takes place later in the century, however, the great hunting days were over for the Chickasaw. Like other Southern nations, most of the tribe had been forcibly removed from Mississippi to Oklahoma at the end of the 1830s. There were only a few descendants—represented by Sam Fathers in the story—who could have learned firsthand the old Chickasaw ways. Sam Fathers is of mixed Chickasaw-black heritage in the story, but his background does not interfere with his being respected for his hunting prowess by the story's white characters. Hunting provided a common ground for men in the South whether they were landed gentry, poor whites, African Americans, American Indians, or mixed bloods:

> [I]n many localities certain Negroes or Indians were numbered among the expert [hunters] of the community, and their society was at times apparently courted.... [H]unting was a factor which promoted integration.
> (Godhes, p. xvi)

A boy's first hunt was commonly associated with his initial forays toward less childish pursuits; it provided a rite of passage that included the assimilation of knowledge, the demonstration of skills, and a show of courage and humility. The intensity of this rite of passage was distinctly Southern in flavor. While Northern boys regarded hunting as a hobby, most Southern boys were raised to view it as an integral part of life. In Faulkner's story, when the young Ike McCaslin kills his first deer, Sam Fathers smears the hot blood on his face, turning the event into an initiation of sorts.

Southern folktales. Tall tales abounded throughout the rural South in the nineteenth century. The origins of the Southern folktale can be traced back to sources from West Africa, France, Ireland, and England, to name just a few. But local scenery and personality types also came to exert a major influence; the South developed its own store of anecdotes and tales that people spun about the characters and deeds of their kinfolk, friends, and neighbors.

The 1830s to 1850s was a golden period for the great folklore tradition of the South. Renowned tellers and writers of tall tales abounded; by profession these folklorists were lawyers, judges, ministers, editors, and sportsmen whose jobs required that they be skilled in rhetorical speech, or else brought them into contact with a great deal of source material.

One story to arise out of this era is a tale called "The Big Bear of Arkansas," which inspired an entire genre of hunting tales. In many ways, the story resembles that of Faulkner's "The Bear." The tale, believed to have been written by Thomas Bangs Thorpe, includes a visit to the big city (New Orleans), an exceptional dog, and also an overeager hound who is killed by the bear. The characters hunt the bear over a period of several years until their prey is finally killed by the dog and a knife-wielding hunter. Whether or not Thorpe's tale actually served as direct source material for Faulkner's story remains uncertain; in any case, the pair of works point out the popularity of bear hunting in a wide variety of Southern literature in the 1800s and early 1900s.

Mixed-race offspring. In the pre-Civil War South, mixed-race offspring were often the product of sexual unions between a slaveholder and one of his slaves. There are different mixtures of races in Faulkner's story. The character Sam Fathers is the offspring of a union between a Chickasaw chief and his black female slave. This same female slave, purchased from the chief by a white planter (Ike's grandfather), later bears a few of the planter's children in a union that mixes the black and white bloodlines. Such sexual relations between a slave owner and his slaves were not uncommon in the Old South, although they were by no means universal. In fact, those slaveowners who indulged in them were often looked upon with scorn by those who did not.

In situations in which slave owners and slaves engaged in sexual liaisons, there is evidence that suggests some of the relations came close to being a form of institutionalized rape. Often the attitude was that the slave woman on the plantation was there for the taking if the master fancied her. Not surprisingly, many young masters indulged, forming a habit that sometimes continued even as they grew older and married. Resistance on the part of the slave woman was considered futile, as the daughter of one slave intimated: "Plenty of the colored women have children by the white man. She know better than to not do what he say" (Eliza Washington in Fox-Genovese, p. 325).

With the master possessing the ultimate authority on the plantation, the possibility existed for even greater iniquities. "[Masters] might have sexual relations with the women they disciplined and who might indeed be their daughters" (Fox-Genovese, p. 315). In part four of *The Bear*, a sixteen-year-old Ike McCaslin discovers precisely this situation in his family's past. He finds that his grandfather, Lucius Quintus Carothers McCaslin, had a daughter with one of his slaves and then proceeded—twenty-two years later—to conceive a child with this same daughter.

The demise of the wilderness. The pre-Civil War plantation system rested on the foundation of frontier conditions, which it did not altogether displace. The system allowed for the maintenance of a certain amount of property as wilderness for use in hunting and other activities. During and after the Civil War, the plantation system foundered, and the conservation of a certain amount of wilderness collapsed as well. There were hopes that the plantations would be divided up for the ex-slaves after the war, but in the end Southern lands became concentrated into larger holdings by even fewer owners than before the war. The end of the war also brought Northerners and Northern industries to the region to take advantage of the situation. All of this resulted in an exploitation of wilderness resources and a loss of the last traces of frontier in the Southern states. John Faulkner, William's brother, described the local effects:

> Hardwood mills began coming in and after them mills that cut almost anything that would make a board. And our wildlife retreated farther and farther into the Big Woods, the still virgin tracts of timber that cloaked the Mississippi Delta.
> (John Faulkner in Utley, p. 95)

William Faulkner brooded about the destruction of the wilderness and wove it into his fiction. In "The Bear," the white landowner Major de Spain begins logging operations on the edges of the hunting grounds, just as real-life timber companies moved into the woods hunted by Faulkner.

"The Bear"

The Short Story in Focus

The plot. One of a series of seven stories in the book *Go Down Moses*, "The Bear" exists in its long form as published in the volume but appeared in a shorter form in *The Saturday Evening Post*. Only the book version includes a lengthy Section IV, summarized below. All seven stories in *Go Down Moses* concern the descendants of the fictional white planter Lucius Quintus Carothers McCaslin (known as Carothers), who moved into northern Mississippi in the early 1800s. He purchased land as well as a part-black slave woman and her son (Sam Fathers) from a Chickasaw chief, then built a plantation and fathered three legitimate white children with his wife and two illegitimate mulatto children by his black slaves. His first illegitimate child, a daughter named Tomey, became the mother of his second illegitimate child, a son. This boy eventually became the father of three children, one of whom was named Tennie's Jim. Meanwhile, Carothers had two white sons and a daughter in his legitimate line of offspring. One of the sons, in turn, had a son named Isaac "Ike" McCaslin. Orphaned at an early age, Ike was being raised by his cousin Cass McCaslin Edmonds and the Chickasaw-black man Sam Fathers.

When "The Bear" opens, Isaac McCaslin is sixteen years old, although the story reaches back to his tenth year and forward to well past his thirty-fifth birthday. To farmers living in the area, the bear Old Ben has become more than a menace with his hungry forays onto their farms for livestock to kill.

Section I opens in 1883 on the day of the final hunt for Old Ben but quickly digresses into the recollection of Isaac's first hunt when he was ten years old. The month is November, and Isaac heads into the woods with Major de Spain, General Compson, Sam Fathers, Ash, Tennie's Jim, Walter Ewell, and Boon Hogganbeck for the first time. Ostensibly, the object of the hunt is Old Ben, a huge bear with a mangled paw who has thus far eluded capture. Isaac shares a stand (a place where hunters stand in wait for game) with Sam Fathers, who serves as his mentor. In the second week of hunting, they hear Old Ben pass their stand. Not long afterward, alone in the stand, Isaac hears Old Ben pass again.

In June of the next summer, during the annual hunt to celebrate Major de Spain's and General Compson's birthdays, Isaac scouts the wilderness for Old Ben and eventually manages to spot the bear and observe him for a few moments.

In Section II, Isaac is thirteen and an excellent woodsman. We learn he has already killed his first buck and a bear. He sees Old Ben again but does not shoot him, despite the opportunity. Later that spring a doe and fawn are killed, and Old Ben is suspected. The culprit turns out to be Lion, a wild mongrel Airedale. Sam captures Lion and tames him. In November of Ike's fifteenth year, the hunters—with Lion—corner Old Ben twice but fail to kill him. Boon shoots at Ben five times at close range and misses. General Compson draws blood.

Section III returns to a cold December in Isaac's sixteenth year. The hunters are waiting in camp for the weather to warm so that Lion and Old Ben can engage in their now-annual confrontation. Boon and Ike are sent to Memphis for whiskey. The morning after their return to camp, the weather thaws and the hunters set out with Lion. They manage to corner the bear. Lion rushes at it, and it retaliates by grabbing the fierce dog with both paws, whereupon Boon jumps on the bear's back and reaches over to plunge his knife in Old Ben's heart. The bear dies, as does Lion—and for no apparent physical reason, Sam Fathers collapses at the scene. Most of the hunters return home. Sam Fathers dies, put out of his misery, the story implies, with Boon's help. The others return to find Isaac and Boon sitting between Lion's grave and Sam's body on a raised funeral platform.

Most of Section IV is set in the commissary on Isaac's twenty-first birthday, though part of the section flashes back a few years. In a conversation with his cousin Cass, Isaac relinquishes his title to the McCaslin farm and accepts a $30 per month pension in return. The flashback covers the time when, while poking through the ledgers at age sixteen, Isaac learned about his grandfather Carothers McCaslin's iniquities—his fathering of illegitimate children with his slaves, and the incest committed with his slave daughter. Later in Section IV, Isaac becomes a carpenter and marries a young woman who urges him to claim his inheritance. He refuses to oblige her, so she refuses to sleep with him and he remains childless.

In Section V, Isaac returns to Major de Spain's land on another hunt before the lumber company moves in and begins to cut the timber. It is 1885, and two years have passed since the hunt detailed in Section III. Eighteen years old, Isaac revisits the land for a final time, going to the graves of Sam Fathers and Lion before meeting Boon. At the end of the story, Isaac finds Boon

"The Bear"

Faulkner at the door of the barn on his farm, Rowan Oak.

under a tree full of squirrels, futilely hammering the breech of his broken gun. Without looking up to see who's approaching, Boon shouts not to touch the gun pieces. They are his. His preoccupation with his possession serves as a symbolic marker for the imminent intrusions of the lumber company on the forests mentioned at the beginning of the section.

Isaac McCaslin's coming-of-age. "The Bear" tells a coming-of-age story that incorporates issues particularly applicable to the South at that time. Isaac goes through an initiation into manhood that is distinctly Southern in several ways. Firstly, his initiation centers around the rite of the hunt. Next, Faulkner gives Isaac a mentor whose ethnic mix reflects the population of the South as well as the egalitarianism among the hunting party. The part-black, part-Chickasaw Indian character, Sam Fathers, introduces Isaac to the wilderness:

> He entered his novitiate to the true wilderness with Sam beside him . . . it seemed to him that at the age of ten he was witnessing his own birth.
> ("The Bear," p. 201)

When he discovers that Isaac has been seeking an encounter with Old Ben, Sam suggests that Isaac leave his gun behind. This advice leads, after the abandonment of two more possessions, to Isaac's true entry into the wilderness, after which he is "permitted" to see Old Ben:

> He stood for a moment—a child, alien and lost in the green and soaring gloom of the markless wilderness. Then he relinquished completely to it. It was the watch and compass. He was still tainted. He removed [them] . . . and hung them on a bush and leaned a stick beside them and entered it.
> ("The Bear," pp. 211-12)

After Isaac is initiated into the wilderness, it becomes the foundation around which he can orient many other things in his life, including his morality. At the opening of Section IV, in which Isaac relinquishes his inheritance, we see him at twenty-one, a man "juxtaposed not against the wilderness but against the tamed land which was to have been his heritage" ("The Bear," p. 252).

Isaac's relinquishment of his inheritance pertains directly to two important issues in the South during the late nineteenth century, issues that were still plaguing Southerners at the time Faulkner wrote "The Bear": first, the white man's guilt in perpetuating slavery and the human exploitation that accompanied it, and second, the rape of the land. The white man's guilt in perpetuating slavery and its inequities is aptly signified by Ike's reaction to the episode of incest and mixed-race sexual relations that he uncovers in his family's past. He finds the ledger entries that lead him to this conclusion during his sixteenth year, the same year in which Old Ben is killed. In his twenty-first year, the ledgers sit on the shelves above him, as a reminder, while he tells his cousin Cass that he will be relinquishing his share of the farm. The rape of the land through the destruction of the wilderness for profit also influences his decision. His mentor, Sam Fathers, has passed on to him the American Indian belief that land is given by a higher power to humans as a whole and is indivisible; people are meant to be stewards, not owners, and defying this truth only brings a curse on the land. At the core, the two issues—exploitation of human as well as geographical property—are inseparable. Carothers, in fact, exploits his slaves by getting them to exploit, or make selfish use of, the land:

> The human beings that [Carothers McCaslin] held in bondage and in the power of life and death had removed the forest from [the land] and in their sweat scratched the surface of it to a depth of perhaps fourteen inches in order to grow something out of it which has not been there before, and which could be translated back into the money he who believed he had bought it had to pay to get it and hold it.
> ("The Bear," pp. 252-53)

Isaac renounces his heritage because of all this exploitation. In his own life Faulkner did not go so far as to renounce his property, but he shared his main character's feelings. He owned two farms, Rowan Oak and Greenfield. His family lived at Rowan Oak, and he was buying more of the nearby woods to isolate his home from the world. Several black tenant families operated his farms, and he let them hold onto the profits because, in his words, "the negroes don't always get a square deal in Mississippi" (Faulkner in Oates, p. 228).

Sources. In addition to the general influence of Southern folktales and American Indian beliefs and rituals, a great deal of "The Bear" comes from Faulkner's recollections of his own childhood experiences in the forest:

> I was taken there as soon as I was big enough to go into the woods with a gun. . . . The three-toed bear was an actual bear. But I don't know that anyone killed him with a knife. And the dog was an actual dog, but I don't know that they ever came into juxtaposition.
> (Faulkner in Utley, p. 97)

Although Faulkner disclaims any basis in fact for the bear's being killed by a dog and a knife, it should be noted that these two elements can be found in the previously mentioned folktale, "The Big Bear of Arkansas," which the writer may have encountered at some point in his life. Regarding its setting, Faulkner's rich and detailed Yoknapatawpha County is based on the region around Oxford, Mississippi, where Faulkner lived much of his life.

Events in History at the Time the Short Story Was Written

Jim Crow laws and World War II. Although they do not apply to "The Bear" directly, Jim Crow laws and World War II are tied to issues that recur throughout the story: white guilt over the legacy of slavery, and the misuse of the environment.

The Jim Crow statutes, or so-called "separate but equal" laws, were coming under fire increasingly in the years approaching World War II. As a result, the legacy of slavery was as much in the public eye in 1942 as it had been in 1882. The continuing industrialization of the South, coupled with the massive waste that accompanies a major war, also brought into focus the rape of the land. Following events from his farm at Rowan Oak, Faulkner worried about the survival of the wilderness in his own seemingly selfish era. He brooded too about bringing a new generation into such a racist, war-torn world; its members, he feared, could be destroyed in a Nazi-Japanese takeover.

Reviews. Two days after *The Saturday Evening Post* published the shortened version of his story, "The Bear" appeared in its long form in the newly released *Go Down, Moses and Other Stories*. (The volume was renamed simply *Go Down, Moses* at Faulkner's request; he wanted the work to be read as a novel, rather than as a collection of short stories.) Faulkner's whole repertoire of writings garnered little critical attention until 1945, when Malcolm Cowley published *The Portable Faulkner*—in response, as Cowley mentions in its introduction, to "the scandalous neglect of his novels" (Cowley in Faulkner, p. xxxi). After the publication of *The Portable Faulkner*, however, Faulkner received considerable critical and academic attention. In their critiques of "The Bear," scholars often focused on the unconventional style of Section IV, and whether or not Isaac's relinquishing his inheritance constituted a heroic act or an escape. Unlike the other sections of "The Bear," which are told in third-person narration, the fourth section uses an experimental style, ignoring rules of capitalization and sentence length, for example, to establish a flow. Some critics, used to Ernest Hemingway's often terse sentences and the works of realist writers that were popular at the time, blasted the experimental style in various writings by Faulkner. As early as 1939, however, the critic Conrad Aiken had disagreed with this assessment. He fathomed a purpose behind the style—"to keep the form—and the idea—fluid and unfinished, still in motion, as it were, and unknown, until the dropping into place of the very last syllable" (Aiken in Tuck, p. 14).

Critics were divided in their estimation of the collection of stories that included "The Bear." "*Go Down Moses,*" said an article in *The Saturday Review of Literature,* "is a mighty wedge of ponderous writing, of Mississippi, of negroes and half-Indians, and great dogs and bears and all kinds of odd 'Deep South'-ers." A *Boston Globe* review was more appreciative, asserting "here are seven stories that represent William Faulkner at his best. Which is equivalent to saying the best we have" (James, p. 245).

For More Information

Faulkner, William. "The Bear." In *The Portable Faulkner*. Edited by Malcolm Cowley. New York: Penguin, 1977.

Fox-Genovese, Elizabeth. *Within the Plantation Household, Black and White Women of the Old South*. Chapel Hill: University of North Carolina Press, 1988.

Godhes, Clarence, ed. *Hunting in the Old South: Original Narratives of the Hunters*. Baton Rouge: Louisiana State University Press, 1967.

James, Mertice M., and Dorothy Brown. *Book Review Digest.* Vol. 38. New York: H. W. Wilson, 1943.

McMillen, Neil R. *Dark Journey: Black Mississippians in the Age of Jim Crow*. Urbana: University of Illinois Press, 1989.

Oates, Stephen B. *William Faulkner: The Man and the Artist*. New York: Harper & Row, 1987.

Tuck, Dorothy. *Crowell's Handbook of Faulkner*. New York: Thomas Y. Crowell, 1964.

Utley, Francis Lee, ed. *Bear, Man, and God: Eight Approaches to Faulkner's "The Bear."* New York: Random House, 1971.

The Belle of Amherst

by
William Luce

Emily Dickinson, a slight and sickly child and teenager, was forced to maintain most of her social contacts through letters, expressing her own feelings in poetry that she mostly kept from public view. William Luce, a late twentieth-century playwright, used Emily Dickinson's letters and poems to create a one-woman play about the poet's life as well as conditions in nineteenth-century New England.

> **THE LITERARY WORK**
>
> A play set in the Dickinson home located in Amherst, Massachusetts, between the years 1845 and 1886; published in 1976.
>
> **SYNOPSIS**
>
> A reclusive poet recounts her life story in the form of a one-woman play.

Events in History at the Time the Play Takes Place

The nineteenth-century family. In the typical New England household of the nineteenth century, each family member generally had his or her own responsibilities. The father's obligations centered around working outside the home and making most decisions. The mother, on the other hand, ran the household—cooking the meals, raising the children, and keeping it clean. Children were expected to behave, work hard in school, and help their parents as needed. As an example, because Emily's mother was ill and restricted to bed, Emily prepared the food at the Dickinson home (the Homestead) while her sister, Lavinia, took care of the other chores. In the play, Emily discusses the many foods that she bakes for the Dickinson family, such as black cake, gingerbread, rhubarb cupcakes, rye bread, and Indian bread.

Religious fervor. In the early 1800s a wave of debate about religion swept the United States. Much of it centered around the differences between Calvinism and Unitarianism. Calvinist beliefs held that God was revealed in three forms and that all good on the earth was God's doing, while all evil was the burden of humans misusing God's grant of human freedom. Unitarians rejected both the belief in a trinity of deity (the Father, Son, and Holy Spirit) and creeds held sacred by other sects. To Unitarians, religion was an individual and a growing process that was hampered by the imposition of firm beliefs and doctrines. The debate between these two systems—and other similar conflicts between organized religions in the era—resulted in a renewed emphasis on religion in the family and in the creation of new and competing Christian sects by the time the play's action begins in the second quarter of the eighteenth century. This religious controversy was further clouded by the appearance of a new philosophy, transcendentalism, a challenge to formal religion that called for faith in an individual's own human intuition rather than reason or subscription to any existing set of religious beliefs. Most New England families were caught up in the religious fervor; nearly everyone was approached to make public demonstration of their beliefs by joining one of the many Christian communities. Many, like the Dickinson family, still held Calvinist beliefs in the tradition of their New England ancestors, the Puritans; they held fast to trust in God and in prayer while disdaining many of the rituals and ceremonies connected with the Catholic Church and its Protestant offshoots.

The Puritan family prayed together twice a day, once in the morning and once in the evening just as in *The Belle of Amherst*. In the play, Emily refers to the family prayers led by her father each morning (Luce, *The Belle of Amherst*, p. 30). Fathers generally led the family prayers, which were often followed by the whole family joining in singing hymns. The family worshipped together in order to work for the conversion of all family members. Father Dickinson, however, was skeptical of most of the organized religions of the time and took many years to take the step toward open conversion.

Education in the nineteenth century. Nineteenth-century education had broken sharply with that of the previous century, a period in which only half of the women in America could even sign their own names (Cott, p. 101). By 1840 most New England men and women knew how to read and write. In many cases, New England children received schooling beyond basic literacy, and in *The Belle of Amherst* all three Dickinson children attended school, although Emily attended only sporadically. She did, however, manage to earn her way into Amherst College, where she studied for a short time.

The nineteenth-century belief was that female education should teach women how to be useful wives, daughters, and mothers. Consequently the curriculum for females emphasized domestic tasks such as housekeeping and cooking. To facilitate this special curriculum, separate schools for boys and girls flourished in New England in the mid-nineteenth century.

Mount Holyoke Female Seminary, the school Emily attended, was caught up in the spiritual fervor of the times. Like other private academies in the nineteenth century, it focused much attention on the religious principles of its students. Mary Lyon, the director of Mount Holyoke, whom Emily refers to as the "Dragon Lady" because of her large nose, tried to help her students experience conversions. Miss Lyon sent those who had not yet converted to Room B (or the dungeon), where they were to read the Bible and discuss issues of religion.

The nineteenth-century woman. During the nineteenth century, some women began to question the assumption that a female should restrict herself to the domestic sphere. They began to lobby for women's political enfranchisement through gaining the right to vote, to sue in court, and to be as able as men to protect their rights under the law. Two advocates of women's rights, Lucretia Mott and Elizabeth Cady Stanton, organized the Seneca Falls Convention in 1848, where they wrote the *Declaration of Sentiments*, a list of desired equal rights for women.

PURITAN CONVERSION

Most nineteenth-century Puritans believed that it was necessary for people to experience a conversion in order to lead religious lives. When someone converted, they generally experienced an emotional religious "awakening" at which time they professed their love for God. This conversion was important to Puritans because they believed that only those who had converted could join God following their death. For a bright young person made a partial recluse by illness, with time to think about serious religious issues, it was a confusing period. Emily Dickinson was torn between her own doubts and family as well as social pressures to acknowledge Christ. Before she was a mature woman, she began to withdraw from the duress into the protection of her home and garden, expressing herself largely through her unpublished poetry.

Women enjoyed strong friendships with other women during this period. A common belief was that women were biologically shaped with certain intellectual, emotional, and character traits and behaviors that made them inherently different from men. Furthermore, many men engaged in professions that required long sojourns away from home, leaving wives to seek companionship among neighboring women in similar situations. Emily Dickinson was molded by these circumstances. In *The Belle of Amherst* she mentions her many close female friends, particularly her sister Lavinia and a childhood companion, Helen Hunt Jackson, with whom she carried on a continuing correspondence. The strength of the two sisters' relationship becomes evident in Lavinia's sadness at the prospect of Emily's mar-

The Belle of Amherst

rying a gentleman caller, a proposal which Emily declines. The author of the play may have been superimposing a more modern slant to the importance of female friendship or lack of it for women in the mid-1800s; in fact, many of Emily Dickinson's letters were addressed to one or two important men in her life.

During the mid-1800s, there were a few women like Lavinia and Emily who remained unmarried. In fact, statistics reveal that approximately 13 percent of New England women remained unmarried in the 1830s. The number of spinsters, or unmarried women, during this period may have been aggravated by the great westward movement of young men seeking land, silver, gold, and fur. Few single women joined in the migration; most stayed in the eastern states, where they were generally viewed as oddities because of their spinsterhood.

Women and writing. A few women poets and writers won renown during Emily's lifetime. Her close childhood friend, Helen Hunt Jackson, wrote poetry and books during her travels across the country. Jackson used her writing ability to lobby for better treatment of Native Americans, while Harriet Beecher Stowe added to the fame of women writers with the publication of *Uncle Tom's Cabin*, a novel about American slavery (also covered in *Literature and Its Times*). In Rhode Island, a group of woman poets including Margaret Fuller, Elizabeth Oakes-Smith, Frances Osgood, and the Carey sisters began to hold poetry meetings for women writers. Emily herself wrote poetry during this period, but, unlike most of the other female writers, did not seem very much interested in seeing it published.

MOUNT HOLYOKE, A SEPARATE GENDER SCHOOL

Zilpah Grant and Mary Lyon opened the Mount Holyoke Female Seminary in 1828, the school that Emily attended as a young girl. Both Lyon and Grant advocated female education and separate schools for girls, arguing that their education for women took into account what they believed to be the female's dissimilar mental capacities as well as their destiny to become housewives. "Along with erudition in anything from philosophy to astronomy, the seminarians acquired preparatory training for the home sphere" as women learned about the "domestic science."

(Ryan, p. 93)

Emily Dickinson

The Play in Focus

The plot. This one-woman play follows the life of Emily Dickinson between 1845 and 1886 at her home in Amherst, Massachusetts. Through a first-person monologue, Emily tells stories about the Dickinson family, her religious crisis, and her romances and unrequited love, also revealing others' perceptions of her.

Emily's family consists of her mother and father and two siblings, her sister Lavinia and a brother named Austin. Theirs is a close family. When Mrs. Dickinson suffers a stroke, Emily and Lavinia take responsibility for maintaining the household. Emily's father holds the children to strict rules that give the impression that he is uncaring and unemotional. However, beneath that veneer, Emily's father shows excitement over such natural events as the aurora borealis and a willingness to bend his rules regarding Emily's bedtime so that she may write. The family bond is revealed again when Austin marries Susan Gilbert. The couple move into the house next door to the Dickinsons' and the family ties are retained.

Emily grows up in a very religious household; her father leads the family in prayers each morning and night. As a young girl, however, Emily finds it difficult to accept Puritanism because she finds it too restrictive. Additionally, she does not like the religion's portrayal of God as strict and threatening, a convention employed to secure moral obedience to its tenets. Emily prefers to think of God as a friend and believes she can relate to him by writing her poetry. Emily admits in the play that she does not feel persuaded to profess herself a Christian even though all of the other members of her family have experienced religious awakenings. At the age of twenty-five, she decides to stop attending church altogether, writing that "Some keep the Sabbath going to Church/ I keep it, staying at Home" (*The Belle of Amherst*, p. 31).

Within the Amherst community, many of Emily's neighbors consider her unbalanced and refer to her as "Squire Edward Dickinson's half-cracked daughter" (*The Belle of Amherst*, p. 3). Emily has earned this reputation because of some bizarre habits—she wears white dresses, drops off poetic notes to neighbors and hides when callers came to visit. According to Emily, this behavior is part of a game in which she likes to portray herself as an eccentric poet.

The influence of nineteenth-century poetry. Emily reveled in the "joys of language and mysteries of poetry" (Chambers-Schiller, p. 100). When she read poetry, she experienced a physical reaction. Her whole body went cold and she felt as if the top of her head had been taken off (*The Belle of Amherst*, p. 7). She particularly enjoyed reading the poems of other mid-nineteenth century writers, especially the works of female British poets such as Elizabeth Barrett Browning. Emily was drawn to Browning, whom she felt demonstrated that women could have talents outside of taking care of the home.

Massachusetts poets like Ralph Waldo Emerson, a leader of the transcendental movement, and Henry David Thoreau also influenced Emily. She read Emerson's *Essays* as a student and received a copy of his *Poems* from Benjamin Newton, her father's law clerk. Emily's father owned two copies of Thoreau's *Walden* in the family library. During a visit to Amherst in 1857, Emerson stayed with her brother, Austin, in the house next door to the Dickinsons. It is probable that Emily spoke with Emerson at that time and attended one or more of his lectures.

In 1862 Thomas Wentworth Higginson, a professor and literary critic, informed Emily that her poems were not publishable because of their irregular meter and problematic style. He had offered the same feedback about the poems of Walt Whitman. Whitman soon had a book of his poems (*Leaves of Grass* [also covered in *Literature and Its Times*]) published under his own name and then republished several times over in the span of his life, but Emily had only seven anonymous poems published during her lifetime.

Sources. After spending many years as a musician and singer, William Luce turned his attention to the writing of "mono-dramas" or one-person plays with a particular interest in female writers. He worked as a composer and playwright for television shows as well as Broadway theater. He enjoyed writing plays about famous literary women, as demonstrated by *The Belle of Amherst*, as well as mono-dramas about Zelda Fitzgerald, Lillian Hellman, and Emily Brontë.

THE "BELLE" OF AMHERST—FACT OR FICTION?

At age fourteen, Emily writes a letter to a school friend stating that she thinks she will be the belle of Amherst by the age of seventeen with scores of admirers. In reality, the young men of Amherst are not enamored of Emily. She receives no valentines and is ignored at the local dances.

Emily never did marry. She however, fell in love with a minister from Philadelphia named Charles Wadsworth. Emily heard Wadsworth preach in the 1850s and began to correspond with him. Ignoring the fact that he was already married, Emily wrote many love poems to Wadsworth and asked him to come to visit her in Amherst. Wadsworth visited Emily in 1860 and then departed for the West Coast to live in San Francisco. She continued to write poems about him: "So We Must keep apart / You there—I here / With just the Door ajar / That Oceans are and Prayer / And that Pale Sustenance / Despair" (*The Belle of Amherst*, p. 60).

To give a full sense of Emily Dickinson, William Luce immersed himself in her poetry and correspondence to her friends. He pieced together various incidents in Emily's life and integrated her poetry to develop a play spanning forty-one years of the poet's life as told from her own perspective. According to Luce, the format of the one-person play worked best for the story of Emily Dickinson because "she was seclusive, an individualist to the highest order" and therefore stood as the best person to tell her story (Introduction to *The Belle of Amherst*, p. xiv).

Events in History at the Time the Play Was Written

Changing role of women. During the 1970s, a strong feminist movement emerged that advocated equality between women and men. In 1966 Betty Friedan, author of *The Feminine Mystique,* and a small group of women founded the National Organization of Women (NOW), a group dedicated to gaining equal rights for women, similar in many ways to the movement born of the Seneca Falls Convention in the mid-nineteenth century. In the 1970s NOW pushed for political changes and lobbied successfully for the passage of the Education Title IX Act (1972), which required that women be given equal opportunities in school admissions, job hiring, and team sports. The next year, the Supreme Court struck down state laws against abortion in the case of *Roe v. Wade.* More significantly, women were choosing to remain single rather than marrying. In 1975, 23 percent of all women were single, a much higher figure than the 13 percent of the 1830s. In short, the 1970s was a decade of increasing freedoms for American women. It was in this atmosphere that William Luce decided to bring to the stage a woman poet who was out of step with most women of her time in terms of religion, marriage, and work and did not receive much attention during her own life.

Reviews of the play. *The Belle of Amherst* opened in Seattle, Washington, in February of 1976 and then moved to Broadway, where it received laudatory reviews. Critics applauded the play for its ability to bring together Emily Dickinson's poetry, letters, family tales, and memories in a way that portrayed her reclusive life. One critic commented that Julie Harris, who acted in the role of Dickinson, actually became her during the play. Luce was lauded for his ability to merge the poetry with the text of the play. In 1987 a television production of *The Belle of Amherst* won an International Emmy Award for its adaptation of the play.

For More Information

Bennett, Paula. *Emily Dickinson: Woman Poet.* New York: Harvester Wheatsheaf, 1990.

Boller, Paul F. *American Transcendentalism, 1830-1860: An Intellectual Inquiry.* New York: G. P. Putnam's Sons, 1974.

Chambers-Schiller, Lee Virginia. *Liberty, a Better Husband: Single Women in America; The Generations of 1780-1840.* New Haven, Conn.: Yale University Press, 1984.

Cott, Nancy F. *The Bonds of Womanhood: "Women's Sphere" in New England, 1780–1835.* New Haven: Yale University Press, 1977.

Johnson, Thomas H., and Theodora Ward, eds. *The Letters of Emily Dickinson.* Cambridge, Mass.: Harvard University Press, 1958.

Luce, William. *The Belle of Amherst: A Play Based on the Life of Emily Dickinson.* Boston: Houghton Mifflin, 1976.

McDannel, Colleen. *The Christian Home in Victorian America, 1840-1900.* Bloomington: Indiana University Press, 1986.

Ryan, Mary. *Womanhood in America: From Colonial Times to the Present.* New York: New Viewpoints, 1975.

Beloved

by
Toni Morrison

Born Chloe Anthony Wofford on February 18, 1931, in Lorain, Ohio, Toni Morrison has emerged as one of the leading voices in American literature since the publication of her first novel, *The Bluest Eye,* (also covered in *Literature and Its Times*), in 1970. Morrison's writings are largely concerned with the African American experience; their author, in fact, declares that her art is inherently political. In 1988 her novel *Beloved* won the Pulitzer Prize in fiction, testimony to the groundbreaking nature of her achievements. This victory was followed by Morrison's winning the Nobel Prize for Literature in 1993.

THE LITERARY WORK

A novel primarily set in Cincinnati, Ohio, in 1873, but also set from 1855 to 1873 and in Kentucky prior to 1855; published in 1987.

SYNOPSIS

Sethe, who was a slave before the Civil War, is now physically free but still bound by the legacy of slavery and haunted by a murder she has committed.

Events in History at the Time the Novel Takes Place

The position of post-Civil War blacks. The Emancipation Proclamation of 1862 and the end of the Civil War brought immediate legal freedom to more than 4 million blacks in the South. The importation of slaves from Africa had ceased after a new law in 1808 curtailed the international slave trade, with the result that the blacks freed at the end of the war were predominately American-born. These ex-slaves had no sustaining support after the Civil War. Trained for few tasks beyond farming and for the most part uneducated (since it was illegal for slaves to learn or be taught to read), many freed blacks found their new situation as equally dismal as the old, but now they possessed no means to survive. Some remained on the old plantations as low-wage workers, but more took advantage of their sudden freedom by moving. A number moved north in search of a new life and still could not escape the legacy of slavery, a problem that plagues the character Sethe in *Beloved.*

Slavery in Kentucky. In *Beloved,* Sethe has escaped from life on a Kentucky farm called *Sweet Home.* Bordering the free states of Ohio, Indiana, and Illinois, Kentucky offered a less sinister environment for slaves than in the Deep South. The products raised in Kentucky—livestock, tobacco, and hemp (manufactured into cotton bagging and rope for tying cotton bales) required relatively small labor forces. Kentucky was thus dotted with medium-sized farms rather than plantations, and in 1850 most of the 38,500 slaveowners of Kentucky possessed fewer than five slaves apiece. Historical records indicate that because of the less vicious form of slavery existing in Kentucky, its slaves lived in terror of being sold into the Deep South. Sale to a Mississippi or Louisiana plantation owner became a justifiable fear after 1820, when there arose a vigorous slave trade between Kentucky and the slave states in the cotton kingdom of the Deep South. One Kentucky judge estimated the yearly number of blacks sold to owners in the Deep South to be 5,000.

Slaves still encountered cruelty at the hands of their masters even in Kentucky. One documented account describes a young female slave. Thinly clad and barefooted, she was severely whipped on a cold winter morning by her white mistress, a Mrs. Maxwell. Maxwell's son later applied his cowhide whip to the young slave with vigor after having her strip down to her waist. A medical examination of her "emaciated body revealed numerous lacerations, bruises, and scars resulting from the searing of her flesh with a red-hot iron" (Coleman, p. 252).

KENTUCKY IN THE CIVIL WAR

Kentucky did not secede from the Union during the Civil War, but its citizens showed a sharp division in their loyalties. Although some 70,000 Kentuckians fought for the Union, around 35,000 volunteered to fight for the Confederacy. Meanwhile, its slaves remained in bondage even after President Abraham Lincoln's Emancipation Proclamation. The Proclamation, which took effect January 1, 1863, freed only the slaves in rebel territory. Kentucky slaves would have to wait until 1865 when the passage of the Thirteenth Amendment outlawed slavery throughout the nation.

With little or no chance of legal retaliation, slaves resisted such cruelty in various ways. Most commonly, a wronged slave would obtain justice by burning down a house, barn, or other structure, a crime for which it was hard to pin down the perpetrator. If caught at such an act, however, the slave faced the death penalty. A few slaves resorted to murdering their masters or overseers and, in some instances, even their own children to prevent them from having to endure the perils and indignities of slavery. One Kentucky slave couple about to be sold down South made a mutual pact "to send their children to heaven" rather than let them "descend to the hell of slavery" (Coleman, p. 269). After killing them, the couple committed suicide. The violence committed by Sethe in *Beloved*, then, while atypical was by no means unique.

Slave women and their children. On Kentucky plantations, as elsewhere, life for the women was replete with emotional as well as physical hardships. Slave women who worked in the fields were separated from their small children, who might be left in the care of older, physically weak women.

A slave woman was regarded not only as a worker but also as a potential breeder of new property—children who would legally belong to her slaveowner. Though most slaveowners did not see this as the primary function of their slave women, childbearing was in some cases encouraged. In fact, a few slave women were promised their own freedom if they would bear as many as ten children. There were also instances of slaveowners who took sexual advantage of their female slaves and then regarded any mulatto children that resulted from these forced couplings as slaves themselves and the owners' property.

Slave mothers had little control over either their children or the destiny of their family. The owner commonly decided whether or not a slave woman could marry and for how long. Taking realistic stock of the slaves' circumstances, some marriage ceremonies declared the vows valid until death or until distance parted the couple. In the novel, Sethe's mother-in-law, Baby Suggs, has endured the pain of such separations:

> In all of Baby's life, as well as Sethe's own, men and women were moved around like checkers. Anyone Baby Suggs knew, let alone loved, who hadn't run off or been hanged, got rented out, loaned out, bought up, brought back, stored up, mortgaged, won, stolen, or seized. So Baby's eight children had six fathers. What she called the nastiness of life was the shock she received upon learning that nobody stopped playing checkers just because the pieces included her children.
>
> (Morrison, Beloved, p. 23)

The Underground Railroad and Ohio. As antislavery sentiment grew in the U.S. in the early 1800s, so did the Underground Railroad, an informal network of people and houses organized to help runaway slaves escape to the North. The Ohio River constituted one of the last boundaries on the pathway to freedom. North of the river lay the free state of Ohio; to the south the slave state of Kentucky. Although Morrison never directly asserts this, characters like Stamp Paid and others who helped in the escape central to *Beloved* might be considered unofficial workers on the Underground Railroad.

The abolitionists who conducted the Railroad never succeeded in rescuing many slaves—at best probably 1,000 a year of the more than 4 million slaves. Yet their network stood as a powerful symbol of the antislavery movement. So greatly did it concern the slaveowners that they

Toni Morrison with a copy of *Beloved*.

lobbied successfully for passage of the 1850 Fugitive Slave Act. The federal law set up a bureaucracy of commissioners to decide cases and penalized Northerners for aiding runaway slaves. The penalty consisted of six months in jail and a $1,000 fine for helping a runaway, as well as another $1,000 in civil damages.

Ohio, where Sethe and Baby Suggs of *Beloved* establish a home of their own, was a free state, but that did not eradicate prejudice on the part of its residents. The status of free blacks is described in the *Ohio House Journal* of 1864. The people of Ohio, it said, regarded blacks as a class to be kept by themselves and barred from social intercourse with whites. As late as 1864, three years into the Civil War, it declared that a black man would not witness any improvement in his social and political rights as long as he lived in Ohio. After the Civil War, improvement was halting at best. It was not until 1870, for example, that black people were allowed to sit on juries in Ohio.

Such were conditions in Ohio at the time when the main character in *Beloved* arrives there to take up residence with her mother-in-law. The nonstatus of free blacks, along with dreadful memories of their former, and even more dismal, slave experience, cast a shadow over number 124, the house in Ohio where the story in *Beloved* begins to unfold.

The Novel in Focus

The plot. Though much of the story prior to the novel's time is told in flashback, the central action of the plot develops out of a single dramatic event. In 1855 a nineteen-year-old pregnant slave girl, Sethe, is brutally beaten and runs away from slavery at Sweet Home, a small family farm in Kentucky. Sweet Home had once been a kinder place; Sethe's original master, Mr. Garner, had been rather good-hearted. He seemed to encourage "a special kind of slavery, teaching [the slaves] what they wanted known" (*Beloved*, p. 140). But conditions changed when Mr. Garner died and the slaves were given to the care of his brother-in-law, known as "schoolteacher." In time, schoolteacher's harsh treatment of his slaves results in the death of one of them, burned alive, and Sethe's sexual attack at the hands of schoolteacher's nephews. Learning that schoolteacher may eventually sell her children prompts Sethe to escape to freedom in the North.

Sethe is helped over the Ohio River, a major thoroughfare on the Underground Railroad. On the journey, she gives birth to her fourth child, a baby girl named Denver. Sethe's husband, Halle, was unable to escape from slavery, but he had previously bought freedom for his own mother, Baby Suggs. Baby Suggs lives in Cincinnati with three of Halle and Sethe's other children, two sons and a daughter sent there by Sethe. She and Denver eventually join them.

After only a month of freedom, Sethe's former owner, schoolteacher, locates her in Ohio and comes to capture her and her children, hoping to profit by having her bear more slave children. Seeing him nearby, Sethe takes her baby Denver and her other children into a shed and tries to kill them to prevent them from being dragged back into the horrors of slavery. She attacks the boys and succeeds in killing Denver's sister by sawing through her throat with a hacksaw, but she is prevented from killing the other children by the character Stamp Paid, who had helped her across the river.

When schoolteacher discovers them, the two boys, who ultimately survive the attack, appear to be dead along with the toddler. Schoolteacher at this point decides that a crazy woman and her one baby are not worth claiming. Buried with a headstone that names her Beloved, the slain baby gives rise to a ghost that haunts Sethe and Baby Suggs. The ghost, in fact, unsettles the entire family, ultimately driving Sethe's two boys away from home.

Many years later, a young woman who calls herself Beloved appears. Near the age Sethe's murdered daughter would be if she had lived, the stranger comes to live with Sethe. Beloved revives Sethe's memories of the past, reopening wounds. A demanding young woman, she overpowers Sethe until Sethe finally becomes incapacitated. Denver must even assume responsibility for finding food to eat; fortunately, the women of the community help out. Ultimately, Beloved leaves and a man from Sethe's past, Paul D, returns to help mend Sethe's broken spirit.

Narrative structure. *Beloved* contains a striking narrative structure that varies from traditional plot designs that contain an initial conflict, rising action, a climax, and a denouement, or resolution. *Beloved*, like Morrison's other novels, begins *in medias res*, or in the midst of the action, using very little exposition, or setting up of the scene. Events from the past intrude upon the present constantly. In fact, to assert the novel is set in a specific time period is misleading since it seems to reside in a period outside measured time—a period in which all moments of the past exist in the present.

In the novel, Sethe's notion of this idea of all time as coexisting simultaneously is expressed in her concept of "rememory," as she explains to Denver:

> It's when you bump into a rememory that belongs to somebody else. Where I was before I came here, that place is real. It's never going away. Even if the whole farm—every tree and grass blade of it dies. The picture is still there and what's more, if you go there—you who never was there—if you go there and stand in the place where it was, it will happen again; it will be there for you. So, Denver, you can't never go there. Never. Because even though it's all over—over and done with—it's always going to be there waiting for you. That's why I had to get all my children out. No matter.
> (*Beloved*, p. 36)

Sethe here expresses the notion of time that both structures the novel and explains reality for her as an ex-slave. The novel is a series of rememories from each character's perspective; the reading of the novel is the reader's attempt to restructure these rememories, thereby entering into them. Morrison's use of memory as a structuring device in *Beloved* allows the reader to experience the novel as an insider. Ultimately, it is this feature of the novel that leads to an understanding of what life is like for its main character.

Spirituality in *Beloved*. Spirits and spirituality haunt Morrison's novel. The house known as 124, where the characters live in Ohio, is haunted, but not in a ghostly way—this haunting is palpable, sensible. When Paul D, a former slave at Sweet Home, comes to visit Sethe in Cincinnati, he describes the sensation upon entering the house: "[He stepped] inside her door smack into a pool of pulsing red light." The description continues, "She was right. It was sad. Walking through it, a wave of grief soaked him so thoroughly he wanted to cry" (*Beloved*, p. 9). The acceptance of the dead baby's spirit as a reality is unquestioned by the characters in the novel. The existence of a spiritual world in the novel parallels Sethe's concept of rememory, and her claim that nothing ever dies.

The reappearance of Beloved as a flesh-and-blood being who is precisely the age Sethe's daughter would have been had she lived touches also on the spiritual beliefs of the characters. It takes them very little time to determine that the young lady who has appeared out of nowhere is the spirit of the baby and to accept this resurrected person without question. Her character can be traced back to African folklore of river spirits with distinctive feet and hands; Beloved emerges from a river and the softness of her skin, specifically of her hands, is frequently noted in the narrative. Such a weaving and melding of African traditions into African American culture helps explain the very real sense taken on by spirits in the novel.

Beyond being a spirit-come-to-life, Beloved represents the spirits of all of the slaves who died on slave ships during the journey from Africa to America. As Morrison explains in an interview with Marsha Darling in 1988:

> She [Beloved] tells them what it was like being where she was on that ship as a child.... The gap between Africa and Afro-America and the gap between the living and the dead and the gap between the past and the present does not exist. It's bridged for us by our assuming responsibility for people no one's ever assumed responsibility for. They are those that died en route. Nobody knew their names, and nobody thinks about them. In addition, they never survived in the lore; there are no songs or dances or tales of these people.
> (Morrison in Taylor-Guthrie, p. 247)

Sources. The most direct source for *Beloved* is a newspaper article Morrison came upon while editing a collection of articles and images called *The Black Book* in 1974. This article, entitled "A Visit to the Black Mother Who Killed Her Child," tells the story of an escaped Kentucky slave, Margaret Garner. In 1850 she attempted to kill her children rather than see them enslaved, and she succeeded in killing one. Morrison deliberately did not look much deeper into the Garner story, but went on to thoroughly research the history of Cincinnati, Sethe's small-town residence in *Beloved,* and to investigate the history of the Underground Railroad and pre-Civil War abolitionist movement.

Beloved draws more indirectly on the slave narrative of the nineteenth century, works such as Frederick Douglass's *My Bondage and My Freedom* (1845) and Harriet Jacobs's **Incidents in the Life of a Slave Girl** (1861) (also covered in *Literature and Its Times*). Such primary sources present a wealth of information about the life of slaves and the institution of slavery. Morrison's novel, however, aims not to recreate a slave narrative that follows a common structure—describing the suffering under slavery, liberation, and the benefits of freedom—but to imaginatively personalize the ex-slave's story and to reconsider the nature of freedom for blacks in the wake of slavery.

Toni Morrison

A third source for *Beloved* relates to its style. Morrison explains the influence of African folk tales.

> What's rich ... is what the reader gets and brings him or herself. That's part of the way in which the tale is told. The folk tales are told in such a way that whoever is listening is in it and can shape it and figure it out. It's not over just because it stops. It lingers and it's passed on.... It has a moment beyond which it doesn't go, but the ending is never like in a Western folktale where they all drop dead or live happily ever after.
> (Morrison in Taylor-Guthrie, p. 253)

Events in History at the Time the Novel Was Written

Morrison, civil rights, and the women's movement. Toni Morrison grew up with a father who was distrustful of other races and a mother who expressed hope for a better future. Morrison entered the work force at age twelve but still managed to graduate from high school with honors. Afterward she chose to attend Howard University, at the time an all-black institution. In 1964, after several years of teaching, she became an editor for Random House, where she managed such notable authors as Muhammad Ali and Angela Davis. Her career coincides with the black civil rights movements of the 1960s and with the late-twentieth-century women's rights movement that began with the publication of Betty Friedan's *The Feminine Mystique* in 1963 and the founding of the National Organization for Women three years later. Morrison was an active participant in both movements.

Morrison was particularly active in the women's movement, as reflected in writings like *Beloved* that feature powerful female characters. From another standpoint, *Beloved* portrays women with very real human emotions and concerns who are trying to shake off the terrible burdens of past enslavement. In some ways, this mirrors what African American civil rights leaders of the 1960s were attempting. It is not surprising that some reviewers have seen *Beloved* as a novel about slavery, while others have described it as a feminist novel. Both positions are certainly supported by the story. It might be most accurate to label *Beloved* a seminal work of black feminism. Importantly, Morrison began publishing her fiction in the early 1970s along with black feminist writers Alice Walker, Audre Lorde, Jane Jordan, Sonia Sanchez, Nikki Giovanni, and Toni Cade Bambera.

Reception. By the time of *Beloved*'s publication in 1987, Morrison was already a prize-winning author. Her *Song of Solomon* had won a National Book Award. Still, when *Beloved* appeared, its strangely organized plot and shockingly vivid detailing of events seemed to confuse the critics. It was described as a book about slavery, a book about the human predicament, and a feminist document. Although critics could not agree on the focus, the work was hailed as another triumph for Morrison. The critics praised the novel for its portrayal of black male characters who are both sympathetic and complex as well as for its powerful female characters. Upon its release, *Beloved* became an instant success; it went on to win the Pulitzer Prize for fiction in 1988.

The legacy of slavery in the 1980s. The damage that slavery did to the United States did not end with the Civil War, Reconstruction, or even the civil rights movement of the 1960s. There is a psychological price still being paid by all Americans, and there are ongoing social problems related to slavery—chronic unemployment among black youth, the economic disparities between minorities and whites, crime and the problems of the inner city, and the large number of fatherless black families. As *Beloved* recognizes, the problems created by slavery do not go away simply because it has been abolished.

African Americans have still not attained an equal economic footing with white Americans. As Mary Frances Berry and John W. Blassingame state in *Long Memory: The Black Experience in America*:

> The black worker was so victimized by the American caste system that it became a truism among economists that while whites generally fluctuate between prosperity and recession, blacks fluctuate between depression and great depression.
>
> (Berry and Blassingame, p. 215)

Even during times of general economic prosperity, standards of living for African Americans have historically decreased. "While the number of poor families in the United States declined by 30 percent between 1947 and 1963, the number of poor black families *increased* by 2 percent" (Berry and Blassingame, p. 215). In the 1980s, as Morrison was writing her novel, such economic circumstances had changed little for African Americans.

Finding strength in family and community. Morrison, who raised her two sons by herself, feels strongly that a family without a father is not a broken family. That many present-day families do exist without a father is clear from statistics concerning the United States. In 1980, at the beginning of the decade in which Morrison wrote her novel, 55.4 percent of black women were unmarried; by 1992 this figure had climbed to 62.1 percent. The divorce rates for blacks as well as for whites has risen greatly, as has the number of households headed by women with no male present. In 1992 the number of female-headed households (46.4 percent) almost equalled the number of married households (47.1 percent) among blacks.

Morrison's hope for the future. In 1989 Toni Morrison was interviewed on television by Bill Moyers. In that interview, Morrison explained a modern message that underlies *Beloved* and her other writings:

> *Moyers:* There is such a gulf between the "inner city" today and the rest of the country in both imagination and reality, in politics and literature. If you were writing for the rest of the country about the "inner city" today, what metaphor would you use?
>
> *Morrison:* Love. We have to embrace ourselves. James Baldwin once said, "You've already been bought and paid for. Your ancestors already gave it up for you. You don't have to do that anymore. Now you can love yourself. It's already possible."
>
> (Taylor-Guthrie, pp. 266–67)

For More Information

Berry, Mary Frances, and John W. Blassingame. *Long Memory: The Black Experience in America*. New York: Oxford University Press, 1982.

Carmean, Karen. *Tony Morrison's World of Fiction*. Troy, N.Y.: Whitston, 1993.

Coleman, J. Winston, Jr. *Slavery Times in Kentucky*. Chapel Hill: University of North Carolina Press, 1940.

Morrison, Toni. *Beloved*. New York: Penguin, 1987.

Sterling, Dorothy. *We Are Your Sisters: Black Women in the Nineteenth Century*. New York: W. W. Norton, 1984.

Taylor-Guthrie, Danille, ed. *Conversations with Toni Morrison*. Jackson: University of Mississippi Press, 1994.

Black Elk Speaks

by
John Neihardt

A collaborative effort, *Black Elk Speaks* was the result of a series of interviews between Nick Black Elk, an American Indian from a Sioux tribe, and John Neihardt, a white poet. Black Elk, a holy man who fought in the Indian wars of the late 1800s, struggled throughout his life with the firm belief that he was supposed to save his people from the encroachment of white settlers. Neihardt wrote the narrative, which is about Black Elk's early years, in the first person, as if the words were spoken by Black Elk himself. Neihardt also added information from his own research and included passages that are represented as the words of other American Indian leaders.

> **THE LITERARY WORK**
> A narrative about the childhood and young manhood of an Oglala Sioux spiritual leader set in the United States, Canada, and Europe from the 1860s through the 1890s; published in 1932.
>
> **SYNOPSIS**
> When he was very young, Black Elk had a powerful vision. The narrative details his struggle to understand and enact that vision, as well as his experiences as a member of a band of Oglala Sioux during the middle and late 1800s.

Events in History at the Time the Narrative Takes Place

The Teton Sioux. Divided into various groups, the Sioux nation occupied a large portion of the Great Plains during the 1800s. Black Elk belonged to the Teton Sioux, a nation of seven tribes that included the Brule, Hunkpapa, Blackfeet, Miniconjou, Sans Arc, Two Kettle, and Oglala Sioux. Black Elk was a member of the Oglala tribe.

Born in 1863, Black Elk grew up during a time when buffalo were vital to the health of the Teton Sioux. In *Black Elk Speaks*, he recalls the great buffalo hunts his tribe engaged in. Buffalo served as the mainstay of the Teton diet and were used to make material for clothing, teepees, and ceremonial objects. Dependent on these animals for survival, the Indians would migrate with the roving herds. Black Elk explains in the book that, as time went on, the buffalo became increasingly scarce and the hunts difficult to conduct. He recalls that Plains tribes were sometimes wasteful of the buffalo in areas where they abounded, but declares that in the end the herds were destroyed by white miners and hunters. As the railroads were built across the Plains region, whites sometimes shot buffalo from train windows for sport, and businessmen used the hides to make such salable commodities as robes and shoes. By 1883 nearly all the buffalo had been exterminated, and the Indians were left without their former means of sustenance.

American Indians did not suffer this destruction without resistance. Black Elk himself participated in major and minor battles as the Sioux fought to protect their land from white settlers and hunters. Bravery, daring, and cleverness in warfare were held in high esteem by the Sioux. In fact, their young men would engage in battle in order to prove their manhood.

The reservation system. Between 1866 and 1891, the population of Western states and territories soared from less than 2 million to 8 million people. Railroads, mines, ranches, farms, and new towns appeared as white settlers moved into the region. Previously, the California gold rush of 1849 had drawn thousands of prospectors across the Great Plains in search of wealth. The settlers and travelers spread disease among the American Indians and decimated the buffalo. In the process, they won the bitter resentment of Plains tribes and clashes between the two peoples became more frequent.

In 1851 a council met in Laramie, Wyoming, to ease the tensions between the Indians and settlers. A number of Sioux participated, signing their first treaty with whites. The Sioux agreed to stay within specific boundaries to minimize subsequent conflict, a stipulation that marked the first time that the nation agreed to give up the complete freedom of movement that had been a hallmark of its existence. Other nations (the Cheyenne, Arapaho, and Shoshone) likewise agreed to stay within specified boundaries under the terms of the first Fort Laramie Treaty, which ultimately led to the inception of the reservation system.

Aside from its intent of taking Indian land, the U.S. government placed tribes on reservations in the hopes that this would help the American Indians assimilate into white society; the theory was that they needed a space in which to undergo a transition. If the Native Americans were installed on the reservations, government officials reasoned, they would learn to speak English, practice the Christian faith, and value private property. The government especially wanted the Indians to cease their dependence on hunting and learn how to farm.

In response to the Fort Laramie Treaty, some of the Oglala Sioux moved onto the Pine Ridge reservation in South Dakota. But the government's expectations conflicted directly with Sioux customs and values. Many warriors could not even conceive of owning land; in their minds, the Great Spirit had provided the land for their use. Dividing it into parcels to be sold to private individuals made no sense. Furthermore, many warriors had little interest in farming, which was regarded as demeaning. Yet assimilation remained the policy pursued by the U.S. government until the 1920s.

Having forced the Sioux to forfeit their land, U.S. officials promised to supply food, clothing, and other necessities until the Sioux could become self-sufficient farmers. In fact, however, Congress repeatedly refused to appropriate enough money for the promised goods. A government commission asked for $1 million to feed twenty thousand Indians, but only received $500,000 to meet all their expenses. Such inadequate provisions only reinforced a popular Native American opinion that whites simply could not be trusted to keep their promises.

By 1872, thirty-one thousand American Indians subsisted entirely on government handouts, while as many as eighty-four thousand depended partially on them. Early treaties had promised to feed reservation populations, but the U.S. agents had mistakenly assumed that, by the time the buffalo herds disappeared, the American Indians would be self-sufficient farmers. Instead, the Sioux grew entirely dependent on the meager governmental rations. The Sioux, meanwhile, had fewer and fewer opportunities to attain prestige in either war or buffalo hunts, and many tribal traditions quickly disappeared.

Laws and land during Black Elk's youth. In the 1860s, Teton Sioux, Northern Cheyenne, and Northern Arapahos fought government soldiers and won control of the Bozeman Trail. Led by the Sioux chief Red Cloud, the tribes signed the important Treaty of 1868, which closed this particular trail to whites and guaranteed the Sioux people domain over the Black Hills, the heart of Sioux territory. The treaty promised that these hills, located in present-day South Dakota and Wyoming, would belong to the Sioux forever.

In 1874, however, a military expedition led by General George A. Custer discovered gold in the Black Hills. News of the gold find spread, drawing streams of miners and new transportation lines to the area. Black Elk recalled the white invasion:

> Up on the Madison Fork the Wasichus [white men] had found much of the yellow metal that they worship and that makes them crazy, and they wanted to have a road up through our country to the place where the yellow metal was; but my people did not want the road. It would scare the bison and make them go away, and also it would let the other Wasichus come in like a river. They told us that they wanted only to use a little land, as much as a wagon

Black Elk Speaks

Chief Crazy Horse (center) at the Battle of Little Big Horn. Pictograph by Amos Bad Heart Bull.

would take between the wheels; but our people knew better. And when you look about you now, you can see what it was they wanted.
(Neihardt, *Black Elk Speaks*, p. 9)

The Sioux rebellion that subsequently took place is now called the Black Hills War of 1876. Their most notable victory was at the Battle of Little Big Horn, which Black Elk witnessed. There, a confederation of tribes destroyed Custer's 7th U.S. Cavalry force, killing the famed general and many of his men. The Little Big Horn proved to be the last major victory for the American Indians, however, and a year later, after more fighting, the Sioux lost the Black Hills.

In 1887 Congress passed the General Allotment Act. Commonly called the Dawes Act after Senator Henry Dawes of Massachusetts, it put into effect a plan that further reduced the size of reservations. The Dawes Act, which intended to eliminate the reservations, divided reservation land into parcels. Each American Indian family would get 160 acres of land, after which the remaining land was to be sold by the U.S. government. The allotted parcels were held in trust by the government for twenty-five years, during which time the Indians could not sell or lease their allotments. This was to prevent them from exchanging their land for cash instead of farming it. The clause proved ineffective, however.

Many of the American Indians who received parcels ignored the clause and sold or leased them. Under this program the government allotted approximately 3,285,000 acres to native peoples and sold off 38,500,000 "surplus" acres between 1887 and 1900. Especially hard hit were the Sioux lands in the northern Plains. By 1910 the American Indians had lost title to some 60 percent of the lands under their control before the Dawes Act took effect.

Buffalo Bill. The late nineteenth century witnessed the close of the American frontier. By 1890 the Census Bureau could no longer distinguish a frontier settlement district on the Western map. The United States had spread its borders from the Atlantic to the Pacific oceans. The once-vast buffalo herds had been hunted to near extinction. Except for a few rebellious bands, the American Indians had been largely confined to reservations, where their populations were declining from war, disease, and starvation. The days of the untamed West were fading into the past.

Buffalo Bill exploited this nostalgic realization by taking the romantic, colorful parts of the West on tour. Born as William F. Cody in 1856, Buffalo Bill had earned his nickname because he supplied workers on the Kansas Pacific Railroad with buffalo meat between 1867 and 1868. He fought in several Indian battles with the 5th U.S. Cavalry between 1868 and 1872. In 1883 Buffalo Bill organized his famous Wild West Show, a traveling show featuring reenactments of buffalo hunts, Indian fights, and stagecoach robberies, all designed to cater to the imagination of those who had never experienced the West.

In 1886 Buffalo Bill entered Pine Ridge Reservation in search of performers. Approximately one hundred American Indians, including Black Elk, decided to join the show, which traveled beyond the United States to Europe, where it eventually performed for Queen Victoria. Black Elk remembered the queen fondly: "We liked Grandmother England, because we could see that she was a fine woman, and she was good to us. Maybe if she had been our Grandmother, it would have been better for our people" (*Black Elk Speaks,* p. 223).

Lonely and homesick much of the time, Black Elk remained away from the reservation for three years. The separation pained him: "All the time I was away from home across the big water, my power was gone, and I was like a dead man moving most of the time" (*Black Elk Speaks,* p. 231).

The Ghost Dance. In despair over the oppressive policies of the U.S. government, American Indians found new hope in a movement that spread from the Sierra Nevada mountains throughout the Great Plains in the late 1800s. Called the Ghost Dance, it was a messianic activity—a religious movement centering on the revelations of a divinely inspired person. The phenomenon began with a Paiute visionary named Wovoka, known to whites as Jack Wilson. Wovoka experienced a series of revelations between 1887 and 1889 that promised a new earth for the native tribes. This new land would cover the old and push whites back across the ocean. Dead ancestors would return, along with the game, the lands, and the old, cherished ways of life that had been lost. During his visions, Wovoka was instructed to teach the Ghost Dance to other American Indians; by performing this dance, the Indians would help bring about the new land.

Although his revelations were interpreted in different ways by various tribes, most agreed that the promised time would arrive in the spring of 1891. Belief in the power of the Ghost Dance spread among the Arapaho, Northern Cheyenne, and Sioux. The dance particularly inspired the Sioux in the Pine Ridge Reservation area, who suffered from disease and starvation. Although the religion was originally pacifist in nature, not calling for violence, the movement concerned many whites, who feared that it might serve to unite the Indians and lead to armed conflict. Government officials were especially concerned about the influence the dance was having on the warlike Sioux.

People who engaged in the Ghost Dance often collapsed and reported spiritual experiences. The vehemence of the dancers frightened Daniel Royer, an inexperienced Bureau of Indian Affairs (BIA) agent who had only been at Pine Ridge a couple of days when he saw it. He called in U.S. troops to quell the dancing, which led to a confrontation and the eventual massacre of a band of Sioux at the Battle of Wounded Knee on December 29, 1890. In this incident, army troops attempted to disarm a group of Indians led by Chief Big Foot who were travelling to the Pine Ridge Reservation. Though neither side expected violence, a scuffle broke out between the soldiers and Indians. A bloody encounter ensued; approximately two hundred and fifty American Indians were killed, including many women and children, while the cavalry lost twenty-five men.

The Narrative in Focus

The contents. Born in 1863, Black Elk remembers Oglala Sioux life before it changed so drastically because of white settlement. He does not see a white person until he is ten years old, but recalls constant rumors that white people are coming to kill all the Sioux and take their lands.

When Black Elk is nine, he has a powerful vision. In this vision, he is surrounded by many horses—black ones with lightning for manes, buckskin ones with manes that grow like grass and trees, sorrel ones with eyes like morning stars, and white ones whose manes flow like blizzards. The horses take Black Elk to his Grandfathers, six spirits who embody the four directions as well as the power of Sky and Earth. They occupy a tepee with a rainbow for a door. In his vision, the Grandfathers show Black Elk the trouble that will befall his people and give him many powers. According to the Grandfathers, Black Elk is given the power to restore the Sioux nation by nurturing a sacred tree and keeping his nation's sacred hoop intact. These images are so powerful that Black Elk does not tell anyone about his vision until he reaches the age of nineteen. He fears that no one will believe that a small boy could experience so awesome a vision.

Meanwhile, life for the Sioux begins to change rapidly. When gold is discovered in the Black Hills in 1874, whites enter Sioux terri-

Black Elk Speaks

tory in large numbers to convince the Sioux to sell or lease the Black Hills. Tension follows, erupting into the Battle of Little Big Horn. Only thirteen years old when the Battle of Little Big Horn takes place, Black Elk is too young to fight in the battle, but he scalps a wounded soldier for the first time.

By this point, the Oglalas have broken up into two divisions. Some bands decide to live with Red Cloud on the reservation, while others, including Black Elk's family, follow Chief Crazy Horse, who wants nothing at all to do with whites.

After the Black Hills are sold in October 1876, Black Elk's band occupies territory that the U.S. government says no longer belongs to them. Government officials try to force the Oglala to live near the reservation, but many refuse. When Black Elk is fifteen, his band follows Sitting Bull and Spotted Tail into Canada to escape persecution. Canadian winters prove harsh, however, and many of the refugees grow homesick and reluctantly return to the United States.

BLACK ELK EXPLAINS THE SACRED HOOP

Imagine a hoop so large that everything is in it—all two-leggeds like us, the four-leggeds, the fish of the streams, the wings of the air, and all green things that grow. Everything is together in this great hoop. Across this hoop, running from the east where the days of men begin to the west where the days of men end, is the hard black road of worldly difficulties.... There is another road ... the good red road of spiritual understanding, and it begins in the south where lives the power to grow and proceeds to the north, the region of white hairs and death. Where this good red road crosses the hard black road, that place is holy, and there springs the sacred tree that shall fill with leaves and blooms and singing birds. And that is the sacred hoop. The power for everything an Indian does comes from the sacred hoop, and the power will not work in anything but a circle.

(Black Elk in Neihardt, *Black Elk and Flaming Rainbow*, pp. 58-9)

Gripped by an overwhelming fear during this time, Black Elk feels that he has to tell somebody about his vision. He confides in a holy man, who decides that Black Elk must perform his vision for others in ritual dances. Black Elk's spiritual power increases after these dances, and he proves able to cure sick people even though he is only nineteen years old.

By 1883 Black Elk's band has returned to the United States and settled in Pine Ridge Reservation housing. The bison herds are gone, and the tribespeople are full of despair. When Buffalo Bill arrives and asks for participants to join his Wild West show, Black Elk volunteers in the hope that the experience will show him some way to help his people. He travels to the eastern United States, London, and Paris. During his stay in Paris in 1889, Black Elk has another vision. He returns at once to the reservation, where he finds more suffering and hunger and further erosion of the Sioux land base.

The same year, rumors of a messiah in the Sierra Nevadas reach the Sioux. The messiah, a Paiute Indian whose name is Wovoka, instructs believers to dance a Ghost Dance. The ceremonial dance spreads like wildfire among the desperate Oglala. In 1890 Black Elk travels to observe some dancers near Wounded Knee Creek on the reservation. He is surprised at the parallels between the scene in front of him and the visions he has experienced, both of which promise that the Indians' dead ancestors will come back to life.

At some of the Ghost Dance ceremonies, such items as a sacred bow and arrows are tied to a tree in the center of the circle. All of these items are important symbols in Black Elk's vision. He dances the next day and receives another vision. In this one, he sees holy shirts to take back to his people. Upon awakening, Black Elk tells the people to create Ghost Dance shirts decorated with symbols of morning stars, eagles, and buffaloes. Many Oglala come to believe that these holy shirts will protect the wearer from bullets in battle. Black Elk, meanwhile, continues to dance, and has many different visions.

That winter, an Oglala chief named Big Foot brings his people down to the reservation from the Badlands because he is sick and his people are starving and freezing to death. American soldiers are waiting to disarm them. On December 29, 1890, during the disarmament process, a gun goes off and the soldiers immediately shoot and kill Big Foot. Suddenly, everybody is shooting and fighting. Black Elk enters the fray and witnesses the slaughter of Big Foot's band at the Battle of Wounded Knee. Although the fighting continues into January, Black Elk and his companions eventually surrender. He settles at Pine Ridge, where he contemplates his belief that he has failed his vision.

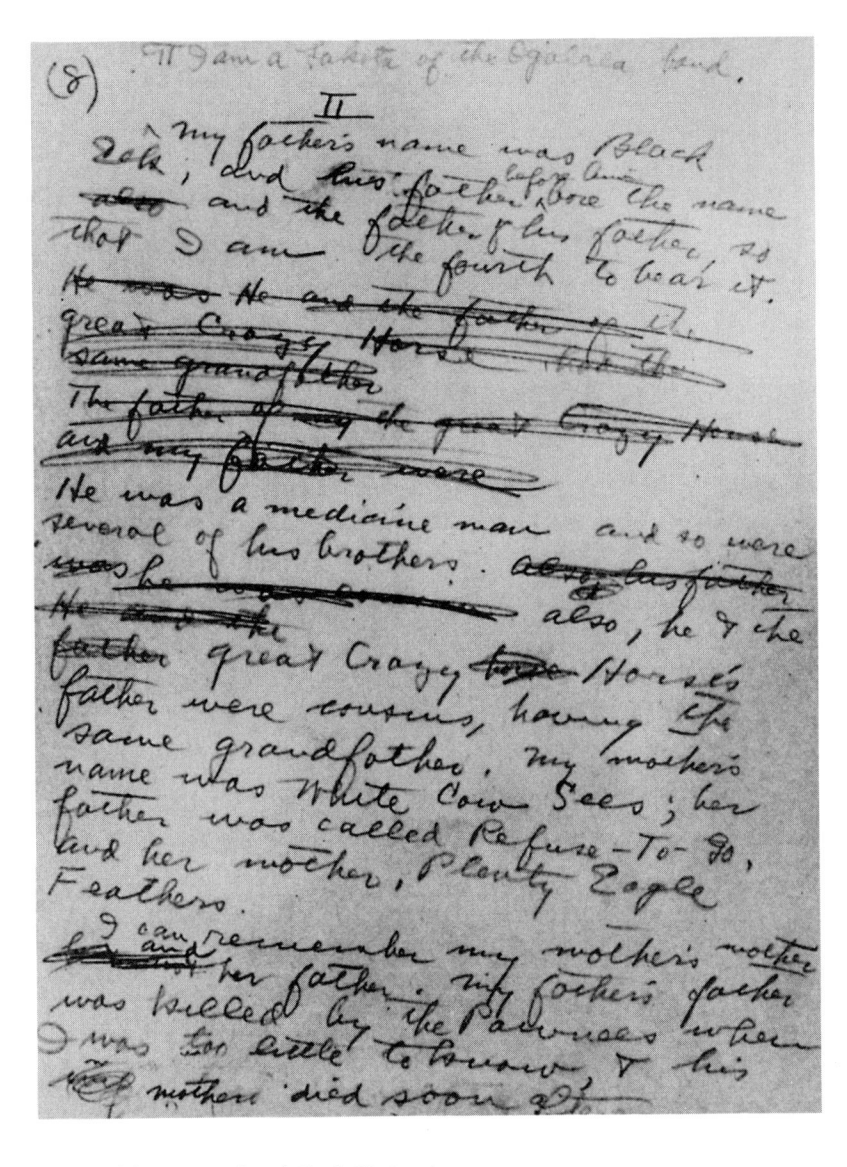

A page of the manuscript of *Black Elk Speaks*.

Black Elk as a holy man. Religion was an important part of the Teton Sioux culture, found in nearly all aspects of life. The *wakantanka* was thought to be the highest holy power to whom Oglalas could appeal for help. People who mediated between the *wakantanka* and commoners were called *wicasa wakan*, or holy men. Holy men attended to the spiritual needs of their tribe, communed with the spirits to ensure a successful hunt or ceremony, and predicted the future. Serving also as teachers, they interpreted myths, dreams, and visions. The *wicasa wakan* also treated sick people in the village. Since they believed that evil spirits often caused sickness, the Oglala called on the *wicasa wakan* to rid the sick of supernatural afflictions.

Black Elk's father had been a medicine man, and the Oglala considered Black Elk a holy man as well. Like many other holy men, he derived his power from his first vision. His quest to understand and act upon this vision lies at the heart of *Black Elk Speaks*. Black Elk believed that his vision gave him the power to restore the broken and scattered Sioux nation. But as he grew to manhood, the Sioux were further weakened until they were transformed from one of the strongest Indian nations into poor governmental charges, subject to hunger and massacre. Black Elk felt personally responsible for the situation. He believed that the potential power of his vision had been ruined by his own weakness and lack of direction.

Black Elk Speaks

In 1883 the Commissioner of Indian Affairs began to stamp out the Oglala religion. He forbade feasts and dances, including the sacred Sun Dance—a ritual in which volunteers were tortured with wooden skewers inserted into the chest or back in the belief that their self-sacrifice would help solve some ongoing problem. The U.S. government outlawed all the practices of Oglala medicine men and holy men. Missionaries, who had worked on reservations since their inception, attempted to make up for this loss by converting the Oglala to the Christian faith. Many Oglalas, including Black Elk, found similarities between Christianity and their own beliefs.

In 1904 Black Elk converted to Catholicism. He preached and administered Christian sacraments when no priest was present. Black Elk did not seem to separate his old faith from his new one; in fact, he applied the term *wicasa wakan* to both Catholic priests and Oglala holy men. He became involved in a period of cultural reinvention for his people, joining together elements of Indian and white ways of life.

Sources. To write *Black Elk Speaks*, John Neihardt interviewed Black Elk and other Oglala survivors. The book reads as one continuous narrative, as if Black Elk and his companions are speaking in turns. While Neihardt makes Black Elk's story appear fluid, the information was actually recorded over many days; indeed, the author indicated his intention to set up multiple interviews in his initial proposal of the project to Black Elk:

> My idea is to come back to the reservation next spring, probably in April, and have a number of meetings with you and your old friends among the Oglalas who have shared the great history of your race, during the past half century or more. I would want you to tell the story of your life beginning at the beginning and going straight through to Wounded Knee.
> (*Black Elk Speaks*, p. 278)

Using Black Elk's memories, Neihardt recorded the Indian's life history all the way up through the notorious Wounded Knee massacre, an incident that symbolized the final conquest of the Oglala. Neihardt's interviews with Black Elk took place thirty years after the Battle of Wounded Knee.

Although Neihardt was a poet, he had a profound interest in the West, having grown up on the frontier in Wayne, Nebraska. Later in his childhood he lived near the Omaha Indian reservation, a situation that allowed him to gain some familiarity with Native American cultures. He probably felt a particular affinity for Oglala holy men since he himself experienced a vision when he was a boy. In 1892, when Neihardt was eleven years old, he suffered a fever and had a vision that instructed him to become a poet.

Events in History at the Time the Narrative Was Written

Early anthropology. During the turn of the twentieth century, anthropology was established as a rigorous discipline in the United States. Early American anthropologists and ethnographers concentrated heavily on Native American populations and worked closely with the Bureau of Indian Affairs and the Smithsonian Institution.

Anthropologists believed that the native cultures were being destroyed and that anthropological records could "preserve" cultural remnants that were in danger of becoming extinct. The anthropologists headed to reservations in droves to gain as much information as possible before the Native American cultures disappeared. The effort inspired a fervor in the general public for "saving" doomed cultures. It was, perhaps, this fervor that prompted John Neihardt to record Black Elk's early life history.

Response to the book. Black Elk himself was not completely satisfied with the book Neihardt wrote about him. He regretted that *Black Elk Speaks* covered only his early life and expressed his wish that Neihardt had mentioned his accomplishments, especially his spiritual development, since the Battle of Wounded Knee.

As far as the larger public was concerned, *Black Elk Speaks* was largely ignored when it was first published. It gained a steady following through the 1940s and 1950s, however, and attracted the attention of famed psychologist Carl Jung. As interest in American Indian spirituality mounted in the 1960s, the book gained widespread popularity.

Despite the fact that Neihardt was a writer and poet by profession, *Black Elk Speaks* was not treated as a literary piece until the early 1970s. As one reviewer noted in 1971, "*Black Elk Speaks* has been many things to many people, and has been studied at various times as anthropology, as sociology, as psychology, and as history. It has been cited as evidence of a religious revival and used as an ecological handbook. But no one, as far as I know, has written about *Black Elk Speaks* as literature" (Stine and Marowski, p. 335). The reviewer remarked that Neihardt's style accounts for the book's fluidity, coherence, and readability.

Policy reform and the Indian New Deal. During the 1920s, Secretary of the Interior Albert B. Fall set out to dissolve federal responsibility for native tribes. He also called for diminishing Indian water and land rights, tried to create a national park out of one reservation, and proposed opening all reservations to oil development. His bills generated enough concern among anthropologists and conservationists to be defeated after long, bitter debates.

Meanwhile, conditions on the reservations steadily worsened, leading to a cry for reform. The government formed a committee to investigate living conditions among American Indians, and in 1928 it published *The Problem of Indian Administration,* also known as the Meriam Report. The report severely criticized current federal policy, blasting the Dawes Act and urging an immediate halt to land allotments. The report also suggested the incorporation of tribes, the granting of limited power to tribal councils, and an increase in appropriations for health and educational programs. Perhaps most importantly, it called for preserving rather than erasing the native peoples' way of life.

A year after *Black Elk Speaks* appeared, John Collier became commissioner of Indian affairs. Collier helped pass the Indian Reorganization Act of 1934, which halted land allotment and reaffirmed the right of the American Indians to operate as tribal entities. Collier appropriated funds for the tribes to buy back native lands, and he helped Indians obtain jobs in soil conservation, irrigation, and road-building projects. Although he would later be criticized for setting up a huge bureaucracy to attain his goals, his efforts followed those of others such as John Neihardt who tried to understand the Native Americans and deal with them on their own terms.

For More Information

Mooney, James. "The Doctrine of the Ghost Dance." In *Teachings from the American Earth.* Edited by Dennis Tedlock and Barbara Tedlock. New York: Liveright, 1975.

Neihardt, Hilda. *Black Elk and Flaming Rainbow.* Lincoln: University of Nebraska Press, 1995.

Neihardt, John. *Black Elk Speaks.* Lincoln: University of Nebraska Press, 1979.

Stine, Jean, and Daniel Marowski, eds. *Contemporary Literary Criticism.* Vol. 32. Detroit: Gale Research, 1985.

Utley, Robert M. *The Last Days of the Sioux Nation.* New Haven, Conn.: Yale University Press, 1963.

Bury My Heart at Wounded Knee

by
Dee Brown

Dee Brown, a librarian by profession, researched and wrote numerous histories of the American West using such primary sources as diaries, letters, recorded speeches, and transcriptions to capture the flavor of the times. Brown published *Bury My Heart at Wounded Knee: An Indian History of the American West* in 1970, a time when the U.S. government was advocating a new policy of self-determination for American Indians, and when Indians themselves had launched their own civil rights movement. *Bury My Heart at Wounded Knee* was warmly received at the time as a much needed alternate perspective of how the West had been "won."

THE LITERARY WORK
A narrative history of the Indian wars in the American West from 1860 to 1890; published in 1970.

SYNOPSIS
Told from the American Indian point of view, this history details how various western tribes fought for and eventually lost their leaders and territory.

Events in History at the Time the Narrative Takes Place

Identity and place. *Bury My Heart at Wounded Knee* details the broken promises, devastating battles, occasional victories, and the loss of leadership and land that western native tribes experienced as they came into contact with whites during the latter half of the nineteenth century. The western tribes are numerous and vary greatly in terms of lifestyle and belief systems. Each group's lifestyle was closely tied to the particular geographical area in which it lived. When whites took tribal lands and the government relocated entire Indian nations, they disrupted the very foundations of each tribe's society. The following examples briefly illustrate the cultural variation among western tribes described in the narrative, as well as their cultural ties to geographical location.

An Apache tribe of the Southwest: the Chiricahua. The term "Apache" designates a language group and refers to tribes that speak Athapascan-based languages, including the Chiricahua, Jicarilla, Kiowa-Apache, Lipan, Mescalero, Navajo, and Western Apache. Unlike some of the southwestern tribes, the Chiricahua Apache did not live in permanent encampments. They avidly hunted deer and gathered wild plants such as yucca, agave, onions, potatoes, piñon nuts, and berries. Raiding was an important element in the Chiricahua economy, as the Chiricahuas plundered neighboring tribes for food, horses, and other goods. Because of this lifestyle, these Apaches lived in small, mobile groups and often dwelled in canyons and mountains, where they could protect themselves from counterattacks.

Dee Brown

Because they lived in small groups, the Apaches often lacked a central authority figure. Among the Chiricahua, a band consisted of three to five local groups, with ten to thirty extended families in each group. Each local group had a leader who earned his position through bravery, generosity, and a demonstration of wisdom. Yet the local leader did not have absolute authority, and he usually did not take action without consulting the group's members. Local group leaders discussed in Brown's narrative include Cochise, Mangas Coloradas, Nana, and Victorio; given their traditional nomadic lifestyle, they resisted confinement to a reservation longer than any other group.

A Plateau tribe: the Nez Percé. The Plateau region spans the area of the northern U.S. between the Cascade and Rocky Mountains. The Columbia River, the area's largest tributary, supplied many tribes such as the Nez Percé with plenty of fish to eat. The Nez Percé also hunted deer, elk, and bear, and ate roots and berries. They snared bison, often traveling far into Idaho, Montana, and Wyoming to find the great herds. The Nez Percé revered a particular location as their place of origin—a hill located near Kamiah, Idaho. Thus when U.S. commissioners asked the Nez Percé in 1876 to move from the Wallowa Valley to a reservation, Chief Joseph replied that the land was "too sacred to be valued by or sold for silver and gold" (Trafzer, p. 70).

The Great Plains: the Cheyenne. Geographically, the Great Plains encompasses the grasslands that stretch from the Mississippi River to the Rocky Mountains, and from southern Canada into Texas. These grasslands supported great herds of buffalo, on which many Plains tribes, such as the Cheyenne, Sioux, and Kiowa, depended for their livelihood.

During the nineteenth century, the Cheyenne ranged as far south as New Mexico and as far north as Montana. They had acquired horses by the middle of the 1700s, which enabled them to become fierce warriors and successful hunters. Although the Cheyenne hunted antelope, deer, and mountain sheep, the buffalo were the Cheyenne's main source of food and materials. The Cheyenne stored buffalo meat for food in summer and winter; used buffalo hide for winter robes, tipi coverings, and clothing; and turned other parts of the buffalo into rope, horse gear, and domestic utensils such as spoons.

Besides food, clothing, and essential supplies, the buffalo also provided the Cheyenne with a means for establishing their social identity as well. Among the men, buffalo hunting was an important test of bravery and a means of gaining status within Cheyenne society. Cheyenne braves spent long hours training their horses to move very close to the buffalo so that the hunter could ride with both hands free.

The herds of buffalo had begun to decline before 1850. Homesteaders plowed up buffalo grazing land, and white hunters shot buffalo indiscriminately. Furthermore, American Indians themselves overhunted buffalo in order to trade the hides for goods. As the buffalo were destroyed, so was the primary resource of Cheyenne culture on the Plains.

American Indian and white relations. Prior to 1871, the federal government pursued a policy of treaty-making with American Indian tribes. Such a strategy considered the Indian nations sovereign entities with whom treaties were to have the same force and dignity as agreements made with foreign nations. Approximately 370 treaties with various American Indian groups were formally passed and ratified by Congress. Roughly 96 treaties had to do with peace-related issues, while 230 treaties dealt with issues of land, especially American Indian removal and resettlement in the West. When the treaty period ended, most indigenous nations viewed their previously concluded treaties as sacred promises made to them by the U.S. government.

Throughout its history of negotiating with American Indians for land, the U.S. repeatedly affirmed that particular areas belonged to the American Indians and that these nations and groups had a right to claim the land. When the United States defined the boundaries of American Indian territory in 1834, for example, it encompassed all lands west of the Mississippi River except Missouri, Louisiana, and the territory of Arkansas. Additionally, the U.S. guaranteed that these lands would be protected from white interests. No white people would be permitted to hunt or trap game. Whites could not allow their cattle to graze without the permission of American Indian authorities, and illegal settlers were supposed to be forcibly removed by agents of the tribes. The U.S. government made these promises in order to induce tribes living in the eastern United States to give up their homelands and relocate in unfamiliar territory further west.

Despite its legal promises, the government did very little to stop white encroachment in the new territories. As the century progressed, a pattern of agreements developed in which American Indians agreed to give up land in order to avoid conflicts with whites. Many of the agreements specified certain areas that were to belong to the American Indian nations alone, and whites were forbidden to enter the areas without their permission. In time, however, whites would appear, conflicts would occur, and the treaty-making process would begin again.

One of the most significant treaties was concluded in 1851 at Fort Laramie with the Northern Plains nations. The United States secured from the various American Indian leaders who entered into the treaty the right to establish roads and military outposts that would aid settlers traveling west. More importantly, for the first time each tribe agreed to stay within specifically defined boundaries in order to avoid further conflicts with whites. This event marks the beginning of the reservation period, which severely restricted the freedom of American Indians to roam as they pleased. By the early 1860s, the U.S. government had decided that the only way the American Indian populace could survive white settlement was to keep them on reservations until they could support themselves.

The purpose of reservations. In 1867 a congressional committee concluded that the best way to guarantee peace was to place all American Indians on reservations. Officials hoped to isolate them from the general population of white settlers and at first closed the reservations to whites to minimize conflict. A reservation was supposed to be large enough so that a tribe could support itself by hunting, but the policy concentrated American Indians on largely worthless land. Ultimately, the government wanted to Christianize the tribes and force them into farming as an economic livelihood. The officials believed the reservations could then be reduced in size. Usually the reservations were reduced well before the American Indians had found alternative ways to support themselves.

In order to entice different tribes into living on reservations, a government body called the Peace Commission promised to provide clothing, education, and rations in the interim. Congress, however, often did not ratify the treaties that contained those promises, or refused to appropriate enough money for the necessary food and supplies. Consequently, the reservations suffered constantly from shortages, which led to more conflicts and feelings of hostility.

The Narrative in Focus

The contents. *Bury My Heart at Wounded Knee* illustrates how various western tribes such as the Apache, Navajo, Nez Percé, Cheyenne, Ute, Commanche, Kiowa and Sioux resisted the American government's effort to place them on reservations

---

MANIFEST DESTINY

In 1846 the United States began to actively pursue a policy known as Manifest Destiny, which held that it was the destiny of the United States and its citizens to expand the country's borders all the way to the Pacific Ocean. By this time, white settlers had filled up most of the territory east of the Mississippi River, and wanted to settle in the Oregon country as well as in southwestern areas between Texas and California, which were claimed by Mexico. The United States secured the Oregon Territory from the British in 1846 and went on to acquire the Southwest from Mexico in 1848. The path to the Pacific Ocean had shifted into American hands, and thus there were few obstacles left beyond the presence of Indian nations on coveted territory.

and release their traditional lands for white settlement. The book is organized both chronologically and geographically. Brown opens with an overview of the early history of western Indian peoples and white explorers and settlers, and briefly outlines some of the tribes detailed later in the book. Chapter 2 describes the plight of the Navajos, who were among the first people to be subdued by harsh U.S. policies. Each chapter opens with several important and well-known political events, followed by a quotation from one or more of the leaders of the tribe about to be discussed. Throughout the book, Brown describes the broken treaties and poignant battles from the perspective of the American Indians themselves, using excerpts from speeches and conversations made by tribal leaders to reinforce this perspective.

Central to *Bury My Heart at Wounded Knee* is the story of the resistance and eventual subordination of the Cheyenne and Sioux tribes of the Great Plains. Although the 1851 Treaty of Fort Laramie clearly stated that these tribes owned the surrounding area, by the late 1850s miners entered the area and soldiers attacked the tribes. Such conflicts culminated in the Sand Creek Massacre of November 28, 1864, in which Major Scott Anthony, Colonel Chivington, and approximately six hundred soldiers attacked a band of peaceful, sleeping Cheyennes. One unwilling observer, George Bent, remembered later:

> There seemed to be indiscriminate slaughter of men, women, and children. There were some thirty or forty squaws collected in a hole for protection. They sent out a little girl about six years old with a white flag on a stick; she had not proceeded but a few steps when she was shot and killed.... I saw quite a number of infants in arms killed with their mothers.
> (Bent in Brown, *Bury My Heart at Wounded Knee,* pp. 89-90)

Although the Cheyenne ceded yet more land after this tragedy, both the Cheyenne and the Sioux were determined to keep the Powder River country, their last great hunting ground. When the tribes discovered that whites were intruding on the Powder River country on their way to the gold mines in Montana, they decided to resist. U.S. officials eventually relented, evacuated the area, and closed the Bozeman Trail. Triumphantly, Chief Red Cloud signed the Treaty of 1868, guaranteeing the Sioux and Cheyenne the Black Hills forever.

Gold, however, was discovered in the Black Hills by prospectors who streamed into the area in 1875, and soon the area swarmed with miners. Again, the government tried to buy and/or lease the land, but the Sioux, led by Crazy Horse, resisted. Although he and like-minded warriors fought bravely, even winning the important Battle of Little Big Horn, the tribes lost the Black Hills and their Nebraska territory in 1877.

SOME TRIBES AND LEADERS IN *BURY MY HEART AT WOUNDED KNEE*

Apache	Cochise
	Mangas Colorado
	Eskiminzin
	Geronimo
	Nana
	Victorio
Cheyenne	Roman Nose
	Black Kettle
	White Antelope
	Dull Knife
Modoc	Kintpuash (Captain Jack)
Navajo	Manuelito
	Barboncito
Nez Percé	Chief Joseph
Sioux	Red Cloud
	Sitting Bull
	Spotted Tail
	Young-Man-Afraid-of-His-Horses
	Crazy Horse
Ute	Ouray
	Nicaagat (Jack)
	Colorow
Kiowa	Satanta
	Kicking Bird

Brown concludes the history by describing the Ghost Dance religious movement among American Indians that began with a Paiute Indian named Wovoka. Wovoka received visions of a time when whites would return to their original home across the ocean. His visions further promised that the dead ancestors of the Indians would reappear, the buffalo would return, and that all American Indians would once again be free. To bring about the revelation, Wovoka instructed American Indians to dance a "ghost dance." The Ghost Dance spread like wildfire from tribe to tribe. In 1890 a Sioux named Kicking Bear brought the news of Wovoka's visions to the Pine Ridge reservation, and by the fall most Oglala Sioux were performing the ceremonial dance.

The Ghost Dance movement frightened white officials and tensions on the reservation increased. When soldiers encountered a Sioux leader named Big Foot on his way to Pine Ridge with a group of Indians, they attempted to disarm the band. A gun went off, and in the next few seconds, soldiers began shooting and fighting. Louise Weasel Bear remembers, "We tried to run, but they shot us like we were a buffalo. I know there are some good white people, but the soldiers must be mean to shoot children and women. Indian soldiers would not do that to white children" (*Bury My Heart at Wounded Knee*, p. 444). By the time the fighting stopped, over half the American Indians involved were dead in what is now remembered as the Battle of Wounded Knee.

Beginning with the Navajo and ending with the Sioux and Cheyenne, *Bury My Heart at Wounded Knee* covers the history of various American Indian peoples and conveys their perspective by using the words of historical figures, those of chiefs as well as soldiers, colonels, and observers.

Conceptions of land. Land was the central source of conflict between American Indians and whites. Settlers demanded American Indian territory, and gained it piece by piece with the help of the government. Such intrusions led to the innumerable treaties and battles that characterize this period. To a large degree the general conflict stemmed from the profoundly differing viewpoints held by American Indians and whites concerning land and its proper use.

Property, especially real estate, has always held an important place in white European culture. Europeans emigrated to the New World partially in hopes of obtaining land, and pioneers settled the western frontier for the same reason. To many American Indians, however, the concept of buying, selling, or owning land was completely foreign. "One does not sell the earth upon which the people walk," said the Oglala Sioux leader Crazy Horse (*Bury My Heart at Wounded Knee*, p. 273).

This difference in outlook rests partly on the spiritual world view of American Indians. Generally American Indians do not recognize boundaries between human and nonhuman elements the way whites do. To many American Indians, people exist as part of a whole, and are not superior to other elements. So power might reside in fish, the sun, moon, birds, or in plants. The land and its environs were tied to American Indian spirituality.

Whites, however, tended to view the land from a much more pragmatic perspective. Land existed for farming or for other practical purposes. Many whites believed that since American Indians did not use the land to accumulate personal wealth, they were not using the land properly. Some even felt that the tribes as a whole were failing to cultivate the land as prescribed by the dictates of the Bible. Furthermore, land acquisition was firmly rooted in ideas brought over from Europe. British writer Thomas More, for example, stated in *Utopia*, "When any people holdeth a piece of ground void and vacant to no good or profitable use: keeping others from the use and possession of it.... [T]his situation ought thereof to be nourished and relieved" (More in Sturtevant, vol. 4, p. 211).

The difference in perspectives led to many clashes before the conception of land promoted by the whites triumphed by force. As one unidentified American Indian stated, "They [the whites] made us many promises, more than I can remember, but they never kept but one; they promised to take our land, and they took it" (*Bury My Heart at Wounded Knee*, p. 49).

Sources. Dee Brown was a professional librarian. He worked both for the U.S. Department of Agriculture and the Department of War, as well as for the College of Agriculture at the University of Illinois in Urbana. Because of his position, Brown had access to many primary sources such as letters, diaries, speeches, anthropological accounts, and historical, congressional, and military documents. *Bury My Heart at Wounded Knee* is based mostly on such primary resources.

Events in History at the Time the Narrative Was Written

Policy changes. The 1960s and 1970s ushered in a new direction for American Indian policy in the U.S. During the 1950s, the government had pursued a devastating directive called "termination," which sought to eliminate American Indians as special citizens. This policy determined that the tribal nations should no longer receive special privileges or undergo continued segregation, but should be treated as citizens of the United States. Under termination, some tribes were no longer recognized and consequently lost their reservations.

By 1961, however, the U.S. Commission on Civil Rights recognized the poverty that was prevalent among American Indian populations. It also noted that Indians suffered from mistreatment by the law both on and off reservations. The government afterward increased spending for American Indian needs. There was at the same time an increase in tribal efforts to have a say in governing their own affairs.

Throughout the late 1960s and 1970s, governmental policy grew more cognizant of American Indian needs. In 1967 the Supreme Court issued a landmark ruling, upholding that the government should pay the Florida Seminole additional monies for land that had been ceded to the government in 1823. In 1968 Congress passed the American Indian Civil Rights Act, which returned jurisdiction over American Indians to the tribes. President Richard Nixon proceeded to request more funding and benefits for American Indians, strengthening their special legal status. In 1970, for example, 48,000 acres were returned to the Taos Pueblo tribe, who had fought to repossess the land for sixty-four years. The government would continue to return land to various Indian peoples as the decade progressed.

Present-day reservations. The following list locates some of the reservations of tribes discussed in the narrative.

> **Navajo:** The Navajo originally lived in northeastern Arizona, northwestern New Mexico, and southeastern Utah during the nineteenth century. Their reservation is located in Arizona, and extends into New Mexico and Utah.
>
> **Modoc:** Traditional Modoc territory encompassed the boundary between present-day California and Oregon. The highest concentrations of Modoc are in the Modoc reservation in Oklahoma and on the Klamath reservation in southwestern Oregon.
>
> **Nez Percé:** The Nez Percé traditionally occupied eastern Oregon, eastern Washington, and western Idaho. They have reservations in the states of Idaho and Washington.
>
> **Cheyenne:** The Cheyenne originally migrated from Minnesota. Traditionally, the Northern Cheyenne occupied Wyoming and southern Montana, while the Southern Cheyenne lived in eastern Colorado and Kansas. The Northern Cheyenne have a reservation in southeast Montana, while the Southern Cheyenne share a reservation with the Arapaho in south-central Oklahoma.
>
> **Ute:** The Utes traditionally occupied the Colorado Plateau and much of eastern Utah. They have reservations in Utah and southern Colorado.

Reviews. *Bury My Heart at Wounded Knee* was well received both popularly and critically, especially because it offered an alternative historical perspective. Brown is not an American Indian, yet his approach of detailing the exact words of the participants was considered a novel way of depicting exactly how the West was won.

PROTEST AND POWER

Taking its cue from the African American civil rights movement of the 1950s and 1960s, a Red Power movement gained momentum during this era. American Indians organized into groups and also mounted individual efforts to have a voice in their own future. In 1968, for example, George Mitchell and Dennis Banks, Chippewa American Indians living in Minneapolis, formed the American Indian Movement (AIM), which concerned itself especially with gaining the same services for urban American Indians that had been made available to those living on reservations. In 1969 American Indians from various tribes took over the former prison of Alcatraz for some eighteen months in an effort to publicize their cause. A number of similar, sometimes violent, incidents involving American Indians would follow in the early 1970s, including their 1973 seizure of Wounded Knee village in South Dakota, a ten-week standoff that resulted in one death.

While some reviewers concentrated on *Bury My Heart at Wounded Knee* as a history told by American Indians, others emphasized the important link between the atrocities committed in the Vietnam War and a growing sense of national guilt over the country's past. N. Scott Momaday, a Pulitzer Prize-winning Kiowa author, stated in 1971, "Having read Mr. Brown, one has a better understanding of what it is that nags at the American conscience at times, and of that morality which informs and fuses events so far apart in time and space as the massacres of Wounded Knee and My Lai [in Vietnam]" (Momaday in Gunton, p. 70). In yet another review, Helen McNeil described Brown's work as the realization of national guilt made manifest by the Vietnam War. McNeil notes:

> Now that Vietnam has brought the United States to the point of accepting national guilt for the first time, this scholarly and passionate chronicle ... has attained U.S. bestsellerdom by fixing the image of the nation's greatest

Bury My Heart

collective wrong: the extermination of the American Indian.... The Indians, one realizes, knew exactly what was being done to them. *Bury My Heart at Wounded Knee* reproduces their words, transcribed at tribal councils or treaty conferences, or dictated in memoirs, indicting the invaders more eloquently than any third-person account could.

(McNeil in Marowski and Matuz, p. 38)

For More Information

Brown, Dee. *Bury My Heart at Wounded Knee: An Indian History of the American West.* New York: Henry Holt, 1970.

Confederation of American Indians. *Indian Reservations: A State and Federal Handbook.* New York: McFarland, 1986.

Gunton, Sharon R., ed. *Contemporary Literary Criticism,* Vol. 18. Detroit: Gale Research, 1981.

Marowski, Daniel G., and Roger Matuz, eds. *Contemporary Literary Criticism,* Vol. 47. Detroit: Gale Research, 1988.

Sturtevant, William C., ed. *Handbook of North American Indians.* 15 vols. Washington, D.C.: Smithsonian Institute, 1978-90.

Taylor, Colin F., and William C. Sturtevant, eds. *The Native Americans.* New York: Smithmark, 1991.

Trafzer, Clifford. *The Nez Percé.* Edited by Frank Porter III. Indians of North America Series. New York: Chelsea House, 1992.

"The Cask of Amontillado"

by
Edgar Allan Poe

Edgar Allan Poe's horror stories have always been associated with his own tragic life, but they are also closely tied to American popular culture in the 1800s. Written in an era that valued sensational subjects, "The Cask of Amontillado" is a perfect example of this link to America. The story's focus—revenge—and its climactic scene—burial of a living man—were chosen in part to fit the American reader's appetite. Poe sets most of the story in the gloomy underground tomb of a European aristocrat, far from the familiar United States. Leading readers there, the narrator relates a mysterious, horrifying story from his past.

> **THE LITERARY WORK**
>
> A short story set in the 1700s or early 1800s in Italy or France; published in 1846.
>
> **SYNOPSIS**
>
> An aristocrat lures his enemy into an underground passageway with an offer of rare wine and buries him alive there.

Events in History at the Time the Short Story Takes Place

An ambiguous setting. One of the rules Poe followed in his writing was to avoid excess. He believed that every detail in a story should be chosen carefully so that it helped to contribute to the mood he was trying to create. Any other details, he thought, should be left out. As a result, many questions raised in "The Cask of Amontillado" go unanswered. It is even uncertain exactly where and when the story takes place. Most critics agree that the story is set somewhere in Italy, as the narrator's references to his "palazzo" (the Italian word for palace) and his knowledge of Italian wines seem to indicate. Some disagree, however, and place the story in France. Although the name of the narrator's enemy, Fortunato, sounds Italian, the narrator himself, Montresor, has a French name. Furthermore, the narrator uses French words like *"flambeaux"* (torches) and *"roquelaire"* (cape), shares two bottles of French wine with Fortunato during their descent into the vaults, and refers in the beginning of the story to the weaknesses of Italians, naming Fortunato and "his countrymen" in the same breath, thus implying that Montresor himself is not Italian.

As for the time in which the story is set, most clues point to the 1700s or early 1800s. The Masons, of whom Fortunato is a member, founded their Italian and French branches in 1726, and the *roquelaire* that Montresor wears was a popular fashion accessory in the 1700s and early 1800s. These uncertainties of time and place may seem frustrating to curious readers, but they add—as perhaps Poe intended—to the aura of mystery in the story.

The carnival season. The carnival season in eighteenth-century Italy and France was the highlight of the year. Usually lasting a week or more, it was a time for parties, feasts, parades, and costumes.

"The Cask of Amontillado"

In these Catholic countries, the carnival season was the last chance to have fun before Lent—a forty-day period of fasting and penitence—so there was a great deal of merriment. Women dressed as male characters from comic plays, and men dressed as female characters. Students wore sailor's uniforms, and sailors dressed as artists. The black mask and cape worn by Poe's Montresor and the court jester's costume favored by Fortunato were both popular as well. Disguised revelers at the carnival threw confetti at the crowd, walked on stilts, ate fine foods, and drank plenty of wine. The festivity of such a carnival setting serves as a stark contrast to the dark underworld of Montresor's vaults in the short story.

> ### ANTIMASONRY IN THE 1800S
>
> The Freemasons, still a practicing society today, were popular in the United States in Poe's era. At the time "The Cask of Amontillado" was written, however, an increasing number of suspicions had been raised about the practices of this secret group. In 1826 three men kidnapped a Masonic prisoner from his jail cell in New York. The prisoner had announced that he would soon publish the Freemasons' secret rituals; outraged citizens therefore assumed that his kidnappers were Masons with something to hide. This crime resulted in a huge backlash against the secret society, including a state legislative investigation, the formation of an "Antimasonic" political party, and the general sense among many that Masons were immoral at best, criminal at worst.

Catacombs and funeral rites. Although it may seem odd for Montresor to store his wine and his family's skeletons in the same underground vaults, it should be noted that burial customs were rather different in eighteenth-century Europe than they are now. In Palermo, Sicily, when someone died, his or her corpse would be walled up in underground tombs known as catacombs. After six months, the flesh having disappeared, the skeleton would be ready for display. The catacombs were brightly lit so that each skeleton could be seen holding a card with the person's name and title. In the case of public officials who died in Sicily, the dead bodies would be displayed in chairs on the main floor of churches, with two officials placed nearby to fan away flies. Elsewhere, human bones were laid in decorated boxes to be viewed by relatives. Clearly, the "long walls of piled skeletons" that greet Montresor and Fortunato during their journey through the catacombs were no oddity in eighteenth-century Europe (Poe, "Cask of Amontillado," p. 466).

The Freemasons. Founded in the Middle Ages as a guild for stone workers, the Masons or "Freemasons" became a powerful social force in eighteenth-century Europe. By mid-century, this former labor union had become a secret society of aristocrats and common people devoted to the ideals of free thought, rationality, and social betterment. Because of the group's secrecy, however, they were suspected of all sorts of evil behavior. One French police code referring to the Masons warned: "Enemies of order seek to weaken in people's spirits the principles of religion and of subordination to the Powers, established by God" (Jacob, p. 6). More specifically, the Masons were often accused of having loose morals, being anti-Christian (which many were, since they valued reason over faith), and threatening the power of various governments.

Most evidence points to the conclusion that Freemasons supported social change, but not in the revolutionary style attributed to them by their critics. Nevertheless, the established institutions in eighteenth-century Italy and France—especially the Catholic church—had reason to be concerned about the spread of this secret society. Most Masons did not hesitate to speak their minds, even if it meant challenging a higher power—or a friend. Perhaps this straightforwardness is what gets Fortunato into trouble with Montresor in Poe's story.

The Short Story in Focus

The plot. "The Cask of Amontillado" is the story of what may be a perfect crime. Narrating events that took place fifty years before, Montresor, a European aristocrat, begins the tale by explaining that Fortunato, a neighboring aristocrat and fellow wine connoisseur, had, after a series of slights, insulted him. Although Montresor never reveals what this insult was, he is angry enough about it to plot Fortunato's murder. The key to Montresor's plan is that he must succeed not only in punishing Fortunato, but also in escaping punishment for the crime himself.

Finding Fortunato on the street one night during the carnival season, Montresor greets him warmly (Fortunato is not aware of his ill feelings) and mentions that he has bought a cask of what he thinks is a fine Spanish wine, Amontillado.

Aware of Fortunato's pride about his wine-tasting abilities, Montresor explains that he is not sure if the wine is truly Amontillado, and that he needs an expert to taste it and decide. Fortunato, already drunk and excited by the chance to display his skill, needs no urging. He rushes off with Montresor to the latter's palace in search of the wine.

Since both Montresor and Fortunato are in carnival disguise, and since Montresor has made sure that his servants will be gone, no one witnesses the two enter the palace together. Carrying torches, they wind through a series of rooms and then descend into Montresor's vault—an underground passageway that serves as both a wine cellar and a burial ground for his ancestors' bodies. The passageway is damp, and when it causes Fortunato to cough, Montresor, pretending to be concerned, tells him he should leave. This reverse psychology works like a charm, for Fortunato becomes even more determined to reach the treasured wine. As they walk through the catacombs, surrounded by the skeletons of Montresor's relatives, they share two bottles of French wine. Fortunato, now in a drunken stupor, makes an obscure sign and explains to Montresor that it is a gesture of the Masons. Montresor, in response, produces a trowel from under his cape, foreshadowing the climax of the story.

Luring Fortunato into a small room, Montresor chains the bewildered man up. Uncovering some stones and mortar buried nearby, he begins to wall up the entrance to the room. Fortunato, still garbed in the costume of a court jester, gradually realizes what is happening to him and screams to be let out. When this fails, he laughs for a moment, guessing that perhaps Montresor is just playing a practical joke on him. Soon, however, his drunken laughter ceases, and aside from the jingling of the bells on his fool's cap, Fortunato falls silent. The last stone finally laid into place, Montresor's carefully planned crime has been committed successfully—except for the possible punishment his conscience deals him.

The criminal mind in the public eye. Although many tales of violent revenge had been written before Poe composed "The Cask of Amontillado," Poe's story is significant because it is a psychological tale. Narrated by a boastful murderer, it opens a window onto the criminal mind as Poe saw it. At the time the story was written, interest in the workings of the criminal mind was significant. Increasingly publicized criminal trials and other literature that featured criminal characters spurred Americans to talk more than ever before about the nature of and reasons for criminal behavior.

Edgar Allan Poe

In the first half of the 1800s, unemotional and self-confident criminals began to appear on the pages of crime magazines. Two brothers, Joseph and Frank Knapp, on trial for murder in 1830, epitomized this personality type. Reflecting on the character of these defendants, their prosecuting attorney, Daniel Webster, declared:

> Here is a new face given to murder, a new character given to the face of Moloch [an Old Testament god to whom children were sacrificed]; no knitted brow, no bloodshot eye of passion disfigured the countenance of the assassin; but all was calm, smooth, and unruffled; . . . all was done in deliberation of purpose, and with consummate skill of execution.
> (Webster in Reynolds, p. 179)

The behavior of these notorious men parallels that of Montresor in Poe's short story. Montresor's calculating mind, skillfully controlled actions, and unrepentant attitude are evident throughout the story. From the beginning of his revenge plot, Montresor takes care to keep his victim unaware of his intentions:

> It must be understood that neither by word or by deed had I given Fortunato cause to doubt my good will. I continued, as was my wont, to

"The Cask of Amontillado"

POSSIBLE SOURCES FOR "THE CASK OF AMONTILLADO"

Title	Year	Author	Similarities
"The Tell-Tale Heart"	1843	Poe	Murder victim is buried under the floorboards of his bedroom.
"The Black Cat"	1843	Poe	Narrator buries his dead wife in a wall.
"La Grande Breteche"	1843	Honoré de Balzac	Husband of unfaithful wife walls up her lover in a closet.
"The Premature Burial"	1844	Poe	Narrator describes numerous incidents of live burial.
"A Man Built in a Wall"	1844	Joel Tyler Headley	Man watches while a hired workman walls up his enemy in a niche of an Italian church.
The Quaker City; or The Monks of Monk Hall	1845	George Lippard	One character attempts to bury a victim alive in a mansion in which the wine cellar and burial vault are combined.

smile in his face, and he did not perceive that my smile *now* was at the thought of his immolation.

("Cask of Amontillado," p. 465)

Indeed, on the night that Montresor seeks his revenge, he shows the depth of control he has over human emotions, cleverly manipulating Fortunato's vanity to ensure that he will accompany Montresor to his palace. Explaining his doubts about the quality of the wine he has bought, Montresor mentions to Fortunato the name of a rival wine-taster:

> "As you are engaged, I am on my way to Luchresi. If any one has a critical turn, it is he. He will tell me—"
> "Luchresi cannot tell Amontillado from Sherry."
> "And yet some fools will have it that his taste is a match for your own."
> "Come, let us go."
> "Whither?"
> "To your vaults."
>
> ("Cask of Amontillado," p. 465)

A master of reverse psychology, Montresor is by far a cleverer man than Fortunato—especially when the latter is drunk. Montresor's criminal success comes not from physical strength or bravery but from shrewd planning and control. Every detail of his revenge plot—from the protection offered by the carnival season to the placement of the stones and mortar—is carefully planned and executed.

At one point near the end of the story, however, Montresor reveals what may be a loss of self-control. For a brief moment, as he finishes the job of walling up Fortunato, Montresor says that his "heart grew sick" ("Cask of Amontillado," p. 468). Although he quickly explains this sickness away, claiming it is due to "the dampness of the catacombs," his comment raises the possibility that Montresor feels a pang of guilt for his actions. This possibility adds another level of intrigue to an already tantalizing portrayal of cold-hearted criminality.

Poe's Montresor must have been constructed with the public imagination in mind. Not only does he represent a familiar character type, but his moment of "sickness" adds a touch of ambiguity to this criminal type. Curious Americans, already debating the finer points of criminality in the 1800s, welcomed this fictional addition to their collection of nonfictional antiheroes.

Sources. Poe once wrote that "the truest and surest test of *originality* is the manner of handling a hackneyed subject" (Poe in Silverman, p. 93). If this is true, then his originality was definitely put to the test when he wrote "The Cask of Amontillado." A work that followed the general trend toward horror and sensationalism in popular literature, Poe's tale drew its plot directly from several recently published stories, including some of his own.

Events in History at the Time the Short Story Was Written

The Gothic tradition and popular sensationalism. Although Poe's stories were unique in many ways, they drew heavily from both literary traditions and popular tastes. A half century before Poe wrote "The Cask of Amontillado," the Gothic tradition of European romantic writers had begun making its way into the stories, novels, and poetry of American writers. Poe took full advantage of this influence; his stories, including "Cask of Amontillado," are some of the best examples of this form of writing.

Gothic fiction, which grew out of England and Germany, created supernatural worlds in which mysterious and unlikely things could happen; paintings came to life, spirits lurked in corridors, and dead bodies rose from their graves. Living in dark mansions or castles, Gothic heroes were often isolated from the rest of the world and suffered from illness, a troubled memory, or some kind of mental disturbance.

One of Poe's favorite types of Gothic story was the "tale of sensation," also quite popular with other Americans at the time. In these stories, characters would describe the sensations they experienced while on the verge of death—usually a particularly gruesome kind of death. By the mid-1800s, the majority of the population in the United States could read. For this reason, printed materials were being produced for the general public rather than an educated elite, as had been the case in the past. Intended for the common reader, "tales of sensation" and their spin-offs became big sellers in the marketplace.

A literary battle. From May to October of 1846, Poe published a series of essays entitled "The Literati of New York City." These essays were often as full of personal gossip as they were of literary critiques. The essays ridiculed many of Poe's former friends, who had shunned him in the wake of a number of unpleasant incidents in which Poe was entangled, including a romantic scandal involving the married poetess Fanny Osgood. Poe's essays included several bitter personal attacks, and many of his victims chose to respond with equally harsh words about him. After satirizing Poe in fiction and challenging him openly in published letters, one respondent, Thomas Dunn English, portrayed Poe in a most unfavorable light in a novel published in 1846:

> Him with the broad, low, receding and deformed forehead, and peculiar expression of conceit on his face.... He never gets drunk more than five days out of the seven; tells the truth sometimes by mistake; has moral courage sufficient to flog his wife.
>
> (English in Meyers, p. 200)

What bothered Poe perhaps even more than these personal slights was a charge of plagiarism—that is, stealing someone else's writing and passing it off as his own—that English also leveled against him. Poe sued English successfully for libel, but not before writing "The Cask of Amontillado," published in November 1846. Many critics claim that English's "insult" drove him to write this revenge story. According to this theory, Poe is the vengeful narrator Montresor, while the role of English is played by Fortunato.

The temperance movement and literature. In August 1849, a month before his death, Edgar Allan Poe joined the Sons of Temperance, a club formed for the purpose of reducing excessive drinking in society. A notorious alcoholic throughout his life, Poe had long remained on the fringes of the temperance movement; he recognized the harm alcohol was doing to him and wanted to stop drinking. As the circumstances of his death indicate, however, he was never able to escape the power of the bottle; Poe fell into a fatal coma after an overdose of alcohol.

In a public announcement about Poe's decision to join their group, the Sons of Temperance wrote: "We trust his pen will sometimes be employed in [our] behalf" (Silverman, p. 97). This comment, voiced too late to have an impact on Poe's work, was probably a reference to the growing popularity of temperance literature at the time. One temperance group, the Washingtonians, had already commissioned an 1842 novel (*Franklin Evans*) from the young Walt Whitman that depicted the evils of alcohol. After being arrested for attempted robbery, the title character, Franklin Evans, laments what drinking has done to his life:

> It were a stale homily, were I to stay here, and remark upon the easy road from intemperance to crime. Those who have investigated those matters, tell us, however, that five out of every six of the cases which our criminal courts have brought before them for adjudication, are to be traced directly or indirectly to that fearful habit.... None know—none can know, but they who have felt it—the burning, withering thirst for drink, which habit forms in the appetite of the wretched victim of intoxication.
>
> (Whitman, pp. 147-48)

"The Cask of Amontillado"

Although Poe would have rejected the "preachy" style of such a novel, many critics have suggested that "The Cask of Amontillado" was a temperance work of another sort. Certainly, Fortunato's drunkenness leads in part to his downfall; he would not have been so slow to discover Montresor's intentions had he been sober. Moreover, it is partly his desire to taste the rare wine that prompts him to follow Montresor to the vaults. These elements may not prove that Poe was a temperance writer, but they do indicate his acknowledgment of the debilitating power of alcohol.

Poe's final chapter. "The Cask of Amontillado" was published after months of literary squabbling with local writers. After its publication, however, Poe did not receive much of a critical response to his story; many people, it seems, could not tolerate Poe the person and so they decided to ignore Poe the writer.

This silence was probably not Poe's main concern, however. His young wife, who suffered from tuberculosis, was on the verge of death. In December 1846, a New York paper reported that Poe, too, was ill and desperately in need of money and food. Poe's health and his wife's death were reported on in great depth in the following months. Meanwhile, the merits of "The Cask of Amontillado" remained largely unremarked upon. Although "The Cask of Amontillado" later came to be recognized as one of his most "unified" works, a story in which every element is essential to the plot and tone, most Poe reviews in the years that followed its publication dwelled on his poetry or on earlier stories.

For More Information

Jacob, Margaret C. *Living the Enlightenment: Freemasonry and Politics in Eighteenth-Century Europe.* New York: Oxford University Press, 1991.

Poe, Edgar Allan. "The Cask of Amontillado." In *The Short Fiction of Edgar Allan Poe.* Edited by Stuart Levine and Susan Levine. Indianapolis: Bobbs-Merrill, 1976.

Myers, Jeffrey. *Edgar Allan Poe: His Life and Legacy.* New York: Charles Scribner's Sons, 1992.

Reynolds, David S. *Beneath the American Renaissance: The Subversive Imagination in the Age of Emerson and Melville.* New York: Alfred A. Knopf, 1988.

Silverman, Kenneth, ed. *New Essays on Poe's Major Tales.* New York: Cambridge University Press, 1993.

Vaussard, Maurice. *Daily Life in Eighteenth Century Italy.* Translated by Michael Heron. London: George Allen & Unwin, 1962.

Whitman, Walter. *Franklin Evans or The Inebriate: A Tale of the Times.* New York: Random House, 1929.

"Civil Disobedience" (Resistance to Civil Government)

by
Henry David Thoreau

> **THE LITERARY WORK**
>
> An essay set in Concord, Massachusetts, in 1846; published in 1849.
>
> **SYNOPSIS**
>
> Upon being jailed for refusing to pay his poll tax—a stance taken to register his protest of the government's support of slavery and the Mexican War—Henry David Thoreau urges Americans to peacefully protest misguided and immoral government policies through various forms of civil disobedience.

Born in 1817, Henry David Thoreau retreated to Walden Pond at the age of twenty-eight to escape a life of "quiet desperation," which he felt that most people led (Knoebel, p. 300). Defying social convention, Thoreau lived at Walden for two years in contemplative solitude. During that time he refused to pay his poll tax in protest of the government's support of slavery and the Mexican War. He was arrested for tax evasion, and the experience prompted lectures and an essay on the subject of civil disobedience, in which he urged Americans to peacefully protest unjust government policies as he had done. Living during the tumultuous era that culminated in the Civil War, he spoke out against what he regarded as misguided and immoral government policies and warned of the imminent dangers they posed to the nation if citizens did not take individual action.

Events in History at the Time of the Essay

American democracy under a microscope. With the adoption of the Constitution in 1788, the United States of America created a government described as the first true democracy in the world and became the "hope of the human race" (Davidson, *Life in America,* p. 315). Many felt that the United States would be the model of political, religious, commercial, and industrial freedom, a democratic experiment without precedent. But as the nation developed and expanded, problems arose that began to turn the international model of freedom and peace into a government that descended into increased restrictiveness and war. By the beginning of the 1800s, the nation was becoming divided over several issues: the rising stream of immigrants from Europe; increased taxation to pay for education, expansion, and defense; conflicts over westward expansion; and the controversial issue of slavery. The government bureaucracy grew, and military confrontations with other nations—particularly with Mexico over territory in the Southwest—occurred with greater frequency.

As America's population and territory increased, emphasis shifted away from the individual and toward the concept of majority rule. Distinct political parties (Whig and Democrat), formed by the presidential election of 1840, further de-emphasized the individual. Collective groups, backed by moneyed interests, exerted

"Civil Disobedience"

control over government policies and ruled through economic and numeric strength rather than through moral conviction. Sensing their devalued role, individuals generally took less personal responsibility for government policies and relegated authority to majority groups who held the reins of power.

As Thoreau saw it, "a government in which the majority rule in all cases cannot be based on justice." He pleaded for a morally responsible government "in which majorities do not virtually decide right and wrong, but conscience" (Thoreau in Knoebel, p. 312). Special interests and political parties in control of the majority were, in Thoreau's view, backing unjust policies—especially regarding the issues of slavery and war with Mexico.

> ### ON THE DANGERS OF POLITICAL PARTIES
>
> In his last public address, President George Washington warned of the potentially poisonous effects of party spirit. He felt that parties chose the most likable rather than the most qualified candidates and tended to take both sides of all issues in order to gain the most public support. In the view of Thoreau as well as Washington, majority rule tends to disempower the individual, discourage dissent, and invite corruption. Party politics, which often involve unqualified, unprincipled leaders, overwhelm individual rights and lead to apathy on the part of the average citizen. Thoreau's essay, "Civil Disobedience," was written to counter this tendency and to spark action on the part of conscientious citizens.

There was a connection between the two issues. Slaveholding Southern interests and the Democratic party supported the war with Mexico for selfish reasons; they wanted to gain more territory in order to increase the number of slave states. This expansion, Southern interests believed, would break the Union or exert enough pressure on the government to keep slavery legal in the United States.

Slavery: the rift widens. Between 1820 and 1850, the issue of slavery increasingly divided the Northern and Southern states. While the morality of slavery was a subject of debate, arguments over slavery were largely framed in economic terms. In the South, where it was legal, slavery was condoned as vital to the economy and considered "a necessary evil" to enable economic prosperity (Davidson, p. 340). In the North, where increasing numbers of working-class immigrants were settling, slavery was seen by workers and manufacturers as an impediment to fair competition. Immigrant workers and Northern manufacturers—who competed directly with Southern businesses that utilized slave labor—wanted the practice abolished, while Southern plantation owners considered slavery necessary to counter the superior technology of Northern manufacturers.

Abolition had been championed on moral grounds primarily by Quakers as early as 1688, but this angle of protest gained little attention until the early 1800s. Through the work of key antislavery activists, such as Wendell Phillips, William Lloyd Garrison, and John Brown, the abolition of slavery became a core political issue by 1846. Thoreau was among the few outspoken abolitionists who attacked the government's endorsement of slavery on moral grounds. In his eyes, the inaction of Northerners to stop slavery was as bad as the Southerners' practice of keeping slaves. Thoreau insisted that citizens should and could effect change through individual actions:

> If one HONEST man, in this state of Massachusetts, ceasing to hold slaves, were actually to withdraw from this copartnership, and be locked up in the county jail thereafter, it would be the abolition of slavery in America. For it matters not how small the beginning may seem to be: what is once done well is done forever.
>
> (Thoreau in Knoebel, p. 317)

Religion and social responsibility. The concepts of individual responsibility and social activism did not begin with Thoreau. Puritans and Quakers were some of America's first civil protesters and activists to act on humanitarian grounds. They began and led the temperance and abolition movements and founded societies dedicated to the concept of peaceful coexistence between man and nature. In fact, Quaker leader William Penn had founded his colony in Pennsylvania (Penn's Holy Experiment) based on ideals of tolerance and equality. Comprised of men and women of all races and creeds, Penn's Quakers did not believe in rule by priests, but rather placed responsibility for moral development on the individual. They practiced humanitarian acts—speaking out against slavery, boycotting slave-produced goods, and sheltering and feeding the oppressed—and regularly demonstrated the power of individual action.

Thoreau drew on many concepts developed by the Quakers and other social reformers who went before him. Thoreau, like Penn's Quakers, escaped mainstream society in his retreat to Walden Pond, and like them he believed it was imperative for the individual to combat immoral policies. "Is there not a sort of blood shed when the conscience is wounded?" Thoreau asks. "Through this wound a man's real manhood and immortality flow out, and he bleeds to an everlasting death" (Thoreau in Knoebel, p. 318). Like the Quakers, Thoreau believed a truly moral person could not stand idly by and be a party to injustice.

Legacy of distrust and protest. Distrust of the government was a natural byproduct of British tyranny and the American Revolution. Since colonists landed on Plymouth Rock in 1620, protest and revolt had been a part of mainstream life in the New World as individuals pressed for freedom and liberty. One of the Founding Fathers, Thomas Jefferson, even described dissent as healthy and vital to democracy. "I like a little rebellion now and then," he said, comparing it to a storm in the atmosphere (Davidson, p. 320).

After the adoption of the Constitution, protests surfaced from time to time throughout the country—for example, against the War of 1812. But Thoreau's concept of civil disobedience, which involved passive resistance, was somewhat new to America. Influenced by Hindu and Buddhist philosophy, Thoreau proclaimed that it was not only legal for Americans to protest immoral government action but that it was their obligation to do so. Like Buddha, who declared that "he who possesses virtue and intelligence, who is just, speaks the truth," Thoreau proclaimed that anyone adhering to God's law, speaking out for what is just and right, constitutes a majority (Weinberg, p. 472).

The Mexican War. In 1845 the annexation of the Republic of Texas became a major source of controversy between the United States and Mexico. Mexico claimed Texas as part of Mexico, while Texas received an offer from the United States to become a state in its union. On July 4 Texas agreed to the United States offer, and diplomatic relations between Mexico and the United States ceased. Approximately six months later, in January 1846, President James Polk ordered General Zachary Taylor to advance to the Rio Grande River and prepare for war. In April hostilities erupted.

Triggered by failed diplomacy and conflicts in other areas of the West as well as the annexation of Texas, the Mexican War lasted approximately two years. It was an unpopular war, fueled largely by Southern slaveholders who wanted to increase the number of slave states and upset the balance of power in the Union. (At the time there was an equal number of slave and free states in the Union.) When France and England refused to come to the aid of Mexico, few doubted that the United States would win the war, though many deplored the action. Ralph Waldo Emerson, a close friend of Thoreau, commented that "the United States will conquer Mexico but it will be as the man swallows the arsenic which brings him down in turn. Mexico will poison us" (Emerson in Devoto, p. 492). The U.S. military had never before invaded a sovereign nation, and people regarded this war as an invasion of Mexico, no matter what official reason was given for the outbreak of hostilities. Many, like Emerson, thought the U.S. invasion was unconscionable, and some, like Thoreau, refused to pay the taxes that supported it. The war ended officially in February 1848, but its effects have lingered (as Emerson and Thoreau predicted) to the present day.

ABOLITION LEADERSHIP

Wendell Phillips, William Lloyd Garrison, and John Brown were three of the nation's best known abolitionists, and all were strongly supported by Henry David Thoreau. Phillips, who presided over the American Antislavery Society from 1865 to 1870, dedicated himself to the abolition of slavery, arguing that it was a sin according to Puritan Christian ideals. Garrison, founder of the first American Antislavery Society, was considered the conscience of the abolition movement. He published an influential abolitionist newspaper, the *Liberator*, to which Thoreau contributed. Brown was a radical abolitionist who is best remembered for inciting slaves to revolt and, with a small band of men, for killing five slaveholders during a raid on Harper's Ferry, Virginia. He was condemned by conservative abolitionists and executed for murder, though he was vehemently defended by Thoreau, who compared Brown to Christ, calling him "an angel of light" (Thoreau in Davidson, p. 383).

The Essay in Focus

The contents. Beginning his essay boldly, Thoreau asserts "that government is best which governs least" or "governs not at all" (Thoreau, "Civil Disobedience," p. 455). He argues that

Thoreau's birthplace in Concord, Massachusetts.

government should function as the will of the people dictates rather than in the interest of a powerful few. Citing the Mexican War as an example of "a few individuals using the standing government as their tool," Thoreau insists that the majority of Americans object to the war ("Civil Disobedience," p. 455). Challenging the notion of what a democracy is, he contends that a democratic government should "let [the people] alone" and allow as much liberty as possible—especially in the area of trade. He calls not for an end to all government, but for a better government, and insists that changes toward that end be implemented immediately.

Thoreau then invites Americans to consider what kind of government would command respect and to insist on obtaining that ideal. He questions why people have consciences if they do not act on them but instead relegate moral authority to their legislators, as the government requires. Referring to the government's endorsement of slavery and the Mexican War, Thoreau insists that people should "be men first, and subjects afterward"; in other words, they should object to such immoral government policies ("Civil Disobedience," p. 456). If the government or companies are run by people of conscience, he continues, then they will become conscientious, responsible institutions.

Challenging another popular notion about democracy and the duties of the citizen, Thoreau cautions against obeying the law for its own sake. He writes that people should not follow leaders blindly, but should instead question authority. The only law one is required to follow, says Thoreau, is the one put forth by God. He warns that when people place absolute faith in mortals "they are as likely to serve the Devil, without intending it, as God" ("Civil Disobedience," p. 457).

It is more important, says Thoreau, to cultivate a respect for what is right than for the law. If the law or government action is unjust, citizens have a moral responsibility to oppose it. Thoreau further insists that those who merely voice opposition to the war or slavery but do nothing to stop these ills are just as guilty as those who propagate them.

Thoreau then questions the notion of majority rule, arguing that it does not ensure that the government will do what is "right," but rather that it will do what is popular. In Thoreau's view, people must be willing to do what is unpopular, to cast independent votes, and to take action against injustice. He contends that, by refusing to challenge the government, citizens promote the war and slavery. "Under the name of Order and Civil Government," Thoreau asserts, everyone is made to support human "meanness" ("Civil Disobedience," p. 462).

Thoreau also examines a call made by a number of abolitionists of his era for Massachusetts and other free states to secede from the Union. Commenting on this proposal, Thoreau asks why these so-called people of conscience do not refuse to pay their taxes, which are being used to support slavery and the Mexican War. He maintains that the only place for a moral person is in jail because it is "the only house in a slave State in which a free man can abide with honor" ("Civil Disobedience," p. 465).

Thoreau next tells of his personal act of civil disobedience. He says he has paid no poll tax for six years in protest of the government's tolerance of slavery and its campaign against Mexico. Finally arrested in Concord for this stance, he gives details of his short prison stay—one night—before someone (presumably his aunt) paid his tax and he was released. He is clearly upset by the action of the person who paid the tax for him. Thoreau realizes his rescuer's intentions were good, but he attempts to show that he lost his opportunity to challenge the government when the tax was paid for him.

Realizing that most men think differently from him, Thoreau decries the actions of politicians such as Daniel Webster, who believed that the Constitution defended the practice of slavery. Saying "no man with a genius for legislation has appeared in America," Thoreau further blasts Thomas Jefferson and the Founding Fathers because they did not outlaw slavery in their initial draft of the Constitution ("Civil Disobedience," p. 478).

Thoreau once again calls for a government truly based on liberty and freedom, and warns that without better leadership or action on the part of the masses, America is sure to decline. He insists that, as Confucius says, the individual is the basis of an empire and should be respected by the government as such. He says that though the United States has taken a big step forward in founding the first multicultural democracy, improvements can be made. It is up to individuals to assert themselves and take control of the government and truly make it a government of the people, as it was intended to be. Thoreau ends the essay optimistically, saying that if individuals respect one another and are regarded by the State as her source of power rather than her slaves, true democracy will occur.

Sources. Thoreau's essay grew out of his personal experiences—his refusal to pay poll taxes

Henry David Thoreau

that would help support the Mexican War and slavery, and his subsequent incarceration. The style of his essay resembles that of one of the leading abolitionists of his day, Wendell Phillips, who was, along with William Lloyd Garrison, Thoreau's personal friend. Thoreau also took cues from Thomas Carlyle, whom he frequently lectured on. In fact, "Civil Disobedience" was first created as a public lecture, which he delivered in Concord in 1848.

Reviews. Thoreau's original "Civil Disobedience" lecture was delivered at the Concord Lyceum in Concord, Massachusetts, on January 26, 1848, under the title "The Relation of the Individual to the State." Nathaniel Hawthorne's niece, Elizabeth Peabody, published the lecture in her periodical, *Aesthetic Papers,* a year later under a new title, "Resistance to Civil Government." Thoreau created the new title for this first publication of his essay. The essay would not be republished until after Thoreau's death in 1862. It was included in the 1866 volume *A Yankee in Canada, with Anti-Slavery and Reform Papers.* In this collection, the essay was titled "Civil Disobedience," the name by which it is often known today. Followers of a recent trend, however, prefer to retain Thoreau's title "Resistance to Civil Government."

"Civil Disobedience"

Hardly anyone read Thoreau's essay in his own lifetime. As a result, it had little impact during the 1800s. At the turn of the century, however, seventy years after it was written, the Russian writer Leo Tolstoy discovered the essay and commented on it in *The North American Review*. Shortly thereafter, Mohandas Gandhi, who was leading a revolution of workers in India, published the tract in his newspaper and later in pamphlet form. Gandhi, who named his movement after Thoreau's essay, was most responsible for making "Civil Disobedience" popular throughout the world. In the 1960s, Dr. Martin Luther King Jr. reintroduced Thoreau's work in the United States, where it became more popular than ever before as people applied its philosophy to the civil rights movement and protests against the Vietnam War. King spoke of the continued relevance of Thoreau's words to this later era. "As a result of his writings ... we are the heirs of a legacy of creative protest. It goes without saying that the teachings of Thoreau are alive today; indeed they are more alive today than ever before" (King in Thoreau, p. 453).

Transcendentalism. Thoreau's life and work challenged the new American nation's notion of progress and industrialization. While the mainstream touted the benefits of expansion and industrialization and moved in droves to the burgeoning cities, Thoreau retreated to the woods and insisted that man was actually regressing and harming the world rather than progressing and improving it through technology. He and a select group of other writers—Emerson, Herman Melville, William Blake, Charles Dickens, and Thomas Carlyle—became known as transcendentalists.

Part of the Romantic movement, transcendentalism fundamentally entails a belief that all wisdom comes from nature; that experience is key to understanding; and, akin to Buddhist philosophy, that knowledge must be acquired firsthand, through individual experience. Transcendentalism places primary emphasis on the individual and on instinct over reason, insisting that every person possesses "divine Reason" (Curti, p. 297). These ideals tended to support the American concept of democracy.

Antimaterialist transcendentalists such as Thoreau cautioned against the potentially corrupting elements of the democratic model, such as basing all decisions on majority rule rather than moral conviction. In "Civil Disobedience," Thoreau breaks ground as a transcendental activist, insisting that it is not enough to merely believe or speak out against injustice—one must act. His essay describes his individual act of disobedience and encourages others of conscience to follow his lead and change America.

For More Information

Curti, Merle. *The Growth of American Thought*. New York: Harper & Row, 1964.

Davidson, Marshall B. *Life in America*, Vols. 1 and 2. Boston: Houghton Mifflin, 1974.

Devoto, Bernard. *The Year of Indecision: 1846*. Boston: Little, Brown, 1943.

Knoebel, Edgar. *Classics of Western Thought*. Vol. 3. San Diego: Harcourt Brace Jovanovich, 1988.

Thoreau, Henry David. "Civil Disobedience." In *The Annotated Walden*. Edited by Philip Van Doren Stern. New York: Clarkson N. Potter, 1970.

Weinberg, Arthur, and Lila Weinberg. *Instead of Violence*. New York: Grossman, 1963.

The Confessions of Nat Turner

by
William Styron

William Styron, a white writer and novelist, was born in 1925 in Newport News, Virginia, the same tidewater region where the real Nat Turner lived one hundred years earlier. Styron's grandmother grew up on a North Carolina plantation, where she owned two slave girls. The hours spent listening to his grandmother's stories about owning slaves haunted the young Styron for years. It troubled him deeply that by his own time racial inequalities still had not been set right. In 1966, during the midst of the growing black civil rights movement, Styron published *The Confessions of Nat Turner,* one of his most controversial novels. The book, which focused on the life and rebellion of a black slave in nineteenth-century Virginia, helped shed light on the racial unrest that persisted into the twentieth century.

Events in History at the Time the Novel Takes Place

Early American slavery. Probably as early as 1619, speculators and slave traders brought Africans across the Atlantic Ocean to the newly established colonial regions. Unlike white indentured servants, who worked for about seven years, blacks became subject to colonial laws passed in 1660 dictating that slaves would serve white owners for life.

The growing plantation-based economy in the South meant that the number of slaves brought from Africa rose dramatically. By the early 1700s, for instance, slaves outnumbered whites by al-

> **THE LITERARY WORK**
> A historical novel set in Southampton County, Virginia, during the years 1800 to 1831; published in 1966.
>
> **SYNOPSIS**
> Nat Turner recounts his life as a slave and his revolt against Virginia slaveowners.

most five to one in South Carolina. As the proportion of blacks increased, white anxiety about possible uprisings grew and more systematic control over slaves became commonplace. Laws were enacted that prohibited slaves from carrying weapons and forbade them from learning to read or write. Some slaves managed to learn these skills anyway, and a few managed to secure weapons.

Free blacks. Although slavery was firmly entrenched in the South, not all blacks were slaves. By the year 1860, the number of free blacks in the South amounted to nearly 500,000. While some blacks were born into freedom, others fled from slave states or bought their liberty after years of saving meager earnings from such menial labor as washing clothes or performing carpentry work. Some masters emancipated their slaves, but this was an unusual occurrence. More common were broken promises of freedom.

Nat Turner, for instance, was a Virginia slave who received assurances from his benevolent owner that he would one day be set free. Cir-

Confessions of Nat Turner

Nat Turner's capture.

cumstances changed, however, and the owner sold Nat. Subsequent and more cruel owners failed to keep the long-ago promise of freedom, a betrayal that only added to Nat's fury and frustration toward all white people.

Free blacks enjoyed relative autonomy compared to slaves, yet they still faced many restrictions designed to keep them subordinate to white people. Free blacks could not vote, serve on juries, or use the same public facilities as white people. In most states, free blacks were prohibited from testifying against whites in court and from marrying or engaging in sexual relations with whites. Despite all these constraints, a number of free blacks managed to save money, accumulate property, and enjoy respectable positions within their communities. In some cases, these "achievements" did little to stem the growing urge to violently resist white society in the South. The slave Gabriel Prosser, the free black Denmark Vesey, and the slave Nat Turner all led slave revolts in the nineteenth century.

Prosser's revolt. On August 30, 1800, under the leadership of Gabriel Prosser, a group of slaves made plans to attack their owners and invade Richmond, Virginia. Meeting secretly with his followers under the guise of funerals and other religious gatherings, Prosser planned for several hundred men to make a surprise attack at midnight. Carrying a flag with the motto "Death or Liberty," the rebels planned to capture arms, burn warehouses, and perhaps even take Virginia's governor as hostage.

On the day of the attack, a horrible storm broke out across the region. As creeks and rivers swelled from the rain, Prosser realized that it would be impossible to cross the waterways into Richmond, and so the attack was called off. By the time the rain stopped, informers had betrayed the mission. White scouting parties searched relentlessly for the rebels, capturing Gabriel Prosser at the end of September in nearby Norfolk, Virginia. Although he would not confess to having committed any crime, Prosser was sentenced to death in October 1800.

Denmark Vesey. Denmark Vesey (1767-1822), a freed black slave, purchased his freedom for $600 using money he had won from a lottery. Soon after buying his freedom, Vesey recruited plantation slaves and free urban blacks to help him carry out his plan to capture the city of Charleston, South Carolina. The revolt was arranged to take place on the second Sunday of July in 1822. Vesey, a carpenter, used a church as a base to meet with his followers.

Among them were a group called the Blacksmiths, who fashioned spikes into bayonets for weapons, while others procured daggers, swords, and ammunition. Before the insurrection took place, though, a slave revealed the plot to white authorities in Charleston. More than a hundred of Vesey's collaborators were captured. Vesey was convicted for planning to overthrow the city and hung along with about thirty-five others.

Nat Turner's Revolt and its aftermath. Nat Turner's Revolt, upon which William Styron's novel is based, is probably the most widely known slave uprising. Like the fictionalized character in William Styron's novel, the real-life Nat Turner, a slave and preacher, heard voices instructing him to rise up against white slaveowners in the South. Nat and his followers carried out these plans, staging a bloody revolt in 1831.

Just prior to Nat Turner's Revolt, the Virginia state legislature had argued extensively about the issue of slavery. Strong antislavery sentiments were expressed in the western counties of Virginia, and it appeared possible that abolition would become a reality. After Nat Turner carried out his plan, however, abolition became an impossibility in Virginia. In fact, life for its slaves grew even worse than it had been.

Like other states across the South, Virginia tightened those laws that regulated the lives of slaves and free blacks. Militias and slave patrols increased, slave churches were prohibited, and black preachers were forbidden to teach. The South began to censor abolitionist literature and even screened the mail. Charity Bowery, a freed black slave, recalled the years after Nat Turner's Revolt:

> On Sundays, I have seen the negroes up in the country going away under large oaks, and in secret places, sitting in the woods with spelling books. The brightest and best men were killed in Nat's time. Such ones are always suspected. All the colored folks were afraid to pray in the time of the old prophet Nat. There was no law about it; but the whites reported it round among themselves, that if a note [of prayer] was heard, we should have some dreadful punishment; and after that, the low whites would fall upon any slaves they heard praying or singing a hymn, and often killed them before their masters or mistress could get to them.
> (Blassingame, *Slave Testimony*, p. 267)

The Novel in Focus

The plot. Styron's novel is a fictionalized recreation of Nat Turner's life and rebellion against white slave masters in Southampton County, Virginia. It is told in the first person by Nat as he sits shackled in his jail cell, where he waits to be hanged for instigating the slave revolt.

Nat Turner is born into slavery in 1800 on the Virginia plantation owned by Benjamin Turner. Nat's father has become a runaway slave; his mother works in the main house as a cook. Raised as a house slave alongside his mother, Nat escapes the grueling work required of the field slaves, and over time comes to feel superior to slaves outside the "big house." His mother reinforces these feelings of superiority, instilling in her son the belief that he possesses special talents and will some day rise to God's great calling.

Upon Benjamin Turner's abrupt death, Nat passes into the hands of Benjamin's brother, Samuel. Impressed by Nat's intelligence and his desire to learn, Samuel encourages Nat to study and teaches him reading, math, and carpentry, promising that he will be freed upon turning twenty-five. Prompted by his master, Nat spends many hours studying from white children's schoolbooks and becomes well versed in Scripture.

As long as Nat lives on Samuel Turner's plantation he enjoys the respect of the Turner family and the privileges of a house slave. Drought and hard times, however, force Samuel Turner to sell his slaves. Nat's next owner, the Reverend Eppes, betrays Samuel Turner's promise of freedom, selling Nat to a cruel fourth master, Thomas Moore.

During the nearly ten years that Nat is owned by Moore, Nat's feelings of frustration and betrayal grow ever stronger and thoughts of revolt are never far from his mind. Nat spends days at a time fasting and praying in a brush arbor built in the nearby woods. Several times he hears voices calling him to God and commanding him to rise up against the white slave master. Inspired by a religious vision, Nat believes he is chosen by God to lead a bloody revolt that will free all slaves.

After the death of Thomas Moore and the marriage of Moore's sister to Joseph Travis, Nat becomes the property of the Travis family. Although Joseph Travis is a kind owner, Nat is not deterred from his plans for rebellion.

In February 1831, Nat begins planning his insurrection. He recruits men from his congregation and together they steal horses, guns, and axes. After fasting and praying in the woods, Nat receives a sign from God in the form of a solar eclipse, and he knows the time for revolt has come. On August 22 Nat's fury is unleashed, with the slaves vowing to kill every white person encountered on their rampage.

The Travis family receives the first blows of the attack. In the midst of the revolt, however, Nat finds that he is unable to murder. His fol-

The building where Nat Turner was held during his trial and until his execution.

lowers begin to lose respect for Nat as a leader as a result. Fearful that he may lose control of his forces, Nat proceeds to murder Margaret Whitehead, a kind young woman who had befriended Nat. Within twenty-four hours at least fifty-five more whites are killed. Local forces soon overcome the insurrection, murdering several of Nat's compatriots on the spot. Nat hides for two months until October 30, when he is captured and brought to jail.

Nat refuses to confess to any crime, saying that he does not feel guilty. Judge Jeremiah Cobb nevertheless convicts Nat and sentences him to be hanged. Lacking any remorse for the revolt, Nat prepares to face his death, still filled with rage toward all white people responsible for slavery and toward slaves who acquiesce to their white masters. Given the choice between freedom and slavery, Nat staunchly claims he would again choose liberty, even if it required him to kill.

The only regret Nat feels is for the death of Margaret Whitehead. Leaning against the cold bars of his jail cell during the final hours before his execution, Nat thinks to himself, "I have no remorse for anything. I would do it all again.... I would destroy them all again, all—But for one..." (Styron, *Confessions of Nat Turner*, p. 403).

Parallels with real-life events. Styron's fictionalized account of Nat Turner's rebellion parallels historical fact in several respects. The novel reflects facts actually known about Nat Turner in regard to his five owners, key events of the rebellion, and his followers. In other respects, however, Styron's novel departs from historical accuracy. Missing from the novel are several key family members from the real Nat Turner's life. In Styron's novel, Nat never lays eyes upon his grandmother. The real-life Nat, however, came from a strong family that included his grandmother. In addition, it was Nat's parents who taught him to read, not the white family who owned him. Moreover, Styron's fictional character is a bachelor, whereas the real-life Nat Turner was married to a woman named Cherry, and together they had a son, Redic. Critics also charged that Styron's use of colloquial language is overdone, bordering on racism rather than accuracy. These critics objected to what they saw as Styron's excessive use of derogatory language when other words would have sufficed.

Sources. Limited historical information about Nat Turner was available to William Styron when he wrote *The Confessions of Nat Turner*. Newspaper accounts of Turner's insurrection were sketchy, and records from the Southampton courthouse where Nat Turner was tried and convicted merely list the names of those involved in the revolt.

An account of the insurrection was told to Nat's court-appointed lawyer, Thomas R. Gray. This account, also called "The Confessions of Nat Turner" was the main historical resource Styron used in writing his novel. There is, however, doubt about the accuracy of Gray's account. It is unclear to what extent facts were omitted or embellished by Gray.

According to Styron, *The Confessions of Nat Turner* rarely departs from the facts that are known about Nat Turner and the revolt of which he was the leader. Historical fact served merely as a loose guideline, though. "In those areas where there is little knowledge in regard to Nat, his early life, and the motivations for the revolt (and such knowledge is lacking most of the time)" wrote Styron in the introduction to the novel, "I have allowed myself the utmost freedom of imagination in reconstructing events" (Styron, p. ii).

In a postscript to his novel, Styron remarked that the stories his paternal grandmother told him about slave ownership strongly influenced him to write *The Confessions of Nat Turner*. Thinking back to these stories, Styron explains, "Nothing so awed me as the fact that this frail and garrulous woman whom I beheld, and who was my own flesh and blood, had been the legal owner of two other human beings. It may have determined, more than anything else, some as-yet-to-be born resolve to write about slavery" (*Confessions of Nat Turner*, p. 437).

As a child growing up in the Virginia tidewater region, Styron was well aware of the racial inequities still in existence in the twentieth century. Ramshackle black schoolhouses with outside privies stood in stark contrast to the well-equipped and up-to-date facilities provided for white students. Disparities such as these were embarrassing evidence to Styron that society was firmly locked in the grip of racial laws that promoted "a separate and thoroughly unequal way of life" (*Confessions of Nat Turner*, p. 435).

Styron's final inspiration for writing his novel came from reading Camus's *The Stranger*, a first-person story told by a convicted murderer while awaiting his execution. Impressed by the framework, he decided that it would be a nice one for his own novel. He would tell the story in the first person and have it end on the day of Nat's execution.

Events in History at the Time the Novel Was Written

The civil rights movement. The 1950s and 1960s saw the growth of a civil rights movement in the United States in which blacks and whites took direct action to defeat segregation and other forms of inequality that persisted in America. These inequalities prompted some people to ignore or challenge rules about segregation of buses, lunch counters, and schools in an effort to gain greater civil rights for blacks.

By 1966, the year Styron's novel was first published, the civil rights movement had achieved several victories for black Americans. In 1954 the U.S. Supreme Court ruled in its *Brown v. Topeka Board of Education* decision that school segregation was illegal and that integration must occur. Pressed by groups such as the National Association for the Advancement of Colored People (NAACP), Congress passed five Civil Rights Acts between 1957 and 1968 that promised equality in education, federal programs, housing, and voting rights. Still, people chafed under continuing inequalities. Just as Nat Turner's anger persisted even after he again became the property of a kind owner, the few civil rights victories would not stem the wave of violence about to break across the nation.

Long Hot Summer. In 1966, during what became known as the "Long Hot Summer," bombings, fires, and assassinations made front-page news. Racial strife erupted in Birmingham and Selma, Alabama, and riots flared in Los Angeles, California; Newark, New Jersey; Detroit, Michigan; and Cleveland, Ohio.

Both blacks and whites participated in the violence, and the consequences were tragic. In July 1966, two people died and more than four hundred were arrested in Chicago, Illinois, after three days of racially motivated rioting. That same summer, a mob of nearly four thousand whites stoned participants in a desegregation march in the Chicago suburb of Cicero. At the head of the march was the black leader Martin Luther King Jr., a champion of nonviolent efforts to garner greater rights for blacks. Also that summer, rioting in the Hough neighborhood of Cleveland, Ohio, left four people dead and fifty injured, and resulted in widespread property damage and 164 arrests.

The Long Hot Summer of 1966 dramatically shifted the tone of the civil rights movement. Many civil rights activists subsequently rejected tactics of multiracial cooperation and nonviolent resistance in favor of a movement called Black Power, which called for blacks to unite, to recognize their common heritage, and to build a sense of community. Whites were no longer welcome, in the eyes of many of these blacks, to join in their struggle for civil rights. The black leader

Confessions of Nat Turner

Malcolm X, who had been assassinated in 1965, would have probably approved of this movement since he had complained that whites, not blacks, were in control of the struggle. More like Nat Turner than Martin Luther King had been, Malcolm at one point urged blacks to use any means necessary to gain equality, including violence. Black leaders who survived him, such as Stokely Carmichael, agreed with this advice. Carmichael urged blacks to carry weapons for self-defense. More separatist than other groups, black radicals rejected the values of white American society and the notion that whites could presume to speak on behalf of the black experience.

Reception. William Styron's novel initially met with some glowing reviews, but controversy soon followed. *The Confessions of Nat Turner* rose to the top of bestseller lists, where it remained for many weeks. Styron was invited to speak at several black colleges, and in 1968 the author received the Pulitzer Prize in fiction for the novel. Meanwhile, though, other critics attacked Styron's novel as a racist version of history. They charged that the author had created a biased version of events. Rather than depicting Nat as a strong black revolutionary, Styron, these critics contended, selectively chose to include certain facts about the real-life Nat while omitting others, thus creating the impression of a weak and ineffectual character. In Styron's novel, for example, Nat, who is portrayed as a bachelor, has violent sexual fantasies about raping Margaret Whitehead, a young white woman. Critics charged that such an episode ignores historical accuracy, instead relying on "stereotypes of ... the revolutionary black man who lusts for the white woman" (Clarke, p. 57).

Some critics objected to Styron's perceived attempt to be a "white authority on blackness" (Clarke, p. 58), arguing that the novel was the product of a racist white man attempting to speak for a black slave. Certain sections in the novel aroused particular attention from critics: "There are occasions," muses Nat in Styron's novel, "when in order to buy some advantage from a white man it is better not even to say 'please' but to silently wrap oneself up in one's niggerness like the blackest of shrouds" (*Confessions of Nat Turner*, p. 269). Such passages, in which Styron's characters convey self-abnegating and self-demeaning traits, were singled out for condemnation. The passages rankled some civil rights activists and flew in the face of the emerging focus on Black Power and black pride.

During the late 1960s Styron received death threats, a development that forced him to stop making public appearances. Styron was shocked and dismayed by the furious response to his book. Once the recipient of thanks and praise for his novel, Styron was now repudiated and his book considered obscenely racist.

Writing *The Confessions of Nat Turner* had allowed Styron to address the guilt and responsibility he felt as a white man living in the South. It was inconceivable, he later recalled, "that in a short time I would experience almost total alienation from black people ... having unwittingly created one of the first politically incorrect texts of our time" (Styron, p. 435).

For More Information

Blassingame, John W. *The Slave Community: Plantation Life in the Antebellum South.* New York: Oxford University Press, 1972.

Blassingame, John W., ed. *Slave Testimony: Two Centuries of Letters, Speeches, Interviews, and Autobiographies.* Baton Rouge: Louisiana State University Press, 1977.

Clarke, John Henrik, ed. *William Styron's Nat Turner: Ten Black Writers Respond.* Boston: Beacon Press, 1968.

Gilmore, Al-Tony. *Revisiting Blassingame's* The Slave Community: *The Scholars Respond.* Westport, Conn.: Greenwood Press, 1978.

Harding, Vincent. *There is a River: The Black Struggle for Freedom in America.* New York: Random House, 1983.

Ruderman, Judith. *William Styron.* New York: Ungar, 1987.

Styron, William. *The Confessions of Nat Turner.* New York: Random House, 1993.

The Count of Monte Cristo

by
Alexandre Dumas

Alexandre Dumas was born in a small village in France in 1802, the son of General Alexandre Dumas, Napoleon's famous mulatto general. The younger Dumas led a life almost as romantic as his novels; he took part in the Revolution of 1830, fought several duels in the course of his life, and fled creditors in France after his excessive spending exhausted his financial resources. Elements of *The Count of Monte Cristo* seem to be drawn from Dumas's own background, working to bring the novel to life.

> **THE LITERARY WORK**
> A novel set primarily in France and Italy between 1815 and 1838; published in 1844.
>
> **SYNOPSIS**
> A young man, falsely imprisoned for aiding the exiled French leader Napoleon, escapes an island on which he is jailed. Posing as the Count of Monte Cristo, he seeks revenge against his enemies.

Events in History at the Time the Novel Takes Place

The rise and fall of Napoleon. Napoleon Bonaparte was born on Corsica, a French island off the west coast of Italy, in 1769. After receiving an education in French military schools, Napoleon became an artillery officer in the French army and eventually climbed the ranks to the position of general. Achieving military victories in Italy and Egypt, Napoleon returned to France in 1799 and used his immense popularity to seize control of the nation from the Directory, a government body that had held power since 1795. In 1804 Napoleon had himself proclaimed Emperor of France and began making plans for a massive invasion of England.

Napoleon's inability to gain control of the English Channel would force him to forfeit this plan before the end of 1805. But leading his "Grand Army" across Europe, he managed to defeat the Austrians at the Battle of Ulm. Two months later, in December 1805, he defeated Austrian and Russian forces at the famous Battle of Austerlitz. In 1807 Napoleon negotiated a peace with the Russians and made plans to turn his armies entirely against Britain. Still unable to gain the control of the Channel, which was crucial to any military campaign against the British, Napoleon engaged in various military and political endeavors throughout Europe.

By 1812 the precarious peace that France had made with Russia had completely deteriorated, and nearly 700,000 French troops marched eastward. Napoleon reached Moscow in September 1812, only to find that much of the city had been burned by retreating Russian soldiers. He decided to return to France in mid-October, but Napoleon's army was pursued by Russian troops throughout the return trip. Nature turned into an enemy as well: the freezing weather of a premature winter decimated the French soldiers, who were also unable to find sufficient food. Only 100,000 survivors returned with Napoleon from the Russian campaign.

Realizing that Napoleon had lost his military might, the armies of Spain, England, and Prussia all turned against France. In April 1814 Napoleon was forced to surrender his army and abdicate his crown. His conquerors exiled him to the tiny island of Elba. One year later, in March 1815, Napoleon returned with a small group of followers and rallied the support of the people and soldiers of France. In June 1815 Napoleon attacked the armies of England and Prussia at the Battle of Waterloo, in which the hastily assembled French army suffered defeat. Thereafter, Napoleon was exiled to the distant island of St. Helena, where he died in 1821.

The novelist Alexandre Dumas was greatly influenced by Napoleon. One of the most memorable moments of his life was seeing Napoleon ride through the small village in which Dumas lived as a young boy. More important was Dumas's connection to the emperor through his father, General Dumas, who had served under Napoleon. Dumas's interest in Napoleon prompted him to use the interaction between his main character, Edmond Dantès, and the exiled emperor on Elba as the incident that sends Dantès to prison and initiates the plot of the novel.

Politics in France, 1815-1830. After the onset of the French Revolution in 1789, French politics was struck by a whirlwind of turbulent events. The rebels executed their king and queen (Louis XVI and Marie Antoinette) in 1793, launched a number of foreign invasions, and saw Napoleon declare himself emperor in 1804. In 1814, the year Napoleon was exiled to Elba, the Bourbon monarchy returned to power with the coronation of Louis XVIII.

The people of France were curious about the kind of government that the new monarch would provide for them. Mindful of the recent rebellion, King Louis promised a liberal constitution that would guarantee civil and religious liberty for all French citizens. This new constitution, the Charter of 1814, guaranteed civil rights to all, established a parliament similar to the one in place in England, abolished military conscription, and gave property rights to all Frenchmen.

One right this constitution did not bestow upon all Frenchmen, however, was the right to vote. Only men aged thirty and older who paid at least three hundred francs in taxes could vote; those who qualified constituted a minority that amounted to only one percent of adult males. In addition, despite the creation of a parliamentary system, all executive power belonged to the king. The unbalanced system gave a large measure of power to the "ultras" or ultra-royalists, conservative supporters of the king. This sudden surge of power on the part of the "ultras" gave rise to the "White Terror" in 1815, during which extreme royalists executed about three hundred of Napoleon's supporters throughout France. It is this sentiment that accounts for Edmond Dantès's severe sentence after he delivers a letter from Napoleon in *The Count of Monte Cristo*.

Five years after the White Terror, in 1820, voting rights were further limited when the government intentionally reduced the taxes so that more citizens would pay less than three hundred francs and thus be disqualified from the voting franchise. Through this ploy, the "ultras" gained more political clout. In 1824 Louis XVIII died and his brother Charles X took over the throne, a development that gave the "ultras" even more influence. King Charles passed laws that promised reparations to noble families who had lost land as a result of the Revolution. In 1827 he disbanded the Paris National Guard (which was made up of middle-class citizens) and replaced it with regular troops. In 1830 Charles X dissolved the Chamber of Deputies (lower house of parliament) after it attempted to defy his authority. He also held new elections and proclaimed several special ordinances. These new ordinances initiated a severe censorship of the press, dissolved the newly elected Chamber before it could even meet, and issued new electoral rules that would have cut the total number of voters from 100,000 to 25,000.

The response to these new ordinances was explosive. Barricades were erected in the streets of Paris, and masses of students demonstrated, joined by middle- and working-class men. After three days of rioting and insurrection, Paris fell into rebel hands. A provisional government was formed and the crown was offered to Louis Philippe, the Duke of Orléans. Considered the ideal candidate, Louis Philippe had fought with the republican armies during the Revolution and could also claim a right to the throne through his great-great-grandfather's uncle, Louis XIV.

Alexandre Dumas played a small role in this rebellion, which became known as the Revolution of 1830. Recognizing that the rebels' supply of gunpowder was extremely low at the start of the insurrection, Dumas left Paris to travel to a small village where large quantities of powder were stored. Carrying an official military order,

Alexandre Dumas

Dumas acquired the powder and returned with it to Paris. Though this action was not a major factor in the revolution, Dumas considered himself very much involved in the movement.

The death of Ali Pasha. Ali Pasha was a Turkish soldier who became responsible for controlling Janina, a city in southern Albania, for the sultan of Turkey. When he received this commission in 1788, his ambition was to become completely independent from the sultan and from Turkey. He hoped to establish himself as, in effect, the leader of his own country. He also planned to add Greece and the Ionian Islands to his budding empire. A great statesman, Ali Pasha courted the powers involved in the Napoleonic wars, obtaining support at various times from Russia, France, Great Britain, and Austria. When the French republic was on the rise, he pledged his support, yet when he heard of the defeat of the French navy by the British admiral Horatio Nelson in 1798, he promised his support to the British and even imprisoned a French general who happened to be in Janina at the time. When Napoleon began his rise to power, Ali Pasha severed his ties with Great Britain and again resumed friendly relations with France.

As the Napoleonic wars ended, a long-running conflict between Russia and Turkey was also coming to a close. This allowed the sultan of Turkey to finally turn his attention back to Ali Pasha, whom he regarded as a traitor. In 1820 the sultan declared Ali Pasha an enemy of the empire and of the Mohammedan religion. Two Turkish armies invaded Albania, and after a two-year siege of Janina, Ali Pasha, betrayed by members of his own army, was captured and subsequently beheaded.

In Dumas's novel *The Count of Monte Cristo*, Ali Pasha is portrayed as a noble hero in the service of France. One of Monte Cristo's greatest enemies, Fernand de Morcerf, is represented as the man who betrayed the Pasha to the Turks, a crime for which he suffers twenty years later. Following the betrayal of Ali Pasha, Monte Cristo buys the Pasha's daughter, Haydee, who has been sold by Fernand to a slave trader. Haydee remains with the Count as his mistress, and it is she who eventually exposes Fernand as a traitor. The shame he faces as a result of this drives Fernand to suicide.

The Novel in Focus

The plot. Edmond Dantès is a sailor who has rapidly climbed the ranks in the merchant shipping business of Morrel and Son. With the death of one of the company's captains, first mate Dantès is in position to be promoted to captain. He is also ready to marry Mercédès, a beautiful girl from a poor family. Dantès's sudden good fortune provokes jealousy in two men: Danglars, a clerk for Morrel and Son who feels he should be promoted over Dantès; and Fernand, Mercédès' cousin, who wishes to marry her himself. Danglars knows that Dantès had delivered a package for the captain who died to the island of Elba, the home of the exiled Napoleon. He reports this action to the royalist authorities. On the day of his wedding, Dantès is arrested and taken to Monsieur Villefort, the public prosecutor.

Acting on information from Danglars, Villefort confronts Dantès concerning his trip to Elba and questions him regarding a letter he received from someone on the island. Dantès replies that he was simply fulfilling the dead captain's last request, and he turns over the letter from Elba to Villefort. Villefort, a staunch royalist, is shocked to see that the letter is addressed to Monsieur Noirtier in Paris, who happens to be his own father, a radical supporter of Napoleon. Realizing that a public reminder of his father's political views would hurt his own aspirations, Villefort burns the letter and sentences Dantès to life in

The Count of Monte Cristo

prison to insure that no one will find out about the correspondence between his father and Napoleon.

Dantès is horrified to find out that the Chateau d'If, an infamous island prison, is to be his new home. Locked in a cell in the dungeon of the prison, Dantès suffers for months and considers suicide to end his miserable plight. As he starves himself to death, Dantès hears a scratching sound coming from within one of the walls. Realizing that it is someone digging for freedom, he resumes eating and determines to dig himself, either to meet the unknown excavator or to escape. The digging escapee turns out to be the Abbé Faria, a priest considered to be insane by the jailers because of his rantings about a buried treasure of incredible value. Faria attempted to dig to a courtyard from which he might have escaped, but through an error of calculation his tunnel instead ends in Dantès's cell. The two become close friends and make plans to flee together.

Unfortunately, Faria suffers a stroke which paralyzes half of his body, leaving him unable to perform the swim necessary for escape from the island. Dantès pledges to stay with his friend and seals the new escape tunnel that they dug together. The priest suffers another stroke. Aware that he is going to die soon, he tells Dantès about the fabled treasure, whose location is known only to him. Faria then dies, and after the jailers sew his body into a shroud, Dantès enters Faria's cell via the adjoining tunnel and substitutes himself for the body of the dead Abbé in the shroud. The jailers haul the "corpse" to the top of the prison wall and hurl it into the sea below. Dantès cuts his way out of the shroud and swims to a small nearby island. With the help of some local smugglers whom he befriends, Dantès eventually makes his way to the tiny island of Monte Cristo, which is the location of the buried treasure. Eluding the smugglers, he uncovers the treasure and, mindful of his new fortune, dubs himself the Count of Monte Cristo.

With his new identity established, the Count returns to European life after a fifteen-year absence. Finding out that Villefort, Danglars, and Fernand have all had great success in life, Dantès begins exacting his revenge upon them. He is especially interested in retaliating against Fernand, who married Mercédès after she thought that Dantès had died in prison. Turning to countless maneuverings, the Count of Monte Cristo enters and ruins the lives of his enemies.

When his final revenge almost takes the life of an innocent young girl, however, Dantès decides that man cannot be the final force of justice; only God has this right. Moreover, Dantès, who has achieved most of his revenge, also realizes that despite the hardships he has suffered, he can still enjoy life through his love for Haydee, his mistress. The Count of Monte Cristo thus leaves Europe behind forever and sails for the East.

Providence and justice in *The Count of Monte Cristo*. At several points in the story, the Count discusses his position as a being whose purpose in the world is to deliver the judgments of providence or justice. In a conversation with Villefort, the Count tells him that he is one of "those men whom God has placed above kings and ministers by giving them a mission to fulfill, rather than a position to occupy" (Dumas, *The Count of Monte Cristo,* p. 176). As they continue talking, the Count goes on to tell Villefort, "I want to be Providence, for the greatest, the most beautiful and the most sublime thing I know of in this world is to reward and punish" (*The Count of Monte Cristo,* p. 178).

The Count goes to a great deal of effort to reward the Morrel family for their good treatment of him as a young man and for their attempts to arrange his release from prison. It is the Count's desire to reward the Morrels that leads to his final understanding of providence and justice. Part of the Count's plan for revenge involves the death of Villefort's daughter Valentine, but when this portion of his scheme has almost come to fruition, the Count realizes that Maximilien Morrel is madly in love with Valentine and has secret plans to marry her. When the Count sees that his plans for revenge almost punished one of the people he loves, he is forced to consider that he might not be capable of delivering judgments of providence and justice. He afterwards allows Danglars, his greatest enemy, to live and, even more importantly, forgives him. By the end of the novel, the Count's realization of his true station is complete. He writes in his letter to Maximilien that he was a man who "believed himself for an instant to be equal to God, but who realized in all humility that supreme power and wisdom are in the hands of God alone" (*The Count of Monte Cristo,* p. 441).

This study of ideas such as judgment, providence, and justice is especially relevant for the period during which Dumas was living. The Reign of Terror, a period during the French Revolution in which royalists were led by the thousands to the guillotines, and the White Terror in 1815, which saw royalists brutally execute several hundred Bonapartists, may have inspired

Dumas's fascination with these concepts. The novel seems to be making the point that the brutal cycles of revenge going on in France were unjust, and that death sentences for political reasons were too extreme. The characters of Villefort and his father, Monsieur Noirtier, show that political opposites can coexist. Villefort is a staunch royalist and Noirtier is a devout Bonapartist, yet the two live together as father and son. Though they still have subtle conflicts, they understand each other and are able to get along.

Sources. Monte Cristo is an obscure island in the Mediterranean Sea that Dumas took note of during a sailing trip. Other influences on Dumas's novel included the real-life experiences of several French citizens.

In constructing the plot for *The Count of Monte Cristo*, Dumas was directly influenced by a true story that he had read in Jacques Peuchet's *Memories from the Archives of the Paris Police*. The story involved a handsome young Paris shoemaker named Picaud who was engaged in 1807 to be married to a beautiful orphan girl who brought with her a 100,000-franc dowry. Some acquaintances of the shoemaker, jealous of his success, told an agent of Napoleon's police that the shoemaker was a spy for the English. Picaud was arrested on his wedding day, though no trial had been held. In 1814, after the fall of Napoleon, Picaud was released from prison, prematurely aged by his suffering and unrecognizable to those who had known him. While in prison, Picaud had cared for an Italian priest who was also imprisoned there. On his deathbed, the priest told Picaud of a treasure hidden near Milan. As soon as he was released, Picaud found the treasure and returned to Paris under a false name. Like the Count of Monte Cristo, Picaud tracked down the men who had betrayed him, and set out to exact revenge, stabbing two men to death and poisoning a third; unlike Monte Cristo, Picaud himself was murdered by the fourth, who later confessed the entire story to a priest who, in turn, related it to the French police. Several subtle acts of revenge enacted by Picaud appear in Dumas's novel. For example, Dumas bestows dishonor on the character of Danglars's daughter by marrying her to a nobleman who was actually an escaped murderer; Picaud had done the same thing to his own enemy's daughter.

Dumas developed the entire plot for his novel by making a few simple changes to this tragic story of the shoemaker and adding his own romantic flourishes. A less direct influence on Dumas's novel seems to have been the classic tale *Arabian Nights*, whose hero Aladdin triumphs over his enemies after finding a fabulous treasure hidden in a cave.

Events in History at the Time the Novel Was Written

Romantic response to the Industrial Age. In the early 1800s, France experienced technological, cultural, and economic changes as well as drastic political changes. Though small workshops and family-operated establishments remained the typical system of production, large factories began to appear in France. Urban areas of the country experienced some growth in population as a result of this industrialization. This new urbanization and industrialization inevitably brought new social ills to France.

> **A FATHER'S INFLUENCE**
>
> During his military career, the author's father, General Alexandre Dumas, had several experiences on expeditions in Italy and Egypt that may have affected his son's writings. While occupying a house in Cairo, Egypt, the general found buried under the floor an immense hoard of treasure that was worth almost two million francs. Unlike Dantès, General Dumas did not keep the treasure; instead he gave it to his commander, Napoleon, to help pay for the army's expenses. The general did, however, resemble Edmond Dantès in another way. General Dumas also experienced life in prison, spending two years in an Italian dungeon. During those two years of imprisonment, the general was repeatedly poisoned with arsenic by his captors, a torment that left him partially paralyzed, blind in one eye, and deaf in one ear. This mistreatment comes to mind when reading several scenes of *The Count of Monte Cristo*, including the poisoning of Valentine and other members of Villefort's household.

City dwellers who lived in close proximity to one another were more susceptible to disease; in Paris, the cholera epidemic of 1832 killed more than 20,000 people. In 1841 the first factory act was passed. It forbade employers from hiring children under the age of eight and limited to eight hours the workday of children from eight to twelve. In actuality this act did nothing, however, largely because the act required that unpaid vol-

The Count of Monte Cristo

unteers serve as inspectors. Poor conditions for industrial workers persisted, leading to riots and strikes throughout the 1830s and into the 1840s.

The Romantic movement, of which Dumas was a central figure in France, reacted in part to the poor conditions of this period. In general the movement celebrated individual emotions, but it also celebrated national traits and heritage. Through their work, some Romantic artists took a reminiscent backward glance at a glorified past.

Elements of this glorification of the past appear throughout Dumas's novels. The high society portrayed in *The Count of Monte Cristo* seems more appropriate to the 1700s than the 1800s. In some instances, the Count himself seems a remnant of the past, with his dramatic gestures of honor and chivalry; even his source of wealth, a treasure from fifteenth-century Italy, forms a connection with the past. Dumas draws attention to the modern age through the Count's fascination with technology; he spends whole afternoons watching the signals of the telegraph operators and shows a great thirst to try every new innovation (such as the steamboat he acquires by the end of the novel). By incorporating the elements of the past in a glorified fashion and his own industrial present in less exaggerated terms, Dumas demonstrates his Romantic sensibilities and at the same time acknowledges his country's movement into the new industrial age.

The critics and *The Count of Monte Cristo*. With the publication of *The Count of Monte Cristo* in 1844, Dumas rose from moderate fame to the status of a worldwide celebrity. Perhaps no other writer of this period enjoyed the universal literary reputation that Dumas did. The fame that *The Count of Monte Cristo* brought its author, enhanced by the publication of *The Three Musketeers* in the same year, forced Dumas to leave Paris because of the constant stream of visitors calling at his door. Literary critics, though, did not share the public's enthusiasm for the novel. Many reviewers condemned *The Count of Monte Cristo* as romantic sensationalism rather than a work of literary merit. In 1848 the *British Quarterly Review* published an article that blasted Dumas's novel:

> Probability is a thing he utterly sets at nought; and this is the great defect and drawback of *Monte Cristo*... Dumas stimulates the vulgarest curiosity, but never stimulates the mind.... Yet no one who knows the frivolous public will wonder at the enormous success of these works; written rapidly, read rapidly, and as rapidly forgotten.
>
> (Harris, p. 52)

In 1870 the *Spectator* expressed a similar sentiment in its review of *Monte Cristo*. "Since the 'Arabian Nights' there has been nothing like 'Monte Christo [sic];' no such revel of improbabilities, no such fandango of absurdities" (Harris, p. 61). These early reviews fail to note that *The Count of Monte Cristo,* though romantic and fantastic on the surface, embraces complicated issues, such as justice and retribution, that were especially relevant during the fifty years following the French Revolution.

For More Information

Bergeron, Louis. *France under Napoleon*. Princeton, N.J.: Princeton University Press, 1981.

Chezrezi, Constantine. *Albania Past and Present*. New York: Macmillan, 1919.

Dumas, Alexandre. *The Count of Monte Cristo*. New York: Bantam, 1981.

Furet, Francois. *Revolutionary France, 1770-1880*. Cambridge: Blackwell, 1988.

Harris, Laurie Lanzen, and Cherie D. Abbey, eds. *Nineteenth-Century Literature Criticism*. Vol. 11. Detroit: Gale Research, 1986.

Ross, Michael. *Alexandre Dumas*. London: David & Charles, 1981.

Daisy Miller

by
Henry James

In the 1800s, Americans took to traveling in Europe in huge numbers. Newspapers across the nation were filled with travel accounts, and many of America's most prominent writers, starting with and including Washington Irving, Nathaniel Hawthorne, Margaret Fuller, and Ralph Waldo Emerson, recorded their impressions of the European people and places that they encountered. Henry James not only traveled but lived abroad for much of his life, attending school in Switzerland (like the young man Winterbourne in *Daisy Miller*) from the age of thirteen. He later used this experience to write stories that pitted American innocence against European sophistication in the context of changing social codes, both in the United States and abroad.

> **THE LITERARY WORK**
>
> A novella set in the late 1800s in Switzerland and Rome; written in London, England, in the spring of 1878, revised in 1909.
>
> **SYNOPSIS**
>
> A young American woman traveling in Europe is courted by an American man living abroad, then shunned by him and others because her behavior does not adhere to the social codes applied to unmarried women by American expatriates of the time.

Events in History at the Time of the Novella

Americans abroad. Why was there a rush to travel to Europe in the 1800s? Historians propose several reasons. First, by the late nineteenth century, Americans who had previously concerned themselves with getting established and procuring food, housing, and employment for themselves, finally had the time and the money to travel. The economic power base shifted from agrarian production to capitalist economics in the late 1870s, creating a new class of Americans able to concentrate on self-improvement and amusement.

Another important factor in the rush to Europe was the stature that the continent occupied in the popular imagination: "Until very late in the century the United States was widely believed to lack almost every element that made up what Henry James called 'the denser, richer, warmer European spectacle'" (Stowe, p. 5). It became increasingly important for those people in America who saw themselves as fashionable to obtain the European cultural benefits (such as art, music, language, and architecture) that would help define them as the privileged class in their own country. Significant numbers of American women were also traveling abroad, women perhaps not unlike Daisy Miller and her mother, wives and daughters of wealthy businessmen who journeyed to Europe to see the sights, to buy goods, and to be seen by other rich Americans. This yearning to become "European" was in conflict with the views held by leading Americans (like Emerson, Walt Whitman, and Mark

Twain) who urged their compatriots to create an indigenous, nonderivative cultural base.

Women in nineteenth-century America. Assessing the social position of American women in James's day is complicated. On one hand, they generally were better educated and enjoyed greater social freedoms than their European counterparts. Government in America provided for the education of girls at an earlier time (1830s) than in England (1870s) or in France (1880s), for example. In addition, "though French demoiselles were still watched and chaperoned as in the past, young American women moved about quite freely, joked about courtship with their friends, and wrote love letters to their suitors" (Hellerstein et al., p. 121). This perhaps explains some of Daisy's reluctance to be chaperoned in Europe; her attitude may stem from the relative lack of social restrictions placed on her at home in Schenectady, New York.

Another factor that shaped the role of women in the United States was their function in the family. While American men pursued an occupation to earn an income, women, who often did not work, took responsibility for ensuring that their families were exposed to "cultural" activities and products, such as theater, literature, and painting. The relatively high position of women in American society was something that was often commented upon in sociological texts of the time. Alexis de Tocqueville, the visiting Frenchman, pointed out in *Democracy in America* (1835) that while the Americans "have allowed the social inferiority of woman to continue, they have done all they could to raise her morally and intellectually to the level of man" (de Tocqueville in Allen, p. 19).

De Tocqueville qualifies his praise, however. No matter how many freedoms American women might have enjoyed in the generations after Tocqueville, by James's day they, like European women, were still denied the right to vote, were educated not for any worldly profession but only for running an efficient and enriching home, and were financially dependent upon the men in their families. There were also certain standards of behavior to which middle-class and upper-class women (particularly the yet-unmarried) were held accountable, standards that did not take into consideration a woman's individual personality or desires. Bluntly speaking, a girl had to retain her virginity, politely referred to as her innocence, until she was safely married.

The ruckus caused by Daisy's flouting of convention in James's novella dramatizes the tension between the freedoms that American women enjoyed by going unchaperoned in male company and the limits on personal independence that bound them. On one hand, Daisy and her mother (who is given no name other than Mrs. Miller) are "allowed" to travel through Europe, enriching and enjoying themselves; on the other hand, society judges them for their failure to adhere to a very narrow definition of respectable womanhood. She appears to be "fast"—that is, sexually experienced, which would cast her outside the bounds of respectable society. The judges are other American women anxious to impress Europeans with their good manners and moral uprightness, which only emphasizes the powerful weight of society's expectations regarding appropriate female behavior.

Victorian women in Europe and America. In a strict sense, the term "Victorian" refers to life in England during the reign of Queen Victoria (1837-1901), but the term has been extended to other nations of the period as well. Certain traits were typical of Victorian societies, including a preoccupation with trying to regulate the behavior of others. For young women of the middle and upper classes, etiquette and household manuals were used to mold them to the purpose society defined for them—serving the family and acting as moral guides to their husbands, since males were believed to need female restraint upon the baser passions a male was expected to have. Although these manuals limited a woman's role, they also focused attention on her and gave her a sense of her own importance. In fact, Victorian women saw themselves as interesting, a view that was shared by their surrounding society. This is certainly true of James's heroine Daisy Miller.

Other factors besides the manuals affected the behavior of young women. In both the United States and Europe, industry continued to displace farming as a means of earning a living. This, in turn, prompted changes in courtship and in marriage. Arranged marriages became a custom of the past in Europe as well as in America, and courtship grew more independent than before. Young factory workers earned wages that allowed couples to get married earlier in life. Meanwhile, the life span of a person grew longer. Earlier marriages and longer lives meant that a woman spent more of her life married than had been true in past societies. This reality probably inspired Victorian women to pay more attention to the likelihood of emotional happiness when considering a marriage. In any case, young Daisy in James's story reflects "a new emphasis [in society] on romantic love as a basis for union" (Hellerstein et al., p. 120). However, she still had to protect her reputation for chastity in order to win herself a husband.

The American girl. The late 1800s saw the appearance of several stereotypical images of American womanhood. They included the American Princess (or heiress), the Temptress, and the New Woman (an independent, strong-minded sort, thirsty for experience of the world)—and these were just some of the labels fastened to certain modes of female behavior in the nation at the time. De Tocqueville's observation about the growing equality of American women was indicative of a growing interest in the nature and characteristics of female life in the thriving society; determining exactly how to think of American women became an important intellectual preoccupation.

To some degree, James's *Daisy Miller* energized the debate about the qualities that constituted an American girl. Was she merely innocent in the sense of being ignorant and lacking in experience, or was she morally loose and sexually adept? James's first effort to publish *Daisy Miller* was rejected by a Philadelphia editor almost instantly and with complete editorial silence, leaving James to ponder what it was about his tale that had met with disapproval. The most famous hypothesis was that the novella brought offense or "outrage upon American girlhood" (James, *Daisy Miller*, p. v), since Daisy appears "vulgar" and morally questionable. This idea—that the nature of all American girls could be captured in the novella's portrait of one particular American girl—demonstrates the power of stereotypes in James's day.

The novella itself questions the validity of labels. On several occasions, the character Winterbourne generalizes about American girls from his experience of Daisy. "How pretty they are!" he marvels over Daisy's beauty (*Daisy Miller*, p. 9). Somewhat later, he decides on the appropriate category in which to place his new acquaintance: "She was only a pretty American flirt. Winterbourne was almost grateful for having found the formula that applied to Miss Daisy Miller" (*Daisy Miller*, p. 17). The idea of such a "formula" was considered intellectually valid at the time; one critic argued that many believed that America in general could best be understood through a study of its women: "Visitors from abroad made a genuine effort to study the young American woman so that they might imbibe 'that intangible quality of Americanism'" (Muirhead in Banta, p. 97). No wonder that conventional Americans were horrified at the thought that James's portrait might lead Europeans to conclude that Americanism was crude at best and corrupt at worst.

The American man. Critics have observed that *Daisy Miller* offers a study not only of American womanhood but also of American manhood. One of the most prominent American men in the novella is Winterbourne, a more or less permanently self-exiled American in Europe who seems to Daisy to be "more like a German" (*Daisy Miller*, p. 12). Living on an inherited income, Winterbourne is a perpetual student, a man who is often in the company of wealthy women—his aunt, the mysterious married lady in Geneva, the Millers. Not only has Winterbourne refrained from becoming involved in business, but he is generally reluctant to compete on any level, either with his rival for Daisy's attention or, more generally, within the newly competitive American culture that he declines to rejoin. Critic Robert Weisbuch comments that "Winterbourne's permanent vacation in Geneva is a choice; he has chosen not to enter into his own time and into the fray of 'competitive individualism'" (Weisbuch, p. 69).

JAMES ON EUROPEAN MANNERS

In a chapter of *Transatlantic Sketches* (1875) entitled "Roman Notebook," James records his impressions of the behavior of European ladies: "The European woman is brought up to the sense of having a definite part (in the way of manners) to play in public. To lie back in a barouche [carriage] alone, balancing a parasol, and seeming to ignore the extremely immediate gaze of two serried [crowded] ranks of male creatures on each side of her path, save here and there to recognize one of them with an imperceptible nod, is one of her daily duties" (James in Fogel, p. 46).

As historians point out, events in the second half of the 1800s challenged traditional notions about respectable men. European standards of aristocracy and inherited wealth gave way to the emergence of the American industrialist or businessman whose wealth was earned and who did not necessarily come from the established upper classes. Winterbourne's failure to understand and eventually win Daisy may point to more than his ignorance of the American girl. It perhaps indicates his unfamiliarity with the new definition of respectable men and the new social and economic rules that accompanied it. Still, however,

Daisy Miller

there was a double standard: sexual "education" was approved for the "new" American male, but not for the maidens he would wish to wed.

Social taboos. To today's reader, and especially, perhaps, to American readers, the scandalous behavior that eventually blackens Daisy's reputation and causes her to be ostracized by "good" society might seem relatively harmless. But young Miss Miller's decisions to meet gentlemen in dark gardens without a chaperon, take unsupervised jaunts to ruined castles with men to whom she is not married, and disregard the social status, religion, and ethnicity of her male companions are all viewed as her flaunting of the traditional European standards of respectability to which women of "good breeding" were expected to adhere.

WITHOUT BLEMISH?

In 1879, a year after James's sensational novella was published, the American John Hay tried to clarify the conflicting standards of female behavior at the heart of *Daisy Miller*: "[Daisy's] conduct is without blemish, according to the rural American standard, and she knows no other.... In every city of the nation young girls of good family, good breeding, and perfect innocence of heart and mind, receive their male acquaintances *tête-a-tête*, and go to parties and concerts with them, unchaperoned" (Hay in Fogel, p. 52).

Respectability for women, married or not, was mostly defined in terms of domesticity. The woman's role was tied to the home and to her relationship with the men—husbands and fathers—in that home. In the highest class of society, a rigid system of chaperonage, whereby young or unmarried women had to be accompanied in public by another, generally older, person, ensured that women did not become derailed from the fast track to marriage and motherhood by inappropriate or fruitless relationships with men who could not advance the woman's family socially or financially. Traveling was, of course, a dangerous activity for women at the best of times, for it took them out of the house and away from responsible masculine influences. In Daisy's case, her willful independence coupled with the ineffectual chaperonage of her mother spelled trouble from the outset, as the novella suggests more than once.

Finally, there is the matter of Daisy's being "an American flirt." She admits to it with grace, and it is important to know that flirting was considered a socially acceptable practice—in America at least. *Godey's Lady's Book and Magazine* of July 1869 has some interesting observations to make on the subject, observations which shed bright light on the central dilemma of *Daisy Miller*:

> Flirting is to marriage what free trade is to commerce. By it the value of a woman is exhibited, tested, her capacities known, her temper displayed, and the opportunity offered of judging what sort of a wife she may probably become.
>
> (*Godey's Lady's Book and Magazine* in Fogel, p. 60)

Daisy runs into trouble because she fails to realize that this American custom is not regarded so benignly in Europe. To be called an "American flirt" was no compliment there, since it signified a girl's frivolous nature, but it was better, as Winterbourne observes, than being a "coquette"—a "dangerous" and calculating European woman intent on seduction.

The Novella in Focus

The plot. Winterbourne, a rather aimless and older American student in Geneva, visits his very proper aunt at the Swiss resort town of Vevey, which is frequented by rich American tourists. Among these tourists are the Millers—young Daisy, her highly jingoistic and bratty little brother, and their vapid and retiring mother. Daisy shocks the traditionally mannered Americans that she meets; her uncultured speech, her straightforward manner, her lack of a chaperon at times, and her willful belief in her own independence cause quite a scandal in the circles in which she travels. Despite the disapproval of Winterbourne's aunt, Daisy and Winterbourne strike up a quick relationship. They part soon after meeting—Daisy travels to Italy, and Winterbourne returns to his studies (or perhaps a married lady) in Geneva—but they promise to meet again in Rome.

By the time that Winterbourne finally arrives in Rome, however, he learns that Daisy has been seen "going around" with a young Italian man named Giovanelli. Her relationship with the Italian is condemned by everyone around her, including Winterbourne. In their eyes, Giovanelli appears to be a penniless seeker of Daisy's fortune, and his willingness to circumvent traditional courtship rituals compromises him and Daisy in the eyes of American society in Rome. Their folly results first in Daisy's exclusion from "good" society and finally in her recklessly exposing herself

The Coliseum in Rome.

to a malaria-infected environment. Winterbourne abandons all hope for Daisy's reform and decides that he need no longer be bothered with trying to understand what type of girl she is. Only after her death does he begin to understand her.

"Roman fever." Daisy's scandalous career comes to a halt in the Roman Coliseum, where she contracts malaria, often referred to as "Roman fever." The word "malaria" is rooted in the Italian language and means "bad air." Although scientists now know that malaria is caused by parasites in the blood stream, in James's day the disease was thought to have been associated with poisonous and damp swamp air. But James chooses to set Daisy's demise in the Coliseum, the ancient Roman site of public execution and trial (the ruins of which still stand in the center of Rome), not just because the Coliseum was famously damp: Daisy seems to die as much from European condemnation as she does of any chill she might have caught in the Italian moonlight. Sitting in the Coliseum, she likens herself and Giovanelli to the early Christians, eyed hungrily by the judgmental Winterbourne, whom she compares to a lion. The allusion is to the ancient Roman pastime of feeding criminals—Christians—to starving packs of wild animals as public entertainment.

***Daisy Miller* in the context of James's career.** *Daisy Miller* changed Henry James's life; his career as a fiction writer (as opposed to more journalistic efforts) began to soar with its 1878 publication in the English *Cornhill Magazine*. The theme of the American abroad, and particularly the American *woman* abroad, fascinated James throughout his life, and turns up again and again in his finest novels, from *The American* to *The Europeans*, *The Portrait of a Lady*, and *The Golden Bowl*. *Daisy Miller*'s exploration of the differences between American and European traditions and manners was not the first of its kind, but it was certainly the most notorious, on both sides of the Atlantic Ocean. The novella also refuted the old idea that American literature was inferior in interest and quality to European works.

James returned to *Daisy Miller* some thirty years after it was first published and made significant changes to it. While he did not meddle with the characters or the plot, he did try to rework his novella at the stylistic level, aiming at a different tone than he had achieved in his earlier effort. The result is that Daisy emerges as much less of an obvious target for the cruel behavior of the Europeanized Americans; rather than a laughably uncultured provincial, she appears more an admirable innocent. James also changed the title; in 1909 he removed the subtitle "A Study," remarking that he could not quite remember why it had been there in the first place, unless, perhaps, it was meant to compensate for a certain flatness in Daisy's character.

Sources. In the preface to *The Novels and Tales of Henry James: New York Edition,* James claims that his inspiration for *Daisy Miller* came from an incident that someone dropped in conversation about a young American girl, "a child of nature and of freedom," who made an embarrassing mistake in her association with a "good-looking Roman, of vague identity" (James, p.v).

A COMEDY IN THREE ACTS

James's first full-length play (he had penned three shorter works previously), entitled "Daisy Miller: A Comedy," was written in Boston in 1882 and has most likely never been produced. Revising the original tragedy, the play tags on a happy ending, closing with Winterbourne and Daisy about to return to America to be married. Try as he might, James could not convince anyone to stage his play, which by all accounts was a rather wooden dramatic effort. His attempts to do so filled him with what he called "deep and unspeakable disgust" for the theatrical world (James in Carlson, p. 78).

In establishing the setting for his novella, James chose the Castle of Chillon as the site of the unescorted Swiss outing undertaken by Winterbourne and Daisy because of his own experience of the place. Chillon, which dates from the thirteenth century, stands on the shores at the east end of Lake Geneva near Montreux. James had written of it in *Transatlantic Sketches* as a packed tourist attraction—which makes Winterbourne's arrangement to see it alone with Daisy something of an expensive proposition. More importantly, though, Chillon was well known in the nineteenth century as a sort of monument to freedom. In the castle, the imprisoned Swiss patriot Francis Bonivard, whose unfortunate history Winterbourne imparts to Daisy, defied the counts of Savoy for six years (1530-1536).

Chillon was familiar to most travelers through two poems that the English Romantic poet Lord Byron wrote about the place. According to Byron's verse about Bonivard, "for my father's faith/ I suffered chains and courted death" (Byron, p. 5). Byron carved his name, visible to this day, on the very pillar to which Bonivard had been chained. There is an unmistakable link between the ideas of political freedom and protest articulated in Byron's poems and Daisy's own unrestrained actions in Europe.

Reviews. An initial review of *Daisy Miller* in the *New York Times* in 1878 reflected the seriousness with which the age regarded the confrontation between American and Old World values: "It is a hackneyed remark that Americans continually shock the prejudices of Europeans. When the prejudices relate to unimportant things, it may be well, to pay no more attention to them than to avoid, as much as possible, hurting their feelings. But when the question relates to the reputation of a young girl, it is worse than folly to persist in defying public opinion" (Stafford, p. 103). *The Nation*'s reviewer also addressed James's work from the point of view of its realism:

> No American who has not been abroad can really appreciate this story.... [O]ne must have painfully struggled between a sense of snobbishness in not acknowledging one's countrypeople and a conviction of untold miseries consequent on the other line of action; in short, one must have suffered in order fully to understand the fine quality of this story.
> (Stafford, p. 106)

For More Information

Allen, Elizabeth. *A Woman's Place in the Novels of Henry James.* London: Macmillan, 1984.

Banta, Martha. *Imaging American Women: Idea and Ideals in Cultural History.* New York: Columbia University Press, 1987.

Byron, Lord. *The Prisoner of Chillon.* Oxford: Woodstock, 1993.

Carlson, Susan. *Women of Grace: James's Plays and the Comedy of Manners.* Ann Arbor, Mich.: UMI Research Press, 1985.

Fogel, Daniel Mark. *Daisy Miller: A Dark Comedy of Manners.* Boston: Twayne, 1994.

James, Henry. *Daisy Miller.* In *The Novels and Tales of Henry James: New York Edition.* Vol. 18. New York: Charles Scribner's Sons, 1909.

Hellerstein, Erna Olafson, Leslie Parker Hume, and Karen M. Offen, eds. *Victorian Women.* Stanford, Calif.: Stanford University Press, 1981.

Stafford, William T. *James's Daisy Miller: The Story, the Play, the Critics.* New York: Charles Scribner's Sons, 1963.

Stowe, William W. *Going Abroad: European Travel in Nineteenth-Century American Culture.* Princeton, N.J.: Princeton University Press, 1994.

Weisbuch, Robert. "Winterbourne and the Doom of Manhood in *Daisy Miller.*" In *New Essays on Daisy Miller and The Turn of the Screw.* Edited by Vivian Pollak. Cambridge: Cambridge University Press, 1993.

A Doll's House

by
Henrik Ibsen

Henrik Ibsen was born on March 20, 1828, in the small town of Skien, Norway. In an effort to escape small-town life and his family's poverty, he later moved to the city of Christiana and began a modest career in journalism and the theater. He was repeatedly denied a writer's stipend because of the way he satirized both the public and the authorities in his writings. Ibsen went into voluntary exile from 1864 to 1891, but even in his absence, his reputation in Norway grew. With the appearance of *A Doll's House*, his fame spread beyond Scandinavia to the rest of Europe and the world.

Events in History at the Time of the Play

Norway in the nineteenth century. Norway was troubled by its share of foreign policy crises and domestic concerns throughout the 1800s. The century had started well enough. Norway was one of the few European states in which the French Revolution of 1789 did not inspire the masses to demand new liberties. While other countries experienced tumultuous times, Norway busily reaped the benefits of supplying exports and shipping services to any country involved in the wars taking place elsewhere. In the summer of 1807, after the British towed home nearly every ship in the Norwegian fleet (which was supplying Britain's enemies), Norway was forced to rethink its foreign policy. The country reluctantly allied itself with Britain's enemy, the French leader Napoleon.

The Norwegian economy, which relied so heavily on the seaports, suffered terribly when

> **THE LITERARY WORK**
> A play set in an upper-middle-class home in an unnamed Norwegian city in the late 1800s; first performed in 1879.
>
> **SYNOPSIS**
> A woman who has committed forgery to save her husband's life reassesses her obligations to her family and her own independent needs.

the British put a naval blockade in place. A combination of factors eventually dissolved the fifty-three-year union between Norway and Denmark; in 1814 Denmark ceded Norway to the Swedish king. Norway was thus united with Sweden in 1880, approximately the time in which the play is set; the union would continue until 1905.

The period of union witnessed the emigration of hundreds of thousands of Norwegians, especially to the United States. As a result of its rugged geography and the trend toward emigration, Norway remained sparsely settled and predominantly rural. In 1850 only 163,000 of Norway's 1,400,000 people lived in urban areas. The population distribution created a small-town mentality that Ibsen loathed and examined repeatedly in his writings.

Christmas in Norway. *A Doll's House* opens on Christmas Eve with Nora Helmer busily making final preparations for the following day. The Christmas season in Norway traditionally called for elaborate celebrations and activities. Beginning well before Christmas Eve, as many as fifteen different kinds of cookies would be baked for the holiday and reserved until about December 23rd, called Little Christmas Eve.

Although customs varied, Christmas Eve itself was traditionally the night a family celebrated Christmas together at home. On that evening, they exchanged gifts and decorated the tree with candles, fruit, raisins, figures made of straw, and heart-shaped paper baskets filled with candy. The next day, December 25th, the tree would look bedraggled after the candles burned low and the celebrants consumed its edibles. Despite its bare appearance, the tree stayed up through the twelve days of Christmas, from Christmas Eve to the feast of Epiphany on January 6th.

December 25th was the "First Day of Christmas," a day to visit neighbors and attend parties like the one given by the Helmers' upstairs neighbors in Ibsen's novel. The "Second Day of Christmas," on the 26th, was also a day to eat and drink well and entertain at home or go visiting.

> **IBSEN ADDRESSES THE NORWEGIAN WOMEN'S RIGHTS LEAGUE IN 1898**
>
> I am not a member of the Women's Rights League. Whatever I have written, has been without any conscious thought of making propaganda. I have been more poet and less social philosopher than people generally seem inclined to believe.... I am not quite clear as to just what the Women's Rights Movement really is. And if you read my books carefully, you will understand that. True enough, it is desirable to solve the problems of Women's Rights along with the others; but that has not been the whole purpose. My task has been the description of humanity.
>
> (Ibsen in Allphin, p. 93)

Norwegian communities also maintained a party tradition that featured a sort of costume ball. This practice could be traced back to an old pagan tradition called *Julebukk,* or "Christmas-buck," in which adults and children put on masks of various animals and moved from house to house, where they would be welcomed with beer, wine, sweets, and special meat dishes.

The tarantella. The scene in *A Doll's House* where Nora dances the Italian tarantella is one of the most famous in the play. Her husband observes, "But Nora darling, you dance as if your life were at stake" (Ibsen, *A Doll's House,* p. 92). He tells her to slow down, but she cannot—she is caught up in the sensual, ecstatic dance. Full of movement, the tarentella involves raising one's arms, running, hopping, whirling, and swinging from side to side.

Though we only see Nora dance alone, the tarantella is a social dance meant for two couples, or even for a long row of men and women. Traditionally the male partner uses two pairs of castanets, while the woman holds a tambourine in her right hand and beats on it with the lower part of her left palm. These instruments are used to keep time and to add to the excitement as the pace of the dance quickens, especially at its conclusion.

The dance itself has a curious history. In sixteenth- and seventeenth-century Italy, the bite of the Apulian spider, also known as the *Lycosa tarentula* or common tarantula, was popularly but mistakenly thought to cause a nervous disease. This sickness, called tarantism, was allegedly marked by hysteria and a mania for dancing. The wild motions of the tarantella dance, which was named after the disease, were thought to be caused by the spider bite.

The women's movement. Ibsen consistently asserted that *A Doll's House* examined issues facing humanity rather than women in particular. Even so, the women's movement embraced him as one of the leading champions of its causes after the publication of the play. Many critics have observed that, regardless of Ibsen's claims, no playwright could have created such an assertive, likable heroine without feeling some sympathy for the challenges facing women at the time.

Camilla Collett became Norway's most celebrated feminist. Her groundbreaking novel, *The District Governor's Daughters* (1854-55), protested the notion that marriage was the all-encompassing goal of a woman's existence. Collett referred to the novel as "the long-suppressed cry from my heart," and it echoed the sentiments of many other women throughout Norway as well (Collett, p. 13). In Collett's view, women had to be educated in order to regard themselves in a new way. She felt sure that once they had more education and greater economic freedom, political privileges would soon follow. At the time, a woman's economic status was tied to her husband, who, for example, had to formally approve any loans for the household. If a woman tried to earn her own money, as Nora and Kristine do in Ibsen's play, her employment opportunities were usually limited to low-paying jobs such as needlepoint, teaching, and menial clerical positions.

The second half of the nineteenth century did witness many changes for women in Norway. In 1854 women received the same inheritance rights as men, and in 1863 the government declared that unmarried women over age twenty-five were legally competent. Educational opportunities expanded in 1882 when women gained the right to take the exams necessary for admittance to the university, although they had to wait until 1884 for the right to earn a university degree. The Women's Rights League was founded in the same year, following the controversy that would result from the performance of *A Doll's House* in 1879. A decade after the play, in 1889, Norway modified the marriage vows, in which a wife professed subservience to her husband, that had been in place since 1688. Finally, more than twenty years after Ibsen's play appeared, women won limited rights to vote in municipal elections (1901); it would take another dozen years for them to win universal suffrage.

Divorce. The Reformation, or separation of the Protestant and Catholic churches begun by Martin Luther in 1517, spread to Norway later in the century. As Protestantism grew in popularity, it spurred the legalization of divorce, which had been more tightly controlled under the Catholic Church. Bigamy, adultery, desertion, and impotence became accepted as valid reasons for a couple to separate. This state of affairs changed in 1909, when the country adopted a new divorce law. More relaxed than the earlier law, it permitted divorce in the case of mutual consent and after a period of separation of at least one year. But while divorce became easier to obtain, it was still frowned upon. The proceedings cost little enough; a poor Norwegian could obtain a divorce almost free of charge. But they were publicized as little as possible; newspapers were forbidden to report divorce cases.

In Ibsen's play the Helmers, who are the drama's central characters, live under the older divorce law. Even if the action had been set after 1909, however, no mutual consent to the dissolution of the marriage existed, since Nora moves out of the house against her husband's wishes.

The Play in Focus

The plot. On Christmas Eve, Nora Helmer returns home with gifts and a Christmas tree she has bought. Her husband Torvald chides her for having once again spent too much. They recall times such as the Christmas before, when money was tighter. Both of them look forward to the

Henrik Ibsen

prestige and secure income Torvald can expect when he becomes bank manager on January 1st. Before Torvald returns to his study, Nora eats macaroons behind his back and lies to him several times about having done so. Her lies suggest an element of dishonesty in their relationship.

Mrs. Kristine Linde, a widow, visits Nora, and Dr. Rank joins Torvald in the study. The two women, once schoolmates, catch up on each other's lives, families, financial hardships, and the jobs they have held. Nora reveals during their conversation that she had secretly "raised" 4,800 crowns without her husband's knowledge or consent; she hopes that this information will make Kristine regard her as a mature adult. Nora explains that the money was spent on a trip she and Torvald took to Italy that supposedly saved her husband's life. Torvald agreed to the trip, mistakenly believing that the money had come from Nora's father. Nora leaves Kristine guessing about how she acquired such a substantial sum on her own.

They are interrupted by the arrival of the bank clerk Nils Krogstad, whom Kristine knew many years earlier. As Krogstad enters the study, Dr. Rank joins the two women. Krogstad eventually leaves quietly and Torvald emerges from the

A Doll's House

The tarantella scene from the world première of *A Doll's House*, at the Royal Theatre in Copenhagen, 1879.

study. He assures Kristine that a position may be opening up for her at the bank.

After Torvald escorts the two guests outside, the children enter. Nora gleefully helps them out of their winter clothes and plays hide-and-seek with them. Their fun ends abruptly when she discovers that Krogstad has reappeared and is watching them. Nora dismisses the children.

Visibly uncomfortable, she speaks rudely; Krogstad has come to see her about business. We learn that Nora borrowed the 4,800 crowns from him, and she reveals that she forged her father's signature to cosign for the loan. Krogstad's own reputation had been ruined by a forgery scandal many years earlier. He is determined to keep his job at the bank, which has begun to reestablish him as a respectable member of society; it is this bank job, however, that Torvald is planning to give Kristine once he becomes bank manager. Krogstad threatens Nora, contending that if she does not intercede on his behalf, he will expose her forgery and ruin her life.

Nora does not grasp fully the legal details, and although she is worried, she refuses to believe her life-saving act has placed the family in danger. Still, she pleads with her husband to retain Krogstad in his position at the bank. Her request only angers Torvald, and he forces her to promise never to raise the subject again.

The next day, on Christmas, the Helmer household prepares for a costume ball to be given by their upstairs neighbors the following evening. Kristine stops by to help repair Nora's costume, and before she leaves, Nora reveals to her the truth about the forgery and the source of the loan. Nora again begs Torvald to let Krogstad keep his job. In a fit of pique, her husband fires Krogstad in a letter sent directly to him by special messenger. In a scene with her long-time friend Dr. Rank, Nora almost asks him for assistance.

Krogstad returns, having received the letter, and implores Nora to do something on his behalf, but she refuses. To Nora's horror, he drops a letter into the Helmer mailbox on his way out that tells Torvald everything. Even her suicide, he explains, would leave him in final control of her reputation. To distract Torvald from the mailbox and bank-related business, Nora insists he help her practice an Italian dance, the tarantella, for the party.

The evening of the ball, Kristine meets Krogstad in private and expresses a desire to join her life to his. After testing her motives, Krogstad is beside himself with joy at this sudden, life-affirming turn of events. He offers to take back the letter to Torvald, but Kristine convinces him it would be best if the Helmers faced Nora's forgery together.

Nora and Torvald return home. Retiring to his study, Torvald reads Krogstad's letter. Nora fantasizes about drowning herself in an icy river, but Torvald stops her by bursting out of the study and demanding that she explain the forgery. His self-absorption, rough behavior, and lack of appreciation for her sacrifice disappoint her profoundly. Once he realizes that Krogstad will not expose Nora's crime, he acts condescending and forgiving, a stance which Nora finds unbearable. She withdraws to change out of her costume.

When Nora reappears, she sits her husband down for the first serious talk in their eight years of marriage. From Torvald's perspective, her manner has changed abruptly. She informs Torvald that she must leave him and the children. For the first time in her life, she explains, she shall be free from the father and husband who has regarded her as merely a doll, not a person. Only by taking such a step does she feel she can become a complete adult, one capable of raising children and participating in a true marriage.

Sources. Nora's crime resembles closely the forgery efforts of a Norwegian woman named Laura Kieler. Already a married man, Ibsen met Kieler in 1871 and called her his "skylark," a pet name that Torvald uses to refer to his wife in the play. Ibsen and Kieler were acquainted for years before she became involved in events that resembled those depicted in *A Doll's House*.

Laura Kieler had been advised that time spent in a warmer climate would save her husband's life. They could not afford a trip south, but Kieler hesitated to broach the subject, since her husband became hysterical at the mention of money. Secretly, with the help of a friend, she secured a loan to finance a trip to Italy. When the loan fell due two years later, however, neither she nor the friend could pay it. Ibsen, unaware at the time of the full circumstances, declined to help her publish an inferior manuscript, which she had hoped would raise money to pay the loan. The day she received his refusal, Kieler forged a check. The crime was soon discovered. She told her husband everything, but he spurned her as a criminal and an unfit mother. Their marriage (and her health) subsequently foundered. He did what he could to take the children away from her, and she suffered a nervous breakdown. Her husband had Kieler committed to a public asylum, but she was released a month later. She pleaded with him to take her back for the sake of the children, and he accepted her proposal unwillingly.

Kieler's misfortune seems to have been a source for Ibsen in other works as well. Selma Brattsberg, a minor character Ibsen had created ten years earlier in the play *The League of Youth,* complains to her husband, "You dressed me up like a doll; you played with me as one plays with a child" (Meyer, p. 298). The critic George Brandes read the play and suggested that Selma was the best thing in it, a character worth developing as the central figure of a later work.

Publication, production, and reaction. While working on *A Doll's House,* Ibsen told his wife, "Now I've seen Nora. She came right up to me and put her hand on my shoulder" (Ibsen in Meyer, p. 447). After concentrating deeply on the likely emotions and feelings of his characters, Ibsen wrote the play quickly.

IBSEN GIVES ADVICE, AND RECONSIDERS

On March 26, 1878, Ibsen sent Laura Kieler a letter in which he indicated his refusal to aid her in her efforts to publish her manuscript. Ibsen had sensed that Kieler was concealing something, and he suggested to her in the letter that, "it is unthinkable that your husband knows everything; so you must tell him; he must take on his shoulders the sorrows and problems which now torment you" (Meyer, p. 444). Later that year, however, his preliminary notes for *A Doll's House* reflect a more pragmatic point of view: "There are two kinds of moral laws, two kinds of conscience, one for men and one, quite different, for women. They don't understand each other; but in practical life, woman is judged by masculine law, as though she weren't a woman but a man.—*Rome, 19 October 1878*" (Ibsen in Salomé, p. 23).

The publication and premiere of *A Doll's House* coincided with the Christmas season, when the play takes place. The first edition of 8,000 copies sold out within a month, and subsequent editions of 3,000 and 2,500 copies sold out as well. No Scandinavian play had ever sold so well, and the impact of *A Doll's House* was immediate and sensational. Ibsen had openly challenged the standard notion of the marriage contract, and as the door slammed shut behind Nora at the end of the play, the controversy began. Debate raged in churches, homes, and newspapers. Nora was discussed as if she were a real woman rather than a character; people even argued over whether society's laws would have convicted her of the forgery. In fact, Nora's declaration of independence in the play prompted such heated discussions among the public that the topic finally had to be declared off-limits at social gatherings.

Despite the warm welcome at home, the first translations and foreign productions of the play were inferior and slow to appear. Ten years passed before a version similar to Ibsen's original play was performed in England or America. In Germany, the lead actress demanded a rewrite on the grounds that *she* would never leave *her* children. Ibsen grudgingly volunteered to adapt the play himself but still refused to have the Helmers reconcile at the end. Instead of leaving, Nora was forced by Torvald to the door of the children's room, where she sank down to her knees as the curtain fell. The "happy ending" failed, however, and the lead actress eventually agreed to perform the play as written.

> **THE PREMIERE IN COPENHAGEN**
>
> It is long since any new play was awaited with such excitement, and even longer since a new play brought so much that is original to the stage, but it is beyond memory since a play so simple in its action and so everyday in its dress made such an impression of artistic mastery.... Not a single declamatory phrase, no high dramatics, no drop of blood, not even a tear ... the mere fact that the author succeeded with the help of only these five characters to keep our interest ... is sufficient proof of Ibsen's technical mastery.
> (Erik Bøghin, in a review of the December 21, 1879, première at the Royal Theatre in Copenhagen, quoted in Meyer, pp. 455-56)

True marriage. "There are some people one loves most and other people that one would almost prefer being with," Nora tells her close friend Dr. Rank (*A Doll's House,* p. 84). Though she and Torvald seem happy together at the beginning of the play, Nora discovers suddenly that they do not have a true marriage. For years, she has been pinning her hopes on a miracle, a grand display of Torvald's love for her in the face of adversity. The conventional religious interpretation of marriage viewed the husband as a shepherd and Christ figure. His wife was regarded as a sheep for whom he should be ready to lay down his life. Torvald, however, is not prepared to make any grand sacrifices. In the moment of crisis, when it is revealed that she committed the crime of forgery, Nora learns that he is primarily concerned with keeping up appearances. She is forced—and she forces him—to reevaluate the nature of their relationship.

According to Nora, the two of them have never had a serious discussion. In fact, Torvald does not treat her as though she is capable of serious conversation. In response to the words she exchanges with Dr. Rank, for instance, Torvald exclaims, "Come now—little Nora talking about scientific research!" (*A Doll's House,* p. 102). Their marriage is based on a mutual acceptance of the idea that Torvald, the man, takes care of Nora, the little girl. Even if Nora believes otherwise, she prefers to maintain an imbalance in their regard for each other as adults. For example, Nora explains why she cannot confide her secret to her husband: "Torvald—with all his masculine pride—how painfully humiliating for him if he ever found out he was in debt to me. That would just ruin our relationship" (*A Doll's House,* p. 54).

On the surface, the Helmers had what would have likely been considered by many people to be a perfect marriage. To outsiders, a portrait emerges of a kind but firmly dominant husband who closely monitors his comfortable home, charming wife, robust children, and secure income. Yet it turns out to be disastrous that Nora has been sheltered so completely by her husband, as she had been by her father.

Kristine and Krogstad offer a slightly different example. Regarding each other as mature adults, they join their lives together for mutual comfort and the good of Krogstad's children. Their future *begins* with a sober discussion. Nevertheless, Kristine enters the union with the same old-world view that Nora rejects.

When we last see the Helmer marriage, Nora's regard for her husband has suffered a major blow, and she realizes that she has never really taken herself seriously. She had once been content to let her father and her husband regard her as a child, as someone too featherbrained to secure a real education. No longer content with such a view, she realizes that she must leave Torvald, at least for a while if not permanently, in order to pursue self-growth. She rejects Torvald's offers to write to her and to give her financial assistance if she needs it. She returns her wedding ring to him and declares that for them to be one day reunited as husband and wife, they must both become so changed that their life together would be a *real* wedlock.

For More Information

Allphin, Clela. *Women in the Plays of Henrik Ibsen.* New York: Revisionist, 1975.

Collett, Camilla. *The District Governor's Daughters.* Translated by Kristen Seaver. Chester Springs, Pa.: Dufour, 1992.

Derry, T. K. *A History of Modern Norway, 1814-1972.* Oxford: Clarendon Press, 1973.

Ibsen, Henrik. *Four Major Plays.* Vol. 1: *A Doll's House.* Translated by Rolf Fjelde. New York: Penguin, 1965.

Meyer, Michael. *Ibsen: A Biography.* Garden City, N.Y.: Doubleday, 1971.

Salomé, Lou. *Ibsen's Heroines.* Edited and translated by Siegfried Mandel. Redding Ridge, Conn.: Black Swan, 1985.

Törnqvist, Egil. *Ibsen: A Doll's House.* New York: Cambridge University Press, 1995.

The Elephant Man

by
Bernard Pomerance

Born in Brooklyn, New York, in 1940, Bernard Pomerance settled in England in the early 1970s with the ambition of becoming a novelist. He soon turned to drama, however, and became involved with various left-wing theater groups, writing and producing plays in London. The first play of his to gain wide recognition was *The Elephant Man*, which is set in the Victorian era and based on a true story. The play portrays the life of Joseph Carey Merrick, an extremely deformed man who was born in 1862. Highlighted in the play are the repressive social attitudes of Victorian society as well as the era's scientific ideas concerning evolution and survival of the fittest.

> **THE LITERARY WORK**
>
> A play based on actual events in London, England, and Brussels, Belgium, spanning the years 1884-1890; published in 1979.
>
> **SYNOPSIS**
>
> A severely deformed man named Joseph Carey ("John") Merrick is rescued from being an exhibit in freak shows by a doctor who introduces him to London society and tries to make him "normal."

Events in History at the Time the Play Takes Place

The Industrial Revolution. From roughly 1780 to 1850, England experienced phenomenal growth in industry. This growth was due to several factors, including a stable British political system, a large population available for work, and ample natural resources. This period, which became known as the Industrial Revolution, was characterized by mechanization and a factory system that led to an increase in per capita production in England. As its industries grew stronger, the country moved from its centuries-old existence as an agrarian nation into an industrial, urbanized society. While other European nations eventually had their own revolutions in industry, England was the first to become fully industrialized. It therefore held an advantage over Europe and the rest of the world. With industrialization came the growth of the middle class in England. Yet the class system that had long divided English society remained firmly in place during the Industrial Revolution, and the nation's population remained segregated.

Colonialism. Due to technological advances of the era, it became easier for the British to successfully dominate larger areas of land. During Joseph Merrick's lifetime alone, England colonized India, South Africa, Zimbabwe, and Zanzibar. The Victorians believed that their political and religious efforts in these colonies brought civilization to the "savages" in these areas, and thus served as a charitable service to mankind.

For the most part, Victorians sought to reshape other peoples in their own image. Victorian missionaries in colonial areas tried to con-

Joseph Carey Merrick

The Elephant Man

The triumph of science. Although high value had been placed on science since the Enlightenment, the period between 1840 and 1890 witnessed a new scientific fervor. Rational thought pervaded all aspects of society, including literature, which shifted its focus from Romanticism to realism. Whereas Romantic novels had dealt with the emotional, mystical, and individual elements of life, realistic ones focused on the accurate portrayal of human existence and events.

Science produced visible material benefits, and as people saw these benefits, they became more accepting of science than they had been earlier in the century. The machines of the Industrial Revolution brought prosperity to a sizeable percentage of the population in England, while advances in medicine helped the British live longer, healthier lives. Along with the triumph of science came a rejection of religious explanations for natural phenomena. While Christianity still played a powerful role in society, the more learned and urbanized Victorians began to see science as the new religion.

The 1800s also saw the sciences become professionalized and specialized. Doctors and other professionals formed organizations and began to lay down guidelines for their practices. Whereas in earlier times scientists had often studied several disciplines at once, in the nineteenth century scientists concentrated more intently on single fields of study, thereby bringing specialization to the scientific world.

The growth in scientific knowledge during this era had a significant impact on many fields of study. Hospitals, for instance, began to take their present-day form at the end of the nineteenth century because of advancements in technology and hygiene. These factors, combined with an overall increase in medical expertise, made successful surgeries more common beginning in the 1880s. While earlier doctors often employed useless treatments such as bloodletting, purgatives, and laxatives, the new medical establishment favored methods based on an empirical approach to science. Both before and after such improvements were introduced, however, the hospital clientele of the Victorian era consisted primarily of the poor, for the wealthy often chose to be treated at home.

Victorian view of the disabled. Until the 1600s, the mentally and physically disabled were viewed in a religious context as being either blessed or damned. They were generally allowed to coexist in a society whose larger population had more respect for them than fear of them. The Enlightenment, a

vert the natives not only to Christianity but to British ways and customs. Meanwhile, the colonized areas added to England's wealth and power, emerging as economic markets for English products and suppliers of raw materials. Through rapid industrialization and rampant colonization, England took its place as the most powerful nation in the world.

Darwinism. In 1859 Charles Darwin's *On the Origin of Species by Means of Natural Selection* was published in England. His work, which concerned plant and animal species, held that life had evolved through natural selection, or "survival of the fittest." Although the text was denounced by the religious community, a large majority of the growing scientific community hailed Darwin as one of its greatest members.

Drawing upon Darwin's idea, colonialists developed an outlook known as "social Darwinism" to justify their domination over native populations of conquered lands. They believed in the superiority of the Anglo-Saxon or white race, which in their minds had reached the highest stage of evolution. Thinking of themselves as the "fittest," they reasoned that it was only natural for them to control the destinies of "less evolved" societies such as those in Africa and India.

The Elephant Man

movement of the 1600s and 1700s that placed high value on the human ability to reason, led increasingly to the separation of the deformed, disabled, and mentally ill from the rest of society. The "Great Confinement" of the 1600s led to the placement of the disabled in workhouses or prison-like asylums. In the Victorian era (1837-1901), in particular, the deformed and deranged were kept out of sight because it was feared that they might upset upper-class Victorian women, who were believed to be sheltered and easily shocked.

> ### DOCTOR TREVES DESCRIBES THE ELEPHANT MAN
>
> The right arm was of enormous size and shapeless. It suggested but was not elephantiasis [a disease in which the affected skin resembles a elephant's hide].... The right hand was large and clumsy—a fin or paddle rather than a hand.... There arose from the fungous skin growths a very sickening stench which was hard to tolerate. To add a further burden to his trouble, the wretched man when a boy developed hip disease which left him permanently lame, so that he could only walk with a stick.
>
> (The Elephant Man, p. 5)

Circuses and freak shows. The increase in wealth that resulted from the Industrial Revolution gave many Londoners a greater amount of discretionary income and leisure time than they had previously enjoyed. For Victorians of the lower classes, the freak show was a favorite pastime. Traveling circus sideshows provided entertainment as well, especially for Londoners. Freak shows and circus sideshows became prominent throughout England, their popularity coinciding with the career of perhaps the greatest known showman: the American P. T. Barnum. In 1889-90 Barnum took his traveling circus, "The Greatest Show on Earth," to London. Just a few years earlier, Joseph Merrick, known as the "Elephant Man," had been put on display in a freak show there. By the time Barnum's circus arrived, Merrick had left the freak show and settled in London.

The Play in Focus

The plot. The play opens with Dr. Frederick Treves's arrival at his new post at the London Hospital and his subsequent discovery of the Elephant Man at a storefront across the road. After paying his two pence to view the "freak of nature" (Pomerance, *The Elephant Man*, p. 3), Treves convinces the showman, known only as Ross, to allow him to examine the creature, an Englishman named John Merrick, at the London Hospital. The Elephant Man, once again on display, is presented to the medical community by Treves, who lectures on his deformities.

After the Elephant Man is returned to Ross, the police deem the showman's exhibition to be a moral disgrace and order him to leave England. The two subsequently venture to the city of Brussels in Belgium. During the Victorian era, Brussels was seen as a place where even the most morally reprehensible activities were accepted. Unfortunately for Ross, his show is viewed as too indecent even for Belgium. Ross takes all of Merrick's money and sends him back to London, alone.

When Merrick arrives in London, the police find Dr. Treves's business card in his coat. Merrick is sent to the London Hospital, where Treves graciously receives him and provides him with an attic room. Treves decides that Merrick must be accepted by society if he is ever to view himself as normal. He believes it is especially important for Merrick to be treated with dignity by women, for they are the members of society who previously showed the greatest fear and loathing in his presence. The doctor invites many of society's elite to see Merrick, including the actress Madge Kendal, Bishop How, the Princess of Wales, and several members of the aristocracy. Each of the visitors claims to see aspects of himself in the Elephant Man.

Merrick and Kendal soon become very close, for they both perform similar functions in society, acting as players on exhibit for others. In Ms. Kendal's case, this is doubly true due to her status as both an actress and a woman.

> Treves: I must warn you, women are not quite real to him—more creatures of his imagination.
> Mrs. Kendal: Then he is already like other men, Mr. Treves.
>
> (*The Elephant Man*, p. 32)

When Merrick discloses that he does not truly consider himself to be a man because he has never seen a nude female, Ms. Kendal disrobes for him in an act of kindness. Dr. Treves enters, misinterprets the act, and condemns them both. Merrick openly questions Treves's beliefs along with the seemingly hypocritical standards of the rest of Victorian society. When Treves retires for the evening, he dreams that he and Merrick have traded places and that he is the one on display. Treves is forced to reexamine his profession along with his beliefs about colonialism, Darwinism, proper behavior, and so forth.

Throughout the play, Merrick is seen constructing a model of a church. The church is symbolic of the fact that science is ultimately unable to save Merrick and make him "normal." Merrick must turn to religion for consolation. In his building of the church, which represents the body of Christ, Merrick seems to be thinking of it as a new body for himself. He completes the model with the words, "It is done" (*The Elephant Man*, p. 66). With this final statement the play refers also to the end of his life and the completion of a transformation within both himself and Dr. Treves. As he falls asleep for the night, he dreams of the Pinheads, two women exhibited alongside him in a freak show in Belgium. Due to Merrick's deformities (his head is too heavy to allow him to breathe while lying down), he sleeps sitting up. In his dream, though, the Pinheads pull him into a normal sleeping position, which cuts off his air flow. Merrick dies, then, still the passive partaker in others' attempts to make him "normal."

Science vs. religion. In the process of criticizing Victorian norms, the play offers some insight into one of the most vigorously debated subjects of the day—the struggle for dominance between religion and science. The two characters who are most furiously embroiled in the debate are the hospital's director, Carr Gomm, and Bishop How. When Carr Gomm makes an offhanded comment to Treves, remarking that "God knows what you will do," the bishop retorts, "God does know, sir, and Darwin does not." Carr Gomm replies, "He'd better, sir, he deformed him" (*The Elephant Man*, p. 20). The exchange between the two men demonstrates the division between the two sides of the debate. Bishop How wants to reiterate God's control over the rules of nature, thereby refuting natural selection. Carr Gomm, although certainly a firm believer in Darwinism due to the nature of his profession, allows the bishop his beliefs. As natural selection would never favor a being such as Merrick, Carr Gomm gives God credit for Merrick's existence.

In a later conversation between the two men, Bishop How argues that Christian duty motivates even men of science:

> Is it science, sir, that motivates us when ... good British churchmen leave hearth and home for missionary hardship in Africa...? Sir, it is not, It is Christian duty. It is the obligation to bring our light and benefices to benighted man. That motivates us, even as it motivates Treves towards Merrick, sir, to bring salvation where none is.
> (*The Elephant Man*, p. 21)

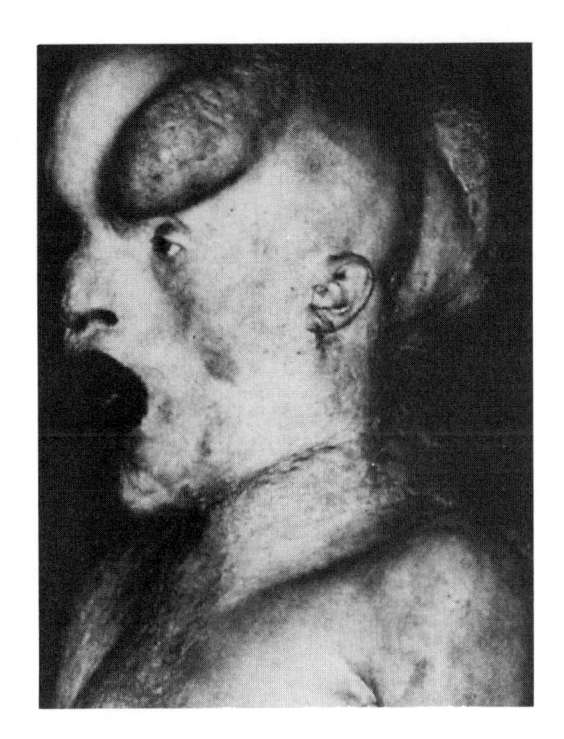

Joseph Carey Merrick

The interaction between Dr. Treves and Merrick shows the transformation of a man who begins the play as a staunch supporter of science. As the play opens, Carr Gomm is explaining to Treves that his ample pay at the hospital will offer some "consolation." This puzzles Treves, who does not feel "a scientist in the Age of Science" should need any consolation (*The Elephant Man*, p. 2). As the play progresses, however, Treves becomes increasingly aware of the limitations of science and even begins to question how beneficial the medical profession is.

Treves first questions his faith in science when he is asked by Merrick if he believes in heaven. While Merrick is soothed by the idea of a place where "the crooked shall be made straight," Treves states that he would settle for "a good general anesthetic" instead of heaven, an indication that he is still concerned with the pursuits of science over those of religion (*The Elephant Man*, p. 54). For Treves, science is on a higher plane than the rest of society. Although he deems it improper for Merrick to see Ms. Kendal nude, Treves does not find it unacceptable to view a female patient in a similar manner. Treves initially believes that the strict morals of society can be transcended only through science, despite Merrick's repeated assertions that Treves's arguments are hypocritical.

By the end of the play, Treves comes to the realization that science does not offer him the

The Elephant Man

consolation that he needs. He sees that science has failed Merrick and he begins to question the very integrity of the medical profession. In the end, Treves finally must turn to the bishop and ask for help, thereby conceding that he needs consolation from a source other than science.

Through the characters' interaction, the play shows that although some people viewed science as the new religion, science could not ultimately console those in need. In calling attention to the demand for an alternative to scientific and rational thought in the Victorian age, the play questions not only the priorities of a bygone era but also the dependence on science in the writer's own time.

Sources. Although every character in the play has a real life counterpart, a degree of artistic liberty was taken by the playwright with their character traits in order to convey certain ideas, and some acquaintances in the life of the Elephant Man were combined into one character for the play. In addition, Pomerance utilized sources such as the memoirs of Frederick Treves when he shaped the play.

In real life the Elephant Man, whom Pomerance calls John Merrick, was actually named Joseph Merrick. Pomerance merely follows the trend, begun by Frederick Treves in his memoirs, of referring to the Elephant Man by a name other than that which appears on his birth certificate. Although the reasons for Treves's error are unclear, the name John was passed down through history without anyone questioning its accuracy until Michael Howell and Peter Ford published *The True History of the Elephant Man*, which appeared in 1980.

Joseph Merrick was born in Leicester, England, in 1862. Although he appeared to be quite normal at birth, his disorder began to make itself manifest by the time he was five. Although Merrick claimed that his deformities were the result of his mother being trampled by an elephant while she was pregnant, his disorder is now thought to have been either a case of neurofibromatosis or Proteus syndrome.

Neurofibromatosis is a relatively common genetic disorder that affects the development of nerve cells and causes massive tumors. The disorder can affect the bones of the afflicted person and result in abnormal skeletal growth. Proteus syndrome is a very rare disease which, among other things, causes gigantism of limbs and hypertrophy (enlargement) of bones. It now seems more likely that Merrick suffered from Proteus syndrome, since neurofibromatosis rarely causes such severe deformities.

Merrick's parents did their best to care for him, but Merrick's mother died when he was only eleven years old, so his father sent the boy to live with relatives. As his illness became increasingly burdensome, Merrick entered himself into a workhouse. He stayed there until he teamed up with various showmen in an effort to earn a living from his misfortune. By this time his deformities were acute. Merrick had an exceedingly large head, covered with tumorous growths that distorted his features almost beyond recognition. His skin looked like cauliflower, and it hung from his body in sacks. Only his left arm was normal; the rest of his limbs were large and unwieldy.

It was at a storefront on Whitechapel Road that the young surgeon Frederick Treves first saw the Elephant Man on display. In his memoirs, Treves referred to Merrick as the "most disgusting specimen of humanity" (Treves in Howell and Ford, p. 171) that he had ever seen. Nonetheless, Treves looked upon Merrick as a curious medical oddity and eventually had him moved to the London Hospital in order to further study his disease. At the London Hospital, Merrick finally had a home.

As Pomerance indicates in his play, Treves thought it very important for Merrick to have visitors who accepted him, and he made a special effort to secure women visitors, since they had previously been the ones who were most afraid of Merrick. During his stay at the hospital, Merrick was visited by numerous members of high society; Alexandra, the princess of Wales, was perhaps his most prestigious guest.

While the actress Dame Kendal has a large role in the play, her actual role in Merrick's life was far less involved. Although Ms. Kendal did send photographs of herself to Merrick and arrange for him to visit the theater, she never actually met Merrick in person. In her memoirs she seems, like Frederick Treves, unable to remember Merrick's first name; initially she calls him John, only to later refer to him as James.

Merrick was found dead in his bed in April 1890. Treves surmised that Merrick had died while attempting to lie down "like other people" (Howell, p. 186). The weight of his head had apparently caused asphyxiation. Although Merrick's life ended at the close of the 1800s, his story did not. Treves recounted the tale of the Elephant Man in his reminiscences of 1923. Almost fifty years later the story was called to the attention of the world once again when the socio-anthropologist Ashley Montagu published the nonfiction book *The Elephant Man: A*

Study in Human Dignity in 1971. Montagu's work focused on Merrick's human development in the face of indignity and suffering and sparked renewed interest in the man's life. Montagu's book inspired not only Pomerance's play but also a film version of Merrick's story directed by David Lynch and a book of poetry by Kenneth Sherman.

Events in History at the Time the Play Was Written

The Postmodern era. Although Bernard Pomerance is an American playwright, he has spent much of his life living abroad in London. Historical events in both England and America, therefore, are relevant to the views expressed by Pomerance in his play, which was first performed in London in 1979.

The Western world of the 1970s was dominated by an almost complete reversal of the ideals of Victorian England. While Victorians saw their time as one of prosperity, the 1970s witnessed a great monetary recession that saw the spread of inflated prices, debt, and unemployment. Events such as the war in Vietnam greatly decreased people's acceptance of authority. The Victorians had put great faith in their leaders, but the 1970s saw a population that openly criticized and questioned authority.

Theater. In the 1970s, instead of viewing theatrical plays solely as entertainment, many playwrights sought to imbue their works with a social message above all else. If a play was not thought-provoking for the audience, they believed, then it had not served its purpose. These writers felt that they needed to draw attention to the fact that a "performance" was taking place in their plays. In this way, the audience would view the play and its actors with a critical eye. Theater began to shift toward an idea developed by the German playwright Bertolt Brecht, which held that actors and the audience should be constantly aware of their status. Playwrights created dramas that, in effect, made the audience part of the play.

Pomerance's use of such techniques is evident in his stage directions for *The Elephant Man,* which state that the actor portraying Merrick is to wear no grotesque makeup. This forces the audience to become part of the play; they must use their imagination without the aid of costumes or makeup that would make it easier for them to immediately empathize with Merrick. Instead, the audience is forced to see the character of the man instead of his deformities.

View of the disabled. In the 1970s a remarkable shift took place in the way the public viewed the disabled. Due to increased education on the subject, people grew less fearful of those who differed from themselves. As a result, the general public became more accepting and inclusive of people outside the mainstream of society.

One example of the kinds of programs developed in the early part of the decade because of this shift of viewpoint was the Independent Living Movement, founded in Berkeley, California. This movement encouraged and provided assistance to those with disabilities who wanted to live and work independently. The disabled no longer had to be completely dependent on others. As a result, they no longer considered themselves to be burdensome, as Merrick had.

The 1970s also saw the passage of numerous laws aimed at facilitating the lives of the disabled. Affirmative action laws, for example, increased employment opportunities for the disabled. In addition, officials passed building access laws that called for ramps in addition to stairs. The institution of these and other improvements made life easier to manage for various disabled people.

Reviews. Bernard Pomerance's *The Elephant Man* was generally lauded by the critics, with one reviewer praising it as "one of the most moving [and] original plays in a decade" (Graham, p. 87). In its first year of performance, the play won three Tony Awards, three Obies, the Drama Desk Award and the New York Drama Critics Circle Award.

The play was not without its critics, however. Martha Bayles of *Harper's* magazine was of the opinion that Pomerance's decision to have the Elephant Man portrayed by an actor without makeup was "avant garde old hat" (Graham, p. 87). Instead of making the audience think about Merrick's position, it made it possible for them to avoid being gawkers, thereby allowing them to view the situation with a certain moral superiority. If they had been forced to view Merrick's deformities, the critic reasoned, they would realize that they were no better than the Victorians whom the play condemns.

Others criticized Pomerance's attempt to use the play as a critique of modern-day society. Randall Craig wrote, "Pomerance locks us up in a Victorian social framework ... while at the same time asking us to accept this as a microcosm of contemporary society.... Let the play be set now instead of coyly sniping at our dubious motives from behind a Victorian barricade" (Craig in Bryfonski, pp. 444-45). Despite such criticisms, a large number of critics found *The Elephant Man* to be an engrossing and thought-provoking work by an extremely gifted playwright.

For More Information

Bryfonski, Dedria, ed. *Contemporary Literary Criticism*. Vol. 13. Detroit: Gale Research, 1980.

Graham, Peter W., and Fritz Oehlschlaeger. *Articulating the Elephant Man: Joseph Merrick and His Interpreters*. Baltimore: Johns Hopkins University Press, 1992.

Howell, Michael, and Peter Ford. *The True History of the Elephant Man*. London: Allison & Busby, 1980.

Kendal, Madge. *Dame Madge Kendal*. London: John Murray, 1933.

Montagu, Ashley. *The Elephant Man: A Study in Human Dignity*. New York: E. P. Dutton, 1971.

Pomerance, Bernard. *The Elephant Man*. New York: Grove Weidenfeld, 1979.

Trombley, Stephen. *Sir Frederick Treves: the Extraordinary Edwardian*. London: Routledge, 1989.

Ethan Frome

by
Edith Wharton

> **THE LITERARY WORK**
>
> A novel set in the fictional community of Starkfield, Massachusetts, from the 1870s to the early 1900s; published in 1911.
>
> **SYNOPSIS**
>
> A farmer's love for his wife's cousin has tragic consequences.

Born in 1862, Edith Wharton grew up in a wealthy New York City family. She married in 1885. By the time she wrote *Ethan Frome*, this marriage, like that of her title character, had begun to deteriorate. In her novel, the unhappy Fromes remain married. Wharton herself, however, became one of the rapidly growing number of Americans who chose to divorce their spouses. While the events in the novel bear some resemblance to its author's personal experiences, *Ethan Frome* also reflects aspects of life near the turn of the century in rural New England, where the population lived very isolated lives.

Events in History at the Time of the Novel

Rural New England. New England changed a great deal during the nineteenth century. In many of its rural communities, both population growth and economic growth slowed, leveled off, and finally declined. Increasing numbers of people moved away from the region's farms in search of greater financial opportunities elsewhere. Others felt drawn to cities by the thought of living in a more diverse, stimulating atmosphere.

There were only limited economic opportunities for farmers in nineteenth-century New England. It had always been somewhat difficult to make a good living farming the rocky soil of the region. A further obstacle was that most of the land in New England had already been settled by this time. Consequently, ambitious farmers had little opportunity to expand their farm holdings. Many chose to leave the area for cheaper, more fertile, and more plentiful farmlands in the Midwest and West. By the last quarter of the century, however, the best farmlands in the West were also taken. An increasing percentage of migrants from rural New England subsequently moved into urban areas.

American cities had expanded a great deal by this time. As the twentieth century approached, employment opportunities became more plentiful and diverse than ever before. The many factories, retail stores, and other types of businesses located in cities needed workers to fill a multitude of positions. In addition, the city offered a much wider array of social and cultural activities than the rural community did. Restaurants, theaters, and museums provided varied sources of stimulation, and a city dweller lived among different types of people. Farm areas had a more homogeneous population than this and far fewer recreational diversions.

Another reason people left for urban areas was the increasing mechanization of the farm. In the

Ethan Frome

Edith Wharton at her desk, 1905.

past, running a farm required a great deal of manual labor. Those who did not own farms could find agricultural employment with others who did. By the end of the nineteenth century, however, farmers had begun to use new inventions, such as mechanical grain drills that planted, fertilized, and covered seed. While such innovations enabled farmers to work faster and more efficiently, they also eliminated jobs previously performed by humans. The number of rural jobs declined substantially.

Farmers who remained behind in rural New England thus lived in smaller, emptier communities by the end of the nineteenth century. A large number of farms stood completely abandoned. In 1891, for example, there were at least 906 abandoned farms in Massachusetts. The majority were located in the central and western counties. In the western county of Berkshire alone, the setting for *Ethan Frome,* 146 farms stood empty in 1891. As rural communities lost residents to the cities, they received few newcomers to take their places. Farming communities became even quieter than before.

Marriage and divorce. Husbands and wives had very distinct marital roles in nineteenth-century America. It was the duty of husbands like Ethan Frome to provide their families with the necessities of life, to treat their wives with courtesy, and to behave responsibly in financial affairs. A wife's responsibilities included maintaining a comfortable home, performing household chores, and bearing and caring for children. She was expected to remain chaste, modest, and frugal in household expenses, and to abstain from conduct that reflected badly on her home or her husband's good name. Divorce was viewed as acceptable only if one of the marriage partners failed to live up to his or her responsibilities.

Divorce remained rare in rural communities through the early twentieth century, in part because of economic considerations. Women in places like *Ethan Frome*'s Starkfield, Massachusetts, often had little knowledge or experience in handling affairs outside the domestic sphere. For the most part, only men learned the skills necessary to run a farm and support themselves and their families. Even if a woman wanted to earn money outside the home, rural communities offered her few opportunities to do so. Women in these areas therefore depended on men for income, food, and shelter. Men, in turn, felt obligated to supply them. This is evident in *Ethan Frome.* The title character's sense of duty to support his sickly wife ultimately overrides his deep desire to leave her behind in order to start a new life out West with the woman he loves.

Outside of rural areas, these traditional attitudes began to change by the early twentieth century. Before the Civil War, divorce in the United States had been rare. In 1860 only 7,380 divorces and annulments were recorded. By 1915, however, America had the highest divorce rate in the world; an average of one out of every seven marriages ended in divorce.

Contributing to the increased divorce rate was the growing independence of women in urban areas. Rapidly developing cities offered a range of jobs to women who wanted to work outside the home. Expanded employment opportunities allowed greater numbers of women to financially support themselves. This freed them from dependence on marriage (and husbands with whom they might be unhappy). Another reason cited for the growing divorce rate was the higher level of expectation that both men and women brought to married life. Individuals began to consider emotional satisfaction at least as important in marriage as the mutual fulfillment of duties and economic obligations.

Ethan Frome struggles with this consideration in Wharton's novel. The companionship and understanding of his love, Mattie, make him realize how unsatisfying his own marriage is. He feels torn between a desire for the emotional compatibility he has with Mattie and a traditional sense of duty toward his wife.

While attitudes toward marriage had begun to change by the turn of the twentieth century, the vast majority of married couples in America did not divorce. Furthermore, most women still chose to remain at home rather than pursue economic independence. Traditional values were still dominant in communities throughout the United States.

The Novel in Focus

The plot. *Ethan Frome* begins in the throes of a bitter New England winter. A young man, the narrator, has traveled to northwestern Massachusetts to take care of an engineering project. He ends up staying in Starkfield when his duties take longer than he expects. One day his interest is piqued by the vision of a solemn man driving a wagon and then limping through the village. He learns the man's name is Ethan Frome, but his neighbors are terse about his story. Only after the narrator has occasion to hire Frome for transportation after a snowstorm does he begin to piece together the story of Frome's tragic life.

This story starts some twenty years earlier, when Ethan is a young man. He has, at this point, been married for seven years to Zeena, a woman from a nearby community. After his mother, a sickly woman cared for by Zeena, had died, he proposed marriage to Zeena because of his loneliness.

Now Frome's marriage to Zeena has begun to deteriorate. Zeena is hypochondriacal and does not speak much to Ethan except to complain. Although Ethan does the best he can for her, it is hard for him to eke out a living on their poor farm. One day Zeena informs Ethan that her cousin Mattie will be coming to stay with them to help take care of the house. Over the course of the year, Ethan and Mattie develop deeply affectionate feelings for each other. They come to cherish the time they spend together.

About a year after Mattie's arrival, Zeena informs the pair that she feels that her health is seriously declining. She takes an overnight trip to a neighboring town to see a new doctor, hopeful that he will be able to provide some treatment for her problems. Ethan and Mattie feel extremely happy to have the house to themselves for the night. Ethan imagines how wonderful it would be if he and Mattie were actually a happily married couple living there.

Soon after her return, her jealous and suspicious nature aroused, Zeena informs Ethan that she has hired a more experienced woman to help take care of her and the house. Mattie's services are therefore no longer needed. Ethan pleads with Zeena to reconsider, but she remains firm. Faced with the impending departure of the woman he loves, an anguished Ethan tries to figure out some way they can remain together. Ultimately, however, his lack of money to support Mattie and himself, along with his sense of duty toward his sick wife, prevents him from leaving Zeena. He insists, however, that he be the one to drive Mattie in the wagon to the railroad station.

NEW ENGLAND WOMEN AND RURAL ISOLATION

The neighbors are so far away. This is especially hard for the women. The men's work takes them away from home—there is feed, wood and coal to be drawn, usually milk to be carried to the creamery, pork and other products to be marketed and even when they are at work on their land, often they can call to their neighbors at work on the other side of the fence. But with women it is different. Their duties compel them to stay at home much of the time. There are the three meals a day to be prepared, dishes and milk things to be washed, and the house to be kept clean and in order, washing, ironing, and sewing.... After the necessary work of the day is done, they feel too tired to walk to a neighbor's. They wish that they might live where neighbors weren't so far away, so they could see somebody once in a while.

(*Fifteenth Vermont Agricultural Report for the Year 1895*, Burlington, Vermont, 1896)

On their drive, they reach the top of a snow-covered hill they had always planned to sled down. They stop and sled down the hill, with Ethan steering them around the huge oak tree that looms at the bottom. As they prepare to sled down once more, they are overwhelmed by the tragedy of their impending separation. They form a suicide pact, and this time coast straight into the oak tree at the bottom of the hill. Their attempt, however, is unsuccessful. Both are severely injured but survive.

The narrator brings the story back to the beginning of the novel. Again it is twenty years later. Entering the Frome household one night, the narrator encounters the three characters. Mattie has

Ethan Frome

become a complaining invalid while Ethan has remained crippled since the accident. They both rely on the recovered Zeena to take care of them.

Rural women. *Ethan Frome* concludes at a time when, despite the rising population of cities, the majority of American women (75 percent) still lived in rural communities. Whereas traditional male duties called for men to work outside and interact with other people, the domestic responsibilities of rural women kept them at home almost all the time. These women often spent entire days doing housework with little human contact. This isolation was intensified in rural communities, where houses were spread far apart. Contact with neighbors was typically infrequent. In fact, if a house sat at the end of a street, almost no one ever passed by it.

NEW TECHNOLOGY AND RURAL ISOLATION

Two late nineteenth-century inventions would help reduce the isolation of rural communities: the telephone and the automobile. The telephone was invented in 1876. For many years it was only an expensive luxury of the upper classes. By 1902, however, 267,000 phones were owned in rural areas across America. Five years later, in 1907, 1,465,000 farms were equipped with phones.

Meanwhile, the first car sale in America took place in 1896. Like the phone, the automobile began as a luxury of the rich. In 1908, however, Henry Ford introduced the Model T, a lower-cost vehicle designed to appeal to a wider market. Ford sold 5,986 Model T automobiles in 1908. By 1912 total sales for the year had skyrocketed to 78,611, and sales continued to climb thereafter.

Both the telephone and automobile would greatly reduce feelings of isolation once they came to rural areas; people would be able to converse with neighbors much more easily and to travel to nearby towns. However, it took a long time for these inventions to reach even middle-class homes in isolated areas such as the one in *Ethan Frome*. In fact, phones and automobiles would not come to many farm families until the mid-1910s, after the time of the novel.

In the early years in which *Ethan Frome* is set, farming families lived without the luxuries that many Americans now take for granted. Farmers did not yet own cars in which to travel away from the house, and there were no radios to bring in news or music from the outside world. Telephones were uncommon as well.

Living in such circumstances was emotionally difficult for rural women, as *Ethan Frome* reveals. Ethan remembers his mother having problems with rural isolation in the house he now inhabits. Referring to the location of his house, he says, "We're kinder side-tracked here now, but there was considerable passing before the railroad was carried through to the Flats.... I've always set down the worst of mother's trouble to that. When she got the rheumatism so bad she couldn't move around she used to sit up there and watch the road by the hour ... after the trains begun running nobody ever come by here to speak of, and mother never could get it through her head what had happened, and it preyed on her right along till she died" (Wharton, *Ethan Frome*, p. 8).

Ethan also muses about his wife's mental health. She spends every day inside the house, and he notes that she has grown increasingly quiet and developed a faraway look in her eyes. He remembers Zeena's attempts to nurse his mother before she herself had fallen ill. "Of late ... her silence had begun to trouble him. He recalled his mother's growing taciturnity, and wondered if Zeena were also turning 'queer'. Women did, he knew. Zeena ... had cited many cases of the kind while she was nursing his mother; and he himself knew of certain lonely farm-houses in the neighbourhood where stricken creatures pined.... At times, looking at Zeena's shut face, he felt the chill of such forebodings" (*Ethan Frome*, p. 30).

Sources. The characters of *Ethan Frome* live a poor, isolated rural existence. The novel's author, in contrast, was born into a wealthy family and spent much of her life in cities. Nonetheless, *Ethan Frome* does have autobiographical elements. Edith Jones married Edward (Teddy) Robbins Wharton in 1885. By the turn of the twentieth century, this marriage had begun to fall apart. Teddy was ten years older than Wharton, and they shared few common interests. Like the Fromes, the couple had no children.

In 1908 Wharton began a passionate affair with journalist Morton Fullerton. This was short-lived, however, and her dissatisfaction with Teddy remained a problem for her. The situation was exacerbated by the fact that Teddy's health, like that of Zeena Frome, had gradually been deteriorating. He was deeply depressed. In 1910 he suffered a nervous collapse and was placed in a sanitarium. Unlike Ethan Frome,

Edith Wharton

Wharton finally chose to end their marriage. She divorced Teddy in 1913.

Wharton's depiction of northwestern Massachusetts in *Ethan Frome* was based on her own observations of the region. Like many wealthy people of the time, she owned a large mansion; hers was *The Mount,* a beautiful home near the town of Lenox in Berkshire County. She spent her summers there between 1902 and 1911. In her own words, "*Ethan Frome* was written after I had spent ten years in the hill-region where the scene is laid, during which years I had come to know well the aspect, dialect, and mental and moral attitude of the hill-people" (Wharton, *A Backward Glance,* p. 296).

The author was also aware of a tragic sledding accident that took place in Lenox. On March 11, 1904, four teenage girls and one boy coasted down a snow-covered slope. They attained a speed of fifty miles per hour before hitting a gaslight pole at the bottom of the hill. The impact of the collision threw the passengers onto the ice. One teen was killed and two were badly hurt. Thus Wharton drew on a mixture of her own marital experience and observations about northwestern Massachusetts to create *Ethan Frome.*

Reviews. *Ethan Frome* was first published serially from August to October of 1911 in *Scribner's Magazine.* It also appeared in book form in 1911, published simultaneously in New York and London. The novel was then translated and retitled *Sous la Neige* for the February 1912 issue of the French periodical *Revue des Deux Mondes.* Most critics greeted the novel with praise, and many credited Wharton with a perceptive description of rural New England. One wrote, "Surely, the melancholy spirit that haunts the remoter byways of rural New England has entered into this chronicle; over all its scenes breathe the benumbing and isolating rigors of her winters, a sense of invisible fetters, a consciousness of depleted resources, a reticence and self-contained endurance that even the houses know how to express" (*The Nation,* pp. 396-97). There were also reviews that praised *Ethan Frome* for superior artistry. "As a piece of artistic workmanship," said one critic, "it would be hard to overstate the quality of this story; it is conceived and executed with a unity of insight, structural skill, and feeling for style which lies only within the reach of an artist who . . . knows every resource of the art" (*Outlook,* p. 405).

For More Information

Banner, Lois W. *Women in Modern America: A Brief History.* San Diego: Harcourt Brace Jovanovich, 1984.

Barron, Hal S. *Those Who Stayed Behind: Rural Society in Nineteenth-Century New England.* Cambridge: Cambridge University Press, 1984.

Lewis, R. W. B. *Edith Wharton: A Biography.* New York: Harper & Row, 1975.

Nation 93, no. 2417 (October 26, 1911): 396-97.

Outlook 99 (October 21, 1911): 405.

Schlereth, Thomas J. *Victorian America: Transformations in Everyday Life, 1876-1915.* New York: HarperCollins, 1991.

Wharton, Edith. *A Backward Glance.* New York: D. Appleton-Century, 1934.

Wharton, Edith. *Ethan Frome.* New York: Dover, 1991.

Gettysburg Address

by
Abraham Lincoln

In July 1863, it was not at all clear to President Abraham Lincoln or the rest of the nation whether the North or South would emerge victorious from the Civil War that threatened to destroy the country. In the midst of all the uncertainty and bloodshed, after a battle that claimed more lives than any until that time, Northerners held a solemn ceremony to consecrate a cemetery for their fallen. In a brief address at the occasion, Lincoln spoke of the larger cause to which both sides had been devoted when founding the nation. Referring to the country's **Declaration of Independence** (also covered in *Literature and Its Times*), his Gettysburg Address turned the idea of equality, rather than the separate causes for which each side fought, into the nation's primary focus.

THE LITERARY WORK
A brief speech delivered at the dedication of the cemetery at Gettysburg, Pennsylvania, on November 19, 1863.

SYNOPSIS
During the Civil War, Abraham Lincoln makes a public address in which he dedicates a cemetery for soldiers that lost their lives in a pivotal conflict of the war.

Events in History at the Time of the Speech

The war prior to Gettysburg. Pitting the Northern states of the Union against the Southern states of the Confederacy, the Civil War was a sobering experience. At an enormous cost not only in money ($20 billion) but also in lives (600,000 killed or dead from disease), the four-year conflict forced the nation to confront issues that threatened its survival.

Although scholars still debate the actual causes of the war, three main areas proved divisive—state rights, economics, and slavery. The Southern states favored state sovereignty over federal regulations, while many Northern ones did not. Tariff arguments pitted Southern plantation owners, who generally wanted low taxes on imported goods, against Northern manufacturers, who pushed for high tariffs on imports in order to protect their own products. Finally, debate escalated over the issue of slavery. Southerners argued that state sovereignty and the sanctity of private property were at stake, growing ever more vehement until they went so far as to tout slavery as a positive good. Meanwhile, Northerners used such publications as Harriet Beecher Stowe's *Uncle Tom's Cabin* (1852) (also covered in *Literature and Its Times*) as an indictment of all slaveowners. Eventually the differences between the two regions congealed into one full-scale conflict of interest. It was a conflict that proved intolerable for the South.

On February 4, 1861, seven Southern states seceded from the Union and adopted a constitution for the Confederate States of America. A

President Lincoln with Union troops at the battlefront.

few months later four more states joined them. With Jefferson Davis as their president, the Confederacy (South Carolina, Mississippi, Florida, Alabama, Georgia, Louisiana, Texas, Virginia, Arkansas, Tennessee, and North Carolina) fought to gain control of federal property in the Southern jurisdiction. They focused their efforts on the acquisition of Fort Sumter on the Charleston Harbor, South Carolina. The fort was a major international port, and the Confederates needed to gain control of it so that they could secure trade with outside nations. On April 12, 1861, after offering Union forces a chance to evacuate the fort, the Confederates fired the first shots of the Civil War.

The conflict continued for two agonizing years before the Battle of Gettysburg. In a seesaw string of battles, the Confederate forces of the South, which had fewer resources and men, nevertheless more than held their own.

The South actually did very well in the first two years of the war. After suffering a temporary setback at Antietam in Maryland, Confederate General Robert E. Lee led his army to victories at Fredericksburg and at Chancellorsville in Virginia. His confidence boosted, Lee decided to go on the offensive and take his troops into the North. His Confederate army seemed close to total victory; another success could woo Great Britain and France into supporting the Southerners. Meanwhile, the Union struggled on, battling not only Lee's army in the East but also other Confederates in the West.

President Lincoln put the Union's eastern army under the command of General George G. Meade; its western troops were headed by General Ulysses S. Grant. In the first week of July 1863, Meade led Union forces into battle at Gettysburg, Pennsylvania, while Grant and his troops were similarly engaged at Vicksburg, Mississippi. At home in the nation's capital, Lincoln anxiously awaited the news from either front; given the recent defeats suffered by the Union army, his administration was being pressured to step down and capitulate altogether.

The Battle of Gettysburg. The Battle of Gettysburg was one of the most important battles in the Civil War and marked a turning point in history. Fought at Gettysburg, Pennsylvania, from July 1 to July 3, 1863, the battle pitted seventy-five thousand Confederate soldiers against ninety thousand Union men. Of these, roughly forty thousand would suffer injury or death in the three days of fighting.

Lee's army had started northward on June 3, 1863, moving slowly because so many men and equipment had to cover so great a distance. Following him were Meade's Union troops. Neither

MAJOR CIVIL WAR BATTLES BEFORE GETTYSBURG

Year	Battle	Victor	Total Killed Union	Total Killed Confederacy
1861	First Battle of Bull Run	Confederacy	460	387
1862	Shiloh	Union	1,723	1,754
1862	Second Battle of Bull Run	Confederacy	1,747	1,553
1862	Battle of Antietam	Union	2,108	1,512
1862	Battle of Fredericksburg	Confederacy	1,284	608
1863	Battle of Chancellorsville	Confederacy	1,606	1,649

side knew exactly where the other's force was. By the end of June, the Confederate army had arrived west and north of Gettysburg, while the Union army was located to the south of the town. The tens of thousands of soldiers dwarfed the town's population of twenty-four hundred.

By chance, some Confederates close to Gettysburg fired on some Union cavalry men on July 1. Neither Lee nor Meade had planned to initiate a fight at that locale, but what began as a small skirmish mushroomed into a full-scale battle. The Confederates captured the town of Gettysburg, pushing the Union troops back to Cemetery Hill. General Lee and his troops charged the right flank of the Union force on July 1. On the following day Lee attacked the left. After both attacks were thwarted, Lee made a frontal attack that was daring, considering the circumstances. Gettysburg was mostly an infantry battle, with soldiers fighting in lines. Both sides used muzzle-loading rifles. Each round took thirty seconds to load and fire, which made a frontal attack a great gamble. The attackers became easy targets.

Nevertheless, on July 3, in what some scholars term the most famous charge in American military history, the Confederates attacked the Union center. The attack turned into a disaster for Lee's forces. By the time the smoke cleared, Lee's army listed 3,903 dead, 18,735 wounded. The North totaled 3,155 dead, 14,529 injured. The number of soldiers killed at Gettysburg thus amounted to more than twice the number of casualties that the armies had endured to that point. On July 5 Lee began his retreat to Virginia, leading his depleted and drastically weakened troops toward the Potomac River, which was swollen due to heavy rains in the area.

Meanwhile, in the West, Grant had laid siege to and won Vicksburg for the Union. With this victory the North gained control of the Mississippi River and cut the Confederacy in two, dividing the Southern states west of the river thoroughfare from those east of it. Lincoln rejoiced. The end of the war seemed near. If Meade's army chased and caught Lee's remaining forces, the Confederacy could be crushed once and for all. But Meade let Lee escape, and the war continued.

Still, Gettysburg had done irreversible damage to the South. Never again would Lee's army be strong enough to take the offensive. There was symbolic value in the battle, too. Out of a ceremony to consecrate a cemetery for the soldiers who perished in the fighting, the primary reason for the war became clear. Ironically, remarked one historian, "out of all this muddle, these missed chances, all the senseless deaths, [Gettysburg] would become a symbol of national purpose, pride, and ideals" because of President Lincoln's brief address (Wills, p. 20).

The cemetery at Gettysburg and the dedication. In his pursuit of Lee, Meade wired Union headquarters that he could not "delay to pick up the debris of the battlefield" (Meade in Wills, p. 20). The "debris" referred to rotting horses and human bodies left to the exposure of the July sun. As they slid the soldiers into shallow graves, spading a little earth over the bodies, the burial crew roughly recorded the names of the Union dead. The same consideration was not shown to the fallen Confederate soldiers. Within a short span of time, these graves suffered from ransacking as anguished family members searched for their missing relatives.

Andrew Curtin, the governor of Pennsylvania, quickly assigned a prominent citizen in Gettysburg, Judge David Wills, to form an interstate commission and gather funding for a proper cemetery. Wills hoped to dedicate the ground for the cemetery before the dead bodies were removed from their scattered, shallow graves and placed into it. In preparing a program, he asked several speakers to attend the ceremony. Poets such as Henry Wadsworth Longfellow, William Cullen Bryant, and John Greenleaf Whittier were invited to speak, but they refused.

Nineteenth-century public oratory addresses typically lasted for several hours, and audiences delighted in the duration. Wills desperately wanted Edward Everett, a noted public speaker, to dedicate the land at Gettysburg. States one scholar, "Everett was that rare thing, a scholar and Ivy-League diplomat who could hold mass audiences in thrall" (Wills, p. 24). As he had already given famous speeches about the Revolutionary War battles of Lexington and Concord and of Bunker Hill, a speech by Everett at Gettysburg would help to soothe some of the local inhabitants' ire over the treatment of their town. Everett agreed to attend, but he required two months from his September 23 invitation to prepare. A commemorating date of November 19, 1863, was set.

At the beginning of November, Wills also issued a rather casual invitation to President Lincoln to speak at the ceremony. The program for the ceremony lists Everett as the orator and Lincoln as the dedicator. The presence of the president was not intended to lend an aesthetic contribution to the ceremony; rather it was for the sake of formality.

While history gives various accounts of the composition of Lincoln's address, more likely than not the president wrote at least one draft of it while still in Washington. He wrote at least six versions of the address in his own hand, making some minor revisions in the drafts. There is uncertainty about the draft that he eventually delivered. It may have been the second version, finished the morning of the ceremony in the house of his host Judge Wills.

The ceremony included band music and a formal procession that had Lincoln riding on horseback in the company of three cabinet members to the commemoration spot. At least fifteen thousand spectators descended on the small town to watch the service. The keynote speaker, Everett, and a consecration hymn were to precede the few ceremonious words to be made by Lincoln.

Everett's speech. Everett, a scholar of classics, peppered his speech with multiple allusions to fallen Greek heroes. He opened by referring to a funeral at which the Greek general Pericles had spoken some twenty-four hundred years earlier. Using a different Greek example, he drew parallels between the dead at Gettysburg and those who had fallen at the Battle of Marathon in 490 B.C. Within this academic rhetoric, Everett more or less gave a retelling of the Battle of Gettysburg's events. In a grand manner he related the battle to the larger war. Ultimately, he condemned the Confederates for their rebellion from the Union and relieved Meade of the blame for letting Lee escape. Everett concluded his speech after almost two hours. Voices then broke out in the consecration hymn.

Delivery of Lincoln's speech. While Everett recited his two-hour speech from memory, Lincoln recited most but not all of his three-minute address from memory. The president delivered his speech in his usual high tenor voice, marked by Lincoln's native Kentucky accent. Although actors impersonating the sixteenth president often lend him a deep baritone, Lincoln's voice was in fact quite shrill. Because Lincoln spent hours poring over Shakespearean speeches, however, he knew how to manipulate the rhythms and inflections of dramatic delivery. Interrupted for applause some five times according to reports, the president's speech was well received by his audience.

FROM THE CONSECRATION HYMN BY BENJAMIN B. FRENCH

'Tis holy ground—
This spot, where, in their graves
We place our Country's braves
Who fell in Freedom's holy cause
Fighting for Liberties and Laws—
Let tears abound.
(Klement, p. 207)

Only 120 known photographs of Abraham Lincoln survive today. It is difficult to piece together how the president might have appeared in a live presentation based on this skimpy evidence. Eyewitnesses usually support the notion that, as a rule, Lincoln gave a fairly negative first impression. His complexion was dark, and his height made him appear gawky. It was his speaking ability that wooed crowds. In 1887 William Herndon recalled that:

When Mr. Lincoln rose up to speak, he rose slowly, steadily, firmly; he never moved much about on the stand or platform when speaking,

Gettysburg Address

trusting no desk, table, railing; he ran his eyes slowly over the crowd.... In his greatest inspiration he held both of his hands out above his head at an angle of about fifty degrees, hands open or clenched, according to his feeling and his ideas.

(Braden, p. 107)

The Speech in Focus

The contents. There is contention about exactly what Lincoln said in the speech he delivered at the ceremony. His written manuscript cannot be relied upon for exact wording, since he relied more on his memory than the written document. One eyewitness, *Boston Advertiser* newsman Charles Hale, declared that he caught every word in the exact language uttered. Hale's claim was confirmed by others in attendance. His version follows:

> Fourscore and seven years ago, our fathers brought forth upon this continent a new nation, conceived in liberty and dedicated to the proposition that all men are created equal.
>
> Now we are engaged in a great civil war, testing whether that nation—or any nation, so conceived and so dedicated—can long endure. We are met on a great battle-field of that war. We are met to dedicate a portion of it as the final resting-place of those who have given their lives that that nation might live. It is altogether fitting and proper that we should do this.
>
> But, in a larger sense, we cannot dedicate, we cannot consecrate, we cannot hallow, this ground. The brave men, living and dead, who struggled here, have consecrated it, far above our power to add or to detract. The world will very little note nor long remember what we say here; but it can never forget what they did here. It is for us, the living, rather, *to be dedicated,* here, to the unfinished work that they have thus far so nobly carried on. It is rather for us to be here dedicated to the great task remaining before us; that from these honored dead we take increased devotion to that cause for which they here gave the last full measure of devotion; that we here highly resolve that these dead shall not have died in vain; that the nation shall, under God, have a new birth of freedom, and that government of the people, by the people, for the people, shall not perish from the earth
>
> (Lincoln in Barton, pp. 81-2)

Lincoln wrote later drafts for publication in the official report of the Gettysburg ceremony, for a New York fair, for a Baltimore fair, and for a book called *Autograph Leaves of Our Country's Authors*. Below is a copy of Lincoln's sixth draft, with revised phrases in bold for purposes of comparison.

> Four score and seven years ago our fathers brought forth **on** this continent, a new nation, conceived in Liberty, and dedicated to the proposition that all men are created equal.
>
> Now we are engaged in a great civil war, testing whether that nation, or any nation so conceived and so dedicated, can long endure. We are met on a great battle-field of that war. We **have come** to dedicate a portion of **that field** as a final resting place for those who **here gave** their lives that **the** nation might live. It is altogether fitting and proper that we should do this.
>
> But in a larger sense, we can not dedicate—we can not consecrate—we can not hallow—this ground. The brave men, living and dead, who struggled here have consecrated it, far above our power to add or detract. The world **will little note**, nor long remember what we say here, but it can never forget what they did here. It is for us the living, rather, to be dedicated here to the unfinished work which they **who fought here** have thus far so nobly **advanced**. It is rather for us to be here dedicated to the great task remaining before us—that from these honored dead we take increased devotion to that cause for which **they gave** the last full measure of devotion—that we here highly resolve that these dead shall not have died in vain—that **this** nation, under God, shall have a new birth of freedom—and that government of the people, by the people, for the people, shall not perish from the earth"
>
> (Lincoln in Barton, pp. 111-12)

Gettysburg Address and Declaration of Independence. Lincoln opened his speech by evoking the words of the Declaration of Independence. Rather than echo the Declaration's exact words, "We hold these Truths to be self-evident, that all Men are created equal" (Thurow in Alvarez, p. 57), the president slightly altered this phrase. Lincoln called the equality of men a "proposition" that the nation is "dedicated" to achieving. He maintained that this achievement had not yet been realized.

The Civil War tested whether the nation could endure and fulfill the principle it set out to achieve—a principle of equality. Unfortunately, equality is not a standard that can be easily measured. During the pre-Civil War era, prejudices ran so deep that many felt blacks did not deserve the freedoms of whites because they were not equal citizens. Furthermore, not all members of society connected equality with justice. That is to say, not all felt it unjust that some members of society were not treated equally. Lincoln understood that the government could not attempt to simply erase this public opinion. As he stated, "A universal feeling, whether well or ill-founded, can not be safely disregarded" (Lincoln in Alvarez, p. 62). His Gettysburg Address attempted to solve this problem of the principle of equality.

Rather than attempting to define the term, Lincoln asserted that the proposition had yet to be achieved. He challenged the nation to find a sense of equality, to prove the Declaration of Independence true. The nation was founded on a belief, but Lincoln asserted that it must be maintained with an acquired knowledge. He forced public opinion away from the moment, focusing it instead on the past and the future. Lincoln insisted that the soldiers' deaths would be in vain unless his audience could renew its commitment to the soldiers' cause.

Lincoln's reliance on the Declaration in his speech cast it in a new light. Long regarded as simply the document in which the thirteen colonies claimed their independence from the British, it was spoken of in his Gettysburg Address as the country's founding law, and it has been regarded as such ever since.

Sources. The 1800s brought with them a revival of interest in Greek history. Archaeologists began uncovering the remains of this ancient democracy, while Romantic poets such as John Keats composed odes to Greek artwork. In his speech, the classicist Everett evoked the image of Pericles speaking over the ashes of fallen Athenians who had fought against Sparta in 431 B.C. But Abraham Lincoln's speech relied more on a Greek format than on evoking images of men like Pericles.

The structure of Grecian funeral orations featured two parts. The "epainesis" refers to the praise of the fallen, while the "parainesis" covers advice to the living. Lincoln's speech, when examined line by line, follows this format almost exactly. He began by referring to the founding fathers and the ideals that they held. He continued with his dedication, noting that "it is altogether fitting and proper" for the living to acknowledge the achievements of the dead. The last half of his speech called on the living to prove themselves worthy of the soldiers who had died.

In many speeches, Lincoln favored the idea of thesis and antithesis, and much of his rhetoric shows these marks of contrast. In his Gettysburg Address, the two poles are death and life. Throughout the speech, Lincoln, like Pericles, called on the living generation to surpass the standards of those who came before.

Lincoln relied not only on classical models, however, for his inspiration. Much of what Lincoln said recast the words of the Declaration of Independence, perhaps to rectify his oversight in composing the Emancipation Proclamation of January 1, 1863, which freed all black slaves in rebel territory. This proclamation was a politically risky move. Lincoln took a gamble in upsetting Northern Democrats who did not support abolitionism. He knew that his Emancipation Proclamation might create turmoil in an already strained Union. In addition, it risked the reputation of the United States around the world. Given the difficulties of the war, European nations could have viewed the Emancipation Proclamation as a desperate attempt to incite a slave rebellion. It could very well have been interpreted as a sign that the Union was losing.

For these reasons, Lincoln walked a middle ground in his Emancipation Proclamation, declaring that it was a purely militaristic move. He would free the slaves using his presidential power of creating a militia troop against a rebellion. His critics noted that his Proclamation made no mention of liberty or the rights of men. Lincoln rectified this with his Gettysburg Address, delivered over ten months later.

Finally, Lincoln's choice of words was probably influenced by other Americans of his day. The renowned congressman and orator Daniel Webster (1782-1852) had defined the American system as "The people's government, made for the people, made by the people, and answerable to the people," for example (Webster in Barton, p. 132). Another American, clergyman Theodore Parker (1810-1860), wrote a sermon that Lincoln is known to have read and underlined. In his sermon, Parker said, "There is what I call the American idea . . . that is, a government of all the people, by all the people, for all the people" (Parker in Barton, p. 135).

Reaction to the speech. As was the custom, newspapers reprinted Lincoln's speech the day after it was delivered. Several newspapers, however, such as Milwaukee's *Daily Wisconsin*, printed an incorrect version of it. Otherwise the press mostly ignored Lincoln's address, focusing instead on Everett's oration.

There were a few negative comments. The *Chicago Times* berated Lincoln for misinterpreting the Constitution in an editorial: "How dare he, then, standing on their graves, misstate the cause for which they died, and libel the statesmen who founded the government?" (Chicago

Times in Wills, p. 39). Many others accused the president of politicking—that is, grandstanding to get re-elected in 1864. The Harrisburg, Pennsylvania, newspaper (*Patriot and Union*) spoke of the "silly remarks" made by the president at Gettysburg, while overseas the *London Times* maintained that "the ceremony was rendered ludicrous by some of the sallies of that poor President Lincoln.... Anything more dull and commonplace it wouldn't be easy to produce (Barton, p. 116).

Not all responses were so caustic, however. The Springfield *Republican* called the speech an absolute gem—deep in meaning, compact in expression, and tasteful in every word and comma. And in 1865 *Macmillan's Magazine* praised the speech's simple structure and rich meaning as true marks of the classical style. Perhaps the greatest compliment, though, came from the keynote speaker, Edward Everett: "I should be glad," he told Lincoln, "if I could flatter myself that I came as near to the central idea of the occasion in two hours as you did in two minutes" (Everett in Barton, p. 195).

For More Information

Alvarez, Leo Paul S., ed. *Abraham Lincoln, The Gettysburg Address and American Constitutionalism.* Dallas: University of Dallas Press, 1976.

Barton, William E. *Lincoln at Gettysburg: What He Intended to Say; What He Said; What He Was Reported to Have Said; What He Wished He Had Said.* New York: Peter Smith, 1950.

Braden, Waldo. *Abraham Lincoln, Public Speaker.* Baton Rouge: Louisiana State University Press, 1988.

Gramm, Kent. *Gettysburg: A Meditation on War and Values.* Indianapolis: Indiana University Press, 1994.

Klement, Frank L. *The Gettysburg Soldiers' Cemetery and Lincoln's Address: Aspects and Angles.* Shippensburg, Pa.: White Mane, 1993.

Wills, Garry. *Lincoln at Gettysburg.* New York: Simon and Schuster, 1992.

Gone with the Wind

by
Margaret Mitchell

Born in 1900, Margaret Mitchell grew up in Atlanta, Georgia. More than thirty years before her birth, Atlanta had been burned to the ground by the Union army during the Civil War. It was rebuilt rather quickly, but memories of that era remained deeply etched in the minds of the Mitchells and other Southern families. As a child, the author heard many stories from older relatives who had lived through the Civil War in northern Georgia. Their stories helped her establish a life-like setting for her best-known work, *Gone with the Wind*.

THE LITERARY WORK
A novel set in northern Georgia, from 1861 to 1874; published in 1936.

SYNOPSIS
A young Southern woman's way of life changes drastically because of the Civil War.

Events in History at the Time the Novel Takes Place

The antebellum South. Agriculture formed the backbone of the Southern economy before the Civil War. The vast majority of Southern whites were modest farmers who worked small tracts of land with their own labor. Only one percent of Southerners owned large plantations with more than fifty slaves. Even so, this "aristocracy" used their wealth and property to exert a power and influence in Southern society far beyond their numbers.

A large plantation, like Tara in *Gone with the Wind*, was nearly self-sufficient. It might employ as many as a hundred slaves to carry out a wide variety of duties. The majority of the slaves—males, females, and children—worked in the fields cultivating tobacco, cotton, and other marketable crops. Others were responsible for growing and preparing food for the plantation's residents to eat, or involved in making clothes for them to wear. Such skilled craftsmen as coopers (barrel-makers), blacksmiths, bricklayers, and carpenters lived on the premises. Inside the Great House, the palatial home of the plantation's owners, a staff of slaves cooked and kept the rooms clean and waited upon the owners, while also nursing and frequently raising the owners' children. Slavery, in short, formed the foundation supporting the Southern plantation owners' way of life before the Civil War.

The culture of the Southern propertied elite. The propertied elite of the antebellum South had a distinct culture, and many of its members believed their way of life to be superior to any other. They prided themselves on what they considered to be their refined and gracious society. Northern "Yankees" were held in disdain. To the Southern elite, it seemed that even the upper classes in the North were always grasping for money, more concerned with rapid economic growth than with a high quality of life. Southerners were happy to be free, or so they told themselves, of such base, materialistic impulses.

The culture of the Southern elite was founded on a value system that revolved around an elaborate code of chivalry. Personal honor, particularly for men, was of the utmost importance, while dishonor, including improper behavior for women, was the ultimate disgrace. No man could passively tolerate an insult without sacrificing his reputation. A man who made disparaging remarks in public about another man, his family, or his property could expect to be challenged to a physical fight, often in the form of a pistol duel. Once challenged, a man could not avoid fighting without appearing to be a coward.

THE LIVES OF UPPER-CLASS SOUTHERN WOMEN

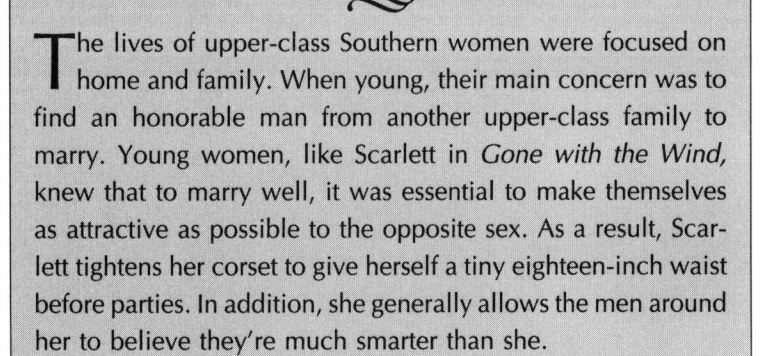

The lives of upper-class Southern women were focused on home and family. When young, their main concern was to find an honorable man from another upper-class family to marry. Young women, like Scarlett in *Gone with the Wind*, knew that to marry well, it was essential to make themselves as attractive as possible to the opposite sex. As a result, Scarlett tightens her corset to give herself a tiny eighteen-inch waist before parties. In addition, she generally allows the men around her to believe they're much smarter than she.

Women filled a special role in upper-class Southern society. The code of honor dictated that men take responsibility for protecting their wives, mothers, and daughters from both physical dangers and the harsh realities of life. In the minds of many Southern patriarchs, females were naturally weak, delicate, and dependent beings in need of such protection. This mindset led to certain unwritten rules. For example, society considered it wrong for women to travel alone without male companionship. This is why, in *Gone with the Wind*, Scarlett is shocked when Rhett Butler leaves her, Melanie, Prissy, and two children to return to Tara from Atlanta by themselves. An "honorable" man would never desert women in the midst of a war. Society also considered it necessary to shelter women from vulgarity. It was ungentlemanly to curse in front of women, or to speak of anything distasteful or disturbing in their presence. A related rule prohibited men from discussing politics with women, since the subject was considered intellectually beyond the understanding of females.

It was understood among the Southern elite that, in exchange for protection, women owed men absolute obedience. Females had an obligation to obey their fathers, husbands, and brothers. Important decisions affecting them, such as the choice of a marriage partner, were ultimately subject to their father's approval. Once married, women became hostesses to visitors in their home. They were also expected to bear their husbands many children, preferably boys. A woman who was not submissive was generally scorned in Southern society. This is demonstrated in *Gone with the Wind*, when Scarlett attempts to oversee the running of a sawmill by herself. She does so in an aggressively masculine manner, ignoring the strong disapproval of her husband, Frank Kennedy. Her actions are seen as disgraceful by Kennedy as well as the people of Atlanta. They are scandalized at her disregard for her husband's wishes and find her involvement in the construction business to be unfeminine.

Despite Southern society's preference for weak and passive women, there were real-life examples of females who took active roles in the business activities of the time. Many, like Ellen O'Hara in *Gone with the Wind*, assumed important managerial positions on the plantation. They took responsibility for accounts, the distribution of food and supplies, the health and housing of slaves, and the activities of cooks, seamstresses, and craftsmen.

Blockade runners. In 1861, at the beginning of the Civil War, President Abraham Lincoln ordered that a 3,500-mile blockade be set up along the Southern coast from Virginia to Texas. Any vessel attempting to enter or leave a blockaded port (Wilmington, North Carolina; Charleston, South Carolina; Mobile, Alabama; New Orleans, Louisiana; or Galveston, Texas), would, after one warning, be captured and its goods confiscated. Because of this blockade, a dangerous but profitable business sprung up—blockade running. Blockade running was the practice of conducting trade between Confederate and foreign ports, which required the trade ships to elude the Union vessels patrolling off-shore. The practice flourished, especially from 1861 through 1863. Of all the blockaded ports, Wilmington proved the best suited for blockade running because it had two widely separated entryways. A runner could estimate which one was least heavily guarded before dashing toward the port. At New

Inlet, the favorite of the two entrances, a vessel could make itself almost invisible by traveling close to the shore.

Some vessels were built especially for blockade running. These vessels had a shallow draft (the amount of vessel below the water line) and could move quickly (at least ten knots). Painted light gray to make their boats as invisible as possible, they used minimal rigging and nonsmoking coal. At first they ran directly from Europe to the American South, but as the blockade tightened, they began to take a safer, less direct route by way of Latin America, especially the Caribbean islands. Using this method, a steamer, usually loaded with luxury goods, such as French wines and silks, but sometimes with rifles and cannons, departed Europe for a foreign port in the Americas, such as Bermuda, Nassau, or Havana. There the cargo was transferred from the steamer to one of the special blockade runners that smuggled the goods to Wilmington or some other Southern port. At the port, the vessel exchanged its goods for cotton, then brought this new cargo back to Nassau, Bermuda, or Havana.

Waiting to make the journey on dark, almost moonless nights, most blockade runners reached their destinations intact. "On the average four out of every six vessels that start to run the blockade succeed, and goods of all kinds are worth ridiculous prices" (Jones, p. 83). Salt worth only $6.50 at Nassau brought $1,700 at Richmond, Virginia. Likewise on the return trip, cotton purchased at $.06 or $.08 a pound at a Southern port brought as much as $1.00 at Nassau or Bermuda. Of course, it was costly to operate a blockade runner. Aside from the expense of the vessel, daring, resourceful captains and pilots had to be paid. The total cost mounted as high as $80,000 a month in 1863. Undaunted, Southern adventurers like *Gone With the Wind*'s Rhett Butler willingly risked the expense since they stood to more than double their investment in a single round trip.

Civil War and Reconstruction in Georgia. During the Civil War, the state of Georgia was surrounded by a buffer zone of other Confederate states that the Union army attacked first. Insulated from the front lines, Georgia was the site of few battles during the first two years of the war.

In 1863, however, Union General William Tecumseh Sherman entered the state of Georgia after subduing rebel forces in Tennessee. He aimed to capture Atlanta, which was an important center of the South's railroad network, as well as Georgia's largest producer of ammunition and army supplies. Sherman's troops gradually moved closer and closer to Atlanta despite the defensive efforts of the Confederate forces. By July 1864 the two sides were engaged in battle just six miles north of Atlanta, and artillery shells began hitting targets in the city itself. Finally, the Confederates were forced to abandon Atlanta, and its remaining inhabitants fled. On November 15, 1864, Sherman set fire to the city. From there he and his 62,000 men began their famous three-hundred-mile "march to the sea." They stripped the countryside from Atlanta to Savannah, taking food and anything else of value they could find, burning homes, and destroying railroad lines. On December 22, Savannah was captured. A few months later, in April 1865, Southern forces surrendered, and the war ended.

Most of the South, including Georgia, was left impoverished and desolate. Sherman's army had destroyed 317 miles of railroad track and $100 million worth of public and private property during its march through the South. Even in areas untouched by the Northern army, years of supporting the war effort through heavy state taxes and numerous contributions of supplies had taken a tremendous toll. Across Georgia, livestock had disappeared, food was in short supply, and buildings sat limply in disrepair. Plantations lost their traditional work force as newly freed slaves left for nearby cities. Thousands of Georgian soldiers had died, or lay wounded or sick, reducing the work force even further. Over five thousand families in Georgia were utterly destitute after the war; they did not even have bread to eat.

The former slaves suddenly had their freedom, but most started out with very little money or property. Faced with obstacles such as racial discrimination, a large number found employment difficult to obtain. Many of the former slaves took up residence in large camps where they lived in terrible conditions, depending on surplus rations provided by the federal government. One such camp outside of Atlanta was home to more than a thousand free blacks.

Most Southern whites were not only poor; they were also bitter about the results of the Civil War. The federal government instituted military rule in Georgia and much of the South. To some extent, this step was taken to ensure that blacks were able to exercise their new right to vote. Meanwhile, white Southerners who refused to take an oath of loyalty to the Union were deprived of their voting rights, an act that prompted further resentment against the federal govern-

Gone with the Wind

Gone with the Wind

General William Tecumseh Sherman

ment and blacks. Resentment mounted as Northerners known as carpetbaggers (for the bags, made of carpeting, with which they traveled) came south and began to influence Georgia's state government. A number of white Southerners, called Scalawags (a term otherwise used to describe very small or diseased cattle), willingly collaborated with the Northerners in the government. This Northern-Southern alliance was largely made up of members of the Republican Party, while the traditional white Southerner was a Democrat. Southern Democrats resented these Republican intrusions into their way of life.

With much of the state impoverished and bitter, reconstruction proved to be a difficult process. As one writer noted in 1866, "There seems to be a complete dearth of money all over the South: never were the people of this country in a more destitute condition.... Another such year as the one we have just passed through and this people will be completely ruined" (Conway, p. 103). Government authorities found it necessary to provide relief for distressed Georgians into the 1870s, foreshadowing a role played by the government some sixty years later in the Great Depression of 1929. In fact, a general depression plagued the nation from 1873 to 1879, introducing widespread unemployment to the country for the first time in its history.

The Novel in Focus

The plot. Young Scarlett O'Hara belongs to a wealthy family that owns Tara, a large plantation in pre-Civil War Georgia. Her life, and that of everyone around her, is forever changed one day when war breaks out against the Northern states. At the time, Scarlett is more preoccupied with the fact that the one man she truly loves, Ashley Wilkes, has just announced his engagement to Melanie Hamilton. To provoke Ashley's jealousy, Scarlett marries Melanie's shy brother, Charles. Charles soon leaves for war and dies, not heroically in the fighting, but in his tent, from a case of measles.

Scarlett, now a widow, grows bored at Tara and moves to Atlanta to live with her new sister-in-law Melanie and Aunt Pitty. Though the intensely jealous Scarlett hates Melanie, Melanie has only love and admiration for Scarlett and acts extremely kindly to her. Rhett Butler, a man that Scarlett had met while living at Tara, frequently visits the young widow. He is a wealthy, outspoken outcast from fashionable Southern society, as well as a blockade runner. Though they frequently have heated arguments, Scarlett grows to enjoy Rhett's attentions. Her love for Ashley Wilkes never diminishes, however.

Over a few years, the fortunes of the Confederacy worsen. Northern troops begin to approach Atlanta. Most of its inhabitants flee the city, but Scarlett feels compelled to stay with Melanie, who is expecting a baby. Soon after Melanie gives birth, she, Scarlett, and their servants must hurriedly leave because the city has been set on fire and Union troops are approaching. They make a harrowing escape one night with the aid of Rhett Butler.

THE BIRTH OF THE KU KLUX KLAN

The majority of white Southerners refused to accept blacks as equals and were opposed to Northern programs to increase civil rights for blacks. Their opposition gave rise to the Ku Klux Klan, founded in Tennessee in 1866 as a social fraternity. Spreading across the South, the Klan became a vigilante group for whites interested in enforcing their own idea of justice. Members of the organization, which was dominated by some elite Southern whites, used intimidation and violence to prevent blacks from exercising new rights, such as voting. Night raiders would roam the countryside in disguise. Dragging people from homes, they whipped, shot, or otherwise assaulted them, and destroyed their property. Eventually, the federal government intervened in these activities, passing congressional legislation against the Klan, making military arrests, and conducting trials in federal courts. In some states, militia units were organized to break up the Klan. The Ku Klux Klan disintegrated under the force of these attacks in the 1870s, but it came back to life in the next century.

Scarlett encounters more misfortune. She returns to Tara, only to discover that her mother has died, her father has suffered a mental breakdown, and her sisters have fallen ill. In addition, the region has been decimated; the Union army swept through the entire countryside, burning and pillaging the property of her neighbors. They left Tara standing, although they stole just about everything of any value, including food. Scarlett and her family face starvation. The former belle takes on the responsibility for managing the entire household. She scours the plantation and desolated countryside for food and works with her hands for the first time in her

Gone with the Wind

life. She vows never to go hungry again, whatever the cost.

The war ends and Tara slowly begins to recover. Before long, however, Scarlett is faced with staggering taxes on the property. She decides to move to Atlanta and plots to steal her sister's modestly secure fiancé Frank Kennedy, whom she marries in order to gain the money to pay the taxes. She surprises him and the rest of Atlanta with her aggressiveness in business, including the purchase of a sawmill. Scarlett becomes a widow once again when Frank, a member of the Ku Klux Klan, dies in a Yankee raid on a Klan meeting.

Scarlett then marries the wealthy Rhett Butler. They have a tempestuous relationship that leads to the birth of a child who dies tragically in a riding accident, a death that sends Rhett into despair. Scarlett, who already has a son and a daughter, respectively, from her two previous marriages, wants no more children, however. This factor, combined with her continued love for Ashley Wilkes, leads her to insist on separate bedrooms. Her marriage with Rhett deteriorates.

In the final part of the book, Melanie dies in childbirth. Scarlett realizes that although she had thought she hated Melanie, the woman had been one of her few true friends over the past years. She also realizes that she now loves Rhett rather than Ashley. It is too late, however, to regain his love. After years of knowing she preferred Ashley to him, Rhett has finally fallen out of love with her. He leaves her, and the novel ends with Scarlett vowing to win him back.

Images of African Americans. *Gone with the Wind* focuses on the changing world of Georgia's white planter elite before, during, and after the Civil War. The changes hinge largely on the roles played by blacks. In *Gone with the Wind,* the majority of black characters are servants of white masters and mistresses. The most frequently cited characteristic of these black slaves is loyalty to their masters. The slave Mammy, for instance, is described as "devoted to her last drop of blood to the O'Haras" (Mitchell, *Gone with the Wind,* p. 25). When the slave Pork gets injured attempting to steal a chicken for the impoverished inhabitants of Tara, Scarlett acknowledges his commitment to the plantation: "Negroes were provoking sometimes and stupid and lazy, but there was a loyalty in them that money couldn't buy" (*Gone with the Wind,* p. 465). These descriptions illustrate a widespread perception of blacks held by Southern whites during the Civil War era.

White Southerners relied on their black servants to meet the most basic of needs. At the same time, white masters considered the black slaves to be biologically and intellectually inferior beings. It was commonly believed that blacks needed the guidance of white masters to survive. They were, according to general misconception, unfit to care for themselves independently. Referring to slaves, Scarlett's mother Ellen told her that "you must realize that they are like children and must be guarded from themselves like children" (*Gone with the Wind,* p. 465).

Blacks were often seen as content with a simpler, more animal-like existence than whites. Some of the descriptions of blacks in *Gone with the Wind* coincide with this stereotypical view. For example, Scarlett meets one of her former slaves in Atlanta as he is on his way home to Tara. He had gotten a taste of life in the North but found it unappealing. His excited greeting is described in terms that might be used to describe a large dog, overcome with simple happiness at seeing his former master: "Sam galloped over to the buggy, his eyes rolling with joy and his white teeth flashing.... His watermelon-pink tongue lapped out, his whole body wiggled and his joyful contortions were as ludicrous as the gamboling of a mastiff" (*Gone with the Wind,* p. 771).

Since blacks were considered intellectually inferior, their desire to exercise their rights as free citizens—in particular, to vote—disturbed Southern whites during the Reconstruction era (1866-1877). This racist attitude is depicted by Mitchell. At one point, for example, Aunt Pitty says to Scarlett, "My dear, they want to let the darkies vote! Did you ever hear of anything more silly?" (*Gone with the Wind,* p. 552). Many Southern whites could hardly imagine blacks being able to handle the responsibilities of freedom, let alone voting. All in all, many white Southerners found it difficult to reconcile themselves to the idea of treating former slaves as equals to themselves. When Scarlett is threatened with the possibility of losing Tara to Jonas Wilkerson, a Scalawag whom she hates intensely, she is upset by the following thought:

> Perhaps they'd even bring negroes here to dine and sleep.... Jonas made a great to-do about being equal with negroes, ate with them, visited in their houses.... When she thought of the possibility of this final insult to Tara, her heart pounded so hard she could scarcely breathe.
> (*Gone with the Wind,* p. 529-30)

Sources. *Gone with the Wind* is a fictional story set in the midst of actual events that took place in northern Georgia around the time of the Civil War. Apparently, none of the characters come directly from real life, although a number of similarities exist between the fictional characters and members of the author's family. Mitchell's ancestors, like the O'Hara family in the novel, were part of Georgia's wealthy planter elite. Some had immigrated from Ireland, as Scarlett's father, Gerald O'Hara, had in the novel.

Mitchell herself was like Scarlett in that she did not always behave in accordance with the norms of the society in which she lived. As a child, she was a tomboy, and later in life she took what was considered an unfeminine job as a journalist. Mitchell also left the Catholic Church, got divorced, and remarried, all at a time when such actions were highly unusual. Even more like Scarlett than the author, however, was the author's grandmother, Annie Stephens. Annie, like Scarlett, lived through the Civil War in northern Georgia. She too was well known for her stubbornness, ruthlessness, and explosive temper. Annie also became involved in business during the Reconstruction era, when such activities were not regarded as fashionable pursuits for a lady; these actions are also undertaken by Scarlett.

To accurately portray life in northern Georgia and Atlanta around the time of the Civil War, Mitchell did a great deal of research. She combed through firsthand accounts available in newspapers and memoirs, interviewed people who experienced the war years, and visited battle sites. Mitchell was personally familiar with Atlanta, the site of much of *Gone with the Wind*'s action, having lived there her entire life. In fact, she spent a number of years in a home on Peachtree Street, just as Scarlett does in the book.

Events in History at the Time the Novel Was Written

The Great Depression. The Reconstruction era that followed the Civil War concerned the Southern states, but the Great Depression of the 1930s swept across not just the South but the entire nation. Both periods were times of widespread poverty in which people faced the threat of unemployment or significant wage reductions.

Georgia was not spared from the damage caused by the Depression, which began in 1929. In America's rural areas—and rural areas covered much of Georgia—farm income declined 60 percent by 1932. Thousands of farmers either lost or abandoned their land. About 500,000 Georgians moved north to search for employment over the course of the decade. Others became migrant workers, traveling from farm to farm, picking crops for extremely low wages. Meanwhile, the situation in cities like Atlanta was not much better. Factory owners cut back on production and laid off workers or reduced their salaries. Many mills closed down. The city government also laid off public employees and reduced social services.

During these years, living patterns emerged that resembled those of the Reconstruction. For example, women once again began to sew clothes for themselves, as they had in the past. Increas-

---

THE REEMERGENCE OF THE KU KLUX KLAN

The Ku Klux Klan reemerged soon after World War I. The strong racial tensions that existed during Reconstruction had never disappeared. On top of that, the early 1920s was a time of great change. Large numbers of immigrants streamed into the United States, and more and more black people moved to northern cities. Minorities in the white population—Jews and Catholics—moved up the economic and social ladder at the same time that labor unions began to gain power. These changes bred fears that led to a new generation of the Ku Klux Klan. The new Klan drew most of its members from the lower and middle classes of white society. Seeing themselves as patriots and defenders of traditional values, the members persecuted anyone they deemed guilty of irreligion, sexual promiscuity, or excessive drunkenness. They terrorized minorities, particularly blacks, through whipping, tarring and feathering, arson, and lynching. Unlike the first Ku Klux Klan, the second one spread beyond the South to become a national organization. At its height in the 1920s, its membership climbed to over 3 million. But it dwindled to about 100,000 during the Depression of the 1930s as fewer people were able or willing to spend money on membership. Since then the strength and size of the Klan has risen and fallen, but it continues to be a force in American society.

---

ing numbers of women turned to preserving their own food rather than buying it in a store. Like some of the Atlanta families in *Gone with the Wind*, Depression-era families often established home businesses wherein they laundered, sold baked goods, or accepted boarders to make ends meet. Conditions improved as the decade progressed. However, many of *Gone with the Wind*'s first readers must have identified with the hard

Gone with the Wind

times faced by Scarlett O'Hara and other Southerners during Reconstruction.

Reviews. *Gone with the Wind* gained almost immediate popularity upon its publication in 1936. Sales topped one million copies by January 1937, more than double what Mitchell had expected. In the spring of 1937, the American Booksellers Association awarded *Gone with the Wind* its annual prize for best fiction of the preceding year. The author won a Pulitzer Prize for the novel in May 1937. Two years later, it was made into a popular film. Since its publication, *Gone with the Wind* has sold over 28 million copies in more than 37 countries.

A number of reviewers have called the book overly sentimental and artistically imperfect, but many have praised it for its vitality and clarity. Stephen Vincent Benét wrote in one review that "the tale of [Scarlett's] adventures and her struggles makes as readable, full-bodied, and consistent a historical novel as we have had in some time—a novel which, in certain passages, as in the flight from burning Atlanta, rises to genuine heights. Miss Mitchell knows her period, her people, and the red hill country of North Georgia" (Benét, p. 5).

For More Information

Benét, Stephen Vincent. *Saturday Review of Literature* (July 4, 1936): 5.

Chalmers, David M. *Hooded Americanism: The First Century of the Ku Klux Klan, 1865-1965.* Garden City, N.Y.: Doubleday, 1965.

Conway, Alan. *The Reconstruction of Georgia.* Minneapolis: University of Minnesota Press, 1966.

Fox-Genovese, Elizabeth. *Within the Plantation Household: Black and White Women of the Old South.* Chapel Hill: University of North Carolina Press, 1988.

Jones, Virgil Carrington. *The Civil War at Sea.* Vol. 3. New York: Holt, Rinehart & Winston, 1960.

Mitchell, Margaret. *Gone With the Wind.* New York: Macmillan, 1964.

Pyron, Darden Asbury. *Southern Daughter: The Life of Margaret Mitchell.* New York: Oxford University Press, 1991.

Smith, Douglas L. *The New Deal in the Urban South.* Baton Rouge: Louisiana State University Press, 1988.

Heart of Darkness

by
Joseph Conrad

Józef Teodor Konrad Korzeniowski was born in Poland in 1857. The son of Polish aristocrats, he changed his name to Joseph Conrad upon becoming an English citizen. In 1890 Conrad went to work in the Congo. Africa had long been ignored by most of Europe, but the end of the 1800s brought a surge of interest in the continent, which experienced great changes as it became the site of rapid colonization.

> **THE LITERARY WORK**
>
> A novella set in the Belgian Congo, about 1890; published in 1899.
>
> **SYNOPSIS**
>
> A sailor relates the story of his journey to Africa and the strange encounters that took place as he voyaged to the farthest reaches of the Congo River.

Events in History at the Time the Novella Takes Place

Kongo kingdom. Located along the equator on the western coast of Africa is one of the largest rivers in the world, the Zaire River. In Joseph Conrad's day it was known as the Congo River. The Congo was first discovered by European explorers in 1482, when a Portuguese expedition found the mouth of the river, which empties into the Atlantic Ocean. They raided the small villages in the surrounding area until they discovered that the villagers were under the protection of a powerful African kingdom, the Kongo kingdom.

After this discovery, the Portuguese carried out trade with the Africans as equals and partners. The Portuguese and Kongolese kings treated one another as fellow monarchs, and the governments exchanged ambassadors. The goodwill between the parties was based on the two countries' commercial relations. The trading had begun with the bartering of European products for African goods, but the Portuguese soon began to buy up slaves. The slave trade expanded rapidly as the Spanish colonies in the New World began to require ever increasing numbers of laborers. By 1525 five to six thousand slaves were being shipped out of Africa each year. The slave trade was made easier by the fact that the Kongo kingdom was well organized. The kingdom had a trade network in place that allowed merchandise, including slaves, to be shipped from deep inland.

Certain local tribes began to gain wealth and power by making their living as slave merchants. They raided small inland villages and carried off the inhabitants to be sold on the coast to the Portuguese. Eventually, though, the constant demand for slaves became generally detrimental to the African kingdom. In 1526 the Kongo king Nzinga Nbemba wrote to the king of Portugal, asking that the slave trade be halted. The king's men "seize upon our subjects, sons of the land and sons of our noblemen and vassals and relatives . . . and cause them to be sold; and so great,

Sir, is their corruption and licentiousness that our country is being utterly depopulated" (Davidson, p. 105). But the slave trade did not cease. The Kingdom of Kongo finally collapsed in 1568 from invasion by neighboring kingdoms, a development that made little difference to the Portuguese merchants. They would continue the slave trade for the next three hundred years, exchanging the Kongolese for new African partners.

Exploring the Congo. Although Europeans maintained a presence on the Congo River for hundreds of years, they had not traveled farther than two hundred miles upstream. At that point, the river became impassable due to waterfalls and strong rapids. In fact, no one knew the exact length of the Congo until Henry Morton Stanley explored the river in the 1870s. Stanley, an English-born American, began a journey across Africa that answered most of the questions about the river.

BRITISH IMPERIALISM IN THE 1800s

The 1870s sparked intense rivalry among Belgium, Germany, the United States, and older colonial powers, especially Great Britain, for world empires. In the last two decades of the century, the scramble for control of Africa stirred heated debate about relations with the continent's natives. Conrad shared a stance taken by others in Great Britain. These Britishers saw themselves as belonging to the highest moral power among nations, and Britain as doing more than ripping Africa's riches from the land the way King Leopold's Belgium was. Britain had long assumed an attitude of responsibility for the so-called betterment of natives. This betterment was thought to involve the replacement of savage customs with so-called civilized ways, although there was some debate about whether or not Africans were capable of being civilized. In any case, a feeling existed in Britain that the shameless greed with which Leopold was operating in Africa called for "intervention by a higher moral power" (Brantlinger, p. 181). Conrad seems to have shared this feeling.

When Stanley began the trip, he was accompanied by a small army of Europeans and African mercenaries—few of whom survived the three-year, seven-thousand-mile journey, which took a heavy toll on the explorers in terms of disease and conflicts with the local inhabitants. Stanley began on the eastern coast of Africa and made his way across the continent to its western edge, where the Congo river emptied into the Atlantic Ocean. He discovered that the Congo River extended some 1,600 miles into the heart of Africa from its mouth at the Atlantic Ocean, and that it was possible to take a boat along nearly its entire length. There was only one stretch of the river that was not navigable, an impassable section between Matadi, two hundred miles in from the mouth of the Congo, and Kinshasa, another two hundred miles further inland. In *Heart of Darkness,* Matadi was known as the Company Station and Kinshasa was referred to as the Central Station. Between Matadi and Kinshasa, it was necessary to take a land rather than a water route. This geographic reality is reflected in *Heart of Darkness,* for the protagonist Marlow has to make a "two hundred-mile tramp" (Conrad, *Heart of Darkness,* p. 20) to get from the Company Station to the Central Station.

Opening up the Congo. Stanley returned to his native England in an attempt to persuade the English government to take advantage of his discoveries. Having noted the vast resources of the Congo River and the surrounding area, he wanted England to be the country to exploit its potential. To Stanley's disappointment, the English were not interested. Nevertheless, his efforts did not go to waste. In 1878 the king of Belgium asked Stanley to found a Belgian colony there.

King Leopold II. The nation of Belgium had been created in 1831. It was a small country surrounded by powerful neighbors when its second king, Leopold II, took the throne in 1865. At that time, Belgium was experiencing strong growth in its economy. The country's small allotment of land was rapidly being used up, however, and Leopold II realized that the country's economy could not expand much farther unless he found some outlet.

Leopold II first tried to secure a foothold in China but was unsuccessful. He then set his sights on Africa. Although the idea of an African colony did not have much popular support in Belgium, Leopold II was a crafty politician. He was able to obtain international backing for his plans, which eventually gained the support of his countrymen.

Leopold II's first step was to put together a private company that would finance explorations in the Congo. When he hired Stanley in 1878, Leopold wanted him to set up the first outposts along the Congo River, particularly at Matadi. While Leopold II was looking mainly for material gains, he hid his motives from the rest of Europe by claiming that his objectives in the Congo were to end slavery and to civilize the native inhabitants. He also promised that all European countries would be able to trade in the Congo. The other heads of state apparently believed in Leopold II's goodwill. At the Congress of Berlin in 1885, an international committee agreed to the formation of a new country that was to be known as the Congo Free State. Leopold II was to be the sole ruler of the huge expanse of land (the Congo Free State was eighty times the size of Belgium). Leopold II, though, never set foot in his new country. Instead, the company he formed, known as the Société Anonyme Belge pour le Commerce du Haut Congo (or SAB), ran the country for him. SAB is the "Company" that Conrad refers to throughout *Heart of Darkness*.

The "white man's burden." Stimulated by the abolitionist movements of the 1800s, Europeans began to ponder with increasing frequency the differences, if any, between African slaves and themselves. Some pro-slavery advocates suggested that the African slaves were not humans at all, or contended that they were subhumans at best, for whom slavery was an appropriate status. They were contradicted by others who maintained that the African slaves were humans and that slavery was wrong. But even these others saw the Africans as a less evolved people.

Many Europeans determined the degree to which a group was evolved by studying differences in technology from group to group. The Africans were not as advanced as the Europeans in technological inventions and were therefore seen as less evolved. Europeans admitted that they too had once been at that lower stage, but they had grown out of it. Many Europeans concluded that all that was necessary to raise up the peoples of Africa was to introduce them to European culture and technology. This perceived responsibility to lift up the nations of Africa came to be known as the "white man's burden." This feeling of responsibility gave rise to a fervor to bring Christianity and commerce to Africa. Missionaries, reasoned the Europeans, would introduce European culture to Africa through religion, and commerce would bring the necessary technological advancements. In fact, many European leaders took advantage of such sentiments to increase their own wealth and power by acquiring products from Africa. King Leopold II was one of those men.

Ivory. By the middle of the 1800s, the slave trade had begun to die out in the Congo River basin. As the slave trade declined, the African traders, who had made high earnings in the slave business, wished to find some new product to sell to the Europeans. Ivory was the answer. Though the Portuguese had been collecting African ivory for hundreds of years, ivory became a symbol of status and wealth in the 1800s, and demand suddenly increased. European artisans used ivory to make jewelry, piano keys, billiard balls, and other small items. From 1888 to 1892, the amount of ivory exported out of the Congo Free State exploded from 12,812 pounds to 261,225 pounds (Nelson, p. 56). In *Heart of Darkness*, finding and gathering ivory was the sole purpose of the Company. One of the story's characters, the enigmatic Kurtz, was by far the best ivory agent in the Company. He collected as much ivory as all the other agents put together.

> **KING LEOPOLD II'S SEARCH TO EXPAND BELGIUM**
>
> Surrounded by the sea, Holland, Prussia, and France, our frontiers can never be extended in Europe. It is far away that we must find compensation.... The sea bathes our coast, the universe lies in front of us, steam and electricity have made distances disappear, all the unappropriated lands on the surface of the globe may become the field of our operations and of our successes.
>
> (Gann and Duignan, p. 29)

A change in tactics. As the Belgians bought up increasing quantities of ivory, the decision was made to stop dealing with the African merchants. In 1892 King Leopold II declared that all natural resources in the Congo Free State were his property. The Belgians no longer needed to trade with the Africans; they could simply take what they wanted. The Belgians began to push deeper and farther into Africa in order to find new sources of ivory, setting up stations all along the Congo River. One of the furthermost stations was located at Stanley Falls, a site that was probably the inspiration for Kurtz's Inner Station in *Heart of Darkness*.

The Novella in Focus

The plot. The story begins on board a ship that is bound down the English river Thames. The ship sits still at anchor, in a calm wind, waiting for the turn of the tide so it can proceed on its journey. The passengers sit in the growing dark-

Heart of Darkness

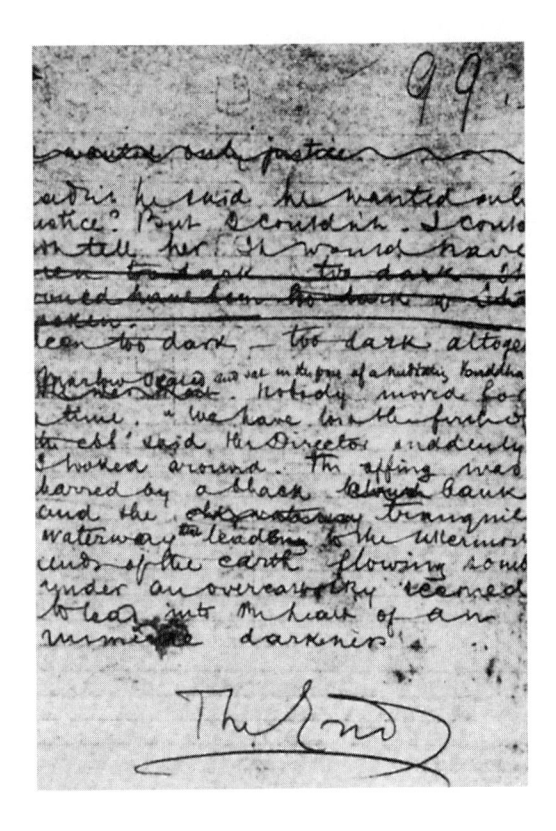

The concluding page of Conrad's manuscript of *Heart of Darkness*.

ness of the evening, waiting for the ship to set sail again. The narrator, who remains unidentified throughout the novel, thinks about all of the great adventurers and explorers of the past who have sailed down the Thames to the Atlantic Ocean, bound for strange, far-off locations. The narrator's thoughts are interrupted by a man named Marlow, described as a seaman and a wanderer. Marlow speaks of how the ancient Roman explorers must have felt as they sailed up the Thames for the first time, when England was still "one of the dark places of the earth" (*Heart of Darkness*, p. 5).

Marlow then proceeds to tell of his journeys to a place of darkness, the Belgian Congo. As a young boy, notes Marlow, he had looked at maps constantly, and had been most intrigued by the maps that were blank and unfinished. Marlow explains that he was drawn to the maps of Africa because the heart of Africa was completely blank—except for the Congo River, which wound all the way from the sea to the middle of the unexplored area. Marlow states that he made a vow to go there one day and discover what lay at the end of the Congo River.

After many years as a seaman, Marlow decides to seek employment with a Belgian company that trades in Africa. Through the influence of an aunt, Marlow is able to obtain command of a steamboat that will sail all the way up the Congo River. To reach the station where his boat is located, Marlow has to undertake a long journey up the Congo. He first stops at the Company Station, where he realizes that the Company's employees have no idea what they are doing. They dig and blast holes in the ground without purpose, and beat the African workers for no apparent reason.

In order to reach the next point of his journey, the Central Station, Marlow makes a long hike overland. When he finally reaches the Central Station, however, Marlow discovers that the steamboat he was supposed to command has sunk to the bottom of the river. In order to continue his journey, Marlow is forced to salvage and rebuild the boat, a daunting task that requires months to complete.

During his stay at the Central Station, Marlow meets the district manager, who complains about a man named Kurtz, a company employee who is stationed deep in the jungle all by himself. The manager disapproves of Kurtz, the most successful ivory agent in the entire company. Since he has not heard from Kurtz in a long time, the manager finally sails with Marlow up the Congo toward Kurtz's post after repairs to Marlow's vessel are completed. The Inner Station, which is where Kurtz is posted, lies in the center of the blankness that had first attracted Marlow to Africa; Marlow would come to call the place the "heart of darkness."

Progress is slow, but eventually Marlow's steamboat nears the Inner Station. The steamer is attacked by local Africans, who kill one of Marlow's workers. Marlow finally scares the attackers away with his steamboat whistle, then docks his boat. He meets a Russian traveler who reports that Kurtz is deathly ill. The Russian also informs Marlow that although Kurtz had aimed to educate the local Africans, the populace of the region had instead stripped him of his civilized ways. Kurtz had turned savage, killing others for ivory. In fact, he had gone so far as to surround his hut with the severed heads of his enemies.

Kurtz had ruthlessly conquered the local inhabitants, who came to view him as a god. Kurtz was also a dying man, however, and it turns out that he had actually ordered the attack on Marlow's boat in hopes that the white men would leave him to perish in the jungle. At last Marlow talks to Kurtz, who reveals that he is aware of

CONRAD'S MODELS FOR CHARACTERS AND PLACES IN *HEART OF DARKNESS*	
Name in the Story	**Real-life Counterpart**
The Company	Société Anonyme Belge pour le Commerce du Haut Congo (SAB)
Company Station	Station at Matadi
Central Station	Station at Kinshasa
Inner Station	Station at Kisangani (formerly Stanley Falls)
Marlow	Conrad himself
Kurtz	Georges Antoine Klein (an SAB agent at Stanley Falls)

how savage he has become. He entrusts Marlow with letters for his fianceé in Belgium and an article Kurtz had written that promotes the idea of educating the African people.

The district manager and Marlow move the dying Kurtz onto the steamer to take him back down the river. Kurtz dies on the trip, uttering in his last moments these final words to Marlow: "The horror! The horror!" (*Heart of Darkness*, p. 71). Marlow sees conviction and judgment in Kurtz's words, which haunt and terrify him. Out of respect to Kurtz, Marlow returns to Europe to inform Kurtz's fiancée of his death. When she asks what Kurtz's last words were, Marlow lies and tells her that Kurtz spent his last breath uttering her name.

How Marlow viewed the benefits of colonization. Even before leaving for the Congo River, Marlow viewed the objectives of the Company with suspicion. After receiving the offer of employment, Marlow visited the aunt who had secured the position for him. He commented sarcastically about his conversation with her:

> I was also one of the Workers.... Something like an emissary of light, something like a lower sort of apostle. There had been a lot of such rot let loose in print and talk just about that time.... She talked about 'weaning those ignorant millions from their horrid ways,' till, upon my word, she made me quite uncomfortable.
> (*Heart of Darkness*, p. 12)

Marlow realized the hypocrisy of the Company's stated mission to help the natives. In his first impression of the Company Station, Marlow saw that colonization had brought the Africans misery. At one point, taking refuge from the merciless heat, Marlow enters a horrible grove of trees. He describes the cost of colonization:

> Black shapes crouched, lay, sat between the trees, leaning against the trunks, clinging to the earth ... in all the attitudes of pain, abandonment, and despair.... The work was going on. The work! And this was the place where some of the helpers had withdrawn to die.
>
> They were dying slowly—it was very clear. They were not enemies, they were not criminals, they were nothing earthly now.... Brought from all recesses of the coast in all the legality of time contracts, lost in uncongenial surroundings, fed on unfamiliar food, they sickened, became inefficient, and were then allowed to crawl away and rest.
> (*Heart of Darkness*, p. 17)

Sources. Probably the single most important influence on *Heart of Darkness* was Conrad's firsthand impressions of the Congo region. In fact, some scholars see the character of Marlow as Conrad himself, in part because the novella's plot closely parallels Conrad's own experiences.

In 1890 Conrad secured a position with the Belgian SAB company as the captain of a steamboat. Like Marlow, Conrad was by profession a sailor. Also like Marlow, Conrad secured the job through the influence of an aunt. In *Heart of Darkness*, Marlow explains that the position had become available because the former captain, Fresleven, had been killed by a native. Conrad received his job for the same reason, and in fact the previous captain's name was Freiesleben. The course that Marlow described as he made his journey up the Congo River can be matched up exactly with Conrad's own trip up the river as documented in Conrad's diary.

Heart of Darkness

The Roi de Belges, Conrad's own steamboat in the Congo.

Conrad's mission was to evacuate a Company agent from Stanley Falls on the steamboat Roi de Belges. The agent, Georges Antoine Klein, was sick and needed treatment. But Klein died on the way back down the river. While historical evidence suggests that Klein was not an extraordinary man like the character of Kurtz, Conrad seemed to have had Klein in mind when he was writing. Conrad's first manuscript of Heart of Darkness originally used "Klein" as the name of the agent from the Inner Station, but Conrad subsequently crossed it out and replaced it with "Kurtz." Other possible real-life models for Kurtz include the ex-missionary Charles Stokes, who became a slave trader and gunrunner before being killed in the Congo. In fact, there were many real-life atrocities in this area under King Leopold's rule. Conrad read about these atrocities after returning to England, and they also influenced his story.

Events in History at the Time the Novella Was Written

The Congo atrocities. Leopold II's plans to found an African colony had gone well. In the years that followed, however, the Congo Free State was constantly on the verge of bankruptcy. In fact, Leopold II was forced to ask the Belgium Parliament to authorize loans to keep the colony from becoming a complete failure. The Congo Free State might have collapsed if it had not been for rubber harvested from the area; rubber trees became a source of great income for the colonists.

By 1901 the Congo Free State had finally established a profitable operation. The harvesting of the rubber trees required laborers, though. In order to meet the demand, all inhabitants of the Congo Basin were forced to work. Any village that refused to send its men was considered to be in revolt and could expect a raid by the military. During these punitive attacks, the troops often brutalized the villagers. In one case the Belgian troops—in order to prove that they had not wasted their rifle ammunition shooting game—severed the hands of all of their victims. In another case, a military commander by the name of Lieutenant Dom decorated his garden with human skulls. A letter by a critic of the Belgian colonial practices, Edmund Morel, describes the plight of a small native boy:

> The youth standing up, with both hands gone—Mola Ekuliti.... His town was attacked by soldiers of the Government post of Bikoro, in 1898, under the command of an officer whom I knew and often met.
>
> Several natives were killed, but Mola was tied up and taken away to the lake-side, where owing to the tightness of the thongs round his wrists, the flesh had swollen. The officer directed the thongs to be beaten off, but his soldiers translated that into beating off the hands—which they did with the butt end of their rifles against a tree. The officer was standing by drinking palm wine.
>
> (Morel, p. 378)

The end of Leopold II's Congo. Beginning in the late 1890s, complaints about the treatment of the natives began to surface. It is said that Leopold II agonized over the reports and immediately ordered that all abuses should cease. Nevertheless, he did nothing to ensure that his directives were followed, and the administrators in the Congo Free State simply ignored the decrees. At the turn of the century, international pressure began to build from groups in England. Yet Leopold II, and even the Belgian people, paid the protesters no heed. It was felt that the English could not comment objectively on events in the Congo because they were interested in the region themselves.

Still, the tales of horror continued until 1908, when, finally, the Belgian Parliament sent its own review board to the Congo to investigate the allegations. They found them all to be true. Heeding the popular outcry, Leopold II turned control of the Congo Free State over to the Belgian Parliament. It took the Belgian government only five years to eliminate the savage abuses that had afflicted the Congo for decades.

The turning point in Conrad's life. Since his teens, Joseph Conrad had been a sailor by profession. He had first served on French ships, but then sought employment on a British vessel in order to secure English citizenship. Between his times at sea, Conrad lived a troubled life. He was constantly in debt, and he frequently asked his wealthy uncle for money. His uncle granted these requests time and time again, albeit grudgingly. Conrad also suffered from emotional instabilities. In 1878 he apparently tried to commit suicide by shooting himself in the chest. Conrad's explanation was that he was wounded in a duel, but even his closest friend did not believe this to be true. This event suggests that he wrestled with some inner darkness of his own.

Conrad's life continued on its uneven course until 1889, the year he began to write his first novel. He began also to search for employment in the Congo, which he secured in 1890. Conrad signed a contract for three years of service in the Congo Free State as the captain of a river steamboat. But he was forced to return home after only six months because of illness, victimized by the unhealthy conditions that apparently struck many employees. Before arriving in Africa, Conrad had confessed: "What makes me rather uneasy is the information that 60 percent of our Company's employés return to Europe before they have completed even six months' service. Fever and dysentery!" (Conrad in Sherry, p. 24).

The illness that Conrad acquired in Africa stayed with him until the end of his life. Strangely, many scholars see that fact as fortunate. Conrad was forced to settle down as a result of his illness. Once he did so, he began to write seriously. In the decade after returning from Africa, Conrad established himself as an important novelist and writer. *Heart of Darkness,* written at the end of that decade, is considered by literary scholars to be some of Conrad's finest writing.

Reception. Some of the earliest English reviews of "Heart of Darkness" appeared in response to its 1902 publication in Conrad's *Youth: A Narrative; and Two Other Stories.* Of the volume's three stories ("Youth," "Heart of Darkness," and "The End of the Tether"), "Heart of Darkness" won high praise for its portrayal of the demoralizing effect that living in the wilderness supposedly had on European white men. Others before Conrad, said Hugh Clifford in *The Spectator* (November 29, 1902), had written of the European's decline in a "barbaric" wilderness, but never "has any writer till now succeeded in bringing ... it all home to sheltered folk as does Mr. Conrad in this wonderful, this magnificent, this terrible study" (Clifford in Dean, pp. 144-45). Another critic called the story "unconvincing" even if the prose was "brilliant" (Masefield in Dean, p. 148). But a third critic described it as an "enthralling" tale, a "masterly analysis of two Continents in conflict," and "the high-water mark of the author's talent" (Garnett in Dean, p. 145-46).

For More Information

Brantlinger, Patrick. *Rule of Darkness: British Literature and Imperialism, 1830-1914.* Ithaca, N.Y.: Cornell, 1988.

Conrad, Joseph. *Heart of Darkness.* Edited by Robert Kimbrough. New York: W. W. Norton, 1971.

Davidson, Basil. *African Kingdoms.* New York: Time-Life Books, 1966.

Dean, Leonard F., ed. *Joseph Conrad's Heart of Darkness: Backgrounds and Criticisms.* Englewood Cliffs, N.J.: Prentice-Hall, 1960.

Gann, L. H., and Peter Duignan. *The Rulers of Belgian Africa, 1884-1914.* Princeton, N.J.: Princeton University Press, 1979.

Morel, Edmund. *King Leopold's Rule in Africa.* London: W. Heinemann, 1904.

Nelson, Samuel H. *Colonialism in the Congo Basin, 1880-1940.* Athens: Ohio University Center for International Studies, 1994.

Sherry, Norman. *Conrad's Western World.* London: Cambridge University Press, 1971.

The Hound of the Baskervilles

by
Arthur Conan Doyle

~

Arthur Conan Doyle was born in Edinburgh, Scotland, in 1859. He began his career as an eye doctor, writing in his spare time to supplement the mediocre income from his struggling practice. Doyle's first Sherlock Holmes story, *A Study in Scarlet*, was published in 1887, and the publication of *The Sign of Four* in 1890 solidified the character's popularity with the reading public and launched Doyle's rise to fame as a writer. Other Sherlock Holmes stories followed until 1893. The publication of *The Hound of the Baskervilles* in 1901 marked the return of Sherlock Holmes after an absence of eight years, a period in which Doyle focused on other literary endeavors. Many consider it the best of the Sherlock Holmes stories.

THE LITERARY WORK

A novel set in London, England, and on the moors surrounding Baskerville Hall in Dartmoor, England, in 1889; published in 1901-1902.

SYNOPSIS

Sherlock Holmes, London's foremost detective, and his assistant, Dr. Watson, investigate the mysterious death of Sir Henry Baskerville, a wealthy landowner, who is believed to be a victim of a deadly curse that hangs over the Baskerville family.

Events in History at the Time the Novel Takes Place

The later Victorian era. The ascension of Queen Victoria to the English throne in 1837 marked the beginning of the Victorian Age in England. Lasting until her death in 1901, the period saw remarkable developments in society, industry, agriculture, religion, and politics. During the first thirty years of Victoria's reign, the popular belief was that these changes all signaled progress and improvement. By the late 1860s, however, confidence in this progress had begun to weaken. Foreign economic and political competition intensified, and it seemed to foster a sense that British influence and power was in decline. Some of this new competition came from the United States, where the Industrial Revolution proceeded apace after the Civil War, producing goods and harnessing resources on such a scale that the U.S. was soon a formidable international economic power. In Europe, Otto Bismarck's unification of the German Empire created another rival. Lastly, a severe economic depression began to weaken Britain's agriculture and industry beginning in the 1870s.

Victorian England's social stratification was perhaps one of the most interesting aspects of the age. The Victorians made clear social and economic divisions between the classes. Railway cars were divided into three different classes of accommodation; seating in churches was segregated into rented pews for the upper classes and free pews for the poor; even drinking establishments were divided into public and private bars.

Many scholars attribute this separation to the Industrial Revolution. Prior to industrialism, society had derived its structure from the ownership of land and the assumed existence of a God-given hierarchy. Linked together, everyone fulfilled whatever function they were responsible for within this communal existence. The emergence of the industrial movement began immediately to separate individuals by creating a constantly changing system of employment that was not based on the land. The rise of the middle class and creation of an enormous working class further separated society.

In *The Hound of the Baskervilles,* Doyle seems to take into account this new social stratification with his characterization of Henry Baskerville. The young Baskerville heir is more the landed gentleman of the past than the stuffy Victorian gentleman of Doyle's time. Even the setting of the novel, the remote and desolate moors, seems chosen to represent the past as it existed before the rise of urban society.

Rise of the detectives. The industrial age and the increasing urbanization that came as a result brought with it a marked increase in all types of criminal activity. Among the many reasons for this sharp increase in crime were the new anonymity that cities offered to their inhabitants and the desperation of the ever-growing number of the extremely poor city dwellers. In London, the number of robberies increased rapidly, and murders also mounted at an alarming rate. Most people believed that the city's magistrates were incapable of preventing further increases in crime.

Finally, in London in December 1811 an incident occurred that served as a tragic turning point in the rising crime epidemic. A family of four died at the hands of a brutal murderer. The city was horrified and the inept police force, which at this time consisted of a loosely organized group of low-paid watchmen known as the Bow Street Runners, scrambled to find the killer. The efforts of the "Runners" proved too slow; on the night of December 19th, the murderer struck again, killing a tavernkeeper, his wife, and their servant. Based on the testimony of several witnesses, a seaman named John Williams was apprehended for the murders; he hung himself in prison the same night. Despite the capture of the killer, there was a strong outcry from the people of London against the judicial authorities and the existing police body. Londoners demanded re-

Arthur Conan Doyle

organization of the night watch system and the formation of an enlarged police body.

Various plans for police reform made their way through the political system over the next twenty years, but most suggested only slight changes. Finally, in 1829, Robert Peel, at this time England's Leader of the House of Commons, proposed and gained support for his Police Bill. Its main focus was the creation of an Office of Police to whose authority every district police station would answer. This central Office of Police would be the Whitehall Division headquarters, which would soon become known as "Scotland Yard," after the name of the street it faced. (This name can, in turn, be traced back to the location's having once been the site of a twelfth-century palace used to house visiting royalty from Scotland.) The officers of this first centralized police force, known as "Peelers" after their founder, gained widespread approval. With the establishment of this law-enforcement body, the path was open for the introduction of a new type of professional—the detective—into nineteenth-century England.

After a serious jewel robbery in 1841, Police Orders requested "an active intelligent man in each Division" (Browne, p. 113), whose duty it

Hound of the Baskervilles

was to trace stolen property. These "active" and "intelligent" men would become England's first detectives. In 1842, after a rise in murders and a series of threats on Queen Victoria's life, an experimental Detective Force was formed. Beginning in 1842 with only six men, this Detective Force had grown to almost eight hundred men by the 1880s, when Doyle created the Sherlock Holmes character. Though Holmes is a "consulting detective" and not a member of Scotland Yard, he seeks aid from members of the "Yard" in many of his cases. In *The Hound of the Baskervilles*, the policeman Lestrade who appears at the end of the novel is a member of Scotland Yard. The rise of the police and the detective force in England and the subsequent interest of the public in the actions of these men undoubtedly influenced Doyle's creation of his famous sleuth.

JACK THE RIPPER

Just a few months after the publication of Doyle's first Sherlock Holmes mystery, London's police force was scrambling to solve its own mystery, the brutal murder of a prostitute in the Whitechapel district. In the next few months, four more prostitutes would be found murdered and similar gruesome details in all the cases would show the killings to be the work of a single murderer. Newspapers roused public fear and fascination with the murders all over the country, and the police force suffered sharp criticism for its inability to apprehend the killer. People speculated that the perpetrator was a privileged member of society and for this reason was not being arrested; numerous public figures were rumored to be responsible for the murders. Called Jack the Ripper after some of the purported letters he sent to the press, his identity was never uncovered.

The British Empire. British claims in foreign lands were stimulated by an interest in the profitable trade of tropical commodities. Known as "an empire upon which the sun never sets" because of its global reach, Britain in 1871 had a population of 235 million people spread across five continents. Vast numbers of British citizens emigrated to the colonies of the empire for various reasons: to find a more pleasant climate, to make their fortune, or to escape disgrace or criminal prosecution at home. In *The Hound of the Baskervilles*, it is the desire for wealth that prompts Sir Charles Baskerville to travel to the goldfields of South Africa, while his brother, fearing criminal prosecution, emigrates to Central America because his actions had made England "too hot to hold him" (Doyle, *The Hound of the Baskervilles*, p. 16). Between 1871 and the end of the century, almost 2 million emigrants departed from the British Isles. In its colonies in Africa, India, and Hong Kong, the ruling British were greatly outnumbered by the indigenous populations; as one writer noted, "the success of white rule in many remote spots depended heavily upon strength of character and bluff" (Read, p. 190). With the remarkable spread of the British Empire came the development of a sense of superiority for the English, who regarded themselves as far more advanced than the natives of the colonies they governed. This superior attitude, while not presented in racist terms, appears in *The Hound of the Baskervilles* in Watson's descriptions of Henry Baskerville and in Baskerville's attachment to his ancestral lands.

The Novel in Focus

The plot. The story begins when a discussion between Sherlock Holmes, England's most famous detective, and his assistant, Dr. John Watson, is interrupted by the appearance of Dr. James Mortimer. Mortimer enlists the aid of Holmes to discover the murderer of his friend Sir Charles Baskerville, whose body was found unmarked except for the expression of incomprehensible terror on its face. Mortimer tells Holmes and Watson of the Baskerville family curse, which he feels may play a part in the murder.

According to the legend of the curse, one of the Baskerville ancestors made a pact with the devil to wreak revenge on a young maiden who escaped his advances. The agreement entailed Baskerville's overtaking the girl and killing her for revenge; in return, the devil would be allowed to claim Baskerville by setting loose a monstrous hound on him. This hound was to haunt every descendant of the Baskerville family, a part of the curse that interests Mortimer because the imprint of a massive paw was found near the corpse of Charles Baskerville.

Intrigued by the details of the case, Holmes agrees to meet with the heir to the Baskerville fortune, Henry Baskerville, who has just arrived from America. After meeting him, the detective agrees to help solve the murder and to determine if there is any danger for the new heir, but because he has another urgent case, he must send Watson to Baskerville Hall in his place. When Mortimer and Baskerville leave, Holmes and Watson follow and observe that someone else is also following Baskerville. Arriving at Baskerville's hotel later, they question Dr. Mortimer and Sir Henry about the man they saw tailing them and learn that he resembles Barrymore, the butler of the late Sir Charles. Watson then leaves with Dr. Mortimer and Sir Henry. Arriving at the edge of the moor, they are surprised to find soldiers looking for an escaped convict in the area.

Baskerville Hall is old and gloomy, and during Watson's first night there he hears the sobs of a woman crying in the house. The next morning, Watson meets Mrs. Barrymore, the butler's wife, and it is obvious that she is the woman who was crying the night before. Watson also meets Stapleton, a naturalist who hunts butterflies on the moor; Stapleton points out the Grimpen Mire, a treacherous swamp of thick vegetation and quicksand pits. Stapleton chases a butterfly off across the moor, and in his absence, his sister Beryl approaches Watson and tells him to leave the moor and go back to London. She stops this discussion as her brother returns and it becomes apparent that she has mistaken Watson for Sir Henry. Watson confronts her later that day on the moor, but she will say nothing further of their previous discussion.

Sir Henry meets Beryl and feels a romantic attraction to her. Another curious development is the behavior of the butler, Barrymore, whom Watson observes staring out at the moor and signaling from a window of the house in the middle of the night. When Watson and Sir Henry catch him in the act, he refuses to explain, but Mrs. Barrymore arrives and explains that her husband was signaling to her brother, who is the escaped convict being pursued by the soldiers. Watson and Sir Henry go out on the moor to catch the fugitive, whose name is Selden, but fail to capture him. In the darkness they hear the cry of a hound, and as they leave the moor they see on a distant hilltop the silhouette of a man who does not seem to be Selden.

Following this incident, Barrymore tells Watson that Sir Charles had gone to meet a woman on the night that he died. Watson determines from the burnt scrap of a letter that the woman in question is a Mrs. Laura Lyons, the daughter of a neighbor. Watson questions Mrs. Lyons, who admits contacting Sir Charles but denies any wrongdoing. Accepting her story, Watson learns through further investigations about the suspicious activity of a young boy who carries a parcel of food onto the moor every day.

Watson follows the boy and discovers a crude camp located in some ancient stone huts. Assuming the camp to be the hiding place of Selden, Watson waits, pistol in hand, for the return of the murderer; instead he is greeted by Sherlock Holmes.

Holmes was the man silhouetted on the hilltop and has been living in the camp for the entire duration of Watson's visit, receiving food from the boy each day. Holmes tells Watson that the Stapletons are actually man and wife, not brother and sister. He also discloses that Laura Lyons is planning a divorce from her husband, and intends to marry Stapleton, whom she believes to be unmarried. As Holmes tells Watson that he believes Stapleton figures prominently in the murder of Sir Charles, they hear a scream and the cry of a hound. They run toward the cry and find the body of a man who has fallen off a cliff in panic. His clothes identify him as Sir Henry, but a closer examination reveals him to be Selden, the escaped convict. As the detectives study the body, Stapleton appears, saying that he also heard the cries and came to help.

Back at Baskerville Hall, Holmes notices the stunning resemblance of a figure in a family portrait with Stapleton, concluding that Stapleton is a Baskerville. Holmes summons officer Lestrade from London and sets a trap for Stapleton by telling everyone that he and Watson are returning to London. Then Holmes calls on Mrs. Lyons and tells her that Stapleton is married. In her anger, Mrs. Lyons tells Holmes that Stapleton, promising her marriage, urged her to arrange the meeting with Sir Charles to ask for financial assistance for her divorce. Once she made the appointment, Stapleton asked her not to keep it.

After hearing this information, Holmes gathers Watson and Lestrade and they prepare to spend an evening on the moor. They wait in the dark outside Stapleton's home, where Sir Henry has been invited for dinner, and from which, on Holmes's advice, Sir Henry intends to walk home. Finally, they hear the sound of a running dog, and Sir Henry bursts through the fog of the moor pursued by a monstrous hound. Holmes empties his revolver at the animal, and the dog, which falls dead, is not the supernatural demon of the legend, but simply a very large dog whose jaws have been painted with phosphorous to give it a ghostly appearance. At Stapleton's, Holmes finds Beryl Stapleton tied up and beaten; her husband has left her there and escaped into the

Hound of the Baskervilles

Jeremy Brett as Holmes and Edward Hardwicke as Watson.

Grimpen Mire. The next day, Holmes and Watson search the mire and find the pen that housed the dog, but not Stapleton, whom, they believe, must have lost his way in the darkness and fallen into the treacherous quicksand.

In the final chapter, Holmes explains the case. He had discovered that Stapleton was in fact Rodger Baskerville, the son of Sir Charles's brother. Rodger Baskerville, alias Stapleton, set out to make the family estate his own by getting rid of the two heirs who preceded him—Sir Charles and Sir Henry. Having learned of the Baskerville curse, Stapleton imported a gigantic dog from France and kept it hidden in the mire. Luring Sir Charles out on the pretext of meeting Laura Lyons, Stapleton painted the dog's face with phosphorous and set the animal loose on Sir Charles, who died of a heart attack when he saw the frightening beast. Stapleton later gave the dog Sir Henry's scent from a stolen boot. He had allowed the romance between his wife and Sir Henry to flourish in the hope that Sir Henry's frequent visits would place him on the moor alone, where it could be made to look like he also perished from the curse.

Nationalism in *The Hound of the Baskervilles*. In Watson's description of Sir Henry Baskerville, Arthur Conan Doyle presents details that illustrate his own nationalistic tendencies and idealistic perception of his country. Upon their arrival at Baskerville Hall, Watson describes Sir Henry's reaction to first seeing his ancestral home, "I read upon his eager face how much it meant to him, this first sight of that strange spot where the men of his blood had held sway so long and left their mark so deep" (*The Hound of the Baskervilles,* p. 39). Watson further describes Sir Henry: "as I looked at his dark and expressive face I felt more than ever how true a descendant he was of that long line of high-blooded, fiery, and masterful men" (*The Hound of the Baskervilles,* p. 39). Through Watson's descriptions, Doyle seems to express his own support of the rights and status of the English aristocracy. This sentiment reflects a position taken by many in the Victorian period, with its growing multitudes of nouveau-riche industrialists who had no connection to the landed nobility. Doyle's mother and father were both extremely interested in their forebears and claimed to be descended from higher-born ancestry, despite their lower middle-class existence. Perhaps influenced by this and by the nostalgia that some Victorians felt for a social structure that was quickly fading in their industrial age, Doyle incorporates elements of England's great national heritage into his story. He weaves this heritage into the character of Sir Henry, and by so doing expresses some regret at the drastic changes affecting his own nineteenth-century England.

Sources. A wide variety of sources influenced Doyle's creation of Sherlock Holmes, not the least of which were Edgar Allan Poe's mystery stories centered around the detective-genius Dupin: "The Murders in the Rue Morgue," "The Mystery of Marie Roget," and "The Purloined Letter." Doyle said of Poe's stories, "each is a root from which a whole literature has developed" (Paul, p. 33).

Sherlock Holmes has many similarities to Poe's Dupin; Dupin's discerning eye and careful reasoning along with his eccentric character are all features that found their way into the Holmes persona. However, Doyle gives credit to Dr. Joseph Bell for being the actual model for Sherlock Holmes. Doyle studied under Dr. Bell at medical school, where Bell's reputation for being a keen and skilled observer was well known among the students. His reputation for these qualities was so great among his former pupils that when the Sherlock Holmes stories became famous, some past students believed they recognized Dr. Bell as the model, and Doyle acknowledged that it was indeed true.

Doyle once related a story concerning Dr. Bell in which the professor, after studying a patient in front of his class, deduced that the man had served in the army in a Highland regiment, was a recently discharged noncommissioned officer, and had been stationed in the West Indies in Barbados. Every detail proved to be true. Bell explained to his class the reasoning behind his hypotheses. The man was respectful but did not remove his hat. They do not remove their hats in the army, and a man recently discharged would likely retain this habit. The man possessed an air of authority and appeared to be Scottish. Finally, the man's illness was Elephantiasis, which is a West Indian ailment. Bell's astute reasoning contains many similarities with Holmes's clever techniques of detection.

The character of Watson resembles Doyle himself in many ways, but also exhibits similarities to a real-life Dr. James Watson, who was known to Doyle.

The setting and story for *The Hound of the Baskervilles* originated from a folktale told by a shipmate of Doyle's on a voyage. The man, who was from the area of Dartmoor, told the story of a devil hound that supposedly haunted the desolate moors of the area. Doyle initially intended to work the story into a novel that did not in-

Hound of the Baskervilles

volve Sherlock Holmes, but after developing much of his tale, found that it provided the perfect background for a Holmes adventure and added the detective and his friend Watson to the narrative.

Events in History at the Time the Novel Was Written

Doyle and divorce reform. Much like the famous detective in his novels, Doyle at several points in his life took up the cause of victims of injustice and oppression. Because of the great fame of his Sherlock Holmes character, Doyle was constantly bombarded by requests from people to help solve crimes and to prove the innocence of prisoners unjustly condemned. Though he had no real detective experience, Doyle did actually prove the innocence of one man who was unjustly accused of a crime, but more often he gave his attention to the social issues of his era. One of the causes which he supported was the reform of the divorce laws.

THE HOUND OF THE BASKERVILLES AND OTHER HOLMES STORIES

Doyle's Sherlock Holmes stories first appeared in the British magazine *The Strand*, which released three sets of short stories and one novel about the famous fictional detective in the following order:

The Adventures of Sherlock Holmes—Twelve short stories appearing from July 1891 to December 1892

The Memoirs of Sherlock Holmes—Published as additional episodes of *The Adventures of Sherlock Holmes;* twelve short stories appearing from December 1892 to November 1893

The Hound of the Baskervilles—A novel published in installments from August 1901 to April 1902

The Return of Sherlock Holmes—Thirteen final short stories appearing from October 1903 to January 1905

The divorce laws enacted in Britain were biased toward the husband. A man could get a divorce merely on the grounds of the infidelity of a wife, but for a woman to obtain a legal divorce, adultery had to be coupled with another wrong, preferably brutality. When circumstances of brutality did exist, the cost of divorce was approximately £700, an incredible amount of money at a time when the average middle-class income was about £400 a year. Brutality and the high cost of divorce are both incorporated by Doyle into *The Hound of the Baskervilles*. It is Mrs. Lyon's desire for a divorce that prompts her to seek financial assistance from Sir Charles. Mrs. Stapleton also is interested in a divorce, but is essentially held prisoner by her husband, who also assaults her, as Sherlock Holmes later discovers. Doyle's use of these themes in his novel shows his strong interest in the subject, and it is not surprising that the writer went on to become president of a society for the reform of the divorce law in 1906. Doyle was also responsible for writing the pamphlet *Divorce Law Reform,* which was influential in the formation of a Royal Commission that began examining the divorce law in 1912.

Popularity of *The Hound of the Baskervilles*. Because it had been eight years since the publication of the last Sherlock Holmes story, Doyle felt that the attitudes of readers might have changed and worried about the reception *The Hound of the Baskervilles* would receive. His fears proved groundless; the reaction to the novel was more positive than he might have hoped. The circulation of *The Strand,* the magazine that carried the serialization of the novel, increased by thirty thousand copies an issue, and people lined up all over London to buy the ones that carried his installments.

A review in another English magazine, *Punch* (April 23, 1902), acknowledged the weirdly imaginative quality of the novel, going on to say that the highest compliment it could pay the book was that the chapter of explanation at the end was the most disappointing one: "The trail is so cleverly laid, incident so generously supplied, and the thing kept going at such a breathless pace, that when the enchanted reader is, as necessarily he must be, dumped down on the common asphalted, unsympathetic earth, a feeling of dissatisfaction steals o'er the mind " (Baron de B.-W. in *Punch,* p. 294).

For More Information

Browne, Douglas G. *The Rise of Scotland Yard.* London: George G. Harrap, 1956.

Cox, Don Richard. *Arthur Conan Doyle.* New York: Frederick Ungar, 1985.

Doyle, Arthur Conan. *The Hound of the Baskervilles.* New York: Dover, 1994.

Paul, Robert S. *Sherlock Holmes: Detective Fiction,*

Popular Theology, and Society. Edwardsville: Southern Illinois University Press, 1991.

Read, Donald. *England 1868-1914: The Age of Urban Democracy*. London: Longman Group, 1979.

Review of *The Hound of the Baskervilles*. *Punch* 122 (April 23, 1902): 294.

Rumbelow, Donald. *Jack the Ripper: The Complete Casebook*. Chicago: Contemporary Books, 1988.

Shanley, Mary Lyndon. *Feminism, Marriage, and the Law in Victorian England*. Princeton, N.J.: Princeton University Press, 1989.

"I Will Fight No More Forever"

by
Chief Joseph

~

Born in Oregon in 1840, Chief Joseph belonged to a Nez Percé band—the white man's name for an Indian tribe that preferred to call itself *Numipu* (meaning "We People"). Joseph grew up in their home territory of the Northwest, becoming a chief when his father passed away in 1871. By then the tribe had split into two factions, its bands differing over their willingness to engage in treaty-making with the whites. Chief Joseph rose to leadership of the renegade bands, who traveled 1,500 miles to escape the dictates of the whites and nearly succeeded. Defeated on the last leg of flight, Joseph issued a surrender statement that conveyed his people's resignation and despair.

> **THE LITERARY WORK**
>
> A statement of surrender made in Montana by Chief Joseph of the Nez Percé to army officer Nelson Miles on October 5, 1877.
>
> **SYNOPSIS**
>
> Resisting a U.S. government order to move to a reservation, the Nez Percé tribe evaded U.S. troops for 1,500 miles. When the tribe finally succumbed to fatigue, sickness, and the relentless pursuit of the troops, their leader, Chief Joseph, ended the chase with a statement of surrender.

Events in History at the Time of the Statement

Territory. The traditional territory of the Nez Percé fell between the forty-fifth and forty-seventh latitude parallels on the North and South, the Bitterroot Mountains to the east, and the Blue Mountains to the west. This area is the region where present-day Washington, Oregon, and Idaho meet. In 1805, when the white explorers Meriwether Lewis and William Clark met the Nez Percé, the tribe had about six thousand members who lived in 130 villages, each housing from ten to seventy-five villagers. This population decreased over the next decades as whites moved west and began to mine the untapped minerals of the mountains.

In 1871 Hinmaton-Yalatkit (Thunder-Traveling-to-Loftier-Mountain-Heights), known also as Joseph, became chief of the Nez Percé band known as the Wallowas. Their village was located in the Wallowa Valley in what is now eastern Oregon. It was a lush country, with hills and mountains surrounding grassy fields, and the village sat at the meeting place of two rivers. Ancestors of the Nez Percé had been buried on this land, and Joseph's father had vowed never to sell it, a promise renewed by his son when he became chief.

Other Nez Percé communities were spread around the territory as well. The villages of chiefs Peopeo Kiskiok (White Bird), Ippakness Wayhayken (Looking Glass), and Toohoolhoolzote (Sound) were neighbors of Joseph's community; eventually all would join him in defending Nez Percé lands.

Nez Percé lifestyle. As one tribal member recalled, "we were raising horses and cattle—fast race horses and many cattle. We had fine lodges, good clothes, plenty to eat, enough of everything. We were living well [before the whites arrived]" (McWhorter, *Yellow Wolf,* p. 35). Time was spent fishing the rivers, traveling to Montana in pursuit of buffaloes, and racing horses for sport.

The Nez Percé placed high value on the right to live as one believed best. They were governed by chiefs, but these men ruled in a democratic style, holding councils before making decisions. The young learned from their elders, who told legends of spirits that lived in the world and recounted the histories of great leaders and relations. Extended families grew up together, and it was in this environment that young boys acquired the skills they would need to become big game hunters and warriors, while young women learned to hunt smaller game and take care of the village.

The Nez Percé were alternately allies and enemies with their American Indian neighbors. No lasting peace or alliance existed between the nations; an alliance with a certain group one season might become a bitter rivalry by the next snow.

Religion. The Nez Percé believed that *Hunyahwat,* the all-powerful being in their religion, had created the world with peace as the primary objective. Furthermore, the creator had made the earth for everything that lived upon it, a belief that inspired the Nez Percé to treat the country with respect. They took no more game than necessary, and carefully used every part of an animal once they had killed it.

The afterlife was thought to be a place of even greater peace. Nez Percé myths claimed that after a member of their community died, spiritual animals would present themselves to the dead. Should the deceased want venison, a deer would appear and the dead could cut off any appetizing part. The spirit deer would not be harmed.

After whites came and destroyed the Nez Percé lifestyle, many members of the tribe who believed in Hunyahwat expected a messiah to come and resurrect all their deceased ancestors, marshaling a powerful band to fight back against the intruders. This belief inspired them to resist white ways, continuing instead to live as their fathers had, hoping for spiritual intervention.

Wyakin. The Nez Percé believed in immortality. Hunyahwat had filled the earth with the spirits of animals, plants, and humans, which could empower and possess the living Nez Percé. Such power was gained during youth as a rite of passage to adulthood.

In accordance with Nez Percé beliefs, each child of the tribe needed to set out from the village on a solitary trek. This journey was undertaken when the child was between the ages of eight and thirteen. The child would spend a night or many nights alone in meditation until a spirit arrived. The spirit might make its presence known by feeling, voice, or vision. After its visit, the spirit then became the child's guardian. Upon receiving the spirit, the child returned toward the village and lost consciousness near the outskirts. A shaman, or spiritual doctor, nursed the child back to health. From then on, the child was known by the name of the spirit encountered on his or her journey.

It was thought that *Wyakin,* the spiritual force, could help in situations requiring extraordinary ability. Many Wounds, a Nez Percé interpreter with great knowledge of his native religion, compared it to the white man's religious beliefs: "You have faith, and ask maybe some saint to help with something where you are probably stalled. It is the same way climbing a mountain. You ask Wyakin to help you" (McWhorter, *Yellow Wolf,* p. 296).

LEWIS AND CLARK ENCOUNTER THE NEZ PERCÉ

The Lewis and Clark expedition was on the verge of collapse when it encountered the Nez Percé tribe, who provided the explorers with food and shelter. The whites found them to be peaceful, helpful, and resourceful, but these characteristics would not prevent them from suffering a dismal fate later in the century.

Missionaries. In September 1834, the Methodist minister Jason Lee became the first white preacher in the Northwest. He was followed in September 1836 by Marcus Whitman and Henry Harmon Spalding, two Presbyterian ministers. Whitman and Spalding began dealing with the Nez Percé and exerted great influence on them. Spalding baptized Joseph's father.

According to biblical readings, God appeared to be more powerful than Hunyahwat. The Bible referred to three domains: heaven, earth, and hell. For the Nez Percé, there were only two domains, heaven and earth. Hunyahwat only created good places. Because the whites' Christian religion also had a place for evil, the Nez Percé

"I Will Fight No More"

General Oliver Howard and Chief Joseph.

considered the God of the whites to be stronger and more vindictive than their own.

According to what they called God's ideals, the Christian ministers created a written law for the whites and Nez Percé. All criminals were supposed to receive equal punishment, but justice was unevenly doled out under the law. As one historian noted, "whites guilty of horse and cattle stealing, fence burning, rape, assault, fraud, and various other crimes were in little danger as long as their accusers were Indians" (Haines, p. 183).

The treaties of 1855 and 1863. The U.S. government and the Nez Percé entered into a treaty in 1855 at Walla Walla, Washington. This treaty allotted five thousand square miles of their customary territory to the Nez Percé, and promised them financial aid. Supported by overwhelming resources, the U.S. government had the power to make these arrangements even though they did not yet own the Nez Percé lands. The treaty was signed in good faith by fifty-six Nez Percé chiefs.

Eight years later, in 1863, the U.S. government decided that more land was needed. Government representatives reopened negotiations and offered the Nez Percé less than six hundred square miles of territory plus some minor financial compensation. Chief Lawyer, respected as the head chief of the Nez Percé, feared the power of the newcomers. He offered to forfeit the northern territories originally guaranteed in 1855. His decision was not agreed upon by all chiefs, though, and the once-united tribe split into two groups—the "Treaty Nez Percé" and the "Non-Treaty Nez Percé." Old Chief Joseph, Chief Joseph's father, was one of the leaders who refused to sign. He died in 1871, passing his chieftainship to his son. Meanwhile, hostilities between whites and Nez Percé mounted as greater numbers of settlers and prospectors entered the homeland of the Non-Treaty Nez Percé.

Soon after Joseph had become chief, U.S. government officials ordered him to relocate his people to the Lapwai reservation in Idaho. Joseph refused, petitioning President Ulysses S. Grant to allow his people to stay in the Wallowa Valley. The President issued an executive order in 1873 supporting Joseph's right to stay there. When gold was discovered in the area, however, and whites began to claim that the Nez Percé were a threat to peace there, Grant sent General Oliver Otis Howard, a Civil War veteran, to force the tribe out of the valley within thirty days. Joseph concluded that they had no choice but to move, and the Nez Percé began the difficult journey to Lapwai.

The spark. On June 15, 1877, Wahlitits (Springtime Ice), a young and powerful Nez Percé, went raiding with his cousins Sarpsis Ilppilp (Red Moccasin Tops) and Wetyetmas Wahyakt (Swan

Necklace). They sought a prospector, Larry Ott, who had killed Wahlitit's father. Unable to find their intended victim, they slaughtered several other miners who had wronged the Nez Percé. Four men were killed, while another man was wounded. After returning to their encampment at Rocky Canyon, the raiders were joined in their manhunt by seventeen more warriors. A number of settlers (variously estimated as between eight and twenty-two) were killed. Chief Joseph moved the tribe onward, to White Bird Canyon.

Thirty Nez Percé had been killed by whites since 1863, and the warriors felt that they were avenging these deaths, but the U.S. government condemned them for the violent spree. Chief Joseph's reaction registered his dismay at both sides:

> I would have given my life if I could have undone the killing of white men by my people. I blame my young men and I blame the white man.... My friends among the white man have blamed me for the war. I am not to blame. When my young men began the killing my heart was hurt. Although I did not justify them, I remembered all the insults I had endured, and my blood was on fire. Still I would have taken my people to the buffalo country without fighting if possible.
> (Joseph in Beal, p. 49)

Retribution. On June 17, 1877, ninety-nine U.S. cavalry men descended from the mountains surrounding White Bird Canyon in Idaho and began an attack on the Indian group, only to find themselves surrounded by entrenched Nez Percé marksmen and warriors. The U.S. troops fired at a Nez Percé peace party carrying a white flag, and a devastating counterattack by the Nez Percé followed. The army quickly retreated, leaving thirty-four dead on the battlefield. Only three Nez Pereé were injured in the fight.

Shortly afterward, a raid involving government soldiers was conducted on the village of Chief Looking Glass. This band had avoided other confrontations, asking only to be left alone. The band fled the village when attacked, and their homes were subsequently burned. Thereafter, Looking Glass's band joined with the other Nez Percé for protection.

Unification of the Non-Treaty Nez Percé was thus achieved. By this time, the total number in the united bands had reached about eight hundred. As the army indiscriminately attacked Nez Percé villages, the chiefs came together and made plans to try and secure safety for their people. They began an escape toward the east, across the Bitterroot Mountains, in an attempt to reach peaceful territory. The U.S. government, furious at the loss of some of its soldiers and at the stubbornness of the Nez Percé people, assigned General Howard to chase the Nez Percé.

The flight. General Howard, known to the Nez Percé as General One-Arm (he had lost an arm in the Civil War), also became known as General Day-After-Tomorrow because he was almost always that far behind in the chase. He was not, however, the only soldier involved in catching the Nez Percé. By using telegraphs and messengers, the U.S. Army involved various commanders occupying points along the escape route.

After a battle at the Clearwater River (in present-day Idaho), the Nez Percé struck out across the Lolo Trail, a perilous route through the Bitterroot Mountains. They had about three thousand horses to aid them in their journey, but were slowed by the sheer size of their group. The band was composed of entire villages of people, including the old, sick, and wounded. At the end of the Lolo trail and the entrance to the Bitterroot Valley, they encountered a blockade called Fort Fizzle, set up by two hundred volunteers and a small number of trained soldiers. The Nez Percé circumvented the blockade by climbing the surrounding hills and bypassing the fort.

CHIEF JOSEPH'S ETHICS

The Nez Percé never make war on women and children; we could have killed a great many ... while the war lasted, but we would feel ashamed to do so.

(Joseph in Beal, p. 129)

Colonel John Gibbon loomed as the next obstacle for the Nez Percé. He was a ruthless soldier, as displayed by his response when asked about the possibility of war prisoners: "We don't want any prisoners" (Gibbon in Beal, p. 114). Gibbon proved able to take advantage of the toll that the journey was exacting on the Nez Percé.

Exhausted, the Nez Percé rested for an extended period at the Big Hole Basin in present-day Montana. Colonel Gibbon's men mounted a sunrise attack upon the sleeping tribe on August 9, 1877. Soldiers charging the village shot men, women, and children until they were beaten back by the regrouped warriors. The Nez Percé were completely unprepared because their "code of

"I Will Fight No More"

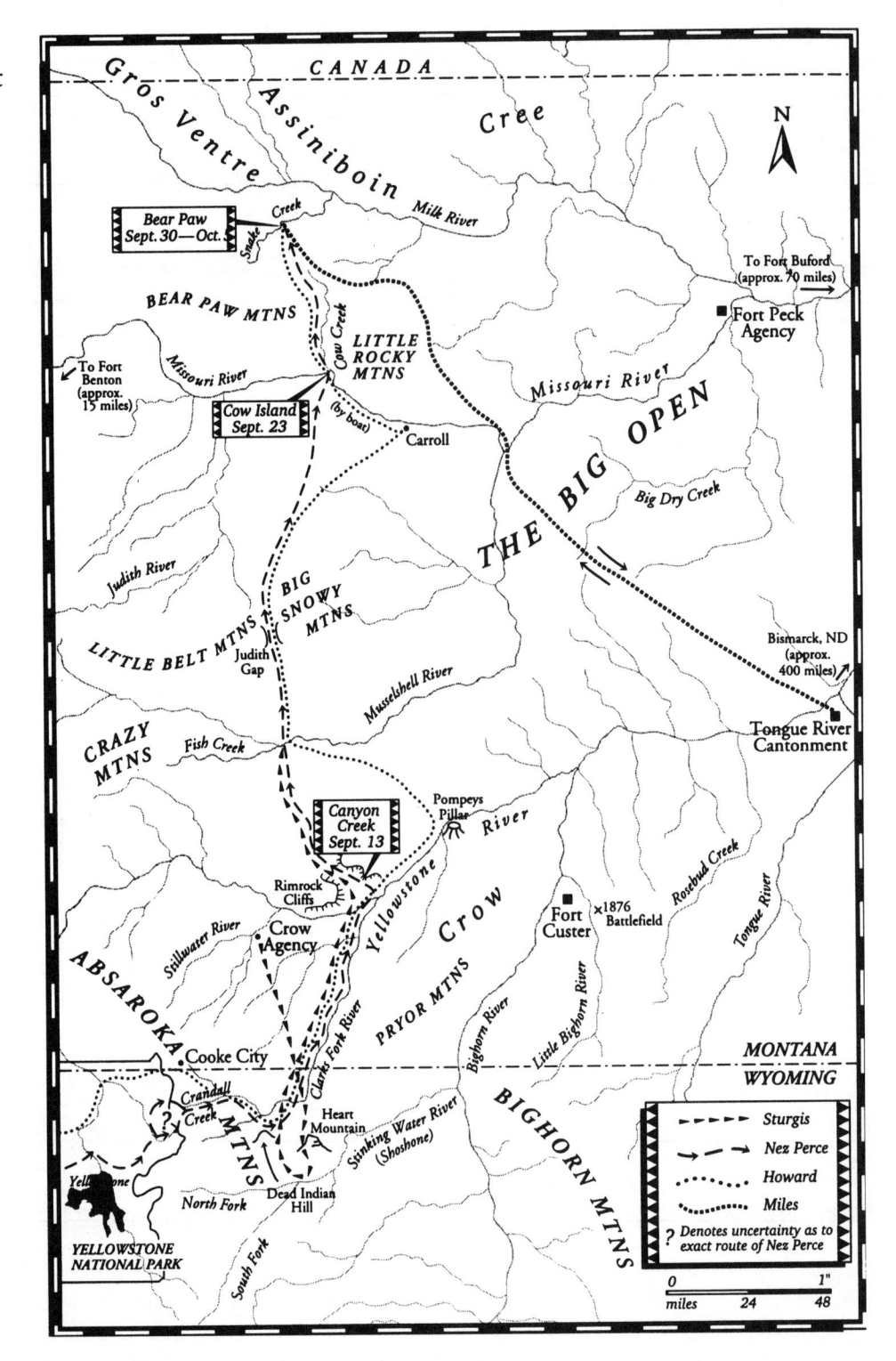

Map of the Nez Percé War of 1877.

ethics convinced them that no one would execute a surprise attack upon a sleeping and undefended camp" (Beal, p. 115). The Battle of Big Hole lasted for five hours. It was followed by a twenty-hour siege on entrenched army soldiers. Approximately ninety Nez Percé were killed by the time the battle concluded; seventy of the dead were women and children. After the battle, the Nez Percé continued their flight.

The continuous travel wore down the sick and the wounded. Many dropped out at safe points along the trail to allow their families to continue on. The number of Nez Percé dwindled considerably as the weak abandoned the tribe to die in peace. Yet the majority continued on, vainly seeking aid from allied tribes stationed farther east on the plains.

Chief Looking Glass, a respected chief of the renegade Nez Percé, hoped that the Crow nation would help the Nez Percé. By combining forces, he felt the two nations could overthrow the U.S. army. But the Crow turned their backs upon the Nez Percé, fearful that such an alliance would bring punishment on themselves from the U.S. government.

During the flight, whites who encountered the Nez Percé were immediately distrusted, and many were killed. The chiefs had control over the group at large, but raids led by small war parties proved impossible to control. Young warriors, vengeful after the Big Hole slaughter, wreaked havoc on whites and white property in and around Bannock City, Birch Creek, and the recently recognized Yellowstone National Park.

Pushed relentlessly by the desire for survival, the Nez Percé kept up a pace too rapid for the chasing soldiers to overtake. Using the supply of fresh horses their large herd afforded them, they could remount continuously; the pursuing troops had no such supply and consequently lost ground. Crow warriors on the side of the U.S. troops chased the fleeing Nez Percé, however, and they were able to steal horses from the herd. In the short run, this only quickened the rate of the Nez Percé escape, but these thefts eventually contributed to the destruction of the united band.

The Nez Percé pushed on, ever conscious of their pursuers. Chief Looking Glass, aware that the group had a lead of several days over Howard and his troops, noted the availability of buffalo close by, the presence of oncoming storms, and the need for the sick and dying to regroup. He recommended a brief rest before making the final push to Canada, only forty miles away. Heeding his advice, the Nez Percé camped at Bear's Paw in present-day Montana.

The final battle. Known as "Bear Coat" by the Nez Percé, Colonel Nelson A. Miles and his troops surrounded the camp and attacked on September 30. The fight lasted five days. Five Nez Percé chiefs died in the battle: Lean Elk, Hahtalekin, Ollokot, Toohoolhoolzote, and Looking Glass. Altogether, twenty-five Nez Percé were killed, while an additional forty-six were injured. U.S. soldiers suffered twenty-three dead and forty-five injured. Though remarkably even, the losses were especially devastating for the Nez Percé. In the words of the Nez Percé, "if we killed one soldier, a thousand would take his place. If we lost one warrior, there was none to take his place" (McWhorter, *Yellow Wolf*, p. 156).

A RESPECTED GENERAL'S PERSPECTIVE

William Tecumseh Sherman, the Civil War general who prepared the Seventh Cavalry to fight the Nez Percé in Yellowstone Park, offered this opinion of resolving conflicts with the native tribes: "The more we can kill this year, the less will have to be killed the next war, for the more I see of these Indians, the more convinced I am that they will all have to be killed or be maintained as a species of paupers" (Sherman in Warren, p. ix). Attempting to flee war altogether, the tribe escaped Sherman and his Seventh Cavalry and headed north toward Canada.

Chief White Bird, who opposed surrender, escaped to Canada with over 230 Nez Percé during the battle. Unanimity was unimportant in Nez Percé policy. Tribal law gave each chief and individual the right of decision, and so White Bird followed his own judgment. After he fled, Joseph was the sole remaining chief. Recognizing the imminent arrival of army reinforcements, Joseph finally surrendered on October 5.

The Statement in Focus

The statement of surrender. At least nine different versions of Chief Joseph's statement of surrender were relayed by eyewitnesses to the event. The version listed here, printed on October 26, 1877, by the *Bismarck Tri-Weekly Tribune*, was the first one released by the press.

"I Will Fight No More"

Tell General Howard I know his heart. What he told me before I have in my heart. I am tired of fighting. Our chiefs are killed. Looking Glass is dead. Ta-hool-hool-shoot is dead. The old men are all dead. It is the young men who say yes or no. He who leads the young men is dead. It is cold and we have no blankets. The little children are freezing to death. My people, some of them, have run away to the hills and have no blankets, no food; no one knows where they are—may be freezing to death. I want time to look for my children and see how many of them I can find. May be I shall find them among the dead. Hear me my chiefs; I am tired. My heart is sick and sad. From where the sun now stands I will fight no more forever.

(Joseph in Aoki, p. 121)

How was the message given? Because of the isolated location in which the Nez Percé surrendered and the lack of reliable communications technology, there has been great debate over the format as well as the exact phrasing of Chief Joseph's famous words.

Whether the statement of surrender was spoken or written by Chief Joseph remains uncertain. Some sources assume that he wrote the majority of the statement and only spoke the words "Hear me my chiefs." The *Chicago Times* of October 26, 1877, contends that the only part spoken was the phrase, "from where the sun stands, forever and ever, I will never fight again," but this phrasing is inconsistent with other accounts (Joseph in Aoki, p. 121). Indeed, the words and phrases in Joseph's message of surrender vary from version to version. The overall meaning, though, is never in question.

Joseph probably communicated verbally to the victorious U.S. generals through an interpreter, and his use of the phrase "Hear me my chiefs" may have been intended for the generals. After a treaty or defeat, American Indians of the 1800s sometimes acknowledged the whites with whom they were dealing as their new chiefs.

How was the statement received? It was Chief Joseph's understanding that by surrendering, the Non-Treaty Nez Percé would be returned to the Northwest and confined to a reservation. These terms were agreed upon by the commanding officers of the U.S. Army, who had an obligation to uphold the terms. Instead, after the surrender, the remaining Nez Percé were sent to Fort Leavenworth in Kansas Territory, a land of swamps in which diseases spread among the tribe. In June 1879, 370 remaining Nez Percé moved from Kansas to Oklahoma Indian Territory, another environment where they had difficulty surviving. By 1884 there were only 282 Nez Percé left.

Chief Joseph traveled to Washington, D.C., a few times over the years to discuss the fate of his people with politicians. He spoke with three presidents over the course of his life, and each leader promised to make efforts to return the Nez Percé to their original environment.

In April 1885, the U.S. government finally returned the Nez Percé to the Northwest. Many went to Lapwai Reservation (in present-day Idaho) to live with the original Treaty Nez Percé; others, including Joseph, went to Colville Reservation (in present-day Washington). These Nez Percé soon moved to the Nespelem Reservation (also in Washington), where conditions were more conducive to survival. Though the three reservations were near their original homeland, the Nez Percé never did resettle in their native Wallowa territory.

Reaction to Chief Joseph's statement. Upon receiving the surrender of the Nez Percé at the Bear's Paw battlefield, Colonel Miles made this report to his superior officers: "I have the honor to recommend that ample provision be made for their civilization, and to enable them to become self-sustaining. They are sufficiently intelligent to appreciate the consideration which, in my opinion, is justly due them from the government" (Miles in Beal, p. 273). Despite his report, the government sent the Nez Percé to Kansas and Oklahoma, where they lost nearly half their number because of climate and conditions.

When he learned of his people's fate, a helpless Chief Joseph said, "I cannot understand how the government sends a man out to fight us, as it did General Miles, and then breaks his word. Such a government has something wrong about it" (Joseph in Beal, p. 273).

Another officer, C. E. S. Wood, the aide to General Howard during the campaign, became so enraged at the treatment of the Nez Percé that he resigned his post. Wood later sent his thirteen-year-old son Erskine to spend time with Chief Joseph at the Nespelem Nez Percé reservation. Erskine Wood later wrote a memoir of Joseph and as an older man made the remark, "I can say truthfully, knowing him was the high spot of my entire life" (Wood in Beal, p. 299).

Joseph was able to put the politics of war in perspective later in life at an address he made with General Howard at the Carlisle School for Indians:

> Here sits a man, Arm-Cut. We were against each other in war, and I used to think I would like to shoot and kill him and would have been happy over it. Today, when we are old, I like him and

he is my friend. If anything happens to him, if he dies, I will be very sad over him. This is the way I feel. Not for anything will I hold thoughts against him again, because that war is over
(Joseph in Aoki, p. 126)

Joseph's words show a loyalty to the oath made in his momentous message of surrender: I will fight no more forever.

For More Information

Aoki, Haruo. *Nez Percé Texts*. Berkeley: University of California Press, 1979.

Beal, Merrill D. "*I Will Fight No More Forever*": *Chief Joseph and the Nez Percé War*. Seattle: University of Washington Press, 1963.

Haines, Francis. *The Nez Percés*. Norman: University of Oklahoma Press, 1955.

Hampton, Bruce. *Children of Grace: The Nez Percé War of 1877*. New York: Henry Holt, 1994.

McWhorter, Lucullus Virgil. *Hear Me, My Chiefs!* Caldwell, Ohio: Caxton, 1952.

McWhorter, Lucullus Virgil. *Yellow Wolf: His Own Story*. Caldwell, Ohio: Caxton, 1940.

Warren, Robert Penn. *Chief Joseph of the Nez Percé*. New York: Random House, 1982.

Incidents in the Life of a Slave Girl Written by Herself

by
Harriet A. Jacobs

Born into bondage in 1813, Harriet Jacobs endured the breakup of her immediate family more than once in her lifetime as a result of slavery. She suffered further from sexual advances made on her by her owner, took highly unusual steps to escape them, then documented her tale in an autobiography written to further the cause of the abolition movement in pre-Civil War America.

Events in History at the Time the Autobiography Takes Place

Slavery in North Carolina. In the early 1800s, the white population outnumbered the slave population in North Carolina by about two to one. Farms in this state tended to be small in comparison to some other parts of the South. Therefore, most of North Carolina's farmers held fewer than ten slaves, although its larger landholders may have possessed up to twenty slaves and occasionally more. In 1827, two years after Harriet Jacobs became his slave, records show that Dr. Norcom submitted a tax statement that listed as his property nineteen blacks. Harriet Jacobs attributes an even larger number to him in her account, saying that he possessed "a fine residence in town, several farms, and about fifty slaves, besides hiring a number by the year" (Jacobs, *Incidents in the Life of a Slave Girl,* p. 15).

North Carolina depended on slave labor mainly to grow cotton, tobacco, rice, grain, and livestock. Cotton was the favorite crop—it enjoyed a relatively long growing season, required

> **THE LITERARY WORK**
>
> An autobiography set mainly in Edenton, North Carolina, but also in the northern United States and in England from 1813 to 1858; published in 1861.
>
> **SYNOPSIS**
>
> A young slave woman runs away to free herself and her two children from bondage. After hiding for seven years in her grandmother's house, she eventually unites with her family in the North and gains freedom.

minimal skill to cultivate, and exploited the labor potential of the entire slave family. Adults usually did the plowing; children as well as adults hoed the fields, all of them working in gangs under the watchful eye of an overseer. The arduous fieldwork sometimes encouraged slaves to seek better positions as house servants for their owners. Especially for women slaves, such a position was a mixed blessing that provided more comfortable living conditions but also brought them into closer proximity to their master and his sexual whims. The situation sometimes resulted in strained relations between a house slave and her mistress, an eventuality that Jacobs experienced.

Free blacks in North Carolina. Harriet Jacobs's grandmother, her uncle, and the man she loved were all free blacks, who, despite the willingness of their former owners to release them, were on the whole feared and disliked. The owners worried that free blacks might help slaves plan revolts or run away. Mostly because of this concern, free blacks were constrained by legal restrictions. An 1826 law stated that a free black could not move into North Carolina. Those born and raised in the state were restricted in their activities. The authorities could arrest "any able-bodied free Negro found spending his or her time in idleness and dissipation, or having no regular or honest employment" (Bassett, p. 36).

By 1844 the North Carolina Supreme Court had ruled that the state would not regard its "free persons of color" as citizens. Free blacks in North Carolina, then, occupied a peculiar position in society—they were not slaves, but since they did not enjoy the rights of a citizen they were not entirely free. Thus, restricted although they were free, Harriet Jacobs's grandmother, uncle, and beloved were nearly helpless in easing the plight of Harriet, a slave.

Seduction, concubinage, and rape. As elsewhere, North Carolina condoned certain standards of conduct among its people, whether they were free or enslaved. Young white women were encouraged to adopt a reserved Victorian standard of dress and social activity, reflected in frocks that barely showed their feet. In contrast, young slave women were often scantily dressed, not by their own choosing but by the nature of the provisions of their masters. As slaves, they could and often were stripped for inspection by possible purchasers (Sterling, p. 19). This double standard helps to explain why young female slaves often fell victim to the lust of their owners.

As in Jacobs's case, often a slaveowner's neighbor as well as the owner himself showed desire for a young slave woman. "The majority—and their sons, neighbors, overseers—held to a double standard that coupled veneration for white womanhood with the disrespect for black. House servants were particularly susceptible to sexual exploitation" (Sterling, p. 20).

Although slave mothers worried about their daughters, they could do very little to protect them. In her autobiography, Harriet Jacobs laments this fact; her own mother had long ago been separated from her children through slave sales. Consequently, as she matured and bore her own first child, Harriet records mixed emotions. She feels a strong love for her new baby daughter, but she also feels depressed at the thought of her anticipated fate.

When they told me my new-born babe was a girl, my heart was heavier that it had ever been before. Slavery is terrible for men; but it is far more terrible for women.
(*Incidents in the Life of a Slave Girl*, p. 71)

Rape of a slave was not considered a crime. White men often justified their actions by claiming that the women were, after all, their "property," or that black women were more passionate than white and hence, more willing to comply with sexual demands. Whatever the justifications, slave women were frequently forced to submit to sexual mistreatment or punished for their refusal or resistance.

Family life. To Jacobs, her family was of the utmost importance. Her grandmother was her pillar of strength. Likewise, she depended on her uncle, aunt, and brother for emotional support. And her children gave her a reason for living. As she wrote, "My life was spared; and I was glad for the sake of my little ones. Had it not been for these ties to life, I should have been glad to be released by death" (*Incidents in the Life of a Slave Girl*, p. 78). The family, in fact, served as an important survival mechanism for slaves. They depended on the family unit for friendship and love, and to maintain their self-esteem.

Probably the most challenging aspect of slavery was the separation of the family. Although, many times, slaveowners tried to keep slave families together, this was not always possible, especially in the event of the death or debt of the slaveowner. In Jacobs's case, her family was broken up when her first mistress died. Slave mothers worried constantly about their families suffering this fate, and in fact nearly one-third of all slave families were dissolved because the members were sold to separate owners. It is for this reason that the slave family was an unstable institution.

Nat Turner's Rebellion. In North Carolina, as throughout the South, Nat Turner's Rebellion marked a very crucial turning point for both slaves and slaveholders alike. Its significance can be measured by the fact that Jacobs's autobiography devotes an entire chapter to this topic. Desperate for better treatment for blacks, a slave named Nat Turner led a band of six bondsmen in revolt in Southampton County, Virginia, in 1831. The slaves agreed to spare no whites and began by murdering Turner's master and family. They then headed towards Jerusalem, the county seat. On the way they attracted seventy more slaves, and together the band killed a total of fifty-seven whites. By August 24, the Virginia

Life of a Slave Girl

militia managed to put down the insurrection. Almost all of Nat Turner's rebels were captured or killed. Nat Turner himself escaped but then was captured on October 30. He was tried and then hung on November 11. The event left a searing impression, alarming slaveowners throughout the South and aggravating their constant fear of slave uprisings. Because of the Turner rebellion, Southern states passed more severe laws in attempts to control slaves. Slave schools, churches, and preachers were forbidden, for example. As one author notes,

> After 1831 ... the conditions of slavery [in North Carolina] became more severe. One law after another was passed which bore hardly on the slave, until at last he was bound hand, foot, and brain in the power of his master.
> (Bassett, p. 7)

Fugitive Slave Law. Jacobs devotes another chapter in her autobiography to a second momentous development of her time—the Fugitive Slave Law. Two such laws had been passed since the inception of the nation, one in 1793 and the other in 1850, both devoted to the recapture and re-enslavement of runaways. Jacobs's concern is with the more stringent 1850 federal law.

The annual number of slave escapes in Jacobs's lifetime was relatively small but growing. By 1850 owners were threatened by as many as 1,000 successful slave escapes a year, with a total slave population of 4 million. This fact, as well as Congress's obsession with preserving the balance between slave states and free states in the Union, had produced the new Fugitive Slave Law. Its stricter provisions gave courts the ability to issue warrants for the arrest of fugitives. Fugitive slaves could not testify on their own behalf nor were they allowed a trial by jury. Any person found aiding an escaped fugitive was subject to fines amounting to $2,000 and six months in jail. The law had a reverse effect in some places. Because its provisions were so stringent, many Northerners became more vigilant in helping runaways and the number of abolitionists increased.

By the time the new Fugitive Slave Law was enacted, Harriet Jacobs had escaped the South and was living as a paid helper to a woman in the North. In her autobiography, Jacobs reports that her employer, Mrs. Bruce (Mrs. Willis in the book) violated the new law to help Jacobs maintain her freedom from her old master. Mrs. Bruce's reaction to the bounty-hunters' pursuit of Jacobs reveals the passion that the Fugitive Slave Law elicited: "I will go to the State's prison, rather than have any poor victim from *my* house, to be carried back to slavery" (*Incidents in the Life of a Slave Girl*, p. 194).

Despite such reactions from many whites, the Fugitive Slave Law of 1850 encouraged a flood of bounty hunters to search relentlessly through the North and South for escaped slaves. The highest rate of capture and return of fugitive slaves to their masters occurred in 1851.

The Autobiography in Focus

The plot. In *Incidents in the Life of a Slave Girl*, Harriet Jacobs tells the story of her life through the character of Linda Brent. Born in 1813, she begins with her "happy" childhood as a house slave to a kind mistress while surrounded by loving parents and other family members. In these early years, her mistress teaches her how to read and sew. But at age twelve, this secure life changes. Both her father and her mistress die (her mother had died when Brent was six years old). Thereafter, Brent becomes the property of her mistress's young niece, Mrs. Flint, and her husband, Dr. Flint. Her brother is purchased by this same family. Brent's grandmother, through a kind benefactress, becomes a free woman.

At age fifteen, Brent becomes subject to Dr. Flint's sexual advances. He is unrelenting in his pursuit of her, and the attention he pays to Brent causes Mrs. Flint to become jealous of the girl. Perhaps the suspicions of Mrs. Flint prevent the doctor from physically forcing himself on Brent. In any event, she is able to fend off her master's attacks. Brent meanwhile falls in love with a free black who is a carpenter and wants to marry her. She asks Dr. Flint for permission and is heartbroken when he denies her request. Brent values her purity, but thinking it will stymie her master's demands on her, she gives herself to a white neighbor, a bachelor named Mr. Sands. By the time Brent is nineteen, she has two children with Mr. Sands, a boy and a girl. Under slave law, the children become property of Dr. Flint.

After the children are born, Dr. Flint renews his interest in Brent. He proposes to set her and her children up in a cottage. Brent refuses his offer and is subsequently sent to the plantation of Flint's son, where she and her children are to be "broken in"—that is, forced to become subservient and submissive. In order to save herself and her children from the degradations of slavery, she devises a plan of escape. After hiding in

SOME MAIN CHARACTERS AND THEIR REAL-LIFE SOURCES

Fictional Name	Actual Name
Linda Brent	Harriet Jacobs
Aunt Martha	Molly Horniblow, Jacobs's grandmother
Willim	John S., Jacobs's brother
Benny	Joseph, Jacobs's son
Ellen	Louisa Matilda, Jacobs's daughter
Dr. Flint	Dr. James Norcom, Jacobs's master from 1825 to 1851
Second Mrs. Bruce	Cornelia Grinnell Willis, second wife of Nathaniel Parker Willis, the woman responsible for liberating Jacobs from bondage

various local places, she settles in a small attic space in a shed attached to her grandmother's house. There she remains for almost seven years, tricking Dr. Flint into believing that she is living in the North. From her small space Brent is able to watch her children grow up. Her hope is that their father will purchase them from Dr. Flint, then set them free. Mr. Sands does, in fact, purchase his children but reneges on his promise to free them.

In 1842 Brent escapes to the North, where she makes several friends, including her new employers, the Bruces. Her children eventually join her in the North for a time, but she lives in continuing uneasiness because slave-hunters pursue her. Brent manages to elude Dr. Flint's slave-hunters for several years; still he continues to search for her and even upon his death his heirs carry on the pursuit of her. Mr. Bruce's first wife, a kind employer, dies, whereupon her husband and young daughter visit England with Brent serving as the child's caretaker. Brent returns to live in Boston for a couple of years, then takes a job again with Mr. Bruce in New York, who has remarried. Finally in 1852, Brent is purchased by Mr. Bruce's second wife and set free.

Slave narratives. During the time in which this autobiography takes place, slave narratives were gaining a wider readership than ever before. The first female slave narrative to be written in the United States was *The History of Mary Prince, a West Indian Slave,* published in 1831. Such narratives were often used by the abolitionist movement to promote their cause and illustrate the cruelties of slavery.

According to the historian Jean Yellin, Jacobs's work resembles other slave narratives in that Jacobs claims "authorship in the subtitle ... uses the first person, and addresses the subject of the oppression of chattel slavery and the struggle for freedom from the viewpoint of one who has been enslaved" (Yellin in Jacobs, p. xxvi). Likewise, as in other tales about slavery, the writer portrays herself as a black person struggling individually for freedom. However, Yellin points out that one striking difference in Jacobs's work is that the main character, Linda Brent, does not quickly flee to the North, but instead spends several years in hiding. Jacobs's narrative also differs from others in that it underscores the importance of family and motherhood, whereas Frederick Douglass's well-known slave narrative, for example, focuses rather on freedom and literacy. The publication of *Incidents in the Life of a Slave Girl* marked a turning point in literary history in another important respect—it discussed the previously taboo subject of a woman's sexual exploitation.

Sources. When this book was first published, there was no doubt about the authenticity of the document and the identity of the author. But as time passed, scholars either began to question the narrative's accuracy or dismissed the tale completely. It was not until 1981 that Yellin discovered Jacobs's letters to Amy Post, the anti-slavery worker who had encouraged Jacobs to share her tale with the public. Yellin authenticated the authorship of these letters, taking six years to document, reconstruct, and identify the characters and events in *Incidents*.

Events in History at the Time the Autobiography Was Written

The controversy over slavery. Harriet Jacobs began to write about her unique experience in anonymous letters to the New York *Tribune* in 1853. Over the next few years, she turned the letters into a manuscript, completing the work in 1858. During this period, Jacobs was purchased by a friendly Northerner and freed. Such acts were inspired by the growing pressure of abolitionists to rid all of the United States of slavery. Proslavery forces remained strong at the same time, however, and tensions mounted that would ultimately lead to the Civil War. Aggravating these divisive strains was the 1852 publication of Harriet Beecher Stowe's novel *Uncle Tom's Cabin* (also covered in *Literature and Its Times*).

HARRIET JACOBS VS. HARRIET BEECHER STOWE

At first Harriet Jacobs proposed that her sensational life story be written by Stowe, but Stowe outraged Jacobs by forwarding a sketch of Jacobs's life (written by Jacobs's Quaker friend Amy Post) to the woman for whom Jacobs worked at the time for verification of the facts. Jacobs had not shared the details of her sexual past with her employer, Mrs. Willis, and felt betrayed. If her story was true, said Stowe, an already renowned author by then, she would include it in her *Key to Uncle Tom's Cabin*, an offer that further outraged Jacobs, who regarded her story as an independent piece. She then decided to write the autobiography herself. "Poor as it may be, I had rather give [my story] from my own hand, than have it said that I employed others to do it for me" (*Incidents in the Life of a Slave Girl*, p. xix).

With the election of Franklin Pierce to the presidency in 1853 came additional strain. Pierce was a strong advocate of expansion of United States territory, and as the territories were settled, they would likely become states. This process created a feverish battle in Congress because a new state could potentially be either "free" or "slave," either prohibiting slavery or allowing it; this determination was important because it threatened to upset the precarious balance of pro- and antislavery states that existed at the time. If there were more free states than slave states represented in Congress, it was thought likely that laws would be passed that were harmful to the institution of slavery—a frightening idea for Southern states. A similar process could take place if slave states became more numerous, with the difference that such an alignment would promote slavery and the other causes favorable to the South.

Congressional leader Stephen A. Douglas responded to this situation by proposing the Kansas-Nebraska Act of 1854. This act, when enacted, split the old Nebraska Territory into two parts and left the issue of slavery up to the inhabitants of each part. The bill's passage soon led to violence in Kansas as both pro- and antislavery supporters entered the state, attempting to influence the vote on slavery, and the two sides clashed. In 1855 the new Kansas Territory opted for slavery, but it was discovered that some of those who voted to permit bondage were actually residents of nearby Missouri. Violent incidents continued in the state, and in 1856 abolitionist John Brown led an attack that resulted in the brutal slaying of five members of the proslavery faction. In 1859 at Harpers Ferry, Virginia, Brown led another violent raid that escalated tensions in the nation to a brittle pitch.

In this atmosphere, Harriet Jacobs found arranging for a publisher difficult. Jacobs first tried to publish her book in England and was initially unsuccessful. The two publishers who expressed interest in publishing it in the United States declared bankruptcy before the job could even be begun. It was not until 1861, therefore, that the book finally appeared in print in Boston, with an introduction by the prominent white abolitionist Lydia Maria Child. The next year, the book was published in England under the title *A Deeper Wrong*. By that time, the Civil War was well under way in the United States.

Reviews. At the time of its publication, *Incidents in the Life of a Slave Girl* was but one of many abolitionist tracts. Edited by Lydia Maria Child, the book reached the public through abolitionist channels. It was sold at the Anti-Slavery Offices in New York and Boston.

Early positive reviews of the work appeared in such abolitionist newspapers as *The Liberator* (February 8, 1861), *Anti-Slavery Bugle* (February 9, 1861), *National Anti-Slavery Standard* (February 16, 1861), and *Weekly Anglo-African* (April 13, 1861). The critic for the *Anti-Slavery Advocate* wrote on May 1, 1861, "We have read this book with no ordinary interest, for we are acquainted with the writer, we have heard of the incidence from her own lips, and have great confidence in her truthfulness and integrity" (Davis and Gates, p. 32). Reviewers generally endorsed Jacobs's book for its truthfulness as well as its intriguing content.

For More Information

Bassett, John Spencer. *Slavery in the State of North Carolina.* Baltimore: Johns Hopkins Press, 1899.

Blassingame, John W. *The Slave Community.* New York: Oxford University Press, 1972.

Campbell, Stanley Wallace. *Enforcement of the Fugitive Slave Law, 1850-1860.* Chapel Hill: University of North Carolina, 1966.

Davis, Charles T. and Henry Louis Gates, Jr. *The Slave's Narrative.* New York: Oxford University Press, 1985.

Jacobs, Harriet A. *Incidents in the Life of a Slave Girl, Written by Herself.* Cambridge, Mass.: Harvard University Press, 1987.

Sterling, Dorothy, ed. *We Are Your Sisters.* New York: W. W. Norton, 1984.

Zafar, Rafia, and Deborah Garfield. *Harriet Jacobs and Incidents in the Life of a Slave Girl.* Cambridge: Cambridge University Press, 1996.

Ishi, Last of His Tribe

by
Theodora Kroeber

Part of a California tribe known as the Yana Indians, Ishi belonged to a subgroup (totaling about 250 before 1848) called the Yahi. From 1860 to 1911, the tribe survived in the southern Cascade Mountains. Achieving distinction as the last-known Yahi, Ishi agreed to move to the University of California Museum of Anthropology in San Francisco, where he lived from 1911 to 1916. He was befriended by the anthropologist Alfred Kroeber during this time. Alfred's wife, Theodora Kroeber, who was twenty years younger than her husband, proceeded to document Ishi's compelling life in biography and in fiction.

> **THE LITERARY WORK**
>
> A novel set in San Francisco and the Mount Lassen area of northern California from roughly 1880 to 1916; published in 1964.
>
> **SYNOPSIS**
>
> As one of the last remaining members of the Yahi tribe of American Indians, Ishi witnesses the extinction of his people and must learn to adapt to the world of white settlers.

Events in History at the Time the Novel Takes Place

Yahi lifestyle. The Yahi drew part of their food supply from the deer, rabbits, and quail they hunted. They also fished for food, using harpoons and spears. Acorns, which were picked in the fall, served as their primary food source. Acorns were prepared for use in making soup, bread, or mush, and the Yahi made a number of dishes that combined the nut with meat or berries. In years when the crop was poor, though, the people tottered on the brink of starvation. The Yahi people cooked with artfully crafted twined baskets, which were also used for other purposes.

In 1848 pioneers began using the Lassen Trail, which crossed Yahi territory, bringing whites into contact with the tribe. From this point on, modern historical developments had a grave impact on the Yahi way of life and eventually led to the complete extinction of the group, which had changed little since the Stone Age.

The California gold rush. As the East Coast of the United States became increasingly overcrowded, many Americans set their sights on the Western frontier. Although it did not yet offer many of the comforts associated with the East, settlers were lured to the West by the promise of spacious, inexpensive land. Interest in the West further accelerated with the gold strike at Sutter's Mill near Sacramento, California, in 1848. The California gold rush attracted those who felt they might be able to quickly and easily acquire riches.

There had been similar rushes for gold in the United States as early as 1830, but none reached the enormous proportions of the California gold rush. The influx of gold seekers reached a peak in

1849. In the first two years of the gold rush alone, California's population increased from 14,000 to 100,000 people. By 1860 California had more than 380,000 residents. The so-called "forty-niners"—a name drawn from the year 1849—came from all over the United States, as well as Europe, South America, Asia, and Australia.

Initially, the process of mining consisted of panning for gold in streams or dried-up riverbeds. As the number of miners increased, however, this supply of gold was exhausted and machines had to be employed to extract the precious metal from the California soil. These machines helped make California one of the most technologically advanced states in the Union. In short, the rush for gold brought wealth and technology to the Western frontier and helped transform San Francisco from a trading post into a major U.S. city. The gold rush also had an effect on Mill Creek Canyon in the southern Cascade foothills, the home territory of the Yahi. While this region was not a center of gold mining or towns, the growing white population used the foothills as grazing lands and sites for hunting cabins. This resulted in greater contact between white settlers and the Yahi.

The railroad. Railroads first appeared in the United States in the late 1820s. The railroads had become a popular means of travel by the 1830s, replacing such earlier methods of transportation as the stagecoach and the steamboat. With the advent of railroads, it became more efficient to travel from the East to the West; people no longer had to depend on the primarily north-south waterways for safe transportation. It was not until 1869, however, that the first transcontinental railroad line was completed, enabling easterners to travel by train to the western coast of the continent. The coming of the railroad, coupled with the gold rush, made California accessible and desirable, and people flocked there by the thousands.

Racist attitudes of the settlers. The construction of the railroad lines had been a daunting task. Railroad companies found it to be in their best interest to hire the cheapest labor possible. As a result, a majority of the railroad laborers were of Chinese origin. Large numbers of Chinese had come to California seeking gold, yet they had been unable to find employment because of the racial attitudes of the white settlers. Those unable to find gold resorted to working on the railroad for low wages in order to survive. Once the railroads were completed, however, the predominately white population displayed little interest in sharing their land with the Chinese immigrants. In fact, they sought to keep such immigrants from coming to California in the future. The Chinese Exclusion Acts, which were passed in 1882, 1892, and 1902, were aimed at preventing any further Chinese immigration. The first two acts suspended immigration from China altogether for ten years each; the 1902 act, which tried to suspend it "permanently," would remain in effect for thirty-one years.

Because tribes of American Indians were already living in California, the white settlers were unable to pass any laws restricting their entry into the state. Instead, laws were passed declaring that all Indians could be indentured. From 1850 to 1863, California Indians were commonly kidnapped and sold or placed into forced servitude (indenture). Estimates place the total number of Native American indentures in California at ten thousand. In some cases, the period of indenture could, by law, last for more than twenty years. More disturbing still, however, was the frequency with which American Indians and other nonwhites were murdered without probable cause and without any form of punishment for their killers. One reason for this was that the laws of the state did not treat American Indians fairly. A state law (Act for the Government and Protection of Indians, passed in 1850 and amended in 1860) provided that "in no case shall a white man be convicted of any offense upon the testimony of an Indian" (Washburn, p. 415).

White settlers and the Yahi. Conflict between the American Indians and the settlers began soon after the gold seekers made their way into California. From 1850 until 1865, the United States government kept a particularly close watch on the Yahi, who were considered a belligerent tribe; they had proven unwilling to accept white domination and refused to move onto reservations. The first documented case of hostility between the two groups occurred in 1857, when the Yahi raided storehouses belonging to the settlers. The end of winter had always been a difficult time for the Yahi, but now, with fewer resources available to them because of the growing white population in the area, they faced a greater likelihood of starvation. Because of this, they looted the food supplies of the whites. Soon after the raid, a party of the settlers led by a well-known "Indian hunter" named Hiram Good set out after the tribe to avenge the raids. They eventually found a band of forty or so Indians and killed them all on sight. The band that they had happened upon were members of another Yana group,

Ishi

Ishi in 1911.

however; they were not the Yahi who had raided their storehouses.

In 1862 a small group of Yahi kidnapped and later killed two of the settlers' children, an event that prompted rage among the settlers. The Yahi who were guilty of the murders reportedly had a distinct hairstyle: their hair had been cut short and covered in tar, a sign that they were in mourning. Historians speculate that their violent act was most likely in retaliation for the earlier murders of Yana children by the settlers, for there is extensive documentation of massacres in which thirty or more Yana were killed. Nevertheless, the 1862 incident prompted a search party to set out for the guilty Yahis, in hopes of exterminating every last Indian in the area. The Yahis, along with other Yana, suffered much loss of life after contact with whites in the mid-1800s. While some eighteen hundred Yana perished after contact, the deaths of fewer than fifty whites can be traced to the Yana.

In 1865, after the murder of three more homesteaders, Hiram Good and his followers set out for the last time to perform a mass execution of the Yahi people. Forty to fifty Yahi, including women and children, were killed. Only a handful of the Yahi people, whom Good's party last saw fleeing into the forest, survived this attack. The remaining Yahi now realized that their only chance at survival was complete concealment.

The Novel in Focus

The plot. *Ishi, Last of his Tribe* is the story of Ishi, a young boy, and the few remaining members of the Yahi people—his "cousin-sister" Tushi, his mother, his uncle, his grandparents, and a slightly older boy from another village named Timawi.

It is revealed at the beginning of the story that despite having spent his life in hiding, Ishi has had numerous encounters with the outside world of the white men, or *saldu*. When he and his family are hunting in the forest, they must continually be on their guard because the saldu could attack at any time. Since all of the rest of the Yahi people have been killed by the saldu, Ishi and his extended family take great care to keep themselves hidden from whites.

Ishi spends a great deal of time at a secret praying place, where he can see the saldu's railway train winding its way through the valley. Ishi believes that the train is a monster that the white men have tamed. While praying, Ishi dreams of traveling into the valley and swimming through the gorge of the canyon into Outer Ocean. There Ishi is greeted by a sacred salmon who brings him back to the Yahi world. Although Ishi is unable to determine the meaning of his dream, he is informed by his Elder Uncle that his vision is a Power Dream and that its message will one day become clear.

Ishi's grandfather tells the story of Ishi's father, who, along with several other members of the tribe, was killed by the saldu while attempting to raid a camp of white settlers. Although the raid was viewed by the settlers as unprovoked, it was seen by the Yahi as retaliation for the murders of their people. As Ishi and Timawi grow into young men, they begin to feel the same desire for vengeance that Ishi's father had. One night, while the two are on a journey together, Timawi leaves Ishi's side. When Ishi finally finds Timawi, he sees that his friend has been killed in an attempt to avenge the wrongful death of his people.

BUFFALO BILL CODY'S WILD WEST SHOW

Through his Wild West Show, William Cody, known as Buffalo Bill, helped mold the image of the American West for the rest of the world. From 1883 through 1913, Buffalo Bill's Wild West Show toured the United States and Europe, staging battles between cowboys and Indians, mock stagecoach robberies, and displays of skill by such well-known sharpshooters as Annie Oakley. Ishi himself often attended performances with his friend Dr. Saxton Pope and is said to have enjoyed them immensely.

The proximity of Ishi's home to the areas populated by the saldu eventually makes it necessary for the remaining Yahi to relocate to a safer site. Ishi finds an abandoned grizzly bear den in a cliff, and the family makes its home there. Soon his grandparents die, leaving only Ishi, his mother, his uncle, and Tushi. Ishi's mother becomes unwell and is unable to move her legs, which further endangers the group.

Despite Ishi's attempt to find a secret home for his family, several saldu men happen upon the cave. Tushi and Elder Uncle flee in one direction while Ishi heads in another. His mother, who is too heavy to carry, remains behind. The saldu do not harm her, but they steal several of the Yahi baskets on the floor of the cave.

After the men have left, Ishi searches for Tushi and his uncle. They have disappeared into the wilderness, never to be heard from again. Ishi returns to his mother, and they decide that they must move on before the saldu return. Then his mother dies and Ishi is left alone—the last of the Yahi. He performs burial rights, shaves off his hair in mourning, and starts wandering without purpose or direction.

Approximately three years later, Ishi arrives at a slaughterhouse outside the city of Oroville. He is arrested and placed in jail. The next day he is visited by a man who, to Ishi's surprise, knows several Yahi words. The man, an anthropologist whom Ishi calls *majapa*, or "the headman," takes Ishi to San Francisco to live in a museum. As Ishi climbs aboard the monster (a train) to venture toward the "Outer Ocean" of San Francisco Bay, he finally understands the meaning of his Power Dream. Ishi lives out the rest of his life at the museum with his newfound saldu friends, returning only once to the Yahi world that he left behind.

The Yahi relationship with nature. One of the reasons the Yahi were able to remain hidden from the saldu for so long was their intimate relationship with nature. The Yahi respect for the natural world contrasts sharply with its treatment by white settlers. The reader is first introduced to the saldu as they are slashing at the brush in an attempt to carve out a trail: "A small berry bush came out by its roots and was thrown into the air, landing, unnoticed except by Ishi, in the top of a clump of manzanita" (Kroeber, *Ishi, Last of His Tribe,* p. 6). In a later passage, as Tushi and Ishi move through the forest, they are careful to only bend the branches when clearing a path. They would not think of breaking them as the saldu have done. This method of travel shows respect for the bushes and the trees, but it also plays a major role in their safety. A path cleared by merely bending the branches does not leave behind a visible sign of their presence.

The Yahi respect for nature can be explained in part by examining their creation myths. Ishi's grandfather explains that the earth, the trees, and the animals were created before man. When man was finally created, the Great God Jupka told the Yahi people that "there [would] be peace [between] the creatures of air and water and brush" (*Ishi, Last of His Tribe,* p. 30). The Yahi regarded animals as the embodiment of the great Yahi gods and heroes. For a person to be disrespectful of nature would be an insult to the gods.

Because of their respect for all living things, the Yahi never took more than they needed, and they were careful to thank the earth during their Harvest Feast for providing them with food. When Tushi asks why the saldu have no Harvest Feast, her grandmother replies, "they do not have a Harvest Feast because those who take the food of others without asking and without courtesy do not give thanks for it" (*Ishi, Last of His Tribe,* p. 10).

Ishi's personal respect for nature is illustrated by Kroeber in two separate instances. When Ishi catches a marmot in a trap, he senses the animal's anguish. "I know now why Elder Uncle says a bow is better than a trap," he states. "The arrow kills; a trap may cause only fear and pain" (*Ishi, Last of His Tribe,* p. 43). Later in the novel, when Ishi is attracting animals using calls that he has learned to imitate, a rabbit walks into his hands. Although he is hungry, Ishi is unable to take the life of an animal that came to him without fear.

Perhaps the greatest misunderstanding between the Yahi and the saldu was over the concept of natural resources as property. The Yahi did not believe that anyone could own nature. Their lives were based on a belief that one should take only what one needed to survive. The homesteaders, on the other hand, saw cattle and grain and land as personal possessions, and they became enraged when property that they regarded as theirs was taken from them by the Yahi. What the settlers did not realize was that through their actions, they were stealing a way of life from the Yahi, one in which man and nature were able to coexist. As settlers encroached on Yahi land and forced them into hiding, hunting became more difficult for the tribe and plundering became a means for survival.

Sources. The man who was known as Ishi by the anthropological community never revealed his Yahi name. The name was given to him by the anthropologist A. L. Kroeber, as *Ishi* was the Yahi word for "man." The Yahi's name is not the only thing that remains lost to history. Encountering an almost insurmountable language barrier, anthropologists found it difficult to learn the true details of Ishi's life. After studying Ishi's own attempts to communicate and examining additional historical documentation, Theodora Kroeber, the wife of A. L. Kroeber and an anthropologist in her own right, was able to assemble bits and pieces of Ishi's life into her biographical work of the Indian. Entitled *Ishi in Two Worlds,* the biography traces what happened to Ishi after making contact with the outside world. In contrast, Kroeber's novel *Ishi, Last of His Tribe* is her attempt to reconstruct the possible nature of Ishi's existence prior to contact with whites. Little is known for certain, however.

Ishi was probably born around 1860. His early childhood was marked by frequent strife between the settlers and the Yahi. Ishi's father is thought to have been killed in the attack of 1865 by Hiram Good and his men. It was difficult, however, for anyone to obtain information from Ishi about his fellow Yahi, for he regarded discussion of the dead as a violation of proper tribal etiquette.

Reports throughout the 1870s and early 1880s attest to the fact that the few Yahi who survived the 1865 attack moved from area to area. Anthropologists believe, however, that this changed in 1885, when Ishi and his family moved into the cave formerly occupied by a grizzly bear. There they remained, virtually invisible to the rest of the world, until the discovery of the cave by surveyors in 1908.

Ishi first encountered the surveyors while he was fishing. Unable to reach the cave before them, he went into hiding. The surveyors, upon approaching the cave, saw an elderly man and a middle-aged woman fleeing. Inside they found an elderly woman who was paralyzed from the waist down. Although they did not harm her, they helped themselves to several baskets. When Ishi returned, he realized that he and his mother had to relocate. His mother, though, was too weak to travel far, and she soon died.

Three years later, in 1911, Ishi was found in the corral of a slaughterhouse in Oroville. He was initially jailed, but when an anthropologist from San Francisco by the name of T. T. Waterman expressed interest in him, Ishi was released into his custody. Waterman and his colleagues A. L. Kroeber and Edward Sapir had been studying the tribes of northern California for some time. Ishi, delighted when Waterman began to speak Yahi words, returned with the anthropologist to San Francisco to live in the University of California Museum of Anthropology. There he spent the rest of his life adjusting to the ways of the white men while still attempting to maintain a link with his past. Although he wore the clothes of the saldu and went to their theaters, he was most content when carving handmade bows at the museum.

Ishi returned to his homeland only once. On the journey, he gave A. L. Kroeber and two others information about the way he had once lived. He did not wish to permanently return to his former home, though, for he felt that the Yahi world had died along with his family. Unable to fight off the diseases of the saldu, Ishi contracted tuberculosis in 1916. He died soon afterward and was buried according to Yahi tradition.

Events in History at the Time the Novel Was Written

Interest in anthropology. The discovery of Ishi came at a time when interest in anthropology in the United States was increasing at a rapid rate. Anthropologists such as A. L. Kroeber and Edward Sapir were instrumental in the establishment of anthropology as an academic discipline, whereas formerly it had been considered a mere gentlemanly interest. Kroeber and his colleagues stressed the importance culture played in shaping the behavior of a group.

By 1964, when the novel was written, anthropology was well established as a course of study in universities throughout the world. The interest created in the field by such pioneers as A. L. Kroeber and Sapir helped create a market for books such as Theodora Kroeber's, which focused on the daily activities of a Native American.

Native American rights. Between the time periods in which *Ishi, Last of His Tribe* was set and written, the United States government went through a fitful string of policies regarding the American Indians. In 1887, under the Dawes Act, the government set out to break up reservations by allotting 160-acre parcels to individual Indian families. In 1934 it switched to a policy of support for the survival of reservations. An about-face in 1953 had the government trying to eliminate reservations once again through a plan wherein American Indians were paid to relocate in cities. Finally, in the 1960s, a decade in which the civil rights of minorities in the United States took center stage, Indian rights groups urged the government to reverse its policy once again and support tribal independence. In 1970 the government agreed to this plan and adopted a policy of "self-determination." Under this policy, which recognized the native peoples' right to independence, tribal groups were given control over money and other benefits received from the U.S. government.

Reviews. *Ishi, Last of His Tribe* was not widely publicized in the literary community because of Kroeber's relative inexperience as a writer of fiction and the book's classification as a work for young people. A few were critical of the tale. A December 1964 review in *Horn Book* faulted the novel for describing the activities of the Yahi in such detail that the book would prove tiresome to those with no special interest in American Indians. But generally Theodora Kroeber's book was warmly received by reviewers, and even the critical December 1964 review acknowledged its importance.

For More Information

Beissel, Henry. *Under Coyote's Eye: A Play about Ishi.* Montreal: Quadrant, 1980.

Heizer, Robert F., ed. *Handbook of North American Indians.* Vol. 8: *California.* Washington, D.C.: Smithsonian, 1978.

Heizer, Robert F., and Theodora Kroeber. *Ishi, the Last Yahi: A Documentary History.* Berkeley: University of California Press, 1961.

Kroeber, Theodora. *Ishi, Last of His Tribe.* Berkeley: Parnassus, 1964.

Washburn, Wilcomb E., ed. *Handbook of North American Indians.* Vol. 4: *History of Indian-White Relations.* Washington, D.C.: Smithsonian, 1988.

Waterman, Thomas Talbot. *The Yana Indians.* Berkeley: University of California Press, 1918.

Jane Eyre

by
Charlotte Brontë

~

Written and set during the Victorian Era, Charlotte Brontë's *Jane Eyre* presents a fictional account of events that take place in the author's native English countryside. Having worked as a teacher and a governess herself, Brontë brings to the story the firsthand perspective of a governess working for a wealthy family.

> **THE LITERARY WORK**
>
> A novel set in northern England during the mid-1840s; published in 1847.
>
> **SYNOPSIS**
>
> Through a first-person narrative, a poor governess tells of the romance and mystery she encounters when she accepts a position at a country manor.

Events in History at the Time of the Novel

Education for girls in Victorian England. For the most part, Victorian English society separated the duties of men and women into completely separate spheres. This meant that the male head of the family assumed the duty of earning an income, while his female counterpart worked within the domestic circle. A woman pursuing a higher education found herself branded with names such as "long-tailed sheep," an allusion to a farm animal that does not garner a high price at a sale. Like the long-tailed sheep, a well-taught woman was not considered a valuable commodity. Charlotte Brontë contradicts these notions in her novel, however. In *Jane Eyre,* the character of Rochester, at whose estate Jane is employed, finds himself attracted to her because of, rather than despite, her acute wit. While Jane does not possess the physical attributes of some of the other females whom Rochester knows, her intellectual capacity makes her a stimulating companion.

In Victorian England, the major barrier facing women was the prevalent belief that the female mind could not sufficiently acquire and retain intellectual material. Traditionalists argued that women were physically and mentally unfit for serious intellectual pursuits. In view of this prevailing attitude, women received only a limited education in certain "appropriate" subjects. According to the traditional curriculum, girls studied English, history, geography, and Scripture. They did not delve into mathematics, science, or the classics. Society expected that its women display a proficiency in art, music, French, sewing, and singing. These talents, people reasoned, would enable a young woman to provide a fitting and cultivated home for her husband.

For the most part, girls received their primary education at home, usually from their mothers. Victorian mothers instructed their young pupils not only in the traditional subjects, but in the skills of housewifery as well. Upper- middle-class families also paid for their daughters to attend special boarding schools. Another breed of boarding school, commonly known as "deplorable schools," acted as dumping grounds for orphans and other unwanted children. These establishments focused less on education than on discipline. Lowood Institution, in Brontë's novel, represents one such establishment.

> ## JOHN STUART MILL
>
> In 1869 John Stuart Mill published his now famous essay, *The Subjection of Women*. His essay stands as one of the earliest examples of the push for domestic reform. Contrary to popular opinion at the time, Mill argued that what people were describing as the nature of women was an artificial concept—the result of forced repression in some respects and excessive stimulation in others. While this essay did not in itself initiate educational reform, it did lend a certain voice to the movement. During the same year that Mill's essay was published, five groundbreaking women persuaded Cambridge University professors to lecture to them. Four years later, they became the first females to pass the university's bachelor's level examinations.

The Victorian governess. Another form of education during the period was provided by female instructors that lived and taught within a family's home. Known as governesses, these women were hired by upper-middle-class and upper-class parents to provide schooling for their children. In the novel, Jane earns her living in this occupation. Because the ability to hire this type of help was regarded as an indication of gentility and membership in elite society, families that could afford the services of a governess were rarely without one. The term *governess* was used to refer to a woman who taught in a school, traveled to her employee's house to teach, or resided with her pupils. By the year 1851, England employed over 750,000 women as domestic servants, 25,000 of whom were governesses. This occupation held a definite appeal for the middle-class woman. Since the variety of "suitable" jobs available to women was limited, a position as a governess provided a working woman with a unique opportunity to maintain a fairly respectable lifestyle. In addition, a woman who had no male supporter to furnish her with a home could find lodgings through such work.

Inherent in the position, however, was a social incongruence. While governesses resided in wealthy homes and were expected to present the outward appearance of affluence, they in fact had little of their own money. In order to make the acquaintance of several of Rochester's wealthy friends, for instance, Jane must wear her "best dress (the silver-gray one, purchased for Miss Temple's wedding, and never worn since) ... [and her] sole ornament, the pearl brooch" (Brontë, *Jane Eyre*, p. 199).

England's holdings in India. For several centuries, England maintained India as one of its colonies. In 1600 Queen Elizabeth I chartered the East India Company, the intent being to dislodge the Dutch from their domination of the trade that flowed out of Asia. Because of the vast wealth of spices from the area, control of the trade out of India was considered a supreme goal. Spices such as cloves, nutmeg, and pepper provided both flavor and partial preservation for meats on European dinner tables.

Originally, the East India Company consisted of four ships that sailed into hostile waters controlled by the Dutch. Upon arrival, the company's British commander offered gifts to the Indian leader in exchange for the freedom to trade with his land. When he returned to England, the commander had charted the most expedient water route to India, acquired over a million pounds of pepper, and established relations with India's government. With a fifteen-year charter that granted it a monopoly on trade with India, the East India Company quickly grew into an influential shipping presence. By 1657 it had obtained the power to mint money and exercise governmental control over British citizens living in India.

The British government originally authorized the presence of soldiers in India to protect its trade posts and warehouses from other European nations. By 1685, however, the East India Company had formally declared its intent to "make ... a nation in India" (Gardner, p. 44). During the late 1700s, under the governorship of Lord Cornwallis, the East India Company initiated a policy of reform based on the idea that Indians should be ruled by Europeans for their own benefit. In the belief that Indian officials were corrupt, Cornwallis excluded all Indians from holding governmental posts worth more than £500 a year, thus ensuring the highest-paying positions for the British.

The widening socioeconomic gap in India, coupled with Britain's insensitivity to native Hindu religious practices, soon led to strife between England and her colony. In 1857 India

A nineteenth-century engraving of Haworth, the town where Charlotte Brontë was raised.

made its first attempt at independence. A popular uprising known as the Indian Mutiny spread across northern India before it was finally put down by the British. The mutiny resulted in the transfer of control of the colony from the British East India Company to the British queen, Victoria.

In Brontë's novel, St. John Rivers departs from England on a missionary trip to India. Although Jane is asked to accompany him, she declines. Like other missionaries, St. John aimed to convert the Hindu Indians to Christianity. Jane says of him, "he clears their [the Indians'] painful way to improvement; he hews down like a giant the prejudices of creed and cast that encumber it" (*Jane Eyre*, p. 477). The caste system to which Jane refers is a Hindu belief in spiritual hierarchy that relegates individuals to different positions in life. According to this religion, once one is born into a certain caste, one may not move out of it in that lifetime. St. John and Jane frown on the system because it separates individuals into rigid social groups. Ironically, British control and suppression of India's peoples caused a similar, perhaps even stricter, separation between the native population and the European colonists.

The West Indies and *Jane Eyre*. In addition to British India, the colonial empire of the British West Indies surfaces in the novel, especially through Rochester's first wife, Bertha Mason. The madwoman in *Jane Eyre*, Bertha is a white Jamaican Creole. In real life, the British settled in

AN OCCUPATIONAL HAZARD—LONELINESS

One of the novel's first readers, Lady Eastlake, faulted *Jane Eyre* for failing to show proper appreciation for employers of governesses. Yet a year after the novel appeared, she wrote an essay in the *Quarterly Review* that expressed a governess's plight: "A governess has no equals, and therefore can have no sympathy.... The servants invariably detest her, for she is a dependent like themselves, and yet, for all that, as much their superior in other respects as the family they both serve. Her pupils may love her ... but they cannot be her friends. She must ... live alone, or she transgresses that invisible but rigid line which alone establishes the distance between herself and her employers." (Perkin, p. 165)

Jamaica in the last quarter of the 1600s, proceeding to establish sugar plantations on the island and making it a lucrative part of their West Indies empire. By 1807 the British had imported some 300,000 African slaves into Jamaica to work its plantations, and a social hierarchy emerged. In the upper classes, from which Bertha comes, were planters, government officials, professionals, and merchants. Bertha is, however, a Creole, a person of European descent born in the West Indies. Viewed as a mixture of two cultures, her character reflects a European fear of contamination—she is portrayed as a crawling, bestial person. Her character also reflects a fear of the harmful effect that tropical climates might have on European women. This same fear is expressed in worry over how Jane might be affected if she voyages to India.

Jane seems in the novel to identify with peoples regarded as inferior in the British Empire. She refers to herself as a slave and compares her own oppression to that suffered by the peoples under colonization. There is evidence that the novel's author shared Jane's apparent sympathy for slaves. Slavery had been abolished in the British Empire in 1833, but there was a movement afoot in the 1840s for worldwide abolition, which Brontë supported as a "glorious deed" (Brontë in Kucich, p. 108). This 1840s movement argued that slavery poisons the character of not only the slave but also the slaveholder—in *Jane Eyre,* the madwoman Bertha becomes a living example of this argument.

WIDE SARGASSO SEA

In 1966 Jean Rhys published her novel *Wide Sargasso Sea,* a work of fiction based on the madwoman in Brontë's novel. Rhys envisions Mrs. Rochester as a young woman on an island in the Caribbean Sea who is virtually sold into marriage with Rochester. In Rhys's novel, Rochester, mean-spirited and snobbish, holds his wife in contempt for the ills he finds in her island society. Upon returning to England, Rochester drives his wife to insanity and locks her away.

Treatment of insane. Before 1845 no codes existed regarding England's treatment of its insane. Run on a charitable basis, hospitals such as St. Mary's of Bethlehem (also called "Bedlam") in London and the Manchester Lunatic Hospital did not need to answer to any city or federal regulations. Equipped with barred windows that would not open and marked with the permanent odor of stale food and human waste, these buildings provided little more than basic physical comfort. In general, many of the nation's twenty thousand known insane received little or no medical attention. They were often placed in prisons or workhouses, while an unknown number of the mentally ill remained confined to their homes under the care of attendants. Known as "single lunatics," these patients could only be interviewed and counted if the Lord Chancellor of the locality suspected a household of detaining one such subject. The mentally ill therefore often failed to receive even the little care that doctors could provide.

In 1890 England passed a Lunacy Act in an attempt to set a standard of care. Under its "Miscellaneous Provisions" heading, the act made it possible for health commissioners to visit the mentally ill members of society under home care and gather regular medical reports on their progress. If substandard home care was being provided, this act allowed for the transfer of a patient to an asylum.

The Novel in Focus

The plot. The opening of the novel finds an orphaned Jane Eyre living with her aunt, Mrs. Reed, and her three cousins, Eliza, John, and Georgiana. Since Mr. Reed, Jane's only blood relation, has recently passed away, the remainder of the family scorns her as a dependent and an outsider. Provoked by a beating from John, Jane fights with her cousin. She consequently suffers a tongue-lashing from her aunt, who needs no further excuse to send Jane away to a boarding school. Although this arrangement would appear to satisfy both the Reeds and Jane, in reality Lowood Institution proves to be more of a nightmare than the Reed household itself.

While Jane does make friends with the pious Helen Burns and comes to love one kind instructor, Lowood generally presents "an irksome struggle with difficulties . . . and unwanted tasks" (*Jane Eyre,* p. 92). The children receive harsh treatment, poor nourishment, and inadequate shelter from the cold. Eventually a typhus fever epidemic takes the lives of several students, and Helen dies of tuberculosis. Nonetheless, Jane remains at Lowood until she reaches age eighteen.

After teaching for a time at Lowood, Jane applies for and obtains a governess position at Thornfield Hall, an estate seventy miles closer to London. There she instructs Adele, the young French ward of Thornfield's master, Mr. Rochester. An orphan as well, Adele easily gets along with Jane. Presently Mr. Rochester visits Thornfield and meets his new employee. Although Jane appears less physically attractive than most of Rochester's women friends, she impresses him with her intelligence and quick wit. To Jane's surprise, Rochester shuns the company of these society women and eventually proposes marriage to her. Strange events, however, begin to occur at Thornfield.

On several occasions Jane is startled by the sounds of someone moaning and by maniacal laughter, which are attributed to a servant, Grace Poole. In the middle of the night, she awakens to the smell of a fire in Rochester's room. Although Jane helps Rochester to escape bodily harm, she remains shaken by the event. The impending wedding only intensifies these occurrences.

On the night before the wedding ceremony, Jane finds a woman, ghastly in appearance, tearing her bridal veil in half. The wedding itself is interrupted by a man bearing the news that Rochester may not marry because he already has a wife. In a flood of anger, Rochester takes Jane back to Thornfield and introduces her to his wife, Bertha Mason, a madwoman whom his father had arranged for him to marry in Jamaica. Hidden in the attic under the care of Grace Poole, this woman is responsible for all of the unnatural events.

Anguished, Jane flees Thornfield for a distant part of England. She falls gravely ill. Only the kindness of the Rivers family, strangers who take her into their care, prevents her from succumbing to death. Although heartbroken, Jane attempts to build a new life in a new town. Through a miraculous turn of events, she discovers that the Rivers are cousins she never knew. Moreover, Jane inherits a small fortune from her Uncle Eyre in Jamaica, who links her with this family. Under these new circumstances, Jane debates whether she should marry St. John Rivers and go with him on a missionary trip to India. However, a supernatural occurrence, in which she hears Rochester's voice, changes Jane's mind.

Worried about her former fiancé, Jane returns to Thornfield to find it burnt to the ground. The local people inform her that the madwoman started a fire, then flung herself to her death from the roof of the mansion. Although Rochester was not killed, he lost his sight and his right hand in the fire. When she encounters him, Jane realizes the power of her feelings for Rochester, and together the two begin rebuilding their love. As their lives begin to brighten, Rochester even regains some of his eyesight.

Brontë and the supernatural. *Jane Eyre* abounds with references to the supernatural. From the ghostly apparition that Jane encounters while locked in one of her aunt's rooms to the final disembodied voice of Rochester, the novel remains full of unnatural events. These were inspired, in part, by the folklore of the Brontës's native Yorkshire. Since her mother died of cancer when Charlotte was only five years old, the Brontë children were raised primarily by a housekeeper, Tabitha (Tabby) Aykroyd. Arriving at the Brontë household in 1824 at the age of fifty-six, Tabby's memory and tales stretched back to the 1780s. The late eighteenth century was a time when the predominantly rural northern England abounded with stories of ghosts and spirits. Through Tabby's stories, the children grew familiar with such characters as the ghost of Holy Trinity Church and the headless woman of White Cross. Both Charlotte and her sister Emily drew from these tales in constructing their novels. Like others in her Victorian society, the character of Jane Eyre sees portents of the unearthly world in the world that surrounds her.

TYPHUS FEVER

In Brontë's novel, a typhus fever epidemic takes the lives of several children at Lowood school. Spread by fleas and rats, the disease usually attacks areas where overcrowded living conditions and poor sanitation invite these types of vermin. Although Brontë herself never battled this illness, England did suffer from several typhus epidemics. By the mid-1800s, however, typhus was on the decline, and after 1850 it surfaced only occasionally. The physician to His Majesty's Hospital at Haslar, Thomas Lind, wrote two essays on the prevention of the disease in the early 1800s. Among other things, he recommended that bedding and clothing of patients be scoured before reuse and that doctors and nurses change their clothing before leaving the hospital. Although seemingly common sense suggestions by later standards, these measures had not yet been employed by Victorian hospitals.

Attitude toward mental illness in Brontë's novel. In the novel, Jane and Rochester both suffer at the hands of Rochester's mentally ill first wife. Brontë makes no attempt to garner sympathy for this mental patient. In fact, her novel reflects a lack of public understanding regarding

Jane Eyre

insanity that was typical of Victorian society. Rochester's first wife, Bertha Mason, remains confined to the attic of the manor under the care of a servant. Not even all members of the household know of her existence. Although "there was some contemporary criticism of Rochester's character directed against the fact that he was a potential bigamist ... [no one noted] his failure to take adequate care of his first wife" (Jones, p. 21). According to Brontë biographers, Charlotte never came into contact with an insane person. More likely than not, she formed her opinions from the widely held views of her day.

CURRER, ELLIS, AND ACTON BELL

Charlotte was not the only Brontë who made her living through writing. Her sisters Emily and Anne received literary recognition with such works as *Wuthering Heights* (also covered in *Literature and Its Times*) and *Agnes Grey*, respectively. Because of the gender bias of the Victorian Age, however, each woman wrote under a pseudonym. Charlotte published as Currer Bell, Anne as Acton Bell, and Emily as Ellis Bell. One publisher, convinced that all three novels were composed by the same author, demanded to meet all three women at once. Although Emily would not attend, Charlotte and Anne did travel to London to allay his misgivings.

Sources. Charlotte Brontë's development of her main characters was inspired at least to some degree by information she learned about actual events. In the 1830s, while teaching at Roe Head, Brontë was exposed to news of a scandalous event nearby. A governess married a gentleman employed by the same family for whom she worked. A year later she discovered that he had another wife who was insane, the excuse given for his bigamy. In the summer of 1839, while working as a governess for a family in Yorkshire, Charlotte Brontë visited Norton Convers, a home said to have an upper-floor room with padded walls, where an insane mistress was confined until her death in a fire.

Various traits in Charlotte Brontë's characters reflect her own life experience. The fictional Helen Burns resembles Charlotte's friend Ellen Nussey in her religious piety. When Charlotte told her of her dislike for governessing, Ellen urged her to steel herself and find consolation in God. But, like her character Jane, Charlotte Brontë had difficulty resigning herself solely to God. In a letter to her friend Ellen, she acknowledges the difference between them when it comes to religion with the cry "I am not like you" (Brontë in Bentley, p. 50). Brontë seemingly adapted Rochester's blindness from her own experiences too. In 1844 her father began losing his sight to cataracts, and Charlotte Brontë acted as his nurse. As Jane "was then his [Rochester's] vision" (*Jane Eyre*, p. 476), so the author helped her father compensate for his loss of sight.

Settings in the novel can be traced back to the author's real life as well. Brontë grew up in the isolated moors of Yorkshire in northern England, and these and nearby environments are incorporated into her novel. Even Lowood Institution was inspired by the author's own experience. Mr. Brontë, whose wife had passed away while their children were young, could not afford to hire a governess. As a result, Charlotte and her sisters attended the Clergy Daughter's School at Cowan Bridge. A boarding institution, Cowan Bridge taught its pupils through fear. In his writings for children, the school director portrays a naughty child, who screamed and cried, as being suddenly struck dead by God and going straight to hell. The school was lacking in many ways, providing poor nourishment and inadequate protection from the cold. In 1825 two of Charlotte's older sisters, Maria and Elizabeth, died of tuberculosis contracted at Cowan Bridge. Afterward Mr. Brontë removed his remaining children from the care of the school.

Reception of the novel. From the first, *Jane Eyre* was an incredibly popular work. Published in 1847 by Messrs. Smith, Elder and Co., the novel acquired a vast assortment of admirers. William Thackeray, the Victorian author of *Vanity Fair*,

A FATHER'S RESPONSE

Of great importance to Charlotte Brontë was her father's opinion of her work. Three months after *Jane Eyre* was published, she ventured into his study, informed him she had written a book, read him some reviews, and asked him to look at it. He said he might. Later he told his daughters Emily and Anne, authors themselves, "Children, Charlotte has been writing a book—and I think it is a better one than I expected" (Gordon, p. 165).

spent a whole day reading the book because he could not put it down. Queen Victoria read the work to her husband, Prince Albert, referring to it as "that intensely interesting novel" (Victoria in Bentley, p. 93). A second edition came out only two months after the original publication, and a third was issued some five months following that.

Journals of the day generally agreed that the novel bore touches of genius, but they faulted as well as praised it. While the *Westminister Review* applauded the characters for being so lifelike, a review in the *Spectator* enraged Brontë, for it criticized the novel for having characters that do not behave the way people act in real life. More than one critic complimented the early portions of the plot, especially the vivid description of Jane's struggles in school, but described later elements, such as Rochester's character, as unnatural. There were also reviewers who regarded the novel as dangerous because Jane Eyre was such an unconventional woman. Actually, says one biographer, the daring part of the novel that made it so revolutionary for its time "lies not in Jane's moments of anger and rebellion, nor in the love-play ... but [rather] in Jane's claim to think for herself" (Gordon, p. 158).

For More Information

Bentley, Phyllis. *The Brontës and Their World.* London: Thames and Hudson, 1969.
Brontë, Charlotte. *Jane Eyre.* New York: Penguin, 1966.
Elliott-Binns, L. E. *Religion in the Victorian Era.* London: Lutterworth, 1953.
Gardner, Brian. *The East India Company.* New York: McCall, 1971.
Gordon, Lyndall. *Charlotte Brontë: A Passionate Life.* New York: W. W. Norton, 1994.
Jones, Kathleen. *Mental Health and Social Policy, 1845-1959.* New York: Humanities Press, 1960.
Kucich, John. "Jane Eyre and Imperialism." In *Approaches to Teaching Brontë's Jane Eyre.* New York: Modern Language Association of America, 1993.
Perkin, Joan. *Victorian Women.* New York: New York University Press, 1995.

John Brown's Final Speech

by
John Brown

John Brown was born in Connecticut in 1800 but raised in Ohio, where his values were shaped by a stern, Puritan upbringing. He was taught that God's will should be carried out without compromise. An antislavery crusader who believed that organized abolitionists were too mild in their tactics, he grew increasingly violent in his own methods. In 1859 he led a raid on the United States Arsenal at Harper's Ferry, Virginia. Killing several citizens, he and his men held the town briefly before their capture by government troops. In his speech defending these acts, Brown claimed that he had been motivated by deep religious and moral beliefs and that his deeds did not amount to murder and treason.

THE LITERARY WORK
A speech given at the courthouse in Charles Town, Virginia (now West Virginia); delivered on Wednesday, November 2, 1859.

SYNOPSIS
On the sixth day of his trial for leading an antislavery raid at Harper's Ferry, Virginia, John Brown made a speech in his defense. He denied the charges of murder and treason and proclaimed his willingness to die to free the slaves.

Events in History at the Time of the Speech

Slavery and abolition. During the 1800s the Northern states fostered the development of commerce and industry, while the Southern economy remained largely an agricultural one. Southern plantation owners relied heavily upon slave labor to produce the sugar, tobacco, wheat, and cotton crops that had become the mainstay of the Southern economy. By mid-century, close to one out of every five Southerners owned slaves.

During the nineteenth century, antislavery sentiments mounted in the North. By the mid-1800s, an organized abolition movement had arisen led by crusaders such as Frederick Douglass, Harriet Beecher Stowe, and William Lloyd Garrison. Many abolitionists hailed from Quaker or other pacifist backgrounds. However, there were also militant abolitionists, such as John Brown, who became increasingly willing to use violence in their fight.

Slave resistance. Though they risked harsh punishments, many slaves did participate in acts of personal resistance. Options ranged from passively neglecting one's chores to openly rebelling. The most famous such insurrection occurred in 1831, when the black slave Nat Turner and his followers rose up against their masters in Southampton County, Virginia. "Nat Turner's Revolt" lasted for two days, during which time he and his followers killed more than fifty whites. In retaliation, local residents captured and killed about seventy slaves. Turner managed to hide in the nearby woods for nearly two months before he was apprehended and hanged.

Most slaves, however, generally lacked the opportunity and the resources necessary to organize a revolt. The Alabama Slave Code of 1852, for example, prohibited slaves from carrying a gun or other weapon, forbade them from owning property or a dog, and made illegal the gathering of more than five male slaves anywhere outside of the plantation.

Although it was difficult for slaves to resist openly, they often defied their lot in covert ways, hiding their actions behind a mask of subservience. Common tactics might involve losing farm tools, damaging equipment, or feigning illness. Arson also became an effective form of slave resistance; it was especially hard to detect who was responsible for setting a fire.

Runaway slaves. Many slaves resisted their owners by running away. Escapes often failed, and the Fugitive Slave Law of 1850 made such flights particularly risky. An affidavit swearing that a black person was not in fact free but a slave was all the legal proof needed to seize a man, woman, or child off the street and have them hauled before a federal commissioner. Commissioners received $10 for each black person returned to slavery and $5 for each one released under the skewed system. The Fugitive Slave Law provided not only a strong incentive to seize and enslave, or re-enslave, black persons, but it also offered them no guarantee of legal protection. Those accused under the law had no access to trial by jury, nor could they give testimony challenging their capture.

Anyone found helping or harboring runaway slaves faced heavy penalties: fines amounting to $2,000 and six months' imprisonment were stipulated under the law. If caught, fugitive slaves might face crippling beatings or maiming by specially trained "Negro dogs." The risk of being sold into even crueler conditions of servitude in the Deep South was never far from a fugitive's mind. Still, several hundred slaves a year were willing to face the risk. Traveling by night and resting by day to avoid detection, some runaways fled to the swamps and mountains in the South. More fled to the free states in the North or Canada. In any case, the majority of these runaways were caught and returned to their owners.

The Underground Railroad. Though most fugitive slaves made the escape on their own, some were fortunate enough to receive help from the "Underground Railroad." Established around 1804, this series of secret routes to freedom ran mostly through Missouri, Illinois, Indiana, and Ohio. Its stops were not, in fact, part of any actual railroad but rather places where fugitives could take shelter along the way. Often moving by night to avoid detection, black or white "conductors" on the "railroad" would guide runaways one leg at a time to safety in the North. Along the way, slaves slept outdoors or rested at hiding places, often in the homes of Quaker abolitionists.

John Brown's friend Harriet Tubman, one of the Underground Railroad's most famous conductors, helped three hundred slaves flee the South, doing so on nineteen separate trips. John Fairfield, another famous conductor, posed as a slaveowner, slavetrader, or peddler to gain the confidence of Southern slave owners, thereby helping large groups of slaves escape without arousing suspicion. In one daring episode, he led twenty-eight slaves to freedom by having them pose as members of a funeral procession.

SLAVE LABOR

Slaves faced physical and emotional hardships on a daily basis. A field slave might easily work ten to fourteen hours a day planting and tending the crops. During harvest time, the workday lasted as long as eighteen hours. Organized into groups under the watchful eye of the driver, slaves often suffered whippings if their work was deemed slow or shoddy. Slaves on cotton plantations were expected to pick approximately 130 pounds of cotton each day. On sugar plantations they worked in snake-infested fields under intense heat from the sun. Cuts and lacerations from the sharp-edged sugar cane were routine, and subsequent infections from these wounds were also common.

The raid at Harper's Ferry. On October 16, 1859, John Brown led a group of twenty-one men in a raid conducted on the federal arsenal at Harper's Ferry. According to modern historians, Brown hoped to seize enough ammunition to stage a massive insurrection against Virginia slaveholders, part of a larger abolition plan he had formulated. Beginning in Northern Virginia, the site of Harper's Ferry, Brown planned to move through the Appalachian Mountains and into the Deep South. He believed the size of his forces would grow along the way until there was strength enough to establish a territory of free black and white people.

This vision of large-scale revolt was swiftly cut short on October 16. Brown and his followers in-

John Brown's Final Speech

vaded the federal arsenal at Harper's Ferry, taking several hostages. The government was quickly alerted and dispatched troops to capture the insurgents. During a siege lasting nearly thirty-six hours, Brown's men shot and killed several local citizens. Ten of Brown's men died, eight during the afternoon fighting and two when a company of marines, led by Robert E. Lee, stormed the arsenal. Among the dead were two of Brown's sons, and Brown himself was beaten, stabbed, arrested, and placed in a prison cell and chained to its floor. Three citizens and one marine had been felled by Brown's men during the standoff.

SLAVE PATROLS

The Alabama Slave Code of 1852 required all free white men to participate in patrol duty at least one night a week. Patrols kept watch for any suspicious slave activity or runaway slaves in their area and exercised the power to enter any plantation to look for subversive activity. Anyone failing to report for patrol duty was fined $10, a significant sum at the time. Wealthy plantation owners might pay for someone to replace them on patrol, but less affluent white men could not afford the expense and so had to appear in person, even if they belonged to the minority of Southern whites who opposed the idea of slavery.

The authorities charged Brown with murder, fomenting slave insurrection, and treason against the state of Virginia. Weak and wounded, he appeared before the court lying on a thin wooden cot. Several of his friends sought a reprieve from Virginia's Governor Wise in order to secure Brown's release from prison, but Brown refused and stated that he "would not walk out of the prison if the door was left open" (Brown in Sanborn, p. 632). Upon hearing his death sentence pronounced, Brown said, "I think that my great object will be nearer to its accomplishment by my death than by my life" (Brown in Sanborn, p. 623).

The aftermath of Harper's Ferry. Although it lasted just a day and a half, the Harper's Ferry raid electrified the nation. While many Northerners hailed John Brown as a hero and a martyr, others voiced strong disapproval of his violent methods. In the South, widespread rumors that abolitionists planned to stage further insurrections surfaced after the Virginia incident. Such hearsay gave Southern slaveowners the impression that abolitionists would stop at nothing to destroy slavery, and thus the entire region went on alert. Troops began drilling and militia leaders demanded more weapons and ammunition, all in escalation of the South's readiness to fight.

The Harper's Ferry raid helped push the nation toward Civil War. One year later, on November 6, 1860, Republican candidate Abraham Lincoln was elected president. Lincoln opposed the spread of slavery but originally had no intention of destroying it altogether. He was nevertheless unpopular in the slave states, ten of which gave him no electoral votes at all. Prior to the election, pro-slavery factions of Democrats charged that important Republican leaders knew about Brown's plan to attack Harper's Ferry before it occurred. As a result of such insinuation, some antislavery Republicans welcomed claims that Brown was insane, which allowed them to distance themselves from the controversy surrounding his actions.

John Brown's final letters home. On November 8, 1859, after receiving his sentence to hang, John Brown wrote a letter to his wife and children. Brown expressed continuing optimism that through his death he was achieving a worthy goal. "P.S." wrote Brown. "Yesterday I was sentenced to be hanged.... I am still quite cheerful" (Brown in Sanborn, p. 580). He comforted his family, asking them not to not feel sad or degraded by the court's sentence. Remember, he wrote, that Jesus "suffered a most excruciating death on the cross as a felon" (Brown in Sanborn, p. 586).

On December 2, 1859, the morning of his execution, Brown handed his final letter to one of his guards. It read, "I, John Brown, am now quite *certain* that the crimes of this *guilty land* will never be purged away but with *blood*. I had, as I now think vainly, flattered myself that without very much bloodshed it might be done" (Brown in Sanborn, p. 620).

The Speech in Focus

The text. The verdict of guilty came back on the sixth day of Brown's trial, on Wednesday, November 2, 1859. The clerk asked him if he had anything to say in response. Brown rose from the cot upon which he had lain throughout his trial and spoke in a clear, strong voice.

> I have, may it please the Court, a few words to say. In the first place, I deny everything but what I have all along admitted, of a design on my part to free slaves. I intended certainly to

have made a clean thing of that matter, as I did last winter when I went into Missouri, and there took slaves without the snapping of a gun on either side, moving them through the country, and finally leaving them in Canada. I designed to have done the same thing again on a larger scale. That was all I intended to do. I never did intend murder or treason, or the destruction of property, or to excite or incite the slaves to rebellion, or to make insurrection.

I have another objection, and that is that it is unjust that I should suffer such a penalty. Had I interfered in the manner which I admit, and which I admit has been fairly proved—for I admire the truthfulness and candor of the greater portion of the witnesses who have testified in this case—had I so interfered in behalf of the rich, the powerful, the intelligent, the so-called great, or in behalf of their friends, either father, mother, brother, sister, wife, or children, or any of that class, and suffered and sacrificed what I have in this interference, it would have been all right, and every man in this Court would have deemed it an act worthy of reward rather than punishment.

The Court acknowledges, too, as I suppose, the validity of the law of God. I see a book kissed, which I suppose to be the Bible, or at least the New Testament, which teaches me that all things whatsoever I would that men should do to me, I should do even so to them. It teaches me further to remember them that are in bonds as bound with them. I endeavored to act up to that instruction.

I say that I am yet too young to understand that God is any respecter of persons. I believe that to have interfered as I have done, as I have always freely admitted I have done in behalf of His despised poor, is no wrong, but right. Now, if it is deemed necessary that I should forfeit my life for the furtherance of the ends of justice, and mingle my blood with the blood of my children and with the blood of millions in this slave country whose rights are disregarded by wicked, cruel, and unjust enactments, I say let it be done.

Let me say one word further. I feel entirely satisfied with the treatment I have received on my trial. Considering all the circumstances, it has been more generous than I expected. But I feel no consciousness of guilt. I have stated from the first what was my intention, and what was not. I never had any design against the liberty of any person, nor any disposition to commit treason or excite slaves to rebel or make any general insurrection. I never encouraged any man to do so, but always discouraged any idea of that kind.

Let me say also in regard to the statements made by some of those who were connected with me, I fear it has been stated by some of them that I have induced them to join me, but the contrary is true. I do not say this to injure them, but as regretting their weakness. Not one but joined me of his own accord, and the greater part at their own expense. A number of them I never saw, and never had a word of conversation with till the day they came to me, and that was for the purpose I stated. Now, I am done.

(Brown, pp. 94-5)

John Brown's motives. As soon as the news of the raid broke, speculation arose about Brown's motives. Such conjecture has continued, and often involves the question of his grasp on reality. In illustrations, he was often portrayed as a wild-eyed man with a mess of hair and an unkempt beard. His supporters at the Harper's Ferry trial urged him to plead insanity, hoping that doing so would insure his acquittal. Others hoped that portraying Brown as unbalanced would discredit his behavior and deny him the "divisive symbolic importance that Brown and his northern sympathizers wanted" (Warch and Fanton, p. 85).

WITNESS TO THE EXECUTION

Present at John Brown's execution was John Wilkes Booth, a member of the Virginia Militia. Booth, who would later assassinate Abraham Lincoln, reportedly marched pompously around the scaffold, delighting in the execution.

However, many regarded Brown as of a fanatically religious bent rather than simply insane. His speech to the court makes one thing clear: his actions came out of a religious background that made them, as he saw it, entirely appropriate; indeed, the speech itself sounds at times like a sermon. Raised according to Christian values, Brown had a Puritan concept of God, one based more on the stern and punishing figure of the Old Testament than on the merciful one of the New Testament. It was said that the abolitionist had committed to memory the entire Bible.

Brown simply saw himself as "acting up to" (living up to) the words that the rest of society claimed to follow—those found on the pages of the Bible. His interpretation of the religious text left him no choice: only by freeing slaves could he follow God's wishes. As he says in his speech, he never meant to kill or cause a revolt or commit treason. He meant only to free slaves and

John Brown's Final Speech

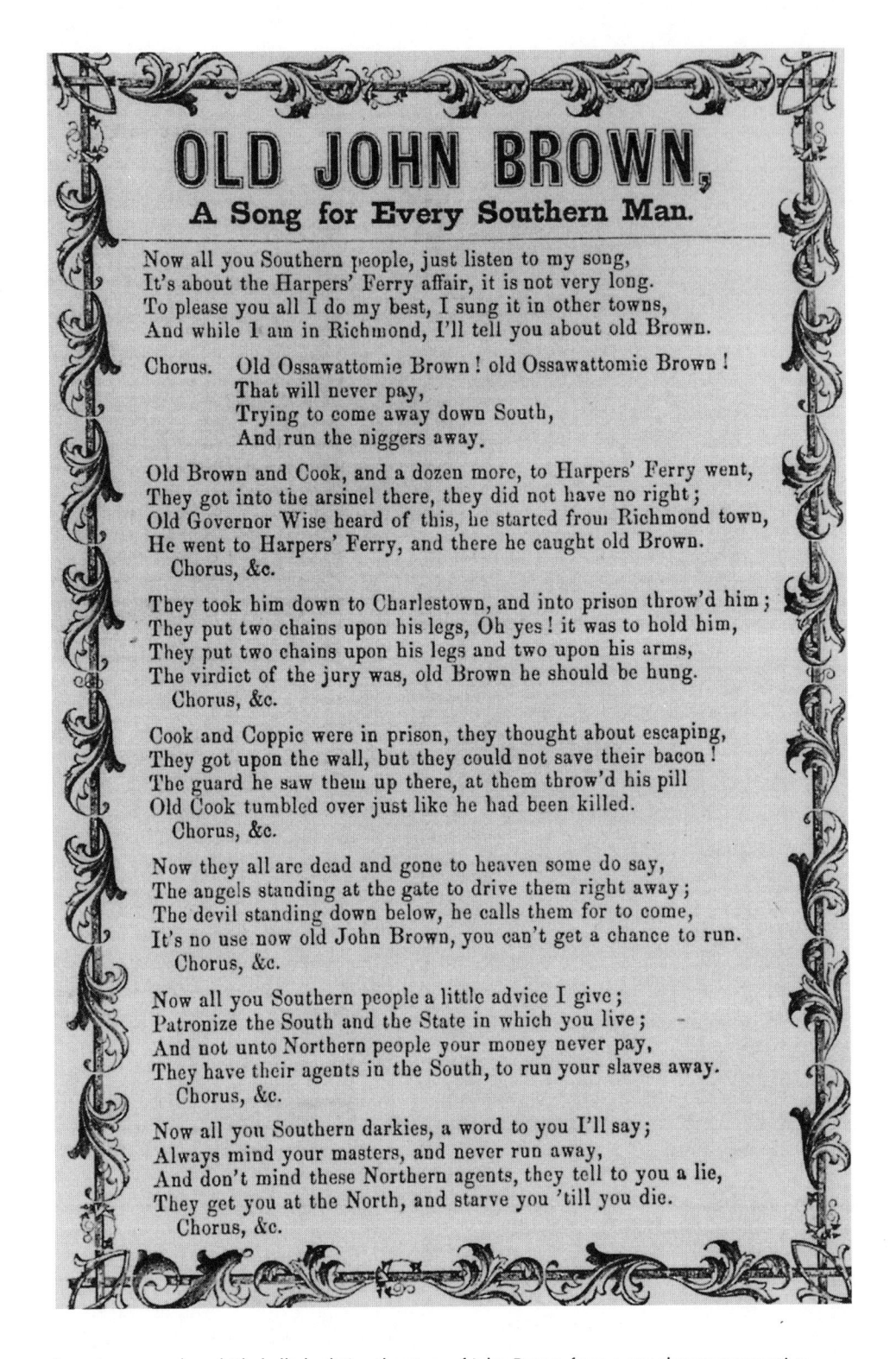

OLD JOHN BROWN,
A Song for Every Southern Man.

Now all you Southern people, just listen to my song,
It's about the Harpers' Ferry affair, it is not very long.
To please you all I do my best, I sung it in other towns,
And while I am in Richmond, I'll tell you about old Brown.

Chorus. Old Ossawattomie Brown! old Ossawattomie Brown!
    That will never pay,
    Trying to come away down South,
    And run the niggers away.

Old Brown and Cook, and a dozen more, to Harpers' Ferry went,
They got into the arsinel there, they did not have no right;
Old Governor Wise heard of this, he started from Richmond town,
He went to Harpers' Ferry, and there he caught old Brown.
  Chorus, &c.

They took him down to Charlestown, and into prison throw'd him;
They put two chains upon his legs, Oh yes! it was to hold him,
They put two chains upon his legs and two upon his arms,
The virdict of the jury was, old Brown he should be hung.
  Chorus, &c.

Cook and Coppic were in prison, they thought about escaping,
They got upon the wall, but they could not save their bacon!
The guard he saw them up there, at them throw'd his pill
Old Cook tumbled over just like he had been killed.
  Chorus, &c.

Now they all are dead and gone to heaven some do say,
The angels standing at the gate to drive them right away;
The devil standing down below, he calls them for to come,
It's no use now old John Brown, you can't get a chance to run.
  Chorus, &c.

Now all you Southern people a little advice I give;
Patronize the South and the State in which you live;
And not unto Northern people your money never pay,
They have their agents in the South, to run your slaves away.
  Chorus, &c.

Now all you Southern darkies, a word to you I'll say;
Always mind your masters, and never run away,
And don't mind these Northern agents, they tell to you a lie,
They get you at the North, and starve you 'till you die.
  Chorus, &c.

A contemporary broadside ballad relating the story of John Brown from a pro-slavery perspective.

nothing more. If others objected, then so be it. He dealt with critics of his goal in the uncompromising terms of an Old Testament prophet, terms by which he not only lived, but also died.

In a deposition given to the court on November 14, 1859, his associate E. N. Smith described John Brown as a fine but peculiar man. Although Smith admired Brown's courage and devotion to his beliefs, he voiced doubts about his sanity. When it came to slavery, Smith said, "he is surely a monomaniac as any inmate of any lunatic asylum in the country" (Smith in Warch and Fanton, p. 86). Others who knew Brown shared this belief. Friends and relatives cited a family history of mental imbalance in their attempts to obtain an acquittal by reason of insanity. Yet John Brown's wife staunchly defended her husband's state of mind, stating that his actions were the result of his strongest convictions. Brown himself firmly rejected the insanity plea.

Sources. Although Brown helped runaway slaves, he never joined any formal abolitionist organizations. He read the works of William Lloyd Garrison's militant followers, and he was influenced by the teachings of Frederick Douglass, whom he met once in Springfield, Massachusetts. Brown even invited him to join in the raid on Harper's Ferry, but Douglass refused.

Brown's own writing and actions can be viewed as sources contributing to his final speech. Masquerading as a black man, John Brown had written an 1847 essay titled "Sambo's Mistakes," published in the black newspaper, *The Ram's Horn*. Allegedly a first-person account of slave resistance, "Sambo's Mistakes" rejected the tactics of peaceful abolitionists. Encouraging slaves to reject their submissive status using whatever means necessary, the essay included some sarcasm: "I have always expected to secure the favor of the whites by tamely submitting to every species of indignity contempt & wrong instead of nobly resisting their brutal aggressions from principle & taking my place as a man & assuming the responsibilities of a man" (Brown in Warch and Fanton, pp. 6-7).

Nine years after writing "Sambo's Mistakes," Brown put his words into action in a violent manner. During the early 1850s, proslavery forces in Missouri had begun invading the neighboring free territory of Kansas, where five of Brown's sons had moved. In letters to their father they described these brutal guerrilla raids, which led the press to call the territory "Bleeding Kansas." At first, he thought merely of settling there with his sons, but their letters soon aroused another aim: to fight alongside the "Free-Soil" Kansas. Collecting weapons from fellow militant abolitionists in New York, Massachusetts, and Ohio, Brown himself went to Kansas in 1855. In response to the sacking of the Free-Soil town of Lawrence, Kansas, Brown led a counter-raid into Missouri in 1856. With four of his sons (one had been slain by proslavery forces), Brown and two others hacked five defenseless proslavers to death with sabers. As was true of his later actions at Harper's Ferry, Brown felt no remorse for this deed.

The single most important foundation for Brown's speech is the Bible. Brown cites passages that would have been well known to his audience, including the golden rule ("Do unto others as you would have them do unto you"). Perhaps most importantly, in Brown's words the Bible taught him "to remember them that are in bonds as bound with them." In other words, Brown believed that the Bible commanded all to feel enslaved as long as slavery existed for some. It should also be noted that his father, Owen Brown, had instilled in his son an unswerving commitment to obeying God's commandments.

How the speech was received. Frederick Douglass praised John Brown, as did Ralph Waldo Emerson, Henry David Thoreau, and Victor Hugo. Brown's influence on transcendentalists such as Emerson and Thoreau was tremendous. They disagreed with the characterization of Brown as insane. In fact, Emerson described Brown as a hero of "simple, artless goodness"; to Thoreau, Brown was "an angel of light" (Emerson and Thoreau in Boyer, p. 3). The French writer Victor Hugo saw Brown's life and death within the context of America's political and moral situation. Brown was executed not by the judge, or the people of Virginia, or the governor, or the hangman, Hugo wrote. Instead, his executor "is the whole American republic.... Politically speaking, the murder of Brown will be an irrevocable mistake" (Hugo in Sanborn, p. 630).

By contrast, editorials in the *New York Times* reflect the conflicting feelings Brown more commonly provoked. On November 3, the day after Brown gave the speech, the *Times* said, "Brown's speech classifies him at once, and in a class of one. He is a fanatic" (Warch and Fanton, p. 124). Yet a month later, after the execution, the *Times* admitted:

> But there is a very wide and profound conviction in the public mind that he was personally honest and sincere,—that his motives were such as he deemed honorable and righteous, and that he believed himself to be

John Brown's Final Speech

doing a religious duty in the work which he undertook.... We do not believe that one-tenth of the people of the Northern States would assent to the justice of Brown's views of duty, or deny that he had merited the penalty which has overtaken his offence. But we have just as little doubt that a majority of them pity his fate and respect his memory, as that of a brave, conscientious and misguided man. (Warch and Fanton, pp. 125-26)

For More Information

Boyer, Richard O. *The Legend of John Brown: A Biography and a History.* New York: Alfred A. Knopf, 1973.

Brown, John. "Speech and Sentence of Brown." In *The Life, Trial and Execution of Captain John Brown, known as "Old Brown of Ossawatomie."* Compiled by R. M. De Witt. New York: Da Capo, 1969.

Furnas, J. C. *The Road to Harper's Ferry.* New York: William Sloane Associates, 1959.

Kolchin, Peter. *American Slavery, 1619-1877.* New York: Hill and Wang, 1993.

Nelson, Truman. *The Old Man: John Brown at Harper's Ferry.* San Francisco: Holt, Rinehart and Winston, 1973.

Sanborn, F. B., ed. *Life and Letters of John Brown, Liberator of Kansas, and Martyr of Virginia.* Boston: Roberts Brothers, 1885.

Warch, Richard, and Jonathan F. Fanton, eds. *John Brown.* Englewood Cliffs, N.J.: Prentice-Hall, 1973.

Leaves of Grass

by
Walt Whitman

> **THE LITERARY WORK**
>
> A collection of poems set in the United States; published from 1855 to 1891-92.
>
> **SYNOPSIS**
>
> As the nation and poet aged, *Leaves of Grass* evolved into a documentary collection of verse that details the American experience during the Civil War era and beyond.

Living during one of the most dynamic, divisive periods in American history, Walt Whitman captured the development of the nation and himself in his masterpiece, *Leaves of Grass*. The collection of poems, written over thirty-seven years, is at once art and documentary, revealing both personal and universal truths. Innovative in both form and substance, *Leaves of Grass* offers a positive yet realistic way of perceiving the world by showing the daily miracle of life.

Events in History at the Time of the Poems

Age of development and dissent. The 1850s in America was a period of reform and rapid change. Cities grew and construction boomed as record numbers of immigrants—250,000 annually—flooded the developing nation. Westward expansion, fueled by the gold rush of 1848-49 and the development of an ever-growing railroad network, seemed to indicate a boundless America, full of prosperity and promise. The publication of Charles Darwin's *Origin of the Species* in 1859 further promoted the concepts of evolution and eternal progress. Darwin's groundbreaking work seemed to back the assertion that American democracy would prevail and technology would continue to improve civilization. Very much a product of his time, Walt Whitman was a firm believer in eternal progress and man's capacity to reform society. Like others around him, he adhered to popular utopian philosophies that a perfect society could be achieved in America through scientific advancement and social reform. In America, thought Whitman, the builders of the nation—the "god-like" common people—could and would create a utopia on earth.

Civil War. Civil war, however, threatened to shatter hopes of achieving utopia. A rift between Northern and Southern states (largely over slavery, commerce, and governmental control) evolved into war in 1861 and served as a sobering check on the utopian ideals of the 1850s.

Still, Whitman, who served in Washington, D.C., as a war nurse (1863-65) and visited the war's battlefields, where he saw firsthand the war's devastating effects—the blood and death—remained optimistic. At war's end the triumph of the North and the preservation of the Union once again bolstered optimism. Whitman and many others felt that America was able to weather this severe storm only because of its foundation of democracy.

Though much of *Leaves of Grass*—and perhaps the best of his poetry—was written before the Civil War, Whitman said the collection could not have been produced without its influence. His stint as a war nurse, tending to wounded and dying young men in makeshift army hospitals, was the most profound experience of his life. He wrote that he felt "horrified and disgusted" seeing "men mutually butchering each other," but at the same time the experience made him feel needed (Whitman in Zweig, p. 20). Sick and dying soldiers, some with amputated limbs, clung and cleaved to him, and he found it "delicious to be the object of so much love and reliance" (Whitman in Zweig, p. 20).

WHITMAN AND LINCOLN

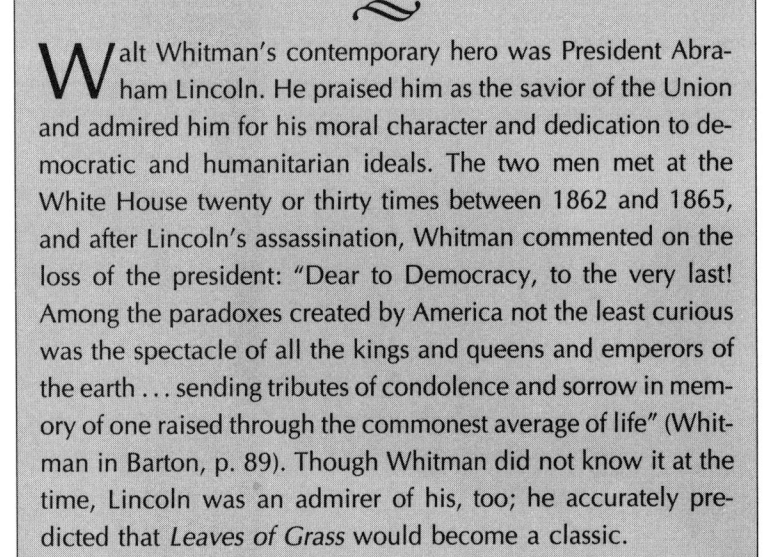

Walt Whitman's contemporary hero was President Abraham Lincoln. He praised him as the savior of the Union and admired him for his moral character and dedication to democratic and humanitarian ideals. The two men met at the White House twenty or thirty times between 1862 and 1865, and after Lincoln's assassination, Whitman commented on the loss of the president: "Dear to Democracy, to the very last! Among the paradoxes created by America not the least curious was the spectacle of all the kings and queens and emperors of the earth ... sending tributes of condolence and sorrow in memory of one raised through the commonest average of life" (Whitman in Barton, p. 89). Though Whitman did not know it at the time, Lincoln was an admirer of his, too; he accurately predicted that *Leaves of Grass* would become a classic.

Reform and religion. Reform movements abounded during the 1800s. Women's rights, temperance, abolition of slavery, and reforms of education, labor, and health were vigorously championed. Accompanying the reform movements was a wave of religious zeal. Evangelical ministers preached atop soapboxes throughout the country, attempting to convert immigrants and Christianize the West. Church leaders joined and sometimes led the temperance and abolition movements.

Whitman was himself both a reformer and spiritual guide. He believed "the real grandeur of these [United] States must be their religion, otherwise there is no real and permanent grandeur." He proposed to "inaugurate a religion" of his own design through the publication of *Leaves of Grass* (Blodgett in Whitman, p. 20). He cast himself in the role of a humanitarian leader, advocating the abolition of slavery and promoting the concept of equality. "I will show of male and female," he wrote in the opening of *Leaves of Grass*, "that either is but the equal of the other"; he asserted that "every atom belonging to me as good [as] belongs to you" (Whitman, *Leaves of Grass*, p. 23).

Victorian Age. The nineteenth century has been named the Victorian Age after Queen Victoria, who was the reigning monarch of England. Exported from Great Britain, Victorian morals and literary styles had a tremendous impact on social behavior and literary content in the United States. Victorian morals dictated a life of restraint, hard work, and avoidance of worldly pleasures, conventions that Whitman daringly defied. In *Leaves of Grass*, he wrote passionate prose and praised the human body and the beauty of lovemaking. He even hinted at homosexual relations in such phrases as "burning for his love whom I love" (*Leaves of Grass*, p. 125). Given the Victorian values of the day, such phrases led government authorities to brand the work as "obscene literature" in 1882.

Democracy. By the turn of the century, America had endured at least four major wars, expanded from thirteen colonies to forty-five states, survived the assassination of President Lincoln and the near-impeachment of President Andrew Johnson, and abolished slavery. The government faced discontented groups from all walks of life: American Indians, African Americans, women, laborers, and ex-Confederates. Still, its democratic structure provided a forum for dissent, which Whitman applauded. In *Leaves of Grass* he contends that the government is for "you" the people and not vice versa. Called the poet of democracy, Whitman authored a guidebook to his concept of democracy when he penned *Leaves of Grass*. By his own confession, he viewed his poetry as a way of giving a new philosophy of body and soul to the American system of government.

The Poems in Focus

The contents. Begun in 1847, *Leaves of Grass* was printed in several different forms and grew tremendously in volume and content over a span of nearly forty years. The final edition of 1891-92 consists of fifteen different sections, beginning with "Starting from Paumanok," reaching a midpoint with "Memories of President Lincoln," and ending with "Good-Bye My Fancy." The final edition of *Leaves of Grass* begins with Whitman identifying himself as the quintessential common man and asserting that we are all linked in our humanity; therefore, he contends, his poems (or "chants" as he calls them) will reveal universal truths.

Whitman then tells the story of his life, beginning with his childhood in Paumanok—the American Indian name for Long Island, New York. Indicating that he has traveled the nation and has lived and worked in a variety of locations, he reveals his love of nature and establishes at the outset his belief in the miracle of daily life. Also immediately established are what Whitman regards as the main issues of his day, such as "union," "identity," "eternal progress," and "the kosmos"; he hints that he will touch upon them all, revealing the flavor of his age (*Leaves of Grass*, p. 16).

Utilizing a loose or free-form style, Whitman tells the story of both America's and his own development. He ends the first section with a vivid image of nineteenth-century life, including its myriad technological achievements—the invention of the printing press (1846), the telegraph (1832), and the steam locomotive (1829)—and beckons his readers to accompany him as he traces his and the country's development.

The second section, "Song of Myself," is probably the most well-known of all the sections within the collection. Originally the first section of the 1855 edition, "Song of Myself" was the first part of *Leaves of Grass* that Whitman wrote. "Song of Myself" announces that Whitman, starting at age thirty-seven, will continue to add to the collection until death. His inspiration, we are told, will be daily life—something few of us take the time to stop and contemplate. He insists that after reading his work, readers will see the miracle of seemingly ordinary events from a fresh perspective. Whitman says he views his collection as an interactive work; he does not see himself strictly as the teacher and the reader exclusively as the pupil, but says rather that both will serve as teacher and pupil educating each other. In a passage that caused others to label the work as vulgar and shocking for the time, Whitman notes that he will write of everything, including sex and the human form. He talks of the beauty of the human body and the wonders of procreation (the reproduction of human life by bearing offspring):

> Urge and urge and urge,
> Always the procreant urge of the world,
> Out of the dimness opposite equals advance,
>   always substance and increase, always sex,
> Always a knit of identity, always distinction,
>   always a breed of life....

Walt Whitman

> Welcome is every organ and attribute of me,
>   and of any man, hearty and clean,
> Not an inch or particle of an inch is vile, and
>   none shall be less familiar than the rest.
>   (*Leaves of Grass*, pp. 30-1)

Whitman makes it clear that he will speak of all aspects of life and will not adhere to the Victorian notion that sex and the human body are shameful. He goes on to show that life is a matter of perspective, and that all things can be viewed in a multitude of ways. This leads him to question popular definitions of luck and misfortune, of progress and regression, and of right and wrong.

Writing that his thoughts "are really the thoughts of all men in all ages and lands," Whitman calls attention to the connectedness among people and claims to speak for "every hue and caste ... every rank and religion" without bias (*Leaves of Grass*, p. 45). Relaying a series of seemingly random events, he praises the beauty of nature in one line and speaks of the horrors seen on battlefields in the next. He gives all the images of his life and times: the good, the bad, the clear, the confusing, the random, and the profound. He becomes "the hounded [fugitive] slave" who winces at the bite of dogs, and then "an old artillerist" telling of his fort's bombardment during the Mexican War (*Leaves of Grass*, pp. 66-7).

Subsequent sections of the work expand on the issues raised in the opening poems and trace Whitman's experiences through age seventy. Examination of the various editions of *Leaves of Grass* gives insight into these experiences.

Evolution of an idea. Whitman produced six editions of *Leaves of Grass* plus three additional reprintings over a period of thirty years. During this time both the nation and Whitman's work underwent rapid change. As Whitman's personal outlook changed because of the passing of events, the tone and content of his poetry also evolved. What began as a highly optimistic treatise on the virtues of democracy and the unquestionable notion of progress turned into a work with a more sober outlook. Whitman himself realized, "no great poem ... can be essentially consider'd without weighing first the age, politics (or want of politics) and aim, visible forms, unseen soul, and the current times, out of the midst of which it rises and is formulated" (Whitman in Reynolds, p. 585).

Optimism and naiveté—1855. The first edition of *Leaves of Grass* was, as noted, substantially optimistic in tone. It celebrated the idea of democracy as Whitman perceived it: a world with no racial, religious, class, or gender barriers; a world of equal opportunity and no formal code of behavior. Whitman did not think that these things were occurring within the United States yet, but he believed that they were within the realm of possibility. All that was preventing Americans from achieving this ideal society, thought Whitman, was a lack of direction, which he was now providing. Whitman felt that he could be the savior of the nation on the strength of his stirring words, a view that echoed the feelings of some nineteenth-century evangelists who felt similarly about their own pronouncements. Whitman himself paid to have the first edition of his work published, supposing that there was a ready audience for his message. While he did receive praise from Ralph Waldo Emerson, premier American man of letters at the time, Whitman won distinction only as a freak and an oddity in the eyes of most American literary critics.

Disappointment begins—1856. Whitman's hopes led to disappointment, and the nation experienced much of the same. Promises that national leadership would overcome inequalities in society and that geographic expansion would lead to eternal progress with no ill effects were destined to bring disillusionment and frustration. By 1856 the nation had begun to divide sharply over the issue of slavery, which had in fact caused intense conflict since the Missouri Compromise. In addition, a disparity of wealth in the country was widening rather than narrowing as the democratic ideal had promised. A series of financial "panics" weakened the economy as well, while the gold rush of 1848-49 and other get-rich-schemes produced far more paupers than wealthy Americans.

Whitman experienced personal disappointment as well. He had dreamed that the demand for his poetry would exceed twenty thousand copies annually and that he would become America's much-needed spiritual guide. Instead, his work was called a "mass of stupid filth," and his publishers insisted on heavily editing "certain objectionable passages" before they would release a second edition (Griswold in Reynolds, p. 348).

The form as well as the substance of the second edition reflected Whitman's growing disillusionment. Whereas the first edition had been ornately bound in a cover inlaid with gold leaf, the second edition was printed in simple typeface and bound in a thick green volume, intended for the average reader to carry and read outdoors. New poems included in the volume illustrated the political turmoil caused by the slavery issue and the lack of substantive national leadership, as well as a poem (later known as "To a foil'd European Revolutionaire") that clearly drew a parallel between failed European revolutions and the American Revolution.

Suffering and distrust—1860. In 1860, with the nation on the brink of civil war, the third edition of *Leaves of Grass* was released. Much speculation has arisen about Whitman's personal life during this period and the possible suffering that may have contributed to the frustrated, confused, and dejected feelings conveyed in the new poetry of this edition. Certainly national events were producing such emotions, while the relative failure of his first two volumes appears also to have contributed to the new tone and content. One addition, "To a President," shows Whitman's disdain for the current leadership (or lack thereof): "All you are doing and saying is to America dangled mirages" (*Leaves of Grass*, p. 272).

Whitman's growing sense of helplessness to do anything to prevent the impending Civil War or to become the spiritual guide of the masses is strongly reflected in "I Sit and Look Out":

> I see the workings of battle, pestilence, tyranny, I see martyrs and prisoners,...

Frontispiece and title page of the first edition of *Leaves of Grass*.

> I observe the slights and depredations cast by
> arrogant persons upon laborers, the poor,
> and upon negroes, and the like;
> All these—all the meanness and agony
> without end I sitting look out upon,
> See, hear, and am silent.
> (*Leaves of Grass*, pp. 272-73)

Conformity and resolution—1881. By the release of the 1881 edition, Whitman had mellowed somewhat. Both he and the nation had experienced a great deal, and much of his former optimism returned. He had endured the Civil War, witnessed Reconstruction and the abolition of slavery, watched the rise and fall (by assassination) of President Abraham Lincoln, and traveled extensively throughout the West and in Canada. His journey to the West was an especially important factor in Whitman's changing views. Offering seemingly limitless natural resources and freedom of access, the West renewed his faith in national progress through expansion and technology. With the economy on the rebound, Whitman's belief in the capitalist system was also restored.

Meanwhile, the mood in the country had changed, becoming more conservative than before the Civil War. The prewar tolerance for individualism and experimentation dwindled, and a new focus on the self-made businessman and the organization emerged. Whitman became a clerk in a government organization, the attorney general's office, helping to process the pardons for former Southern rebels. Affected by the nation's mood as well as his job, Whitman changed his style. His verse became more conventional, meeting popular expectations oftener than before—"poems like 'O Captain!' and 'Pioneers!' had a buoyant driving militarism sure to please the postwar crowd" (Reynolds, p. 458).

Whitman was finally becoming a respected public figure, and his goals of leading the country and promoting democracy were in part being fulfilled. Based on his poem "O Captain!" he had begun to lecture on President Lincoln. Whitman's poetry gained stature, and by the time the 1881 *Leaves of Grass* was published, he was being widely applauded by the literary establishment.

The only officially sanctioned edition of *Leaves of Grass* was published in 1881 by one of Boston's finest publishing houses (James R. Osgood and Company). Because of the sexual nature of some of the poems, the Boston district attorney ordered Osgood to stop publishing the book on the ground that it was obscene literature. In the end, Whitman would not agree to all the changes Osgood demanded, and their publishing arrangement collapsed. But the controversy only helped Whitman. As one observer commented, "the book has been advertised more widely than ever by the attempt to suppress it." (Reynolds, p. 543). A Philadelphia firm, Rees Welsh, took over the publication, and *Leaves of Grass* experienced its best sales yet; the one thousand-copy run of the edition reportedly sold out in a single day.

Whitman's renewed optimism was not of the naive brand of his earliest poetry. His was a new voice, a fresh perspective. In "As I Walk These Broad Majestic Days," Whitman shows his ultimate expression of hope for the future, citing the growth of cities and the spread of inventions:

> I see the ships, (they will last a few years,)
> The vast factories with their foremen and workmen,
> And hear the indorsement of all, and do not object to it.
> But I too announce solid things,
> Science, ships, politics, cities, factories, are not nothing,
> They stand for realities he says, and all is as it should be. Then he turns to his own realities, those of a poet, because
> What else is so real as mine?
> Libertad and the divine average, freedom to every slave on the face of the earth,
> The rapt promises and luminé of seers, the spiritual world, these centuries-lasting songs.
> And our visions, the visions of poets, the most solid announcements of any.
> (*Leaves of Grass*, pp. 486-87)

The 1881 edition of *Leaves of Grass* combined the substance and structure that Whitman had been struggling to achieve since he had begun the work. Though additions were made later, the basic structure of the work was established with this version and was not altered.

Deathbed edition—1891. The final or "deathbed" edition of *Leaves of Grass* was the most optimistic in tone. Whitman added thirty-five new poems in a final section called "Good-Bye My Fancy." Mostly about religion or the afterlife, the poems reflected his happy outlook at the time. "Is there anything better in this world anywhere," he asked, "than cheer...? Any religion better?"; explaining himself, he said "I stand for the sunny point of view—stand for the joyful conclusions" (Whitman in Reynolds, p. 585). Though his health was failing, the poet's vision had become truly positive.

In this final edition, Whitman touches on his own life, then traces human development from the Garden of Eden through America's westward expansion, the Civil War, and the rise and fall of President Lincoln, taking detours down various other roads. The poet winds up his collection commenting on death—but in an unconventional way. Whitman welcomes death, portraying it as an event as joyous as birth. With "Good-bye My Fancy" he concludes a lifetime work regarded as a dialogue with his soul. Whitman does not profess to know what death means, or whether his soul is immortal or dies with his physical self, but he is happy for the time they have shared together: "Long have we lived, joy'd, caress'd together; Delightful!—now separation—Good-bye my Fancy" (*Leaves of Grass*, p. 558).

Whitman conveyed a sense of contentment at having completed the work of his life. "*L. of G. at last complete*—after 33 y'rs of hackling at it, all times & moods of my life," he wrote at one point (Whitman in Reynolds, p. 586). He seemed to know he had produced a masterpiece that would last forever. In contrast to the 1881 edition, however, this final deathbed edition sold reasonably but not marvelously well.

Sources. Whitman derived the subject matter for *Leaves of Grass* from a compilation of newspaper accounts (he worked the bulk of his early life as a journalist), from personal observations, and from a lifetime of experience. Many of the events discussed in the work that he did not personally witness he identified with as a humanitarian. For example, he used well-known newspaper reports as the source for his depiction of fugitive slaves being captured. Whitman also emulated the style of evangelical ministers and wrote his "leaves" as gospels.

Reviews. Even the deathbed edition of Whitman's "songs," though they celebrated the pains and pleasures of average citizens, found only a small audience among them. A review of the time, as one biographer notes, aptly summarized the response from Whitman's primary audience, the American people: "The poet of the people is neglected by the people, while the works of scholarly singers like Longfellow and Bryant find a place in every farmer's library" (Reynolds, p. 589).

Whitman's work was well-received in Europe, where it had a profound impact on realism, a literary movement of the time. In stark contrast to writers of the Romantic movement, *Leaves of Grass* was based in realism and shunned all literary conventions of the era. Whitman's work signaled a shift from a reserved, overeducated, European style of literature to a more colloquial, formless, and freer style that reflected the new nation of the United States. Yet the work, although well-received in Europe, would not become popular in the United States for close to forty years.

For More Information

Barton, William E. *Abraham Lincoln and Walt Whitman.* Port Washington, N.Y.: Kennikat Press, 1955.

Bowers, Fredson. *Whitman's Manuscripts.* Chicago: University of Chicago Press, 1955.

Callow, Philip. *From Noon to Starry Night: A Life of Walt Whitman.* Chicago: Ivan R. Dee, 1992.

Davis, William C. *The Civil War.* Alexandria, Va.: Time-Life, 1983.

Reynolds, David S. *Walt Whitman's America.* New York: Alfred A. Knopf, 1995.

Whitman, Walt. *Leaves of Grass.* Edited by Harold W. Blodgett. New York: New York University Press, 1965.

Zweig, Paul. *Walt Whitman: The Making of the Poet.* New York: Basic Books, 1984.

Little Women

by
Louisa May Alcott

Born in 1832, Louisa May Alcott grew up in Concord, Massachusetts, which later became the setting of her most famous novel, *Little Women*. Most of the characters depicted in this highly autobiographical story resemble people Alcott knew as a young girl. Moreover, many of the March sisters' experiences in that novel are similar to those of Alcott and her own three sisters. In addition to these autobiographical elements, *Little Women* reflects much about the daily lives of nineteenth-century Americans growing up in New England during the heyday of philosophical and social reform.

> **THE LITERARY WORK**
>
> A novel set in Concord, Massachusetts, in the 1860s; published in two volumes in 1868 and 1869.
>
> **SYNOPSIS**
>
> Four sisters grow into young women in the northern United States during and after the Civil War.

Events in History at the Time of the Novel

Nineteenth-century women. For most females in nineteenth-century America, life centered around the home. A woman's time was largely spent providing a pleasant and comfortable place in which her family could live. Women who did not manage to achieve this contented domesticity were judged failures. They were also to a great extent blamed for wrongdoings of other household members. For example, if a man took to excessive drinking or gambling outside the home, it was often assumed to be his wife's fault. People supposed that she had not provided for him a peaceful home where he felt comfortable spending his time.

The task of keeping one's home clean and pleasant was tremendously time-consuming in nineteenth-century America. Some families were wealthy enough to hire domestic servants, but most were not. Even when a woman could afford to hire outside help, as the Marches do in *Little Women,* there was so much to accomplish that she was still kept quite busy. First, women were responsible for cooking three somewhat elaborate meals every day. Breakfast alone typically consisted of fresh bread, cooked potatoes, cooked or raw fruit, and beef, ham, or fish. These had to be prepared from scratch with the exception of cured meats. Very little could be bought already prepared, although smokehouses and cellars commonly housed the preserved fruits from a harvest and the cured meats. At the time, most stoves were fueled by coal or wood, so a woman had to deal with more than just the food in preparing a warm meal.

In addition to cooking, women were also responsible for cleaning the furniture and clothing of the household. Often an entire day was devoted to doing a family's laundry, since clothes had to be washed by hand and hung to dry. Also done by hand were the chores of sewing, mending, and pressing the clothes.

Girls such as the March sisters of *Little Women* were expected to help their mothers with such household chores until they learned to perform these tasks themselves. This domestic apprenticeship prepared them for the time when they would marry and tend families of their own. In *Little Women,* Marmee tells her daughters to "make this home happy, so that you may be fit for homes of your own, if they are offered to you" (Alcott, *Little Women,* p. 95). Aside from homemaking skills, girls were taught the traits that would help them become suitable companions for their husbands and good influences on their children. They were supposed to be polite, kind, cheerful, selfless, and industrious, and to avoid the display of disagreeable traits such as stubbornness at all times. Generally speaking, women in the 1800s were expected to work hard to make those around them healthier and happier than they would otherwise be.

Women and employment. Given the domestic responsibilities assigned to American women in the 1800s, it was uncommon for any woman to pursue a career separate from her domestic duties. At the same time, financial hardship made it necessary for hundreds of women to find ways of supplementing their meager family income. Poor married women usually tried to find work that they could do at home. Sewing, laundering, or ironing for wealthier families, for example, allowed them to take care of their own families while supplementing the household income.

Unmarried women, such as Meg and Jo of *Little Women,* typically lived with their mothers. Since they were not ultimately in charge of running the household, they might have had some time to spend in search of employment. Like married women, however, the majority of single women took jobs in which they relied on the domestic skills they had been developing since childhood. The most common female occupations involved taking care of others—some women became governesses or teachers of children, for example; others took jobs as companions to the elderly.

Women writers of the nineteenth century. While domestic and caretaking positions were the most common types of employment, some women of the 1800s did earn money in such creative pursuits as writing. Louisa May Alcott, for example, supported herself and eventually her parents, sisters, nephews, and nieces by writing novels and articles for magazines and newspapers.

In the 1800s, women who chose to become authors faced obstacles that male writers did not face. One problem that all female authors faced was that women's writing was generally assumed to be inferior to that of men. The vigorous, forceful, "masculine" style that many men employed was respected, and men were believed to be the only ones capable of truly great writing. Women were expected to write in a less powerful, more "feminine" way that was delicate, warm, and morally uplifting. A woman was criticized for being unfeminine if she did not write in this style, even though it was deemed inferior to more "masculine" styles. Furthermore, the best writers supposedly had a wide knowledge of the world and were familiar with a variety of people and places. As one article written in 1864 stated:

> To understand by long experience the meannesses of the world, to comprehend the various ways in which men undergo moral declension and decay . . . is part of the necessary qualification for a great writer. The women who attain to it must attain to it by undergoing a defeminizing process; after which they gain much strength and breadth of view at the sacrifice of that nameless beauty of innocence which is by nature the glory of the woman."
> (*The Living Age,* pp. 609-10)

BOARDING HOUSES

In *Little Women,* Jo spends a winter in a New York City boarding house. Boarding was a common way for single and sometimes married people to deal with the housing shortages that existed in cities in the mid-1800s. Running a boarding house was also regarded as a respectable way for married women who owned a building to earn extra money. It allowed them to be at home and care for their own family while they cooked, cleaned, and laundered clothes for their boarders.

Proper women were not expected to be familiar with much of the world outside their own homes. Those who were knowledgeable about the world were judged as improper and overly masculine if they showed this worldliness in their writing. While such societal views made it difficult for women to be taken seriously as authors in the 1800s, Louisa May Alcott numbered among the few who nevertheless became successful authors.

Nineteenth-century feminism. While women's roles as wives and mothers gave them an important place in the eyes of nineteenth-century American society, men were thought to hold a naturally superior place. They therefore enjoyed a host of privileges that were denied to women, such as access to higher education and the right to vote.

In the early 1800s, however, an increasing number of American women challenged their inferior social and political status. Many of the first feminists were those involved in the abolitionist movement to end slavery. As that struggle unfolded, these activists came to realize that while a large number of women were members of the movement, only men held leadership positions and made the important decisions. They also could identify to some extent with the feelings of the slaves for whose freedom they were fighting. Women, like slaves, were subjugated to the rule of others—namely, the men in their lives who insisted the women obey decisions made for them.

In 1848 a number of dissatisfied women gathered at a Women's Rights Convention in Seneca Falls, New York. The group produced a "Declaration of Sentiments and Resolutions" that declared men and women to be fully equal. The document also demanded suffrage, or the right to vote. Suffrage would permit women to protect their own political and social interests so that they would no longer be dependent on the will of men. For the remainder of the 1800s, gaining suffrage became the main goal of the women's movement.

Many opposed women's suffrage because they believed that women's proper sphere was in the home and that their responsibilities in that regard precluded them from becoming politically informed or sophisticated enough to be trusted with the right to vote. Suffragists argued that such assumptions were untrue and that the female voice needed to be heard in government.

Louisa May Alcott became involved in the women's movement, joining the New England Women's Suffrage Association in 1868. She attended a series of debates at the Boston State House on women's suffrage in 1874. She also contributed articles to the *Woman's Journal,* which was founded in 1870 and dealt with the rights of women and girls. Some of Alcott's unconventional views on women are reflected in her novel through the character Jo, and the tension between traditional and newer views of women's rights and roles surfaces through her sisters' reaction to her behavior. The character of Jo is criticized, for instance, for such unfeminine behavior as using slang words, putting her hands in her pockets, and whistling. Meg says, "You are old enough to leave off boyish tricks, and behave better, Josephine. It didn't matter so much when you were a little girl; but now you are so tall ... you should remember that you are a young lady" (*Little Women,* p. 7).

Nineteenth-century education. In 1860 there were only one hundred public high schools in the United States. A greater number of elementary schools existed, but even these institutions, which were open for only a short part of the year, were attended by only 57 percent of the nation's children in 1870. The average elementary student attended school forty-five days a year.

The typical curriculum of this period involved basic reading, writing, spelling, and arithmetic skills. Other areas of study might include geography, history, and grammar. In many of these subjects, a student proved his or her comprehension by memorizing lessons and reciting them before the class. Multiplication tables, poems, and capital cities were some of the items to be memorized. Discipline for students who misbehaved was often strict, sometimes involving humiliation of the student. Such harsh treatment is illustrated in *Little Women,* when Amy is ordered to stand on a platform facing her class for disobeying her teacher. Corporal or bodily punishment was also used, and *Little Women* reflects this reality as well. At one point, Amy's teacher strikes disobedient students on the hand. Such corporal punishment remained common, though some people, like Marmee in the novel, opposed its use in the classroom.

Learning at home was one option for those who were dissatisfied with the quality of public education or for whom a public school was unavailable. In *Little Women,* Beth and Amy are both educated in this way. In addition, wealthy families often hired one or more private tutors for their children, as Mr. Laurence does when he hires John Brooke to be his grandson Laurie's tutor.

For young people of all social classes, formal education frequently stopped by age fourteen or fifteen. Females, in particular, were not expected to pursue higher education because academic knowledge was thought unnecessary for their preordained lives as homemakers. In *Little Women,* sixteen-year-old Meg and fifteen-year-old Jo are no longer attending school, a normal situation for young women at the time. For the most part, American colleges educated

Louisa May Alcott at her desk in the mid-1870s.

only young men whose families could afford the expense.

The Novel in Focus

The plot. The novel opens during the Civil War (1861-65) as Christmas approaches. The four March sisters—Meg, Jo, Beth, and Amy—live with their mother, whom they call Marmee. Their father serves as a chaplain in the Union army and is therefore away from home for much of the novel. The family is somewhat poor, but relatively happy. On Christmas morning the sisters decide to give up their special holiday breakfast and proceed to take it to a poorer family in the neighborhood. Later that day, their kindness is unexpectedly rewarded when a sumptuous dinner feast is delivered to them by their wealthy neighbor, Mr. Laurence. Jo meets Mr. Laurence's grandson, Laurie, the following week at a New Year's Dance. The two quickly become best friends.

While Meg spends her days as a governess for the children of a wealthy family, Jo works as a companion to her elderly Aunt March. Shy Beth stays home most of the time helping her mother with domestic work. Amy, the youngest, attends school until one day Marmee learns that Amy's teacher struck the girl on the hand for disobedience. Strongly opposed to corporal punishment, Marmee withdraws Amy from the school permanently to pursue her education at home, as Beth has been doing.

Much of each sister's time is spent trying to overcome what she believes to be her greatest fault. For Meg, it is vanity. She greatly envies her wealthier girlfriends who are able to afford expensive dresses and jewelry. Jo's problem is controlling her temper. Beth is most concerned with her shyness, and Amy, with her selfishness. The girls learn moral lessons as they grow up. For example, Jo stops Amy from accompanying her to a play one night. In revenge, Amy burns a book of stories Jo has been writing. Furious at her sister's actions, Jo refuses to forgive her sister. Weeks later, Amy nearly drowns when she steps onto one end of the icy pond where Jo, who had been angrily ignoring her, is ice skating. After rescuing Amy, Jo realizes the importance of controlling her temper and being willing to forgive. She and Amy reconcile.

SCARLET FEVER

Scarlet fever was one of the most common childhood diseases of the 1800s. In *Little Women*, scarlet fever infects Beth; she never fully regains her health and eventually dies. She first comes down with the illness within a week of exposure to an infected person. This was typical of the illness, as was her development of a severe sore throat, high fever, and the eruption of a bright red skin rash. Scarlet fever was highly contagious, but only to those who had never had it. This factor makes it necessary for Amy to leave at once to live with Aunt March, but Jo and Meg safely remain at home. Doctors visited infected patients like Beth at home, but did not have many remedies beyond herbal cures, bed rest, high fluid intake, and the strength of the patient's own constitution. Scarlet fever was potentially fatal for anyone infected, although most eventually recovered from the disease. Since the 1800s, scarlet fever has become a much less frequent and dangerous disease because of the new methods of immunization and effective treatments such as penicillin.

When the family learns that Mr. March is seriously ill in Washington, D.C., Marmee immediately leaves to care for him. During her absence, Beth grows ill with scarlet fever. Her sisters, fearing she will die, send for Marmee to come home immediately. The fever finally slackens just as she arrives. Beth makes a gradual recovery, but she never fully regains her strength.

In the meantime, Laurie's tutor, John Brooke, and Meg have fallen in love. They get engaged, then wait three years to get married. By this time, the Civil War is over and Mr. March has returned home to his family. Laurie has gone on to college. Jo is starting to get her writing published in newspapers and magazines. Amy, who has become Aunt March's companion, prepares to accompany her aunt to Europe.

Moving away from home, Jo spends a winter in New York City as a governess to the children of the owner of a boarding house. She does a great deal of writing and becomes friends with Professor Bhaer, a fellow boarder. Soon after Jo returns home, Laurie asks her to marry him. She refuses, insisting that they would not make a good couple. The rejection leaves Laurie miserable and he leaves for Europe, where he meets Amy. The two become close friends, fall in love, marry, and become the parents of a sickly child.

Beth's health, in decline since her bout with scarlet fever, reaches a critical stage. She finally dies in the springtime. The loss grieves the family deeply. Jo grows lonely, but is overjoyed when Professor Bhaer arrives in town for a visit. When he asks her to marry him, she accepts. Within a year of their marriage, Aunt March dies and leaves her large estate to Jo. She decides to open a boys' school on the estate with her new husband. Though Beth is still sorely missed, the March family is otherwise happy.

Jo's struggles with femininity. In the first chapter of *Little Women*, Jo declares, "I like boy's games, and work, and manners. I can't get over my disappointment in not being a boy," (*Little Women*, p. 7). Unlike her sisters, Jo has a very hard time behaving like a proper female. She frequently uses slang and enjoys whistling, both of which were viewed as strictly masculine mannerisms in the 1800s. She takes little interest in fashion or her appearance; her hair is frequently unkempt, and she tends to be careless with her clothes. Mishaps, such as getting the back of her party dress burned and spilling lemonade on her nice white gloves, do not bother her. In fact, she dresses nicely when necessary for her sisters' sake rather than for herself. They care more about what others might think of her than she does.

Jo becomes less rambunctious as she grows older, but she never fits the ideal that nineteenth-century society espoused for females. She is not soft-spoken, nor is she submissive, passive, or reliant on men. Instead, Jo expresses her feelings and opinions without fear of what others, male or female, might think of her. She even says to Laurie, "I'm not afraid of anything" (*Little Women*, p. 51). Her friendship with him is one of equality; she does not automatically submit to his opinions just because she is female. Moreover, unlike most other women of her day, she does not spend her time doting on men and marriage. Independence seems to be a higher priority to her: "To be independent, and earn the praise of those she loved, were the dearest wishes of her heart" (*Little Women*, p. 153). In fact, she pursues her interest in writing in part because she views it as an avenue to future financial independence. Finally, while other young women make marriage the focal point of their lives, Jo doesn't feel that she absolutely needs to marry. Such attitudes set Jo apart from the majority of girls and women in nineteenth-century America.

Sources. *Little Women* is a highly autobiographical novel. Most of the main characters had counterparts in real life. Louisa May Alcott, like Jo in the book, was one of four sisters who grew up in Concord, Massachusetts.

Each of the fictional characters shared personality traits with their real-life counterparts. Anna Alcott, like Meg, was attracted to wealth, yet married a schoolteacher. Jo very much resembled Louisa May Alcott: both had independent spirits and fiery tempers, and both began writing at an early age. Like Beth, Elizabeth (Lizzie) Alcott was a shy homebody. She died at age twenty-three, her body weakened by scarlet fever. Like the character Amy, May Alcott was somewhat vain, highly proper, and interested in the arts. In fact, May contributed her own illustrations to the first edition of *Little Women*.

The Alcott family was among the genteel poor, just like the March family depicted in the novel, and most of the events in the lives of the March sisters were actually experienced by the Alcott sisters. Louisa, Anna, Elizabeth, and May, for example, gave away their holiday breakfast one Christmas morning to a poorer family just as the Marches do for the Hummels at the beginning of *Little Women*.

Other elements of the novel are purely fictional. Alcott did not grow up with a close male friend like Laurie. Her characterization of him in the book seems to have been drawn from a combination of young men she knew. Professor Bhaer also had no single counterpart in real life. Although he is a philosopher, he seems to be modeled in part on the Alcotts' neighbor and Louisa May Alcott's lifelong friend, Ralph Waldo Emerson, an eminent transcendentalist who, like Louisa's father Bronson Alcott, was a social reformer and educator.

Alcott also relied on her imagination to describe the marriages of Meg, Jo, and Amy, for only Meg's counterpart, Anna Alcott, was actually married. Alcott herself never married.

Reception. *Little Women* was originally published in two separate parts. The first section, which appeared in 1868, told of the lives of the March sisters up until the time of Meg's engagement to John Brooke. It gained immediate popularity among a young female audience. Alcott received a great many letters from readers of the novel begging for a sequel which would tell about the later lives of the sisters.

Characters	Real-Life Counterparts
Meg March	Anna Alcott
Jo March	Louisa May Alcott
Beth March	Elizabeth Alcott
Amy March	May Alcott
Marmee	Abigail Alcott
Mr. March	Bronson Alcott

The second part, which appeared in 1869, was originally called *Good Wives* since it focuses largely on the path each sister takes to marriage. Released for sale on April 14, *Good Wives* sold 13,000 copies by the end of May, a tremendous showing in nineteenth-century America. The entire story not only brought its author national fame and money but also set a new precedent for girls' books. At the time that *Little Women* was first published, many books were available that were geared toward a young female audience. The majority of these, however, focused on the adventures of nearly perfect young girls and featured somewhat one-dimensional characters. *Little Women* was unique because its characters were more well-rounded. Each of the March sisters had faults. They wanted to be good and moral people, but like real human beings, they sometimes found this a struggle. One reason often cited for the enduring popularity of this book is that its young female readers readily identify with Alcott's three-dimensional characters.

Since its first publication, *Little Women* has never been out of print. It has been published in twenty-seven different languages and has remained popular to the present day.

For More Information

Alcott, Louisa May. *Little Women*. 1868-69. Reprint. New York: Oxford University Press, 1994.

Cogan, Frances B. *All American Girl: The Ideal of Real Womanhood in Mid-Nineteenth Century America*. Athens: University of Georgia Press, 1989.

Cremin, Lawrence A. *Traditions of American Education*. New York: Basic Books, 1977.

DuBois, Ellen Carol. *Feminism and Suffrage: The Emergence of an Independent Women's Movement in America, 1848-1869*. Ithaca, N.Y.: Cornell University Press, 1978.

The Living Age (June 25, 1864): 609-10.

MacDonald, Ruth. *Louisa May Alcott*. Boston: Twayne, 1983.

Madame Bovary

by
Gustave Flaubert

B orn on December 12, 1821, Gustave Flaubert was the second son of Achille-Cléophas Flaubert, the chief physician of the main hospital in Rouen. The novelist's older brother, Achille, succeeded their father in the medical profession, while Gustave studied law in Paris and sought other avenues of advancement. In 1844 an illness resembling epilepsy left him a semi-invalid, and he proceeded to pursue a literary career. He set his first novel, *Madame Bovary*, in the Caux region, in northwest France, where he had grown up and would spend most of the rest of his life.

Events in History at the Time of the Novel

The bourgeoisie. The time between the onset of the French Revolution (1789) and World War I is often described as the era of the middle class. Flaubert's novel reflects this by featuring characters with shifting monetary profiles. As one scholar noted, "The main impression is one of mobility, money on the move, an economic and social transformation" of a true middle class in which positions and power are gained through commerce and finance (Heath, p. 56). In fact, with the growth of commerce and industry, a low-born Frenchman could gain wealth and prestige rapidly. This wealth helped propel him up the social ladder, whereas in the past heredity had determined one's position in French society. But financial changeability was not the only volatile aspect of French life in the first half of the 1800s.

> **THE LITERARY WORK**
>
> A novel set in and near the Caux region of Normandy, France, from the 1830s to 1856; published in 1856.
>
> **SYNOPSIS**
>
> Disillusioned with her marriage, a young woman in provincial France turns to adultery to fulfill her romantic notions of life.

A stormy political period also set the scene for the rise of the bourgeoisie, or middle class.

The turbulent years after the Revolution of 1789 witnessed the reign of Emperor Napoleon Bonaparte I (1805-1814), the restoration of King Charles X (1815-1830), and the revolution that dethroned him. His reign was followed by the July Monarchy (1830-1848), a constitutional monarchy that would also be overthrown by a revolution. The king abdicated, and another Bonaparte, Napoleon III, again assumed the title of emperor in 1852.

Amidst this political turmoil, the peasants migrated to the cities in great numbers. They were accompanied by a swelling working class of people seeking to take part in France's delayed participation in the Industrial Revolution sweeping through Europe. A burst of railway- and road-building under the July Monarchy gave the cities unprecedented contact with the countryside. The improvements in overland transportation facilitated the exchange of information, goods, and laborers, especially between Paris and the regions to the south. It was in towns and cities that bourgeois culture flourished, since rural areas rarely provided the clubs, associations, and cultural events preferred by this aspiring social class.

In Flaubert's novel, the Bovarys struggle to maintain a modest bourgeois lifestyle. Emma Bovary is continually preoccupied with the symbolic trappings of success that are so important to the bourgeoisie, such as having good table manners, quoting literature, possessing titles, and dressing well. Situated outside Paris in a couple of villages and a provincial capital, the plot seems to develop outside the context of the political tumult of these volatile years. It progresses from Charles Bovary's first marriage in the 1830s to his married life with Emma in the 1840s, to the undefined present time of the story's narration. The novel, except for one brief scene at an agricultural fair, contains no mention of the political revolutions of 1830 and 1848 or various aspects of industrial progress such as the railway. Far from Paris, the characters in Flaubert's novel wrestle with changes that are able to reach their tentacles into such distant rural areas—the construction of a cotton mill, for example, is one of the few reflections of the Industrial Revolution that finds its way into the plot.

VIEWPOINTS ON EDUCATION FOR WOMEN—NAPOLEON I AND ROUSSEAU

"What we ask of education is not that girls should think but that they should believe."
Napoleon I (Bidelman, p. 4)

"All education of women should be relative to men. To please them, to be useful to them, to be loved and honored by them, to counsel them, to console them, to render their lives agreeable and sweet; these are the duties of women at all times."
Jean Jacques Rousseau (Bidelman, p. 25)

The Catholic Church and religious education. Early in the eighteenth century, the Catholic Church had overseen literally all of the educational institutions in France, for even the lay teachers received their permission to teach from a bishop or his representative. Around 1750, however, society began to become more secular. The people and the lower clergy increasingly resented the wealthy, tax-exempt upper clergy.

Even before the Revolution of 1789, the liberal ideas of the Enlightenment era had begun to disrupt the union of church and state. Even so, control of education by the church lingered on in the post-1789 era, and leaders continued to distinguish between the kinds of education advisable for boys and girls. Napoleon I took a particularly dim view of arguments that contended that women should be included in the redefinition of France's educational system, and he reached back to the statements of anti-feminist philosophers of the Enlightenment such as Jean Jacques Rousseau to find support for his beliefs.

This attitude persisted even after Napoleon's downfall so that the nationwide system of primary education that was created in 1833 catered exclusively to boys. Girls, meanwhile, had to content themselves with a convent education. This sort of education contributed to the sense of refinement possessed by the character of Emma Bovary; officially her training was focused on geography and tapestry work. Unofficially, it also became a haven for the reading of romantic novels; these books excited Emma's imagination and tragically affected the rest of her life.

Romantic novels. Emma Bovary's entire perception of life was colored by the romantic novels that she read. The books ignited Emma's imagination and convinced her that her future should be filled with passion, gentlemen in velvet, glorious kisses, dark forests, and excitement. Instead she marries an ordinary doctor whose advances repulse her, and despite his devotion to her, she despairs. *Madame Bovary*, writes one perceptive critic, is in fact "the novel of Emma's attempt to live her novel," and its tragic consequences reflect the antiromantic stance taken by Flaubert in his own writing (Heath, p. 84).

Romantic novels enjoyed an immense readership in France during the 1830s and 1840s. Most popular was *The Mysteries of Paris* (*Les Mystères de Paris*) by Eugène Sue, published serially in 1842 and 1843. Readers waited with excited anticipation for the next installment of Sue's tale in their daily newspapers. The story concerned a Prince Rodolphe, whose name is used in *Madame Bovary*; his daughter was kidnapped in childhood only to be found by her father many years later on a street in Paris.

Despite the popularity of the Romantic novel, the focus on reason continued to dominate some French minds. The character of the pharmacist Homais in *Madame Bovary* defends the writings of the philosopher Voltaire, for example. The Romantics, on the other hand, showed faith in the church. While the novel portrays a realistic view of the times, Flaubert forges new ground by finding fault with the Romantics and the consequences that their works have on Emma Bovary.

Professional and popular medicine. The 1840s saw the growth of an "official science" in France, a more empirical approach than had been taken in the past. Earlier "scientists" held that tendencies to murderousness, lust, or thievery could be detected by examining the cranium of an individual. Phrenology, the study of the relationship between the shape of a person's skull and his or her character traits, began to lose intellectual support over time, though it remained popular throughout the 1800s. In the novel, Charles Bovary is characterized as a well-meaning doctor who never quite mastered his medical training, even in comparison with his colleagues. In Charles's office, a model skull for phrenological study is on proud display.

Folk theories about disease abounded during the nineteenth century, and these theories encouraged belief in traditional cures, such as bloodletting. Religion continued to offer alternate explanations and methods of healing, and misinformation was sometimes spread deliberately by charlatans. As literacy and scientific knowledge increased, however, all strata of society began to benefit from the spread of more accurate information. France joined Europe in the development and use of one "modern" medical convenience, contraceptives, in the form of the condom known today. Thought to have been invented sometime in the 1700s, possibly by a doctor after whom the device was named, this method of birth control became more or less popular in France, depending to some degree on a person's social status.

Wet-nursing. In eighteenth- and nineteenth-century France, it was common practice to allow a woman who had recently given birth to suckle and board someone else's child. Such a woman, called a wet-nurse, cares for Madame Bovary's child in the novel. In real life, an intermediary often made the arrangements between parents and wet-nurses, getting the parents to pay the wet-nurse, a modest fee—for example, ten to twelve francs a month. It was an income the wet-nurses, or *nourrices*, often tried to cultivate for as long as possible.

Parents who lived in Paris and other rapidly growing cities often contracted wet-nurses. Until the road-building of the July Monarchy and the Second Empire, the wet-nursing needs of the Parisian bourgeoisie were met almost exclusively by women in rural areas in the Normandy and Picardy regions, where *Madame Bovary* takes place. About 1760, however, Enlightenment philosophers, physicians, and statesmen launched a broad critique of wet-nursing, and class attitudes began to diverge. Patronage by the well-to-do fell off sharply during the French Revolution and again in the 1870s, after the closure of the Bureau of Wet Nurses in 1876. Business suffered further with the passage of the Roussel Law in 1874, which strove to document the business and investigate the welfare of the infants. Instead of a wet nurse, wealthier families came to prefer maternal feeding or at least closely supervised live-in nurses. They wished to distinguish themselves from the families of tradesmen and artisans who had to use wet nurses because the husband's low income necessitated that the wife work as well.

DOMINANT MOVEMENTS IN FRENCH LITERATURE

1715-1830: Rational thinking and a return to the classics of Greece and Rome held the highest esteem. As elsewhere, France favored writers of the Enlightenment such as Voltaire and Montesquieu, who were concerned with philosophy and reasoning.

1830-1850s: Romantic thinking and the creation of emotional, imaginative writings gained dominance. Most notably, the Romantics embodied a spirit of revolt against established ways wherein men and women were encouraged to let themselves be guided by the warm passion of the heart rather than the cold logic of the head.

1850s-1870: Scientific thinking and the heyday of realism in French fiction prevailed. Following the revolution of 1848, this movement affected literature in the 1850s, as demonstrated in the fiction of Flaubert, whose *Madame Bovary* has been credited with ushering in the change. Suppressing his own instinct to indulge in Romantic fiction, Flaubert instead dissects the characters and society portrayed in his stories in an objective manner.

Suicide and debt. Unable to pay her creditors, the character of Emma Bovary receives official notice that she must pay her bills or all her household furniture will be sold. Hardship and financial ruin threatened many bourgeois and lower-class families in this period. Under the threat of imprisonment, bankrupt individuals

Gustave Flaubert's notebooks.

suffered the seizure and public sale of all their possessions. Afterward they might resort to prostitution, beggary, migration, thievery, or worse. Rates of suicide and infanticide rose as some saw no alternative.

Women were generally less likely than men to commit suicide, since they were more strongly encouraged than men to avoid excess, to tolerate suffering, and to fear scandal, death, and religious damnation. In addition, a Christian upbringing prompted a woman to feel shame at the idea of her dead body being examined by the prying eyes of the public and the coroner.

Masculinism. The Napoleonic Code (1804), also called the French Civil Code, reflected Napoleon I's imperial approach to the organization of society. He reasoned that fathers and husbands should lead the family with the same unquestioned authority with which he led the empire. As a result, women were completely excluded from politics, higher education, and the professions. A wife could not work without her husband's permission, and anything she earned belonged to him. Motherhood was celebrated with intense fervor throughout the 1800s. Yet in the private sphere, a mother had no legal authority over her children while her husband was alive. If he wished to do so, the husband had the option of making arrangements to assign guardianship of the children to a third party in the event of his death.

Attention was paid to the sexual dimension of marriage during this era. There was an attempt to counsel marriage partners to engage in sex for the good of their health and union. In a popular marriage manual, a Dr. Auguste Debay counseled husbands to please their wives in bed so they would remain faithful. Likewise, the wives were advised to submit to the demands of their husbands.

Divorce was available from 1792 to 1816 and again after 1884. Outlawed in 1816, it represented to conservatives of the period an extension of the anarchy into which the revolution had descended. Divorce, in their eyes, carried this anarchy into the home, and so they outlawed it. Some women took refuge from bad marriages in adultery, as Emma does in Flaubert's novel. There was, however, an alternative. In 1835 the female novelist Amantine-Lucile-Aurore Dupin (who wrote under the pseudonym George Sand) filed for legal separation from her spouse. After the outlawing of divorce in 1816, this was the only legal recourse left for an unhappily married woman. Sand was a friend and mentor of Flaubert's, although they had literary differences—she wrote popular Romantic novels in contrast to Flaubert's anti-Romantic stories.

Rouen in 1847.

The Novel in Focus

The plot. Trapped in a miserable, arranged marriage to an older woman, Dr. Charles Bovary meets the charming young Emma Rouault when he is summoned to set her father's broken leg. The physician's nagging wife, Héloise, resents his keen interest in the patient's recovery and finally makes her husband promise to discontinue his frequent visits to the Rouault farm. Charles soon learns that Héloise has lied to him about her fortune, and bitter scenes follow, bringing on a relapse of her old illness; Héloise dies quickly.

At Monsieur Rouault's invitation, Charles resumes his visits to the farm, where he gradually finds favor in the eyes of Emma and her father. She and Charles are married, and Emma quickly immerses herself in household tasks to compensate for her disappointment in the marriage. She mistakenly thought she was in love with Charles; now she resents him because their union has failed to spark the bliss and passion she has read about in romantic novels.

On the verge of giving up hope, Emma finds diversion and a new chance for happiness when she and Charles are invited to a ball. The glamour of the event and the lifestyle of their host, a nobleman whom Charles has doctored, contrasts sharply with the daily life of the Bovarys, and upon returning home, Emma feels more miserable than ever. Her husband's sincere but clumsy efforts to please her only irritate her further. She grows ill, and Charles decides that a move from their village to the town of Yonville might brighten her days.

In Yonville Emma gives birth to a daughter, which delights Charles but depresses his wife, who has been hoping for a son. Little Berthe is sent to a wet-nurse; Emma makes infrequent visits to her baby, alternating between fitful indifference to Berthe and sudden, showy displays of maternal concern. On her arrival in Yonville, Emma made the acquaintance of Léon Dupuis, a young law clerk who shares her romantic ideas about life. Months of flirtation lead nowhere, however, and a frustrated Léon moves to Paris to study law, leaving Emma to regret her hesitation and to sink back into misery and illness.

Before long, however, Emma meets Rodolphe Boulanger, a suave stranger who sets out to seduce her. After resisting, Emma capitulates, telling herself that nothing as romantic and beautiful as love can be sinful. Her initial feelings of guilt vanish when she identifies herself with the adulterous heroines of fiction, whom she believes have known true romance. Meanwhile, Charles and Homais, the town pharmacist, fail miserably in a highly publicized attempt to cure a young man of clubfoot. Disgusted with her husband and desperate to keep the interest of her lover, Emma begins to squander her husband's money. Rodolphe leaves her nevertheless, and Emma nearly throws herself from the attic window in despair. Instead she falls ill and lays near death for several months.

> ### EMMA AND BERTHE
>
> The moment Little Berthe is born, she almost ceases to exist for Emma: "She wanted a son. He would be strong and dark; she would call him Georges; and this idea of having a male child was like a promise of compensation for all her past frustrations. A man is free ... whereas woman is continually thwarted" (Flaubert, *Madame Bovary*, pp. 84-5). As Berthe grows into a cheerful little girl, Emma can hardly be bothered to look at her, much less look at her affectionately. This lack of motherly regard only added to the controversy surrounding the novel. Considering the great emphasis that nineteenth-century France placed on a woman's domestic role, it is hardly surprising that Emma's indifference to her only child scandalized conservative readers. Her behavior, as both a mother and a wife, was unacceptably abominable in their eyes.

When she recovers, Charles takes her to the city of Rouen for a change of pace, and there they meet Léon unexpectedly. Soon Emma arranges regular trips to Rouen, where she and Léon indulge their passion and spend money freely. Charles worries about Emma's growing debts but hesitates to broach the subject, even though he has granted her a power of attorney. His mother advises him to destroy the power of attorney, but the Bovary finances are already ruined. Charles returns from a trip to find his wife's name posted publicly for a debt of several thousand francs. Emma throws herself on the mercy of everyone she knows but fails to raise any money. Desperate, she finally takes arsenic in an attempt to die a heroine's death. Her attempt succeeds, devastating her husband. Years after her death, Charles discovers love letters to his wife from Léon and Rodolphe. Broken with grief and disillusion, he dies soon after, leaving only twelve francs for the support of his young daughter.

Madame Bovary on trial. In 1857 the lawyer Jules Sénard defended Flaubert against the charge that *Madame Bovary* was an "outrage to public and religious morals" (Heath, p. 47).

Flaubert won the case, for the court recognized that readers could draw a moral lesson from the novel. Still, the court admonished the novelist for his refusal to condemn Emma's adultery outright in the novel. The legal controversy won the painstakingly constructed work and its author widespread fame and readership, and Flaubert later dedicated the novel to Sénard in gratitude.

In addition to the novel's shocking content, Flaubert's narrative technique contributed to the uproar. Critics and admirers alike pointed out that he had achieved a sense of impartiality or impersonality through his style of writing. His use of past tenses, shifting points of view, and the technique of "free indirect discourse" achieved a tone that reviewers at first condemned as cold and impersonal. In fact, Flaubert uses this technique to humanize Emma in the novel. Instead of her saying "How I envy the ineffable feelings of love that I used to try to picture from my readings," the novel describes her thoughts this way:

> She sat down on a bench in the shadow of the elms. How calm things used to be! How she envied the ineffable feelings of love which she used to try to picture from her readings. She was not happy, she never had been ... if there were, somewhere, a being strong and handsome, ... why should she not find him?
> (Flaubert in Bart, p. 344)

This reporting of the flow of a person's thoughts had never been used to so great an extent in a French novel before.

Since Flaubert became known for the extraordinary pains he took in revising his manuscripts, his style, though objectionable to some readers, could not be dismissed easily. The editors of the *Revue de Paris* magazine, which printed the novel in installments in 1856, responded to widespread criticism and appealed to Flaubert for drastic changes. Having already made adjustments, the novelist lashed out at the editors in a letter written on December 7, 1856:

> I consider that I have already done a great deal, and the *Revue* thinks that I should do still more. I will do nothing: I will not make a correction, not a cut; I will not suppress a comma; nothing, nothing! But if the *Revue de Paris* thinks that I am compromising it, if it is afraid, the simple thing to do is to stop publication of *Madame Bovary* at once. I wouldn't give a damn.
> (Flaubert, *Letters of Gustave Flaubert*, p. 221)

Sources. In memoirs written long after the event, Maxime du Camp takes perhaps more than his share of credit for the success of Flaubert's literary career, for he claims that he directed the au-

SOME PEOPLE AND PLACES IN *MADAME BOVARY*	
Fictional Name	**Real-life Source**
Yonville-l'Abbaye	Town of Ry, approximately 30 miles from Rouen
Charles Bovary	Louis Delamarre, a young physician
Monsieur Rouault	Monsieur Couturier, owner of a heavily mortgaged farm
Emma Bovary	Delphine Couturier, the farmer's daughter
Homais	Jouanne, a druggist in Ry
Léon Dupuis	Louis Bottet, a law clerk
Rodolphe Boulanger	Monsieur Campion, a proprietor

thor to events that inspired *Madame Bovary*. At his prompting, he writes, his friend Flaubert drew on the Delamarre affair, a local scandal in the town of Ry outside Rouen. There a young physician named Louis Delamarre courted and won the pretty Delphine Couturier, who only secured her father's reluctant permission to marry by feigning pregnancy. She soon regretted her marriage, even though her dull husband economized so that she could indulge her whims. Straying into adultery, she became involved with a Monsieur Campion, Rodolphe Boulanger's real-life counterpart.

Delphine stole poison from a local pharmacist named Jouanne and killed herself on March 6, 1848. Delamarre, who, unlike Charles Bovary in the novel, never discovered his wife's infidelity, ordered this epitaph for her tombstone: "She was a good mother, a good wife" (Huneker, p. 128). Campion lost his farm and fortune after Delphine's death and tried unsuccessfully to make something of himself in the United States. He returned to Paris and shot himself on the street about 1852.

Other possible sources for the plot include the case of a Mademoiselle de Bovery, who was involved in adultery and the death by poisoning of a chemist's wife in a Normandy village in 1844.

Reviews. Many reviewers were vehement in their condemnation of the novel. The *Saturday Review* called it "one of the most revolting productions that ever issued from a novelist's brain" (Heath, p. 49). Less harsh was a review in *Le Moniteur* by Sainte-Beuve, who praised the work for its truthfulness and saw in it a new type of literature: "The work bears the imprint of the time of its publication.... I detect signs of a new literary manner: science, observation, maturity, strength, a little harshness" (Sainte-Beuve in Heath, pp. 49-50). Regardless of the critics, the trial had given enormous publicity to the work. The publicity surrounding the novel made its author a celebrity and the book a popular success.

For More Information

Bart, Benjamin F. *Flaubert*. Syracuse, N.Y.: Syracuse University Press, 1967.

Bidelman, Patrick Kay. *Pariahs Stand Up! The Founding of the Liberal Feminist Movement, 1858-1889*. Westport, Conn.: Greenwood Press, 1982.

Flaubert, Gustave. *The Letters of Gustave Flaubert, 1830-1857*. Translated by Francis Steegmuller. Cambridge, Mass.: Harvard University Press, 1980.

Flaubert, Gustave. *Madame Bovary: Patterns of Provincial Life*. Translated by Francis Steegmuller. New York: Alfred A. Knopf, 1957.

Heath, Stephen. *Gustave Flaubert: Madame Bovary*. Cambridge: Cambridge University Press, 1991.

Huneker, James. *Egoists: A Book of Supermen*. New York: Charles Scribner's Sons, 1909.

Ramsey, Matthew. *Professional and Popular Medicine in France, 1770-1830: The Social World of Medical Practice*. New York: Cambridge University Press, 1988.

Wright, Gordon. *France in Modern Times: The Enlightenment to the Present*. New York: W. W. Norton, 1987.

The Miracle Worker

by
William Gibson

~

William Gibson was born in the Bronx, a borough in New York City, in 1914. As an adult, he became fascinated with Anne Sullivan's famous triumph as the teacher of a deaf and blind girl named Helen Keller. Sullivan had herself been half-blind as a child and had experienced obstacles that confronted the disabled. Through Sullivan's letters, Gibson learned about the almshouses to which disabled children were often abandoned. Anne Sullivan's subsequent achievements, especially her heroic efforts to communicate with Helen Keller, served as the cornerstone of Gibson's play *The Miracle Worker*.

Events in History at the Time the Play Takes Place

Almshouses. Institutions called "almshouses" or "asylums" sprang up in eighteenth-century America to house a wide-ranging collection of society's outcasts. Modeled on the English workhouse system, most almshouses tried to defray their costs by using inmates for forced labor. Male and female inmates took on chores in the daily maintenance of the asylum, which paid for some expenses, but other practices met with less success. Forcing youngsters into labor contracts with outside employers generally failed, and small enterprises (manufacturing sheets and towels in almshouse factories, for example) proved unprofitable in all but the most depressed economic times.

Despite the shocking living and working conditions in the average poorhouse, some children

---

THE LITERARY WORK

A play set primarily in and around the Keller home in Tuscumbia, Alabama, in the 1880s; published in 1959.

SYNOPSIS

A deaf-blind girl learns to communicate with the outside world, thanks to the efforts of a spirited young teacher.

---

received a limited education. But even asylums that provided some basic schooling considered it their chief duty to provide food, shelter, and a place where the inmates would not bother the rest of society. Buildings were surrounded by fences, and in most asylums, parents were only permitted to visit their children once a week in special visiting rooms. Normally, whatever schooling might be provided in such an asylum did little to meet the needs of the visually or aurally impaired.

Education for the deaf and blind. From the early 1700s educators in the United States worked to develop successful methods for teaching the deaf and the blind. European models offered several starting points. Basing his efforts on French methods, Thomas Hopkins Gallaudet founded the American Asylum for the Education of the Deaf and Dumb in 1817. Elsewhere, a form of sign language, allegedly developed by Spanish monks who had taken a vow of silence, found its way into the United States. This form of communication met significant resistance, however. Scholar Joseph Shapiro points out some of the reasons for this opposition:

> As Arden Neisser notes in her history of sign language, "gesturing was something that Italians did, and Jews, and Frenchmen: it reflected the poverty of their cultures and the immaturity of their personalities. Sign language became a code word with strong racial overtones." Speech was God given. It was what separated men from beasts. If one did not have speech, then one did not have language and was presumably unable to reason. This type of logic, a set of long-standing ideas, dated back to Aristotle.
> (Shapiro, p. 90)

At an international conference in Milan, Italy, in 1880, delegates voted in favor of lip-reading and oralism (enunciating words) over sign language by a count of 116 to 4. Three schools of nongesticulating speech gained prominence: the Hollando-German, the Spanish-French, and the Anglo-American.

Meanwhile, debate about educating the disabled was affected by two works: Gregor Mendel's theory of heredity and Charles Darwin's *On the Origin of Species* (1856-1858). Mendel developed the idea that many characteristics are inherited through genes, while Darwin argued that plants and animals evolved through a process of natural selection. In the struggle to exist, explained Darwin, life either adapted to its environment and survived or failed to adapt and perished. Popular interpretations of the work of Mendel and Darwin led to a view of the disabled as hopeless beings who were not fit for survival.

Dr. Samuel Gridley Howe, who founded the Perkins Institution for the Blind in 1832, objected to this view. In his mind, every human life, whether disabled or not, had spiritual integrity. Howe's limited success with Laura Bridgman—who was deaf, blind, mute, and nearly devoid of the sense of smell—gained wide renown and opened the way to further experimentation.

The Battle of Vicksburg. Vicksburg, Mississippi, was the site of a bitterly contested battle in the Civil War. Under siege for forty-seven days by Northern troops who penned in the city, Vicksburg's defenders surrendered on July 4, 1863, to General Ulysses S. Grant. As a result, Grant emerged as a hero of the Union cause with a reputation for ruthless determination. After further battlefield victories, he became the commander of all the Union forces in the war. *The Miracle Worker* notes that the determination of the teacher Annie Sullivan resembles that shown by Grant. When Helen's father, Captain Keller, watches Annie and Helen in a physical brawl, he observes, "Ha. You see why they [the Northerners] took Vicksburg?" (Gibson, *The Miracle Worker*, p. 221).

Cultural conflict in the South. Dr. Howe opened his institute in Boston, a city in the North. A handful of Northern schools like his introduced new methods of education for the deaf and blind into the nation. In the South, the new methods spread slowly after the Civil War because many Southerners were suspicious of changes that were imposed by the North.

EDUCATIONAL TOOLS FOR THE BLIND

Like educators of the deaf, teachers of the blind used various tools: single wooden or metal letters, raised letters on a page (linear type), and varieties of the braille dot system invented by Louis Braille, a French musician, educator, and inventor. Braille, who had been blinded in an accident at age three, adapted his system from a method devised by Charles Barbier. In Braille's system, sixty-three different arrangements of six raised dots—identifiable by touch—represented various letters and numerals. This system continues to be used, in modified form, today.

Social relations between Southerners and Northerners remained tense long after federal troops had defeated the Confederacy and left the South. Especially during the period of Reconstruction (1865-77) that followed the war, Southerners turned a cold shoulder to Northern ideas and government. They felt the Northerners were wrongly interfering in the domestic affairs of the South. Southern heads of household and employers resented being told how to treat the former slaves who now acted as servants and employees, while Southerners in general chafed at Northern officers who belittled and violated Southern social graces. Southern resentment of the conditions imposed by the North after the war surfaced in the elections of 1874. These elections restored to power the old Democratic party, whose leaders continued to hold values of the pre-Civil War South. *The Miracle Worker* acknowledges the tension between Northerners and Southerners after the war in its depiction of the relationship between Captain

The Miracle Worker

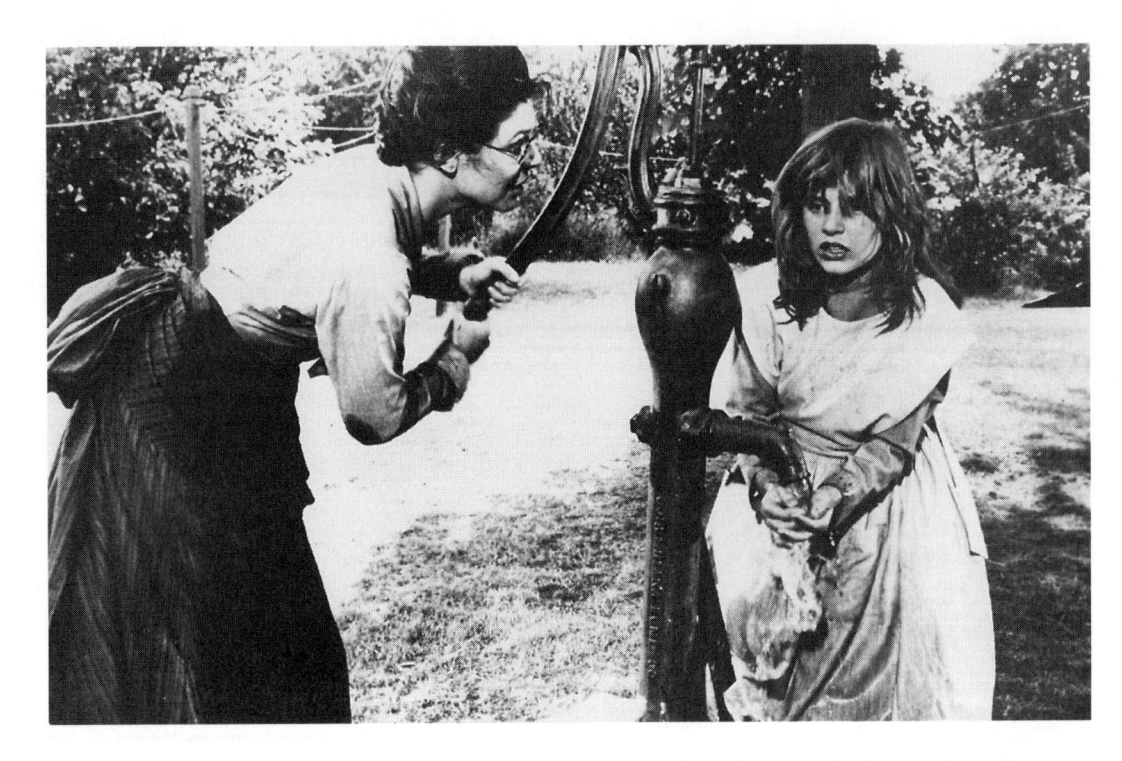

Anne Bancroft as Annie Sullivan and Patty Duke as Helen Keller in the film adaptation of *The Miracle Worker*.

Keller, a product of the Old South, and Annie Sullivan, a seemingly impertinent teacher from the North.

The Play in Focus

The plot. Captain Keller and Kate Keller give thanks for the recovery of their baby daughter Helen from acute congestion of the stomach and brain. Their relief turns to horror, however, when they discover that the fever has left the child unresponsive to light and sounds.

The play continues when Helen is six and a half years old. Her spoiled behavior goes unchecked by the adults in the family, who discuss, for the hundredth time, what should be done with Helen. Exhausted by the persistent optimism of the women of the household, Captain Keller agrees to follow yet another lead in the search for a solution.

Help arrives in the person of Annie Sullivan, who has taken leave of her fellow students and of her teacher Anagnos at the Perkins Institution in Boston. Kate Keller takes an immediate liking to the twenty-year-old Annie, quelling reservations about her youth and inexperience. But Captain Keller is openly skeptical, as he confides to his wife: "Here's a houseful of grownups can't cope with the child, how can an inexperienced half-blind Yankee schoolgirl manage her?" (*The Miracle Worker*, p. 195).

Annie's presence disrupts the Keller home from the outset. The young governess refuses to tolerate Helen's inconsiderate behavior and objects openly to the family's indulgence of the child's whims. Only by secluding herself with Helen can Annie begin to make progress with her young charge. The members of the Keller family alternately express both mistrust and interest in Annie's methods, while the young teacher's correspondence reveals her own doubts. Intrigued by Helen's spirit and intelligence, though, Annie refuses to give up. She and Helen wage battle after battle, each enjoying small victories.

Helen's progress is threatened by the low expectations, pity, and indulgence of her family. Not until Annie arranges to live with Helen in complete seclusion for two weeks does the final breakthrough come, in the last hour of the fourteenth day. At long last, the child gains an inkling of the connection between the manual alphabet and the names of the objects that Annie spells into her hand. This climax crowns one of the play's several violent, nearly nonverbal scenes.

Overcoming more than disability. As an adult, Helen Keller often noted that it was not blindness, but the attitude of the seeing to the blind, that proved to be the hardest burden to bear. In

The Miracle Worker, Gibson portrays the way in which pity, no matter how well-intended, can hamper the development and quality of life of a disabled person. For instance, when Helen throws a tantrum, the Captain admonishes Annie to have more pity for the child. Instead, Annie loses her patience:

> Pity? For this tyrant?... I'll tell you what I pity, that the sun won't rise and set for her all her life, and every day you're telling her it will, what good will your pity do her when you're under the strawberries, Captain Keller?
> (*The Miracle Worker,* p. 222)

Annie does not mince words in her effort to convince the Kellers that Helen needs language more than she needs to learn politeness: "All of you here are so sorry for her you've kept her—like a pet, why, even a dog you housebreak" (*The Miracle Worker,* p. 245). Annie encourages the Keller family to think of Helen as a complete human being. Yet even after the two-week period of seclusion, Helen's parents insist on a limited view of their daughter. As Helen spells into the paw of the family dog, Captain Keller struggles to achieve perspective, turning even to religion:

> Teaching a dog to spell. (A pause) The dog doesn't know what she means, any more than she knows what you mean, Miss Sullivan. I think you ask too much, of her and yourself. God may not have meant Helen to have the—eyes you speak of.... You make us see how we indulge her for our sake. Is the opposite true, for you?
> (*The Miracle Worker,* pp. 276-77)

The Captain's words do not necessarily convey malicious intent. Like most people of their day, the members of the Keller family are unfamiliar with the experimental methods in use at the time to try to reach those persons suffering from double disability. They reflect the characteristics of a society attempting to find a more compassionate place for its disabled than the almshouse. The family members display not only pity but also ignorance, fear, curiosity, and prejudice. These are probably the same impulses that drove audiences to see a photo-play of Helen Keller and Anne Sullivan when it appeared in the early 1900s. This photo-play, a kind of short film, toured America's finest theaters, with its two heroines making special in-person appearances at the showings.

Sources. Relying heavily on the letters Anne Sullivan wrote in 1887, William Gibson worked into his play real exchanges between Helen and Anne, fictionalizing almost none of their interaction. But he did take some liberties, joining together certain incidents separated in time and making minor adjustments to other events in order to show more clearly how "everyone in the family was to be significantly affected by the work with the child, and we were to see it liberate the teacher from her past as much as the pupil from her present" (Preface to *The Miracle Worker,* p. 15).

Anne Sullivan had battled her way through a difficult past indeed. Half-blinded in childhood by trachoma (a viral disease of the eye), the neglected girl had been forced to depend on her alcoholic father after her mother died at age twenty-eight. When Anne was ten, he abandoned her to Tewksbury Almshouse in Massachusetts, where she and her younger brother struggled to survive and to stay together. She talked her way into the Perkins Institution at age fourteen. After six years, nine eye operations, and innumerable confrontations with Michael Anagnos, the head of the school, Anne left in order to earn her way in the world.

ANNE SULLIVAN'S EXPERIENCE IN TEWKSBURY ALMSHOUSE

[Anne Sullivan] had seen evil enough as a child of the Irish "famine poor" who was placed in the women's ward of this squalid institution, where all the twenty-seven foundlings received that year had died and seventy out of eighty had died the year before. She had been surrounded from the age of ten with crazy old bedridden women, tubercular, cancerous, perverted, crippled, grotesque, and with ignorant unmarried girls whose babies were covered with sores and whose talk was all of seduction, starvation and rape. The only playroom for herself and her brother, who was finally wheeled away himself, was the dead-house at the end of the ward where big gray rats scurried about with cockroaches during the night.

(Brooks, pp. 12-13)

In preparation for her first job as Helen's teacher, Anne studied the account of the work done at Perkins with Laura Bridgman. Anne pressed Laura, who lived at Perkins, for as much information as possible. The aging pupil, who enjoyed sewing, may be the Laura referred to in the play, a background figure who provided doll clothes for Helen's doll.

The play's other main character is based on the real Helen Keller, who survived her childhood

The Miracle Worker

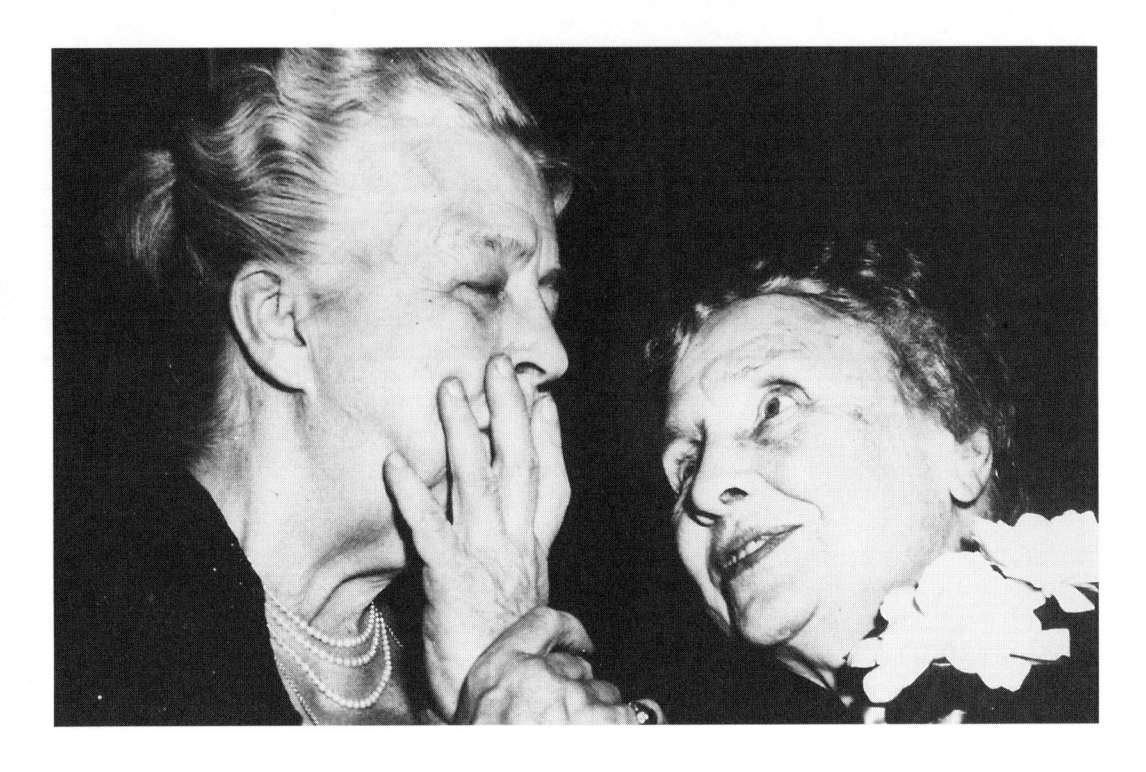

Helen Keller (right) conversing with Eleanor Roosevelt, 1955.

isolation to become one of the most celebrated women in American history. Born in Tuscumbia, Alabama, she lost her hearing and sight to illness at eighteen months. In his *American Notes* (1842), Charles Dickens described movingly his visit to Perkins Institution and an encounter with Laura Bridgman. The *Notes* inspired Helen's mother, Kate Keller, to contact the school for help. Another famous author, Mark Twain, would come to know Helen Keller personally. Twain, in fact, referred to Helen as a "Miracle" and to Anne as the "Miracle Worker," which later became the title of Gibson's play (Koestler, p. 95).

With the help of several teachers and a tremendous amount of personal drive, Helen learned to sign, write, and speak, graduating from Radcliffe in 1904 and earning international fame as a lecturer and author. The adult Helen was invited to meet presidents, royalty, and entertainers. With the passing of Anne Sullivan on October 20, 1936, Helen Keller lost her closest companion, whom she continued to call Teacher until she herself died on June 1, 1968.

Events in History at the Time the Play Was Written

The civil rights movement in Alabama. In the 1950s, Alabama attracted international attention as the birthplace of the campaign for desegregation and voting rights for African Americans. The Southern Christian Leadership Conference (SCLC), led by Martin Luther King Jr., helped mobilize the black community to plan an effective long-term strategy to realize these goals.

Segregation on Montgomery's public buses was challenged by Claudette Colvin on March 2, 1955, and again on October 21, by Mary Louise Smith. After Rosa Parks refused to surrender her seat to a white man on December 1, the SCLC launched a widespread bus boycott, which succeeded more than a year later. Marches in Selma, Alabama, including dangerous night marches, continued to call attention to the seg-

---

THE HEROINE OF THE STORY

The Miracle Worker is invariably identified as "the play about Helen Keller," and I have been asked a hundred times how I came to be so interested in her. I reply patiently I was never interested in her, the play is about her teacher, and for that reason is not named *The Miracle Workee*.

(Gibson, *Monday after the Miracle*, p. viii)

regation of public facilities and to the voting rights campaign. Television viewers nationwide saw graphic footage of dogs and hoses turned on protesters in Birmingham, Alabama, in April and May of 1963.

Slowly, federal legislation and Supreme Court decisions began to reflect a change in official policy. Back in 1954, in the case of *Brown v. Board of Education of Topeka,* the Supreme Court had ruled unanimously that segregation in public schools was unconstitutional. Ten years later, after exhaustive congressional debate, President Lyndon B. Johnson signed into law the Civil Rights Act of 1964, which was soon followed by the Voting Rights Act of 1965 and the Fair Housing Act of 1968. Many people in the South opposed these mandates of the federal government, however, just as they had opposed Northern interference in the post-Civil War years. In 1959, in the midst of these mandates, *The Miracle Worker* first appeared on stage.

Production and reviews. After opening the play on Broadway in 1959, William Gibson restricted the release of *The Miracle Worker* to amateur groups whose audiences were nonsegregated. The decision reflected Gibson's careful marketing of the moving story that had captivated him eleven years earlier.

Gibson had first attempted to tell the story of *The Miracle Worker* as a solo dance piece. He then shaped the story as a television script. The television broadcast, which aired on February 7, 1957, was warmly received. Gibson subsequently received offers to do more with the script, and he chose to turn the story into a stage play rather than a film.

> During rehearsals [for *Two for the Seesaw*] another movie offer for *The Miracle Worker* came my way, this one giving me some control of casting, but now I could not think of that first act [written for a stage show] going to waste; I declined the movie, and exercised my right to cancel a second telecast, by way of keeping some audience [for the stage show] at least theoretically available.
> (Preface to *The Miracle Worker,* p. 11)

On October 19, 1959, the stage play opened at the Playhouse Theater on Broadway. Throughout the length of the play's run at that venue, it had no trouble attracting a thousand theatergoers a night. *New York Times* critic Brooks Atkinson had high praise for the compelling story and for the cast, noting especially the performances of Anne Bancroft as Annie Sullivan and of Patty Duke as Helen Keller. But he condemned certain aspects of the production—such as, in his view, its embarrassing use of offstage voices. Nevertheless, he acknowledged the popularity of *The Miracle Worker.*

> Nothing in the theater this season is so overwhelming as the last inarticulate but eloquent scene in which a frantic little girl for the first time understands the meaning of a word and realizes that the teacher is not a fiend but a friend.
> (Atkinson, p. 1)

DISCRIMINATION IN SCHOOLS FOR THE DISABLED

In 1945 an inspector of the Alabama Institute for the Deaf and Blind observed, "most of the buildings for the white students are satisfactory or excellent.... The unit of the institute for Negro deaf and blind, located near the buildings for the white pupils, has very unsatisfactory buildings which are both overcrowded and hazardous.... Although the Negro pupils receive the same food as the white pupils, their housing is worse and their training appears to be much less adequate" (Alabama Educational Survey Commission, p. 419).

Changing attitudes and technology. The turn of the twentieth century witnessed a trend wherein blind and deaf students were brought

WHAT IS IT ACTUALLY LIKE TO BE DEAF-BLIND?

A man who lost his hearing as a young adult and his sight in an accident twelve years later described his double disability in the following terms: "What is it actually like to be deaf-blind? I can only tell you what it is like for me. What it's like for a person who has never seen or heard, I do not know. First, it is neither 'dark' nor 'silent.' If you were to go out into a London fog—one of the thick yellow variety—and then close your eyes, you would see what I see. A dull, flesh-colored opacity.... Nor is my world 'silent' (most of us wish it were so!). You have all put a shell to your ear as children and 'listened to the waves.' ... Cracklings, squeakings, rumblings—what I hear is the machinery of my being working. The blood rushing through my veins, and little cracklings of nerves and muscles as they expand and contract. In short, my hearing has 'turned inwards'" (Koestler, p. 452).

out of the isolation of specialized institutions and into public schools with seeing and hearing students. Some educators argued that the move was inefficient, especially for students with double disability, since teachers at regular schools often felt unable to meet their needs. As a result, special day and residential schools continued to receive funding in many states. In Alabama in 1926, for instance, the state government allocated $159,040 per year for the Deaf, Dumb, and Blind Institute at Talladega, and an additional $300,000 for the construction and repair of Institute buildings.

Over time, American society began to regard the disabled as productive citizens rather than as charity cases. Workshops for the blind demonstrated the economic potential of one sector of the disabled population. The handmade items produced in these workshops received more respect and a larger market than the almshouse products of the 1800s had. The first sizable employment opportunities for the blind came during World War I; during World War II, the federal government ordered mops, brooms, mats, mattresses, mail bags, and pillow cases from the workshops. This accomplishment was aided by the Wagner-O'Day Act of 1938, which provided for a committee to set a fair market price for goods produced in the workshops.

Beginning in 1941, childhood epidemics caused tens of thousands of young people to go blind in the United States, greatly adding to the population of sight-impaired citizens. Given the large number of children, elderly, and veterans affected by blindness, increasing attention was paid to the ways in which the quality of life of disabled Americans could be improved. "One pack" hearing aids began to appear on the market in the early 1940s; their compact design helped to make hearing aids light enough to be usable even by children. In addition, the invention in 1954 of the Tellatouch—one of several telephone innovations—enabled a sighted caller to communicate with a deaf-blind person who could read Braille.

More technological advances followed, along with new legislation (such as the 1990 Americans with Disabilities Act) to address the needs of the disabled in all areas of life, from employment to public services to telecommunications.

For More Information

Alabama Educational Survey Commission. *Public Education in Alabama.* Washington, D.C.: American Council on Education, 1945.

Atkinson, Brooks. Review of *The Miracle Worker. The New York Times* (November 1, 1959): II, 1.

Brooks, Van Wyck. *Helen Keller: Sketch for a Portrait.* New York: Dutton, 1956.

Fleming, Walter Lynwood. *Civil War and Reconstruction in Alabama.* Gloucester, Mass.: Peter Smith, 1905.

Gibson, William. *The Miracle Worker.* In *Dinny and the Witches and The Miracle Worker.* New York: Atheneum, 1960.

Gibson, William. *Monday after the Miracle.* New York: Atheneum, 1983.

Koestler, Frances A. *The Unseen Minority: A Social History of Blindness in the United States.* New York: David McKay, 1976.

Lash, Joseph P. *Helen and Teacher: The Story of Helen Keller and Anne Sullivan Macy.* New York: Delacorte, 1980.

Shapiro, Joseph P. *No Pity: People with Disabilities Forging a New Civil Rights Movement.* New York: Times Books, 1993.

Les Misérables

by
Victor Hugo

> **THE LITERARY WORK**
>
> A novel set in France from 1815 to 1832; published in 1862.
>
> **SYNOPSIS**
>
> A repentant ex-convict saves an orphan girl, who matures and marries.

Victor Hugo, the son of a general in Napoleon's empire, was born in 1802 in Besançon, France. Although raised by his mother to be a royalist, Hugo's inclination to republican ideals and his mild nostalgia for his father shaped his political and literary career.

Events in History at the Time the Novel Takes Place

The French Revolution. The thirteen American colonies won their independence from Great Britain in part because of support from France. Although French involvement was more an effort to frustrate Britain than a defense of a constitutional democracy, the principles of the American Revolution, along with the ideas of Enlightenment philosophers, who extolled the virtues of tolerance and reason and dismissed the notion of divine right to rule, influenced the French people's quest for a more liberal constitution in their own land.

The financial burden of their involvement in the American Revolution left France bankrupt. While the French Parliament insisted that the royal court could curtail its lavish spending and eliminate the deficit, the court argued that the nobles should lose their tax exemptions and pay their share of the country's debt. Negotiations were cut short when King Louis XVI, outraged by demands that finances be administered by a new commission independent of the crown, dismissed the Assembly, the portion of the Parliament that was active. But the opposition of the nobles to the king's reforms forced the king in 1789 to summon the entire Parliament, known as the Estates-General, which had not been active since 1614. He convened it now, after so long a hiatus, to resolve the squabbling over taxation and other economic and administrative problems.

The Estates-General traditionally included three groups of equal size: deputies of the church, the nobility, and the so-called Third Estate, the group that represented the 25 million common people of France. Since the Third Estate comprised the vast majority of the population, there was great debate over whether it should receive more representation in the Estates-General. The king ruled in favor of giving the Third Estate twice as many deputies as each of the other two groups. When the nobility and clergy, outraged by the change, refused to convene with the newly enlarged Third Estate, the Third Estate took power into its own hands and declared itself a National Assembly, swearing an oath to continue meeting until it had drawn up a constitution for France. After a failed attempt to suspend the sessions, the king ordered troops into Paris. This use of force infuriated the people, who stormed the Bastille, a former prison and a symbol of despotism, on July 14, 1789.

The troops withdrew and a draft of a new constitution was begun by the Assembly, limiting the powers of the crown; it was not finished until 1791. On August 27, 1789, however, its basic tenets were set forth in the Declaration of the Rights of Man, a document that established every citizen's right to liberty, equality, property, and security, adding that it was the duty of every citizen to defend the rights of all citizens. Louis XVI fled, hoping to rally troops and win back the throne; instead he was captured and executed.

FRENCH POLITICAL TERMS AND THEIR MEANINGS

Royalists or Ultras: Supported the right of the king to absolute power.
Constitutionalists: Advocated a Parliamentary monarchy.
Republicans: Favored a constitutional democracy with no king.
Bonapartists: Supported the French empire created by Napoleon Bonaparte.
Bourbons: Ruled France from 1589 to the Revolution; royal family included Louis XVI, executed in 1793; his son Louis XVII, who died in prison in 1795; and Louis XVIII, brother of Louis XVI.
Legitimists: Opposed Louis Philippe, who was not a Bourbon king.

The years following the king's execution were marked by turmoil and brutality. In June 1794 a new law denied an accused man defense counsel and allowed "moral proof" to replace tangible evidence in trials. Such a law doomed even a petty thief, like the novel's Jean Valjean, since one transgression was considered sufficient evidence that the accused was corrupt and irredeemable. In the forty-nine days following the enactment of this law, nearly 1,400 people were executed.

Napoleon. In 1795 the Directory, a five-man board elected by the legislature, came to power, assuming much of the authority once held by the king. A small group of conspirators, including Napoleon Bonaparte, dislodged the Directory in a *coup d'état* in 1799. Napoleon afterward became dictator, a position he retained until 1814, when he abdicated after the surrender of Paris to invaders. Napoleon returned in 1815 from exile on the island of Elba, only to be thoroughly routed at Waterloo. It is in this year that the plot of Hugo's novel, which refers to preceding events of the French Revolution, begins.

The Restoration. A Bourbon king—Louis XVIII—had briefly ruled prior to Napoleon's return from Elba. After Waterloo, Louis XVIII again took the throne, though his powers were more limited than previous kings. Since he was forced to rule by dictates of a charter and to share power with the Parliament, France became a constitutional monarchy. This was a form of government that many revolutionaries had sought in the uprising of 1789. Political divisions within the country continued, however. In elections held in 1815, Royalists won power in the assembly. Their success among voters reflected discontent with Napoleon's actions, which had left France saddled with debt and occupied by foreign troops. Three distinct political groups emerged during this time: Ultras, representatives of the aristocracy who supported the crown; Constitutionalists, determined to make the Parliamentary monarchy a success; and Republicans, who sought to eliminate the monarchy altogether.

The 1816 elections left the Constitutionalists with a majority. Putting aside political squabbles, they focused on paying France's debts and freeing the country of foreign occupation. France entered a period that was relatively calm and prosperous until 1830, despite minor uprisings.

Charles X. Louis XVIII was succeeded in 1824 by his brother Charles X, an Ultra whose policies inflamed the Parliament and the people. On July 26, 1830, the country was rocked by the publication of three ordinances backed by Charles. They called for the dissolution of Parliamentary bodies, abolition of freedom of the press, and the reduction of the electorate to 25,000 landed proprietors. Armed demonstrations broke out in Paris, and Charles X was replaced by the duc d'Orleans, Louis Philippe, who had fought in the revolution and was hailed as the "citizen king."

Louis Philippe and the Revolution of 1832. The revolution of 1830 was a victory for the middle class. But economic hardship among the poor led to insurrections in Lyons and Paris. Louis Philippe had to contend with the Legitimists, who thought him a traitor, and the Republicans, who opposed the citizen king and found enthusiastic recruits among workers and students.

Although often ignored by historians, the insurrection of 1832 is regarded as the first Republican uprising since the great French Revolution of 1789. The Republicans chose the burial of Lamarque, a hero of the Revolution, as the occasion of the uprising. The funeral procession was interrupted by Republicans who cried "Down with Louis Philippe!" No one knows who fired the first shot, but in the ensuing pandemonium the rebels managed to secure large parts of the center of Paris before being eventually overpowered.

Republican ideals were more popular in Paris than elsewhere in the country. Much of France remained sympathetic to the crown. This reality is reflected in the novel by Bishop Myriel's parishioners, who regard his meeting a former revolutionary as "far more dangerous than his excursion across bandit infested mountains" (*Les Misérables*, p. 35).

Penal codes. The barbaric penal laws of the pre-Revolutionary or *ancien* regime prescribed various methods of execution depending on the social class of the condemned. Nobles were beheaded, while commoners were hanged or subjected to torture. In 1791, pressured by public outrage and influenced by English institutions, French legislators adopted penal reforms with milder punishments, including education for petty criminals. While Jean Valjean's initial sentence of five years in prison for petty theft in *Les Misérables* may seem excessive, the fact that he was allowed to learn to read and write in jail indicates that he was imprisoned under progressive reforms.

The Novel in Focus

The plot. After spending five years in prison for stealing a loaf of bread to feed his sister's children, and then fourteen more years for trying to escape, Jean Valjean is finally released. He is required by law when entering a village or town to show his convict's passport to the local police, so his past handicaps his chances for a brighter future. In the village of Digne, he is refused both shelter and food. On the brink of despair he listens to the advice of a sympathetic local and seeks the aid of the Bishop Myriel, whose door is always open to the needy. The pious bishop offers him food and a bed, but Valjean repays his kindness by stealing his silverware and two silver candlesticks. Quickly apprehended, he is brought back by the police only to be freed again by the benevolent bishop, who insists that the silver was a gift.

With the bishop's parting words "use this silver to become an honest man" echoing in his ears, Valjean leaves Digne (*Les Misérables*, p. 106). Shortly thereafter he robs a child of a coin, then reflects on this petty theft. Valjean passes judgment on himself, deciding he is a miserable man, and becomes truly repentant. This small crime, though, will haunt him in the future; Valjean becomes a wanted criminal because of this petty theft.

NAPOLEON REMEMBERED

During the Restoration, many French regarded Napoleon's empire as a corrupt dictatorship. Mention of Napoleon often sparked disputes, as is illustrated in the following anecdote from Hugo's novel. The word *L'aigle* means "the eagle," which was a Bonapartist symbol, and the conversation illustrates how sensitive the topic of Napoleon was.

"What is your name?"
"L'Aigle."
The King scowled, looked at the signature of the petition, and saw the name written as LESGLE. This spelling, *anything but Bonapartist,* pleased the King, and he began to smile.
"Sire," resumed the man with the petition, "my ancestor was a dog trainer surnamed Lesgueules.... My name is Lesgueules, by contraction Lesgle, and by corruption L'Aigle." This topped off the King's smile.

(Hugo, *Les Misérables,* p. 655)

Elsewhere, the romances of four young girls end abruptly when their whimsical beaus abandon them. One of the girls, Fantine, has become pregnant and has an illegitimate child. She makes her way back to her home town, Montreuil, to find a job. Fantine is scared about the fate of her infant daughter, and certain that she herself, as an unwed mother, will not be welcomed in her hometown. She decides to entrust her child, Cosette, to the care of a Montfermeil innkeeper, Thenardier, and his wife, agreeing to pay them each month for their help.

Her hometown, Montreuil, has prospered, as has Jean Valjean, who happened to settle here. He has taken another name to avoid arrest, since he is still wanted for the theft of the coin. The reformed Jean Valjean, under the assumed name Monsieur Madeleine, has revitalized the local industry of Montreuil by suggesting that shellac be substituted for resin to make jet beads, thus lowering the price of the raw materials. He has become mayor, and the townspeople call him Father Madeleine.

Les Misérables

Victor Hugo

Fantine easily finds a factory job in Montreuil. But her letters to the Thenardiers, which include money for her daughter (but which the Thenardiers squander on their own children, treating Cosette like a servant), arouse suspicion among local gossips. When it is discovered that she has an illegitimate child, she is fired. Desperate for money, she first sells her hair, then her two front teeth, and then her body. Riled by a troublemaker who stuffs ice down her frock, she retaliates and gets arrested for assault by Javert, a policeman who is insistent that everyone obey the letter of the law.

Fantine is brought before the mayor, Jean Valjean, who immediately orders her release. Javert, the policeman, is amazed but bows to the mayor's authority. Fantine catches a fever and is taken to the infirmary. Valjean discovers she has a daughter in a nearby town and writes to the Thenardiers, requesting the return of Cosette. Sensing an opportunity for profit, the Thenardiers demand more money, which Valjean immediately sends. But as it becomes clear that they have no intention of relinquishing the child, Valjean himself resolves to fetch her.

Valjean's intervention on behalf of a prostitute, meanwhile, arouses the policeman's suspicion that Valjean is not the honest man he seems to be. Javert suspects Valjean is a convict. He reports his suspicions to the higher authorities, only to find that a man mistaken for Valjean has already been arrested for the petty theft of the coin. The man awaits trial.

Now Jean Valjean, still hiding his true identity, is in a quandary. Rather than allow an innocent man to be condemned, he himself goes to Arras, the seat of the trial, and identifies himself before a thunderstruck court as the wanted criminal. The amazed authorities fail to apprehend him. A few days later, however, Javert arrests Valjean in Fantine's quarters. Fantine, already in the grips of a fever, dies.

Valjean escapes and, by feigning a fall into the sea, convinces the authorities he is dead. He goes to Montfermeil to free Cosette from the Thenardiers, and he flees with her to Paris. Here he finds an inconspicuous house in a district outside Paris. Javert, however, tracks him down, and he is forced again to flee. After a feverish chase, he confounds Javert by scaling the walls of a convent. Here he and Cosette take refuge and enjoy many happy years together.

The novel then introduces Marius, who will eventually meet and marry Cosette. His grandfather, a Royalist, has disinherited his father, a hero of the Napoleonic wars. Having grown up in his grandfather's house, Marius never knew his father, who has just died, leaving him a note that asks Marius to do whatever service he can for Monsieur Thenardier, who saved his father's life at the Battle of Waterloo.

Marius, convinced that his father loved him, becomes fascinated by the Revolution, which he had always regarded as unprincipled brutality. Leaving his grandfather's house to take up residence in the Latin Quarter of Paris, he is befriended by a group of radical intellectuals whose political banter fuels his confusion about the empire, the republic, and the monarchy. He finds a modest job and lives in a detached state of reverie. Romance soon upsets his tranquility. He falls passionately in love with a girl (Cosette) he sees often in the Luxembourg Gardens, yet is wary of her companion, a grey-haired old man (Valjean).

One day, through a hole in the wall of his shabby abode, Marius sees the girl and Jean Valjean in his neighbor's squalid apartment. His neighbor, the villainous Thenardier, posing as a beggar, appeals to Jean Valjean for aid. Valjean promises to return with money. After he leaves, Marius overhears Thenardier's plan to kidnap or rob Valjean and rushes to the police, unwittingly drawing Javert back on the trail of Valjean. But before Javert can capture him, Valjean stealthily slips out the window and escapes.

Thenardier's daughter, Eponine, has fallen in love with Marius and, out of love for him, helps him find Cosette's address. Marius overcomes his timidity and confesses his love to Cosette, who reciprocates but keeps their relationship secret.

Valjean's fears are aroused by an anonymous warning (from Eponine, who has already thwarted her father's plans to capture Valjean once before), and he makes plans to move with Cosette to England. This threatens to shatter Marius's dreams. The emotional turmoil of Marius is paralleled by the political turmoil that surfaces in Paris. His radical friends become involved in the Revolution of 1832, taking refuge behind a barricade in a dead-end street and capturing Javert as a spy. In his despair, Marius seeks a romantic death in the insurrection. Valjean joins the insurrection to defend Marius, whom he knows his adopted daughter loves.

Javert's detention in the clutches of the radicals ends when Valjean manages to save the ruthless inspector's life. Returning to the barricade, he sees that the insurgents are doomed, grabs the wounded and unconscious Marius, and disappears into the Paris sewers. After an exhausting journey, he reaches an opening, but he finds that it is locked. Thenardier appears and demands money for opening the grating. Valjean turns over all his money, and Thenardier unlocks the opening. Before Thenardier leaves, he tears off a pocket from Marius's clothes, believing that Valjean has wronged Marius and that this material evidence will one day come in handy.

Valjean emerges from the sewers only to be apprehended by Javert. Javert eventually releases Valjean, though. Unable to forgive himself for this breach of duty, he flings himself into the Seine River.

Marius and Cosette are married, and Marius and his aristocratic grandfather reconcile. Valjean confesses his past sins to Marius, without once mentioning his selfless magnanimity, and Marius encourages his estrangement from Cosette. When Thenardier turns up to beg Marius for money, he describes Valjean as a murderer. He recounts his meeting with Valjean in the sewer, insisting that Valjean carried the body of one of his victims with him. As proof of this claim, he produces the torn rag from Marius's clothing. Marius realizes that Valjean was his savior, and he curtly dismisses Thenardier. He then goes with Cosette to console Valjean moments before his death from a lingering illness.

Gillenormand, Pontmercy, and Marius. Marius's grandfather, Monsieur Gillenormand, is a relic of the *ancien* regime who regards the revolutionaries of 1789 as a bunch of rogues and his own son as an outlaw. He places high value on appearances, as shown by the fine tapestries and magnificent hangings that decorate his house. He also insists on frivolous touches at his grandson's wedding, believing that "the useless is needed in happiness" (*Les Misérables*, p. 1352).

Under his grandfather's influence, Marius had been indoctrinated with all the biases of the Restoration, which denounced and abhorred Napoleon. Marius, though, discovers that his father, Pontmercy, fought with distinction for Napoleon in the Napoleonic Wars. This discovery inspires him to research the past, and his image of Napoleon as an ogre is replaced by "a suffused brilliance and radiance in which from an inaccessible height the pale and marble phantom of Caesar shone out" (*Les Misérables*, p. 633). Marius's radical friends, however, are opposed to Napoleon. They diffuse but they do not destroy Marius's newfound respect for Bonaparte.

NOBLE TITLES—WERE THEY COVETED OR SHUNNED?

While it may seem contradictory for a nation that fought a revolution against privilege to embrace noble titles, they became highly valued under Napoleon. These new titles were awarded on the basis of merit rather than inheritance. A member of the middle class could gain a noble title through money, political office, or, as Marius's father does in the novel, military deeds. In 1815, when the monarchy was restored, the noble titles that had been awarded during the Napoleonic era were delegitimized.

Passions of allegiance divide the Pontmercy family as they did French society. Although ideologically opposed, Marius's father and grandfather share many characteristics. His father refuses to answer a letter addressed to "Monsieur Commandant Pontmercy" instead of "Baron" Pontmercy, a title awarded to him for fighting so gallantly in the Wars. His stubborn insistence on the proper title resembles Marius's grandfather's insistence on frivolous show. At one point the grandfather grows alarmed at Marius's wounds, exclaiming "he got himself riddled like a brute ... for the Republic ... instead of going to dance

Les Misérables

... as young people should" (*Les Misérables*, p. 1316). This reaction reveals both his upper-class heritage and his love for his rebellious grandson. Overcome with joy at Marius's wedding, the two finally put aside their political differences.

Sources. Hugo's main character, Jean Valjean, was inspired by a real person. In 1801 the petty thief Pierre Maurin was condemned to five years in prison for stealing bread to feed his sister's starving children. A nonfiction description of the meeting between Maurin and the bishop is echoed in Hugo's novel. The ex-convict, "driven away by the innkeepers ... follow[ed] the advice of an old woman and knocked on the bishop's door" (Simon, p. 335). The bishop's welcome inspired him to "become an honest man" (Simon, p. 337). He later joined Napoleon's army and died in the Battle of Waterloo.

Hugo's use of historical detail in the novel implies a wealth of knowledge. He, in fact, often drew on secondary sources in his writing. The convent in the Rue Neuve-Sainte-Geneviève is real, and Hugo himself carefully examined the exterior, which he describes in the novel. But for details about the inside of the convent he relied on his mistresses, Juliette Drouet and Léonie Biard. Drouet had stayed in a convent herself and possessed an autographed manuscript of an old resident of the convent of Sainte Madeleine. Biard, thanks to her aunt's memories, had intimate knowledge of convent life between 1819 and 1823.

Events in History at the Time the Novel Was Written

The French economy and crime. In the 1850s and 1860s, France became a more industrialized country. This change in manufacturing processes made France a wealthier country, but led to an increase in unemployment, which, in turn, led to a rise in crime. Hugo's definition of "les misérables" as "the unfortunate and the infamous" (*Les Misérables*, p. 744) draws a distinction between those who choose degradation and those who are driven to it. Both Valjean and Fantine are pictured less as villains than victims, for they were denied work and ostracized as criminals. They are representative of outcasts in the author's own era as well as earlier times. Investigations by sociologists of the period showed that the scarcity of employment drove thousands of poor women in the 1800s to resort to prostitution for survival. Regarding them as corrupt, authorities in Paris founded a Police Morals Bureau that attempted to record the names of all prostitutes and subject them to regular physical examinations. The object was to protect larger society, but the very existence of the Morals Bureau suggests how prevalent the occupation was.

Prison conditions in the mid-1800s. Instructed to remain silent at all times, prisoners were utterly depersonalized. One observer noted that "we do not want inmates to talk to each other, but we cannot help it if they hear each other scream" (O'Brien, p. 75). There were suicides and riots in prison, yet most inmates managed to adapt, forming relationships and communities. Argot, a criminals' dialect that helped the convicts develop a sense of solidarity, is discussed by Hugo in the novel.

Some criminology theories of the time stressed the connection between biology and moral development, and concluded that criminals were irredeemable. In *Les Misérables*, Valjean, tormented by both guilt and anger after committing his crime, questions this theory: "Can man, created good by God, be made wicked by man?" (*Les Misérables*, p. 89).

Other philosophies insisted that environment was crucial to the development of a person's character. In the eighteenth century, Voltaire and other philosophers had called for a prison system that rehabilitates rather than punishes, and these ideas resonate through Hugo's introduction to the novel:

> So long as there shall exist, by reason of law and custom, a social condemnation which, in the midst of civilization, artificially creates a hell on earth, and complicates with human fatality a destiny that is divine ... there should be a need for books such as this.
> (*Les Misérables*, p. xvii)

Hugo's political life. In 1848, Louis Napoleon was elected president of the French republic. Three years later, he staged a military *coup d'etat* that allowed him to assume control of the country, effectively ending the republic. The popular support for Louis Napoleon's actions was indicated in 1852, when the French voted to disband the republic and restore the empire. Apparently a sufficient number of French voters were willing to sacrifice liberties in favor of a strong authoritarian government that would provide stability. This disheartened Hugo, who used his literary talents to preach the virtues of a republic.

Hugo delivered pompous harangues idealizing the revolution of 1789. Sensing danger, he fled to Brussels, Belgium. Incensed by the dissolution of the republic, he wrote the invective "Napoleon the Small," which belittled the emperor Napoleon III, nephew of the renowned Napoleon Bonaparte. Belgium, which was concerned about irritating France, expelled Hugo, who moved to the Channel Islands—first to Jersey and then to Guernsey—where he finished *Les Misérables*.

Reception. *Les Misérables* was cheered by eager readers, and one review praised Hugo's realism, insisting that "historical personages pass along these pages as breathing and earnest flesh and blood" (*Boston Review* in Harris, p. 359). A review in the *Southern Literary Messenger* extolled Hugo's moral and philosophical intentions, and described the novel as a Bible among the fictional works of the nineteenth century. Yet many critics were less enthusiastic. They criticized Hugo's digressive style, his unlikely plot and characters, and his moral diatribes. Some complained that a man would not be condemned to five years in prison for stealing bread and that Valjean's transformation into a morally uplifting humanitarian was beyond belief. Despite critical controversy over the novel, high sales attested to its popularity, and translations of the work spread Hugo's fame abroad.

For More Information

Goubert, Pierre. *The Course of French History.* Translated by Maarten Ultee. New York: Franklin Watts, 1988.

Harris, Laurie Lanzen, ed. *Nineteenth Century Literature Criticism,* Vol. 10. Detroit: Gale Research, 1985.

Hugo, Victor. *Les Misérables.* Translated by C. E. Wilbour. New York: Penguin, 1987.

Maurois, Andre. *Victor Hugo and His World.* London: Thames and Hudson, 1966.

O'Brien, Patricia. *The Promise of Punishment: Prisons in 19th Century France.* Princeton, N.J.: Princeton University Press, 1982.

Simon, Gustave. "Les Origines des Misérables." *La Revue de Paris* (January 1909): 327-48.

Moby Dick

by
Herman Melville

~

Herman Melville was born in New York City in 1819. Because of his family's financial instability, Melville was forced to go to work at an early age. After a variety of jobs, Melville signed onto a whaling ship at age twenty. Through this employment he learned firsthand about the rigors and rewards of the burgeoning whaling industry, gaining experience that he would later apply in the writing of his mid-nineteenth-century novel *Moby Dick*.

THE LITERARY WORK

A novel set on the high seas during the 1840s; published in 1851.

SYNOPSIS

The captain of an American whaling ship seeks revenge against the whale that bit off his leg during an earlier voyage.

Events in History at the Time the Novel Takes Place

An expanding nation. The first half of the nineteenth century was an important time in the development of the United States. In the War of 1812, the country had succeeded in defending its borders against the British. This victory created a strong new sense of patriotism among Americans, and the country finally began to form a solid identity completely separate from its European roots. To maintain this new identity, it became necessary to keep the foreign powers at bay. American leaders realized that the best way to deter aggression was to expand and strengthen the nation from the inside. In 1816 trade barriers were erected to promote domestic industry and keep foreign products from American markets. Federal and state governments financed improvements in the infrastructure of the nation by granting loans to pay for the construction of new systems of transportation. The building of the Erie Canal in the 1820s and the expansion of railway lines in the 1830s are examples of these improvements. Besides discouraging aggression against the United States, this internal strengthening led to rapid economic growth. Factories sprang up to supply the widespread demand for products that could for the first time be carried to distant consumers via new avenues of transportation. The young nation soon found itself in the throes of a bustling period of economic growth.

The American whaling industry. The advent of whaling in the United States began in the early 1600s with some of the first colonists. Most of these early whalers launched their expeditions from the island of Nantucket, off the Massachusetts coast, and from the colonies at New York and Connecticut. The whalers stayed close to shore searching for humpback, right, and grey whales. A turning point for the American whaling industry came in 1712 when a whaleship was blown off course into deeper waters and right into a 'pod' or group of sperm whales. One of the whales was killed and hauled ashore. The whalers discovered that the oil from the sperm whale was of superior quality, burning brighter and steadier than the other whale oils. Eager to obtain more of the valuable sperm whale oil, Americans began to venture farther out to sea and to stay longer. Soon American whaling ships were sailing all over the world in search of sperm whales.

The height of American whaling came in 1846 when the United States was still in the early stage of expansion and industrialization. At this point three-quarters of the world's whale ships were American-owned. America consumers propelled the industry with their demands for greater supplies of the sperm whale oil, which they used as a lubricant for machinery as well as for illumination.

The hunt. When a whale was spotted from the whaling ship, smaller whaling boats were immediately launched to pursue the massive animals. Built from half-inch thick cedar planks, the boats were 26 to 30 feet in length and built for speed. Commonly they were manned by a crew of six: the headsman, an officer of the ship who steered the vessel; the harpooner; and four rowers. A harpoon was a long wooden shaft connected to a barbed point that would embed itself inextricably in the whale's body. When the crew came within range, its harpooner would throw his harpoon into the whale. The harpoon was attached to one thousand feet of durable hemp rope that was coiled tightly in round tubs aboard the small whaling boat. When the whale was struck, it would immediately dive, pulling the rope from the tubs at an amazing speed, and also pulling the boat along briskly in what came to be known as "the Nantucket sleigh-ride." The rapidly pulled rope was one of the most dangerous elements of the whale hunt and could easily tear off a man's arm or whip him out of the boat if he were not careful. In 1803 Captain Gardner of the *Venus* was dragged overboard when his leg became entangled in the line. Gardner survived, but Captain Palmer, an American whaling master, was not so lucky. Palmer was pulled out of the boat and never seen again. In the novel, Melville writes of a final confrontation with Moby Dick as the line catches Captain Ahab around the neck and drags him down into the ocean's depths—like Palmer, never to be seen again.

Whales and extinction. In *Moby Dick,* the character Ishmael ponders the fate of the whale. He discusses the large numbers of whaling expeditions and wonders if the whale population can endure this relentless hunting. Ishmael questions, "Whether Leviathan [the whale] can long endure so wide a chase, and so remorseless a havoc; whether he must not at last be exterminated from the waters, and the last whale, like the last man, smoke his last pipe, and then himself evaporate in the final puff" (Melville, *Moby Dick,* pp. 470-71). Ishmael goes on to consider this possible extinction and compares it to the near vanquishment of other animals at the hands of overzealous hunters:

> Comparing the humped herds of whales with the humped herds of buffalo, which, not forty years ago, overspread by tens of thousands the prairies of Illinois and Missouri, and shook their iron manes and scowled with their thunder-clotted brows upon the sites of populous river-capitals, where now the polite broker sells you land at a dollar an inch, in such a comparison an irresistible argument seems furnished, to show that the hunted whale cannot now escape speedy extinction.
>
> (*Moby Dick*, p. 471)

WHALERS AND EXPLORERS

Whalers traveled all over the known world in pursuit of whales and sometimes into uncharted territory. In *Moby Dick*, Melville points out the debt that the world owes to whalers: "For many years past the whale-ship has been the pioneer in ferreting out the remotest and least known parts of the earth. She has explored seas and archipelagoes which had no chart. . . . If American and European men-of-war now peacefully ride in once savage harbors, let them fire salutes to the honor . . . of the whale-ship, which originally showed them the way, and first interpreted between them and the savages."

(*Moby Dick*, p. 111)

Despite this preamble, which seems to indicate a belief that whales will inevitably become extinct, Ishmael goes on to reason that because the waters of the ocean are so vast and the number of whales killed by each expedition are so few, whales will never face extinction. As the twentieth century was later to reveal, modern whaling techniques would prove Ishmael wrong as some species of whales neared extinction.

The Novel in Focus

The plot. The novel opens in New York City, home to the restless narrator Ishmael. Growing more and more depressed because he is living on land, Ishmael decides to return to the sea, where he feels more at home. He makes his way to the island of Nantucket in order to sign aboard a whaling ship. Because he misses the ferry, Ishmael is forced to spend a night at the Spouter Inn. All the beds are taken at the inn, so Ishmael finally decides to share a bed with Queequeg, a Polynesian harpooneer whom he regards as a cannibal. Though Ishmael is at first terrified by his strange bedfellow, the two soon become close companions. Queequeg believes that they should remain together and leaves Ishmael the responsibility of choosing a ship for them to join. Ishmael finds them positions aboard the *Pequod*, which is about to leave on a four-year whaling expedition.

ATTRIBUTES OF A SPERM WHALE

The largest-toothed of all whales, the sperm whale can grow up to sixty feet in length. It is a predator, feeding off giant squid that live in the deepest regions of the ocean. The sperm whale was the most dangerous whale for the nineteenth-century whalers to hunt, which is illustrated by their old saying: "For every barrel of [whale] oil, at least a drop of human blood" (Whipple, p. 43). Despite this drawback, the sperm whale was still a profitable quarry, providing four sources of income: the blubber, which was turned into whale oil; spermaceti, a waxy liquid that was made into candles; ambergris, a lumpy, foul-smelling substance that was used in perfumes and cosmetics; and ivory from the jawbone of the whale, which was carved by sailors in an artistic medium known as scrimshaw.

The *Pequod* is under the supervision of Captain Ahab. Ishmael soon learns that Ahab had once gone slightly insane after his leg was bitten off by a legendary white whale the whalers call Moby Dick. Ishmael is assured that the madness was only temporary and that Ahab has returned to complete control of his faculties. But as soon as the *Pequod* sets sail, it becomes obvious that Ahab's malady has not been completely cured. Ahab plans to use the *Pequod* and its crew to hunt down and kill Moby Dick no matter what the cost. Over the objections of the first mate, Starbuck, Ahab convinces the crew to aid him in his revenge. Though Starbuck sees the folly of his captain's plans, he is too loyal to Ahab to stop him.

While searching for Moby Dick, the *Pequod* charts a course that takes it through the world's prime whaling grounds. Some of the finest whaling waters are located in the Sea of Japan, and this is where Ahab believes he will have the best chance of finding Moby Dick.

Along the way, the *Pequod* encounters several other whaling ships, all returning home from long voyages at sea. Ahab asks the captain of every ship if he has seen the white whale. As it nears the Sea of Japan, the *Pequod* meets two ships that tried to capture Moby Dick. Both of the vessels lost crew members in their battles with the whale. One ship, the *Rachel,* is still looking for one boatload of men who disappeared during the encounter with the white whale.

Shortly after meeting the *Rachel,* the crew spots Moby Dick. For three consecutive days Ahab sends out small boats to capture the whale. On the first day, Moby Dick crushes Ahab's boat between his jaws. The entire crew of the small boat escapes unharmed. On the second day, Moby Dick once again destroys Ahab's boat, this time killing one of the sailors. On the third and final day, Moby Dick ignores the pursuing Ahab and rams the *Pequod* itself. The awesome power of the whale is too much for the ship and it sinks with a shattered hull. As the ship sinks, Captain Ahab finally harpoons Moby Dick. The harpoon line catches Ahab around the neck and he is pulled into the deep as the white whale dives beneath the surface, never to be seen again. Every member of the Pequod's crew is killed, except for Ishmael, who was thrown clear of the wreck. The *Rachel,* still searching for its missing crew, discovers Ishmael and rescues him.

Race and prejudice in Melville's America. Though some scholars argue that *Moby Dick* is a novel almost devoid of political messages and symbolism, others have suggested that a number of the novel's episodes pertain strongly to the political and social issues affecting the United States during this period. With the Civil War less than a decade away, the national debate over slavery was reaching a crisis point. The issue of race became a topic of great importance. In the Southern states, proslavery factions tried to justify their enslavement of Africans with the argument that blacks were inferior to whites and actually thrived under slave conditions. In the late 1840s, the proslavery factions introduced the science of ethnology to validate their position on the slavery issue. According to Dr. Josiah C. Nott, the principle aims of ethnology were to "know what was the primitive organic structure of each race... and what position in the social scale Providence has assigned to each type of man" (Nott in

Depiction of a whale hunt from *The Naturalist's Library, Volume 7: The Natural History of the Ordinary Cetacea or Whales*, 1837.

Karcher, p. 22). These "ethnologists" directed their study of race to proving the biological inferiority of blacks. Their study placed whites at the top of the order and blacks at the very bottom.

Some scholars believe that Melville attacks these notions of superiority and inferiority in *Moby Dick*, using Ishmael's experiences with people of greatly varying racial and cultural backgrounds. The greatest example of this authorial stance appears during Ishmael's first encounter with Queequeg. Though at first terrified by the appearance of the "cannibal," Ishmael immediately realizes that Queequeg is neither a "savage" nor so different from himself. When Queequeg invites Ishmael to share his bed, Ishmael says, "He really did this in not only a civil but a really kind and charitable way" (*Moby Dick*, p. 25). Ishmael makes further realizations about racial equality when he says of his first apprehensions of Queequeg, "What's all this fuss I have been making about, thought I to myself—the man's a human being just as I am" (*Moby Dick*, p. 25). These types of ideas were directly opposed to the proslavery ethnologists who postulated that there had been a separate creation for each race and that the races were not in the slightest way connected.

Phrenology was another so-called science of the time and is mentioned in *Moby Dick*. Phrenologists examined the formation of the head, claiming that each detail of cranial formation precisely defined the nature of the person. According to this theory, criminals, for example, could be detected simply by the shape of their heads. Ishmael's observations in the novel further disparage the proslavery viewpoint by using the ideas of phrenology. Ishmael judges that Queequeg's head was "phrenologically an excellent one" (*Moby Dick*, p. 51) and further states that Queequeg's head "reminded me of George Washington's" (*Moby Dick*, p. 51). This comparison of the head of the nonwhite Queequeg to that of George Washington, respected as a supreme figure of European-American achievement, uses one "science" of the era—phrenology—to dislodge a basic argument of another—ethnology—which justified the proslavery stance that blacks belonged in an inferior position.

Sources. Though scholars have found that Melville drew on a wide variety of material to write *Moby Dick*, three particular sources stand out. One is a book written by Owen Chase, the first mate on the whaling ship *Essex*. In November 1820, during a routine attempt to harpoon a sperm whale, the whale escaped from the small pursuing boats and headed straight for the 238-ton *Essex*. The whale rammed the ship and smashed a great gouge into the hull. Then, even as the ship was taking on water, the whale struck again. Within minutes the ship began sinking. Out of almost forty crew men, only eight survived, one of whom was Owen Chase. While at sea, Melville met Chase's son, who lent Melville a copy of a book by his father. In *Moby Dick,* Melville's narrator describes the *Essex* disaster and confirms that it indeed happened: "I have seen Owen Chase, who was chief mate of the *Essex* at the time of the tragedy; I have read his plain and faithful narrative; I have conversed with his son; and all this within a few miles of the scene of the catastrophe" (*Moby Dick,* p. 211).

A STRANGE COINCIDENCE

In the same year that *Moby Dick* was published, the whaler *Ann Alexander* met up with a particularly vicious sperm whale. The whale destroyed two of the three pursuing whale boats and then rammed the *Ann Alexander,* causing her to sink. The survivors were rescued the next day. When the news of the incident made its way back to the United States, one of Melville's friends wrote him about the remarkable coincidence between his book and the real-life event. Melville replied: "I make no doubt it is Moby Dick himself.... I wonder if my evil art has raised the monster?" (Whipple, p. 72).

The second and perhaps most significant source for the novel was Melville's own experience aboard whaling ships. In 1841, Melville signed onto the whaler *Acushnet* and began his own voyage through the world's whaling territory. He learned firsthand the difficulties of life aboard a whaling ship and came to understand the incredible amount of courage and skill necessary to hunt and kill sperm whales. It was most likely during Melville's time at sea that he heard stories of Mocha Dick. Mocha Dick was the name given to a sperm whale that had repeatedly attacked whaling ships. The whale looked distinctive because though most sperm whales were black Mocha Dick was said to be all white. The tally attributed to Mocha Dick was fourteen whaleboats destroyed and thirty men killed, although there is some doubt about whether the same whale was responsible for all these attacks since they occurred across the globe.

The final source for many elements in *Moby Dick* comes from the stories of the Bible. Many of the characters in the novel have the same names as characters in the Bible, and certain aspects of the novel resemble biblical tales. Melville used the Bible as a source knowing that many readers of his time were thoroughly versed in it and would easily make the connection between the characters in his novel and their biblical counterparts.

The Ahab of the Bible is mentioned in Kings I of the Old Testament and is said to have ruled Israel from 869 to 850 B.C. He was presented to nineteenth-century churchgoers as a wicked king because he permitted his wife Jezebel to stray from the worship of the one supreme God and join the cult of Baal of Tyre. In Melville's naming of the narrator Ishmael, he may have been inspired by the Old Testament book of Genesis, which mentions an Ishmael, who is the son of Abraham and one of his wife's slaves, Hagar. Ishmael and his mother are banished from the household after Abraham and his wife Sarah bear their own son, Isaac.

The biblical story of Jonah was perhaps also an important influence upon the plot of *Moby Dick.* Jonah is commanded by God to convince the people of Nineveh to abandon their wicked ways. In an attempt to escape this difficult task, Jonah boards a ship heading out to sea. On the voyage, he is thrown overboard and swallowed by a great fish. Realizing his error in defying God, Jonah proceeds to rectify it. Spat onto the shore by the fish, Jonah goes to speak to the people of Nineveh as God commanded. Ashamed at their own wickedness, the people repent, proclaim a fast, and avert their own destruction. This conclusion is different than the one presented in *Moby Dick.* Melville's Captain Ahab never repents his maniacal desire for revenge against Moby Dick, and so dooms himself and his crew to death.

Events in History at the Time the Novel Was Written

A new American literature. One of the many technological advancements of the Industrial Revolution was the improvement of printing and publishing techniques. Whereas previously only the wealthy could afford to keep a library of books, the sudden low cost of printing in the 1830s meant that the majority of Americans could now buy books. This revolution in publishing coincided with and supported the expansion of American literature.

In the 1840s and '50s a debate raged among American intellectuals regarding the development of American literature. Many simply wanted to expand on the literary traditions inherited from Europe. Others, Melville among them, argued for a completely new literature, wholly American and unconnected with European literary traditions.

In 1850, Melville took out time from writing *Moby Dick* to produce an essay on the subject of American literature. He wrote that to assume that no author might surpass Shakespeare was an unworthy belief, insisting instead that an American was bound to carry republican progressiveness into literature, as well as other parts of life. *Moby Dick* has since been held up as one of the finest contributions to the new American literature for which Melville argued.

Critics have argued that *Moby Dick* presents a uniquely American style because of the novel's innovations that are unconnected to European literary traditions. In the novel, Melville experiments with a wide variety of narrative techniques. Some chapters simply use prose to describe the events aboard ship, but there are also elaborate descriptions of whales and the whaling industry, resembling an article in a scientific journal or factual book rather than a novel. Several chapters of Melville's novel even portray events in the form of a drama, with each character coming forward to offer their own soliloquy about the pursuit of Moby Dick. This wide variety of methods showed readers of Melville's day that American literature was far from constrained by more rigid European literary traditions.

Mediocre reception. Before *Moby Dick* was published in London (under the original title of *The Whale*) in 1851, Melville was a moderately successful writer with four published novels. His first book, *Typee,* had been a great success, but with the publication of each successive novel, Melville's reputation declined. The release of *Moby Dick* did not seriously help or harm Melville's career as a writer at the time. There were some good reviews of the novel, but many critics were simply confused and many were disappointed by *Moby Dick*. One disparaging critic, Henry F. Chorley, wrote: "[*The Whale* by Herman Melville] is an ill-compounded mixture of romance and matter-of-fact. The idea of a connected and collected story has obviously visited and abandoned its writer again and again in the course of composition" (Chorley in Harris, p. 329). Another critic, George Ripley, considered the novel a great success. He wrote: "[In] point of richness and variety of incident, originality of conception, and splendor of description, [Herman Melville's *Moby Dick*] surpasses any of the former productions of this highly successful author" (Ripley in Harris, p. 329). Ripley continued his high praise of the novel in noting that "certain it is that the rapid, pointed hints which are often thrown out, with the keenness and velocity of a harpoon, penetrate deep into the heart of things, showing that the genius of the author for moral analysis is scarcely surpassed by his wizard power of description" (Ripley in Harris, p. 239).

For More Information

Allen, Gay Wilson. *Melville and His World.* New York: Viking, 1971.

Burton, Robert. *The Life and Death of Whales.* London: Andre Deutsch, 1980.

Harris, Laurie Lanzen, ed. *Nineteenth-Century Literature Criticism.* Vol. 3. Detroit: Gale Research, 1983.

Karcher, Carolyn L. *Shadow over the Promised Land: Slavery, Race, and Violence in Melville's America.* Baton Rouge: Louisiana State University Press, 1980.

Melville, Herman. *Moby Dick.* Oxford: Oxford University Press, 1988.

Whipple, A. B. C. *Yankee Whalers in the South Seas.* Garden City, N.Y.: Doubleday, 1954.

Narrative of the Life of Frederick Douglass, An American Slave

by
Frederick Douglass

Frederick Douglass was born Frederick Augustus Washington Bailey in the cabin of his grandmother, Betsey Bailey, on Tuckahoe Creek in Talbot County, Maryland, sometime around February of 1818. Born of a slave mother and white father (who was probably his master), Douglass tells a powerful tale of the beatings and mistreatment that he observed and endured. The story spans Douglass's twenty years in slavery, his success in escaping it, and his initial involvement in the abolitionist movement.

> **THE LITERARY WORK**
>
> An autobiography set mainly in Maryland from 1818 to 1838; published in Massachusetts in 1845.
>
> **SYNOPSIS**
>
> Douglass's story is a firsthand account of the brutal treatment and continual oppression of slavery that takes place in a border state in the first half of the nineteenth century.

Events in History at the Time the Autobiography Takes Place

Slavery in Maryland. Maryland, where Frederick Douglass was born and where he spent his years in slavery, was one of the so-called border states that marked the boundary between North and South prior to the Civil War. Though a slaveholding state, it contained an unusually large number of free blacks prior to the Civil War.

As Douglass grew up, he witnessed a reversal of sorts in voting rights in Maryland. By 1810 the state had abandoned racial barriers to voting; to qualify for this right, however, people had to own property, an impossibility for the majority of blacks. Twenty years later these property qualifications had largely disappeared, but there was a return of racial restrictions on the right to vote.

A divided state. Maryland is a geographically divided state with the large water mass of Chesapeake Bay nearly cutting the state into two parts. In the second quarter of the 1800s, the time Douglass writes of in his autobiography, the state had a population of fewer than half a million people. Nearly one-fourth of the population was centered in and around Baltimore at the northern end of the Bay. Baltimore, a prosperous and congested city of eighty thousand, was the base of the state's commerce. Other, less prosperous parts of the state were largely dependent on the city. Slaveholding was legal throughout the state, but conditions faced by slaves were significantly different depending on whether they lived in Baltimore or on rural plantations.

Most slaves in the city were either domestic servants or were hired out by their master to work as artisans, craftsmen, or laborers—with all their earnings going to their masters. Slaves on the plantations were frequently involved in agricultural work. Furthermore, the treatment slaves received from their owners tended to be different depending on the location where they lived. Though slavery existed in Baltimore, there was considerable opposition to the practice among some residents of the city. In view of this opposition, a slaveholder in Baltimore might be less inclined to administer brutal punishment to his slaves for fear of upsetting his neighbors. While a slave, Frederick Douglass experienced both the harsh conditions of rural slavery and the somewhat milder urban variety. He served as a houseboy and a hired-out worker in Baltimore, but lived on an eastern Maryland plantation for the first years of his life, as well as some of his teenage years.

East-shore plantations. The eastern shore between Chesapeake Bay and the Atlantic Ocean was the poorest part of Maryland and the most isolated. Douglass was born a slave on one of the small-scale plantations in eastern Maryland and served under a master who owned three small farms and about thirty slaves. The land in this part of the state was flat and broken by offshoots of the Chesapeake Bay, and roads in the region were poor; only a small number of surfaced thoroughfares existed in the early 1800s. The area was comprised mostly of small plantations that supplied Baltimore with raw materials and produce. A slave in this less populated area could encounter harsh treatment from masters undeterred by the judgment of a neighbor with antislavery sentiments. Nor could the slave easily attempt to escape from the isolated region.

Life for slaves on the small-scale plantations of the eastern shore was insecure. The failure of the farm or the death of the owner could and usually did lead to the selling of slaves and consequent breakup of some slave families. Those sold were usually destined for Georgia and other areas of the Deep South, where they often faced harsher treatment.

Physical conditions on the plantation. Away from the city, a slave's monthly allowance of food typically amounted to about eight pounds of pork, or the equivalent in fish, and one bushel of corn meal. Adults were issued two coarse linen shirts, one pair of linen trousers, one jacket, one pair of winter trousers, one pair of socks, and one pair of shoes annually; this all amounted to about seven dollars' worth of clothing per year. Children received only two linen shirts per year. If their clothes wore out, as often happened, they would go naked. Children were fed as a group—slopped like hogs, as Douglass describes it. Both the children and the adults slept on floors with only blankets; no mattresses were provided. But the slaves were so physically exhausted by laboring from dawn to dusk that lack of proper bedding was less of a problem for them than lack of enough sleep.

> **DOUGLASS ON THE VARIATIONS IN SLAVERY**
>
> I had resided but a short time in Baltimore before I observed a marked difference, in the treatment of slaves, from that which I had witnessed in the plantation. A city slave is almost a freeman, compared with a slave on the plantation.... There is a vestige of decency, a sense of shame, that does much to curb and check those outbreaks of atrocious cruelty so commonly enacted upon the plantation. He is a desperate slaveholder, who will shock the humanity of his nonslaveholding neighbors with the cries of his lacerated slave.
> (Douglass, *Narrative of the Life of Frederick Douglass*, p. 38)

The slave family. The conditions faced by slaves often threatened their family structure. When captured in Africa, many family members were separated from one another; the Middle Passage, the voyage on slave ships to an initial port of entry in the Americas, saw huge numbers of slaves die in transport; at the auction block, families that had remained intact were sometimes arbitrarily broken apart and sold to different slaveowners. Many first-generation slaves saw their family lives disintegrate, and those born into slavery in this country lived with the constant threat of forcible separation. About one third of all Southern slave families were torn apart by a husband's sale away from a wife—or worse, when a child was separated from a parent—and the fear of this eventuality was constant.

Families also experienced disunion even when living on the same plantation. As soon as they were able to work, mothers were frequently parted from their infants and made to resume their labor in the fields. Elderly women usually nursed the children, who, if they were fortunate, could see their exhausted mothers at night. Dou-

BLACKS IN BALTIMORE, 1790-1860

	Total Population	Slaves	Free Blacks
1790	13,503	1,255	323
1800	26,514	2,843	2,771
1810	46,555	4,672	5,671
1820	62,738	4,357	10,326
1830	80,620	4,120	14,790
1840	102,313	3,212	17,980

glass only saw his mother four or five times in his life since she had been hired out to a master who lived twelve miles from the plantation where Douglass was raised. She died when Douglass was around seven years old. He knew little about his father beyond the fact that he was a white man. There were rumors that his father was the slaveowner on the plantation where Douglass lived. At least fifteen of Douglass's surviving relatives were sold and sent farther south into other states during his boyhood.

At age seven or eight, Douglass was transferred from his plantation to a houseboy position in Baltimore. In the *Narrative*, he sums up his feelings about his move to the city:

> The ties that ordinarily bind children to their homes were all suspended in my case. I found no severe trial in my departure. My home was charmless; it was not home to me.... My mother was dead, my grandmother lived far off.... I had two sisters and one brother that lived in the same house with me; but the early separation of us from our mother had well nigh blotted the fact of our relationship from our memories.
>
> (*Narrative of the Life of Frederick Douglass*, p. 34)

Slaves and free blacks. The social conditions of the slave's life in cities like Baltimore were a source of discontent. The urban slave lived side-by-side with freed blacks, a condition unknown in the countryside. When manumitted (freed), ex-slaves were required to leave the state, but frequently they did not. Their presence served as a constant reminder to the enslaved like Douglass that there was a possibility of freedom. The fact that freed blacks vastly outnumbered slaves in Baltimore further emphasized the disparity in conditions, becoming both an irritant and an inspiration to those in bondage.

The intellectual atmosphere for city slaves was more stimulating than the countryside. Here they were inadvertently exposed to discussions about those politically organized against slavery and the drive in the North to abolish it. Douglass describes the mixture of despair and hope that such talk evoked in him:

> I often found myself regretting my own existence, and wishing myself dead; and but for the hope of being free, I have no doubt but that I should have killed myself, or done something for which I should have been killed. While in this state of mind, I was eager to hear any one speak of slavery.... Every little while I could hear something about the abolitionists.
>
> (*Narrative of the Life of Frederick Douglass*, p. 43)

The abolitionists. There were abolitionists in every state of the Union. Some of them were secretly organized into an escape network known as the Underground Railroad, in which homes and other buildings served as stations that sheltered fugitive slaves as they fled to the North. Although the Railroad was more active for those slaves from Southern states crossing the Ohio River into Ohio, activists were willing to help farther east in Maryland. Douglass, however, mistrusted the Underground Railroad workers. He found them well-meaning but too vocal. His autobiography does not indicate that there was any formal help in his escape. Indeed, he writes little of the actual route, since at the time of its publication in 1845 there were still slaves trying to escape bondage. To protect them and those who helped them, Douglass does not elaborate on the route or mechanism of his own flight.

Cover of the sheet music of an antislavery song about Frederick Douglass.

Frederick Douglass

EVENTS IN DOUGLASS'S LIFE AS A SLAVE

1818: Born on eastern Maryland farm of Aaron Anthony

1824: Sent twelve miles away to farm of Anthony's daughter, Lucretia Anthony Auld, whose husband is Thomas Auld.

1826: Sent to Thomas Auld's brother, Hugh Auld, in Baltimore

1833: Sent back to Thomas Auld

1834: Rented out as field hand to slave breaker Edward Covey

1835: Rented out as a field hand to William Freeland

1836: Makes failed attempt to escape slavery; jailed, then returned to Hugh Auld in Baltimore; trained as ship's caulker

1838: Agrees with Hugh Auld to hire out his own labor, paying Auld $3 a week; saves money and escapes to New York; marries; moves to Massachusetts

The Autobiography in Focus

The contents. Frederick Douglass taught himself to read and write with a little help from one of his kinder owners. When approached to write his story, he insisted on doing it alone and in his own words. The autobiography delivers a straightforward account of Douglass's own experiences as a child and young man under slavery.

Beginning with a brief description of his family, Douglass quickly launches into the first powerful account of mistreatment he witnesses, the beating of the slave "Aunt Hester." Aunt Hester had been warned by Master Anthony not to go out in the evening and not to associate with Mr. Lloyd's servant, Ned. Upon finding her out one evening in the company of Ned, Anthony ties her hands to a rafter of the roof, stands her on tiptoe atop a stool, and whips her mercilessly while cursing her. Douglass describes the punishment:

> He then said to her, "Now, you d———d b———h, I'll learn you how to disobey my orders!" and ... he commenced to lay on the heavy cowskin [whip], and soon the warm, red blood (amid heart-rending shrieks from her, and horrid oaths from him) came dripping to the floor. I was so terrified and horror-stricken at the sight, that I hid myself in a closet.
> (*Narrative of the Life of Frederick Douglass*, p. 19)

In another case, one of the overseers, the aptly named Mr. Gore, whips a slave named Demby, who runs to a creek to relieve the pain of the whipping. Ordered to come out of the creek, Demby refuses, and Mr. Gore pursues him, finally shooting him in the face with his musket as he stands in the water. Even Master Anthony is surprised at the severity of this punishment. When asked by Anthony why he had resorted to such violence, Gore replies that Demby has become unmanageable and is setting a bad example for other slaves.

Along with such incidents, Douglass describes the evil effect that slavery has on the personality of even a kind owner. When sent to live with Hugh Auld in Baltimore, Douglass sees his first friendly white face, that of his new master's wife, Sophia Auld; she begins to teach Douglass to read but is later chastised by her husband for doing so. Teaching slaves to read and write, he reminds her, is illegal in Maryland. In the end, she becomes more violently opposed to Douglass's reading than her husband. Douglass, however, who has already learned the alphabet from her, resolves to read regardless of her and her husband's opposition. He gets white boys to teach him, trading bread for reading lessons while on errands for his mistress.

Having been sent to Baltimore at age seven, Douglass is returned to the eastern shore plantation at age fifteen. He tries teaching other slaves to read at a Sabbath school, a Sunday school where students learned religion as well as basic skills, but some white men quickly put an end to it. His master, who concludes that city life has ruined Douglass, sends him to Edward Covey, a

Frederick Douglass

and Douglass has begun to subscribe to the abolitionist journal *The Liberator*. He has been persuaded to speak at an 1841 antislavery meeting and begins his important work in the movement.

Breaking the spirit. As his autobiography describes, Douglass's life took a turn for the worse at fifteen, when deaths in his owner's family resulted in his return to the plantation. Douglass came to know his first real physical suffering as a slave. His new master, Thomas Auld, did not feed his slaves adequately and was exceptionally cruel. Douglass rebelled and was sent to the nearby farmer Mr. Covey, to be "broke," or made submissive. Covey's strict rules and cruel punishments finally began to break Douglass's spirit. As Douglass expresses it, "a few months of his discipline tamed me. Mr. Covey succeeded in breaking me. I was broken in body, soul, and spirit. My natural elasticity was crushed, my intellect languished, the disposition to read departed, the cheerful spark that lingered about my eye died; the dark night of slavery closed in upon me, and behold a man transformed into a brute!" (*Narrative of the Life of Frederick Douglass*, p. 58).

Douglass did not give in completely, though. Running away after having been beaten senseless, Douglass returned determined that his next beating would be resisted to the death. In his next encounter with Covey, the men fought for two hours, hand-to-hand. After that, Covey did not bother him for the six months remaining of his servitude. Douglass maintains that when a male slave resisted a flogging, an overseer rarely ever tried to beat that slave again. The historian John Blassingame agrees. "The relationship of the planters and overseers to the recalcitrant slave was a strange one. Generally, they feared him, particularly if he were noted for his strength" (Blassingame, p. 212). Generally, the owners and overseers refrained from punishing such a slave unless they could take him by surprise, get him drunk, or coerce other slaves or whites to help. The only other alternative was to shoot such a slave, but owners often considered their slaves too valuable to exact this type of punishment. Aware of this dilemma, many slaves threatened to fight, flee, or stop working if they were beaten, and the power they derived from standing up to the planter or overseer heightened their own self-esteem. As Douglass puts it,

> I now resolved that, however long I might remain a slave in form, the day had passed forever when I could be a slave in fact. I did not hesitate to let it be known of me, that the white

slave breaker who beats recalcitrant slaves into docility. After countless whippings and an attempt to leave the farm, Douglass fights back and Covey backs down.

Douglass's first attempt to escape slavery is foiled, though it helps indirectly in his later success. Upon being captured, he is briefly imprisoned, then released to his former owner, Master Hugh. Back in Baltimore, Douglass is hired out to a shipbuilder and learns the trade of a ship-caulker. After a time Master Hugh is persuaded to let Douglass hire out his own time. This allows him to save money for another attempt to escape slavery, which succeeds.

Because of his desire to protect those active in assisting runaways, Douglass provides virtually no details about his escape. Upon arriving in New York, he is all alone: he knows and trusts no one. He is soon taken in by David Ruggles, a man known for helping fugitive slaves. Ruggles suggests that Douglass relocate to New Bedford, Massachusetts, where he can ply his trade as a ship-caulker and enjoy greater safety from being seized as a fugitive. First, however, Douglass sends for his fiancée, Anna Murray, and marries her on September 15, 1838. By the story's end, they have established themselves in New Bedford,

man who expected to succeed in whipping, must also succeed in killing me.

(*Narrative of the Life of Frederick Douglass*, p. 65)

Sources. Around the age of twelve Douglass encountered a copy of *The Columbian Orator*, a collection of speeches ranging from the classical era to Douglass's time. Of particular interest to the young slave was the "Dialogue between a Master and Slave." The incident in the narrative apparently transpired upon a slave's being recaptured after having attempted to flee for the third time. In the dialogue, the slave convinces his master, through reasoned argument, to free him. Douglass at this time had begun to reflect upon the whole concept of his enslavement, and *The Columbian Orator* provided him with much encouragement and food for thought. Among the other items it included were "Dialogue between a White Man and an Indian," "Oration on the Manumission of Slaves," and "Slaves in Barbary, a Drama in Two Acts." Beside stimulating thoughts about human relations and mistreatment, the collection provided Douglass with models for speaking and writing.

When he reached freedom and had settled in New Bedford, Douglass was introduced to William Lloyd Garrison's abolitionist newspaper, *The Liberator*. The paper and its cause kindled a fire in Douglass. He attended abolitionist meetings and was urged to speak on slavery. On the Massachusetts island of Nantucket on August 11, 1841, Douglass spoke so vigorously at a meeting of the Massachusetts Anti-Slavery Society that he was hired by the organization as a lecturer. His fame as an impassioned orator spread quickly, and his speeches helped him shape the material that is included in the autobiography.

The Christian Bible was another rich source for Douglass's writing. His work is infused with the rolling cadences of the American Protestant sermon. He quotes from the Bible and in an appendix to the autobiography, condemns slaveholding America for hypocrisy in religion. His appendix ends with a contemporary source, a parody by a Northern preacher who visited the South. The first stanza reads:

> Come, saints and sinners, hear me tell
> How pious priests whip Jack and Nell,
> And women buy and children sell,
> And preach all sinners down to hell,
> And Sing of Heavenly union.
>
> (*Narrative of the Life of Frederick Douglass*, p. 100)

Events in History at the Time the Autobiography Was Written

The slavery debate. By 1845 William Lloyd Garrison's journal, *The Liberator*, had been the public voice of the most radical American abolitionists for fourteen years; Theodore D. Weld's more reasoned but equally effective *Slavery As It Is* had been circulating for six years. Antislavery sentiments were growing, and the issue demanded more attention as the United States expanded westward. In 1843 a new member of Congress, Stephen A. Douglas, became deeply involved in trying to keep a balance between slavery and antislavery factions in the Union. Douglas led the congressional Committee on Territories for two years and then assumed the same position in the Senate. During this period, the United States was nearing war with Mexico and the subsequent acquisition of Texas. These prospects fanned the competition in Congress between slave-state and free-state advocates. It was during this period of bitter jockeying for dominance by the states that Frederick Douglass wrote and published his *Narrative of the Life of Frederick Douglass*.

Personal and public life. When Frederick Douglass and his new wife first settled in New Bedford, Massachusetts, Douglass adopted a new name. He had been born Frederick Augustus Washington Bailey, by which name he was known in the countryside of Maryland; in Baltimore he had adopted the last name "Stanley"; during his brief stay in New York he had used the name "Johnson." Settling into his new life of freedom, he took the name of Douglass, since there were so many Johnsons in New Bedford.

Douglass was surprised that the nonslaveholding North was more prosperous than he had imagined; he thought that the Northerners must be much poorer since they did not have the economic advantages provided by slavery. He got hired as a ship-caulker, a job normally reserved for whites, and he found plenty of work doing odd jobs. In 1839 Douglass joined an antislavery society in New Bedford. He began speaking at meetings, arguing against plans to colonize American blacks outside the United States. Douglass was an impressive figure, six feet in height, and he spoke in a smooth, flowing style. He became a regular speaker on the antislavery circuit. The job took him away from his wife and children for long periods and it exposed him to hostile audiences. By becoming a public figure, he was also at greater risk of being captured, sent back to his former master, and re-enslaved.

Despite these dangers, Douglass continued his work. When some critics expressed doubts that a man possessing his intelligence and speaking ability could have ever actually been a slave, Douglass began the *Narrative of the Life of Frederick Douglass* as an answer. His abolitionist friends were mindful of the fact that Douglass was still legally a slave. They feared that publishing his autobiography would result in his capture by Southern slave catchers. With their help, Douglass fled to England, where he would remain for two years and where English admirers raised the money to buy his freedom legally.

Reception. *Narrative of the Life of Frederick Douglass, An American Slave* was an instant success, selling five thousand copies in its first four months of publication. It especially appealed to both Americans and Europeans opposed to slavery. They found in Douglass's descriptions of the slave's life and the conditions of enforced servitude more reason for their opposition. Douglass was now famous and had formed his own views about how to attack slavery. Upon his return from Europe, he broke with Garrison and his extremely radical approach; for instance, Garrison frowned on political action, or negotiating with slave states, and called for disunion. Douglass pursued a different route, supporting political action, and in 1847 he started his own newspaper, *The North Star*. In subsequent years, he wrote two more autobiographies: *My Bondage and My Freedom* (1855) and the *Life and Times of Frederick Douglass* (1881).

For More Information

Blassingame, John W. *The Slave Community: Plantation Life in the Antebellum South*. New York: Oxford University Press, 1972.

Davis, Charles T., and Henry Louis Gates, Jr., eds. *The Slave's Narrative*. Oxford: Oxford University Press, 1985.

Douglass, Frederick. *Narrative of the Life of Frederick Douglass, An American Slave*. In *Frederick Douglass: Autobiographies*. New York: Penguin, 1994.

Douglass, Frederick. *My Bondage and My Freedom*. In *Frederick Douglass: Autobiographies*. New York: Library of America, 1994.

Fields, Barbara Jeanne. *Slavery and Freedom on the Middle Ground: Maryland during the Nineteenth Century*. New Haven, Conn.: Yale University Press, 1985.

Sundquist, Eric J., ed. *Frederick Douglass: New Literary and Historical Essays*. Cambridge: Cambridge University Press, 1990.

"The Necklace"

by
Guy de Maupassant

Guy de Maupassant was the child of an unhappy marriage. His mother has been described as neurotic and his father as a man who sought relief from his wife in the arms of other women. Perhaps the collapse of his parents' marriage engendered de Maupassant's pessimism, reflected particularly in his stories about infidelity and failed relationships. It certainly influenced his own attitude toward women, which, in turn, affected his creation of characters in stories such as "The Necklace."

> **THE LITERARY WORK**
>
> A short story set in France in about 1885; published in 1885.
>
> **SYNOPSIS**
>
> A young woman wastes away her youth working to replace a lost diamond necklace, only to discover that the necklace was a fake.

Events in History at the Time of the Short Story

The purpose of women. De Maupassant's attitude toward women was ambivalent. He was one of few nineteenth-century authors to recognize and celebrate women's sensuality rather than regard it as a sign of corruption. He was also, however, devastatingly cruel to women, whether in his own life or in his fiction. He recommended that the French Academy commission a treatise on how to "break decently, properly, politely, without noise, scene or violence, with a woman who adores you and with whom you are fed up" (de Maupassant in Steegmuller, p. 178). He scoffed at monogamy, insisting that he could not understand how two women could not be better than one, three better than two, and ten better than three. Moreover, he sarcastically dismissed the women's rights movement as nothing more than an uprising of skirts. With no effort to hide his scorn, the author suggested that men recognize only one right in women: the right to please. He approvingly kissed the rosy fingertips of ladies who aimed, above all, to be beautiful and seductive.

These glib opinions, which were published in French journals, reflect a type of scrutiny applied to women that put the less wealthy, such as Madame Loisel in "The Necklace," at a disadvantage. Women with limited financial resources found it much more difficult to attain the level of appearance expected in French society. It is not surprising, then, that the main character in "The Necklace" hesitates to be seen in plain clothing. Anything other than vain and shallow pretensions would meet with disapproval. In de Maupassant's opinion, the female should strive to be a charming and an eye-pleasing ornament for the pleasure of male existence.

De Maupassant's lifestyle reflected his dismissive view of women. He became famous for his casual sexual relationships, and eventually died of syphilis, a common sexually transmitted disease in the nineteenth century.

French feminism. When a German historian said the women's rights movement was "the child of the revolution of 1789" (Schirmacher, p. 175), she certainly spoke of ideology, not practice. The National Assembly, eager to limit the powers of the Crown, had proclaimed the Rights of Man, but dismissed the rights of women, denying a petition for universal suffrage. This was in fact a step backward for women, some of whom had actually been able to vote in local elections under the monarchy. The Napoleonic Code (1804)—a national code of law that spelled out civil, marriage, and other rights—demanded a wife's total obedience to her husband, denying her property rights and authority over her children. The penal code even allowed the acquittal of men who killed their wives for committing adultery. Conditions improved little for women after Napoleon's defeat in 1814, when the male-dominated monarchy was restored. It was not until the reestablishment of a republican form of government (the Third Republic in 1870) that feminists gained some favor in government.

During the first tumultuous decade of the Third Republic (1870-1880), some feminists opposed universal suffrage. Their paramount concern was to insure the survival of the republic, and some were afraid that if they gained the vote, conservative provincial women would add enough support to the monarchists to bring them back to power. Although feminists managed to help achieve the legalization of divorce and the passage of reforms in female education, women were practically excluded from political life.

Women's education. Many of the French believed in women's natural domesticity. They therefore favored an education for girls that was centered on providing them instruction in the areas of family values and morality. France based the achievement of this goal largely on religious instruction. Catholic schools, which stressed character development at the expense of intellectual learning, provided the only secondary education available to girls.

If the republican government made progress in broadening women's schooling, it was partially because the desire for general reforms in education harmonized with feminists' wishes to expand their opportunities. In 1880 nonreligious state schools for girls were founded. Although these state schools offered a more liberal education than the Catholic schools, girls learned neither Latin nor mathematics, and so were practically excluded from the hard sciences. Moreover, the high value placed on handicraft classes often overpowered or reduced the importance of courses in history or composition. Vocational training was regarded as beneficial for lower-class women, who could make use of these practical skills. This emphasis met with approval from the bourgeois or middle class as well, which judged that domestic training produced better housewives and mothers. In any case, the introduction of state education in 1880 came too late to impact the short story's main character, a grown woman at the time such tentative reforms were implemented.

Middle-class women, who were generally confined to the home, often grew frustrated by the narrow boundaries within which they were able to tread. In "The Necklace," Madame Loisel complains to her friend about the abject poverty she suffered while working to replace the lost necklace, but she never actually held a job herself. Instead, she had to dismiss her domestic help and do her own housework—something her Catholic education would certainly have prepared her to handle. Such chores would have been but a fraction of the responsibilities faced by women of lower economic classes. The confinement to the home, which so frustrated women of the bourgeoisie, must have been envied by lower-class women.

Undereducated and underfed, lower-class women provided cheap labor as domestics or seamstresses. In 1866 working-class women earned an average of 2.41 francs per day, whereas male industrial workers earned an average of 4.51 francs per day. Since they all competed for a few miserable yet precious jobs, women could hardly haggle for better wages. One woman even bribed the proprietor of a store with gifts to secure a job of hemming two meters of fabric for one sou (a five-cent coin).

The Industrial Revolution, the new republic, and conspicuous consumption. Industrialization during the mid-1800s created new opportunities for the French labor force. Peasants abandoned the small towns and villages for larger cities, seeking factory jobs or employment in banks, post offices, commercial offices, government bureaus, and department stores. Here they became a part of an emerging class of so-called petty bourgeoisie, who displayed an interest in education and an ability to buy goods on store credit. This distinguished them from the less financially able and, for the most part, less educationally involved working class.

Curiously, the elimination of the monarchy and the establishment of a republic in 1870

Luxurious furnishings from the late 19th century.

heightened class consciousness in France. In the new state, money tended to blur the differences in position attained as a result of heritage. Wealthy bourgeoisie were thus able to assume all the pretensions of the aristocracy. Displays of wealth affirmed one's social status, and the bourgeoisie enjoyed lifestyles that before had been accessible almost exclusively to the aristocracy. Displaying evidence of one's upward mobility became so important that "many got into debt seeking to keep up appearances" (Magraw, p. 14).

The French came to see conspicuous consumption as a means to maintain some sort of individual identity. Many artisans had been forced to leave their trades for mundane clerical work or monotonous jobs in the more productive factories during the Industrial Revolution from the 1850s to the 1870s. No longer able to express themselves through their work, they spent their extra earnings on articles that might reflect their personal tastes.

Fashion as a symbol of status. While many artisans were forced to abandon their trades, craftsmen continued to produce jewelry, felt hats, and other popular frivolities. Inventories of household possessions indicate that jewels were a widespread symbol of bourgeois status and that "in wealthy families this might be accompanied by a diamond necklace" (Walton, p. 100). Jewelry not only reflected the wealth of female consumers, but also mirrored a woman's tastes, desires, and concern for current fashion trends.

This need to prove social status and create individual identity was strong for bourgeois women, who, often jobless and confined to the home, had few outlets for self-expression. "Through consumption they could express something of their personalities," notes one authority, "and could satisfy a great deal of their ambition for social status and recognition" (Walton, p. 53). This consumption was less an opportunity for expression than an obligation to prove one's position, however. Since even the poor could attend some public functions, like the theater, it was necessary to turn to other means to demonstrate one's social station. Making it clear that one could afford costly frivolities was one way to do so.

As a woman's status depended largely on her access to money, she was usually dependent on her husband's income. Young women therefore often sought rich men. Women were expected, however, to provide a dowry—money or property given to the husband by the bride's family after the marriage—and rich men sought large dowries. As a daughter of a poor artisan, Madame Loisel had no dowry and therefore had to content herself with marrying a clerk.

The Short Story in Focus

The plot. Madame Loisel, an attractive young woman married to a clerk, longs to enjoy the luxuries and romance of aristocratic life. Her husband receives an invitation to a select ball given by the minister of education, and she, eager to impress the ministers and undersecretaries who will be present, borrows a diamond necklace from a rich old school friend. After a delightful evening of merrymaking, she loses the necklace by some unexplained misfortune. Her husband takes out an enormous loan to replace the jewels, and he and she then slave away for ten years to repay the debt. Then she happens to see her old friend, who still appears young and pretty. Her friend hardly recognizes the haggard Madame Loisel, who explains, "I've had some hard times since I saw you last; and many sorrows ... and all on your account" (de Maupassant, "The Necklace," p. 163). When her friend asks for further explanation, Madame Loisel admits that she lost the original necklace and worked for ten years to replace it. Her bewildered friend reveals that the original necklace was a convincing but worthless fake.

Convincing fakes. At one point de Maupassant interrupts his tale with the statement that "women have no caste nor class, their beauty, grace, and charm service them for birth or family ... [and] are their only mark of rank" ("The Necklace," p. 153). Madame Loisel's concerns reflect this awareness of the importance of outward appearances in shaping identity in French society. She knows that her appearance, accented by costly clothes and adornments, will transform her, a clerk's wife, into a lady of distinction. Disguised as a rich lady, she is "in the triumph of her beauty, in the pride of her success" ("The Necklace," p. 158) and wins the attention of undersecretaries and ministers. But her overcoat, which she has to go home in, is a modest garment of ordinary quality, and she longs to flee from the other women who are wrapping themselves in costly furs. Encouraged by social pressure to assume the air and guise of a lady, she pretends to be what she is not. The diamond necklace she wears, a fake, is also not what it appears to be. As a result, Madame Loisel mistakes it for a genuine piece. She, like the undersecretaries and the minister, is unable to distinguish between the real and the false.

Sources. De Maupassant worked, often under assumed names, for two Parisian newspapers, the *Gil Blas* and the *Gaulois*. He often borrowed content from his newspaper articles in the creation of his stories and novels. A prolific writer (he published nearly three hundred short stories and six novels), de Maupassant often transposed ideas or plots from one story to another. "The Necklace" is an inversion of another of de Maupassant's stories, "The False Jewels." The surprise of the latter story is that the jewels are in fact real. A bereaved clerk discovers that his late wife's supposedly fake jewels are actually treasures lavished on her by her wealthy lovers. In "The Necklace" de Maupassant merely reversed the revelation to create a different tragedy.

WOMEN'S ENVIRONMENT

Often excluded from public life, bourgeois women not surprisingly became obsessed with their homes. They grew attached to furnishings, which they believed reflected their tastes. In an article from *Le Conseiller des dames et demoiselles* (*The Adviser for Ladies and Maidens*), a woman wrote affectionately of her desk, "How many sheets have I blackened on your green baize! How you would laugh, patient piece of furniture, if you could express your thoughts, remembering the compositions ... that have seen the light of day since your arrival in my room" (Walton, p. 52). Another woman, having ordered a new piano, could hardly wait for the arrival of her "new friend." In contrast, Madame Loisel "suffered from the shabbiness of her house, from its mean walls, worn chairs and ugly curtains" ("The Necklace," p. 154). As a lower middle-class woman unable to spend money freely, she is denied one of the few outlets for self-expression available to women.

Reception. Among the tales in the collection *Contes du jour et de la nuit* (*Stories of Day and Night*), "The Necklace" was a favorite. Its surprise ending won the story popularity among nonliterary readers, whose reproach, "it makes you feel too bad" (Steegmuller, p. 204), is a tribute to de Maupassant's talents. A critic for *Harper's Magazine* spoke for many when he praised the heartbreaking pathos and sad tone of the story.

But the story's popularity eclipsed much of de Maupassant's other work and earned him an unfair reputation as a specialist in cheap trick endings. In fact, among de Maupassant's numerous short stories, only a handful have trick endings. The story is now viewed as one featuring a skillful plot that has long served as a model for professional short story writers (Steegmuller, p. 209). Although particularly popular in the United States, "The Necklace" is less well known in France than de Maupassant's other stories.

A version of the story was televised in America in 1949, but it only hurt de Maupassant's reputation as a commercial writer. It included a made-for-Hollywood happy ending in which the couple, as a result of their trials, rediscover a wealth of love for each other. The shock of de Maupassant's brutal irony, the reason for the story's original distinction, is traded for a maudlin love story and a trite moral: that love is priceless.

For More Information

Hause, Steven, and Anne Kenny. *Women's Suffrage and Social Politics in the French Third Republic.* Princeton, N.J.: Princeton University Press, 1984.

Magraw, Roger. *Workers and the Bourgeois Republic.* Oxford: Blackwell, 1992.

Maupassant, Guy de. "The Necklace." In *The Portable Maupassant.* Edited by Lewis Galantienre. New York: Viking, 1947.

Quartararo, Anne. *Women Teachers and Popular Education in Nineteenth Century France.* Newark: University of Delaware Press, 1995.

Schirmacher, Kaethe, and Conrad Eckhardt. *The Modern Women's Rights Movement.* New York: Macmillan, 1912.

Steegmuller, Francis. *A Lion in the Path.* New York: Random House, 1949.

Walton, Whitney. *France at the Crystal Palace.* Berkeley: University of California Press, 1992.

"The Notorious Jumping Frog of Calaveras County"

by
Mark Twain

Mark Twain first earned his reputation as a fiction writer with the publication of "The Notorious Jumping Frog of Calaveras County," originally entitled "Jim Smiley and His Jumping Frog." Trained as a journalist, Twain lived in the West for most of the Civil War. In 1864 and 1865, he spent several months mining around Angel's Camp, California, where he supposedly heard a version of the story from a camp bartender. Like a true journalist, Twain noted the anecdote. He developed it into a fictional piece less than a year later, gaining nationwide recognition as a premier humorist and short-story writer from its publication.

> **THE LITERARY WORK**
>
> A short story about an event that allegedly occurred in California during the gold rush days; published in 1865.
>
> **SYNOPSIS**
>
> A local man bets a stranger that his frog will win a jumping contest. At an opportune moment, the stranger pours small bullets into the mouth of the man's frog. The bullets make the frog so heavy that it cannot jump, and the stranger's frog wins the contest.

Events in History at the Time of the Short Story

Mining camps and the "forty-niners." In 1848, two weeks before Mexico signed the Treaty of Guadalupe Hidalgo ceding California to the United States, gold was discovered at Sutter's Mill. The discovery enticed 100,000 people to California within a year and induced 250,000 more people to emigrate within the next three years. By the summer of 1849, 40,000 gold-seekers, or "forty-niners," as they were called, headed west. By 1850, 80,000 gold-seekers reached the West Coast; these early fortune-hunters shaped the history and settlement patterns of early California.

Angel's Camp was the site of several important gold discoveries. One of the richest finds occurred in November 1854 at the Morgan Mine, which was located about four miles south of Angel's Camp. Discovered there was a mass of gold weighing 195 pounds, the largest nugget known to have been found in the United States.

Such discoveries lured people of all races and nationalities. Among those who rushed to California were miners from the Mississippi River Valley called "Pikes," East Coast Yankees, Australians, Irishmen, Englishmen, Hawaiians, Mexicans, and Frenchmen. Mining towns and camps sprang up overnight, quickly gaining distinctive characters as revealed by their names: Whiskey Bar, Humbug Creek, Gouge Eye, Lousy Level, Devil's Retreat, Flapjack Canyon, You Bet, Git-Up-and-Git, and Chicken-Thief Flat.

Despite their colorful names, however, most mining camps were rather ugly places, extremely dusty during the summer and muddy during the winter. People threw garbage everywhere; empty sardine boxes, old boots, and bottles littered the ground. Not surprisingly, dysentery, scurvy, diarrhea, malaria, and other maladies flourished in these camps.

Early miners lived in shanties, often made from shirts tacked onto wooden frames. So exorbitant were food and living expenses that meals generally consisted of hard bread, beans, pork, and strong coffee. In the winter of 1849-50, for example, potatoes cost $1 a pound; eggs cost $.50 each and apples cost $.75 for two. Tobacco sold for $2 a pound and a box of sardines cost as much as $16. Laundry cleaners charged $8 to wash twelve shirts; some miners found it cheaper to send their dirty clothes to China.

Social life differed greatly from the East. Women were rare and the few who lived in the camps and towns were usually prostitutes. In fact, women were so scarce that in one camp a man exhibited a lady's bonnet and boots for $1 a look. Typically men in the camps spent their leisure time drinking and gambling; otherwise they turned to singing, dancing, fiddle-playing, cockfights, bear and bullfights, and traveling shows for entertainment.

Gambling. Gambling became one of the most common pastimes in nineteenth-century mining camps. Almost everybody gambled, even children as young as ten or twelve years old. Furthermore, gambling was not restricted to miners alone; loggers, cowboys, railroad workers, and American Indians all took part in the games of chance. Gamblers wagered gold by the ounce and quickly lost and won fortunes. One reason for this careless wagering was that many people assumed that there was a large amount of gold yet to be discovered in the area. They reasoned that what was lost in gambling would soon be recovered in prospecting. Gamblers in California soon became famous for their recklessness; in 1849 one New York reporter described them as "mad, stark mad" (Hicks, p. 83).

Con men and entrepreneurs quickly took advantage of the gambling fever in the mining camps. "Lucky Bill" Thorington was one such opportunist. A master of the "shell game," Thorington invited people to correctly pick the shell that contained a hidden pea. Using trickery, he won one hundred pounds of gold in two months. Saloons and gambling halls sprang up anywhere gold was discovered, and proprietors eagerly helped part the miners from their riches. Many gambling establishments in the 1850s were quite elegant, as this description of a typical saloon shows:

> The roof, rich with giltwork, is supported by pillars of glass; and the walls are hung with French paintings of great merit.... Green tables are scattered over the room, at each of which sit two "monte" dealers surrounded by a betting crowd. The centers of the tables are covered with gold ounces and rich specimens from the diggings, and these heaps accumulate very rapidly in the course of the evening.
> (Cummings and White, p. 116)

Not all gambling establishments were quite so refined, however. Monte tables were often set up in the streets of less ostentatious towns and camps. Faro, roulette, rondo, and blackjack were also commonly played. Even the most modest gambling halls, however, had something in common with the more refined establishments: cheating was rampant.

Of course, not all gambling revolved around formal games, as "The Notorious Jumping Frog of Calaveras County" implies. People placed bets on the most ridiculous situations; the consequences were apparently unimportant. One miner, for example, bragged about his throwing abilities. In response, his partner bet him $1.50 that he couldn't hit the bar mirror with a beer glass. The miner threw the glass, won the bet, and paid the bartender $175 for a new mirror. In another example, two Marysville ice dealers bet on whose block of ice could last longer in the summer heat. Twain's humorous story thus portrays the devil-may-care attitude that existed in the West in the mid-1800s.

Western humor. During the nineteenth century, the West developed its own particular brand of humor, which included generous doses of tall tales and practical jokes. On the Great Plains of the Old West, for example, cowboys put bull snakes in their companions' bedrolls or burrs under the saddles of other riders' horses. By such standards, Eastern humor was considered rather stodgy. Eastern publications followed a British-style humor, and often had to explain to their audience which sections of their publications were funny and why. Needless to say, this audience often did not "get" Western humor, much to the delight of the Westerners.

Tall tales were widely printed in almanacs and newspapers during the early 1800s and reached their peak between 1850 and 1865. Early Western newspapers played a particularly large role in developing and perpetuating these humorous stories. More personal and colorful than their modern-day counterparts, early newspaper names included the *Cripple Creek Crusher,* the *Arizona Kicker,* the *Gringo and Greaser,* and the *Boomerang* of Wyoming. Newspapers commonly invented hoaxes to boost sales and to keep their readership interested when there was nothing newsworthy to report. Since most people knew the local news before the newspaper was distributed, hoaxes served as huge sources of amusement for readers. Many Westerners assumed that people knew when they were being lied to; those who did not obviously did not belong out West.

During part of his stay in the West, Mark Twain worked with William Wight, the chief reporter and staff writer for the *Territorial Enterprise* in Virginia City, Nevada. Wight, whose pen name was DeQuille, was a master hoaxer. On one occasion, DeQuille reported the discovery of small stones that, when scattered, suddenly rushed together towards a center and huddled up like a bunch of eggs in a nest. DeQuille's hoax traveled around the world, and for the next fifteen years he was plagued by hundreds of curious letters from scientists, circuses, and vendors. Another time, DeQuille published the alleged discovery of the rare "Shoo Fly," a bug that the Indians ate as a delicacy. DeQuille received a letter from an entomologist in San Francisco who informed him that he would receive credit for the discovery if he packed a specimen and sent it to the Smithsonian Institution. DeQuille reprinted the scholar's advice in his paper, as well as his response:

> What the professor says may be true, but when we view the insect and consider its cuspidated tentacles and the scarabaeus formation of the thoracic pellicle, we are inclined to think it a genuine bug of the genus 'hum'.
> (Emrich, p. 289)

Mark Twain's first hoax, which appeared on October 5, 1862, concerned a claim that a petrified man had been discovered:

> The body was in a sitting posture, and leaning against a huge mass of croppings; the attitude was pensive, the right thumb resting against the side of the nose; the left thumb partially supported the chin, the forefinger pressing the inner corner of the left eye and drawing it partly open; the right eye was closed, and the fingers of the right hand spread apart.
> (Twain in Brown, pp. 60-1)

Only the careful reader discerned that Twain's "discovery" was found thumbing his nose.

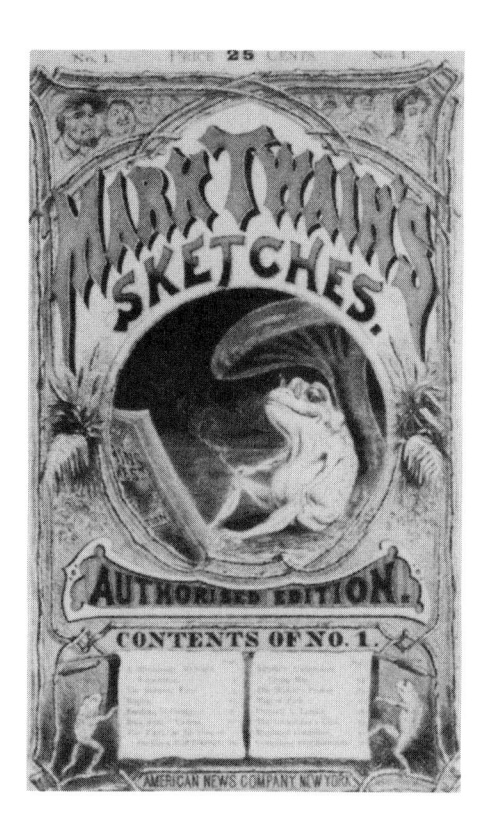

Cover of an early collection of Twain stories, featuring the "Notorious Jumping Frog." Illustration by Daniel Webster.

Twain's hoax was probably based on another story that claimed some strange, live animals were found in the Western Territory. This story was reprinted in New York without any indication that it was supposed to be humorous.

Nobody knows whether or not Easterners actually believed such stories, but Western journalists delighted in presenting made-up tales as if they were factual, perhaps believing that they could fool Eastern readers. Likewise, oral storytellers often employed a similar technique, relating their exaggerated and humorous tales as if they were serious and truthful accounts. Such a "straight-faced" delivery made the telling even more funny. Such oral stories, and their written counterparts, proved popular, and the spinning of tall tales soon developed into an art form.

Frog jumping. Scholars remain unsure whether or not frog-jumping contests actually occurred in Angel's Camp during Mark Twain's era. Today, Angel's Camp city officials like to claim that such contests took place, but little evidence exists to support their contention. The only indication that frog jumping contests were common in the area in the 1860s stems from an interview with

Angel's Camp resident Jess May in the late 1920s. May claimed to have seen the frog jumping contest that Twain featured in his short story. According to May, the participants were "city slickers" and the contest occurred about one year before Twain arrived at the camp.

The first official frog jumping contest, however, took place in 1928. The city of Angel's Camp made plans to celebrate their newly paved streets. Planned festivities included a rodeo, races, and mining contests. Two of the planners, Carl Mills and Harry Barden, decided to call the festivities the "Jumping Frog Jubilee" and to hold a frog jumping contest. Although they initially encountered difficulties persuading the city officials, their idea caught the imagination of others, and newspapers all over the West carried the story. The contest was held on May 28, 1928. There were 51 entries from all over the state, and nearly 15,000 people came to cheer the jumpers. Although many of the frogs unexpectedly jumped sideways, the winner was the "Jumping Frog of the San Joaquin," which jumped three feet, six inches. The next year, 20,000 people showed up for the contest and 500 frogs were entered, including one shipped from France.

The Short Story in Focus

The plot. As the story begins, Simon Wheeler, an old, garrulous resident of Angel's Camp, is in a store in the settlement. An unnamed Eastern man asks Simon about a friend of a friend. Wheeler does not know the whereabouts of the person, but instead launches into a comic story about another man with a similar name. Wheeler tells about Jim Smiley, a camp resident in approximately 1850. A man who liked to bet, Smiley gambled on nearly everything. He bet on standard gambling contests such as chicken fights and dog fights as well as more unusual things. Smiley bet on the most minor aspects of everyday life, wagering on when a bird might fly away, for instance. While Smiley didn't seem to care which side he took, he often ended up winning anyway.

One day, Smiley caught a frog. He named the frog Daniel Webster and taught it to jump. The frog learned to jump so well that he could jump and catch flies long-distance. All Jim Smiley had to do was yell, "Flies, Dan'l, flies!" and the frog would jump (Twain, "The Notorious Jumping Frog," p. 4). Soon he was betting regularly on Daniel's jumping capabilities. Jim Smiley felt very proud of his pet, noting that "all a frog wanted was education, and he could do 'most anything'" ("The Notorious Jumping Frog," p. 4).

One day a stranger entered the camp. The stranger observed Jim Smiley's frog and asked what the frog could do. Jim proudly replied that Daniel could outjump any frog in Calaveras County, and offered to bet $40 on his claim. The stranger replied that if he had a frog, he'd take the bet; so Jim offered to catch one for him. While Jim busily set out to catch a frog for his challenger, the stranger opened Daniel Webster's mouth and filled him with quail-shot "pretty near up to his chin" ("The Notorious Jumping Frog," p. 5).

After a while, Jim returned with the stranger's frog. "Now, if you're ready, set him alongside of Dan'l, with his fore paws just even with Dan'l's, and I'll give the word" ("The Notorious Jumping Frog," p. 5). Each man touched his frog's behind to make it jump. The stranger's frog leaped high, while poor Daniel gave a push and went nowhere. The stranger took the money and departed, leaving Jim confused. A few moments later, however, Jim picked up Daniel and realized something was wrong. When he turned the frog upside down, out poured several handfuls of quail-shot. Furious, Jim chased after the stranger, but he was unable to catch him.

Simon Wheeler, the narrator, is about to continue with more adventures concerning Jim Smiley's amazing animals, but a voice from the back of the store interrupts him and he excuses himself. Bored by the story, the hapless Easterner quickly takes advantage of the momentary interruption to exit rather indignantly.

Twain's politics and writing. Twain's early hoaxes and other writings were humorous. Yet, unlike the writings of many of his colleagues, they also contained traces of political and social criticism. "The Notorious Jumping Frog of Calaveras County" contains several hints of social and political satire. Twain not only depicts the polished Easterner as something of a buffoon, but he also uses the vernacular Western dialect to enhance his story. During Twain's time this was not a common practice, and some critics considered it a rebellious stance against stuffy Eastern writing standards.

Furthermore, Twain named the pets owned by the character Jim Smiley after political figures of the era. Smiley's dog, called Andrew Jackson, is characterized by Twain as a feisty fighting bulldog who overcomes his opponents by biting their hind leg and grimly holding on. When the dog encounters an opponent without hind legs, he loses the fight and dies soon after. Smiley's frog is named Daniel Webster, a prominent politician and occasional opponent of Andrew Jackson. Webster was instrumental in helping pass the Compromise of 1850, which admitted California into the nation as a free state. Twain was obviously having fun at the expense of public figures of the day.

Sources. Most sources appear to agree that Mark Twain heard a version of this story while visiting Angel's Camp in 1865. Furthermore, most agree that a bartender at the Tryon Hotel, a man named either Ben or Ross Coon, told Twain the narrative. Apparently, Mr. Coon was an excellent storyteller who claimed to have first heard the tale in Mississippi. The main characters in Coon's story were allegedly African American. Mark Twain himself claimed that the story took place at Angel's Camp in the spring of 1849 and that the tale was told to him as history. Furthermore, two versions of the jumping frog story can be found in newspapers of that area prior to 1864, one in the *San Andreas Independent* (December 11, 1858) and the following one in the *Sonora Herald* (June 11, 1853):

> A Toad Story.—A long stupid looking fellow [a Yankee] used to frequent a gambling saloon, some time since, and was in the habit of promenading up and down, but never speaking.... One day he came in with an important air, and said:
>
> "I have got a toad that'll leap further than any toad you can scare up.... I'll bet money on it. Barkeeper, give me a cigar box to hold my toad in."
>
> The fun was great, and the oddity was the talk of all hands. A gambler, in the evening, happened to come across a very big frog, fetched him to the gaming house and offered to jump him against the Yankee's toad.
>
> "Well," says Yank, "I'll bet liquors on it." A chalk line was made and the toad put down. They struck the boards behind the toad and he leaped six feet, then the frog leaped seven.
>
> [The Yank paid the gambler but, refusing to be bested, challenged him again the next morning and won. The story continues:]
>
> "My frog is darned heavy this morning," says the gambler.
>
> "I reckoned it would be, stranger," says the Yankee, "for I rolled a pound of shot into him last night."
>
> (Appendix to Lewis, pp. 31-2)

Twain also found a version of the jumping frog story in Dr. Henry Sidgwick's textbook *Greek Prose Composition*. In this version, the contest occurred between an Athenian and a Boethian. Many excited people, upon hearing of this version, thought that the story might actually stem from a Greek fable, while Twain hypothesized that similar stories had developed separately. Dr. Sidgwick eventually wrote to Twain and explained that he had found Twain's story so charming that he translated it into Greek with minor alterations and included it in his book.

Reviews. Mark Twain originally sent his story to Artemus Ward in New York for inclusion in a book of humor. The story's arrival in New York was tardy, however, so Ward sent it to another publication. Originally entitled "Jim Smiley and His Jumping Frog," the piece was published in *New York Saturday Press* on November 18, 1865. A humorous, Western story, it provided a welcome relief to readers who were weary of Civil War news. An article in the *Alta Californian* on January 10, 1866, reported how New Yorkers reacted to the story:

> Mark Twain's story in the *Saturday Press* on November 18, called "Jim Smiley's Jumping Frog," has set all New York in a roar, and he may be said to have made his mark. I have been asked fifty times about it and its author, and the papers are copying it far and near. It is voted the best thing of its day.
>
> (Lewis, p. 19)

The story became an immediate hit, securing Twain's reputation as a fiction writer. Yet Twain himself appeared ambivalent about the story's reception. He later wrote:

> To think that, after writing many an article a man might be excused for thinking tolerably good, those New York people should single out a villainous backwoods sketch to compliment me on—a squib which would never have been written but to please Artemus Ward, and then it reached New York too late to appear in his book.
>
> (Twain in Lewis, p. 18)

The success of "Jim Smiley and His Jumping Frog" brought Twain offers to publish a book of his short stories, a project enthusiastically embraced by editor Charles Henry Webb. Twain and Webb combined to prepare Twain's first book, *The Celebrated Jumping Frog, and Other Sketches,* with Webb editing Twain's writing. Twain announced its price in the *Alta California*—$1.50 a copy. "It will have a truly gorgeous gold frog on the back of it and that frog alone will be worth the money. I don't know but what it would be well to publish the frog and leave the book out" (Twain in David, p. 9).

For More Information

Cummins, Duane D., and William Gee White. *The American Frontier.* Encino, Calif.: Glencoe, 1980.

David, Beverly R. *Mark Twain and His Illustrators,* Vol. 1. Troy, N.Y.: Whitston, 1986.

Emrich, Duncan. *It's an Old Wild West Custom.* New York: Vanguard, 1949.

Hicks, Jim, ed. *The Gamblers.* Alexandria, Va.: Time-Life Books, 1978.

Lewis, Oscar. *The Origin of the Celebrated Jumping Frog of Calaveras County.* San Francisco: Book Club of California, 1931.

Twain, Mark. "The Notorious Jumping Frog of Calaveras County." In *The Complete Short Stories of Mark Twain.* Edited by Charles Neider. New York: Bantam, 1990.

"An Occurrence at Owl Creek Bridge"

by
Ambrose Bierce

> **THE LITERARY WORK**
>
> A short story set in Alabama during the American Civil War, around 1863; published in 1891.
>
> **SYNOPSIS**
>
> A Confederate civilian being hung by Union soldiers vividly imagines making an escape.

In September 1861, just a few months after the Civil War broke out, nineteen-year-old Ambrose Bierce joined the Union army in Indiana. By the time the war ended in 1865, he had fought in numerous major battles, worked as a military mapmaker, and been severely wounded in the head. He had also stored up enough memories to provide material for nineteen short stories about the war. "An Occurrence at Owl Creek Bridge" is the most famous of these stories. Despite its unconventional style, this story provided one of the first realistic portrayals of the horrors of the war.

Events in History at the Time the Short Story Takes Place

Railroads in the Civil War. Peyton Farquhar, the main character in Bierce's short story, is slated to be hung not for murder, rape, or some other violent crime, but for attempting to destroy a railroad bridge. A civilian, Farquhar hoped to protect Confederate soldiers from attack by tampering with the railroad line. The idea of using railroads to fight a war may seem strange today, but at the time of the American Civil War, tracks and locomotives played an extremely important role in military maneuvers. Used to transport troops, supplies, and food, railroads were usually the most efficient route from one site to another. Many famous battles were won or lost because of the use or destruction of railroads.

In the spring of 1864, for example, Union general William T. Sherman tried to cut off supplies to the Confederate army. He ordered one of his generals to cut the rail line that connected Decatur, Alabama, to Atlanta, Georgia, which was a Confederate stronghold. Union soldiers burned the wooden railroad ties until they were hot enough to allow the iron rails above them to be bent. With thirty miles of track destroyed in this way, rail contact with Atlanta was eliminated. Atlanta Confederates suffered greatly from lack of supplies as a result. By September, the weakened city had been captured by the Union, and shortly after this the war ended. Union destruction of southern rail lines like the Decatur-Atlanta route was partly responsible for the North's victory.

Civil War spies. Several key battles of the Civil War hinged on the activities of individuals who did not appear on the battlefield. Many of the war's great victories were won in part because of the information gathered in enemy camps by spies. In Bierce's story, a soldier disguised in Confederate uniform is actually a Union spy.

Railroad bridge destroyed in the Civil War Battle of Fredericksburg, 1863.

This subterfuge was used by both sides in the war; soldiers would dress in the uniform of the other side and slip into enemy territory, reporting battle plans and strategic locations when they returned to the home camp. Others would impersonate civilians and cross enemy lines to observe the nature and deployment of enemy military equipment. Many spies were not soldiers at all.

Peyton Farquhar's readiness to burn a Union bridge was typical of the military fervor felt by some civilians. One young woman, Belle Boyd—who could observe the movements of Union officers from her home in West Virginia—risked her life time and again to carry messages to Confederate officers about Union plans. Although her fate was less tragic than the one suffered by Peyton Farquhar, she spent more than a few days in prison and sometimes found herself crossing battlefields in the midst of fierce fighting. She was only one of a devoted body of spies—both soldiers and civilians—who affected the course of the Civil War.

A civilian planter in the midst of war. In the spring of 1862, the South's Confederate government passed a law requiring all white men aged eighteen to thirty-five to serve for three years in the military. Although this law had a great impact on the lives of most Southerners, those who owned plantations, like Peyton Farquhar, had two ways to escape it. Wealthy men had the option of hiring substitutes (new immigrants or people too young or old to be directly affected by the law) to serve in their stead. In addition, an amendment passed the following September stipulated that planters who owned at least twenty slaves were automatically exempt from service. Although this amendment was added to protect the farming economy of the South, it was perceived as unfair and caused a rift between rich planters and poorer Confederates. Soon soldiers began to believe that they were involved in "a rich man's war and a poor man's fight" (Rogers et al., p. 206).

Peyton Farquhar, whom Bierce describes as a civilian of about thirty-five, may have avoided military service for a few different reasons. He probably owned enough slaves to qualify for the planter exemption (since he was well-to-do), and if he did not, he may have been exempt anyway because of his age. For Farquhar, however, these exemptions were probably not his only reasons for remaining a civilian. As the story points out, part of him wanted to fight for the South. In fact, he "chafed under the inglorious restraint" of everyday life, longing for "the larger life of the soldier" (Bierce, "An Occurrence at Owl Creek Bridge," p. 12). Perhaps Farquhar thought he should stay home to protect his farm and family, then decided to justify this decision (and quench his own thirst for military involvement) by acting as a Confederate assistant on the side. In any case, by the summer of 1862, the northern Alabama city of Huntsville had been captured by the Union army, so that even the Confederate civilians in this area lived in danger. Most residents of northern Alabama moved south to avoid the Union troops, but Peyton Farquhar stayed where he was.

Brutal battles. Ambrose Bierce fought for the Union, or the North, in the Civil War. One of the first battles in which the young Ambrose Bierce fought was at Shiloh, near the Mississippi/Tennessee border, in April 1862. There the twenty-year-old Bierce became one of 100,000 soldiers who took part in what was then the bloodiest battle ever fought in North America; almost one-fourth of the participants were killed. Although Bierce survived, and his side was victorious, this battle must have had a powerful effect on him. In an essay entitled "What I Saw at Shiloh," he describes a scene from the battlefield:

> There were men enough; all dead, apparently, except one, who lay near where I had halted my platoon to await the slower movement of the line—a Federal sergeant, variously hurt, who had been a fine giant in his time. He lay face upward, taking in his breath in convulsive, rattling snorts, and blowing it out in sputters of froth which crawled creamily down his cheeks, piling itself alongside his neck and ears. A bullet had clipped a groove in his skull, above the temple; from this the brain protruded in bosses, dropping off in flakes and strings
> (Bierce in Woodruff, p. 63)

Bierce was not the only one to witness such a scene or to be affected by it. At Shiloh and on other battlefields, soldiers faced horrors they had never imagined before. One soldier from Iowa, unable to describe the details of the battle he had fought, wrote that the best way to experience his feelings without enduring the battle was to "call to mind all the horrible scenes of which you ever saw or heard, then put them all together and you can form some faint conception of the scene I witnessed" (Mitchell, p. 77). Many soldiers became paralyzed with fear at the first sight of battle. Others felt exhilarated by their brushes with death. In any case, most of them had to face what might have been the most horrific truth of war—that they were not just victims of the enemy's guns, but killers themselves.

The Short Story in Focus

The plot. "An Occurrence at Owl Creek Bridge" is the story of the hanging of a Confederate civilian, Peyton Farquhar, as punishment for his efforts to sabotage a Union bridge. The story is divided into three sections. The first describes the scene of the hanging, the second provides background to explain how Farquhar came to such a point, and the third details his imagined escape.

The first section of the story is told mostly in the detached language of an objective observer. A man's hands are tied behind him and a noose encircles his neck. He stands on a railroad bridge, where he is flanked by Union soldiers quietly preparing to put him to death. The man makes no motion of protest, but remains quiet during the preparations. He is described as a civilian gentleman of thirty-five, a Confederate planter. As the time of his hanging approaches, he begins to consider a way to escape; but in the next moment, the plank he has been standing on is removed.

Before more details of the hanging can be described, the story abruptly shifts to the next section, a flashback into Farquhar's recent life. An ardent supporter of the Confederacy, he is always eager to hear news of the war. When a soldier stops by his plantation one evening, Farquhar presses him for details from the battlefront. This soldier, a Union spy disguised as a Confederate soldier, tells Farquhar about a nearby railroad bridge that is strategically important for the Union. Any civilian caught interfering with it, he says, will be hanged. At Farquhar's urging, however, he explains that one side of the creek that runs under it is not very well guarded, and that the bridge could easily be destroyed by fire.

Instead of telling the story of Farquhar's attempt to burn the bridge, the narrative returns to the scene of the hanging. When the plank that has supported his weight is removed, Farquhar falls straight through the railroad ties of the bridge (the same bridge he had attempted to destroy) and is, Bierce writes, "as one already dead" ("An Occurrence at Owl Creek Bridge," p. 13). He is not dead, however; he awakens after losing consciousness, aware of agonizing pains throughout his body. He falls into the rushing creek below, for the rope that his captors sought to hang him with has broken. After a long struggle, he frees his hands from the cord that tied them and is able to swim to the surface for air. Within moments, the soldiers standing on the bridge begin firing at him, but he manages to dodge their bullets and swim to shore. The rest

"Owl Creek Bridge"

of his escape takes him through a thick forest to a road he follows all the way to his home. He passes through the gate and sees his beautiful wife waiting for him in front of the house. Just as he reaches to touch her, he feels a blow to his neck and all goes dark. He is dead. Though his mind led him home, his body, with a broken neck, has not escaped from the noose. It hangs from the Owl Creek Bridge.

Glorified war vs. reality. The American Civil War was the subject of great numbers of songs, novels, and stories long before "An Occurrence at Owl Creek Bridge" was written. Almost all of these works, however, painted a picture of the war as a glorious period in American history, a time when courageous soldiers fought for honorable ideals. The horrors of battle were ignored or glossed over so the romantic vision of war could be portrayed. One typical Civil War writer, John Esten Cooke, describes his branch of the Confederate army in the 1868 novel *Mohun*:

> Army of Northern Virginia!—old soldiers of Lee, who fought beside your captain until your frames were wasted ... —you are greater to me in your wretchedness, more splendid in your rags, than the Old Guard of Napoleon, or the three hundred of Thermopylae! Neither famine, nor nakedness, nor suffering, could break your spirit. You were tattered and half-starved; your forms were war-worn; but you still had faith in Lee, and the great cause which you bore aloft on the points of your bayonets.
> (Cooke, p. 241)

In the second section of "An Occurrence at Owl Creek Bridge," Peyton Farquhar's devotion to the "great cause" of the Confederates is described. Although he is not a member of the military, Farquhar feels that "no service [is] too humble for him to perform in aid of the South, no adventure too perilous for him to undertake" since he is "at heart a soldier" ("An Occurrence at Owl Creek Bridge," p. 12). His eagerness to burn down Owl Creek Bridge betrays his hunger for military action and the opportunity for distinction that comes with it. Farquhar's initial vision of the war, then, is very much in keeping with the sentiments toward the conflict portrayed by Cooke.

Soon, however, this vision abruptly changes. Farquhar's transformation from an idealistic military dreamer to a man desperate to escape the horror of death is typical of the transformation most Civil War soldiers went through after their first battle. One Union soldier, after being promoted early in the war to a position that did not require much fighting, complained to his wife in a letter that safety "is not what I came for[;] I came to fight & kill and come back[.]" After a year and a half, he wrote his wife again: "it makes me laugh to see the papers talk about this regiment and that[,] and that the men are eager for a chance to get at the enemy all in your eyes, there is none that wants to fight or will if they can keep clear of it" (Mitchell, p. 76).

Most Civil War soldiers, however noble their reasons for fighting, wanted desperately to stay alive. This desire often led them to less-than-noble acts, like deserting their posts to return home. Farquhar's imagined escape alludes to such realistic reactions instead of romantic ones. Farquhar allows his desperation to take control of his sensations; his desire to live is so powerful that his mind concocts an illusion of escape that feels real. Early literary accounts of the war such as those provided by Cooke may not have dwelled on such desperate feelings, but Bierce's story may relate a more honest version of the way most real Civil War soldiers died—feeling fear and desperation, not honor and courage, in their hearts.

Sources. Like many of Bierce's war stories, "An Occurrence at Owl Creek Bridge" is based largely on the writer's own experiences as a Civil War soldier. In fact, the battle at Shiloh at which Bierce was present was fought next to a Tennessee waterway known as "Owl Creek." Why Bierce shifted Owl Creek to Alabama in his story is unknown, although some evidence suggests that it might have been because of another experience he had during the war. In his *Bits of Autobiography*, Bierce recounts an adventure he had while stationed in Alabama. Bored with life at the camp where they were confined for a few days, Bierce and some fellow soldiers decided to explore the nearby Confederate territory. Soon Bierce found himself separated from his friends and imprisoned by Confederate soldiers. In a daring escape, however, Bierce made his way back to the Union camp. A comparison of Bierce's autobiographical escape and Farquhar's fictional one shows their similarities:

> *Bits of Autobiography*
>
> I now took my course by the north star (which I can never sufficiently bless), avoiding all roads and open places about houses, laboriously boring my way through forests, driving myself like a wedge into brush and bramble, swimming every stream I came to (some of them more than once, probably), and

pulling myself out of the water by boughs and briars—whatever could be grasped.
(Bierce, *The Collected Works,* pp. 312-13)

"An Occurrence at Owl Creek Bridge"

All that day he traveled, laying his course by the rounding sun. The forest seemed interminable; nowhere did he discover a break in it, not even a woodman's road.... By nightfall he was fatigued, footsore, famishing. The thought of his wife and children urged him on. At last he found a road which led him in what he knew to be the right direction. It was as wide and straight as a city street, yet it seemed untraveled. No fields bordered it, no dwelling anywhere.
("An Occurrence at Owl Creek Bridge," p. 17)

Both Bierce and Farquhar journey through the streams and forests of Alabama while military men pursue them. Both eventually reach "home" —for Bierce, his Union camp; for Farquhar, his plantation. But Farquhar's safe return is just an illusion, while Bierce's return (according to his autobiography) is real.

Events in History at the Time the Short Story Was Written

Postwar cynicism. In the decades after the Civil War, the United States entered into a prosperous era. Cities grew, industries flourished, and many people became very wealthy. San Francisco, the city in which Bierce settled after the war, was home to a number of "forty-niners," prospectors who had struck it rich in the gold rush of 1848-1849, and railroad executives, whose monopoly on California transportation made them among the wealthiest men in the country. Not everyone in San Francisco was a member of this new wealthy class, however. After a depression that began in 1873, jobs were extremely hard to find. The very rich grew richer and the poor grew poorer. Soon working people began to unleash their frustration on one another.

Bierce, a keen observer of the social injustices in San Francisco, wrote newspaper columns that were harshly critical of hypocritical businessmen and political figures, but these bitter pieces did little to brighten the prospects for most of San Francisco's residents. The idealism that had flourished in the East during the Civil War—the support for the values of the region, whether North or South—was almost nonexistent in postwar California. Bierce, though a valiant Union veteran, became the spokesperson for cynicism in the West. He, as well as many of his fellow citizens, had lost faith in humanity and in the prospects for a better life. This pessimistic view persisted not only in his columns but also in the dark world of stories such as "An Occurrence at Owl Creek Bridge."

Realism, Romanticism, and reader response. In the 1880s, a few years before Bierce began writing his war stories, American writers started experimenting with a new way of portraying life in their fiction. This new movement, called realism, stressed the importance of characters who resemble real people, not idealized figments of a writer's imagination. For many real-

TWO TRAGEDIES

Bierce's disillusionment with society may have had its roots in his Civil War experiences or in events in his life during his stay in San Francisco. Shortly before writing "An Occurrence at Owl Creek Bridge," his life was rocked by two personal tragedies that must have added to his pessimism. The first had been long in coming. His troubled marriage (to the daughter of a forty-niner) ended in 1887 when Bierce found a love letter written to his wife by a wealthy bachelor. Despite his wife's probable innocence in the matter (and his own previous love affairs), Bierce's ego was wounded, and he left his wife forever. "I don't take part in competitions—even in love," he explained to a friend (Bierce in Saunders, p. 51). Far more shocking an event was the death of Bierce's son, Day, at the age of sixteen. Enraged at the marriage of his girlfriend to a rival, Day went on a shooting rampage in 1889 that ended with his own suicide. Apparently proud of his son's tragic attempt to protect his honor, Bierce remarked on seeing his son's body: "You are a noble son, Day. You did just right" (Bierce in Saunders, p. 56).

ists, this meant recreating the lives of common men and women, including their everyday speech and their moral weaknesses. Although Bierce is known for creating a more realistic picture of the horrors of war than any Civil War writer before him, he detested realism as a movement. Bierce commented on the issue in his written work:

We human insects care for nothing but ourselves, and think that is best which most closely touches such emotions and sentiments as grow out of our relations, the one with another. I don't share this preference and a few others do not, believing that there are things more interesting than men and women.

(Bierce in Grattan, p. 115)

Rather than recreating life as everyone (and everything) else perceived it, Bierce wanted to explore what life could be. Consequently, his stories usually focus on extraordinary things happening in the midst of "real" life. Rejecting realism, Bierce thought of himself as a "Romantic" writer, an adherent to an older tradition of American writing that stressed the importance of imagination over all else.

Partly because of Bierce's refusal to follow the trend of the times, "An Occurrence at Owl Creek Bridge" and his other stories were not very popular at the time they were written. Ironically, however, their vivid, honest descriptions of war and the believable sensations of their characters led later literary critics to point to Bierce as one of the first American realists.

For More Information

Bierce, Ambrose. *The Collected Works of Ambrose Bierce*. Vol. 1. New York: Neale, 1909.

Bierce, Ambrose. "An Occurrence at Owl Creek Bridge." In *The Collected Writings of Ambrose Bierce*. New York: Citadel, 1946.

Cooke, John Esten. *Mohun or, The Last Days of Lee and His Paladins*. Ridgewood, N.J.: Gregg, 1968.

Grattan, C. Hartley. *Bitter Bierce: A Mystery of American Letters*. Garden City, N.Y.: Doubleday, Doran, 1929.

Mitchell, Reid. *Civil War Soldiers*. New York: Simon & Shuster, 1988.

Rogers, William Warren, Robert David Ward, Leah Rawls Atkins, and Wayne Flynt. *Alabama: The History of a Deep South State*. Tuscaloosa: University of Alabama Press, 1994.

Saunders, Richard. *Ambrose Bierce: The Making of a Misanthrope*. San Francisco: Chronicle Books, 1985.

Woodruff, Stuart C. *The Short Stories of Ambrose Bierce, a Study in Polarity*. Pittsburgh: University of Pittsburgh Press, 1964.

Oliver Twist

by
Charles Dickens

At age twelve, Charles Dickens worked in a shoe blacking factory apart from his family for reasons beyond his or their control. In the process, he met a working-class boy, an orphan named Bob Fagin, whose name Dickens would use for the villain in *Oliver Twist*. As a boy, Dickens dreamed of growing up to be an educated and distinguished man, but his dreams were troubled by fears that he might become permanently stationed among the poor, where he might be reduced to a life as a desperate robber or vagabond. These fears are reflected in the novel, for such a fate almost befalls young Oliver Twist.

> **THE LITERARY WORK**
>
> A novel set in London and in rural England in the 1830s; written and published in 1837-38.
>
> **SYNOPSIS**
>
> A young orphan, Oliver Twist, escapes a harsh apprenticeship in a rural town and travels to London, where he becomes involved with a gang of thieves. Fortunately for Oliver, he is befriended by a wealthy family whose members protect him from the robbers, investigate his mysterious past, and discover his parentage.

Events in History at the Time of the Novel

The New Poor Law of 1834. Since the 1600s, England had worked to relieve the burdens faced by the poorest segment of its population through a system known as the Poor Laws. These laws provided small supplements of food and money to men who worked in seasonal occupations such as agriculture and assisted the lowest ranks of the working classes when food prices rose. For members of society who could not earn any kind of a living, such as children, young women, the elderly, the handicapped, or the insane, the Poor Laws provided them with food and a place to live. Known as poorhouses or workhouses, these shelters became the focus for new changes in the Poor Laws in the early 1800s.

Lawmakers in England felt that because the country's system of relief, which had been in place for over two centuries, had not remedied the poverty situation in England, the system needed to be changed. In 1834 a New Poor Law went into effect. The main thrust of the Poor Law Amendment Act, or so-called New Poor Law, was that every local system of relief throughout England would operate under a uniform set of regulations. This detail alone caused innumerable problems, including a political one—local authorities felt that their powers were being subordinated and their judgment questioned. Perhaps the greatest problem with the New Poor Law was that it focused more on the systems and institutions for the poor rather than the poor themselves.

The New Poor Law guaranteed food and shelter to anyone who had no money. This was a

Oliver Twist

drastic change from the old Poor Laws, which had helped supplement the meager incomes of outdoor workers (for example, construction workers or miners) who needed just a little help to get by. The New Poor Law would not allow this. It gave out small allowances of bread but no money to outdoor workers. This new arrangement ultimately had a significant impact on English workhouses, where the poor were supported by public funds and put to work. The new stipulation in the Poor Law caused workhouse populations to swell with the addition of outdoor workers who had been cut off from the monetary aid they had received in the past. Unable to survive on their own, they moved into the workhouses to receive support.

> ### APPRENTICES AND THE POOR LAW AMENDMENT ACT
>
> Apprenticeship had been used in England for centuries as a way of teaching young men a trade. Under this arrangement, a boy was apprenticed to a master craftsman who prepared him for an occupation and provided him with food and shelter in exchange for the boy's assistance. The repeal of the Statute of Apprentices in 1814 removed all government regulation of the apprentice system, and the conditions for apprentices worsened tremendously. Even more harmful to apprentices was the Poor Law Amendment Act of 1834. This new law gave absolute authority to employers and took away the few freedoms of choice that remained to apprentices at the time. Thereafter most apprentices were forced to work long hours under poor conditions. This virtual slavery generally lasted until the apprentice was twenty-one or twenty-four years old. In the novel, Oliver serves as an apprentice to the undertaker Mr. Sowerberry; his service illustrates the abusive nature of the system under the 1834 act.

Another troublesome element of the New Poor Law was the theory that strong discipline and harsh conditions within the workhouse would discourage the less fortunate from unnecessarily seeking relief and encourage them to find whatever work they could. The new workhouse discipline segregated inmates by sex and age. Following this rule to the letter, the workhouses separated mothers from children and husbands from their wives. Many critics of the new system attacked this measure as an attempt to solve the problem of poverty by prohibiting the poor from having children.

Though food and shelter were guaranteed under the New Poor Law, the quality of this food and shelter dropped significantly. This was a result of the prevailing philosophy at the time, which held that it would be unjust for the unemployed poor to live under better conditions than the most impoverished members of the working class. As a result, food allowances shriveled and the conditions within the workhouses declined. A well-known reference to these small food rations appears in *Oliver Twist*. When Oliver asks for a second helping of gruel, he is severely reprimanded and the authorities attempt to have him removed from the workhouse because of his ungratefulness.

Able-bodied poor were treated in an especially harsh manner. Officials made their living conditions miserable in an effort to encourage them to find employment, even though such work did not exist. Unfortunately for the poor, the government only made small adjustments to the system during the following years in hopes that it would eventually surmount its initial difficulties and begin solving the problem of the poor in England. In fact, the only effect the new system had was to increase the numbers of the poor in the workhouses, worsen their conditions, and raise the crime rate, as able-bodied men and women turned to illegal activities for subsistence.

Crime in London. During Dickens's lifetime, crime ran rampant in the city of London. Dickens seemed to have a strong interest in the criminal aspects of the city, kindled perhaps by his stint as a court reporter, a position that exposed him to the characters and incidents of the London underworld. Even before Dickens, London had been rife with criminal activity. In the 1700s, guidebooks informed readers, "a man who saunters about the capital with pockets on the outside of his coat deserves no pity," and a foreign visitor wrote that "pickpockets are legion. With extraordinary dexterity they will steal handkerchiefs, snuff-boxes, watches—in short, anything they can find in your pockets. Their profession is practiced in the streets, in churches, at the play, and especially in crowds" (Babington, pp. 16-17). In Dickens's novel, Oliver becomes involved with a gang of pickpockets who are supervised by a criminal named Fagin. According to historians, such an arrangement was not uncommon.

Pickpockets usually started learning their skills early in life; children as young as five years

Illustration by George Cruikshank of Oliver's reception by Fagin and the boys.

old learned the trade from their parents, their companions at the cheap lodging houses that were so common during this period, or from a recognized "thief-trainer." Sometimes fledgling pickpockets would practice by attempting to remove objects from the pocket of a coat to which bells were attached. When they could remove these objects without ringing the bells, they practiced picking the pockets of their teacher as he walked up and down the room. Once pickpockets successfully passed these tests, they were ready to try their skills on the street. In addition to picking pockets, young boys in London also stole money from small children who had been sent on errands by their parents. All these aspects of the pickpocket "profession" are on display in *Oliver Twist*.

Another popular crime of the era in which Oliver becomes involved was housebreaking. Many housebreakers used young boys such as Oliver in their crimes. The boys would enter houses through fanlights or small windows. Once inside, they would then open a door for the other members of the gang.

Crime was not the exclusive province of the male members of London during this period. Young girls committed numerous crimes during this period. Primary among them, and almost exclusively limited to young women, was the crime of shoplifting. Young women would enter a shop and ask to see certain articles. When the shopkeeper turned his back to retrieve the article in question, the shoplifter would grab whatever she could. An even less savory endeavor practiced by young women was prostitution. The women either worked for themselves or were forced into the profession by someone else. Called dress-lodgers, women who were forced into prostitution were generally kept in captivity through violence or a debt to their "employer," who threatened to have them thrown in prison if they did not work to repay what they owed.

> ### THE *HUE AND CRY*
>
> In 1772 John Fielding, the Justice of the Peace for Westminster and Middlesex and the half brother of the novelist Henry Fielding, began to circulate a publication called *Extraordinary Pursuit* to magistrates throughout England. This bulletin, which was distributed free of charge, contained details on all criminals who had run away from London. In 1773 the name of the bulletin was changed to *Public Hue and Cry,* then to *Hue and Cry,* and eventually to *Police Gazette.* By the end of the eighteenth century, the publication had been expanded by Sir Sampson Wright to include four pages and was published twice a week. It contained accounts of crimes, descriptions of criminals and stolen property, and reports on the examinations of suspects from the city magistrates' offices. In one of Fagin's first appearances in *Oliver Twist,* he is intently reading a copy of *Hue and Cry.*

Charity in the Victorian age. As conditions worsened for the poor in England, groups and individuals interested in providing charity for the impoverished slowly emerged. The era saw the appearance of groups such as the Society for Bettering the Condition of the Poor and the Strangers' Friend Society, whose members set out to improve the lives of the poorest classes. Dickens took great interest in charity efforts, but felt that the poor should be helped by individuals rather than by institutions like workhouses. In *Oliver Twist,* Dickens presents two examples of upper-class members of society taking pity on the destitute and friendless Oliver—Mr. Brownlow and the Maylie family. The charity of these characters seems intended to encourage upper-class readers to make individual efforts to alleviate the misery of the poor and helpless. Dickens also goes to great lengths to portray the atrocious conditions of the workhouses and to show that they are filled with not just unworthy and lazy paupers but with innocent women and children as well.

Jews in England. During the Middle Ages Jews existed on the fringes of English society. The primary force behind this alienation was the Catholic Church, which forbade any social relationships between Christians and Jews. There was a prevalent belief that Jews had betrayed Christ and by so doing were linked somehow to the devil. Following this reasoning, the larger English population began to believe that Jews were intent on destroying Christian society. Charges that Jews had poisoned wells, helped spread the Black Plague, and slaughtered Christian children during Jewish religious rituals became commonplace.

The only reason the Christian community tolerated Jews at all was because of the economic benefits the Jews provided. Centuries of forced exclusion from trade, as well as laws against Jews owning land, had taught them to deal and barter in other arenas. While the Christian population focused on land, the Jews learned the principles of banking and finance. Since the Catholic Church believed that moneylending was a despicable practice fit only for nonbelievers, Jews found their niche as the moneylenders of the Middle Ages. Yet religious hatred against the Jews mounted, and in 1290 King Edward I banished all Jews from England. For the next few hundred years, there were only tiny communities of Jews in England, and they kept their religious faith hidden.

In 1656, during Oliver Cromwell's government, Jews from Holland and elsewhere in Europe were allowed into England and were finally able to admit their faith without fear of reprisals and expulsion. Though their legal and economic fortunes began to improve, Jews remained subject to social and cultural persecution. Even the most liberal-minded members of society considered Jews to be greedy, lowly people whose primary desire was to use money as a tool against Christian society. A 1777 engraving called "Jews Receiving Stolen Property" illustrates the popular image of the group in England. Dickens reflects this attitude in *Oliver Twist* through the character of the Jew Fagin, a thief who exploits children and women to pursue his hunger for financial gain.

How closely Fagin represents a real-life character remains open to question. Certainly there were Jewish criminals in England. In 1771 a gang of eight Jews committed some brutal murders at Chelsea that contributed to general hatred of the Jews and physical violence against members of their faith. The Jewish community dissociated itself from the criminals, refusing to bury the four who were executed for the crime in sacred ground. The majority of Jews engaged in legitimate occupations, working as used clothing dealers, domestic servants, necklace makers, printers, perfumers, butchers, doctors, and sailors. Still, social discontent resulted in crime by Jews as well as non-Jews. Among the convicts shipped to Australia from 1788 to 1852, there were at least one thousand Jews. One of these men was Ikey Solomon, the "Prince of Fences," who may have been Dickens's model for Fagin in *Oliver Twist*.

The Novel in Focus

The plot. When the novel begins, the young orphan Oliver Twist is trapped within the miserable parish workhouse. He lives under deplorable conditions, suffering from lack of food, care, and most of all, compassion. After causing a disturbance by asking for a second helping at mealtime, Oliver is sent out of the workhouse to serve an apprenticeship with a coffin-maker. This experience leads to further abuse, and Oliver finally decides to run away to London.

On the way, he meets Jack Dawkins, a strange young man who is also known as the Artful Dodger. The Dodger takes Oliver into London and introduces him to several other young boys and their employer Fagin, an old Jewish man. Oliver is astonished to discover that the boys are employed to pick pockets, and upon first witnessing the Artful Dodger and Charley Bates pick the pocket of an elderly gentleman, Oliver is mistakenly arrested as the thief while the Dodger and Charley run away.

The elderly gentleman, Mr. Brownlow, takes pity on the innocent-looking Oliver, and when evidence proves that Oliver did not commit the crime, he takes the boy home with him. Oliver spends a short, happy period with Mr. Brownlow, but while performing an errand for his savior, he is kidnapped by Bill Sikes and Nancy, two confederates of Fagin.

For a brief period Oliver is held captive by Fagin; then Bill Sikes takes him on a mysterious expedition. Oliver arrives at a house in the country, where he is to be a participant in a burglary. After being forced into the house through a tiny window, Oliver is shot by one of the household servants. Sikes flees, abandoning Oliver in a ditch. The wounded Oliver then stumbles to the same house they had attempted to rob and seeks assistance. Its owner, Mrs. Maylie, makes sure that Oliver is carefully nursed back to health by her young housemate Rose and their good friend Dr. Losberne. After Oliver tells them of his horrifying experiences, Mrs. Maylie decides to make him a member of her family, and Oliver accompanies them when the family relocates to a cottage farther out in the country.

In a town near the cottage, Oliver encounters a strange man who speaks harshly to him. A few days later he is startled to see Fagin and the stranger peering into the window of the Maylie cottage. Oliver rouses the household, but the two men mysteriously disappear.

The family then leaves to spend some time in London, where Oliver again meets Mr. Brownlow. When Brownlow hears the tale of Oliver's earlier kidnapping, he is relieved that the boy had not left him by choice. Meanwhile, Nancy visits Mrs. Maylie's companion Rose at her hotel. She tells Rose about Fagin's interest in Oliver and about a man named Monks, who is also quite interested in the young orphan. Rose relates this to Mrs. Maylie, one of her cousins, and Dr. Losberne. Mr. Brownlow also becomes involved in the mystery.

After another meeting with Nancy, they discover that Oliver is a half-brother to Monks, who is trying to prevent Oliver from receiving an inheritance that he desires for himself. Mr. Brownlow sheds some light on the story when he realizes from the description of Monks that he is the son of one of Mr. Brownlow's good friends. The friend had died almost ten years earlier after leaving Monks's mother and beginning a relationship with Oliver's mother. Monks had been watching for Oliver, and when the boy surfaced in London, Monks had enlisted Fagin to train Oliver as a pickpocket, for any illegal activities performed by the boy would invalidate his claim to the inheritance.

Another unexpected surprise is that Rose turns out to be the youngest sister of Oliver's mother, whose family fell on hard times. The charitable Mrs. Maylie had taken Rose into her home just as she later took in Oliver. Rose is therefore revealed as Oliver's aunt.

Mr. Brownlow corners Monks and threatens to turn him into the authorities for fraud unless he signs documents explaining his bad faith. At this point, Sikes kills Nancy, realizing that she has betrayed the gang. After eluding the authorities for several days, he is surrounded by the police and in trying to escape accidentally hangs himself. Fagin is punished for his actions as well. Captured by the police, he is executed for his criminal behavior. Mr. Brownlow adopts Oliver as his son and the entire group, including Dr. Losberne, the Maylies, and Mr. Brownlow, settle in a small town in the country.

Social commentary in *Oliver Twist*. One of the most powerful elements of *Oliver Twist* is Dickens's witty commentary on the social conditions of his time and his attack on the government institutions he felt were responsible for these deplorable conditions. His commentary begins from the first pages of the novel. When Oliver is born in the workhouse, Dickens reveals how the boy will be regarded: "the orphan of a workhouse—the humble, half-starved drudge—to be cuffed and buffeted through the world—despised by all, and pitied by none" (Dickens, *Oliver Twist*, p. 3).

ECHOES OF DICKENS'S REALITY

Adored by Dickens, his sister-in-law Mary Hogarth died in his arms during the months he was writing *Oliver Twist*. The author explained her death by saying that "the medical men imagine it was a disease of the heart" (Dickens in Slater, p. 82). Dickens was so grief-stricken he could not continue his writing for a time, and some scholars see his longing for Mary's presence reflected in *Oliver Twist*. The character Rose Maylie in the novel has some similarities to the author's sister-in-law. Like Mary, Rose totters on the brink of death due to a consuming illness. In the novel, however, the character miraculously recovers.

Oliver's poor condition is elaborated on in the next chapter, where Dickens first begins his open criticism of the Poor Law Amendment Act of 1834. It was the passage of this law that actually gave Dickens the idea to write *Oliver Twist*, his intention being to ridicule the New Poor Law. Dickens begins this attack by describing the Poor Law Commission with scathing sarcasm: "The members of this board were very sage, deep, philosophical men; and when they came to turn their attention to the workhouse, they found out at once ... the poor people liked it! It was a regular place of public entertainment for the poorer classes" (*Oliver Twist*, p. 11). Discussing the actual creation of the New Poor Law, Dickens writes that the Commission "established the rule, that all poor people should have the alternative of being starved by a gradual process in the house, or by a quick one out of it" (*Oliver Twist*, p. 11). This statement refers to the new stipulations which, since they did not provide any supplementary relief to outdoor workers, forced poor people to live in the workhouse if they wished to receive relief.

Dickens continues his attack on other aspects of the Poor Law Amendment Act as well, all the while aiming his anger at the officials who were responsible for the legislation: "They made a great many other wise and humane regulations, ... kindly undertook to divorce poor married people, ... and, instead of compelling a man to support his family, as they had theretofore done, took his family away from him, and made him a bachelor" (*Oliver Twist*, p. 11). This passage is a commentary on the new practice of segregating men and women, even married couples, when they entered the workhouse, as well as the rules that created a dynamic wherein families would enter the institution while the husbands remained outside working. Previously the families could remain together, supported by a combination of the man's wages and outdoor relief.

Of the initial adoption of the Poor Law Amendment Act, Dickens writes cynically: "It was rather expensive at first, in consequence of the increase in the undertaker's bill, and the necessity of taking in the clothes of all the paupers, which fluttered loosely on their wasted, shrunken forms, after a week or two's gruel" (*Oliver Twist*, p. 12). Dickens thus makes clear his scorn for the New Poor Law belief that conditions within the workhouses should not be as good as the conditions of the poorest and lowest working classes outside the workhouses. The author alludes to this aspect of the law elsewhere as well. In a conversation between Mr. Bumble and the undertaker, Mr. Sowerberry, for instance, the undertaker explains that "there's no denying that, since the new system of feeding has come in, the coffins are something narrower and more shallow than they used to be" (*Oliver Twist*, p. 24).

Though it launches a powerful attack on the Poor Law Amendment Act, the novel in no way condones the increased crime that accompanies this new system. Dickens's novel shows crime to be truly despicable. The condition of the character Nancy and her death at the hands of Sikes are some of the most powerful moments in the story and show in graphic terms the cruelties and horrible realities of London's criminal underworld.

In the second half of the novel, Dickens indicates that there is still hope for the future of the poor by introducing the noble-minded characters who help Oliver escape poverty and discover the identity of his parents.

Sources. While Dickens's primary motivation for writing *Oliver Twist* was a desire to attack the Poor Law Amendment Act of 1834, several other factors influenced the creation of the novel. Among them was Dickens's own experiences in childhood. When Dickens was twelve years old, his father's debts forced the family into debtor's prison. At the time, Dickens had a job in a factory that produced black paste for polishing boots; his father felt that instead of joining the family in prison, young Dickens should live with a woman who took in homeless boys. This arrangement would allow the boy to continue working at his job. For three months, while the family was in prison, the twelve-year-old Dickens worked twelve-hour days in the factory and visited his family on the weekends. This traumatic period of separation was an experience Dickens would never forget. Though it was not so severe as Oliver's predicament in the novel, these painful childhood memories most certainly influenced aspects of the novel such as its commentary on the "wisdom" of separating fathers who worked outside the poorhouses from their families who lived inside.

Another character who diverges from a real-life source is the villain Fagin, the namesake of Dickens's boyhood workmate Bob Fagin. By all accounts, the real-life Fagin behaved kindly toward Dickens. Dickens, however, had a horror of the other boy, recoiling from his poverty as if it were contagious.

Another influence on Dickens in his creation of *Oliver Twist* may have been the emergence of crime novels in the early nineteenth century. Known as "Newgate Novels," these stories were filled with highwaymen, robbers, and murderers. The highwayman became an incredibly romantic figure at the time. Though *Oliver Twist* did not romanticize crime as many of the "Newgate Novels" did, this trend may have given him the freedom to freely write about characters and incidents that had previously been considered inappropriate for literary purposes.

Reception. *Oliver Twist* was first published in serial form in 1837 and became an instant success. Dickens had gathered a strong following through the serialization of his novel the *Pickwick Papers,* and though the darker undertones of *Oliver Twist* were nothing like the comical *Pickwick Papers,* the reading public was equally intrigued. Just prior to the publication of the hardcover *Oliver Twist* in November 1838, an article in the *Edinburgh Review* praised Dickens's entire career, especially focusing on his *Pickwick Papers* and *Oliver Twist*.

The book version of *Oliver Twist* was such a success that it prompted William Harrison Ainsworth, a fellow author and good friend of Dickens, to write, "I need not enlarge on the merits of Mr. Dickens as by common consent he has been installed in the throne of letters vacated by [Sir Walter] Scott" (Ainsworth in MacKenzie, p. 75). Even higher praise came from Queen Victoria, who described *Oliver Twist* as excessively interesting; the queen recommended the book to her prime minister, Lord Melbourne. This great success, combined with the popularity of the *Pickwick Papers,* cemented Dickens's position in the literary world and enabled him to negotiate for higher payments from his publishers on future projects. After enduring his family's turbulent financial status during his childhood, this rise to wealth was a tremendous triumph for Dickens.

For More Information

Babington, Anthony. *A House in Bow Street: Crime and the Magistracy, London, 1740-1881.* London: MacDonald, 1969.

Dickens, Charles. *Oliver Twist.* New York: Bantam, 1982.

Driver, Felix. *Power and Pauperism: The Workhouse System, 1834-1884.* Cambridge: Cambridge University Press, 1993.

MacKenzie, Norman, and Jeanne MacKenzie. *Dickens: A Life.* Oxford: Oxford University Press, 1979.

Pollins, Harold. *Economic History of the Jews in England.* London: Associated University Presses, 1982.

Slater, Michael. *Dickens and Women.* London: J. M. Dent & Sons, 1983.

One Hundred Years of Solitude

by
Gabriel García Márquez

~

Gabriel García Márquez spent his childhood in Aracataca, Colombia, near where the fictional town of Macondo was placed in *One Hundred Years of Solitude*. Born in the late 1920s, he learned the history of his family and country through the stories of his grandparents, who raised him until he was eight years old. His grandfather, a colonel in one of Colombia's bloodiest civil wars, and his grandmother, a storyteller with a love of the fantastic, shared memories and insights that helped to shape the novel he wrote some forty years later. *One Hundred Years of Solitude* portrays the horrors and wonders in the lives of a fictional family in northern Colombia against a backdrop of recorded history—exploration and discovery, war, poverty, wealth, political conflict, natural disasters, and national lies.

Events in History at the Time the Novel Takes Place

Early unrest: Liberals vs. Conservatives. After winning independence from Spain in the early 1800s, Colombia became embroiled in a long series of internal battles. In the 1800s alone there were probably eighty or more of these struggles, which ranged from small revolts to full-scale civil wars. These conflicts did not end with the turn of the century. Rather, they established a pattern of violence that has continued in Colombia until today.

In addition to causing the deaths of hundreds of thousands of Colombians, the nineteenth-century battles widened the rift between Colombia's two emerging political parties, the Liberals and the Conservatives. In their early stages, the Conservatives sought to recreate certain aspects of Spanish society in Colombia. They favored a strong central government, a powerful church (almost all residents of Colombia were then, and still are, Catholic), and limited voting rights. The Liberals, on the other hand, espoused many of the ideals that had been fought for in the French and American Revolutions of the late 1700s. They supported stronger local government, limits on church authority (including the freedom to marry without the church's involvement), and greater public rights, such as freedom of the press and universal suffrage.

As the fighting between Conservatives and Liberals continued, however, these ideological differences became less relevant to soldiers, party

---

THE LITERARY WORK

A novel set in northern Colombia from the 1830s to the 1930s; published in 1967.

SYNOPSIS

A young couple founds a village and settles there to raise a family. The family's story, interwoven with the history of Colombia, covers a century of births, deaths, love, violence, and encounters with the supernatural.

officials, and the public in general. Although disagreements about the role of the church remained, party leaders did not establish a permanent position on most other issues. Often, differences between political parties seemed no greater than differences within a party, leading one observer of Colombian politics to joke that the only difference between Liberals and Conservatives is "the Liberals drink in public and pray in private, while Conservatives pray in public and drink in private" (Fluharty, p. 48).

Their platforms may have been similar in a number of respects, but the Liberals and Conservatives fought serious—and bloody—civil wars. The most destructive of these, the Thousand Days' War, lasted from 1899 to 1902 and claimed 100,000 lives. The Liberal forces, strong in the northern region of the country, where the fictional town of Macondo was placed in *One Hundred Years of Solitude,* used guerrilla tactics to fight the national (Conservative) army for control of the government. The two sides eventually arrived at a treaty, but the agreement came too late to save the devastated economy.

Other scars from the conflict were slow to heal as well. Even though the two parties remained more or less on peaceful terms for the next few decades, hostilities between them persisted. García Márquez's grandfather, for example—a Liberal colonel in the war—tried hard to prevent the marriage between the author's mother and father because the latter was a Conservative. The conflict between Liberals and Conservatives was to last well into the twentieth century.

***Cachacos* and *costeños*.** In addition to the political divide between Liberals and Conservatives, the geography of Colombia also fostered a cultural divide. *Costeños,* those who lived on or near the Caribbean coast, were a different breed from *cachacos,* residents of the inland capital city of Bogotá. Coastal dwellers like the fictional residents of Macondo considered themselves more easygoing and informal than the cold, stuffy big-city types of Bogotá. Because of the slave trade that was common in their region, coastal dwellers also tended to have more African blood in their veins and, consequently, a more African culture, including a unique style of music and a folklore tradition.

These differences explain why the gypsy character Melquíades felt more at home in the easygoing atmosphere of the coastal community of Macondo than in a city such as Bogotá. Coastal dwellers, such as the Buendía family, looked down on cachacos like the novel's Fernanda del Carpio; her aloofness, her fanatical religiosity, even her insistence on using fine china and table linen marked her as a member of this inland culture. As with the divide between Conservatives and Liberals, the differences between Fernanda and the Buendías—as with most costeños and cachacos—were almost impossible to resolve.

The United Fruit Company and the Ciénaga massacre. Gabriel García Márquez was born in the midst of Colombia's "banana fever." In 1900 United Fruit Company of Boston (UFC) began buying bananas from plantation owners in north central Colombia. Soon the UFC had converted this region into a unified network of banana plantations. This network, which eventually included García Márquez's hometown of Aracataca, was governed by executives from the United States who, like the fictional Jack Brown, isolated themselves from the local residents they employed. This isolation was not just brought about by the wire fences separating United States compounds from native villages; it was also enforced by the UFC's hiring practices. Since they hired plantation workers indirectly (through subcontractors), UFC executives were able to avoid Colombian labor laws. As a result, the working conditions for the more than thirty thousand workers who grew, cut, and packed UFC bananas were very poor.

> ### RACE IN COLOMBIA
>
> Like the fictional Buendía family, which descended both from South American Indians and from Spanish immigrants, the great majority of the Colombian population shared ancestry from more than one racial group. Although costeños generally had more African blood than cachacos, members of both groups had Indian and European ancestors. Also present in Colombia were small numbers of pureblooded natives—such as the Guajiro Indians who, in the novel, live with the Buendía family—and people with predominantly African backgrounds, like the fictional prostitute Nigromanta.

The labor arrangement led United Fruit Company officials to claim that no Columbian employees were on the company's payroll, even though the company's banana trade constituted 6 percent of the Colombian economy. This claim, argued successfully in Colombian courts, may explain García Márquez's reference to a seemingly ridiculous court decision "set down in

100 Years of Solitude

Gabriel García Márquez

solemn decrees" in *One Hundred Years of Solitude* wherein it was declared that "the workers did not exist" (García Márquez, *One Hundred Years of Solitude*, p. 307).

By October 1928, when García Márquez was eighteen months old, the UFC's banana workers had grown sick and tired of the unjust treatment they received. They tried to negotiate with UFC officials, but their requests for better working conditions were ignored. Their demands were simple: higher wages; decent health care; clean, safe housing; one day off per week; payment in cash rather than credit at the company store; and, most importantly, the UFC's recognition that its banana workers were legal employees. In November, after the United Fruit Company declined to discuss the workers' demands, a strike was called—the third in ten years.

Worried that a prolonged strike might drive the banana business out of their country, the Conservative government sent troops into north central Colombia to replace the workers, some of whom were jailed. By early December strikers had grown more frustrated, although they still sought to resolve their dispute with the UFC through negotiation. On December 6, in the town of Ciénaga (thirty miles north of Aracataca), a large group of striking workers gathered by the railway station to wait for the arrival of a government mediator. The army general who had been sent in to break the strike became concerned about the size of the gathering and announced that the crowd must disperse. In the ensuing confusion, gunfire broke out, and a number of strikers were killed in the ensuing violence. Government officials claimed that between nine and forty strikers were killed, but one union leader claimed that the number of those slain in the incident reached four hundred. The story told in history classrooms across Colombia was merely that "public order had been disturbed" in Ciénaga, then had been restored by government troops (Janes, p. 12). Just as the massacre in *One Hundred Years of Solitude* was treated by fellow villagers as a figment of José Arcadio Segundo's imagination, the real Ciénaga massacre was written out of high school textbooks and soon forgotten by much of the public.

The Novel in Focus

The plot. José Arcadio Buendía and his wife Úrsula are the first in a long line of Buendías to inhabit the village of Macondo. After founding the village and settling into his new life, the young José Arcadio becomes fascinated by the magic tricks of the gypsies who pass through town from time to time. He befriends the gypsy Melquíades who, after roaming the world with his troupe, comes to live with the Buendías. Melquíades reveals that he has already died once, in Singapore, but has come back to life because he was lonely. The resurrected Melquíades then dies again by drowning in a river. Melquíades's presence continues to influence the family even after his death; his ghost haunts the room where he wrote a series of manuscripts, and these manuscripts become an object of study for members of each generation of Buendías.

José Arcadio's two sons, who bear their own sons by the same woman, a prophet/prostitute, soon go their separate ways, one to follow the gypsies and one to lead local Liberal troops in a war against the Conservatives. Aureliano, the soldier, fights years of losing battles and is finally forced to end the war by signing a peace treaty containing humiliating terms. Before he reaches this point, however, a son, a nephew, and countless friends and enemies die in the conflict.

At home, José Arcadio has gone mad and Úrsula has taken control of the family's well-being. A rivalry surfaces between her daughter and an adopted orphan, both of whom fall in love with the same man. Their conflict is the first of many complex romantic situations. As time passes, Buendía descendants experience passion, rejection, love, and disappointment in a series of relationships that occasionally border on incest. In the midst of these relationships, Remedios the Beauty, José Arcadio's great-granddaughter, ascends to heaven one day on her sister-in-law's sheets.

Meanwhile, the train has come to Macondo. After the town's first railroad tracks are laid, a visitor from the United States arrives. He samples the bananas at the Buendías' table, considers their marketability, and establishes a banana business just outside of town. Although the business brings work to the village, its officials mistreat their employees, who eventually decide to strike. José Arcadio Segundo, great-grandson of the original José Arcadio, leads banana workers in a demonstration and is the sole survivor of a bloody army massacre of three thousand striking workers.

After this massive destruction of life (which all of the townspeople deny ever happened) comes destruction of property. A natural disaster—five years of rain—wreaks havoc on Macondo and reduces the Buendías to poverty. When the sun finally reappears, Úrsula (now well over one hundred years old) dies. Within the next few years, most of her remaining relatives either leave or die. Soon the only Buendías left in Macondo are Aureliano Babilonia, Úrsula's bastard great-great-great grandson, and Amaranta Úrsula, her great-great-granddaughter. These two fall passionately in love while Aureliano Babilonia studies Melquíades's cryptic manuscripts. Amaranta gives birth to a child with a pig's tail, a tragic sign of their incestuous relationship, and soon dies. Aureliano, left alone with Melquíades's papers, finally deciphers their meaning just as he and his village are swept away by a hurricane. The papers tell the story of his family's life before, during, and after the time in which they were written.

Unreal reality. Gabriel García Márquez once remarked to interviewers who questioned the realism of his style that "reality is not restricted to the price of tomatoes" (García Márquez in Bell-Villada, p. 12). Although he calls himself a realist writer, "reality" for García Márquez includes not just daily events but myths, superstitious beliefs, and miracles. For this reason, many critics have given García Márquez's style the name "magical realism." A clear example of this style, *One Hundred Years of Solitude* contains a resurrection (that of Melquíades), a woman who lives to be over 145 years old (Pilar Ternera), an ascension to heaven (by Remedios), a five-year-long rainstorm, and numerous ghosts who haunt the Buendía house. García Márquez's decision to include such events in his novel reflects his own upbringing, in which—judging from the stories he has told about his grandmother—imagination and open-mindedness must have been greatly valued. But his willingness to stretch the truth also displays a tragic side of Colombian life.

Considered in the context of Colombian history, García Márquez's novel takes on a more plausible appearance. In a country overrun with violence, in which events can be erased from public consciousness and obvious truths distorted, the unthinkable becomes believable: A banana company denies that it employs workers; a government massacre is written out of the history books; men play soccer with the heads of their rivals. These are not inventions of a fantastical novelist, but real occurrences in the history of the country. By weaving Colombia's own troubled history into the Buendías' lives, García Márquez reminds his readers of the elusive nature of their own reality.

Sources. García Márquez started *One Hundred Years of Solitude* after a three-year period of writer's block. He had been working in Mexico City for an advertising agency and writing film scripts for melodramas, but he was not able to produce any stories or novels. The experience that pulled him out of this creative slump was so fantastic that it could have been a scene in one of his books. He was driving with his family on a Mexican highway in 1945 when a powerful inspiration struck him; suddenly he knew exactly what to write. "It was so ripe in me," he later explained, "that I could have dictated the first chapter, word by word, to a typist" (García Márquez in Bell-Villada, p. 56).

Taking advantage of his personal history as he wrote the novel, García Márquez relied on many of his friends and relatives—and Colombia's political events—as models for characters and plot.

García Márquez's emphasis, however, was on the lives of the generations that came before him. His grandmother (whom he knew for little over a decade) was recreated as Úrsula, whose life spanned a century, and who progresses from an ambitious young wife to a blind old woman too stubborn to die over the course of the novel. Similarly, he chooses Liberal General Uribe

Fictional Name	Real-life Source
Macondo (the town)	Macondo—a banana plantation near Aracataca; *macondo* means "banana" in Bantu, an African dialect spoken by Colombian slaves
Colonel Aureliano Buendía	General Rafael Uribe Uribe—legendary Liberal leader in the Thousand Days' War; Colonel Buendía also resembles the author's grandfather, Colonel Nicolás Márquez, who fought under Uribe
Úrsula Iguarán (Buendía)	Tranquilina Iguarán—García Márquez's grandmother
Fernanda's hometown	Zipaquirá—the cold, somber cachaco town where García Márquez went to boarding school
The wise Catalonian	Ramón Vinyes—a book dealer and writer in Barranquilla, Colombia; young García Márquez's mentor
Nigromanta	Eufemia—an Afro-Hispanic prostitute who worked in the brothel where García Márquez lodged in Barranquilla

Uribe, who fought at the turn of the twentieth century, as one of his models for Colonel Buendía. Nevertheless, as the novel shifts back and forth from one era to another, it becomes clear that the specific time in which its events take place is not so important after all. Just as the names and traits of the novel's characters are repeated again and again in successive generations, the characters display timeless qualities inspired by contemporary sources. The issues raised in *One Hundred Years of Solitude*—and the characters that raise them—are rooted both in the past and the present.

Events in History at the Time the Novel Was Written

La Violencia. On April 9, 1948, Jorge Eliécer Gaitán, a Liberal presidential candidate who had been an outspoken critic of the Ciénaga massacre, was assassinated in Bogotá, Colombia's capital city. Although he had been disliked by many high officials of the Liberal party, he was immensely popular among middle- and lower-class Liberals. As word of his death spread through the country, Colombia's already unstable social situation turned into a nightmare. Rioters looted stores and overturned trolley cars, often with the help of Liberal police. In Cali, a city in western Colombia, angry Liberals murdered several prominent Conservatives, beheaded them, and then played soccer with their heads.

As the unrest spread to the countryside, Conservative police and soldiers were sent to quell Liberal violence. Their brutal methods included cutting off the testicles of Liberal sympathizers, slashing the wombs of pregnant Liberal women, and throwing babies of Liberals into the air to land on the sharp points of Conservative soldiers' bayonets. The worst acts of savagery continued until 1953 and resulted in the deaths of some 200,000 Colombians, but this period of national butchery known as "La Violencia" ("the violence") lasted well into the 1960s. What began as a knee-jerk reaction to the shock of Gaitán's murder became an almost twenty-year-long era of bloody revenge and senseless violence.

Some of the slaughter was carried out by organized units. Peasant guerrilla groups formed to fight the Conservative army, while government forces, even in periods of comparative peace, sanctioned "official" murders of political opponents. In fact, although the brutal acts of this period often seemed arbitrary and pointless, La Violencia did have some political roots. Many Liberals believed that Gaitán was assassinated by Conservative politicians to ensure their victory in the next election. Conservatives, on the other hand, blamed communists for instigating the violence so that they could more easily take over the Conservative government. Ironically, however, most evidence supports the theory that Gaitán's assassin was actually a lone gunman without clear political affiliations.

Cover of *One Hundred Years of Solitude*.

The Boom and the Cuban Revolution. García Márquez is one of a number of Latin American writers who won fame for their work in the 1960s. This group, which shared many of García Márquez's interests and stylistic techniques, included Julio Cortazar of Argentina, Carlos Fuentes of Mexico, Guillermo Cabrera Infante of Cuba, and Mario Vargas Llosa of Peru. Together, their work comprised what was labeled a "Boom" in Latin American fiction.

Many of the group's predecessors in Latin America had written in the popular style of "realism" and dealt with the everyday lives of common people, but "Boom" writers were more interested in creating a style that dealt with "real life" in a new way—a way that fit Latin American culture. One of the concepts that grew out of their experimentation was "magical realism," the mingling of supernatural or fantastical events with commonplace ones. Magical realism focused on the power of imagination, not the limited view of practical reality.

Why was this style uniquely Latin American? First, myth and folklore played a more significant role in Central and South America than in much of Europe and North America. In addition, many Latin American countries, like Colombia, had a history of political unrest and deceptive governments; as a result, "official" reality had lost its credibility.

But perhaps the biggest inspiration for this new style was the Cuban Revolution. In the late 1950s, the young law student Fidel Castro led a revolt that ended in the exile of Cuba's tyrannical dictator, Fulgencio Batista. Castro immediately became Cuba's leader and proceeded to redistribute the land, taking it from the wealthy and giving it to peasants. Though opinions differ about Castro's effectiveness as a ruler, his successful takeover astonished Latin America. Onlookers across Central and South America saw Castro as a symbol that even the impossible was possible: a young student tired of oppression had radically changed the course of his country. The precise effect of the Cuban Revolution on the "Boom" writers is difficult to determine, but at the very least, it opened the eyes of these and other Latin Americans to the possibility of change and the ability to create new realities.

For his part, García Márquez had direct ties to revolutionary Cuba. From 1959 to 1961, he worked for *Prensa Latina,* a Cuban news agency, first in Havana, Cuba, and later in New York City. His ties to Cuba extended beyond journalism, however. An outspoken supporter of the Cuban Revolution since it began, he and Castro became friends. His literary concerns may even reflect Castro's influence.

Impact of the novel. *One Hundred Years of Solitude* was a huge popular and critical success. The eight thousand copies first printed by its Argentine publisher sold out in a week. Eventually, sales of the Spanish version of the novel reached over 10 million, while translations were sold in thirty different languages. Its popularity was due in no small measure to its attraction of a wide range of readers from all social and economic classes. García Márquez even tells of a group of farmers he met in Cuba who, when they found out who he was, cried out, "Macondo!" (Bell-Villada, p. 5).

The novel was not just a favorite of the general public, however. It attracted the praise of literary critics and won numerous international awards as well. Pablo Neruda, the Nobel prizewinning Chilean poet, spoke for many of his colleagues when he called it "the greatest revelation in the Spanish language since the **Don Quixote** (also covered in *Literature and Its Times*) of Cervantes" (Neruda in Marowski, p. 142). As Neruda's comment suggests, this century-long

100 Years of Solitude

chronicle of one family's life in Colombia became an instant classic.

For More Information

Bell-Villada, Gene H. *García Márquez: The Man and His Work*. Chapel Hill: University of North Carolina Press, 1990.

Bushnell, David. *The Making of Modern Colombia: A Nation in Spite of Itself*. Berkeley: University of California Press, 1993.

Fluharty, Vernon Lee. *Dance of the Millions: Military Rule and the Social Revolution in Colombia, 1930-1956*. Pittsburgh: University of Pittsburgh Press, 1957.

García Márquez, Gabriel. *One Hundred Years of Solitude*. Translated by Gregory Rabassa. New York: Harper & Row, 1970.

Janes, Regina. *Gabriel García Márquez: Revolutions in Wonderland*. Columbia, Mo.: University of Missouri Press, 1981.

Marowski, Daniel G., and Roger Matuz, eds. *Contemporary Literary Criticism*. Vol. 47. Detroit: Gale Research, 1988.

"The Open Window"

by Saki

THE LITERARY WORK

A short story set in an upper-class home in the English countryside sometime between 1880 and 1905; published in 1914.

SYNOPSIS

As a prank, an English girl of the upper class fabricates a tale about ghosts and madness in her family for a gentleman visitor suffering from a nervous condition.

H. H. Munro (born in 1879 in Burma) took the pen name "Saki" (after the cup-bearer in the immensely popular *Rubaiyat* of Omar Khayyám) when his first work was published in the *Westminster Gazette,* a London literary journal. He had a tendency to display dark humor in most of his writing, as reflected in "The Open Window" and in most of his other short stories. Saki's morbid storytelling was due in large part to his secluded upbringing by his grandmother and two unmarried aunts in the countryside of west England in the 1870s and 1880s as well as to his conservative social and political philosophies, increasingly under seige in an age of striking social changes. H. H. Munro was to die, like many young men of his generation and class, on a battlefield in France; he was killed November 14, 1916, near Beaumont Hamel.

Events in History at the Time of the Short Story

Decay. Saki's characters tend to be drawn from the milieu he knew best, the English upper class, of which he was a member. Not particularly wealthy, Munro's family was nevertheless of solid social standing and he moved in elite circles. During his writing career, England was experiencing a series of social shifts, the most prominent of which was the gradual rejection of Tory or conservative politics in favor of more liberal approaches to governing a changing society. In 1906, the Liberal party defeated the Tories in national elections, a change in allegiance that had been developing slowly over the past few years. The long-standing class system that divided the privileged from the masses was being destabilized by the growth of the middle class and by an increased social mobility that resulted from the new wealth and influence created by the country's successful industrialization.

When Queen Victoria died in 1901, ending a reign that spanned 64 years, many of her grieving subjects mourned not only the death of a beloved monarch but the passing of England's greatness. The word "decay" perhaps best characterizes a widespread feeling of enfeeblement and defeat that coursed through the nation in the early years of the new King Edward's reign. In January 1902, General Sir Frederick Maurice reported in the *Contemporary Review* that fully 60 percent of Englishmen were so physically unfit as to disqualify them from service in the country's armed forces. Of course, a great number of

"The Open Window"

such men came from Britain's teeming urban poor, who lived in deplorable conditions, suffering, among other things, from malnutrition and disease. Nevertheless, the idea that the English people as a whole had somehow become dissipated took hold in conservative circles unprepared to establish social programs to improve the living conditions of the poor. The problem was a matter of morality, rather than sociology or economics —how had such a problem been allowed to grow in the first place? Further alarming statistics concerning a lack of mental acuity among the English did not help the general feeling of decline; between 1891 and 1901, it was reported, England saw a 21.44 percent increase in the number of "mentally defective" citizens, a whopping 18 percent increase over the number cited for the previous decade (Hynes, p. 23).

> ## A BREATH OF FRESH AIR
>
> Saki's aunt's estate in Devonshire, where he grew up, had large French windows in the drawing room leading out to a large yard, reminiscent of those in "The Open Window." However, unlike the aunt in the short story, Saki's aunt Augusta would not allow the windows to be open because she believed fresh air to be hazardous to a person's health. Saki and his siblings were not allowed to go into the yard, and the drawing room windows and those throughout the house were barred. When Colonel Munro, Saki's father, finally finished his military duty overseas and resumed care of his children, he bought an estate only four miles from his sisters. Colonel Munro nailed open the windows in the bedrooms of his new home, and Saki finally was allowed to breathe fresh air.

Saki himself was politically and socially conservative, and when he parodies the upper classes, as he does in "The Open Window," it is less because of his devotion to a revised social order than because, in his opinion, the ruling class should never have been so ill-prepared as to allow such a predicament to arise in the first place. Increased poverty, disease, economic expansion, powerful weapons, and the threat of war were the reward for complacency and clinging to luxurious habits in the face of a changing world.

The other half. A variety of surveys on the living conditions of the lower classes in London and York were widely circulated during the same broad period in which Saki was writing his short fiction. Sociologist Seebohm Rowntree, a wealthy businessman concerned about the widening gap between social classes in the cities, conducted a highly publicized investigation into the daily lives of the nation's urban poor. Published in 1901, Rowntree's study, *Poverty, a Study of Town Life,* concluded that 25 to 30 percent of the urban population of the nation was living in poverty. By linking the poverty problem to living conditions, Rowntree's study focused attention on public health. Slum conditions included residences where inhabitants lived sometimes more than two to a room "which provided inadequate air space" (Bentley, p. 41). Rowntree also discussed the fact that so many of the army recruits from major British cities were rejected on medical grounds. There was, the study indicated, a national health crisis, not just because urban men were unwell, but because they were incapable of military action. The British political maneuvers that would eventually lead the country into World War I were already taking shape in the early years of the century; that England would need a standing army was growing more and more obvious by the day. A national health crisis could not be ignored if it threatened to weaken Britain's military effectiveness. The government appointed a committee whose efforts would lead to the adoption of numerous social reforms to improve public health as well as education, employment conditions, and welfare.

British military occupation of India. The British presence in India is reflected in "The Open Window." Saki and his father both served in the British forces in the area, and Vera, the young woman with the rather cruel imagination in the short story, invents a tragic Indian episode to explain Mr. Nuttel's precipitous flight from the house of her aunt. There had been a strong British presence on the Indian subcontinent since the first decade of the seventeenth century, when the East India Company, a British trading conglomerate, set up its first post on India's northwest coast. The Company controlled trade, law and order, and education in India until 1859, when Queen Victoria proclaimed that India would be governed directly by the British sovereign. What changed the Company's fortunes in India was the Indian Mutiny, or the First Indian War of Independence, depending on which side one stands. The chain of events leading to the bloodshed is convoluted, but perhaps the overarching reason for the uprising was the suspicion that the British intended to dispense with basic Indian social and religious customs and replace them with British traditions. Economic and legal reform was one thing, but to threaten ancient customs and taboos was quite another. The single event that precipitated the fighting was the arrival from Britain of a new kind of cartridge for the rifles carried by Indian soldiers in the ranks of the East India Company's army. This cartridge required greasing with a mixture of animal fats. The British, however, failed to recall the taboo in Hindu culture against touching any product made from cattle, and the Muslim taboo against pork. Company officials were careful to specify to *British* manufacturers of the cartridge lubricants that only goat or sheep fat was to be used, but once subcontractors in India itself began to produce the stuff, the directions got less precise.

A rumor spread among the Indian ranks that the British purposely used animal fats that would, according to Indian customs, contaminate the men who used them; this fear grew rapidly, fed by the more general suspicion that the British intended to flout religious standards important to the Indian soldiers. Discontent spread like wildfire. Eighty-five Indian soldiers stationed at Delhi refused to grease their rifle cartridges, and for their disobedience were immediately sent to jail for ten years. This touched a raw nerve among the thousands of Indians in British regiments, who took up arms against the British. Within days, beginning on May 10, 1957, the British colony at Delhi was butchered in its entirety, including women and children, and the violence spread to many parts of the country. A year of savage fighting had begun, with the British response matching the Indian in terms of atrocities. Saki's own grandfather, George Munro, was killed during this time.

As both a child and as an adult, Saki lived with the legacy and landmarks of the Indian Mutiny. He heard many details of the murders and open graves of British military victims of the uprisings. In the short story, Vera's account of Mr. Nuttel's night spent in a newly dug grave on the banks of the Ganges River brings to mind such a disaster.

Class distinction in social practices. In "The Open Window," Mr. Nuttel has arrived with a letter of introduction to Vera's aunt, Mrs. Sappleton, from his sister. A letter of introduction was a means by which members of the upper class distinguished themselves as such to one another; it served as a sort of social glue. Such a letter would verify the family background and connections of an individual to assure the host of their status and class.

H. H. Munro

The social sphere to which Saki belonged and which he often mocked maintained an intricate system of etiquette throughout the nineteenth and early twentieth centuries. Such social practices as letters of introduction, calling cards, parlor regulations, formal address, and provisions for seating at table were adhered to with a sort of religious scrupulousness. Many of these practices involved comparing or connecting individuals through their family titles, which enabled the upper class to maintain an elitist hierarchy whose members would always recognize each other's social status.

In "The Open Window" Saki calls these upper-class practices into question. Although coming to the country to rest his nerves, Mr. Nuttel feels obligated to first follow the protocol required of a gentleman by making the appropriate set of social contacts. Although she advises him to establish himself as a gentleman for the sake of his nerves, Mr. Nuttel's sister has forced him into a situation that is uncomfortable for him and ironically shatters his nerves.

Saki's story focuses first on the formalities that concern the characters. Mr. Nuttel is worried

"The Open Window"

about his letter of introduction and his conversation with Vera. He feels he must "endeavor... to say the correct something which should duly flatter the niece of the moment without unduly discounting the aunt that was to come" ("The Open Window," p. 288). Mrs. Sappleton apologizes for having him wait, and when she speaks with him she must "replace... a yawn at the last moment" ("The Open Window," p. 291) so as not to offend him.

The polite concerns at the beginning of the story contrast greatly with Vera's outlandish prank and its consequences. The story's tone and climax seem to celebrate the mischievous way in which Vera undermines the social conventions that govern Mr. Nuttel's visit.

The Short Story in Focus

The plot. Vera, a girl of fifteen, must entertain and converse with a gentleman, Mr. Framton Nuttel, who has arrived to visit her aunt, Mrs. Sappleton, at their country home. Mr. Nuttel has come to the country on the advice of his doctors, seeking rest and relaxation as a cure for his nerves.

Mr. Nuttel comes prepared with Mrs. Sappleton's name, address, and a letter of introduction, given to him by his sister, who stayed in the neighborhood four years earlier. He silently doubts whether meeting his sister's acquaintances in the country will be beneficial to him. However, his sister has insisted that if he remains alone and secluded, his nervous condition will only worsen.

Vera discovers that Mr. Nuttel knows nothing more about her aunt than her name and residence. She then mysteriously announces that her aunt's "tragedy" occurred since his sister's stay. She alerts him to the open French windows that lead to the yard and tells him that exactly three years ago her aunt's husband and two brothers went out into the yard with their spaniel to go shooting.

Vera tells Mr. Nuttel that the three were engulfed in a "treacherous bog" and that their bodies were never found. She claims that her deluded aunt believes that they will return and so she keeps the window open every day until evening.

Mr. Nuttel is alarmed even further when Vera's aunt arrives in the room and indeed begins to talk of how her husband and brothers are out hunting. Mrs. Sappleton says she expects them to return momentarily. Mr. Nuttel looks over at Vera to acknowledge her aunt's delusion, but Vera stares in horror at the window through which three muddy figures then arrive.

Mr. Nuttel runs wildly from the house and into the street. Vera explains to her aunt and family that the dog must have frightened Mr. Nuttel. She says he confessed to having a horror of dogs due to being chased and surrounded by wild dogs in India. The tale ends with the following sly remark: "Romance at short notice was her specialty" ("The Open Window," p. 291).

Mr. Nuttel's cure. Mr. Nuttel has been advised to seek relief for his nervous condition by spending time in the country. The little bit of conversation he attempts to make is entirely devoted to his health concerns:

> "The doctors agree in ordering me complete rest, an absence of mental excitement, and avoidance of anything in the nature of violent physical exercise," announced Framton, who laboured under the tolerably wide-spread delusion that total strangers and chance acquaintances are hungry for the least detail of one's ailments and infirmities, their cause and cure. "On the matter of diet they are not so much in agreement."
> ("The Open Window," p. 290)

Mr. Nuttel's concerns and his doctor's prescriptions reflect the trend at the time of the story toward natural and holistic therapies, some of which resemble modern New Age therapies. During Saki's era, many health professionals, social theorists, and evangelical entrepreneurs set up health spas in country locales. They advocated hydrotherapies (immersion in and absorption of mineral waters), vegetarian diets, heat treatments, exercise programs, and meditation.

Throughout the nineteenth century, health practices underwent much speculation and scrutiny. Many philosophers of the day, including John Stuart Mill, promoted the ideal *mens sana in corpore sano,* which means "a sound mind in a sound body." The widespread epidemics of cholera, typhus, and influenza in the 1830s and 1840s killed hundreds of thousands. It was in the wake of such traumatic disease that many suffered ailments labeled "hypochondria" or "neuroses," labels that did not carry the stigma they later came to acquire.

Before the age of psychoanalysis, mental conditions and complaints were treated physically. People suffering from stress and depression were seen as having physical problems with their nervous system, and retreats to the country were sometimes recommended to such patients as "nerve cures." The physical ailments of a hypochondriac were taken seriously. They were treated along with their mood and seen as early stages of what could become a deteriorating or even fatal condition.

It was further thought that the ideal of "a sound mind in a sound body" could be achieved through proper exercise of the will. Those who failed to achieve it seemed frequently to be individuals of artistic temperament; writers, for example, appeared to often become afflicted with mental ailments. Physicians, as well as literary critics, determined this fact to be the result of the authors' overactive and "morbid" imaginations and intellectual solitude (Haley, p. 60). Thus, while a "change of air" and "scenery" were recommended cures, all intellectual and artistic enterprises were discouraged during the period of recovery.

While Victorian fiction usually attributed nervous ailments to solitude, Saki turns this concept around in "The Open Window." He creates great irony by having a patient attempt to quietly socialize in the country in order to rest his nerves and instead be traumatized by a seemingly delusional woman and a conniving girl.

As psychoanalysis began to become more familiar — Freud's *The Psychopathology of Everyday Life* was published in 1904 and *On Psychotherapy* in 1905 — nerve cures and rural retreats started to look more like pseudo-science. It is in this kind of light that Saki presents Mr. Nuttel's cure. Both in the way he describes Nuttel and in the fate he constructs for him, Saki pokes fun at the idea of a superficial social visit in the country curing anyone's nervous condition.

Sources. Saki, along with his sister, Ethel, and his older brother, Charlie, was left in the care of his grandmother and his two aunts, Augusta and Charlotte, after his mother died in 1872. Saki's father, Colonel Charles Augustus Munro, was stationed in west Burma as an officer in the British military police. "The Open Window," like many of Saki's short stories, involves a mischievous child rebelling against an aunt with whom the child lives. Many of the circumstances and characters in the story resemble those of Saki's childhood growing up at his aunts' estate. While Saki himself never admitted to any direct correlation between his fiction and real-life experiences, his biographers, including his sister, have commented on the similarities.

Saki planned many practical jokes to amuse himself and his sister when he was a boy, just as in "The Open Window" Vera plays an imaginative prank on her aunt and her visitor.

Saki's sister, Ethel, may have inspired references in the story to Mr. Nuttel's sister. Saki carried on a consistent correspondence with Ethel. And just as Mr. Nuttel's sister does in "The Open Window," Ethel Munro offered her brother plenty of advice in her letters.

Saki's older brother, Charlie, was sent to boarding school very soon after moving in with his aunts. Augusta and Charlotte found him too loud and active to handle. Charlie sometimes returned for holidays. When his return coincided with visits from his uncle Wellesley Munro, the boys were taken out around the grounds by their uncle with a dog that was otherwise constantly tied to a post at the estate. In "The Open Window," Vera describes her aunt's husband and younger brothers going out to hunt with an eager spaniel. Vera says her aunt's youngest brother, Ronnie Sappleton, used to sing loudly and got on her aunt's nerves. It may be memories of the outings with his brother Charlie and Uncle Wellesley that inspired Saki's depiction of boisterous Ronnie Sappleton enjoying the chance to roam the grounds with his brother and the dog.

Fictional Name	Real-life Source
Mrs. Sappleton	Augusta Munro (Saki's aunt)
Vera	Saki as a child
Framton's sister	Ethel Munro (Saki's sister)
Mr. Sappleton	Wellesley Munro (Saki's uncle)
Ronnie Sappleton	Charlie Munro (Saki's brother)

In 1872 Saki's mother was pregnant with her fourth child. Although all three of her previous births had been successful in Burma, her husband decided to send her back to England for her health and nerves. Walking along a quiet lane soon after arriving, she was charged by a cow and killed. The brutal irony of his mother's death may have been the inspiration for many of Saki's stories, especially "The Open Window," in which a retreat to the country leads to crisis instead of relief.

Reviews. In 1912 Saki began regularly submitting his short stories to different newspapers and periodicals, including the *Westminster Gazette* and *The Morning Post*. In June of 1914, John Lane published a collection of these short stories. Entitled *Beasts and Super-Beasts,* the collection contained "The Open Window."

Editors in the early 1900s were particularly impressed by the surprise ending. Another author, O. Henry, was famous for using this literary device. Certain publishers who worked with Saki began to nearly demand it of him after "The Open Window" was specifically praised for it in a review in the London periodical *Spectator.*

> [Saki] has the complementary ... quality of knowing how to leave off. Perhaps the best instance of this is to be found in that extraordinary fantasia, "The Open Window," which we well remember reading in the *Westminster Gazette.* Here, after an almost intolerable situation has been suddenly converted into comedy with a jerk like that of a cinematograph, the strange conduct of the young lady is ... summed up ... in seven words: "romance at short notice was her specialty." It may be added that it is a formidable specialty.
> (*Spectator,* p. 60)

For More Information

Bentley, Nicolas. *Edwardian Album.* New York: Viking Press, 1974.

Haley, Bruce. *The Healthy Body and Victorian Culture.* Cambridge, Mass.: Harvard University Press, 1978.

Hibbert, Christopher. *Daily Life in Victorian England.* New York: American Heritage, 1975.

Hynes, Samuel. *The Edwardian Turn of Mind.* Princeton, N.J.: Princeton University Press, 1968.

Langguth, A. J. *Saki: A Life of Hector Hugh Munro.* New York: Simon and Schuster, 1981.

Moorhouse, Geoffrey. *India Britannica.* New York: Harper & Row, 1983.

Munro, H. H. "The Open Window." *The Short Stories of Saki.* New York: Random House/Viking Press, 1958.

Spectator 113 (July 11, 1914): 60.

"The Outcasts of Poker Flat"

by
Bret Harte

Francis Bret Harte was born in 1836 in Albany, New York. After moving to San Francisco with his family in 1854, Harte began his literary career as a "printer's devil," a person who set the type for the printing presses of local newspapers. Harte wrote articles for several small newspapers, then left San Francisco to teach school in a Sierra mining town. He may have spent a short time prospecting during this period. Harte eventually returned to San Francisco, where he was encouraged by the editor of a local periodical, the *Overland Monthly*, to write stories about the gold rush mining camps that he had seen firsthand. In 1868 Harte's story, "The Outcasts of Poker Flat," was published in the *Overland Monthly* and became an instant success.

> **THE LITERARY WORK**
>
> A short story set in the Sierra Mountains of northern California in the 1850s; published in 1868.
>
> **SYNOPSIS**
>
> A small group of ne'er-do-wells are exiled from the town of Poker Flat. Attempting to reach the next town, they take shelter together when a snowstorm catches them unprepared. The challenges of this predicament bring out the best qualities of the characters as each sacrifices himself or herself for the benefit of others in the group.

Events in History at the Time the Short Story Takes Place

The California gold rush. The first major discovery of gold in California occurred in February 1848, at Sutter's Mill. John Sutter was a cattle rancher and entrepreneur who had plans for establishing a community on the Sacramento River in northern California. During the construction of a saw mill on the American River, Sutter's chief carpenter, James Marshall, discovered gold while digging into the river bottom. The news of the discovery spread quickly, but few people were interested in the finding initially. There had been rumors of gold in California since Sir Francis Drake first landed there in the late 1500s, yet by early 1848, little gold had actually been found. It was not until Samuel Brannan took interest in Marshall's discovery that belief in the gold find began to take hold.

Brannan was a San Francisco merchant and real estate speculator who was a part owner in a general store at Sutter's Mill. When his customers began to offer gold in payment for goods, Brannan realized the rumor of gold was a reality. Brannan purchased goods and equipment that would be in demand by gold hunters in the future and moved these goods to his store at Sutter's Mill. On May 12, 1848, Brannan went to San Francisco, where he displayed a bottle of gold dust and spread the news that gold was being found on the American River.

"Outcasts of Poker Flat"

Shortly after Brannan's announcement, nearly every town in California lost a majority of its population to the Sutter's Mill region. On May 29 the *San Francisco Californian* complained that "the whole country, from San Francisco to Los Angeles, and from the sea shore to the base of the Sierra Nevadas, resounds with the sordid cry of gold, GOLD, GOLD! while the field is left half-planted, the house half-built, and everything neglected but the manufacture of shovels and pickaxes" (Bean, p. 91). The paper also announced that it was suspending publication as a result of a loss of staff, subscribers, and advertisers.

> ### THE DONNER PARTY
>
> Though their expedition took place before the gold rush of 1849, the experience of the Donner Party is a good example of the rigors faced by travelers trying to reach California by the overland routes. The Donner Party was organized for the journey west in Springfield, Illinois, in 1846 by George Donner and James Reed, two successful businessmen who were curious about life in California. The expedition began with nine wagons and approximately 30 people, but grew to include 87 pioneers by the time the wagon train reached the Sierra Mountains. The party endured more than six months of arduous travel through dry deserts and rough terrain before reaching the mountain range. On November 2, just a few miles short of the summit, the party decided to stop for the night. During the night, though, a snowstorm blocked the pass and the pioneers found themselves trapped in the mountains as winter set in. The majority of the party was snowed in until February, and many survived only by eating the flesh of the dead. Of the 87 migrants, 40 died.

News of the gold discovery, as well as actual gold specimens, finally spread to Washington, D.C., in September 1948. President Polk incorporated this news into his message to Congress on December 5, using it as further justification for his acquisition of California from Mexico. Further samples of gold arrived in Washington and were put on display at the War Department. The display drew excited crowds, and the Philadelphia Mint soon announced that the samples were of a quality equal to the standards of United States gold coins. With this announcement the gold rush truly began.

Aspiring prospectors relied on three main routes to the goldfields: by way of the Isthmus of Panama, around South America's Cape Horn, or overland. The sea routes drew the initial crowds in the winter and early spring of 1849 because they were open all year. Eventually, however, more than twice as many gold seekers would venture to California by land as by sea.

The crowds attracted by the gold rush had a massive impact on the population of California. In 1848 the state's population numbered less than 15,000 people; by 1852 the state census counted 223,856 California residents. The first year of this incredible westward rush for gold was 1849, during which more than 40,000 miners uncovered almost $30 million worth of gold. This incredible surge in population and frenzied activity created the scenarios that inspired Bret Harte in his writing.

Gamblers and the gold rush. The lure of quick wealth attracted more than just would-be prospectors to California. The abundance of ready money also brought gamblers to the state. Many of these gamblers were seeking a new base of operations, as the emergence of railroad transportation had forced Mississippi riverboat gambling into decline. Those gamblers who made the journey were not disappointed. The propensity for gambling among prospectors was so great that many of the rapidly appearing casinos featured tiny scales on the tables to weigh the gold dust and nuggets used for betting. When seventeen-year-old Bret Harte arrived in San Francisco in 1854, he entered a city that supported as many as one thousand gaming houses featuring a countless variety of games of chance.

The favorite games of the period included roulette, rouge et noir, and vingt-et-un (twenty-one, which soon became known as "blackjack"). Faro, however, was perhaps the single most popular game. A game in which players bet on the value of cards as the dealer exposed them one at a time, Faro had been popular in Paris since the 1600s.

Not satisfied with the laws of probability, many gamblers took to cheating to better their odds. Gamblers employed a vast array of techniques to cheat at cards, perhaps the most simple of which was to mark cards. This practice involved marking cards with symbols hidden amid the intricate patterns on their faces or by shaving one side of a card so that a gambler could detect by its feel which card he was dealing. Marking the cards was usually only half of the cheating process, though. After marking cards, the gambler had to be dexterous enough to manipulate the deck to further improve his chances of winning. Finally, a gambler had to be able to cheat under pressure. Otherwise, his marked cards and quick hands were useless. Poker Alice, a famous woman gambler, recalled one South Dakota cheater who could manipulate cards with amazing skill except when it really mattered: "When he got into a game, with the sharp eyes of professional gamblers upon him, the courage necessary to that crooked skill wilted and he became only an honest, frightened, exceedingly bad player who lost his stack of chips almost as soon as they were set before him" (Poker Alice in Hicks, p. 123).

Coolness under pressure was the quality relied upon by most cheaters who sought to make a living at the tables. A professional card cheat could earn $1,000 for one night's gaming. On an incredibly good night, a gambler could earn several thousand dollars. "The Outcasts of Poker Flat" reflects this reality, for it features the character of John Oakhurst, who wins a large sum of money from the inhabitants of Poker Flat before a grim-faced group of armed men escort him from the town.

Women in the gold rush. In many ways, the California gold rush was a male-dominated phenomenon. In the early 1850s, more than three times as many men as women immigrated to California, and in San Francisco men outnumbered women by as many as ten to one. Still, there were a number of women who played a role in the gold rush and left their mark on the period. Elizabeth Bays Wimmer, for instance, played a significant role in the initial discovery of gold.

When James Marshall made his find on the American River, he was at first unsure if it was a discovery at all. No one in the camp knew what gold looked like in its natural state. Elizabeth Wimmer, who was working as the camp cook and laundress, suggested a clever test to determine whether the substance was, in fact, gold. Wimmer recorded her thoughts at the time in her journal: "I said, 'This is gold, and I will throw it into my lye kettle ... and if it is gold, it will be gold when it comes out.' At the bottom of the pot was a double handful of potash, which I lifted in my two hands, and there was my gold as bright as could be" (Wimmer in Levy, pp. xx-xxi).

Many of the women in California were not destined to play so dramatic a part in the rush for gold. The combination of quick wealth and the small number of women in the region made California a prime market for prostitutes. Almost as soon as miners began digging the first nuggets from the ground, prostitutes flocked to California. The miners received these new migrants with open arms. In one instance, a passenger ship from Panama arrived in San Francisco with two women, described by one observer as "two daughters of Eve of the sort called 'liberated'" (Levy, p. 150). These women wanted to debark, but instead became engaged in a lengthy argument with one of the ship's crew concerning the payment for their passage. One account of the incident describes what ensued as the dispute continued: "Two of the waiting crowd, tired of marking time, clambered on board the ship, throwing a bag of gold at the feet of the greedy purser, [then] came back to land with the girls to a general 'Hooray!' from the crowd" (Levy, p. 150).

LOSING HANDS

~

Pat Hogan, who began his gambling career in California during the gold rush, hit a run of bad luck at the tables in San Francisco. Much like Harte's character John Oakhurst, Hogan could not accept his own run of bad luck. His fortunes dwindle to a point where he, like Oakhurst, commits suicide. The similarity between the two also appears in their suicide notes. Hogan left in his pocket a single card—an ace of hearts—on which he had written:

> Life is only a game of poker, played well or ill;
> Some hold four aces, some draw or fill;
> Some make a bluff and oft get there,
> While others ante, and never hold a pair.
>
> (Hogan in DeArment, p. 155)

Also written on a card, the deuce of clubs, was the suicide letter by Oakhurst. He left a less poetic but equally metaphoric note:

> Beneath this tree lies the body of John Oakhurst, who struck a streak of bad luck on the 23rd of November, 1850, and handed in his checks on the 7th December, 1850.
>
> ("The Outcasts of Poker Flats," p. 21)

Although this exuberant acceptance of prostitutes was common, in some cases prostitutes were less welcome. From Rich Bar, California, for example, Louisa Clapp wrote to her sister in 1851, "Yes! these thousand men—many of

"Outcasts of Poker Flat"

Bret Harte

whom had been for years absent from the softening amenities of female society ... looked only with contempt or pity upon these [prostitutes] ... [who] left in a few weeks, absolutely driven away by public opinion" (Levy, p. 155). In "The Outcasts of Poker Flat," the prostitutes known as Duchess and Mother Shipton receive much the same treatment from the townspeople.

Other women in California sized up the situation in the region and carved out profitable businesses for themselves. For example, Luzena Stanley Wilson arrived in California in 1849 and quickly recognized that a fortune could be made by providing meals and lodging for miners. She subsequently set up a cooking operation for miners in Nevada City, California. Wilson wrote of her cooking operation, "from the first day it was well patronized, and I shortly after took my husband into partnership" (Wilson in Levy, p. 102). Armed with the profits from her cooking enterprise, Wilson had a small house built and gradually added rooms to accommodate lodgers. As profits mounted, the Wilsons opened a store and within six months they had $10,000 invested in the hotel and the store, and owned goods worth perhaps $10,000 more.

Many women, though, took menial positions washing clothes and working in saloons. Some women who washed clothes for miners were able to earn $15 to $20 a week, a substantial sum for the period, and women who served drinks and dealt cards in saloons and gambling houses were easily able to support themselves with their earnings. In "The Outcasts of Poker Flat," Piney Woods, the only woman in the story who is not a prostitute, works as a waitress in a restaurant.

The Short Story in Focus

The plot. As the story begins, the small town of Poker Flat is attempting to rid itself of its most undesirable citizens. Two of the worst are hung outside of town, and four others are simply exiled from the city. These four characters are John Oakhurst, a shady gambler whose success at fleecing the townspeople made him very unpopular; the Duchess and Mother Shipton, a pair of prostitutes; and Uncle Billy, a thief and drunkard. Connected through their exile, the four outcasts decide to travel together to Sandy Bar, a small town on the other side of the mountains. When the journey is half finished, the group encounters Tom Simson, a young man from Sandy Bar who is also known as "the Innocent." Tom is accompanied by Piney Woods, a young girl with whom he has eloped. The newlyweds have decided to seek a fresh start in Poker Flat. After discovering a dilapidated log cabin nearby, the two parties decide to camp together for the night in the remains of the shack. When the group awakens in the morning, they discover that an early winter storm has dropped a substantial amount of snow on the area during the night. Even worse, Uncle Billy has stolen the horses and most of the supplies and disappeared, an act that severely reduces the chances of the group making it through the storm, which continues unabated.

Fortunately, Uncle Billy was unable to steal all of the provisions. A small store of food has been left with the party. Hoping that the storm will soon blow over, the outcasts and their two new comrades stay together in the cabin, sharing the small quantity of food left to them. Through this forced fellowship the outcasts realize for the first time in their lives what it feels like to care about others. Oakhurst works diligently at making a pair of snowshoes, which he hopes will prove to be the salvation of the group. Mother Shipton starves herself to death, sacrificing her needs for young Piney, who will have a better chance of survival with her portion of the food. The Duchess, previously a

"Outcasts of Poker Flat"

The undesirables are exiled from Poker Flat. Illustration by John Keely.

selfish and solitary character, does all she can to comfort and console the fearful Piney.

Finally, when the food supply is almost entirely depleted, Oakhurst's snowshoes are finished and he gives them to Tom in the belief that the young man has the best chance of reaching Poker Flat and summoning aid for his young bride. Oakhurst leaves with Tom, telling the Duchess and Piney that he is going to accompany him as far as a nearby canyon. When Oakhurst does not return, the young women look outside the cabin and find that though he has not come back, he left them a pile of firewood to help them stay alive in the freezing weather. Unfortunately for Piney and the Duchess, Tom does not return quickly enough with rescuers, and the two young women freeze to death in each other's arms. In a nearby gulch, the body of John Oakhurst is found lying beneath a tree. The man is dead from a self-inflicted gunshot wound.

The use of sentiment in "The Outcasts of Poker Flat." Bret Harte is best known for his use of sentimentalism to propel his works and for the "heart of gold" aspect of his most famous characters. "The Outcasts of Poker Flat" is no exception to this rule, for it relies heavily on both of these devices to keep its action moving. As soon as the outcasts are trapped together, the story becomes a sentimental tale. The hardened facades of the Duchess and Mother Shipton crumble and they work together to keep the innocent Piney from knowing that they are prostitutes, for they worry that the knowledge of this fact might tarnish her innocence. All three of the outcasts from Poker Flat also keep Uncle Billy's thievery a secret from Tom and Piney, reasoning that the information might only frighten them more. Mother Shipton's sacrifice of her own life so that Piney might live, the peak of the sentimental side of the story, is the perfect example of the heart-of-gold element in Harte's work. Coarse in the beginning of the story, Mother Shipton becomes the kindest and most selfless of the characters.

Harte uses his characterizations to attack the judgmental society of the period. As a writer, he would become well known for his courageous stands against the injustices perpetrated against the Indians, the Chinese, and the slaves of the South. His depiction of the inner goodness of his characters was meant to show that it is unjust to judge and condemn on the basis of appearance alone. One of the final lines in "The Outcasts of Poker Flat" highlights this theme. When Piney and the Duchess are found lying dead together, Harte writes, "you could scarcely have told from the equal peace that dwelt upon them which was she that had sinned" ("The Outcasts of Poker Flat," p. 21).

Sources. According to most scholars, the writings of Bret Harte were created primarily in response to his environment. When Bret Harte arrived in northern California in 1854, he found himself in a part of the world rife with subject matter. During his ramblings though the gold mining towns, Harte was inspired by the characters he encountered. Harte was also impressed by the breathtaking scenery of northern California and is well known for his descriptions of the Sierra Mountains, in which many of his stories, including "The Outcasts of Poker Flat," were set.

Another likely influence on "The Outcasts of Poker Flat" is the real-life story of the Donner Party. Harte's tale and the actual tale of the Donner Party are similar in several respects. The party of outcasts from Poker Flat, just like the Donner Party, are doomed because of their decision to stop overnight instead of finishing their journey; for both groups the span of one day becomes the difference between life and death. Another similarity lies in the behavior of certain members of the stranded groups. Tamsen Donner, whose husband was injured and unable to travel, refused to leave him when a rescue party arrived at Donner Lake. As a result of her selflessness, Tamsen died with her husband, just as Mother Shipton dies due to her selfless devotion to Piney in the short story.

Events in History at the Time the Short Story Was Written

Vigilantes and lynch mobs in San Francisco. When the rush of gold-seekers headed west in 1849, San Francisco was in a state of lawlessness. Throughout the 1850s, vigilance committees were formed under the pretense of keeping order, but they often contributed to the chaos. The vigilante movement reached its greatest heights in 1856 under the leadership of William Tell Coleman. Coleman was a successful businessman who, according to historian Walton Bean, believed strongly in the benefits of "prompt and summary punishment" (Bean, p. 127). The cause for the resurgence of this vigilante group was the shooting by James P. Casey of James King, the editor of the *Daily Evening Bulletin*.

King had used his newspaper to criticize and condemn the corrupt politicians of San Francisco's Bay Area. During King's journalistic crusade, Casey was elected to the position of county supervisor in an election believed by most to be corrupt. In response to this dishonest election,

King noted in the *Bulletin* that Casey had served a term in the New York state penitentiary at Sing Sing prison. Infuriated by this public denunciation, Casey threatened King in the *Bulletin* office and shot him on the street an hour later.

As Casey sat in the county jail, William Coleman prepared his vigilantes for action. Four days after the shooting, 2,500 armed vigilantes marched on the county jail and removed Casey. They also captured Charles Cora, a notorious gambler who had shot and killed a U.S. Marshal. Both men were given a trial before a tribunal of vigilantes, who condemned Casey unanimously and Cora by a slim majority. Both men were hanged with public ceremony on May 22, 1856. Though Coleman's vigilance committee disbanded under threat from federal authorities later in 1856, vigilante punishment continued to resurface sporadically in San Francisco throughout the 1860s and after. Rather than controlling crime, though, the vigilance committees seemed to create an even greater atmosphere of lawlessness. This is perhaps a factor in Harte's description of Poker Flat and its vigilantes: "It [Poker Flat] was experiencing a spasm of public reaction, quite as lawless and ungovernable as any of the acts that had provoked it" ("The Outcasts of Poker Flat," p. 7).

The champion of outcasts. Throughout the two decades following the discovery of gold in California, certain segments of the population faced harsh treatment and persecution. The victims of this persecution found a defender in Bret Harte. Harte's first battle against injustice occurred when he was the junior editor of the *Northern Californian* in Arcata. In February 1860 a gang of locals invaded the peaceful Indian village on Gunther's Island in Humboldt Bay and brutally murdered sixty Indians, mostly women and children, with axes and hatchets. The attack was made in reaction to the actions of a completely separate tribe of Indians located a hundred miles away.

In charge of the paper while his editor was away on business, Harte bitterly denounced the incident in an article titled "Indiscriminate Massacre of Indians—Women and Children butchered" (Bean, p. 154). The article angered the public so greatly that Harte and his editor agreed it would be best for the paper if Harte moved back to San Francisco.

Once in the Bay area, Harte fought against the racism directed at the growing population of Chinese in San Francisco. In 1867 he wrote an article for the *San Francisco News Letter* describing the celebration of St. Patrick's Day. He satirically recounted how the Irish had boasted of their love of liberty and freedom just after beating up a negro and chasing several Chinese out of the neighborhood. Harte biographer Richard O'Connor noted that he also paraphrased one of the slogans of the celebration to read, "Ireland for the Irish, America for the Naturalized, and Hell for Niggers and Chinese" (O'Connor, p. 96). His attitude indicates a strong respect for the individual person, regardless of outward appearance; it is this respect that underlies Harte's characters in "The Outcasts of Poker Flat."

Bret Harte and the critics. After the 1868 publication of "The Outcasts of Poker Flat" in the *Overland Monthly,* Bret Harte became an international celebrity. In England a dying Charles Dickens sent for the edition of the *Overland* that featured Harte's stories "The Luck of Roaring Camp" and "The Outcasts of Poker Flat." Some readers were less impressed by Harte's work. The American critic E. S. Nadal wrote in 1877, "The Outcasts of Poker Flat is very nearly spoiled by the absurd manner of Oakhurst's death.... Mr. Harte shows his want in judgment by admiring his characters in the wrong places" (Nadal in Poupard, p. 192). Henry Seidel Canby was more complimentary of Harte's work, although he also questioned its realism. "What gives these characters their lasting power? Why does that highly melodramatic tragedy in the hills above Poker Flat ... hold you spell-bound at the thirtieth as at the first reading?" Canby continued, "Bret Harte believed, apparently, that it was his realism that did it. He had put the western miner into literature as he was—hence the applause.... Not the realism, but the idealization, of this life was the prize Bret Harte gained" (Canby in Poupard, p. 197).

For More Information

Bean, Walton. *California: An Interpretive History.* New York: McGraw-Hill, 1978.

DeArment, Robert K. *Knights of the Green Cloth: The Saga of Frontier Gamblers.* Norman: University of Oklahoma Press, 1982.

Harte, Bret. "The Outcasts of Poker Flat." In *The Luck of Roaring Camp & Other Stories.* New York: Lancer, 1968.

Hicks, Jim, ed. *The Gamblers.* Alexandria, Va.: Time-Life, 1978.

Levy, Jo Ann. *They Saw the Elephant: Women in the California Gold Rush.* Hamden, Conn.: Archon, 1990.

O'Connor, Richard. *Bret Harte: A Biography.* Boston: Little, Brown, 1966.

Poupard, Dennis, ed. *Twentieth-Century Literary Criticism.* Vol. 25. Detroit: Gale Research, 1988.

The Ox-Bow Incident

by
Walter Van Tilburg Clark

Although Walter Van Tilburg Clark was born into a family of academics, he was raised in an environment notorious for its lack of civilized behavior. From the moment his family moved to Reno, Nevada, in 1917, the eight-year-old Clark felt an immense appreciation for this region commonly known as the Great Basin. It would be an affinity he would constantly return to throughout the course of his life, both physically as well as in his writings. Of the books Clark has penned, many believe *The Ox-Bow Incident* to be one of the best examples of the unique relationship that Clark shared with his surroundings.

Events in History at the Time the Novel Takes Place

Nevada in the 1800s. In the early part of the nineteenth century, the land now known as Nevada was nothing more than a barren region sparsely inhabited by American Indians. Occasionally Spanish missionaries and Hudson Bay Company fur traders would traverse its plains, but it wasn't until the 1830s and '40s that American settlers and gold seekers began to cross the land en route to California.

With the 1848 Treaty of Guadalupe Hidalgo, which ended the Mexican-American War, the United States acquired 1.2 million square miles of western territory. Included was much of the land that would later comprise the state of Nevada. Under U.S. sovereignty, the area gradually began to prosper, luring in settlers who wished to try their luck in agriculture or cattle-raising. After the discovery of the Comstock Lode in 1859, however, the population in the region soared; it grew so rapidly that on March 2, 1861, Nevada gained recognition as an autonomous territory. Three years later, on October 31, 1864, the U.S. Congress, in need of silver and votes for the Northern cause during the Civil War, voted to admit Nevada as the thirty-sixth state.

For the next decade and a half, the history of Nevada was dominated by the presence of the Comstock Lode. Thousands continued to flock to the area in search of their share of the record amounts of silver being mined daily, and temporary cities, called "boom" towns, emerged to accommodate the steadily rising population. Outside representatives from banks and investment enterprises also surfaced to profit from the silver others found. Unfortunately, for every bonanza the Comstock produced, a period of depression would inevitably follow in a boom-and-bust cycle that plagued the Nevada economy.

> **THE LITERARY WORK**
> A novel set in Nevada during the spring of 1885; published in 1940.
>
> **SYNOPSIS**
> After hearing the news that one of the local cowhands has been shot, several townspeople form a posse and set out on their own to find those responsible.

During the 1880s Nevada experienced its worst depression to date. Because of its dependence on the precarious mining industry, the state found itself in dire straits when the Comstock Lode failed to produce another bonanza. In order to circumvent this problem, many Nevadans began to shift their focus elsewhere, particularly toward their meager agricultural markets. Despite efforts to expand its economy, Nevada would remain in a state of depression until the next century, when a combination of several factors—like legalized gambling, reduced divorce requirements, and the construction of the Hoover Dam—would reestablish its basis for economic growth.

Frontier justice. With the occurrence of the first American vigilante movement in the back country of South Carolina in 1767, this convoluted form of justice would provide an option to more conventional methods of deciding guilt or innocence. This system found particular support from those in the western region, where large expanses of land and lax adherence to the law made many believe that taking matters into one's own hands was the only correct way to exact justice. As a result of this ideology, between 1767 and 1910 at least 326 vigilante movements or episodes occurred across the United States, with the bulk of these taking place in the region west of the Appalachian Mountains.

Many of the vigilante movements in the West were formally organized, with a constitution or declaration to which the members would subscribe. Oftentimes, they would even provide the accused with a formal (albeit illegal) trial, complete with both prosecuting and defense attorneys who would regulate the proceedings in a fair manner. Despite its vague resemblance to law and order, the number of accused who were acquitted following their "trial" was extremely low; the majority of these hearings resulted in death. Overall, in the period between 1860 and 1909, these movements claimed over five hundred lives, most of them by hanging.

The boom town. As the amount of silver extracted from the Comstock Lode steadily increased, so too did the quantity of prospectors. In order to accommodate this quick rise in the population, boom towns sprung up practically overnight. Since the average wage of the Nevada miner was only $5 a day, the boom towns provided few commodities, usually made available in only a general store and saloon. Boarding was also provided—at the rate of $4 a day. Many chose to erect their own form of shelter rather than pay such a sum. When the quantity of settlers had risen enough to demand some permanent institutions, schools and churches appeared.

> **COMSTOCK LODE**
>
> The Comstock Lode refers to a series of profitable silver mines located in the Sierra Nevada Mountains and named after "Pancake" Henry Comstock, an unsuccessful gold miner who alleged ownership of the land on which the first vein was discovered in 1859. During the peak period of 1876-78, the mines yielded approximately $36 million annually and immortalized Nevada on the map.

When the boom towns first appeared, the only road through town consisted of a dirt pathway defined by the steady tracks of countless wagons. In the summer, this pathway was dust-laden except for the slim trenches made by the wheels. In the winter, this same thoroughfare would become a mud bog after the rains. Nevertheless, many settlers continued to flock to the area in search of riches, prompting the construction of more and more buildings to accommodate the flow. Eventually some towns, like Virginia City, grew large enough to sustain themselves following the departure of their temporary citizens. As was often the case, however, many others were simply vacated, leaving behind only a hollow shell of the prosperity they once enjoyed.

> **LIFE IN THE BOOM TOWN**
>
> Above C Street in Virginia City, the ornate homes of the merchants and bankers looked down on the gaudy, vulgar town, which had swelled to twenty-thousand people by the mid-1870s. While the Irishmen, Cornishmen, Germans, Mexicans, and a polyglot of miners labored in the tunnels far below, town matrons sat on their porches eating ice cream and drinking champagne.
>
> (Milner et al., p. 201)

The Novel in Focus

The plot. As *The Ox-Bow Incident* opens, the reader is introduced to two rugged cowboys, Gil Carter and Art Croft, who are returning to the

The Ox-Bow Incident

town of Bridger's Wells after a long period of isolation on the range. Like many of the boom towns that existed at the time, Bridger's Wells offered travelers the basic necessities: a general store, a land and mining claims office, an inn, a saloon, and a church. Both men soon join the town's other visitors in Canby's saloon.

WHO REALLY DISCOVERED THE COMSTOCK LODE?

Because of the immense wealth spawned by the discovery of the Comstock Lode, the region loosely known as Nevada gained enough national recognition to earn itself statehood. But who should be credited with this landmark discovery? One suggestion offered by historians is the two Grosh brothers. Like many of the miners who prospected in the area known as Gold Canyon during the winter, these brothers would spend the summer months at Carson City searching for precious minerals. After several years of this, their hard work finally reached fruition with the discovery of a ledge of silver ore. Unfortunately, before either of the brothers could capitalize on their find, tragedy struck. On August 19, 1857, Hosea Grosh accidentally struck a pick into his foot, a wound that would lead to his death less than a month later on September 2. Shortly thereafter, while returning to California, his brother Allan and a companion met harsh storms that left both men with badly frozen legs. After refusing to allow amputation, Allan died from the wound on December 19. Although critics claim that the ledge these two brothers discovered was merely the Silver City branch of the Comstock Lode, many believe that had they lived a few more years, further discovery was imminent.

Once inside the dark and cool interior, the two order whiskey and begin talking. Based on the conversations that take place, the reader discovers two key points. The first is that Rose Mapen, Gil's love prior to departing for the range, has been run out of town because of her overtly flirtatious manner. The second point is that cows have been rustled and the culprits are still at large. This last bit of news proves to be particularly upsetting to those in attendance. As the time passes, the men continue to drink and unwind by engaging in a high-strung game of poker. Before tempers explode beyond control, however, the mood is interrupted by the arrival of unfortunate news. It seems that the rustlers have struck again and this time a man has been shot. Upon hearing this everyone files out of the saloon, led by Jeff Farnley, a close companion of the victim.

Outside in the open, feelings of anger quickly replace anxiety as the men begin to organize a vigilante posse. For the next few hours, people and horses scurry about frantically while those in possession of weapons return home to collect them. Thanks to the words of the storeowner, Davies, several of those in attendance begin to question the wisdom of their actions. Despite his efforts, any doubts sparked in the men's minds are quickly put to rest by the appearance of Major Tetley, a retired officer in the Confederate army, and his scholarly son, Gerald. Shortly after their arrival, the group, now numbering twenty-eight in all, exit the town in pursuit of the rustlers.

After riding for several hours, the sky darkens and snow begins to fall, causing some of those present to reconsider their actions once again. As the weather continues to worsen, so too does the morale of the men, until they are startled back to reality by the arrival of a stagecoach. When the stagecoach finally comes into view, one of the men, a former guard and driver for Wells Fargo named Winder, recognizes the vehicle as one of their own. Unfortunately, his efforts to attract the coach's attention are stifled by the wind, causing the driver to mistakenly believe that his coach is being attacked.

In the confusion that ensues, the driver fires shots at the posse. At first, nobody appears to be hit, but as the coach quickly comes to a stop, it becomes evident that Art has taken a bullet in the shoulder. While those around him see to his wound, the passengers in the stagecoach gradually emerge. To everyone's surprise, out comes Rose Mapen, Gil's former love, and her husband, a Mr. Swanson from San Francisco. After several moments of astonishment, the men saddle up again to renew their quest.

As the night progresses, the weather grows increasingly worse. By now, the wind is swirling with snow and even the warmest of posse riders cannot help but to feel the chill. Before the elements become too harsh, the men find temporary sanctuary in a valley, where it is rumored that the rustlers had last been seen. Sure enough, sleeping around a fire are the silhouettes of three men, clueless to the fate that awaits them.

After the first awakens—a large man resembling "a Mex playing a Navajo" (*The Ox-Bow Incident*, p. 190)—it is not long before all three are alert and demand an explanation. Still failing to

The Ox-Bow Incident

The hanging scene from William Wellman's film adaptation of *The Ox-Bow Incident*.

realize their situation, the three men adamantly declare their innocence in whatever offense the others are accusing them of committing.

Over the course of the next several hours, the posse acts as judge, jury, and executioner for the three men. The defendants are confronted with a barrage of questions, to which they provide competent answers. Unfortunately, because of the lack of evidence present—and fueled by the men's insatiable desire to exact justice—the story provided by the three men is ruled to be untrue. They are declared guilty, and after further consideration it is decided that they will be hung at dawn.

When morning arrives, the three men are led to the middle of the valley to the site of their execution, "a big pine with its top shot away by lightning" (*The Ox-Bow Incident,* p. 218). There, the accused lose all sense of composure. "My God," cries one, in disbelief, "you aren't going to, really!" (*The Ox-Bow Incident,* p. 217). As before, their cries go unheeded, and the posse proceeds with the hanging.

Before they can ride out of view of the swaying bodies, however, the posse is met by Risley, the sheriff, and four companions, one of whom is the man thought to have been killed by the rustlers. It seems that the rumors surrounding his murder had been just that. Upon hearing this news, those in the posse immediately realize the magnitude of their mistake. Scarcely a word is spoken or a head raised as they continue their ride into town.

Back in Bridger's Wells, the men slowly disband, still reflecting on their actions. Major Tetley and his son, Gerald, later commit suicide.

As the novel comes to a close, Gil and Art are conversing about their desire to return to the isolation of the range. Despite the amenities of the town, they are anxious to escape from the events that have unfolded. "I'll be glad to get out of here," Gil acknowledges, as if the act of leaving would provide a catharsis for what occurred. (*The Ox-Bow Incident*, p. 287).

AN EYEWITNESS ACCOUNT

One night as I was making my run, my horse shied out to one side and would not pass a clump of several juniper trees along the road. I finally forced him back into the road and then I discovered why the horse had shied. From each of these small trees was suspended a man with a rope around his neck, and on each of their chests was pinned a notice from the Vigilance Committee. You should have seen the clearing out of Virginia City after that lynching bee.

(Dosch in Lockley, p. 6)

What Davies thinks. Although the story in *The Ox-Bow Incident* is told from the point of view of Art Croft, it is the storeowner Davies who represents the conscience of the men. Through his eyes, the reader is led along a path that delves into the paradox of frontier justice.

From the moment the men begin to organize a posse in the absence of the law, Davies remains sternly opposed, though he accompanies them. He repeatedly questions the men about the nature of their feelings and challenges them to consider more deeply what they are about to do. "We desire justice," he declares emphatically, "and justice has never been attained in haste and strong feeling" (*The Ox-Bow Incident*, p. 41).

At the conclusion of the story, those in the posse finally realize the tragedy in their mistake. None, however, is as upset as Davies, who places the blame for the entire episode upon his own shoulders. According to him, his inability to stop the hanging is far worse than the crime committed by those who proceeded. In a personal confession to Art, Davies makes the following statement:

> I had everything, justice, pity, even the backing—and I knew it—and I let those three men hang because I was afraid. The lowest kind of virtue, the quality dogs have when they need it, the only thing Tetley had, guts, plain guts, and I didn't have it.
>
> (*The Ox-Bow Incident*, p. 278)

The sort of indecision that plagues Davies was not uncommon throughout the West. Given a lax and ineffectual legal system, many turned to vigilantism as a means to establish order and stability in the region. Eventually many men came to view personal justice outside the law as the only masculine way to combat criminality. As a result, those who opposed such measures often kept their opinions to themselves out of fear of being labeled weak or unmanly. This may account for Davies's reticence in stopping the hanging.

Sources. According to a collection of notes acquired after Clark's death, the original draft of *The Ox-Bow Incident* was not based on any particular event, past or present. The novel merely arose out of Clark's dissatisfaction with the conventional Western. In a lecture given on the modern American novel, Clark made this admission:

> I had become irked at the way the West was treated in popular fiction and the moving pictures, with two-gun cowboys stuffed with Sunday-school virtues, and heroines who could go through a knock-down without getting a curl misplaced.
>
> (Laird, p. 74-5)

Clark originally sought to satirize the entire genre in the hope that "people would stop writing or reading such junk" (Laird, p. 75). In time Clark realized the triviality in his mission and instead chose to deal with a theme very real to Amer-

---

HIGH PRAISE

Walter Van Tilburg Clark's *The Ox-Bow Incident* is your correspondent's unwavering choice for the year's finest first novel. It has many of the elements of an old-fashioned horse opera—monosyllabic cowpunchers, cattle rustlers, a Mae Western lady, barroom brawls, shootings, lynchings, a villainous Mexican. But it bears about the same relation to a Western that *The Maltese Falcon* does to a hack detective story. Not to put too fine a point on it, I think it's sort of what you might call a masterpiece.

(Clifton Fadiman in James and Brown, p. 177)

ican security: the spread of fascism in Europe.

Once Clark had decided on his new topic, he "dumped the stuff [he] had written into the wastebasket and started over" (Laird, p. 75). This time, calling upon people and images from his past, as well as those in the present, he created a new set of characters, each assigned a counterpart based on descriptions received from Nazi Germany. For example, in the novel, the militant leader Tetley is portrayed as a former officer in the Confederate army; in Clark's mind, he was a combination of Adolf Hitler and Hitler's predecessor German chancellor Paul von Hindenburg and symbolized the Prussian officer tradition. Clark also modeled his novel on personalities whom he had known from his days in Virginia City, Reno, and Carson. Sometimes he would use real-life sources to inspire characters. Other times, the real-life sources would come to symbolize entire institutions.

Because of his intellectual upbringing, many scholars believe Clark patterned the character Davies upon himself, portraying the author's own concerns about good and evil.

Events in History at the Time the Novel Was Written

Fascism and *The Ox-Bow Incident*. Although written in the Western genre, many readers viewed *The Ox-Bow Incident* as an allegory for fascism and demagoguery. In their own time, Benito Mussolini's Fascist Party, founded in Milan, Italy, in March of 1919, gradually gained recognition for its extreme right-wing policies and dictatorial style of government. At its inception, the Fascist Party served as a movement bent on exposing the faults of Italy's other parties, though it provided no clear solution of its own to cure the country's ills. Eventually, as the years progressed, it gained support from powerful industrialists who feared the communist alternative, and from less fortunate citizens such as unemployed war veterans and members of the lower-middle class. This latter group proved to be extremely supportive of Mussolini.

By the time Clark began his work on *The Ox-Bow Incident* in the late 1930s, Mussolini's party was gaining global attention for its aggressive participation in the European arena. In the summer of 1936, Italy had entered the Spanish Civil War on behalf of Generalissimo Francisco Franco, a fellow fascist dictator seeking to assume control over Spain. Additionally, in 1935-36, and later, in 1939, Italian forces initiated attacks on Ethiopia and Albania. These blatant acts of aggression incited feelings of both shock and discomfort, and Clark was one of many who were of the opinion that the events overseas were an

---

WELLS FARGO

Founded on March 18, 1852, by Henry Wells and William George Fargo out of the back room of a bookstore in Syracuse, New York, Wells, Fargo & Company soon became the premier transportation and banking service in the West. Its original advertisement offered not only to "forward packages, parcels, and freights of all descriptions between the City of New York and City of San Francisco" but also to "purchase and sell Gold Dust, Bullion and Bills of change" (Stone, p. 163). In the decade following 1855, the company expanded its holdings to include a series of stagecoach lines from the Midwest to the Rocky Mountains. In 1866, in what would later be called the "Grand Consolidation," they gained control of almost all stagecoach and express services west of the Missouri. By the time the novel takes place in 1885, most of the Wells Fargo stage lines had been relegated to secondary routes by the advent of the transcontinental railroad in 1869, although several operations continued to run in remote areas of the region even after 1900.

FROM MEMORY TO PRINT

Of all the characters mentioned in *The Ox-Bow Incident*, few are as interesting as Ma Grier, the burly proprietor of a boarding house, who is chosen as Tetley's lieutenant. Like many of Clark's characters in the novel, Ma was based on a real person.

One day, while riding his bike home from an excursion in the mountains, Clark decided to stop at a roadside diner for a beer. Unfortunately, the diner had been shut down for some unknown legal reason and those present were in the process of loading equipment onto a truck. When the time came to load the huge cook stove used to fry burgers, the owner, a large woman simply known as "Ma", wrapped her portly hands around its base and, giving it a subtle hoist with her hips, lifted it onto the truck by herself. Later, when searching his mind for a female character who would command the respect of other men, it was the image of "Ma" that popped into Clark's mind.

enormous threat to both world security and American democracy. Although it would take the Japanese bombing of Pearl Harbor in December of 1941 for America to be lured into war against Italy and its Axis allies of Germany and Japan, the atrocities committed by Mussolini and his supporters prior to Pearl Harbor were grave enough to inspire Clark to begin work on what would later be recognized as his finest literary achievement.

Reviews. When *The Ox-Bow Incident* was published in 1940, it was soon regarded as one of the greatest Western novels of all time. Critics lauded it for its crisp storytelling, engaging characters, and courage in dealing with a theme not commonly found in the average cowboy tale. The reviewer G. G. Stevens further praised the novel for its "high grade of psychological insight" (Stevens in James and Brown, p. 176). In the months and years following the novel's publication, similar positive appraisals could be found in nearly every literary review in the country. Occasionally, some extolled Clark's work merely for its skillful writing, but more often it was Clark's mastery in dealing with a complex theme that earned him many accolades.

For More Information

Clark, Walter Van Tilburg. *The Ox-Bow Incident*. New York: Random House, 1940.

Elliott, Russell R. *History of Nevada*. 2nd ed., revised. Lincoln: University of Nebraska Press, 1987.

James, Mertice M., and Dorothy Brown, eds. *The Book Review Digest*. Vol. 36. New York: H. W. Wilson, 1941.

Laird, Charlton, ed. *Walter Van Tilburg Clark: Critiques*. Reno: University of Nevada Press, 1983.

Lockley, Fred. *Vigilante Days at Virginia City: Personal Narrative of Col. Henry E. Dosch, Member of Fremont's Body Guard and Onetime Pony Express Rider*. Portland: Koke-Tiffany, 1924.

Milner, Clyde A., Carol A. O'Connor and Martha A. Sandweiss, eds. *The Oxford History of the American West*. New York: Oxford University Press, 1994.

Stone, Irving. *Men to Match My Mountains: The Opening of the Far West, 1840-1900*. New York: Berkley Books, 1956.

Westbrook, Max. *Walter Van Tilburg Clark*. New York: Twayne, 1969.

Pride and Prejudice

by
Jane Austen

Despite her popularity, critics have argued that Jane Austen's works remain apart from the political, intellectual, and artistic revolutions of her era. Her *Pride and Prejudice* does not, in fact, make any direct reference to political events. The development of the novel, however, does reflect changes in English society. Rewritten over a period of years from 1797 to 1813, Austen's story begins with strict observance of the social codes that dominated her society. Its conclusion, however, inspired perhaps by the French Revolution and its aftereffects (1789-1815), shows some defiance of these codes.

Events in History at the Time of the Novel

The French Revolution. The French Revolution began in 1789, a number of years prior to the publication of Austen's work, but its social impact was felt long after its inception. Before the Revolution, social boundaries in England, as in the rest of Europe, were rigidly drawn and not easily crossed. The Revolution, which began with the storming of the Bastille prison in Paris on July 14, 1789, changed all of that.

Toward the end of the 1700s, population growth in France had led to a shortage of food supplies. Living hand to mouth, much of the population grew increasingly upset by a monarchy that lived in splendor, ignoring the needs of the masses. Simultaneously, the emerging middle class was gaining importance in political affairs. The monarchy of King Louis XVI seemed

> **THE LITERARY WORK**
> A novel set in the English countryside during the beginning of the 1800s; published in 1813.
>
> **SYNOPSIS**
> A love story unfolds between two young people who come from different social and economic classes.

in danger of crumbling. The Estates-General, the governing body of France, attempted to settle the unrest with a meeting in May and June of 1789. But the dissension of the Third Estate, the subbody made up of the middle and lower classes, deadlocked the talks. Inspired by this show of power, citizens in Paris convened and stormed the Bastille, a national prison. Soon revolts erupted throughout the nation. In many instances, peasants burned the homes of wealthy aristocrats and demanded greater social equality. Although the Revolution passed through several phases, key events included the beheading of the king in 1793 and the ascension of Napoleon as the crown emperor in 1804.

Napoleon's reign marked a period of nationalism for France. By embarking on foreign military excursions, the emperor set France up to become leader of the world. He had fought England once before—from 1793 to 1802—and made preparations to attack it again after becoming emperor, but England's Admiral Horatio Nelson prevented the invasion, defeating a combined fleet of Frenchmen and Spaniards at the Battle of Trafalgar in 1805. The presence of militia in Austen's novel alludes to this militaristic atmosphere on the European continent at the time, while the novel's treatment of social classes reflects the growing power of commoners after the French Revolution. Until the defeat of Napoleon at Waterloo in 1815, France's revolutionary climate threatened to envelope all of Europe.

England's landed gentry and social ladder. During the late 1700s, the English population showed high regard for land ownership. Owning property brought not only the promise of an income but a social position as well. The landed gentry dominated the political life of the nation, occupying seats in Parliament and positions in the church, and serving as officers in the army.

ENTAILMENT

In English laws of inheritance, land passed from father to son. If a family had no male offspring, the estate would move into the hands of the eldest living male of the extended family. This process was known as entailment. In *Pride and Prejudice*, the Bennets are by no means a wealthy family, but they do command some social status due to their ownership of property. Since Mr. Bennet has only daughters, however, his land is entailed to their male cousin, Mr. Collins. Upon the death of Mr. Bennet, Mr. Collins would have the legal right to oust Mrs. Bennet and her five daughters from their home and assume its ownership.

The landed gentry observed strict social rules. In order to maintain its standing in society, this class took a guarded approach to marriage matches. Marriage linked the inheritance of the groom to the dowry of the bride, and it was felt that the two partners needed to be of a similar economic stature to ensure the continued prominence of both families. In *Pride and Prejudice,* for instance, the character of Lady Catherine, herself a member of the landed gentry, mentions Darcy's betrothal to an economic and social equal. Speaking to Elizabeth Bennet, a commoner, she states that "their fortune on both sides is splendid. They are destined for each other by the voice of every member of their respective houses; and what is to divide them? The upstart pretensions of a young woman without . . . fortune" (Austen, *Pride and Prejudice,* p. 316). She dismisses the idea of a union between two people of different social rank, voicing objections that were by no means rare. Climbing the social ladder was not an easy feat to accomplish in such an environment.

Still, a new class of gentry—made up of successful merchants, bankers, and manufacturers—began to emerge at the start of the 1800s. They did not draw their income from their property or inheritance but rather from the increasing trade and manufacturing that England had begun to participate in with the onset of the Industrial Revolution. Members of this class came from a variety of backgrounds and crossed social boundaries more easily than the old aristocrats. As the new gentry's wealth and power expanded, its membership demanded increased political clout. In *Pride and Prejudice,* Mr. Bingley represents a member of this new gentry. While he does not himself hold a job, his family acquired its wealth and status through trade, not birthright. As a result, while Bingley's sisters do not necessarily approve of his marriage to a woman of an inferior class, they do not object as strongly as Lady Catherine does to such a match.

London vs. the country. Throughout Austen's novel, the disparity between the classes is underscored by the debate between city and country living. Upon his first introduction to the country town of Longbourn, Darcy remarks, "the country . . . can in general supply but few subjects for such a study [of amusement]. In a country neighborhood you move in a very confined and unvarying society" (*Pride and Prejudice,* p. 37).

In England during the late 1700s, country towns existed as virtually isolated and independent islands. The social centers of such towns were usually the local churches. Here members congregated weekly for both spiritual worship and social exchange. Other country amusements included dances, fairs, and such sporting events as cricket matches. Along with all of its apparent simplicity, the English country provided the scenery that increasingly enthralled artists of the late 1700s. Painters such as J. M. W. Turner popularized the beauty of this land.

London, however, provided the only "real" society for the upper classes. It was reputed to be both the most beautiful and the most populous of Europe's cities. The night life, noted one historian, included "theaters, balls, assemblies, wax works, taverns, gardens, thousands of grog [liquor] shops, bawdy houses from the fashionable bagnios [brothels] of Covent Garden . . . to the cheap cat houses of London's underworld"

(Burton, p. 10). The greatest injustice suffered by one of Austen's characters is to reside in London for a few weeks without being allowed to "put [her] foot out of doors . . . not [for] one party, or scheme, or anything" (*Pride and Prejudice,* p. 282). Along with London's appeal, however, came its vices. The growth of industry led to an increase in traffic and smoke, leading one visitor to observe that "there were not so many fine streets as in Berlin and these not-so-fine streets were always crowded with a tumult of people" (Burton, p. 13).

Women's education and conduct. The beginning of the nineteenth century saw a surge in the popularity of etiquette books. With a new middle class emerging, old upper-class social manners needed to be taught to the inexperienced. Young women, according to the conservative teachers, should present themselves "as neat as the strictest delicacy demands, and as fashionable as the strictest delicacy permits" (Quinlan, p. 144). Formality reigned, and even husbands and wives referred to each other by their last names using the prefix "Mr." or "Mrs." In Austen's novel, Mrs. Bennet always calls her husband "My dear Mr. Bennet." At one point, their neighbor Miss Bingley addresses Elizabeth Bennet as "Miss Eliza," which would have been considered a shocking and rude breach of etiquette.

Acceptable standards of behavior differed between the sexes. While "gaming," or gambling, was discouraged but permitted for men, it was generally frowned upon for females. The reading of fiction also met with disapproval, for society thought it to be fraught with vice. One teacher of the era, for instance, questioned "whether any sort of fictitious representation of life and manners ought to be put into the hands of youth" (Quinlan, p. 145). Even in correspondence, women encountered social barriers. They were not allowed to write to a man unless they were engaged to the recipient of the letter.

Similarly, a woman's education differed greatly from that of a man. While boys were schooled away from home in such subjects as Latin, mathematics, and science, until the 1870s girls were generally taught at home by governesses. Their subjects consisted of "accomplishments" that would lead to the maintenance of good homes and social contacts. Young girls learned music, singing, drawing, and sewing, along with reading and writing. Oftentimes the arts were taught by masters whom young women would visit, an arrangement that Austen alludes to in her novel. A character from Austen's novel remarks to a girl that "your mother should have taken you to town every spring for the benefit of masters" (*Pride and Prejudice,* p. 147). Only with such an education, it was thought, could women hope to provide welcoming homes for future husbands.

Mary Wollstonecraft. With the 1792 publication of her book *A Vindication of the Rights of Woman,* (also covered in *Literature and Its Times*) Mary Wollstonecraft shook the foundations of gender inequality in England. She asserted the equal intellectual abilities of women and demanded equal education and social opportunities for her gender. Until this point, popular opinion had maintained that women were simply incapable of learning the same skills as men. Women were thus raised to become accomplished and self-sacrificing companions and childbearers, not individual thinkers.

> **MARRIAGE AND SPINSTERHOOD IN THE EARLY 1800S**
>
> Only a small minority of women remained unmarried in England during the 1800s. Spinsterhood—remaining single—usually meant suffering the hardship of having to survive on too little income. As Jane Austen once observed, spinsters had an unhappy tendency to be poor. She herself remained unmarried throughout her lifetime, remaining true to her belief that it was dishonorable to enter into wedlock "without affection" (Austen in Perkin, p. 154). She was fortunate, though, to have a family to help support her, for Austen could not have survived on the small earnings from her writings.

Although Austen never credited Wollstonecraft's ideas as an inspiration for her novel, her character Elizabeth, an independent spirit, has many of the qualities that were championed by Wollstonecraft. Unlike her younger sisters, who choose to sit idly all day long, Elizabeth reads voraciously and educates herself. Her continual challenging of Mr. Darcy shows a defiance not often expressed by women in nineteenth-century England.

The Novel in Focus

The plot. Jane Austen's novel opens with the promise of a new neighbor, Mr. Bingley, for her main characters, the Bennet family. A single man who plans to reside at the nearby home of Netherfield, Bingley unwittingly notifies the busybodies of Longbourn that he "must be in want of a wife" (*Pride and Prejudice*, p. 1). Bingley's wealth and social prominence make him the perfect candidate for young, single women, and although her family is from a lower social class, Mrs. Bennet joins several others in trying to secure Bingley as a husband for one of her five daughters. To the delight of Mrs. Bennet, the eldest daughter, Jane, soon finds favor with the popular Bingley. In no time the town begins buzzing with gossip of an impending engagement.

More independent and outspoken than her sister Jane, Elizabeth Bennet wants nothing to do with the new neighbors. Although she enjoys the company of Bingley, she finds his family and his close friend Mr. Darcy too disdainful for her taste. Elizabeth's acquaintance with the dashing, young Mr. Wickham intensifies her dislike for Darcy, for Wickham tells her how Darcy robbed him of an inheritance. Aside from Wickham, Elizabeth finds little interest in the men of Longbourn. And unlike her younger sisters, Catherine and Lydia, she remains equally indifferent to the military men stationed in a nearby town. To the dismay of Mrs. Bennet, Elizabeth's future seems to be that of an old maid. The arrival of a previously unseen cousin, William Collins, appears to improve Elizabeth's marital prospects, however.

Because the Bennets' estate is entailed to Mr. Collins, the family lives with the knowledge that upon Mr. Bennet's demise, Mr. Collins will acquire ownership of their property. Aware of his strong position, Collins visits the Bennets with the hope of selecting a wife from among the sisters. Such a match promises mutual satisfaction for both households. Collins will gain a spouse, and the Bennet family will secure its future living arrangements. Unfortunately, Collins proves to be an incredibly boring man who talks of little besides his admiration for his patroness, Lady Catherine de Bourgh. Elizabeth sees no cause for celebration when her cousin William asks for her hand in marriage; her refusal both shocks and enrages her mother.

Not stung too badly by Elizabeth's rejection, Collins quickly becomes engaged to and marries Elizabeth's friend Charlotte. As if the dismay of losing one potential husband were not enough for Mrs. Bennet, Bingley and his entourage leave Netherfield that same week without even the hint of an engagement for Jane. Heartbroken, Jane leaves to stay with an aunt in London, while Elizabeth heads to Hertfordshire to visit Charlotte in her new home.

While in Hertfordshire, Elizabeth is forced, through Collins, to make the acquaintance of the pompous Lady Catherine de Bourgh. Lady Catherine lives in a splendid home with her daughter and relishes every opportunity to tell others how they might improve their own lives. Coincidentally, Lady Catherine is also the aunt of Darcy, and during Elizabeth's stay with Charlotte, Darcy stops in Hertfordshire as well. Over the next few weeks, he visits frequently with Elizabeth, and eventually makes a proposal of marriage. Elizabeth not only refuses Darcy but she also accuses him of ruining Jane's happiness with Bingley and grievously wronging her friend Mr. Wickham, whom Darcy supposedly robbed of his inheritance. Darcy departs the next morning, leaving Elizabeth a letter that explains his past.

In his correspondence, Darcy relates that although he did encourage Bingley to forget Jane, it was with the best intentions. Due to the inferior social status of the Bennets, a marriage between the two families would not fare well in the current social circles of England. He felt it for the best that the young couple separate. Moreover, while Bingley showed an affection for Jane, Darcy did not perceive that the sentiments were returned with the same intensity. As for Wickham, Darcy explained that the young man squandered his inheritance, forced Darcy to financially support him for a number of years, and then attempted to elope with Darcy's sister.

Although ashamed of her hasty judgment of Darcy, Elizabeth decides to forget about him, assuming that she will never see him again. She departs from Hertfordshire to join her aunt and uncle in a tour of northern England. At her aunt's insistence, the party stops in Derbyshire to visit Pemberley, a famous mansion that is the residence of the Darcy family.

While at Pemberley, Elizabeth encounters Darcy, who had stopped by unexpectedly. His demeanor, she notices, is much changed since their last meeting. No longer does he exhibit a pompous and curt attitude; she instead finds him an enchanting companion. Distressing news from home, however, cuts short the family's visit to Derbyshire. Elizabeth, along with her aunt and uncle, rush back to Longbourn when told that Lydia has eloped with the infamous Wickham.

Knowing Wickham's greed, the Bennets fear that the man's interest in Lydia is not for marriage but simply for sexual companionship. When they receive word that the couple is living together out of wedlock in London, these fears appear to have materialized. This state of

Depiction of eighteenth-century English family life.

affairs threatens to ruin the Bennet family's reputation, but Darcy takes action to set matters right. He makes secret plans to pay a dowry for Lydia and arranges a marriage between the girl and Wickham. Only Elizabeth knows of his hand in helping the Bennets with their narrow escape from scandal.

Fortune smiles on the family again when Bingley returns to Longbourn to resume his courtship of Jane. Darcy, having realized his error in misjudging the level of Jane's affections, wholeheartedly supports the union. Soon the couple becomes engaged. With her sister united to Darcy's close friend, Elizabeth begins seeing this former suitor with greater frequency. To the absolute delight of Mrs. Bennet, Elizabeth and Darcy soon announce their own plans to marry.

The anti-revolution. Although Austen's novel does deal with two rather revolutionary upsets of social order, they are accomplished in a peaceful rather than an antagonistic manner. The marriage of the two Bennet girls to men far above their own social stature represents a shift in thinking for the nineteenth-century English audience. As mentioned earlier, this shift might have stemmed from the ideals promoted in the French Revolution. Without bloodshed or war, Austen's characters deny the old social code, and there are no tragic consequences. According to the view of University of London's Professor Isabel Armstrong, presented in the introduction to *Pride and Prejudice,* the novel is the story of how the French Revolution could have been avoided.

Certainly, the social clashes in the novel nearly lead to unhappy outcomes. Darcy's skepticism almost divides Bingley and Jane, while Elizabeth's blanket condemnation of the upper classes nearly costs her her own love. But the characters resolve their differences peacefully, bending their own positions to allow for the other person's point of view. As Darcy explains at one point, "I have been a selfish being all my life, in practice, though not in principle.... I might still have been but for you, dearest, loveliest Elizabeth!" (*Pride and Prejudice,* p. 328). Concerning a quarrel when their differences came to a head, the couple cannot decide with whom the greater fault lies. They eventually decide "we will not quarrel for the greater share of blame annexed to that evening ... the conduct of neither, if strictly examined, will be irreproachable" (*Pride and Prejudice,* p. 326).

By the time the novel was published in 1813, Austen's audience would have been well aware of the destruction caused overseas by the French Revolution. Many could have come to the conclusion that horrible destruction and death might have been prevented had Louis XVI of France

Pride and Prejudice

only come to his senses as Darcy did, and had the populace of France shown the understanding of Austen's Elizabeth Bennet.

The Romantic period. For the most part, Austen chose not to refer in her novels to contemporary political and social events. Evidence of her sensitivity to these events nevertheless finds its way into *Pride and Prejudice*. The aftermath of the French Revolution led to an artistic freedom felt throughout Europe. No longer troubled by rigid social constraints, English artists and writers began exploring their world with an experimental boldness that signaled a literary renaissance. Earlier in the 1700s, a scattering of writers had broken away from custom, focusing on the spontaneous, the emotional, and the natural, as opposed to the political world. Their numbers grew after the French Revolution. In England, authors William Wordsworth and Samuel Taylor Coleridge published their *Lyrical Ballads* in 1798, initiating what became known as the Romantic movement in English literature.

In *Pride and Prejudice*, Austen echoes these sentiments. Indeed, as one Austen biographer noted, "the temple, the hermitage, the wilderness which Longbourn ... possesses are signs of the enthusiasm [for nature] growing up in the latter part of the eighteenth century" (Craik, p. 160). Other allusions to the Romantic movement, such as Elizabeth's desire to visit the Lake District, an area from which many great Romantic poets hailed, are also conveyed in the novel.

Sources. While the majority of Austen's novel comes from her own imagination, its setting and tone were derived from autobiographical sources. Reared in the English countryside in northern Hampshire, Jane Austen found inspiration for her novels within her immediate environment. Although Jane's father was not a wealthy man, his income did allow him to maintain horses and a carriage similar to the ones the Bennets employed. Like the fictional family, however, the Austens' horses were more often used for farming than as transportation.

The preference for country living shown in *Pride and Prejudice* probably stems from Austen's mother. Mrs. Austen once called London "a sad place. I would not live in it on any account, one has not time to do one's duty either to God or to man" (Laski, p. 16). Similarly, Elizabeth Bennet's penchant for reading probably finds its roots in Austen's own upbringing. Her father maintained a vast library and even schooled several pupils in the classics. Austen's social calendar as a young woman was similar to the one enjoyed by the Bennets as well, for it was filled with balls and other events and featured a number of suitors.

Reception of the novel. From the beginning, Austen's novel found favor among readers and critics alike. Robert Louis Stevenson, author of the novel *Treasure Island* (also covered in *Literature and Its Times*), remarked that "when Elizabeth Bennet opened her mouth, he wanted to go down on his knees" (Laski, p. 86). The first edition of the work sold out within seven months, and a second one came less than four months later. An 1813 review in *The British Critic* noted that Elizabeth Bennet's character was developed with great spirit and consistency, but said that the same was not true of her lover, Darcy, whose character changed rather abruptly from indifferent gentleman to ardent lover. Still the review declared the novel to be far superior to other such publications of the day, a well-told story with well-drawn characters and energetic writing. It also praised certain details for being remarkably true to life at the time: "The picture of the younger Miss Bennets, their perpetual visits to the market town where officers are quartered, and the result, is perhaps exemplified in every provincial town in the kingdom" (*The British Critic* in Harris, p. 30).

For More Information

Austen, Jane. *Pride and Prejudice*. Edited by James Kinsley. New York: Oxford University Press, 1970.

Burton, Elizabeth. *The Pageant of Georgian England*. New York: Charles Scribner's Sons, 1967.

Craik, W. A. *Jane Austen in Her Time*. London: William Clowes and Sons, 1969.

Harris, Laurie Lanzen. *Nineteenth-Century Literature Criticism*, Vol. 1. Detroit: Gale Research, 1981.

Laski, Marghanita. *Jane Austen and Her World*. London: Thames and Hudson, 1969.

Perkin, Joan. *Victorian Women*. London: John Murray, 1993.

Quinlan, Maurice. *Victorian Prelude*. Hamden, Conn.: Archon, 1965.

Ragged Dick; or, Street Life in New York with the Boot-Blacks

by
Horatio Alger

> **THE LITERARY WORK**
> A novel set in New York City in the late 1850s; published in 1867.
>
> **SYNOPSIS**
> A fourteen-year-old orphan transforms himself from a homeless boot-black into a "respectable" young man through a combination of self-reliance and the help of friends.

Horatio Alger began a long career as a popular novelist for boys with the publication of *Ragged Dick,* his most successful book. So widely known were Alger's 119 books in the late 1800s and early 1900s that a "Horatio Alger story" became a synonym for a person, real or fictional, who rises in life from rags to riches. Actually a story about the rise from rags to respectability rather than riches, *Ragged Dick* is set at a time when two interrelated trends were shaping American lives. Both urbanization, or the growth of cities, and the spread of industry posed new challenges to society. People moving from the countryside to cities were confronted with different ways of living and working than in the past. Mixing fact with fiction, *Ragged Dick* describes this new urban world and advises young boys how to best succeed in it.

Events in History at the Time the Novel Takes Place

Urbanization. In 1830 fewer than one in ten Americans lived in towns or cities; thirty years later approximately two in ten did. New York itself more than doubled in population between 1830 and 1860 to become a city of half a million residents. Like other cities, its growth was related to trade, manufacturing, and the internal improvements being made to move raw materials and finished goods from producer to consumer.

Improvements in transportation modes were essential to this change. Ragged Dick jokes in the novel about his "Erie shares," referring to the Erie Railroad, which ran through southern New York state by mid-century. In the north of the state, the Erie Canal had provided water transport since its completion in 1825. Four feet deep and 363 miles long, it connected the Great Lakes with the Hudson River, which flowed into the Atlantic Ocean at New York City. After the canal opened, the cost of moving a ton of goods from New York to Lake Erie fell from $100 to $8 per ton. Such advances encouraged domestic trade between the lands being settled in the West and the urban East. As trade between these regions grew, New York developed into a thriving commercial center.

New York in the late 1850s was a dynamic city. In *Ragged Dick,* Alger mentions numerous buildings that illustrate the city's commercial vitality. One is the Customs House, described as a massive structure reminiscent of the Parthenon in Athens. Customs—or taxes on imported goods—were a major source of government revenue in the 1800s. New York's position as the nation's leading port made its Customs House prominent. Another symbol of the city's financial role is Wall Street, "a street not very wide or very long, but of very great importance" (Alger, *Ragged Dick*, p. 101). But in some ways New York still had a great deal of growing to do. The use of elevators was just making high-rises practical, and the only transportation between Manhattan and the nearby city of Brooklyn was the ferry that Dick rides in the novel.

Moreover, there were a great number of New Yorkers who did not share in the growing prosperity. The city's rapid growth made it difficult to provide all its residents with adequate housing, health care, sanitation, and public safety. In fact, city government only slowly took responsibility for services intended to address the needs of its growing urban population. In its place, private efforts attempted to provide these services. Companies, for example, supplied water and collected garbage for people who could afford to pay. Despite such attempts, those people with little money tended to be crowded into tightly packed, unclean neighborhoods.

> **NEWSBOYS' LODGING HOUSE**
>
> The Newsboys' Lodging House provided 140 beds in three rooms connected by folding doors. Lodging cost 5¢ a night, in contrast to the 25¢ charged elsewhere in the city. Another 5¢ bought a boy a plain meal of coffee and bread, sometimes with soup. In 1866 the lodging house providing housing for 8,192 boys.

Ragged Dick belongs to a group of New Yorkers who endure a marginal existence: homeless street boys earning their own living. No child labor laws regulated their work, and the government offered them no support. Ragged Dick mentions an actual institution, the Newsboys' Lodging House, where dinner and bed for a night cost what he could earn by shining one pair of shoes.

Despite its name, the lodging house also served two other types of young "street" workers—matchsellers and boot-blacks (shoeshine boys). The house was associated with the Children's Aid Society established by Charles L. Brace and other private philanthropists in 1853. Its goals included giving street boys a basic education as well as "habits of industry and self-control and neatness" (Bender, pp. 197-99).

Immigration. America's new urban population was both native-born and immigrant. Until the 1840s, cities consisted primarily of American-born residents, but after that date a large number of immigrants began to arrive. In the 1840s and 1850s, most of these immigrants were Irish. Ireland had been suffering from a long economic depression that worsened in 1845 because of a disease that destroyed the country's main food crop, potatoes. The resulting famine killed approximately one million people. Those who could afford the travel expenses emigrated to America. Extremely poor when they arrived, the Irish remained in eastern ports such as New York and Boston, where they made up a large part of the new industrial work force. Only one boy in *Ragged Dick* has an obvious ethnic identity—Micky Maguire, whose name marks him as Irish.

Individualism. The mid-nineteenth century urban world saw a decline in the traditional willingness to defer to one's social "betters," those members of wealthy and/or prominent families. Displacing this old attitude was the egalitarian ideal, the notion that every individual deserves respect. Even without good clothes and manners, one's character could earn one respect, as shown in the novel by the acceptance Ragged Dick receives from those more affluent than he. Though raggedly robed, the novel's hero refrains from stealing, cheating, or bullying younger boys. "His nature," in Alger's words, "was a noble one" (*Ragged Dick*, p. 44).

The influence of individualism on politics is evident in the growing numbers of men who became eligible to vote. In 1821 the state of New York abolished all property qualifications for voting. In economics the government adopted a hands-off or "laissez-faire" approach that showed respect for individualism. The belief was that as individuals worked to increase their personal well-being, public prosperity would follow.

A laissez-faire economic policy encouraged people to live according to the work ethic, the notion that hard work and frugal living should be central activities of one's life. According to this ethic, economic well-being reflected an individual's own efforts. Success was within everyone's grasp and those who worked hard could achieve it. This was not a new idea in Alger's day. In colonial America, Benjamin Franklin had lived by the work ethic and had advocated it in a variety of his publications. Nor did the work ethic extend to merely economic realms; it also reflected Protestant religious values that viewed work as pleasing to God. Valued by society and religion, work was regarded as a key part of a moral life.

The changing world of work. By the mid-nineteenth century, the nation had begun to industrialize. Industrialization involved more than the use of machinery for manufacturing goods; it changed the nature of business by bringing workers together into ever larger workplaces. These eventually grew into sprawling factories. Industrialization also broke manufacturing down into ever smaller steps. Before industrialization, a skilled artisan might make an entire product from start to finish. In a factory, a product was put together by many workers, each doing one specific task.

Industrialization led to a distinct separation between business owners and workers, despite society's discussion about the equality of all individuals. The process also influenced the formation of a distinct middle class. Larger in scale than previous systems, industrial manufacturing and commerce created a need for managers and professionals who could serve as factory supervisors, accountants, and clerks. These jobs offered higher pay, cleaner and safer working conditions, and greater social standing than the average, machine-operating factory position. But they also required a higher level of education. "Save your money, my lad," advised a character in *Ragged Dick*. "Buy books, and determine to be somebody, and you may yet fill an honorable position" (*Ragged Dick,* p. 109). The link between education and middle-class employment helped create a new understanding of childhood as a time of training for adult work. Families sought to keep their children in school long enough for them to gain sufficient skills for at least an entry-level position in a middle-class profession. In *Ragged Dick*, the characters' different levels of education influence the work available to them.

Efforts were also made to give those already in the work force an education. But instead of emphasizing such traditional college subjects as Latin and Greek, these efforts sought to provide established members of the work force with a more practical education in the arts and sciences. On an excursion through the city, Ragged Dick mentions one such effort, known as the Cooper Institute. The institute, also known as Cooper Union, was established by Peter Cooper, a New York millionaire who began work as a mechanic. Opened in 1859, it offered public lectures and made available rooms for discussion and formal instruction.

The absence of women. Women hardly appear in *Ragged Dick*. In part, this reflects the nineteenth-century divide between the worlds of men and women. Society placed the highest value on

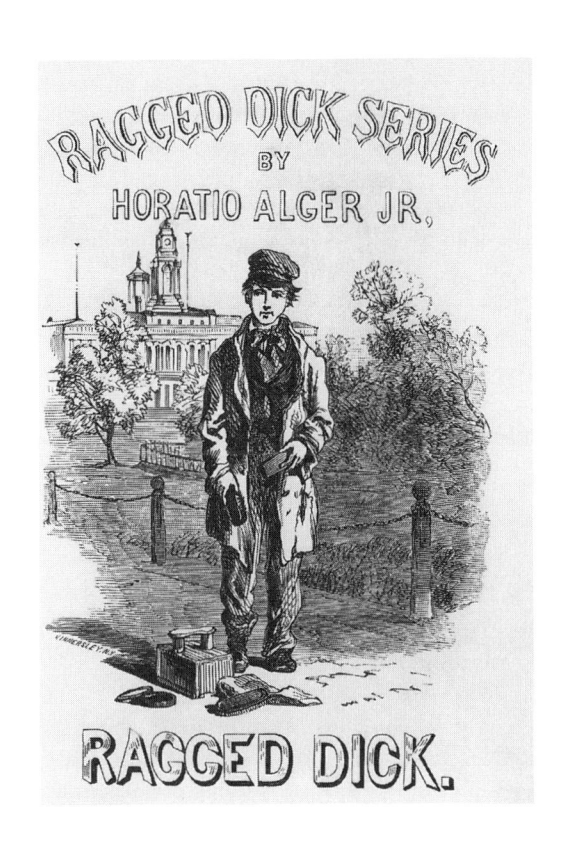

Cover of an early edition of *Ragged Dick*.

those women who embraced a domestic existence. Women were expected to limit themselves to the private sphere of family life, where their reputedly high moral character could be separated from the rougher world of business.

One reference in *Ragged Dick*—to Alexander T. Stewart's department store—alludes to an aspect of women's urban existence that became increasingly evident in the nineteenth century: the emergence of the department store. The burgeoning availability of goods helped create this innovation in selling. Whereas most urban stores in the 1850s were specialty shops (like the one in which Dick's friend Harry Fosdick finds work), department stores began to offer a wide variety of goods. Their larger size and diversity led them to establish fixed prices, a practice that differed from smaller stores, where customers often bargained over price. Department stores also tried to create a pleasant environment in which customers felt free to adopt a more leisurely approach to shopping. Located in the center of the city, the stores became a destination for middle-class women. Stewart's New York store was one of the earliest and largest in the nation.

Popular entertainment. Differences between middle- and working-class life also appeared in the types of entertainment each class supported. The middle class supported efforts to make urban life more refined. They were key supporters, for example, of efforts to establish public parks in which people would experience nature in an aesthetically pleasing design. Working-class entertainment, by contrast, centered around saloons and the theater. In the early 1800s, staged entertainment appealed to all classes, but as the century progressed, music and theater began to separate into genteel "highbrow" and popular "lowbrow" forms.

As Ragged Dick's activities reveal, the city offered both types of entertainment. The Bowery is the site of Dick's inexpensive nightly entertainment during his life as a boot-black. There he is able to enjoy a melodrama at the Old Bowery Theatre, followed by a feast of oyster stew or a bit of smoking and gambling.

The trees and meadows of Central Park, which was under construction at the time, would soon provide New Yorkers with more "wholesome" relaxation options. Prior to the construction of Central Park, New York had small parks that served their immediate area. Central Park was a bolder vision: five times as large as all other city parks combined, it would be easily accessible to all. One of its two designers, Frederick Law Olmsted, believed the shared experience it would provide New Yorkers would help create a sense of community among them. Construction began in the late 1850s and the first attraction, a skating rink, opened in the winter of 1858-59. By 1863 the park was completed.

The Novel in Focus

The plot. Ragged Dick, as the novel's hero is initially called, is a fourteen-year-old orphan who works as a boot-black, polishing customers' boots on the sidewalks of the city's avenues. The plot advances, over a period of about ten months, through three stages in Dick's life. The first describes life as a boot-black and how Dick is encouraged to leave it behind. The second part of the novel details the use he makes of this advice, while the third tells of his successful search for a new job. The novel does not focus on Ragged Dick's character, which changes very little; it concentrates instead on the outward signs of his progress. By the novel's end, he has completed a transition from life as an illiterate boot-black to that of an educated accountant's clerk, boosted by his own efforts and the support of a circle of friends and acquaintances.

Dick's life as a boot-black is characterized by an easy-going, live-for-today attitude. By using his wits, he earns enough to rent a room, but he prefers instead to pass his evenings in the Bowery, where he spends his extra money on good times. His only complaint is the discomfort of sleeping outside in bad weather; otherwise he feels that little is lacking from his life.

An appealing character, Ragged Dick is honest, humorous, alert, energetic, capable, and generous. He lives as he does because no one has ever suggested that he do otherwise. This changes when Dick meets Frank Whitney, a boy slightly younger than he. Frank stops in New York on his way to boarding school, and Ragged Dick offers to show him the city. Frank agrees but persuades Dick to first clean up and change his ragged clothes for a suit that Frank gives him.

The following chapters describe their tour of New York. Ragged Dick shows Frank the prosperous new urban life of the city. But he also points out the shady side of urban life, like the scams that city people pull on newcomers from the countryside. Highlighted in these chapters is Dick's honesty, a marked contrast from the con men around him.

The day proves unusual for Dick in several ways. He finds that he is treated well by others because he looks "respectable," and is swayed by his companion's views of education. Committed to preparing himself for adult life, Frank regards education as the key to his future success. He urges Dick to apply himself in the same way—that is, to change himself from a working-class to middle-class person. Dick is appreciative of Frank's comments, for his new friend is the first person ever to encourage him in this way. There is one obstacle to making this change, however: entry-level wages in a middle-class profession are too low to live on. Without some savings or other support, the transition from worker to middle-class employee is out of reach.

The second part of the novel shows how Dick puts Frank's advice to use. As the young boot-black and Frank part, Frank's father gives Dick five dollars, remarking that Dick can repay the loan by helping someone less fortunate someday. Dick decides to rent a room and open a savings account. Having made these decisions, he has two meetings that further fix him on his new path. An affluent businessman, Mr. Greyson, whose shoes he shines, invites Dick to attend his Sunday School class. Later that day, Dick treats a fellow boot-black, Harry Fosdick, to dinner. Fosdick is an educated boy who is new to the streets, having been recently orphaned. Dick proposes that Fosdick teach him to read and write in return for sharing his room. In a few weeks, Dick helps Fosdick get a job, using his own savings to buy Fosdick a respectable suit. Fosdick applies to many jobs. Finally, with the timely help of Mr. Greyson, who provides him with a desperately needed reference, the boy secures a position as a shop clerk.

The novel then skips nine months ahead. Dick has learned to read and write; he continues to save money, living frugally with Fosdick. The final episode of the novel focuses on Dick's decision to find a new job. He has enough education and has learned to behave respectably (by, for example, controlling his use of slang in conversation). He joins Fosdick on an afternoon's errand that takes them on the Brooklyn Ferry. When a young boy falls overboard, Dick leaps to his rescue. After an interview the following day in which Dick refers to himself for the first time as "Richard," the boy's father offers him a job as a clerk in his accounting firm—at more than triple the usual starting salary. Shortly thereafter, Dick finds that his ragged old suit has been stolen. He decides to keep his boot-black equipment to remind himself of his humble beginnings.

Alger's messengers. Alger uses the characters in *Ragged Dick* to illustrate the qualities and circumstances that he believes are necessary for success. He emphasizes Dick's honesty and *pluck,* the energy and alertness that win him opportunities to get ahead. By contrast, two other boot-blacks, Johnny Nolan and Micky Maguire, lack these qualities and are therefore less successful. Nolan is an honest but lazy boy: he lacks the necessary energy to work his way up the economic ladder; Maguire is energetic enough but dishonest.

The novel's middle-class boys do not display the range of personalities that the lower-class boys do. Rather, they come to Ragged Dick's aid. Frank Whitney introduces Dick to a new attitude toward life. Harry Fosdick, a boy who has suffered downward mobility that Dick helps reverse, has the education to help Dick move up. These boys illustrate another of Alger's messages: those more fortunate should help those who are less fortunate. Adults, in their brief appearances, also contribute to Ragged Dick's ascension in society; Mr. Whitney's financial gift starts Dick on his way, while a nameless policeman points out a prosperous bookstore owner who began life as a newsboy.

The moral. Although *Ragged Dick* mixes humor and drama with moral instruction, its focus is always on showing its readers how to get ahead in life. Alger had been a teacher and minister, and these experiences carry over into his writing. He infuses his plot with the personal belief that "success" requires not only self-discipline but also the timely intervention of others. The individualism that Alger advocates is generous, not coldhearted. Dick benefits from the aid of others, and he, in turn, uses his savings to assist those in need, at one point helping a friend's family pay their rent.

In keeping with the work ethic, Alger points to all labor as valuable. Any job, even boot-blacking, offers the dignity of labor, the chance to prove oneself an honest man. It bears repeating that Dick's journey to prove himself and achieve success is not one of the "rags-to-riches" stories with which Alger is so often associated. Instead, it is the rise to a respected middle-class position that matters in the novel.

Sources. *Ragged Dick* mentions actual sites in New York, such as the Bowery, Central Park, and the Newsboys' Lodging House. Researching his subject, the author himself spent time with boys on the street and at the Newsboys' Lodging House. He often named his fictional characters after people in his own life. Johnny Nolan was the name of a street boy Alger knew, and the fictional Micky Maguire can be traced back to a real street tough named Paddy Shea. Details in the plot hark back to real-life models as well. In fact, the Newsboys' Lodging House improvised a savings plan for its residents—a table that held over a hundred individually assigned boxes with slits at the top, into which the boys could drop their extra earnings. Ragged Dick's "rise" in the novel begins with the opening of a savings account that brings to mind these makeshift banks.

Events in History at the Time the Novel Was Written

Reception. Released first in twelve installments in a magazine, *Ragged Dick* became Alger's best-selling book. The *Providence Evening Press* praised the book as charming, while the *Boston Transcript* applauded Alger for exposing the struggling nobility of street boys. Some liked the liveliness with which Alger delivered his message; others thought the message naive. Hardly anyone believed Alger's books had literary merit. Later, in the 1870s and 1880s, a movement to remove Alger's books from public libraries developed. The movement rested on growing concern over the sensationalism of dime novels and other cheap forms of children's writings.

Dime novels. Industrialization contributed to the development of a new form of entertainment—the dime novel, so called because a copy cost 10¢. Beginning in the 1840s, innovations in printing had made it possible to print materials more quickly and inexpensively. Subsequent lower prices helped expand the market for books and magazines that appealed to the general public. The impact spread into children's literature, the market for which Alger wrote. Before the advent of lower prices, the market had been filled by books that aimed to guide children in the development of proper social attitudes. The plots of these works unfolded in family settings, with parents serving as the source of lessons and instruction. The dilemmas that children faced were the ordinary ones of daily life.

In contrast, dime novels usually featured romance, historical incidents, and violent action. Dime novels for children told tales that were concerned with adventure (such as boy-heroes living on their own) rather than moral edification. Dime novels first became popular around 1860, a few years before *Ragged Dick* appeared, and continued to enjoy a widespread readership until about 1895.

Horatio Alger's combination of moral messages and dramatic events actually places him between the earlier and later types of young people's literature. As a series of lessons on how to succeed in the working world, *Ragged Dick* remains tied to the earlier literature. Yet its characters live independently of adults, and its incidents often form a humorous mix of adventure and travelogue. Like the dime novels of the period, Alger's tales celebrate individualism.

Gilded Age. Between 1865 and 1901 the United States underwent a transformation from a country of small isolated communities into a vast industrial network, its regions linked by transportation and communication advances. Railways expanded from 35,000 miles of track in 1865 to a whopping 53,000 miles in 1870. In 1867, the year *Ragged Dick* was published, George Pullman founded the Pullman Palace Car Company, introducing a luxury dining and sleeping car for train travelers. Pullman's innovation reflected a focus on opulence during an era that became known as the Gilded Age, a period known for its spectacular splendor and the promise of affluence. The extreme poverty of the era received less attention, and the desperate condition of the masses was often overshadowed by the emphasis on luxuriant living.

Several American businessmen managed to accumulate tremendous wealth during this period. John D. Rockefeller and Andrew Carnegie are two of the best-known examples. The son of a peddler, Rockefeller rose to dominate the oil industry. Carnegie, the son of Scottish immigrants, climbed from factory worker to factory owner. These two were exceptions, though, for most of the nation's wealthiest citizens inherited their riches and the network of opportunity that such holdings provided. Still, they generally worked hard to improve their positions. Elsewhere, more moderately successful men moved up from the lower to the middle class in sufficient numbers to justify the hopes that Alger must have raised in his young readers. In fact, these hopes were not at all far-fetched, since Alger's hero strives not for "riches" but for a "respectable" steady job.

Survival of the fittest. Social mobility, people's movement from one economic class into another, usually meant upward mobility. Yet downward mobility, of which there are several examples in *Ragged Dick*, was also possible. Many people explained this reality by referring to a theory called "survival of the fittest."

In 1864 a book by Herbert Spencer, who coined the phrase "survival of the fittest," appeared in New York. The book, *Social Statics*, maintained that the pressure to survive had a positive effect on the human race. Proponents of the theory argued that it led to social progress, for those with intelligence, self-control, and skill were more likely to survive (and thrive), while those without such qualities were eliminated. The phrase, adopted by the scientist Charles Darwin, spread through society and confirmed the laissez-faire attitude of government to the poor. Reinforcing this attitude were books such as those by Horatio Alger, which preached about self-improvement through hard work.

There were 942,292 people in New York in 1870; certainly not all of them would succeed. While Alger's books suggest that those with sterling characters would have the best chance, *Ragged Dick* also shows an awareness that unethical men sometimes succeed in politics. The street-tough Micky Maguire is described as a fine prospect for the political profession. If he were fifteen years older, says the novel, he would have "been prominent at ward meetings, and a terror to respectable voters on election day" (*Ragged Dick*, p. 123). The allusion here is to groups like the Tweed Ring, a small group of men led by William Tweed, who controlled politics in New York from 1866 to 1871. For years the ring embezzled millions of dollars earmarked for the building of a new city courthouse. The *New York Times* finally exposed the theft in 1870, and a year later Boss Tweed and his ring were defeated in city and state elections.

For More Information

Alger, Horatio. *Ragged Dick and Mark, the Match Boy*. New York: Crowell-Collier, 1962.

Bender, Thomas. *New York Intellect: A History of Intellectual Life in New York, from 1750 to the Beginnings of Our Own Time*. Baltimore: Johns Hopkins University Press, 1987.

Cashmand, Sean Dennis. *America in the Gilded Age: From the Death of Lincoln to the Rise of Theodore Roosevelt*. New York: New York University Press, 1984.

Hemstreet, Charles. *Nooks and Corners of Old New York*. New York: Charles Scribner's Sons, 1899.

Scharnhorst, Gary, with Jack Bales. *The Lost Life of Horatio Alger, Jr.* Bloomington: Indiana University Press, 1985.

The Red Badge of Courage

by
Stephen Crane

Born six years after the close of the Civil War, Stephen Crane was fascinated by the subject and read all materials he could find on the conflict. He found, however, that the accounts of battle were rather superficial; based solely on action, they lacked feeling. As a writer keenly attuned to human experience and emotions, Crane wanted to explore the soldiers' emotions during battle. He created *The Red Badge of Courage* to expose the human side of warfare. Written when Crane was twenty-three, the novel is a realistic account of a young man's struggle to come to terms with the brutality of war and his own fear of death and cowardice, as contrasted with romantic notions of glory through battle. Published just before the nation began the Spanish-American War, *The Red Badge of Courage* served as testimony to the horrors of battle on any front.

Events in History at the Time the Novel Takes Place

Civil War. The Civil War began in April 1861 and lasted through May 1865. The conflict between the Northern and Southern sections of the United States arose in 1860 when seven Southern states seceded from the Union to form the Confederate States of America. While the North fought to preserve the Union, the South fought for independence. Though often romanticized, the war was one of the bloodiest and most divisive events in U.S. history. The conflict claimed the lives of more than half a million soldiers, wounded four hundred thousand, and cost $20 billion.

> **THE LITERARY WORK**
> A novel set on the East Coast of the United States, probably in 1863; published in 1895.
>
> **SYNOPSIS**
> A naive young man who joins the Union army during the Civil War confronts not only the Confederates but also his own fears and romantic notions of heroism. In battle, he faces the grim reality of warfare and gains self-knowledge.

The Civil War raged for four years, with little movement toward victory on one side or the other for the first two years. Though the Northern or Union army outmanned the Confederate army nearly three to one (2.2 million Union troops vs. 800,000 Confederate troops), it lacked strong leadership and a cohesive battle plan. The Confederates, on the other hand, had the gifted General Robert E. Lee at the helm and the strength of conviction on their side. Southerners believed firmly in their right to secede and—much like the colonists of the American Revolution—fought for their right to independent rule.

Before the issuance of the Emancipation Proclamation in January 1863, the North had little moral ground or rationale to bolster their effort except for preservation of the Union. For this and other reasons, patriotism in the North waned after the onset of battle. This aspect of the war is illustrated in *The Red Badge of Courage* in Crane's account of discontented Union soldiers who lack confidence in their leaders. The novel depicts the Union regiments in constant disarray, with troops making little or no military gains despite the ever growing body count.

After President Abraham Lincoln issued the Emancipation Proclamation, which outlawed slavery in all areas in rebellion against the Union, there was an abrupt shift in the war and an increase in momentum for the Union army. The North began to make significant gains on the battlefield, and public support for its war effort sharply increased. Morale lifted among the Northerners, who could view themselves as champions of abolition and freedom fighters.

Poor drafted. President Lincoln instituted the first military draft in U.S. history during the Civil War. First passed in 1862, the law as rewritten in 1863 allowed men to buy their way out of service by paying $300 or hiring replacement soldiers. The inclusion of this loophole for wealthier citizens meant that the Union army was comprised primarily of the poor and lower classes. Crane makes note of this in the novel, describing a dead soldier obviously of humble origins:

> Once the line encountered the body of a dead soldier. He lay upon his back staring at the sky. He was dressed in an awkward suit of yellowish brown. The youth could see that the soles of his shoes had been worn to the thinness of writing paper, and from a great rent in one the dead foot projected piteously. It was as if fate betrayed the soldier. In death it exposed to his enemies that poverty which in life he had perhaps concealed from his friends.
> (Crane, *Red Badge of Courage*, p. 134)

Battle of Chancellorsville. Henry Fleming, the main character in *The Red Badge of Courage*, also appears in Crane's short story "The Veteran," a work that identifies the battle in which Fleming fought in the novel. As one scholar noted, "the name of the battle in which Henry Fleming achieved his manhood is never given in *The Red Badge of Courage*. Scholars have not agreed that the battle even ought to have a name.... Yet an examination of the evidence leads to the conclusion that the battle does have a name—Chancellorsville" (Hungerford, p. 520).

The Battle of Chancellorsville pitted 130,000 Union soldiers under General Joseph Hooker against 60,000 Confederates under General Robert E. Lee. It erupted on May 1, 1863, in Virginia, a state that had seceded, and eventually resulted in a resounding loss for the Union troops despite their superior numbers.

Strategic decisions proved to be a pivotal factor in the battle's outcome. On the Union side, Hooker crossed the Rappahannock River and advanced to attack the Confederate forces from behind Chancellorsville. Lee and another Confederate general, T. J. "Stonewall" Jackson, meanwhile split their troops. Surprising Hooker, Jackson's forces attacked the extreme right of the Union forces, far from the ongoing fighting. The Union soldiers panicked, and many fled in terrified mayhem. This opened the way for an attack on the rear of the Union army. A small contingent of Union cavalrymen saved the day, however, and prevented a rout. The cavalry force held off Jackson until the Union side could drag over some artillery and lay down a blast of cannonfire.

THE "GLORY OF WAR" MYTH

Posters and newspaper propaganda touting the glory of war inspired hundreds of thousands of young men to join the Union army. Exaggerated accounts of victories and pictures of dashing men in bright uniforms convinced many that war was honorable and would make men—even heroes—out of ordinary young boys. In the novel, Henry Fleming, Crane's main character, is lured by these inducements and overwhelmed by romantic notions of the glory of battle—until he experiences the brutal reality of armed conflict for himself.

The Union cavalry charge took place around 6:30 p.m. on May 2, and while it slowed the momentum of the Confederate army, it did not change the outcome. The Union forces were forced to withdraw north of the river and lost the battle. The Union casualties in the Battle of Chancellorsville included 1,606 killed and 9,762 wounded. Nearly six thousand others were missing, but it is uncertain how many of those may have deserted.

Union troubles at the top. Inept leadership contributed heavily to the losses on the Union side. A string of Union generals, including George McClellan, Ambrose Burnside, Joseph Hooker, and George Gordon Meade, were fired by President Lincoln after suffering huge losses and failing to pursue Lee's Confederate forces when opportunities arose. The war dragged on in part because of the Union forces' inability to settle on a cohesive

Red Badge of Courage

Title page of the first edition of *The Red Badge of Courage*.

battle plan. Finally, though, President Lincoln and General Ulysses S. Grant devised a plan of all-out assault in 1864. Even with the strategy in place, however, casualties mounted, and from an infantryman's perspective, it must have been difficult to see the sense of the Union's military plan. The assault on all fronts was chaotic, and as Crane details, "the men dropped here and there like bundles" (*Red Badge of Courage,* p. 145). There were too few supplies for the Union army and regiments had a difficult time communicating with each other. Messages were carried by horseback, which meant long delays between battle reports. These delays led to further chaos, as generals could not accurately gauge victories or defeats in a timely fashion, nor could they send in reinforcements or order retreats as needed. As time passed, however, the Union army became a more cohesive body. It emerged victorious in 1865 when the Confederates surrendered at Appomattox.

The Novel in Focus

The plot. As the novel opens, Henry Fleming, a young farm boy who has enlisted in the Union army against his mother's wishes, awaits his first battle. Henry, a naive young man, is filled with romantic notions of the glory of warfare, but he is also a little terror-stricken.

The rumors of battle reverberate throughout the camp in which Henry waits, as do overinflated stories of bravery, victory, cowardice, and defeat. When armed conflict becomes imminent, Henry questions whether he will be able to perform in battle. He grapples with his conscience, wondering if he can be courageous and heroic, or if he will be a coward and flee. He has the same questions about his fellow soldiers—many of whom he has known since boyhood. Furthermore, he questions the ability of the generals, who are virtually in control of his destiny:

> In his great anxiety his heart was continually clamoring at what he considered the intolerable slowness of the generals. They seemed content to perch tranquilly on the river bank, and leave him bowed down by the weight of a great problem.
> (*The Red Badge of Courage,* p. 125)

As Fleming wavers between moods of confidence and self-doubt, he both wants the battle to ensue and hopes it will never happen.

Finally, the battle commences and Henry becomes "not a man but a member" (*Red Badge of Courage,* p. 143). He loses himself in battle and is at once transformed into "a driven beast" as he fights not individuals but "battle phantoms" (*Red Badge of Courage,* p. 144). As the conflict increases in intensity, he feels the full impact of the atmosphere of war, its horrific smells and scenes of death and destruction. He survives the initial battle, but just as he begins to feel relieved at his survival, the fighting begins anew, which "to the youth ... was an onslaught of redoubtable dragons" (*Red Badge of Courage,* p. 149). Fear and panic consume him, and as the regiment is attacked he runs into the woods and away from the artillery fire.

Fleming tries to find a rationale for his actions, searching for a way to define himself as a brave soldier who was smart enough to preserve himself rather than a coward who fled the scene of battle and abandoned his fellow men. Unable to resolve this inner conflict, he flees further into the forest and at his first opportunity falls into line with a retreating group of wounded soldiers. As the soldiers march he is questioned by one who asks innocently where he has been wounded. An overwhelming wave of guilt passes over Fleming and he extricates himself from the scene. As he leaves, he encounters a member of his regiment who has been mortally wounded. The wounded man dies before Fleming's eyes, deepening his sense of guilt as he retreats even further into the woods. As he continues his miserable flight, he comes to feel that he cannot go back, and begins to wonder what will become of him.

Fleming settles into a hiding place where he watches the battle around him. As he watches other Union soldiers who had previously been in flight turn to join the battle, Fleming contemplates whether they are heroes or fools. He convinces himself that those Union soldiers who turn to engage the enemy are fools, and that the inept generals are leading his regiment to certain death. As he watches from his position of safety, though, he realizes that his comrades are indeed winning the battle and that he is no longer able to justify leaving the battle himself.

By chance Fleming stumbles into a line of men rapidly fleeing through the woods. He grasps at one to ascertain the cause of their deployment and succeeds in irritating the soldier beyond measure. The upset soldier butts Fleming in the head with his rifle and sends him crashing to the ground. The blow, though, turns out to be a great stroke of luck for Fleming, for the injury makes it appear as if he has been injured in battle. He thus rejoins his regiment without reproach.

Finding his regiment camped in the woods, Henry is warmly greeted by fellow soldiers who had given him up for dead. He tells them he has been hit and, after examining him, they determine he has been shot in the head. They bandage him and give him a place to sleep, treating him as a hero. At first, Henry feels guilty and is certain that others will discover his lie. As time passes, though, his tale continues to be accepted. The respect accorded him as one who is a brave soldier continues as well, and Fleming begins to believe his story himself.

The regiment regroups and is sent, once again, into battle. This time, Fleming stands and fights with his comrades, distinguishing himself as one of the bravest of all. He continues to charge when he is called back, and his commanders openly wish all their men fought like him, like "wild cats" (Red Badge of Courage, p. 199).

Henry is next sent into a final skirmish, in which his regiment is to lead a charge into enemy lines. By chance he overhears the generals denigrating his division, calling them nothing more than "mule drivers" to be sacrificed at the front (Red Badge of Courage, p. 202). Henry realizes how insignificant his life is to the army, and feelings of hatred for his superiors well up in him. The generals' low regard also spurs him to prove his worth, however, and he valiantly stands and fights when his regiment charges. He and his friend Wilson, who are lauded as heroes following their strong performance in battle, are subsequently recommended for promotion.

Stephen Crane

After the battle, Fleming soon forgets his hatred for the generals and the horrible nature of combat. In hindsight, the gruesome fighting becomes glorious and heinous deeds are transformed into valiant efforts. But gradually, as Henry distances himself from the fighting, "his eyes seemed to open to some new ways. He found that he could look back upon the brass and bombast of his earlier gospels and see them truly. He was gleeful when he discovered that he despised them" (Red Badge of Courage, p. 230). As he recalls the total picture of his war experience, from desertion to facing the danger of the front lines, from flight to fight, he truly becomes a man. He realizes that events—particularly in war—can be shaded any color and that, though he was ultimately successful as a soldier, the war experience is an abominable one. He no longer wishes to be any kind of soldier; instead he seeks "an existence of soft and eternal peace" (Red Badge of Courage, p. 231).

How typical was Henry Fleming? Early in the novel, Fleming's fear leads him to consider deserting from the army. If he had in fact become a deserter, he would have had a great deal of company. Desertion was a huge problem for much of the Civil War. Fear, disenchantment, and discouragement at the chaos and lack of leadership were all factors in the high desertion rates, but other reasons included the lack of arms and clothing (especially shoes), the empty months of waiting for pay that never came, and the seemingly endless marching through knee-deep mud. Still another contributor to the desertion rate was the attraction of bounties. Volunteers were offered a bounty—a financial reward—if they enlisted. This led some to join an outfit, collect the bounty, then desert and reenlist in another state under an assumed name.

By the time Hooker took command of the Union forces on January 26, 1863, the number of deserters had mounted to several hundred a day. An average of more than 4,600 soldiers a month deserted from the Union's Army of the Potomac in 1863. Slipping to the rear and from the field during battle was a common trick, and one that Fleming almost employs in the novel.

The beginning of 1863 saw sharper measures taken against deserters. General Hooker instituted strict rules about taking leaves and arresting stragglers. Those who joined the enemy army or persisted in attempting to desert would be shot or hung. The executions mounted after Chancellorsville, in the winter of 1863-64. Earlier penalties had been less severe. If Fleming had been found guilty of desertion, possible punishments would have included being tied up during marches or hard labor on forts or in trenches. Certainly he would have lost at least six months' pay.

Sources. Crane based his realistic tale on accounts of the Civil War that he read in magazines and books, especially texts about Civil War leaders. The author relied on two historical sources in particular. He specifically drew on *Corporal Si Klegg and His Pard*, a book by Colonel W. F. Hinman published in 1887. His other main source, *Battles and Leaders of the Civil War* (1887) was a collection written by Civil War veterans, who at the request of *Century Magazine* recorded their memories of major battles. Crane also drew on his own feelings. A twenty-three-year-old man when he wrote the novel, he was of draft age and could relate to how a young man might greet the war experience.

Events in History at the Time the Novel Was Written

The temper of the times. In the eyes of many, the 1890s was a pivotal decade in American history. Prior to that time, the United States had been a rural country full of individual spirit. The 1890s saw the growth of an urban and industrial society that displaced the older, largely agrarian one. At the same time, the country's western frontier was becoming settled and offered fewer opportunities to those hoping to find wealth and adventure. People began to eye territory outside United States borders.

Domestic unrest was visible during the decade as well. Strikes such as the 1892 Homestead Steel strike and the 1894 Pullman railroad strike erupted, while a financial depression also took place between 1892 and 1894. Meanwhile, the philosophy of social Darwinism replaced some of the idealistic notions that had formerly been central to the American identity. According to the social Darwinist philosophy, poverty was an inevitable byproduct of the struggle for existence, and attempts to wipe it out were doomed to failure. A new hopelessness surfaced. Coupled with it were attempts to glamorize the past.

Literature of the decade glorified heroism and the courage of soldiers on both sides of the Civil War. It was in this vein that the editors of *Century Magazine* had designed *Battles and Leaders of the Civil War*, one of Crane's primary sources in writing *The Red Badge of Courage*. The editors hoped to foster mutual respect for both armies, focusing on the bonds forged by soldiers in the field rather than the horrors they endured.

Crane's novel challenged these popular tales, which often featured heroes on the battlefield rewarded by the love of an awed heroine at home. In *The Red Badge of Courage*, Henry Fleming has similar romantic notions of warfare, but they are dispelled when he encounters the grim reality of the battlefield. Crane believed fiction should present a slice out of life, a goal he attempted to achieve in his novel. He was apparently successful in this regard, for many readers had a difficult time believing he had not yet experienced war firsthand.

Crane attempted to capture the reality of war in a certain way, employing a methodology similar to the artists of his era who produced impressionistic paintings: to record the way an experience affects the senses before the mind intervenes to analyze it. At least one reviewer argues that in doing so, Crane had no intention of writing an antiwar novel:

> It is difficult to see *Red Badge*, written in a militaristic decade like the 1890s as upholding antiwar sentiments.... Deeply located in its own historical period, [the text] ... points not

to antiwar feelings but to the martial spirit of its times.... [It simply] makes no attempt to hide the carnage that is war.... In *Red Badge* the romantic, old-fashioned approach to war and violence which dominated popular literature is contrasted with an impressionistic, spectacular descriptive mode

(Mariani, p. 142-43)

It has been further suggested that Crane used this same style of describing battles in his later assignments as a war correspondent for American newspapers, first in Greece during the Greco-Turkish War in 1897, then in Cuba during the Spanish-American War a year later. He apparently secured his correspondent positions specifically because of his ability to create vivid fictional descriptions of battles. This provides further support for the claim that readers of his day did not regard his literary output as antiwar in tone.

New York City street life. Crane spent much of his early adult life living among the urban poor and "fringe element" of New York City. He frequently kept company with prostitutes and street people, even disguising himself as a transient in order to learn how they lived and were treated by society. He was one of the first "literary bohemians," so-called because he cavorted with and wrote about these outcast members of society (Chase in Crane, p. xi). In this way he was ahead of his time, although he was often criticized for his choice of subject matter. Many did not consider the lower classes to be a fitting topic for literary endeavors. Crane was able to use his city experiences in the novel by drawing on the grim parallels between poverty-stricken urban streets and bloody war zones. In the novel, he refers to the approaching army as a train and speaks of soldiers as mobs, linking the urban battlefield to the military one. His observations of poor residents in the city also helped him to imagine the mindset of soldiers; both the urban poor and the men in battle faced seemingly insurmountable odds as they attempted to survive.

The "progress" of civilization. As the nineteenth century drew to a close, it was assumed that humankind was steadily progressing. Advancements in technology, rapid industrialization, and improved education made some people feel that humans—and in particular Americans—had evolved beyond the destruction and ignorance that had taken place in the past. Yet wars continued to be fought and, with the improvement of weapons technology, became bloodier and more deadly. Crane points out in his novel that though education and religion were supposed to have "civilized"

men and "checked" their passions, war continued to rage, and violence had only increased (*Red Badge of Courage*, p. 120). His words proved visionary when the United States engaged in its first international conflict, the Spanish-American War, in 1898. Working in Cuba for Joseph Pulitzer's *New York World* and later for the Hearst newspapers, Crane covered the conflict as a full-fledged war correspondent. His real-life experience confirmed the disenchantment captured in his earlier *The Red Badge of Courage*.

THE SONG OF RAPPAHANNOCK

One of the best-selling novels during the Spanish-American War was *The Song of Rappahannock*, a patriotic story that challenged *The Red Badge of Courage*, declaring that recruits did not behave like the unsteady Henry Fleming.

Reviews. *The Red Badge of Courage* was an overwhelming success when it was published. It was the first war novel of its kind, a work in which the psychology rather than just the physical activity of war was examined. Reviewers hailed the novel as a great work, and the only major criticisms leveled against the novel were that it at times lacked unity and that it featured an ending that was overly moralistic. The novel made Crane famous and led to a series of related war stories, including a follow-up short story, "The Veteran" (1896), which detailed the later life and death of Henry Fleming.

For More Information

Benfey, Christopher. *The Double Life of Stephen Crane: A Biography*. New York: Alfred A. Knopf, 1992.

Cady, Edwin. *Stephen Crane*. New York: Twayne, 1962.

Crane, Stephen. *The Red Badge of Courage*. Edited by Richard Chase. Boston: Houghton Mifflin, 1960.

Hungerford, Harold R. "'That Was at Chancellorsville': The Factual Framework of *The Red Badge of Courage*." *American Literature* 34 (January 1963): 520-31.

Lonn, Ella. *Desertion during the Civil War*. New York: Century, 1928.

Mariani, Giorgio. *Spectacular Narratives: Representations of Class and War in Stephen Crane and the American 1890s*. New York: Peter Lang, 1992.

Wheeler, Richard. *Voices of the Civil War*. New York: Thomas Crowell, 1976.

"Self-Reliance"

by
Ralph Waldo Emerson

Ralph Waldo Emerson (1803-1882) was one of the most influential thinkers in nineteenth-century America. Like his father, he became a Unitarian minister in Boston, but he later left the church, whose doctrines he could not embrace fully. He traveled briefly in Europe, and after returning became a lecturer, an essayist, a poet, and a leader of the transcendentalist school of thought in America. His philosophy embraced individuality, optimism, and a belief in the presence of God in all things and persons. He is best remembered for his essay "Self-Reliance" and other early works that champion these ideals.

Events in History at the Time of the Essay

The Jackson administration. Andrew Jackson's presidency (1829-1837) dominated America in the decade before Emerson wrote "Self-Reliance." Through the essay Emerson tried to help individuals renew themselves and throw off the burden of "dead" institutions. In many ways, the nation under Andrew Jackson was also trying to free itself from its past and re-establish its identity in the 1830s.

The United States had entered a period of redefinition in which it tried to prove its autonomy and national character to the world. To achieve these goals, Jackson built on several key developments that had strengthened American sovereignty earlier in the century. Treaties had provided for the acquisition of the Louisiana Territory

THE LITERARY WORK
An essay written in Concord, Massachusetts, synthesizing ideas from Emerson's journals and lectures of the 1830s; published in 1841.

SYNOPSIS
Emerson expresses his outrage at the reluctance of Americans to trust in themselves and take action based on a recognition of God in all creation.

from France (1803), the assurance of commercial independence and freedom from meddling by foreign powers (1814), and the acquisition of East Florida from Spain (1819). A few years later, in 1823, the Monroe Doctrine had declared the whole Western Hemisphere off limits to interference by European powers. These changes allowed the young republic to focus on domestic issues with renewed zeal. Emerson's essay, with its emphasis on looking inward for guidance, seems to be addressing both the growing nation and the individual.

The federal government encouraged settlement in its newly acquired territories, and the country expanded rapidly. In the first half of the century, fourteen new states were admitted to the Union, and in the 1820s alone, the total U.S. population increased by a third. Across the country, as well as in Congress, people seriously debated how much power the federal government should have over the states, given that each state seemed to have its own interests, problems, and history. Jackson's presidency itself represented a break with tradition, since Jackson's rural Southern background contrasted sharply with that of the elite New England politicians who had dominated the government until then.

Andrew Jackson was known as the "people's president," and he enjoyed most of his support among the common people in the South and West. Not surprisingly, he favored their interests and tried to expand their voting rights. For example, he advocated the abolition of property requirements and religious tests for eligibility to vote and hold public office. He also favored the South by claiming to be powerless to uphold federal orders that went against its economic interests. Jackson's style suited many Americans who longed for a new approach to government. Meanwhile, others struck out on their own to effect social change.

Unitarianism. Emerson resigned his position as a Unitarian minister in 1832 after only three years of service. He felt unable to administer the Lord's Supper in good conscience, since he was no longer sure the ritual was valid. Instead he devoted himself to a re-evaluation of Christian beliefs in America, often incurring the disapproval of his former fellows in the Unitarian church.

The Unitarian faith that shaped Emerson's youth and early adulthood was, to be sure, the most progressive form of Christianity in its day. Although the Unitarians still believed that the Bible revealed God's plan for humankind, they had come to reject the Puritan idea that people were inherently depraved. Also, contrary to almost all other Christian churches, they viewed Jesus Christ as the highest representative of mankind rather than as the son of God. In his sermons, Emerson struggled to put forward his own ideas while staying within the limits of Unitarian doctrine. Some of his subsequent essays, such as "Self-Reliance," echo his early sermons, as the following indicates:

> Nor on the other hand let it be thought that there is in this self-reliance anything of presumption, anything inconsistent with a spirit of dependence and piety toward God. In listening more intently to our own soul we are not becoming in the ordinary sense more selfish, but are departing farther from what is low and falling back upon truth and upon God. For the whole value of the soul depends on the fact that it contains a divine principle, that it is a house of God, and the voice of the eternal inhabitant may always be heard within it. —
> *From a sermon Emerson delivered four times,*

Ralph Waldo Emerson

beginning on 30 December 1830.
(Emerson in McGiffert, p. 110)

The Unitarian church in Boston attracted elites and members of the upper middle class, who were often reluctant to commit themselves openly to controversial causes such as abolition. Many were content to follow the path to salvation cleared by their forefathers, who had seen no need to abolish slavery. Some Unitarian businessmen had lucrative contracts with the South and chose to overlook the dire conditions under which slaves suffered. Other Unitarians—and religious groups in general—preferred moral suasion to political activism, arguing that legislation would address only the symptoms of the problems, not the causes. Lasting reform, they were convinced, could only come through a genuine change of heart. Emerson remained detached from the slave controversy in the 1830s and 1840s, preoccupied instead with promoting new ways of thinking. It was only later that events like the adoption of the Fugitive Slave Law in 1850 drove him into the camp of the radical abolitionists.

Religious revivals and the Age of Reform. A wave of religious revivals called the Second Great Awakening swept across New England from the

"Self-Reliance"

1790s through the 1830s. Fiery preachers tried to convert and save as many people as possible, since society showed signs of rejecting organized religion in the years after the American Revolution. Those who participated in the revivals often tried to practice and spread the faith by taking up a social cause.

As a result, the period between 1830 and 1860 was truly an age of reform in New England. Movements addressed a variety of social ills, such as slavery, drinking, war, inadequate rights for women, prostitution, and neglect of the deaf, blind, and insane. The reform impulse was strengthened by the ideas of European Romanticism, which emphasized the dignity and worth of every person and recognized feeling rather than rationality as the source of truth. In "Self-Reliance" too, Emerson encourages his readers to give their emotions primary consideration.

> **EMERSON SEEKS GREATER "DEPTH OF INTEREST" IN REFORM MEETINGS**
>
> As far as I notice what happens in philanthropic meetings and holy hurrahs there is very little depth of interest.... [A]n observer new to such scenes would say, Here was true fire; the assembly were all ready to be martyred, and the effect of such a spirit on the community would be irresistible; but they separate and go to the shop, to a dance, to bed, and an hour afterwards they care so little for the matter that on the slightest temptation each one would disclaim the meeting. "Yes, he went, but they were for carrying it too far," etc., etc.
> —26 April 1838.
>
> (Emerson, *Journals*, p. 431)

Some revivalists turned away from the emphasis on sin in traditional Calvinism, choosing instead to preach about the doctrine of free will. The notion that every person could choose to do good and be saved reinforced Emerson's idea that each person was close to God and capable of self-improvement. Emerson remained ambivalent about getting personally involved in reform causes, though he was occasionally persuaded to support one by writing a letter or delivering a speech. He preferred to spend his time in contemplation, although he did write and lecture in the late 1830s. His two major addresses were "The American Scholar" (1837), which has been described as America's intellectual declaration of independence from Europe, and "The Divinity School Address" (1838), which caused an uproar in religious circles. Listeners branded him as an infidel and atheist because he denied the special authority of Jesus Christ and spoke of the supreme authority of the spiritual intuition inside every individual.

Two issues attract Emerson's attention. In the late 1830s, Emerson was struck by the plight of the slaves and that of the Native Americans facing forcible removal to the West. He agreed to speak out in support of these two groups. Some Northerners considered slavery a morally corrupt institution but only showed concern for the welfare of slaves overseas in the Caribbean islands of Haiti and Barbados. Emerson voiced his disdain for the hypocrisy shown by people who restricted themselves to becoming sentimental at the plight of slaves "a thousand miles off" (Emerson, "Self-Reliance," p. 51).

Meanwhile, President Jackson was leading the fight for an aggressive plan to relocate the entire Native American population to territory west of the Mississippi River. The Removal Act of 1830 became one of the first pieces of legislation passed under the Jackson administration, and the authorities moved quickly to enforce it. The affected tribes had no legal recourse against relocation since Indian testimony was not admissible in court. Occasionally, they received a little help from prominent Americans such as Emerson, who spoke out on their behalf.

Romanticism and transcendentalism. Through Emerson's contact with English poets such as Thomas Carlyle, European Romanticism found a direct avenue into America and into transcendentalist thought. Romanticism rejected what it considered to be the overemphasis of the earlier Enlightenment movement on science and factual knowledge. Instead, the Romantic movement recognized feeling and intuition as surer guides to the truth. Like the Romantics, the transcendentalists held that one should seek knowledge through introspection and a thoughtful examination of nature. The transcendentalists further believed that people were basically good and capable of bettering themselves. In their view, self-reliance was essential to social improvement.

Emerson served as the most powerful spokesman of the transcendental movement, defining its basic principles in his essay *Nature* (1836) and continuing to spread these ideals in his lectures and writings. An informal club met for the first time in 1836 to discuss what came to be called Transcendentalism, and Emerson later wrote, "I suppose all of them were surprised at this rumor of a school or sect, and certainly at the name of Transcendentalism, given nobody knows by whom, or when it was first applied" (Emerson in Swift, pp. 6-7). Other sources say the name started as a joke originated by some of the members. The movement reached its height in the years between 1830 and the 1850s, and it had an impact on American thought out of proportion to the small number of intellectuals who identified themselves with it. Emerson himself is usually credited with making popular to Americans the ideas of self-reliance and freedom of thought, which were basic to the movement.

The Essay in Focus

The contents. Although "Self-Reliance" is sometimes criticized for its loose style, the essay in fact follows a fairly straight course. Emerson encourages self-trust, reminding us of the need for nonconformists and the reasons why it is reprehensible to conform. He acknowledges the harsh consequences of a self-reliant approach to life and offers practical suggestions. At the same time, he broadens his argument by considering the historical and religious significance of his ideas.

Emerson introduces his essay with three quotations. The first ("Do not search outside yourself") is from the ancient satirist Persius, the second from the play *Honest Man's Fortune* by two dramatists of the English Renaissance, and the third from one of Emerson's own poems. By recalling the work of writers from other times and places, Emerson makes it clear that he values other sources. Ultimately, however, he looks into his own heart for answers and shares them with others.

Emerson first encourages the reader to trust and respect the self. One must begin, he says, by listening to one's own thoughts instead of passing them over automatically. The next essential steps are to speak those thoughts with conviction and translate them into action. Peace of mind, he warns, will elude the person who does not testify to the divine idea that he or she represents. Emerson suggests we look to infants, children, and adolescents for fresh examples of honesty and nonconformity. What would it be like, he wonders, if an adult could recapture these qualities of youth!

Society desperately needs nonconformists, Emerson assures us. Moreover, one's choices need not be explained to others, who have no right to tell one how to fit into society. Devotion to "dead" institutions, such as church societies or the dominant political parties, is a waste of time. If a man simply attaches himself to a group, Emerson has trouble defining who that person really is. Emerson maintains that adopting the opinions of even one group infects a person's ability to utter any truth at all.

The consequences of nonconformity provide Emerson with two reasons why people are afraid to embrace self-reliance. First, the world rejects a nonconformist. Emerson acknowledges that "when the unintelligent brute force that lies at the bottom of society is made to growl and mow," it is difficult to act as if society's disapproval does not matter to us ("Self-Reliance," p. 56). Second, we are terrified of contradicting ourselves because we do not want to disappoint others, who rely on our past record to figure out who we are. Emerson is not convinced: "Suppose you should contradict yourself; what then?" ("Self-Reliance," p. 57). Ultimately, he writes, you are who you are, and your actions (provided each is genuine) all have one thing in common: you.

"THE SOUL OF MAN...DOES ABHOR THIS BUSINESS"

At the prompting of friends, Emerson wrote a letter (a "shriek" of indignation, as he called it) to President Jackson's successor, Martin Van Buren, protesting the impending removal of the Cherokees: "Such a dereliction of all faith and virtue, such a denial of justice, and such a deafness to screams for mercy, were never heard of in times of peace, and in the dealing of a nation with its own allies and wards, since the earth was made." —*From Emerson's letter of protest to President Van Buren; sent 25 April 1838* (Emerson in Cooke, pp. 64-5).

The historical significance of these ideas captures Emerson's attention next. He assures us that we are as much at the center of things today as anyone ever was in the past. To be great, a person must commit himself fully to the age in which he finds himself. Those people who seize upon this fact never have time to accomplish their goals within a lifetime, but their actions are so compelling that others follow in their footsteps for centuries.

In examining the past, Emerson urges us not to feel intimidated by the accomplishments of others. Artifacts may be impressive, but they depend on our praise to make them celebrated. Heroes are put on pedestals, as though they were the only ones capable of virtuous deeds. The way we document leaders in our histories exaggerates their authority, and we lose sight of the fact that the actions of the commoner today are just as important.

Emerson then becomes more philosophical and abstract, examining the source of self-trust. Each of us has the wisdom of intuition, he says, and everything else we know is taught to us. In our calm hours, we can and do get in touch with this original knowledge common to all creation. An absolute respect is due to these involuntary perceptions, the things we and all people know to be indisputably true.

> **A CRITIC TAKES ISSUE WITH EMERSON'S "DIVINITY SCHOOL ADDRESS"**
>
> Why not be satisfied with the strong language of Jesus and John, and say that if [a man] love, God dwells *in* him, and he *in* God? or that he *partakes* of the divine nature, as Peter declares. Why go further, and seem to destroy the personality either of God or man by saying that he *is* God?—*The transcendental reformer James Freeman Clarke, in response to unorthodox religious ideas in Emerson's "Divinity School Address.*
>
> (Harris, p. 276)

As he explores the religious significance of self-reliance, Emerson claims that our intuition should even play a leading role in the way we relate to God. When God speaks, he communicates not one idea at a time, but rather all things at once. If our minds are open to this sort of communication and we hear him, our established notions fall away, as they should. Emerson stresses the potential for religious insight in his own time, claiming that to be a slave to the past is to miss the point. To exist with God, each of us must live fully in the present moment and listen for Him. But again, we are trapped: we dare not think that we ourselves hear the voice of God unless it sounds like the phrases familiar to us from the Bible.

The essay advises its readers to start on the road to nonconformity by achieving a state of spiritual isolation and calm. Even if the changes do not come all at once, people must at least begin to reorient their lives. Practically speaking, we must renounce our old ways, inform our friends and family of our commitment to truth, and be willing to part with our loved ones if they cannot make the same commitment. Again, Emerson knows that the task is difficult, that it demands something godlike in the person who takes it to heart. Instead, most of us cower before our fears of truth, failure, death, and each other. As a result, he explains, an entirely new outlook is needed in all areas of human activity. Religion, education, social interaction, and our pursuit of material goods must be re-evaluated from the perspective of self-reliance and respect for the divinity in each of us. Ultimately, according to Emerson, nothing will bring us peace but the triumph of such principles.

"God is here within." The religious implications of the ideas in "Self-Reliance" were much too radical for many New Englanders. Most religious groups believed God and his creation to have very little in common, and that if one were able to communicate with the other, it would be through a minister or the Bible. Emerson, however, was prepared to stir up controversy in his attempt to convince the reader that each person is directly linked to divinity, and as such should take himself or herself seriously. "God is here within," he declares ("Self-Reliance," p. 71). Emerson boldly asserts that "man is the word made flesh," which would have been recognized by most New Englanders as an echo of the biblical idea that God is the Word, and Christ is the Word made flesh ("Self-Reliance," p. 76). In short, Emerson sets the average person equal to Christ. According to Emerson, man represents the divine idea but is usually too afraid or too committed to institutional religion to truly do God's work.

Many of the religious principles in "Self-Reliance" had been set forth in the already mentioned "Divinity School Address" three years earlier. It, too, had offended many believers, particularly by instructing Harvard College's Divinity School students (who were about to graduate and become ministers) that it is more prudent to stay home and reflect on the Sabbath than to attend a lifeless church service. The chapel seated about a hundred persons, and the front pews were filled with Emerson's conservative Unitarian adversaries. One of them later savaged Emerson in a lengthy article, and many newspapers labeled him an infidel and an atheist. According to one source, Emerson even worried whether he could continue to supplement his income by lecturing. Despite the outcry, or perhaps because of it, Emerson reiterated many of these ideas in "Self-Reliance."

Emerson was well aware of the arguments against his liberal outlook on religion. He openly defied the opposition's compelling claim that the miracles described in the Bible proved that Christ, unlike the rest of us, had been sent by God. Emerson was convinced that God's message is undeniable not because of the "evidence" of the miracles, but rather because any careful listener can hear God's message whenever He speaks. As a result, each of us has direct access to divine truth. One radical implication of this philosophy is that someone in communion with God today could write an equally legitimate Bible. Another is that believers are thoroughly justified in bypassing organized religion. Conservative and mainstream Christians opposed these implications vehemently, however carefully Emerson had thought them out and in whatever terms he presented them.

Sources. "Self-Reliance" draws on the ideas set forth in Emerson's previous lectures and pamphlets, especially *Nature* (1836), "The American Scholar" (1837), and the "Divinity School Address" (1838). Emerson relied heavily on his journal when composing these early works, often quoting from it word for word.

In addition to the influence of Unitarianism on Emerson's cosmology, several schools of philosophy helped shape his understanding of the place of people in the universe. He relied on a book called *On Germany*, by Germaine de Staël, for an overview of intellectual activity in Europe. In the German philosopher Immanuel Kant, Emerson found a polar opposite to John Locke, an Englishman who insisted that all knowledge is gained through the five senses. Like Kant, Emerson believed that all men's knowledge was shaped by intuition, which "transcended" sensory experience. Such a belief, in turn, fueled Emerson's respect for the private insights each person could achieve in moments of calm. His decision not to place too much faith in the material world also harked back to Plato and Hindu beliefs as well. Both spoke of the illusory nature of the world. While a student at Harvard, Emerson studied the Hindu concept of an illusory world from which each person must break free in order to discover and trust the godliness of the inner self. His agreement with this concept is evident in "Self-Reliance."

Two movements in literature also had a profound impact on Emerson. His interest in European Romanticism was brought into sharper focus by a visit to his heroes William Wordsworth, Samuel Taylor Coleridge, and Thomas Carlyle, all leaders of the Romantic movement in England. He and Carlyle kept up a warm correspondence for many years. At the same time, the writings of scholars called the German "Higher Critics" supported Emerson's unorthodox approach to Christianity. Promoting a nontraditional interpretation of the Bible, these critics regarded the religious text as a purely historical document and refused to accept miracles as proof of Christ's divinity. By being open to their ideas, Emerson was able to nurture his belief that anyone could communicate with God directly.

Reception. "Self-Reliance" was one of the texts that made Emerson famous. The controversial essay had a significant impact in the author's own day, answering a spiritual need for many people in a time of change. Contained in his first full-length volume, *Essays*, the piece helped attract a circle of devoted New England readers, many of whom had heard Emerson speak in the 1830s. More and more admirers started to visit Emerson at his home in Concord, Massachusetts.

Supporters and detractors commented on Emerson's content as well as his style. Some attacked Emerson's unorthodox religious views and his idealism. As a general comment on Emerson's lectures, one critic had written in 1838 that their style "has been so different from the usual one, so completely Emersonian, as to confound and puzzle some, and disgust others" (Harris, p. 275). The observation probably held true for "Self-Reliance" in 1841 since even his supporter Carlyle acknowledged in a preface to the *Essays* that "the utterance is abrupt, fitful; the great idea not yet embodied struggles towards an embodiment. Yet," continues Carlyle, "everywhere there is the true heart of a man.... Sharp gleams of insight arrest us by their pure intellectuality" (Carlyle in Harris, p. 276).

Although readers debated whether Emerson was optimistic or simply naive, few doubted that he had written from the heart. After observing people's reactions to *Essays* for three years, Emerson's fellow writer Margaret Fuller attested to his sincerity: "You have his thought just as it found place in the life of his own soul. Thus, however near or relatively distant its approximation to absolute truth, its action on you cannot fail to be healthful" (Fuller in Harris, p. 277).

For More Information

Cooke, George Willis. *Ralph Waldo Emerson: His Life, Writings, and Philosophy*, 5th ed. Boston: James R. Osgood, 1882.

Emerson, Ralph Waldo. *Journals of Ralph Waldo Emerson*, Vol. 4: *Journals of Ralph Waldo Emerson, 1836-1838*. Edited by Edward Waldo Emerson and Waldo Emerson Forbes. Boston: Houghton Mifflin, 1910.

Emerson, Ralph Waldo. "Self Reliance." In *The Complete Works of Ralph Waldo Emerson*. Vol. 2: *Essays, First Series*. Boston: Houghton Mifflin, 1903.

Harris, Laurie Lanzen, ed. *Nineteenth-Century Literature Criticism*, Vol. 1. Detroit: Gale Research, 1981.

Jacobs, Donald M., ed. *Courage and Conscience: Black and White Abolitionists in Boston*. Bloomington: Indiana University Press, 1993.

McGiffert, Arthur Cushman, Jr. *Young Emerson Speaks: Unpublished Discourses on Many Subjects by Ralph Waldo Emerson*. Boston: Houghton Mifflin, 1938.

Swift, Lindsay. *Brook Farm: Its Members, Scholars, and Visitors*. New York: Corinth, 1961.

Shane

by
Jack Schaefer

Born in 1907 in Cleveland, Ohio, Jack Schaefer studied history as well as classical and American literature throughout his life. He was especially drawn to the history of the western United States, although he did not travel to that area until after he published *Shane*. His first novel, *Shane* appeared as a magazine serial before being published in its final hardback version in 1949. It is considered a classic representative of a distinct literary genre, the Western.

Events in History at the Time the Novel Takes Place

Cattle barons. Cattlemen generally moved into frontier territory after explorers and trappers, but before farmers. After the Civil War, many ranchers occupied the Great Plains, moving large cattle herds from Texas to markets up north. During this time the Great Plains was a largely unsettled region with vast expanses of open land claimed by the U.S. government. Ranchers, especially in the 1870s, enjoyed free use of this government land to graze their cattle. The open range cattle herds required thousands of acres in order to survive, since ranchers left the tough breeds to fend for themselves during the winter. Depending on the quality of the grazing land, each animal required from 20 to 130 acres.

Such large land requirements compelled the ranchers to occupy more land than they could legally own. Under law, ranchers might only obtain as much as 1,100 acres. Some ranchers obtained extra land by convincing their cowboy employees to file for homesteads with the federal government and subsequently transfer the titles

> **THE LITERARY WORK**
>
> A novel set in the Wyoming Territory in 1889; published in 1949.
>
> **SYNOPSIS**
>
> A strange gunfighter with a mysterious past suddenly appears in a small Wyoming valley. After siding with a local homesteading family in their fight against a cattle baron, the gunfighter is forced to partake in a life-or-death shootout on the homesteaders' behalf.

to the ranchers. These claims were usually fraudulent since the cowboys neither settled nor cultivated the land as required. Ranchers also obtained prime grazing land under other laws such as the Desert Act, which allowed people to purchase up to 640 acres of desert. Only one-seventh of the Wyoming Territory had been surveyed, so cattlemen easily claimed prime grazing lands as desert there. Most ranchers, however, simply squatted—that is, settled on the land without permission to do so and without paying rent—a practice considered legal until the government decided to use the surplus land. The cattle baron in Schaefer's novel, Luke Fletcher, acquires his land in this way.

Open range grazing practices were tolerated only because there was plenty of space. During the 1880s, however, the region became overstocked and overgrazed. In 1879 Wyoming supported 450,000 cattle; only six years later, the number of cattle roaming the territory had increased to 1.5 million.

Shane

Jack Schaefer

Harsh weather during the winter of 1886-87 decimated the cattle population, leaving the survivors nearly unfit for market. Some historians estimate the loss at three or four hundred thousand out of two million cattle. During this time of economic hardship, homesteaders started moving into Wyoming, placing further land pressures upon the hard-pressed cattlemen. *Shane* refers to the mounting tension caused by their arrival:

> He [Fletcher] had been running cattle through the whole valley at the time the miners arrived, having bought or bulldozed the few small ranchers there ahead of him. A series of bad years working up to the dry summer and terrible winter of '86 had cut his herds about the time the first of the homesteaders moved in and he had not objected too much. But now there were seven of us in all and the number was rising each year.
> (Schaefer, *Shane*, p. 46)

Such conflicts of interest eventually generated severe hostilities between the cattle barons and the small ranchers, sheepherders, and farmers of the region. These hostilities culminated in the Johnson County War of 1892, a three-day battle in which the cattlemen and their hired gunfighters declared open warfare on the entire county in order to evict small interests.

Homesteaders. The Homestead Act of 1862 granted 160 acres of land as a homestead in the West to the head of a family or to anyone twenty-one years of age. The act endured, with various modifications, until 1977. In order to obtain the land, the government required the homesteader to pay a small fee, live on the land for five years, and improve the property in particular ways.

Homesteading on the Great Plains proved difficult. The better lands fell into the hands of the railroads and speculators, leaving poorer, hard-to-farm land for the homesteaders. In the rainy East, farmers easily profited from 160 acres. A farm of equal size on the dry plains, however, left many homesteaders impoverished. People often referred to the Homestead Act as the government's bet: 160 acres of land against the homesteader's survival skills.

Although the act entitling them to land was passed in 1862, homesteaders did not settle the Great Plains for several years. After 1870, however, settlers quickly spread throughout the region. Between 1870 and 1900, homesteaders occupied 430 million acres of public land. Often called "nesters," these homesteaders comprised an important civilizing force in frontier society. Their predecessors, the trappers, explorers, and ranchers, had generally not established permanent settlements. The farmers, however, brought wives, children, and the trappings of eastern civilization. The novel *Shane* features a settlement in which "there were several stores, a harness and a blacksmith shop, and nearly a dozen houses. Just the year before, the men had put together a one-room schoolhouse" (*Shane*, p. 46).

The nesters often clashed with ranchers when they laid claim to the public lands. Accustomed to grazing their herds on these lands, the ranchers resented the homesteader's intrusion and considered them a threat. Meanwhile, many homesteaders, such as the novel's Joe Starrett, recognized the wastefulness of open range ranching:

> Listen to me, Shane. The thing to do is pick your spot, get your land, your own land. Put in enough crops to carry you and make your money play with a small herd, not all horns and bone, but bred for meat and fenced in and fed right. I haven't been at it long, but already I've raised stock that averages three hundred pounds more than that long-legged stuff Fletcher runs on the other side of the river and it's better beef, and that's only a beginning.
> (*Shane*, p. 7)

Sometimes, the ranchers and homesteaders quarreled over water sources. Settlers often claimed areas near streams, thereby separating the cattle from water. Cattlemen, in turn, diverted whole streams under the pretense of irrigation in order to provide water for their cattle and thus cut off the homesteader's water supply. In fact, access to water is one reason why Luke Fletcher wants to buy the homesteaders' land. "I'll be wanting all the range I can get from now on. Even without that, I can't let a bunch of nesters keep coming in here and choke me off from my water rights" (*Shane*, p. 95).

Women on the frontier. Although cooking and other domestic skills played an important and time-consuming role in the life of pioneer women, western life also liberated women from many traditional roles they occupied in the East. Wyoming, for example, shocked the East when it became the first state or territory in the nation to enfranchise women in 1869. On the frontier, women often worked in nontraditional roles; they labored in the fields, rode horses in pants or split skirts, and drove cattle. Many learned to shoot and hunt. At times women took up arms to protect land claims; some even turned into gunslinging outlaws. Thousands of women homesteaded their own land; in fact, by 1900, 10 percent of all homesteaders were women.

Law in the Wyoming Territory. Many forms of popular culture portray the frontier as a violence-ridden place. In reality, it was often quite peaceful. Theft was rare, since resources were plentiful and neighbors were scarce. Settlers, cowboys, and others generally welcomed strange travelers like Shane into their houses or settlements to eat and spend the night. Many left the doors to their houses or businesses unlocked. In fact, many houses and business lacked doors altogether. The owner assumed people were honest until proven otherwise, and society respected a person's word as a solid bond. Vendors often sold goods on credit to both regular customers and strangers, and sometimes people rode hundreds of miles in order to pay a debt.

Formal government, however, was loose and often unavailable. As the character Bob Starrett notes in the novel:

> We knew, too, how far away the government was from our valley way up there in the Territory. The nearest marshal was a good hundred miles away. We did not even have a sheriff in our town. There never had been any reason for one. When folks had any lawing to do, they would head for Sheridan, nearly a full day's ride away.
>
> (*Shane*, p. 45)

Furthermore, local governments were easily influenced by local strongmen, such as the novel's Luke Fletcher: "Even if we had had a sheriff, he would have been Fletcher's man. Fletcher was the power in the valley in those days" (*Shane*, p. 46). Under such conditions, the line between criminals and law enforcers was often blurry.

Some residents reacted by taking the law into their own hands. Such incidents in the novel as the killing (at Fletcher's behest) of Ernie, a homesteader who refuses to sell his land, were not unusual. In 1889, for example, cattle king Albert Bothwell lynched a man and a woman, accusing them of cattle rustling. In reality, the couple had claimed a homestead on Bothwell's open range along an important water source.

People sometimes formed vigilante groups when they thought the judicial system failed, such as on occasions when courts ignored or freed people who had allegedly committed homicide. In such instances, vigilante groups sometimes took it upon themselves to enact the death penalty. Besides punishing criminals, these groups sometimes stepped in to settle personal disputes under the guise of "justice." When Wyoming gained statehood in 1890, vigilante groups remained active despite the burgeoning judicial system.

Gunfighters. During the settlement of the frontier, gun ownership was much more common in the West than in the East. Some westerners became expert shooters, willing to risk their lives in gunfights for any number of reasons. These gunfighters play a prominent role in the history and legends of the West and include such infamous names as Doc Holliday, the Earp brothers, Jesse James, and Butch Cassidy.

Certain attributes became associated with gunfighters. While they came from all types of backgrounds, many, like Shane, were Southerners, since ex-soldiers from the Confederate Army headed West in great numbers after their defeat in the Civil War. Found on both sides of the law, gunfighters were admired as well as hated. They could be cattle rustlers or sheriffs; often they were both. Most preferred to cultivate an aura of mystery in order to intimidate their enemies.

Even in their own time, gunfighters inspired the mixture of fear and awe that the Starretts felt in Shane's presence. The public often exaggerated the gunfighters' skills and reputations. In reality, smoky gunpowder and woefully inaccurate firearms often handicapped the gunfighters. Despite wild claims, a man was considered a good shot if he could hit another man fifteen yards away.

Illustration by John McCormack from an edition of *Shane*.

Since gunfighters often did not care on which side of the law they fought, many worked as mercenaries. During the 1880s, cattlemen hired gunfighters such as Stark Wilson to protect their range interests from sheepherders, small ranchers, homesteaders, and rustlers. These hired men earned good wages, taking in approximately $100 to $150 a month, three times the salary of a U.S. marshal. Some earned as much as $200 a month, while one Wyoming fighter charged a flat rate of $500 per rustler caught.

The Novel in Focus

The plot. In the summer of 1889, Bob Starrett, the young son of homesteaders Joe and Marian Starrett, observes a mysterious, well-dressed stranger riding into the small Wyoming valley in which his family lives. The stranger's worn yet elegant appearance and his courteous behavior impress the Starrett family. Although the stranger merely requests the use of their water pump, Joe invites him to dinner and to spend the night. The stranger, who introduces himself simply as "Shane," accepts the invitation. Although Shane is amiable, the Starretts also perceive him as a mysterious and somewhat dangerous man. Despite this impression, however, they and Shane take an immediate liking to one another. Shane converses with Marian about the latest fashions in Cheyenne, Wyoming, and talks with Joe about the farm. Bob simply holds Shane in awe.

The following day, Joe shows Shane his farm, pointing out a particularly strong and heavy stump that he has not yet uprooted. "That was the one bad spot on our place. It stuck out like an old scarred sore in the cleared space back of the barn—a big old stump, all jagged across the top" (*Shane*, p. 12). Ledyard, the local salesman, arrives and attempts to sell Joe a cultivator (a farm tool used to break up the soil) at an unfair price. Shane says that he has recently seen the same cultivator for sale at a much cheaper price. Taking Shane at his word, Joe refuses to buy the cultivator at Ledyard's inflated price. The incident begins a long-lasting friendship between Shane and Joe. Ledyard huffily leaves, and soon afterward Shane picks up an ax and starts to hack at the stubborn stump. Joe picks up a second ax, and the two men cement their friendship by working together the entire day to uproot the old stump.

As Shane prepares to leave the next day, Joe tells him of the current land disputes between homesteaders, such as himself, and Luke Fletcher, a large rancher who grazes his cattle on public land. Noting that his previous farmhand left town after a brawl with Fletcher's men, Joe asks Shane to help him for the summer. Shane agrees.

Tensions between Fletcher and the homesteaders mount toward the end of the summer, when Fletcher obtains a beef contract and insists on his right to graze his cattle on the homesteaders' land. He offers to buy their farms, but the homesteaders, several of whom now own their land, decide not to sell. Shane comes to represent the homesteaders' resistance, and the group rallies around Joe Starrett, their reluctant leader.

One day, as Shane sits in the town saloon, one of Luke Fletcher's cowboys insults him and challenges him to a fight. Shane realizes that Chris, the young cowboy, is only acting on Fletcher's orders, and he leaves the saloon in order to avoid fighting. Both sides misinterpret Shane's reaction. Convinced that Shane does not have the stomach for a fight, Fletcher and his men begin to harass and insult the farmers with greater frequency, and the farmers soon resent Shane. Their resentment forces him to return to the saloon to face Chris. Shane demonstrates his deadly prowess by breaking Chris's arm and knocking him out cold in approximately thirty seconds.

Although Shane's quick disposal of Fletcher's henchman brings temporary peace to the valley, violence soon flares again. Five of Fletcher's men attack Shane at the saloon. The din of the pitched battle attracts Joe, who helps Shane win the brawl. The victory, however, only further angers Fletcher, who realizes that none of his men can beat Shane. Fletcher finally hires Stark Wilson, a gunslinger with a murderous reputation, to intimidate and even kill the homesteaders if necessary.

Eventually Wilson and Fletcher arrive at the Starrett farm. Fletcher offers to buy Joe's farm and hire him on at his ranch, stating that he will wait for Joe's answer at the saloon. Shane recognizes that if Joe refuses the offer, Fletcher and Wilson may kill him. Shane subsequently knocks Joe out and goes in his stead to meet Wilson and Fletcher.

The climax of the novel is a classic gunfight. Wilson accepts Shane's challenge to a duel in the saloon. When the smoke clears, Wilson is dead and Shane is wounded. Fletcher shoots at Shane from a hiding place on the balcony, but misses. Shane promptly kills him too. He then leaves the saloon, remarking to the stunned crowd that "I'll be riding on now. And there's not one of you that will follow" (*Shane,* p. 112). Young Bob, who witnessed the whole scene, realizes that Shane is badly hurt and runs after him. But Shane simply and gently says good-bye, and rides off.

Sources. Jack Schaefer worked as a journalist and edited a small magazine when he wrote *Shane* in 1945 and 1946. He often relaxed by reading American history as well as writing short stories. Schaefer noted, "I was getting books to review, and I was happiest and felt most at home west of the Mississippi River. Out here it is so neglected—one of the greatest periods in history, neglected by historians and writers alike.... I was not reading Westerns then. I read history" (Schaefer in Nuwer, p. 278). Schaefer decided to write a basic legend about the West. The characters are fictitious and little information is available about their possible origins. Shane, however, is similar in character to Schaefer's father, and may have been based on him.

Events in History at the Time the Novel Was Written

Westerns and pulp literature. During the early 1900s, popular fiction became widely available to the reading public in the form of cheap fiction magazines, commonly known as pulp magazines. In 1896 Frank Munsey established his magazine *Argosy* as one that would carry only adult fiction. Printed on wood-pulp paper, the magazine sold for a dime on the newsstands and ushered in the era of pulp fiction. Generally, pulps were slick-covered magazines that contained illustrations. Their stories were often sensational, exploiting themes of sex and violence. Detective stories and Westerns quickly became standard pulp fare in the early 1900s, while later pulps developed the genres of romance, horror, fantasy, and science fiction.

The popularity of pulps declined rapidly after World War II, when paperbacks emerged as a cheap alternative to hard-bound books. In 1945 *Argosy* changed into an adventure magazine, but it continued to publish books in traditional pulp genres such as the Western. *Shane* was originally published in *Argosy* in 1946 as a three-part serial called *Rider from Nowhere.* *Argosy* marketed *Rider from Nowhere* as a pulp Western, using traditional pulp illustrations and captions designed to sell magazines and capture the reader's attention. *Shane* was released as a hardback in 1949 and maintained a prominent place in Western literature thereafter.

Reviews. Although *Shane* has been translated into over thirty languages and more than seventy editions have been published, it has never been classified as a bestseller. Yet the novel has continually received praise when reviewed. Over the years many authors and critics have cited *Shane* as one of the best representatives of the Western genre. In 1985 the Western Writers Association voted *Shane* one of a handful of the most important Westerns of all time. The comments of Al Chase of the *Chicago Sunday Times,* writing in 1949, typify reaction to Schaefer's novel:

> Altho 'Shane' is not another 'Virginian,' it has the same quality, dignity and appeal which made Owen Wister's famous novel of years ago read by people who scoffed at 'Westerns.' It's a tragic, taut little tale of a grim, unforgettable, mysterious and at times sinister figure of a man.
> (Chase in Jones, p. 813)

Postwar domesticity. World War II constituted a time of great uncertainty and change for many Americans. Not surprisingly, at the end of the war Americans renewed their focus on home and family, values that permeated the late 1940s and 1950s. People emphasized materialism and consumerism as well as social and familial stability. The age at which the average woman married dropped nearly a full year, from twenty-one to twenty. Between 1940 and 1960 the birthrate rose rapidly, creating the baby-boom generation. Advertisers and other shapers of popular culture cultivated the image of the housewife, and public figures extolled the virtues of motherhood and the importance of a woman's devotion to house and home. Jack Schaefer's Marian Starrett character seems to directly reflect the domestic emphasis of this period. Marian's chief occupation and first love is cooking, an activity that keeps her close to home.

Despite the emphasis on domestic roles, however, greater numbers of older married women began to enter the labor force in the post-World War II period. By 1950 the number of American wives working outside the home had risen to 21 percent. Unlike the mavericks on the 1880s frontier, however, most of these working women stepped into jobs considered appropriate for females, securing employment as garment workers, salespersons, teachers, or nurses.

For More Information

Etulain, Richard W., and Michael T. Marsden. *The Popular Western*. Bowling Green, Ohio: Bowling Green University Popular Press, 1974.

Jones, Mertice M., Dorothy Brown, and Gladys M. Dunn, eds. *The Book Review Digest*. Vol. 45. New York: H. W. Wilson, 1950.

Larson, T. A. *Wyoming: A Bicentennial History*. New York: W. W. Norton, 1977.

Myres, Sandra L. *Westering Women and the Frontier Experience, 1800-1915*. Albuquerque: University of New Mexico Press, 1982.

Nuwer, Henry Joseph. "An Interview with Jack Schaefer: May 1972." In *Shane: The Critical Edition*. Edited by James C. Work. Lincoln: University of Nebraska Press, 1984.

Shaefer, Jack. *Shane: The Critical Edition*. Edited by James C. Work. Lincoln: University of Nebraska Press, 1984.

Trachtman, Paul. *The Gunfighters*. New York: Time-Life Books, 1974.

Sister Carrie

by
Theodore Dreiser

Theodore Dreiser was born in Terre Haute, Indiana in 1871. After a difficult childhood spent in poverty, Dreiser began writing for Chicago newspapers in 1892. After nearly a decade of success in journalism, Dreiser composed his first novel, *Sister Carrie,* in 1900. In the work, Dreiser realistically portrays the social and economic factors of his society. It is for this quality of realism that he has become best known.

Events in History at the Time of the Novel

The growth of Chicago. Though the Great Chicago Fire of 1871 had destroyed most of the city's newer buildings, subsequent decades saw a rebuilt Chicago rise dramatically from the ashes. By 1890 the territorial confines of Chicago stretched to 165 square miles. The growth of American industry had made it a city of wealthy tycoons such as Philip Armour, the pork-packing magnate, and George Pullman, the builder of railroad cars. As industries continued to grow, young men and women poured into Chicago and other major cities from rural communities across the Midwest, hoping to earn their fortunes. The railroads provided the major impetus for growth. In 1860 there were only 60,000 miles of track in the United States, but by 1900 that figure had multiplied to 250,000, leaving hardly a single major community outside the railroad system.

Supporting the rise of industry was an increase in nonagricultural jobs; about 4.6 million Americans worked in factories and 3 million in

> **THE LITERARY WORK**
>
> A novel set in Chicago, Montreal, and New York City in the late 1880s and early 1890s; published in 1900.
>
> **SYNOPSIS**
>
> A young woman becomes involved in illicit affairs with two different men as she pursues her dreams of success and fortune. With the financial decline of her second lover, Carrie rises to wealth and fame on the New York stage.

construction and transportation by the end of the century. This industrial work force was fed by a steady stream of immigration, which brought 5 million people to the United States between 1880 and 1890 alone. Meanwhile, there was a major internal migration of workers from rural areas to urban centers. By 1920 nearly half the population of the United States was living in cities.

The main attraction of the cities was employment. Chicago was home to many large enterprises, including major weaving and cloth production facilities, an enormous meat-packing industry, and countless clothing and shoe factories.

Many of the immigrants were soon disappointed with the sprawling city, finding that the work was difficult and the pay low. Other negative factors included the dense cloud of coal smoke that continuously poured from factory chimneys.

Sister Carrie

This heavy smoke settled over everything and even prompted city lawmakers to pass ordinances against the nuisance. Unfortunately, few paid any attention to the ordinances and the city's industries continued to pollute the atmosphere.

Dreiser's interest in this rapid growth is presented in one of *Sister Carrie*'s early chapters. Dreiser writes, "Streetcar lines had been extended far out into the open country in anticipation of rapid growth. The city had laid miles and miles of streets and sewers through regions where perhaps one solitary house stood out alone—a pioneer of the populous days to be" (Dreiser, *Sister Carrie*, p. 16). Dreiser had come to Chicago in circumstances very similar to Carrie's, seeking work in a variety of industries, all with limited success. His intimate familiarity with Chicago's commercial workings and his own problems finding employment there most certainly influenced his use of the city as the setting for Carrie's early failures and feelings of alienation and desperation.

> **MEAT PACKERS IN CHICAGO**
>
> One of Chicago's largest enterprises was the pork- and beef-packing industry, which expanded astronomically following the Civil War due to increased railroad shipping after the invention of the refrigerated car. The innovation made possible widespread shipping of meat from a centrally located facility. Dreiser's older brother, Rome, worked for a time in the Chicago stockyards, where cattle and pigs were kept. Most likely he served as the model for Sven Hanson, Carrie's brother-in-law in the novel, who cleans refrigerator cars at the stockyards.

Labor uprisings and *Sister Carrie*. With the growth of industry in the nation, there came inevitable conflicts between labor and employers. As factory owners continued their search for the highest profits, they attempted to keep the wages of their workers as low as possible. This was made easier by the constant supply of impoverished and desperate labor arriving by the thousands from Europe. The workers' only defense against low wages and the harsh conditions of employment was the formation of labor unions, collective organizations of workers who could affect the production and profits of employers by threatening to walk off the job.

Between 1870 and 1900, there were countless confrontations between labor and management, especially in larger centers of industry like Chicago. The railroad business was an industry especially prone to labor conflicts. One of the greatest railroad strikes occurred in 1877, when most of the railroad traffic in Chicago, Illinois, St. Louis, Missouri, and several other major cities stopped completely for a matter of weeks. Dreiser portrays a similar strike in *Sister Carrie*, when the workers of the Brooklyn City Railroad of New York go on strike. The character Hurstwood becomes a "scab," or nonunion worker for the railroad, and shows amazement at the fury of the labor dispute when he is hit with a rock thrown by one of the union strikers. In this episode Dreiser also depicts the strong sympathies felt for strikers by other working-class members in society. Though responsible for protecting the nonunion workers like Hurstwood, a policeman in the novel does not feel that he is being true to himself in performing the duty. "In his heart of hearts he sympathized with the strikers and hated this scab.... Strip him of his uniform and he would have soon picked his side" (*Sister Carrie*, p. 413).

Gilded Age. The late nineteenth century was the Gilded Age in America, when a few men made vast fortunes from the tremendous growth of industrial enterprises. The glitter associated with the age was a sham of sorts, though; beneath the few stories of stupendous fortunes lay the sixty-hour-plus workweeks of men and women who labored at a grinding pace in dangerous factories day after sweat-filled day for miserable wages. For many, their earnings barely kept pace with their expenses. In 1891, for example, the monthly expenses of one family—a laborer, his wife, and a child—totaled $28.01 for food, rent, and other necessities. His monthly income was $23.67 (Nash, p. 629).

Prostitution. There were few jobs open to females in the late 1800s: teaching, factory work, and household service positions summed up the range of possibilities. A recession hit the nation in 1884, which resulted in fewer openings even in these limited positions. Factory work, an option chosen by Carrie in the novel, offered at best the paltry sum of $6 a week, a dismal prospect that drove some working women into prostitution. Other females became mistresses, or "kept women"; such a woman had one lover from whom she received financial support. Like Carrie in the novel, mistresses capitalized on their sexual traits to enjoy the glitter that would otherwise have been denied them.

As for Carrie, her understanding of the moral significance of money was the popular understanding, nothing more. The old definition, "money: something everybody else has, and I must get," would have expressed her understanding of it thoroughly.
(*Sister Carrie,* p. 62)

Apparently there was a rise in the number of prostitutes in the late 1800s. Circumstances at the time were conducive to prostitution. Various forms of entertainment had appeared by the 1880s: movie houses, dance halls, concert saloons, penny arcades. Some of these places had begun to feature erotic content. Major movie houses advertised sensual pleasure and penny arcades displayed pornographic pictures. Concert saloons of the era catered to males. While these saloons did not support open prostitution, it was understood that their waitresses would be available for after-hours activities. Patrons of Harry's Hill, the classiest dance hall-concert saloon in New York City, regarded any woman who entered the place as a prostitute. Other young prostitutes put themselves on display at amusement parks, waiting to be picked up by young men. While statistics are unavailable, this type of working woman was probably a minority compared to the number who took respectable jobs. She did, nevertheless, exist, and her presence was encouraged by certain entertainments of the era. Meanwhile, women on stage, even in respectable shows such as the musical comedies in which Carrie performs in the novel, were thought to be morally lax, even though they weren't classed as prostitutes.

All the world's a stage. Workers had experienced some advances in the late nineteenth century. In agricultural areas, the work week decreased from 66 to 56 hours after 1880. In nonfarm occupations, it declined from 60 or more hours to roughly 54 hours per week. This resulted in an increase in leisure time that, in turn, contributed to the expansion of recreation and amusement. There was also a decline in the influence of organized religion, which alleviated one of the primary restraints on amusements. These factors and others contributed to a widespread growth in the entertainment industry. By the 1880s show business had begun to show huge profits. In 1883 P. T. Barnum's circus known as "The Greatest Show on Earth" earned $1.4 million. This growing economic promise led to an increase in theaters and other recreational establishments. By 1880 New York City had twenty-five theaters and over 7,000 saloons, beer gardens, and concert halls. This sharp rise in the popularity of the stage and its financial possibilities also translated into rising salaries for performers.

In the 1880s the most successful performers would be lucky to make $50 per week. By 1900 average performers salaries had quadrupled, and in some cases increased tenfold. Top-of-the-line stars could expect to earn even more as seen in the cases of Eva Tanguay, Nora Bates, and Elsie Janis, top actresses who earned between $2,500 and $3,500 per week. In Dreiser's novel, Carrie begins her stage career at $12 per week, still a sizable income considering that she earned $4.50 per week at her earlier job in the shoe factory. As her success on the stage begins to mount, her salary increases to $150 per week with the promise of much more to come.

A STAR IS BORN

An article in *Cosmopolitan* magazine at the turn of the century describes the incredible financial potential for rising young actresses: A young girl who had been in the chorus of musical shows for a couple of years without attracting too much attention decided she would give imitations of the kind that made the actress Elsie Janis famous. For weeks she besieged managers for a chance at any salary at all. Finally William Hammerstein, being short of an act for a Sunday afternoon concert, gave her an opportunity. Within seven days Belle Blanch, as she called herself, was booked for a whole year at $500 a week (*Cosmopolitan* in Auster, p. 37).

Actresses who had risen out of the working class served as models for all kinds of women in late nineteenth-century America. By the turn of the century, the chorus girl had captured the American imagination. She was more talked about, claimed the *Denver Post,* than the president of the United States. The world of glamour in which a chorus girl supposedly moved was the fascination; her life was envisioned as one replete with limousines, diamonds, furs, champagne, and rich suitors. Daily newspapers encouraged such talk, printing stories of chorus girls who married millionaires. In fact, chorus girls earned enough to become self-reliant and independent of men, as Carrie does at the end of the novel.

Late nineteenth-century view of Chicago.

The Novel in Focus

The plot. Caroline Meeber, called Sister Carrie by her family, leaves her home in rural Wisconsin by train to seek her fortune in Chicago. Carrie is immediately impressed by a fellow passenger on the train, Charles Drouet, a traveling salesman who speaks with her for the duration of the trip. Once in Chicago, the two separate, but not before Drouet takes Carrie's address and promises to visit her. Carrie goes to live with her sister Minnie and her husband, Sven Hanson, who live in a working-class neighborhood. Sven, who cleans refrigerator cars at the stockyard, makes it clear to Carrie that she must work and pay her share of the bills.

After a difficult job search, Carrie finds a position in a shoe factory and feels that she has made a great start in Chicago. But she catches a bad cold and loses her job when she misses work. While looking for a new position, she meets Drouet by chance. He treats her to lunch at an expensive restaurant. When he hears of her unemployment and meager living conditions, he insists on helping her. He gives Carrie money to buy warm clothes, and when they meet again, she accepts additional gifts of expensive clothing from him. Eventually Carrie allows Drouet to rent a room for her and realizes that she is straying from the values of her traditional upbringing, but she feels powerless to resist the chance to improve her lifestyle.

Carrie leaves the Hansons and becomes Drouet's mistress, moving with him to a comfortable apartment. Drouet frequents a popular saloon managed by George Hurstwood, a well-to-do friend. During a visit to the saloon, Drouet invites Hurstwood to call on him at home. He accepts the offer and when he meets Carrie at Drouet's apartment, he is immediately attracted to her. Carrie is also impressed with the impeccably dressed saloonkeeper. When Hurstwood realizes that Drouet and Carrie are not married, he begins to think of how he might obtain her for himself.

While Drouet is out of town, Carrie begins to spend time with Hurstwood. Drouet's Elks Lodge (a charitable men's club) sponsors an amateur theatrical production and he encourages Carrie to audition for a role. She agrees and gets the part. During the performance, she shows a natural aptitude for the stage, captivating the audience and especially Hurstwood.

Hurstwood's marriage begins to deteriorate as his wife slowly realizes that he is spending time with another woman. Mrs. Hurstwood threatens to create a public scandal by divorcing her husband. Instead of facing this blow to his reputation, Hurstwood separates from his wife. That night as he closes up the saloon, Hurstwood finds that the safe—to which he does not have the combination—has been left unlocked and $10,000 from the bank has not been put away. After accidentally closing the door to the safe before putting in the money, Hurstwood decides to take the $10,000 rather than explain the embarrassing circumstances of how it arrived in his possession.

Hurstwood goes to Carrie and tells her that Drouet is hospitalized across town and that they must go by train to see him. Carrie goes with him, not suspecting that they are actually boarding a train that will eventually land them in Montreal. When detectives pursue them, Hurstwood returns the bulk of the money and takes Carrie with him to New York.

Hurstwood uses the money he has kept to buy a part interest in a saloon, and for two years he and Carrie live in a comfortable apartment building. When profits from the saloon plummet, Carrie and Hurstwood are forced to move into a shabbier apartment in a less refined part of New York. Hurstwood loses his stake in the business, and being a middle-aged man with no capital, has difficulties finding work.

Carrie, realizing that she must fend for herself, pursues a career on the stage, encouraged by her former success. She finally gets a small part as a chorus girl and begins working her way up while Hurstwood's fortunes continue to fall. As Carrie makes further progress, she becomes unwilling to support Hurstwood and leaves him. Carrie gradually becomes a celebrity as Hurstwood declines further and finally commits suicide.

Realism, commerce, and capitalism in *Sister Carrie*. One of the most compelling elements of Dreiser's *Sister Carrie* is the realism used in describing the topics of commerce. Employment, money, and industry are presented in thorough detail. During Carrie's initial search for employment, every aspect of the job hunting process is covered. Setting the mood even before Carrie begins her job search, Dreiser's novel presents a complete background on the commercial history of Chicago. Instead of discussing the scenery of the city, the novel describes it in terms of commercial resources, giving its population, key industries, and municipal improvements. Likewise the novel presents its characters strictly in commercial terms. For example, it tells the reader what Carrie's brother-in-law, Sven, does for a living and what time he must get up for work in the morning, not what type of person he is. The only thoughts of Sven's divulged to the reader are his ambitions for making enough money to invest in real estate. Similarly, Carrie's feelings about her relationships, her home, or her life never surface; instead her dreams of future wealth and purchasing power propel her through the story.

The novel goes into detailed quantitative descriptions of money itself. When Carrie finally gets a job offer at a clothing factory, Dreiser gives precise information about the salary she would be earning, $3.50 per week. When she later locates her job at the shoe factory, she is excited to learn that the salary here is higher, $4.50 per week. This technique of providing the exact dollar figures continues throughout the novel. When Hurstwood spirals into the depths of poverty, the novel counts out every penny.

> **MALE CHARACTER TYPES IN *SISTER CARRIE***
>
> Charles Drouet, the traveling salesman in *Sister Carrie*, is a masher—a man who tries to force his romantic intentions on a woman. The term *masher*, says the novel, "sprung into general use among Americans in 1880" (*Sister Carrie*, p. 5). As Dreiser explains, such a man behaved boldly from the start. If he were to catch the attention of some susceptible young woman in a department store, before leaving he would discover her name, her favorite flower, and an address where he could send her a note. "As much as the businessman and frontiersman, he [the masher] was a major example of male appearance and behavior in the late nineteenth century" (Banner, p. 240).

There are several reasons for Dreiser's intense focus on commerce and financial matters. The first is that Dreiser himself, much like Carrie, was preoccupied with fantasies and thoughts about money throughout most of his life. Having grown up in extreme poverty, Dreiser was very interested in the security and comfort that money could provide. The era in which Dreiser wrote also prompted him to focus on money. During Dreiser's young adulthood, financial giants pursuing the rewards of American capitalism were building the nation and helping to foster the myth of the Gilded Age—that riches were within anyone's grasp in this land of opportunity known as the United States. Yet in reality, the era featured deprivation and poverty for most American laborers. Dreiser's novel emphasizes both the difficulties and possibilities presented by the

Sister Carrie

Theodore Dreiser

rapid expansion of American commerce at the end of the nineteenth century.

Sources. Most of Dreiser's sources for *Sister Carrie* came from his own personal and family life. The exploits of Dreiser's sister Emma supplied the basic framework for a great deal of the novel. Emma moved from the Dreiser home in rural Warsaw, Indiana, to Chicago, Illinois, after a falling-out with her fanatically religious father, John Paul Dreiser. In Chicago, Emma lived under an assumed name and fell in love with L. A. Hopkins, a suave forty-year-old, then discovered he was married. Hopkins was a cashier at Chapin & Gore, a fashionable downtown bar, and was obviously the model for George Hurstwood, the dapper saloon manager in *Sister Carrie*. Despite his being married, Emma eloped with Hopkins to Montreal, where he admitted to her that while drunk he had stolen $3,500 from the Chapin & Gore safe. Realizing that the police were on his trail, he returned all but $800 of the money in a letter to his former employers, begging them not to prosecute him. They granted his wish, but the scandal made the headlines in the Chicago papers; the Dreiser family escaped mention only because Emma had taken another name. Fearful of returning to Chicago, Emma moved with her lover to New York, where they rented out rooms to women of questionable character and profession. The only major difference between Emma's story and Carrie's story in the novel is the amount of the money stolen, and Dreiser's embellishment of the theft itself.

The career of Dreiser's older brother also influenced the novel. Much like Carrie in the novel, his older brother Paul had an aptitude for the stage. Paul worked his way up from traveling minstrel shows, becoming a national celebrity through his winning stage performances and sentimental ballads. When Dreiser was still young and living at home, Paul would take him to the theater, give him tours backstage, and introduce him to the actors. This experience undoubtedly played a part in Dreiser's creation of Carrie's stage career.

Finally, Dreiser's own life provided a great deal of source material for *Sister Carrie*. The author's introduction to Chicago as a young man bears a strong resemblance to Carrie's arrival in the big city. Just like Carrie, Dreiser struggled desperately to find a decent job there, trying his hand at everything from cleaning second-hand stoves to working in a railroad yard tracking cars. Dreiser lost the well-paying railroad job after a winter cold kept him from going to work, the same circumstance that costs Carrie her job at the shoe factory. Similarly, Dreiser's habit of lounging in hotel lobbies when he felt depressed became Hurstwood's habit as this character descends into poverty and eventual suicide near the end of the novel.

Dreiser, the publishers, and the critics. When Frank Norris, the famous American novelist and an editor for the Doubleday publishing house, read *Sister Carrie*, he realized immediately that he had found something exceptional. In a letter to Dreiser, Norris described his conversation with other Doubleday editors regarding the book: "I said, and it gives me great pleasure to repeat it, that it was the best novel I had read in M. S. [manuscript] since I had been reading for the firm, and that it pleased me as well as any novel I have read in any form, published or otherwise" (Norris in Swanberg, p. 86). With Frank Doubleday in Europe, Walter Hines Page, a partner in the firm and the boss during Doubleday's absence, signed an agreement with Dreiser to publish the book.

When Doubleday returned from Europe, he was not as enthusiastic about the novel as Norris and Page had been. According to Doubleday's moral policies, lust and vice were acceptable in fiction only if they were punished in the end to provide the reader with a wholesome moral lesson. Carrie, not punished in the slightest, enjoyed a frivolous existence with two lovers and became a successful actress living a life of luxury, a plot that could be construed as promoting unchastity as a way of life. Doubleday also disapproved of the book because he found it vulgar in its portrayal of rude and uneducated characters, and also because he felt its pessimism was offensive. Despite Doubleday's dislike of the novel, an agreement had been signed and Dreiser had no intention of letting his first novel go unpublished. After extensive wrangling over the terms of the contract, *Sister Carrie* was published on November 8, 1900.

Despite the high hopes of Norris and Dreiser, the novel was blasted by critics as "depressing," "inelegant," and "unpleasant" (Swanberg, p. 92). After more than a year on the racks, Doubleday reported that only 456 copies had been sold. As realistic fiction became more widely accepted, critics still questioned Dreiser's themes and characters, but were forced to acknowledge his powerful style and artistic excellence. The critic Granville Hicks wrote "one feels his [Dreiser's] effort, as he laboriously amasses detail, as he clumsily probes into motives, as he ponderously gropes for words. And one feels his honesty, his determination to present life exactly as he sees it.... One cries out against the author's clumsiness, his sheer stupidity, and yet one surrenders to his honesty and acknowledges in the end that he is a master" (Hicks in Poupard, pp. 176-77).

For More Information

Auster, Albert. *Actresses and Suffragists: Women in the American Theater, 1890-1920*. New York: Praeger, 1984.

Banner, Lois W. *American Beauty*. New York: Alfred A. Knopf, 1983.

Dreiser, Theodore. *Sister Carrie*. New York: Penguin, 1994.

Nash, Gary B., et al., eds. *The American People: Creating a Nation and a Society*. Vol. 2. New York: Harper & Row, 1990.

Poupard, Dennis, ed. *Twentieth-Century Literary Criticism*. Vol. 10. Detroit: Gale Research, 1983.

Swanberg, W. A. *Dreiser*. New York, Scribner's, 1965.

Wade, Louise Carroll. *Chicago's Pride: The Stockyards, Packingtown, and Environs in the Nineteenth Century*. Chicago: University of Illinois Press, 1987.

Sons and Lovers

by
D. H. Lawrence

~

Born in 1885, D. H. (David Herbert) Lawrence grew up during the end of the Victorian age in England. A period of rapid growth, the era was marked by both progress and repression. Industrialism fueled the economy and secondary education became more accessible to the masses, but these benefits were not without cost. Families such as the Lawrences were divided by the rapid changes. While parents often remained in the working class, their educated children rose to the middle and upper classes, creating cultural and economic rifts. Queen Victoria, moreover, promoted a strict "moral" code that advocated sexual abstinence and utterly chaste behavior. As the age came to a close, writers such as D. H. Lawrence and Sigmund Freud began to discuss the taboo subject of sex and to challenge typical Victorian notions of proper male-female relationships. *Sons and Lovers* examines human relationships during this era, shedding light on Lawrence's unique life experience as well as those of thousands of young Englishmen who came of age at this time.

Events in History at the Time of the Novel

Progress at a price. The Victorian age signaled England's emergence as the world's leading economic power. Coal, of which the nation was a major producer, literally fueled the Industrial Revolution and enabled Great Britain to become a leading manufacturer and exporter. Cities grew, populated by factories and factory workers, while

> **THE LITERARY WORK**
>
> A novel set in England at the turn of the twentieth century; published in 1913.
>
> **SYNOPSIS**
>
> *Sons and Lovers* traces the struggles of Paul Morel, the youngest son of a working-class British family, in his relationships with his parents and lovers at the end of the Victorian age.

mines throughout the countryside churned out the black fuel that stoked the fires of industry.

The Industrial Revolution was accompanied by a shift toward democracy and capitalism. Though England remained a limited monarchy, the lower classes were able to rise in standing through education and work. Primary and secondary schools opened across the nation, training people to staff the new industries. Previously, only the upper classes typically attended secondary school and class status was relatively fixed; a working-class family remained in the working class and a landed family remained in the nobility, regardless of income bracket. As the children of the lower and middle classes began attending college and achieving financial success in the cities, class lines blurred.

While creating changes for the better in many respects, heavy industry and the capitalist economy also produced its share of casualties. Accidents as well as respiratory diseases contributed to a high rate of premature death among miners, and illness victimized the larger population as well. Because of the coal smoke, polluted black skies became the norm in the cities, and lung diseases grew common. Meanwhile, the eager embrace of capitalism contributed to the breakup of the family and a mass exodus to the cities. Upon completing their education, young men would leave for the cities, where they could advance their stations in life by doggedly pursuing a career. In *Sons and Lovers*, this trend is exemplified by William, the eldest of the Morel boys. Apprenticed to a lawyer for a shipping firm in London, he rapidly rises up the corporate ladder—but at the cost of forsaking his family and health. He is so determined to get ahead that he spends all his time working and courting an aristocratic young woman. In his mother's view, he forgets his obligations to the family and also neglects his own health. At just eighteen, he dies of erysipelas (an infectious disease also known as St. Anthony's Fire). His father blames his death on London, the symbol of capitalism and the modern way of life. From his perspective, it has literally torn his family apart.

Disease. Epidemics broke out frequently in Victorian England. By the late 1800s, though many technological and scientific advancements had been made, respiratory ailments were common, as were infectious diseases. Tuberculosis and bronchitis accounted for 17 percent of all deaths in Eastwood, home of the Lawrences and the fictional Morels. As a child, D. H. Lawrence contracted tuberculosis and battled it his entire life, finally dying from the disease in 1930 at age forty-four. Diagnosis of disease at this point greatly outpaced treatment. Opium-based pain medication such as morphine was commonly prescribed for long-term diseases such as cancer, for which there was no remedy. Though occasionally tumors could be removed surgically if detected early enough and located in remote areas (not near any vital organs or arteries), most cancer treatment consisted of pain minimization. As in the case of the novel's ailing Mrs. Morel, doctors could only try to lessen the pain of cancer patients, for they had no therapy or cure.

Women's rights and roles. Although a woman reigned over England, the cause of women's rights benefited little from her rule. Queen Victoria vehemently opposed women's suffrage and property rights, and repeatedly thwarted passage of reform bills proposed in Parliament. Victorian culture denounced women for becoming public figures or for assuming traditional male roles outside the home. Women's rights advocates, known as suffragettes, were sharply criticized by the government, ostracized, and viewed as militant agitators. The stifling climate in which most women lived their lives during this century can be seen in the person of the novel's Mrs. Gertrude Morel. She harbors a desperate desire to pursue goals outside the home, to be educated and independent, but for her those goals are impossible to achieve. She repeatedly laments that her personal dreams have died and can only be fulfilled through her sons, who keenly feel this obligation. As the novel explains,

> Now she had two sons in the world. She could think of two places, two centers of industry, and feel that she had put a man into each of them, that these men would work out what *she* wanted; they were derived from her, they were of her, and their works would also be hers.
> (Lawrence, *Sons and Lovers*, p. 127)

CHILD LABOR IN MINES

Children as young as seven—D. H. Lawrence's father among them—worked in the deep, dirty coal pits, risking health and longevity. Most had little choice, however. It was a necessity for children of the working class to begin adding to the family income as soon as possible. Because they were employed at such an early age, these children—including Mr. Lawrence and the fictional Mr. Morel—were uneducated. They spent their lives in the mines, as had their fathers and most of the neighbors in the community. Therefore, when their sons were not only afforded secondary education but also went off to the cities to work at desk jobs, earning far more with their intellect than the miners could earn with their muscle, it sometimes caused friction and animosity within the family. Fathers felt slighted because their sons were breaking with family tradition, and considered it "unmasculine" to make a living indoors.

In contrast, Clara Dawes represents the next generation of women, the suffragettes who can and will agitate for change. Ironically enabled by Queen Victoria's death in 1901, women began making great strides at the turn of the century, entering the work force and education in greater numbers than ever before. In 1903 Mrs. Emmeline Pankhurst founded the Women's Social and

Political Union, and with her daughter, Christabel Pankhurst, led violent demonstrations, smashing store windows and burning down buildings in the early 1910s to agitate for the right to vote. Though still on the fringe rather than in mainstream society, suffragettes like Clara in the novel symbolized the new British woman who would live to see voting rights granted in 1918, a few years after the novel's publication.

Women's Literary Guild. During the Victorian age women were generally discouraged from assuming public roles or even gathering in public places. Whereas men could congregate in pubs (public houses), women had few places to socialize or meet among themselves. One of the few options was the Woman's Literary Guild. A setting where women could exchange intellectual ideas, the Guild served as both an educational center and a political breeding ground for female activists. Both the novel's Mrs. Morel and the author's mother were instrumental in the organization, each helping to found their local chapters.

DEMOCRATIC TACTICS

Taking direct action to win higher wages and better working conditions, dock and railway workers as well as coal miners staged major strikes in 1911 and 1912. Intervening in the labor disputes, the government finally granted the coal miners' demand for a minimum wage guaranteed by an act of Parliament. Labor unrest continued in the years that followed. In 1913, when Lawrence's novel was published, England's three large unions—the miners, railway workers, and transport employees—agreed to join forces by making demands on all their employers at the same time, figuring that the threat of all three of them going on strike at once would increase the likelihood of their demands being met.

Challenges to Victorian stereotypes. Victorian culture dictated clearly defined roles for men and women and discouraged public discussion of male-female relationships. Women were to live within the domestic sphere and find fulfillment as wives and mothers, while men were to be the monetary providers and the source of physical strength for the family. While women could be emotional and sensitive, men were to remain stoic and hardy. Extramarital affairs and premarital sex were vehemently opposed. Sex within marriage was not discussed and its primary importance was to produce children.

These black-and-white role definitions, combined with a lack of communication and sexual frustration, hampered relationships during the era. In the novel, the Morels have virtually no communication and therefore develop no bond as husband and wife. For the most part, Mrs. Morel operates strictly within the realm of house and home, Mr. Morel exclusively outside of it, and their lives and interests rarely overlap. Paul, marked by his sensitivity and emotional nature, is ostracized by his father and other working-class men who consider him either a snob or a wimp. D. H. Lawrence personally struggled with his role as a man of feeling. Rather small and weak, and endowed with an artist's sensitivity as well, Lawrence found it difficult to gain acceptance from his male peers—including his own father—and went through several unfulfilling relationships until he finally found his equal in a mate.

While the novel includes unconventional male and female characters—Clara Dawes, the suffragette, and Paul Morel, the sensitive artist—and relationships that begin to challenge tradition, it presents no positive male-female relationship. The book suggests that more open and intimate relationships between the sexes will develop at some point in the future, though achieving that sort of intimacy at the current time is nearly impossible. Lawrence did find his own long-term relationship just as he was finalizing *Sons and Lovers* (1912) and, as the end of this novel suggests, it bucked tradition. He fell in love with a married, liberated woman, Frieda Weekley, with whom he spent the rest of his life.

Psychological and literary challenges. Like D. H. Lawrence, other prominent personalities of the day were challenging Victorian social conventions. Sigmund Freud wrote his essays on sexuality in 1905 and defined what he called the "Oedipus Complex." Though Lawrence had probably never read this essay himself but rather heard of it only secondhand through his companion Frieda Weekley, some scholars see a reflection of Freud's "Oedipus Complex" in *Sons and Lovers;* they think Paul and his mother have the type of relationship described by Freud. In his theory, at a certain point in sexual development, children have an unconscious desire to have the exclusive love of the parent of the opposite sex. The child is jealous of the physical affection between his parents and can even come to hate the parent of the same sex.

In the novel Paul repeatedly states that while his mother lives, he cannot truly love another woman. He is generally fearful of and angry toward his father and has a relationship with his mother that is closer to that of husband and wife—though nonsexual—than child and parent. Lawrence personally experienced this phenomenon with his own mother. In fact, as he later stated, the writing of *Sons and Lovers* was a cathartic exercise that helped him to resolve these feelings. After completing the novel, Lawrence could finally achieve a closer relationship with his father and find fulfillment with another woman.

The Novel in Focus

The plot. The novel opens with a disclosure of details about the early life of the Morels. Gertrude Coppard has married "beneath her" by wedding Walter Morel, a coal miner. They settle in Nottinghamshire, lowlands mining country that lies close to Derbyshire. The area is also known as "Hell Row."

Gertrude comes from an upper-middle-class family that has recently gone bankrupt. Though Walter Morel makes a good living and literally rescues her from a life of poverty, he is still considered of lower status since his family is of the working class. While she is staunchly Puritan, intellectual, and emotionally undemonstrative, he is not religious, visceral, and sensual. A teetotaler, she prefers to read books while he loves to drink and dance. They are extreme opposites, and for a while that attracts them to each other. But Gertrude has greater aspirations than he, and more than her age will allow. She dreams of being a schoolteacher, of expounding on the literature she loves and philosophizing with fellow intellectuals. Unfortunately her dreams are destined to remain unrealized, especially after she bears five children. As she remarks, "I wait, I wait, and what I wait for can never come" (*Sons and Lovers*, p. 14). Ultimately, rather than live life herself, she lives it vicariously through her children—particularly through her sons who can fulfill the dreams she cannot.

Though her plight is not his fault, Mrs. Morel blames it on her husband and alienates him from the family. A domineering woman, she runs the household and pits the children against their father, a hard-working miner who likes to drink and socialize in the pubs after a long day.

Mrs. Morel resents her husband's freedom, and their fights become a regular spectacle for the children. As the parents grow further apart, Gertrude latches on to her sons. She transfers to

Jessie Chambers, the model for Miriam in *Sons and Lovers*.

them her personal aspirations and also tries to shape them into ideal husbands, or men who will finally fulfill her and take care of her as she would like. This greatly affects the feelings and behavior of her two elder sons, particularly Paul. First William is to be her savior. He is in superb physical shape and excels in school. The first of the family to be sent to secondary school, upon graduating he lands a prestigious job in London, earning far more than his father. This leads to a major rift between the father and son. The father cannot comprehend how a man can earn that much money without physical labor, simply by sitting at a desk all day.

William is the perfect example of the eager young capitalist. He is given all the opportunities to succeed that his father was denied, and he is going to work doggedly to make the most of them. He dates an upper-class young woman and puts in long hours at the office. He promises to take care of his mother financially and visit regularly, but his contributions to the family coffer steadily decrease, as do his visits home. He neglects his health and that becomes a fatal mistake when erysipelas, an acute skin and tissue disease, fells him at just eighteen.

Fictional Character	Real-life Source
Paul Morel	D. H. Lawrence
Walter Morel	Arthur Lawrence
Gertrude Morel	Lydia Lawrence
Miriam	Jessie Chambers

Fictional Event	Real-life Source
Death of brother, William	Death of brother, William
Paul nearly dies of pneumonia	D. H. nearly dies of pneumonia
Paul caught in a love triangle (with Miriam and Clara)	D. H. caught in a love triangle (with Jessie Chambers and Louie Burrows)
Paul leaves lovers and mother	D. H. leaves lovers and mother

After William's death, Mrs. Morel falls into a deep depression and virtually withdraws from life. During this time, Paul nearly dies of pneumonia. Mrs. Morel realizes that she has neglected him, and his near-death experience prods her back to life. Paul now begins to emerge as a personality in his own right. He gets a job at a surgical appliance factory in Nottingham and begins expressing himself in earnest as an artist. He and Miriam, a girl he has grown up with, spend a great deal of time together. He teaches her French and gives her books to read. Although they care deeply for each other, for a long time their relationship does not go beyond friendship. A major obstacle is Mrs. Morel, who feels Miriam will steal Paul's soul if the two young people get too close. Their relationship is further complicated by society's view that it is improper for a young man and woman to spend so much time together without becoming engaged. Torn between platonic friendship and their desire for each other, Paul and Miriam finally consummate their relationship. They discuss marriage but conclude that it would not work between them. Yet they continue to sleep together. Paul is relieved of sexual frustration and feels he has finally become a man, but he still finds a deep void in his life, as does Miriam. He wants his physical and emotional passion to be satisfied by one person, which does not happen with Miriam. She, in turn, is dismayed by the distance he projects when they are together.

In the meantime, Miriam introduces him to Clara Dawes, an older, liberated woman, a suffragette who is currently separated from her husband. She eventually attracts Paul's eye. When he and Miriam break up, he begins seeing Clara. She educates him in many ways, and he feels very happy with her—yet there is still something missing. In fact, she is not free to be with him. She is still technically married, and this prevents them from publicly acknowledging their relationship. A second obstacle, again, is Mrs. Morel. Though she likes Clara, Paul's mother still dominates his life. Until she dies, there can be no other woman for Paul.

Actually, Mrs. Morel is dying. She has cancer, a much more advanced case of it than anyone knows. When her large tumor is finally discovered, it has grown well beyond the point of surgical treatment. All the doctors can do is minimize her pain through morphine. Drugged nearly all the time, she still cannot sleep. Paul and his sister, Annie, care for her, but this constant attendance begins to take its toll. They cannot stand to see their mother suffer so. Finally, the children want to end their mother's suffering. When her nurse is away one night, they add extra morphine into her nightly sleep remedy. She seems to know what is happening. She comments on how bitter it is yet drinks it down eagerly. For the first time in months, she sleeps through the night. She lasts through the next day and finally dies with Paul and Annie by her side. After her death, Paul goes into a depression of sorts. He feels truly alone and then proceeds to sever all of his worldly ties. First, he breaks off with Clara, reuniting her with her husband, Baxter. Then he tells Miriam once and for all that they will never marry. He seems to contemplate suicide but at the last looks toward the lights of the city and walks toward them. Though he wants to join his mother in the dark, he resolves to live on, for her and for himself.

The imagery of nature as sexual expression. In Victorian England, it was not acceptable to discuss sex openly. Even in the early 1910s,

Lawrence had to be very delicate in approaching the subject of a young man's—in fact, his own—development and entry into adulthood. Lawrence accomplished this feat by using the imagery of nature and clever metaphors. The text of *Sons and Lovers* is replete with sensual descriptions of nature, of budding flowers and dew speckled grass, as well as of passion expressed through art. The imagery is clearly erotic, as the following passage indicates:

> She saw the dark yews and the golden crocuses, then she looked at him gratefully.... And now he asked her to look at this garden, wanting the contact with her again. Impatient of the set in the field, she turned to the quiet lawn surrounded by sheaves of shut-up crocuses. A feeling of stillness, almost ecstasy came over her. It felt almost as if she were alone with him in this garden.
> (*Sons and Lovers,* p. 201)

Similarly the novel describes a discussion of Paul's art as if the talk were a form of sexual rather than intellectual intercourse:

> They began to talk about the design. There was for him the most intense pleasure in talking about his work to Miriam. All his passion, all his wild blood went into this intercourse with her, when he talked and conceived his work. She did not understand, any more than a woman understands when she conceives a child in her womb. But this was life for her, and for him.
> (*Sons and Lovers,* p. 241)

In these passages Lawrence illustrates both the repressive climate in which he grew up and his cleverness in evading restrictive social conventions to express underlying and overt feelings of sexual passion. Just as Paul expresses his sexuality through his work, so does Lawrence.

Sources. Lawrence based *Sons and Lovers* on his own experiences and those of his contemporaries. Characters as well as events in the novel coincide with the author's life. Clara Dawes, for example, is based partly on Lawrence's wife, Frieda, and partly on Alice Dax. Seven years older than Lawrence, Dax was a woman with whom he had an affair.

In addition to fictionalizing real-life events, Lawrence also based the book on Frieda's impressions of how female characters in the book might have felt. When revising it while abroad with Frieda in 1912, he used much of her input to flesh out the characters—especially Mrs. Morel.

Reviews. When *Sons and Lovers* first appeared in print, it was greeted with poor sales and general

The Lawrence family. From left to right, top row: Emily, George, and Ernest; bottom row: Ada; mother, Lydia; David Herbert; and father, Arthur.

disinterest or shock. The subject matter was considered too racy for general consumption and the book was exceedingly long—even by turn-of-the-century standards. Over a hundred pages were cut before its publication in 1913, but even that did not help sales. In fact, it probably hurt because the censorship drastically altered the meaning and content of the book by all but eliminating the first section, which makes the book truly about "sons" and not a single son. Today the original content seems tame, but in his own time Lawrence was breaking new ground. Though the work went on to sell several million copies after Lawrence's death, its author only received his original advance of £100.

For More Information

Burgess, Anthony. *Flame into Being: The Life and Work of D. H. Lawrence.* New York: Arbor House, 1985.
DeLaura, David. *Victorian Prose.* New York: Modern Language Association of America, 1973.
Lawrence, D. H. *Sons and Lovers.* Cambridge: Cambridge University Press, 1992.
Worthen, John. *D. H. Lawrence: The Early Years.* Cambridge: Cambridge University Press, 1991.

The Souls of Black Folk

by
W. E. B. Du Bois

Born in 1868 in the small Massachusetts town of Great Barrington, William Edward Burghardt (known as W. E. B.) Du Bois was physically far removed from the South, where slavery had only recently been abolished. Nevertheless, Du Bois, a superior student and the first African American to earn a Ph.D. from Harvard University, would make it his life's mission to promote true equality for African Americans. *The Souls of Black Folk* is a collection of fourteen of Du Bois's essays that discuss what emancipation meant to blacks, how contemporary black leadership was going astray, and how difficult it was for blacks to escape slavery's turbulent legacy and obtain equality in white society.

Events in History at the Time of the Essays

Slavery's legacy. Though black slaves in the South had been freed by the Emancipation Proclamation in 1863 and their liberty was confirmed by the Thirteenth Amendment in 1865, their new status brought few of the benefits most had expected it would. During Reconstruction (1865-77), when the United States Army occupied the South, blacks did make numerous gains. The Fourteenth Amendment to the Constitution guaranteed them their rights as American citizens and the Fifteenth Amendment prohibited discrimination in voting. Schools and colleges for blacks were opened, and under the auspices of the Republican-led federal government, blacks were even elected to high offices in the South.

THE LITERARY WORK
A collection of essays about race relations in the United States, some previously published in the 1890s; published as a collection in 1903.

SYNOPSIS
Du Bois addresses the problem of the "color line," which he contends will be the world's most serious dilemma in the twentieth century.

Nonetheless, many remained poor and illiterate, and hostility toward them in the North as well as the South began to increase. Among the roots of this renewed hostility was a competition for jobs that occurred with the influx of an entire populace of former slaves into the labor market.

When Reconstruction ended in 1877, Southern state and local governments once more fell into the hands of the conservative white majority. The Civil War and its aftermath had embittered many white Southerners, many of whom resented the ex-slaves' enfranchisement all the more since they themselves were denied voting rights as a result of their support of the Confederacy. After Reconstruction these conservative whites returned to power and black political gains became a thing of history.

Although blacks in the South continued to vote in large numbers throughout the 1880s, state governments in the South increasingly restricted their right to vote through obstacles such as poll taxes and literacy tests. Administered when blacks registered to vote, the tests might require them to read and copy a difficult section of the state constitution, then interpret it. Southern governments also began to pass Jim Crow laws (named after a mid-nineteenth century children's rhyme that later became a minstrel song and dance) that mandated racial segregation. In 1896 the Supreme Court upheld these laws in *Plessy v. Ferguson,* ruling that segregated railroad cars were not unconstitutional as long as facilities for both races were "separate but equal." This decision opened the way for a flood of Jim Crow laws in the South (many were based on earlier statutes that had been used to regulate free blacks in Northern states before the Civil War). By 1910 post offices, prisons, restaurants, theaters, zoos, bowling alleys, swimming pools, and churches were among those places segregated by law throughout much of the South.

Social Darwinism and racist theory. Contemporary scientific opinion contributed to white racism. Beginning in the seventeenth century, European scientists had devised theories to rank humans by race, seeking genetic reasons for cultural and technological differences among societies. The trend was reinforced by misinterpretations of the work of mid-nineteenth century biologist Charles Darwin, whose ideas, so successful in the realm of science, appealed to social theorists as well. Spawned by the writings of English social conservative Herbert Spencer (who coined the phrase "survival of the fittest"), the application of Darwin's evolutionary theory to society is called social Darwinism. It should be stressed that Darwin himself had nothing to do with this application. It was Spencer who maintained that society advanced as a result of competition by which the weak were filtered out or eliminated while the strong rose to the top. Spencer's belief was that nature worked to rid the world of the weak and make space for the fit. The social Darwinism based on his ideas held that "higher" races such as whites would further "evolve" into a "superior" species, while "inferior" races such as blacks would eventually disappear.

Social Darwinism enjoyed great popularity in America, where it was first embraced by a business community eager to give to ruthless practices the legitimacy of "natural law." Soon racist assumptions also pervaded American scholarship. Du Bois himself reports encountering such assumptions at Harvard University, where "it was continually stressed in the community and in classes that there was a vast difference in the development of the whites and the 'lower' races; that this could be seen in the physical development of the Negro" (Du Bois, *Dusk of Dawn,* p. 98).

Of course, Du Bois refuted such talk, but it filtered down to the popular level, bolstering racism by providing a supposedly scientific basis for it. As a result, race relations worsened during the 1890s and early 1900s. In the South, racist demagogues such as Senator James K. Vardaman rose to prominence, supported in part by an influx of low-income whites from the Populist Party into the Democratic Party, which dominated the region after 1892. By the mid-1890s, lynchings—when a black was killed by a white mob—increased to an estimated hundred deaths each year. The actual number may be far greater than this figure, however, since no accurate records of black deaths were kept.

Economic exclusion. Despite increasing racial tensions, other events overshadowed the plight of black Americans near the end of the century. Victory in the Spanish American War (1898) made the United States into a world power for the first time. Farm lands and agricultural production had increased dramatically and would continue to escalate through the first decade of the twentieth century. Industrial output also expanded, but at the cost of poor working conditions for many workers. The American Federation of Labor (A. F. of L.) had begun to increase its influence as an umbrella organization of unions in supporting workers' causes. Union membership rose to nearly 1.5 million, and the factory workers' lot gradually improved in many sectors. Yet blacks did not benefit much from the economic expansion. In fact, they were generally barred from organized labor; the A. F. of L. of 1903 did not encourage black membership.

Booker T. Washington, the most influential black of the late 1890s, accepted segregation in the labor movement, as he did in society in general. Washington called on blacks to prepare themselves vocationally, endorsing occupational education for African Americans but downplaying other higher education for them as something almost frivolous during his day. Washington proposed that blacks move slowly toward equality with whites; the first step, he maintained, must be preparation to work in the growing factory society.

Black progress. Despite adversity, conditions in black communities began slowly to improve. Southern conservatives (those who were not radical racists), Northern philanthropists, black

Souls of Black Folk

W. E. B. Du Bois at the Congress of Partisans of Peace in Paris, 1949.

churches, and various voluntary organizations supported black education, and the literacy rate among blacks rose. Also some of the black entrepreneurs and professionals, by catering to the needs of their own communities, were becoming more prosperous.

In 1901 Booker T. Washington became the first black invited to the White House. He used his influence in the Theodore Roosevelt and William Howard Taft administrations to bring about the appointment of blacks to positions in the federal government. Washington, who had founded the Tuskegee Institute in Alabama and built it into a major educational institution for blacks, promoted "industrial" or vocational-technical education. His consistent message was that blacks had to improve themselves in industry, competence, and virtue, and he considered higher academic education inappropriate for most poor blacks. Washington generally refused to speak out in favor of civil rights, though he worked behind the scenes to fight discrimination and prejudice. He secretly financed lawsuits challenging Jim Crow laws, and wrote anonymous articles denouncing racial injustice.

W. E. B. Du Bois stirred controversy by challenging Washington's views and leadership. While Washington stressed economic improvement as a necessary first step toward political equality, Du Bois demanded political equality immediately and unconditionally. When Du Bois published *The Souls of Black Folk* in 1903, Washington's views were understood to be those of the black leadership. Yet by 1910, largely through the influence of his essays, Du Bois won the philosophical war between his own and Washington's ideas and went on to help establish the National Association for the Advancement of Colored People (NAACP), a leading black political organization.

Academic and literary career. A man of impressive versatility, Du Bois had studied at Harvard University and the University of Berlin, and he had published two highly respected works of history and sociology before writing *The Souls of Black Folk*. *The Suppression of the African Slave Trade* (1896), his Harvard Ph.D. thesis published in book form, was the first historical analysis of the slave trade. *The Philadelphia Negro* (1899) examines black life and culture in Philadelphia, and became a pioneering work in black studies as well as in the field of sociology. These two books firmly established Du Bois's academic credentials and won him several teaching posts at major universities. A university professor most of his life, Du Bois was also a novelist, poet, and the founder and editor (for twenty-five years) of the NAACP's journal, *Crisis,* which reached a readership of 100,000 by 1920.

The Essays in Focus

The contents. Throughout the fourteen essays in this collection, Du Bois addresses the "problem of the color line" (Du Bois, *The Souls of Black Folk,* p. 1). Blacks, he argues, are shut out of the white-dominated world by an impenetrable veil of race prejudice and discrimination. Du Bois seeks to describe the spiritual world behind this veil, the world in which 10 million black Americans live and strive. In so doing, he set out to "provide a massive dose of racial truth whites have refused to accept" (Byerman, p. 12).

Each essay is preceded by an epigraph containing a few lines of poetry, usually from an acclaimed source such as Johann Schiller or John Greenleaf Whittier, along with a few bars from a Negro spiritual. The essays themselves are a mix: studies on racial segregation, acclamations for the black contributions to American culture, exaltations of education as a means of progress, and personal sentiments about the situation of blacks in white society.

The first essay in the collection, "Of Our Spiritual Strivings," traces the development of the black community from emancipation to the twentieth century. The history of American blacks, he contends, is the story of a struggle between two souls—American and Negro.

> [It] is the history of this strife—the longing to merge [the black person's] double self into a better and truer self. He would not Africanize America ... he would not bleach his Negro soul in a flood of white Americanism.... He simply wishes to make it possible to be both a Negro and an American without being cursed and spit upon by his fellows, without having the doors of Opportunity closed roughly in his face.
> (*The Souls of Black Folk,* p. 5)

In perhaps the most famous essay in the collection, "Of Mr. Booker T. Washington and Others." Du Bois addresses the attitudes of the influential black educator, which Du Bois feels promote the subservience and inferiority of blacks:

> Mr. Washington's programme practically accepts the alleged inferiority of the Negro races ... and [he] withdraws many of the high demands of Negroes as men and American citizens. In other periods of intensified prejudice all the Negro's tendency to self-assertion has been called forth; at this period a policy of submission is advocated.
> (*The Souls of Black Folk,* p. 43)

Du Bois outlines what he sees as the flaws in Washington's philosophy and in the course of the essay encourages his readers to disagree with the respected Mr. Washington and follow their duty to act on behalf of true liberty and equality for blacks. He criticizes Washington's approach to education and civil rights extensively and in detail. Weaving economic, historical, and humanistic analysis, he defends the value of education for its own sake, referring to a passage from Washington's famous autobiography, *Up from Slavery* (also covered in *Literature and Its Times*):

> So thoroughly did he [Washington] learn the speech and thought of triumphant commercialism, and the ideals of material prosperity, that the picture of a lone black boy poring over a French grammar amid the weeds and dirt of a neglected home soon seemed to him the acme of absurdities. One wonders what Socrates and St. Francis of Assisi would say to this.
> (*The Souls of Black Folk,* p. 38)

Du Bois accuses Washington of preaching a "gospel of Work and Money" (*The Souls of Black Folk,* p. 43) and calling on blacks to give up the struggle for civil rights, political power, and higher education. He charges that Washington's efforts are contributing to segregation, disenfranchisement, and the closing off of educational opportunities for blacks.

Other essays in the collection document the difficulties of poor blacks. In "Of the Quest for the Golden Fleece," Du Bois comments that the homes of laborers in Dougherty County, Georgia, are wretched, and the lives of the people there are more or less the same as they had been in the days of slavery. In "Of the Meaning of Progress" Du Bois recalls his days as a schoolteacher in the Tennessee hills. The schoolhouse was a log hut with rough benches, and despite the harsh conditions and dullness of his surroundings Du Bois grew to appreciate the community. Ten years later, Du Bois writes, when he revisited the area, he found his favorite student dead. The local people, said the student's mother, had encountered trying times since Du Bois had left. At the end of the essay, Du Bois muses on the nature of progress, and how hard life can be for the lowly.

The remainder of the book discusses economic and social conditions in the black community, black leadership and education, and black contributions to American culture. Du Bois's observations reflect not only his subject, the "souls" of black Americans, but also his own passion in striving to portray that subject.

Souls of Black Folk

Du Bois addressing the Congress of Partisans of Peace.

Du Bois's perspectives amplified. Du Bois's views were momentous for his era because they offered blacks an alternative to Booker T. Washington's more passive ideologies. Du Bois, moreover, communicated his ideas in a way that would appeal to both the politically and the artistically inclined. Bringing his academic training to bear in one of the book's early essays, for example, Du Bois comments on racial segregation:

> The Negroes are a subjugated, servile caste with restricted rights and privileges. Before the courts, both in law and custom, they stand on a different and peculiar basis. Taxation without representation is the rule of their political life.
> (*The Souls of Black Folk*, p. 34)

This hard-edged political analysis contains a historical allusion to the founding fathers' famous complaint against British rule. Compare it with the poetically expressed indignation of the following passage, taken from an essay about the death of Du Bois's first child as an infant:

> He knew no color line.... No bitter meanness now shall sicken his baby heart 'til it die a living death, no taunt shall madden his happy boyhood.... Well sped, my boy, before the world had dubbed your ambition insolence, had held your ideals unattainable, and taught you to cringe and bow.
> (*The Souls of Black Folk*, pp. 173-74)

While the two passages differ in style, they share outrage at the double standard to which blacks are subjected in society. Explaining this outrage are other passages that assess blacks' contributions to American culture. Their gift of story and song, Du Bois writes, softened an ill-harmonized and unmelodious land, while their gift of sweat and brawn helped push back the wilderness and laid the foundation of America's growing economic empire. A third gift, a gift of the spirit, provided oases of simple faith and reverence to bolster the soul. Black people were, Du Bois claims, America's most religious citizens.

Du Bois also attacks the racist notions that sprang from social Darwinism and infected the attitudes of many scientists and much of the public during the 1890s. He rejects the "silently growing assumption of this age that the probation of races is past, and that the backward races of today are of proven inefficiency and not worth the saving" (*The Souls of Black Folk*, p. 214). Giving black people an alternative to the course of action advocated by Booker T. Washington, he calls on them to resist all forms of racism. He enjoins them to fight Jim Crow laws and voting restrictions, and recognize the importance of education, particularly university education.

In one of his sharpest attacks, Du Bois states that Washington's approach is detrimental and must be resisted.

> So far as Mr. Washington apologizes for injustice, North or South, does not rightly value the privilege and duty of voting, belittles the emasculating effects of caste distinctions, and opposes the higher training and ambition of our brighter minds,—so far as he, the South or the Nation does this,—we must unceasingly and firmly oppose them. By every civilized and peaceful method we must strive for the rights which the world accords to men, clinging unwaveringly to those great words which the sons of the Fathers would fain forget: "We hold these truths to be self-evident: That all men are created equal; that they are endowed by their Creator with certain unalienable rights; that among these are life, liberty and the pursuit of happiness."
> (*The Souls of Black Folk*, p. 50)

Shortly after the publication of *The Souls of Black Folk*, Washington answered Du Bois in a letter to a coal contractor (January 1904):

> The main difference between Dr. Du Bois' position and that of my own is that he believes that what the race is entitled to can be secured by making demands and asserting grievances. My belief is that we will secure more quickly, and have in our possession more permanently the rights we should possess through the more slow but sure channel of development along commercial lines in connection with education, morality, and religion. I believe that one successful Negro owning a bank is more potent in securing respect and justice for the race than a hundred men making abstract speeches and demands for justice.
> (Washington in Harlan, pp. 416-17)

Sources. *The Souls of Black Folk* began as an idea from the publishing company that first issued it, A. C. McClurg & Co. of Chicago. In 1902, the company asked Du Bois to write a small number of essays that they could publish as a book. At first, Du Bois resisted, claiming that "books of essays always fall so flat" (Du Bois in Lewis, p. 277). Later, however, he agreed to a collection of some of his essays that had appeared in magazines and academic journals. Of the book's fourteen essays, nine had appeared previously elsewhere; Du Bois, however, rewrote them extensively to fit his idea for the book, which was, as he put it, to "show the strange meaning of being black here in the dawning of the Twentieth Century" (*The Souls of Black Folk*, p. 1).

The chapter on Booker T. Washington was based on a review of Washington's book *Up from Slavery* that Du Bois wrote for *Dial* magazine. For the book, Du Bois expanded the brief review into a full-scale attack on Washington's philosophy of accommodation. He also added sections that filled out Washington's historical context as a black leader, comparing him with figures such as Frederick Douglass and (with bitter irony) Jefferson Davis, President of the Confederacy.

A DIFFERENCE IN BACKGROUNDS

The dispute between Du Bois and Washington was partly rooted in their backgrounds. Du Bois was born free, grew up in rural Massachusetts, earned a Ph.D. at Harvard University, and studied in Europe. His only extensive exposure to Southern blacks—at that time the vast majority of American blacks—came during his years as a student at Fisk University, a black university in Tennessee. When *The Souls of Black Folk* was published, he had been a university teacher for ten years, teaching such wide-ranging subjects as Greek, Latin, history, and sociology. In 1903, he was a professor of economics at the University of Atlanta. Washington, by contrast, was born a slave in Virginia and was a lifelong resident of the South, having graduated from Hampton Institute, a vocational college for blacks. Du Bois had little experience of the unwritten rules by which most blacks and whites interacted, and no tolerance for the inequalities generated by those rules. Washington, who grew up with them, saw the rules as a safety valve for racial tensions. But in the first decade of the new century, fewer blacks were willing to heed Washington's message of patience, and Du Bois came to represent the new black leadership.

Du Bois's extensive education shows itself in the many references throughout the essays to literary and historical figures from many cultures. His studies in Berlin, for example, gave him a love of the German Romantic poets Goethe and Schiller, who are among those borrowed from in the brief poetic quotations that precede each essay. Other Romantic poets quoted by Du Bois include America's James Russell Lowell and John Greenleaf Whittier and England's Alfred Lord Tennyson, Lord Byron, Algernon Swinburne, and Elizabeth Barrett Browning. Brief musical quotations from Negro spirituals, also presented at the start of each chapter, reinforce the Romantic tone incurred by the poetic references.

Reception. Du Bois hoped that his book would raise public awareness of racial injustice and inspire reforms. "Let the ears of a guilty people tingle with truth," he writes as an afterword, "and seventy millions sigh for the righteousness which exalteth nations, in this drear day when human brotherhood is mockery and a snare" (*The Souls of Black Folk,* p. 217). In fact, *The Souls of Black Folk* reached a wide readership. Sales of the book were steady and strong, rising to nearly 10,000 copies within five years, a fine number for a black author of a controversial work on black culture. England published an edition in 1905, and plans (ultimately unsuccessful) were made for a German version as well. Since then, *The Souls of Black Folk* has appeared in many languages and has attained the rank of an international classic.

The book provoked predictable reactions from the white South, ranging from hostility—"this book is indeed dangerous for the Negro to read"—to disgust—a demand that the author be arrested for "inciting rape" (Lewis, p. 293). Black and white Northern responses were more ambivalent. While Washington's informal influence served to stymie some of the attention it might have received in the black press, several notable black reviewers praised it strongly. Novelist James Weldon Johnson, for example, attributed to it an impact "greater upon and within the Negro race than any other single book published in this country since *Uncle Tom's Cabin*" (Johnson in Lewis, p. 277). Wendell Phillips Dabney, editor of the black *Ohio Enterprise,* ran this uppercase headline over a review of it: "SHOULD BE READ AND STUDIED BY EVERY PERSON, WHITE AND BLACK" (Dabney in Lewis, p. 292).

White reviewers in the North often expressed regret at Du Bois's impatience while expressing sympathy for his aims. By contrast, John Daniels in *Alexander's Magazine* praised the book's poetic tone as an important part of Du Bois's message:

> Take his sadness and bitterness for granted, then feel it with him, its power, its justice. Judge his book not as an argument, as an anti-Washingtonian protest, but as a poem, a spiritual, not intellectual offering, an appeal not to the head but to the heart. Give the book its highest place; not that of a polemic, a transient thing, but that of a poem, a thing permanent.
> (Andrews, p. 38)

For More Information

Andrews, William L., ed. *Critical Essays on W. E. B. Du Bois.* Boston: G. K. Hall, 1985.

Byerman, Keith. *Seizing the Word—History, Art, and Self in the Work of W. E. B. Du Bois.* Athens: University of Georgia Press, 1994.

Du Bois, W. E. Burghardt. *The Souls of Black Folk.* 1903. Reprint. New York: Penguin, 1989.

Harlan, Louis R. and Raymond Smock, eds. *The Booker T. Washington Papers.* Vol. 7: *1903-04.* Urbana: University of Illinois Press, 1977.

Lewis, David Levering. *W. E. B. Du Bois: Biography of a Race, 1868-1919.* New York: Henry Holt, 1993.

Powers, Richard H. "An American Tragedy: The Transformation of Booker T. Washington from Hero to Whipping Boy." *Lincoln Review* 11, no. 1 (Winter-Spring 1993): 19-39.

Sundquist, Eric. *To Wake the Nations.* Cambridge, Mass.: Harvard University Press, 1993.

"The Souls of Black Folk." *The Outlook* 74, no. 11 (July 11, 1903): 669-71.

The Story Catcher

by Mari Sandoz

M ari Sandoz was born to a Swiss German-speaking family on a homestead in northwestern Nebraska in 1896. As a child, she was exposed to the Cheyenne and Sioux tribes, who lived on neighboring reservations and often pitched their tepees near her house when visiting the area. She later became a scholar of the Great Plains, researching and writing about American Indian history in that area, especially on the turbulent events of the nineteenth century.

> **THE LITERARY WORK**
> A novel set in the Great Plains during the 1840s; published in 1963.
>
> **SYNOPSIS**
> After many adventures, a young Oglala Sioux boy finally comes of age, gaining the wisdom and insight necessary to be the tribal historian.

Events in History at the Time the Novel Takes Place

Plains Indians during the 1840s. *The Story Catcher* takes place on the High Plains north and west of the Bighorn Mountains, which cross from present-day Montana into Wyoming. Although many American Indians considered the encroaching settlement of whites a threat by this time, the most serious of the battles against the U.S. military had not yet taken place. There was, however, another threat brought by whites during this period—the smallpox epidemic that struck in 1837. Some tribes lost as many as 80 percent of their population to this devastating illness. The main character of the novel, Lance, has his important dream while sick with smallpox.

Second parents. Every child in traditional Sioux society had a second mother and father. Lance's blood mother plays a relatively small role in the book, and he instead turns to his second mother, Feather Woman, during the many trials that he experiences as he grows into adulthood. Often the second parents were friends or relatives of the blood parents. Ideally, the second father was an excellent warrior, hunter, or healer, while his wife, the second mother, was warm-hearted, loving, and able to take over much of the child's care.

The Sioux believed that by having two sets of parents a person avoided familial conflicts. A mother, for example, would not become overly attached to her sons and incur the jealousy of the father, nor would she feel pangs of resentment against her daughters as they matured. After the age of seven, Sioux boys were not allowed to directly speak to their mother or sisters but could only send messages through a third party. The second mother, however, was free to demonstrate affection directly to the boy, and he generally felt freer in her presence. He could talk and laugh more easily than in his blood home, where such actions were considered improper.

Courting. During this period, the Sioux believed that if their young women were not virtuous, the

The Story Catcher

Picture by Amos Bad Heart Bull (1869-1913), an Oglala Sioux, depicting the death of Crazy Horse in 1877.

buffalo would disappear. Thus, the very well-being of the tribe hinged on the behavior of the girls. Sioux maidens lived under the guardianship of the old woman of their lodge, who usually accompanied them wherever they went in order to ensure proper conduct.

Courting was a formal process. Initially, a suitor might tie a "courting horse" outside his sweetheart's lodge. If the girl's family favored the young man, they led the horse away and added it to the family herd. This sign of approval, however, was only the beginning. Once the family accepted the courting horse, the youth found an elderly person to act as a go-between. This go-between would communicate with the family to discover what was further required of the suitor in order for him to marry his love. Some men worked for years to prove themselves. In *The Story Catcher*, Lance ties his mare in a suitor's offering only at the very end of the book, after he has already won many honors:

> In the first morning light he looked out, afraid that the mare would still be tied there, rejected, left for him to lead away. But she was gone, taken to the family herd, and he was publicly accepted as a suitor. Now he had the right to present his formal wooing, try to persuade the girl and her family that he would make an acceptable husband. This might take years, as

it sometimes did, but in his gratitude Lance turned his eyes to the sky, the earth and the four directions—to the Powers in which all things are brothers.
(Sandoz, *The Story Catcher*, p. 174)

Picture-history. Art was an integral part of Sioux life, serving as both a means of adornment and a method for communicating and recording history. Picture-writing was "utilized for messages ranging from love letters to directions to new camp sites to warnings to those who might venture into an unsafe area" (Szabo, p. 7). Anybody was allowed to draw, and throughout the story, Young Lance draws pictures of events. His depictions serve either as remembrances for himself or as signals to others. To draw them, Lance sometimes uses blood, charcoal, or the colorsticks someone had given him. Sioux artists often worked with red, blue, green, yellow, black, and white clay powders.

Despite the fact that anybody could draw pictures, only the official historian recorded the tribal history for everyone. The Oglala Sioux preserved much of their history through art, so the tribal historian filled an essential role in their nation. In the eyes of the Oglala, tribal historians were as important as medicine men and great warriors. Each band had only one historian and this historian chose his successor. It was a very difficult position to attain, as Lance discovers when he tells Paint Maker of his secret desire. Paint Maker replies, "This is not for one who was not given the dreaming and the wisdom." When Lance protests that he indeed had the dreaming, Paint Maker asks, "That may be the dreaming, but the wisdom?" (*The Story Catcher*, p. 156).

Tribal historians needed two vital skills. First, they required the ability to observe events objectively, even if they had participated in their occurrence. They had to be able to look closely at what happened and include exact detail, since tribal historians would say, "The picture is the rope that ties memory solidly to the stake of truth" (Blish, p. xxi). Secondly, the historian needed the ability to render the picture both comprehensible and meaningful, to "grasp the action and the meaning, with something beyond the factual content, something broader, more, as the Sioux liked to say, of the sky and the great directions, a meaning more elevated, more profound" (Blish, p. xxi). The pictures recorded hunts, moves, ceremonial rites, and natural disasters, among other events. Including individual participants, the pictures made people distinguishable—by their depicting them in their regalia, for example. Formal histories had to be approved by band leaders and uncontested by anyone involved in the recorded event.

The Novel in Focus

The plot. *The Story Catcher* depicts the adventures and development of a young Oglala Indian named Young Lance who draws pictures of various events in his life throughout the novel. The plot opens as Lance, hovering near a recent battle site, discovers an Arikara ("Ree") Indian child hidden terrified in the bushes. Lance captures the lost and starving child and decides to take the "little Ree" back to his village and raise him as a Sioux. When Lance returns, however, village members are angry at him for endangering them. They remind him that he is forever responsible for the little Ree's actions, and that their Ree enemies will probably attack the Sioux upon discovering that the youth is alive.

Many people ostracize Lance for his foolish act. The next day, some leave to hunt buffalo but do not invite him along since he might bring bad luck. Despondent, Lance spots an eagle flying overhead. He leaves the camp, climbs to the eagle's nest, and captures the bird with his bare hands. This news spreads quickly throughout the village. Everyone comes to see the bird, and Lance gains some respect since, "It was a solemn thing that this Young Lance who was not permitted to go with the hunt today should take an eagle in the old pit, without a vision, a medicine guidance, a leader, or anyone to tell him how it was done" (*The Story Catcher*, p. 27).

Lance has other adventures: he participates in buffalo hunts and even serves as a war scout. Not yet considered adults, Lance and his friends seek to gain status by capturing enemy horses. Against tribal wishes, the three young boys steal out of the village and travel for five days into enemy territory. All they find, however, are well-guarded enemy camps that are too strong to attack. As they turn back, their Ree enemies discover and pursue them. One arrow strikes Lance in the knee and he hides in a big hole left by a dead tree. Undiscovered, he lays thirsty and feverish for days. Lance spends the entire winter in the hole as his wound slowly heals; occasionally he draws pictures using skin, charcoal, and blood to depict his predicament. "On an antelope skin were pictures telling the winter's story, drawn in charcoal and blood paint.... They told of the events beginning with the wounding, pictured in the center" (*The Story Catcher*, p. 72).

THE SUN DANCE

A sacred ceremony, the Sun Dance was performed by male volunteers who sought spiritual help to cure a relative's illness, for example, or to solve an ongoing problem like the one the novel chronicles when Lance's brother disappears in a flood. Sacrifice, the dancers believed, would right disharmony in the world and bring favor from the spirits. The Sun Dance, geared around this concept, included torturing the dancers. Their chests and backs were pierced with wooden skewers, which had leather ropes attached to them. Another part of the ropes would be fastened to the top of a Sun Lodge, and the dancers would dangle in the air until the skewers broke their flesh free and the ritual ended.

When Lance finally goes home, his village celebrates his return from the dead. His knee is still lame, and he cannot easily participate in the dancing and hunting. Because of his handicap, he grows shy, especially around the beautiful Blue Dawn, a childhood friend who has become quite womanly.

The Story Catcher

Lance continues to mature and witnesses many happenings, which he draws on skins. In one instance, his adopted brother, the little Ree, is captured by Crow Indians. Since little Ree is Lance's responsibility, Lance sets out after him alone, leaving only a small picture of what has happened as a message to others. After capturing Lance, the Crows take him to the little Ree, who cries, "My brother has come!" (*The Story Catcher*, p. 103). Lance and the little Ree manage to escape when the Crow settlement is swept away in a flood. In the ensuing panic, Lance cannot find his adopted brother. He vows to dance in the Sun Dance if his brother escapes. Eventually Lance discovers the little Ree alive in a washed-out patch of earth.

Lance's spiritual advisor deems that Lance is not yet old enough to fulfill such a solemn vow. Disappointed, Lance continues to draw and participate in tribal activities such as the annual great council, a meeting of over twenty thousand Indians. At one point he catches smallpox, and dreams of red, blue, yellow, and green figures, no bigger than his fingers, which float down to him. Lance later interprets this dream as a call to become the tribal historian. He also begins to pursue Blue Dawn more earnestly, and on one occasion even tries to convince her to come away with him without following the proper courting procedures.

Lance eventually approaches Paint Maker, the old tribal historian, explaining to the old man how he saw and drew events. When Paint Maker points out that anybody is allowed to draw pictures, Lance replies that he wants to make pictures for the tribe. Paint Maker notes:

> A recorder of what has been done is equal to the greatest hunter, the bravest warrior, or even the holy man. To be such a historian, such a recorder, you must learn to see all things, to know how they look, and how they are done.
> (*The Story Catcher*, p. 157)

Paint Maker initially rejects Lance's drawings. Lance reacts by participating bravely in a battle against the Pawnees, and learning to record the horrors of battle with an objective and keen eye. When his Ree enemies enter the village and offer gifts in exchange for his adopted brother, he wisely allows the little Ree to make his own decision. Lance also overcomes his shyness and offers Blue Dawn a courting horse captured in battle. Eventually both his own father and Paint Maker acknowledge Lance's abilities and maturation and accept Lance as the next tribal historian. Together they sing his song of praise: "Now he will be the picture maker of the deeds of the people; / Now he will no longer be called Lance; / Now he is the Story Catcher" (*The Story Catcher*, p. 175).

Individual vs. tribe. Lance often acts according to his personal desires, sometimes imperiling the village. He steals away from a scout camp, for example, placing the entire party in danger. Additionally, instead of killing the little enemy Ree at the battle site, Lance feels for the child and takes him into captivity. Many tribal members, however, do not agree with Lance's decision. In fact, they are angry because Lance's action might prompt the Rees to attack if they find out the child is living in the village. Lance's decision is potentially dangerous to the whole community.

In nineteenth-century Sioux society, the welfare of the community was more important than individual desires. Even infants were not allowed to endanger the village. When newborns began to cry, their mothers would gently pinch the babies' noses and close their mouths. The mothers would interrupt their hold to let the baby breathe, then close off the air again if the baby continued to make noise. As Sandoz notes:

> During the newborn minutes, that newborn hour, Indian children, boy and girl, were taught the first and greatest lesson of their lives: that no one could be permitted to endanger the people by even one cry to guide a roving enemy to the village or to spoil a hunt.
> (Sandoz, *These Were the Sioux*, p. 24)

Throughout the story, Lance struggles with his personal desires on one hand and his tribal obligations on the other. Village elders forbade the boys to steal enemy horses because if the boys are killed, others will be obligated to avenge their deaths, bringing trouble and discord to the community. Yet Lance and his friends attempt to steal horses anyway, in order to gain personal status. Lance also acts on his sexual desire, urging Blue Dawn to come away with him. According to Sioux belief, the buffalo would not come if the young women did not remain virtuous, and so Lance's desires again imperil the tribe. Luckily, Blue Dawn refuses, and the next day Lance regrets his action.

> He wanted to offer his handsome mule to the girl as a gift of apology, an apology for his impulsiveness of last night. His face burned at the thought of the humiliation he would have brought upon her, her parents, and her grandfather ... upon his own people too, particularly Good Axe, the honored bearer of the holy lance, and his mother and his sisters.
> (*The Story Catcher*, p. 155)

Sources. According to Helen Stauffer, who has written extensively on Mari Sandoz, the events and characters found in *The Story Catcher* stem from a variety of sources, including Sandoz's earlier writings. The capture of the eagle, for example, derives from an earlier story called "The Birdman," while other events and characters can be traced back to legend, literature, and history. Stauffer writes, "The influence of ***Black Elk Speaks*** (also covered in *Literature and Its Times*) can be seen in details of the young boys' training and games, such as burning sunflower seeds on the wrist, stealing dried meat from racks, or the Throwing-Them-off-Their-Horses contests" (Stauffer, p. 245).

Sandoz drew extensively from purely historical events as well. Lance's winter survival story, for example, appears to be based on an actual happening. Also Sandoz was intimately familiar with the life of Amos Bad Heart Bull, a famous Oglala historian: *The Story Catcher* is dedicated to him. Amos Bad Heart Bull had another name, Eagle Lance, possibly the inspiration for the protagonist's name.

Events in History at the Time the Novel Was Written

Mari Sandoz and the American Indian civil rights movement. Throughout her life, Mari Sandoz took an active interest in the political affairs of American Indians. For example, she fought the 1953 Eisenhower Administration policy of termination, which sought to eliminate reservations as political organizations. As a part of this effort, the federal government encouraged American Indians to assimilate into white society by paying them small sums of money to relocate to cities. That same year, without the consent of native tribes, the government passed Public Law 280, which extended state controls over offenses committed by or against Indians on reservations.

Sandoz wrote to cabinet members and congressmen, including Senator Sam Ervin, chairman of the Senate Judiciary Subcommittee on Constitutional Rights. She argued that many American Indians still did not have basic civil rights. In 1961 the federal government agreed with her, its United States Commission on Civil Rights concluding that for the vast majority of American Indians living in the United States, "poverty and deprivation are common. Social acceptance is not the rule. In addition, Indians seem to suffer more than occasional mistreatment by the instruments of law and order on and off the reservations" (Nash, p. 929). In fact, Indians faced obstacles similar to African Americans and other minorities during that era.

In the end, the black civil rights movement affected federal direction. The policy of termination was abandoned in 1961, and instead the government pursued "self-determination" for the American Indians, a concept embracing tribal restoration, self-government, cultural renewal, and self-sufficiency. This approach, along with the Civil Rights Act, desegregation efforts, and the growing youth movement, furthered American Indian political awareness and cultural pride, especially among younger generations. The sit-ins of the early 1960s, for example, inspired fish-ins beginning in 1964 among West Coast American Indians who claimed ancestral fishing rights.

CIVIL RIGHTS ACT OF 1964

Passed after almost a decade of direct action (sit-ins, demonstrations, and other forms of protest), the Civil Rights Act of 1964 outlawed racial discrimination in places of public accommodation and gave the U.S. Justice Department more authority in schools and elections to ensure fair treatment of minorities in both. The act also prohibited discrimination in hiring workers in businesses, and the benefits of the legislation affected all minorities, including American Indians.

Advocate and youth groups were also organized during the 1950s and 1960s. The American Indian Chicago Conference in 1961, for example, outlined a program for Indian affairs that addressed health, welfare, education, and economic issues. Interested individuals sponsored Pan-Indian organizations, which began to lobby Congress, and American Indian groups increasingly sought grant money from the government to achieve their purposes.

American Indian art in the 1950s and 1960s. Conceptions of self-determination infused American Indian art as well. During the 1930s and 1940s, American Indian art grew in popularity, and artists sometimes found white patrons who encouraged their pursuits. Sandoz herself served on the board for the American Indian Society for Creative Artists and sent money to the Northern Cheyenne reservation for the Little Finger Nail Art Award. Often, however, patrons such as the

Philbrook Art Center in Tulsa, Oklahoma, advanced a particular style, encouraging romantic, nostalgic paintings depicting buffalo hunts and costumed warriors. Indian painting from these schools of the 1930s and 1940s used techniques that rendered their subjects two dimensionally. Artists portrayed specific events and emphasized detail in ceremonial and warrior costumes.

During the late 1950s, however, new artists challenged the boundaries of these old styles. Oscar Howe, a Sioux artist, as well as other American Indians began portraying emotion and drama in their paintings, and generalizing the subject matter in order to convey spiritual and mystical impressions. Howe, for example, often alluded to ceremonies and customs in his paintings but did not literally illustrate them. In 1958, when the Philbrook Museum rejected Howe's work as "nontraditional," he protested. His protest led to a broader definition of traditional Indian art and the eventual acceptance of new subject matter and styles that included cubism and realism.

American Indian arts developed further in the early 1960s, when the Institute of American Indian and Alaska Native American Culture and Arts was founded in 1962 on the recommendation of the Indian Arts and Crafts Board. Designed to help develop artistically talented youths, the Institute served to promote the advancement and appreciation of American Indian culture through the arts. The Institute emphasized a contemporary approach to native art, incorporating American and European styles, as well as the inclusion of social issues such as political activism.

Reviews. Mari Sandoz's *The Story Catcher* was well received. Published in 1963, it won the Levi Strauss Golden Saddleman Award that year and the Western Writers of America Spur Award for best juvenile literature in 1964. A review in the *Chicago Tribune* (November 10, 1963) praised the novel for showing deep knowledge and understanding of the Plains Indians, and for having rhythmic prose that was beautifully suited to the epic quality of the tale.

For More Information

Blish, Helen. *A Pictographic History of the Oglala Sioux*. Lincoln: University of Nebraska Press, 1967.

Nash, Gary. *The American People: Creating a Nation and a Society*. Vol 2. New York: Harper & Row, 1986.

Sandoz, Mari. *These Were the Sioux*. New York: Hastings House, 1961.

Sandoz, Mari. *The Story Catcher*. Lincoln: University of Nebraska Press, 1963.

Stauffer, Helen. *Mari Sandoz: Storyteller of the Plains*. Lincoln: University of Nebraska Press, 1982.

Szabo, Joyce. *Howling Wolf and the History of Ledger Art*. Albuquerque: New Mexico Press, 1994.

Tess of the D'Urbervilles

by
Thomas Hardy

Written toward the end of the Victorian era, *Tess of the D'Urbervilles* reflects the confusion of Thomas Hardy's changing society. The novel explores not only the hypocrisy of England's moral standards, but also the nature of that country's changing agricultural economy. As an inhabitant of a rural village himself, Hardy relates from firsthand experience a tale of the declining landed gentry and rural communities undergoing turbulent events.

> **THE LITERARY WORK**
>
> A novel set in the countryside of Wessex, England, during the late 1800s; published in 1891.
>
> **SYNOPSIS**
>
> A beautiful country girl is sexually assaulted and later suffers the consequences of Victorian England's moral codes, which make her an unsuitable wife because she is no longer pure.

Events in History at the Time of the Novel

The changing face of country life. The latter half of the Victorian era—the years between 1860 and 1900—constituted a period of transformation for rural England. More and more country villages lost their inhabitants to job opportunities in industrialized cities such as London and Manchester. Encouraging this "drift from the land," as the migration was frequently termed, was an agricultural depression in the last quarter of the century.

Hardy's novel takes place in southwest England, a rural region in which he was born. In real life, farm wages remained low here partly because this region, in contrast to the middle and northern parts of England, had little industry. Without factories to compete for workers, the farm employer did not feel pressed to raise wages. Circumstances grew especially grim for farm workers toward the end of the 1800s when the number of unemployed men was on the rise. One result was that it grew harder for women to find work in the fields; another was that the income earned by women in rural industries (for example, dairying, glovemaking, or plaiting straw) became vital to family survival.

While there was little industry in southwest England, life there was nevertheless affected by inventions and developments in the nation. The early 1800s had witnessed the growth of mass transportation. With villages more readily accessible to one another, trade within the nation boomed. Railways transported goods in a matter of hours instead of days. For many country dwellers, this meant an increase in commerce and trade. The dairy industry grew rapidly because fresh milk was now able to survive a quick daily journey to towns hundreds of miles away. In Hardy's novel, Tess finds plenty of work on a dairy farm although her own village suffers an agricultural slump; this seeming contradiction is explained by the boom in transportation.

Other industrial developments affected rural life as well. There is an episode in the novel that involves Tess's employment at a steam threshing machine, which causes her suffering. The machine requires several workers to perform small repetitive tasks for hours at a time. Tess, placed on the platform with the machine and rick (cornstack), unties each sheaf given to her before it is seized by the man who feeds it to the machine. Introduced as early as 1803, the steam threshing machine was no longer new by Tess's day; in fact, Hardy was probably drawing on his memory of it to create the scene. It was once thought that such scenes reflected his sorrow at the passing of old rural ways (in this case, the flailing of corn by hand with a wooden tool to separate it from the stalk). But as one biographer suggests and the not-so-new threshing machine indicates, such a scene may instead be showing Hardy's nostalgia for and "normal attachment" to the environment of his youth (Seymour-Smith, p. 20). In any case, the scene exposes a few of the rural hardships of the era.

Some of these hardships were suffered by the rural industries. Though the invention of better methods of transport benefited a number of rural industries, it brought a decrease in productivity for others. Once goods could be more easily shipped in from distant areas, most village craftsman, such as shoemakers and carpenters, lost their business to the cheaper, more efficient factory labor of the towns. This decline in job opportunity drove many young workers from the country into the city.

The departure of its youth upset not only the economic structure of the countryside, but the social one as well. Firstly, there was a change in the landowning class. In reaction to the agricultural decline of the period, the old gentry abandoned lands that had belonged to their families for several generations. Almost 6 million acres of agricultural property would change hands in the early 1900s. The majority of this land came from the breakups and sales of old family estates. In the process, as is the case with the D'Urbervilles, to whom Tess may be related, these once-powerful landowners lost not only their estates but also their economic and social influence.

Despite the ominous foreboding of this decline, English villages did not turn into ghost towns during this period. Newcomers arrived, but in localities that had once boasted only three surnames in an entire village (in other words, had been occupied by only three families), these new arrivals unleashed great commotion. Suddenly news of popular trends and current events from the big cities began to reach the previously isolated villagers. Most of newcomers hailed from England's middle class. They built new homes, brought urban tastes to the rural areas, and replaced the figure of the landed country squire with that of the wealthy modern businessman. Old pastimes, such as the folk dancing in which Tess participates at the opening of the novel, soon seemed outdated. More disciplined activities like English football (known in America as soccer) replaced these archaic recreational pursuits. Yet despite the losses it suffered, the English village also benefited from the influx. The rural standard of living improved, and communication with other regions increased. Furthermore, country living gained a new attractiveness. With the population boom in the cities, the close-knit community and calm surroundings of the country village seemed a commodity worth having.

Marriage for the Victorians. In the novel, the character Angel comes from a traditional middle-class family that, not surprisingly, expects the youngest son to marry a woman of similar socioeconomic status. When he announces that he has found "a woman who possessed every qualification to be the helpmate of an agriculturist" (Hardy, *Tess of the D'Urbervilles,* p. 28), his mother's initial response is to ask, "Is she of a family such as you would care to marry into—a lady, in short?" (*Tess of the D'Urbervilles,* p. 28). As reflected by her question, marriage, in the eyes of the Victorian gentry, served as a union of more than mere love.

In the Victorian era most members of the upper classes obtained their earnings from their land. The Duke of Westminster, for instance, drew an annual salary of £250,000 (the equivalent of $1,215,000 at a time when the pound equaled approximately $4.80), and his was not even England's largest holding. As the Victorian era progressed, however, such grand estates grew more and more difficult to maintain as one parcel. In time, primarily because of the advent of foreign economic competition, there was a general collapse in British agriculture, as wool, grains, and produce could be obtained cheaply from foreign sources. Many of the gentry were forced to sell off their acreage and thus looked to marriage to provide them with the necessary means of survival. In the case of the Ninth Duke of Marlborough, a relationship of love was forsaken for a more profitable match with Consuelo Vanderbilt, the great-granddaughter of the American tycoon Cornelius Vanderbilt. The

Scene from a 1924 film version of *Tess of the D'Urbervilles,* starring Conrad Nagel and Blanche Sweet.

duke was not alone in his preference for money over love.

The minimal relevance of love in marriage was further reinforced by Victorian ideas of sexuality. One medical textbook claimed that sexual indulgence "not only retards the development of the genital organs, but of the whole body, impairs the strength, injures the constitution and shortens life" (Hibbert, p. 112). As a topic, sexuality did not arise in the company of polite society. Even with the sanction of marriage, the experts warned that excess should be avoided, "and sensual feelings in the man gradually sobered down" (Hibbert, p. 112). Given such restrained ideas about sexuality, Angel's outrage toward Tess for her past sexual encounter in the novel seems more understandable. This is not to say, however, that Victorians had no sexual feelings or unapproved relations—only that they hid them from view. While health manuals of the age did warn against excess, they also warned that abstaining from sex altogether was as harmful to one's health as overindulging in it. And the prevalence of prostitutes indicated that Victorian men did not, in fact, abstain. The *Pall Mall Gazette* estimated in 1885 that London alone housed over sixty thousand prostitutes. In the novel Angel confesses his own "eight-and-forty hours' dissipation with a stranger" (*Tess of the D'Urbervilles,* p. 177). It seems that what Victorian men often deemed as improper at home they actively sought on the streets or, as the novel demonstrates, in the woods. Meanwhile, society expected women of the upper classes to be passionless creatures and ascribed sexual longings only to lower-class females.

The Victorian woman. Tess the milkmaid, with her means of financial independence, represents a minority of Victorian women. The 1861 census records just one percent of the English labor force as female. By 1881 this number had advanced to three percent, and a few improvements occurred for women in the job market during the twenty-year interval. Almost 100,000 women held jobs as teachers by 1871, and other professions showed growth as well. In 1865 Elizabeth Garrett became the first women to obtain a medical qualification; by 1881 England could boast twenty-five female doctors. Yet many of these working women were subjected to a double standard, holding positions identical to those of men but being paid only half of what their male colleagues earned.

The law, like other societal institutions of the era, also treated women unfairly. Although England legalized divorce in 1857, its limited scope enabled men to divorce their wives more easily than women could divorce their husbands. For

Tess of the D'Urbervilles

instance, while a husband could file for separation on the ground of adultery alone, a woman needed to prove both adultery and cruelty or desertion by her husband. And if a woman sought redress by getting a divorce, she often found herself socially ostracized for her efforts. In any case, whether the man or woman filed for separation, grounds for divorce remained difficult to prove, and the termination of the marriage was often not granted. When in the novel Tess tells Angel that she had once been raped, she assumes that with this knowledge, he would be able to divorce her should he wish to do so. He replies, however, in a most definitive tone, "Indeed I cannot" (*Tess of the D'Urbervilles,* p. 187). The rape occurred before the marriage and so did not constitute a violation of it. Although the qualifications for divorce expanded in 1868, the procedure nonetheless still proved to be arduous.

Women also suffered inequality in marriages of the time. As the writer T. H. Huxley observed, "Women ... were brought up to be either drudges or toys beneath man or `a sort of angel above him'" (Huxley in Hibbert, p. 38). There existed no common ground. Upon marriage, a woman surrendered all assets over to her husband; until the late 1880s, she held no legal claim to her own belongings. Women who did not marry were hardly better off: in Victorian society, an unmarried woman was regarded as a failure in some way. The commonplace belief was that a woman's place was in the home, and in any case, most women could not afford, in the financial sense, to leave it.

Hardy's novel comments on the difficult position of the Victorian woman. Although Tess attempts to make moral and wise decisions throughout the book, she remains bound, by virtue of her gender, to the role of the social deviant. Society shoulders her with blame for becoming the victim of sexual assault and calmly accepts her husband's desertion of her on the basis of this knowledge. The full title that Hardy gives the book, *Tess of the D'Urbervilles: A Pure Woman Faithfully Presented,* attests to the author's sympathy for the plight of his heroine.

The Novel in Focus

The plot. Tess Durbeyfield arrives at her village cottage in Marlott one evening to find her father in an excited state. He has learned that day, via the village parson, that his family name hails from a noble line of gentlemen known as the D'Urbervilles. Although the family proper has long since died out, John Durbeyfield and his family represent the last of this great lineage. Dreaming of the riches that he will collect, John and his wife, Joan, conspire to find any remaining D'Urbervilles, however remote their kinship might be. That evening Joan reveals her discovery of a rich woman in the nearby town of Trantridge who uses the surname d'Urberville. Well aware of her daughter's physical and social charms, Joan decides to send Tess to Trantridge to make the acquaintance of the supposed relative.

Although Tess initially refuses to take part in the mission, a turn of events changes her mind. While delivering goods for her peddler father, Tess has an accident with an oncoming carriage. When her horse dies at the scene, Tess realizes that she has killed the family's primary source of income. Feelings of guilt compel her to go along with her mother's plan. When she arrives at the Trantridge mansion, Tess meets Alec D'Urberville, the son of the rich woman. Unbeknownst to Tess, Alec's family simply stole the surname upon their arrival in the area. They bear no relation to either Tess or the true D'Urberville line. Alec refuses to allow Tess to meet his mother, as the old woman is an invalid. Taken with Tess's beauty, however, he secures a position for Tess at the mansion caring for his mother's fowls. Tess's family, ecstatic at the prospect of Tess obtaining luxuries for the lot of them, willingly grants her permission to move to the new town.

Tess's seeming good fortune soon turns into a nightmare. Alec, a well-known rogue, hotly pursues Tess despite her rebuffs. Although Tess does make new acquaintances in Trantridge, Alec's presence taints every social event. One night after a neighborhood dance, Alec follows Tess on her walk home. Offering her a ride on his horse, he takes her to a remote part of the woods where she can no longer find her way on her own. In the cover of darkness and isolation, he forces himself on her. The next morning, Tess flees Trantridge and returns home to Marlott.

Within the year Tess gives birth to a baby that does not survive. With her name tainted and her chastity sullied, Tess decides to leave her village and find work elsewhere. Eventually she makes her way to Blackmoor Vale, an area known for its dairy farms. There she finds a post at Talbothay's Dairy working as a milkmaid. The dairyman and his wife provide a warm, comfortable home for their employees. Tess shares lodgings with three other milkmaids, Retty, Marian, and Izz. Together the four girls enjoy an idyllic sum-

Alec presses his attentions on an unwilling Tess. Illustration by Hubert Herkomer, 1891.

mer. They spend their days milking the cows, and their evenings dreaming of the dairyman's apprentice, Angel Clare.

The son of a well-to-do parson, Angel, unlike his brothers, opts for a career outside the church. Hoping to become a gentleman farmer, he travels across England learning various aspects of the trade. Tess and Angel experience love at first sight. Although they come from vastly different economic backgrounds, the two attempt to forge a relationship. Tess, however, feeling that because of the rape she is by nature the wife of another man, has difficulty entering into a relationship with Angel. In time his kindness and constant pressure win her over, and a wedding is planned. On the morning of her nuptials, Tess attempts to confess the incident to her betrothed, but Angel insists that she wait until later to talk of faults.

That night he confesses that in a period of recklessness, he spent two days sexually involved with a woman. Tess gladly forgives him, and in relief that their pasts indeed share a similarity, recounts her own tale. Angel, however, cannot likewise forgive Tess. He tells her that she is no longer the pure bride that he married, and refuses to remain with her. Within days, Angel leaves for Brazil and Tess returns home.

At home in Marlott, John Durbeyfield dies, leaving his family without the means to maintain their lodgings. It is during this desperate period that Alec D'Urberville returns to Tess's life. Under his intense pressure and promise of money for her family, Tess agrees to live with him as his wife. Soon after these arrangements come to fruition, Angel returns home to find his Tess. During his sojourn, he has come to realize his error and has forgiven her. He catches up with Tess and Alec at a hotel where they live. His return throws Tess into a state of wild desperation in which she kills Alec and flees with Angel. Reunited with her true love, Tess seems not to care that her life might soon come to an end. The couple travels to Stonehenge before the authorities apprehend them. The close of the novel finds Tess punished with death by hanging.

A society in flux. From religion to economic and social details, *Tess of the D'Urbervilles* brings alive changes of the late Victorian era. In religion, for example, a reactionary movement against laxness in the Church of England had sprung up in England during the 1700s. It was a back-to-the-Bible movement, spearheaded by John Wesley, whose followers separated from the mainstream to form the Methodist Church. Its focus on hellfire and damnation made outsiders identify it as a grim, fanatical sect. Yet it persisted into the 1800s, in which the writings of various novelists, Hardy among them, showed strong disapproval for the

Tess of the D'Urbervilles

sect. In Hardy's novel, the villainous Alec d'Urberville becomes a preacher for a Methodist group (the "Ranters"), an experience that fails in any way to redeem his base character.

Shifts in England's rural economy and social order likewise surface in the novel. While the early 1800s had seen great herds of sheep and cattle driven to market, the advent of the railroad made this kind of transport unnecessary. Rather than raising cattle, or corn, or sheep for various purposes, it became possible, in fact, to devote a farm entirely to dairy products, as Tess's workplace does. Tess explains this one day as she and Angel Clare drive some milk cans to a train, observing that Londoners would drink the milk at breakfast on the morrow, a formerly unheard-of feat. Railroads, in other words, made specializations such as dairy farming possible by quickly transporting perishable goods.

But if nineteenth-century changes brought some advantages to rural society, they also brought disadvantages. Large landowners were not a segment of society adversely affected by all the changes. The beginning of the 1800s had seen a hierarchy of relatively stable rural classes:

1. Landed aristocracy—old families with large estates, each consisting of ten thousand or more acres
2. Gentry—landowners with less property than the aristocracy (one thousand to three thousand acres), who often rented out their holdings to others to farm
3. Yeomen—gentlemen farmers who owned nearly as much property as the gentry but worked the land themselves, a class that disappeared toward the end of the century
4. Laborers or cottagers—the lowest rural class, who inhabited one- to four-room thatch or slate dwellings and owned or leased the same small plot for generations, using common lands for grazing their livestock.

Tess's family, of course, belongs to the lowest group of rural laborers. When her mother was a child, such laborers had often stayed on the same farm all their lives, renewing their lease from one generation to the next. As the century passed, however, the rural focus shifted to large-scale farming, another consequence of new transportation and mechanization. One result was that instead of renewing leases, as had been the custom, landowners would now send cottagers packing when their leases expired, a calamity that befalls Tess's family. In the end, Tess herself "spends her brief life as an itinerant farm laborer, working here for a dairy farm, there cutting turnips—but always moving on when the season is over and the task is done. We are made witness in the tale of her life to the story of an itinerant laborer whose own destruction is meant to mirror the disappearance of the traditional English countryside" (Pool, p. 166).

Sources. Hardy seems to have drawn his portrait of Tess using several different models. As far as the circumstances of Tess's "undoing," the author relied heavily on the life of his servant, Jane Phillips. During the summer of 1877, the young servant girl disappeared from her home. Genuinely concerned for Jane's welfare, Hardy and his wife sought out her whereabouts only to discover that she had run off with a lover. Later, in December of the same year, a church registry recorded the death of an infant son born to the same Jane Phillips. The child, like Tess's in the novel, was baptized by its mother, and had no legal father to list in the record book. For Tess's occupation, Hardy found inspiration in the milkmaid Augusta May—an eighteen-year-old who worked at a dairy run by her father.

For the physical Tess, Hardy turned to an idealized model—the wife of the sculptor Hamo Thornycroft. Hardy once commented, "I think [Mrs. Thornycroft] the most beautiful woman in England; [it was] her on whom I thought when I wrote *Tess of the D'Urbervilles*" (Hardy, p. 363).

For the decline of the D'Urberville family, Hardy had to search no further than his own ancestry for inspiration. In 1888 the author traveled to Earshot to visit Woolcombe, an estate that once belonged to family members, the Dorset-Hardys. As pointed out in the back matter following the novel, there on the grounds of the old estate he found evidence of the "decline and fall of the Hardys" (Hardy, p. 356). He concluded as his novel does, "so we [old families] go down, down, down, down" (Hardy, p. 356).

Hardy's fictitious "Wessex" county is modeled on his hometown region of Dorset in southwest England. Hardy originally created the Wessex area in 1874 for his novel *Far from the Madding Crowd*. He renames many of the Dorset towns for their appearance in his works. The real town of Shaftsbury becomes Marlott, and Manhull likewise becomes Vale of Blakemore.

Fascinated by country lore and events, Hardy took some key episodes in the novel from the pages of the *Dorset County Chronicle*. An article from an issue dated October 17, 1872, tells of a vehicle collision between a mail cart and a wagon. The incident bears a striking resemblance to Tess's own accident on her family's horse cart. As for the novel's opening scene, where John Durbeyfield learns of his esteemed ancestry, Hardy states that the event "occurred under my own eyes. I was standing at the street corner of a little town in this county when a tipsy man swaggered past me singing 'I've-got a-great family vault...'." (Hardy, p. 361). Through bystanders Hardy learned that the man hailed from one of England's oldest Norman families.

Reception of the novel. As material in the critical edition of Hardy's novel indicates, the novel received conflicting reviews. The *Pall Mall Gazette* (December 31, 1891) states that Hardy "never exercised [his art] more powerfully—never, certainly, more tragically—than in this most moving presentment of a 'pure woman'" (Hardy, p. 381). Another paper, *The Athenaeum*, remarks, "*Tess of the D'Urbervilles* is well in front of Mr. Hardy's previous work, and is destined, there can be no doubt, to rank high among the achievements of Victorian novelists" (Hardy, p. 382). One of Hardy's fellow novelists, however, had less pleasant things to say about the opus. Robert Louis Stevenson wrote to his friend Henry James, "Tess is one of the worst, weakest, least sane ... books I have yet read.... I should tell you in fairness I could never finish it" (Stevenson in Hardy, p. 387). Particularly irksome to Hardy was a piece in the *Saturday Review* that spoke of the characters as unnatural and the whole tale as dreary. Citing the praise the work garnered, Hardy's friends tried to convince him not to be so distressed by unfavorable comments. Indeed, in light of the overall response, *Tess of the D'Urbervilles* was a critical and commercial success. The novel would elevate Hardy to a new career plateau, financially enabling him to become a full-time novelist.

For More Information

Brown, Jonathan. *Village Life in England, 1860-1940*. London: B. T. Batsford, 1985.

Hardy, Thomas. *Tess of the d'Urbervilles*. Norton Critical Edition. Edited by Scott Elledge. New York: W. W. Norton, 1991.

Hibbert, Christopher. *Daily Life in Victorian England*. New York: McGraw Hill, 1975.

Kauvar, Gerald B. *The Victorian Mind*. New York: G. P. Putnam's Sons, 1969.

McCord, Norman. *British History, 1815-1906*. London: Oxford University Press, 1991.

Millgate, Michael. *Thomas Hardy: A Biography*. New York: Random House, 1982.

Pool, Daniel. *What Jane Austen Ate and Charles Dickens Knew: From Fox Hunting To Whist—the Facts of Daily Life in Nineteenth-Century England*. New York: Touchstone, 1993.

Seymour-Smith, Martin. *Hardy*. New York: St. Martin's Press, 1994.

Things Fall Apart

by
Chinua Achebe

Chinua Achebe was born in 1930 in eastern Nigeria, the son of devout Christian parents. He was baptized Albert Chinualumogu, but dropped this Victorian name when he began his studies. At the university in Nigeria, his frustrations with some of the narrow or distorted portrayals of Africa in European novels (specifically Joyce Cary's *Mister Johnson*) motivated him to write *Things Fall Apart*. Also motivating Achebe was a personal reality. After World War II, many Nigerians sought a reconciliation with their past, which they had abandoned for Christianity and the industrialization brought by Europeans to the British colonies in West Africa. Although Achebe had spoken Igbo, not English, as a child, he and his family celebrated Christian, not Igbo, festivals. His writing of *Things Fall Apart* when he reached manhood was Achebe's "act of atonement with [his] past, the ritual return and homage of a prodigal son" (Achebe, *Morning Yet on Creation Day*, p. 123).

Events in History at the Time the Novel Takes Place

Structure of a nineteenth-century Igbo community. Until the late nineteenth century, the Igbo dwelled in small independent villages linked to one another by trade but not by politics. Living in sedentary agricultural communities, they relied from year to year on the success of their harvest. Yams were the staple crop of the Igbo diet. To facilitate trade among the villages,

> **THE LITERARY WORK**
>
> A novel set among an Igbo (Ibo) tribe in mainland Nigeria between 1850 and 1900; published in 1958.
>
> **SYNOPSIS**
>
> Christian missionaries to Nigeria disrupt traditional Igbo life and drive one village leader, Okonkwo, to suicide.

the Igbo used small seashells called cowries as a unit of currency.

The Igbo believed in a hierarchy of gods, ranging from Chukwu, the all-powerful, to the *chi*, an individual's personal god. A malevolent chi would thwart a man's ambitions, whereas a kind one would ensure success. But the Igbo did not believe that a man's fate was entirely determined by his chi. "When a man says yes," they declared, "his chi says yes also" (Achebe, *Things Fall Apart*, p. 28). In other words, a man's will and his chi work together. The saying resembles the Christian adage that the Lord helps those who help themselves. The Igbo believed also in the importance of their ancestors. Failure to preserve traditions might anger the spirits of their forefathers.

Within the independent villages, political organization was based on ancestry. The smallest unit, the nuclear family, was under the rule of the husband, who often lived in a hut separate from his wife or wives and their children. The

Chinua Achebe

extended family of relatives on the husband's side was ruled by the oldest surviving man because it was believed he could communicate with revered ancestors.

An assembly of adult men debated concerns that affected the entire village, such as a decision to go to war. A man won influence in these assemblies by acquiring titles, which could be purchased from a council of titled elders with yams. This system of purchasing titles served as a method of rewarding hard work and encouraged the spread of wealth.

Secret societies, such as the masked "egwugwu" in Achebe's fictional village (Umuofia), helped enforce unwritten codes of conduct. Crimes included the slaying of a clansman, whether accidentally or intentionally; theft; assault; slander; and disrespect for the gods. Members of the secret societies would disguise themselves as the spirits of ancestors. They denounced offenders and arbitrated disputes; their anonymity and their supernatural air lent them a sense of authority. In Achebe's novel, a convert to Christianity unmasks an egwugwu, an unpardonable offense. In doing so, the convert threatens the survival of a revered tribal tradition.

The arrival of European missionaries and traders in West Africa in the mid-eighteenth century radically changed Igbo life. The missionaries challenged traditional laws and persuaded some of the Igbo to convert to Christianity. There was also a new unity among the independent villages as confrontations with colonial authority motivated them to cooperate against a common threat. At the same time, by tampering with the traditional religion, the missionaries had broken a bond that united the Igbo. In the novel, Okonkwo's perceptive friend, Obierika, says

> The white man is very clever. He came quietly and peaceably with his religion. We were amused at his foolishness and allowed him to stay. Now he has won our brothers, and our clan can no longer act like one. He has put a knife on the things that held us together and we have fallen apart.
> (*Things Fall Apart*, p. 162)

The slave trade and the Christian missionaries. At the end of the eighteenth century, the slave trade off the coast of Africa had been active for more than three hundred years. At this time, a humanitarian outcry against slavery arose in Great Britain and reached its Parliament. The legislative body responded in 1807 by passing the Abolition Act, which made the trade in African slaves illegal for British subjects. A British navy detachment was deployed off the coast of West Africa to intercept slave ships, but this effort proved costly and not entirely effective. There was another, less direct method, suggested Thomas Buxton, the leader of the British antislavery movement: let the freed slaves in England who had been converted to Christianity return to Africa as missionaries and encourage other blacks to end their participation in the barbarous slave trade.

White missionaries of the era regarded the conversion and salvation of distant peoples such as the Igbo the duty of a Christian. The missionaries who arrived in Africa in the nineteenth century intended to atone for the horrors of slavery, to which in the past whites had so grievously contributed, by educating and Christianizing the African. The assumption was that European Christianity would heal the wounds that had been inflicted by white European as well as other slave traders. But because of their ignorance and intolerance of African customs, the missionaries often only deepened old scars.

African natives were frequently apprehensive about the missionaries and, although they sent their children to missionary schools, they re-

Things Fall Apart

stricted what the missionaries could teach. Parents were aware of the benefits of education and wanted their children to be competitive applicants for the jobs in emerging fields like civil service, which required proficiency in spoken and written English. They did not, however, desire or expect any moral or religious teaching, contending that the proverbs and fables of tribal history imparted the morals of their own native religion. European education was supposed to provide a supplement to tribal teachings, not a substitute for them.

> ### THE "OGBANJE" PHENOMENON
>
> When an infant died, it was suspected that the spirit of the child would enter its mother's womb so that it might be reborn, and then die again to torment its mother. Such a child was called "ogbanje" and was thought to have the power to return any number of times in this vicious cycle. To discourage the wicked spirit, the Igbo would mutilate the infant's body and throw it into the forest. Another explanation for the high death rate of Igbo infants is that it may have been caused in part by the disease known as sickle cell anemia. The recessive gene that causes sickle cell anemia and thereby kills infants occurred with unusual frequency among the Igbo.

The missionaries, however, sprinkled the lessons with Christian morals and proverbs. An essay on Igbo farm work, for example, concluded with the statement "When God created the first man, the occupation he bequeathed to him was farming, as we learn from the Bible" (Emenyonu, p. 26). An essay about trading began with "trading is a good occupation when embarked upon with the fear of God and honesty," and ended with "To cheat your customer is bad. One who fears God should desist from such. Jesus Christ urges you to do unto others as you would that they do unto you" (Emenyonu, p. 26). The trusting children were learning Christianity just as they would have with more formal instruction.

In other areas, however, the missionaries easily won the favor of Igbo villagers who had suffered from precolonial practices. Lepers, for example, who lived as outcasts and were not given proper burial, embraced Christianity as an alternative to Igbo religion. Having endured persecution under tribal law, such outcasts antagonized the more traditional Igbo, denouncing their rituals, art, music, and clothing.

When violence erupted, British soldiers came to enforce British laws. They interceded in disputes between villagers, practically replacing tribal authority. The Igbo often had to rely on interpreters who themselves were African Christian converts disdainful of traditional customs. They suffered the treachery of unscrupulous officials like the district commissioner in the novel, who invites the leaders of Umuofia to his office in seeming friendship but then arrests them. In 1900 a British major warned, "The practice of calling chiefs to meetings and then seizing them and of calling in guns to mark and then destroy them has resulted in a general distrust of the government and its policy" (Wren, p. 29). Government corruption clashed with the maxims of pious missionaries and spread suspicion of Europeans among natives, intensifying already existing conflicts.

Resistance to European authority resulted in what was called "collective punishment." Rather than identify and punish guilty individuals, British "peacemakers" slaughtered whole villages. The Collective Punishment Ordinance of 1912, as noted in the records, "legalize[d] [in the West] what in practice has always been done in the Central and Eastern provinces" (Wren, p. 28). Archives record an uprising in 1915 during which outraged clan members destroyed a church near Enugu, a village not far from where Achebe's father was working. The British retaliation killed more than forty natives to compensate for one dead and one wounded British soldier. Although the alleged intent was "pacification," colonialism, in fact, caused more violence than it prevented.

The Novel in Focus

The plot. Okonkwo, the child of an idle man who bequeathed his son nothing but debts and a poor reputation, struggles to rise above his father's disgrace and become a man of wealth and influence. He wins respect through his prowess in physical combat, both in wrestling and at war, and works to amass barns full of yams, a sign of wealth.

When a woman from Umuofia is killed by a man in the neighboring village of Mbaino, the tribe demands recompense or threatens war. To avert bloodshed, the people of Mbaino offer a young virgin and the son of the killer to the people of Umuofia. The virgin is given to the husband of the slain woman to replace his wife, and the boy to the clan as a whole to replace the lost life. As a leader in his village, Okonkwo is asked to take the boy, Ikemefuma, into his household.

Ikemefuma slowly forgets his previous life and becomes a part of Okonkwo's family, even calling Okonkwo "father." The friendship that develops between Ikemefuma and Okonkwo's timid son, Nwoye, emboldens Nwoye and delights Okonkwo. But their happiness is shattered when, after three years, the implacable village oracle demands Ikemefuma's death in retribution for the earlier murder, now that the boy has grown up and can pay the penalty. A clan leader comes to Okonkwo's house and warns, "That boy calls you father. Do not bear a hand in his death" (*Things Fall Apart*, p. 55).

Okonkwo, too eager to prove that he is not like his poorly-thought-of father, ignores his friend's advice to stay at home and accompanies the party leading Ikemefuma to his death in the forest. As a man raises his blade to slay the boy, Okonkwo turns away. But when Ikemefuma cries out "My father, they have killed me!" (*Things Fall Apart*, p. 59), Okonkwo draws his machete and finishes off the killing by slicing the boy in half. Okonkwo does this because he was "afraid of being thought weak" (*Things Fall Apart*, p. 59).

Obierika, a friend of Okonkwo, announces his daughter's engagement, helping to lift Okonkwo out of his depression. But his first peaceful sleep since Ikemefuma's death is disturbed by one of his wives, Ekwefi, whose only child, a daughter named Ezinma, has fallen ill. Ekwefi had borne ten children, nine of whom had died in infancy. She had seen the bodies of her "ogbanje" infants mutilated and thrown into the forest. She expressed her despair in names that she choose for her children, such as Onwumbiko ("Death, I implore you"), Ozoemena ("May it not happen again"), and Onwuman ("Death may please himself") (*Things Fall Apart*, p. 74). Although sickly, her tenth child, Ezinma, has survived, but the slightest sign of illness upsets Ekwefi. Fortunately, the girl withstands the sickness, and the trial revives Okonkwo, reminding him of his love for his daughter, whom he often insists should have been a boy. His happiness is, however, short-lived.

A village leader dies and during the funeral rites Okonkwo's gun discharges and kills the dead man's youngest son. Although the death was an accident, Okonkwo is forced into exile for seven years. A crowd of men destroy his house and barns and kill his animals. Although they bear Okonkwo no ill will, they feel they must cleanse the land of his sin.

Okonkwo has fled with his family to the village where his mother was born, Mbanta; its people have welcomed him. During the second year of Okonkwo's exile, his friend Obierika brings him news of the village Abame, which was decimated. A white man riding what Obierika describes as an iron horse had ventured near the village. The villagers had approached him, but found him incomprehensible. The village oracle warned that the white man would destroy their clan, so they killed him. Soon after, on a market day, white men surrounded the villagers and shot into the crowd. Obierika concludes that the men of Abame were foolish to kill a stranger, but warns "I am greatly afraid. We have heard stories about white men who made the powerful guns and the strong drinks and took slaves away across the seas, but no one thought the stories were true" (*Things Fall Apart*, p. 130).

By the time Obierika returns to visit Okonkwo two years later, white missionaries have established a church and won converts back in Umuofia. The converts are the outcasts from the clan, and no one considers the crazy new faith of Christianity a serious threat. Obierika is distressed, however, by the bond that has developed between the missionaries and Okonkwo's son, Nwoye. Nwoye had left his father after a violent encounter and returned to Umuofia. Now Obierika reports that Nwoye has been moved by the Christians' rhetoric, particularly their insistence that the Igbo gods were "gods of deceit who tell you to kill your fellows and destroy innocent children" (*Things Fall Apart*, p. 136).

As Okonkwo's seventh year of exile comes to an end, he eagerly looks forward to his return home. Arriving in Umuofia, he discovers to his amazement that the Christians have flourished and recruited more converts, even men who were influential in the clan. More importantly, the white men have built a district court and now arbitrate village disputes. Okonkwo is outraged, but few seem to share his anger.

Mr. Brown, a white missionary, had befriended members of the clan, who even presented him with a carved elephant tusk as a sign of dignity. His attempts to explain the differences between Christianity and the native religion were sometimes futile, but his willingness to discuss Igbo traditions won him the villagers' respect.

Mr. Brown's health deteriorated, though, and he was succeeded by the Reverend James Smith, a different breed of preacher. Smith's intolerance of local customs encourage the more fervent converts to provoke the tribe. During an annual ceremony, one convert boldly unmasks one of the costumed men portraying the ancestral spirits, a deliberate attempt to reveal the identity of the person beneath the mask. In retaliation the tribesmen burn the church.

Pleased that his tribe has acted to drive the Christians from their village, Okonkwo agrees to accompany the other village leaders summoned before the district commissioner. They are cautious and take their machetes, but in the commissioner's office they are nevertheless caught unaware and handcuffed. The commissioner demands a fine of two hundred bags of cowries and leaves the men alone with guards, who taunt and abuse them. Rather than await their decision, the commissioner sends messengers to Umuofia to extort the money from the villagers. The villagers quickly gather the two hundred and fifty bags of cowries, fifty of which the messengers have added on for themselves, and the leaders are released.

The village convenes to discuss the threat of the white men, but their meeting is interrupted by messengers who insist the people disperse. Okonkwo draws his machete and slays one of the messengers, expecting the crowd to cheer and join him. But when he turns, he sees nothing but a fearful tumult. He leaves the people, returns to his compound, and hangs himself. When the district commissioner arrives, Obierika must ask him to attend to the burial of Okonkwo. It is an abomination for a man to take his own life, and such a man cannot be buried by his clan. The district commissioner orders a messenger to take down the body, and then ponders how the story of this man's suicide will make a reasonable paragraph in his memoirs.

Colonial justice. In the novel, when a woman of Umuofia flees her brutal husband, the man calls on her family to pay him some recompense. The *egwugwu*, or assembly of clan members dressed as spirits, convene to hear his arguments. Responding to his wife's charge that her husband beat her, the egwugwu order that the man beg his wife for forgiveness and that he offer her family gifts to atone for his crime.

The entire proceeding demonstrates that the people of Umuofia were neither lawless nor ungoverned before the arrival of the European colonists. Although the colonial authorities contended that they were bringing justice to unruly savages, they often only spread corruption. In the novel, they intercede in a dispute concerning land and award the area in question to the family which "ha[d] given much money to the white man's messengers and interpreter" (*Things Fall Apart*, p. 162). Okonkwo is incredulous, and asks his friend Obierika, "Does the white man understand our custom about land?" Obierika replies, "How can he when he does not even speak our tongue?" (*Things Fall Apart*, p. 162).

Sources. Achebe's frustration with European novels about Africa motivated him to write *Things Fall Apart*. He was particularly bothered by the works of Joyce Cary, a British novelist who had lived in Nigeria for six years. Cary believed that "life in a primitive tribe is monotonous and boring. It survives, when it does survive, only because people who suffer it have no idea of anything better" (Cary in Killam, p. 131). He claimed his novels set in Africa "were meant to show certain men and their problems in the tragic background of a continent still little advanced from the Stone Age" (Cary in Killam, p. 124). Achebe described these novels as "a most superficial picture of—not only of the country but even of the Nigerian character." He then concluded that "perhaps someone ought to try and look at this from the inside" (Achebe in Okoye, p. 10).

Although the use of detail in *Things Fall Apart* would suggest a thorough knowledge of the Igbo traditions and culture, Achebe conceded,

> it was all sort of picked up here and there. There was no research in the library [because] there wasn't really anything to read. The Ibos are perhaps the least studied of all major tribes in Africa.
> (Achebe in Okoye, p. 160)

Although Achebe's parents were Christian, they were by no means intolerant or critical of the traditional religion. Their explanations helped Achebe create an authentic picture of the Igbo past. Achebe's grandfather had been a leader in the village and indeed had welcomed some of the first Christian missionaries. Among these missionaries was G. T. Basden, an inquisitive pioneer whom the village honored with an ivory tusk. He became Achebe's father's teacher and friend and wrote extensively of his experiences. Although Achebe denies he consciously modeled any character on Basden, he admits "it seems likely that the legend of Basden must have informed my conception of Brown" (Achebe in Okoye, p. 18).

Events in History at the Time the Novel Was Written

Nigerian politics. Up until the World War II, the British made few concessions to Nigerians' petitions for self-rule. During the war Britain's prime minister, Winston Churchill, promised to "respect the right of all peoples to choose the form of government under which they will live" (Ezera, p. 39). Having pledged to fight for self-rule in Nazi-occupied Europe, Churchill could not continue to ignore the demand for independence in Nigeria.

The Richards Constitution of 1946 was the first attempt to superimpose federalism on the diverse peoples of Nigeria. The three regions (northern, southern and western) were brought under the administration of one legislative council composed of twenty-eight Nigerians and seventeen British officers. Regional councils, however, guaranteed some independence from the national council and forged a link between local authorities, such as tribal chiefs, and the national government.

There were three major tribes (the Hausa, the Yoruba and the Igbo) and more than eight smaller ones living in Nigeria. This diversity complicated the creation of a unified Nigeria. Between 1946 and 1960 the country went through several different constitutions, each one attempting to balance power between the regional and the national bodies of government.

On October 1, 1960, Nigeria attained full status as a sovereign state and a member of the British Commonwealth. But under the Constitution of 1960 the Queen of England was still the head of state. She remained the commander-in-chief of Nigeria's armed forces, and the Nigerian navy operated as part of Britain's Royal Navy. Nigerians felt frustrated by the implication that they were the subjects of a monarch living over four thousand miles away. In 1963, five years after the publication of Achebe's novel, a new constitution would replace the British monarch with a Nigerian president as head of state in Nigeria.

Neglected traditions. In 1958, while Nigerians were striving toward political freedom, Achebe was looking back to the traditions almost extinguished by colonialism. Colonialism had sometimes fostered a sense of inferiority among Africans that made them suspicious or even disdainful of their past. Achebe wrote:

> I would be quite satisfied if my novels (especially the ones I set in the past) did no more than teach my readers that their past—with all its imperfections—was not one long night of savagery from which the first Europeans acting on God's behalf delivered them.
> (Achebe, *Morning Yet on Creation Day*, p. 72)

Achebe's decision to write in English was by no means an estrangement from his ethnic roots. Rather, it was a guarantee that his novels would be accessible to almost all of the many peoples of Nigeria, who speak several different languages. Achebe pointed out "the only reason why we can even talk about African unity is that when we get together we can have a manageable number of languages to talk in—English, French, Arabic" (Achebe, *Morning Yet on Creation Day*, p. 95). English, he believed, could be a valuable tool in forging Nigerian unity.

Reception. Some critics felt that Achebe's novel unjustly faulted colonialists. Africans, they alleged, should be grateful for the introduction of western culture and technology. Soon after the publication of *Things Fall Apart*, Honor Tracy, a British critic, in an article entitled "Three Cheers for Mere Anarchy!" wrote:

> These bright Negro barristers who talk so glibly about African culture, how would they like to return to wearing raffia skirts? How would novelist Achebe like to go back to the mindless times of his grandfather instead of holding the modern job he has in broadcasting in Lagos?
> (Achebe, *Morning Yet on Creation Day*, p. 5)

On the other hand, *Things Fall Apart* won praise as a "vivid account of tribal beliefs and culture" (Allen, p. 814). Critics commended Achebe's ability to include Igbo proverbs in a novel in English and to preserve in his narrative the neglected customs of an almost forgotten past. They stressed his talents not just as a historian, but as a novelist whose portrayal of a proud man's fall invites comparison with Greek tragedies.

For More Information

Achebe, Chinua. *Morning Yet on Creation Day*. Garden City, N.Y.: Anchor Press/Doubleday, 1975.

Achebe, Chinua. *Things Fall Apart*. New York: Fawcett Crest, 1959.

Allen, Walter. "New Novels." *New Statesman* 55 (June 21, 1958): 814-15.

Emenyonu, Ernest. *The Rise of the Igbo Novel*. Ibadan, Nigeria: Oxford University Press, 1978.

Ezera, Kalu. *Constitutional Developments in Nigeria*. London: Cambridge University Press, 1960.

Killam, G. D. *Africa in English Fiction*. Ibadan, Nigeria: Ibadan University Press, 1968.

Okoye, Emmanuel Meziemadu. *The Traditional Religion and its Encounter with Christianity in Achebe's Novels*. Bern: Peter Lang, 1987.

Wren, Robert. *Achebe's World: The Historical and Cultural Context of the Novels*. Washington: Three Continents Press, 1980.

Thousand Pieces of Gold

by
Ruthanne Lum McCunn

~

Ruthanne Lum McCunn has written several books about the role of the Chinese in American history. A Chinese American herself, McCunn lived in Boise, Idaho—the state in which her novel is set—with her father's family. She later moved to San Francisco, where she wrote *Thousand Pieces of Gold*. The well-researched biographical novel serves as a depiction of the life of a typical female Asian immigrant in Idaho during the gold rush era.

Events in History at the Time the Novel Takes Place

Prostitution. While McCunn's novel does not expressly state that its main character Lalu had to work as a prostitute, many Chinese barmaids did. Chinese prostitution became common in the United States during the latter half of the nineteenth century. While whites entered the profession too, conditions for the Chinese were vastly different from those of their white counterparts. White prostitutes usually worked independently or for wages, whereas Chinese prostitutes were bought and sold as slaves. In 1860, approximately 85 percent of the Chinese women in San Francisco worked as prostitutes, and by 1870 the figure had dropped only slightly—to 71 percent.

Most of the Chinese prostitutes came from rural families in China. Chinese families sometimes sold their daughters into slavery when they could no longer afford to keep them. Others were captured or tricked into immigrating. Using deceit and bribery, importers smuggled these women into the United States. Some women signed contracts in China that bound them to a life of prostitution for a particular owner or brothel. Mostly illiterate, these women often misunderstood the contract, believing they had signed a marriage agreement. Other women were simply auctioned off without the formality of a contract. They were taken to a barracoon, a large auction room that held up to a hundred women, and sold to the highest bidders as prostitutes, mistresses, or concubines. Some, like Lalu, wound up in mining camps, where they often suffered harsher treatment than prostitutes in the cities; a few women committed suicide in order to escape their terrible fate.

The life of a Chinese prostitute was a bleak one. Brothel owners generally forced the females to

---

THE LITERARY WORK

A novel about a Chinese slave girl set in China and Idaho from the late 1850s to the 1930s; published in 1981.

SYNOPSIS

A Chinese girl is sold into slavery and brought to America in the late nineteenth century. Beginning as a barmaid in a mining-town saloon in Idaho, Lalu eventually wins her freedom through a poker game. She manages a boarding house and later marries the man who won the poker game.

work steadily for approximately four to five years, after which the women obtained positions as cooks or housekeepers for the enterprise. Others continued working as lower-class prostitutes, sitting in tiny rooms, calling out to solicit passersby through barred windows. Most prostitutes had no medical care and died early; many were beaten and some were murdered. Perhaps most striking is the case of "The Yellow Doll," a prostitute in Deadwood, South Dakota, who was chopped up into tiny pieces. The mistreatment of prostitutes persisted even after death. When male Chinese laborers died, their bodies would often be sent back to China for a proper burial. When female Chinese prostitutes died, their bodies might be dumped on the streets of the local Chinatown.

Foot-binding. The practice of foot-binding served various purposes in Chinese society. On one hand, the practice controlled women because a woman with bound feet could not run away. Most could not even walk short distances without enduring extreme pain. On the other hand, foot-binding served as a status symbol, since females with bound feet could not carry a full workload and often required extra care. In fact, peasants who hoped to marry a daughter into the upper classes would bind her feet in order to make her more attractive. In the novel Lalu's family bound her feet for this reason, but halted the process because they needed Lalu in the fields. Although her feet remained small, they still looked larger than completely bound feet, and Lalu suffered the consequences. She was continually chastised for their size throughout her childhood.

Chinese in Idaho mining towns. The Chinese constituted a large portion of the mining population in Idaho during the latter half of the nineteenth century. By the late 1860s, whites had worked the easiest areas and sold the leftover, low-grade or abandoned mines to the Chinese, who paid as much as $8,000 for a claim. The 1870 census lists 4,274 people of Chinese descent in Idaho, most of whom were miners. These people constituted more than one-third of Idaho's population and almost 60 percent of the miners. A number of the mining camps were almost exclusively Chinese, and, according to some sources, in the year 1872 the Chinese worked two-thirds of all the gold claims in Idaho.

In the novel, Lalu arrives in Warrens, Idaho, in the early 1870s. At that time Warrens contained a sizable Chinese population. By 1881 there were approximately 100 white miners and about 400 Chinese miners in a town that, like others of its kind, was quite remote. Often only one or two trails led to the town, and visitors were infrequent. For the Chinese prostitutes and servants who lived in such towns, life was in some ways more difficult, in others more flexible, than for the urban servants in San Francisco. Chinese women in rural areas tended to suffer much more abuse than their urban counterparts. As illustrated in the saloon featured in the novel, the customers behaved more roughly and the ethnic tension was greater because the clientele was more racially mixed. Yet the rural women enjoyed a higher degree of relative freedom. They could, for example, walk alone in their areas, which was an impossibility in the cities.

SLAVERY AFTER THE AMERICAN CIVIL WAR

After the United States abolished slavery in 1865, aspects of it persisted for certain minorities through contract labor arrangements and other schemes. Chinese prostitution enterprises existed in the western regions of the country. Most of the potential prostitutes were either kidnapped or lured into such arrangements. A few entered into contracts in which they knowingly consented to become prostitutes for a time, but loopholes trapped them into the contract forever. If a prostitute became pregnant or sick, for example, an extra year could be added to her contract period. In fact, life proved so harsh for the prostitutes that many did not even live out the terms of their contracts. A Chinese prostitute was not allowed to keep any wages a client might give her, although she could sometimes keep gifts. She was locked into a position of slavery or, at best, semislavery in America.

Prejudice. The late 1800s witnessed rampant anti-Chinese sentiment throughout the West. The economy had slowed, and many whites found it easy to blame their economic woes on the Chinese. In 1869 the railroad was completed and, suddenly jobless, tens of thousands of its former Chinese laborers spread throughout the West looking for work. The Chinese were often willing to work for lower wages than whites, so employers hired them as strikebreakers, a practice that fueled anti-Chinese resentment among white workers. Other economic factors further aggravated the situation. In 1875 the price of gold dropped in California. Unemployment spread, and wages dropped. In San Francisco, especially, people blamed the Chinese for the lower standards of living. Most of the immigrants flocked first to this city, where other residents considered the Chinese newcomers a "Yellow Peril." There was strong fear that hoards of Chinese immigrants would swoop down on America to grab the country's shrinking riches.

During this period, citizens passed a significant number of anti-Chinese laws. Californians were usually the first to adopt such laws, but they quickly spread throughout the West. The 1850 California Foreign Miner's Tax, for example, increased the price of a mining license and was initially aimed at discouraging European, Mexican, and South American miners. In 1852 it was specifically renewed to include the Chinese, whom it charged a monthly tax of $3. In 1870 the California state legislature refused to let any Chinese woman into the country who was not of "good moral character." In 1879 the U.S. Congress restricted the number of Chinese vessels that could arrive, and later it signed a treaty limiting the number of immigrants. Most devastating was the Chinese Exclusion Act of 1882, which banned the immigration of Chinese laborers for the next ten years and forbade the immigration of any woman who was not American-born (even those born overseas but conceived by American immigrants); it also forbade the immigration of unmarried women. The Geary Act in 1892 extended the Exclusion Act for another ten years, and in 1904 Chinese laborers were barred from entering the United States indefinitely. In 1922 a non-Chinese American woman who married a Chinese man would lose her U.S. citizenship, and in 1924 all Chinese women were barred from entering the United States for permanent residence. Additionally, Alien Land Laws throughout the West prohibited the Chinese from owning property and forbade interracial marriages in many Western states.

Numerous instances of racial violence occurred as well; the lynching incident described in *Thousand Pieces of Gold* was not uncommon. Over a hundred Chinese people were killed in Idaho between 1866 and 1867. In San Francisco's Chinatown, many Chinese people were beaten or murdered in a riot in 1871. The year 1885 proved especially violent. In an act that sparked racial riots across the West, twenty-eight Chinese people were murdered in Rock Springs, Wyoming, eleven of the bodies being burned and dismembered. On the same day, eleven Chinese were murdered at a farm in Puget Sound, Washington. An additional thirty-two Chinese people were killed at Douglas Bar, Oregon, that same year. The Chinese had no recourse to counter such attacks; bringing cases to court was useless. "He doesn't have a Chinaman's chance" became an expression that aptly summed up the plight of the Chinese during this time.

Chinese women did not escape the violence. During the 1880s, it escalated to such a degree that 1,163 Chinese women set out to return home to China, and only 917 women arrived. The women who remained in the United States meanwhile suffered discrimination in a number of ways. Not recognized as persons of individual worth, most were assigned generic nicknames such as "China Mary" or "Polly." One Boise newspaper editorial described the Chinese mining camp women as "Ye pining, lolling, screwed-up, wasp-waisted, putty-faced, consumption-mortgaged and novel-devouring daughters of fashion and idleness, you are no more fit for matrimony than a pullet is to look after a family of fifteen chickens" (Peterson, p. 60).

FOOT-BINDING

Throughout the novel, the narrator refers to Lalu's feet and, in so doing, reflects a Chinese preoccupation with the female foot. The Chinese considered tiny feet a sign of great beauty; the ideal length of a woman's foot was supposedly three inches long. Foot-binding was a common practice in China during the nineteenth century. A custom which dates to the tenth century, it entailed tightly wrapping a young woman's feet in cloth in order to make them small. Over time the fabric was wrapped tighter and tighter until the arches of the feet were broken and the toes permanently bent underneath.

The Novel in Focus

The plot. *Thousand Pieces of Gold* tells the story of a young Chinese girl named Lalu Nathoy, a farmer's daughter whose family is dependent on their crops for survival. One year when the crop is extremely poor, Lalu's family nearly starves to death. Although they consider selling Lalu in order to save themselves, they instead decide to unbind her feet so she can help her father work in the fields, an uncommon activity for women in Lalu's village. Five years later, Lalu's region is hit by a severe drought and many of its residents resort to crime in order to survive. The village is

Thousand Pieces of Gold

A Chinese miner turned peddler, in nineteenth-century Idaho.

attacked by bandits. They catch Lalu, give her father two small bags of seed in exchange for her, and then sell her into slavery in America.

The boat ride to America is cramped and dirty. Lalu and many other girls like herself are smuggled through customs with fake identification papers and bribes. The slave traders divide the girls into two groups; those with contracts and those without. Girls with contracts have unwittingly signed a paper agreeing to the use of their bodies for prostitution. Lalu and the other girls without contracts are stripped and sold on an auction block as prostitutes, concubines, or slaves. Lalu is sold as a slave to a man she will meet in Idaho weeks later.

Lalu journeys with a guide to Warrens, Idaho, where her owner, Hong King, runs a saloon. Since there are few Chinese or American women in Warrens at that time, Hong King intends to use Lalu as a business attraction. He first tells Lalu, "A slave does not choose her own name. From now on you are Polly. Is that understood?" (McCunn, *Thousand Pieces of Gold*, p. 117). "Polly" spends years working in the bar for Hong

King. She is initially afraid of the rough men who frequent the saloon and who eagerly gather around to stare at her. Eventually she befriends Charlie Bemis, a white saloon-owner next door who protects her as best he can from the abusive atmosphere in which she lives.

Polly dreams of attaining her freedom. She realizes that her family considers her dead and that she can never return to China. But not giving up hope, she hoards the gold dust that falls between the cracks in the saloon, hoping to one day buy herself from Hong King. She decides that if she wins her freedom, she will never marry. As a Chinese woman, her whole life has belonged either to her father or her owner. As a married woman, she would belong to her husband. She therefore resolves never to give up her freedom by marrying.

THE ROLE OF ANTI-CHINESE SENTIMENT IN THE NOVEL

Polly struggles against anti-Chinese sentiment in Idaho. After Charlie wins her in the poker game, she tells him that she intends to start a boarding house, whereupon he informs her that only Americans, not Chinese, can own land in the United States. Polly counters that she intends to become an American, to which Charlie replies that the only way for a Chinese person to become a citizen is to be born in the United States. Such racial obstacles affect Polly's major life decisions. Charlie tries to convince her to marry him for her own protection. If they marry, she could not be deported, and she could retain their property if Charlie dies. After almost twenty years of living with him, Polly agrees to marry Charlie on the condition that they will never have children. She does not want racially mixed offspring, whom, she has observed, are treated as outcasts in American society.

Polly learns that Hong King has no intention of ever selling her and if she tries to flee, he plans to doggedly track her down, so one night she decides to kill him. When she enters the saloon, however, she discovers Charlie Bemis and Hong King playing a very serious game of poker. Each man bets everything he owns, and Hong King eventually bets Polly herself. Hong King turns over a straight, but Charlie turns over a full house and it wins him the game. Polly is angry at the manner in which the men carelessly play with her life. "But this is my life," she tells Charlie. "Not Jim life. Not yours. Mine." (*Thousand Pieces of Gold*, p. 159).

Charlie loves Polly. Although she refuses to marry him, they remain intimate friends and he builds her a boarding house with her gold dust savings. For the next fifteen years, Polly manages a respectable boarding house and earns the admiration of the community. On one occasion, a man shoots Charlie in the face and Polly gains further respect by dislodging a bullet fragment from the back of his neck and nursing him back to life.

After Charlie regains his health, he finds a beautiful spot along the River of No Return (Salmon River) and plans to build a homestead there. Polly loves the place and finally agrees to marry him. They claim their ranch in Charlie's name since Polly cannot own land. One day, the house catches fire. Bedridden with tuberculosis, Charlie thinks only of the ownership papers that Polly will need if he perishes. She manages to rescue Charlie from the flames, but he suffers smoke inhalation and dies shortly thereafter.

After Charlie's death, Polly feels a need to leave the homestead. She travels to Warrens and Boise, but returns after about a year to live her final days at the homestead.

Chinese women in the nineteenth century. Polly's attitudes toward marriage stem directly from the limited social position that women in China occupied during the nineteenth century. Chinese society considered women distinctly inferior to men and expected women to obey males at all times. Confucian philosophy dictated that women act in accordance to the "Three Obediences" and the "Four Virtues." The "Three Obediences" ordained that Chinese women must obey their fathers while living at home, their husbands after marriage, and their eldest son if they were widowed. The "Four Virtues" dictated that women should follow such ethical codes as obedience and chastity, along with rules such as speaking rarely and always in a pleasing manner, taking care of their appearance, and excelling in domestic tasks.

Chinese women did not choose their husbands. Instead, marriages were arranged by a matchmaker or by the family. Often a young girl was promised to a particular boy as a child, and the couple met for the first time on their wedding night. Although men could both divorce and remarry, women were not allowed to do either. New wives served their in-laws as virtual slaves and were often abused. The Chinese valued sons highly, and if a new wife produced sons, the family considered her valuable, whereas if she produced daughters, she was seen as a failure. In the words of one Chinese proverb, the feeling was that "eighteen gifted daughters are not equal to one lame son" (Yung, p. 13). Families strove to marry their daughters early, and in times of extreme poverty daughters were often sold like Lalu, and small girl babies were sometimes drowned or abandoned.

Sources. Ruthanne Lum McCunn was born in San Francisco, California, and raised in Hong Kong. The child of a mixed marriage, she lived briefly with her father's family in Boise, Idaho, where she experienced severe racial prejudice, a shock to her after her life in Hong Kong. She then returned to San Francisco and resolved to write about the Chinese-American experience.

Polly Bemis was a real-life Chinese girl who was sold as a slave and lived in Warrens, Idaho, during the latter half of the nineteenth century. Although *Thousand Pieces of Gold* is a novel, the author attempted to reconstruct Bemis's life story. Ruthanne McCunn used newspapers, journals, private papers, and oral histories to piece together the novel. She was able also to interview people who knew and remembered Polly Bemis.

Events in History at the Time the Novel Was Written

Women in China. Since Lalu's time, the position of women in China has seen some important gains. The practice of foot binding, for example, was abandoned early in the twentieth century. Child-brides have also been forbidden, as has the practice of drowning female children.

Even more dramatic changes for women began in China in the early 1950s when the new communist government enacted laws to improve their social and economic status. The government guaranteed equality between the sexes as well as the right of women to own land and work for wages. One edict, the Marriage Law, granted women freedom in a variety of ways by restricting the power of men to control them through marriage. Reissued in 1980, this law discouraged arranged marriages. Women could choose whom they wanted to marry, and if their parents opposed them, the law granted women access to support organizations and even court trials. The Marriage Law also prohibited the transaction of money in marriage, in order to limit the buying and selling of brides. The reissued law raised the legal age of marriage to twenty-two years for men, and to twenty years for women. It also reaffirmed a woman's right to a divorce.

Beginning in the 1950s, other laws gave women the right to participate in the work force. Yet despite these advances many traditional beliefs regarding the inferiority of women have continued to affect behavior, especially in the rural areas of China. The birth of a son, for example, is still considered by many to be a greater honor than the birth of a daughter. Moreover, while more women have entered the work force in recent times, their position there is often inferior to that of men. Just before the writing of the novel, in the late 1970s, women were performing the least skilled, most repetitive jobs in Chinese society.

Chinese and Chinese American women. The Immigration Act of 1965 abandoned the quota system, which had limited the number of immigrants according to their nation of origin. One result was a dramatic increase in the number of female Chinese immigrants to the United States. In 1950, for example, there were only 100 Chinese women for every 162 Chinese men, but by 1970 the ratio was 100 Chinese women for every 107 Chinese men. Chinese American women also made significant economic and social advances during the past century. In 1970, 58 percent of women of Chinese ancestry between the ages of eighteen and twenty-four were enrolled in school, and throughout the 1970s they continued to enter universities in record numbers. According to a 1980 census, Chinese American women were generally better educated than many other sectors of the population.

Yet such generalizations do not portray a complete picture. During the time the novel was written, many Chinese American women still encountered sexism, racism, and exploitation in the work force. In the 1970s garment workers in a U.S. Chinatown, for example, often labored overtime for below the minimum wage and received no benefits such as time off for moving or illness.

For More Information

McCunn, Ruthanne Lum. *An Illustrated History of the Chinese in America.* San Francisco: Design Enterprises of San Francisco, 1979.

McCunn, Ruthanne Lum. *Thousand Pieces of Gold.* San Francisco: Design Enterprises of San Francisco, 1981.

Peterson, Ross F. *Idaho: A Bicentennial History.* New York: W. W. Norton, 1976.

Yung, Judy. *Chinese Women of America: A Pictorial History.* Seattle: University of Washington Press, 1986.

Tom Brown's Schooldays

by
Thomas Hughes

During his youth, Thomas Hughes, a descendant of a prestigious family, was shuffled here and there in search of a suitable education institution. He finally settled at the English Public School in Rugby, where a transformation of education was taking place. Young Thomas matured under the watchful guidance of Thomas Arnold, a man known as the Doctor. Long regarded as an educational reformer and the savior of the historic Christian public school, Arnold helped Hughes and myriad other students to mature during his lifelong quest to produce good, moral, and Christian Englishmen. The experiences of a student in one of the public schools later became the subject of Hughes's novel *Tom Brown's Schooldays*.

Events in History at the Time of the Novel

The English public school system. In their present forms, English and American public schools differ. In the United States, public schools provide free education for the masses and are responsible for the general education of the country's children. In England, this kind of school is called a board school. Today's English public schools bear a closer resemblance to the college preparatory schools in the United States. They admit both males and females, and are designed to mold the males into proper Englishmen. Some public schools are directly related to the colleges at Cambridge and Oxford, preparing students for those institutions.

THE LITERARY WORK
A novel set in Rugby, England, sometime between 1827 and 1842; published in 1857.

SYNOPSIS
An English country boy comes of age in a historic public school.

The earliest public schools were created to educate students along strictly religious lines. William of Wykeham, who in 1387 founded England's first public school at Winchester, was a member of the clergy more interested in establishing an institution that was subject to the church than in creating a school with a broad educational basis. The first schools maintained a strong allegiance to their original benefactors, the church and the king. At this point, intellectual development was not the main focus. Rather, the schools promoted an acceptance and understanding of established powers.

The public school at Rugby, however, began on a different educational foundation. In 1567 Lawrence Sheriffe, a merchant in London, donated a sum of money to found a school in Rugby, his native home. The school had no specific religious principle to promote; instead, its main purpose was to provide a free education for children living in that part of the country. Sheriffe also insisted that it would be headed by "an honeste, discreete, and learned man" (Reddall, p.

198). Armed with these two ideals, the school survived a turbulent history of mismanagement and reformation before developing into one of England's great public schools.

In a similar manner, each public school acquired an individual identity over the years. Their philosophies generally reflected the founder's ideals and the personality of the headmaster (principal). Many public schools aimed to provide a superior education for the poorer members of society, a costly goal to maintain. The government provided no funding, so the institutions were forced to turn to money from private endowments. As wealthier families became important financial supporters of schools, the institutions began to cater to the children of these families and to attach a higher priority to educating the rich. Many poorer children, though, could not even afford the transportation costs to the relatively isolated schools. Over time, the havens for poor scholars became playgrounds for the rich.

Public schools in the 1700s and 1800s. Some general characteristics can be attributed to the public school around the time of *Tom Brown's Schooldays*:

1. It was a class school, catering to a well-to-do clientele.
2. It was expensive.
3. It educated boys between the ages of about eight and twenty years old.
4. It was predominantly a boarding school.
5. It was independent of the government, yet was not privately owned or operated for a profit.

A great distinction existed between the students and the teachers (known as schoolmasters), and this chasm widened even more as time passed. Students were at the public schools not to think, but to learn—to accept the teachings of the church and accept the will of the king.

Should the students prove difficult or unwilling, schoolmasters could apply other "teaching" methods beyond simple verbal instruction or lessons by rote. "Learning of a sort was more often beaten into a boy by blows than willingly acquired and a perpetual feud seems to have been in existence between the boys and the masters," remarked one historian (Warner, p. 9). It was accepted practice for students to be flogged, sometimes publicly, and not only by the teachers but also by the headmaster.

The historical events of the late 1700s and early 1800s also played a part in changing the English educational system. The political and social revolutions in America and France inspired calls for reformation in the schools. Institutions that had existed unchanged for centuries now faced a questioning student body. Many students embraced the spirit of liberty that they felt was embodied in the revolutions, and some were inspired to hoist the new tricolored flag of France over their schoolyards. Witnessing the changes occurring in other countries, students demanded development in education.

Thomas Arnold and Rugby School. Given these conditions, Thomas Arnold of Rugby made several important innovations that had a significant impact on English education. It was once said that "if Mr. Arnold were elected to the Headmastership of Rugby, he would change the face of education all through the public schools of England" (Warner, p. 25). This prophecy took seed in 1828, when he was named to the position. Through his passionate efforts over the next fourteen years, he reformed Rugby and influenced the entire public school system, setting up an education that reflected Christian standards.

Arnold took steps to forge a better relationship between the teachers and the students. His efforts contributed to a drop in incidents of phys-

Thomas Hughes

ical abuse. However, even his model school used a variety of physical punishments.

Arnold took on his responsibilities with very clear goals in mind. "What we must look for here is, first, religious and moral principles; secondly, gentlemanly conduct; thirdly, intellectual ability" (Arnold in Warner, p. 25). Arnold aimed to provide the boys at Rugby with the foundation to become Christian men, and he took a direct role in this by serving as the chaplain for the school as well as the headmaster. He was able to communicate his moral and religious philosophies to every student who attended Rugby through personal communications and his weekly sermons. Arnold also influenced his schoolmasters and more responsible older students, urging them to pay close attention to every individual enrolled in the school. Every three weeks Arnold held meetings with his schoolmasters to review the work and behavior of his students and to keep tabs on any potential problems within the school. Using the knowledge he gathered, he sent monthly reports home to the parents regarding the progress of every child.

ARNOLD'S PUNISHMENTS

When Arnold administered punishment, he was swift and severe. He wasted no time with repeat offenders of his school's policies on drinking, swearing, and lying. Before he received the title of Rugby headmaster, he had stated to his superiors that he would expel students more easily than had been previously done, and in fact he did. After one instance in which he expelled several students, he stood before the assembled school and said, "It is *not* necessary that this should be a school of three hundred, or one hundred, or of fifty boys; but it *is* necessary that it should be a school of Christian gentlemen" (Arnold in Findlay, p. 60).

The students themselves gained more responsibility under Arnold's individualized system as well. He believed that students learned best if they could work, study, and think for themselves rather than have their education created for them by their schoolmasters. The teachers were used as guides and experts, but ultimately the children were responsible for their own education. This philosophy extended to the government of Rugby school. Arnold developed an environment in which the children ran their own dorms and study areas and controlled their own free time and responsibilities. The schoolmasters, leaders of the sixth form (the oldest students), and Arnold provided guidance and stood ready to extend punishment or remedies as needed. For the most part, however, the students were allowed great freedom.

Under Arnold's tenure, Rugby became a highly respected institution. But Arnold also proved to be influential in shaping other public schools in England. Many were founded in the years following Arnold's reforms, whereas earlier the public school had been a dying institution. These new schools were modeled after Arnold's ideals, though none succeeded quite like Rugby.

Curriculum. Latin and Greek were traditionally emphasized at the public school, with some attention paid to Scripture, history, mathematics, and French. Usually a different schoolmaster taught each subject. A common weekday schedule looked something like this:

7:00-7:45 a.m.	**Latin and Greek** (1st language lesson)
8:00-9:45 a.m.	Breakfast and prepare 2nd language lesson
10:00-11:30 a.m.	**Latin and Greek** (2nd language lesson)
12:15-1:15 p.m.	**Arithmetic**
1:30-3:15 p.m.	Dinner and prepare 3rd language lesson
3:30-4:15 p.m.	**Latin and Greek** (3rd language lesson)
4:30-5:30 p.m.	**Arithmetic**
5:45-7:30 p.m.	Tea and free time
7:45-10:00 p.m.	Prayers and prepare 1st language lesson for next day

Religious studies formed only a small part of the weekly curriculum, but students devoted Sunday to biblical study. They learned the gospel and psalms on Sunday mornings. A weekly sermon by Thomas Arnold followed in the chapel. After an early dinner, students would study chapters of the Bible and then listen to a second sermon. They had free time every other weekday afternoon and after Sunday's second sermon.

School sports. The most popular sport at Rugby was, and continues to be, the game of football. Football has been associated with Rugby School because of the game's development and enormous popularity at the institution. A plaque at the school commemorates William Webb Ellis as the inspiration for the game; it states that in 1823 he was the first to pick up the ball and run with it, thus originating the Rugby style of football. The game was a consistent conversation piece among students, and an almost fanatical pastime during the Christmas term. One historian notes that some of the games at Rugby were "really pitched battles, and more than once the masters had to interfere to prevent serious physical injuries" (Reddall, p. 212). The various schoolhouses at Rugby played intrasquad matches. There was even a game featuring active students against alumni, but no games with other public schools took place until many years later.

While a student at Rugby, Thomas Hughes became captain of the football and cricket teams; both sports are described in positive terms in *Tom Brown's Schooldays*. Played on a large, circular outdoor field, cricket features ten players spread out on defense as a hurler pitches a ball at three wooden sticks, called wickets. One batter from the opposing team protects the wickets by swinging at the hurled ball. A batter scores a run by hitting the ball onto the playing field and running to another set of wickets, behind the hurler. Every player receives two turns at bat in a game that can last from a few hours in duration to as long as six days.

Another popular game at the school was fives. Rugby fives is a handball game played within four walls by two or four players. The object is to smash a ball off the front wall, leaving the opponent unable to return a shot.

Critics of public schools often charged that their students spent an inordinate amount of time playing sports and games. In fact, the amount of time most boys spent just thinking about sports, as mentioned in many firsthand accounts of various public schools, far outweighed the amount of time spent on studies.

Pastimes. Some of the more traditional English sports and activities are mentioned in the novel at the "Veast day" (Feast day) celebration that occurs in the main character's home county of Berkshire. Jingling matches, a spectator sport at the veast, involved about a dozen blindfolded men in a roped-off ring. A man with no blindfold but with a bell around his neck then entered the ring. The blindfolded men would subsequently stagger around in frantic efforts to catch the bell-carrying noisemaker, a sight that provided fine entertainment for the watching crowd.

Another pastime, backswording, featured two men who faced off against one another with cudgels, or clubs. The object of the contest was to open a bleeding wound on the head of one's opponent, which required only a slight scrape with the weapon. While description of the pastime makes it sound as if the contest was one of simple violence, it actually took great skill—competitors were encouraged to use strategy instead of brute force.

Pastimes at Rugby differed from those in Berkshire County. Aside from some of the schoolboy pastimes mentioned in *Tom Brown's Schooldays*, including hiking, fishing, collecting birds' eggs, and annoying local farmers, the boys read novels and Charles Dickens' Pickwick serials. Much to the dismay of their schoolmasters, students became obsessed with reading these unscholarly weekly serials, known as *The Posthumous Papers of the Pickwick Club*.

Fagging. A tradition passed down throughout public school history, fagging has long been a controversial topic. Younger children are required by unwritten rule to perform menial tasks for the school's oldest students, those in the sixth form. These tasks include polishing boots and cooking breakfast. In *Tom Brown's Schooldays*, the fifth form also attempts to garner favors from the younger children, but the attempt is unsuccessful.

PRAEPOSTERS

A praeposter was a student of the sixth form whose duties included watching out for school members of younger ages, regulating fagging duties, and serving as a liaison between the student body and the headmaster. Thomas Arnold developed trusting personal relationships with his older schoolboys, choosing the more responsible students to be praeposters.

Defenders of the practice have pointed to the benefits of fagging. They contend that the practice results in the development of a relationship between newer students and their respected schoolmates. Older students are able, through the interaction, to keep close tabs on the greener students. Fagging also has been said to foster teamwork, mutual respect, and responsibility. However, fagging leaves the use of younger boys to the discretion of older boys.ABuse of the privilege resulted in the bullying of younger students. At Rugby, Arnold would not tolerate repeat offenses of bullying. Under the theory that others would imitate troublemakers, he would expel students for persisting in this as well as other forms of misbehavior.

Tom Brown's Schooldays

The Novel in Focus

The plot. The novel begins with the narrator supplying background information on the widespread and famous Brown family. Explaining in part the origins, accomplishments, and respect enjoyed by its members, a scenario is created of a proud family.

Out of this extended family emerges the young Tom Brown. Tom is educated in the country style, by tutors instructed to bring up the robust and combative boy as a well-rounded young man. His early childhood develops along traditional English lines, involving exploration, physical activity, and innocent mischief.

Interspersed with Hughes's account of Tom Brown, though, are passages that outline the author's own personal beliefs. At one point, for example, the narrator laments the lack of understanding that many young people have about their country:

> Oh Young England! Young England! You who are born into these racing railroad times, when there's a Great Exhibition, or some monster sight, every year, and you can get over a couple thousand miles of ground for three pounds ten, in a five weeks' holiday; why don't you know more of your own birth-places?
> (Hughes, *Tom Brown's Schooldays*, p. 9)

Many of Tom's friends attend a small boarding school, but Squire Brown seeks a better education for his son. Unfortunately, Tom first attends a school that is run by an overworked schoolmaster and a pair of poorly educated, disinterested assistant teachers. Tom grows discouraged, and when an outbreak of fever plagues the school in mid-semester, Squire Brown packs his boy off to a public school.

Upon his arrival at Rugby, Tom makes a friend named East, who informs him on the particulars of proper dress and gives him preliminary instructions on the rules of football. The bright-eyed Tom soon finds himself on the playing field, adjusting easily to becoming a real Rugby schoolboy.

East and Tom prove themselves thorough ragamuffins, ignoring school boundaries, fishing in private holes, and pirating poultry. The Doctor, Rugby's headmaster, is informed of the antics of the charismatic troublemakers through a praeposter and decides to pair up a timid newcomer with the boisterous Tom Brown. At this point, Tom's character begins to undergo a dramatic change. He is increasingly influenced by his very pious young charge, Arthur.

Tom's charismatic and physical gifts aid Arthur's adjustment to Rugby, while the younger boy's spiritual and emotional purity help guide Tom on the path into adulthood and responsibility. Previously in his educational career, Tom had taken shortcuts to better grades, but witnessing Arthur's passion for learning kindles Tom's own intellectual interests. He, East, and Arthur engage in religious and philosophical discussions, exercising their minds. Previously only Tom's body had received real training.

An eccentric nature lover befriends Arthur, Tom, and East, and the four adventure through the neighboring communities, encountering some minor trouble along the way. Further difficulties arise when Tom hazards a fight against a class brute to defend Arthur's honor. His troubles appear to be worth the effort, for he gains the respect of his challenger.

Near the end of the semester, Arthur and many other students take to sick-beds during a fever epidemic. The sickness is so severe that one child dies, and Arthur contemplates his own mortality. His subsequent discussions with Tom are enlightening for both and display the genuine affection and camaraderie they feel for one another. A later discussion with East shows the distance the friends have traveled from their initial days as troublemakers to their present status as role models.

The novel concludes with a sixth-form Tom Brown, captain of the cricket team, discussing school with a schoolmaster and the now mature Arthur. The master recalls the days of Tom's youth and mentions the decision made by the Doctor to have Tom sponsor Arthur. The revelation shows Tom how he has been blessed by the caring guidance of authority figures, who molded him into a respected member of the sixth form and a student bound for Oxford and manhood.

A monumental relationship. Tom's introduction to Rugby is eased by the playful East, who entices young Brown to fun and trouble. His real maturation, however, comes later in the book from a boy younger than himself.

The relationship forged between Tom and Arthur is important for two reasons. First, it gives an example of the impact the headmaster had on the lives of Rugby schoolboys. Though the Doctor demands respect from and even inspires fear in his students, he always makes the effort to get to know and keep tabs on the hundreds of boys left in his charge. By heeding the information offered by his network of schoolmasters and sixth formers, he remains aware of the problems of individuals and is able to institute changes that deeply affect their lives.

Pairing Arthur with Tom benefits both children. The isolated, frail newcomer is physically empowered by the active Tom, who, in turn, gains the desire and courage to fulfill his academic potential because of Arthur's influence. The relationship serves as a perfect counterbalance for the two boys; each gains strengths that round out his personality.

A behind-the-scenes influence on both boys surfaces through the character of Arthur. Arthur mentions his father, a clergyman and Christian Socialist who devotes his life to helping the poor laborer. Interestingly, the Christian Socialist movement (a short-lived effort to bring Christianity to less-educated people) did not occur in England until 1848, about fifteen years *after* the novel takes place. When Thomas Hughes wrote the book, he was immersed within the movement and greatly interested in the common worker. He took the opportunity during his writing of the book to introduce Christian Socialism to readers, though no such movement existed at the time the story was set.

Sources. Thomas Hughes attended the public school at Rugby from 1834 until 1842, where he achieved more respect for his athletic feats than his academic accomplishments. Though he never openly admitted that *Tom Brown's Schooldays* was based on his own school experience, the story is regarded as autobiographical. Many characters in the novel are based on influential people from Hughes's life.

Thomas Arnold, the model for the Doctor in the book, served as the headmaster of the Rugby School when Hughes was a student there. An excerpt from a speech Thomas Hughes gave at Rugby near the end of his life illustrates the author's high regard for Thomas Arnold's efforts on his behalf: "I passed all those years under the spell of this place and Arnold, and for half a century have never ceased to thank God for it" (Hughes in Worth, p. 4).

Thomas Hughes's older brother, who died during the author's youth, is probably represented by Old Brooke, a well-respected sixth former during Tom Brown's early schooldays.

Perhaps the most significant character in the novel is Tom's friend Arthur, whose father is a Christian Socialist. These characters are based on Frederick Denison Maurice and Charles Kingsley, who along with Hughes founded the Christian Socialist movement. Hughes dedicated nine years of his life to the movement, and his depiction of the nobility of Arthur's family was indicative of his high regard for Christian Socialism.

Reviews. *Tom Brown's Schooldays* was by and large regarded as a realistic portrayal of life under the Arnold administration. Immediately well received, it has become the accepted interpretation of life at the English public school in the 1800s.

Some readers have attributed its popularity at least partly to the attention Hughes pays to recreation rather than to academics. Worried that this focus would damage the image of the public schools, Matthew Arnold, Thomas Arnold's son, showed concern over the book's lack of concentration on academics:

> [The novel] gives the reader the impression that it is the chief business at a public school to produce a healthy animal, to supply him with pleasant companions and faithful friends, to foster in him courage and truthfulness, and for the rest to teach as much as the regulations enforce, but no more.
> (Arnold in Worth, p. 105)

Another criticism of Hughes's novel has concerned the number of asides that appear throughout the book. The narrator stops to share his religious and moral views directly with the reader on many occasions, and this practice has alienated some readers. "We feel now and then that he is slapping us on the back with altogether too encouraging and muscularly Christian a hand" (Darwin, p. 159). Yet, despite its asides, the novel has a remained a popular favorite.

For More Information

Darwin, Bernard. *English Public School*. London: Longmans, Green, 1929.
Findlay, J. J. *Arnold of Rugby*. Cambridge: Cambridge University Press, 1897.
Hughes, Thomas. *Tom Brown's Schooldays*. London: J.M. Dent & Sons, 1857.
Reddall, Henry Frederic. *School-Boy Life in Merrie England*. New York: Phillips & Hunt, 1888.
Warner, Rex. *English Public Schools*. London: Collins, 1946.
Worth, George J. *Thomas Hughes*. Boston: Twayne, 1984.

The Turn of the Screw

by
Henry James

Henry James was born in New York City, the second son of well-to-do, liberal parents. He spent much of his youth traveling in the United States and Europe, an experience that would influence many of his greatest works. After an unsuccessful attempt at writing in the United States, James moved in 1875 to Europe. Settling first in Rome, then Paris, James finally found England most to his liking. He settled in a red-brick house in the community of Rye, in Sussex, England, a home that he had felt destined to lease. He created *The Turn of the Screw* there between September and December 1897. James carefully set the tale in the 1840s, the decade of his own youth. He used his surroundings for inspiration in his writing, for the house brought back memories of his boyhood, a time when he, like the boy Miles in the story, experienced demanding governesses and a confining environment.

Events in History at the Time of the Novel

Society in Victorian England. The society of Victorian England was governed by strict rules of decorum. Many of these rules of behavior applied to the interactions between men and women. For example, eye contact between men and women who did not know each other and were of different classes was considered indecent. This helps the reader understand the discomfort of the governess in *The Turn of the Screw* when she sees the figure of a man atop a tower.

THE LITERARY WORK
A novel set in rural England during the 1840s; written in 1897 and published in 1898.

SYNOPSIS
A young governess travels to a rural estate to take care of two children; shortly after her arrival she believes she sees the ghosts of the former governess and one of the house servants, both of whom recently died. Determined to protect the children from the apparitions, the governess becomes increasingly obsessed with the ghosts, which leads to tragic results.

The man stares at her, and disconcerted by this she reflects on how propriety could have been restored to the moment: "Some challenge between us, breaking the hush, would have been the right result of our straight mutual stare" (James, *Turn of the Screw*, pp. 311-12). Another major breach of social decorum stems from the man's lack of a hat in the presence of a stranger. The governess says of this: "and there was a touch of the strange freedom, as I remember, in the sign of familiarity of his wearing no hat" (*Turn of the Screw*, p. 311). In real life, this last breach might also be considered an insult because of the difference in their social classes since she has been bred as a member of the upper class and he is a lowly servant.

Any romantic relationship between men and women of different social standing was considered indecent. Indeed, the plot of James's novel turns in part on the repercussions of indulging such a forbidden attraction. When the new governess learns that the former governess, Miss Jessel, had had a relationship with Quint, the valet of the house, she is shocked and asks, "In spite of the difference——?" (*Turn of the Screw*, p. 331). The housekeeper who tells her the story sadly responds, "Oh, of their rank, their condition. She was a lady . . . And he so dreadfully below" (*Turn of the Screw*, p. 331). This improper relationship is described as the reason that Miss Jessel was dismissed from her duty as governess at Bly House. It is implied that she became pregnant, evidencing an immoral act made even worse by the class differences between the governess and the valet.

According to the social code of the time, governesses were not supposed to interact socially with the men and women of the house, or with persons from the surrounding areas. In one historical account, for instance, a governess describes her conduct in relation to the local minister, to whom she was attracted: "I avoided him as much as I could without appearing singular, during his stay. I was as reserved as possible, lest he should perceive my sentiments" (Weeton in Renton, p. 101). Though this governess had strong feelings for the minister, she put aside any thoughts of a relationship; the governess realized that if she acted too friendly toward him she would be in danger of losing not only her position, but also a good reference from her employer, which would be needed when she sought her next job.

Education and the role of the governess. Since the 1500s, England has relied on governesses to educate many of its children. The position of governess was specifically created for the purpose of educating young girls at home. Usually boys were sent away to school for their education.

Altogether there were some twenty-one thousand governesses registered in England in 1850. The education they provided was generally a poor one. Because the purpose in educating young girls was to make them suitable for marriage, governesses focused on needlework and social skills rather than on serious academic subjects. They taught dancing, singing, piano, English, a smattering of French or Italian, and perhaps drawing. Few were equipped to teach Latin, mathematics, history, or the sciences. When a young girl learned anything of this sort, her lessons usually came from such textbooks as *Miss Richmal Mangnall's Historical and Miscellaneous Questions for the Use of Young People*. Rather than provide a thorough understanding of a subject, *Mangnall's Questions*, as it was commonly called, merely listed hundreds of questions and answers on wide varieties of information that students would have to memorize.

A governess typically came from a middle-class or lower-middle-class family that needed her supplemental income. She generally worked for upper-class families, though by the second half of the 1800s, some middle-class families were hiring governesses as well. The governess usually lived in the home of her employer; in many cases she was forced to share a bedroom with the youngest children, the care of whom became an additional responsibility. Generally her salary was very low, about twelve pounds a year (the average farm worker earned thirty pounds annually). For this small wage she took responsibility for her employer's children from morning until night, enjoying only one day off every other week. Though most governesses received room and board, unlike other servants they did not wear uniforms and so had to provide their own attire.

Turn of the Screw

AN EXAMPLE OF A LESSON FROM *MISS MANGNALL'S QUESTIONS*

Q. What is whalebone?
A. A sort of gristle found inside the whale in long, flat pieces three to four yards long; it supplies the place of teeth.
Q. Are there not four hundred or five hundred of them in one whale?
A. Yes; they stick to the upper jaw and form a kind of strainer to keep in sea snails and other small creatures on which whales live.
Q. What is whalebone used for?
A. To stiffen stays, umbrellas, and whips.
Q. Are not umbrellas of great antiquity?
A. Yes; the Greeks, Romans, and all eastern nations used them to keep off the sun; ombrello, in Italian, signifies a little shade.

The life of the average governess was incredibly lonely. Most governesses would not associate with the other servants of the household, believing this to be beneath their dignity, and yet most families would not associate with their governesses, regarding them as servants. Governesses consequently endured a life of solitude, which was viewed as one of the chief drawbacks of the profession. The loneliness of her position greatly affects the governess in *The Turn of the Screw* and deserves consideration when evaluating her actions.

A governess's job was not easy, yet there was much competition for her position because there were few other occupations open to young, unmarried women. Employment agencies began exploiting governesses, charging a fee to find them work, and then giving them interviews for positions for which they were unqualified. In 1843 the plight of governesses attracted public attention, resulting in the formation of the Governesses' Benevolent Institution. This institution provided inexpensive room and board for governesses who were between jobs and had no place to stay. In 1848 the Governesses' Benevolent Institution set up a college that awarded certificates of proficiency to governesses, intending to help them find jobs more easily. Both the college and the institution were established on Harley Street in London. It is therefore ironic that Harley Street is mentioned in *The Turn of the Screw* as the place where the governess's employer lives for most of the year.

Women in the Victorian Age. Women, who received an inferior education in the Victorian period, also suffered from the popular attitude that a female should not show her knowledge. In *Advice to Young Ladies on the Improvement of the Mind*, published in 1808, Thomas Broadhurst congratulated women on living in an age during which education was available to them. But he also warned against "any display of literary attainments; since of all objects that are disagreeable to the other sex, a pedantic female is, I believe, the most confessedly so" (Broadhurst in Renton, p. 50). His statement reflects a common regard for women not as individuals in their own right but only in relation to men.

Many of Henry James's works examine the plight of women in a male-dominated society. He is especially well known for novels that deal with the loss of innocence in young women as a result of their involvement with men. In *The Turn of the Screw*, two of the primary characters in the story are women, and they develop a bond that allows the housekeeper, Mrs. Grose, to believe the governess's statements even though the things she describes seem impossible. This again is partly a function of social class. Mrs. Grose, an illiterate domestic of the lowest social class, is deferential to her social superior, the governess. The primary male characters include the master of the house, who is the dominant force in the novel. He never fully becomes part of the action, however, because he does not want to be bothered by any obligations.

The Novel in Focus

The plot. The novel begins with a framing episode in which a group of men and women are telling each other ghost stories. One of the men, Douglas, proposes to read a supposedly factual ghost story written by his sister's former governess. The narrative he presents is inscribed in the first person, as told by the governess, who recalls events that happened many years before.

The daughter of a country parson, the girl arrives in London to answer an advertisement placed by someone who wants a governess for an orphaned nephew and niece. The employer turns out to be a gentleman, a bachelor with whom the young governess becomes immediately infatuated, notwithstanding his vanity and irresponsible behavior toward his wards. He gives her the job on the condition that she take full responsibility for the children and not bother him about them.

Upon arriving at the country house where the children live, the governess finds that the boy has been expelled from school for unknown reasons and so now must be taught with his sister at home. She also learns that the former governess left her position and subsequently died, though the circumstances of her death remain unclear. The new governess establishes herself at the country house with the housekeeper, Mrs. Grose, and the two seemingly angelic children, Miles and Flora.

One day, while walking on the estate, the governess sees a figure upon one of the towers looking down at her. She describes the suspicious character to the housekeeper, who tells her the description of the man matches that of the former valet, Peter Quint, an unsavory character who died some months earlier. The governess believes that he has come back to haunt the children.

Not long afterwards, the governess sees the figure of another stranger, this time a woman dressed in black, whom she concludes must be the former governess. When she asks the housekeeper about the woman, she discovers that Miss Jessel, the previous governess, though a lady, had a love affair with the servant Quint. She also discovers that the children knew about the liaison but lied about it. At this point she determines that they had been corrupted in this way by Miss Jessel and Quint. After learning of these prior events, the governess begins to see the apparitions at night and becomes convinced that the children are getting up to meet them, even though the children give plausible explanations for what seems to her to be suspicious behavior on their part. Readers are left unsure about the appearance of the ghosts; it is unclear whether the governess is really seeing them or whether she is entering upon an insane obsession that causes her to hallucinate the ghostly presences.

The housekeeper suggests telling the master about the strange happenings, but the governess refuses, deciding that her employer would think she was insane. (Also, her vanity takes over. She proudly wants to take credit for saving the children on her own.) Seeing the ghost of Miss Jessel again, the governess believes that the ghost is damned and that it wants the little girl, Flora, to share her damnation. The little girl runs away shortly after this sighting, and the governess finds her on the shore of a nearby lake. When the governess asks Flora where Miss Jessel is, the little girl replies "there," pointing to a spot where nothing appears, then turns angrily upon the governess.

Afterward, Flora grows feverish and expresses her desire to be taken away from the governess. The housekeeper becomes worried and urges the governess to leave, but the governess convinces the housekeeper to take the little girl away and leave the boy at home. Alone with the boy, the governess questions him about his expulsion from school. He answers cryptically that he was expelled because he said certain things, and the entire situation sounds harmless to the governess. But again she sees the ghost of Peter Quint, and her panic proves to be contagious. The boy becomes frightened and asks where the ghost is. When the governess shrieks that he is there, the boy cries out "you devil" and dies from fright. Here the story ends, without the reader ever knowing for certain just who "the devil" is in this case.

Ghosts vs. psychology in *The Turn of the Screw*. There are two opposing theories concerning James's *The Turn of the Screw*. The first theory holds that the tale is a straightforward ghost story about guilt and the corruption of the innocent. The second theory argues that there are really no ghosts at all in this story, and that the apparitions are actually delusions of the governess, whose solitude and infatuation with her employer drive her to insanity.

Those who support the theory that the ghosts in *The Turn of the Screw* are real cite James's use of the character Douglas, who introduces and reads the story to the assembled listeners. Douglas describes the governess as "the most agreeable woman I've ever known in her position; she would have been worthy of any whatever" (*Turn of the Screw*, p. 293). By introducing the character and her story in this way, James gives the governess complete credibility, which suggests that her story of the ghosts should be believed. In addition, the fact that she had never seen the valet, yet describes him so perfectly that the housekeeper immediately identifies him, seems to suggest that she did truly see the apparition on the tower.

Proponents of the other theory argue that the ghosts do not exist because no one sees them but the governess. This argument attempts to refute the theory that she identified the ghost of Quint by stating that she could easily have been given a description of him from one of the other servants or from any of the local townspeople. It has also been suggested that though she describes the apparition on the tower as Quint, she is really describing the master. Moments before discerning the specter upon the battlements, the governess had been thinking how charming it would be to suddenly see the master of the house appear from around a corner or from the garden. Another argument holds that the story's placement among James's works suggests that it is a tale of psychological rather than ghostly terror. *The Turn of the Screw* is grouped with *The Aspern Papers* and *The Liar*, both stories that deal with unreliable narrators and psychological plots. His ghost stories (he wrote fifteen altogether) are grouped separately. Though the story presents enough ambiguities to strengthen either argument, James himself claims that he sat down determined to write a ghost story, and insists that he did not create the governess as a character tormented by delusions.

James's interest in ghosts was not uncommon for his time; many other writers in England and in the United States were fascinated by psychic phenomena. For example, Sir Arthur Conan Doyle devoted a great deal of time and money to psychic research in the later part of his life.

Henry James and women. Like the master of the house in *The Turn of the Screw*, James preferred to keep women at an emotional distance.

Turn of the Screw

Henry James (left) and his brother William.

Leon Edel, one of James's premier biographers, writes that while studying at Cambridge James "saw a goodly number of women, saw them as creatures to be observed and chatted with at tea" (Edel, p. 84). Edel goes on to describe James's writing and its view of women: "He wrote of the mystery of womankind, of young men trapped by wily females, of sad heroes betrayed" (Edel, pp. 84-5).

Perhaps fearing entrapment by "wily females" himself, James decided at age thirty-five never to marry. When James reviewed the book *Modern Women* in 1868, it became apparent that he was not so much opposed to women as he was to society as a whole. In his review James concluded that it was impossible to discuss and condemn modern women apart from modern men. He contended that their faults were "part and parcel of the follies of modern civilization" (Edel, p. 86).

Sources. James was first inspired to write *The Turn of the Screw* during a visit with the Archbishop of Canterbury, Edward White Benson, in 1895. The two had been discussing ghost stories, and the Archbishop spoke of an incident he had heard of wherein two small children, living in some remote area, were visited by the spirits of certain "bad" servants. These spirits had beckoned the children into dangerous situations and seemed to desire that the children destroy themselves. James made some notes concerning the Archbishop's tale and set it aside in his notebook.

The actual structure of the story, as well as the names of some of the principle characters, came from Frank Leslie's "Temptation," a tale that had been published in 1855. It centers on a struggle for possession of an inheritance and also incorporates a series of subplots involving valets, housekeepers, and governesses. Leslie's tale also includes two children who are victims of unknown horrors and a prime villain named Peter Quin. James simply added one letter to get the name of his villain, and he also took the name Miles from Quin's henchman in "Temptation." Leslie's tale is set in a house on Harley Street, and James borrowed the street name for the London home of the master in *The Turn of the Screw*.

Reviews. *The Turn of the Screw* first appeared in a serialization in *Collier's* magazine from January to April 1898. The story instantly caught the interest of the public and became a great success. James received high acclaim for his clever manipulation of the ghosts' actions. In response to questions concerning the mysterious ambiguities of the ghosts, James made the following observation: "So long as the events are veiled the imagination will run riot and depict all sorts of horrors, but as soon as the veil is lifted, all mystery disappears and with it the sense of terror" (James in Edel, p. 256). He preferred to leave his readers wondering.

PSYCHOLOGY, GHOSTS, AND WILLIAM JAMES

Henry James's brother, William James, was one of the most famous and well-respected psychologists of the late 1800s and early 1900s. His two major works, *Principles of Psychology* and *Pragmatism*, attempted to describe human life as it is actually experienced, rather than formulating models of abstract reality far removed from the real details of life. In the mid-1890s William James's greatest interest was in the field of psychical research, the study of the human mind, and the supernatural. During this period, William James conducted a survey of hallucinations for the British Society for Psychical Research, of which he was president for two years. This survey involved spending a great deal of time with people who claimed to have seen ghosts and other supernatural phenomena. Henry James was a great admirer of his brother's work and would have been completely familiar with his research during this period.

For More Information

Bryfonski, Dedria, and Sharon K. Hall, eds. *Twentieth-Century Literary Criticism*. Vol. 2. Detroit: Gale Research Company, 1979.

Edel, Leon. *The Life of Henry James*. New York: Penguin, 1977.

James, Henry. *The Turn of the Screw*. New York: Signet, 1980.

Lustig, T. J. *Henry James and the Ghostly*. New York: Cambridge University Press, 1994.

Renton, Alice. *Tyrant or Victim? A History of the British Governess*. London: Weidenfield and Nicolson, 1991.

Twenty Thousand Leagues under the Sea

by
Jules Verne

~

Born in the seaport town of Nantes, France, Jules Verne reached his thirties before settling into the life of a science fiction writer, the occupation of his choice. He had begun writing in his teens, creating unremarkable plays, articles, and stories. His father groomed him to become a lawyer but regularly read the latest science news to his five children. Meanwhile, his mother showed her fast-paced imagination, which Verne later compared to his own. In his early teens, he ran away and worked for a day on a sailing vessel before his father fetched him home. The fact that young Verne took refuge at sea reflected his deep love for the watery depths, and his interest in the ocean later resurfaced in *Twenty Thousand Leagues under the Sea,* a remarkably prophetic novel. Added to this love was a passionate feeling about current events that would greatly affect the development of character and action in the novel.

Events in History at the Time of the Novel

Polish-Russian strife. In 1863 the Polish people rose up against the Russian czar who had become their dictator. Poland had experienced a long and troubled relationship with the Russian nation on its borders, and the situation came to a violent head shortly before Verne wrote *Twenty Thousand Leagues under the Sea.*

The political tensions of Verne's day had their roots about a century earlier in 1772, when Russia, Austria, and Prussia began to divide

> **THE LITERARY WORK**
> A novel set in the depths of the world's oceans around 1869, first published in France as a magazine serial in 1869 and as a book in 1870.
>
> **SYNOPSIS**
> Verne combines adventure and learning in a study of freedom, revenge, and scientific discovery beneath the waves.

Poland among themselves in a series of three partitions that slowly but surely consumed the entire country. By 1795 there was no country of "Poland" left.

Foreign powers dominated the land in the 1800s. After defeating the Austro-Russian army in December 1805, Napoleon I of France established the Grand Duchy of Warsaw (Poland's major city) in 1807; after Napoleon's eventual defeat in 1814, the Russians turned the Duchy into a constitutional monarchy that was ruled by the Russian czar. In 1830 the Poles successfully threw their Russian overlords out of power, but the Russians were back within the year. Another Polish attempt to regain control in 1863 was even less successful. Led by the czar, the Russians brutally repressed the uprising, disgusting France with their merciless bloodshed. The Russians, moreover, were fed up with Polish attempts to reclaim their nation; among many cruel and bloody measures, they imposed the rule that the

Russian tongue, not Polish, was to be the official language of Poland.

Captain Nemo, the troubled sea captain of *Twenty Thousand Leagues under the Sea,* has a dark past that is mysteriously alluded to throughout the novel. Verne reveals, however, that he originally thought of Nemo as a wronged Polish aristocrat:

> Remember what the original idea for the book was all about: a Polish aristocrat whose daughters have been raped, whose wife has been hacked to death, whose father has been tortured and murdered, whose friends have died in Siberia and whose nationality is due to vanish from Europe under the tyranny of the Russians.
>
> (Verne in Jules-Verne, p. 88)

Nemo's pitiless destruction of the many lives aboard a warship at the novel's close is explained in part by the long history of strife between the Russians and the Poles. Verne, like many in France, objected passionately to the Russians' brutal punishment of the Poles for the 1863 uprisings. To avoid censorship of his book, Verne agreed not to reveal details about Nemo's dark past, but he clearly had the suffering of the Poles in mind.

Censorship in France. Verne's publisher, Pierre-Jules Hetzel, was aghast at the violent retribution that Captain Nemo exacts from others on the warship at the end of *Twenty Thousand Leagues under the Sea.* By way of explanation, Verne in 1867 wrote a letter to Hetzel, drawing out the political ramifications of the *Nautilus*'s last battle:

> Supposing the situation were as I intended it to be, and as my readers will feel it to be; supposing Nemo were a Pole, and the sunk ship a Russian ship, could anyone raise the shadow of an objection? No! A hundred times no!... [D]o not forget what the original, true, logical and watertight idea for the book was all about: a Pole versus Russia. Since we cannot make it explicit, which is in some ways unfortunate, let us leave people to suppose that this may be the case.
>
> (Verne in Jules-Verne, p. 87)

Verne's determination to lend *Twenty Thousand Leagues under the Sea* a contemporary dimension by very specifically recalling the Polish struggle for independence ran headfirst into censorship concerns. His publisher predicted that if the book offended the Russians, it would be banned in France.

Since 1852, when Louis Napoleon, or Napoleon III, proclaimed himself the emperor—

Illustration by Edouard Riou for the first edition of *Twenty Thousand Leagues under the Sea.*

he was still in power when Verne was writing his underwater adventure—literature had come under rather strict censorship policies. For example, writers could not speak negatively about the emperor's politics or about his government, and after a while conservative republicans (like Victor Hugo) were not allowed to publish very much, if at all. Writers were watched closely for any possible political commentary that they might be making, so the concerns of Verne's publisher were reasonable.

Meanwhile, events elsewhere in Europe contributed to French concern about offending Russia. While Verne was finishing *Twenty Thousand Leagues under the Sea,* the Prussians were on the move in Denmark and Austria, and many in the French government feared that France would be next on their list. If this turned out to be the case, the French would need the Russians as allies. France subsequently took precautionary steps to court them. Hetzel's caution was merited, as shown by the events that followed. In fact, the Franco-Prussian war broke out in 1870, shortly after the initial publication of Verne's novel.

Submarines. The immediate predecessor of Nemo's fictional submarine *Nautilus* is Robert

20,000 Leagues under the Sea

Fulton's actual submarine of the same name, a twenty-one-foot-long vessel built in 1800. The first underwater vessel had been built almost two centuries earlier, around 1620, by the Dutch inventor Cornelius van Drebbel. The American Revolution saw the first real use of the submarine in military operations, when David Bushnell created a tiny one-man version called the *Turtle*. In 1776 the *Turtle* made a failed attempt to sink a British ship in the New York harbor; its effort, however, has gone down in history as the first submarine attack on another vessel of war. The earliest successful attack also occurred in an American struggle; during the Civil War, a Confederate submarine tried to blow up a Union ship in the Charleston harbor. Both vessels sank.

A LESSON IN UNDERWATER BOTANY

A good example of Verne's encyclopedic explanations in his novel may be found in the underwater trek through "the forest of the island of Crespo": "A light network of marine plants, of that inexhaustible family of seaweeds, of which more than two thousand kinds are known, grew on the surface of the water. I [the character Aronnax] saw long ribbons of fucus floating, some globular, others tuberous; laurenciae and cladostephi of most delicate foliage, and some rhodomeniae palmatae resembling the fan of a cactus. I observed that the green plants kept nearer the top of the sea, while the red were at a medium depth, leaving to the black or brown hydrophytes the care of forming the gardens and parterres of the remote beds of the ocean" (Verne, *Twenty Thousand Leagues under the Sea*, p. 211).

Closer to home, many local French inventors were working out the complications of building submarines. From Nantes, Verne's birthplace, came Brutus Villeroi, who described his own attempts to build an underwater vessel in an 1832 scientific journal. A few decades later, in the city of Amiens, Verne met Jacques François Conseil (after whom Verne named one of the characters in *Twenty Thousand Leagues under the Sea*), who had successfully made a submarine dive in 1858. That same year, the French Ministry of Marine called for bids on building a submarine to be financed by the government. In 1863, a few years before Verne wrote his novel, *Le Plongeur,* a 140-foot submarine, was completed. *Le Plongeur* was to carry a crew of twelve men, but it had problems with underwater pressure and buoyancy. A model of *Le Plongeur* appeared on display at the Paris Exhibition in 1867; Verne consulted the model for his own literary purposes.

Scientific education in France. Verne played an important part in Pierre-Jules Hetzel's dream of producing science-based literature for the edification of French children. Perhaps because education was largely in the hands of the Roman Catholic Church, and many of the claims of science seemed to run counter to theologically based ideas of creation and knowledge, science took a back seat to such disciplines as theology and philosophy in mid-nineteenth-century French schools. Whenever more liberal elements in French politics controlled the government, scientific education was given a boost, but that lasted only while the liberals were in power. The exposure that French schoolchildren had to science therefore varied widely in quality and quantity.

In 1850 the French minister of education passed a law that granted control of primary education solely to the Catholic Church, and France rapidly fell behind other nations in technological developments. Hertzel hired Verne specifically to write for his new French journal (the English translation of which is *The Magazine of Education and Recreation*). The magazine's role was, according to Hetzel, "to complement the education offered in the schools and not to replace it" (Evans, p. 14). Verne also contracted to write two volumes of scientific fiction a year, and to write about science, technology, and adventure in such a way that people of all ages, especially children, would learn from it. This aim explains the presence in *Twenty Thousand Leagues under the Sea* of lists of different sea creatures, encyclopedic explanations of electricity, and histories of nineteenth-century explorers.

Verne became a huge success in France, producing one bestseller after another for a while. Once France began to adopt a more rigorous program of scientific education, however, his popularity temporarily plummeted. In 1882 a secularization of elementary education was launched under the auspices of Jules Ferry, the French minister of culture since 1879. The intention was to redress France's lag behind other European nations in scientific knowledge. In keeping with this intention, the movement away from a church-centered education initiated a trend toward a more science-oriented curriculum.

A difference of opinion. In the novel, in his study aboard the *Nautilus,* Captain Nemo has hung portraits of his role models, men associated with acts of bravery and rebellion the world over. Two of these portraits are of American leaders of the antislavery movement: President Abraham Lincoln and John Brown, leader of the ill-fated 1859 raid on Harpers Ferry. A radical abolitionist, Brown planned to raid a federal arsenal at Harpers Ferry in what is today West Virginia. Brown then planned to flee to the cover of nearby mountains and encourage slaves to rebel against their masters. Brown never made it past the first stage of his plan. He seized the federal arsenal, then fought the townspeople of Harpers Ferry, taking refuge with some hostages and fellow rebels in the arsenal. He was eventually captured and hanged for treason.

Hetzel encouraged Verne to play up the connection between Nemo and the antislavery movement, but Verne cautioned him in a letter against a too-easy identification of Nemo with abolition: "You tell me the abolition of slavery is the greatest economic event of our times. I agree. But I cannot see what that has to do here.... [I]f Nemo wanted revenge on the slavers, all he had to do was join Grant's army and that was it" (Verne in Jules-Verne, p. 89). Verne's intention seems to have been to make Nemo a despiser of tyranny in general, not just a man opposed to the American slave trade, even if it was the "greatest economic event" of his time.

"The Sea Does Not Belong to Despots." In 1888 Jules Verne was elected as a radical socialist to the town council of Amiens. Broadly, socialism at the time promised to attend to the issues of workers and to support programs to aid the underprivileged. To some, this may come as a surprise, for Verne is commonly regarded as a "nice, quiet middle-class gentleman," in the words of Aristide Briand, a friend of Verne's son who later became the French prime minister (Chesneaux, p. 11). In fact, however, many of the socialist leaders of the time were widely held to be "mere bourgeois idealists" (Cobban, p. 45). Verne had money in his own family and married a wealthy widow; both families were associated with the "pseudo-nobility" in France, people who through their wealth were able to acquire all the trappings of the aristocracy, complete with surnames that alluded to land or property (the prefix "de" often signifies a person's geographic origins, for example) and could thus signify their social position. Verne owned a yacht on which he sailed whenever he could, had a comfortable home in Amiens, and knew that he would be paid handsomely for his writing. Some historians even question whether the platform upon which Verne was elected to the town council was all that radical; his personal letters and public speeches consistently place him among moderate or even conservative politicians.

Yet this same Verne created the tortured and darkly heroic Captain Nemo, despiser of society at large and would-be champion of the oppressed:

> The sea does not belong to despots. On the surface, they can still exercise their iniquitous rights.... But thirty feet beneath this level, their authority ceases, their influence is extinguished, their power disappears. Ah! Monsieur, come and live at the bottom of the sea! Only there can true independence be found. There I recognize no Master. There I am free.
> (*Twenty Thousand Leagues under the Sea*, pp. 162-63)

TYRANNY VS. LIBERTY

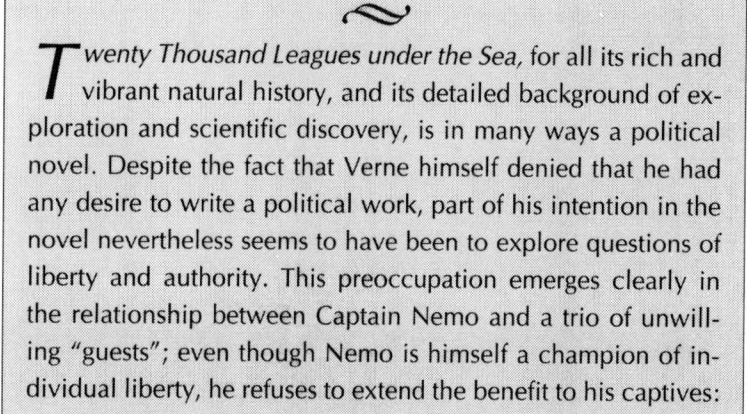

Twenty Thousand Leagues under the Sea, for all its rich and vibrant natural history, and its detailed background of exploration and scientific discovery, is in many ways a political novel. Despite the fact that Verne himself denied that he had any desire to write a political work, part of his intention in the novel nevertheless seems to have been to explore questions of liberty and authority. This preoccupation emerges clearly in the relationship between Captain Nemo and a trio of unwilling "guests"; even though Nemo is himself a champion of individual liberty, he refuses to extend the benefit to his captives:

> "For seven months we have been here on board, and I ask you today, in the name of my companions, and in my own, if your intention is to keep us here always?"
> "Monsieur Aronnax, I will answer you today as I did seven months ago: Whoever enters the Nautilus must never leave it."
> "You impose actual slavery on us!"
> "Give it what name you please."
> (*Twenty Thousand Leagues under the Sea*, p. 469)

Only if Nemo is to be regarded as an evil or insane person can this impassioned speech, and others like it throughout the novel, be regarded as running counter to Verne's own purposes. But Nemo is in many ways a heroic man, and his support of individual rights and freedoms speaks to a time in which people all over the world were struggling for independence. A solitary and an independent human being, Nemo represents the strong current of anarchism and resistance to all forms of government. The principle tenets of his philosophy included the guaranteed freedom of each individual, suspicion of monetary standards, and the sanctity of private property. The extent to which Verne himself supported such ideas remains uncertain.

The Novel in Focus

The plot. *Twenty Thousand Leagues under the Sea* takes place between July 1866 and June 2, 1868. A "monster" is sighted time and again in various waters all over the earth: "a long object, spindle-shaped, at times phosphorescent, and infinitely larger and more rapid in its movements than a whale" (*Twenty Thousand Leagues under the Sea*, p. 91). The maritime and scientific communities are intrigued and the popular community entranced by these mysterious sightings. Suggestions concerning its nature range from a floating island to a huge sea monster to ... a submarine. The last possibility is dismissed as impossible; skeptics insist that no one man or government could have built such a thing unnoticed. Public opinion instead holds that a horrible sea monster is on the loose. An American ship, the *Abraham Lincoln*, is dispatched to hunt down the creature in the interests of safe sea-trade. Pierre Aronnax, an assistant professor of natural history at the Museum of Paris, and his servant Conseil are invited along.

The *Abraham Lincoln* sets out from New York on July 3 and explores the Atlantic Ocean, making its way eventually around Cape Horn (the southernmost point of South America) and into the Pacific Ocean. By October the American vessel has not spotted the monster and the crew feels discouraged. But on November 5, 1867, some two hundred miles from Japan, the *Abraham Lincoln*'s Canadian harpoonist, Ned Land, catches sight of the creature, and the chase begins. The pursuit ends abruptly, when a collision pitches Land, Aronnax, and Conseil into the sea; they soon discover that the monster they have been chasing is in fact a metal ship of some kind.

The novel now follows the exploits of the "monster," a submarine named *Nautilus*, and her mysterious captain, Nemo. Silent, driven, and at times cruel, the cultivated and politically radical Nemo is on a terrible mission. He imprisons Aronnax, Land, and Conseil within the ship. They are not told Nemo's purpose but they do

Jules Verne

learn much of the natural history and geography of the lands past which they voyage. The seas teem with unknown wonders, and the professor takes some comfort in the new knowledge he is gaining. Still, the drive to be free prevails, and the three captives plot their escape.

The three men do escape the confines of the submarine, but not according to their plan. Instead, they watch the outcome of Nemo's journey in fascinated horror. His submarine succeeds in sinking a mysterious ship that attacks it, but then gets drawn into a deadly maelstrom (whirlpool). When Professor Aronnax and his friends regain their senses, they find themselves on a Norwegian island without Captain Nemo, his ship, or his crew. While Nemo disappears from the vicinity of Professor Aronnax, readers meet him five years later in another of Verne's novels.

Father of "science fiction"? Jules Verne has very often been referred to as the inventor of the literary genre of science fiction, but at least one critic points out that this is not strictly true. If science fiction operates essentially in the realm of the fantastic, then Verne is not really a science fiction writer, for most of the scientific gadgets, machines, and methods of which he writes were feasible in his day. He should perhaps be referred to more accurately as the father of "scientific fiction" (Evans, p. 2). Others suggest that Verne is not really an inventor of new machines or a maker of scientific breakthroughs, but an adept engineer who cleverly works with what already exists, improving upon, rather than creating. He is, in fact, rather careful not to go too far beyond the realm of what has been proven or at least speculated upon responsibly, reining in his imagination in favor of representing scientific truths. H. G. Wells, another man often credited as the father of science fiction, said of Verne that "The interest he invoked was a practical one; he wrote and believed and told that this thing or that could be done, which was not at that time done. He helped his readers imagine it done and to realize what fun, excitement or mischief might ensue" (Wells in Costello, pp. 185-86).

Nemo. In Latin, the word "nemo" means "no man" or "no one." By this cryptic name, Verne apparently intended for the reader to understand more deeply the extent to which the captain of the Nautilus has cut himself off from all human society, choosing to sink beneath the waves with his library, his art, and his anger.

The mysterious captain reappears in Verne's The Mysterious Island (1875), telling a story that completely contradicts what we learn of him in Twenty Thousand Leagues under the Sea and from Verne's letters to Hetzel. In the later novel, Nemo holds himself out as an Indian prince whose family was slaughtered by the British during the Indian Mutiny (also known as the Sepoy Rebellion) of 1857-1859. The rebellion occurred when officers of the East India Company, a British trading monopoly that took political control of India in 1757, ordered Indian soldiers to break certain religious taboos in the interests of battle. The Indians refused and discontent spread rapidly. The British suppressed the rebellion by mid-1858, with political control of the region passing into the hands of the British Crown (Queen Victoria) rather than the East India Company. The Indian Mutiny left both the rebels and the victors feeling bitter, and increased the tension between the two sides.

The hero of The Mysterious Island, Cyrus Smith, informs Nemo that Professor Aronnax has written a novel about him, entitled Twenty Thousand Leagues under the Sea. Nemo anticipates the way in which Aronnax would have characterized him: "As a great public enemy, no doubt.... Yes, a rebel, banished perhaps from humanity!" (Martin, p. 100). In The Mysterious Island, all the mystery and horror of Nemo's past is explained away—here, he is portrayed as a colonizer, and a defender of a well-run society. What remains constant is his hatred for political oppression: "Scientist and artist though he was, he remained Indian at heart, Indian in his desire for vengeance, Indian in the hope he nourished of being able one day to assert his country's right to independence and to throw out the foreigners" (Chesneaux, p. 117).

Sources. For his oceanic adventure story, Verne drew on his own lifelong attraction to navigation. In his young adulthood, Verne made three significant voyages, one to Scotland, another to Norway and Denmark, and a third, in 1867, to the United States aboard the *Great Eastern,* a ship that appears in *Twenty Thousand Leagues under the Sea.* The *Great Eastern* achieved renown as the ship that laid the transatlantic cable that connected North America with Europe.

AUTHOR, AUTHOR

A rumor regarding the identity of the author of *Twenty Thousand Leagues under the Sea* has endured for years. Some critics have suggested that the tale of submarine adventure was not really the work of Jules Verne, but of the Communist insurrectionist Louise Michel, a French woman who sold the manuscript to Verne for the measly sum of 100 francs because she was broke. The idea that Verne bought the novel is highly suspect, however. *Twenty Thousand Leagues under the Sea* was given to Verne's publisher in 1868, and mentioned in correspondence earlier still, but the story surrounding Michel claims that she handed over her work sometime later than that.

When he was a boy, Verne read all the seafaring adventure stories that abounded during the period, including Daniel Defoe's *Robinson Crusoe,* James Fenimore Cooper's *The Pilot,* and Sir Walter Scott's *The Pirate.* Some thirty years later, armed with the money that he earned from *Twenty Thousand Leagues under the Sea* and other novels, Verne bought himself a sumptuous yacht and sailed as far as Ireland, Italy, and the Baltic region. Literary predecessors of *Twenty Thousand Leagues under the Sea* include several French books on submarine voyages, including an 1864 oceanographic work entitled *Les Mystères de l'Ocean* (*Mysteries of the Ocean*) and *Voyages sous les Flots* (*Voyage under the Waves*), written in 1868 by Aristide Roger (the pen name of Jules Rengade).

20,000 Leagues under the Sea

Verne was a tireless researcher of marine life as well as underwater craft, and he became familiar with twenty-five different failed experiments with submersibles. He also turned to his brother Paul, a naval officer who supplied him with a wealth of information and advice. Farther from home were the scientists whom he met at the residence of the renowned world traveler Jacques Arago. Perhaps some of these discussions contributed to his remarkably accurate predictions in the novel: the invention of scuba gear and the feat of sailing under the South Pole, for example.

Abridged versions surface. Verne was an immensely popular writer, not only at home, but also in England and America, where his books were translated into English. His 1871 illustrated version of *Twenty Thousand Leagues under the Sea* was subject to rather extensive cutting when the novel was reprinted in France in 1928. The extensive scientific discussions that were central to Verne's and Hetzel's conception of the novel were eliminated, and the resulting book was more purely an adventure novel for children than an edifying work on science and discovery. English translations of Aronnax's adventures were also radically truncated; it was not until 1976 that the full version appeared in English.

For More Information

Chesneaux, Jean. *The Political and Social Ideas of Jules Verne*. Translated by Thomas Wikeley. London: Thames and Hudson, 1971.

Cobban, Alfred. *A History of Modern France, 1871-1962*. Vol. 3. New York: Penguin, 1982.

Costello, Peter. *Jules Verne: Inventor of Science Fiction*. London: Hodder and Stoughton, 1978.

Evans, Arthur B. *Jules Verne Rediscovered: Didacticism and the Scientific Novel*. New York: Greenwood Press, 1988.

Jules-Verne, Jean. *Jules Verne: A Biography*. Translated and adapted by Roger Greaves. New York: Taplinger, 1976.

Martin, Andrew. *The Mask of the Prophet: The Extraordinary Fictions of Jules Verne*. Oxford: Clarendon Press, 1990.

Verne, Jules. *The Complete Twenty Thousand Leagues under the Sea*. Translated by Emanuel J. Mickel. Bloomington: Indiana University Press, 1991.

Two Years before the Mast

by
Richard Henry Dana, Jr.

> **THE LITERARY WORK**
>
> Narrative set along the California coast from 1834 to 1836; published in 1840.
>
> **SYNOPSIS**
>
> Richard Henry Dana, Jr. chronicles two years of his life as a merchant seaman on board a trade vessel voyaging from Boston to California and back.

Born into an illustrious and prosperous family, Richard Henry Dana, Jr. resisted an inclination to join the navy and instead entered Harvard College at age sixteen, in 1831. He, however, interrupted his studies after three years, leaving Harvard because of an eye ailment. At the time, New England merchant ships were sailing to California to take advantage of a recent trade boom along the Pacific Coast. Dana decided to become a seaman on one of these merchant ships. Two years later he returned to his studies at Harvard, graduated, and took up teaching and the study of law. It was while he was in law school that Dana completed *Two Years before the Mast*, a narrative in which he reported in vivid detail what day-to-day life was like for a merchant seaman of his era.

Events in History at the Time the Narrative Takes Place

Merchant ships of the 1830s. The period in which Dana grew up was one of marked changes in world shipping. The steamship was gradually being tested, improved, and put to use for longer voyages. Most of the world trade was still transported by sailing vessels, but these vessels, too, were changing, becoming larger and faster. In the 1830s, by far the largest number of ships visiting or leaving New England's ports were brigs, two-masted, square-rigged wooden vessels. But various factors combined to push the brigs from their preeminent position. The competition for trade with China, which included transporting furs from the West Coast of North America, stimulated the development of a larger, slimmer ship, the clipper. A three-masted vessel outfitted with triangular sails, the clipper competed favorably with the steam-powered ships and could be managed by fewer crewmen. In Dana's time, clippers of wood and metal were rapidly replacing the older brigs. These clippers were later replaced by steam-powered vessels.

The *Pilgrim*, the vessel on which Dana served, was a brig of considerable size, but at that time did not technically qualify as a "ship." The ship designation was reserved for vessels with three or more masts. Richard Dana therefore sailed on a less than up-to-date vessel for his time, and one that required constant labor by its crew.

Sea trade in the 1830s. By the early 1800s, trade possibilities on the West Coast were well established. California was still a part of Mexico, but American fur traders had long moved about in the region and shipped furs to New England mer-

Two Years before the Mast

chants and to China. As the fur trade began to be exhausted, new possibilities arose. Spain had claimed much of California by establishing a series of missions that stretched from San Diego in the south to Sonoma in the north. These missions, fueled largely by Indian labor, grew into agricultural and industrial centers operated by the Catholic Church. Twenty-one thriving missions were established between 1769 and 1830.

> **FROM COLONIZATION TO INDEPENDENCE IN CALIFORNIA**
>
> **1769:** Spain founds the first of a string of twenty-one missions, visible evidence of its claim to the territory
> **1821:** Mexico gains independence from Spain
> **1822:** Control of California shifts from Spain to Mexico
> **1834-40:** Mexican government sells its large mission lands to private individuals, a process known as secularization.

Meanwhile, in 1810, Mexico made attempts to withdraw from Spanish rule. By 1821 Mexico was an independent nation that assumed control of California, which was soon divided into two provinces with capitals at Monterey and San Diego. The former rulers of the region, the Spanish, had established market centers at

> **THE MISSION INDIANS**
>
> In *Two Years before the Mast*, Dana recalls the conditions among the workers at one California mission: "We rode out to the Indian huts. The little children were running about amongst the huts, stark naked, and the men were not much better; but the women had generally coarse gowns, of a sort of tow cloth. The men are employed, most of the time, in tending the cattle of the mission, and in working in the garden, which is a very large one, including several acres, and filled, it is said, with the best fruits of the climate" (Dana, *Two Years before the Mast*, p. 173).

the missions and protected them with presidios (military bases). The new Mexican nation had little time to be concerned with the missions initially, but they soon realized their economic value and pushed for their military to succeed the Catholic Church as administrators of the missions. By the 1830s, the missions were beginning to fall under the control of the Mexican military and Mexican civilians. In 1831 Mexican Governor José María Encheandía officially placed the rule of the missions in government rather than church hands. The secularization of the missions had been ordered only two years before the *Pilgrim* appeared on the California coast. When the vessel arrived in California, it found a region beset by military-church tensions, and the influence of the church's long-time rule was still very much evident.

New England leather. Back in New England, leather businesses were growing and in need of more raw material. The missions operated cattle enterprises that provided a good, if distant, source of leather for the New Englanders. Ships sailed from Boston, Massachusetts, around South America's southern tip, Cape Horn, and back north to the coast of California. There they stopped at San Diego, Santa Barbara, and Monterey to bring back thousands of hides from the mission cattle ranches.

These voyages were high-risk ventures. The trip from Boston to California might take six or seven months, to which stops in ports for trading had to be added. Part of the journey was spent in the treacherous waters around the southern tip of South America, and the vessels had to stop for supplies at little-known South American ports. It was one of these long, hazardous trips for which Richard Dana signed on as a deck hand on the *Pilgrim*.

Two-way trade. The brigs left Boston heavily laden with trade goods. Much of the outgoing cargo consisted of leather goods that the New Englanders sold to Californians—shoes, belts, and hats manufactured from hides obtained in previous trading voyages. Californians bought not only leather goods but a variety of manufactured items, including coffees and teas, spices, jewelry, textiles, clothes, tools, and building materials, paying for the products in cattle hides rather than silver. In return the Californians sold more than cattle hides. Their mission cattle also produced tallow, a fat used to manufacture soaps, lubricants, candles, and margarine. California exported about a million hides and more than 60 million pounds of tallow between 1826 and 1848. California's business leaders depended on the cheap, mostly forced labor of area Indians. The low cost of labor made their businesses very profitable.

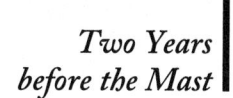

Richard Henry Dana, Jr.

must stay on constant watch. As the ship travels further into southern waters, dipping below the equator and around Cape Horn, more squalls occur. Dana recalls the leaky forecastle (a section of the upper deck, located at the bow in front of the foremast) and the misery of being soaked through to the skin for days on end. He remembers removing and putting on wet clothing as the storms persist. On one of the blackest days of the journey, two months into the voyage, a crew member falls overboard and disappears at sea. Aside from such danger, the crew members deal with daily hardships as well. So carefully rationed is the food that if the ship rocks and a sailor happens to drop his portion, there is no food available to replace it. In sympathy, though, fellow sailors shared their portions with any such unfortunate ones.

Despite the hard work and the sometimes unbearable weather, Dana records a few beautiful moments at sea:

> The first time that I had heard the near breathing of whales.... Some of the watch were asleep, and the others were perfectly still, so that there was nothing to break the illusion, and I stood leaning over the bulwarks, listening to the slow breathings of the mighty creatures.
> (*Two Years before the Mast*, p. 69)

The Narrative in Focus

The contents. On August 14, 1834, the merchant ship *Pilgrim* sets sail from Boston around the southernmost tip of South America, Cape Horn, to the coast of California. On board is Richard Henry Dana Jr., taking a two-year break from his college studies at Harvard to experience the life of a merchant sailor. Dana will later recount in painstaking detail what is expected of each and every man on board, explaining the duties of the officers and sailors alike.

Dana grows extremely ill during his first few days of sea life, but eventually adjusts to being on the merchant brig. He quickly realizes that a vessel needs constant maintenance and that a sailor's work is never finished. Among the daily tasks are washing down the decks, coiling up the rigging, making and setting the sails, tarring the holes in the hull, and greasing, oiling, varnishing, scraping, and painting various portions of the vessel. Even when all major tasks are accomplished, the first mate keeps the sailors busy by having them spin yarn and ropes.

Besides the continual work, the seamen contend with the weather. A few days into the voyage the *Pilgrim* experiences a squall and the sailors

> ### A SAILOR'S LIFE
>
> Yet a sailor's life is at best but a mixture of a little good with much evil, and a little pleasure with much pain. The beautiful is linked with the revolting, the sublime with the commonplace, and the solemn with the ludicrous.
> (*Two Years before the Mast*, p. 94)

After a voyage of 150 days from Boston, the *Pilgrim* drops anchor off Santa Barbara on January 14, 1835. Dana describes the mission community's adobe houses and tile roofs. At the *Pilgrim*'s next stop, Monterey, the trading begins. Dana gives detailed descriptions of the Californian men and women who are taken in small boats to the ships and allowed to browse through the cargo of merchandise from New England. He marvels at how easily the Californians pay for common goods that are priced far above what any Bostonian would pay.

The vessel spends several months traveling up and down the California coast, trading manufactured goods for silver and hides. Dana's work

Two Years before the Mast

changes when he goes ashore near the port of San Diego to live and cure hides for a time. It is at this point that he grows familiar with daily life in California, native peoples such as the Kanakan Indians, and the missions.

Dana observes that mission society is largely paternal, with the missionaries adopting a fatherly attitude to the Indians. The missionaries, though, resort to physical punishment when the mission Indians commit various offenses, defending this form of discipline as the only way they have of exerting control. In describing the Indians themselves, Dana reflects biases of his time. He notices that the Indian women and children perform much of the drudgery at the missions, but ignores the hunting and herding skills of the men, describing them as a lazy bunch that is more prone to drinking than the Mexicans of the area.

> ### HAZING
>
> Haze is a word of frequent use on board ship.... It is very expressive to a sailor, and means to punish by hard work. Let an officer once say, "I'll haze you," and your fate is fixed. You will be "worked up," if you are not a better man than he is.
> (*Two Years before the Mast,* p. 94)

Dana and other crew members continue to cure hides at the port while their ship gathers additional hides along the coast. After several weeks, Dana grows anxious about when he will return home. It is rumored that the *Pilgrim* will not be returning to Boston soon. But its chief officer, Captain Thompson, gets assigned to the helm of another ship, the *Alert,* which plans to sail to Boston, carrying a full cargo of hides and tallow. Dana arranges to join the crew of the *Alert,* and it voyages around the treacherous Cape Horn in record time. Not only is the *Alert* much larger and better equipped than the *Pilgrim,* but it also enjoys a more harmonious crew; both the captain and the seamen respect the first mate, which was not the case on the *Pilgrim.* Just 135 days after leaving San Diego, California, the *Alert* arrives in Boston. On September 19, 1836, the crew leaves the ship. A year later, Dana begins to write his narrative.

Officers vs. the crew. In *Two Years before the Mast,* Dana notes that the camaraderie among the members of the crew was notable. Because these seamen were perpetually subjected to the mood swings of the captain and any disharmony that may or may not have existed between him and the first and second mates, they sustained a silent brotherhood among themselves. Their unity was also strengthened by the fact that officers exercised the right to discipline sailors on a whim.

To disobey an order, no matter how unreasonable, was regarded as pure insubordination or mutiny. A seaman would not disobey his superiors under any circumstances unless he was prepared to pay the price. In some cases, insubordination was punished by flogging (whipping). Dana's narrative reports Captain Thompson as being in a particularly bad humor not long after entering Californian waters. Sam, a crew member who was slow in speech and motions but in Dana's view a good sailor nonetheless, suffered the consequences of the captain's bad mood. He was hazed for insignificant mistakes.

On one occasion the captain, already in a foul mood, was preparing to go ashore when he encountered Sam and became irate with him for no reason. When Sam protested, the captain decided to flog him. At hearing the shocking news, another sailor, John the Swede, asked the captain in earnest, "What are you going to flog this man for?" (*Two Years before the Mast,* p. 153). This questioning of the captain's authority was enough to have John immediately thrown in irons and flogged following Sam. Dana expressed horror at the sound of the painful cries coming from his fellow sailors, whom the captain mercilessly whipped. Dana's description of this flogging proved very influential in changing the maritime laws to better protect a sailor's human rights.

Sources. There are no fictional characters in Dana's narrative. All the people he wrote about were real, and he did not use pseudonyms. Drawn from his own personal experience, his narrative became a major source for later writers. Herman Melville drew from Dana's account of his experiences as a sailor in order to compose his masterpiece *Moby Dick.* Other, less enduring works that were influenced by Dana's narrative include *Forty Years at Sea* by William Nevens and *A Voice from the Main Deck* by Samuel Leech.

Events in History at the Time the Narrative Was Written

Change. Four years after Dana's return from sea, *Two Years before the Mast* was published. In that short period both shipping and California had changed drastically. Steamships had begun to travel across the Atlantic Ocean, although continued reservations about the reliability of steam power led many to fully rig their steamships as sailing vessels as well. Faster and trimmer sailboats appeared. By the start of the 1840s, easier-to-handle triangular sails were in use and experiments were underway to create metal hulls. Soon sailing vessels were strong enough to carry as many as seven masts. Such developments made a seaman's work a little less difficult, and the size of the crews smaller. *Two Years before the Mast* thus documented an already disappearing era in which square-rigged sailing vessels had been dominant.

In California, control of the mission lands and cattle had shifted from the Catholic administrators to a few hundred ranchers. Mexico still ruled the region, but the westward movement of U.S. citizens was stimulating the growth of its non-Mexican population. The growing American population in the area, coupled with the country's hunger to expand its land holdings, set the stage for the takeover of the area by the United States. In 1846 America declared war on Mexico. Two years later, in February 1848, the U.S. received California and a vast block of additional land at the conclusion of the Mexican War.

Life at sea. Conditions of the seamen had improved only slightly by 1840. Few land dwellers knew or cared about their plight. Dana, however, embarked on a mission to bring their working conditions to the attention of the public. In 1840 he began a law practice in Boston, and in 1841 he published *The Seaman's Friend*, a book about the legal rights and duties of sailors. In fact, this was only one of Dana's many writings concerning the rights of seamen. He became known as a sympathetic supporter of sailors, and seamen sometimes trooped into his law office for legal aid. These sailors sought help in a variety of areas. Some hoped to recover wages owed to them or sought to punish a captain who had flogged them, while others looked to Dana after fights with shipmates.

Dana's *Two Years before the Mast* became one of the strongest weapons in the effort to publicize the plight of the journeyman sailor. During the early 1840s there was an increasing movement toward seamen's reform. Public speakers promoted antiflogging legislation, and seaman's aid societies praised *Two Years before the Mast* to further their cause. Dana's book was touted as perhaps the only sea narrative based totally on fact and as one that portrayed sea life from the perspective of a seaman rather than a tourist or ship's officer. For these reasons, it had an immediate impact.

The narrative as propaganda. The historian Robert F. Lucid addresses the issue of whether *Two Years before the Mast* truly influenced the reforms of maritime laws, or just simply served as propaganda for the reformists. He points out that although Dana describes the harsh action of flogging and the humiliation of the flogged sailors in sympathetic terms, he in no way makes a judgment regarding the actual legitimacy of flogging in his narrative. Nor does Dana ever advocate the abolishment of flogging. Yet Lucid notes that Dana's reputation as a champion of seamen's rights was fostered to a great extent by the publication of his personal narrative.

> **FROM *THE SEAMAN'S FRIEND***
>
> The laws of the United States provide that if any master or officer shall unjustifiably beat, wound, or imprison any of the crew, or withhold from them suitable food and nourishment, or inflict upon them any cruel or unusual punishment, he shall be imprisoned not exceeding five years and fined not exceeding $1000 for each offense.
>
> (Dana, *The Seaman's Friend*, p. 201)

Thanks largely to the publication of his book, Dana was lionized by various reform societies.... His career at the bar, furthermore, identified him to many as the champion of the rights of seamen ... and the reputation which he made this way undoubtedly became inextricably bound up with his literary reputation.... He accomplished much. Credit for his accomplishments should go to him, and should not confuse the already vexing question of literature's influence upon society.

(Lucid, pp. 402-03)

Reform took many years. Flogging continued to be administered at the discretion of the seaman's superiors even after Dana's death in 1882. Not until the passage of an act of Congress in 1898 were flogging and all other forms of physical punishment by a ship's officers outlawed. The penalty for violating the new legislation was imprisonment.

Reviews. The popularity and success of *Two Years before the Mast* was immediate, and the book went on to become one of the most highly regarded narratives in American history. Dana's document was praised for its clean, lyrical literary style as well as for its powerful social commentary.

Ralph Waldo Emerson, who had conducted the grammar school in Cambridge that Dana attended in 1826, lavished praise for the work in the journal the *Dial* in 1840:

> It will open the eyes of many to the conditions of the sailor, to the fearful waste of man, by which the luxuries of foreign climes are made to increase the amount of commercial wealth.... It will serve to hasten the day of reckoning between society and the sailor, which though late, will not fail to come.
>
> (Emerson in Lucid, p. 392)

In 1869 Dana supplemented the narrative with a closing chapter entitled "Twenty Four Years After," in which he recounts a trip back to the California coast in 1860. Continuing to revise the book, Dana issued three more amended versions of the manuscript. But his original 1840 version is the one lauded as a classic in narrative American literature.

For More Information

Adams, Charles Francis. *Richard Henry Dana: A Biography.* Boston: Houghton Mifflin, 1890.

Bauer, K. Jack. *A Maritime History of the United States: The Role of America's Seas and Waterways.* Columbia: University of South Carolina Press, 1988.

Brooks, Van Wyck. *The Flowering of New England, 1815-1865.* New York: World, 1936.

Dana, Richard Henry, Jr. *Two Years before the Mast.* Boston: Harper & Bros., 1840.

Dana, Richard Henry, Jr. *The Seaman's Friend.* 1851. Reprint. Delmar, N.Y.: Scholar's Facsimiles & Reprints, 1979.

Lucid, Robert F. "Two Years before the Mast as Propaganda." *American Quarterly* (December 1960): 392-403.

Rolle, Andrew. *California History.* Arlington Heights, Ill.: Harlan Davidson, 1963.

Uncle Remus: His Songs and His Sayings

by
Joel Chandler Harris

Joel Chandler Harris was born on December 9, 1848, in Putnam County, Georgia. As a young white man, he became apprenticed to a printer on the Turnwold plantation. He felt comfortable among the plantation slaves and spent much of his spare time in the slave quarters. Harris believed that it was ethnologically important to record their verbal art and speech patterns. With the publication of *Uncle Remus*, he established himself as one of the earliest collectors of plantation dialect and folklore.

> **THE LITERARY WORK**
>
> A collection of antebellum folklore from Georgia; published in 1880.
>
> **SYNOPSIS**
>
> Uncle Remus, an aged ex-slave, recounts the tales, songs, and proverbs of plantation blacks to a young white boy. Also included in the collection are character sketches about a second Uncle Remus, who lives in Atlanta.

Events in History at the Time of the Collection

The collecting of folklore. The active collecting of folklore and development of compilations such as *Uncle Remus* became common in the late nineteenth and early twentieth centuries. There was a feeling that folklore from previous times was in danger of dying out, just as earlier ways of life, like the plantation system, had ended. To prevent the folk stories and songs from disappearing, scholars and hobbyists placed an emphasis on collecting them in written form. They believed the tales had historical value and wanted to preserve them for the future. Harris himself, in addition to feeling some nostalgia for the past, strongly believed that it was ethnologically important to preserve the folklore of former slaves, and so set about his collecting.

Uncle Remus is primarily a collection of tales, songs, and proverbs that Joel Chandler Harris recorded from the oral tradition of former slaves. Since many slaves could not read or write, oral folklore played an essential role in the creative expression of their daily lives. Tale-telling, for example, formed an integral part of the slave's life, and *Uncle Remus* became the first major publication to record slave tales. Although the collection primarily records the tricksterlike stories about Brer Rabbit, slaves also narrated tall tales, legends, humorous anecdotes, outrageous yarns, animal stories, other kinds of trickster tales, origin narratives, and many others.

Scholars have debated and puzzled over what these stories actually meant to the slaves. Most academics agree that the stories were told for entertainment, but some have also hypothesized that the stories provided a metaphor for the master/slave relationship, or even that the stories contained didactic elements that taught the slaves important lessons. Most likely, however, the tale-tellings contained multiple layers of meaning, depending on the intent of the teller, the situation, and the teller's audience. Harris himself remained ambivalent about assigning universal meaning to the stories and, in the end, admitted his own ignorance of any subtle purposes.

The various songs recorded in *Uncle Remus* demonstrate the important place of music in nearly all aspects of a slave's life. Though some slaveowners forbade singing, music filled the daily routine of most slaves and some were even forced to sing whether they wanted to or not. Many songs reflected the slaves' oppression, mood, and daily experiences. Work songs, for example, related to specific plantation duties, and partially served to pass time and ease labor by dictating a particular work pace. Many songs were satirical or contained double meanings that poked fun at an unknowing slaveowner. Sometimes slaves sang one version of a song in the master's presence and another more subversive version while he was away. Songs also served as a way to convey secret warnings or messages to other slaves, to preserve history, and to achieve a variety of other purposes. Black spirituals, or religious folk songs, drew upon several sources, including traditional hymns, psalms, and biblical images. Generally improvisational, these songs were communally re-created at each performance and were characterized by complex rhythms, body movements, and repeat phrasings. Like the secular songs, spirituals often contained hidden meanings. Slaves who sang for heavenly freedom and deliverance, for example, also sought earthly liberation from the condition of slavery in their daily lives.

Many peoples of Africa are given to speaking indirectly or using proverbs as comparisons in everyday life. It is not surprising, then, that proverbial usage was fairly common among slaves and that many of the proverbs in Harris's collection comment upon the nature of work. Proverbs such as "Looks won't do ter split rails wid" (Harris, *Uncle Remus*, p. 157) help to motivate, while "Rails split 'fo 'bre'kfus' 'll season de dinner" (*Uncle Remus*, p. 156) comment on the benefits of an early start to one's day. Many, such as "Good luck say: 'Op'n yo' mouf en shet yo' eyes,'" "Better de gravy dan no grease 'tall," and "Hit's a mighty deaf nigger dat don't year de dinner-ho'n" (*Uncle Remus*, pp. 157, 156, and 158) relate to both food and hunger, important facets of slave life. Still others simply comment on general human nature, such as "Licker talks mighty loud w'en it git loose fum de jug" (*Uncle Remus*, p. 157).

Minstrel shows and misrepresentations. As a printer's apprentice on the plantation, Joel Chandler Harris worked for a man named Joseph Addison Turnwold, a planter, lawyer, scholar, and aspiring author who sought to develop a literature of the South, and who encouraged Harris to write. Turnwold's perspective greatly influenced Harris, who himself had a natural ear for the black dialect of his region and once bragged that "he could 'think in Negro dialect,' that if necessary he could speak whole passages of Emerson as a Negro would" (Hemenway, p. 16). After he left Turnwold, Harris felt frustrated by the imprecise renditions of black dialect and plantation lore that he saw in the minstrel shows and in written publications. Minstrel theater, which featured white actors who blackened their faces and then proceeded to sing, dance, and tell jokes to white audiences, had begun in 1843. At first the shows made an effort to portray black people realistically, but by Harris's time they had dropped any attempt at honest representation. The shows came to feature a lazy, loud-mouthed, flashily dressed, wide-grinning black who used poor grammar. Neither the stereotype nor the dialect was true to life. Published articles also included misrepresentations, unintentional but inaccurate nonetheless. One article in particular motivated Harris to publish his own work. According to his own knowledgeable ear, the word the author expressed as "Buh" should have been "Brer"; Harris decided that he could do a better job of preservation himself. As he notes in the introduction, "The dialect, it will be observed, is ... different also from the intolerable misrepresentations of the minstrel stage, but it is at least phonetically genuine" (*Uncle Remus*, p. 39).

The black Southern vernacular of the late nineteenth century varied widely, ranging from minor linguistic variations of standard English to distinctive African American languages such as Gullah. Much of the linguistic misrepresentation that frustrated Harris stemmed from white prejudices and misunderstandings. Often, whites would transcribe a word into "dialect" even if in black English it sounded exactly like the standard one. For example, someone might write "w'en" for "when" or "fokes" for "folks," a practice of which Harris was also occasionally guilty. Although some scholars in the twentieth century have criticized Harris's dialect writing as simply a product of racial prejudice, historically Harris's publications have been considered some of the most successful early attempts at transcribing the black vernacular of Middle Georgia. More recently, linguistic scholars have offered evidence that the vernacular English found in Harris's

Joel Chandler Harris

writings was not simply a black dialect, but contained elements shared by both blacks and whites who spoke the southern Piedmont dialect. Whether or not future evidence will confirm this, Harris's transcriptions are acknowledged as some of the most accurate renditions of the area's dialect at that time.

Racism in the New South. Joel Chandler Harris also wrote for the *Atlanta Constitution,* where he served under a man named Henry Grady. Grady was a famous spokesman for the New South, a term for a small group of merchants, industrialists, and planters who advocated rapid change and industrialization as a means of reorienting and rebuilding the South after the Civil War. Grady and many other New Southerners advocated not only reconciliation with the North, but racial reconciliation as well. They supported freedom for blacks and blamed slavery as a cause of Southern "backwardness." Furthermore, Grady and his followers envisioned blacks as playing an important role in the region's transformation from an agricultural to an industrial society. Partly in order to win sympathy for their political aims, the New Southerners often romanticized the South's antebellum past.

Some scholars suggest that Uncle Remus, who embodied a romantic, peaceful, and mythical past, served to promote New South political aims. Harris's collection eliminated the cruel white plantation owner and replaced the blackfaced minstrel's grin with a loving persona of a black man who would not be frightening to whites. He furthermore created a romantic framework that reminded whites of a time when relations between the races had been calm, and around which the South could reunite. "Uncle Remus, immensely popular, witnessed that black people would turn the other cheek, would continue to love, despite all the broken promises of American history" (Hemenway, p. 20). Through Uncle Remus, blacks were further portrayed as a people with natural intelligence. The argument that such portrayals helped serve a political end is supported by the fact that Uncle Remus originally appeared as a series of character sketches in the *Atlanta Constitution,* in which he is depicted as a streetwise customer who discusses topical issues for a white readership. Furthermore, Uncle Remus became more politically oriented over the course of the more than thirty years in which Harris wrote stories about him.

Grady, Harris, and others supported full legal rights for blacks, a radical position at that time. But many New Southerners did not support *social* equality. They still regarded blacks as inferior to whites, and this perspective, coupled with the fact that the Remus character probably served to further the political purposes of Harris and likeminded Southerners, might partially explain both the rural and urban Remus's subservient nature and his inoffensive—in some cases, even reactionary—political positions.

Despite Grady's attempts at reconciliation, however, by the end of the 1880s, racial hostilities and open discrimination against blacks were growing in the South. Along with the stereotypes that portrayed blacks as lazy, foolish, and clownlike were ones that depicted them as angry and violent, and all of these images permeated the media. The original cover illustration to *Uncle Remus,* a comical-looking rendering that Harris certainly did not select, demonstrates this tendency. Laws were passed with the intention of keeping blacks in the position of second-class citizens. In 1883, for example, the U.S. Supreme Court made a series of rulings concerning provisions in the Civil Rights Act of 1875. The legislation had assured blacks of equal rights in public places, but the court found that parts of the act were unconstitutional. Segregation laws became institutionalized especially after 1896, when the Supreme Court's *Plessy vs. Ferguson* rul-

Brer Rabbit and the Tar-Baby. Illustration from the *English Lilliput Series*.

ing held that it was legal to maintain separate but equal accommodations for blacks and whites. The ruling sanctioned the separation of the two races in public facilities such as schools, hotels, restaurants, and libraries. Meanwhile, propaganda suggesting that blacks were thieves, liars, and rapists spread throughout the South, increasing white fear and hostility. Such propaganda proposed that the only way to control blacks was to lynch or burn them, thereby deterring other blacks from committing similar actions. In fact, most of the so-called "crimes" committed by blacks were either totally invented or clearly trivial. The truth, though, proved less important than the rumors. In the 1890s, over 1,400 black men were burned alive or lynched in this atmosphere of hatred and fear. Harris, who advocated humanitarian treatment and education of blacks and who worked as a writer during this unfortunate era, might have been seeking a way to change public perceptions about blacks without directly addressing the issues of equality and hate crimes. Because of this, one scholar has explained, Harris used the figure of Uncle Remus as well as his other writings "to do by indirection what ... [he] never could accomplish by direct methods" (Mixon, p. 474).

The Collection in Focus

The contents. *Uncle Remus: His Songs and His Sayings* is an anthology of plantation slave lore written in dialect. Depicted in the anthology are two Uncle Remuses. One lives in rural Georgia in the vicinity of a "big house," and the other lives in the city of Atlanta. The collection contains thirty-four tales told by the rural Uncle Remus, seventy proverbs, and ten songs. The songs consist of work songs, play songs, religious songs, and a revival hymn. Additionally, the collection contains twenty-one sketches about the Atlanta Uncle Remus and a tale about the rural Uncle Remus during the Civil War.

The majority of the tales are animal stories centering on such characters as Brer Rabbit, Brer Fox, Brer Wolf, and Brer Terrapin. The animals steal, lie, cheat, and sometimes kill one another. Brer Rabbit is the weakest of all the animals, yet through trickery and cunning he manages to gain the upper hand in most situations. For example, in "The Wonderful Tar-Baby Story," Brer Fox sets out to catch Brer Rabbit by making a tar doll. Brer Rabbit becomes infuriated when he greets the doll and it doesn't answer; punching the doll, he becomes trapped in the sticky tar. Instead of becoming Brer Fox's dinner, however, Brer Rabbit pleads with Brer Fox: "Skin me, Brer Fox,... snatch out my eyeballs, t'ar out my years by de roots, en cut off my legs,... but don't please, Brer Fox, don't fling me in dat brier-patch" (*Uncle Remus*, pp. 18-19). Of course, Brer Fox does just that, freeing the clever rabbit.

The proverbs and sketches found in the rest of the book reveal Uncle Remus's character and personal beliefs. The Atlanta and rural versions of Remus share similar viewpoints; both advocate humility, dignity, integrity, and hard work as socially correct behavior. An example of the proverbs is "Lazy fokes' stummucks don't git tired" (*Uncle Remus*, p. 175). In the sketches, the urban Uncle Remus sometimes chides younger blacks for their sloth or plainly states his opinions on matters of race, religion, and superstition.

Use of story. The Uncle Remus stories are partially tales of cunning and trickery. The weak triumph over the strong because the stronger animals are infinitely gullible. Brer Rabbit is not overwhelmingly smart. It is rather the case that his enemies are overwhelmingly stupid, and Brer Rabbit delights in their ineptitude. Whether or not these stories are direct analogies to slavery, parallels can be drawn between the stories and the slave-master relationship.

The cunning emphasized in the tales was an essential survival technique for many slaves. Their existence depended on the whim of slavemasters; thus slaves became skillful at reading their masters' emotions. They learned what to say and how to act in order to avoid beatings or to satisfy particular needs of their own. Putting their intentions aside for a moment, many masters demanded that slaves behave in particular ways. Some wanted their slaves to act happy; others wanted the slaves to act humble and subservient. Given such expectations, it is hardly surprising that a number of owners stated that their slaves never revealed their true feelings or character, even those slaves who had lived with the same masters all their lives. Whites noted that their slaves acted one way before them, and another way with other slaves. As one rice plantation owner admitted, "I used to try to learn the ways of these Negroes, but I could never divest myself of the suspicion that they were learning my ways faster than I was learning theirs" (Levine, p. 101). These practices enhanced a slave's chances for survival.

Evidence of such manipulation is found in the narrative frame that Harris sets up in his collection—specifically in the way Uncle Remus treats his eager listener. The young boy has access to the fine foods of the "big house," and Uncle Remus uses a number of devices to obtain handouts, including refusing to tell another story until he is placated. He also uses the stories to teach the boy lessons. In "Mr. Fox Is Again Victimized," for example, Uncle Remus informs the boy, "I ain't tellin' no tales ter bad chilluns," (*Uncle Remus*, p. 70). His rebuke follows some misbehavior on the boy's part; the boy has thrown stones at people with a slingshot and sicced the dog on Remus's pig. Eager to hear the stories, the young boy immediately apologizes for his misbehavior, promises never to do these things again, and placates Remus with some tea cakes. Only after he receives the cakes does Remus continue telling the story. Similarly, in "Mr. Wolf Makes a Failure," the boy brings Remus a mince pie. Remus says, "Dish yer pie ... will gimme strenk fer ter persoo on atter Brer Fox en Brer Rabbit en de udder beastesses w'at dey roped in 'long wid um" (*Uncle Remus*, p. 84). He eats the pie, and then proceeds with the story.

Sources. The stories, songs, and proverbs in *Uncle Remus* stem from Harris's own memory as well as interviews and conversations with ex-slaves. Harris spent several of his teenage years in his

Uncle Remus

job as a newspaper apprentice on the Turnwold plantation. He notes that "it was on this and neighboring plantations that I became familiar with the curious myths and animal stories that form the basis of the volumes credited to Uncle Remus" (Harris in Baer, p. 186). After work, Harris and some other boys would visit the slaves' quarters to hear stories. Uncle Remus is a combination of "Uncle" George Terrell, "Old" Harbert, and "Aunt" Crissy, slaves whom Harris knew. As Harris explains, "Remus was not an invention of my own, but a human syndicate, three or four old darkies I had known. I just walloped them together into one person and called him Uncle Remus" (Harris in Trosky, p. 193).

Harris published the first Uncle Remus animal tale while employed at the *Atlanta Constitution* in 1879. By then, he already had a widespread reputation as a Southern humorist, and had been writing popular black dialect sketches for quite some time. His natural ear for accurately writing dialect was quickly recognized by the public. Harris developed sketches into vehicles using proverbs, animal tales, and character descriptions to comment upon various topics to white audiences. Uncle Remus first appeared in these sketches.

The source of the tales, proverbs, and songs has been a matter of academic debate since the publication of the book. In his introduction to *Uncle Remus*, Harris states that he believes the tales stem from Africa. While some academics agree, others insist that India is the source of some tales, such as the widely known and popular Tar Baby tale. Still others suggest that the plantation slaves borrowed themes and motifs from Native Americans or whites, and the debate has never really been resolved. Whatever their origin, most scholars agree that the plantation slaves modified the tales and songs to fit their own lives, producing lore specific to their own experience.

Reception. *Uncle Remus* was an immediate hit with both popular and academic audiences who tended to view it as one of the first "true" portrayals of antebellum life. It sold 7,500 copies in the first month and helped generate tremendous interest in African American culture. The *New York Times* labeled the publication as the first real book of American folklore, while one of Harris's Northern correspondents wrote him that the stories "are, to people here, the first graphic pictures of genuine Negro life in the South" (Hemenway, p. 14).

After the publication of *Uncle Remus*, animal stories such as the Brer Rabbit tales grew increasingly popular, as did the whole field of black American folklore. Black spirituals generated even greater public excitement than the tales among both the public and academics. By the end of the 1880s, African American culture had become an important new area for formal research.

In response to such favorable reaction, Joel Chandler Harris continued to write Uncle Remus tales for nearly thirty years. The later books differ from the earlier ones in several ways. Over time, for example, the relationship between Uncle Remus and the young white boy grows cooler. Remus does not play the role of teacher and moral escort as often, and the young white boy in later books (who is the son of the young white boy in the original book) shows less understanding of the magical realms about which Remus narrates.

Furthermore, Remus himself becomes more critical of the white world, which, in the wake of progressive efforts toward industrialization and modernization, he sees as antiseptic, unimaginative, and rationalistic. "By the time the last major Remus book was published, when radical racism had reached the peak of its frenzy, Remus himself in the frame narratives wages all-out war on a white world characterized by materialism, scientism, and disdain for the imaginative sensibility" (Mixon, p. 473). Despite these changes, later critics would accuse Harris of acting superior or showing a paternalism toward his Uncle Remus character. Others would retort that if any paternalistic touches crept into his writing—Uncle Remus's subservient behavior, for example—one must remember that Harris as well as his characters are, to some degree, a reflection of their times.

For More Information

Baer, Florence E. "Joel Chandler Harris: An 'Accidental' Folklorist." In *Critical Essays on Joel Chandler Harris*. Edited by R. Bruce Bickley. Boston: G. K. Hall, 1981.

Bickley, R. Bruce. *Joel Chandler Harris*. Boston: Twayne, 1978.

Hemenway, Robert. Introduction to *Uncle Remus: His Songs and His Sayings*, by Joel Chandler Harris. New York: Penguin, 1982.

Harris, Joel Chandler. *Uncle Remus: His Songs and His Sayings*. New York: Grosset & Dunlap, 1880.

Levine, Lawrence W. *Black Culture and Black Consciousness*. London: Oxford University Press, 1977.

Mixon, Wayne. "The Ultimate Irrelevance of Race: Joel Chandler Harris and Uncle Remus in Their Time." *The Journal of Southern History* 61, no. 3 (1990): 457-78.

Montenyohl, Eric L. "The Origins of Uncle Remus." *Folklore Forum* 18, no. 2 (Spring 1986): 136-37.

Trosky, Susan M., and Donna Olendorf, eds. *Contemporary Authors*. Vol. 137. Detroit: Gale Research, 1992.

Uncle Tom's Cabin or, Life among the Lowly

by
Harriet Beecher Stowe

According to many, Harriet Beecher Stowe's *Uncle Tom's Cabin* did not just reflect the author's era. They contend that the novel actually affected the history of that era. When President Abraham Lincoln met Stowe during the Civil War, he reportedly exclaimed, "So this is the little lady who made this big war" (Lincoln in Gerson, p. 163).

Events in History at the Time of the Novel

Conflict over slavery mounts: 1830-1850. In 1830 the United States, a land of different subcultures, had been united for barely fifty years. During this time its two settled regions, the North and the South, headed in increasingly different directions. The North, consisting mainly of family farms and reliant on an economic system of free labor, began to industrialize and urbanize. Meanwhile, the South, made up of great plantations as well as family farms, became committed to large-scale agriculture and the use of black slave labor.

Until the 1830s the two regions shared some common ground concerning slavery. Southern liberals, who hoped the practice would die out naturally, had begun to push for emancipation. In 1831-32, the Virginia legislature openly debated such a proposal, and it was defeated by only fifteen votes. But afterward, opinions polarized. Southerners silenced their liberal neighbors and began to defend slavery not just as a necessary evil but as a positive good. Legal restrictions mounted against freeing slaves.

> **THE LITERARY WORK**
> A novel set in the slave states of Kentucky and Louisiana and the free state of Ohio in 1850; published in 1852.
>
> **SYNOPSIS**
> The plot traces the fates of three slaves from the upper South. Two of them escape north to freedom, while the third is sold into bondage in the lower South.

Southerners went on the offensive in part because the invention of the cotton gin in 1793 had revived slavery's profitability. The cotton gin made it possible to prepare short-grain cotton for market. This strain of cotton could be grown anywhere south of Kentucky and Virginia, and Americans who flocked to the lower South to establish plantations spread westward into Louisiana and east Texas. The upper South, which had a climate that did not lend itself to widespread cotton production, began to diversify its agriculture. To raise money for this purpose, or sometimes simply to get out of debt, residents of the Upper South—such as the novel's Mr. Shelby—often resorted to the sale of slaves, now in great demand in the Lower South. By 1850 the price of a good field hand had climbed to $1,500, which led one Southern reviewer to criticize Stowe's novel for having the slaveowner Mr. Shelby collect only about $1,000 for the sale of Uncle Tom.

Uncle Tom's Cabin

Southerners defended slavery as a positive good on two grounds. First, they maintained that Africans were childlike and needed the protection of paternalistic masters. More commonly, Southerners argued that their system was more humane than the factory labor system prevalent in Europe and the northern United States. Indeed, there were serious inequities in the economic system of the North. In factories, men, women, and children worked six days a week from dawn until dark in dangerous, unhealthy conditions. Their employers paid them low wages, could fire them during slack seasons, and had no obligation to support them during illness or old age. In contrast, argued Southerners, most slaveowners treated their chattel with fatherly kindness, ministered to them in sickness, and provided for them in old age. In Stowe's novel, the first slaveowners, the Shelbys, appear to fit this description.

> **COMPROMISE OF 1850**
>
> Included in the Compromise of 1850 were five provisions: 1) the admission of California to the Union as a free state; 2) the abolition of slave trading in the District of Columbia; 3) the establishment of Utah and New Mexico as territories that could determine the issue of slavery for themselves; 4) the transfer of some lands claimed by Texas to New Mexico; and 5) a harsher Fugitive Slave Law.

Northern antislavery sentiment. After 1830 Northerners attacked the very principle of human bondage with increasing frequency. Inspiring the Northerners were worldwide struggles for individual liberty—the French Revolution of 1789, the Haitian Revolution led by blacks in 1791, and the wave of European revolutions in 1830. Common people seemed to be rising up everywhere, demanding equality and fairer working conditions. Indeed, these world events are alluded to in the novel; two characters, George Harris and Augustine St. Clare, refer to these political and social currents, which make slavery seem patently unjust and doomed to expire.

Also fueling the Northern attacks on slavery was the Second Great Awakening, a religious movement of the era. Influenced by Puritan traditions, evangelical leaders called for people to find salvation through Christ, and to act with Christian love, morality, and humility. People felt tormented by the questions of whether their souls were damned or saved and whether they had honestly tried to perfect society by stamping out sin. The religious impulse inspired a wave of reform movements to wipe out alcoholism, prostitution, and slavery. As noted in Stowe's novel, religious leaders of the day hotly debated whether or not the Bible condoned slavery.

Stowe's family history. Stowe, a mother of six and the wife of a struggling professor, lived in the center of this fervor. Her father, Lyman Beecher, was one of the era's greatest evangelical preachers. Her brothers, meanwhile, were nationally prominent preachers, while her sisters were famous reformers. Her eldest sister, Catherine, spearheaded the cause of "true womanhood," the notion that women were more spiritual and virtuous than men and could perfect the world through their influence inside and outside the home. Dominating the era was an idealized image of white women bearing intense mother-love for their children, and a new sentimentality about the young, especially about those who died early in life. These views are reflected in, for example, the moral purity and gentle but unmistakable power of Mrs. Shelby in *Uncle Tom's Cabin*.

Racial attitudes. Despite the North's distaste for slavery, strong antislavery sentiment was not widespread in the region. Abolitionists remained a radical fringe there, and some felt that obstacles to eliminating slavery were insurmountable. Issues such as reimbursement of slaveowners for their losses—slaves were an expensive investment—seemed insoluble. Moreover, many in the North shared the South's racial prejudices, and some feared that once freed, the ex-slaves would move North, flooding the job market and reducing everyone's wages.

Stowe saw firsthand the effects of such Northern racial prejudice when living in Cincinnati. Located on the Ohio River just across from the slave state of Kentucky, the city became a destination for both runaway slaves and free blacks. Prejudice against them erupted into mob violence in 1829 and again in 1841. Such outbreaks led to the belief that whites and blacks were simply incompatible; some argued that the only solution was to send the freed slaves back to Africa. In 1821 the American Colonization Society established Liberia, a colony in West Africa for this purpose, and at the end of *Uncle Tom's Cabin*, the Harrises set out for Liberia in the hopes of establishing a new and better society there.

Compromise of 1850 and the Fugitive Slave Act. The North and South might have co-existed in an uneasy equilibrium were it not for Amer-

Harriet Beecher Stowe

ica's westward expansion. After the Mexican War (1846-1848), America's size increased by 20 percent, and tensions mounted as Congress debated which areas would be free states and which would be slave states.

The Compromise of 1850 temporarily resolved the question, but one aspect of it caused a furor. As a concession to the slave states, a harsher Fugitive Slave Law was passed. It denied blacks accused as fugitives the right of trial by jury and the right to testify on their own behalf. Free blacks falsely fingered as runaways had no way to protect themselves. Particularly galling to antislavery groups was a provision in the new law that made those who aided runaways liable to a fine of $1,000 and six months in prison.

One biographer maintains that late in 1850, outraged by the Fugitive Slave Act, Stowe swore she would take action: "I will write something. I will if I live" (Stowe in Hedrick, p. 207). Stowe later said she wrote with such feverish inspiration that it was as though God had written the book, using her as the instrument.

In March 1852 *Uncle Tom's Cabin* appeared in book form and quickly made publishing history. Presses ran twenty-four hours a day to keep up with the demand. In less than a year, 300,000 copies had been purchased in the United States, while another 1.5 million copies were sold in Great Britain. President Lincoln's observation about the novel's sparking the Civil War appears, to some degree, credible. The novel helped rouse the uninvolved and fueled passions that erupted into warfare.

Life under slavery. Contrary to the image of the South as a region of plantation slaveholders, only 30 percent of all white families owned slaves in 1860, and most possessed twenty slaves or less; only one percent owned large plantations with more than fifty slaves. Yet this tiny minority of planters dominated Southern culture and politics.

Living patterns for the slaves varied considerably: those on small farms often lived under the same roof as their owners and worked side by side with them in the fields; those on the larger farms and plantations had their own slave quarters and worked under an overseer or, more commonly, directly under their owners.

There were laws against excessive punishment of blacks. But more effective in checking excesses was public opinion: slaveowners known for their cruelty were shunned by polite society. Whippings and other brutal punishments occurred, but this was an era when people believed in the value of corporal punishment for black and white alike. A parent, said society, who spared the rod would be spoiling the child. Despite such ideas, slaveowners often refrained from bodily punishment for selfish reasons: slaves were expensive property, and scars reduced their value.

In many cases, at prescribed times slaves could visit with spouses on neighboring plantations, fish and hunt to supplement their diets, or hire themselves out to earn cash, as Uncle Tom's wife did. Some were even able to save up enough money to buy their freedom. Owners encouraged marriage-type relationships since they produced children (new slaves), and weddings such as the one Mrs. Shelby organized for Eliza in the novel were not uncommon. Many masters tried not to separate families when they sold slaves. Approximately two-thirds of slave marriages remained intact in the prewar period, and it was supposedly illegal to sell children younger than ten separately from their mothers (though this law was sometimes ignored).

Southerners admitted that the horrors Stowe described in her novel sometimes occurred, but they claimed that these cases were exceptions. Nonetheless, their constant terror of slave revolts suggests that in their hearts they knew slavery was brutalizing and oppressive. Under slavery 94

135,000 SETS, 270,000 VOLUMES SOLD.

UNCLE TOM'S CABIN

FOR SALE HERE.

AN EDITION FOR THE MILLION, COMPLETE IN 1 Vol., PRICE 37 1-2 CENTS.
" " IN GERMAN, IN 1 Vol., PRICE 50 CENTS.
" " IN 2 Vols., CLOTH, 6 PLATES, PRICE $1.50.
SUPERB ILLUSTRATED EDITION, IN 1 Vol., WITH 153 ENGRAVINGS,
PRICES FROM $2.50 TO $5.00.

The Greatest Book of the Age.

Early advertisement for Stowe's famous book.

percent of America's 4 million blacks had no civil rights. They could not even choose where to live, much less their occupations. They were bought and sold like cattle and subjected to humiliating slave auctions. Slaves sold "down South" experienced hard labor on large, isolated plantations, far from the free states.

Other abuses abounded. Slave marriages had no legal status. Many marriages ended when a slaveowner decided to sell a husband or wife, and slaves lived with the anxiety that their families might at any moment be separated against their will. Moreover, slave women lacked the power and, in the eyes of some owners, the right to resist their sexual advances. Despite the law, children younger than ten were sometimes sold away from their mothers. Finally, slaves were constantly reminded that their black skin rendered them inferior in American society.

While few rose up in open rebellion, there were slaves who attempted to escape. Between 1830 and 1860, an estimated fifty thousand slaves escaped through the "underground railroad," a term used to describe the various routes to freedom in the North and Canada. Fugitive slaves took refuge in the woods or with other friendly slaves or, if they were light-skinned, escaped by passing as white. Once they crossed into the North, guides, usually free blacks, would shelter them and assist in their northward journey. The route that the characters George and Eliza take from Kentucky, across the Ohio River to Ohio and on up to Canada, was among the most commonly traveled.

Other slaves resisted their plight by embracing a rich culture they created out of their African and American roots. Close slave communities developed on many plantations. Members of these communities regarded themselves as one family and called all the older slaves "uncle" or "auntie," a practice that explains how the character of Tom came to be known as "Uncle" Tom. From one generation to the next, the slave community passed on dances, songs, funeral rites, and oral lore such as folktales about Br'er Rabbit, who always outsmarted his powerful adversary, the fox. Like the slave, the rabbit only *seemed* to be weak.

Religion was another cornerstone that sustained the slaves. Though mostly Baptists, they mixed their Christianity with elements of traditional African religions. Like Uncle Tom, many of the slaves became preachers, and a few preached so powerfully that they even earned the respect of whites, who sometimes attended their services. Their sermons and especially their gospel songs drew upon biblical images of the Jews who had once been in bondage and, like the slaves, longed for freedom. Eloquently expressed in the spirituals of the slaves were sorrows and hopes for freedom—in this world or the next. For many, the biblical River Jordan represented the rivers that separated the American slave states from the free states, and the biblical Promised Land symbolized the North.

The Novel in Focus

The plot. The novel opens with an incident that brings out one of the worst pitfalls of the slave system. A kind Kentucky slaveowner, Mr. Shelby, has fallen into debt. The only way he can save his home is to sell two slaves for whom his family has great affection. The coarse slave trader, Haley, will accept only Uncle Tom and little Harry, the son of the genteel mulatto Eliza. Shelby feels forced to agree to this arrangement and, despite his good intentions, capitulates.

When Eliza and Uncle Tom discover the bargain, they react quite differently. Eliza has just learned that her husband George, who lives on a neighboring plantation, has planned his own escape. He can no longer bear the cruelty of his master. Eliza has no one to turn to for help, but she will not, as a mother, tolerate having her child torn from her. She resolves to escape and in the middle of the night carries young Harry to the Ohio River. When she finally reaches the river, it is so choked with ice that no boats can cross. But the slave trader Haley has caught up with her. In desperation and with grim determination, Eliza grabs her son, leaps onto the ice floes, and crosses to the Ohio shore.

Eliza first seeks refuge in the home of Senator Bird, who has just voted "yes" on the Fugitive Slave Act. When he is actually confronted with the sight of this poor woman and her son, though, he realizes he must disobey the very law he helped pass. As Eliza travels further north, she is protected by whites of the Quaker faith. Finally, she is reunited with George, and they head north to Canada.

Uncle Tom reacts quite differently to the news that he is being sold. A pious Christian, he submits to his fate and sadly bids farewell to his wife and children. He is taken south down the Ohio and then the Mississippi rivers to the big slave auctions in New Orleans. On the way, he witnesses the anguish of fellow blacks in bondage. He sees children torn from their mothers and virginal young women being sold into prostitution during grim slave auctions taking place at various landings.

Uncle Tom and little Eva St. Clare, the five-year-old daughter of a rich planter, develop a friendship on the boat, and Eva persuades her father to buy Tom. She is an angelic child, full of Christian faith and sweetness, who recoils at the evils of slavery. Her father, a sophisticated man named Augustine St. Clare, realizes that slavery is wrong but does nothing about this conviction. Eva develops tuberculosis and dies. Her father has promised Uncle Tom his freedom, but shortly after Eva's death he is killed in a brawl, and Tom's fate hinges on his widow. The callous Mrs. St. Clare proceeds to sell him.

Uncle Tom now descends into the deepest hell of slavery, a remote Red River plantation devoid of the saving influence of women or the Christian faith. His new owner is the cruel Simon Legree. Enraged by Uncle Tom's piety and goodness, Legree tries to destroy both traits. His other slaves have already been defeated in spirit and dehumanized, but Uncle Tom struggles against this fate and finally marshals the spiritual strength to

Uncle Tom's Cabin

Fictional Name	Real-life Source
Uncle Tom	Rev. Josiah Henson, an ex-slave whose master finally freed him, but whose life and character resemble that of Uncle Tom
George Harris	Lewis Clark, an escaped slave educated in the home of Stowe's brother
Simeon Halliday	John Hunn and Tho's Garrett, Quakers convicted of helping a fugitive slave family escape in Maryland in 1846; John Van Zandt, Stowe's neighbor
Senator Bird	Stowe's neighbor, Professor Upham, who believed the Fugitive Slave Law should be followed yet aided a fugitive when he appeared at his door

resist. When Legree's embittered slave-mistress, Cassie, begs Uncle Tom to help her murder Legree, he refuses to sink into such sin. Legree finally has Tom beaten mercilessly until the old slave loses all strength. Just as Eliza and George step onto the free shores of Canada, Uncle Tom, pummeled to death, rises in triumph to heaven like a Christian saint.

An antislavery tract. Stowe's novel does not condemn all Southerners, for it represents them as a mix of both good and bad people. The practice of slavery, though, is roundly condemned. Through the story of St. Clare's father and uncle, the novel suggests that circumstances, not character, make slaveholders. Both of the older men were upright Yankees, but one settled in New England and the other on the Louisiana frontier. The same qualities that made one a successful pillar of the community in Vermont turned the other into a rich, stern slaveholder.

Nor does the novel let Northerners off the hook, for it laments that "[b]oth North and South have been guilty before God" (*Uncle Tom's Cabin*, p. 629). As a national institution, the novel argues, slavery requires the collusion of all Americans. Indeed, the ugliest slave drivers and traders, Simon Legree and Haley, hail from the North.

The novel examines how slavery affects people's characters and souls. Slavery corrupts whites who, either by chance as in Mr. Shelby's case, or by intention as in the case of Simon Legree, fall into the sin of treating human beings as animals. More important are the effects of the institution on the slaves themselves. Stowe's novel was one of the first works to present the slaves' points of view and to show that they, too, were God's children. Like whites, they cared intensely for their families, and mother-love flowed strongly for them as well. They also felt driven to maintain their dignity and self-respect, and they too sought religious salvation. The novel, though, reflected the fear that slavery would destroy blacks' chance for salvation. The slaves Topsy and Cassie are so brutalized that they are almost lost to religious belief. Even noble George Harris is so embittered that he cries out, "O, I've seen things all my life that have made me feel that there can't be a God" (*Uncle Tom's Cabin*, p. 191).

Most importantly, the novel addresses the question of what people should do when their "nation carries in its bosom great and unredressed injustice" (*Uncle Tom's Cabin*, p. 629). Its answer is clear: The novel advocates active resistance, even violence if necessary, as when George and his party shoot it out with the slave catchers.

Sources. Stowe's only direct contact with the South was a brief visit to Kentucky, but she read widely and was especially familiar with narratives of escaped slaves, antislavery tracts, and religious debates about slavery between various ministers.

Stowe also knew freed and runaway slaves when she lived in Cincinnati. Stories circulated about women who had fled across the ice-choked river, their children in their arms, and Stowe herself helped a female runaway in 1839. These personal experiences became sources for the characterization of Eliza. Stowe also learned about slave life from ex-slaves who worked in middle-class homes. A cook in Stowe's household, Eliza Buck, told how she had been abruptly sold to a Louisiana planter, how she had sneaked out at night to care for slaves "mangled and lacerated by the whip," and how her next owner, a Kentuckian, had fathered all her children (Hedrick, p. 219). She became the inspiration for Cassie and other female characters. From her brother

Charles, who had worked in New Orleans for a year, Stowe heard detailed descriptions of slave auctions and plantation life. Charles had met an overseer who had boasted that his fists were hard from "knockin' down niggers." Stowe used her image of this overseer to develop the cruel character of Simon Legree (Hedrick, p. 222). Above all, Stowe was inspired by the death of her own two-year-old. "It was at his dying bed ... that I learnt what a poor slave mother may feel when her child is torn away from her" (Stowe in Hedrick, p. 193).

Although each one of the novel's characters was based on several different real people, Stowe singled out some specific individuals whom she used as models.

Reviews of *Uncle Tom's Cabin*. Stowe's novel unleashed a storm of responses. The great Russian writer Leo Tolstoy hailed it as one of the greatest productions of the human mind; the black abolitionist Frederick Douglass described it as a beacon of light. Others warned that it was subversive, for it idealized those who disobeyed the law. Some antislavery supporters objected to its apparent support for colonization in Liberia and claimed that it made demeaning generalizations about blacks as a race. The London *Times* warned that it would "keep ill blood at the boiling point" and make slavery more difficult to abolish (Bailey, p. 399).

Southerners cursed the novel, and in a flood of reviews, articles, and books of their own, raged that it was slanderous, a "wild and unreal" portrayal (Bailey, p. 397). They complained that Stowe's slaves were impossibly idealized, that she had portrayed them as if black skin automatically graced a person with beauty, nobility, and goodness. They also railed against its "unladylike" qualities, contending that no decent woman would have her characters speak in dialect or refer to the unmentionable topics of sexual relations and prostitution. Nationally, some readers praised its realism. Others criticized it as artistically sloppy. But all agreed on its power as a gripping tale of daring escapes and conflict between good and evil.

To critics who stormed about the novel's inaccuracy, Stowe marshaled together instances from her own experiences along with new evidence to create a book much lengthier than the novel. *A Key to Uncle Tom's Cabin* (1853) cited laws, legal cases, books, and newspaper articles that supported her claim that her novel depicted slavery in a realistic way. To those who protested that Uncle Tom's murder was unrealistic, Stowe cited law cases, particularly *Souther vs. The Commonwealth,* which described a slave torture and murder far worse than the one endured by Uncle Tom (Hedrick, p. 231). She also found ready support for other details in her novel—for example, a $500 reward in a newspaper notice about a runaway who sounded very much like George Harris in her novel. The runaway "without close observation, might pass himself for a white man, as he is very bright—has sandy hair, blue eyes, and a fine set of teeth" (Stowe, *Key to Uncle Tom's Cabin,* p. 17). Stowe's research for the *Key to Uncle Tom's Cabin* horrified her. Slavery was "worse than I supposed or dreamed" (Stowe in Hedrick, p. 231).

The novel's popularity, and the stir it caused among critics, faded after the Civil War. But the images of Eliza clutching her child and crossing the icy river survived, as did the images of little Eva's and Uncle Tom's saintly deaths. "Simon Legree" and "Uncle Tom" went on to become permanent expressions in the English language, and Stowe's little work of fiction assumed its acknowledged place as a book that helped spark the Civil War. Ironically the term "Uncle Tom" would later take on a negative meaning—indicating a black who shows humiliating subservience to whites. The irony is that the source of this expression, Stowe's novel, in fact aimed, and to a great extent managed, to dismantle a similar image of her own time—that of the contented slave.

For More Information

Bailey, Thomas A., and David M. Kennedy. *The American Spirit: United States History as Seen by Contemporaries.* Vol. 1. Lexington: D. C. Heath, 1987.

Blassingame, John W. *The Slave Community: Plantation Life in the Antebellum South.* New York: Oxford University Press, 1979.

Gerson, Noel. *Harriet Beecher Stowe.* New York: Praeger, 1976.

Hedrick, Joan D. *Harriet Beecher Stowe: A Life.* New York: Oxford University Press, 1994.

Stowe, Harriet Beecher. *The Key to Uncle Tom's Cabin.* Salem, N.H.: Ayer, 1987.

Stowe, Harriet Beecher. *Uncle Tom's Cabin, or Life among the Lowly.* Edited by Ann Douglas. New York: Penguin, 1981.

Up from Slavery

by
Booker T. Washington

~

A teacher and former slave, Booker T. Washington founded and ran the Tuskegee Institute beginning in 1881, a school for African Americans in rural Alabama. Building on the school's success, Washington rose to prominence in the 1890s, winning recognition as the nation's leading African American spokesperson after the death of Frederick Douglass in 1895. In 1901 Washington published his autobiography, *Up from Slavery*. The book conveys his practical approach to black self-improvement, an approach that called for cooperation and compromise with white society.

> **THE LITERARY WORK**
>
> An autobiography set in Alabama from the late 1850s to 1900; published in 1901.
>
> **SYNOPSIS**
>
> A self-trained African American leader recounts his early slave experience and his faith and beliefs as reflected in the Tuskegee Institute, a vocational school that he established for African Americans.

Events in History at the Time of the Autobiography

Slavery. In the years before the Civil War, slaveowners (who amounted to about one-fourth of Southern whites) controlled every aspect of the slave's life. Slaves were considered property and lived in often squalid conditions in shacks or barracks on the large plantations. They worked the fields, did the laundry, cooked the food, and served their masters in whatever capacity was demanded. Owners sometimes punished slaves severely, most commonly by whipping. The law forbade slaves from traveling except as directed by their owners. Slave families routinely suffered the pain of being broken up by the sale of children or spouses. Runaways were often tracked down and beaten harshly. The Fugitive Slave Law, passed in 1850, allowed the apprehension of any black suspected of being a runaway. Even in Northern states, those accused had no legal recourse.

Solomon Northup, a free black from upstate New York, was abducted in this way and enslaved. He describes the humiliation of the slave sale in his account, *Twelve Years a Slave*:

> Next day many customers called to examine Freeman's [the owner of the slave market] "new lot." ... He [Freeman] would make us hold up our heads, walk briskly back and forth, while customers would feel of our hands and arms and bodies, turn us about, ask us what we could do, make us open our mouths and show our teeth, precisely as a jockey examines a horse which he is about to barter for or purchase.
>
> (Northup in Meltzer, p. 48)

War and freedom. Through the four years of the Civil War, Southern blacks waited and watched. As parts of the South came under Northern rule, some black men were recruited to serve in the Union Army. Many, however, remained loyal to their masters as a matter of survival. Slaves protected the plantations, hid white owners from mistreatment by soldiers of either side, and suffered with their white masters when war reduced provisions.

Despite the Emancipation Proclamation of 1863, which freed slaves in rebel territory, slavery for most blacks ended only with Northern victory in 1865. Generations of oppression left the majority of these former slaves ill-prepared for freedom. Southern states had legally banned their slave populations from even the most elementary education; not surprisingly, a preponderance of the ex-slaves emerged from bondage untrained for any occupation other than farm work. Still, blacks embraced their freedom at the end of the war with joy.

Black options. Many former slaves at first signed contracts that permitted them to labor in gangs under overseers, much as they had during slavery. Filled with desire to own their own land, however, they rapidly abandoned wage labor for sharecropping or tenant farming. Sharecroppers "borrowed" a plot of land, seed, tools, food, and clothing from a landowner, to whom, in return, they pledged as much as 50 percent of their harvest. They often had to buy other necessities on credit and at high cost from the landowner at his designated store, which made it nearly impossible for them to get out of debt and increase their earnings. Tenant farming differed slightly. In exchange for "borrowing" land, tools, and other items from a merchant, tenants promised to sell their entire crop to him. Forced before harvest-time to buy goods on credit at the merchant's store, they too became debt-ridden to a white landlord.

African Americans in the South thus faced severely limited options in the years immediately after the war. Despite the economic disadvantages, many preferred the nominal independence of sharecropping or tenant farming to the contract system, which reminded them too much of slavery. White overseers, for example, sometimes used whips just as they had before the war.

Freedmen's Bureau. The postwar era known as Reconstruction (1865-1877) brought an upheaval to Southern society that matched that of the war itself. In 1865, as part of Reconstruction, Congress established the Bureau of Refugees, Freedmen, and Abandoned Lands, usually known as the Freedman's Bureau. One of its purposes was to aid former slaves in the transition to freedom. Officially the bureau operated through 1868, though its education division and its efforts to collect money owed to black veterans continued until mid-1872. For the initial years of its stormy existence, the Freedmen's Bureau pro-

Booker T. Washington

vided food, housing, medical care, and farm supplies to both blacks and whites in the war-ravaged South. It also oversaw labor relations, settling disputes that arose between black laborers and white employers. The bureau's longest lasting legacy, as reflected in its continuing activities in this field after 1868, was in education.

Education. By 1869 the bureau had set up hundreds of schools that ultimately taught 200,000 ex-slaves to read. The bureau also helped establish black institutions of higher learning such as Howard University, the Hampton Institute, Fisk University, and Atlanta University. By the late 1860s, ex-slaves were flocking to educational opportunities wherever they arose. Classrooms across the South filled up with students of all ages seeking to escape illiteracy. Some classes taught a student population that spanned four generations; as Washington writes, "it was a whole race trying to go to school" (Washington, *Up from Slavery,* p. 21).

Along with their eager students, the new schools were distinguished by the teachers who led them. Beginning in Reconstruction's earliest days, a wave of enthusiastic Northern whites, many of them unmarried women and a good number highly religious in character, came south to teach the ex-slaves. These "Yankee" teachers brought their Puritan values of hard work, thrift, and cleanliness with them, influencing a whole generation of African Americans. Washington encountered such men and women at the Hampton Institute in Virginia, where he spent three years. Washington's time at Hampton proved to be the single most decisive influence in his life; he repeatedly praises "the part that the Yankee teachers played in the education of the Negro after the war" (*Up from Slavery*, p. 42).

Against the desire for learning was balanced the need to make a living. Children usually helped supplement the income of African American families, contributing either labor at home or wages from a job. As a child, Washington, for example, worked at the salt and coal mines in the early mornings, going to school when he could snatch time in the afternoons and evenings.

African Americans in politics. African Americans played a greater part in Southern politics during Reconstruction than at any time until the 1960s. Allied with Northern Republicans who had come south, African Americans were elected to political positions and achieved a measure of control in many state governments after 1867. Referring to their occupations outside politics, Washington's autobiography reflects the popular conception that these officials were unprepared for the offices in which they found themselves:

> I heard some brick-masons calling out, from the top of a two-story building on which they were working, for the "Governor" to "hurry up and bring up some more bricks." ... I made inquiry as to who the "Governor" was, and soon found that he was a coloured man who at one time had held the position of Lieutenant-Governor of his state.
>
> (*Up from Slavery*, p. 57)

But Washington also acknowledges that "some of them ... were strong, upright, useful men" (*Up from Slavery*, pp. 57-8). Educated Northerners of African descent—preachers, teachers, soldiers and businessmen—numbered among the new black leaders. Others were Southerners from the small class of African American landowners and merchants. These newly elected officials focused more on advancing education and commerce than on the economic plight of their race. There was some discussion of land redistribution, which alarmed Southern whites, but in the end it came to little more than talk. Land ownership, on the contrary, became concentrated into a smaller number of holdings, and larger ones, than had existed before the war.

Southern white backlash. Southern whites responded to the changes Reconstruction wrought in several ways. Laws called Black Codes, passed by Southern states in the 1860s, set restrictive conditions for the right to vote and seek public office. In 1866 the Ku Klux Klan organized in Pulaski, Tennessee, to combat the new policies introduced by Reconstruction and to reestablish the dominant position of whites in Southern society. Its presence was soon felt throughout the South. The Klan and its supporters tried to intimidate blacks into not voting, or into voting for Klan-supported candidates. In 1868 efforts to control the vote resulted in the deaths of at least 25 people and injury to 175 others in two days of fighting. The Klan attempted to force the ex-slaves to vote for its candidates by threatening—and sometimes carrying out—mutilations, beatings, and even murders.

Outraged, the Republican Congress imposed the harsh Force Acts of 1871 and 1872. Five military regions replaced state governments until such time as the states could be legally readmitted to the Union by becoming certified for the statehood they held before the Civil War. In some cases, restoration of statehood did not come until 1874. Under the Reconstruction Acts, a slow-moving Congress was responsible for determining which Southerners could hold office, and what conditions must be met for enfranchisement and for statehood.

The end of Reconstruction. The tug-of-war between Congress and Southern whites gradually lost its hold on the nation's attention, and by the late 1870s public support for Reconstruction had waned in the North. Reconstruction ended in 1877 with the election of Rutherford B. Hayes to the presidency. The Klan stepped up its terrorization, the old white power brokers of the South returned to office, and the plight of African Americans in the region worsened. Though the plantation system had come to an end, members of the pre-Civil War planter class returned to power, controlling the land, towns, and factories of the post-Civil War South. Under the contract system of farm labor that developed immediately after the war, no matter how oppressive the work, ex-slaves were bound to their jobs. They could not break their contracts without facing floggings or prison. Wages were held dismally low, and African Americans flocking to the cities found housing as abominable as on their former plantations.

In the 1880s the Supreme Court began overturning civil rights acts and other Reconstruction-era legislation. Encouraged, whites who had resumed control of the Southern states enacted a series of "Jim Crow" laws that restricted African American voting rights and the use of public facilities. The Supreme Court affirmed such laws in 1896 with its decision in *Plessy vs. Ferguson,* which allowed "separate but equal" facilities for whites and blacks. In reality, separate meant anything but equal.

African American responses to Jim Crow. Even before the end of Reconstruction, African Americans rose up in their own defense. Some, like T. Thomas Fortune, argued for black separatism, calling for African Americans to found their own banks and other institutions to support the freedmen and preserve their identity. Carrying this even further, a number of others—such as "Pap" Singleton in the 1870s—advocated and founded towns for "blacks only" in Tennessee and Kansas as well as in Oklahoma Territory. Others stayed in the South and protested the systematic deprivation of their rights by whites. J. C. Price organized the Citizens Equal Rights Association in 1887 to petition against and protest segregation. Using the press, Ida B. Wells denounced lynching in her Memphis, Tennessee, newspaper *Free Speech.* These heated responses represented a minority reaction on the part of blacks, however. Most opted to follow the quieter path forged by Booker T. Washington, who advised adjusting to white racism for the present time and staying out of politics (though secretly he backed activists who fought for African American rights). Washington counseled fellow blacks to help themselves economically by learning skills they could profit from, a message that won the approval of even Southern whites.

The Autobiography in Focus

The contents. *Up from Slavery* begins with Washington's birth to a slave woman named Jane on a day, according to his own estimate, in 1858 or 1859. Growing up a slave, he was put to work in the fields by the age of three. He never knew his father's name, going only by the name Booker until he took his stepfather's first name on enrolling in school. His mother married Washington Ferguson after the Civil War and moved the family to Malden, West Virginia, where Ferguson had previously worked as a slave in the salt mines. Ferguson again found work there, and Booker and his brother, John, soon were working in the mines as well.

Booker, however, showed an early interest in education. Just as early, he began to form opinions about the roles of blacks and how they might rise within the system. He obtained another job working as a servant for $5 a month in the home of General Lewis Ruffner and his wife Viola. Though the strict Viola Ruffner frightened Washington at first, she eventually befriended him and continually encouraged him to pursue his schooling. While living in the Ruffner house, Washington recalls, he gathered together his first "library"—comprised of a dry goods box that held every book he could get his hands on.

Washington's dream was to attend Hampton Institute, a vocational school for African Americans, but his mother considered the notion a "wild goose chase" (*Up from Slavery,* p. 32). Washington had no clear idea of exactly where Hampton was or how much it would cost to travel there, and although he had very little money—mostly small contributions from family and acquaintances, he struck out on his own. A few hours into the journey, he realized that he did not have enough money to make the five-hundred-mile journey by rail or stagecoach. Undaunted, he walked and begged rides in wagons and cars to reach his destination. He ran out of money in Richmond, but found work loading cargo off a ship and eventually saved enough earnings to finish the trip.

Washington did well at Hampton and eventually became a teacher there himself. He opened a night school at Hampton that became very popular. His reputation grew, and eventually the founder of Hampton Institute, General Samuel Chapman Armstrong, selected Washington to establish a school similar to Hampton in Tuskegee, Alabama.

Arriving in Tuskegee in June of 1881, Washington found that not only was funding minimal, but there was not even a school building in which to conduct classes. Though he had to begin classes in an old church, he eventually succeeded in raising money to buy an abandoned plantation at a cost of $500. His main strategy was to use the building of the school as a learning experience for his students. Washington and his forty pupils learned brick-making, bricklaying, and other necessary skills to construct the first permanent building. As the student enrollment grew and faculty members were added, the Tuskegee students continued to build and make bricks for sale. By the end of the century, Tuskegee boasted more than forty brick buildings—all but four of them constructed by the students.

As Tuskegee became a leading vocational school for African Americans, Washington's reputation grew as well. Through his campaigns to

Up from Slavery

gain funding, he developed skills as a public speaker, and in 1895 a speech he gave at the Atlanta Exposition in Georgia brought him national prominence. The fifteen-minute speech, delivered before an audience of several thousand, summarized his views. He counseled accepting the white call for segregation while insisting on black self-improvement. "In all things that are purely social," he assured listeners, "we can be as separate as the fingers, yet one as the hand in all things essential to mutual progress" (*Up from Slavery*, p. 147). It was vitally important now, he continued, for everyone to put their efforts into the training and growth of useful, intelligent black citizens. Over the next five years, as the autobiography relates, Washington's messages brought him recognition from both blacks and whites as America's leading black voice.

WASHINGTON'S VIEW OF EDUCATION

We wanted to teach the students how to bathe; how to care for their teeth and clothing. We wanted to teach them what to eat, and how to eat it properly, and how to care for their rooms. Aside from this, we wanted to give them such a practical knowledge of some one industry, together with a spirit of industry, thrift, and economy, that they would be sure of making a living after they had left us. We wanted to teach them to study actual things instead of mere books alone.... We wanted to give them such an education as would fit a large proportion to be teachers, and at the same time cause them to return to the plantation districts and show the people there how to put new energy and new ideas into farming, as well as into the intellectual and moral and religious life of the people.

(*Up from Slavery*, pp. 84-5)

Washington's aims and methods. Washington believed that African Americans, having suffered under slavery for so long, had to begin at the bottom and work their way up in society by degrees. He thus stressed basic training in areas such as personal hygiene, good manners, and manual labor as a foundation for the study of other subjects. Above all, he believed, blacks needed qualified teachers who could teach the ex-slaves lessons that they could use to improve their daily lives.

Washington's educational philosophy was based on that of General Armstrong, the headmaster of the Hampton Institute during Washington's stint there. Armstrong's ideas were a natural fit with Washington's own character. A practical man, Washington believed in doing the best he could with the tools he was given. His viewpoint in this respect matched that of a number of white New Englanders who had come south, which explains why he got along so well with no-nonsense people like Mrs. Ruffner and General Armstrong. It also explains why Washington tried to cooperate with Southern whites in public, an approach that brought him criticism from some other African Americans. Not in his autobiography but important to gaining an understanding of Washington's methods is the story of his friend Thomas Harris. A black man living in Tuskegee, Harris wished to become a lawyer. For the town's whites, a black carpenter or builder may have been acceptable, but a lawyer or doctor was not. Southerners (and many Northerners too) expected blacks to "know their place" in society—that is, to have ambitions only for jobs involving manual labor. When hostile whites attacked Harris and shot him in the leg, the town's white doctors refused to treat him. The wounded man's friends brought him to Washington and asked him to have the school doctor treat Harris's leg. Washington turned them away, claiming that he could not allow the school to be endangered by a white mob.

This was the story told by the white newspapers, which endorsed Washington's behavior. The story caused other African American leaders to attack Washington bitterly. Yet in reality, while pretending to turn the man away, Washington had secretly arranged and paid for him to be taken to another town and treated there in safety. This solution saved the man *and* managed to preserve the receptive attitude of the whites toward Washington and the school, an attitude necessary for the school's survival. In this same way, Washington later secretly assisted blacks who challenged white restrictions in court, while on the surface preaching cooperation with white society.

By the 1890s, with the Tuskegee Institute's success to his credit, Washington began to win financial support from millionaires in the white community, people like Andrew Carnegie and the railroad king Collis P. Huntington. He impressed these hard-headed businessmen by telling them exactly how much he needed and what it would be used for, and then by providing an account of every dollar spent. As in other areas of his life, in raising money for the school Washington's own personality—practical and businesslike—appealed to white values. His approach would change somewhat in the decade following the publication of his autobiography. After 1910 or so, he saw evidence that the jobs he had wanted African Americans to fill were being taken over by machines. Washington also became less accepting of existing prejudices, and he grew closer to those who emphasized political equality over cooperation.

Sources. *Up from Slavery* was compiled from articles written by Washington for the journal *Outlook*. As a book, though, it also has roots in what had by the end of the century become a well-defined genre of literature, the black slave autobiography. The best known of these is **The Narrative of the Life of Frederick Douglass** (1845) (also covered in *Literature and Its Times*), but other slaves or former slaves had also published accounts of their lives and struggles, for example, *The Narrative of Sojourner Truth*, published in 1850.

Obviously, Washington's main source was his life experience and the lessons he gleaned from it. Throughout the book, he expresses gratitude to and appreciation for the personalities who guided him. Chief among them were Mrs. Ruffner, the "Yankee" lady for whom he worked during his boyhood, and General Samuel Armstrong, who ran the Hampton Institute. "The lessons," declares Washington, "I learned in the home of Mrs. Ruffner were as valuable as any education I have ever gotten anywhere since" (*Up from Slavery*, p. 30). The General was, in Washington's words, simply "the noblest, rarest human being that it has ever been my privilege to meet" (*Up from Slavery*, p. 37).

Reception. *Up from Slavery* won praise from both blacks and whites. Even before its publication, however, a growing number of African American leaders had begun to question Washington's approach. W. E. B. Du Bois, a Northerner from Massachusetts and the first African American to earn a Ph.D. from Harvard University, led the attack. Why, these critics demanded, should blacks wait to win economic and political equality? They had waited for more than thirty years already. By what law or principle should blacks be relegated to manual labor? Du Bois was by 1901 becoming an outspoken advocate of a more aggressive challenge to the status quo.

While Du Bois and others objected to Washington's doctrine of cooperation with whites as presented in *Up from Slavery*, the book was not all they criticized. They also resented what Du Bois called the "Tuskegee Machine," referring to Washington's extensive if informal political influence. Presidents Theodore Roosevelt and William Howard Taft, for example, sought Washington's approval when appointing blacks (and some whites) to office. Two years after *Up from Slavery* appeared, Du Bois would respond to Washington's ideas with a passionately argued book of his own, **The Souls of Black Folk** (also covered in *Literature and Its Times*). And in 1909, with other prominent African Americans, Du Bois would aid in establishing the National Association for the Advancement of Colored People (NAACP), an organization that developed into the most vocal opponent of the ideas presented in Washington's autobiography.

For More Information

Faulkner, Audrey, et al. *When I Was Comin' Up: An Oral History of Aged Blacks*. New York: Archon, 1983.

Kolchin, Peter. *First Freedom: The Responses of Alabama's Blacks to Emancipation and Reconstruction*. Westport, Conn.: Greenwood Press, 1972.

Litwack, Leon F. *Been in the Storm So Long: The Aftermath of Slavery*. New York: Alfred A. Knopf, 1979.

Meltzer, Milton. *The Black Americans: A History in Their Own Words*. New York: Thomas Y. Crowell, 1984.

Rawick, George P. *The American Slave: A Composite Autobiography*. Westport, Conn.: Greenwood Press, 1970.

Sundquist, Eric. *To Wake the Nations*. Cambridge, Mass.: Harvard University Press, 1993.

Washington, Booker T. *Up from Slavery*. New York: Heritage, 1970.

Walden

by
Henry David Thoreau

Henry David Thoreau was born in Concord, Massachusetts, in 1817. His family moved away several times but always returned to the small New England town. In the 1830s and 1840s, Concord was a hotbed of activity for reformers of all types. Thoreau himself became a member of a group of thinkers and reformers called the Transcendentalists. Thoreau devoted his life to living out Transcendentalist ideas, which reacted against perceived negative changes taking place in the United States.

> **THE LITERARY WORK**
>
> A narrative set in Concord, Massachusetts, in 1845; published in 1854.
>
> **SYNOPSIS**
>
> The author describes how and why he lived alone in the woods next to Walden Pond for a year.

Events in History at the Time of the Narrative

The young United States. The early 1800s was an exciting period for Americans. The United States had not lost to the British in the War of 1812, regarded by some as the "Second War of American Independence" (Nash, p. 324). After the war, England's influence dimmed and a new sense of patriotism enveloped Americans, who began to form their own identity separate from the Europeans. In 1816 trade barriers were erected to keep foreign products from American markets. The federal and state governments, meanwhile, began to finance improvements within the United States by funding the construction of advanced forms of transportation such as manmade canals and railroads. This stimulated strong economic growth that caused a number of drastic changes in American society.

The American Enlightenment. One force that strongly shaped the early years of the United States was an intellectual movement called the American Enlightenment. It was based on the notion that through systematic investigation of the universe (which largely meant through science), all of its laws could be discovered. The knowledge gained from investigation could then be used to improve human affairs. Enlightenment thinkers viewed science, and the technological advancements that were derived from science, in a positive light. In fact, science came to be so important that religion became a subordinate concern for many people. The movement was limited to the elite portion of the American population during the 1700s, but the Industrial Revolution of the nineteenth century spurred a massive spreading of Enlightenment ideals to the general population. Science and technology emerged as national symbols of American progress.

The Industrial Revolution. When Thoreau wrote *Walden* in the 1840s, the railroad was still a relatively new invention. Several passages are devoted to the train, which Thoreau describes as an "iron horse" and a "fire-steed." While Thoreau marvels at the power of the train, he views it ultimately as degrading to the human character: "Our inventions," he says, "are wont to be pretty toys, which distract our attention from serious things. They are but improved means to an unimproved end" (Thoreau, *Walden*, p. 306).

Henry David Thoreau

The advent of the railroad was a turning point in American history. Before the railroad, land transportation had been expensive and slow. It cost more to move a ton of iron ten miles than it did to ship it across the Atlantic Ocean. Transporting products from one section of the nation to another had been prohibitively expensive. All this changed with the coming of the railroad, a quicker and less expensive alternative to other modes of transportation.

Perhaps most greatly affected by the appearance of the railroads were the nation's farmers, who made up the majority of the American work force in 1820. Prior to the railroad, farmers cultivated only the crops their families needed to survive, but the new transportation option allowed them to raise one or two crops and sell them to distant markets to earn a good living. Families became more prosperous, which enabled them to afford more luxury items like chinaware, furniture, and manufactured textiles.

In response to the increasing buying power of Americans, manufacturers began to turn out greater numbers of products. The cycle escalated as new factories were built. The Industrial Revolution, in turn, triggered a transformation in American society. More and more people moved from rural areas to the cities to work in the newly built factories. Most Americans saw the changes as positive because they signaled the nation's economic growth.

A consequence of the newly industrialized society was the fact that Americans started to specialize in certain areas of work. They ceased being self-reliant. Frowning on the increasing division of labor, Thoreau foresaw it as a negative trend with a debilitating effect on humanity: "We belong to the community. It is not the tailor alone who is the ninth part of a man; it is as much the preacher, and the merchant, and the farmer. Where is this division of labor to end? and what object does it finally serve? No doubt another *may* also think for me; but it is not therefore desirable that he do so to the exclusion of my thinking for myself" (*Walden*, p. 301).

EMERSON AND THOREAU

Emerson, a member of the first generation of American transcendentalists, inspired younger men such as Thoreau, who belonged to the second generation. In fact, Emerson was a close friend and neighbor of Thoreau. When Thoreau was looking for work, Emerson hired him as a handyman and helped him to find tutoring jobs. Emerson also helped get Thoreau's writings published. Finally, Emerson was the one who granted Thoreau permission to live on the land next to Walden Pond, which Emerson had purchased in order to save its trees from being cut down. When some contemporaries accused Thoreau of imitating Emerson's writing. Emerson dismissed the accusation: "In reading him [Thoreau], I find the same thought, the same spirit that is in me, but he takes a step beyond, and illustrates by excellent images that which I should have conveyed in a sleepy generality" (Emerson in Harding, p. 117).

Reform movements. The 1830s and 1840s were marked by a religious revival called the Second Great Awakening (the first had taken place in the 1730s). According to some scholars, this Second Great Awakening was a response to the rapid changes of the Industrial Revolution. People, the scholars argue, wanted to find some stability in their unstable world. Ministers played an important part in the movement. Many traveled around the country preaching to huge crowds, delivering the message that humankind had the ability to choose between good and evil. This was

Walden

A recreation of Thoreau's room at Walden.

contrary to the doctrine of Calvinism, the dominant form of Protestantism at the time, which held that each person's fate was predetermined before birth. Furthermore, the ministers who were active in the Second Great Awakening held that it was possible to remove sin from the world and improve society. This could be accomplished, they believed, if a person who chose the right path would convince others to do the same.

In response to these new ideas, reform movements began to spring up all over the country. There were movements against the consumption of alcohol and against slavery; other movements promoted improvements in health and diet, education, or labor rights. Shared by the various members of these movements was the belief that the world could become a better place.

The Utopian societies. Arising from the reform movements were groups who believed the best way to change the world would be to begin again. In the 1840s over a hundred different groups established their own separate societies. While some were founded for religious reasons, others were based on new concepts of social cooperation. In 1841 a group of intellectuals from a local transcendentalist movement called New England Transcendentalism attempted to found a community at Brook Farm in Massachusetts. Life at Brook Farm was based on the equal division of physical labor and intellectual pursuits. The utopian community lasted six years before collapsing due to financial problems.

When Brook Farm was established, Thoreau was invited to join. He declined. A few years later, some of Thoreau's friends tried to establish yet another utopia. Thoreau once again said that he wanted no part of it, explaining that he was suspicious of any enterprise that involved more than one person. In *Walden,* Thoreau writes: "I find it wholesome to be alone the greater part of the time. To be in company, even with the best, is soon wearisome and dissipating.... I never found the companion that was so companionable as solitude" (*Walden,* p. 386).

The transcendentalists. In 1836 a Massachusetts reformer named Ralph Waldo Emerson wrote a short essay entitled "Nature." Along with a few like-minded individuals, Emerson, through the ideas he presented in this essay, began the American Transcendental Movement, a reaction against the cold rationality of the Age of Enlightenment. Transcendental ideas had originated earlier, however, with the German philosopher Immanuel Kant. Kant, in turn, had based his concepts on those of the ancient Greek philosopher Plato.

Transcendentalist theory states that truth can only be known through each person's intuition.

Describing and measuring the characteristics of something, as scientists do, is a superficial act. For the transcendentalists, the physical world is not real; it is only the manifestation of some deeper truth. By using intuition, a person may see the truth that is hidden behind a physical form. Emerson, for example, said that on a certain occasion he saw a rock drop into a pond, and as he watched the concentric ripples of water he intuitively knew that it represented the idea of influence.

The individual is central to transcendentalist thought, which holds that change begins inside the individual, works its way out, and so reforms society. In Thoreau's words, "Things do not change; we change" (*Walden*, p. 567). But by its very nature, the transcendentalists believed, society forces people to conform to its customs and become a part of the masses. Individuality is lost in the process, presenting transcendentalists, like Thoreau, with a dilemma they struggled to overcome.

The birth of American literature. One of the technological advances of the Industrial Revolution was the improvement of printing and publishing techniques. Prior to the 1830s, only the wealthy could afford to own a library, but advances in printing and publishing dropped the cost of all printed material so rapidly that nearly everyone could afford to buy books. A minor information revolution began as Americans gained access to all sorts of books and periodicals.

One result of the new publishing environment was that reformers were able to spread their ideas more efficiently. In 1840 the Transcendentalists began a journal entitled the *Dial*. It was in the *Dial* that Thoreau was first published—a poem of his appeared in the premier issue.

Coinciding with the revolution in publishing was the beginning of an American literary movement. There was a call for Americans to begin to explore new themes and writing styles that were uniquely American in nature, to prove that the United States was indeed the equal of any nation. This was a contrast to earlier writers who mimicked European themes and styles. The first generation of the truly American writers, such as Hawthorne, Melville, Emerson, and Thoreau, would eventually gain international recognition for the whole of American literature.

The Narrative in Focus

The contents. Thoreau begins his essay with an explanation of why he went out to live in the wilderness by himself—to demonstrate that it is possible to live comfortably while still living within one's means. Thoreau believes that too many of his fellow townsmen are overburdened by their possessions. They are so preoccupied with earning money to pay for their worldly goods that they have no time to devote to intellectual pursuits. Thoreau elaborates: "Most men ... through mere ignorance and mistake, are so occupied with the factitious cares and superfluously coarse labors of life that its finer fruits cannot be plucked by them" (*Walden*, p. 261). Through disuse, humankind's ability to think has become dormant; it is because of this intellectual slumber that the world is in such pitiful shape. All it takes to make the world a better place is to reform the individual, and individual reform can be attained only by reawakening the intellect. Thoreau hopes to wake his neighbors up so that they may help in changing the world.

> **WEALTH VS. EXPERIENCE**
>
> Thoreau had the opportunity to become rich soon after his graduation from Harvard College. Helping in his father's pencil factory, Thoreau created a new type of pencil that was superior to all others. He immediately quit, however. When asked why he did not continue in the pencil-making business, where he could earn a fortune, Thoreau replied, "Why should I? I would not do again what I have done once" (Emerson, p. 379).

To demonstrate that every person can live simply, Thoreau sets out to build a house in the wilderness and live there for a year. All Thoreau has as he begins his enterprise is permission to live next to Walden Pond and an ax that he borrowed from a friend. With the ax he begins constructing his home. Thoreau describes all of the steps he takes in building his house, even giving the prices of all the materials that he uses in order to demonstrate that it is cheaper to build one's house than rent one. Thoreau finishes the construction and moves in on July 4, 1845. To earn money he works as a day laborer and cultivates a bean field. However, Thoreau works only long enough to cover his expenses, about six weeks during the year.

As the essay progresses, Thoreau describes his neighbors, which include the animals and plants, the people, and the ponds in the surrounding area. Thoreau becomes increasingly familiar with

Walden

nature and unfamiliar with human society. He relates the way a wild mouse takes food from his hands or how a bird sometimes lands on his shoulder. In contrast, Thoreau views the townspeople of Concord as somewhat hostile. Indeed, it was during his time at Walden that Thoreau was jailed for refusing to pay a general poll tax. He had refused to pay because he chose not to support a government that permitted slavery to exist. In discussing the experience, Thoreau reveals a general antipathy for social institutions and policies: "Wherever a man goes, men will pursue and paw him with their dirty institutions, and, if they can, constrain him to belong to their desperate odd-fellow society" (*Walden,* p. 420). In contrast, when Thoreau speaks of nature's ponds, he does so with admiration. He views the ponds as pure, sacred wells and as places for spiritual renewal.

BATHING

Though Thoreau maintained strong ideas of morality that would seem prudish nowadays, it is known that Thoreau bathed nude in Walden Pond every morning. He considered the ritual to be a spiritual cleansing. It is because of this daily practice that he came to be described as the pioneer American nudist.

Holding high regard for Walden Pond, Thoreau makes it his job to study the body of water. He notes how the water is green at certain angles and blue from others. He describes in detail how the ice forms in the winter and how it breaks up in the spring. Walden Pond is the object of Thoreau's scientific and spiritual inquiries during his stay along its shores.

In the final section of *Walden,* Thoreau calls on his neighbors to begin to live according to their own ideas. He demands: "Let everyone mind his own business, and endeavor to be what he was made" (*Walden,* p. 564).

Thoreau the individual. Since his death in 1862, scholars have tried to determine Thoreau's nature and personality. The descriptions vary widely, even by people who personally knew Thoreau. In the eulogy prepared by Emerson, Thoreau was painted as a cold stoic. Emerson quoted one of Thoreau's friends as saying, "I love Henry, but I cannot like him; and as for taking his arm, I should as soon think of taking the arm of an elm-tree" (Emerson, p. 381).

Emerson's son wrote a book about his memories of Thoreau, which were quite different from those of his father. He portrayed Thoreau as beloved by children and appreciated by his neighbors. This view is supported by the fact that, on the day of Thoreau's burial, the Concord schools were closed so that the children could bring wildflowers to his grave. Yet it is also a fact that Thoreau was not greatly appreciated by his fellow townspeople. Indeed, he had a bad reputation with his neighbors as the man who accidentally set fire to 300 acres of the Concord woods.

All who knew Thoreau, though, agreed that he possessed a deep and abiding love of nature. He was said to have spent most of his time walking through the woods. During those walks Thoreau closely observed and recorded the birds, plants and animals he found. In fact, Thoreau eventually became a land surveyor to support himself, for the occupation enabled him to visit the woods on a daily basis.

Sources. Where Thoreau received the inspiration for his writing is a subject of much speculation by scholars. Some have retrieved the records from Thoreau's college and secondary school in order to study Thoreau's reading list during his schooling. They have also reviewed the records at the Harvard College library, poring over the lists of books that Thoreau checked out on his own accord.

While they are too numerous to list, three general types of literature are visible in Thoreau's writing of *Walden:* Eastern religious texts, such as the Bhagavad-Gita; works of ancient Greek and Roman writers, such as Homer; and biblical passages. In the opening of the essay, Thoreau compares the hardships of his townsmen with the trials of self-imposed penance undertaken by Hindu Brahmins. Later in the text, he talks about causing the transmigration of the soul of a woodchuck when he killed it. This concept comes from Hinduism, which holds that souls repeatedly reincarnate after death in a variety of creatures, including human, animal, and insect; through good karma (deeds), one's soul obtains rebirth in more highly evolved life forms. Throughout *Walden* Thoreau also refers to the Greek and Roman classics, particularly through mythological allusions. Furthermore, Thoreau states that the only book he brought with him to Walden Pond was Homer's *Iliad,* which he could read in Greek. While Thoreau often downplayed the impact that the Bible had upon his writing, *Walden* is full of biblical allusions. He comments, for example, that "perhaps on that spring morning when Adam and Eve were driven out of Eden Walden Pond was already in existence" (*Walden,* p. 428).

Composition and reception. When Thoreau moved out to Walden Pond in 1845, his reasons were more varied than he states. While he did desire to live in a more simple manner, he also went to Walden to write. Thoreau had a brother, John, who died of lockjaw in 1842. In memory of his brother, Thoreau decided to write a book about a boating trip that he took with John in 1839. Thoreau's friend, Ellery Channing, suggested that Walden Pond would be an ideal location for him to write the book. Thoreau took his friend's advice.

In *Walden,* Thoreau describes only a year of his life at the pond. In reality, however, he lived there for two years, two months, and two days. During that time, Thoreau wrote most of the book about his brother, entitled *A Week on the Concord and Merrimack Rivers.* He also finished the initial version of *Walden,* the first of seven drafts he would write. Originally, Thoreau had not planned to write about his experience at Walden. He took note of the large number of Concord residents who were interested in his decision to live there, however, and began to realize the impact such an account might have.

In 1849 Thoreau was able to get *A Week on the Concord and Merrimack Rivers* published, but it was a dismal failure. As a result, the publishers were unwilling to take another chance on Thoreau with *Walden.* It was not until 1854, with the help of some powerful friends, that Thoreau had *Walden* published. It was a mild success, though few critics gave it much acclaim. It was not until after Thoreau's death in 1862 that *Walden* gained wider recognition.

For More Information

Emerson, Ralph Waldo. *Selections from Ralph Waldo Emerson.* Edited by Stephen E. Whicher. Boston: Houghton Mifflin, 1957.

Harding, Walter. *A Thoreau Handbook.* New York: New York University Press, 1959.

Nash, Gary B., et al. *The American People: Creating a Nation and Society.* New York: Harper & Row, 1986.

Sayre, Robert F. *New Essays on Walden.* Cambridge: Cambridge University Press, 1992.

Thoreau, Henry David. *Walden.* In *The Portable Thoreau.* Edited by Carl Bode. New York: Penguin Classics, 1975.

"The Yellow Wallpaper"

by
Charlotte Perkins Gilman

An autobiographical tale, "The Yellow Wallpaper" details Charlotte Perkins Gilman's personal battle with depression and the disastrous "Rest Cure" treatment she received. Living during the restrictive Victorian Age and the "golden age of hysteria," Gilman experienced firsthand the frustrating limitations placed on women in her era, many of whom were victimized by society's complete misunderstanding of postpartum depression and other psychological maladies. Gilman, however, was born into a family of outspoken women. Her great-aunts Catherine Beecher and the novelist Harriet Beecher Stowe both championed social causes of their era. Two generations later Gilman proved equally outspoken. "The Yellow Wallpaper" is Gilman's attempt to show the ill effects of cultural restrictions and forced inactivity on women's lives during the late Victorian age.

Events in History at the Time of the Short Story

Women's roles and rights. The Victorian Age, which began in Great Britain with Queen Victoria (who ruled from 1837 to 1901), had a profound impact on social values in the United States—particularly on the values associated with women. The Victorian ideal stressed female chastity and innocence and held that a woman's ultimate roles were those of wife and mother. She was thus discouraged from aspiring to other occupations. Women were to behave demurely and remain within the domestic sphere, learning only

> **THE LITERARY WORK**
> A short story set in New England in the 1880s; published in 1892.
>
> **SYNOPSIS**
> A woman suffering from depression is subjected to a "Rest Cure." Relegated to an isolated country house and forbidden to work or exercise, she goes insane.

what was necessary to become competent mothers and charming wives.

Despite this ideal, education for women did gain ground. State-funded schooling for both boys and girls began to spread in the East at the primary level in the 1830s and at the secondary level in the 1850s. Gilman's own schooling consisted of four years of education, part of them spent in the Young Ladies School of Providence, where she earned above-average grades in spelling (88) and composition (83) but below-average marks in arithmetic (69) and grammar (57).

Far more appealing to Gilman than any of these subjects were the physical fitness classes run by Dr. John P. Brooks, who advocated the healthful effects of physical movement for women. Gilman's great-aunt, Catherine Beecher, echoed this advice. But it was a minority viewpoint. Generally, the underlying idea of how to educate a woman remained the same as it had been earlier in the century. It was, as the majority saw it, necessary to educate women not for their own benefit but for the sake of increasing their value to men. To be attractive to men, to win the respect of men, to care for, advise, and comfort husbands, to raise children—these were considered the womanly duties that dictated the nature of a girl's education.

As adults, American women did not have the right to vote, and they held only limited property rights. As they became increasingly active in the temperance and abolition movements, they began to realize that their citizenship was of an inferior quality. They subsequently began to lobby for their own rights. In 1848 the first women's rights convention was held in Seneca Falls, New York. Activists called for voting and property rights for women as well as greater educational and professional opportunities. Women emerged as public speakers and writers as the women's rights movement grew, and they slowly began to challenge Victorian ideals and social conventions.

The struggle to gain the vote formed only one part of the women's movement, though. Wives and mothers also stepped out of their homes to reform society in various ways, by joining the Women's Christian Temperance Union, establishing social settlement houses aimed at alleviating poverty, and joining women's trade unions that sought better factory and working conditions. In 1890 an assortment of women's clubs formed the General Federation of Women's Clubs, gaining national strength. Meanwhile, many women cast off their tight-laced dresses and adopted a new fashion, the looser shirtwaist blouse and ankle-length skirt.

The members of the social purity movement also sought to improve society. Feeling that sex could be a source of joy but too often became a major source of evil, Gilman took an active part in this movement. Its members advocated sex education, hygiene, and the right of women to make decisions about their own bodies rather than simply submit to the whims of men. In 1890, the year she wrote "The Yellow Wallpaper," Gilman joined the lecture circuit in California, partly to champion the social purity movement.

Evolution, industrialism, and the "Woman Question." Women began to play a more public role in society with the growth of industrialization. Along with an abundance of factory jobs in the post-Civil War era, positions opened up in the east as men left to join the great westward expansion. The situation created a demand for a sharp increase in the labor force. Women consequently went to work in greater numbers than in the past, and the need arose for them to gain more educational skills than they had customarily obtained. Great Britain opened its first women's college in 1848, following the opening of Mount Holyoke Seminary, an American college for women in 1837. But while numbers of women in public roles increased, the vast majority remained confined to the domestic sphere, and an earnest debate ensued over the wisdom of allowing women to enter professions and receive higher education.

LOOKING BACKWARD

In 1888 Edward Bellamy wrote a runaway bestseller called *Looking Backward*. The hero in Bellamy's novel wakes up in the year 2000 in a utopia where citizens coexist comfortably and happily. Everyone works for one gigantic trust operated by the national government. Women, though they work fewer hours than men, fill positions along with them in the industrial labor force. Captivated by the book, Gilman embraced its ideas. She not only promoted a woman's right to control her own body but also encouraged women to gain economic independence from men in their private lives.

Catherine Beecher, Gilman's great-aunt, felt that women and men should retain separate roles (she argued that women held more power this way); in her view, women should care for home and family, while men should tend to politics and business. Gilman, on the other hand, advocated that women needed mental and physical challenges and the opportunity to work and create outside the home. She demonstrated through her work and life that women need a wide range of choices and opportunities in order to live a full life; some of those denied such opportunities were at risk of falling into severe depression. The debate, which became known as the "Woman Question," persisted into the next century.

The publication of Charles Darwin's *Origin of the Species* (1859) further incited controversy over women's roles and issues. His theory of evolution flouted conventional wisdom, contending that women were actually the hardier and more necessary sex, the one able to preserve the species; because women were mothers, they were vital to survival. Darwin's theory was used to promote both sides of the "Woman Question."

Charlotte Perkins Gilman addresses the Federation of Women's Clubs, 1916.

Proponents of expanded roles for women could argue that because women were hardier, they were fully capable of being mothers and professionals in the work world. On the other hand, advocates of women's domesticity could say that Darwin's theory called attention to the necessity of motherhood and its supreme priority in a woman's life. Gilman believed Darwin's theories validated both arguments. In her view, women could be both mothers and professionals but needed economic independence and freedom from domestic chores in order to successfully manage these dual roles. Through her books, *Women and Economics, Concerning Children, The Home,* and *Herland,* as well as "The Yellow Wallpaper," Gilman became known as "the first comprehensive feminist philosopher" in the United States (Sochen, pp. 34-5).

Women's rights movement. By 1892 the women's rights movement had scored some mild successes. In 1860 New York State granted property rights to married women, and in 1861 Kansas allowed its women limited voting rights on school issues. Eighteen more states extended such limited voting rights to women by 1890. But women were still greatly restricted: they could not vote for public officials or hold public office themselves; they were vastly underpaid compared to men; occupations other than teaching, nursing, low-level factory labor, or domestic service were closed to them; and most colleges and professional training institutions continued to admit men only. In "The Yellow Wallpaper," the protagonist, who is suffering from depression, observes: "I believe that congenial work, with excitement and change, would do me good" (Gilman, "The Yellow Wallpaper," p. 152). Society's restrictions, however, minimize her opportunities and limit her options, with devastating consequences.

Gilman used the story to illustrate her belief in the great need for social reform in the Victorian Age and the potentially crippling effects that lack of opportunity has on women. Gilman saw herself as a member of the larger women's rights movement and spoke of the costs involved in being a female rebel—the loneliness, the loss of loving relationships with men, and the scorn of the larger society.

Covert writing. Though the Victorian Age is known as a time of tremendous creative energy, women were by and large excluded from participation in most literary activities. There were some successful women writers, but in general, writing was not seen as a proper profession for a lady. British poet laureate Robert Southey summed up the common viewpoint:

> Literature cannot be the business of a woman's life and it ought not to be. The more she is engaged in her proper duties, the less leisure she will have for it, even as an accomplishment and a recreation.
>
> (Southey in Cahill, p. xii)

A few women in America, such as Louisa May Alcott and Edith Wharton, wrote novels that earned favorable reviews, though male critics of the time often dismissed the works of female writers as inconsequential. In England women resorted to taking on male pen names to secure publication and recognition as serious writers, such as Mary Ann Evans (who wrote under the name George Eliot) and Emily Brontë (as Ellis Bell). For subject matter, most published women authors stuck to traditional "female" genres, such as romance or Gothic novels, in order to gain publication and a steady readership.

In "The Yellow Wallpaper," the protagonist is forbidden to write upon the advice of her doctor husband, John. Writing is seen as detrimental to her health, when actually it is the only activity that keeps her from going mad. Indeed, the woman realizes that her writing is a necessary release: "But I must say what I feel and think in some way—it is such a relief!" ("Yellow Wallpaper," p. 156). Like the modern-day writer Elizabeth Bowen, who said, "I only feel half-alive when I'm not writing," Gilman and her character demonstrate that there are psychological—in addition to economic—reasons for women to work and create (Cahill, p. xii).

The protagonist of "The Yellow Wallpaper" cries out for a man who will encourage her in her literary efforts instead of maligning them. In the course of the story, Gilman shows that the real "Rest Cure" is activity, and suggests that writing, for her protagonist as well as herself, produces rest. "I think sometimes," says the woman, "that if I were only well enough to write a little it would relieve the press of ideas and rest me" ("The Yellow Wallpaper," p. 154).

The golden age of hysteria. Rooted largely in women's thwarted ambitions and limited opportunities, a rash of so-called "hysteria" cases occurred during the late 1800s and early 1900s. Because of the rise in this type of mental illness, the period became known as the "golden age of hysteria." Authorities of the time defined the malady in terms of femininity and female sexuality. Rooted in the Greek term *hysteron*, meaning "womb," hysteria was known as a strictly female illness that was caused by women's "delicate constitutions" and "emotionality." Many doctors, in fact, believed it to be caused by the uterus, which was why they concluded that men could not become hysterical (Showalter, p. 129).

Hysteria was assumed to be a largely self-created or imagined illness. People did not generally take it (or mental illness) seriously, though hysteria became a focal point of study by physicians throughout the world (leading, in fact, to Sigmund Freud's development of psychoanalysis). Symptoms included fainting, vomiting, choking, sobbing, laughing, paralysis, and temperamental fits. Reflecting the belief that women were prone to hysteria because they were less rational and stable than men, Dr. Edward Tilt, in a typical Victorian textbook definition, wrote: "mutability [changeability] is characteristic of hysteria, because it is characteristic of women" (Showalter, p. 129). As more studies were conducted, however, some doctors began to link hysteria with restricted activity and sexual repression. One doctor wrote in 1879:

> The range of activity of women is so limited, and their available paths of work in life so few, compared with those which men have in the present social arrangements, that they have not, like men, vicarious outlets for feelings in a variety of healthy aims and pursuits.
>
> (Showalter, p. 130)

Strong women who exhibited more than the usual amount of forceful, confident, and fearless behavior were particularly prone to hysteria, according to F. C. Skey, a Victorian Age physician. In fact, as shown in "The Yellow Wallpaper," strong and creative women, forbidden from exercising their minds and bodies, often struck out with fits of hysteria or became exceedingly depressed because they could not find constructive outlets for their energy.

In addition, postpartum depression—depression that follows childbirth—was not diagnosed as a legitimate condition during Gilman's time. Motherhood brings significant hormonal and other changes that require psychological adjustment. After giving birth, some women become extremely depressed. Postpartum depression, coupled with the stifling social constraints of the Victorian Era, drove some women mad, causing serious mental illness and even suicide.

The Rest Cure. Cures and remedies for mental illness abounded during the golden age of hysteria. The most accepted "cure" was Dr. Silas Weir Mitchell's "Rest Cure," which required complete isolation from family and friends, forbade any type of mental or physical exertion, and re-

"The Yellow Wallpaper"

quired a milk-fed diet and total bedrest. In effect, the cure was as much a punishment for hysterical women as an attempt at a cure. "When they are bidden to stay in bed a month," Mitchell wrote, "and neither to read, write, nor sew ... then rest becomes for some women a rather bitter medicine, and they are glad enough to accept the order to rise and go about when the doctor issues a mandate which has become pleasantly welcome and eagerly looked for" (Showalter, p. 139). His attitude illustrated the general belief that women feigned hysteria and that they could stop their outbursts at will.

The Rest Cure had devastating effects on many women. Treated by Mitchell, Gilman herself came precariously close to losing her mind after three weeks under his care. Fellow writers Jane Addams and Edith Wharton experienced similar results from Mitchell's treatment. Only when they resumed writing and active participation in their lives did they emerge from their depressed states. "The Yellow Wallpaper" was Gilman's attempt to show the detrimental effects of the Rest Cure (she specifically wrote it to convince Mitchell that his treatment was flawed) and the vital importance of mental and physical stimulation for all human beings, including women. Her story vividly illustrated the emotional torture that women suffered when denied the right to fully express themselves through meaningful work.

The Short Story in Focus

The plot. "The Yellow Wallpaper" is a short story about a woman literally trapped on a country estate as she undergoes the Rest Cure. In its opening lines, the story reveals the author's personal distrust of the medical profession after her experience with Dr. Mitchell. It also touches on the prevailing attitude that mental illness—particularly in the case of women—was not real. In the story John, the protagonist's husband and a doctor, reflects this attitude. He is a physician, says the protagonist, who scoffs at the intangible in life and does not believe that his wife is sick.

The woman being treated has recently had a baby. She is not allowed to work, exercise, or have any outside contact, and she is expressly forbidden to write—her only creative outlet. She is placed in the children's nursery upstairs, which resembles an insane asylum. There are bars on the windows and rings in the walls. The bed is chained to the floor, and the walls are adorned with a dreadful peeling yellow wallpaper. She realizes that she might recover more quickly if she had more interaction with others and a more stimulating environment, but her husband forbids it. She is even prevented from caring for her infant son while in this "hysterical" state.

Slowly, as the story progresses, the woman begins to go mad. The story describes the protagonist as a creative person who "could get more entertainment and terror out of blank walls and plain furniture than most children could find in a toy-store" ("The Yellow Wallpaper," p. 155). Without any other outlet for her imagination, her creativity is applied to her surroundings. She becomes obsessed with the yellow wallpaper in her room. She sees a woman trapped in its complex pattern and becomes determined to help her find a way out of the maze. She rips and tears at the paper when no one is around, keenly aware that she will be perceived as crazy if anyone sees her doing so. But she cannot stop. The pattern of the paper—like her restricted life—is torturing her, and she "must follow that pointless pattern to some sort of conclusion" ("The Yellow Wallpaper," p. 44).

Meanwhile, her husband pressures her to get well. She begs for some diversion or outside stimulation, but he tells her that such stimulation is not in her best interest and insists that if she follows his prescription, she will recover. When it becomes apparent that her condition is in fact worsening, he threatens to send her to Dr. Mitchell. Petrified by that threat, she pretends that she is recovering when her husband is around.

With nothing else to occupy her mind and time, the wallpaper begins to consume her life. She sees the woman creeping through its pattern night and day, and she starts to creep along with her. Even when John is present, she creeps and peels at the paper, an indication that she is nearing the edge of sanity. Finally, when John is gone for the night, she determines to rip all the wallpaper down, ending once and for all its torturous effects. She locks herself in the nursery and throws the key out the window. She contemplates suicide—jumping from the window or hanging herself with a piece of rope—but reasons: "I know well enough that a step like that is improper and might be misconstrued" ("The Yellow Wallpaper," p. 52). Instead of committing suicide, she begins circling the room, following the pattern in the wallpaper. In essence, she becomes the woman in the wallpaper, trapped in its endless maze. John comes home to find her locked in the room and becomes frantic. He threatens to beat the door down, but she refuses to open it, taunting him: "I've got out at last ... in spite of you.... And I've pulled off most of the paper so you can't put me back!" ("The Yellow Wallpaper," p. 53). When John finally breaks through the door and finds her compulsively, perpetually circling the room, he faints. She only laughs, noting that since his slumped body is blocking her path by the wall, she will have to creep over him every time she circles the room.

Sources. The inspiration for "The Yellow Wallpaper" was Gilman's own bout with depression and the complete misunderstanding of her condition by Victorian doctors. Gilman suffered from depression for much of her adult life. Her illness seems to have surfaced during her engagement to the painter Walter Stetson. It intensified in 1885 after she gave birth to a daughter. Gilman "found herself unable to perform routine household duties and spent much of her time in bed, weeping" (James, p. 39). At her husband's urging, she received treatment from Dr. Mitchell, who prescribed the most domestic life possible. According to Mitchell, who believed that her depression was contrived in order to get out of performing her wifely duties, she should not touch a pen or pencil for the rest of her days and should keep the baby with her always.

As a result of the Rest Cure, Gilman had a complete nervous collapse in 1885. Only after ignoring Mitchell's advice did her condition improve. She left her husband, resumed writing, and ventured to California to recuperate. As a result of her own self-treatment, she realized that it was intellectual stimulation, physical exercise, and her devotion to meaningful work that kept her sane. In 1887 she and Walter agreed to separate; it would take seven more years to finalize their divorce. In commenting on the separation and its effects on her daughter, Gilman observed that it seemed "better for the child to have separated parents [who were sane] than a lunatic mother" (Gilman in Hill, p. 152). In 1894 Gilman sent her daughter to live with her ex-husband, though the two women were happily reunited later in Pasadena, California.

In 1900 Gilman married her first cousin, New York attorney Houghton Gilman. This marriage, apparently a happy one, was to last until his death in 1934, although Gilman continued to battle depression throughout her life, and some contemporary specialists speculate that she may have suffered from the form of mental illness known as chronic manic depression.

Gilman's decision to ignore Mitchell's Rest Cure in favor of writing resulted in a period of great output. By the end of 1890, Gilman had written or delivered an impressive collection of plays, articles, and lectures, along with short stories such as "The Yellow Wallpaper." These writings attacked and unmasked myths of the day about so-called happy marriages, and promoted the idea that women were entitled to a separate existence from men in body, mind, and spirit. "The Yellow Wallpaper" warns of the possible consequences if a woman is not given these rights.

GILMAN'S OWN REACTION

Gilman herself relished the short story, taking satisfaction in the horror of it. "When my awful story 'The Yellow Wallpaper' comes out," she told a friend, "you must try and read it. Walter [Gilman's first husband] says he has read it *four* times, and thinks it the most ghastly tale he ever read. Says it beats Poe" (Gilman in Hill, p. 186).

Reaction to Gilman's ideas. "The Yellow Wallpaper" was published in 1892 in *New England Magazine*. The story received little notice at the time, but launched Gilman on a literary career. Her divorce, on the other hand, received a considerable amount of attention. At the end of 1892 the San Francisco *Examiner* blasted Gilman for her unconventional choices: "There are not many women, fortunately for humanity, who agree that 'any' work ... is higher than that of being a good wife and mother" (Hill, p. 198). The paper suspected some hidden agenda in Gilman's actions. It seemed unbelievable to the writer of the article that a woman would have more powerful instincts than devotion to husband and child.

Though Gilman went on to write many books and treatises on women's issues, "The Yellow Wallpaper" became her most famous and critically acclaimed short story. More recently, her work and life have become the subject of intense study, especially among feminist scholars at major universities.

For More Information

Cahill, Susan, ed. *Women and Fiction 2: Short Stories by and about Women*. New York: New American Library, 1978.

Gilman, Charlotte Perkins. *"The Yellow Wallpaper" and Selected Stories of Charlotte Perkins Gilman*. Edited by Denise D. Knight. Newark: University of Delaware Press, 1994.

Hill, Mary A. *Charlotte Perkins Gilman: The Making of a Radical Feminist, 1860-1896*. Philadelphia: Temple University Press, 1980.

James, Edward. *Notable American Women*. Cambridge, Mass.: Belknap, 1971.

Showalter, Elaine. *The Female Malady*. New York: Random House, 1985.

Sochen, June. *Movers and Shakers*. New York: Quadrangle, 1973.

Index

A

Aaron, Hank   4:*145, 148*
Abernathy, Ralph   5:*89 (illus.)*
Abolitionists/Abolition of slavery
  John Brown's raid on Harper's Ferry   2:*188–94*
  changing little for freed slaves   5:*19–20*
  controversy and disagreement with, in North   2:*9, 315, 404*
  as core political issue by mid-19th century   2:*88, 242*
  early efforts   2:*22–24*
  Emancipation Proclamation (1862)   2:*59, 60 (sidebar), 135, 308, 309*
  Liberia   2:*404*
  proposals for land for freed slaves   2:*41*
  and Underground Railroad   2:*16, 60, 62, 189, 238, 406–7*
  women's role in   2:*23–24*
  (*See also* African Americans; Jim Crow laws; Reconstruction)
Abortion   5:*51, 136*
Abraham Lincoln: The Prairie Years, Sandburg, Carl   2:*1–7*
Achebe, Chinua, *Things Fall Apart*   2:*360–65*
Acheson, Dean   5:*101*
Achilles   1:*169–70*
Across Five Aprils, Hunt, Irene   2:*8–14*
Adam and Eve   1:*301–2*
Adams, John   1:*29, 72, 94*
Adams, John Quincy   1:*209*
Adams, Richard, *Watership Down*   5:*346–51*
Addison, Joseph   1:*307*
Adoption of children, by African Americans   4:*33*
Adultery/infidelity   5:*273, 287*
  in *Anna Karenina*   2:*34–40*
  in *Ethan Frome*   2:*125–29*
  in *Madame Bovary*   2:*209–15*
  in *Medea*   1:*238–41*
  in *Scarlet Letter*   1:*351–57*
Adventures of Don Quixote, The, Cervantes Saavedra, Miguel de   1:*1–7*
Adventures of Huckleberry Finn, The, Twain, Mark   2:*15–21*
Advertising
  fostering consumer culture   3:*26*
  targeting teenagers   4:*392*
  WWII-related ads excluding minorities   4:*197*
Advise and Consent   5:*4*
Aegean Sea   1:*60 (map)*
Aeneas. *See Aeneid, The*
Aeneid, The, Virgil   1:*8–13*
  parallels to *Beowulf*   1:*49*
  parallels to Shakespeare's *The Tempest*   1:*383*
Affirmative action   5:*181, 183–84, 342*
AFL (American Federation of Labor)   3:*44*
Africa and Africans
  in 16th-century England   1:*299*
  Algeria   3:*212*
  apartheid in South Africa   1:*63*; 3:*86*
  Belgian Congo   2:*145–46, 150–51*
  Ethiopia   4:*67*
  Gambia   5:*298*
  Ghana   4:*314*
  impact of WWI   3:*292–93*
  independence movements   4:*314*
  ivory trade   2:*147*
  Kenya   3:*290–96*
  Liberia   2:*404*
  Maasai   3:*295*
  Medea as Egyptian "woman of color"   1:*240 (sidebar)*

Index

Moors 1:*297, 299*
natives as "squatters" 3:*293–94*
Nigeria 2:*360–62, 364–65;* 3:*84;* 4:*314*
oral tradition and griots 5:*298–300, 301–2*
post-WWI economic problems 3:*293*
racism of colonial powers 2:*360–65;* 3:*291*
Rhodesia 4:*165–66*
slave trade 1:*37, 39, 103, 274, 299, 337–38;* 2:*361*
Tanzania 3:*290*
(*See also* Colonialism, imperialism, and interventionism)

African American men
"humiliations, emasculation" faced by 4:*53–54;* 5:*146, 328–29*
physicians in Georgia 3:*154–55, 156–57*
relationship of class, race, and manhood 4:*313–14*
as soldiers in Vietnam War 5:*102–3*

African American women
accused of black male-bashing 3:*87;* 5:*121*
African-style clothing and hairdos 4:*56;* 5:*145, 300*
and black feminism 2:*64;* 3:*86–87;* 4:*56*
cosmetics for 4:*50, 56*
devaluation of 3:*80–82;* 4:*54;* 5:*115–16*
differences with white women in civil rights and feminist movements 3:*354–55;* 5:*92–93, 117*
employment in South 3:*418–19*
as heads of families 3:*355, 375, 423*
as "mammies" 3:*392*
race- and gender-based limitations upon 5:*115–16*
sexual abuse of 2:*49, 60, 169, 406;* 4:*54;* 5:*117*
as single heads of households 2:*65;* 3:*80, 423;* 4:*2;* 5:*68, 117, 328–29*

African Americans in 19th century
churches as cornerstones of community 5:*189*
exodus from South to West 3:*249–50*
gospel songs and black spirituals 2:*398, 402, 407;* 4:*258*
mixed race offspring and color prejudice 5:*21*
(*See also* Civil War; Jim Crow laws; Segregation; Slavery in America; Slaves)

African Americans in 20th century
adopting white society's values 4:*52*
adoption of children 4:*33*
in black ghettos. *See* Ghettos
class/social stratification among 4:*2–3, 30*
communism and 1:*398–99;* 3:*164, 238–39*
community, kinship, and closeness 2:*341–42;* 3:*383–84, 394;* 4:*52*
crime, some turning to 4:*145*
crime, victims of 4:*31;* 5:*340–41*
during Great Depression 3:*154, 236–37*
education 4:*3;* 5:*342*
employment opportunities and limitations 4:*311;* 5:*341 (sidebar)*
family life 3:*80, 84–86, 353–55, 375, 422–23;* 4:*33;* 5:*68, 145–46, 329–30*
Harlem Renaissance 3:*159–65, 256, 321, 384–85, 421;* 4:*204 (sidebar), 207*
Hollywood's stereotypical images of 2:*142;* 4:*50, 369*
middle class, rise of 3:*252, 255, 387–88;* 4:*2, 51*
mixed race offspring and color prejudice 2:*49;* 3:*17–18, 81, 83, 387–88;* 4:*3, 50, 51–52;* 5:*130*
oral tradition 5:*298–300, 301–2*
poverty of many 3:*37;* 4:*5 (sidebar), 145;* 5:*329*
race colonies 3:*383*
religion's importance to 3:*372*
riot following assassination of King (1968) 5:*112 (sidebar)*
riots in central Los Angeles (1992) 5:*340*
riots in Watts (1965) 5:*340*
(*See also* Great Migration; Jim Crow laws; Segregation)

African Americans' civil rights/reform/power movements
activism for FEPC (Fair Employment Practices Commission) 3:*42*
anti-integrationist 5:*15*
assassinations of leaders 4:*54;* 5:*112 (sidebar)*
autobiographies as genre 4:*205;* 5:*304*
Black arts movement 4:*207*
black feminism 2:*64;* 3:*86–87*
"Black is Beautiful" slogan 4:*54, 56*
Black Muslims and Nation of Islam 3:*238, 325;* 4:*56, 248–50;* 5:*12–13, 69, 110–11, 302*
black nationalism, separatism, and Pan-Africanism 3:*160, 238, 325;* 4:*56, 211, 311–12*
Black Panther Party 4:*54, 56, 207*
Black Power movement 2:*97–98;* 3:*43, 325;* 4:*56, 207;* 5:*143–44*
CORE (Congress of Racial Equality) 3:*42;* 4:*376*
efforts of 1940s and '50s 4:*28–29, 255*
emphasizing African heritage 5:*300–302*
fostered by Harlem Renaissance 3:*163–64, 256*
King's approach, compared to Malcolm X's 4:*250;* 5:*13, 15, 111*
militancy and Malcolm X 2:*98;* 3:*324–25;* 4:*54, 249–50;* 5:*69–70, 110, 111*
in Missouri 4:*28–29*
NAACP 2:*342, 415;* 3:*250, 320, 396;* 4:*195, 255, 310;* 5:*88, 120 (sidebar)*
Niagara Movement (1905) 3:*250, 320*
OAAU (Organization of Afro-American Unity) 5:*16–17*
pacifist versus outspoken, sometimes violent protest 4:*205, 207*
passive resistance and nonviolence 5:*11–12, 108, 189, 192*
SCLC (Southern Christian Leadership Conference) 5:*189*
seeking African roots 3:*86;* 5:*145*
self-empowerment philosophies 3:*325*
SNCC (Student Nonviolent Coordinating Committee) 4:*56;* 5:*300*

Index

UNIA (United Negro Improvement Association) 3:160; 4:211
    urban blacks' involvement in 5:143
    WPC (Women's Political Council) 5:88
African Americans, literary works concerning
    Adventures of Huckleberry Finn, The 2:15–21
    "Ain't I a Woman?" 2:22–27
    Almos' a Man 4:1–6
    Autobiography of Malcolm X, The 5:11–18
    Bear, The 2:47–53
    Beloved 2:59–65
    Benito Cereno 1:37–43
    Betsey Brown 4:28–34
    Black Boy 3:36–43
    Bluest Eye, The 4:49–57
    Color Purple, The 3:80–87
    Confessions of Nat Turner, The 2:93–98
    Cry, the Beloved Country 4:94–100
    Fences 4:144–50
    Fire Next Time, The 5:107–14
    for colored girls who have considered suicide / when the rainbow is enuf 5:115–21
    Gathering of Old Men, A 5:129–34
    Gone with the Wind 2:137–44
    Hero Ain't Nothin' but a Sandwich, A 5:143–48
    His Own Where 5:149–55
    Home to Harlem 3:159–65
    "I Have a Dream" 5:185–93
    I Know Why the Caged Bird Sings 4:201–8
    Incidents in the Life of a Slave Girl 2:168–73
    Invisible Man 4:209–15
    John Brown's Final Speech 2:188–94
    Leaves of Grass 2:197
    Manchild in the Promised Land 4:247–53
    Member of the Wedding, The 4:254–59
    Narrative of the Life of Frederick Douglass 2:236–41
    Native Son 3:236–42
    Not without Laughter 3:249–56
    Raisin in the Sun, A 4:309–15
    Roots 5:298–305
    Souls of Black Folk, The 2:340–46
    Sounder 3:370–76
    Sweet Whispers, Brother Rush 5:328–32
    Their Eyes Were Watching God 3:383–89
    Tituba of Salem Village 1:393–99
    Uncle Remus 2:397–402
    Uncle Tom's Cabin 2:403–9
    Understand This 5:339–45
    Up From Slavery 2:410–15
    Worn Path, A 3:418–24
African Methodist Episcopal Church 3:83
Age of Reason 1:268–69, 272
Agee, James, *Death in the Family, A* 3:100–105
Agnosticism 3:265
AIDS (Acquired Immune Deficiency Syndrome) 5:9
Aiken, Conrad 3:414
AIM (American Indian Movement) 2:79 (sidebar); 5:246–47

"Ain't I a Woman?" Truth, Sojourner 2:22–27
Air pollution 4:9
Alaska 3:52–56, 261 (sidebar)
Albania 2:101
Albee, Edward, *Zoo Story, The* 4:397–402
Alchemy 1:384, 385 (sidebar)
Alcohol and alcoholism
    among American Indians 1:220; 4:83, 189 (sidebar); 5:361
    among Irish 3:220, 398, 400
    among war wives 4:317
    among Welsh 3:65–66
    Anti-Saloon League and temperance movements 2:25 (sidebar), 85–86; 3:69, 75, 147, 401
    Prohibition 3:22–23
    saloons as social halls 3:219, 398, 400
    as woman's issue 2:25 (sidebar); 3:219
    (See also Prohibition)
Alcott, Louisa May, *Little Women* 2:202–8
Aldrin, Edwin E. ("Buzz") Jr. 5:82, 292, 295 (illus.)
Aleichem, Sholom 3:123
Alexander the Great, Czar of Russia 1:169 (sidebar)
Alexander II, Czar of Russia 3:57, 120
Alexander III, Czar of Russia 3:120
Alger, Horatio, *Ragged Dick* 2:301–7
Ali, Muhammad 5:70 (sidebar), 72 (illus.), 307–8
Alianza, La 4:175–76, 321
Alice's Adventures in Wonderland, Carroll, Lewis 2:28–33
All Creatures Great and Small, Herriott, James 3:1–7
All Quiet on the Western Front, Remarque, Erich Maria 3:8–14
Allegory, *Animal Farm*, Orwell, George 4:14–20
Allen, Ethan 3:98 (sidebar)
Allende, Isabel, *House of the Spirits, The* 5:163–70
Allende, Salvador 5:164–65, 166 (illus.), 168–69
Almanacs, *Poor Richard's Almanac*, Franklin, Benjamin 1:309–15
Almos' a Man, Wright, Richard 4:1–6
Amadis of Gaul 1:6
Amazons 1:58–59, 61–62, 258, 259–60
America. See Colonial America; United States
American Childhood, An, Dillard, Annie 4:7–13
American Communist Party
    popularity of, during Great Depression 3:45
    standing against racism 3:40
    (See also Communism)
American Dream
    achievement as impossible for black men 4:313
    achieving through hard work and frugality 2:302, 305; 4:111
    achieving through salesmanship in 1950s 4:111
    Ben Franklin as embodiment of 1:26–27, 309
    in colonial times 1:97
    Dreiser's preoccupation with 2:331–32
    merit rather than rank determining success 1:72

Index

American Indians in 16th century, decimated by smallpox   5:214
American Indians in 17th century, displayed in Renaissance Europe   1:383
American Indians in 18th century
   as allies of British in Revolutionary War   1:108
   as allies of French in French and Indian War   1:204–5
   decimated by smallpox   1:220, 352
   enslaved   1:103; 2:175
   French and Indian War (Seven Years' War)   1:93, 123, 204–6
   land/natural resources as considered by   1:220; 2:78, 178
   legends and Folk, Thelore   1:332
   Paxton Boys massacre   1:220–21
   pressure of westward expansion of American colonists   1:108, 204, 220–21
   Puritans' view of   1:102, 422
   Uncas   1:207 (sidebar), 208
   "walking purchase" of land from   1:220 (sidebar)
American Indians in 19th century
   art   2:348–49, 351–52
   Battle of Wounded Knee   2:69, 78
   BIA (Bureau of Indian Affairs)   5:246
   Black Hills War (1876)   2:67–68, 77
   buffalo, Great Plains tribes' dependency on   2:66–67, 75
   Crazy Horse   2:348 (illus.)
   and Dawes Act (1887)   2:68, 179; 4:186
   decimated by smallpox   2:347
   defended by Bret Harte   2:287
   family and family life   2:347
   Ghost Dance   2:69, 77–78
   holy men   2:71–72
   horse culture of Plains tribes   5:364 (sidebar)
   missions/missionaries and   2:161–62, 392 (sidebar)
   national guilt felt by whites   2:79
   Ongpatonga   1:209 (illus.)
   parallels to Anglo-Saxons after Norman Conquest   1:257
   peyote religion   4:188
   religion of   2:71–72, 78
   Removal Act (1830)   1:208–10; 2:316, 317 (sidebar)
   reservations policies of U.S. gov't.   1:224; 2:67, 68, 73, 76, 79, 179, 316, 317 (sidebar), 351; 4:186–87
   Sand Creek Massacre   2:77
   "second parents" among Sioux   2:347
   spirituality of   2:72, 161; 5:246
   Sun Dance   2:349 (sidebar); 4:187–88
   "Trail of Tears"   5:29–30
   treaties and U.S. gov't.'s failure to enforce   2:75–76, 162
American Indians in 20th century
   AIM (American Indian Movement)   2:79 (sidebar); 5:246–47
   alcoholism   1:220; 4:83, 189 (sidebar); 5:361
   BIA (Bureau of Indian Affairs)   5:246
   Catholic Church   5:244, 361–62
   citizenship status   4:80
   Civil Rights Act of 1964 affecting   2:351 (sidebar)
   cultural mixture of American Southwest   4:320–21
   Indian Reorganization Act (1934)   2:73; 4:186
   matrilineal cultures   4:82 (sidebar)
   military service   4:80, 185–87; 5:362–63
   mission school of Anglican Church   5:195
   Navajo Night Chant   4:188
   poverty of   5:360–61
   prestige factor of Indian ancestry   5:30
   Red Power and rights movements   2:79 (sidebar), 179, 351
   relocation program (1952)   4:186–87
   self-determination policies (1961 and 1970)   2:351; 4:190–91
   storytelling, powers of   4:83 (sidebar), 85, 188, 189, 192
   and tribal rights (1934)   2:73
American Indians, literary works concerning
   Bear, The (Chickasaw)   2:47–53
   Black Elk Speaks (Oglala Sioux)   2:66–73
   Bury My Heart at Wounded Knee (Western tribes)   2:74–80
   Ceremony (Laguna Pueblo)   4:79–86
   Drums Along the Mohawk (Iroquois)   1:108
   House Made of Dawn (Navajo, Jemez Pueblo, and WWII veterans)   4:185–92
   I Heard the Owl Call My Name (Kwakiutl)   5:194–200
   "I Will Fight No More Forever" (Nez Percé)   2:160–67
   Ishi, Last of His Tribe (Yahi)   2:174–80
   Last of the Mohicans, The (Delaware and Iroquois)   1:204–10
   Leaves of Grass (America's Indian heritage)   2:195–201
   Light in the Forest, The (Delaware)   1:219–24
   Love Medicine (Chippewa)   5:243–50
   Story Catcher, The (Oglala Sioux)   2:347–52
   Tempest, The (Europeans' explorations of New World)   1:383
   Yellow Raft in Blue Water, A (Cree)   5:360–66
American Indians by tribe
   Arawak (Taino)   5:214
   Cherokee   5:29–30
   Cheyenne   2:75, 79
   Chippewa   5:243–50
   Chiricahua Apache   2:74–75
   Cree   5:361 (sidebar), 362 (illus.), 364 (sidebar)
   Delaware (Lenape)   1:206, 219–20
   Iroquois   1:108, 110, 205–6
   Jemez Pueblo   4:187, 189–90, 191
   Kiowa   4:186, 187–88
   Kwakiutl (Canada)   5:194–200
   Laguna Pueblo   4:79–86

métis 5:244
Modoc 2:79
Mohegan 1:352
Narragansett 1:352
Navajo 2:79; 4:80, 186, 188; 5:360
Nez Percé 2:75, 79, 160–67
Pequot 1:352
Pueblo 4:47
Sioux 2:66–67, 347–50; 5:360
Ute 2:79
Yahi 2:174, 175, 177
Zuni Pueblo 4:186
American Revolution
  Continental Congress 1:125
  Declaration of Independence 1:93–100
  in *Drums Along the Mohawk* 1:107–14
  influence of *Common Sense* 1:71–77, 94
  influence of "Give Me Liberty or Give Me Death" speech 1:122–28
Amistad mutiny 1:43
Anaya, Rudolfo A.
  Bless Me, Ultima 4:42–48
  Heart of Aztlán 4:171–76
Anderson, Robert, *I Never Sang for My Father* 5:201–7
Anderson, Sherwood, on *Babbitt* 3:27
André, Major John 1:213 (sidebar)
Angelou, Maya, *I Know Why the Caged Bird Sings* 4:201–8
Angels in America, Kushner, Tony 5:1–10
Anglican Church (Church of England) 1:78, 123, 129, 232, 233 (sidebar), 306, 351, 393
  Dissenters 1:129, 338, 342, 407, 411; 3:265
Anglo-Saxon England 1:44–45, 153, 181
  Norman Conquest of 1:181, 250–51, 290
Animal Farm, Orwell, George 4:14–20
  politically motivated rejection by publishers 5:252–53
Animals, stories concerning
  All Creatures Great and Small 3:1–7
  Bless the Beasts and Children 5:34–38
  Call of the Wild, The 3:51–56
  Day No Pigs Would Die, A 3:94–99
  Red Pony, The 3:334–37
  Sounder 3:370–76
  Watership Down 5:346–51
Anna Karenina, Tolstoy, Leo 2:34–40
Anne, Queen of England 1:130–31, 342
Anne, Queen of France 1:389
Annesley, Brian 1:201
Anonymous, *Beowulf* 1:44–50
Anthropology
  comparative 5:42
  interest in Polynesian peoples' origins 4:221–27
  researchers' interest in American Indians 2:72, 179
Antigone, Sophocles 1:14–21
Antinomians 1:352, 357
Anti-Semitism
  in accusations of fix of 1919 World Series 4:261
  of African Americans 4:376–77
  of Argentina's "dirty war" 5:210
  in Brooklyn 3:402
  of Charles Lindbergh 4:373
  contributing to generation gap 5:203
  diminishing in 1950s and '60s 5:203
  and Dreyfus affair 1:91–92, 364 (sidebar)
  in England 1:182–83; 2:264–65
  of Father Charles Coughlin 4:373
  in Germany 1:370; 4:157–59
  holocaust denial 4:40
  in Italy 1:243–44, 246
  Kristallnacht 4:159, 162–63
  and moneylending 1:182–83; 2:264
  and nationalism 1:364
  origins of "ghetto" 1:244, 249
  Pale of Settlement 3:119–20, 121
  pogroms 1:364; 3:120–21
  in Poland 1:364
  in Russia 1:364; 3:119–21
  in Soviet Union 3:124–25; 5:122
  in U.S. of 1940s 4:236–37, 373
  in U.S. military 4:36–37
  in Wharton's works 3:170
  (*See also* Holocaust)
Antiwar literature
  All Quiet on the Western Front 3:8–14
  Catch-22 4:66–72
  Fallen Angels 5:101–6
  Farewell to Arms, A 3:112–18
  Red Badge of Courage, The 2:308–13
  Slaughterhouse Five 4:343–48
  Waste Land, The 3:411–17
Appalachian Trail 5:278–79
Arabs, anti-Zionism 4:107
Archery 1:253
Argentina 5:208–11, 212–13
Aristotle
  commenting upon *Republic* 1:328
  influence in 16th century 1:233
  influence on Jefferson 1:100
  woodcut of 1:326 (illus.)
Armenia 3:338–43; 4:199
Arms control 4:71; 5:126, 225, 239, 252 (sidebar)
  prohibiting military use of space 5:239
Armstrong, Neil A. 5:82, 292
Armstrong, William H., *Sounder* 3:370–76
Army. *See* Military
Arnold, Benedict 1:213 (sidebar)
Arnold, Thomas 2:373–74
Art
  African 4:56
  artists benefitting from New Deal's WPA 3:391, 424
  as barrier against chaos and loss of faith 3:117
  Black arts movement 4:207
  Carnegie Institute of Pittsburgh 4:9
  first International Exhibition for 4:8 (sidebar)
  French atelier system of teaching 3:266
  Modernism 3:411; 5:42

Index

Paris as western capital of 3:265–66
patrons for artists 1:88
Primitivism 3:385 (sidebar)
(See also Literature)
Arthur, King of Celtic England 1:288, 290
in *Once and Future King, The* 1:288–94
Asians. See Chinese and Chinese Americans; Japanese and Japanese Americans
Asimov, Isaac, *Foundation* 5:122–28
Astrology 1:346, 350
ASWPL (Association of Southern Women for the Prevention of Lynching) 3:391–92
Athena 1:282, 283
Athens. See under Greece in ancient times
Atom bomb
  creating "atomic anxiety" 4:255; 5:126
  decision to use 4:178–79
  Hiroshima and Nagasaki as targets 4:179–82, 180 (illus.), 181 (sidebar)
  Manhattan Project 4:71, 81–82, 316; 5:123
  Soviets' capability 4:183; 5:96, 126
  test site at Bikini atoll 5:124 (illus.)
  UN attempts to regulate 5:96
  (See also Nuclear weapons)
Atomic energy. See Nuclear energy
Atwood, Margaret, *Handmaid's Tale, The* 5:135–42
Austen, Jane, *Pride and Prejudice* 2:295–300
Austria-Hungary 3:11 (sidebar)
Autobiography
  American Childhood, An, Dillard, Annie 4:7–13
  Autobiography of Benjamin Franklin, The 1:22–29
  Autobiography of Malcolm X, The, X, Malcolm and Haley, Alex 5:11–18
  Barrio Boy, Galarza, Ernesto 3:28–35
  Black Boy, Wright, Richard 3:36–43
  Bound for Glory, Guthrie, Woody 3:44–50
  Diary of a Young Girl, The, Frank, Anne 4:116–23
  Endless Steppe, The: Growing Up in Siberia, Hautzig, Esther 4:131–36
  Farewell to Manzanar, Houston, Jeanne W. and James D. Houston 4:137–43
  Hiroshima Diary, Hachiya, Michihiko 4:177–84
  Hunger of Memory, Rodriquez, Richard 5:178–84
  I Know Why the Caged Bird Sings, Angelou, Maya 4:201–8
  Incidents in the Life of a Slave Girl, The, Jacobs, Harriet 2:168–73
  Manchild in the Promised Land, Brown, Claude 4:247–53
  Narrative of the Life of Frederick Douglass, Douglass, Frederick 2:16, 236–41
  Out of Africa, Dinesen, Isak 3:290–96
  So Far from the Bamboo Grove, Watkins, Yoko K. 4:349–55
  Up From Slavery, Washington, Booker T. 2:410–15
  Woman Warrior, The, Kingston, Maxine Hong 5:352–59

Autobiography of Benjamin Franklin, The, Franklin, Benjamin 1:22–29
Autobiography of Malcolm X, The, X, Malcolm and Haley, Alex 5:11–18
Autobiography of Miss Jane Pittman, The (a novel), Gaines, Ernest J. 5:19–26
Aviation
  breaking sound barrier 5:293–94
  golden age of 3:211–12
  Lindbergh and 3:367
  Right Stuff, The 5:291–97
  and UFOs (unidentified flying objects) 4:347–48; 5:59 (illus.)
  (See also Space Age; War weaponry)
Awakening, The, Chopin, Kate 3:15–20
Azerbaijan 3:343
Aztlán 4:173, 174–75, 176

B

Ba'al Shem Tov 4:87
Babbitt, Lewis, Sinclair 3:21–27
Babe Ruth 4:262, 265
Babi Yar massacre 4:120
Baby boom 1:224; 2:325–26; 4:38, 74, 240
Backswording 2:375
Baer, Dov 4:89
Bakke, Allan 5:181
Baldwin, James, *Fire Next Time, The* 5:107–14
Baptists 5:19, 188
Baraka, Amiri (Leroi Jones) 4:207
Barbed wire 3:113, 260
Barn Burning, Faulkner, William 2:41–46
Barrio Boy, Galarza, Ernesto 3:28–35
Baseball
  Aaron, Hank 4:145, 148
  Babe Ruth 4:262, 265
  changing strategies of play 4:261–62
  creation of two-league system 4:261
  growing popularity leading to scouts 3:284
  history of scandals 4:260–61, 265
  Jackie Robinson 4:146
  minor leagues and decrease in college-educated players 4:261
  Negro League 4:145, 148
  Pittsburgh Pirates 4:10
  segregation in 4:146, 147
  White ("Black") Sox fix of 1919 World Series 3:149–50; 4:260–61
  (See also Shoeless Joe)
Bay of Pigs fiasco 5:226
Bean Trees, The, Kingsolver, Barbara 5:27–33
Bear, The, Faulkner, William 2:47–53
Beat movement 4:75
  (See also Counterculture)
Beauty: A Retelling of the Story of Beauty and the Beast, McKinley, Robin 1:30–36
Becker, Charles 3:149
Becket, Thomas 1:146
Begin, Menachem 4:103, 105, 107

Index

Behavior modification and conditioning   5:*156–57*
Behaviorism   5:*45*
Behn, Aphra   3:*361–62*
Belaúnde, Fernando   5:*334*
Belgium   2:*146–47, 150–51*; 3:*9*; 4:*254, 357, 359*
Bell, Clive   3:*356*
Bell Jar, The, Plath, Sylvia   4:*21–27*
Bellamy, Edward   2:*423*
Belle of Amherst, The, Luce, William   2:*54–58*
Belle Glade, Florida   3:*383–84*
Bellecourt, Clyde   5:*247 (illus.)*
Belleforest, François de   1:*139, 141 (sidebar)*
Beloved, Morrison, Toni   2:*59–65*
Benito Cereno, Melville, Herman   1:*37–43*
Beowulf, Anonymous   1:*44–50*
    influence upon Tolkien   1:*153*
Bergson, Henri   3:*213*
Betsey Brown, Shange, Ntozake   4:*28–34*
Bible, source for Milton's *Paradise Lost*   1:*301*
Bierce, Ambrose
    as character in *The Old Gringo*   3:*279, 280, 281*
    Occurrence at Owl Creek Bridge, An   2:*255–60*
Bilingual education   4:*45*; 5:*172, 179–81, 183, 217*
Billy Budd, Melville, Herman   1:*51–56*
Biloxi Blues, Simon, Neil   4:*35–41*
Biography (and autobiography)
    Abraham Lincoln: The Prairie Years, Sandburg, Carl   2:*1–7*
    American Childhood, An, Dillard, Annie   4:*7–13*
    Autobiography of Benjamin Franklin, The, Franklin, Benjamin   1:*22–29*
    Autobiography of Malcolm X, The, Malcolm X as told to Alex Haley   5:*11–18*
    Barrio Boy, Galarza, Ernesto   3:*28–35*
    Belle of Amherst, The (Emily Dickinson), Luce, William   2:*54–58*
    Black Boy, Wright, Richard   3:*36–43*
    Black Elk Speaks, Neihardt, John G.   2:*66–73*
    Bound for Glory, Guthrie, Woody   3:*44–50*
    Diary of a Young Girl, The, Frank, Anne   4:*116–23*
    Endless Steppe, The: Growing Up in Siberia, Hautzig, Esther   4:*131–36*
    Farewell to Manzanar, Houston, Jeanne W. and James D. Houston   4:*137–43*
    Hiroshima Diary, Hachiya, Michihiko   4:*177–84*
    Hunger of Memory, Rodriquez, Richard   5:*178–84*
    I Know Why the Caged Bird Sings, Angelou, Maya   4:*201–8*
    Incidents in the Life of a Slave Girl, Jacobs, Harriet   2:*168–73*
    Manchild in the Promised Land, Brown, Claude   4:*247–53*
    Narrative of the Life of Frederick Douglass, Douglass, Frederick   2:*16, 236–41*
    Out of Africa, Dinesen, Isak   3:*290–96*
    Up From Slavery, Washington, Booker T.   2:*410–15*
    Woman Warrior, The, Kingston, Maxine Hong   5:*352–59*

Black Boy, Wright, Richard   3:*36–43*
Black Death. *See* Bubonic plague (Black Death)
Black Elk Speaks, Neihardt, John G.   2:*66–73*
Black feminism   2:*64*; 3:*86–87*
Black Muslims and Nation of Islam   3:*238, 325*; 4:*56, 248–50*; 5:*12–13, 69, 110–11, 302*
Black Panther Party   4:*54, 56, 207*
Black Power movement   2:*97–98*; 3:*43, 325*; 4:*56, 207*; 5:*143–44*
Blacks. *See* African Americans
Blair, Eric Arthur. *See* Orwell, George
Blake, William   1:*410 (sidebar), 416*; 2:*92*
Bless the Beasts and Children, Swarthout, Glendon   5:*34–38*
Bless Me, Ultima, Anaya, Rudolfo A.   4:*42–48*
Bligh, Cap't. William   1:*273–74, 276–77*; 4:*64–65*
Blindness. *See* Disabled persons
Blixen, Karen. *See* Dinesen, Isak
Bloomsbury Group   3:*356, 358–59*
Blue Ridge Mountains   5:*278*
Blues, the   3:*254 (sidebar)*; 4:*258*
Bluest Eye, The, Morrison, Toni   4:*49–57*
Boethius   1:*344, 345–46, 350*
Boleyn, Anne   1:*149, 150, 231*
Bolt, Robert, *Man for All Seasons, A*   1:*231–37*
Booth, John Wilkes   2:*191*
Bosnia   2:*37–39*
Boston   3:*43*
Bound for Glory, Guthrie, Woody   3:*44–50*
Bouquet, Col. Henry   1:*221*
Bowling   1:*335 (sidebar)*
Boxer Rebellion in China (1900)   3:*205*; 5:*354*
Boxing   5:*68–69*
Bracero Program (1942–1964)   3:*34*; 4:*44*
Bradbury, Ray
    Dandelion Wine   3:*88–93*
    Fahrenheit 451   5:*95–100*
Braddock, Gen'l. Edward   1:*205*
Bradford, Richard, *Red Sky at Morning*   4:*316–22*
Brahmans   1:*365, 367 (sidebar)*
Brave New World, Huxley, Aldous   5:*39–45, 141, 157, 252*
Britain. *See* England
Brontë, Charlotte, *Jane Eyre*   1:*415 (sidebar)*; 2:*181–87*
Brontë, Emily, *Wuthering Heights*   1:*413–19*
Bronze Age of ancient Greece   1:*14, 258, 280, 283 (sidebar)*
Brook Farm (utopian community)   1:*357*; 2:*418*
Brooke, Arthur   1:*347, 349 (sidebar)*
Brooklyn, New York   3:*397–98*; 4:*88*; 5:*149–51*
Brotherhood of Sleeping Car Porters   3:*42*
Brown, Claude, *Manchild in the Promised Land*   4:*247–53*
Brown, Clifford   4:*376*
Brown, Dee, *Bury My Heart at Wounded Knee*   2:*74–80*
Brown, John   2:*89 (sidebar), 172*
    Final Speech   2:*188–94*

Index

Brown v. Board of Education   3:375; 4:29–30, 314; 5:90, 108, 180, 181
Brutus (Marcus Junius Brutus)   1:190, 191, 192–93
Bubonic plague (Black Death)   1:159, 160, 344, 345, 350
Buck, Pearl S., *Good Earth, The*   3:131–37
Buckingham, Duke of (George Villiers)   1:388, 389
Buddhism   1:365–69; 3:186–87; 5:48
Buffalo Bill (William F. Cody)   2:68, 177
Buffalo (bison)   2:66, 67, 75; 5:34–35
Bull from the Sea, The, Renault, Mary   1:57–63
Bunche, Ralph   4:255; 5:54
Burial customs
   among Canadian Kwakiutl   5:197
   in ancient Greece   1:18–19
   catacombs in Sicily   2:82
   mourning traditions in Victorian England   1:414–15
Burke, Edmund   1:52–53, 359, 362, 373 (sidebar), 408
Burns, Olive Ann, *Cold Sassy Tree*   3:75–79
Bury My Heart at Wounded Knee, Brown, Dee   2:74–80
Byron, George Gordon Noel (Lord Byron)   1:115, 116, 119, 120; 2:110

C

Caen, Herb   3:226
Caesar, Julius   1:12, 13
Caine Mutiny, The, Wouk, Herman   4:58–65
Cajuns   4:365; 5:21, 130
California
   Clear Lake   4:340–41
   farming and migrant workers   3:29–30, 49, 140–42, 269–71, 275, 335, 337; 4:297 (sidebar)
   gold rushes   2:174–75, 195, 249–50, 281–84
   Sacramento   3:30
   Salinas Valley   3:334–35
   South Central Los Angeles   5:339–42
   Spanish mission system   2:392, 394, 395
   timeline: colonization to independence   2:392 (sidebar)
   (*See also* San Francisco)
Call of the Wild, The, London, Jack   3:51–56
Calvin, John, and Calvinism   2:54, 55; 3:377–78; 4:10, 304
Canada, Kwakiutl of British Columbia   5:194–200
Canals
   Panama   3:231–32, 270
   Suez   3:184; 4:107
   U.S. system of   2:230
Canterbury Tales, The, Chaucer, Geoffrey   1:64–70
   Shakespeare influenced by   1:262
Capital punishment   4:379–80; 5:131
Capitalism
   in America's Gilded Age   2:20, 306, 328
   ethics and regulation, lack of   4:9
   failures of, enhancing appeal of communism   3:208, 210
   Hellman's attack on excesses of   3:207, 210
   Steinbeck's warning about   3:144
   versus socialism and Marxism   3:321; 4:18–19
   (*See also* Industrialization)
Capone, Alphonse   3:366
Capote, Truman
   as basis for character in *To Kill a Mockingbird*   3:395
   Christmas Memory, A   3:68–74
Caribbean islands
   Dominican Republic   5:220
   Haiti (formerly Saint-Domingue)   5:116–17
   Puerto Rico   3:277; 4:385–86, 388–89, 401; 5:214–21
   slavery in   1:39
   (*See also* Cuba)
Carlyle, Thomas   1:375; 2:92
Carmichael, Stokely   2:98; 3:325; 4:55 (illus.), 56; 5:145 (illus.)
Carnegie, Andrew   2:306; 4:8, 9
Carranza, Venustiana   3:279
Carrie, King, Stephen   5:46–52
Carroll, Lewis, *Alice's Adventures in Wonderland*   2:28–33
Carson, Rachel, *Silent Spring*   4:337–42
Carthage   1:10, 12
Carver, George Washington   3:418
Cask of Amontillado, The, Poe, Edgar Allan   2:81–86
Castro, Fidel   2:273; 4:279; 5:225
Catch-22, Heller, Joseph   4:66–72; 5:318 (sidebar)
Catcher in the Rye, Salinger, J. D.   4:73–78; 5:318 (sidebar)
Catesby, Robert   1:229 (sidebar)
Cather, Willa, *O Pioneers!*   3:257–63
Catholicism and Catholic Church
   among American Indians   5:244, 361–62, 365–66
   anti-Semitism of   2:264
   comparison to Anglican Church   1:233 (sidebar)
   conflict with English Protestants   1:131, 132, 229, 305–6
   control of education in France   2:210
   criticisms by
      Cervantes   1:6–7
      Chaucer   1:65
      Dante   1:174–75; 3:111
      Joyce   3:111
   Crusades   1:182, 291
   cult of Our Lady of Fatima   5:365–66
   decline in Scotland   4:304–5
   equivocation doctrine   1:230
   Inquisition   1:2, 3
   in Ireland   1:269; 3:107–8, 109–10, 305–7
   Jesuits   3:307–8
   in medieval England and Europe   1:49–50, 65
   Merton, Thomas   5:280–81
   monasticism   3:186–87; 5:280
   opposition to contraception   4:304 (sidebar)
   parochial schools   5:62–63
   Penitentes   4:318 (sidebar)

perpetuation of machismo sentiment   5:*173*
pilgrimages   1:*64–70, 145–46*
popes   1:*174, 176, 296, 344, 345*
Reformation   1:*231*
Trappist monks   5:*280*
(*See also* Protestantism)
Cattle ranching
  on Great Plains   2:*321–22*
  and leather trade on California missions   2:*392*
  on reservations   4:*79*
  (*See also* Farming)
Celts
  Britons (Gauls)   1:*196–97*
  Scotland   1:*187*
Censorship and banning of literary works
  in 14th- and 15th-century Europe   1:*349*
  Adventures of Don Quixote, The   1:*4*
  blacklisting by McCarthyites   3:*178*; 4:*72*; 5:*96*
  Brave New World   5:*45*
  Catcher in the Rye   4:*78*; 5:*62*
  in Communist China   5:*98*
  Flowers for Algernon   4:*156*
  Hero Ain't Nothin' but a Sandwich, A   5:*148*
  His Own Where   5:*154*
  by Nazis   3:*13*; 5:*99*
  One Day in the Life of Ivan Denisovich   4:*285*
  by Smith Act (1940)   5:*97*
  by Soviet dictatorship   4:*286*; 5:*96*
Central America
  Guatemala and refugees   5:*27–29*
  Panama Canal   3:*231–32, 270*
  (*See also* Mexico)
Central Intelligence Agency (CIA)   4:*293*
Ceremonies and celebrations
  Chinese New Year   5:*75, 76 (illus.)*
  Christmas
    A Doll's House   2:*111–17*
    Child's Christmas in Wales, A   3:*63–67*
    Christmas Memory, A   3:*68–74*
    Worn Path, A   3:*418–24*
  Indian healing ceremonies   4:*82–83*; 5:*249*
  Kwakiutl Candlefish   5:*196 (sidebar)*
  Kwakiutl *hamatsa* (Cannibal Dance)   5:*196–97*
  Kwakiutl potlatch   5:*198 (illus.), 199*
  (*See also* Burial customs)
Ceremony, Silko, Leslie Marmon   4:*79–86*
Cervantes Saavedra, Miguel de
  Adventures of Don Quixote, The   1:*1–7*
  in Battle of Lepanto   1:*296 (sidebar)*
Chagall, Marc   3:*123*
Chamberlain, Neville   4:*357, 359*
Chambers, Whittaker   5:*96*
Chaplin, Charlie   3:*101*
Charles I of England   1:*299, 303, 304 (illus.), 305, 306*
Charles II of England   1:*129, 130, 306, 337, 338*
Charles X of France   1:*391*
Chateaubriand, François René de   1:*165*
Chaucer, Geoffrey, *Canterbury Tales, The*   1:*64–70*

Chávez, César   3:*33 (illus.), 34*; 4:*47, 175, 300–302, 301 (illus.),409*
Chekhov, Anton, *Cherry Orchard, The*   3:*57–62*
Chennault, Claire   3:*190*
Chernobyl disaster   5:*286, 287 (illus.)*
Cherry Orchard, The, Chekhov, Anton   3:*57–62*
Chesapeake Bay   4:*216–17, 219*
Chiang Kai-shek   3:*189, 190 (illus.)*
Chicago
  in 1920s   3:*89–90*
  barrios of   5:*174*
  black activism   3:*238*
  ethnic makeup   3:*176*
  and King's northern civil rights campaign   5:*174*
  in late 19th century   2:*327–28, 330 (illus.)*
  meat-packing industry   2:*328 (sidebar)*
  South Side and Black Belt   3:*237–38*; 4:*309–11*
  streetcars   2:*328*
  suburbs of   5:*261–62*
Chicanos
  affirmative action programs   5:*181, 183–84*
  César Chávez   3:*33 (illus.), 34*; 4:*47, 175, 300–302, 409*
  discrimination   5:*178*
    zoot suit riots of 1940s   4:*295–97, 403–10*
  education dropout rates and reform efforts   5:*179*
  family life   4:*45*
  folk healing (*curanderos*)   4:*45*
  immigration to U.S. from Mexico   3:*282*; 4:*44–48*
  life in New Mexico   4:*45*
  literary Renaissance of 1960s and '70s   5:*172–73*
  Luna (land) and Marez (sea)   4:*47*
  mestizo (mixed-race) heritage   5:*172*
  myth of Aztlán   4:*174*
  origin of term   5:*171*
  pachuco zoot-suit culture of 1950s   4:*173, 295–97, 403*
  post-WWII community   5:*178–79*
  rights movement   4:*47–48, 300–302*; 5:*171–72, 179*
    Brown Berets   4:*176*
    Chicanas   3:*202*; 5:*174*
    Community Service Organization (CSO)   4:*300*
    El Teatro Campesino   4:*409*; 5:*172*
    G.I. Forum   4:*300*
    impact of military service on   4:*44*
    La Alianza   4:*175–76, 321*
    La Raza Unida   4:*176*
    League of United Latin American Citizens (LULAC)   4:*300*
    Mexican American Legal Defense and Education Fund (MALDEF)   5:*179*
    table grape boycott   4:*175, 301 (illus.), 409*
    United Farm Workers   4:*175, 300–302, 409*; 5:*171*

Richard Rodriguez's autobiography 5:178–84
Rubén Salazar 4:410
Vietnam War protesters 4:409–10
WWII military service 4:44
(See also Latinos)
Child abuse
    Fetal Alcohol Syndrome 5:361
    relationship to poverty 5:329 (sidebar)
    and suicide 5:288, 289–90
Child labor 2:103–4, 335 (sidebar); 3:76 (sidebar), 77 (illus.), 285
Childbearing
    abortion 5:51, 136
    midwifery 4:218
    by unwed couples 5:267
    in vitro 5:42–43
    (See also Family and family life)
Childhood's End, Clarke, Arthur 5:53–60
Childress, Alice, *Hero Ain't Nothin' but a Sandwich, A* 5:143–48
Child's Christmas in Wales, A, Thomas, Dylan 3:63–67
Chile 5:163–70
Chin, Frank, *Donald Duk* 5:74–80
China
    Boxer Rebellion (1900) 3:205; 5:354
    civil strife (1911–49) 3:189–90; 5:229, 254
    communist victory in civil war (1949) 5:254, 354–55
    communists' land reform 5:355
    communists' purge of opponents 5:254–55
    Confucius 3:193 (sidebar)
    divorce in 2:370, 371; 3:132, 193; 5:230
    dynasties and alien invaders 3:189
    footbinding of girls 3:135; 5:230 (sidebar)
    Guomindang 4:126 (sidebar); 5:230, 254
    Hong Kong conceded to Great Britain 5:354
    Japanese invasion (1930s–40s) 3:189–90; 4:59; 5:229–30
    marriages as business deals 3:192–93
    missionaries 3:133
    Nixon's visit (1972) 5:358
    opium addiction 3:134 (sidebar)
    Opium Wars (1839–42 and 1856–60) 5:354
    peasant farmers 3:131–32
    prostitution in 3:135
    Republican era (1912–49) 5:229–30, 354
    superstition and syncretism 3:133, 190–91
    Taiping Rebellion (1851–64) 5:354
    and Taiwan 3:190; 5:254
    women in 2:366–67, 368 (sidebar), 370–71; 3:132–33, 134–35; 5:352, 355
Chinese and Chinese Americans
    assimilation of second generation 5:231–32, 234–35
    Chinese New Year festival 5:75, 76 (illus.)
    defended by Bret Harte 2:287
    immigration in 19th century 2:367–68, 370 (sidebar), 371; 4:124–27
    immigration in 20th century 2:368; 4:125, 127, 129
    as miners in Old West 2:367–68, 369 (illus.)
    as "model minority" 3:194
    in New York's Chinatown 4:126
    racism and prejudice against 2:175, 287, 367–68, 370 (sidebar), 371; 3:30; 4:124–27, 194, 330; 5:230–31
    in San Francisco's Chinatown 3:226; 5:74–75, 77–79
    tongs 4:129
Chinese and Chinese Americans, literary works concerning
    Donald Duk 5:74–80
    Eat a Bowl of Tea 4:124–30
    Joy Luck Club, The 5:229–35
    Kitchen God's Wife, The 3:189–95
    Thousand Pieces of Gold, McCunn, Ruthanne Lum 2:366–71
    Woman Warrior, The 5:352–59
Chivalry 1:2, 66, 291
Chocolate War, The, Cormier, Robert 5:61–66
Chopin, Kate, *Awakening, The* 3:15–20
Chorus in Greek drama 1:10
Chosen, The, Potok, Chaim 4:87–93
Christian, Fletcher 1:273, 274
Christianity
    among pioneers of midwest 3:259
    Baldwin on "racist hypocrisy" of 5:112
    clergymen extolling WWI 3:10
    missionaries 2:118–19, 147, 161–62, 361–62; 3:133, 280; 5:195
    suicide as sin 4:22
    (See also Catholicism and Catholic Church; Protestantism; Puritanism)
Christmas Memory, A, Capote, Truman 3:68–74
Chu, Luis, *Eat a Bowl of Tea* 4:124–30
Churchill, Winston 1:237; 5:53, 95
    Speech on the Evacuation at Dunkirk 4:356–63
CIA (Central Intelligence Agency)
    experiments with drugs 4:293–94
    role in Cuba's Bay of Pigs "invasion" 5:226
Cicero 1:327
Cicotte, Eddie 3:149; 4:260
Ciénaga massacre (Colombia) 2:270
Cinema. See Hollywood and motion picture industry
CIO (Congress of Industrial Organizations) 3:44
Cisneros, Sandra, *House on Mango Street, The* 5:171–77
Citizenship
    in ancient Athens 1:241
    for Chinese immigrants 5:231
    for Puerto Ricans 5:215
City-states
    of ancient Greece 1:286, 327–28
    of Italy 1:379–80
Civil Disobedience, Thoreau, Henry David 2:87–92
Civil rights movements
    affirmative action 5:181, 183–84, 342
    American Indians 4:190–91; 5:246–47

assassination of King   4:*54*; 5:*112 (sidebar)*
Chicano. *See* Chicanos
Civil Rights Acts of 1957, '64, and '65   2:*97*; 3:*354, 375*; 4:*148*; 5:*91*
    FBI & J. Edgar Hoover's theory of communist inspiration of   1:*399*
    focus on South, then North   2:*13*; 5:*25*
    fostering literary efforts
        autobiographies   4:*205*; 5:*304*
        ethnic and cultural explorations   4:*92–93, 207*; 5:*15, 62, 145, 217, 300–302*
        women's studies programs   5:*117*
    Freedom Rides   5:*88–90*
    gay rights movement   4:*241*
    judicial opposition in 1980s to   5:*1–2*
    in Louisiana   5:*25*
    March on Washington (1963)   5:*110, 186–88*
    origins and growth of   2:*97*; 3:*42–43*; 4:*28–29, 155–56, 255, 314–15*; 5:*185, 192, 300*
        Alabama as testing ground   2:*220–21*; 3:*73, 395–96*; 4:*314–15*; 5:*11, 88–90, 185–86*
    race riots in "long hot summer" of 1966   2:*97–98*; 4:*207*
    students' free speech movement   5:*311*
    TV's role in creating public support for   5:*108*
    women's involvement in   5:*92–93*
    (*See also* African Americans' civil rights/reform/power movements)
Civil War
    blockade runners   2:*138–39*
    causes of   2:*130–31*
    Chancellorsville   2:*309*
    demise of plantations and wilderness   2:*49, 53*
    desertion from armies   2:*10–11, 312*
    draft of mostly poor and lower classes   2:*256, 309*
    and Emancipation Proclamation (1862)   2:*59, 60 (sidebar), 135, 308, 309*
    families torn by conflicting loyalties   2:*10*
    in Georgia   2:*139, 140 (illus.)*
    Gettysburg   2:*131–32*
    glorification vs. reality of battle   2:*257, 258, 308, 309 (sidebar), 312, 313*
    and industrialization of meat-packing   3:*175*
    John Brown's raid at Harper's Ferry contributing to   2:*190*
    major battles of   2:*131 (sidebar)*
    Northerners' point of view   2:*11, 22*
    overview of   2:*308–10*
    railroads' importance   2:*255, 256 (illus.)*
    Shiloh   2:*257*
    in southern Illinois   2:*9–10*
    Southerners' point of view   2:*11, 22*
    spies   2:*255–56*
    Union Army leadership troubles and poor morale   2:*308–10*
    Vicksburg   2:*217*
    western migration and Mexican War contributing to   2:*88, 89, 395, 405*
    Walt Whitman, impact on   2:*195–96*
    (*See also* Reconstruction)
Clairvoyance   5:*239*
Clark, Walter Van Tilburg, *Ox-Bow Incident, The*   2:*288–94*
Clarke, Arthur, *Childhood's End*   5:*53–60*
Clay, Cassius. *See* Ali, Muhammad
Clemens, Samuel. *See* Twain, Mark
Cleopatra   1:*190*
Clipper ships   2:*391*
Clothing
    for slaves   2:*237*
    (*See also* Fashions)
Coal mining   3:*63, 64*
Cody, William F. (Buffalo Bill)   2:*68, 177*
Cohn, Roy   5:*2–4*
Cold Sassy Tree, Burns, Olive Ann   3:*75–79*
Cold War
    arms race   5:*252 (sidebar)*
    Berlin Wall   5:*238, 293*
    Cuban missile crisis and Bay of Pigs   4:*135*; 5:*225, 226, 238–39, 293*
    and "domino" theory   2:*13–14*
    FBI investigations   4:*129*; 5:*127*
    fear of Communist China and Chinese immigrants   4:*129*
    fear of nuclear war   4:*12, 13 (illus.)*; 5:*53, 59, 225*
    fear of "radicalism"   1:*399*; 4:*236*
    fear of "socialized" medicine   4:*12*
    fear of Soviet strength   4:*110*; 5:*225, 292*
    fostering American interventions in third world   1:*223*
    as indirect, hostile competition of ideologies   5:*225, 254, 292*
    iron curtain for Eastern Europe   5:*95–96*
    Kennedy's olive branch with militancy   5:*224–26*
    and McCarthyism   1:*84, 398*; 3:*208, 209 (illus.)*; 4:*71, 110, 398*; 5:*2, 3 (illus.), 96, 97, 127*
    NATO (North Atlantic Treaty Organization)   5:*124, 224, 292*
    and "Red Scare"   1:*84–86*; 3:*105*; 4:*71–72*; 5:*2, 127*
    reflected in United Nations   5:*254*
    trade as weapon in   5:*126*
    Truman Doctrine (1947–49)   4:*110*; 5:*123–24*
    Truman's loyalty program for federal employees   4:*72, 236*
    U.S. support for oppressive Latin American military dictatorships   5:*27–28*
    U.S.-Soviet competition for global influence   5:*95–96*
    U.S.-Soviet competition in space   5:*53*
    (*See also* Communism)
Coleridge, Samuel Taylor   1:*116, 416*
Colombia, South America   2:*268–70, 272–73*
Colonial America
    American Revolution   1:*122–27*
    Boston Tea Party   1:*125*
    class and economic stratification   1:*97, 102, 108*

Index

democracy and revolutionary fervor   1:71–72, 74, 76–77, 93–94, 96–97, 108
Dutch in New Netherland (New York)   1:211, 212, 330–32, 333 (illus.), 335 (sidebar), 336
French and Indian War (Seven Years' War)   1:93, 123, 204–6
indentured servants   1:394
materialism   1:102, 105, 311
militias and Continental Army   1:110 (sidebar)
money, credit, and inflation   1:103–4
New England area   1:78–80
New York area   1:107–8, 110, 112 (illus.)
population and economic growth   1:310
reactions to Stamp/Tea/Townshend/Intolerable/Molasses Acts   1:93, 94 (sidebar), 102, 123–25
regional conflicts   1:211–12
rhetoric in   1:123
smuggling   1:102–3
towns and cities   1:102
westward expansion   1:102, 103, 107, 204
Yankee stereotype   1:217
(See also American Indians; American Revolution; Slavery in America; United States)
Colonialism, imperialism, and interventionism
American
bolstered by social Darwinism   3:234–35
Chile   5:164–65
Cuba   3:231, 278; 4:135; 5:225, 226, 238–39, 293
Domican Republic   5:220
El Salvador   3:282
Guam   3:277
Guatemala   5:27–28
Latin America   3:231, 277–78, 280–81
Liberia   2:404
Monroe Doctrine (1823) and "big stick" corollary (1904)   3:277
Nicaragua   3:282
Panama Canal   3:231–32
Philippines   3:101, 278
Puerto Rico   3:277; 4:385–86; 5:215
Spanish-American War (1898)   3:101, 278
Belgian   2:145–46, 150–51
British   2:118–19
in America. See Colonial America
bolstered by overseas commerce   1:337
criticized by H. G. Wells   3:406, 410
and decolonization of late 1940s   4:165
East Africa   3:290–91
end of   5:107
fostering sense of superiority   2:154
India   2:182–84, 276–77; 3:181–82, 297–98
Ireland. See Ireland
Nigeria and Igbo people   2:362, 364; 3:84
Palestine   4:102–5
Rhodesia   4:165–66
Tasmania   3:406
viewed as "bettering" and "civilizing" native peoples   1:118; 2:146; 3:84

Wales   1:149
West Indies   2:183–84
in China   3:205
Dutch   1:338
French
Algeria   3:211–13
Indochina (Vietnam)   5:101, 306
Saint-Domingue (Haiti)   5:116–17
German   3:290
Italian   4:67
Japanese   4:58–59, 92, 177–78, 349–54
missionaries   2:118–19, 147, 161–62, 183, 361–62; 3:133, 280
segregation of rulers and ruled   3:182
Spanish
Colombia   2:268
Mexico   5:172
Puerto Rico   5:214–15
Color Purple, The, Walker, Alice   3:80–87
Comiskey, Charles   3:149; 5:314, 316
Common Sense, Paine, Thomas   1:71–77
effectiveness of   1:94
Communal movements
Communards and Paris Commune   1:363
Shakerism   3:95, 99
Twin Oaks colony   5:279
Communism
and anti-Bolshevik reactions of 1920s   3:21–22, 44
appeal of, to blacks   3:164, 238–39
in China   3:136, 194
communists as targets of Holocaust   4:160, 267
contrast with capitalism   4:166
global disillusion with, following revelations of Stalin's purges   4:166
Great Depression enhancing appeal of   3:39–40, 45, 129, 208–10
influence on Jack London   3:52
labor organizers accused of   3:144
landowners as "capitalist" enemies of   4:282
and Marxism   3:59, 179, 321; 4:18–19
opposition to racism and prejudice   3:40; 4:211
as theory   4:166
use of folksongs   3:47, 50
(See also Cold War; Soviet Union)
Communist Manifesto   1:376
Computers   5:97, 127
Comstock Lode (Nevada silver mines)   2:288–89, 290 (sidebar)
Comte, Auguste   3:213
Confessions of Nat Turner, The, Styron, William   2:93–98
Confucius   3:193 (sidebar)
Congregationalists   1:357, 424–25
Connell, Richard, *Most Dangerous Game, The*   3:231–35
Conrad, Joseph, *Heart of Darkness*   2:145–51
Conroy, Pat, *Prince of Tides, The*   5:285–90
Conservatism

fundamentalism and New/Religious Right   5:137–39
pro-business policies of Reagan presidency   5:1
Contender, The, Lipsyte, Robert   5:67–73
Copernicus, Nicolaus   1:24, 94, 305
Corcoran, Thomas "Tommy the Cork" Gardiner   3:402
CORE (Congress of Racial Equality)   3:42; 4:376
Corey, Giles   1:83 (sidebar), 395
Corinth   1:238, 241
Cormier, Robert, *Chocolate War, The*   5:61–66
Cossacks   3:233
Cotton
 causing soil exhaustion   3:390
 crop failures from boll weevil   4:2
 as "King" Cotton   2:15, 22, 44 (illus.), 168, 403
 North-South contention over trade in   3:203–4
 plummeting of prices for farmers in 1920s and '30s   3:153, 390, 391
 for typhus prevention, advantages of clothing and bedding of   1:115
Cotton, John   1:352
Coughlin, Father Charles   4:373
Count of Monte-Cristo, The, Dumas, Alexandre   2:99–104
Counterculture (beatniks, hippies, and protesters)
 in 1950s   4:75, 289, 293, 399–400
 in 1960s   5:37, 64 (sidebar), 83, 158, 237, 272, 279, 308–10, 323–25
Coxey, Jacob S. and Coxey's Army   3:51–52
Crane, Stephen, *Red Badge of Courage, The*   2:308–13
Craven, Margaret, *I Heard the Owl Call My Name*   5:194–200
Creationism   2:30
Creoles   3:15–18; 4:365; 5:21, 130
Creon   1:15, 17, 18, 19
Crime
 blacks and Latinos as victims of   4:31; 5:340–41
 blacks turning to   4:145
 and capital punishment   4:379–80; 5:131
 by Chinese American tongs   4:129
 and creation of police detectives   2:153–54
 drug-related   4:250–51
 during Reconstruction, violence and unequal justice for freed slaves   5:20–21
 gang truce in Los Angeles   5:341
 by gangs, juvenile delinquents   4:251, 386, 387–89
 gangsters (*tsotsi*) of South Africa   4:97
 outlaws on American western frontier   1:256–57
 outlaws in medieval England   1:252–53
 and Pinkerton's National Detective Agency   3:225–26
 Prohibition fostering corruption, bootlegging, and gangsterism   3:69, 147–48, 366–67, 401
 in slums, ghettos   5:13, 67–68, 112, 146, 150, 339–42

(*See also* Law enforcement; Lynching)
Cromwell, Oliver   1:299, 306
Crucible, The, Miller, Arthur   1:78–86
Crusades   1:182, 291
Cry, the Beloved Country, Paton, Alan   4:94–100
Cuba
 American interventions of 1898 and 1901   3:231, 278
 Bay of Pigs and missile crisis   4:135; 5:225, 226, 238–39, 293
 personalismo   4:275
 religion   4:274–75
 Revolution of 1950s   2:273
 role of luck   4:275–76
Cultural conflict. *See* Ethnic and cultural conflicts
Cyprus   1:296
Cyrano de Bergerac, Rostand, Edmond   1:87–92
Cyrano de Bergerac, Savinien de   1:87, 88 (sidebar), 89–90

D

Daisy Miller, James, Henry   2:105–10
Daly, Carroll John   3:227
Damnation. *See* Sin and damnation
Dana, Richard Henry, Jr., *Two Years before the Mast*   2:391–96
Dance   4:387
Dandelion Wine, Bradbury, Ray   3:88–93
Dante Alighieri
 Divine Comedy   1:175 (sidebar), 178
 Inferno   1:174–80
 influence on Joyce   3:111
Daoism (also Taoism)   5:237
D'Artagnan (Charles-Ogier de Batz de Castelmore)   1:387
Darwin, Charles   2:29, 119
Darwin, Erasmus   1:116
Darwinism. *See* Evolution
Dawes Act (1887)   2:68, 179; 4:186
Dawn, Wiesel, Elie   4:101–8
Day No Pigs Would Die, A, Peck, Robert Newton   3:94–99
DDT   4:338–39
De Beauvoir, Simone   4:167
De Gaulle, Charles   3:214
De Tocqueville, Alexis   2:106
Deafness. *See* Disabled persons
Dean, James   4:392, 400
Dean, John   5:159 (illus.)
Death in the Family, A, Agee, James   3:100–105
Death of a Salesman, Miller, Arthur   4:109–15
Debs, Eugene V.   3:54, 175
Declaration of Independence, The, Jefferson, Thomas   1:93–100
 comparison to language in *Common Sense*   1:76
 evoked in King's "I Have Dream" speech   5:191
 evoked in Lincoln's Gettysburg Address   2:134–35

Declaration of the Rights of Man (French Revolution) 1:372
Declaration of Sentiments (for women's rights) 2:24, 55, 204; 3:16
Dee, John 1:385 (sidebar)
Defoe, Daniel 1:131, 268, 342
   Robinson Crusoe 1:337–43
Delamere, Hugh Cholmondeley, Baron 3:295
Delaware (Lenape) Indians 1:206, 219–20
Democracy
   in 19th-century America 2:87–88, 89–91
   in ancient Greece 1:18, 321, 322
   before and after publication of *Common Sense* 1:74
   individualism and egalitarianism contributing to 2:302
   influence of Declaration of Independence upon 1:100
   Kennedy's call for defense of freedom 5:226–27
   at King Arthur's round table 1:292
   rise of common people as political force in France 1:164, 165
   role of printing press in promoting 1:162 (sidebar)
   Whitman as poet of 2:196
   (See also Suffrage)
Denmark 1:136–38, 141
Depression, The Great 2:45
Detective fiction. *See* Mystery and detective stories
Developmental disabilities. *See* Disabled persons
Devil (Satan)
   comparative conceptions of 5:57 (sidebar)
   in Dante's *Inferno* 1:177, 179 (illus.)
   Lucifer in Milton's *Paradise Lost* 1:301–3, 305
   Puritans' belief in 1:79–81, 102, 393, 394
Devil and Tom Walker, The, Irving, Washington 1:101–6
DeWitt, John 4:138
Diary of a Young Girl, The, Frank, Anne 4:116–23
Diaspora 4:101
Díaz, Porfirio 3:28, 29, 197, 278
Dickens, Charles 2:92, 375
   Oliver Twist 2:261–67
   Tale of Two Cities, A 1:371–78
Dickinson, Emily 2:54–58
Dictatorship
   of Argentina's military rulers 5:208–11, 212–13
   of Chile's military junta 5:169
   in Communist China 5:254–55
   and "divine right" of Charles I of England 1:303
   of Japan's prewar military 4:178, 183
   opposition to, in *Twenty-Thousand Leagues under the Sea* 2:387
   Orwell's attacks upon 5:254 (sidebar)
   of Peru's military junta 5:333–34
   warnings against 1:18
   (See also Fascism; Hitler, Adolf; Soviet Union; Stalin, Josef)

Diem, Ngo Dinh 5:102
Diet
   of concentration camp inmates 4:268
   of poor farmers 3:371
   of Siberian work camp inmates 4:283–84
   of slaves 2:237
Dillard, Annie
   American Childhood, An 4:7–13
   Pilgrim at Tinker Creek 5:278–84
Dinesen, Isak, *Out of Africa* 3:290–96
Disabled persons
   in almshouses in 18th-century America 2:216, 219 (sidebar)
   Clubfooted 3:264
   education for 2:216–17, 221–22
   Independent Living movement 2:123
   overcoming pity 2:218–19
   views of, in 1970s 2:123
   views of, in Victorian Age 2:119–20
   (See also Mental and emotional disabilities)
Diseases
   AIDS 5:9
   atomic radiation sickness 4:181
   bronchitis 2:335
   bubonic plague (Black Death) 1:159, 160, 344, 345, 350
   cancer 2:335; 4:340
   cholera 2:103
   "fainting" 3:420
   "hysteria" 2:425
   leprosy 2:362
   measles 1:220
   "nerves" (stress, depression) 2:278–79
   neurofibromatosis 2:122
   polio 4:9–10
   postcombat syndrome 4:80 (sidebar)
   postpartum depression 2:425
   Proteus syndrome 2:122
   puerperal fever 3:285
   rabies 3:387, 406
   radioactive poisoning 4:85
   respiratory 2:335; 3:2, 76, 219, 223
   resulting from depression 5:273
   scarlet fever 2:206 (sidebar)
   sickle cell anemia 2:362 (sidebar)
   smallpox 1:220, 352; 2:347; 5:214
   trench foot and trench fever 3:9, 115 (sidebar)
   tuberculosis 2:335; 3:2, 219, 223
   typhoid, typhus 2:185 (sidebar); 3:2
   venereal 4:37
   (See also Alcohol and alcoholism; Drug/substance abuse; Medicine; Mental and emotional disabilities)
Dissenters. *See* Anglican Church
Divine Comedy. *See* Inferno
Divorce
   in 1800s 2:126, 127, 158, 212, 355–56
   among Issei couples 4:332
   in China 2:370, 371; 3:132, 193; 5:230
   in czarist Russia 2:37, 39

Doyle's support for reform   2:*158*
·in early 20th-century America   3:*167–68, 272, 368*
for Jews   3:*427, 429 (sidebar)*
legalization spurred by Protestantism   2:*113*
and remarriage   4:*242*
soaring rate of, in late 20th century   2:*65;* 4:*241–42;* 5:*36, 138, 267, 273, 286–88*
Dix, Dorothy   3:*17*
Doctorow, E. L., *Ragtime*   3:*319–25*
Doctors. *See* Diseases; Medicine
Documents
  Declaration of Independence (American Revolution)   1:*93–100*
  Declaration of the Rights of Man (French Revolution)   1:*372*
  Declaration of Sentiments (for women's rights in America)   2:*24, 55, 204;* 3:*16*
  (*See also* Essays; Narratives; Speeches)
Dodgson, Charles Lutwidge. *See* Carroll, Lewis
Doll's House, A, Ibsen, Henrik   2:*111–17*
Dominican Republic   5:*220*
Don Quixote. See Adventures of Don Quixote, The
Donald Duk, Chin, Frank   5:*74–80*
Doolittle, James "Jimmy"   4:*68*
Dorris, Michael, *Yellow Raft in Blue Water, A*   5:*360–66*
Douglas, Stephen A.   2:*2, 242*
Douglass, Frederick
  influence upon Toni Morrison   2:*63*
  Narrative of the Life of Frederick Douglass   2:*236–41*
  on *Uncle Tom's Cabin*   2:*409*
Doyle, Arthur Conan, *Hound of the Baskervilles*   2:*152–59*
Drama. *See* Plays; Theater
Dreiser, Theodore, *Sister Carrie*   2:*327–33*
Dreyfus, Alfred   1:*91–92, 364 (sidebar)*
Drug/substance abuse
  among African Americans   4:*250–51*
  among American Indians   4:*83*
  attitudes of 1950s   5:*99 (sidebar)*
  among beatniks   4:*75*
  dealers' self-concept as respectable and superior   5:*341–42*
  experiments by CIA   4:*293–94*
  fines and prison required by Boggs Act (1951)   5:*99 (sidebar)*
  LSD   4:*288, 289, 292, 293–94;* 5:*82–83, 324–25*
  morphine addiction   3:*218–19, 223*
  Narcotics Control Act (1956)   4:*250*
  opium addiction in China   3:*134 (sidebar)*
  opium products   3:*379*
  in prep schools   4:*74*
  psychedelic   5:*82–83*
  by Puerto Ricans   5:*217*
  risk of AIDS   5:*342*
  suspicions of conspiracy by white officials to allow in ghettos   5:*144*
  unequal, unjust penalties for dealing   5:*342*
  aomng youth of 1950s   4:*173*
  (*See also* Alcohol and alcoholism)
Drums Along the Mohawk, Edmonds, Walter D.   1:*107–14*
Drury, Allen   5:*4*
Du Bois, W. E. B.
  advocating education for "talented tenth"   3:*250, 385*
  advocating no toleration of segregation or inequality   3:*320*
  compared to Booker T. Washington   2:*345 (sidebar);* 3:*250, 320, 385*
  criticism of *Up from Slavery*   2:*415*
  Souls of Black Folk, The   2:*340–46;* 3:*162–63*
Du Maurier, Daphne, *Rebecca*   3:*326–33*
Dubliners, Joyce, James   3:*106–11*
Dueling   1:*389 (sidebar)*
Dumas, Alexandre
  Count of Monte-Cristo, The   2:*99–104*
  Three Musketeers, The   1:*386–92*
Duncan, King of Scotland   1:*225*
Dune, Herbert, Frank   5:*81–87*
Dunkirk evacuation   4:*356, 359–63*
Dust Bowl, The   3:*34, 46, 138–40;* 4:*297*
Dutch in New Netherland (New York)   1:*211, 212, 330–32, 333 (illus.), 335 (sidebar), 336*
Dutch Reformed Church   1:*331, 425*
Dystopian literature
  Brave New World as   5:*141, 252*
  described   5:*100, 141, 252*
  Handmaid's Tale, The as   5:*141*
  Nineteen Eighty-Four as   5:*100, 141*

E

Earthquakes, in Chile   5:*168 (sidebar)*
Eat a Bowl of Tea, Chu, Luis   4:*124–30*
Eatonville, Florida   3:*383*
Edmonds, Walter D., *Drums Along the Mohawk*   1:*107–14*
Education
  in 19th-century America   2:*42–43, 204–5*
  for African Americans
    in blacks-only schools   2:*413;* 3:*371, 375*
    and *Brown v. Board of Education*   3:*375;* 4:*29–30, 314;* 5:*90, 108, 180, 181*
    demand for more control by   5:*144*
    dropout rates of   5:*342*
    forbidden use of libraries   3:*40, 371*
    freed slaves   2:*411–12, 413, 414*
    improvements in   3:*375, 420*
    integrated   3:*43, 396;* 4:*29–30, 31 (illus.), 314;* 5:*116, 131–32, 181*
    in "Movable School"   3:*380*
    negative effects of segregation on   4:*33*
  of American Indian children   5:*244, 246, 361–62*
  bilingual   4:*45;* 5:*172, 179–81, 183, 217*
  of black South Africans   4:*97*
  creating generation gap   5:*182, 198, 244, 246*

Index

criticality for Jews 3:425
for disabled persons 2:216–17, 221–22; 4:151–52
by governesses in Victorian Age 2:182, 183 (sidebar), 378–80
increases in school attendance during Depression 3:153–54
in Japanese schools in 1930s California 4:333
and *Lau v. Nichols* 5:180
of migrant farm workers' children 3:144 (sidebar)
minority studies programs
    African American history 5:147–48
    in Black English or Ebonics 5:145, 154, 342
    increasing college enrollments 5:217
    Puerto Rican history and culture 5:217
    women's studies 5:117
at prep schools 4:74
promoted by G.I. Bill 3:92; 4:73
schools handling contentious issues 5:311–12
in small communities 4:217
in Southern mill towns 3:78; 4:256
in Southern rural towns during Depression 3:352
textbook content reviewed by Religious Right 5:138
through Americorps program 5:340
University of California v. Bakke 5:181

Education, of men
  apprenticeship system 2:262
  in boarding schools 4:240
  boys' street gangs 3:400–401
  in colonial America 1:23, 123
  in czarist Russia 3:58
  English schools 2:372–77; 3:346
  fagging 2:375
  G.I. Bill (1944) 3:92; 4:73
  hunting as rite of passage 2:48
  importance for achieving middle-class status 2:303
  in New Netherland 1:212–13
  in private/prep schools 4:325–27; 5:62–63
  reforms in 19th-century England 3:265
  scientific, in France 2:386
  in skills of knighthood 1:182 (sidebar), 290–91
  in traditional Jewish communities of Eastern Europe 3:425–26
  Wollstonecraft on 1:410

Education, of women
  in 17th-century England (Tudor era) 1:232–33, 236
  in 17th-century France 1:30
  in 18th-century France 1:32
  in 18th-century New Netherland 1:212–13
  in 19th-century America vs. Europe 2:106
  in 19th-century England 1:412; 2:30, 181–82, 297, 422–23
  in 19th-century France 1:408; 2:210, 245
  in 19th-century New England 2:55, 56 (sidebar), 203
  in 19th-century South 2:42
  in 20th-century America 1:35
  in 20th-century Scotland 4:303–4
  Ben Franklin on 1:24 (sidebar)
  blacks on athletic scholarships 4:149
  college and increased opportunities for 5:174
  Jewish 3:427, 430
  skepticism for 1:236
  in Victorian Age 1:412; 2:30, 181–82, 422–23
  Wollstonecraft on 1:409–10; 2:297

Edward I of England 1:244, 291
Egypt, Six-Day War with Israel 4:107
Eichmann, Adolf 4:107 (sidebar), 269, 270, 272, 273; 5:210
Eisenhower, Dwight D. 4:398; 5:53, 91
Eleanor of Aquitaine 1:250
Elephant Man, The, Pomerance, Bernard 2:118–24
Eliezer, Israel Ben 4:87
Eliot, T.S. 5:42
  Waste Land, The 3:411–17
Elizabeth I of England
  bolstering national pride 1:349
  Catholic faction's opposition to 1:149, 349
  conspiracy of Earl of Essex 1:194, 349
  courtiers 1:263
  proving effectiveness of female monarch 1:233, 236
  rivalry with, execution of Mary, Queen of Scots 1:141, 149, 150, 349
  succession of crown to James of Scotland 1:201
  unification and commercial strengthening of England 1:150, 201, 263
  as virgin queen 1:201, 261, 262–63, 350

Elizabethan Age
  belief in supernatural 1:4, 141, 142 (sidebar), 194–95, 227–28, 262, 346, 350
  bubonic plague 1:344, 350
  concepts of sin and damnation 1:143
  education of women in Tudor era 1:232–33, 236
  family life and obligations 1:203
  foreign influence/corruption 1:150
  growth of American colonies 1:149
  kinship ties 1:141, 145
  popularity of history plays 1:150
  popularity of revenge tragedies 1:142
  popularity of satire and puns 1:349
  treatment of insane 1:203
  wars with Spain 1:1–2

Ellison, Ralph, *Invisible Man* 4:209–15
Emancipation
  Emancipation Proclamation (1862) 2:59, 60 (sidebar), 135, 308, 309
  life little changed for freed slaves 5:19–20
  (*See also* Abolitionists/Abolition of slavery)
Embrey, Sue Kunitomi 4:143
Emerson, Ralph Waldo
  influence on Dickinson 2:57
  on John Brown 2:193

as model for Prof. Bhaer in *Little Women*   2:*207*
opposition to war with Mexico   2:*89*
Self-Reliance   2:*314–20*
support for abolition   2:*315*, *316*
support for American Indians   2:*316*, *317*
support for Thoreau   2:*417*
as transcendentalist   1:*356*; 2:*92*, *314*
on *Two Years before the Mast*   2:*396*
Endless Steppe, The: Growing Up in Siberia, Hautzig, Esther   4:*131–36*
Engels, Friedrich   1:*376*
England in medieval times
  Anglo-Saxons   1:*44–45*, *153*, *181*
  Celts, Britons, and Arthurian legends   1:*196–97*, *288*, *289* (illus.), *290*
  expulsion of Jews   1:*244*, *246*, *248*
  feudalism   1:*65–66*, *153*
  Magna Carta   1:*255*
  Norman Conquest   1:*181*, *251–53*
  relations with Scotland   1:*145*, *149–50*
  Romans   1:*288*
  royal forests   1:*251–52*
  Saxon invaders and Wales   1:*288*
  wars with France   1:*159*, *160*
England in 16th century
  Henry VIII   1:*149*, *150*, *231*, *232*, *234* (illus.)
  (See also Elizabeth I; Elizabethan Age)
England in 17th century
  civil war, execution of King Charles I, and Restoration   1:*129*, *303*, *305–6*
  class consciousness   1:*338*
  foreign influences upon   1:*150*
  Glorious Revolution and William of Orange   1:*130*, *338–39*, *342–43*
  growth of tolerance   1:*299–300*
  Gunpowder Plot   1:*229*
  slave trading by   1:*337–38*; 2:*361*
  wars with France   1:*130–31*, *305*
  wars with Spain   1:*87*, *201*
England in 18th century
  British Royal Navy   1:*273–79*
  class consciousness   1:*342*
  Dissenters and Test Act   1:*129*, *338*, *342*, *407*, *411*
  French and Indian War   1:*93*, *123*
  historic rivalry with France   1:*391–92*
  London vs. country living   2:*296–97*
  as power in foreign trade   1:*400*, *401*
  publishing industry's growth   1:*342*
  reactions to French Revolution   1:*359–60*, *372–73*, *373* (sidebar), *376*, *408*
  Tories vs. Whigs   1:*129–31*, *305–6*, *311*, *337*, *342*
  wars with France   1:*51–52*, *93*, *123*, *204–6*, *220–21*
  wars with Spain   1:*130–31*
England in 19th century
  apprenticeship system   2:*262*
  British Royal Navy   1:*51–56*, *404–5*
  class consciousness   1:*376*, *413–14*; 2:*152–53*, *157*, *277–78*, *296–97*

and *nouveaux riches*   3:*327*
War of 1812   1:*53*
(See also Victorian Age; Victorian women)
England in 20th century
  birthrate/population decline   3:*347*; 5:*348*
  British Library   3:*360*
  British Royal Navy   4:*229*
  classes, and fading of social hierarchies   3:*312*, *315–16*, *326–27*; 5:*347–48*
  consumerism, materialism, conspciuous consumption   1:*237*; 3:*344–45*, *348*
  as cultural superpower in 1950s   4:*307* (sidebar)
  despair, decay, and decline   2:*275–76*; 3:*344–45*, *348*; 5:*39–40*
  fascism in 1930s   4:*304*
  General Strike of 1926   5:*40*
  London "season"   3:*312*
  nationalism and socialism   4:*231*
  post-WWII decline and recovery   3:*66*; 4:*229*, *231*; 5:*256–57*
  Scotland   4:*305*
  Wales   3:*63–64*, *66*
  in WWI   3:*9*, *11* (sidebar)
  Yorkshire   3:*1–3*
Enlightenment, The (Age of Reason)
  American   2:*416*
  and American "moral sense"   1:*94*, *96*
  backlash as Romantic movement   1:*106*
  as belief in reason, science, and "progress": perfectibility of humankind and its institutions   1:*24–25*, *268*; 2:*416*
  decline of religious influence and increase of materialism   1:*102*, *311*
  early scientific discoveries fostering   1:*24–25*, *94*, *96*
  failures of, fostering fierce satires   1:*272*
  Franklin's common sense approach to experimentation   1:*25–26*
  influence on Patrick Henry   1:*123*
  Jewish (*Haskalah*)   3:*120*, *426*; 4:*88*
  "natural rights" theories of John Locke   1:*100*
  treatment of disabled persons   2:*119–20*
Entailment   2:*296* (sidebar)
Entertainment
  carnival season of Italy and France   2:*81–82*
  circuses and freak shows   2:*33*, *120*, *329*
  dancing   3:*23*
  drive-in restaurants of 1950s   4:*392* (sidebar)
  illicit wartime amusements   4:*37*, *38*
  as industry   2:*329*
  jazz clubs   3:*161*
  lotteries   4:*235–36*
  minstrel shows   2:*16–17*, *21*, *398*
  ouija board   5:*56*
  practical jokes   1:*212*
  pubs in England   3:*3*
  radio   3:*154*, *364–65*; 4:*386*, *391*
  standardization of, in 1920s   3:*101*

Index

tale-telling and storytelling   1:49, 66–68, 70; 2:397; 3:421; 4:83 (sidebar), 85
taverns   1:331; 3:219, 398, 400
theaters and concert halls   2:329
for troops of WWII   4:38, 68–69
of working and middle classes   2:303–4
(See also Games and sports; Hollywood and motion picture industry; Television)
Environment
air pollution   4:9
Chernobyl disaster   5:286, 287 (illus.)
concerns reflected in Dune   5:85–86
conservation of buffalo   5:34–35
destruction of wilderness   2:49, 53
first Earth Day (April 22, 1970)   5:279 (sidebar)
nuclear waste disposal   5:286
pesticides ("biocides") and DDT   4:337–42; 5:347, 351
rabbit population in England   5:347
Walden movement and Twin Oaks colony   5:279
Epic poems   1:49, 153, 172, 173, 282 (sidebar), 285
(See also Poetry)
Equal Rights Amendment (ERA)   3:79; 5:51, 136, 358–59
"Equality" in America
Emancipation Proclamation (1862)   2:59, 60 (sidebar), 135, 308, 309
on eve of Revolution   1:99
individualism and egalitarian ideals of late 19th century   2:302
(See also African Americans' civil rights/reform/power movements; Civil rights movements; Segregation; Women's rights movement)
Equivocation doctrine   1:230
Erasmus, Desiderius   1:2, 6
Erdrich, Louise, Love Medicine   5:243–50
Escapism
fantasies of African American youths   4:4 (sidebar)
as response to despair   5:40
and Thurber's Walter Mitty   3:364, 369
Espionage
Civil War spies   2:255–56
Cold War spies   4:71–72
Rosenbergs executed for   4:72, 380, 381 (illus.); 5:2, 127
Esquivel, Laura, Like Water for Chocolate   3:196–202
Essays
Civil Disobedience, Thoreau, Henry David   2:87–92
Common Sense, Paine, Thomas   1:71–77, 94
Fire Next Time, The, Baldwin, James   5:107–14
Modest Proposal, A, Swift, Jonathan   1:266–72
Pilgrim at Tinker Creek, Dillard, Annie   5:278–84
Prince, The, Machiavelli, Niccolò   1:316–20
Republic, Plato   1:321–29

Room of One's Own, A, Woolf, Virginia   3:356–63
Self-Reliance, Emerson, Ralph Waldo   2:314–20
Silent Spring, Carson, Rachel   4:337–42
Souls of Black Folk, The, Du Bois, W. E. B.   2:340–46
Vindication of the Rights of Woman, A, Wollstonecraft, Mary   1:406–12
Walden, Thoreau, Henry David   2:416–21
Essex (Robert Devereaux, Earl of Essex)   1:194, 248, 349
Ethan Frome, Wharton, Edith   2:125–29
Ethiopia   4:67
Ethnicities. See African Americans; American Indians; Chinese and Chinese Americans; Japanese and Japanese Americans; Jews; Latinos; Puerto Rico and Puerto Ricans)
Ethnic and cultural conflicts
American Indian versus white. See American Indians
Anglo-Saxon English versus Norman   1:181
Asian versus white. See under Racism and prejudice
Christian versus modern-day secular in U.S.   3:102; 5:138
Christian versus warrior, in England   1:49–50
Dutch versus English in New Netherland   1:330–32, 334–35
Eastern (Muslim, Hindu) versus Western   3:303
Latino versus white. See Chicanos; Latinos
male-dominated versus ancient matriarchal   1:61–62
rural versus urban in U.S.   3:101–2, 140–41
Scottish Highlanders versus English   1:187
Southern versus Southwestern U.S.   4:320–21
Southern versus Yankee in U.S.   2:217–18
(See also Multiculturalism; Racism and prejudice)
Ethnology   2:232–33
Eugenics   3:272; 4:152; 5:41–42
Euripides, Medea   1:238–41
Europe, appeal of, to American upper class   2:105–6
Europe, James Reese   3:162 (sidebar), 163 (illus.)
Everything That Rises Must Converge, O'Connor, Flannery   5:88–94
Evolution
as Darwin's theory of (Darwinism)   1:293; 2:29, 121
fostering belief in progress and man's capacity to reform   2:195; 3:378
fostering doubt of man's divine nature   3:378
interest of H. G. Wells in   3:404–5
opposed by religious-minded   3:102, 404; 5:138
and Scopes Trial   3:102 (sidebar)
as social Darwinism ("survival of the fittest")
contributing to racism   2:341
impact on views of poor and disabled   2:217, 306, 312; 3:207, 410
H. G. Wells' criticism of   3:410

white superiority, Manifest Destiny, and "white man's burden"   **2**:*119, 147, 341;* **3**:*170, 172, 182 (sidebar)*
Extrasensory perception (ESP)   **5**:*47, 239*

F

Fabre, Jean Henri Casimer   **5**:*282*
Facism
   depression of 1930s enhancing appeal of   **3**:*129*
   (*See also* Nazis)
Fahrenheit 451, Bradbury, Ray   **5**:*95–100*
Fairfield, John   **2**:*189*
Fallen Angels, Myers, Walter Dean   **5**:*101–6*
Falwell, Jerry   **5**:*137–38, 140 (illus.)*
Family and family life
   in 19th-century New England   **2**:*54, 126–27*
   in 20th-century England   **3**:*347*
   of African Americans   **3**:*80, 84–86, 353–55, 375, 422–23;* **4**:*33;* **5**:*68, 145–46, 329–30*
   for Truman Capote   **3**:*72*
   in Celtic society   **1**:*197*
   changing roles within   **5**:*139*
   Chicano   **4**:*45*
   in China   **3**:*131–32, 192–93*
   in colonial America   **1**:*207–8, 217, 221, 334*
   in Elizabethan/Jacobean England   **1**:*141, 150, 203*
   of gang members, and gangs as substitutes for   **5**:*266–67*
   intergenerational conflicts
      among African Americans   **3**:*255;* **4**:*252*
      among American Indians   **5**:*244, 246*
      among Canadian Kwakiutl   **5**:*198*
      among Chicanos   **5**:*182*
      among Chinese Americans   **5**:*358*
      over marriage to person of differing ethnicity   **5**:*203–4, 232*
      over WWII   **4**:*327*
   of Mexican Americans   **4**:*172–73*
   pro-family movement of religious right   **5**:*138–39*
   role of black female servants in   **4**:*257–58*
   in sharecropper families   **3**:*370–71, 373, 375*
   single-female heads of households   **2**:*65;* **3**:*80, 423;* **4**:*2;* **5**:*68, 117, 136, 138, 267, 328–29*
   in slave families   **2**:*60, 169, 237–38, 405, 406, 410;* **4**:*204–5*
   in South   **3**:*78, 80*
   in stepfamilies   **5**:*36*
   in Dylan Thomas's work   **3**:*65*
   (*See also* Divorce; Love and marriage)
Family and family life: literary works depicting
   Beloved   **2**:*59–65*
   Betsey Brown   **4**:*28–34*
   Bless Me, Ultima   **4**:*42–48*
   Bluest Eye, The   **4**:*49–57*
   Cold Sassy Tree   **3**:*75–79*
   Color Purple, The   **3**:*80–87*
   Dandelion Wine   **3**:*88–93*
   Death in the Family, A   **3**:*100–105*
   Death of a Salesman   **4**:*109–15*
   Doll's House, A   **2**:*111–17*
   Ethan Frome   **2**:*125–29*
   Fences   **4**:*144–50*
   Fiddler on the Roof   **3**:*119–24*
   Gone with the Wind   **2**:*137–44*
   Good Earth, The   **3**:*131–37*
   Hamlet   **1**:*136–43*
   Heart of Aztlán   **4**:*171–76*
   Hero Ain't Nothin' but a Sandwich, A   **5**:*143–48*
   His Own Where   **5**:*149–55*
   Human Comedy, The   **4**:*193–200*
   I Never Sang for My Father   **5**:*201–7*
   In Nueva York   **5**:*214–21*
   Jacob Have I Loved   **4**:*216–20*
   King Lear   **1**:*196–203*
   Like Water for Chocolate   **3**:*196–202*
   Little Foxes, The   **3**:*203–10*
   Little Women   **2**:*202–8*
   Long Day's Journey into Night   **3**:*218–24*
   Love Medicine   **5**:*243–50*
   Man without a Face, The   **4**:*240–46*
   Member of the Wedding, The   **4**:*254–59*
   Not without Laughter   **3**:*249–56*
   Ordinary People   **5**:*259–64*
   Pocho   **4**:*295–302*
   Prince of Tides, The   **5**:*285–90*
   Raisin in the Sun, A   **4**:*309–15*
   Red Sky at Morning   **4**:*316–22*
   Roll of Thunder, Hear My Cry   **3**:*350–55*
   Runner, The   **5**:*306–13*
   Seventeen Syllables   **4**:*330–36*
   Sons and Lovers   **2**:*334–39*
   Sounder   **3**:*370–76*
   Sweet Whispers, Brother Rush   **5**:*328–32*
   Tree Grows in Brooklyn, A   **3**:*397–403*
   Yellow Raft in Blue Water, A   **5**:*360–66*
   (*See also* Autobiography)
Fantasy
   Alice's Adventures in Wonderland   **2**:*28–33*
   Beauty: A Retelling of the Story of Beauty and the Beast   **1**:*30–36*
   Devil and Tom Walker, The   **1**:*101–6*
   Handmaid's Tale, The   **5**:*135–42*
   Hobbit, The   **1**:*152–58*
   Rip Van Winkle   **1**:*330–36*
   Secret Life of Walter Mitty, The   **3**:*364–69*
   (*See also* Folklore and fairy tales; Science fiction)
Fard, W. D.   **5**:*12–13, 110*
Farewell to Arms, A, Hemingway, Ernest   **3**:*112–18*
Farewell to Manzanar, Houston, Jeanne W. and James D. Houston   **4**:*137–43*
Farley, James Aloysius   **3**:*402*
Farming
   Bracero Program (1942–1964)   **3**:*34;* **4**:*44*
   in California   **3**:*269–71, 275, 334–35*
   chemicalization of, in 1950s   **4**:*203*
   by Cherokee   **5**:*29*
   in Chile   **5**:*163–64, 165*

Index

Dust Bowl of 1930s 3:34, 46, 138–40; 4:297
in England 2:353–54, 358; 3:2, 5–6
families displaced by large corporations 3:92, 269
hard times in 1920s 3:25, 94–95
Homestead Act (1870) 2:322–23; 3:244, 257
mechanization of, in 1930s and '40s 4:203 (sidebar)
in Mexico's *ejidos* system 3:282
in Mexico's hacienda system 3:29, 278, 282
migrant workers and discrimination 3:29–30, 49, 140–42, 269–71, 275, 335, 337; 4:297 (sidebar)
in New England 1:102, 217; 2:125
nurture versus exploitation debate 3:262
racism against Japanese farmers 4:331
skyrocketing production and surpluses of 1960s 4:338
social stratification of owners versus workers 3:336
in South Africa 4:94
Spreckels sugar interests 3:269, 270 (sidebar), 319
tenant farming and sharecropping 2:42, 411; 3:80, 249, 370–71
in Texas of 1900s 3:244
training in, of and by blacks in "Movable School" 3:380
under Soviet Five-Year Plans 4:132
unions for farm workers 3:34, 49–50, 141, 275; 4:175–76
United Farm Workers 4:175, 300–302, 409
and use of pesticides ("biocides") 4:337–42
working conditions, long hours 3:244 (sidebar)
(*See also* Cattle ranching; Cotton)
Fascism
characteristics of 4:304, 306–7
described 1:293–94
neo-fascists 4:40
origins in Italy 4:66
and *Ox-Bow Incident* 2:293
Fashions
African-style clothing and hairdos 4:56; 5:145, 300
American Indian style 5:247
cosmetics for African American women 4:50, 56
global popularity of American 1:223
as symbols of generational conflict 5:271–72
women's
daring styles of 1920s 3:23
"New Look" of 1940s and '50s 4:22
restrictiveness in Victorian era 3:420
as status symbol 2:246, 247 (sidebar)
in youth culture of 1950s 4:172, 392
"zoot suits" 4:173, 403, 404–5, 408–9
(*See also* Clothing)
Fate
in ancient Greece 1:169
in Middle Ages 1:160

portents in Elizabethan era 1:194–95
Faulkner, William
Barn Burning 2:41–46
Bear, The 2:47–53
FDR. *See* Roosevelt, Franklin Delano
Federal Writers' Project 3:237
Felsch, Oscar "Happy" 3:149
Feltre, Fra Bernardino de 1:244
Feminine Mystique, The, and Betty Friedan 1:62; 2:58; 3:430; 4:11 (sidebar), 167, 241, 394; 5:51 (illus.), 136
Feminism. *See* Women's rights movement (and feminism)
Fences, Wilson, August 4:144–50
Fencing 1:141
FEPC (Fair Employment Practices Commission) 3:42
Feudalism 1:65–66, 159–61, 187, 290
Fiddler on the Roof, Stein, Joseph 3:119–24
Film. *See* Hollywood and motion picture industry
Fire Next Time, The, Baldwin, James 5:107–14
First Inaugural Address, Roosevelt, Franklin D. 3:125–30
Fishing
aquaculture 5:285–86
crabs and oysters 4:216–17, 219
game fish 4:274, 275 (sidebar), 279 (sidebar)
by Kwakiutl of British Columbia 5:195
shrimping 5:285–86
Fitzgerald, F. Scott, *Great Gatsby, The* 3:146–52
Flaubert, Gustave, *Madame Bovary* 2:209–15
Fleming, Alexander 3:365–66
Florence, Italy 1:174–76, 316–18
Florida
Belle Glade 3:383–84
Eatonville 3:383
Flowers for Algernon, Keyes, Daniel 4:151–56
Folklore and fairy tales 1:31–32, 36, 106
adapted to American themes 1:335
African 2:63, 64
American Indian 1:332
of American South 2:48–49
Beauty: A Retelling of the Story of Beauty and the Beast, McKinley, Robin 1:30–36
Dutch 1:332
efforts to collect in late 19th century 2:397
Germanic 1:105, 106
impact of Disney fairy tales on socialization of girls 1:36
Merry Adventures of Robin Hood, The, Pyle, Howard 1:250–57
mixed with Judeo-Christian beliefs 1:50, 138
origins of *Beowulf* in 1:49
as social commentary and criticism 1:31–32, 36
Uncle Remus, Harris, Joel Chandler 2:397–402
in Yorkshire, England 1:418–19
(*See also* Myth)
Football 4:145–46, 147; 5:63
for colored girls who have considered suicide / when the rainbow is enuf, Shange, Ntozake 5:115–21

Ford, Henry and Ford Motor Company   3:23, 77, 88, 101; 5:43 (illus.), 44–45
Fordism   5:46
Forster, E. M.   3:356
   Passage to India, A   3:297–304
Fort William Henry Massacre   1:205
Foundation, Asimov, Isaac   5:122–28
France in 15th century   1:159–61
France in 16th century, invasion of Italy   1:317
France in 17th century
   dueling   1:389 (sidebar)
   Gascons   1:386, 391
   musketeers   1:386, 387
   wars and civil turmoil   1:87–89, 305, 386–89
   women's position in   1:30
France in 18th century
   class hatred   1:358–60, 361, 371–72
   love and marriage   1:31
   wars with England   1:51–52, 93, 123, 130–31, 204–6, 220–21, 360
   women's position in   1:408, 409
France in 18th century: French Revolution
   American Revolution's contributions to   2:223–24
   echoes in *Frankenstein*   1:116
   emigrés fleeing   1:360–61, 372
   English reactions to   1:359–60, 372–73, 373 (sidebar), 376, 408
   guillotine   1:360 (sidebar), 373
   Jacobins   1:372
   origins of   1:51, 358–60, 371–72; 2:223–24, 295
   Paris Commune and Communards   1:363
   Reign of Terror   1:372; 2:102, 224
   storming of Bastille   1:358, 362 (illus.), 372; 2:224
   women ignored in proposals for education reform   1:408
France in 19th century
   bourgeoisie   2:209–10
   censorship in   2:383
   class hatred   2:224
   Dreyfus affair   1:91–92, 364 (sidebar)
   historic rivalry with England   1:391–92
   Industrial Age in   2:103–4
   landmark historical dates   1:160 (sidebar)
   Louis Napoleon and end of republic (1848)   2:228–29
   Napoleonic era and wars   2:99–100, 224, 227 (sidebar), 245, 295–96
   Paris as capital of Western art   3:265–66
   Republican government of 1870s   1:91
   Restoration of monarchy after Napoleon (1816)   2:100–101, 224
   Revolution of 1830   1:163–65, 391; 2:100
   Revolution of 1832   2:224–25
   wars with England   1:123, 130–31, 159, 160, 204–6, 220–21, 305, 360
   White Terror (1815)   2:102
   women, education and rights   1:32; 2:210, 245
France in 20th century
   African colonies   3:211–13
   as nonracist haven for Richard Wright   4:4
   in WWI   3:9, 11 (sidebar)
Franco, Francisco   4:67
Frank, Anne, *Diary of a Young Girl, The*   4:116–23
Frankenstein, Shelley, Mary   1:115–21
Franklin, Benjamin
   Autobiography of Benjamin Franklin, The   1:22–29
   as embodiment of American Dream   1:26–27, 309
   Poor Richard's Almanac   1:309–15
Freedom Rides   5:88–90
Freemasons (Masons)   2:82
French and Indian War (Seven Years' War)   1:93, 123, 204–6, 220–21
Freud, Sigmund   2:336; 5:260, 261
   and psychoanalysis   4:168 (sidebar); 5:42, 260–61, 263
Frick, Henry Clay   4:8
Friedan, Betty   1:62; 2:58; 3:430; 4:11 (sidebar), 167, 241, 394; 5:51 (illus.), 136
Friedrich, Richter, Hans Peter   4:157–64
Fuchs, Klaus   4:72
Fuentes, Carlos, *Old Gringo, The*   3:277–83
Fugitive Slave Acts (1793 and 1850)   1:42; 2:16, 62, 170, 189, 410
Fujimori, Alberto   5:334
Fuller, Edward   3:149
Fuller, Margaret   1:356, 357
Fundamentalism and New/Religious Right   5:137–39

G

G.I. Bill (1944)   3:92; 4:73
Gaelic League   3:109, 308–9
Gaines, Ernest J.
   Autobiography of Miss Jane Pittman, The   5:19–26
   Gathering of Old Men, A   5:129–34
Galarza, Ernesto, *Barrio Boy*   3:28–35
Galileo   1:305
Games and sports
   archery and quarterstaff fencing   1:253
   backswording   2:375
   bowling   1:335 (sidebar)
   boxing   5:68–69
   "chicken"   4:172
   fencing   1:141
   football   4:145–46, 147; 5:63
   frog-jumping contests   2:251–52
   gambling in mining camps   2:250, 282–83
   hero-worship of players   4:262
   horseracing in England   3:345–46
   hunting   2:47–48; 3:232
   hurling   3:109, 309
   involving animals   1:212
   jingling matches   2:375
   mahjong   5:232 (sidebar)
   racism continuing into 1980s   4:149

Index

rodeo   5:362, 364 (sidebar)
rugby in England   2:374–75
running feats of Jemez Pueblo   4:191
tournaments of knights' skills   1:291
values inculcated in students   5:63
(See also Baseball; Entertainment)
Gandhi, (Mahatma) Mohandas Karamchand   2:92; 3:298–300, 302; 5:192
Gandil, Arnold "Chick"   3:149; 4:260; 5:314, 315
García Márquez, Gabriel, *One Hundred Years of Solitude*   2:268–74
Garden of Eden   1:301–2
Garnet, Father Henry   1:230
Garrison, William Lloyd   2:23, 89 (sidebar), 242
Garvey, Marcus   3:160, 163; 4:211, 312
Gathering of Old Men, A, Gaines, Ernest J.   5:129–34
Gay rights movement   4:241
Geller, Uri   5:48
Gematriya   4:89
General literature, *Poor Richard's Almanac*, Franklin, Benjamin   1:309–15
Geoffrey of Monmouth   1:290
George I of England   1:131, 266, 342
George II of England   1:130, 269, 270 (illus.)
George III of England   1:93, 95 (illus.), 97
Germany
    Berlin Wall   5:238, 293
    early 20th century   1:370
    education in post-WWII period ignoring Third Reich   4:163
    fascism in   1:293–94
    Tripartite Pact (Japan, Germany, Italy; 1940)   4:59
    WWI   1:277–78; 3:8, 11 (sidebar)
    (See also Hitler; Nazis)
Gettysburg Address, Lincoln, Abraham   2:130–36
    influence on white South Africans of 20th century   4:99
Ghana   4:314
Ghettos
    black   4:30–31; 5:71–72, 143, 149–51
        Bedford-Stuyvesant   5:149–51
        crime in   5:13, 67–68, 112, 146, 150, 339–42
        drugs, suspicions of conspiracy by white officials to allow   5:144
        South Central Los Angeles   5:339–42
    Brooklyn   3:397–98; 4:88
    Jewish   1:244, 249; 4:118
    schools in, as overcrowded and inadequate   5:151–52
Ghibellines   1:174, 175, 345
Ghosts. See Supernatural
Gibson, William, *Miracle Worker, The*   2:216–22
Gilded Age (late 19th-century America)   2:20, 306, 328, 331
Gilman, Charlotte Perkins   3:168–69
    Yellow Wallpaper, The   2:422–28
Ginsberg, Allen   4:75; 5:83, 84 (illus.), 324
"Give Me Liberty or Give Me Death," Henry, Patrick   1:122–28
Glenn, John   5:292, 296
Glover, Goodwife (Goody)   1:79
Goddard, Robert   5:54
Godwin, William   1:115, 119, 407, 411 (illus.), 411–12
Gold rushes and silver strikes
    in Black Hills of Dakota   2:67–68
    boom towns   2:289
    in California   2:174–75, 195, 249–50, 281–84
    on Cherokee land in Oklahoma   5:29
    Chinese immigration for   4:124; 5:74, 352
    Klondike   3:52–56, 261 (sidebar)
    miners subject to robbers   1:256
    in Nevada   2:288–89, 290 (sidebar)
    in Nez Percé territory   2:162
    (See also Mining industry)
Golden Notebook, The, Lessing, Doris   4:165–70
Golding, William, *Lord of the Flies*   4:228–34
Goldman, Emma   3:321
Gone with the Wind, Mitchell, Margaret   2:137–44
Good Earth, The, Buck, Pearl S.   3:131–37
Good, Sarah   1:79, 395, 396
Good versus evil. See Sin and damnation
Gorbachev, Mikhail   5:8
Gothic horror stories and romances   2:81, 85, 185; 3:338
    Jane Eyre   1:415 (sidebar), 419; 2:181–87
    Rebecca   3:326–33
Gouzenko, Igor   4:72
Governesses in Victorian Age   2:182, 183 (sidebar), 378–80
Gowrie Conspiracy   1:229
Grady, Henry   2:399
Graetz, Heinrich   4:89
Grant, Duncan   3:356
Grant, Ulysses S.   2:217
Grapes of Wrath, The, Steinbeck, John   3:138–45
"Graying" of America   5:202–4
Great Awakenings
    in American colonies   1:73, 106, 122
    in early 19th-century America   1:424–25
Great Britain. See England
"Great Chain of Being"   1:201, 203
Great Depression, The (1930s)
    in agriculture   3:32, 34, 138–40, 153, 247, 350–51
    causes of   3:125, 138
    comparisons to hard times of Reconstruction   2:143–44
    Coxey's Army   3:51–52
    Dust Bowl   3:34, 46, 138–40; 4:297
    in England   5:39–40
    enhancing appeal of communism   3:39–40, 45, 129, 208–10
    hobo tradition   3:46, 270
    homelessness   3:126, 140, 142

impact on African Americans   3:*154*, 236–37
impact on South   3:*68–69*
New Deal programs
   Farm Relief Act (Agricultural Adjustment Act) (1933)   3:*247*
   Federal Writers' Project   3:*237*
   FERA (Federal Emergency Relief Administration)   1:*113*
   FLSA (Fair Labor Standards Act) (1938)   3:*49*
   FSA (Farm Security Administration) (1937)   3:*142*
   NLRA (National Labor Relations Act) (1933)   3:*128*
   NRA (National Recovery Act) (1933)   3:*390–91*
   purposes of   3:*45, 142*
   questionable effectiveness   3:*69, 128*
   Social Security System   3:*49, 128*
   WPA (Works Progress Administration)   3:*128, 391, 423–24*; 4:*44*
Okies   3:*140*
plight of sharecroppers and tenant farmers   3:*105, 350–51*
rural Southern education   3:*352*
soup kitchens   3:*45 (illus.)*
stock market crash and bank failures   3:*125–26, 208*
teamwork, as preoccupation of Steinbeck   3:*337*
widespread unemployment and poverty   3:*68, 126, 350*
WWII helping to end   2:*45*; 3:*424*
Great Gatsby, The, Fitzgerald, F. Scott   3:*146–52*
Great Goddess (ancient Greece)   1:*59, 61–62*
Great Migration (1915–1960)
   affecting Harlem Renaissance   3:*159–65, 256, 321, 384, 421*
   blacks and issue of union membership   3:*39*; 4:*210*
   causing increase of single female-headed families   3:*80, 423*; 4:*2*
   estimates of numbers of   4:*2, 50, 203*
   exacerbating racial tensions in Northern cities   2:*6*
   housing discrimination in North   3:*39, 159*; 4:*30–31*
   increasing with WWI   3:*236, 384*
   increasing with WWII   4:*51*
   making race a national question   4:*209–10*
   offering hope, then disillusion   3:*39, 80, 159, 236*; 4:*50–51*
   to Pittsburgh's steel and coal industries   4:*144*
   reasons for   4:*202–3*
   sharecroppers fleeing economic and racial oppression   3:*351*
   targeting Chicago and New York City   4:*309*
   transforming African Americans' sense of identity   4:*210*

   two phases of   4:*309*
Great War, The. *See* World War I
Greece, invasion of Turkey (1920)   3:*340*
Greece in ancient times
   Athens
      citizenship law   1:*241*
      Parthenon   1:*240*
      Pericles   1:*17, 18, 240, 241, 322*
      Plato   1:*321–22, 328*
      Socrates   1:*240, 322, 323 (illus.), 324, 327*
      Sophists   1:*19, 240*
      Theseus   1:*57, 61 (sidebar), 258, 259*
   Bronze Age   1:*14, 258, 280, 283 (sidebar)*
   burial rites   1:*18–19*
   civic/human laws versus divine   1:*17, 20*
   and concept of barbarians   1:*173*
   Corinth   1:*238, 241*
   "Dark Ages"   1:*167, 172, 283 (sidebar), 286*
   Mycenaean Age   1:*57–59, 167, 258, 281–82, 283 (sidebar)*
   Peloponnesian War   1:*241, 324, 328*
   position of women in   1:*17, 20, 58–59, 230–40, 259*
   ritual sacrifice   1:*283*
   Sparta   1:*324–25, 328*
   suicide as honorable   4:*22*
   Thebes   1:*14*
   Thirty Tyrants   1:*322, 324, 325 (sidebar)*
   Trojan War   1:*8, 14, 166–69, 281, 283 (sidebar)*
Greek myths
   basis of *Aeneid* in   1:*9*
   basis of *Antigone* in   1:*14*
   basis of *Medea* in   1:*238*
   basis of *Midsummer Night's Dream* in   1:*259 (sidebar)*
   Great Goddess and Amazons   1:*58–59, 61–62, 258, 259–60*
   Ovid's *Metamorphoses* as source of   1:*262*
   as sources of ideas for humanists   1:*380*
   as sources for Milton's *Paradise Lost*   1:*301*
   Zeus   1:*9, 59, 61, 170, 282, 283, 301*
Green Mountain Boys   3:*98 (sidebar)*
Greene, Bette, *Summer of My German Soldier*   4:*371–77*
Griffes   3:*18*
Grissom, Gus   5:*296*
Guatemala and refugees   5:*27–29*
Guelphs   1:*174, 175, 345*
Guest, Judith, *Ordinary People*   5:*259–64*
Guillotine   1:*360 (sidebar), 373*
Guillotine, Dr. Joseph Ignace   1:*360*
Gulliver's Travels
   Swift, Jonathan   1:*129–35*
   War of the Worlds compared to   3:*410*
Gunpowder Plot   1:*229*
Guthrie, Woody
   Bound for Glory   3:*44–50*
   on songs of New Deal era   3:*128 (sidebar)*
Gypsies

Index

in England   3:3
as victims of holocaust   4:119, 160, 267

H

Hachiya, Michihiko, *Hiroshima Diary*   4:177–84
Hades   1:283, 285
Haiti (formerly Saint-Domingue)   5:116–17
Haley, Alex
   Autobiography of Malcolm X, The (with Malcolm X)   5:11–18
   Roots   5:298–305
Hall, James Norman, *Mutiny on the Bounty*   1:273–79
Hamer, Fanny Lou   3:354
Hamilton, Virginia, *Sweet Whispers, Brother Rush*   5:328–32
Hamlet, Shakespeare, William   1:136–43
Hammett, Dashiell
   influence upon Hellman   3:210
   Maltese Falcon, The   3:225–30
Handmaid's Tale, The, Atwood, Margaret   5:135–42
Hansberry, Lorraine, *Raisin in the Sun, A*   4:309–15
Harding, Warren G.   3:22 (illus.)
Hardy, Thomas, *Tess of the D'Urbervilles*   2:353–59
Harlem, New York   4:247–48; 5:67–68
Harlem Renaissance   3:159–65, 256, 321, 384–85, 421; 4:204 (sidebar), 207
Harrington, Michael   5:266 (sidebar)
Harris, Joel Chandler, *Uncle Remus*   2:397–402
Hart, Leo   3:144 (sidebar)
Harte, Bret, *Outcasts of Poker Flat, The*   2:281–87
Harwood, Richard   4:40
Hasidim   3:425, 426; 4:87–90
Hate groups
   Knights of the White Camellia   5:21 (sidebar)
   (*See also* Ku Klux Klan)
Hathorne, John   1:83 (sidebar), 396, 420, 422, 424 (sidebar), 425 (sidebar)
Hathorne, William   1:420, 424 (sidebar)
Hautzig, Esther, *Endless Steppe, The: Growing Up in Siberia*   4:131–36
Hawthorne, Nathaniel
   Scarlet Letter, The   1:351–57
   Young Goodman Brown   1:420–26
Haya de la Torre, Raul   5:333, 334
Hays, Mary   1:412
Health issues
   Medicaid   5:68
   overcrowding of hospitals in ghettos   5:150
   scientific improvements in Victorian Age   1:115; 2:119
   (*See also* Disabled persons; Diseases; Drug/substance abuse; Mental and emotional disabilities)
Heart of Aztlán, Anaya, Rudolfo A.   4:171–76
Heart of Darkness, Conrad, Joseph   2:145–51
Heart Is a Lonely Hunter, The, McCullers, Carson   3:153–58
Hebrides   1:226

Hector   1:170
Heinlein, Robert A., *Stranger in a Strange Land*   5:321–27
Heinz, Henry   4:8
Heisenberg, Werner   5:283
Helen of Troy   1:8, 166, 168 (illus.), 281
Hell. *See* Devil (Satan); *Inferno*; *Paradise Lost*; Sin and damnation
Heller, Joseph, *Catch-22*   4:66–72
Hellman, Lillian, *Little Foxes, The*   3:203–10
Hemingway, Ernest
   Farewell to Arms, A   3:112–18
   Old Man and the Sea, The   4:274–80
Henry II of England   1:250, 251, 254–55
Henry IV of England   1:144
Henry IV, Part I, Shakespeare, William   1:144–51
Henry, Patrick
   as "American, not Virginian"   1:96–97
   "Give Me Liberty or Give Me Death" speech   1:122–28
Henry V of England   1:146
Henry VIII of England   1:149, 150, 231, 232, 234 (illus.)
Herbert, Frank, *Dune*   5:81–87
Hero Ain't Nothin' but a Sandwich, A, Childress, Alice   5:143–48
Herodotus   1:286
Herriott, James, *All Creatures Great and Small*   3:1–7
Herzl, Theodore   4:102
Hesse, Hermann, *Siddhartha*   1:365–70
Heyerdahl, Thor, *Kon-Tiki*   4:221–27
Hidalgos   1:2–3
Highlanders of Scotland   1:187
Hinduism   3:300, 302
Hine, Lewis   3:285
Hinton, S. E., *Outsiders, The*   5:265–70
Hippies. *See* Counterculture
Hippolyta and Amazons   1:58–59, 61–62, 258, 259–60
Hirohito, Emperor of Japan   4:178, 183
Hiroshima Diary, Hachiya, Michihiko   4:177–84
Hirsch, Samson Raphael   4:90 (sidebar)
His Own Where, Jordan, June   5:149–55
Hispanics. *See* Chicanos; Latinos
Hiss, Alger   4:110; 5:96
Histories
   Bury My Heart at Wounded Knee, Brown, Dee   2:74–80
   Two Years before the Mast, Dana, Richard Henry, Jr.   2:391–96
Hitler, Adolf   1:113–14, 294; 3:210; 4:157–58, 305 (illus.), 356–57; 5:122–23
Hobbit, The, Tolkien, J.R.R.   1:152–58
Holinshed, Raphael   1:148, 227
Holland   4:116–19
Holland, Isabelle, *Man without a Face, The*   4:240–46
Hollywood and motion picture industry
   Caucasian ideal of beauty reinforced by   4:50

development of   3:3, 89, 101
end of golden age of (1920s–45)   4:75–76
ethnic stereotypes used by   2:142; 4:50, 369
female as sex object   4:393
late 1940s attempts to address real issues
    4:75–76
patriotic films for WWII   4:325
reflecting and influencing teenagers and
    generation gap   4:392, 394
as target of witch hunts for "Reds"   4:236
"thrillers" as new genre   3:329
(See also Television)
Holocaust
adding to urgency of Zionist appeal   4:102
beginnings within Germany (1933–38)
    3:401–3; 4:267
collusion of some Jews in   4:269–70, 272–73
concentration camps   4:160–61, 194, 267–73
delayed U.S. acceptance of proof   3:403
denial by anti-Semites and neo-fascists   4:40
described   4:119–20
estimates of number of victims   4:194
extension outside German borders (1939)
    3:403; 4:267
as "final solution"   4:267
Israel exacting justice for atrocities   4:107
    (sidebar)
Jews in Siberia "spared"   4:134
Kristallnacht   4:159, 162–63
liberation of Buchenwald   4:269, 272
made easier by Nazis' deceptions and some Jews'
    willingness to be deceived   4:272, 273
Nazi "scapegoating" of Jews (1933–39)
    4:159–60
in occupied Holland   4:117–18
reactions of Germans to   4:194
subsequent pressure upon Jewish women to bear
    children   3:430
Vrba-Wetzler report and warnings to Hungarian
    Jews   4:269, 272
war crimes trials   4:272–73
(See also Diary of a Young Girl, The; Friedrich;
    Night)
Holy Grail legends   4:264–65
Holy League   1:296
Holy Roman Empire   1:87, 174, 176, 344, 345
Home to Harlem, McKay, Claude   3:159–65
Homelessness
of deinstitutionalized mental patients   4:289
during The Great Depression of 1930s   3:126,
    140, 142
in South Africa   4:97
of Vietnam veterans   5:106
Homer
Iliad   1:166–73
Odyssey   1:280–87
Homosexuality
in *Angels in America*   5:1–10
in *Biloxi Blues*   4:38
in *Catcher in the Rye*   4:74

growth of gay subculture   4:241, 245–46
and lesbianism   3:327–28, 357, 362
in *Man without a Face, The*   4:244
in military   4:38, 39–40
and Mormonism   5:4–5
as reported by Kinsey   4:398 (sidebar); 5:324
seen as pathological deviance   4:77
targeted by Nazis in Holocaust   4:119, 160
targeted by New/Religious Right   5:136, 137–38
Hood, Robin   1:188, 255 (sidebar)
(See also *Merry Adventures of Robin Hood*)
Hoover, Herbert   3:126–27
Hoover, J. Edgar   1:84 (sidebar), 399
Horror fiction
Carrie   5:46–52
Frankenstein   1:115–21
Psycho   5:46–47
Hound of the Baskervilles, Doyle, Arthur Conan
    2:152–59
House Made of Dawn, Momaday, N. Scott
    4:185–92
House of Mirth, The, Wharton, Edith   3:166–73
House of Stairs, Sleator, William   5:156–62
House of the Spirits, The, Allende, Isabel   5:163–70
House on Mango Street, The, Cisneros, Sandra
    5:171–77
Housing
adobes   4:318
in barrios   5:174
in black ghettos. See Ghettos
discrimination against African Americans   2:13;
    3:39, 237; 4:30–31, 310; 5:13
in middle-class suburbs   5:261–62
postwar prosperity, G.I. Bill, and home
    ownership   4:73
and racial violence   4:310 (sidebar)
racist restrictions ruled illegal   4:201
rent control ordinances   4:384, 400
rent supplements   5:68
shacks of sharecropper families   3:371
in slum tenements of New York   3:397–98;
    4:384–85, 401; 5:67–68, 149–50
in South Africa   4:95, 96–97
streetcars' impact on   4:366
"white flight" to suburbs   4:384, 385
Houston, Jeanne W. and James D. Houston, *Farewell
to Manzanar*   4:137–43
Howe, Samuel Gridley   2:217
Huerta, Dolores   4:47
Huerta, Victoriano   3:278–79
Hughes, Langston   3:164
Not without Laughter   3:249–56
Hughes, Thomas, *Tom Brown's Schooldays*
    2:372–77
Hugo, Victor
Hunchback of Notre Dame, The   1:159–65
on John Brown   2:193
Les Misérables   2:223–29
Human Comedy, The, Saroyan, William   4:193–200
Humanism   1:2, 142, 233, 380, 381

Index

Hunchback of Notre Dame, The, Hugo, Victor   1:*159–65*
Hundred Years' War   1:*159, 160*
Hungary   4:*166*
Hunger of Memory, Rodriguez, Richard   5:*178–84*
Hunt, Irene, *Across Five Aprils*   2:*8–14*
Hurston, Zora Neale, *Their Eyes Were Watching God*   3:*383–89*
Hutchinson, Anne   1:*352 (sidebar), 352–53*
Huxley, Aldous, *Brave New World*   5:*39–45*
Huxley, Thomas Henry   3:*265, 404*; 5:*324–25*
Hydrogen bomb   4:*183*

I

"I Have a Dream," King, Martin Luther, Jr.   5:*185–93*
I Heard the Owl Call My Name, Craven, Margaret   5:*194–200*
I Know Why the Caged Bird Sings, Angelou, Maya   4:*201–8*
I Never Sang for My Father, Anderson, Robert   5:*201–7*
"I Will Fight No More Forever," Chief Joseph   2:*160–67*
Ibsen, Henrik   3:*406*
    Doll's House, A   2:*111–17*
Idaho   2:*367*
Igbo of Africa, late 19th century   2:*360–62*
Iliad, Homer   1:*9, 166–73*
Illinois. *See* Chicago
Imagining Argentina, Thornton, Laurence   5:*208–13*
Imagism   3:*413–14*
Imlay, Gilbert   1:*410*
Immigration in 19th century
    Chinese   2:*367–68, 370 (sidebar), 371*; 4:*124–27*; 5:*74*
    Chinese Exclusion Acts (1882 and 1902)   2:*368*; 4:*125*; 5:*74, 231*
    Geary Act (1892)   2:*368*; 4:*125*
    Irish   3:*107, 398–99*
    Jewish   3:*121*
    to steel mills   4:*8*
    Swedish   3:*243–44, 259–60*
    urbanization with   2:*302, 327*; 3:*166*
    to Western homesteads   3:*258–61*
Immigration in 20th century
    America as "salad bowl" rather than melting pot   5:*176*
    anti-immigrant bigotry and fears   3:*233, 402*; 4:*330–31*; 5:*180*
    Armenian   4:*199*
    California Alien Land Act (1913)   4:*331*
    Chinese   2:*368*; 4:*125, 127, 129*; 5:*229, 352–54*
    Chinese Exclusion Act and Geary Acts (1904, 1922, 1924)   2:*368*; 5:*231*
    feelings of shame and inferiority among children of   5:*78–79*
    generational conflicts between children and parents   4:*385*; 5:*78–79, 182, 358*
    Guatemalan political refugees   5:*28–29*
    Immigration Acts (1924, 1965, 1980)   4:*331*; 5:*28, 75 (sidebar)*
    Irish   3:*401–2*
    Japanese   3:*30*; 4:*137, 143, 330–31*
    Japanese "picture brides"   4:*331–32*
    Jewish   3:*121*; 4:*92, 102–3, 104 (illus.), 106*
    Literacy Test (1917)   3:*233*
    Mexican   3:*29–30*; 4:*44–48*
    National Origins Act (1924)   3:*233*
    of Puerto Ricans   4:*385*; 5:*215–16*
    restrictions of 1920s enhancing opportunity for blacks   4:*203*
    Russian   3:*233*
    Sanctuary Movement   5:*29*
    urbanization with   3:*101, 102*
    War Brides Act (1945)   4:*124, 127*; 5:*231*
Imperialism. *See* Colonialism, imperialism, and interventionism
Impressment of sailors by Royal Navy   1:*52*
In medias res   2:*62*
In Nueva York, Mohr, Nicholasa   5:*214–21*
Inaugural Address
    Kennedy, John F.   5:*222–28*
    Roosevelt, Franklin D.   3:*125–30*
Incest   4:*52*
Incidents in the Life of a Slave Girl, Jacobs, Harriet   2:*168–73*
    influence upon Toni Morrison   2:*63*
Independent Living Movement   2:*123*
Indeterminacy, principle of   5:*283*
India
    500s to 300s b.c.   1:*365*
    Amritsar massacre   3:*298*
    Buddhism   1:*365–69*; 3:*186–87*; 5:*48*
    caste system   1:*366*; 3:*182, 184*
    civil service   3:*185*
    infrastructure   3:*184–85*
    map of   3:*183 (illus.)*
    nationalism   3:*298–300*
    religions   1:*366*; 3:*300–301, 302*
    under British rule   2:*182–84, 276–77*; 3:*181–82, 297–98*
Indians. *See* American Indians
Individualism
    and classical liberalism   3:*268*
    criticism of "cult" of   5:*2 (sidebar)*
    decline in, during 1950s era of conformity   4:*382*; 5:*323–24*
    and egalitarian ideals in 19th-century America   2:*302*
    machine age as debasing   5:*41, 46*
    Teddy Roosevelt popularizing "Old West" myth of   5:*206*
    of Thoreau   2:*88–89*
Industrialization
    allowing growth of middle class   2:*118, 153*
    democracy and capitalism, shift toward   2:*334–35*
    in France   2:*103–4, 245–46*

leading to Romantic movement   1:*106, 115–16*
leading to worker/owner class distinctions
   2:*303*
reaction of Luddites   1:*119–20, 120 (illus.)*
social and economic improvement and upheaval
   1:*106*; 2:*417*
stimulants of   1:*115, 336, 417*
women's increasing opportunities for jobs
   2:*423*
working conditions and attempts to improve
   3:*174–75, 178–79*
working conditions and worker's revolts   1:*363*;
   2:*328, 329, 404*
(*See also* Capitalism; Labor unions; Urbanization)
Inferno, Dante Alighieri   1:*174–80*
Inheritance, by entailment   2:*296 (sidebar)*
Integration
   Baldwin on moral standards of   5:*113*
   Brown v. Board of Education   3:*375*; 4:*29–30,
      314*; 5:*90, 108, 180, 181*
   opposition of Malcolm X to   5:*15*
   of schools   3:*43, 396*; 4:*29–30, 31 (illus.), 314*;
      5:*116, 131–32, 181*
   slow pace of   4:*33–34*
   of University of Mississippi   5:*19*
Internment of Japanese Americans (1942–44)
   4:*138–43, 195, 335–36*
Interventionism. *See* Colonialism, imperialism, and
   interventionism
Invisible Man, Ellison, Ralph   4:*209–15*
Ionesco, Eugène   4:*400*
Ireland
   Absentees   1:*266, 269 (sidebar), 269*
   Catholicism in   1:*269*; 3:*107–8, 109–10, 305–7*
   concessions by James I   1:*131*
   cultural revival   3:*108–9, 308–9*
   English subjugation of   1:*131–32, 267*; 3:*106–7,
      305–6*
   famine and emigration in mid-19th century
      2:*302*
   Home Rule movement   3:*109, 307*
   Irishness as depicted in *Kim*   3:*187*
   misgovernment and economic decline in 18th
      century   1:*266–69*
   Parnell, Charles   3:*109–10*
   Potato Famine of 1845   3:*107*
   Protestants and Patriots   1:*267*
   (*See also* England)
Irish Americans
   growing acceptance of   3:*401–2*
   sense of community   3:*400–401*
   stereotypes of heavy drinking   3:*220, 398, 400*
Irving, Washington
   Devil and Tom Walker, The   1:*101–6*
   Legend of Sleepy Hollow, The   1:*211–18*
   Rip Van Winkle   1:*330–36*
   The Sketch Book   1:*335–36*
   on slavery   1:*103*
Ishi, Last of His Tribe, Kroeber, Theodora   2:*174–80*
Islam   1:*296*; 3:*300*

and Nation of Islam   3:*238, 325*; 4:*56, 248–50*;
   5:*12–13, 69, 110–11, 302*
Israel
   Biblical history of   4:*101*
   as British mandate of Palestine   4:*102–3, 105*
   conflicts with Arabs   4:*106–8*
   Hasidic opposition to   4:*88*
   immigration to
      denied by Soviet government   3:*124*
      from Europe of 1880s   3:*121*
   Six-Day War (1967)   4:*93*
   War of Independence (1948–49)   4:*106*
   Women's Equal Rights Law (1951)   3:*430*
Italy
   in 16th century   1:*316*
   in ancient times   1:*9*
   fascism in   1:*293–94*
   Florence   1:*174–76, 316–18*
   Jews in   1:*246, 248–49*
   map of   1:*345 (illus.)*
   Milan   1:*379–80*
   Mussolini, Benito   2:*293–94*
   Venice   1:*242–46, 295–97*
   Verona   1:*344–45*
   in and after WWI   3:*11 (sidebar), 113–14*; 4:*66*
   in WWII   4:*66–67*
Ithaca   1:*281*
Ivanhoe, Scott, Sir Walter   1:*181–88*

J

Jackson, Andrew   1:*209–10*
Jackson, Shirley, *Lottery, The*   4:*235–39*
Jackson, "Shoeless" Joe   3:*149*; 4:*265*; 5:*314, 316*
Jacob Have I Loved, Paterson, Katherine   4:*216–20*
Jacobs, Harriet, *Incidents in the Life of a Slave Girl*
   2:*168–73*
James, Henry
   Daisy Miller   2:*105–10*
   on *Dr Jekyll and Mr. Hyde*   3:*382*
   Turn of the Screw, The   2:*378–83*
James I of England (James IV of Scotland)
   belief in supernatural and witchcraft   1:*228,
      384, 385*
   concessions to Irish   1:*131*
   daughter's marriage subject to her own approval
      1:*385*
   increase of political and religious factions
      1:*299*
   parallels to life of Hamlet   1:*141*
   subject of regicidal conspiracies   1:*229, 230*
   succession to throne of England   1:*141, 149,
      150, 201*
   support for theater and arts   1:*299*
James II of England   1:*130*
Jamestown, Virginia   1:*379, 384, 394*
Jane Eyre, Brontë, Charlotte   1:*415 (sidebar), 419*;
   2:*181–87*
Japan
   in 19th century   4:*177*

Index

countries conquered during WWII   5:123 (sidebar)
dictatorship of prewar military   4:178, 183
Emperor Hirohito   4:178, 183
frosty relations with Korea   4:353–54
furor over textbooks' coverage of WWII   4:354
Hiroshima as first atom bomb target   4:179–82
imperialism of   4:58–59
invasion of China (1930s and '40s)   3:189–90; 5:229–30
invasion and occupation of Korea (1894-95, 1904-05, 1910-45)   4:59, 177, 349–54
Korean laborers in   4:353
Nagasaki as second atom bomb target   4:180 (illus.), 181 (sidebar)
rapprochement with South Korea   4:354
Russo-Japanese War (1904–05)   4:59
WWII   4:58–61

Japanese and Japanese Americans
  as farm workers   3:30
  immigration   3:30; 4:137, 143, 330–31
  Issei and Nisei   4:137

Japanese and Japanese Americans, works concerning
  Farewell to Manzanar   4:137–43
  Hiroshima Diary   4:177–84
  Seventeen Syllables   4:330–36
  So Far from the Bamboo Grove   4:349–55

Jara, Victor   5:164, 168
Jason   1:238–39
Jazz   3:162 (sidebar); 4:258
Jefferson, Thomas
  Declaration of Independence, The   1:93–100
  on Patrick Henry   1:127
Jerusalem   1:182
Jesuits   3:307–8
Jews
  in America   3:430
  assimilation, threat of   3:120, 123, 430; 4:88, 90 (sidebar), 91
  British offer of homeland in Africa   3:291
  criticality of education for   3:425
  Diaspora   4:101
  divorce   3:427, 429 (sidebar)
  education of women   3:427, 430
  in England   1:182–83, 185; 2:264–65
  expulsion or conversion to Christianity   1:244, 246; 2:264
  Gematriya   4:89
  in ghettos   1:244, 249; 4:118
  Hasidim   3:425, 426; 4:87–90; 5:283 (sidebar)
  immigrating to America and Israel   3:121
  immigration in 20th century   3:121; 4:92, 102–4, 106
  in Italy   1:243, 246, 248–49
  Jewish Enlightenment (*Haskalah*)   3:120, 426; 4:88
  Levantines   1:248
  Marranos   1:248, 249
  marriage-bed custom   3:428 (sidebar)
  Mitnagdim   3:426
  and moneylending   1:182–83; 2:264
  Orthodox   4:93
  of Poland   4:131–32
  revival of American   4:91–92, 93
  role and rights of women   3:427–30
  suicide and   3:428; 4:22
  traditional marriage   3:119
  Zionism   3:121; 4:88, 101–2
  (See also Anti-Semitism; Holocaust)

Jews, literary works concerning
  Biloxi Blues   4:35–41
  Chosen, The   4:87–93
  Dawn   4:101–8
  Diary of a Young Girl, The   4:116–23
  Endless Steppe, The: Growing Up in Siberia   4:131–36
  Fiddler on the Roof   3:119–24
  Friedrich   4:157–64
  Night   4:267–73
  Summer of My German Soldier   4:371–77
  A Tree Grows in Brooklyn   3:402
  Yentl, the Yeshiva Boy   3:425–31

Jim Crow laws
  African American responses to   2:413
  challenges to, by black soldiers of WWI   3:252
  coming under fire in 1930s and '40s   2:53
  described   3:81, 351; 5:90
  federal authorities ignoring   4:1
  origins of term   2:21, 341; 3:351
  upheld by *Plessy v. Ferguson*   2:21, 341, 399–400, 413; 3:351, 375, 419; 4:1; 5:90, 107–8

John Brown's Final Speech, Brown, John   2:188–94
John I of England   1:251
Johnson, Lyndon Baines   3:324; 4:347, 375; 5:68, 102
Johnson, Samuel   1:307
Jolly Roger (pirates' flag)   1:401
Jones, Leroi (Amiri Baraka)   4:207
Jonson, Ben   1:150, 300
Jordan, June, *His Own Where*   5:149–55
Joseph, Chief of Wallowa Nez Percé, "I Will Fight No More Forever"   2:160–67
Joy Luck Club, The, Tan, Amy   5:229–35
Joyce, James   5:42
  Dubliners   3:106–11
  Portrait of the Artist as a Young Man, A   3:305–11
Julius Caesar   1:169 (sidebar), 189–91
Julius Caesar, Shakespeare, William   1:189–95
Jung, Carl Gustav   3:329
Jungle, The, Sinclair, Upton   3:174–80
Jupiter   1:191

K

Kansas-Nebraska Act (1854)   1:42; 2:5 (sidebar), 172, 193
Karma   1:367
Kasztner, Rezso   4:269–70, 272–73
Katherine of Aragon   1:231

Keats, John   **1**:*406*
Keller, Helen   **2**:*220 (illus.)*
   (*See also Miracle Worker, The*)
Kelly, Charles T. and Kelly's Army   **3**:*51–52*
Kennedy, John F.
   appeal to, by King for civil rights   **5**:*186*
   Bay of Pigs and Cuban Missile Crisis   **4**:*135*;
      5:*225, 226, 238–39, 293*
   environmental concerns   **4**:*338, 341 (sidebar)*
   expanding U.S. role in Vietnam   **4**:*375*
   Inaugural Address   **5**:*222–28*
   intervention on behalf of civil rights protesters in
      Alabama   **5**:*12*
   moon walk goal launching space race   **5**:*81,
      292, 293 (sidebar), 321–22*
   opposing Nixon for president   **5**:*321–22*
   President's Panel on Mental Retardation   **4**:*152*
   sending "advisors" to Vietnam   **5**:*158, 307*
Kennedy, Joseph P.   **3**:*402*
Kennedy, Robert   **5**:*90*
Kentucky
   in Civil War   **2**:*60 (sidebar)*
   slavery in   **2**:*59–60*
Kenya   **3**:*290–96*
Kerensky, Alexander   **3**:*232*
Kerouac, Jack   **4**:*75*
Kesey, Ken, *One Flew over the Cuckoo's Nest*
   4:*288–94*
Keyes, Daniel, *Flowers for Algernon*   **4**:*151–56*
Keynes, John Maynard   **3**:*356*
Kherdian, David, *Road from Home, The*   **3**:*338–43*
Khrushchev, Nikita   **4**:*135, 166, 286, 398, 399
   (illus.);* **5**:*225*
Kim, Kipling, Rudyard   **3**:*181–88*
King, Dr. Martin Luther, Jr.   **5**:*14 (illus.), 89 (illus.),
   109 (illus.)*
   appeal to Kennedy for help in civil rights
      movement   **5**:*12, 186*
   assassination of   **4**:*54*; **5**:*112 (sidebar)*
   criticism of, by Malcolm X   **4**:*250*; **5**:*13, 15, 111*
   education and pastorate   **5**:*108*
   influenced by Ghandi and passive resistance
      2:*92*; **5**:*108, 189, 192*
   influenced by Thoreau   **2**:*92*
   organization of Montgomery bus boycott   **5**:*11,
      88, 108*
   protesting residential segregation   **2**:*12 (illus.),
      13, 97*
   speech: "I Have a Dream"   **5**:*185–93*
King Lear, Shakespeare, William   **1**:*196–203*
King, Rodney   **5**:*340*
King, Stephen, *Carrie*   **5**:*46–52*
Kingsolver, Barbara, *Bean Trees, The*   **5**:*27–33*
Kingston, Maxine Hong, *Woman Warrior, The*
   5:*352–59*
Kinsella, W. P., *Shoeless Joe*   **5**:*314–20*
Kinsey, Alfred Charles and Kinsey Report   **4**:*75,
   241, 398–99 (sidebar);* **5**:*324*
Kipling, Rudyard, *Kim*   **3**:*181–88*
Kitchen God's Wife, The, Tan, Amy   **3**:*189–95*

Klondike   **3**:*52–56, 261 (sidebar)*
Knights and knighthood   **1**:*182 (sidebar), 290–91*
Knights of the White Camellia   **5**:*21 (sidebar)*
Knowles, John, *Separate Peace, A*   **4**:*323–29*
Knox, John   **4**:*304*
Kon-Tiki, Heyerdahl, Thor   **4**:*221–27*
Korea
   frosty relations with Japan   **4**:*353–54*
   invasion by Japan (1894–95 and 1904–05)
      4:*59, 177*
   occupation by Japan (1910–45)   **4**:*349–50*
   reprisals against fleeing Japanese (1944–45)
      4:*350, 352 (sidebar)*
Korean War   **1**:*223*; **3**:*73*; **4**:*92*
Kristallnacht   **4**:*159, 162–63*
Kroeber, Theodora, *Ishi, Last of His Tribe*   **2**:*174–80*
Ku Klux Klan
   birth of, in 1865–66   **2**:*141 (sidebar), 412*;
      3:*102*; **5**:*21*
   law enforcement officers enlisting in   **4**:*4, 202*
   lynchings and violence against blacks   **2**:*141
      (sidebar), 143 (sidebar), 412*; **3**:*419*; **5**:*25, 130*
   re-emergence during
      1920s xenophobic, anti-Bolshevik era   **2**:*143
         (sidebar)*; **3**:*22*; **4**:*201–2*
      1940s   **4**:*201–2*
      1960s civil rights era   **5**:*21 (sidebar), 25*
Kushner, Tony, *Angels in America*   **5**:*1–10*

L

Labor unions
   accused of being "red" (communist or socialist)
      3:*144*
   AFL (American Federation of Labor)   **3**:*44*
   African Americans excluded, then included
      2:*341*; **3**:*250*; **4**:*210–11*
   Agricultural Labor Relations Act (1975)   **4**:*48*
   anti-labor and anti-Bolshevik reactions of 1920s
      3:*21–22*
   attempts to limit power of, Taft-Hartley Act
      (1947)   **4**:*172, 173 (sidebar)*
   Brotherhoood of Sleeping Car Porters   **3**:*42*
   Carnegie Steel and Homestead Strike (1892)
      3:*321*
   CIO (Congress of Industrial Organizations)
      3:*44*
   "closed" and "union" shops   **4**:*173 (sidebar)*
   conflicts with management   **2**:*328, 336 (sidebar)*
   and Debs, Eugene V.   **3**:*54*
   for farm workers   **3**:*34, 49–50, 141, 275*
   growth of   **2**:*328, 336 (sidebar), 341*; **3**:*176
      (sidebar)*
   leaders cooperating with business owners
      4:*172*
   leaders' corruption   **4**:*145*
   and Mexican Americans   **4**:*172, 175–76*
   National Labor Relations Act (1933)   **3**:*128*
   opposition to   **3**:*44, 141, 155 (sidebar), 208*
   Pinkerton's detectives hired to thwart   **3**:*225*

Index

STFU (Southern Tenant Farmers' Union)   3:*208*
strikes and violence   3:*176 (sidebar), 179*; 4:*109*
table grape boycott   4:*175*
Language. *See* Linguistic considerations
Lasch, Christopher   4:*111*
Last of the Mohicans, The, Cooper, James Fenimore   1:*204–10*
Latinos
   Chicanos. *See* Chicanos
   concepts of *machismo* and *marianismo*   3:*201*; 4:*278–79, 299*; 5:*167, 173–74, 337*
   curanderos   3:*199*; 4:*45*
   decline of paternal authority   4:*172–73*
   enlisting in military for WWII   4:*44*
   help to Dust Bowl migrants   4:*297 (sidebar)*
   life in barrios   4:*172 (sidebar)*
   men admired for adultery   5:*337*
   mestizo or mixed-race heritage   5:*172, 334*
   Puerto Rico and Puerto Ricans   3:*277*; 4:*385–86, 388–89, 401*; 5:*214–21*
   the Virgin de Guadalupe and La Malinche   5:*173*
   women's roles   4:*299*; 5:*167–68, 173–74*
   in WWII   4:*295, 406*
   (*See also* Cuba; Mexico)
Latinos, literary works concerning
   Barrio Boy   3:*28–35*
   Bless Me, Ultima   4:*42–48*
   Heart of Aztlán   4:*171–76*
   House of the Spirits, The   5:*163–70*
   House on Mango Street, The   5:*171–77*
   Hunger of Memory   5:*178–84*
   Imagining Argentina   5:*208–13*
   In Nueva York   5:*214–21*
   Like Water for Chocolate   3:*196–202*
   Old Gringo, The   3:*277–83*
   Old Man and the Sea, The   4:*274–80*
   One Hundred Years of Solitude   2:*268–74*
   Pocho   4:*295–302*
   Time of the Hero, The   5:*333–38*
Laudanum   3:*379*
Laurents, Arthur, et al., *West Side Story*   4:*384–90*
Law
   American jury system   4:*378–79*
   capital punishment   4:*379–80*; 5:*131*
   conviction, then successful appeal in Sleepy Lagoon murder case   4:*405*
   judicial opposition in 1980s to civil rights legislation   5:*1–2*
   Jury Selection and Service Act   4:*379*
   lawyers' apprenticeships and circuit riding   2:*1–2*
   legal challenges to internment of Japanese   4:*140–41*
   legal challenges to restrictive housing covenants   4:*310*
   as legislation. *See under individual topics, e. g.* Civil rights movements; Great Depression; Labor unions; Segregation
   weakness of Prohibition as legislation   3:*22–23, 69*

Law enforcement
   absence on American frontier   2:*323*
   absence on rural California farms   3:*274*
   attacking civil rights protesters   5:*23 (illus.)*
   at Democratic National Convention of 1968   5:*271*
   officers enlisting in Ku Klux Klan   4:*4, 202*
   prisons   3:*371, 374 (illus.)*
   slave patrols   2:*190 (sidebar)*
   (*See also* Crime; Vigilantism)
Lawrence, D. H.
   Rocking-Horse Winner, The   3:*344–49*
   Sons and Lovers   2:*334–39*
Leary, Timothy   5:*82–83, 324*
Leaves of Grass, Whitman, Walt   2:*195–201*
Lee, Ann   3:*95*
Lee, Harper, *To Kill a Mockingbird*   3:*390–96*
Left Hand of Darkness, The, LeGuin, Ursula   5:*236–42*
Legend of Sleepy Hollow, The, Irving, Washington   1:*211–18*
Legends. *See* Myth
Legislation. *See under individual topics, e. g.* Civil rights movements; Great Depression; Labor unions; Segregation
LeGuin, Ursula, *Left Hand of Darkness, The*   5:*236–42*
Lenape (Delaware) Indians   1:*206, 219–20*
Lenin, Vladimir   4:*14, 15 (illus.)*
Leopold, King of Belgium   2:*146–47, 150–51*
Lepanto, Battle of   1:*296*
Lesbianism
   and bisexuality of Woolf   3:*357*
   hints in *Rebecca* and concern for du Maurier   3:*327–28*
Lessing, Doris, *Golden Notebook, The*   4:*165–70*
Leuchter, Fred. A.   4:*40*
Levantine Jews   1:*248*
Levellers   1:*359*
Lewis, C. S.   1:*158*
Lewis, John L.   3:*155 (sidebar)*
Lewis, Oscar   5:*266*
Lewis, Sinclair, *Babbitt*   3:*21–27*
Liberalism, classical
   and individualism   3:*268*
   targeted by New Right   5:*136*
Liberia   2:*404*
Liddell, Alice   2:*29 (illus.)*
Light in the Forest, The, Richter, Conrad   1:*219–24*
Like Water for Chocolate, Esquivel, Laura   3:*196–202*
Lincoln, Abraham
   biography of   2:*1–7*
   Emancipation Proclamation (1862)   2:*59, 60 (sidebar), 135, 308, 309*
   Gettysburg Address   2:*130–36*
   influence on white South Africans of 20th century   4:*99*
   quote from *Declaration of Independence*   1:*99*
   on race   2:*3, 5*

Walt Whitman on   2:*196 (sidebar)*
Lindbergh, Charles   3:*367;* 4:*373*
Lindner, Robert   4:*77–78*
Linguistic considerations
   alliteration   5:*223*
   Black English, or Ebonics   5:*145, 154, 342*
   Churchill's rhetoric   4:*361–62*
   colloquial prose of Lardner   4:*262 (sidebar)*
   Dutch place-names in New York   1:*331 (sidebar)*
   English accents   3:*4–5, 313–14*
   English as melding of French and Old English   1:*183 (sidebar)*
   ethnic idioms, street slang, and group identification   4:*249 (sidebar), 386*
   ethnic/racist slurs   4:*32, 386*
   fading/loss of native or immigrants' languages   4:*85, 142*
   Gaelic League   3:*109, 308–9*
   ghetto street slang   5:*17*
   Kennedy's rhetoric   5:*186*
   King's rhetoric   5:*223–24*
   metaphor   5:*186*
   Mycenaean alphabet   1:*172 (sidebar)*
   "naming", power of   5:*176*
   non-Greek-speakers as barbarians   1:*173 (sidebar)*
   oratory, rhetoric of speeches   5:*186, 223*
   Phoenician alphabet   1:*286–87*
   plain, simple language of common men   1:*72–73, 76, 163, 342*
   pronouns, inclusive   5:*186*
   puns in Shakespeare   1:*348–49*
   puns in Victorian Age   2:*30*
   repetition   5:*186*
   rhyme   5:*223*
   rhythm   5:*223*
   Roman names   1:*190*
   Roosevelt's (Franklin Delano) rhetoric   3:*127*
   Southern dialect
      in *Cold Sassy Tree*   3:*79*
      in *Color Purple, The*   3:*87*
      in *Gathering of Old Men, A*   5:*133*
      in *Huckleberry Finn*   2:*17*
      in *Uncle Remus*   2:*397, 398–99*
   Southwestern dialects   4:*321 (sidebar)*
   suppression of native languages by colonialists   4:*350*
   Western dialect in *Notorious Jumping Frog*   2:*252*
   Yiddish   3:*120*
Linguistic considerations: etymological
   "acid and acid heads"   5:*83*
   barrios   4:*44*
   "bindlestiffs"   3:*269–70, 275*
   "blackamoor"   4:*54*
   "blacklisting"   3:*178;* 4:*72*
   "Catch-22"   4:*70 (sidebar)*
   "Chinaman's chance"   2:*368*
   "colored", "Negro", "African American" and "black"   5:*120 (sidebar)*
   "coolies"   4:*124*
   "democracy", Paine's redefinition of   1:*74*
   "dry" years and "Drys"   3:*69, 75*
   "Dust Bowl"   3:*46*
   "flappers"   3:*147*
   "flipping" trains   3:*46*
   "freaking out"   5:*83*
   "gas him"   5:*37 (sidebar)*
   "ghetto"   1:*244*
   "greasers"   5:*266*
   "Hoovervilles"   3:*126*
   "Jim Crow"   2:*21, 341*
   "lost generation" (post-WWI)   3:*13, 112, 116–17*
   "mashers"   2:*331*
   "moonshine"   3:*69*
   "no man's land"   3:*9, 113*
   "octoroons"   3:*18*
   "Okies"   3:*46*
   "pachuco"   4:*173, 296*
   "quadroons"   3:*17–18*
   "revolution," Paine's redefinition of   1:*74*
   "runrummers"   3:*147*
   "Say it ain't so, Joe"   3:*150*
   "Simon Legree"   2:*409*
   "skid row"   3:*46*
   "speakeasies"   3:*69, 147*
   "Tenderloin"   4:*37*
   "trench foot"   3:*9*
   "trips and bad trips"   5:*83*
   "Uncle Tom"   2:*409*
   "wage slavery"   3:*179*
   "Walter Mitty"   3:*369*
Lipsyte, Robert, *Contender, The*   5:*67–73*
Literature
   for adolescents and young adults, as genre   5:*61–62, 265–66, 268–70, 331*
   allegory and fable   4:*16 (sidebar), 19*
   almanacs (*Poor Richard's Almanac*)   1:*309–15*
   bildungsroman   3:*264, 311;* 4:*47*
   calendarios de las señoritas (Mexican magazines for women)   3:*196–97*
   choreopoems   5:*117–18*
   crime stories and "Newgate Novels"   2:*83, 267*
   detective fiction   2:*325;* 3:*226–27*
   development in 17th-century French salons   1:*88*
   "dime" novels with romance, adventure, and violence   2:*306;* 3:*226–27*
   dystopian   5:*100, 141, 252*
   of Enlightenment   2:*211 (sidebar)*
   for ethnic groups, minorities   5:*62*
   future history   5:*127*
   Gothic horror stories and romances   2:*81, 85, 185;* 3:*338*
   horror fiction   5:*46–47*
   Imagism   3:*413–14*
   Latin American   2:*273*
   "magical" realism   2:*271, 273;* 3:*196, 202;* 4:*48;* 5:*169, 213, 330*

Index

novels, birth of 1:*341–42*
pornographic 3:*381*
printing and publishing, impact of advances in 1:*160, 162 (sidebar)*; 2:*234, 306, 419*
pulp magazines 2:*325*; 3:*226–27*
realism. *See* Realism
repetition as literary device 4:*70*
romance novels of 1980s 5:*331*
romances 2:*210*
of Romantic era. *See* Romantic movement
satirical. *See* Satire
science fiction. *See* Science fiction
slave narratives. *See* Slave narratives
Southern renaissance in 3:*421*
stream of consciousness technique 3:*111, 358*
thrillers, psychological 3:*328–29*
utopian 5:*251–52*
westerns 2:*321, 325*
Wilder's view of importance of 3:*288*
writers
    benefitting from New Deal's Federal Writers' Project 3:*237*
    patrons for 1:*88*
    prejudice against women as 2:*186, 203, 212, 424–25*; 5:*282 (sidebar)*
(*See also* Biography (and autobiography); Censorship and banning of literary works; Documents; Essays; Narratives; Novels; Plays; Short stories; Speeches)
Little Foxes, The, Hellman, Lillian 3:*203–10*
Little Prince, The, Saint-Exupéry, Antoine de 3:*210–17*
Little Women, Alcott, Louisa May 2:*202–8*
Locke, Alain 3:*256, 389*
Locke, John 1:*100*
London, England 1:*417*
London, Jack, *Call of the Wild, The* 3:*51–56*
Long Day's Journey into Night, O'Neill, Eugene 3:*218–24*
López, Dr. Roderigo 1:*248*
Lord of the Flies, Golding, William 4:*228–34*
"Lost generation" (post-WWI) 3:*13, 112, 116–17*
Lotteries 4:*235–36*
Lottery, The, Jackson, Shirley 4:*235–39*
Louis Napoleon 2:*228–29*
Louis Phillippe of France 1:*164*
Louis XI of France 1:*160*
Louis XIII of France 1:*386, 387, 388*
Louis XIV of France 1:*31, 87, 88, 130, 386, 387*; 3:*212*
Louis XVI of France 1:*51, 358, 359, 372*
Louis XVIII of France 1:*391*
Louisiana 3:*15–18*; 4:*365–66*; 5:*21, 22, 25, 130, 131–32*
L'Ouverture, Toussaint 5:*116–17*
Love and marriage
    in 18th-century France 1:*31*
    according to Thurber 3:*367–68*
    adultery/infidelity 5:*273, 287*
    in ancient Greece 1:*285*
    children of immigrants marrying Caucasians 5:*232*
    in China and Chinese culture 3:*132, 192–93, 194*; 4:*128*
    in colonial America 1:*24*
    debutantes' "coming out" 3:*326–27*
    in early 17th-century England 1:*263–64, 385*
    for Emily Dickinson 2:*55–56, 57*
    for England's landed gentry 1:*414*; 2:*296, 354–55*; 3:*326–27*
    happiness versus duty in 3:*271–72*
    Japanese "picture brides" 4:*331–32*
    polygamy 5:*4*
    problems of adjustment to retirement 5:*203, 273*
    sexual dimension of, in 19th century 2:*212, 423*
    or spinsterhood 2:*297*
    for traditional Jews 3:*119, 123*
    for underage teens 5:*151*
    in Victorian Age 2:*116, 336*
    War Brides Act (1945) 4:*124, 127*; 5:*231*
    Wollstonecraft on 1:*410–11*
    for women of 1970s 2:*58*
(*See also* Divorce; Family and family life)
Love and marriage, works emphasizing
    Anna Karenina 2:*34–40*
    Beauty: A Retelling of the Story of Beauty and the Beast 1:*30–36*
    Color Purple, The 3:*80–87*
    Daisy Miller 2:*105–10*
    Doll's House, A 2:*111–17*
    Ethan Frome 2:*125–29*
    Farewell to Arms, A 3:*112–18*
    Gone with the Wind 2:*137–44*
    Handmaid's Tale, The 5:*135–42*
    His Own Where 5:*149–55*
    House of Mirth, The 3:*166–73*
    Jane Eyre 2:*181–87*
    Kitchen God's Wife, The 3:*189–95*
    Like Water for Chocolate 3:*196–202*
    Love Medicine 5:*243–50*
    Madame Bovary 2:*209–15*
    Merchant of Venice, The 1:*247*
    Othello 1:*297*
    Pride and Prejudice 2:*295–300*
    Romeo and Juliet 1:*346*
    Scarlet Letter 1:*351–57*
    Seventeen Syllables 4:*330–36*
    Sons and Lovers 2:*334–39*
    Tess of the D'Urbervilles 2:*353–59*
    Wuthering Heights 1:*413–19*
Love Medicine, Erdrich, Louise 5:*243–50*
Lower classes 1:*363, 366 (sidebar), 366*
LSD (lysergic acid diethylamide) 4:*288, 289, 292, 293–94*; 5:*82–83, 324–25*
Luce, William, *Belle of Amherst, The* 2:*54–58*
Lucifer. *See* Devil (Satan)
Luddite movement 1:*119–20, 120 (illus.)*
Luther, Martin 1:*231–32, 232 (illus.)*; 2:*113*

Luxembourg   4:254–55
Lynching
  advocation of, by racist propaganda   2:400
  anti-lynching crusader Ida B. Wells-Barnett   3:83, 238
  ASWPL (Association of Southern Women for the Prevention of Lynching)   3:391–92; 5:133
  of black soldiers during WWII   4:197
  "defense of white womanhood" excuse   5:133
  Dyer Antilynching Bill   3:392
  economic aspect of excuses for   3:83, 391
  estimates of deaths from   2:341; 3:37, 83, 238, 419; 4:202; 5:131
  FDR's reason for refusal to sign Dyer Antilynching Bill   3:154, 392; 4:202
  horrific cruelties of   2:412; 3:274, 391
  increasing with desperation of Great Depression (1930s)   3:45
  by Ku Klux Klan   2:141 (sidebar), 143 (sidebar), 412; 3:419; 5:130–31
  in Northern states   3:238
  perpetrators generally escaping punishment   3:274
  police joining mobs   4:4, 202
  to prevent exercise of voting rights   2:412; 3:419
  sexual aspect of excuses for   3:83, 238, 273
  as Southern phenomenon   3:238
  of whites   3:273–74

M

MacArthur, Douglas   4:80–81, 350
Macbeth, Shakespeare, William   1:225–30
McCarthy, Joseph and McCarthyism   1:84, 398; 3:208, 209 (illus.); 4:71, 110, 398; 5:2, 3 (illus.), 96, 97, 127
McCullers, Carson
  Heart Is a Lonely Hunter, The   3:153–58
  Member of the Wedding, The   4:254–59
McCunn, Ruthanne Lum, *Thousand Pieces of Gold*   2:366–71
Machiavelli, Niccolò, *Prince, The*   1:316–20
McKay, Claude, *Home to Harlem*   3:159–65
McKinley, Robin, *Beauty: A Retelling of the Story of Beauty and the Beast*   1:30–36
McMullin, Fred   3:149
Madame Bovary, Flaubert, Gustave   2:209–15
Madero, Francisco   3:29, 197, 278
"Magical" realism   2:271, 273; 3:196, 202; 4:48; 5:169, 213, 330
Magna Carta   1:255
Maimon, Solomon   4:88
Malamud, Bernard, *Natural, The*   4:260–66
Malcolm II of Scotland   1:225
Malcolm III of Scotland   1:226
Mallory, Thomas   1:290, 293
Maltese Falcon, The, Hammett, Dashiell   3:225–30
Man for All Seasons, A, Bolt, Robert   1:231–37
Man without a Face, The, Holland, Isabelle   4:240–46

Manchild in the Promised Land, Brown, Claude   4:247–53
Manchuria   4:59, 178, 350; 5:230
Manhattan Project   4:71, 81–82, 316
Manifest Destiny   2:76 (sidebar); 3:234
Manorial system   1:251
Mao Zedong   3:136, 189; 5:254
Mark Antony   1:13, 189, 191
Marooning   1:401–2
Marranos   1:248, 249
Marsh, Ngaio   3:329
Marshall Plan   5:123–24, 224, 292
Martinez, Vilma   5:179
Marx, Karl   1:376; 3:232
Marxism
  concept of capitalists versus proletariat   3:321
  concepts of "wage slavery" and "estranged labor"   3:179; 4:18–19
  in Czarist Russia   3:59
  (See also Communism)
Mary Stuart, Queen of Scots   1:141, 149–50, 349
Masons (Freemasons)   2:82
Mather, Cotton
  associated with Puritan excess   1:213
  comparison to J. Edgar Hoover   1:84 (sidebar)
  excerpt from *Bonifacius*   1:28
  impact of *Memorable Providences*   1:79, 80, 396
  impact of *The Wonders of the Invisible World*   1:80 (illus.), 80, 422, 424
Mather, Increase   1:424
Matlovich, Leonard Jr.   4:39
Maugham, W. Somerset, *Of Human Bondage*   3:264–68
Maupassant, Guy de, *Necklace, The*   2:244–48
Meat-packing industry   3:175
Medea, Euripides   1:238–41
Media
  black press airing grievances of black soldiers in WWII   4:195
  contributing to anti-Japanese hysteria of WWII   4:138, 140, 141, 194
  creating crime-ridden image of Central Park   4:401
  decrying racial violence   4:310 (sidebar)
  fanning 1940s hysteria over zoot suiters and "Mexican goon squads"   4:296, 404, 405
  FDR's popularity with and concealment of disability   3:127
  misrepresentation of "black power"   4:56
  misrepresentation of Malcolm X   5:16
  muckraking journalists   3:176, 320
  "New Journalism"   5:293
  overlooking violence against minorities and homeless   4:401
  patriotic emphasis during WWII   4:371
  role in consolidation of Japanese culture in California   4:332
  use of, for propaganda   4:66–67
  and "yellow journalism"   3:279
  (See also Television)

Index

Medici, House of 1:316, 317, 318
Medici, Marie de' 1:387
Medicine
  ambulances of WWI 3:114
  Chinese 3:194 (sidebar)
  Chippewa "love medicine" 5:249
  homeopathy 3:68–69
  Indian remedies 3:68–69; 5:249
  Latino *curanderos* 3:199; 4:45
  as male dominated 4:218
  midwifery 4:218
  Navajo Night Chant 4:188
  opium products 3:379
  penicillin 3:366
  polio vaccines 4:10
  "socialized", 1950s fear of 4:12
  (*See also* Diseases)
Mediterranean
  Albania 2:101
  in ancient times 1:9
  Egypt 4:107
  Ethiopia 4:67
  Palestine 4:102–3, 105; 5:54
  Peloponnesian War 1:241, 324, 328
  Sicily 4:67
  Suez Canal 3:184; 4:107
  (*See also* Greece in ancient times; Israel; Italy; Turkey)
Melanesia 4:222
Melville, Herman 2:92
  Benito Cereno 1:37–43
  Billy Budd 1:51–56
  Moby Dick 2:230–35
  praise for *Young Goodman Brown* 1:425
Member of the Wedding, The, McCullers, Carson 4:254–59
Mencken, H. L.
  on *Babbitt* 3:25, 27
  influence on Sinclair Lewis 3:26–27
  on Scopes Trial 3:102 (sidebar)
  on Southern culture 3:40 (sidebar)
Mendel, Gregor 2:217
Mendelssohn, Moses 4:88
Menelaus 1:281
Mental and emotional disabilities
  association with pressure to conform 4:74
  asylums/institutions
    abuses in 3:244–45
    and deinstitutionalization 4:289
    as fashionable "resorts" 3:413
    hospitalization in 3:272; 4:77
  changing attitudes in 1950s and '60s 4:151–56
  connectedness of mental health and human relationships 4:153
  developments in psychology 3:329, 378; 4:77
  education for children 4:151–52
  effects of childhood abuse 5:289–90
  eugenic sterilization of retarded 3:272; 4:152; 5:41, 42
  Fetal Alcohol Syndrome 5:361
  "frontier madness" 3:259
  history of 4:288–89
  National Association for Retarded Children (NARC) 4:151
  in Shakespeare's time 1:139 (sidebar), 203
  stigma of 5:262–63
  targeted by Nazis in Holocaust 4:119
  treatments for
    electroconvulsive therapy (ECT) 4:24 (sidebar), 289–90
    lobotomy 4:290
    methods of 1940s and '50s 4:289–90
    pyschosurgery 4:290
    "rest cure" 2:425–26
    tranquilizing drugs 4:289
  in Victorian Age 2:119–20, 184, 185–86, 278–79
  writers suffering from
    T. S. Eliot's wife 3:412–13
    Gilman 2:427
    Plath 4:21–26
    Woolf 3:358
  of WWII veterans 4:80 (sidebar), 325
Merchant of Venice, Shakespeare, William 1:242–49
  parallels to *Ivanhoe* 1:187
Meredith, James 5:19
Merry Adventures of Robin Hood, The, Pyle, Howard 1:250–57
Merton, Thomas 5:280–81
Metamorphoses, Ovid 1:262
Methodism 2:357–58
Mexican Americans. *See* Chicanos; Latinos
Mexican War 2:88, 89, 242; 5:172
Mexico
  Bracero Program (1942–1964) 3:34; 4:44
  close ties to U.S. 3:282
  dictatorship of Díaz (1876–1910) 3:28–30
  ejidos system 3:282
  hacienda system 3:29, 278, 282
  immigration to U.S. from 3:282; 4:44–48
  mining industry 3:28
  PRI and one-party democracy 3:282
  Revolution (1910–20) 3:29, 278–79; 4:295, 296 (sidebar)
  women in 3:197–98, 200–202
Micronesia 4:222
Middle Ages
  as depicted in *Beowulf* 1:44–50
  as depicted in Chaucer 1:64–70
  importance of kings and kinship 1:153
Middle class, rise of
  African Americans in 20th century 3:252, 255, 387–88; 4:2, 51
  in American East 2:303, 306
  bourgeoisie of France 2:209–10, 245–46
  in England 1:66, 72, 338, 342, 371; 2:118, 153, 354; 3:312
  importance of proper manners 2:297
  moving to suburbs 4:73

replacing aristocray of Old South   4:364–65
Midsummer Night's Dream, A, Shakespeare, William   1:258–65
Midwifery   4:218
Migrant farm workers   3:29–30, 34, 49, 140–42, 143 (sidebar), 269–71, 275, 335, 337; 4:297 (sidebar)
   braceros   3:34; 4:44
Milan, Italy   1:379–80
Military
   African Americans in   3:160, 424
   American Indians in   4:80, 185–87; 5:362–63
   anti-Semitism in   4:36–37
   Army training camps   4:36
   authority and mutiny   4:63–64
   British "batmen"   3:348
   Claire Chennault and American Volunteer Group   3:190
   desertion during Civil War   2:10–11, 312
   desertion in Vietnam   2:13 (sidebar)
   and "Flying Tigers"   3:190
   homosexuals in   4:38, 39–40
   illicit wartime amusements   4:37, 38
   Latinos in   4:44
   racial discrimination in   3:41–42; 4:195, 197, 212
   reservists and regulars   4:63 (sidebar)
   United Service Organizations (USO)   4:38
   (*See also* War)
Military draft
   of American Indians for WWII   4:80
   of blacks for Vietnam   5:102–3
   of Chicanos for Vietnam   4:176
   of Chinese Americans for WWII   4:127
   of disadvantaged for Vietnam (Project 100,000)   5:102–3, 158, 307
   dodging and avoiding   2:256, 309; 4:324, 327
   induction process   4:35–36
   of Nisei for WWII   4:140 (sidebar)
   of poor/lower classes for Civil War   2:256, 309
   of Puerto Ricans for WWI   5:215
   as target of blacks' protest   4:213
   for WWII in 1940   4:35, 324–25
Mill, John Stuart   2:182 (sidebar)
Miller, Arthur
   Crucible, The   1:78–86
   Death of a Salesman   4:109–15
   importance in American theater   1:85
Mills, C. Wright   4:74
Milton, John, *Paradise Lost*   1:301–8
Minh, Ho Chi   5:101
Mining industry
   accidents and disease   2:335
   child labor   2:335 (sidebar)
   in Chile   5:163, 164
   Chinese in   2:367; 5:352
   coal   3:63, 64; 4:9; 5:39–40
   in Mexico   3:28
   (*See also* Gold rushes and silver strikes; *Thousand Pieces of Gold*)

Minotaur   1:259
Minstrel shows   2:16–17, 21
Miracle Worker, The, Gibson, William   2:216–22
Les Misérables, Hugo, Victor   2:223–29
Missionaries   2:118–19, 147, 161–62, 361–62; 3:133, 280; 5:195
Mississippi River   2:16, 17
Missouri Compromise (1820)   2:5 (sidebar), 15–16, 22
Mitchell, Margaret, *Gone with the Wind*   2:137–44
Mitnagdim   3:426
Moby Dick, Melville, Herman   2:230–35
Modernism   3:411; 5:42
Modest Proposal, A, Swift, Jonathan   1:266–72
Mohammed, Sufi Abdul   4:211
Mohr, Nicholasa, *In Nueva York*   5:214–21
Momaday, N. Scott, *House Made of Dawn*   4:185–92
Monasticism   3:186–87
   Trappist monks   5:280
Money
   in colonial America   1:103–4, 310
   "Wood's Coins" in Ireland   1:268
Moneylending (usury)   1:103–4, 182–83, 243 (sidebar), 243, 247
Monro, Lt. Col. George   1:205
Monroe, James   1:209
Moors   1:297, 299; 3:212, 213
More, Sir Thomas   1:232, 233, 237
Mormonism   5:4
Morrison, Toni
   Beloved   2:59–65
   Bluest Eye, The   4:49–57
Mortimer family   1:144, 145
Most Dangerous Game, The, Connell, Richard   3:231–35
Motion pictures. *See* Hollywood and motion picture industry
Mott, Lucretia Coffin   2:24, 55; 3:16
Moynihan, Daniel
   Moynihan Report (1965)   3:355, 375
   on Project 100,000   5:103
Muhammad, Elijah   3:239 (illus.); 4:249; 5:13, 69, 110–11
Mulattos   3:18
Multiculturalism
   America as "salad bowl" rather than melting pot   5:176
   encouraging autobiographies   3:32, 34
   ethnic studies programs
      African American history   5:147–48
      in Black English, or Ebonics   5:145, 154, 342
      increasing college enrollments   5:217
      Puerto Rican history and culture   5:217
   and women's studies   5:117
   (*See also* African Americans; American Indians; Chinese and Chinese Americans; Japanese and Japanese Americans; Jews; Latinos; Puerto Rico and Puerto Ricans)

Murphy, Charles F.   3:*148, 399*
Music
   blues   3:*254 (sidebar);* 4:*258*
   Chinese opera   5:*75*
   and dance   4:*387*
   effectiveness in theatrical productions   4:*258*
   folksongs of 1930s and 1940s   3:*47, 128*
   gospel songs and black spirituals   2:*398, 402, 407;* 4:*258*
   importance to slaves   2:*398*
   jazz   3:*162 (sidebar);* 4:*258*
   New Chilean Song   5:*164*
   ragtime   3:*321 (sidebar)*
   reflecting generation gap   4:*386*
   rock 'n' roll   4:*172, 386, 391–92*
   Smith, Bessie   3:*253 (illus.)*
   Welsh regard for   3:*65*
Musicals
   for colored girls who have considered suicide / when the rainbow is enuf, Shange, Ntozake   5:*115–21*
   golden age on Broadway   4:*387*
   West Side Story, Laurents, Arthur, *et al.*   4:*384–90*
Musketeers   1:*386, 387*
Muslim Turks   1:*296*
Mussolini, Benito   2:*293–94;* 4:*66–67, 305 (illus.)*
Mutiny
   aboard *Amistad*   1:*43*
   aboard HMS *Bounty*   1:*273–79, 276 (illus.)*
   aboard USS *Somers*   1:*56*
   in *Benito Cereno*   1:*37–43*
   in *Billy Budd*   1:*51–56*
   in *Caine Mutiny, The*   4:*58–65*
   at Spithead and Nore   1:*53*
Mutiny on the Bounty, Nordhoff, Charles and James Norman Hall   1:*273–79*
Mycenaean Age of ancient Greece   1:*57–59, 167, 258, 281–82, 283 (sidebar)*
Myers, Walter Dean, *Fallen Angels*   5:*101–6*
Mystery and detective stories
   Hound of the Baskervilles   2:*152–59*
   Jane Eyre   1:*415 (sidebar), 419;* 2:*181–87*
   Maltese Falcon, The   3:*225–30*
   rise of   2:*325;* 3:*226–27*
Mysticism   1:*416*
   Hasidic Jews   3:*425, 426*
Myth
   Arthurian   1:*288, 290*
   Chinese   5:*77 (sidebar), 358*
   and comparative anthropology   5:*42*
   creation of   1:*152*
   disguising contemporary social criticism   1:*15, 63*
   founding of Rome   1:*10 (sidebar)*
   Holy Grail legends   4:*264–65*
   Irish   3:*109*
   Mexican and Aztlán   4:*173, 174–75, 176*
   Norse   1:*50, 152, 153, 156*
   (See also Folklore and fairy tales; Greek myth)

N

NAACP (National Association for the Advancement of Colored People)   2:*342, 415;* 3:*250, 320, 396;* 4:*195, 255, 310;* 5:*88, 120 (sidebar)*
Nairobi   3:*293*
"Naming", power of   5:*176*
Napoleon Bonaparte   1:*163, 391;* 2:*99–100, 224, 225 (sidebar), 295–96*
Napoleonic code   4:*365*
Narrative of the Life of Frederick Douglass, Douglass, Frederick   2:*236–41*
   inspiring resistance on part of slaves   2:*16*
Narratives
   Black Elk Speaks, Neihardt, John G.   2:*66–73*
   Bury My Heart at Wounded Knee, Brown, Dee   2:*74–80*
   Kon-Tiki, Heyerdahl, Thor   4:*221–27*
   Two Years before the Mast, Dana, Richard Henry, Jr.   2:*391–96*
   (See also Slave narratives)
NASA (National Aeronautics and Space Administration)   5:*81, 291*
Nation of Islam   3:*238, 325;* 4:*56, 248–50;* 5:*12–13, 69, 110–11, 302*
National Labor Relations Act (1933)   3:*128*
National Organization of Women (NOW)   1:*62;* 4:*22, 394;* 5:*136, 237*
Nationalism
   and anti-Semitism   1:*364*
   as aspect of fascism   4:*304*
   of Black Muslims and Nation of Islam   3:*238, 325;* 4:*56, 248–50;* 5:*12–13, 69, 110–11, 302*
   of black separatists   3:*160*
   caused by economic hardship   1:*113*
   ethnic movements   1:*363–64*
   extremes of   1:*292, 293–94*
   in *Hound of the Baskervilles*   2:*157*
   under Young Turks   3:*339*
Native Americans. *See* American Indians
Native Son, Wright, Richard   3:*236–42*
NATO (North Atlantic Treaty Organization)   5:*124, 224, 292*
Natural, The, Malamud, Bernard   4:*260–66*
Naturalism   1:*293*
Nature
   celebration of   1:*413, 416*
   (See also Romantic movement)
Nazis
   achieving dictatorship   4:*158*
   anti-Semitism fostering emigration of Jews   4:*102*
   condemnation of *All Quiet on the Western Front*   3:*13*
   countries conquered by   5:*123 (sidebar)*
   escaping to Argentina   5:*210*
   execution of Remarque's sister   3:*14*
   Great Depression enhancing appeal of facism   3:*129*
   nationalism of   1:*294*

Index

neo-nazis 4:163–64
   plans for extermination of Jews and "undesirables" 3:124
   rabid racism and belief in Aryan superiority 4:158, 193; 5:42
   remilitarization of Germany 4:356–57
   rise of and consolidation of power 4:157, 158, 356–57
   (*See also* Holocaust; World War II)
Nebraska 3:257–58, 260
Necklace, The, Maupassant, Guy de 2:244–48
Neihardt, John G., *Black Elk Speaks* 2:66–73
Neruda, Pablo 5:164, 168
New Deal. *See under* Great Depression, The
New England
   agricultural decline 2:125–26
   Boston 3:43
   Boston Tea Party 1:125
   Massachusetts 1:78–80, 355, 395–97
"New Journalism" 5:293
New Mexico
   Chicano life in 4:45, 171
   Gallup 4:83
   Laguna Pueblo 4:79–80, 85
   Los Alamos 4:81, 316–17
   Manhattan Project 4:71, 81–82, 316–17
   Sagrado 4:318
   Tierra Amarilla 4:174
   Trinity Site detonation of atom bomb 4:81–82
   Walatowa (Jemez Pueblo) 4:187
   WWII village life 4:318–21
New Netherland (New York) 1:211, 212
New Orleans 3:15
New York
   Brooklyn 3:397–98; 4:88; 5:149–51
   Chinatown 4:126
   Dutch in (New Netherland) 1:211, 212, 330–32, 333 (illus.), 335 (sidebar), 336
   Hudson Valley 1:330–32, 333 (illus.), 334–35, 336
   in late 18th century 1:107–8, 110
   Mohawk Valley 1:108, 110, 112 (illus.)
   New York City 2:301–7, 313; 3:146–47
      Central Park 4:401
      "garbage riots" (1969) 5:220 (sidebar)
      Harlem 4:247–48; 5:67–68
      Harlem and Harlem Renaissance 3:159–65, 256, 321, 384–85, 421; 4:204 (sidebar), 207
      Harlem Renaissance 3:159–65, 256, 384–85, 421
      Manhattan's West Side 4:384–89, 400–401
      Puerto Ricans 4:385–86, 388–89, 401; 5:214–21
      Spanish Harlem (El Barrio) 5:214, 216–17
      Tweed Ring 2:306–7
      Tammany Hall 3:148–49, 398–99
Newspapers
   origins of 1:268
   "yellow journalism" 3:279
Newton, Huey P. 4:54

Newton, Sir Isaac 1:24, 94
Niagara Movement (1905) 3:250, 320
Nicholas II, Czar of Russia 3:121, 232
Nietzsche, Friedrich 3:54
Nigeria 2:360–62, 364–65; 3:84; 4:314
Night, Wiesel, Elie 4:267–73
Nineteen Eighty-Four, Orwell, George 5:251–58
   as dystopian 5:100
Nirvana 1:366, 367
Nixon, Richard
   "kitchen debate" with Khrushchev 4:398, 399 (illus.); 5:321–22
   loss to Kennedy attributed to poor appearance on TV 5:223
   use of anti-communism for campaign 5:96
   visit to Communist China 5:358
   Watergate scandal 3:99; 5:158–59, 263, 317
Nonfiction
   almanacs (*Poor Richard's Almanac*) 1:309–15
   Kon-Tiki, Heyerdahl, Thor
   Right Stuff, The, Wolfe, Tom 5:291–97
   Two Years before the Mast, Dana, Richard Henry, Jr. 2:391–96
   (*See also* Biography (and autobiography); Documents; Essays; Slave narratives; Speeches)
Noon Wine, Porter, Katherine Anne 3:243–48
Nordhoff, Charles, *Mutiny on the Bounty* 1:273–79
Norman Conquest of Anglo-Saxon England 1:181, 250–51, 290
Norse myths 1:50, 152, 153, 156
North Carolina 2:168
North Dakota 5:244
Norway 1:137–38; 2:111–13
Not without Laughter, Hughes, Langston 3:249–56
Notorious Jumping Frog of Calaveras County, The, Twain, Mark 2:249–54
Notre Dame cathedral 1:161, 162 (illus.), 163, 164 (sidebar)
Novellas
   Awakening, The, Chopin, Kate 3:15–20
   Daisy Miller, James, Henry 2:105–10
   Heart of Darkness, The, Conrad, Joseph 2:145–51
   Of Mice and Men, Steinbeck, John 3:269–76
   Turn of the Screw, The, James, Henry 2:378–83
Novels
   birth of 1:341–42
   Across Five Aprils, Hunt, Irene 2:8–14
   Adventures of Don Quixote, The, Cervantes Saavedra, Miguel de 1:1–7
   Adventures of Huckleberry Finn, The, Twain, Mark 2:15–21
   Alice's Adventures in Wonderland, Carroll, Lewis 2:28–33
   All Creatures Great and Small, Herriott, James 3:1–7
   All Quiet on the Western Front, Remarque, Erich Maria 3:8–14
   Animal Farm, Orwell, George 4:14–20
   Anna Karenina, Tolstoy, Leo 2:34–40

Index

Autobiography of Miss Jane Pittman, The, Gaines, Ernest J.   5:19–26
Babbitt, Lewis, Sinclair   3:21–27
Bean Trees, The, Kingsolver, Barbara   5:27–33
Beauty: A Retelling of the Story of Beauty and the Beast, McKinley, Robin   1:30–36
Bell Jar, The, Plath, Sylvia   4:21–27
Beloved, Morrison, Toni   2:59–65
Benito Cereno, Melville, Herman   1:37–43
Betsey Brown, Shange, Ntozake   4:28–34
Billy Budd, Melville, Herman   1:51–56
Bless the Beasts and Children, Swarthout, Glendon   5:34–38
Bless Me, Ultima, Anaya, Rudolfo A.   4:42–48
Bluest Eye, The, Morrison, Toni   4:49–57
Brave New World, Huxley, Aldous   5:39–45
Bull from the Sea, The, Renault, Mary   1:57–63
Caine Mutiny, The, Wouk, Herman   4:58–65
Call of the Wild, The, London, Jack   3:51–56
Carrie, King, Stephen   5:46–52
Catch-22, Heller, Joseph   4:66–72
Catcher in the Rye, Salinger, J. D.   4:73–78
Ceremony, Silko, Leslie Marmon   4:79–86
Childhood's End, Clarke, Arthur   5:53–60
Chocolate War, The, Cormier, Robert   5:61–66
Chosen, The, Potok, Chaim   4:87–93
Cold Sassy Tree, Burns, Olive Ann   3:75–79
Color Purple, The, Walker, Alice   3:80–87
Confessions of Nat Turner, The, Styron, William   2:93–98
Contender, The, Lipsyte, Robert   5:67–73
Count of Monte-Cristo, The, Dumas, Alexandre   2:99–104
Cry, the Beloved Country, Paton, Alan   4:94–100
Dandelion Wine, Bradbury, Ray   3:88–93
Dawn, Wiesel, Elie   4:101–8
Day No Pigs Would Die, A, Peck, Robert Newton   3:94–99
Death in the Family, A, Agee, James   3:100–105
Donald Duk, Chin, Frank   5:74–80
Drums Along the Mohawk, Edmonds, Walter D.   1:107–14
Dune, Herbert, Frank   5:81–87
Eat a Bowl of Tea, Chu, Luis   4:124–30
Ethan Frome, Wharton, Edith   2:125–29
Fahrenheit 451, Bradbury, Ray   5:95–100
Fallen Angels, Myers, Walter Dean   5:101–6
Farewell to Arms, A, Hemingway, Ernest   3:112–18
Flowers for Algernon, Keyes, Daniel   4:151–56
Foundation, Asimov, Isaac   5:122–28
Frankenstein, Shelley, Mary   1:115–21
Friedrich, Richter, Hans Peter   4:157–64
Gathering of Old Men, A, Gaines, Ernest J.   5:129–34
Golden Notebook, The, Lessing, Doris   4:165–70
Gone with the Wind, Mitchell, Margaret   2:137–44
Good Earth, The, Buck, Pearl S.   3:131–37
Grapes of Wrath, The, Steinbeck, John   3:138–45

Great Gatsby, The, Fitzgerald, F. Scott   3:146–52
Gulliver's Travels, Swift, Jonathan   1:129–35
Handmaid's Tale, The, Atwood, Margaret   5:135–42
Heart of Aztlán, Anaya, Rudolfo A.   4:171–76
Heart Is a Lonely Hunter, The, McCullers, Carson   3:153–58
Hero Ain't Nothin' but a Sandwich, A, Childress, Alice   5:143–48
His Own Where, Jordan, June   5:149–55
Hobbit, The, Tolkien, J.R.R.   1:152–58
Home to Harlem, McKay, Claude   3:159–65
Hound of the Baskervilles, Doyle, Arthur Conan   2:152–59
House Made of Dawn, Momaday, N. Scott   4:185–92
House of Mirth, The, Wharton, Edith   3:166–73
House of Stairs, Sleator, William   5:156–62
House of the Spirits, The, Allende, Isabel   5:163–70
House on Mango Street, The, Cisneros, Sandra   5:171–77
Human Comedy, The, Saroyan, William   4:193–200
Hunchback of Notre Dame, The, Hugo, Victor   1:159–65
I Heard the Owl Call My Name, Craven, Margaret   5:194–200
Imagining Argentina, Thornton, Laurence   5:208–13
In Nueva York, Mohr, Nicholasa   5:214–21
Invisible Man, Ellison, Ralph   4:209–15
Ishi, Last of His Tribe, Kroeber, Theodora   2:174–80
Ivanhoe, Scott, Sir Walter   1:181–88
Jacob Have I Loved, Paterson, Katherine   4:216–20
Jane Eyre, Brontë, Charlotte   2:181–87
Joy Luck Club, The, Tan, Amy   5:229–35
Jungle, The, Sinclair, Upton   3:174–80
Kim, Kipling, Rudyard   3:181–88
Kitchen God's Wife, The, Tan, Amy   3:189–95
Last of the Mohicans, The, Cooper, James Fenimore   1:204–10
Left Hand of Darkness, The, LeGuin, Ursula   5:236–42
Light in the Forest, The, Richter, Conrad   1:219–24
Like Water for Chocolate, Esquivel, Laura   3:196–202
Little Prince, The, Saint-Exupéry, Antoine de   3:210–17
Little Women, Alcott, Louisa May   2:202–8
Lord of the Flies, Golding, William   4:228–34
Love Medicine, Erdrich, Louise   5:243–50
Madame Bovary, Flaubert, Gustave   2:209–15
Maltese Falcon, The, Hammett, Dashiell   3:225–30
Man without a Face, The, Holland, Isabelle   4:240–46

Merry Adventures of Robin Hood, The, Pyle, Howard   1:250–57
Les Misérables, Hugo, Victor   2:223–29
Moby Dick, Melville, Herman   2:230–35
Mutiny on the Bounty, Nordhoff, Charles and James Norman Hall   1:273–79
Native Son, Wright, Richard   3:236–42
Natural, The, Malamud, Bernard   4:260–66
Night, Wiesel, Elie   4:267–73
Nineteen Eighty-Four, Orwell, George   5:251–58
Not without Laughter, Hughes, Langston   3:249–56
O Pioneers!, Cather, Willa   3:257–63
Of Human Bondage, Maugham, W. Somerset   3:264–68
Old Gringo, The, Fuentes, Carlos   3:277–83
Old Man and the Sea, The, Hemingway, Ernest   4:274–80
Oliver Twist, Dickens, Charles   2:261–67
One Day in the Life of Ivan Denisovich, Solzhenitsyn, Alexander   4:281–87
One Flew over the Cuckoo's Nest, Kesey, Ken   4:288–94
One Hundred Years of Solitude, García Márquez, Gabriel   2:268–74
Ordinary People, Guest, Judith   5:259–64
Outsiders, The, Hinton, S. E.   5:265–70
Ox-Bow Incident, The, Clark, Walter Van Tilburg   2:288–94
Passage to India, A, Forster, E.M.   3:297–304
Pigman, The, Zindel, Paul   5:271–77
Pocho, Villarreal, José Antonio   4:295–302
Portrait of the Artist as a Young Man, A, Joyce, James   3:305–11
Pride and Prejudice, Austen, Jane   2:295–300
Prime of Miss Jean Brodie, The, Spark, Muriel   4:303–8
Prince of Tides, The, Conroy, Pat   5:285–90
Ragged Dick, Alger, Horatio   2:301–7
Ragtime, Doctorow, E. L.   3:319–25
Rebecca, du Maurier, Daphne   3:326–33
Red Badge of Courage, The, Crane, Stephen   2:308–13
Red Pony, The, Steinbeck, John   3:334–37
Red Sky at Morning, Bradford, Richard   4:316–22
Road from Home, The, Kherdian, David   3:338–43
Robinson Crusoe, Defoe, Daniel   1:337–43
Roll of Thunder, Hear My Cry, Taylor, Mildred   3:350–55
Roots, Haley, Alex   5:298–305
Runner, The, Voigt, Cynthia   5:306–13
Scarlet Letter, The, Hawthorne, Nathaniel   1:351–57
Scarlet Pimpernel, The, Orczy, Baroness Emmuska   1:358–64
Separate Peace, A, Knowles, John   4:323–29
Shane, Schaefer, Jack   2:321–26
Shoeless Joe, Kinsella, W. P.   5:314–20
Siddhartha, Hesse, Hermann   1:365–70
Sister Carrie, Dreiser, Theodore   2:327–33
Slaughterhouse Five, Vonnegut, Kurt, Jr.   4:343–48
Sons and Lovers, Lawrence, D. H.   2:334–39
Sounder, Armstrong, William H.   3:370–76
Story Catcher, The, Sandoz, Mari   2:347–52
Strange Case of Dr. Jekyll and Mr. Hyde, The, Stevenson, Robert Louis   3:377–82
Stranger in a Strange Land, Heinlein, Robert A.   5:321–27
Summer of My German Soldier, Greene, Bette   4:371–77
Sweet Whispers, Brother Rush, Hamilton, Virginia   5:328–32
Tale of Two Cities, A, Dickens, Charles   1:371–78
Tess of the D'Urbervilles, Hardy, Thomas   2:353–59
Their Eyes Were Watching God, Hurston, Zora Neale   3:383–89
Things Fall Apart, Achebe, Chinua   2:360–65
Thousand Pieces of Gold, McCunn, Ruthanne Lum   2:366–71
Three Musketeers, The, Dumas, Alexandre   1:386–92
Time of the Hero, The, Vargas Llosa, Mario   5:333–38
Tituba of Salem Village, Petry, Ann   1:393–99
To Kill a Mockingbird, Lee, Harper   3:390–96
Tom Brown's Schooldays, Hughes, Thomas   2:372–77
Treasure Island, Stevenson, Robert Louis   1:400–405
Tree Grows in Brooklyn, A, Smith, Betty   3:397–403
Twenty-Thousand Leagues under the Sea, Verne, Jules   2:384–90
Uncle Tom's Cabin, Stowe, Harriet Beecher   2:403–9
Understand This, Tervalon, Jervey   5:339–45
War of the Worlds, The, Wells, H.G.   3:404–10
Watership Down, Adams, Richard   5:346–51
Wuthering Heights, Brontë, Emily   1:413–19
Yellow Raft in Blue Water, A, Dorris, Michael   5:360–66
NOW (National Organization of Women)   1:62; 4:22, 394; 5:136, 237
Nuclear energy   5:124, 127, 286
   Chernobyl disaster   5:286, 287 (illus.)
Nuclear weapons
   and arms control   4:71; 5:126, 225, 239, 252 (sidebar)
   arms race   5:252 (sidebar)
   hydrogen bomb   4:183
   (*See also* Atom bomb)

O

O Pioneers!, Cather, Willa   3:257–63
Oates, Joyce Carol, *Where Are You Going, Where*

Have You Been? 4:391–96
Occurrence at Owl Creek Bridge, An, Bierce, Ambrose 2:255–60; 3:281
O'Connor, Flannery, *Everything That Rises Must Converge* 5:88–94
Octavian (Octavius Caesar) 1:12 (sidebar), 13
Octoroons 3:18
Odria, Manuel 5:333–34
Odyssey, Homer 1:280–87
    Odysseus and the Sirens 1:284 (illus.)
    parallels to *Ivanhoe* 1:187
Oedipus complex (Freud) 2:336–37
Of Human Bondage, Maugham, W. Somerset 3:264–68
Of Mice and Men, Steinbeck, John 3:269–76
Ohio River, and Underground Railroad 2:16, 60
Oil booms of 1920s 3:45–46
"Okies" 3:46, 47, 49
Oklahoma 5:29, 269
Old age. *See* Senior citizens
Old Gringo, The, Fuentes, Carlos 3:277–83
Old Man and the Sea, The, Hemingway, Ernest 4:274–80
Oliver Twist, Dickens, Charles 2:261–67
Olympians 1:301
Once and Future King, The, White, T.H. 1:288–94
One Day in the Life of Ivan Denisovich, Solzhenitsyn, Alexander 4:281–87
One Flew over the Cuckoo's Nest, Kesey, Ken 4:288–94; 5:318 (sidebar)
One Hundred Years of Solitude, García Márquez, Gabriel 2:268–74
O'Neill, Eugene, *Long Day's Journey into Night* 3:218–24
Ongpatonga 1:209 (illus.)
Open Window, The, Saki 2:275–80
Oppenheimer, Robert 4:316
Orczy, Baroness Emmuska, *Scarlet Pimpernel, The* 1:358–64
Ordinary People, Guest, Judith 5:259–64
Orwell, George
    Animal Farm 4:14–20
    Nineteen Eighty-Four 5:251–58
Osborne, Sarah 1:79, 395, 396
Othello, Shakespeare, William 1:295–300
Ottoman Turks 1:295–96; 3:338–40
Our Town, Wilder, Thornton 3:284–89
Out of Africa, Dinesen, Isak 3:290–96
Outcasts of Poker Flat, The, Harte, Bret 2:281–87
Outsiders, The, Hinton, S. E. 5:265–70
Ovid, *Metamorphoses* 1:262
Ox-Bow Incident, The, Clark, Walter Van Tilburg 2:288–94

P

Pabel, Reinhold 4:373 (sidebar)
Pacificism 1:23 (sidebar), 142, 365, 369, 370
Paine, Thomas
    Common Sense 1:71–77, 94
    opposition to slavery 1:72 (sidebar)
    The Rights of Man 1:52
Pakistan 3:300, 301
Palestine 4:102–3, 105; 5:54
    (*See also* Israel)
Pamphlets
    Common Sense, Paine, Thomas 1:71–77
    Modest Proposal, A, Swift, Jonathan 1:266–72
    popularity in England 1:268
    popularity and limitations in colonies 1:72–73, 122
    by Swift 1:132
Panama Canal 3:231–32, 270
Pankhurst, Emmeline 2:335–36; 3:359
Paradise Lost, Milton, John 1:301–8
    influence on Herman Melville 1:54
    popularity in America 1:307
Paranormal phenomena 2:383 (sidebar); 5:47–48, 56, 239
Paredes, Américo 5:172
Paris, France
    as capital of western art 3:265–66
    Notre Dame cathedral 1:161, 162 (illus.), 163, 164 (sidebar)
Paris (Trojan prince) 1:8, 166, 281
Parks, Rosa 3:73; 5:11, 88, 185
Parnell, Charles 3:109–10
Parody 1:4
Parris, Rev. Samuel 1:79, 83 (sidebar), 394, 395, 421
Parthenon 1:240
Passage to India, A, Forster, E.M. 3:297–304
Pastoral novels 1:6
Paterson, Katherine, *Jacob Have I Loved* 4:216–20
Paton, Alan, *Cry, the Beloved Country* 4:94–100
Paxton Boys massacre 1:220–21
Peck, Robert Newton, *Day No Pigs Would Die, A* 3:94–99
Peloponnesian War 1:241, 324, 328
Pennsylvania 1:22, 71–72, 310
    Pittsburgh 4:7–9, 144, 149
Percy family 1:144–45, 149
Pericles of ancient Athens 1:17, 18, 240, 241, 322
Perón, Juan and Eva 5:208–9, 210
Persephone 1:283
Peru 4:221, 222; 5:333–38
Pesticides ("biocides") 4:337–42; 5:347, 351
Petrarch 1:345, 348
Petry, Ann, *Tituba of Salem Village* 1:393–99
Philadelphia, Pennsylvania 1:71–72, 310
Philippines 3:101
    Bataan Death March 4:81
Phillips, Wendell 2:89 (sidebar)
Phoenician alphabet 1:286–87
"Phrenology" 2:211
Pigman, The, Zindel, Paul 5:271–77
Pilgrim at Tinker Creek, Dillard, Annie 5:278–84
Pilgrimages 1:64–70, 145–46, 182
Pinkerton's National Detective Agency 3:225–26
Pinochet, August 5:169 (illus.)

Index

Piracy 1:400–402, 405
Pittsburgh, Pennsylvania 4:7–9
Plath, Sylvia, *Bell Jar, The* 4:21–27
Plato
    Academy 1:328
    complaining of Homer 1:285, 286 (sidebar)
    Republic 1:321–29
Plays
    Angels in America, Kushner, Tony 5:1–10
    Antigone, Sophocles 1:14–21
    Belle of Amherst, The, Luce, William 2:54–58
    Biloxi Blues, Simon, Neil 4:35–41
    Cherry Orchard, The, Chekhov, Anton 3:57–62
    Crucible, The, Miller, Arthur 1:78–86
    Cyrano de Bergerac, Rostand, Edmond 1:87–92
    Death of a Salesman, Miller, Arthur 4:109–15
    Doll's House, A, Ibsen, Henrik 2:111–17
    Elephant Man, The, Pomerance, Bernard 2:118–24
    Fences, Wilson, August 4:144–50
    Fiddler on the Roof, Stein, Joseph 3:119–24
    for colored girls who have considered suicide / when the rainbow is enuf, Shange, Ntozake 5:115–21
    Hamlet, Shakespeare, William 1:136–43
    Henry IV, Part I, Shakespeare, William 1:144–51
    I Never Sang for My Father, Anderson, Robert 5:201–7
    Julius Caesar, Shakespeare, William 1:189–95
    King Lear, Shakespeare, William 1:196–203
    Little Foxes, The, Hellman, Lillian 3:203–10
    Long Day's Journey into Night, O'Neill, Eugene 3:218–24
    Macbeth, Shakespeare, William 1:225–30
    Man for All Seasons, A, Bolt, Robert 1:231–37
    Medea, Euripides 1:238–41
    Member of the Wedding, The, McCullers, Carson 4:254–59
    Merchant of Venice, The Shakespeare, William 1:242–49
    Midsummer Night's Dream, A, Shakespeare, William 1:258–65
    Miracle Worker, The, Gibson, William 2:216–22
    Othello, Shakespeare, William 1:295–300
    Our Town, Wilder, Thornton 3:284–89
    Pygmalion, Shaw, George Bernard 3:312–18
    Raisin in the Sun, A, Hansberry, Lorraine 4:309–15
    Romeo and Juliet, Shakespeare, William 1:344–50
    Streetcar Named Desire, A, Williams, Tennessee 4:364–70
    Tempest, The, Shakespeare, William 1:379–85
    Twelve Angry Men, Rose, Reginald (screenplay) 4:378–83
    West Side Story, Laurents, Arthur, et al. 4:384–90
    Zoo Story, The, Albee, Edward 4:397–402
    Zoot Suit, Valdez, Luis 4:403–10
Plays, descriptions by type
    choreopoems 5:115, 117–18, 120–21
    histories 1:150
    morality plays 1:148
    revenge tragedies 1:142
Plessy v. Ferguson (Supreme Court ruling allowing segregation) 2:21, 399–400, 413; 3:351, 375, 419; 4:1; 5:90, 107–8
Plutarch 1:193–94
Pocho, Villarreal, José Antonio 4:295–302
Poe, Edgar Allan, *Cask of Amontillado, The* 2:81–86
Poetry
    Welsh regard for 3:64
    Aeneid, The, Virgil 1:8–13
    Beowulf, Anonymous 1:44–50
    Canterbury Tales, The, Chaucer, Geoffrey 1:64–70
    haiku 4:333, 334
    Iliad, Homer 1:166–73
    Inferno, Dante Alighieri 1:174–80
    Leaves of Grass, Whitman, Walt 2:195–201
    Odyssey, Homer 1:280–87
    Paradise Lost, Milton, John 1:301–8
    Waste Land, The, Eliot, T.S. 3:411–17
Poetry, types of
    blank verse 1:303 (sidebar)
    choreopoems 5:117–18
    epic poems 1:49, 153, 172, 173, 282 (sidebar), 285
Pogroms
    against Armenians 3:342
    against Jews 1:364
Poland
    of 1800s 2:384–85
    "capitalists" deported from, by Soviets 4:131–32
    Nazi invasion of 3:214; 4:193
    Stalin/Hitler partition agreement 4:17, 131
"Polis" or Greek city-state 1:286, 327–28
Political parties in America
    American Communist Party 3:40
    Democratic, as party of Irish Americans 3:401–2
    Democratic South becoming Republican 3:79
    Republicans of Progressive era 3:286
    Socialist Labor Party 3:174–75
    ward bosses 3:398
    Whigs, Democrats, and Republicans 2:2, 87
Politics in America
    campaigning in mid-19th century 2:2
    Chinese American influence on 4:126–27
    during Reconstruction, African Americans in 2:412
    enactment of income tax 3:285, 320
    enactment of referenda provisions 3:285
    first recall act 3:319
    Irish American neighborhoods 3:398–99
    New York's Tammany Hall 3:148–49, 398–99
    politicians' invocation of Lincoln 2:7
    Teapot Dome scandal 3:25
    televised debates costing Nixon 1960 presidential election 5:223

Polynesia   4:222
Pomerance, Bernard, *Elephant Man, The*   2:118–24
Poor Richard's Almanac, Franklin, Benjamin   1:309–15
Poorhouses, almshouses in 18th-century America   2:216, 219 (sidebar)
Pope, Alexander   1:343
Pope Boniface VIII   1:176, 177
Popes
   competing for control of Tuscany   1:174
   conflicts with Holy Roman Emperors   1:174, 176, 344, 345
   fathering children   1:296
Pornography, prevalence in Victorian Age   3:381
Porter, Katherine Anne, *Noon Wine*   3:243–48
Portrait of the Artist as a Young Man, A, Joyce, James   3:305–11
   as example of bildungsroman   3:264, 311
"Positivism"   3:213
Post-traumatic stress disorder   5:106
Potlatch ceremony of Kwakiutl   5:198 (illus.), 199
Potok, Chaim, *Chosen, The*   4:87–93
Pound, Ezra   3:413–14, 416; 5:42
Poverty
   of African American families   3:37; 4:5 (sidebar), 145; 5:329
   of American Indians   5:360–61
   and child abuse   5:329 (sidebar)
   as deserved, in Hinduism   3:300
   of Great Depression years   3:68, 126, 350
   and Johnson's War on Poverty   3:324; 5:68, 150, 266
   linked to emotional depression and pessimism   5:266 (sidebar)
   of Puerto Ricans   5:215–16
   and Reagan's welfare cuts   5:1, 329
   in South Central Los Angeles   5:339–42
   studies of, in 1960s   5:266
Poynings Law   1:267
Prairie Years, The. *See Abraham Lincoln: The Prairie Years*
Predestination   4:304
Prejudice. *See* Racism and prejudice
Premarital sex   5:324
Presbyterianism   4:10, 304
Presley, Elvis   4:172, 386
Pride and Prejudice, Austen, Jane   2:295–300
Prime of Miss Jean Brodie, The, Spark, Muriel   4:303–8
Primitivism   3:385 (sidebar)
Prince, The, Machiavelli, Niccolò   1:316–20
   influence in early 16th century   1:233
   influence upon Shakespeare   1:200, 380
Prince of Tides, The, Conroy, Pat   5:285–90
Printing and publishing
   advances in   1:160, 162 (sidebar); 2:234, 306, 419
   muckraking magazines   3:176
   paperback books   2:325
   pulp magazines   2:325; 3:226–27

Prisons   3:371, 374 (illus.)
Privateers   1:400
Proctor, John   1:81 (sidebar), 83 (sidebar)
Progress, belief in
   Stephen Crane's objections to   2:313
   destroyed by WWI   3:412
   fostered by Enlightenment (Age of Reason)   1:24–25, 268; 2:416
   reality belying   3:217, 227
   science and technology ("positivism") as 19th century's evidence for   2:416; 3:213
   Second Great Awakening contributing to   2:417–18
   tempered by Victorians' doubt   3:314
   and utopian philosophies of 19th century   2:195
   H. G. Wells's objections to   3:409
   (*See also* Evolution; Science/technology)
Prohibition
   disillusionment with   3:69, 227, 401
   fostering corruption, bootlegging, and gangsterism   3:69, 147–48, 366–67, 401
   restrictions retained in South   4:207 (sidebar)
   in San Francisco   3:226
   support by Anti-Saloon League and temperance movements   2:25 (sidebar), 85–86; 3:69, 75, 147, 401
   support from rural, anti-urban areas   3:69–70
   Volstead Act   3:147, 151, 401
   weaknesses of, as legislation   3:22–23, 69
   (*See also* Alcohol and alcoholism)
Project 100,000, draft of disadvantaged for Vietnam   5:102–3, 158, 307
Propaganda
   as aspect of fascism   4:304; 5:253
   pro-war, from Hollywood   4:325
   use by British   5:252, 257
   use of media for   4:66–67
   use by Soviets   5:252
Prosser, Gabriel   1:39, 42; 2:94
Prostitution
   in China   3:135
   of female Chinese immigrants   2:366–67
   near military installations   4:37
   serving gold miners of California   2:283–84
   women driven to, by lack of work
      America of 1880s   2:328–29
      France of 1800s   2:228
      Victorian England   2:264, 355
   women kept as, for repayment of debts (Victorian London)   2:264
Protest movements. *See* Civil rights movements; Counterculture
Protestantism
   African Methodist Episcopal Church   3:83
   all-black churches   3:250, 252
   Anglican Church (Church of England)   1:78, 123, 129, 232, 233 (sidebar), 306, 351, 393
   and anti-Catholic prejudice and policies   1:74, 132, 230, 269

Index

Baptists   5:*19*, *188*
Christian Socialist movement   2:*377*
clergymen denouncing women's rights activists   2:*25*
creationism   2:*30*
decline of influence in late 18th century   1:*102*
decline of influence in late 19th century   2:*329*
Dutch Reformed Church   1:*331, 425*
establishment of distinct denominations in colonial America   1:*106*
fundamentalists and New/Religious Right   5:*137–39*
Great Awakening in American colonies   1:*73, 106, 122, 424–25*
in Ireland   1:*267, 269*
Methodism   2:*357–58*
Presbyterianism   4:*10, 304*
as protest against abuses of Catholic Church   1:*231*
Quakerism   1:*23*; 2:*22, 25, 88–89*
as Reformation of Catholic Church   1:*231*; 2:*113*
revival meetings   1:*425*; 2:*315–16*
Second Great Awakening in America   1:*424–25*; 2:*23, 315–16, 404, 417–18*
segregation of churches   5:*189*
Shakerism   3:*95–99*
spread of, spurring legalization of divorce   2:*113*
television evangelists   5:*31–32*
Unitarianism   2:*54, 315*
(*See also* Puritanism)
Psychology
behavior modification and conditioning   5:*156–57*
changing views of mental illness   4:*289*
conceptions of intelligence   4:*152–53*
conflicting theories of nature of mankind   4:*233–34*
connectedness of mental health and human relationships   4:*153*
development of   3:*329, 378*; 4:*77*
ethical considerations of experimentation   4:*153*
insistence on domesticity and dependence for women   4:*167*
as means of rehabilitation of nonconformists   4:*399*
and paranormal phenomena   2:*383* (sidebar); 5:*47–48, 56, 239*
psychiatry   4:*289* (sidebar)
psychoanalysis   4:*168* (sidebar); 5:*42, 260–61, 262*
PTSD (post-traumatic stress disorder)   5:*106*
theories of absent father   4:*244–45*
theories of community collusion in evil   4:*238*
twins and struggle for identity   4:*219*
(*See also* Mental and emotional disabilities; Suicide)
Ptolemy   1:*305*
Puerto Rico and Puerto Ricans   3:*277*; 4:*385–86, 388–89, 401*; 5:*214–21*

Punishments
in 19th-century America   2:*17*
in 19th-century France   2:*225, 228*
aboard ships of Royal Navy   1:*273–74, 275* (illus.)
branding   1:*420*
capital   4:*379–80*; 5:*131*
collective, in British colonies   2:*362*
of drug users, racial inequality of   4:*250*
dueling   1:*389* (sidebar)
in Elizabethan England   1:*198* (sidebar)
of English schoolboys   2:*373–74*
feuds   2:*17* (sidebar)
flogging   2:*394, 395*
guillotining   1:*373*
hazing on ship   2:*394*
inequality of, for blacks   5:*16*
marooning   1:*401–2*
prisons   3:*371, 374* (illus.)
public hanging   1:*374*
quartering   1:*373–74*
of seamen   2:*394, 395*
in Southern prisons and road/chain gangs   3:*371, 374* (illus.)
in Soviet Union, Siberian exile and forced labor   4:*132, 282*
tarring and feathering   2:*17* (sidebar)
Puns
in Shakespeare   1:*348–49*
in Victorian Age   2:*30*
Puritanism
and Antinomians   1:*352, 357*
austerity and discipline   1:*78, 101, 393–94*
belief in witchcraft and Satan   1:*79–81, 394, 395–96, 421–23*
Calvinism   2:*54, 55*; 3:*377–78*; 4:*304*
concept of conversion   2:*55* (sidebar)
and Congregationalists   1:*357, 424–25*
Defoe influenced by   1:*338*
doctrines of   1:*23, 101–2, 352, 393–94*
Franklin influenced by   1:*311*
good works and redemption   1:*23, 101–2, 352*
Half-Way Covenant   1:*421*
hardships faced by colonists in New England   1:*351*
immigration to New England   1:*421*
intolerance   1:*102, 394*
Milton influenced by   1:*307*
as "purifiers" of Church of England   1:*299, 420*
Putnam, Ann   1:*79, 83* (sidebar), *396*
Pygmalion, Shaw, George Bernard   3:*312–18*
Pyle, Howard, *Merry Adventures of Robin Hood, The*   1:*250–57*
Pyramus and Thisbe   1:*259* (sidebar)

Q

Quadroons   3:*17–18*
Quakerism   1:*23*; 2:*22, 25, 88–89*
Quarterstaff fencing   1:*253*
Quixote. *See Adventures of Don Quixote, The*

Index

R

Rabbits 5:336–37, 348 (illus.)
Racism and prejudice
   American Communist Party's stand against 3:40; 4:211
   in American jury system before 1969 4:379 (sidebar)
   of Aryans, neo-Nazis, and neo-fascists 4:40, 50; 5:42
   in concept of "white man's burden" 2:147; 3:170, 172, 182 (sidebar)
   eliminating through claiming of identity 5:176
   of eugenics movement 5:42
   FEPC (Fair Employment Practices Commission) to investigate 3:42
   (See also Holocaust)
Racism and prejudice, against
   African Americans
      among immigrants 4:52
      antiblack propaganda 2:400
      Baldwin's condemnation of 5:111, 113
      in Caucasian standards of beauty 4:49–50
      combated by Du Bois 2:343–46
      covert 4:314
      creating self-hatred 4:53–54; 5:116
      economic 4:30–31, 33
      exacerbated by economic competition 2:43
      housing discrimination 2:13; 3:39, 237; 4:30–31
      by Ku Klux Klan 2:141 (sidebar), 143 (sidebar), 412; 3:419; 5:25, 130
      by labor unions 2:341
      in legal and prison systems 3:371
      Lincoln on 2:3, 5
      in minstrel shows 2:16–17, 21, 398
      in New South 2:399–400; 3:36–37, 41, 203, 320
      in professional sports 4:149
      race riots of early 19th century 2:6, 404; 3:160, 252, 321; 4:310
      race riots of 1940s 4:197, 201, 213, 247, 248 (illus.)
      "science" of ethnology contributing to 2:232–33
      Scottsboro case 3:39, 239
      sexual taboos 3:391
      social Darwinism contributing to 2:341
      soldiers in WWII 4:212–13
      stereotyping justifying slavery 1:39, 41, 42, 394; 2:403, 404
      as viewed by Styron 2:97
      by white supremacists 3:352
      (See also Lynching; Segregation; Slavery)
   African blacks 1:63; 2:360–65; 3:291; 4:94–100
   American Indians. See American Indians
   Anglos 4:320
   Armenians 4:200
   Chinese 2:175, 287, 367–68, 370 (sidebar), 371; 3:30; 4:124–27, 194, 330; 5:230–31
   Germans during WWII 4:375
   immigrants in general 4:194
   Irish 3:220, 221 (sidebar)
   Japanese 3:30; 4:137, 138–43, 194, 195, 330–31
   Jews. See Anti-Semitism
   Latinos
      deportations of braceros in 1930s 4:44
      mestizos or *criollos* 5:334–36
      in Southwest 4:320
      zoot suit riots of 1940s 4:295–97, 403–10
   lower castes in India 1:366; 2:183; 3:182, 184, 300
   migrant farm workers 3:29–30, 34, 49, 140–42, 143 (sidebar), 269–71, 275, 335, 337; 4:297 (sidebar)
   Moors 1:297, 299, 300
   Poles 4:369
   users of sign language 2:217
Radio
   Dylan Thomas's broadcasts 3:66–67
   FDR taking advantage of 3:127
   new teenage audience of 1950s 4:386, 391
   popularity of 3:3, 45
   "thrillers" produced on 3:329
Ragged Dick, Alger, Horatio 2:301–7
Ragtime, Doctorow, E. L. 3:319–25
Railroads
   in England 2:353, 354, 358
   in France 2:209–10
   in India 3:184–85
Railroads in U.S.
   California population boom and 2:175, 195
   Chinese workers on 4:124, 125; 5:75–77, 78 (illus.)
   contributing to western migration 2:327
   federal and state funding for expansion of 2:230
   hobo tradition of 1930s 3:46
   importance in Civil War 2:255, 256 (illus.)
   importance to travelers 2:175
   luxury travel in Pullman cars 2:306
   raising farm incomes 2:417
   refrigerated cars for transport of perishables 2:328; 3:175
   Thoreau's disapproval of 2:416
Raisin in the Sun, A, Hansberry, Lorraine 4:309–15
Randolph, A. Philip 3:42, 159–60; 4:255; 5:186, 188
Realism
   Bierce on 2:259–60
   of Crane 2:312
   described 2:259
   of Dreiser 2:327, 331
   of Joyce, as "slice of life" 3:111
   levels of 1:4, 6 (sidebar)
   in literature for young adults 5:265–66, 276
   "magical" 2:271, 273; 3:196, 202; 4:48; 5:169, 213, 330
   of *Les Misérables* 2:229

versus stereotypes   1:42
Whitman's impact on   2:200
Rebecca, du Maurier, Daphne   3:326–33
Reconnaissance planes   5:96
Reconstruction
   African Americans in politics   2:412
   Black Codes   2:412; 5:21
   carpetbaggers and scalawags   2:141
   civil rights granted, then ignored   2:21, 340–41, 412
   demise of plantations and wilderness   2:49, 53
   economy of South   2:41–42
   education of freed slaves   2:411–12, 413, 414
   end of   2:412–13
   Force Acts (1871 and 1872)   2:412
   Freedman's Bureau   2:411
   in Georgia   2:139–40
   Ku Klux Klan   2:141 (sidebar), 143 (sidebar), 412
   lack of training or means of survival for freed slaves   2:59, 411
   sharecropping and tenant farming   2:42, 411
   violence and unequal justice for freed slaves   5:20–21
   white backlash following   2:340–41, 412–13
   (See also Jim Crow laws; Segregation)
Red Badge of Courage, The, Crane, Stephen   2:308–13
Red Pony, The, Steinbeck, John   3:334–37
Red Power movement   2:79 (sidebar)
"Red Scare"   1:84–86; 3:105; 4:71–72; 5:2, 127
   (See also Cold War)
Red Sky at Morning, Bradford, Richard   4:316–22
Reform movements of 19th century
   child labor laws   2:103–4
   encouraged by belief in progress   2:195, 196
   multifaceted nature of   2:23
   as response to rapid change of Industrial Revolution   2:417
   settlement houses   3:397–98
   strengthened by Romantic movement   2:316
   temperance movement   2:25 (sidebar), 85; 3:147
   utopian societies of 1840s   2:418
   women's involvement in   2:423
Reform movements of 20th century
   against child labor   3:76 (sidebar), 77 (illus.)
   during Progressive Era   3:75–76
   Independent Living Movement   2:123
   Pure Food and Drug Act (1906)   3:179
   temperance movement   3:69, 75, 147
   (See also Civil rights movements; Prohibition)
Reformation   1:231; 2:113
Refugees   5:28–29
Reincarnation   3:300
Reisman, David   4:75, 111, 382
Religion
   and agnosticism   3:265
   of American Indians   2:71–72, 78, 178; 4:188
      healing ceremonies for returning war veterans   5:363

   in ancient Greece   1:15–16, 169
   ancient sacrificial rites   4:238
   Buddhism   1:365–69; 3:186–87; 5:48
   in China   3:133, 190, 193
   Chippewa *manitou*   5:246, 249 (sidebar)
   comparative conceptions of   5:57 (sidebar)
   conflicts with Darwinists   3:102, 404
   conflicts with non-believers in 20th century   3:102
   cults   5:83–84
   Daoism (also Taoism)   5:237
   Eastern, in America   5:237
   freedom of, in America   1:73–74
   "Great Chain of Being"   1:201, 203
   Hinduism   3:300, 302
   in India   1:366; 3:300–301
   Islam   1:296; 3:300
   miracles and paranormal phenomena   5:48
   monasticism   3:186–87
   moral sense directed toward political issues   1:96
   Mormonism   5:4
   Nation of Islam   3:238, 325; 4:56, 248–50; 5:12–13, 69, 110–11, 302
   of Nez Percé   2:161
   People's Temple and Jim Jones   5:84
   pilgrimages   1:64
   of Pueblo Indians   4:79
   rationalistic versus mystical/emotional   1:425; 3:426
   reincarnation   3:300
   vs. science in Victorian Age   2:29–30, 121–22
   syncretism   3:190–91; 4:44 (sidebar)
   transcendentalism   1:356–57; 2:54, 92, 314, 316–19, 416, 418–19
   Unification Church   5:83
   Zen Buddhism   4:334
   (See also Christianity; Greek myth; Jews; Sin and damnation)
Remarque, Erich Maria, *All Quiet on the Western Front*   3:8–14
Renaissance   1:2, 380
Renan, Ernest   3:213
Renault, Mary, *Bull from the Sea, The*   1:57–63
Republic, Plato   1:321–29
Republican Party of 1830s   2:2
"Resurrection men"   1:120–21
Retirement, problems of adjustment to   5:203, 273
Revival meetings   1:425
Revolution, French. *See* France in 18th century: French Revolution
Revolutions of 1848   1:376
Rhetoric
   of Churchill's speeches   4:361–62
   in colonial America   1:123
   of Kennedy's speeches   5:223
   of King's oratory   5:186
Rhodesia   4:165–66
Richard I of England (the Lion-Hearted)   1:181–82, 184 (illus.), 188, 251

Index

Richard II of England 1:144
Richelieu, Cardinal Duc de 1:387–89
Richter, Conrad, *Light in the Forest, The* 1:219–24
Richter, Hans Peter, *Friedrich* 4:157–64
Riegner, Gerhardt, 3:403
Right Stuff, The, Wolfe, Tom 5:291–97
Riis, Jacob 3:169 (sidebar), 285, 320
Rip Van Winkle, Irving, Washington 1:330–36
Risberg, Charles "Swede" 3:149
Road from Home, The, Kherdian, David 3:338–43
Roberts, Oral 5:31–32
Robeson, Paul 1:389–90
Robespierre, Maximilien 1:359 (illus.), 372
Robinson Crusoe, Defoe, Daniel 1:337–43
Rock 'n' roll 4:172, 386, 391–92
Rockefeller, John D. 2:306
Rocking-Horse Winner, The, Lawrence, D.H. 3:344–49
Rodeo 5:362, 364 (sidebar)
Rodriguez, Richard, *Hunger of Memory* 5:178–84
Roll of Thunder, Hear My Cry, Taylor, Mildred 3:350–55
Romantic movement
  Darwin's influence on 1:116
  disapproval of Industrial Revolution 1:115–16, 120
  emphasizing emotion, imagination, mystery, individuality, and nationalism 1:106, 115, 118–19, 217, 406
  favoring plain speech of common people 1:163
  influence on Dumas 2:104
  influence on Emerson 2:316–17, 319
  influence of French Revolution 1:116
  influence on Hermann Hesse 1:365, 370
  interest in medieval romance 1:413
  interest in past 2:104
  as reaction against rationality of Enlightenment 1:106, 217, 406
  reflections in Emily Brontë's works 1:413
  reflections in Jane Austen's works 2:300
  and transcendentalism 1:356–57; 2:54, 92, 314, 316–19, 416, 418–19
Rome, Italy
  in ancient times 1:9, 12–13, 189–92
  civil war, republic, and dictatorship 1:190
  mythical founding of 1:10 (sidebar)
  religious holidays 1:191–92
Romeo and Juliet, Shakespeare, William 1:344–50
  as model for *West Side Story* 4:384
Room of One's Own, A, Woolf, Virginia 3:356–63
Roosevelt, Eleanor 3:154, 392, 395, 424; 4:297
Roosevelt, Franklin Delano
  authorizing internment of Japanese Americans 4:138
  First Inaugural Address 3:125–30
  invocation of Lincoln 2:7
  New Deal 1:113; 3:45, 69, 128, 141
  political appointments of Irish Americans 3:401–2
  political support from Sandburg 2:7

reason for refusal to sign Dyer Antilynching Bill 3:154, 392
  support for equal rights 4:255
Roosevelt, Theodore
  as big game hunter 3:232 (sidebar)
  "big stick" corollary to Monroe Doctrine 3:277
  coining term "muckrakers" 3:176
  expansionism of 3:101, 231
  popularizing "Old West" myth of individualism 5:206
  as Progressive reformer 3:284–85
  support for preservation of buffalo 5:34
  support for trade union movement 3:420
  as trust buster 3:167
Roots, Haley, Alex 5:298–305
Rose, Reginald, *Twelve Angry Men* (screenplay) 4:378–83
Rosenberg, Julius and Ethel 4:72, 380, 381 (illus.); 5:2, 127
Rostand, Edmond, *Cyrano de Bergerac* 1:87–92
Rotarians 5:202
Rothstein, Arnold 3:149–50; 4:261; 5:315, 316 (illus.)
Rousseau, Jean-Jacques 1:409 (sidebar)
Runner, The, Voigt, Cynthia 5:306–13
Rush, Benjamin 4:289
Russia, czarist
  anti-Semitism and pogroms 1:364; 3:119–21
  Bolshevik Revolution 4:14, 16
  Bolsheviks and Mensheviks 4:14
  Cossacks 3:233
  decline of nobility 2:35–36; 3:57
  education reform 3:58
  emancipation of serfs 2:34
  industrialization 4:14
  intelligentsia 3:58
  land ownership 3:57–58, 60
  local government 2:35
  marriage and divorce 2:37, 39
  oppression of Poland 2:384–85
  peasants and intelligentsia 4:14
  revolution of 1905 1:363; 3:59, 232
  Russo-Japanese War (1904–05) 4:59
  Russo-Turkish war 2:37–39
  as threat to British-controlled Punjab 3:184, 185
  women's rights movement 2:37, 39
  WWI 3:8, 11 (sidebar)
  (*See also* Soviet Union)
Rustin, Bayard 5:188

S

Sacatras 3:18
Sackville-West, Vita 3:361–62
Sailboats 2:395
Saint-Domingue (Haiti) 5:116–17
Saint-Exupéry, Antoine de, *Little Prince, The* 3:210–17
Saki, *Open Window, The* 2:275–80

Salazar, Rubén   4:47, 410
Salem, Massachusetts   1:78–80, 355, 395–97
Salinas Valley, California   3:334–35
Salinger, J. D.
    Catcher in the Rye   4:73–78
    as reclusive   5:319
Salk, Jonas Edward   4:10
San Francisco
    in 1920s   3:226
    Chinatown   3:226; 5:74–75, 77–79
    prejudice against Chinese   2:367–68
    vigilantes   2:286–87
Sand, George (Amantine-Aurore-Lucile Dupin)
    2:212; 3:406
Sandburg, Carl
    Abraham Lincoln: The Prairie Years   2:1–7
    on *Call of the Wild*   3:56
Sandoz, Mari, *Story Catcher, The*   2:347–52
Saroyan, William, *Human Comedy, The*   4:193–200
Satan. *See* Devil (Satan)
Satire
    Adventures of Don Quixote, The   1:4, 6–7
    Devil and Tom Walker, The   1:101–6
    Gulliver's Travels   1:129–35
    Modest Proposal, A   1:266–72
    use in Shakespeare's time   1:349
Saxo Grammaticus   1:136, 139, 141 (sidebar)
Scarlet Letter, The, Hawthorne, Nathaniel   1:351–57
Scarlet Pimpernel, The, Orczy, Baroness Emmuska
    1:358–64
Schaefer, Jack, *Shane*   2:321–26
Schlafly, Phyllis   5:136–37, 138 (illus.)
Schooners   1:401
Science fiction   2:388–89; 4:347; 5:54–56, 126
    (sidebar)
    Brave New World   5:39–45
    Childhood's End   5:53–60
    Dune   5:81–87
    episodes in *Slaughterhouse Five*   4:347
    Fahrenheit 451   5:95–100
    Foundation   5:122–28
    House of Stairs   5:156–62
    Left Hand of Darkness, The   5:236–42
    Nineteen Eighty-Four   5:251–58
    and purported UFOs   4:347–48; 5:59 (illus.)
    as "speculative fiction"   5:141
    Stranger in a Strange Land   5:321–27
    Jules Verne as father of   2:388–89
    War of the Worlds, The   3:404–10
    H. G. Wells as father of   2:389
    women writers of   5:239
    (*See also* Fantasy)
Science/technology
    American Enlightenment   2:416
    anthropology   2:72, 179; 4:221–27; 5:42
    assembly line production and mass production
        3:89, 100–101, 102
    automobile   2:128 (sidebar); 3:23, 77, 88–89,
        94, 101; 5:40 (illus.)
    aviation   3:211–12, 367; 5:96, 293–94

    behaviorism   5:45
    civilian applications of war technology   4:236
    computers   5:97, 127
    contraceptives   2:211; 5:272, 324
    cotton gin   2:403
    drugs and pharmaceuticals   3:379
    electricity   3:89
    in Elizabethan Age   1:142 (sidebar), 200
    in Enlightenment   1:24–26, 268–69, 272
    "ethnology"   2:232–33
    eugenics   3:272; 4:152; 5:41–42
    explorations   1:118 (sidebar)
    explosives   5:76
    extrasensory perception (ESP)   5:47, 239
    on farms   3:5–6
    in Franklin's day   1:24–26
    Galileo, Copernicus, and Newton   1:24, 94, 305
    indoor plumbing   3:77
    Industrial Revolution   1:115, 336; 2:119
    influence on H. G. Wells   3:404–5
    innoculations against disease   3:378, 406
    jet engine   4:71
    motion pictures   3:3, 89, 101
    nuclear energy   5:124, 127, 286
    Pasteur's discoveries   3:285, 406
    penicillin   3:366
    pesticides ("biocides") and DDT   4:337–42
    "phrenology"   2:211
    physics and principle of indeterminacy   5:283
    printing and publishing   1:160, 162 (sidebar);
        2:234, 306, 419
    professionalization and specialization of   2:119
    psychiatry   4:289 (sidebar)
    psychoanalysis   4:168 (sidebar); 5:42, 260–61,
        263
    psychokinesis and telekinesis   5:47–48
    radio   3:3, 45, 89
    religion and   2:29–30, 121–22
    and "resurrection men"   1:120–21
    in Romantic period   1:116
    satellites in space   5:54
    space exploration   5:53, 54, 81–82
    steam threshing machine   2:354
    steamships   2:391, 394–95
    submarines   2:385–86
    telecommunications   5:54
    telephone   2:128 (sidebar); 3:77
    tractors   3:6, 92
    (*See also* Evolution; Progress, belief in;
        Psychology; Railroads; Television; War
        weaponry)
Scopes Trial   3:102 (sidebar)
Scotland
    Calvinism in   3:377; 4:304
    education of women in 1930s   4:303–4
    Gowrie Conspiracy   1:229
    Hebrides   1:226
    Highlanders   1:187
    as Presbyterians   4:10, 304
    status of women in 11th century   1:226

Index

    in time of *Macbeth* (11th century)   **1**:*225–26*
    troubled relations with England   **1**:*145, 150, 181, 187, 201*
Scott, Sir Walter
    emulated by Cooper   **1**:*208*
    friend of Washington Irving   **1**:*105*
    influencing Hugo   **1**:*165*
    Ivanhoe   **1**:*181–88*
Scottsboro case   **3**:*39, 239*
Seale, Bobby   **4**:*54*
Second Great Awakening   **1**:*424–25*; **2**:*23, 404, 417–18*
Secret Life of Walter Mitty, The, Thurber, James   **3**:*364–69*
Secular humanism   **5**:*138*
Segregation
    acceptance for time being by Booker T. Washington   **2**:*341, 342, 343, 344, 345, 410, 413, 414*; **3**:*162, 250, 320, 385*
    of churches   **5**:*189*
    documentation of negative effects   **4**:*32–33*
    in New Orleans   **3**:*17–18*; **5**:*22*
    protest by (multiracial) high school football team   **4**:*29*
    in public facilities   **3**:*38* (illus.), *42* (illus.); **4**:*29* (illus.)
    in public transportation   **5**:*88–90, 185–86*
    in schools for disabled   **2**:*221* (sidebar)
    in South   **1**:*399*; **2**:*97*; **3**:*419*; **4**:*28–29, 373–74*; **5**:*22*
    in Supreme Court rulings
        overturned for residential housing, interstate bus travel   **4**:*201*
        overturned for schools in *Brown v. Board of Education*   **3**:*375*; **4**:*29–30, 314*; **5**:*90, 108, 180, 181*
        sanctioned by *Plessy v. Ferguson*   **2**:*21, 399–400, 413*; **3**:*351, 375, 419*; **4**:*1*; **5**:*90, 107–8*
    of U.S. military during WWII   **3**:*41–42*; **4**:*195, 197, 374* (sidebar)
    (*See also* African Americans' civil rights/reform/power movements; Integration; Jim Crow laws)
Self-Reliance, Emerson, Ralph Waldo   **2**:*314–20*
Senior citizens
    loneliness, depression, serious illness, and suicide   **5**:*273, 275* (illus.)
    problems of adjustment to retirement   **5**:*203, 273*
Separate Peace, A, Knowles, John   **4**:*323–29*
Serbia   **3**:*8, 11* (sidebar)
Serling, Rod   **4**:*379*
Seventeen Syllables, Yamamoto, Hisaye   **4**:*330–36*
Sex education
    for mentally handicapped   **4**:*152*
    programs of 1960s   **5**:*153* (sidebar)
    social purity movement of late 19th century   **2**:*423*
Sexual dimension of life

    in 19th century   **2**:*212, 423*
    abuse of African American women   **4**:*54*
    abuse of female slaves   **2**:*49, 60, 169, 406*
    adultery/infidelity   **5**:*273, 287*
    AIDS   **5**:*9*
    Catholic and Presbyterian views on   **4**:*304* (sidebar)
    changing mores   **5**:*272–73*
    contraceptives   **2**:*211*; **5**:*272, 324*
    effects of childhood abuse   **5**:*289–90*
    "free love" movement of 1960s   **5**:*272*
    Freud's arguments against repression   **3**:*23*
    harassment of women in workplace   **1**:*35*
    hypocrisy of public attitudes   **4**:*75*
    impotence   **4**:*128*
    incest   **4**:*52*
    interracial taboos, miscegenation   **3**:*391*
    Kinsey Report   **4**:*75, 241, 398–99* (sidebar); **5**:*324*
    rape   **4**:*395*; **5**:*117, 136, 141*
    sexual revolution of 1960s and '70s   **5**:*151*
    treatment in literature as shocking   **4**:*74*
    Victorians' repression of   **2**:*334, 336, 338–39, 355*; **3**:*18, 380–81*
    (*See also* Homosexuality; Love and marriage; Prostitution)
Shakerism   **3**:*95–99*
Shakespeare, William
    Hamlet   **1**:*136–43*
    Henry IV, Part I   **1**:*144–51*
    Julius Caesar   **1**:*189–95*
    King Lear   **1**:*196–203*
    Macbeth   **1**:*225–30*
    Merchant of Venice, The   **1**:*242–49*
    Midsummer Night's Dream, A   **1**:*258–65*
    Othello   **1**:*295–300*
    Romeo and Juliet   **1**:*344–50*
    Tempest, The   **1**:*379–85*
Shane, Schaefer, Jack   **2**:*321–26*
Shange, Ntozake
    Betsey Brown   **4**:*28–34*
    for colored girls who have considered suicide / when the rainbow is enuf   **5**:*115–21*
Sharecropping and tenant farming   **2**:*42, 411*; **3**:*80, 104, 105, 249, 350–51, 370–71, 418*; **4**:*2*
    STFU (Southern Tenant Farmers' Union)   **3**:*208*
Shaw, George Bernard, *Pygmalion*   **3**:*312–18*
Shelley, Mary
    daughter of Mary Wollstonecraft   **1**:*115, 116, 407*
    Frankenstein   **1**:*115–21*
Shelley, Percy Bysshe   **1**:*115, 116, 119*
Shepard, Alan   **5**:*292, 296*
Sherman, William Tecumseh   **2**:*139, 140* (illus.), *165* (sidebar)
Shipping industry
    of early 19th century   **2**:*391–92, 393, 394–95*
    longshoremen   **3**:*161* (sidebar)
Ships
    privateers   **1**:*400*

sailboats 2:*395*
schooners 1:*401*
steam-powered 1:*404 (sidebar)*; 2:*394-95*
Shoeless Joe, Kinsella, W. P. 5:*314-20*
Short stories
   Almos' a Man, Wright, Richard 4:*1-6*
   Barn Burning, Faulkner, William 2:*41-46*
   Bear, The, Faulkner, William 2:*47-53*
   Cask of Amontillado, The, Poe, Edgar Allan
     2:*81-86*
   Child's Christmas in Wales, A, Thomas, Dylan
     3:*63-67*
   Christmas Memory, A, Capote, Truman 3:*68-74*
   Devil and Tom Walker, The, Irving, Washington
     1:*101-6*
   Dubliners, Joyce, James 3:*106-11*
   Everything That Rises Must Converge, O'Connor,
     Flannery 5:*88-94*
   Legend of Sleepy Hollow, The, Irving, Washington
     1:*211-18*
   Lottery, The, Jackson, Shirley 4:*235-39*
   Most Dangerous Game, The, Connell, Richard
     3:*231-35*
   Necklace, The, Maupassant, Guy de 2:*244-48*
   Noon Wine, Porter, Katherine Anne 3:*243-48*
   Notorious Jumping Frog of Calaveras County, The,
     Twain, Mark 2:*249-54*
   Occurrence at Owl Creek Bridge, An, Bierce,
     Ambrose 2:*255-60*
   Open Window, The, Saki 2:*275-80*
   Outcasts of Poker Flat, The, Harte, Bret
     2:*281-87*
   Rip Van Winkle, Irving, Washington 1:*330-36*
   Rocking-Horse Winner, The, Lawrence, D.H.
     3:*344-49*
   Secret Life of Walter Mitty, The, Thurber, James
     3:*364-69*
   Seventeen Syllables, Yamamoto, Hisaye
     4:*330-36*
   Where Are You Going, Where Have You Been?,
     Oates, Joyce Carol 4:*391-96*
   Worn Path, A, Welty, Eudora 3:*418-24*
   Yellow Wallpaper, The, Gilman, Charlotte Perkins
     2:*422-28*
   Yentl, the Yeshiva Boy, Singer, Isaac Bashevis
     3:*425-31*
   Young Goodman Brown, Hawthorne, Nathaniel
     1:*420-26*
Siberia 4:*133-35*
Sicily 4:*67*
Siddartha Gautama 1:*365-68*
Siddhartha, Hesse, Hermann 1:*365-70*
Silent Spring, Carson, Rachel 4:*337-42*; 5:*35*
Silko, Leslie Marmon, *Ceremony* 4:*79-86*
Silver. *See* Gold rushes and silver strikes
Simon, Neil, *Biloxi Blues* 4:*35-41*
Sin and damnation
   beliefs of Calvinists 3:*377*; 4:*304*
   beliefs of Puritans 1:*23, 393, 421*
   beliefs in Shakespeare's time 1:*143*
   depictions in morality plays 1:*148*
   and guilt in *The Scarlet Letter* 1:*351, 355-56*
   in *Paradise Lost* 1:*301, 306*
   and predestination 4:*304*
   in *Young Goodman Brown* 1:*420-26*
Sinclair, Upton, *Jungle, The* 3:*174-80, 320*
Singer, Isaac Bashevis, *Yentl, the Yeshiva Boy*
   3:*425-31*
Sister Carrie, Dreiser, Theodore 2:*327-33*
Skinner, B. F. 5:*156, 279*
Slaughterhouse Five, Vonnegut, Kurt, Jr. 4:*343-48*
Slave narratives
   described 2:*171*; 4:*205*
   Douglass, Frederick (*Narrative of the Life of
     Frederick Douglass*) 2:*236-41*
   Jacobs, Harriet (*Incidents in the Life of a Slave Girl*)
     2:*168-73*
   by Northrup, Solomon 2:*410*
   Roots as 5:*305*
Slave trade
   auction block 1:*40 (illus.)*
   diagram of slave ship 1:*38 (illus.)*
   English involvement in/prohibition of
     1:*274-75, 299, 337-38*; 2:*361*
   impelled by need for labor 1:*103*
   missionaries' attempts to atone for 2:*361-62*
   overview 1:*37, 103*
   traders despised 1:*103*
Slavery in America
   of American Indians by forced indenture
     2:*175*
   causing rift between North and South 2:*88,
     172, 188, 403-4*
   of Chinese prostitutes 2:*366-67*
   in colonial America 1:*394*; 2:*93, 175*
   Compromise of 1850 2:*404-5*
   as depicted in *Tituba of Salem Village* 1:*397-98*
   extent of, in Old South 2:*188, 405, 410*
   Fugitive Slave Acts (1793 and 1850) 1:*42*;
     2:*16, 62, 170, 189, 404-5, 410*
   Kansas-Nebraska Act (1854) 1:*42*; 2:*5
     (sidebar), 172, 193*
   in Kentucky 2:*59-60*
   Kongo kingdom and 2:*145*
   legacy of, in late 20th century 2:*65*
   in Maryland 2:*236-37*
   Missouri Compromise (1820) 2:*5 (sidebar),
     15-16, 22*
   Nat Turner's Rebellion 2:*169-70*
   in North Carolina 2:*168*
   opposition of
     Patrick Henry 1:*126 (sidebar)*
     Thomas Paine 1:*72 (sidebar)*
     Henry David Thoreau 1:*88, 89 (sidebar)*
   racist justifications of 1:*39, 41, 42, 394*; 2:*403,
     404*
   references to, deleted from Declaration of
     Independence 1:*98*
   reliance upon, for harvesting of cotton 2:*15,
     22, 44 (illus.), 59, 168, 403*

Index

slave codes and patrols   1:103; 2:189, 190 (sidebar)
  as soul-corrupting for whites   2:52, 408
  Southern states avoiding mention in state constitutions   1:99 (sidebar)
  and Underground Railroad   2:16, 60, 62, 189, 238, 406–7
  whites' feelings of guilt at   2:52, 53
  (See also Abolitionists/Abolition of slavery; African Americans)
Slavery in North America
  among Canadian Kwakiutl   5:194–95
  brought by Spaniards to Puerto Rico   5:214
Slaves
  Amistad mutiny   1:43
  arson by   2:189
  cimaroons   1:401–2
  communities and culture   2:407
  escapes, rebellions, and resistance   1:39, 43, 401–2; 2:60, 93, 94–95, 169–70, 188–89, 406–7
  family life   2:60, 169, 237–38, 405, 406, 410; 3:423; 4:204–5
  female, sexual abuse of   2:49, 60, 169, 406
  food and clothing   2:237
  freed before Emancipation Proclamation   2:93–94, 168–69, 238
  ill-prepared for freedom   2:411
  literacy   2:16, 24–25
  living and working conditions   2:189 (sidebar), 237, 405, 410
  loyalty of some to white masters during Civil War   2:410–11
  music   2:398, 407
  punishment   2:240–42, 405, 410
  religion   2:407; 3:83
  social distinctions between   3:387
  use of cunning and manipulative behavior   2:401
Sleator, William, *House of Stairs*   5:156–62
Smith, Bessie   3:253 (illus.)
Smith, Betty, *Tree Grows in Brooklyn, A*   3:397–403
Smith, Henry Nash   3:226
Smith, Joseph Jr.   5:4
Smoking. *See* Tobacco
So Far from the Bamboo Grove, Watkins, Yoko K.   4:349–55
Social Darwinism. *See under* Evolution
Social Security System   3:128
Socialism
  American, birth of   3:174–75
  labor unions accused of   3:144
  opposed by fascism   4:66
  popular among European immigrants   3:321
  utopian   5:251–52
Socrates   1:240, 322–24, 327
Solzhenitsyn, Alexander, *One Day in the Life of Ivan Denisovich*   4:281–87
Sons and Lovers, Lawrence, D. H.   2:334–39
  as example of bildungsroman   3:264
Sophists   1:19, 240

Sophocles, *Antigone*   1:14–21
Souls of Black Folk, The, Du Bois, W. E. B.   2:340–46; 3:320
Sounder, Armstrong, William H.   3:370–76
South, The
  of 1980s   3:78–79
  anti-Yankee bias   3:76
  Christmas traditions   3:69
  folklore in   2:48–49
  homeopathy and Indian remedies   3:68–69
  hunting in   2:47–48
  Illinois' ties to   2:8–9
  industrialization/decline of agriculture and aristocracy   3:76, 203; 4:364–65, 368; 5:91, 129–30
  and "King" Cotton   2:15, 22, 44 (illus.), 168, 403
  mixed race offspring   2:49; 3:17–18, 81, 83
  "New"   3:72–73, 203
  plantation life   2:137–38
  religious influences   3:76–77
  segregation in   1:399; 2:97; 3:419; 4:28–29, 373–74; 5:22
  social stratification in rural areas and small towns   3:393
  storytelling tradition   3:421
  textile mills and mill towns   3:76, 153, 203–4; 4:256
  womanhood, ideal of   3:19, 392–93; 4:366–67
  (See also Civil War; Jim Crow laws; Reconstruction)
South Africa, racism and apartheid   1:63; 3:86; 4:94–100
South America
  Argentina   5:208–11, 212–13
  Chile   5:163–70
  Colombia   2:268–70, 272–73
  Peru   4:221, 222; 5:333–38
South Carolina   5:285–86
South Pacific
  climate   4:231 (sidebar)
  island fighting and major sea battles (1942–45)   4:60–61
  island peoples' origins   4:221–22
  Japanese conquests in WWII   4:178
  Philippines   3:101; 4:81
Southey, Robert   1:121
Soviet Union
  anti-Semitism   3:124–25; 5:122
  anti-Zionism   4:107–8
  atomic bomb capability   4:183; 5:96, 126
  centralized planning and control of means of production   5:124
  de-Stalinization   4:285–86
  European conquests and sphere of influence   5:123 (sidebar), 224, 253–54
  Five-Year Plans and forced labor   4:16, 132
  forced collectivization of agriculture   4:281–85
  Gorbachev and "perestroika"   5:8
  gulag system of labor camp prisons   4:282–85; 5:239 (sidebar)

Index

invasion of Armenia   3:*340*
invasion of Poland   3:*340*; 4:*131*
propaganda   5:*252*
reprisals against Japanese in Korea and Manchuria   4:*350*
seen as "controlling" international communism   4:*166*
Siberia   4:*133–35*
Sputniks and space program   5:*81, 291, 292, 293, 294, 321*
Stalin/Hitler non-aggression pact (1939)   3:*210, 214*; 4:*17*
Stalin's reign of terror and purges   4:*16–17, 166*
suppression of Hungarian uprising (1956)   4:*166*
totalitarianism   4:*16*
Ukraine, Babi Yar massacre   4:*120*
(See also Russia)
Space Age
 Dillard's musings   5:*279–80, 281* (sidebar)
 manned space flight highlights   5:*294* (sidebar)
 moon landing   5:*81–82*
 NASA (National Aeronautics and Space Administration)   5:*81, 291*
 Right Stuff, The   5:*291–97*
 satellites for communications   5:*54*
 treaty prohibiting military use of space   5:*239*
 U.S.-Soviet competition in space race   5:*53, 81, 321–22*
 (See also Aviation; War weaponry)
Spain
 Civil War   4:*67*
 decline of empire   1:*1–3*
 fascism in   1:*293–94*; 4:*67*
 Inquisition   1:*2–3*
 invasion of Italy   1:*317*
 wars with England and France   1:*1–2, 87, 88, 130–31, 201, 305*
Spanish-American War (1898)   3:*101, 278*
Spark, Muriel, *Prime of Miss Jean Brodie, The*   4:*303–8*
Sparta   1:*324–25, 328*
Speech on the Evacuation at Dunkirk, Churchill, Winston   4:*356–63*
Speeches
 "Ain't I a Woman?", Truth, Sojourner   2:*22–27*
 John Brown's Final Speech, Brown, John   2:*188–94*
 First Inaugural Address, Roosevelt, Franklin D.   3:*125–30*
 Gettysburg Address, Lincoln, Abraham   2:*130–36*
 "Give Me Liberty or Give Me Death", Henry, Patrick   1:*122–28*
 "I Have a Dream", King, Martin Luther, Jr.   5:*185–93*
 "I Will Fight No More Forever", Joseph, Chief   2:*160–67*
 Inaugural Address, Kennedy, John F.   5:*222–28*
 On the Evacuation at Dunkirk, Churchill, Winston   4:*356–63*

Spencer, Herbert   2:*341*
Spinsterhood, in early 19th-century England   2:*297*
Spock, Benjamin   4:*21–22*
Sports. See Entertainment; Games and sports
Spreckels, Claus and sugar interests   3:*269, 270* (sidebar), *319*
Sputnik   5:*81, 291, 292, 293, 294, 321*
Stalin, Josef
 banning books depicting life in West   5:*96*
 British outrage at   4:*17*
 Five-Year Plans for economic development   4:*16, 282*
 forced collectivization of agriculture   4:*281–82*; 5:*122*
 as Marxist Party member   4:*14, 15* (illus.)
 non-aggression pact with Hitler   3:*210, 213–14*; 4:*17*
 oppression or extermination of Jews   3:*123–24*
 political prisoners exiled to Siberian gulags   4:*282–85*; 5:*239* (sidebar)
 purges of opponents   4:*16–17*; 5:*122, 254*
 (See also Soviet Union)
Stanley, Henry Morton   2:*146*
Stanton, Elizabeth Cady   2:*24, 55*; 3:*16*
Steamships   1:*404* (sidebar); 2:*391, 394–95*
Stein, Joseph, *Fiddler on the Roof*   3:*119–24*
Steinbeck, John
 Grapes of Wrath, The   3:*138–45*
 Of Mice and Men   3:*269–76*
 Red Pony, The   3:*334–37*
Stevenson, Robert Louis
 on *Pride and Prejudice*   2:*300*
 Strange Case of Dr. Jekyll and Mr. Hyde, The   3:*377–82*
 on *Tess of the D'Urbervilles*   2:*359*
 Treasure Island   1:*400–405*
STFU (Southern Tenant Farmers' Union)   3:*208*
Stock market
 1929 crash and bank failures   3:*125–26, 208*
 speculation fever of 1920s   3:*146*
 speculations in trusts and railroads of 1900   3:*167* (sidebar)
 (See also Great Depression)
Stoicism   1:*192–93*
Stoneham, C. A.   3:*149*
Story Catcher, The, Sandoz, Mari   2:*347–52*
Stowe, Harriet Beecher
 relationship with Harriet Jacobs   2:*172*
 Uncle Tom's Cabin   2:*403–9*
Strachey, Lytton   3:*356*
Strange Case of Dr. Jekyll and Mr. Hyde, The, Stevenson, Robert Louis   3:*377–82*
Stranger in a Strange Land, Heinlein, Robert A.   5:*321–27*
"Stream of consciousness" writing   3:*111, 358*
Streetcar Named Desire, A, Williams, Tennesse   4:*364–70*
Streetcars   2:*328*; 3:*25*; 4:*366*
Stuyvesant, Peter   1:*331*

LITERATURE AND ITS TIMES   ∼   VOLUME 2   479

Index

Styron, William, *Confessions of Nat Turner, The* 2:93–98
Submarines 2:385–86
Suburbia 4:73
Suez Canal 3:184; 4:107
Suffrage (right to vote)
   for African Americans 4:148
      granted by 14th and 15th Amendments 5:21
      Jim Crow laws restricting 3:37, 352, 419; 4:1; 5:22
      Mississippi Plan (1890) preventing 5:22
      protected by Civil Rights and Voting Rights Acts (1957 and 1965) 5:22, 186
   for American Indians 4:80
   expansion by elimination of property qualifications 2:302
   hindered for freed blacks 2:341
   Nationality Act (1940) 4:80
   for women. *See* Women's suffrage
Suicide
   by American Indians 4:83
   attempts by Shange 5:120
   effects of childhood abuse 5:288, 289–90
   of interned Japanese Americans 4:140
   of Japanese girls in Korea (1944–45) 4:350, 353
   of Jim Jones and 911 members of People's Temple 5:84
   by kamikazi pilots 4:61 (sidebar), 62 (illus.)
   in *Madame Bovary* 2:211–12
   by men 4:23, 114 (sidebar)
   of prep school students 4:74
   as response to depression 5:259–60
   of Sylvia Plath 4:22–26
   of teenagers 5:259–60, 261
   by Vietnam War veterans 5:106
   by white males 5:273
Sullivan, Joseph 3:149
Summer of My German Soldier, Greene, Bette 4:371–77
Sumner, William 3:207
Sun Yat-Sen, Dr. 4:126; 5:229
Supernatural
   alchemy 1:384, 385 (sidebar)
   astrology 1:346, 350
   belief in, by American Indians 4:83
   belief in *curanderismo* 4:45
   belief in, in China 3:133
   belief in, in Elizabethan/Jacobean era 1:194–95, 227–28, 262, 346, 350
   belief in, in Victorian England 1:418–19; 2:185, 383
   in *Beloved* 2:63
   in *Beowulf* 1:46–48, 49
   brujas (witches) 4:46
   dreams related to 1:424
   in *Hamlet* 1:138, 141, 142 (sidebar)
   in *The Hobbit* 1:153
   in *Julius Caesar* 1:195
   in *Legend of Sleepy Hollow, The* 1:213, 215, 217
   and "mysteriousness" of African and African American culture 5:330
   and mysticism 1:416
   and paranormal phenomena 2:383 (sidebar); 5:47–48, 56, 239
   in *Romeo and Juliet* 1:346, 350
   superstitions associated with Chinese New Year 5:75, 76 (illus.)
   in *Tempest, The* 1:381, 383
   in *Turn of the Screw, The* 2:381
   (*See also* Witchcraft)
Swarthout, Glendon, *Bless the Beasts and Children* 5:34–38
Sweden, immigration to U.S. 3:243–44, 259–60
Sweet Whispers, Brother Rush, Hamilton, Virginia 5:328–32
Swift, Jonathan
   criticism of *Robinson Crusoe* 1:343
   Gulliver's Travels 1:129–35
   Modest Proposal, A 1:266–72
Syncretism 3:190–91; 4:44 (sidebar)

T

Tahiti, 1:274, 278, 392
Taine, Hippolyte 3:213
Taiwan 3:190; 5:254
Tale of Two Cities, A, Dickens, Charles 1:371–78
Tammany Hall, New York 3:148–49, 398–99
Tan, Amy
   Joy Luck Club, The 5:229–35
   Kitchen God's Wife, The 3:189–95
Tasmania 3:406
Taverns 1:331
Taylor, Mildred, *Roll of Thunder, Hear My Cry* 3:350–55
Teapot Dome scandal 3:25
Technology. *See* Science/technology
Teilhard de Chardin, Pierre 5:93
Telecommunications 5:54
Telekinesis 5:47–48
Telepathy 5:239
Television
   as babysitter 5:36–37
   Bonanza creating sense of family security 5:203 (sidebar)
   debates costing Nixon 1960 presidential election 5:223
   development of 3:92; 5:96–97
   golden age of TV drama 4:379
   impact on conduct of Vietnam War and antiwar sentiment 5:37
   impact on public support for civil rights protesters 5:108
   interconnectedness versus loneliness of viewers 4:398
   spreading conformity 4:236
   violent content of programming 5:62

westerns 5:201–2
(See also Media)
Television evangelists 5:31–32, 137–38, 140 (illus.)
Temperance movement 2:25 (sidebar), 85–86; 3:69, 75, 147
Tempest, The, Shakespeare, William 1:379–85
Templars 1:182, 185 (sidebar)
Tenant farming and sharecropping 2:42, 411; 3:80, 104, 105, 249, 350–51, 370–71, 418; 4:2
Terrorism
    Arab against Israel 4:106
    by Argentine military junta 5:209–10, 212–13
    by Chilean military junta 5:169
    by Guatemalan military 5:28
    of Herut Party in Israel 4:107
    of Irgun in British Mandatory Palestine 4:103
    (See also Ku Klux Klan)
Tervalon, Jervey, *Understand This* 5:339–45
Tess of the D'Urbervilles, Hardy, Thomas 2:353–59
Theater
    Chinese opera 5:75
    in early 1900s in America 3:220–21
    El Teatro Campesino 4:409; 5:172
    Elizabethan 1:261–62, 263
    golden age of television drama 3:92; 4:236, 379
    importance in ancient Greece 1:19–20, 240
    innovations of Wilder 3:287–88
    musicals 4:387
    in postmodern era 2:123
    realism in 1:92
    supported by James I 1:299
    Teatro Rodante Puertorriqueño 5:216
    and Theater of the Absurd 4:400
    (See also Plays)
Thebes (in ancient Greece) 1:14
Their Eyes Were Watching God, Hurston, Zora Neale 3:383–89
Theseus 1:57, 61 (sidebar), 258, 259
Things Fall Apart, Achebe, Chinua 2:360–65
Thirty Years War 1:87, 88, 388 (sidebar), 388
Thisbe 1:259 (sidebar)
Thomas, Dylan, *Child's Christmas in Wales, A* 3:63–67
Thoreau, Henry David
    Civil Disobedience 2:87–92
    influence on Dickinson 2:57
    influence on King 5:192
    on John Brown 2:193
    as transcendentalist 1:356; 2:92, 416
    Walden 2:416–21
Thornton, Laurence, *Imagining Argentina* 5:208–13
Thousand Pieces of Gold, McCunn, Ruthanne Lum 2:366–71
Three Musketeers, The, Dumas, Alexandre 1:386–92
Thucydides 1:14
Thurber, James, *Secret Life of Walter Mitty, The* 3:364–69
Tijerina, Lopez Reies 4:175, 176, 321

Time of the Hero, The, Vargas Llosa, Mario 5:333–38
Titans 1:301
Tituba (in real life) 1:79, 83 (sidebar), 394–96, 422–23
Tituba of Salem Village, Petry, Ann 1:393–99
To Kill a Mockingbird, Lee, Harper 3:390–96
Tobacco
    cigars 3:65
    rise during 1920s in popularity of smoking 3:89
    snuff 3:71 (sidebar)
    for women 3:19, 23, 167, 168 (illus.)
Tolkien, J.R.R., *Hobbit, The* 1:152–58
Tolstoy, Leo
    Anna Karenina 2:34–40
    on *Uncle Tom's Cabin* 2:409
Tom Brown's Schooldays, Hughes, Thomas 2:372–77
Totalitarianism. See Dictatorship
Tournaments 1:291
Towns and cities, growth of. See Urbanization
Transcendentalism 1:356–57; 2:54, 92, 314, 316–19, 416, 418–19
Transportation
    Appalachian Trail 5:278–79
    automobiles 2:128 (sidebar); 3:23, 77, 88–89, 94, 101; 5:40 (illus.)
    aviation 3:211–12
    canals 2:230; 3:184, 231–32, 270; 4:107
    public, segregation of 5:88–90, 185–86
    roads and highways 3:77, 91
        Blue Ridge Parkway 5:278
        creating suburbs 5:262
        National System of Interstate and Defense Highways (1956) 3:73
        Route 66 3:140
    sled dogs 3:52–56
    streetcars 2:328; 3:25; 4:366
    (See also Railroads in U.S.)
Treasure Island, Stevenson, Robert Louis 1:400–405
Tree Grows in Brooklyn, A, Smith, Betty 3:397–403
Trojan War 1:8, 14, 166–69, 281, 283 (sidebar)
Trotsky, Leon 4:16; 5:254
Truman Doctrine (1947–49) 4:110; 5:123–24
Truman, Harry S 4:72, 173 (sidebar); 5:96, 123
Truth, Sojourner, "Ain't I a Woman?" 2:22–27
Tubman, Harriet 2:189
Turkey
    Ali Pasha 2:101
    genocide of Armenians 3:338–43; 4:199
    "guest" workers from, in Europe 4:163–64
    under Ottoman Turks 1:295–96; 3:338–40
    WWI and British occupation of former holdings 4:102
    and Young Turks 3:339, 340, 342
Turn of the Screw, The, James, Henry 2:378–83
Turner, Nat 2:93–94, 95, 169–70, 188
    (See also *Confessions of Nat Turner, The*)

Index

Tuskegee Institute   2:413, 414
Twain, Mark
   Adventures of Huckleberry Finn, The   2:15–21
   Notorious Jumping Frog of Calaveras County, The
   2:249–54
Twelve Angry Men, Rose, Reginald (screenplay)
   4:378–83
Twenty-Thousand Leagues under the Sea, Verne, Jules
   2:384–90
Twinship   4:219
Two Years before the Mast, Dana, Richard Henry, Jr.
   2:391–96
Tyler, Wat (Peasant's Revolt of 1381)   1:65

U

UFOs (unidentified flying objects)   4:347–48; 5:59
   (illus.)
Ukraine, Babi Yar massacre   4:120
Uncas   1:207 (sidebar), 208
Uncle Remus, Harris, Joel Chandler   2:397–402
Uncle Tom's Cabin, Stowe, Harriet Beecher   2:403–9
   aggravating North-South rift over slavery   2:172
Underground Railroad   2:16, 60, 62, 189, 238,
   406–7
Understand This, Tervalon, Jervey   5:339–45
UNIA (United Negro Improvement Association)
   3:160; 4:211
Unions. See Labor unions
Unitarianism   2:54, 315
United Nations   4:103, 107–8
   birth of   5:53–54
   Cold War reflected in   5:254
   "Convention Relating to Status of Refugees"
      5:28–29
   and Declaration of Women's Rights (1967)
      5:174
United Service Organizations (USO)   4:38
United States in 19th century
   American Enlightenment   2:416
   American literature, birth of   1:210, 211, 217,
      218, 335–36; 2:419
   American literature, maturation of   2:109,
      234–35
   appeal of European travel to middle- to upper-
      class Americans   2:105–6
   belief in progress   2:195, 196, 313, 416
   canal system   2:230
   conservatism and commerce   2:199, 306, 312,
      328, 331
   democracy, growth of   2:87–88, 89–91
   depressions in later years   3:51, 169
   dissent, protest, and civil disobedience   2:87,
      89, 90, 312
   economic growth   2:195, 230, 416
   Gilded Age   2:20, 199, 306, 312, 328, 331
   Jackson administration   2:314–15
   Mexican War   2:88, 89, 242
   rural New England   2:125–26
   War of 1812   1:53; 2:416

   whaling industry   2:230, 232–34
   (See also Civil War; Railroads in U.S.;
      Reconstruction; Slavery in America; West, The;
      Western migration)
United States in 20th century: Progressive Era
   (1900–1919)
   as era of reform   3:75–76, 284–85
   labor unions, support for   3:420
   muckraking journalists   3:176, 320
   multifaceted agenda of   3:285, 319–20
   postwar return to (probusiness) normalcy
      3:21
   reformers as elitist   3:319
   reforming zeal carried to other countries   3:280
   trust busters and Teddy Roosevelt   3:167
   women's roles changing   3:271–72, 280
      (sidebar)
   Woodrow Wilson   3:279–80, 319
   World War I (1917–18). See World War I
United States in 20th century: Roaring Twenties
   (1920–1929)
   assembly line/mass production   3:89, 100–101,
      102
   boomtowns   3:25
   buying on credit   3:89
   car culture   3:23
   consumer/mass culture, advertising   3:26, 89,
      100–101, 102
   gangsters and St. Valentine's Day Massacre
      3:366–67
   hard times for farmers   3:94–95, 138–40
   machine age as degrading individualism and
      culture   5:41
   modern morals and changing status of women
      3:23, 228–29
   postwar economic boom   3:146
   Prohibition. See Prohibition
   race riots (1919)   2:6, 404; 3:160, 252, 321;
      4:310
   San Francisco's corruption   3:226
   stock market speculation fever   3:146
   Teapot Dome scandal   3:25
   and United Fruit Company in South America
      2:269–70
United States in 20th century: Thirties (1930–1940).
   See Great Depression, The
United States in 20th century: World War II
   (1941–45). See World War II
United States in 20th century: 1946–1959
   age of big government   4:110
   baby boom   1:224; 2:325–26; 4:38, 74, 240
   beatniks, counterculture, hippies, and protesters
      4:75, 289, 293, 399–400
   Cold War. See Cold War
   consumerism, credit buying, and conformity
      3:2, 91; 4:73–74, 110–11, 236, 328, 397–401;
      5:322–23
   disillusion, dehumanization, and dystopian
      literature   5:252
   divorce rate increase   4:38

Index

global commercial and cultural influence 1:223; 3:92
"heroes" as powerful and nonconformist 4:262, 292, 381–82
inflation and anxiety 4:109–10
mass culture and influence of television 4:111, 379, 398
postwar boom, prosperity 4:109–10, 328
teenage culture 4:391–93, 394–95
War Brides Act 4:124, 127; 5:231
white male economic dominance 4:397
women and cult of domesticity 4:237, 240–41
women as sex objects 4:393

United States in 20th century: 1960s
appeal of Eastern religions 5:237, 281
civil rights protests. *See* Civil rights movements
counterculture, hippies, and protesters 5:37, 64 (sidebar), 83, 158, 237, 272, 279, 308–10, 323–25
cults, iconoclasm, rebels as heros 5:83–84, 318 (sidebar), 323–24
decade of tumult 5:309 (sidebar)
environment, concern for 4:337–42; 5:85–86, 279
feminism. *See* Women's rights movement (and feminism)
"free love" movement 5:272
"graying" of America 5:202–4
Johnson's Great Society and War on Poverty 3:324; 5:68, 150, 266
riots 2:97–98; 3:324; 4:207; 5:112 (sidebar), 340
self-fulfillment and human potential movement 5:204, 287–88
(*See also* Vietnam War)

United States in 20th century: 1970s–1980s
antibusing incidents 3:324
disillusion with government after Nixon and Watergate 3:99; 5:158–59, 263, 317
environment, concern for 5:279 (sidebar)
feminism. *See* Women's rights movement (and feminism)
judicial opposition to civil rights legislation 5:1–2
"me" generation and self-help movements 5:263, 287–88
official apology and monetary compensation to Japanese Americans for WWII internment 4:143, 195
probusiness conservatism (Reagan presidency) 5:1
recession, unemployment, and welfare cuts 5:1, 329
rise of New Right and religious fundamentalists 5:136–39
sexual revolution 5:151
(*See also* Vietnam War)

U.S. Army. *See* Military
United States Military. *See* Military
U.S.S.R. *See* Soviet Union

Up From Slavery, Washington, Booker T. 2:410–15

Urbanization
in 19th-century America 2:125, 195, 301–4
of 19th-century England 1:106, 217, 417; 2:118, 353, 354, 358
in 19th-century France 2:103–4, 209
in 20th-century America 3:25, 73, 88–89; 4:171–72
in 20th-century South 5:91
in 20th-century South Africa 4:95
by American Indians in 20th century 4:186
in Chile 5:164
cities viewed as hotbeds of sin 3:69
of colonial America 1:102
department stores made possible by 2:303
with immigration 2:302, 327; 3:101, 102, 166
and Mexican Americans 4:171
promoting individualism 2:302
replacing rural, agrarian society 2:312, 327; 5:91
rise of crime and police detectives 2:153–54
(*See also* Ghettos; Housing)

USS *Somers* 1:56
Usury (moneylending) 1:103–4, 182–83, 243, 247

Utopian societies
depicted in literature 5:251–52
in novel *Looking Backward* (1888) 2:423
of 1840s 2:418
Shakers 3:95–99
Twin Oaks colony 5:279
Walden movement 5:279

V

Valdez, Luis 5:172
  Zoot Suit 4:403–10
Van Dine, S. S. 3:227
Vargas Llosa, Mario 5:211 (sidebar)
  Time of the Hero, The 5:333–38
Veblen, Thorstein 3:169
Venice, Italy 1:242–46, 295–97
Verne, Jules
  Twenty-Thousand Leagues under the Sea 2:384–90
  H. G. Wells compared to 3:410
Verona, Italy 1:344–45
Verrall, Richard 4:40
Vesey, Denmark 2:94–95
Veterinarians 3:1
Victor Emmanuel III, King of Italy 4:66, 67
Victoria, Queen of England 2:28, 335
Victorian Age
  agricultural depression 2:353
  charity 2:264
  circuses and freak shows 2:33, 120, 329
  class divisions and social stratification 2:152–53, 157, 358
  crime in London 2:262–64
  debt, bankruptcy, and poorhouses 2:211–12, 261–62, 266

Index

divorce 2:158, 355–56
education, progress in 1:412; 2:334
England as world's leading economic power 2:334
foreign competition and economic depression 2:152
humor and puns 2:30
hypocrisy of 3:381
imperialism 2:118–19
landed gentry's decline 2:354–55
London as center of 1:417; 2:20, 196
love and marriage in 2:106, 116, 336
men's roles in 2:107–8, 336
mining industry 2:335
mourning traditions 1:414–15
police, reorganization of 2:153–54
pride plus anxiety 3:405–6, 408–9
public school system 2:372–77
science vs. religion 2:29–30; 3:404
sexual repression 2:334, 336, 338–39, 355; 3:18, 380–81
urbanization with industrialization 1:417; 2:118, 353, 354, 358
work ethic and circumscribed codes of behavior/decorum 2:20, 108, 196, 378–79; 3:381
Yorkshire 1:417–18
(*See also* Colonialism, imperialism, and interventionism)
Victorian women
American stereotype of 2:107
divorce 2:158, 355–56
dowries for 2:246
education of 1:412; 2:30, 181–82, 422–23
emancipation of, opponents and proponents 1:356; 3:167
employment
denial of meaningful work 2:426, 427
as governesses 2:182, 183 (sidebar), 378–80
limited opportunities for 2:203, 355
need to supplement husband's income 3:168–69
in prostitution 2:228, 264, 328–29, 355
evolution and the "Woman Question" 2:423–24
fashion and home furnishings for status 2:246, 247 (sidebar); 3:420
fashionable clothing as restricting 3:420
as "feminine" 2:204, 206–7
as "helpless" 3:19
as "hysterical" 2:425
ignorant preferred to educated, by men 2:380
as innocent and chaste 2:422–25
lack of rights 2:356
marriage and domestic roles for 2:106–7, 108, 116, 202, 303, 336; 3:167
as "maternal" 2:212, 404
prejudice against as writers 1:415 (sidebar); 2:56, 186, 203, 212, 424–25
shopping and department stores 2:303
social calls 3:321–23
as spinsters in England 2:297
supposed moral superiority of 2:106; 3:16, 18, 167, 228
view of themselves as "interesting" 2:106
Vidocq, François-Eugène 3:226
Vietnam War
American Indian soldiers in 5:362–63
anti-Vietnam war movements 3:98, 324
arising from Cold War's "domino theory" 4:347, 375; 5:101–2, 158
arising from French hopes to recolonize Indochina 5:306–7
atrocities, compared to those inflicted upon American Indians 2:79
black soldiers in 5:102–3
combat against jungle guerillas 5:103
draft of disadvantaged for (Project 100,000) 5:102–3, 158, 307
fall of South Vietnam to communist North 5:307
Johnson's escalation of involvement 5:158, 307
Kennedy's sending of "advisors" 5:158, 307
protested by
antiwar forces in U.S. 2:13–14; 4:347; 5:105–6, 158, 307–8
blacks 4:207; 5:103 (sidebar)
Chicanos 4:409–10
students at Kent State University 5:158
women and mothers 5:308
young men subject to draft 5:307–8
young people 5:271
return of POWs 4:376
seen as West's failure to contain communism 4:135
U.S. forces withdrawn from 4:375–76
U.S. soldiers questioning purposes of 5:104–5
U.S. soldiers' reasons for enlisting 5:307 (sidebar)
veterans' postwar experience 5:105–6
Vietnam Memorial 5:105 (illus.), 106, 312
as world's first "television" war 5:3–7, 37
Vigilantism
in frontier West 1:256–57; 2:323–24
in rural California 3:273–74
in San Francisco of 1850s 2:286–87
tarring and feathering by mobs 2:17 (sidebar)
(*See also* Ku Klux Klan; Lynching)
Vikings 1:49, 138, 226
Villa, Pancho (Doroteo Arango) 3:197, 279
Villarreal, José Antonio 5:172
Pocho 4:295–302
Vindication of the Rights of Woman, A, Wollstonecraft, Mary 1:406–12; 2:297
Viracocha people 4:221, 222
Virgil
Aeneid, The 1:8–13
as character in Dante's *Inferno* 1:176–77, 178–79
Virginia 1:379, 384, 394; 5:278–84

Index

Voigt, Cynthia, *Runner, The*   5:306–13
Vonnegut, Kurt, Jr., *Slaughterhouse Five*   4:343–48

W

Walden, Thoreau, Henry David   2:416–21
Wales   1:288; 3:63–64, 66
Walker, Alice, *Color Purple, The*   3:80–87
Walpole, Robert   1:266, 269
War
   and antiwar sentiment. *See* Antiwar literature
   Arab-Israeli Six-Day War (1967)   4:93
   Cold War   1:84, 223, 388–89
   England's civil war   1:303, 305–6
   England's wars with France   1:51–52, 93, 123, 130–31, 159, 160, 204–6, 220–21, 305
   England's wars with Spain   1:1–2, 87, 88, 130–31, 201, 306
   French and Indian War (Seven Years' War)   1:93, 123, 204–6, 220–21
   glorification vs. reality of battle   2:257, 258, 308, 309 (sidebar), 312, 313; 3:9–11, 12–13; 4:69–70
   Korean   1:223; 3:73; 4:92
   Mexican   2:88, 89, 242; 5:172
   Napoleonic   2:99–100, 295–96
   Peloponnesian   1:241, 324, 328
   Revolutions of 1848   1:376
   Russo-Turkish   2:37–39
   Spanish-American (1898)   3:101, 278
   Thirty Years   1:87, 88, 388 (sidebar), 388
   Trojan   1:8, 14, 166–69, 281 (illus.), 281, 283 (sidebar)
   Vietnam. *See* Vietnam War
   War of 1812   1:53; 2:416
   (*See also* American Revolution; Antiwar literature; Civil War; France in 18th century: French Revolution; Military; World War I; World War II)
War on Poverty   3:324; 5:68, 150, 266
War weaponry
   aircraft
      bombers   4:67–68
      dive-bombers   4:359
      fighter bombers   4:67
      fighters   4:361
      helicopters   4:71
      jets   4:71
   aircraft carriers   4:59
   atomic/nuclear   4:71
      arms control proposals   4:71; 5:126, 225, 239, 252 (sidebar)
      hydrogen bomb   4:183; 5:126
      Manhattan Project   4:71, 81–82, 316
      missiles   5:124
      (*See also* Atom bomb)
   barbed wire used as   3:113
   in *Beowulf*   1:46 (illus.)
   field artillery   3:113
   incendiary bombs   4:179
   landing craft   4:60
   machine gun   3:9, 113
   minesweepers   4:61
   rockets   5:54, 96
   submarines   1:277–78
   technological enhancements during WWI   3:113
   technology causing anxiety   3:406; 4:255
War of the Worlds, The, Wells, H.G.   3:404–10
   Orson Welles' October 1938 broadcast of   3:154, 365, 408 (sidebar)
Warren, Mary   1:81 (sidebar), 83 (sidebar)
Washington, Booker T.
   advocating (temporary) acceptance of segregation   2:341, 342, 343, 344, 345, 410, 413, 414; 3:162, 250, 320, 385
   autobiography: *Up From Slavery*   2:410–15
   compared to Du Bois   2:345 (sidebar); 3:162, 250, 320, 385
Waste Land, The, Eliot, T.S.   3:357, 411–17
Watergate scandal   3:99; 5:158–59, 263, 317
Watership Down, Adams, Richard   5:346–51
Watkins, Yoko K., *So Far from the Bamboo Grove*   4:349–55
Watson, John Boradus   5:45
Weaver, George "Buck"   3:149
Weizmann, Chaim   4:102, 103
Weld, Theodore D.   2:242
Welles, Orson   3:365, 408
Wells Fargo   2:293
Wells, H. G.
   influenced by science and Darwinism   3:404–5
   on *Portrait of the Artist as a Young Man*   3:309 (sidebar), 311
   rejection of Christianity   3:404
   War of the Worlds, The   3:404–10
Wells-Barnett, Ida B.   3:83, 420
Welty, Eudora, *Worn Path, A*   3:418–24
West, The
   California gold rush   2:174–75, 195, 249–50, 281–84
   Chinese prostitutes   2:366–67
   gunfighters   2:323–24
   homesteaders   2:127 (sidebar), 128, 322–23; 3:244, 257, 259, 260–61
   humor, practical jokes, and tall tales   2:250–51
   Nebraska   3:257–58, 260
   racism against Chinese   2:175, 287, 367–68, 370 (sidebar), 371
   ranching and cattle barons on Great Plains   2:321–22
   Teddy Roosevelt popularizing "Old West" myth of individualism   5:206
   settling and demise of frontier   2:312
   Wells Fargo   2:293
   women on frontier   2:323
West Side Story, Laurents, Arthur, et al.   4:384–90
Western migration
   beginning in colonial times   1:102, 103, 107
   California gold rush   2:174–75, 195, 249–50

Index

Donner Party 2:282 (sidebar)
encouraged by Homestead Act (1870) 2:322–23; 3:244, 257
encouraged by U.S. gov't. 2:314
end of western frontier 2:68
hardship and survivalism 3:259–60
increasing job opportunities for women in East 2:423
land speculators 3:258
and Manifest Destiny 2:76 (sidebar); 3:234
and Mexican War 2:88, 395
to Nebraska 3:257–58
Nevada silver strikes 2:288–89, 290 (sidebar)
pressures upon American Indians 2:67, 74
railroads 2:175, 195
single women absent from 2:56, 250
(See also Gold rushes and silver strikes)
Weston, Jessie L. 3:415
Wet-nurses 2:211
Whaling industry 2:230, 232–34
Wharton, Edith
    Ethan Frome 2:125–29
    House of Mirth, The 3:166–73
Where Are You Going, Where Have You Been?, Oates, Joyce Carol 4:391–96
"White man's burden" and white supremacy 2:119, 147, 341; 3:170, 172, 182 (sidebar)
Whitman, Walt
    on imperialism 3:300 (sidebar)
    Leaves of Grass 2:195–201
Whyte, William 4:75, 382
Wiesel, Elie
    Dawn 4:101–8
    Night 4:267–73
Wiesenthal, Simon 4:273
Wight, James Alfred. See Herriott, James
Wilder, Thornton, Our Town 3:284–89
Wilhelm II, Kaiser (Germany) 3:8
Wilkins, Roy 5:186, 188
William the Conqueror 1:250, 290
William of Orange 1:130
Williams, Claude "Lefty" 3:149; 4:260, 261; 5:316
Williams, Paulette Linda. See Shange, Ntozake
Williams, Tennesse, Streetcar Named Desire, A 4:364–70
Williamson, Joel 3:387
Wilson, August, Fences 4:144–50
Wilson, Edmund
    praise for Animal Farm 4:19–20
    praise for The Waste Land 3:417
Wilson, Woodrow 3:279–80, 319
Winthrop, Gov. John 1:78, 352 (sidebar)
Witchcraft
    belief in, in medieval Scotland 1:227–28
    belief in, by Latinos (brujas) 4:46
    belief in, by Puritans 1:79–81, 102, 393, 394
    in The Crucible 1:78–86
    in The Devil and Tom Walker 1:101–6
    interest of James I in 1:228
    in Macbeth 1:227–28
    spectral evidence of 1:421–22
    in Tituba of Salem Village 1:394–97
    witch trials 1:79, 83, 85 (illus.), 355, 395–96, 397 (illus.), 423 (illus.)
    in Young Goodman Brown 1:420–26
    (See also Supernatural)
Wolfe, Tom, Right Stuff, The 5:291–97
Wollstonecraft, Mary
    as first English feminist 3:359
    mother of Mary Shelley 1:115, 116, 407
    similarities to, in Elizabeth Bennet 2:297
    tribute by William Blake 1:410 (sidebar)
    Vindication of the Rights of Woman, A 1:406–12
Woman Warrior, The, Kingston, Maxine Hong 5:352–59
Women, (See also Education of women; Love and marriage)
Women in ancient times
    as "Great Goddesses" and Amazons 1:58–59, 61–62, 258, 259–60
    in Greece 1:17, 20, 58–59, 259, 327
    names in Rome 1:190 (sidebar)
    Plato on leadership roles for 1:325, 327
    as rulers in Celtic England 1:197
    as spoils of war 1:8, 169, 170–71
Women in medieval times
    as depicted by Chaucer 1:69
    in Scotland 1:226
Women in 15th century, in salons of Paris 1:31, 88–89
Women in 16th century
    prejudice against, as leaders 1:236
    in Tudor and Elizabethan England 1:232–33, 236, 263–64
Women in 17th century, targeted in witchhunts 1:80
Women in 18th century
    on colonial farms 1:334
    defiance of convention 1:406, 407, 409
    urging education and rights for 1:406, 408–11
    as wet-nurses 2:211
Women in 19th century
    American Southern ideal of, 2.138, 3.19m 3:392–93
    Chinese 2:366–67, 368 (sidebar), 370–71
    in France 2:212, 244, 247
    involvement in abolition of slavery 2:23–24
    involvement in reform movements 2:423
    isolation of farms and homesteads 2:127 (sidebar), 128; 3:259, 260–61
    in prostitution 2:228, 264, 283–84, 328–29, 355; 4:37
    teaching freed slaves 2:411–12
    as wet-nurses 2:211
    (See also Victorian women)
Women in 20th century
    Chinese 3:132–33, 134–35, 191–93; 4:128
    dangers of childbirth 3:285–86
    as domestic, passive, and "feminine" 1:33–34, 35–36; 2:326; 4:22, 74, 167, 237, 240–41

emancipation of
  negative portrayals in detective fiction of 1920s   3:228–29
  new freedoms of 1920s   3:147
  opponents and proponents   3:167
  single mothers of 1950s as "irrational"   4:169 (sidebar)
employment for   2:326; 3:271; 5:138
  as chorus girls   2:329
  as midwives   4:218
  as repugnant to Religious Right   5:137
  in wartime and afterwards   4:21–22, 74, 166–67, 196 (illus.), 197–98
fashions for. *See* Fashions
importance of marriage   3:168
Jewish   3:427–30
in Maoist thought   3:136
Mexican   3:197–98, 200–202
participation in Progressive Era's reform movements   3:75, 76
protesting Vietnam War   5:308
rural life
  isolation of   3:271
  for sharecropper families   3:370–71
  on Texas frontier   3:246
as sexual goddesses, sex objects   4:74, 393
as single heads of households   2:65; 3:80, 423; 4:2; 5:68, 117, 136, 138, 267, 328–29
subject to sexual double standard   4:38, 74, 395
and suicide   4:22–26
(*See also* African American women)
Women's rights movement (and feminism)
  abortion and *Roe v. Wade*   5:51, 136
  advocating self-determination   5:138–39
  antifeminist backlash   5:136
  authors active in
    Gilman   2:424
    Le Guin's take on   5:237–38
    Morrison   2:64
    Renault's sympathy with   1:62
    Woolf   3:330–32
  battered wives shelters   5:136
  and black feminism   2:64; 3:86–87, 354–55; 5:92–93, 117
  in Britain   3:359
  Chicana women's movement   3:202
  in czarist Russia   2:37, 39
  educated women at core of   5:135
  hiatus between 1918 and 1960s   5:135–36
  legislation affecting
    Civil Rights Act (1964), Title VII   1:35; 5:136
    Equal Pay Act (1963)   1:35; 5:237
    Equal Rights Amendment (ERA)   3:79; 5:51 (illus.), 136, 358–59
    Higher Education Act (1972), Title IX   5:136
  in Mexico   3:201–2
  National Organization of Women (NOW)   1:62; 4:22, 394; 5:136, 237

  in Norway   2:112–13
  origins in
    19th century   2:22, 24, 25, 27, 55, 204, 423; 3:16
    abolitionist movement   2:24, 204
    civil rights movement of 20th century   1:35; 2:58
    discontent of women in 1950s   4:167–70; 5:136
    EEOC's refusal to enforce Title VII   5:237
    Friedan's *Feminine Mystique*   1:62; 2:58; 3:430; 4:11 (sidebar), 167, 241, 394; 5: 136
    gender discrimination in workplace   1:35; 5:136
    myths of women's selfless inclination to serve and nurture   5:136, 288
    objections to sexual double standard   4:38, 74, 395
    oppression and discrimination   2:23–24, 355–56, 380, 422, 423–26
    sexual harassment in workplace   1:35
    women's subordination to men   4:169, 170
  rape crisis centers   5:136
  role of women's clubs   2:336; 3:16–17, 287 (sidebar)
  in Victorian England   2:335
  women's studies programs resulting   5:117
Women's rights and roles, discussion pertaining to
  Antigone   1:14–21
  Canterbury Tales, The   1:68–69
  Ethan Frome   2:126–27, 128–29
  Left Hand of Darkness, The   5:237–38, 239–40, 242
  Lottery, The   4:237
  Macbeth   1:226
  Maltese Falcon, The   3:228–29
  Midsummer Night's Dream, A   1:259–60, 261–64
  Noon Wine   3:246–47
  Odyssey   1:282, 285
  Of Mice and Men   3:271–72
  Passage to India, A   3:301–2
  Sweet Whispers, Brother Rush   5:329
  Turn of the Screw, The   2:378–83
  Worn Path, A   3:420–21
Women's rights and roles, literary works emphasizing
  "Ain't I a Woman?"   2:22–27
  Anna Karenina   2:34–40
  Awakening, The   3:15–20
  Beauty: A Retelling of the Story of Beauty and the Beast   1:30–36
  Bell Jar, The   4:21–27
  Belle of Amherst, The   2:54–58
  Beloved   2:59–65
  Bluest Eye, The   4:49–57
  Carrie   5:46–52
  Color Purple, The   3:80–87
  Daisy Miller   2:105–10
  Doll's House, A   2:111–17

Index

For Colored Girls Who Have Considered Suicide When the Rainbow Is Enuf   5:115–21
Golden Notebook, The   4:165–70
Gone with the Wind   2:137–44
Handmaid's Tale, The   5:135–42
House of Mirth, The   3:166–73
House of the Spirits, The   5:163–70
House on Mango Street, The   5:171–77
I Know Why the Caged Bird Sings   4:201–8
Incidents in the Life of a Slave Girl   2:168–73
Jacob Have I Loved   4:216–20
Jane Eyre   1:415; 2:181–87
Joy Luck Club, The   5:229–35
Kitchen God's Wife, The   3:189–95
Like Water for Chocolate   3:196–202
Little Women   2:202–8
Madame Bovary   2:209–15
Medea   1:238–41
Member of the Wedding, The   4:254–59
O Pioneers!   3:257–63
Out of Africa   3:290–96
Pride and Prejudice   2:295–300
Prime of Miss Jean Brodie, The   4:303–8
Pygmalion   3:312–18
Rebecca   3:326–33
Room of One's Own, A   3:356–63
Scarlet Letter, The   1:351–57
Seventeen Syllables   4:330–36
Sister Carrie   2:327–33
Streetcar Named Desire, A   4:364–70
Sweet Whispers, Brother Rush (portions of)   5:329
Tess of the D'Urbervilles   2:353–59
Their Eyes Were Watching God   3:383–89
Thousand Pieces of Gold   2:366–71
Turn of the Screw, The   2:378–83
Vindication of the Rights of Woman, A   1:406–12; 2:297
Where Are You Going, Where Have You Been?   4:391–96
Woman Warrior, The   5:352–59
Wuthering Heights   1:413–19
Yellow Raft in Blue Water, A   5:360–66
Yellow Wallpaper, The   2:422–28
Yentl, the Yeshiva Boy   3:425–31

Women's suffrage
  achieved in 1919 and 1930 in Britain   3:359
  achieved in 1920 in U.S.   3:76, 287
  agitation for change   2:335–36; 3:16
  in California by 1911   3:271
  in Chile in 1952   5:167
  defeated in many states of U.S.   3:286–87
  denounced in Victorian Age   2:335
  expanding by 1890   2:424
  in Kansas (1861), although limited   2:424
  ratification denied in Alabama   3:392
  in Wyoming in 1869   2:323
Woodstock Music and Art Fair (1969)   5:65 (illus.), 324
Woolf, Virginia   5:42

Room of One's Own, A   3:356–63
Wordsworth, William   1:416
World War I
  Africa, impact on   3:292–93
  ambulance service   3:114
  British occupation of former Ottoman Empire   4:102
  casualties of   3:11 (sidebar)
  causes and outbreak   1:157–58; 3:8–9, 112–13, 411
  Italy's role in   3:113–14
  losses, destruction   1:157–58; 3:11 (sidebar), 411–12
  "lost generation"   3:13, 112, 116–17
  navies' roles in   1:277–78
  older generations supporting   3:9–11, 12–13
  Ottoman slaughter of Armenians   3:339–40
  postwar issues
    disillusionment and despair   3:227, 412
    German reparations, inflation, and unemployment   4:157
    global expansion   1:223; 3:21, 88
  proving H. G. Wells's fiction as prophetic   3:406
  racial issues
    African Americans as employees and soldiers   3:160, 252; 4:144, 145, 212–13
    segregation of U.S. military   4:212–13
  reasons for joining   1:278
  Russian defeats, civil war, revolution (1917)   3:232–33
  sacrifices on German home front   3:11
  technological enhancements of weaponry   3:113
  Treaty of Berlin (1921)   3:88
  trench warfare   3:9, 113, 115 (sidebar)
World War II
  American mobilization for   2:45; 3:424; 4:325
  America's prewar isolationism   4:323, 362
  aviation
    bomber crews   4:68–70
    Lindbergh's contributions to   3:367
  causes of   1:113–14; 4:157, 356–57
  chronology
    Nazi precursor conquests in Europe (1935–366)   1:113–14; 3:213, 214; 4:357
    British "appeasements" of Hitler (1936–39)   4:356, 357, 362
    Rome-Berlin Axis (1936)   4:67
    Stalin/Hitler nonaggression pact (1939)   3:210, 214; 4:357
    Poland partitioned by Germany and Soviet Union (1939)   4:131
    France and England declare war on Germany (1939)   3:214
    French unpreparedness (1939)   3:213–14
    Tripartite Pact (Japan, Germany, Italy; 1940)   4:59
    standoff at Maginot Line   4:357
    "blitzkrieg"; Germany invades Belgium, Luxembourg, and France   4:254–55, 357, 359

Index

first American peacetime draft (1940)   4:35, 324–25
Italy helps Nazis (1940)   4:67
German occupation of Holland (1940)   4:116–19
Dunkirk, evacuation of (May 1940)   4:356, 359–63
German invasion of Russia, (1941)   3:124; 4:131
Pearl Harbor (1941)   4:59, 178, 323
Lend-Lease (1941–45)   4:228–29, 363
Pacific theater (1942–45)   4:60–61, 80–81, 178
Philippines' Bataan Death March   4:81
Aleutian islands, battles for (1942–43)   4:254
Allies establish North African base (1942–44)   3:214
emergence of De Gaulle (1943)   3:214
Allied invasion of Sicily (1943)   4:67
Italy declares war on Germany (1943)   4:67
kamikazi missions (1944)   4:61 (sidebar), 62 (illus.)
liberation of France (1944)   3:214
Battle of the Bulge (Dec. '44)   4:343
Yalta Conference (Feb. '45)   4:344
Dresden, firebombing by Allies (Feb. '45)   4:343–44
founding of United Nations   5:54
atomic bombing of Japan (Aug. '45)   4:178–82, 180 (illus.), 181 (sidebar)
Nuremberg war crimes trials of former Nazis   4:272–73
conquests by dictatorships   5:123 (sidebar), 224, 253–54
on home front
    for American South, industrialization and economic recovery from Depression   2:53; 3:72–73
    cynicism and opportunism   4:371
    families of servicemen   4:317–18
    German prisoners of war   4:371–73
    intergenerational conflict   4:327
    media's partiotic emphasis on war issues   4:371
    persecution and internment of Japanese Americans (1942–44)   4:137–43, 194–95, 335–36
    race riots of 1940s   4:197, 201, 213, 247, 248 (illus.), 295–97, 403–10
    racism   4:199, 200
    rationing and inflation   3:424; 5:256–57
    women at work   4:21–22, 74, 166–67, 196 (illus.), 197–98
importance of Churchill's rhetoric and determination   4:361–62
Palestine   4:102–5
postwar issues
    baby boom   1:224; 2:325–26; 4:38, 74, 240
    Britain   4:229, 231; 5:256–57
    emphasis on home and materialism   2:325–26
    Marshall Plan   5:123–24, 224, 292
    (See also Cold War)
psychological casualties and postcombat syndrome   4:80 (sidebar), 325
racial issues
    African Americans as employees and soldiers   3:424
    American Indians in   4:80–81
    Chicano rights movement watershed   4:44
    Latinos in   4:295, 406
    segregation of U.S. military   3:41–42; 4:195, 197, 374 (sidebar)
    (See also Holocaust)
reservists and regulars   4:63 (sidebar)
(See also Nazis)
Worn Path, A, Welty, Eudora   3:418–24
Wouk, Herman, *Caine Mutiny, The*   4:58–65
WPA (Works Progress Administration)   3:128, 391, 423–24; 4:44
Wright, Richard
    Almos' a Man   4:1–6
    on anti-Semitism of his youth   4:376
    Black Boy   3:36–43
    as critic of Hurston   3:385, 389
    Native Son   3:236–42
    on *The Heart Is a Lonely Hunter*   3:157
Wuthering Heights, Brontë, Emily   1:413–19
Wyoming, women's suffrage in 1869   2:323

X

X, Malcolm   2:98; 3:324–25; 4:54, 249–50; 5:69–70, 111
    with Alex Haley, *Autobiography of Malcolm X, The*   5:11–18

Y

Yamamoto, Hisaye, *Seventeen Syllables*   4:330–36
Yankees   1:217, 332, 334, 335; 2:8–9, 137
Yeager, Chuck   5:293
Yellow Raft in Blue Water, A, Dorris, Michael   5:360–66
Yellow Wallpaper, The, Gilman, Charlotte Perkins   2:422–28
Yentl, the Yeshiva Boy, Singer, Isaac Bashevis   3:425–31
Yorkshire, England   1:417–18; 3:1–3, 5–6
Young Goodman Brown, Hawthorne, Nathaniel   1:420–26
Young Turks   3:339, 340, 342
Youth
    adolescence in hiding from Holocaust   4:121–22
    antiestablishment rebellion   5:272
    and dance   4:387
    distinctive *pachuco* culture of 1950s   4:173, 296
    distinctive teenage culture of 1950s   4:172, 391–93, 394–95

Index

facing conflict and violence 5:268–69
gang membership 4:251, 386, 387–89; 5:216
gang truce in Los Angeles 5:341
and generation gap 4:386, 394; 5:198
juvenile delinquency 4:251, 386, 387–89; 5:37
literature for adolescents, as genre 5:61–62, 265–66, 268–70
moral laxity of war years 4:37
peer pressure and negativity 5:65–66, 71–72, 217
protesting against Vietnam War 5:271
psychotherapy for 5:260–61
students' free speech movement 5:311
suicide by teenagers 5:259–60, 261
television as babysitter 5:36–37
television as too violent 5:62

Yukon territory and Klondike River 3:52–56, 261 (sidebar)

Z

Zapata, Emiliano 3:197, 198 (illus.)
Zen Buddhism 4:334
Zeus 1:9, 59, 61, 170, 282, 283, 301
Zindel, Paul, *Pigman, The* 5:271–77
Zionism 3:121; 4:88, 101–2
  and Arabic anti-Zionism 4:107
  and Soviet anti-Zionism 4:107–8
Zoo Story, The, Albee, Edward 4:397–402
Zoot Suit, Valdez, Luis 4:403–10
Zundel, Ernst 4:40

102984

MAGNIFICAT HIGH SCHOOL
RESOURCE CENTER
ROCKY RIVER, OH 44116-3397

FOR REFERENCE

Do Not Take From This Room